THIRD EDITION

The Paralegal
Profess...

W9-BML-880

Thomas F. Goldman, JD
Professor Emeritus
Bucks County Community College

Henry R. Cheeseman, JD, LLM
Clinical Professor of Law
University of Southern California

Prentice Hall
Boston   Columbus   Indianapolis   New York   San Francisco   Upper Saddle River
Amsterdam   Cape Town   Dubai   London   Madrid   Milan   Munich   Paris   Montreal   Toronto
Delhi   Mexico City   Sao Paulo   Sydney   Hong Kong   Seoul   Singapore   Taipei   Tokyo

Dedicated to the memory of my parents,
Morris and Ethel Goldman, who guided me through life,
encouraged me to pursue an education,
and delighted in my becoming a teacher.

—Thomas F. Goldman

In memory of Henry B. and Florence Cheeseman
A grain of sand has been ten thousand mountains.
Who are we to hold it?

—Henry R. Cheeseman

Editor in Chief: Vernon Anthony
Senior Acquisitions Editor: Gary Bauer
Developmental Editor: Linda Cupp
Editorial Assistant: Megan Heintz
Director of Marketing: David Gesell
Senior Marketing Manager: Leigh Ann Sims
Marketing Assistant: Les Roberts
Senior Managing Editor: JoEllen Gohr
Project Manager: Christina Taylor
Operations Specialist: Deidra Skahill

Senior Art Director: Diane Ernsberger
Cover Designer: Wanda Espana
Cover Art: Franz Jantzen/U.S. Supreme Court
Full-Service Project Management: Mary Jo Graham
and Barb Tucker, S4Carlisle Publishing Services
Composition: S4Carlisle Publishing Services
Printer/Binder: Webcrafters, Inc.
Cover Printer: Coral Graphics
Text Font: Janson Text

Credits: Cover: The Supreme Court of the United States/Franz Jantzen; Page 1: SuperStock, Inc./Ingram Publishing; Page 2: iStockphoto; Page 38: Pearson Education/David Graham; Page 74: Photos.com/Tanya Constantine; Page 126: Shutterstock; Page 175: Getty Images Inc. -Stone Allstock/Bruce Ayres; Page 176: Henry Cheeseman; Page 206: Pearson Education/David Graham; Page 240: Pearson Education/David Graham; Page 284: Photos.com/Image Source; Pages 325, 326: Pearson Education/David Graham; Page 366: Photos.com/Dave and Les Jacobs; Page 410: iStockphoto; Page 445: Getty Images/Yellow Dog Productions/The Image Bank; Pearson Education/David Graham; Page 488: iStockphoto; Page 520: Dreamstime LLC-Royalty Free/Stephen Coburn/Dreamstome.com; Page 554: Getty Images Inc. -PhotoDisc/Triangle Images/Digital Vision; Page 446: CORBIS-NY/Creasource; Page 614: Photos.com/Image Source; Page 656: Photos.com/Steve Allen; Page 708: Fotosearch.Com, LLC/Royalty Free; Page 732: iStockphoto

Library of Congress Cataloging-in-Publication Data
Goldman, Thomas F.
    The paralegal professional / Thomas F. Goldman, Henry R. Cheeseman, — 3rd ed.
        p. cm.
    Rev. ed. of: The paralegal professional / Henry R. Cheeseman, Thomas F. Goldman. 2nd ed. 2008.
    Includes bibliographical references and index.
    ISBN 978-0-13-506392-7
    1. Legal assistants—United States—Handbooks, manuals, etc. I. Cheeseman, Henry R. II.
    KF320.L4C445 2011
    340.023'73—dc22   2009046203

Prentice Hall
is an imprint of

www.pearsonhighered.com

ISBN 10:   0-13-506392-2
ISBN 13: 978-0-13-506392-7

BRIEF CONTENTS

CONTENTS

CHAPTER 6
The Court System and Alternative Dispute Resolution   206

PART III
PARALEGAL SKILLS 325

CHAPTER 9
Interviewing and Investigation Skills 326

CHAPTER 14

Property Law *520*

PART IV   LEGAL SUBJECTS

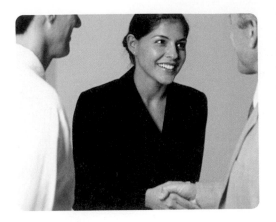

Welcome to the third edition of *The Paralegal Professional*. The paralegal profession is a dynamic, evolving, and growing field that requires developing not only concept knowledge, but also professional and analytical skills, and a firm understanding of the ethical values and obligations of the profession to be competitive in an increasingly challenging work environment. Our goal in the third edition is to provide paralegal students and professionals with the foundation on which to grow and excel in this field today and in the future.

In this edition, we have incorporated comments and suggestions from a wide range of adopters of the text, non-users, and our students. Their feedback resulted in several important changes to the Table of Contents and the introduction of several new features that help bring paralegal practice alive and illuminate the roles and tasks paralegals are asked to assume in the legal working environment.

In the third edition we have divided the book into 4 sections that provide a logical grouping of topics and flexibility as to coverage of the most commonly practiced substantive areas of law.

Part I: The Paralegal Profession focuses on introducing students to the paralegal profession, career opportunities, the paralegal workplace, ethics, regulation, and the use of technology on the job.

Part II: Introduction to Law provides an overview of law and the American legal system and now introduces students to the three area of procedure: civil, criminal, and administrative procedure in succession. This treatment helps students understand the differences between these three legal arenas early in the course.

Part III: Paralegal Skills focuses on introducing students to interviewing, investigation, traditional and online legal research, and writing and critical thinking in the legal field.

Part IV: Legal Subjects provides an overview of the most common individual legal areas of practice. New sections in each of these chapters inform students of employment opportunities related to the field of practice.

We are particularly excited about the new video case studies that are integrated into the third edition. The third edition includes 44 video scenarios that make it easy to bring the world of the practicing paralegal into the classroom. Videos cover topics such as resume writing and interviewing for a job, working in a small family firm, the courtroom players and their roles, and paralegals performing various procedures and duties. Many of the segments present scenarios dealing with common ethical situations that paralegals will encounter on the job making it easy to integrate ethics education throughout the course.

Our book has been carefully and thoroughly designed to meet the requirements as set forth by the American Bar Association (ABA) and the American Association for Paralegal Education (AAfPE) regarding coverage of paralegal topics, ethical issues, professional skill development, and other educational requirements for an introductory paralegal education course.

Thomas Goldman
Henry Cheeseman

Thomas F. Goldman, JD, is Professor Emeritus of Bucks County Community College, where he was a professor of Law and Management and Director of the Center for Legal Studies and the Paralegal Studies Program. He is currently a member of the Paralegal Studies Advisory Board and mentor at Thomas Edison State College, where he has developed the Advanced Litigation Support and Technology Certificate Program in the School of Professional Studies.

He is an author of textbooks in paralegal studies and technology, including *Technology in the Law Office, Accounting and Taxation for Paralegals, Civil Litigation: Process and Procedures,* and *SmartDraw Tutorial and Guide.*

An accounting and economics graduate of Boston University and of Temple University School of Law, Professor Goldman has an active international law, technology law, and litigation practice. He has worked extensively with paralegals and received the award of the Legal Support Staff Guild. He was elected the Legal Secretaries Association Boss of the Year for his contribution to cooperative education by encouraging the use of paralegals and legal assistants in law offices. He also received the Bucks County Community College Alumni Association Professional Achievement Award. He has been an educational consultant on technology to educational institutions and major corporations and is a frequent speaker and lecturer on educational, legal, and technology issues.

Henry R. Cheeseman is an award-winning author of several business law textbooks published by Prentice Hall, including the definitive, highly regarded *Business Law.* Other textbooks by Professor Cheeseman published by Prentice Hall are *Contemporary Business and Online Commerce Law, The Legal Environment of Business and Online Commerce, Essential of Business and Online Commerce,* and *Introduction to Law.* He has earned six degrees, including a Juris Doctor degree from the UCLA School of Law, an LLM degree from Boston University, and an MBA degree from the University of Chicago. Professor Cheeseman is a Clinical Professor of Law and the Director of Legal Studies at the Marshall School of Business, University of Southern California. Students there voted him the best teacher of the year on many occasions, earning him the "Golden Apple" Teacher Award. He has also served at the Center for Excellence in Teaching at the University. Professor Cheeseman recognizes the importance of the paralegal to the practice of law, and has co-authored this new and exciting edition of *The Paralegal Professional.*

BUILD A SOLID FOUNDATION FOR YOUR PARALEGAL CAREER!

Written by an award-winning team, *The Paralegal Professional*, Third Edition, builds the foundation in substantive and procedural legal knowledge and real-world skills you will need throughout your course of study. The book emphasizes the following:

DEVELOP CRITICAL THINKING AND PROCEDURAL SKILLS!

End-of-chapter material in this edition has been greatly expanded to focus on developing critical thinking and hands-on skills, including the following exercises and assignments:

- Critical thinking and writing case exercises
- Web research exercises
- Ethics analysis and discussion questions
- Collaborative exercises
- Legal analysis and writing cases, cases for briefing
- New portfolio building exercises

LEARN ABOUT TECHNOLOGY APPLICATIONS IN THE LAW OFFICE

To be effective on the job, you will need to become comfortable using computers and common legal office software. Chapter 4, Technology and the Paralegal, introduces you to the types of application programs and their uses commonly found in law offices today.

UNDERSTAND HOW TO HANDLE ETHICAL SITUATIONS IN THE WORKPLACE

The Paralegal Professional, Third Edition, text and package is designed to build a strong foundational understanding of ethical principles for paralegals in the introductory course. Resources include Chapter 2: Ethics and Professional Responsibility, new ethical perspectives boxes integrated throughout the textbook, and 24 ethics-related video segments from the new Paralegal Professional Classroom Video Series Segments.

KEY NEW AND RETAINED FEATURES OF THE TEXTBOOK

▶ **PARALEGALS AT WORK CHAPTER OPENERS**

These opening scenarios offer a hypothetical fact situation that a professional paralegal could encounter on the job. They are designed to stimulate a student's interest in the material to be covered in the chapter.

▶ **ETHICAL PERSPECTIVE BOXES**

These new boxes present hypothetical fact situations and ethical dilemmas that paralegals might face in their professional careers.

ETHICAL PERSPECTIVE
Paralegal's Duty to Report Sexual Harassment Conduct

Ms. Heath is hired as a paralegal for the law firm of White, Cassel, and Smith, a large law firm. Ms. Heath is assigned as a paralegal professional to assist Mr. White, a partner of the law firm. During the first couple of weeks on the job, on numerous occasions when Ms. Heath was in attorney Mr. White's office on legal and paralegal matters, Mr. White made rude comments such as talking about people having sex, how good he is in bed, making obscene gestures, and touching Ms. Heath on the

▶ **NEW! SIDEBAR BOXES**

These new boxes provide additional information and commentary on chapter topics.

DIVISION OF MARITAL PROPERTY

Law	Description
Equitable distribution	The marital property is distributed fairly. This does not necessarily mean the equal distribution of the property.

▶ **NEW! PARALEGALS IN PRACTICE BOXES**

For the third edition, we have added profiles of paralegals practicing in a variety of types of practices. Their commentaries provide students with insight into the world of practicing paralegals.

Paralegals *in* Practice
PARALEGAL PROFILE
Annette R. Brown

Annette R. Brown, ACP has been employed by the Rocky Mountain Elk Foundation, Inc. virtually since the creation of its in-house legal department in 1995. The Elk Foundation is a charitable non-profit corporation in Missoula, Montana, with a mission to protect habitat for elk and other wildlife. In addition to her paralegal degree, Annette also has Advanced Paralegal Certifications in Real Estate, Trademarks, and Contracts Administration/Contracts Management from the National Association of Legal Assistants (NALA). She is currently serving as NALA's Region VIII Director which includes the states of Alaska, Idaho, Montana, Oregon, and Washington.

▶ **ADVICE FROM THE FIELD ARTICLES**

These articles feature professional advice straight from the experts on interviewing skills, developing your portfolio, professional development, handling clients, and more.

Advice *from the* Field
GETTING CASE ANALYSIS OFF TO A FAST START
by DecisionQuest

From your first conversation with a prospective client, you're learning about the dispute that led the individual or corporation to seek counsel. There are many benefits to taking a systematic approach to analyzing this knowledge. Not least of these is the favorable impression you'll make on those who retain you.

The following article presents a method for organizing and evaluating the facts about any case. And it illustrates how the early results of this dispute analy-

CHRONOLOGY

A chronology of key facts is a critical tool for analyzing any dispute. As you create the chronology, important factual disputes and areas of strength and weakness become obvious.

Begin by listing the fact and the date on which it occurred. As you enter each fact, be sure to make the important details about the fact explicit. For example,

▶ **IN THE WORDS OF THE COURT BOXES**

Excerpts from key court cases are presented to familiarize students with important legal decisions.

IN THE WORDS OF THE COURT

Alaska Case Law
WHITING V. STATE, A-8755 (ALASKA APP. 10-12-2005)

MANNHEIMER, Judge.

Michael T. Whiting appeals his conviction for felony driving under the influence, . . . the facts . . . : Whiting and his girlfriend and his girlfriend's six-year-old son decided to go fishing in Gastineau Channel. Whiting piloted a skiff into the channel and then turned the motor off. The three occupants of the skiff fished while the skiff drifted in the channel; Whiting sat in the rear of the skiff near the motor. While Whiting was fishing, he was also drinking alcoholic beverages.

▶ **PARALEGAL CHECKLISTS**

Checklists help students track their personal progress as well as class and job details.

CHECKLIST Website Profile

☐ Address (URL):
☐ Name of organization or site:
☐ Key subject:

THE PARALEGAL PROFESSIONAL
VIDEO SERIES ONLINE AND ON DVD

Free to Adopters of Paralegal Professional 3e

The third edition of *The Paralegal Professional* is supported by 44 scenario-based video segments that allow you to bring the world of the practicing paralegal into the classroom. Videos cover topics such as resume writing and interviewing for a job, working in a small family firm, the courtroom players and their roles, and paralegals performing various procedures and duties. All are assignable and can be shown in the classroom from a DVD or viewed online at the Companion Website. For a complete listing of the videos by chapter, consult the Video Case Study Index on pages xviii and xix following the Table of Contents.

Getting a Job and Related Video Segments:

These include segments on preparing for a job interview, interviewing advice, and an engaging interview scenario enactment.

Paralegal Practice and Ethics-Related Video Segments:

Many of the segments present situations involving paralegal ethics, such as common UPL, confidentiality, conflict of interest, billing, and zealous representation issues.

PARALEGAL PROFESSIONAL VIDEO CASE STUDIES ON DVD (ISBN:0-13-506610-7)

View the video cases online on the Companion Website: www.pearson highered.com/goldman.

Paralegal Practice Video Segments:

These segments include a combination of interviews with members of the legal team and law office practice scenario-based sections. Topics covered include interviewing and deposition, electronic discovery, legal research, courtroom procedures, courtroom players and etiquette, the independent paralegal, small family practice, and many other topics.

Teaching notes for the videos are in the Instructor's Manual!

INTEGRATE ETHICS INSTRUCTION
INTO THE INTRODUCTORY COURSE!

Many paralegal programs struggle with the question of how to integrate dedicated ethics instruction into a paralegal curriculum already packed with coursework. *The Paralegal Professional 3e* text and package is designed to build a strong foundational understanding of ethical principles for paralegals in the introductory course. Resources include:

Chapter 2: Ethics, Regulation, and Professional Responsibility

The fundamental ethics issues and principles are presented in chapter 2.

New Ethical Perspectives Boxes Integrated throughout the Textbook

These new boxes present hypothetical fact situations and ethical dilemmas that highlight situations paralegals might face in their professional careers.

> **ETHICAL PERSPECTIVE**
> *Paralegal Loses $900,000 for Failing to Get a Contract in Writing*
>
> Paralegals are sometimes themselves involved in contract disputes. Consider the following case. Barbara Lucinda Sawyer worked as a paralegal for Melbourne Mills, Jr., an attorney at a law firm. Ms. Sawyer proposed that Mr. Mills and the law firm become engaged in class-action lawsuits. Mr. Mills agreed to pay Ms. Sawyer an unspecified bonus when "the ship comes in." After Ms. Sawyer's assistance and persistence, the law firm became involved in class-action litigation—primarily the Fen-Phen class-action litigation. After the law firm received millions of dollars in fees from the Fen-Phen class-action lawsuits, Ms. Sawyer and her husband Steve met with Mills to discuss Ms. Sawyer's bonus. Mr. Mills orally agreed to pay

Paralegal Practice and Ethics-Related Video Segments

Many of the segments present situations involving paralegal ethics, such as common UPL, confidentiality, conflict of interest, billing, and zealous representation issues.

Need More Coverage of Ethics in a Handy Supplemental Guide?

TOP 10 RULES OF ETHICS FOR PARALEGALS, SECOND EDITION
by Deborah Orlik

If more depth in dealing with ethical issues is desired, this handy guide can be packaged with the textbook at low cost.
(ISBN: 0-13-506393-0)

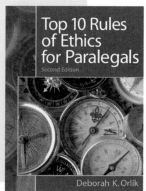

▶ ## THE PARALEGAL PROFESSIONAL COMPANION WEBSITE:

YOUR 24/7 STUDY AND RESOURCE SITE

At: www.pearsonhighered.com/goldman
Use this book-specific Website to prepare for tests, do online research, read full versions of cases discussed in the book, and view the video case studies discussed in your textbook.

- Learning Objectives
- Chapter Summary
- Key Term Flashcards
- Web Exercises
- Video Case Studies Online
- Full Case Versions of Cases in the Book
- Quizzes

▶ ## TOP 10 RULES OF ETHICS FOR PARALEGALS, SECOND EDITION

by Deborah Orlik

If more depth in dealing with ethical issues is desired, this handy guide can be packaged with the textbook at low cost. (ISBN: 0-13-506393-0)

▶ ## MOVIE GUIDE FOR LEGAL STUDIES, SECOND EDITION

by Kent Kauffman

This supplemental movie guide to 33 of the most popular movies that deal with legal issues can be packaged with *The Paralegal Professional*, Third Edition. It includes a synopsis of each movie with notes on key scenes and discussion questions that can be assigned or discussed in class. Teaching notes are included in the Instructor's Manual. (ISBN: 0-13-506375-2)

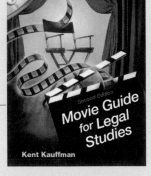

▶ ## PEARSON ENGLISH/SPANISH LEGAL DICTIONARY

by Antonio Figueroa, Norma C. Connolly

(2004, 464 pp., Paper) The approximately 1,200 terms presented in this book are up-to-date in their use and interpretation. They are easy to find, use, and correlate in both languages. (ISBN: 0-13-113738-7)

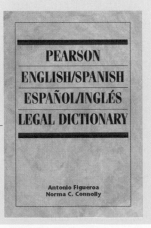

INSTRUCTOR'S MANUAL WITH TOOLKIT

FOR NEW INSTRUCTORS

The Instructor's Manual has been dramatically expanded to accommodate the needs of instructors with any level of experience. Whether you are a first-time instructor or an experienced hand, this manual contains a wealth of teaching materials:

- **New Instructor's Toolkit:**
    - Preparing for Class
    - *"First Day of Class"* Notes and PowerPoints

- **Sample Syllabi: 10-, 12-, 15-, 16-Week Courses with Templates on CD**
    - Weekly Assignments
    - Weekly Deadlines
    - Drop-Box Formatted Assignments also on CD

- **Using PowerPoint Quick Guide**

- **Using WebCT and BlackBoard Notes**

- **Transition Notes for Users of Miller 3e and Statsky 6e**

- By Chapter
    - **Chapter Outline**
    - **Teaching Notes**
    - **New! Law in the Movies Teaching Notes**
    - **New! Outcome Assessment Tools**

- ## TEST GENERATOR

    This computerized test generation system gives you maximum flexibility in preparing tests. You can create custom tests and print scrambled versions of a test at one time, as well as build tests randomly by chapter, level of difficulty, or question type. The software also allows online testing and record-keeping and the ability to add problems to the database.

- ## POWERPOINT LECTURE PRESENTATION PACKAGE

    Lecture Presentation screens for each chapter are available online and on the Instructor Resource CD.

- ## INSTRUCTOR RESOURCE CENTER

    The Instructor's Manual, Test Generator, and PPT Package can be downloaded from our Instructor Resource Center. To access supplementary materials online, instructors need to request an instructor access code. Go to www.pearsonhighered.com/irc, where you can register for an instructor access code. Within 48 hours of registering you will receive a confirming e-mail including an instructor access code. Once you have received your code, locate your text in the online catalog and click on the Instructor Resources button on the left side of the catalog product page. Select a supplement and a log-in page will appear. Once you have logged in, you can access instructor material for all Pearson textbooks.

- ## THE PARALEGAL PROFESSIONAL VIDEO CASE STUDIES ON DVD

    All video cases are available for in-class use on DVD free to adopters. Ask your local representative for more information or call 1-800-922-0579 (ISBN: 0-13-506610-7).

COMPLETE ONLINE COURSES: COURSECONNECT!

COURSECONNECT INTRODUCTION TO PARALEGAL STUDIES

ONLINE COURSES

Looking for robust online course content to reinforce and enhance your student learning? We have the solution: CourseConnect! CourseConnect courses contain customizable modules of content mapped to major learning outcomes. Each learning objective contains interactive tutorials, rich media, discussion questions, MP3 downloadable lectures, assessments, and interactive activities that address different learning styles. CourseConnect courses follow a consistent 21-step instructional design process, yet each course is developed individually by instructional designers and instructors who have taught the course online. Test questions, created by assessment professionals, were developed at all levels of Bloom's Taxonomy. When you buy a CourseConnect course, you purchase a complete package that provides you with detailed documentation you can use for your accreditation reviews. CourseConnect courses can be delivered in any commercial platform such as WebCT, BlackBoard, Angel, or eCollege.

TWO CHOICES IN COURSECONNECT COURSES

Introduction to Paralegal Studies (covers the first 3 parts of the textbook)
Introduction to Paralegal Studies and the Law (covers all 4 parts of the textbook)

For more information regarding which course and platform application is right for your school, please contact your representative or call 800-635-1579.

VERSUSLAW® ONLINE LEGAL RESEARCH ACCESS

Pearson Education has teamed-up with VersusLaw® to provide paralegal and legal studies students with online legal research access. One-semester subscription access code cards (ISBN: 0-13-118514-4) can be packaged with any Pearson Paralegal Studies title. The VersusLaw® subscription allows students to work from the dorm, home, library, or anywhere there is an Internet connection. Receive online access to archives and current opinions from the following courts:

- U.S. Supreme Court
- U.S. Circuit Court of Appeals
- Federal District Court
- State Appellate Court
- Tribal Courts
- Foreign Courts

ACKNOWLEDGMENTS

A round of applause to those whose insights contributed to the learning aspects of the book. Special thanks to:

Michael Fitch, for his guidance and encouragement early in the development of the project.

Kathryn Myers, for her generosity and kindness in allowing the use of material on portfolios and for the guidance she unknowingly gave by her example of enthusiasm, dedication, and hard work in support of paralegal education.

Lilian Harris for her constant encouragement and help in developing materials on family law and the needs of tireless paralegal program directors and faculty to teach students the real-world approach.

Richard Opie for sharing his ideas and materials.

Joy Smucker for her encouragement in developing soft skills materials.

Deborah Orlik for help in really understanding the ethics of the paralegal profession.

Bill Mulkeen for his encouragement and insights to the educational needs of students.

Don Swanson, an independent paralegal, for his expertise in the role of the paralegal in e-discovery and total dedication to help paralegal students by volunteering endless hours to help paralegal educators and authors with real-life experiences and paralegal educational needs.

Members of the AAfPE board who have shared ideas and material and offer guidance in developing the materials for this book to meet the needs of the paralegal student and faculty, including Pamela Bailey, Marissa Campbell, Christine Lissitzyn, Bob LeClair, Ed Husted, and Carolyn Smoot.

The inspiring panelists and speakers at the AAfPE annual and regional meetings over the past eleven years, who provided insights, guidance, suggestions, and encouragement.

To the officers and members of the local and national professional associations, including NALA, NFPA, NALS, and ALA, for allowing the use of materials but mostly for their suggestions regarding topics and real-life issues to be covered.

Paralegal Edie Hannah of Tom Goldman's law office, for tireless reviews, detail checking, encouragement and support, countless hours on the phone getting materials, and networking with other professionals to obtain comments and input to make this textbook relevant to working paralegals as well as to students preparing for the profession.

The students in Tom Goldman's classes, for testing the text and online materials in a class setting and graciously providing suggestions and feedback.

Vivi Wang, Tiffany Lee, and Ashley Anderson, Professor Henry Cheeseman's research assistants at the Marshall School of Business at the University of Southern California, for their excellent assistance in conducting legal and paralegal research for this book.

Finally, much gratitude to the reviewers of the second edition, whose thorough comments helped to complete this edition:

Hakim Ben Adjoua, Columbus State Community College
Laura C. Barnard, Lakeland Community College

Karen Betancourt, University of Texas at Brownsville and Texas Southmost College
Carol Brady, Milwaukee Area Tech—Milwaukee
Belinda Clifton, IIA College
Karen Cook, Anne Arundel Community College
Subrina Cooper, University of Southern Mississippi
Jennifer Cote, Madonna University
Brian Craig, Minnesota School of Business—Richfield
Steven A. Dayton, Fullerton College
Robert Donley, Central Pennsylvania College
Jameka Ellison, Florida Metro University—Lakeland
Linda Gassaway, McLennan Community College
Katherine Greenwood, Loyola University
Jennifer Jenkins, South College—Knoxville
Alan Katz, Cape Fear Community College
Elaine Lerner, Kaplan College—Online
Robert McDonald, Franciscan University
Alan Mege, LeHigh Valley College
Hillary Michaud, Stevenson University
Sharla Miller-Fowler, Amarillo College
Anne Murphy Brown, J.D., Ursuline College
Kathryn L. Myers, Saint Mary-of-the-Woods College
Lisa Newman, Brown Mackie College—Atlanta
Deborah Periman, University of Alaska-Anchorage
Beth Pless, Northeast Wisconsin Technical College
Pat Roberson, New Mexico Junior College
Labron Shuman, Delaware County Community College
Kathy Smith, Community College of Philadelphia

REVIEWERS OF THE FIRST EDITION

Mercedes P. Alonso-Knapp, Florida International University
Sue Armstrong, Central Washington University
Linda Cabral Marrero, Mercy College
Chelsea Campbell, Lehman College CUNY
Anderson Castro, Florida International University
Mark A. Ciccarelli, Kent State University, OH
Ernest Davila, San Jacinto College North, Texas
Stephanie Delaney, Highline Community College
Tara L. Duncan, Everest College, Phoenix, AZ
Katharine Greenwood, Loyola University
Louise B. Gussin, University of Maryland University College
Laura J. Hansen-Brown, Kaplan University, Florida
P. Darrel Harrison, Miramar College, San Diego, CA
Linda Hornsby, Florida International University
Dee Janssen Lammers, Pima Community College, Tucson, AZ
Pierre A. Kleff, Jr., The University of Texas at Brownsville
Nance Kriscenski, Manchester Community College
Victoria H. Lopez, Southwestern College, California
Margaret Lovig, Coastline Community College, California
Leslie Miron, Mercy College
R. Eileen Mitchell, University of New Orleans
Kathryn L. Myers, Saint Mary-of-the-Woods, IN
Mary People, Arapahoe Community College, Colorado

Anthony Piazza, Dan N. Myers University
Robin Rossenfeld, Community College of Aurora, Colorado
Wesley K. Sasano, Everest College—Rancho Cucamonga, California
Deborah Vinecour, SUNY Rockland Community College
Alex A. Yarborough, Virginia College at Birmingham

Thomas F. Goldman
Henry R. Cheeseman

The Paralegal Profession

The paralegal, or legal assistant, profession has seen explosive growth since the late 1960s. In recent years it has evolved into a profession that demands strong professional skills, a firm foundation in ethics, and increasingly higher degrees of knowledge including knowledge of technology applications. Opportunities and career choices for the paralegal have never been better. Possible employers are as diverse as the duties paralegals are asked to perform. Today's paralegals need specialized skills in many areas. Formal programs of study and continuing education programs have developed to help individuals obtain needed skills. As with other professions, ethical rules and regulations have evolved to help paralegals avoid conflicts and possible malpractice. These topics will be discussed in Part I.

The Paralegal Profession

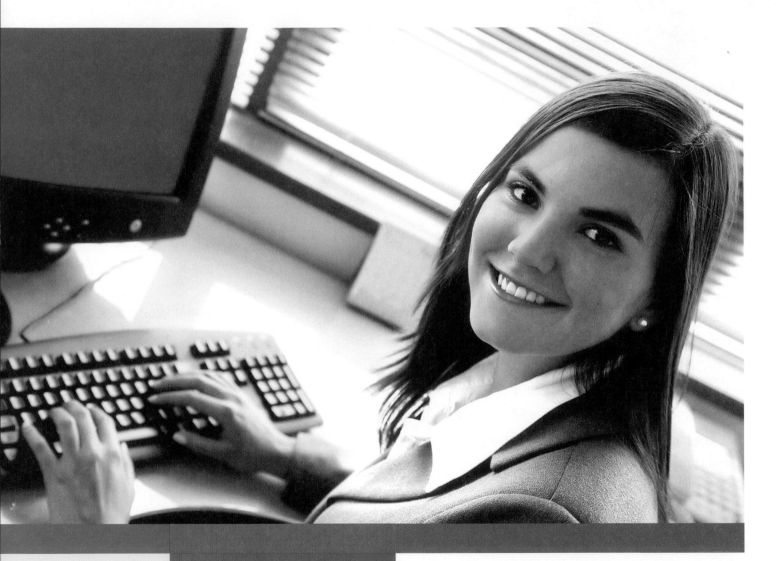

DIGITAL RESOURCES

Chapter 1 Digital Resources at *www.pearsonhighered.com/goldman*

- Video Case Studies:
  - When Friends Ask for Legal Advice
  - Resume Writing Do's and Don'ts
  - Independent Paralegal
- Chapter Summary • Web Links • Court Opinions • Glossary • Comprehension Quizzes
- Technology Resources

> " The great can protect themselves, but the poor and humble require the arm and shield of the law. "
>
> *Andrew Jackson*

Paralegals at Work

On the Friday before Thanksgiving, Ariel sits in the bleachers watching her high school alma mater, Lincoln High, take on Newtown. Ariel's brother, Ethan, is a linebacker on the football team and this is his last high school football game.

Ariel graduated from Lincoln in 1995 and went on to get her bachelor's degree with a major in English and a minor in Languages. She spots Mr. Marshall, her high school guidance counselor, and goes over to greet him.

As their conversation continues, Ariel asks Mr. Marshall about the career advice he's given to her brother. Ethan is thinking about a legal career but isn't interested in criminal justice or law enforcement. He's not sure about the time and dedication it takes to get through law school. Mr. Marshall gave Ethan information on local paralegal programs.

Ariel has been working as an editorial assistant for a small publisher of medical books. Although she always has plenty of work to do, she's not challenged in her job. She wants to use the language and writing skills she's developed, as well as have more autonomy and control over her work. Ariel asks Mr. Marshall whether a paralegal career makes sense for her.

Consider the issue involved in this scenario as you read the chapter.

INTRODUCTION TO THE PARALEGAL PROFESSION

Prior to the late 1960s, many of the functions of paralegals today were performed by those with titles such as legal secretary, lay assistant, and legal clerk or law clerk (the latter of which usually was reserved for the recent law school graduate who had not yet passed the bar exam). Members of the legal profession and the legal community increasingly see the paralegal as a member of the legal services delivery team. As paralegals' educational level increases, so will the responsibility given to them. In many areas of law, the cost of legal services has increased. The use of paralegals in many cases permits the delivery of quality legal services at a reduced cost to the client.

Opportunities and career choices for the paralegal have never been better. Paralegals are employed in every area of the delivery of legal services. They interview clients, conduct factual investigations, do legal research, prepare legal documents, assist at the counsel table in trials, and even represent clients in some administrative hearings. They are employed in law firms of all sizes, federal, state, and local government, insurance companies, and corporations.

What Is a Paralegal?

Paralegal (legal assistant)
A person qualified by education, training, or work experience who is employed or retained by a lawyer, law office, corporation, governmental agency, or other entity who performs specifically delegated substantive legal work for which a lawyer is responsible; equivalent term is legal assistant.

American Bar Association (ABA) Largest professional legal organization in the United States.

National Federation of Paralegal Associations (NFPA) Professional organization of state and local paralegal associations founded in 1974.

National Association of Legal Assistants (NALA) Professional organization for legal assistants that provides continuing education and professional certification for paralegals, incorporated in 1975.

A great deal of confusion has arisen as to what the professional in this field should be called or what the professionals should call themselves. The most popular terms, **paralegal** and **legal assistant,** have been used in most of the United States. These terms were used interchangeably by the **American Bar Association (ABA),** the **National Federation of Paralegal Associations (NFPA),** and the **National Association of Legal Assistants (NALA).** The confusion stems in part from the shift from the title of "secretary" to "administrative assistant" and, in some offices and educational institutions, "law office assistant."

The exact definition of legal assistant has been the subject of discussions by national organizations including the ABA, NFPA, and NALA, as well as many state legislatures, supreme courts, and bar associations. The trend is toward the use of the term *paralegal* and away from using the term *legal assistant*. Originally called the Standing Committee on Legal Assistants, the American Bar Association changed its name to the Standing Committee on Paralegals, in recognition of this trend.

The American Bar Association's 1997 version of the definition, which also has been adopted by the National Association of Legal Assistants, is:

> A legal assistant or paralegal is a person, qualified by education, training, or work experience who is employed or retained by a lawyer, law office, corporation, governmental agency or other entity and who performs specifically delegated substantive legal work for which a lawyer is responsible.

The National Federation of Paralegal Associations adopted a resolution in 2002 eliminating the term *legal assistant* from its definition of *paralegal* because that term now is being used to refer to positions outside the paralegal definition. Accordingly, NFPA defines a paralegal as follows:

> A paralegal is a person qualified through education, training or work experience to perform substantive legal work that requires knowledge of legal concepts as customarily, but not exclusively performed by a lawyer. This person may be retained or employed by a lawyer, law office, governmental agency or other entity or may be authorized by administrative, statutory or court authority to perform this work.

Web Exploration

Check the current definition approved by the American Bar Association at www.abanet.org.

Web Exploration

Review the full NFPA resolution at www.paralegals.org.

What Do Paralegals Do?

The primary function of paralegals is to assist attorneys in preparing for hearings, trials, meetings, and real estate closings. In many cases paralegals do the preparatory work, helping to draft documents, assisting in the preparation of other documents and

Paralegals *in* Practice

PARALEGAL PROFILE
Vicki L. Karayan

During her 12-year paralegal career, Vicki L. Karayan has worked for both law firms and business corporations. She is currently employed in Camarillo, California, at WellPoint, Inc., the nation's second largest company in the health care industry. As an Advanced Certified Paralegal, her present position of Business Change Advisor focuses on compliance reporting and legal research for the company's consumer marketing department.

I became inspired to pursue a paralegal career after going through a difficult, personal legal battle. After graduating with an Associate's degree in Applied Science with a Legal Studies emphasis, I worked in a general practice firm. Later, I worked for a bankruptcy law firm where I eventually became the trainer/staff manager of seven offices. A family move led to a new job in a nationwide bankruptcy firm where I learned to track federal and state regulatory requirements.

In order to work closer to home, I took an Administrative Assistant position in the Medicaid Marketing department for a corporate health care company. What started as an entry level job grew into a whole new position, as I offered better ways to tackle the company's market compliance reporting and legal research, and also helped improve office efficiency and staff training. Three promotions later, I believe I owe much of my career success to actively looking for opportunities to apply knowledge and skills learned from previous jobs and experiences, and from learning how to network with people, building strong working relationships based on ethical practices.

My advice is: try not to limit yourself to traditional paralegal job descriptions. Some of the best opportunities are found by looking "outside the box" and obtaining as many business and technology skills as possible. Finally, find what you love to do, and then network by making new business connections through individuals you already know and others you meet. These contacts can help your work go more smoothly and provide invaluable information in the future.

forms, coordinating the activities and functions required in some cases, and in many offices maintaining the financial records of the firm.

People tend to think of paralegals as working in a private law office directly under the supervision of attorneys. Actually, employers of the paralegal are just as diverse as the duties they are asked to perform. Many paralegals are employed by the federal government, as well as state and local governments including regulatory bodies. The paralegal's activities might include analyzing legal material for internal use and collecting and analyzing data, as well as preparing information and explanatory material, for use by the general public.

More and more paralegals are coming to the profession from other professions. For example, they may come from nursing, bringing with them a specialized body of knowledge that they combine with the legal skills they learned in a paralegal program. With this expertise they frequently are hired to analyze case materials for trial attorneys, both plaintiff and defense, and also are employed as case analysts and as claims representatives for health insurance companies. Their knowledge of medicine, combined with their legal knowledge, gives them a unique ability to analyze specialized material.

Other specialties can take the same career path. Those with engineering and other Bachelor of Science degrees bring specialized expertise to the law, such as patent and intellectual property law. A paralegal with a criminal justice or a forensic science background, for example, may well be the ideal paralegal to work with criminal defense attorneys and prosecutors.

Prior to the recognition of a separate paralegal profession, individuals typically had acquired specialized knowledge of a narrow legal field through on-the-job training. Someone working with a lawyer—usually a secretary—learned the daily routine tasks and become knowledgeable about that specific area of law. Many of these individuals became resource sources of information, such as the documentation requirements for real estate settlements, the preparation and filing of estate and trust accountings, and the procedures for preparing and filing cases and appeals. These were the first paralegals. Today, many of the skills and procedures formerly acquired over an

Web Exploration

Review the Model Standards and Guidelines of the National Association of Legal Assistants at http://www.nala.org/stand.htm.

Advice *from the* Field

Kathleen Call is executive director of Robert Half Legal, a leading staffing service specializing in the placement of legal professionals ranging from project attorneys and paralegals to administrators, legal secretaries and other support staff. Robert Half Legal, which works with law firms and corporate legal departments, has offices throughout the United States and Canada.

When you think of which skills will be most important to your career advancement over the next five years, chances are "proficiency with technology" ranks high on your list. Knowledge of key software applications has become a critical success factor in the legal profession. However, to be considered for the best job opportunities in the future, you'll not only need technical competency, but also solid interpersonal skills and problem-solving abilities.

Audio- and video-conferencing, email, corporate Intranets and, of course, the Internet have increased exponentially the amount—and speed—of day-to-day professional communication. The expanded use of technology will make it more important for legal professionals to be able to communicate effectively and articulately.

Another significant development driving the need for strong soft skills is the trend toward a more collaborative workplace. In a team-based office environment, diplomacy, flexibility, persuasiveness and management skills are critical. In a survey we commissioned among executives at the nation's 1,000 largest companies, 79 percent of respondents said self-managed employee work teams will increase productivity for U.S. companies. These productivity gains will only be realized, however, if team members can work together effectively. As a result, firms are placing a premium on excellent interpersonal skills.

WHAT ARE PEOPLE SKILLS?

Since soft skills are intangible and therefore hard to quantify, how do you determine whether you have what it takes to succeed? Our firm has identified a composite of key interpersonal traits represented by the acronym "PEOPLE":

Problem-solving abilities (organization, judgment, logic, creativity, conflict resolution)

Ethics (diplomacy, courtesy, honesty, professionalism)

Open-mindedness (flexibility, open to new business ideas, positive outlook)

Persuasiveness (excellent communication and listening skills)

Leadership (accountability, management and motivational skills)

Educational interests (continuous thirst for knowledge and skills development)

A deficiency in these skills can seriously limit your career prospects, whether you're applying for a new job as a legal assistant or seeking to move upward as an attorney within your current firm. Just as workers who failed to enhance their technical skills were left behind by the digital revolution, those who dismiss the significance of PEOPLE skills can find themselves stagnating in dead-end jobs.

ASSESS YOUR STRENGTHS AND WEAKNESSES

While it's relatively easy to measure the development of your proficiency with technology, it's much more challenging to gauge your progress in enhancing your PEOPLE skills. Again, this is primarily because these qualities are more subjective in nature. Since there are no classes on "flexibility" or "positive outlook" at the typical college or university, how do you acquire and upgrade your interpersonal abilities?

The following steps will help you take an accurate inventory of your strengths and weaknesses:

Honestly evaluate your aptitude in each of the PEOPLE skills. Which seem to come naturally? Is there room for improvement in any area?

Ask trusted friends, family members and coworkers for their opinions. How would they rate your PEOPLE skills?

COMMIT TO LEARNING

It takes time and experience to fully develop interpersonal skills, so don't expect to see improvement overnight. Here are some effective strategies to help you continue your progress:

Develop a list of the characteristics you'd most like to develop in yourself. Then brainstorm specific activities that will boost your abilities in your selected areas. For example, if you'd like to refine your leadership skills, volunteer to work on cases that provide the opportunity to supervise others or manage a project from start to finish.

Observe those who demonstrate strong PEOPLE skills in the areas you'd like to improve. How do they apply their abilities in various situations? How are their responses different than what yours would be?

Select a mentor. The best candidate is someone in the legal field whom you admire. Ask your prospective mentor if he or she would advise you, particularly in those PEOPLE skills that you've determined require enhancement. Since it's difficult to see yourself objectively, a mentor's ongoing support and feedback can be invaluable.

Enhance your listening skills. Concentrate on paying close attention to what others are saying. In general, avoid interrupting but ask for clarification when necessary. To prevent misunderstandings, paraphrase information in your own words when you are given complex instructions.

Become a better writer. Read books on effective writing so that you can develop a more concise style, or consider taking a journalism or business writing course. Proofread everything you write, especially e-mail. Because electronic messages are prepared and sent quickly, they can be inadvertently filled with typographical and grammatical errors. In addition, it's important to employ PEOPLE skills in your writing, explaining yourself diplomatically and courteously.

Refine your verbal communication. Know what you want to say before you speak, and use a tone and style appropriate to the audience. When leaving a voice-mail message, organize your thoughts in advance to avoid being vague or rambling. If you're presenting a report to an attorney or client, rehearse a few times so your delivery will be smooth and your message clear.

Become a volunteer. You can acquire stronger leadership and organizational skills through volunteer work. Whether it's becoming involved in a trade association or helping your favorite charity, the skills you develop can be used on the job in a variety of situations.

Seek growth opportunities outside the workplace. Hobbies and leisure-time activities are an enjoyable way to enrich your PEOPLE skills. By coaching your child's soccer team, for example, you'll develop motivational and managerial skills, and become better at dealing with diverse personalities. If you'd like to enhance your creativity, consider taking an art or music class.

extended time on the job are taught at institutions specializing in the education of paralegals or legal assistants, offering a certificate program, a two-year associate degree program, or a four-year bachelor's degree program.

In 1968 the American Bar Association formed a committee to investigate the use of lay assistants in the legal office. The result was the American Bar Association's forming the Standing Committee on Legal Assistants, later changed to Standing Committee on Paralegals. The ABA gave this committee jurisdiction over training and standards for the education of legal assistants. Within this jurisdiction the Standing Committee on Paralegals monitors trends in the field and recommends to the House of Delegates—the policymaking body of the American Bar Association—training programs that meet its standards for quality education.

Professional Skills

The skills needed by a paralegal are varied and depend, in some cases, on the nature of the legal specialty in which one works. Common to all paralegals are certain professional skills, also known as soft skills, including communication skills, initiative, resourcefulness, problem solving, commitment or "stick-to-itiveness," team working, leadership, and self-motivation, among others.

Everyone has goals in life. You might be an accomplished jogger who longs to win the Boston Marathon, or a skilled writer who has visions of writing the great American novel. Achieving most goals requires some set of skills. If your goal is to be a successful paralegal, you will need certain basic skills. You may possess some of these already, and may need to acquire others. Some of the basic skills you already have are:

- the ability to read English—unless someone is reading this book to you
- the ability to communicate at some level in writing or speaking
- initiative—because you have signed up for this course or have picked up this book to read and learn about the paralegal profession

In addition, you may have skills such as

- facility with computers and the Internet
- the ability to speak a second or third language
- a background in medicine, engineering, business, or other academic or occupational area

Some other skills are less obvious—resourcefulness, commitment or stick-to-itiveness, analytical skills and interpersonal skills including cultural sensitivity—so we will explore them in more depth. We cannot all run a marathon or type 160 words a minute, but we all can acquire most of the basic skills by making an effort to improve ourselves and attain the knowledge base to achieve most, if not all, of our goals.

Many people achieve much more than they, themselves, and others believed they were capable of achieving—by just plain hard work. If you want something bad enough and are willing to work hard enough, you can achieve your personal and professional goals. A good starting point in achieving your goals is to understand your strengths and weaknesses, capitalize on the strengths, and work on improving the weaknesses.

NATIONAL ASSOCIATION OF LEGAL ASSISTANTS MODEL STANDARDS AND GUIDELINES FOR UTILIZATION OF LEGAL ASSISTANTS PARALEGALS

Preamble

Proper utilization of the services of legal assistants contributes to the delivery of cost effective, high-quality legal services. Legal assistants and the legal profession should be assured that measures exist for identifying legal assistants and their role in assisting attorneys in the delivery of legal services. Therefore, the National Association of Legal Assistants, Inc., hereby adopts these Standards and Guidelines as an educational document for the benefit of legal assistants and the legal profession. . . .

III Standards

A legal assistant should meet certain minimum qualifications. The following standards may be used to determine an individual's qualifications as a legal assistant:

(1) Successful completion of the Certified Legal Assistant (CLA)/Certified Paralegal (CP) certifying examination of the National Association of Legal Assistants, Inc.;

(2) Graduation from an ABA approved program of study for legal assistants;

(3) Graduation from a course of study for legal assistants which is institutionally accredited but not ABA approved, and which requires not less than the equivalent of 60 semester hours of classroom study;

(4) Graduation from a course of study for legal assistants, other than those set forth in (2) and (3) above, plus not less than six months of in-house training as a legal assistant;

(5) A baccalaureate degree in any field, plus not less than six months in-house training as a legal assistant;

(6) A minimum of three years of law-related experience under the supervision of an attorney, including at least six months of in-house training as a legal assistant; or

(7) Two years of in-house training as a legal assistant.

For purposes of these Standards, "in-house training as a legal assistant" means attorney education of the employee concerning legal assistant duties and these Guidelines. In addition to review and analysis of assignments, the legal assistant should receive a reasonable amount of instruction directly related to the duties and obligations of the legal assistant.

SOURCE: Copyright 1984, adopted 1984; revised 1991, 1997, 2005. Reprinted with permission of the National Association of Legal Assistants, www.nala.org, 1516 S. Boston, #200, Tulsa, OK 74119.

CHECKLIST Strengths and Weaknesses

- ☐ My strengths:
- ☐ How can I capitalize on my strengths?
- ☐ My weaknesses:
- ☐ How can I overcome my weaknesses?

Resourcefulness

Resourcefulness is the ability to meet and handle a situation and find solutions to problems. It is one of the most valuable skills anyone can have—and one that is not easily taught. A resourceful person in the office is sometimes referred to as the "can-do" person on the team. This is the person who usually finds some creative way to accomplish what everyone else has given up on. Certainly, creativity is involved— solving the problem by thinking outside the box and not limiting the solution to tried-and-true methods.

The skill of organizing includes the ability to

- categorize
- prioritize
- organize
- utilize time efficiently

When everyone else says, "I can't find this witness," the resourceful person tries a new approach and finds the witness. When others use only the standard telephone directories, the resourceful person uses the cross-reference directory. When local telephone directories do not yield results, resourceful people use the national telephone directories on CD and the online Internet telephone directories.

In the legal workplace the person who gets noticed is the one who finds a way to get the job done in time for the hearing, meeting, or arbitration. This is the person who is willing to use unconventional ways to get the job finished, such as when the power goes out or the computer system crashes just before a deadline. Lawyers want resourceful people on their team and reward them to keep them on the team.

Commitment

Commitment means finishing what one starts out to do or complete. From our childhood we remember the story of the tortoise and the hare (rabbit), in which the tortoise wins the race by being "slow and steady." The tortoise wins in part because of commitment—putting everything into the race and not stopping until the job is done. Many people start jobs and don't finish them. Others start what seems to be an insurmountable task and—to their amazement and maybe ours—finish, and finish well. Taking on an assignment in a law office requires commitment. Team members are expected to finish the task, whether it is researching a case, writing a brief, filing a pleading, or organizing a file.

As a professional, you are expected to finish the tasks within the assigned timeframe. There is no excuse for not doing some tasks, such as filing the complaint with the court before the statute of limitations expires, or getting the brief to the court by the court-imposed deadline. Even a simple thing like getting to court on time requires commitment.

Not everyone has the necessary commitment or wants to take on the responsibility of meeting commitments. You have to decide whether you are willing to make the commitment. Others will be depending on you, and if you do not want to commit, admit it to yourself and to the others who are depending on you, and then choose some other activity or profession. Choosing a profession, whether it is the legal profession, the paralegal profession, the medical profession, or the accounting profession, requires a commitment to serve others. As a professional, you are making a commitment to your clients that you will provide the best professional advice, skill, and effort. They depend on this professionalism and the necessary commitment.

Analytical Skills

Analytical skills allow one to follow a step-by-step process to solve a problem. It could be finding a missing witness by looking in telephone books, or determining that the person is part of a group, such as a professional society or an organization that publishes a membership directory. Solving these types of problems requires analytical skills to figure out, for instance, what made a bottle explode, injuring a client. Determining the actual cause requires a step-by-step analysis of the potential reasons and the narrowing down of possible causes.

CREATING AN IMPRESSION

Unless you are intentionally trying to create a different impression, try to

- have a positive attitude
- be diplomatic
- be flexible
- establish good rapport with others
- be a team player
- be resourceful
- be adaptable
- be thorough

One of the basic skills that law students and paralegal students are taught is legal analysis, the ability to identify the facts and legal issues and contrast and compare them to the law and to other cases. This is a skill that develops with time. As you learn the elements of crimes, torts, and other areas of law, you will learn the individual parts of each. In contracts law, you will learn what conduct is a valid acceptance of a contract offer, and in tort law, what constitutes reasonable conduct under the circumstances.

Interpersonal Skills

Vital to paralegal success, as well as to success in other endeavors, is the ability to work with people. To categorize people, coworkers, colleagues, and employers might be unfair, but we all do it. We think—and sometimes say—things like, "He's a pleasure to work with" or, "She has clients eating out of her hand." Conversely, we might say things like, "She's the most negative person I know," or "He's only out for himself." These comments reflect the other person's interpersonal skills (or lack thereof), the ability to work with and communicate with others.

How we relate to others can make the job easier or harder. These others include not just coworkers as members of the legal team but also clients, witnesses, and opposing parties. Obviously, everyone in the firm or on the team must have a level of trust and confidence in the others on the team. People who have a good working relationship accomplish more and enjoy doing it. By contrast, conflict and tension make the job harder and can cause people to take shortcuts and avoid contact, which can result in poor performance and potential malpractice.

Not everyone has the personality to deal with every type of situation and every type of personality—for example, dealing with clients. But everyone on the legal team has to develop the skills to work with people and recognize when they may have to have someone else handle certain aspects of a case or client. The skill is in recognizing when and how they can affect relationships and results. Some might call this "sensitivity"— to other people's needs, desires, wants, likes, and dislikes.

Cultural differences are discussed later, but in the American culture, for example, people tend to be sensitive to odors—breath, body, environmental. We do not want to offend. Our use of language is another area of sensitivity. We try to avoid using words that we believe will offend the other person in a specific circumstance, such as telling off-color jokes in a religious setting in front of a person of the cloth.

The starting point in working with attorneys, paralegals, and support staff, clients and opposing counsel, court personnel and others, is to be sensitive to issues such as these. What offends you probably offends others. Being sensitive to how others react to your words, conduct, and actions can provide good clues as to what is acceptable and what is not.

In the past, how we related to others and how others perceived us was measured by direct face-to-face contact, telephone contact, and written communications. Today we have to add to those forms of communication the way we write emails and use electronic communications. These technological advances make our communications more immediate. Too many happy faces and frowning faces, such as:) or :(in an email could be interpreted as overfamiliarity. THE USE OF ALL CAPITAL LETTERS might be interpreted as shouting at the reader. Poor spelling and bad grammar in emails are likely to be seen as less than professional or pure sloppiness or carelessness. In the past, letters were dictated, typed, proofread, and then signed. Today we dash off an email without much thought—and sometimes it reflects just that. How our clients view our capabilities and skill now might be measured by that quick email response.

Communication Skills

Communication means expressing ideas effectively. The practice of law requires good communication, both oral and written. The lawyer and the paralegal who work together must be able to communicate assignments and information with clarity and, frequently, brevity. Over time, communication will improve, as each person comes to understand what the other is really asking or saying.

Communication is made complex by subtleties, nuances, and expressions that may require interpretation or explanation. For example, older attorneys who are used to using traditional methods of research may ask the new paralegal (who has a deep understanding of computer research methods and little traditional book experience) to "check the pocket parts." This means checking for the latest update or change to a statute or case law. Or asking a paralegal to "Shepardize" a case may have no meaning to one who has learned only the West system, in which the method for checking other cases is called KeyCiting, or the Loislaw system, which refers to this as GlobalCiting.

Communication can be a major problem in the fast-paced office when the litigation attorney sends a message from court in the middle of a case to the support paralegal at the office, by a two-way pager, after the other side has brought up an unexpected case in argument to the court. Nowadays, we rarely have the luxury of time to develop a common written and oral language base for communication among the paralegal, clients, opposing attorneys, and court personnel. Letters, pleadings, contracts, and other written documents must be clear and accurate. In many situations, only one document must carefully communicate the idea, request, or demand.

Oral communication also must be clear and precise. The old adage still holds true: First impressions matter. If a first discussion in person or by telephone is filled with slang and poor grammar, the impression may affect the client's or court's view of the firm's professionalism, ability, and legal skills. It can influence the client's decision to stay with the firm or not, the judge's granting the request, or the court clerk's giving you the help you need.

Career Planning

Career planning should include educational planning and a plan for perfecting professional skills. A sound educational plan builds on a sound foundation, at the base of which are general education courses that will assist in any occupational choice and are acceptable in meeting basic core requirements either for an associate's degree or a bachelor's degree. Occupation-related courses such as paralegal specialty courses should be selected with an eye toward transferability and suitability in a higher-level educational pursuit.

This is not to say that all courses must be transferable from school to school or from associate-degree program to bachelor's- or master's-degree program. Something can be learned from every course you take, including the realization that you do not wish to pursue this area of study further. Think of the people you know who have pursued a career only to discover later that they are not interested in this line of work. One of your early educational goals should be to explore areas of your actual or potential interest. Many students even find a career goal after taking one of the dreaded required courses.

Therefore, you should be prepared to explore new areas of specialty and new technology. It is clearer today than ever that successful paralegals have a good foundation in computer skills. Further, you will have to maintain and build upon these skills as ever more sophisticated online service and resources continues.

COMMUNICATION SKILLS

Do I:

- read with comprehension?
- listen effectively and accurately and interpret nonverbal communication?
- write in clear, concise, and grammatically correct English?
- speak in clear, concise, and grammatically correct English?
- use language to persuade?
- tailor the nature of the communication to maximize understanding in the intended audience, including people with different levels of education and different cultural backgrounds?

Source: American Association for Paralegal Education

SIDEBAR

Web Exploration

Check the available resources for paralegal students at the different national paralegal organizations:

National Federation of Paralegal Associations
http://www.paralegals.org

National Association of Legal Assistants
http://www.nala.org

Association of Legal Administrators
http://www.alanet.org

International Paralegal Management Association
http://www.paralegal management.org/ipma/

NALS.... the Association for Legal Professionals
http://www.nals.org

CHECKLIST My Career Roadmap

- ☐ Skills I need to acquire:
- ☐ Skills I need to strengthen:
- ☐ Courses I should take:
- ☐ Extracurricular activities for the resume:

- ☐ Interim work experience I should seek:
- ☐ Volunteer activities:
- ☐ Short-term career goals:
- ☐ Long-term career goals:

Paralegal Education in the United States

According to the Department of Labor, occupations requiring a postsecondary vocational award or an academic degree accounted for 25 percent of all jobs in 1998, 29 percent of all jobs in 2000, and will account for 42 percent of total job growth from 2000 to 2010.

The best trained, most skilled individual clearly will be the one to get the job. The challenge in obtaining your first job is to demonstrate that you are the best person for the job. Consider the prospective employer comparing the resumes of a number of paralegal job applicants. One paralegal has a high school diploma and a paralegal certificate. Another applicant has an associate degree or even a bachelor's degree in paralegal studies. Which would you hire?

An estimated 1000 paralegal education programs are available in the United States. These programs are offered in on-site, online, and hybrid format combining online and on-site instruction. Some of these programs have obtained ABA approval of their paralegal education program. Many of the institutions offering these programs are members of the American Association for Paralegal Education (AAfPE), which, as a condition of institutional membership, requires substantial compliance with the ABA guidelines for approval of a paralegal program.

What are the qualifications that permit one to call oneself a paralegal or a legal assistant, and to be billed as a paralegal? The answer is not easy to come by. Just as the practice of law falls to the individual states for regulation, so does regulation of the paralegal profession. Presently regulations lack uniformity, either by statute or by court rules. Without a state law such as the California Statute shown in Exhibit 1.2 on page 23 or a court rule, perhaps the most consistent and universal recognition of minimum qualifications are those established by the educational guidelines of the American Bar Association's Standing Committee on Paralegals and the **American Association for Paralegal Education (AAfPE),** a national association of legal educators. The minimum educational requirements for certification of the educational institutions' program of study have become the de facto standard of the minimum qualifications to call one a paralegal or legal assistant.

The ABA Standing Committee Guidelines require that instruction be at the postsecondary level and contain at least 60 semester hours including general educational and legal specialty courses. Of these 60 hours, at least 18 must be general education courses and at least 18 must be legal specialty courses.

For purposes of the Guidelines, a "legal specialty course" is interpreted in Guideline G-303(c)d as a course (1) in a specific area of law, procedure, or legal process, (2) which has been developed for legal assistants and emphasizes legal assistant skills, forms, documents, procedures, and legal principles and theories, and (3) which is pertinent to the legal assistants' performance of a job.

The American Bar Association and the American Association for Paralegal Education are voluntary programs. As stated by the ABA,

> Seeking approval from the American Bar Association is a voluntary process initiated by the institution offering the program. Therefore, the lack of approval does not necessarily mean a paralegal program is not of good quality and reputable.

The majority of programs may have chosen not to undergo the cost or process for approval by the ABA or for membership in the AAfPE, or offer a majority of courses in online or hybrid format that do not meet the ABA guidelines, which limit the number of such courses that may be offered as part of the program of study.

Types of Educational Programs

The goal of the educational experience is to get a job and be able to perform at a professional level. The demands on paralegals today require them to have higher-level skills and ability than in the past. Whereas basic typing, office, and business communications skills might have been acceptable for a starting position in a law firm

American Association for Paralegal Education (AAfPE) National organization of paralegal educators and institutions offering paralegal education programs.

RELEVANT PARALEGAL SKILLS

Skill Development

- Critical thinking skills
- Organizational skills
- General communication skills
- Interpersonal skills
- Legal research skills
- Legal writing skills
- Computer skills
- Interviewing and investigation skills

Acquisition of Knowledge

- Organization and operation of the legal system
- Organization and operation of law offices
- The paralegal profession and ethical obligations
- Contracts
- Torts
- Business organizations
- Litigation procedures

twenty years ago, these are not the skills demanded for those looking for a paralegal position today.

More and more employers today also are asking for transcripts showing the courses taken and the minimum number of hours of study as spelled out in the ABA guidelines, even for graduates of educational institutions that have not obtained ABA certification of their programs. The reality is that many attorneys do not know the educational requirements to obtain a paralegal degree or certificate. And in many cases they do not know the elements of the ABA, NFPA, or NALA definitions of paralegal or legal assistant.

Paralegal/legal assistant educational programs generally fall into two categories: (a) those offering a certificate, and (b) those offering a degree, either an **associate's degree** or a **bachelor's degree.** These programs of study may be offered by a two-year community college or junior college or a four-year college or university. A number of business and private **(proprietary)** schools also offer paralegal/legal assistant programs of study.

Students' educational and professional backgrounds will determine, in many cases, which of the programs to select. Those with bachelor's and higher academic degrees may need only the legal specialty courses. Those who come from a specialty background, such as nursing or one heavy in science courses, may want to broaden their education by taking courses of a general nature in addition to the legal specialty courses.

Certificate Programs

Most educational institutions with paralegal/legal assistant programs, both public and private, offer a certificate. The **certificate** recognizes completion of a program of study that requires less than is required to receive a degree. Some certificates award college credits; some do not. For students who already possess a baccalaureate degree, obtaining additional college credits probably isn't an issue. For students without an undergraduate degree, programs that do not offer college credit still can be valuable but should be considered carefully. At the very least, the actual time spent in the classroom should be equivalent to the minimums of college credit courses.

Students' concerns should be for what is acceptable in the community in which they intend to work. Those planning to transfer should consider the acceptability of the course for transferring credit to another credit-granting institution. Even if they have no immediate intent to continue in school, they would be wise to plan ahead and not lose the hours and credits they have earned, in the event they later decide to transfer or go on to obtain a degree.

Many professional paralegal organizations are reporting that a bachelor's degree is becoming more necessary to enter the paralegal field and some programs. The U.S. Attorney's Office, for example, is requiring at least a four-year degree to consider individuals for a paralegal position.

Associate's degree A college degree in science (AS) arts (AA), or applied arts (AAS), generally requiring two years of full-time study.

Bachelor's degree A college degree generally requiring four years of full-time study.

Proprietary school Private, as opposed to public, institution, generally for profit, offering training and education.

Certificate A recognition of the completion of a program of study that requires less than that needed for a degree.

Associate Degree Programs

Many community colleges and junior colleges offer an associate degree in science (AS degree) or in arts (AA degree) or applied arts (AAS degree) in paralegal or legal assistant studies. For many students the two-year community college or junior college programs offer a community-based transition into higher education. For others it is a way of getting back into higher education while working at a full-time job or after being in another occupation.

Support services for returning students or students who need additional help are often available. Many of these schools offer English courses for those for whom English is a second language and those returning to school who need a refresher course or help with study skills after years away from school. This also tends to be a cost-effective educational environment for trying different areas of study before finding an area of concentration.

Baccalaureate Programs

Web Exploration

IPMA Position Paper is available at www.paralegalmanagement
.org/ipmadocs/education%
20position%20paper.pdf.

Some of the earliest paralegal programs were built on a model in which a bachelor's degree was the prerequisite for entering the paralegal program of study. A number of programs now offer a bachelor's degree in paralegal studies. One national organization—the International Paralegal Management Association (IPMA)—has recommended the bachelor's degree as the minimum qualification to enter the profession. The increase in professional recognition of paralegals has resulted in their gaining more responsibility, as well as a growing demand for the skills required to perform the assigned tasks. As the standing of the paralegal on the legal team rises, so will the demand for those with a broad-based educational background to serve in those positions. Four-year programs of study are attempting to meet that demand by merging traditional four-year study core requirements and legal specialty courses.

Consider the family law attorney or paralegal. In the frequently highly charged emotional environment of custody and divorce, knowledge of family and child psychology is essential. For those in an intellectual-property practice, an understanding of science and engineering is a basic requirement. The four-year timeframe allows more flexibility to explore and build skills and knowledge, as well as to meet the increasing demand for more education for paralegals.

Graduate Programs

A few colleges and universities now offer graduate degrees in legal studies. Others offer advanced degrees in related areas such as legal administration.

Specialty Certificates

Specialty certificates, such as the paralegal certificate or the legal nurse consultant certificate, offer an excellent entry point into a paralegal career. Specialty certificates combined with degrees in other fields of study, such as nursing, journalism, and computer science, are like a capstone program preparing a person for entry into a new career. One of the greatest demands has been for those with a background in nursing combined with a paralegal education. A growing number of colleges are offering a certificate in Legal Nurse Consulting.

Paralegal Advanced Competency Exam (PACE) National Federation of Paralegal Association's certification program that requires the paralegal to have two years of experience and a bachelor's degree and have completed a paralegal course at an accredited school.

Paralegal Certification

The National Federation of Paralegal Associations (NFPA) administers an exam to test the competency level of experienced paralegals known as **Paralegal Advance Competency Exam (PACE),** which requires that:

> . . . the paralegal cannot have been convicted of a felony nor be under suspension, termination, or revocation of a certificate, registration, or license by any entity.

- An associates degree in paralegal studies obtained from an institutionally accredited and/or ABA approved paralegal education program; and six (6) years substantive paralegal experience; OR
- A bachelor's degree in any course of study obtained from an institutionally accredited school and three (3) years of substantive paralegal experience; OR
- A bachelor's degree and completion of a paralegal program with an institutionally accredited school; said paralegal program may be embodied in a bachelor's degree; and two (2) years substantive paralegal experience; OR
- four (4) years substantive paralegal experience on or before December 31, 2000.

Those who successfully pass the exam may use the designation "PACE-Registered Paralegal, or RP." Continued use of the designation requires 12 additional hours of continuing legal or specialty education every 2 years, with at least one hour of legal ethics.

Since 1976, the National Association of Legal Assistants has conferred the **Certified Legal Assistant (CLA)** designation on those who pass its national certification program's two-day comprehensive examination. In 2004, NALA registered the certification mark CP with the U.S. Patent and Trademark Office for those who prefer the term Certified Paralegal. To be eligible to take the exam requires the following.

1. Graduation from a legal assistant program that is:
   - approved by the American Bar Association; or
   - an associate degree program; or
   - a post-baccalaureate certificate program in legal assistant studies; or
   - a bachelor's degree program in legal assistant studies; or
   - a legal assistant program which consists of a minimum of 60 semester hours (900 clock hours or 90 quarter hours) of which at least 15 semester hours (225 clock hours or 22.5 quarter hours) are substantive legal courses.
2. A bachelor's degree in any field plus one year's experience as a legal assistant. Successful completion of at least 15 semester hours (or 22.5 quarter hours or 225 clock hours) of substantive legal assistant courses will be considered equivalent to one year's experience as a legal assistant.
3. A high school diploma or equivalent plus seven (7) year's experience as a legal assistant under the supervision of a member of the Bar, plus evidence of a minimum of twenty (20) hours of continuing legal education credit to have been completed within a two (2) year period prior to the examination date.

To maintain use of the CLA designation, evidence must be submitted of completion of 50 hours of continuing legal assistant education every five years. For those who have achieved the initial designation, NALA also offers specialist credentials for those practicing in a specific area of law, such as bankruptcy, intellectual property, civil litigation, probate, and estate planning. Successful completion of these examinations permits the additional designation CLAS, Certified Legal Assistant–Specialty.

NALS offers members and nonmembers the opportunity to sit for three unique certifications dedicated to the legal services profession—ALS, PLS, and PP. The exams are of varying levels and are developed by professionals in the industry.

1. **ALS**—the basic certification for legal professionals exam—covers:
   Part 1: Written Communications
   Part 2: Office Procedures and Legal Knowledge
   Part 3: Ethics, Human Relations, and Judgment
2. **PLS**—the advanced certification for legal professionals exam—covers:
   Part 1: Written Communications
   Part 2: Office Procedures and Technology
   Part 3: Ethics and Judgment
   Part 4: Legal Knowledge and Skills

Web Exploration

Detailed information on PACE can be obtained at http://www .paralegals.org/displaycommon .cfm?an517.

Certified Legal Assistant (CLA) Designation by National Association of Legal Assistants for those who take and pass NALA certification program two-day comprehensive examination.

Web Exploration

General information about paralegal certification, including requirements, exam subjects, and testing schedule can be found at http://www.nala .org/cert.htm.

ALS (Accredited Legal Secretary) The basic certification for legal professionals from NALS.

PLS (Professional Legal Secretary) The advanced certification for legal professionals from NALS.

3. **PP** (Professional Paralegal)—professionals performing paralegal duties. Examination eligibility requires five years' experience performing paralegal/legal assistant duties (a candidate may receive a partial waiver of one year if he or she has a postsecondary degree, other certification, or a paralegal certificate; a candidate with a paralegal degree may receive a two-year partial waiver). The exam covers:

Part 1: Written Communications
Part 2: Legal Knowledge and Skills
Part 3: Ethics and Judgment Skills
Part 4: Substantive Law

A comparison of the various exams—NALS, NALA, and NFPA—is presented in Exhibit 1.1

Minimum Education

The **International Paralegal Management Association (IPMA)** is an organization for paralegal management professionals. In its position paper on paralegal education it states that "nearly 80% of IPMA member organizations require the bachelor's degree when hiring, and many require specific paralegal education and/or give credit for professional certifications."

Legal assistants have assumed many responsibilities formerly handled by lawyers. Working with complex legal issues requires that a legal assistant possess clear writing, researching, and critical thinking abilities.

Making a Personal Assessment and Setting Goals

If you are reading this book, you probably have made at least a tentative career goal to enter the paralegal profession, with the ultimate goal of obtaining a job. It should not be "just a job" but, rather, a job that will give you satisfaction and one that you will get up and go to with anticipation, not dread. The paralegal field offers many and varied specialties. An early goal should be to take courses that will introduce you to the specialty you would enjoy most. Maybe you already are well versed in something that will lead to a specialty, such as nursing, one of the sciences, or law enforcement.

One of the first steps is to assess your own skills. What are your other educational skills? What are your personality traits? Do you like working under deadlines or working with certain groups of people, such as elderly people or those with disabilities?

As you will find out, the paralegal profession offers opportunities in many areas of legal specialty and in many types of working environments. Understanding your interests, skills, and desired working conditions and job locations will help you select the best educational path toward achieving your professional goals.

Selecting a Specialty

It is never too early to set career goals; although you will find that your final career path will take many bends and turns as you start your first job and learn about the various areas of practice that are available to you. Your ultimate specialty or employer might result from your educational background, such as journalism or medicine, or an area of special interest such as environmental issues, or possibly just a preference to work with certain types of clients such as the elderly or infirm.

And it is never too late to make a career adjustment. Many successful individuals begin a career later in life. Colonel Sanders started Kentucky Fried Chicken late in life. Schools are full of nontraditional students seeking a career change. In the paralegal field we are seeing more and more nurses who, having worked in the medical field for years, are making a career change to the legal field.

Your decision should be based on a self-evaluation of your likes and dislikes, interests, passions, and any physical or geographic limitations. If you hate to fly, you probably will not want a job that requires travel. If you are not comfortable with

Exhibit 1.1 Legal certification comparison chart

Compares the certification exams offered by: NALS . . . the association for legal professionals National Association for Legal Assistants (NALA), National Federation of Paralegal Associations, Inc. (NFPA)

	Professional Paralegal (PP)—NALS	PLS . . . the advanced certification for legal professionals (PLS)—NALS	Certified Legal Assistant (CLA)—or Paralegal (CP)—NALA	Paralegal (RP)—Paralegal Advanced Competency Exam (PACE) Registered
Organization Established	1929, incorporated in 1949	1929, incorporated in 1949	1975	1974
Certification Established	2004	1960	1976	1996
Membership	5,000 individual members Regular Member = $135.00 per year (includes state and local dues) International Member = $135.00 per year Retired Member = $45.00 per year National Associate Member = $45.00 per year (educators, judges and attorneys) National Student Member = $19.00 per year (must be a full-time student) Lifetime Member = $750.00 (one time fee) (annual billing for state and local dues)	5,000 individual members	18,000 individual members Active Membership Annual Dues: $125 Associate Membership Annual Dues: $100 Student Membership Annual Dues: $50 Sustaining Membership Annual Dues: $70	11,000 individual members and 50 member associations
Number Certified	402 (eff 03/08)	5,482 (eff 03/08)	over 15,000 (2008)	
Eligibility to Test Education and/or Employment			A paralegal must meet one of the following alternate requirements: 1. Graduation from a paralegal program that is: (a) Approved by the American Bar Association; or (b) An associate degree program; or (c) A post-baccalaureate certificate program in legal assistant studies; or (d) A bachelor's degree program in legal assistant studies; or (e) A legal assistant program which consists of a minimum of 60 semester hours (900 clock hours or 90 quarter hours) of which at least 15 semester hours (225 clock hours or 22.5 quarter hours) are substantive legal courses.	• An associate degree in paralegal studies obtained from an institutionally accredited and/or ABA approved paralegal program; and six (6) years of substantive paralegal experience; or, • A bachelor's degree in any course of study obtained from an institutionally accredited school; and three (3) years of substantive paralegal experience; or, • A bachelor's degree and completion of a paralegal program from an institutionally accredited school,

(continued)

Exhibit 1.1   Legal certification comparison chart *(continued)*

	Professional Paralegal (PP)— NALS	PLS . . . the advanced certification for legal professionals (PLS)—NALS	Certified Legal Assistant (CLA)— or Paralegal (CP)—NALA	Paralegal (RP)— Paralegal Advanced Competency Exam (PACE) Registered
				said paralegal program may be imbedded in a bachelor's degree; and two (2) years of substantive paralegal experience; OR, • Four (4) years substantive paralegal experience on or before December 31, 2000; and, • The paralegal cannot have been convicted of a felony nor be under suspension, termination or revocation of a certificate, registration or license by any entity.
Examination Topics	Part 1—Written Communications: Grammar and word usage, spelling, punctuation, number usage, capitalization, composition, and expression Part 2—Legal Knowledge and Skills: Legal research, citations, legal terminology, the court system and ADR, and the legal skills of interviewing clients and witnesses, planning and conducting investigations, and docketing Part 3—Ethics and Judgment: Ethical situations involving contact with clients, the public, coworkers, and subordinates; other ethical considerations for the legal profession; decisionmaking and analytical ability; and ability to recognize priorities Part 4—All areas of substantive law, including	Part 1—Written Communications: Grammar and word usage, punctuation, number usage, capitalization, spelling, and composition and expression Part 2—Office Procedures and Technology: records management, computer information systems, equipment/ information services, office procedures and practices, office accounting Part 3—Ethics and Judgment: Ethical situations involving contact with clients, the public, coworkers; ethical considerations for legal profession; decisionmaking and analytical ability; ability to recognize priorities	**Communications** • Word usage and vocabulary • Grammar/punctuation • Writing skills • Nonverbal communications • General communications related to interviewing and client communications • General communications related to interoffice office situations This section contains a writing exercise. *The Elements of Style,* Strunk & White, has been adopted by the NALA Certifying Board as the authority for the Communications section. **Ethics** • Ethical responsibilities centering on performance of delegated work including confidentiality, unauthorized practice of law, legal advice, conflict of interest, billing and client communications • Client/public contact including identification as a non-lawyer, advertising and initial client contact • Professional Integrity/ competence including knowledge of legal assistant codes of ethics • Relationships with co-workers and support staff • Attorney codes/discipline	Domain I—Administration of Client Legal Matters: Conflict checks; develop, organize and maintain client files; develop and maintain calendar/tickler systems; develop and maintain databases; coordinate client services. Domain II—Development of Client Legal Matters: Client interviews; analyze information; collaborate with counsel; prepare, file, and serve legal documents and exhibits; prepare clients and witnesses for legal proceedings. Domain III—Factual/Legal Research: Obtain factual and legal information; investigate and compile facts; inspect, evaluate, and analyze evidence; ascertain and analyze legal authority. Domain IV—Factual/Legal Writing: Communicate with client/counsel; draft legal analytical documents. Domain V—Office Administration: Personnel management; acquire technology; coordinate and utilize vendor

Exhibit 1.1 Legal certification comparison chart *(continued)*

Professional Paralegal (PP)— NALS	PLS . . . the advanced certification for legal professionals (PLS)—NALS	Certified Legal Assistant (CLA)— or Paralegal (CP)—NALA	Paralegal (RP)— Paralegal Advanced Competency Exam (PACE) Registered
administrative; business organizations and contracts; civil procedure and litigation; criminal; family; real property; torts; wills, trusts, and estates; admiralty and maritime; antitrust; bankruptcy; environmental; federal civil rights and employment discrimination; immigration; intellectual property; labor; oil and gas; pension and profit sharing; taxation; water; workers' compensation	Part 4—Legal Knowledge and Skills: Legal Knowledge: citations, legal research, and the ability to prepare legal documents based on oral instructions and materials; all areas of substantive law	• Knowledge of the American Bar Association's Rules of Professional Conduct and the NALA Code of Ethics and Professional Responsibility is required by this examination. **Legal Research** • Sources of law including primary authority, secondary authority; understanding how law is recorded • Research skills including citing the law; shepardizing, updating decisions; procedural rules of citations • Analysis of research problem including identification of relevant facts and legal issues *A Uniform System of Citation,* Harvard Law Review Association, has been adopted by the NALA Certifying Board as the authority for the Legal Research section. **Judgment and Analytical Ability** • Comprehension of data—identifying and understanding a problem • Application of knowledge—ability to link facts or legal issues from other cases to the problem at hand, recognizing similarities and differences by analogy • Evaluating and categorizing data • Organizing data and findings in a written document This section contains an essay question which requires analysis of a research request, finding applicable law, and writing a responsive memo. Examinees will be graded on the ability to: • Identify which facts are relevant and state them concisely and accurately; • Identify the threshold or main issue and any secondary issue(s); • Identify the relevant legal authority and apply it to the facts; and • Draw persuasive logical conclusions. **Substantive Law** The substantive law section of the examination is composed of five subsections. The first section, Substantive Law-General covers concepts of the American legal system. **All examinees are required to take this section.**	services; create and maintain library and legal resources; develop and maintain billing system.

(continued)

Exhibit 1.1 **Legal certification comparison chart** *(continued)*

	Professional Paralegal (PP)— NALS	PLS . . . the advanced certification for legal professionals (PLS)—NALS	Certified Legal Assistant (CLA)— or Paralegal (CP)—NALA	Paralegal (RP)— Paralegal Advanced Competency Exam (PACE) Registered
			Subjects covered within this section include: • Court system including their structure and jurisdiction • Branches of government, agencies, and concepts such as separation of powers • Legal concepts and principles including sources of law, judicial decision making, appellate process • Sources and classifications of law including the constitution, statutes, common law, civil law, statutory law, and equity law The other four sub-sections are selected by the applicants from a list of nine substantive areas of the law. These tests cover general knowledge of the following practice areas: • Administrative Law • Bankruptcy • Business Organizations • Civil Litigation • Contracts • Criminal Law and Procedure • Estate Planning and Probate • Family Law • Real Estate The skills required by these tests involve recall of facts and principles that form the basis of the specialty area. Examinees must also demonstrate an understanding of the structure of the law and procedures to be followed in each specialty area. © 2008, National Association of Legal Assistants 1516 S. Boston, #200, Tulsa, OK 74119 nalanet@nala.org	
Cost	$200 (retake $50/section) $250 (retake $60/section) PLS Members Part 4: $150 (retake $50) PLS Nonmember Part 4: $200 (retake $60)		The fee for the CLA/CP examination is $250 for NALA members and $275 for nonmembers	
CLE Required			50 hours (five hours legal ethics)	12 hours continuing legal education including at least one hour in ethics every two (2) years.

Legal Certification Comparison Chart prepared by Kathleen L. McRae, PLS, RP and Lyn M. Hurlbutt, PP, PLS, CLA, RP, CPS. NALS is dedicated to enhancing the competencies and contributions of members in the legal services profession. NALS Resource Center, 314 East Third Street, Suite 210, Tulsa, OK 74120 918.582.5188, 918.582.5907 (fax) © NALS, Inc. Reprinted with permission. All rights reserved.

CHECKLIST Career Planning

☐ My current paralegal job-related skills are:

☐ My special interests are:

☐ My passions are:

☐ My personality traits are:

☐ My geographical work and living desires are:

☐ My willingness to accept responsibility is:

☐ My level of self-motivation is:

strangers, you probably will not want a job as a paralegal investigator for a litigation firm. If you like books and research, you might want to work as the firm's librarian or researcher.

Assessing Your Background

As the law has become more specialized, so has the demand for paralegals with more than just paralegal skills. Law firms specializing in an area such as medical malpractice frequently look for paralegals who also have a medical background such as nursing. Firms with large, complex litigation cases often look for someone with computer database skills who can manage the files. Paralegals with journalism experience and training frequently are sought out for their interviewing and writing skills.

Your personal background can be an asset when added to your paralegal certificate or degree. As you begin your professional training, take stock of your entire educational background, special skills, and talents, as well as personal areas of interest.

Doing a self-assessment early in your studies offers you an opportunity to recognize your strengths and develop them and to acknowledge weaknesses that you need to work on to permit your personal and professional growth.

Assessing Your Skills

You may well have a number of personal skills that will benefit you in the future as a paralegal. You might have great interpersonal skills, communicate well orally and in writing, and be a highly motivated person—all qualities of a good paralegal.

Individuals with language skills are particularly in demand in international law, as well as in working with clients who lack English-language skills. The paralegal who understands a second language and the cultural nuances of the client's background can be invaluable.

Assessing Your Interests

What are your personal interests? Are you an active outdoors person in your free time, for whom working on environmental issues would be of high interest and satisfaction? Do you find yourself drawn to volunteering or working in your free time with shut-ins and elderly people?

Selecting Your Electives

Becoming aware of your interests and background knowledge enables you to select the elective course that can qualify you for work in a specialty field of law. Taking electives is a good way to explore an area in which you think you might be interested, without committing to more than one semester or a few credits of study. Many students find new interests and a potential career direction after taking courses in areas they had not considered previously. For example, you may have been reading in newspapers and magazines, and following on television, stories about the high-technology industries and wondered how your career goal as a paralegal might fit into this growth area.

One of the fastest growing fields is that of intellectual property law. In an age of dot coms, computers, and a growing global marketplace, protection of intellectual property has become a critical concern for individuals and companies alike. Taking a three-credit course in intellectual property may well introduce the paralegal student to a new area of interest in a potential growth area of the paralegal profession. This is also true for other emerging areas in the paralegal profession, such as environmental law and legal nurse consulting.

Regulating the Practice of Law

To protect the public, certain professions, such as law, require state licensure as a method of regulating who can practice. For the lawyer, the rules that must be followed to continue practice are found in the individual states' code or canon of ethics for lawyers, such as the Model Rules of Professional Conduct of the American Bar Association as adopted by many states' highest courts, serious violation of which can result in the loss of the license or right to practice law.

Paralegals, with a few exceptions, have no state license requirement to enter the profession, and no unified code of ethics. State regulations and ethics opinions are neither uniform nor mandatory. At worst, a paralegal runs the risk of a charge of unauthorized practice of law under the state criminal code, which will be discussed in more detail in Chapter 2, and at best the violation of a professional organization's ethics code results in a loss of membership in the organization.

Regulating the Paralegal Profession

Unauthorized Practice of Law (UPL) Giving legal advice, if legal rights may be affected, by anyone not licensed to practice law.

Regulation and licensing of the paralegal profession has been one of the hottest topics in the legal and paralegal communities. Each state, through its respective legislature and court, regulates and licenses the practice of law. The original **Unauthorized Practice of Law (UPL)** issues were simply those of the licensing of attorneys and laws preventing the unauthorized practice of law. With the development of the paralegal profession has come a new set of concerns and controversy surrounding what constitutes the unauthorized practice of law, who should be permitted to render legal services, and under what conditions.

The conflict is between the paralegal profession and the bar organizations, such as the American Bar Association, which does not see the need for the additional time, effort, and cost for certification of paralegals. The ABA position is broadly based on the argument that the public is protected by the attorney's obligation to supervise the paralegal and responsibility to the public.

For the most part, the paralegal profession has sought some level of regulation, certification, or licensure. Somewhere in the middle are increasing numbers of employers of paralegals who want some level of assurance that those they hire who claim to be paralegals are qualified for those positions. As the responsibilities undertaken by paralegals have increased, so have the educational requirements. Within the profession has come a concern that those who hold themselves out as paralegals are truly qualified to perform the work they have undertaken. This is no different from the organized bar monitoring the activities of those holding themselves out as being lawyers.

State Licensing

Some states and others have attempted to set up licensing systems or defining who may use the title paralegal. A case in point is the proposal rejected in 1999 by the New Jersey Supreme Court to license traditional paralegals, which had been developed after five years of study by that court's committee on paralegal education and regulation. If it had been approved, this proposal would have made New Jersey the first state to license traditional paralegals. Another state's approach is that of North Carolina's plan shown below.

- California leads the nation in setting stringent educational requirements that may become a model for other states. In 2000 California amended its Business and Professional Code requiring minimum educational standards for paralegals. See Exhibit 1.2.

Exhibit 1.2 California regulation of paralegals

While other state legislatures and courts wrestle with the minimum standards, California addressed the requirements in a 2000 amendment to the Business and Professional Code that requires a paralegal to possess at least one of the following:

(1) A certificate of completion of a paralegal program approved by the American Bar Association.
(2) A certificate of completion of a paralegal program at an institution that requires a minimum of 24 semester, or equivalent, units in law-related courses, accredited by a national or regional accreditation organization or approved by the Bureau for Private Postsecondary and Vocational Education.
(3) A baccalaureate or advanced degree and minimum of one year of law-related experience under an attorney who is an active member of the State Bar of California.
(4) A high school diploma or general equivalency diploma and a minimum of three years' law-related experience under the supervision of a California attorney, with this training being completed before December 31, 2003.

Other states might look to the California statute in deciding the question of who is qualified by education, training, or work experience.

- After a number of efforts, a Hawaii State Bar Association task force on paralegal certification developed a compromise voluntary certification proposal for consideration by the Hawaii Supreme Court, which recognized the opposition from some segments of the bar.

To some observers it is obvious that the organized bar is fearful in many cases of the incursion of the paralegal profession into the practice of law. For some, the issue is loss of income. Others are concerned for the delivery of quality legal services by all those who hold themselves out as being members of the legal profession.

Florida and Ohio are among the states that have addressed the issue of certification of paralegals.

Florida Registered Paralegal

A Florida Registered Paralegal is a person with education, training, or work experience, who works under the direction and supervision of a member of The Florida Bar and who performs specifically delegated substantive legal work for which a member of The Florida Bar is responsible and who has met the requirements of registration as set forth in Chapter 20 of the Rules Regulating The Florida Bar. A Florida Registered Paralegal is not a member of The Florida Bar and may not give legal advice or practice law. Florida Registered Paralegal and FRP are trademarks of The Florida Bar.

Source: www.floridabar.org

Ohio State Bar Association Certified Paralegal

The Ohio State Bar Association offers a voluntary credentialing program for paralegals. Individuals meeting the OSBA definition of "paralegal," meeting the eligibility requirements and passing a written examination will be designated as an "OSBA Certified Paralegal." This credential, along with a logo provided for the purpose may be used by the paralegal to the extent permitted by the Supreme Court of Ohio's Rules for the Government of the Bar and Rules of Professional Conduct.

OSBA Paralegal Certification provides a valuable credential for paralegals in Ohio through the use of objective standards which measure the training, knowledge, experience and skill of paralegals. It requires a commitment to excellence and will assist lawyers and law firms in identifying the highly qualified paralegal professionals.

Source: http://www.ohiobar.org/pub/?articleid=785

For the paralegal, it is a question of status as well as job opportunities. With the establishment of minimum standards for holding oneself out as a paralegal comes a

Advice *from the* Field

I recommend a visit to the North Carolina State Bar's Paralegal website (http://www.nccertifiedparalegal.org), for information on the benefits of paralegal certification. The first page is shown below.

PLAN FOR CERTIFICATION OF PARALEGALS

The State Bar's interest in the paralegal profession promotes proper utilization of paralegals and assures that legal services are professionally and ethically offered to the public. The Plan for Certification of Paralegals approved by the NC State Bar and adopted by the NC Supreme Court in 2004 will assist in the development of paralegal standards, raise the profile of the paralegal profession, and standardize the expectations of the public and other legal professionals.

The State Bar has worked diligently with attorneys and paralegals across our state to establish a voluntary North Carolina certification program with requirements that are properly defined and that will ensure the credential has value. Through education and experience, the North Carolina certification plan will assist lawyers and administrators in distinguishing paralegals that meet or exceed the skills required for certification. As multi-skilled professionals, paralegals have a diverse knowledge base and must practice

effective interpersonal communication skills to maintain collaborative relationships within the legal team. Paralegals, like attorneys, will continue to be held accountable to the highest of ethical and professional standards.

Paralegals certified by the State Bar may use the following designations:

- North Carolina Certified Paralegal
- North Carolina State Bar Certified Paralegal
- Paralegal Certified by the North Carolina State Bar Board of Paralegal Certification
- NCCP

This site has two brochures that may be downloaded,

NC Certified Paralegal—A Primer for Paralegals

NC Certified Paralegal—A Primer for Attorney

Both brochures review the benefits to the public, to the profession, to attorneys and to paralegals. I think that they give a great overall response to "why" become certified. North Carolina began their certification program July 1, 2005, as of February 2006, the Board received 1489 applications and had certified 762. The current applicants are qualifying under the grandfather clause which ends June 30, 2007.

status that members of a profession are entitled to enjoy. For those who have worked hard to develop the necessary paralegal skills by way of education and experience, it eliminates unqualified individuals from taking jobs that should be performed by qualified individuals. The stated goals of the different groups are not that far apart: delivery of quality legal services at affordable prices with a reasonable standard of living for the legal profession and the paralegal profession.

The traditional role of the attorney in advising and representing clients is limited to those who are admitted to practice as lawyers under the applicable state law. Some exemptions do exist that allow nonlawyers to perform certain services under state law, such as document preparation under California law.

Federal Practice

Under federal regulations, nonlawyers may represent parties before the Social Security Administration, the Patent Office, and other agencies. A conflict may arise between the federal law and state law that limit the activity. For example, Florida sought unsuccessfully to enjoin a practitioner authorized to practice before the Patent Office, alleging UPL (*Sperry v. Florida*, 373 U.S. 379 (1963)).

Under federal regulation, a paralegal can, without supervision, represent individuals before the Social Security Administration, including appearing before Administrative Law Judges on behalf of clients. Paralegals may appear as representatives of claimants for disability claims; Medicare parts A, B, and C; and cases of overpayment and underpayment.

As representative of a claimant, the paralegal in practice before the Social Security Administration may obtain information, submit evidence, and make statements and arguments. The difference between the paralegal and the attorney is only in the matter of direct versus indirect payment for services. The Social Security Administration pays the attorney directly, whereas the paralegal must bill the client for services rendered. Within the Social Security Administration, paralegals are employed as decision writers and case technicians.

Opportunities for Paralegals

The U.S. Department of Labor has included the paralegal profession among the fastest growing occupations with employment projected to grow 22 percent between 2006 and 2016, much faster than the average for all occupations. This encompasses additional growth of the occupation as well as the need for individuals to replace existing employees. The Labor Department estimates might be increased further by the de facto requirement found in the court opinions that more paralegals be used to perform services instead of attorneys performing the services.

Web Exploration

Check the latest paralegal statistics in the *Occupational Outlook Handbook* from the Department of Labor, Bureau of Labor Statistics at http://www .bls.gov/oco/home.htm.

Projections data from the National Employment Matrix					
				Change, 2006–16	
Occupational title	SOC Code	Employment, 2006	Projected employment, 2016	Number	Percent
Paralegals and legal assistants	23-2011	238,000	291,000	53,000	22

Source: Occupational Outlook Handbook, 2008–09 Edition, U.S. Department of Labor, Bureau of Labor Statistics

Paralegals held about 238,000 jobs in 2006, according to the Bureau of Labor Statistics, U.S. Department of Labor, *Occupational Outlook Handbook*, 2008–09 Edition. In May 2006, full-time wage-and-salary paralegals and legal assistants had median annual earnings, including bonuses, of $43,040. The middle 50 percent earned between $33,920 and $54,690. The top 10 percent earned more than $67,540, and the bottom 10 percent earned less than $27,450. Median annual earnings in the industries employing the largest numbers of paralegals were:

Federal government	$56,080
Management of companies and enterprises	52,220
Local government	42,170
Legal services	41,460
State government	38,020

Source: *Occupational Outlook Handbook*, 2008-09 Edition, U.S. Department of Labor, Bureau of Labor Statistics

In a 1998 survey by the American Bar Association:

- Almost two-thirds of the lawyers who responded, 65.5 percent, employ legal assistants at their firms; 60.2 percent of respondents actively work with paralegals.
- The general responsibilities most often assigned to paralegals are maintaining client files, drafting correspondence, and performing factual research.

- Legal assistants are more likely to be employed by large firms than small firms.
- Lawyers in smaller firms delegate a wider array of responsibilities to legal assistants than do lawyers in bigger firms.
- Lawyers with business/corporate, probate/estate planning, and litigation practices make more extensive use of paralegals than do lawyers in other practice areas.

The ABA survey demonstrates that clients who choose to work with larger firms are much more likely to have a portion of their work completed by paralegals than those who choose a lawyer from a small firm. Almost all (99 percent) of the lawyers practicing in firms with more than 100 lawyers reported that their firms use legal assistants. By contrast, only 34.8 percent of those working at firms of three or fewer lawyers employ paralegals. Of the lawyers who indicated that their firms do not employ paralegals, 56.8 percent reported that the size of their firm would not support legal assistants, and 44.1 percent said that their secretaries assume tasks that otherwise would be assigned to legal assistants.

Compensation for paralegals is as varied as the working environments and regional locations. As with most jobs and professions, salaries tend to be higher in large metropolitan areas and lower in small and rural areas. Large firms tend to pay more, and small firms tend to pay less. At times, these variations in compensation can be justified by the costs of working in certain locations, such as higher taxation and the cost of commuting.

The Future

The future of the paralegal profession may be determined by clients who are unwilling or unable to pay what they see as inflated fees for lawyers. The future also could be dictated by the courts, which, looking at the fairness of charging higher rates for attorneys' tasks that could properly be delegated to a paralegal would result in a lower charge to the client. Two of the future concerns involving paralegals and billings are the following:

1. The cases in which secretarial or clerical tasks are charged to the client as paralegal fees. These tasks are considered overhead (part of the cost of running the office) and should be performed at no additional cost to the client. This is one of the areas in which the definition of paralegal has come into play in the courts. Courts are allowing charges for paralegal fees but not for secretarial fees.
2. The fairness of charging higher rates for attorneys' performing tasks that could properly be delegated to a paralegal, thereby resulting in a lower charge to the client.

For instance, summarizing depositions traditionally has been a task delegated to paralegals. Assume that the paralegal takes two hours to complete the task and the paralegal's time is billed to the client at $75 per hour (don't get excited—that doesn't necessarily have any bearing on what you may be paid); the client would be charged $150. For a lawyer to do the same work, if billed out at $175 per hour, the client would be charged $350. Unless there is good reason for the lawyer to do the work, the decision not to delegate the work to a paralegal seems unfair to the client. A number of court decisions are beginning to draw upon these fundamental questions of the fairness and propriety of attorney billings for their services. As other federal and state courts weigh in on this line of decisions, law firms may have to hire more paralegals.

Getting Started

As you start your legal studies and paralegal career, consider the suggestions and advice in the following *Advice from the Field* by a leading paralegal educator.

Web Exploration

Full article available at the website of NFPA at http://www
.paralegals.org/displaycommon
.cfm?am=1&subarticlenbr=564.

Web Exploration

The Kathryn Myers' student portfolio article and other information for students can be found on the American Association for Paralegal Education website at www.aafpe.org.

Advice *from the* Field

A portfolio is a purposeful collection of student work that is accumulated over time. The material reveals the extent of student learning, achievement, and development. The "portfolio system" is intended to specify knowledge and competence in areas considered necessary to successfully work as a paralegal/legal assistant while leaving the selection of means of documentation of competency to the individual student. Documentation of knowledge and skill acquisition can take a variety of forms including, but not limited to,

- letters of support
- diaries
- videotapes and audiotapes of work
- pleadings
- memoranda
- course projects
- registration receipts from continuing education and other conferences attended
- proof of membership in professional organizations
- subscriptions to legal publications

Typically, much of the material can be compiled from projects and activities required within courses.

PROCEDURE

The portfolio shall contain documentation of knowledge and skill acquisition based on the Core Competencies established by the American Association for Paralegal Education. Those core competencies are divided into two areas—skill development and acquisition of knowledge. Within those areas are competencies based on:

SKILL DEVELOPMENT

- critical thinking skills
- organizational skills
- general communication skills
- interpersonal skills
- legal research skills
- legal writing skills
- computer skills
- interviewing and investigation skills

ACQUISITION OF KNOWLEDGE

- organization and operation of the legal system
- organization and operation of law offices
- the paralegal profession and ethical obligations
- contracts
- torts
- business organizations
- litigation procedures

It is understood that the areas may overlap somewhat and that these areas do not cover all competencies associated with the program, student growth, or professional success. However, students who perfect these competencies and who perform from this educational base have a foundation for success.

It is suggested that the student purchase a secure container to collect and organize the material [such as] a hanging file folder or file box. This portfolio may be maintained on computer disk; however, you will not have any graded materials if this is the only method of collection you use.

Students should keep a log of all materials completed. When completing each assignment, [they should] enter the document in the log, with a column to check for inclusion in the campus portfolio and another to check for inclusion in the professional portfolio. Some documents may, of course, overlap in their application.

Students are responsible for the contents of their portfolios. The student should periodically review the contents of the portfolio and add or remove materials based on decisions as to the extent to which the contents adequately represent knowledge and skill acquisition in each of the areas outlined below. This portfolio is not intended to be a compilation of senior level work; rather, it is useful to provide work of varying levels of efficiency to show, among other things, growth and improvement.

CONTENT

To be a successful paralegal/legal assistant, the student must possess a common core of legal knowledge as well as acquire vital critical thinking, organizational, communication, and interpersonal skills. Courses in a student's program should provide the student with

(continued)

the means to develop the competencies, which have been divided into the following sections:

Area 1 Understanding the Profession and Its Ethical Obligations

Area 2 Research

Area 3 Legal Writing

Area 4 Basic Skills

Area 5 Acquisition of Legal Knowledge

Area 6 Professional Commitment Beyond Coursework

Area 7 Evaluation of Professional Growth/ Evaluation of Program

Appendix

GUIDELINES FOR SELECTING ENTRIES

When selecting entries, students should bear in mind that each piece is part of a much larger whole and that, together, the artifacts and rationale make a powerful statement about individual professional development. Asking the following questions may help with decision making.

1. What do I want my portfolio to show about me as a paralegal? What are my attributes as a paralegal?
2. What do I want my portfolio to demonstrate about me as a learner? How and what have I learned?
3. What directions for my future growth and development does my self-evaluation suggest? How can I show them in my portfolio?
4. What points have been made by others about me as a paralegal and learner? How can I show them in my portfolio?
5. What effect does my professionalism have upon my peers? How can I show this in my portfolio?
6. What overall impression do I want my portfolio to give a reviewer about me as a learner and as a paralegal?

When decision-making about what to include becomes a challenge, it may be helpful to look at each artifact and ask yourself, "What would including this item add that has not already been said or shown?" Remember that portfolios create representative records of your professional development; they are not intended to be comprehensive.

VALUES AND ATTITUDES

Values and attitudes determine the choices we make in our lives. They cross the boundaries of subject-matter areas. Thus, in this final section of your portfolio, you are asked to look at your own values and attitudes and then write a one- to three-page paper in which you reflect upon your own values. Identify one or more values that are important to you. Explain how they influence your choices as a person, parent, future paralegal, voter, and/or citizen of the global community. Include specific examples.

The following questions may help you choose a topic for your essay: What does it mean to be honest? fair? tolerant? open to new ideas and experiences? respect evidence? Which is more important—decreasing the production of greenhouse gases or preserving jobs?

The right to choose how many children we want or controlling world population growth? Freedom to produce pornographic art or the right of children to be sheltered from such experiences? Spending more time with your children or getting a second job so you can buy things you want?

There are no easy answers to these questions. Have fun thinking about your own values. Remember to include specific examples from your own life!

TRANSCRIPTS

Include copies of unofficial transcripts from all colleges and universities that you have attended.

Degree evaluation

Graduation evaluation

Awards or recognitions

Include a copy of your degree evaluation, if you received one.

Include a copy of your graduation evaluation.

Include copies of awards or recognitions you have received.

PROFESSIONAL PORTFOLIO

Modify this inclusive portfolio into a professional portfolio. This professional portfolio will be representative, not comprehensive. Each artifact chosen for inclusion should represent at least one significant aspect of you and/or your accomplishments that can be translated into employability. Use these guidelines to prepare your professional portfolio:

1. Prepare your portfolio as a showcase of your best work—your highest achievements. This will involve selecting from artifacts in your portfolio and adding new ones.
2. Do not send your portfolio when you apply for a job. Rather, include in your cover letter a statement concerning your portfolio. For example: "Throughout my paralegal studies program at _____ College, I developed a professional portfolio that clearly and concisely exhibits my attributes as a paralegal. I would be pleased to share this portfolio with you during an interview."
3. If granted an interview, take your portfolio with you. Be prepared to present the highlights. Practice presenting it effectively. In some instances, you might be asked to present it at the beginning of the interview, and in other instances you might

use it as a source of evidence or enhancement of a point you make in the interview. Interviewing practices vary widely from employer to employer. Portfolios are most likely to be reviewed in situations where the employer is familiar with the abilities of a paralegal.

4. If the interviewer(s) is particularly interested and would like to examine your portfolio more closely, offer to leave it if at all possible. You should make explicit arrangements for collecting it and, of course, follow through as planned. It could be that your portfolio will create the impression that tips the scales in your favor.

5. Remember—it is likely that some people in a position to hire are not familiar with professional portfolios as you know them. Take time to concisely explain that developing your portfolio has been a process of reflection and evaluation that has helped you to know yourself as a paralegal and to establish a foundation for career-long professional development. To some extent, presenting

your portfolio will inform the interviewer about both you and the portfolio concept and process.

6. Keep your portfolio up to date. As you continue to gain experience and to grow professionally, alter it to reflect your development. It is not only your first job application that may be enhanced by a well prepared and presented portfolio but developing your portfolio is an excellent foundation for meeting any expectation of continuing legal education.

CONCLUSION

It is my hope and intention that by your creating this portfolio, you have an opportunity to reflect upon your education and to emphasize to yourself and others that you are capable and qualified to perform as a paralegal. It is time to believe in you. Good luck!

Reproduced with permission of Kathryn Myers.

Concept Review *and* Reinforcement

LEGAL TERMINOLOGY

ALS (Accredited Legal Secretary) 15
American Association for Paralegal Education (AAfPE) 12
American Bar Association (ABA) 4
Associate's degree 13
Bachelor's degree 13
Certificate 13
Certified Legal Assistant (CLA) 15

International Paralegal Management Association (IPMA) 16
Legal assistant 4
National Association of Legal Assistants (NALA) 4
National Association of Legal Secretaries (NALS) 16
National Federation of Paralegal Associations (NFPA) 4

Paralegal 4
Paralegal Advanced Competency Exam (PACE) 14
PLS (Professional Legal Secretary) 15
PP (Professional Paralegal) 16
Proprietary school 13
Unauthorized Practice of Law (UPL) 22

SUMMARY OF KEY CONCEPTS

What Is a Paralegal?

Definition	A paralegal, or legal assistant, is "a person qualified by education, training, or work experience who is employed or retained by a lawyer, law office, corporation, governmental agency or other entity who performs specifically delegated substantive legal work for which a lawyer is responsible."

What Do Paralegals Do?

Functions of Paralegals	The primary function of paralegals is to assist attorneys in preparing for hearings, trials, meetings, and closings.

Professional Skills

Definition	Professional skills are also called soft skills. These include communication skills, initiative, resourcefulness, problem solving, commitment, team work, leadership, and self-motivation.
Resourcefulness	The ability to meet and handle a situation and find solutions to problems.
Commitment	The ability to complete what one starts out to do.
Analytical Skills	Analytical skills allow one to follow a step-by-step process to solve a problem.
Interpersonal Skills	The ability to work with people.
Communication Skills	Communication means expressing ideas effectively—both oral and written.

Career Planning

Career Planning	Career planning includes educational planning and a plan for perfecting professional skills.
Paralegal Education in the United States	An estimated 1,000 paralegal education programs are available in the United States. These programs are offered in onsite, online, and hybrid format combining online and on site instruction. Some of these programs have obtained ABA.
Qualifications of a Paralegal	Qualifications were established by the educational guidelines of the American Bar Association's Standing Committee on Paralegals and American Association for Paralegal Education.
Types of Educational Programs	1. Certificate programs 2. Associate degree programs 3. Baccalaureate programs 4. Graduate programs 5. Specialty certificates
Paralegal Certification	PACE (Paralegal Advance Competency Exam) of the National Federation of Paralegal Associations CLA (Certified Legal Assistant) of the National Association of Legal Assistants ALS (the basic certification for legal professionals of NALS) PLS (the advanced certification for legal professionals of NALS) PP (Professional Paralegal certification of NALS)
Making a Personal Assessment and Setting Goals	1. What are your other educational skills? 2. What are your personality traits? 3. Do you like working under deadlines? 4. Do you like working with certain groups of people? 5. What are your personal interests? 6. Recognize your strengths 7. Acknowledge weaknesses
Selecting a Specialty	Your decision should be based on a self-evaluation of your likes and dislikes, interests, passions, and any physical or geographic limitations.
Assessing Your Background	Doing a self-assessment early in your studies offers you an opportunity to recognize your strengths and develop them and to acknowledge weaknesses that you need to address in order to permit your personal and professional growth.

Regulating the Practice of Law

Reasons for Regulating the Practice of Law	The practice of law is regulated by state government and court rule to protect the public from incompetent and unscrupulous practitioners.
Regulating the Paralegal Profession	The traditional role of the attorney in advising and representing clients is limited to those who are admitted to practice as lawyers under the applicable state law. Some exemptions do exist that allow nonlawyers to perform certain services under state law.
State Licensing	Some states have enacted legislation establishing licensure to perform certain paralegal functions to address the issues of the unauthorized practice of law.
Federal Practice	Under federal regulations, nonlawyers may represent parties before the Social Security Administration, the Patent Office, and other agencies.

Opportunities for Paralegals

Compensation Issues for the Paralegal	In 2006, paralegals held about 238,000 jobs in the United States, with median annual earnings of $43,040. The U.S. Department of Labor projects that this profession will continue to be among the fastest growing through the year 2016.

The Future

Career Planning	As courts require the use of paralegals to reduce legal costs, law firms may have to hire more paralegals and delegate work to them in fairness to clients and propriety in billing practice.

WORKING THE WEB

1. Download a copy of the latest edition of the ABA Standing Committee on Paralegals *Update Newsletter* at www.abanet.org/legalservices/paralegals/home.html.
2. What advice does the ABA Standing Committee on Paralegals offer in its publication on *Getting Started As a Pro Bono Legal Assistant?* www.abanet.org/legalservices/paralegals/publications.html
3. The *Occupational Outlook Handbook* is updated regularly. Download a copy of the current version on Paralegals and Legal Assistants and compare the salary ranges with those in this text. Have they changed? www.bls.gov/oco/ocos114.htm
4. One of the significant issues for paralegals over the past years has been whether paralegals are classified as exempt or nonexempt according to the U.S. Department of Labor regulations. Download a copy of the current Overview for Executive, Administrative, Professional, Computer, & Outside Sales Employees, and highlight the information that applies to paralegals. www.dol.gov/esa/regs/compliance/whd/fairpay/main.htm
5. Print out a copy of the Mission Statement or Homepage of each of the major national paralegal associations.
   a. International Paralegal Management Association www.paralegalmanagement.org
   b. NALS . . . the Association for Legal Professionals http://www.nals.org
   c. National Federation of Paralegal Associations www.paralegals.org
   d. National Association of Legal Assistants www.nala.org
   e. Association of Legal Administrators www.alanet.org
6. Compare your skills with the list of knowledge or competencies required of principal legal administrators at http://www.alanet.org/education/knowledgelist.html.

CRITICAL THINKING & WRITING QUESTIONS

1. How does the American Bar Association define the term "paralegal"?
2. What are the minimum qualifications that a paralegal should meet?
3. What is the role of the paralegal in the legal system?
4. Why should those planning to become paralegals or legal assistants get a well-grounded education and develop the necessary skills?
5. How can one satisfy the court that he or she is qualified as a paralegal and not as a legal secretary?
6. What is the advantage to the paralegal in obtaining the PACE or CLA designation?
7. What educational plan makes the most sense for you? Why?
8. How can a paralegal demonstrate the qualifications for employment as a paralegal?
9. Why would an employer, such as the U.S. Attorney's office, require a four-year degree for those seeking a paralegal position?
10. Complete the checklist "Career Planning" and assess your personal skills and professional goals. Based on your answers, how well prepared are you for a career as a paralegal? What skills need development?
11. How does assessing your interests and skills help in choosing a career path?
12. What skills are required to be a paralegal and why are they important?
13. Complete the "Strengths & Weaknesses" checklist in this chapter.
14. Why are good English writing and speaking skills important for the paralegal?
15. Complete the "My Career Roadmap" checklist in this chapter.
16. How can you use the "Strengths & Weaknesses" checklist in preparing your personal career roadmap?
17. What advantages might a person have in entering the paralegal profession later in life?
18. What actions have you observed in other people that demonstrated their resourcefulness? Have others ever told you that you are resourceful?
19. How can you demonstrate the characteristic of commitment?
20. Start to network by setting up a meeting with a working paralegal and preparing a list of questions to ask at that meeting.

Building Paralegal Skills

VIDEO CASE STUDIES

When Friends Ask for Legal Advice

Dante, a paralegal is approached by a friend for legal advice about his apartment lease. His landlord is refusing to allow him to have a dog in his apartment.

After viewing the video case study at www.pearsonhighered.com/goldman answer the following:

1. Would a paralegal working in a real estate office be able to give advice as an incidental activity?
2. Is advising the person that you are a paralegal enough to avoid UPL?
3. What is the law in your state on UPL?

Resume Writing Do's and Don'ts

Two law office human resource directors review some of the resumes they have received and discuss the errors people often make in submitting job applications.

After viewing the video case study at www.pearsonhighered.com/goldman answer the following:

1. Why is a good resume and cover letter so important in getting a paralegal position?
2. What are some of the skills human resource directors look for in new hires?
3. Make a list of skills you need to acquire and courses you should take in pursuing your paralegal studies.

Independent Paralegal

Don Swanson, President of Five Star Legal, an independent paralegal discusses the pros and cons of being an independent paralegal.

After viewing the video case study at www.pearsonhighered.com/goldman answer the following:

1. What are the advantages and disadvantages of working as an independent paralegal?
2. Are there any regulatory issues in your jurisdiction on working as an independent paralegal?

ETHICS ANALYSIS & DISCUSSION QUESTIONS

1. Does your state by statute, regulation, code, ethics rule, or court rule define "Paralegal" or "Legal Assistant"? If it does, what is that definition and where is it so defined? If not, should it formally define the term?
2. Does your state have a statute or court rule on the regulation of the paralegal or legal assistant practice? What are the requirements to practice as a paralegal or legal assistant? Does the law define the practice in some other terminology?
3. Does your state have minimum educational requirements for paralegals? Should there be a set of minimum qualifications?
4. Does having a set of minimum educational requirements eliminate the need for a set of ethical guidelines?

DEVELOPING YOUR COLLABORATION SKILLS

Working on your own or with a group of other students assigned by your instructor, review the scenario at the beginning of the chapter discussing the employment options and educational issues involved.

1. Discuss why or why not Ethan and Ariel should consider a paralegal career. What are the advantages or disadvantages? What strengths or skills do Ethan and Ariel bring to this type of career choice?
2. Working individually or in a group, complete the following:
   a. Summarize, in writing, your career advice to Ethan and/or Ariel.
   b. Share your advice with other students or groups. Does your group have any additional advice or recommendations?
   c. Take on the role of Ethan and/or Ariel. Might they have any other questions for Mr. Marshall about the paralegal profession? Make a list of additional questions. Where might Ethan and Ariel get additional information about the paralegal profession?
3. Select a spokesperson that can summarize and present your recommendations in class.

PARALEGAL PORTFOLIO EXERCISE

Using a three-ring binder with the following tabbed sections listed, start to create a hardcopy portfolio of your work and accomplishments in this course. Please also include any work you are doing in other courses that best represents your growing "skill set." Prepare binder tabs with the following headings listed and insert into your three-ring binder:

A. Understanding the Profession and Its Ethical Obligations
B. Research
C. Legal Writing
D. Basic Skills
E. Acquisition of Legal Knowledge
F. Professional Commitment Beyond Coursework
G. Evaluation of Professional Growth/Evaluation of Program
H. Appendix

LEGAL ANALYSIS & WRITING CASES

Doe v. Condon   532 S.E.2d 879(S.C. 2000)

The Unauthorized Practice of Law and the Paralegal
A paralegal asked the court if he could conduct unsupervised "wills and trusts" seminars for the public, "emphasizing" living trusts during the course of his presentation and answering estate-planning questions from the audience. He proposed a fee-splitting arrangement with his attorney–employer.

The South Carolina Supreme Court ruled: "The activities of a paralegal do not constitute the practice of law as long as they are limited to work of a preparatory nature, such as legal research, investigation, or the composition of legal documents, which enables licensed attorney–employer to carry a given matter to a conclusion through his own examination, approval, or additional effort.

" . . . The paralegal plays a supporting role to the supervising attorney. Here the roles are reversed. The attorney would support the paralegal. Petitioner would play the lead role, with no meaningful attorney supervision and the attorney's presence and involvement only surfaces on the back end. Meaningful attorney supervision must be present throughout the process. The line between what is and what is not permissible conduct by a non-attorney is sometimes unclear as a potential trap for the unsuspecting client. . . . It is well settled the paralegal may not give legal advice, consult, offer legal explanations, or make legal recommendations."

Questions

1. Why is the practice of law limited to licensed attorneys?
2. What tasks may a paralegal perform?

Sperry v. Florida   373 U.S. 379 (1963)

Petitioner, not a lawyer and not admitted to practice in Florida as a lawyer, was nevertheless authorized to practice before the U.S. Patent Office pursuant to federal statute (35 U.S.C. Sec. 31). The Florida Bar sued to prevent him from representing patent applicants, preparing and prosecuting the patent claims and advising them in the State of Florida.

The Supreme Court, in holding that the Petitioner was permitted to perform tasks incident to prosecuting of patent claims, said, ". . . by virtue of the Supremacy Clause, Florida may not deny to those failing to meet its own qualifications the right to perform the functions within the scope of the federal authority." The Court further stated, ". . . since patent

3. What tasks may a paralegal not perform?
4. Why is the answering of legal questions about the need for a will or a trust the unauthorized practice of law (UPL)?
5. Why is a fee-splitting arrangement between a lawyer and a paralegal prohibited?

Note: If in South Carolina, include the parallel citation: 341 S.C. 22. The Lexis citation for this case is 2000 S.C. LEXIS 125.

practitioners are authorized to practice before the Patent Office, the State maintains control over the practice of law within its borders except to the limited extent for the accomplishment of the federal objective."

Questions

1. Does this decision allow anyone to practice before any federal agency without being licensed?
2. What are the prerequisites for nonlawyers to act on behalf of others before federal agencies?
3. What steps would a paralegal have to take to prosecute patent claims?

WORKING WITH THE LANGUAGE OF THE COURT CASE

Missouri v. Jenkins

491 U.S. 274 (1989)
Supreme Court of the United States

Read the following case excerpts. Information on preparing a briefing is provided in Appendix A: How to Brief a Case. In your brief, prepare a written answer to each of the following questions.

1. What is the difference between "market rates" for paralegals and cost to the attorney for paralegal service?
2. Does billing for paralegal services at market rates unfairly benefit the law firm?
3. According to this court, how is a reasonable attorney's fee calculated?

4. How does the public benefit from allowing paralegals to be billed at market rates?
5. Does this court believe that a reasonable attorney's fee should include paralegal fees?

Brennan, J., delivered the opinion of the Court.

This is the attorney's fee aftermath of major school desegregation litigation in Kansas City, Missouri. We [are hearing this case to decide] should the fee award compensate the work of paralegals and law clerks by applying the market rate for their work?

I

This litigation began in 1977 as a suit by the Kansas City Missouri School District (KCMSD), the school board, and the children of two school board members,

against the State of Missouri and other defendants. The plaintiffs alleged that the State, surrounding school districts, and various federal agencies had caused and perpetuated a system of racial segregation in the schools of the Kansas City metropolitan area. . . . After lengthy proceedings, including a trial that lasted 7½ months during 1983 and 1984, the District Court found the State of Missouri and KCMSD liable. . . . It ordered various intradistrict remedies, to be paid for by the State and KCMSD, including $260 million in capital improvements and a magnet-school plan costing over $200 million.

The plaintiff class has been represented, since 1979, by Kansas City lawyer Arthur Benson and, since 1982, by the NAACP Legal Defense and Educational Fund, Inc. (LDF). Benson and the LDF requested attorney's fees under the Civil Rights Attorney's Fees Awards Act of 1976, 42 U.S.C. § 1988. Benson and his associates had devoted 10,875 attorney hours to the litigation, as well as 8,108 hours of paralegal and law clerk time. For the LDF, the corresponding figures were 10,854 hours for attorneys and 15,517 hours for paralegals and law clerks. Their fee applications deleted from these totals 3,628 attorney hours and 7,046 paralegal hours allocable to unsuccessful claims against the suburban school districts. With additions for postjudgment monitoring and for preparation of the fee application, the District Court awarded Benson a total of approximately $1.7 million and the LDF $2.3 million. . . .

Both Benson and the LDF employed numerous paralegals, law clerks (generally law students working part-time), and recent law graduates in this litigation. The court awarded fees for their work based on Kansas City market rates for those categories. As in the case of the attorneys, it used current rather than historic market rates in order to compensate for the delay in payment. It therefore awarded fees based on hourly rates of $35 for law clerks, $40 for paralegals, and $50 for recent law graduates. [. . .]

III

Missouri's second contention is that the District Court erred in compensating the work of law clerks and paralegals (hereinafter collectively "paralegals") at the market rates for their services, rather than at their cost to the attorney. While Missouri agrees that compensation for the cost of these personnel should be included in the fee award, it suggests that an hourly rate of $15—which it argued below corresponded to their salaries, benefits, and overhead—would be appropriate, rather than the market rates of $35 to $50. According to Missouri, § 1988 does not authorize billing paralegals' hours at market rates, and doing so produces a "windfall" for the attorney.

We begin with the statutory language, which provides simply for "a reasonable attorney's fee as part of the costs." Clearly, a "reasonable attorney's fee" cannot have been meant to compensate only work performed personally by members of the bar. Rather, the term must refer to a reasonable fee for the work product of an attorney.

Thus, the fee must take into account the work not only of attorneys but also of secretaries, messengers, librarians, janitors, and others whose labor contributes to the work product for which an attorney bills her client; and it also must take account of other expenses and profit. The parties have suggested no reason why the work of paralegals should not be similarly compensated, nor can we think of any. We thus take as our starting point the self-evident proposition that the "reasonable attorney's fee" provided for by statute should compensate the work of paralegals, as well as that of attorneys.

The more difficult question is how the work of paralegals is to be valuated in calculating the overall attorney's fee.

The statute specifies a "reasonable" fee for the attorney's work product. In determining how other elements of the attorney's fee are to be calculated, we have consistently looked to the marketplace as our guide to what is "reasonable." In *Blum v. Stenson*, 465 U.S. 886 (1984), for example, we rejected an argument that attorney's fees for nonprofit legal service organizations should be based on cost. We said: "The statute and legislative history establish that 'reasonable fees' under § 1988 are to be calculated according to the prevailing market rates in the relevant community. . . ." A reasonable attorney's fee under § 1988 is one calculated on the basis of rates and practices prevailing in the relevant market, i.e., "in line with those [rates] prevailing in the community for similar services by lawyers of reasonably comparable skill, experience, and reputation," and one that grants the successful civil rights plaintiff a "fully compensatory fee," comparable to what "is traditional with attorneys compensated by a fee-paying client."

If an attorney's fee awarded under § 1988 is to yield the same level of compensation that would be available from the market, the "increasingly widespread custom of separately billing for the services of paralegals and law students who serve as clerks," all else being equal, the hourly fee charged by an attorney whose rates include paralegal work in her hourly fee, or who bills separately for the work of paralegals at cost, will be higher than the hourly fee charged by an attorney competing in the same market who bills separately for the work of paralegals at "market rates." In other words, the prevailing "market rate" for attorney time is not independent of the manner in which paralegal time is accounted for. Thus, if the prevailing practice in a given community were to bill paralegal time separately at market rates, fees awarded the attorney at market rates for attorney time would not be fully compensatory if the court refused to compensate hours billed by paralegals or did so only at "cost." Similarly, the fee awarded would be too high if the court accepted separate billing for paralegal hours in a market where that was not the custom.

(continued)

We reject the argument that compensation for paralegals at rates above "cost" would yield a "windfall" for the prevailing attorney. Neither petitioners nor anyone else, to our knowledge, has ever suggested that the hourly rate applied to the work of an associate attorney in a law firm creates a windfall for the firm's partners or is otherwise improper under § 1988, merely because it exceeds the cost of the attorney's services. If the fees are consistent with market rates and practices, the "windfall" argument has no more force with regard to paralegals than it does for associates. And it would hardly accord with Congress' intent to provide a "fully compensatory fee" if the prevailing plaintiff's attorney in a civil rights lawsuit were not permitted to bill separately for paralegals, while the defense attorney in the same litigation was able to take advantage of the prevailing practice and obtain market rates for such work. Yet that is precisely the result sought in this case by the State of Missouri, which appears to have paid its own outside counsel for the work of paralegals at the hourly rate of $35.

Nothing in § 1988 requires that the work of paralegals invariably be billed separately. If it is the practice in the relevant market not to do so, or to bill the work of paralegals only at cost, that is all that § 1988 requires. Where, however, the prevailing practice is to bill paralegal work at market rates, treating civil rights lawyers' fee requests in the same way is not only permitted by § 1988, but also makes economic sense. By encouraging the use of lower cost paralegals rather than attorneys wherever possible, permitting market-rate billing of paralegal hours "encourages cost-effective delivery of legal services and, by reducing the spiraling cost of civil rights litigation, furthers the policies underlying civil rights statutes."

Such separate billing appears to be the practice in most communities today. In the present case, Missouri concedes that "the local market typically bills separately for paralegal services," and the District Court found that the requested hourly rates of $35 for law clerks, $40 for paralegals, and $50 for recent law graduates were the prevailing rates for such services in the Kansas City area. Under these circumstances, the court's decision to award separate compensation at these rates was fully in accord with § 1988.

IV

The courts correctly granted a fee enhancement to compensate for delay in payment and approved compensation of paralegals and law clerks at market rates. The judgment of the Court of Appeals is therefore Affirmed.

2

Ethics and Professional Responsibility

DIGITAL RESOURCES

Chapter 2 Digital Resources at *www.pearsonhighered.com/goldman*

- Video Case Studies:
  - Disclosure of Status
  - Confidentiality Issue: Family Exception?
  - Confidentiality Issue: Public Information
- Chapter Summary • Web Links • Court Opinions • Glossary • Comprehension Quizzes
- Technology Resources

LEARNING OBJECTIVES

After studying this chapter, you should be able to:

1. Understand the difference between the attorney's rules of ethics and the paralegal's rules of ethics and the obligations of each profession.

2. Analyze a situation to determine if it involves the unauthorized practice of law.

3. Understand the concept of confidentiality of client communications and the attorney–client privilege.

4. Understand the concept of conflict of interest for the legal profession and methods to protect client confidentiality.

5. Explain the difference between attorney–client privilege and the work-product doctrine.

6. Explain the issues in making inadvertent disclosure of confidential information.

Paralegals at Work

Kelsey and Kathryn became friends when they were studying to be paralegals. Kathryn now works for a large national law firm while Kelsey does freelance paralegal work. They have over the years met frequently for lunch to discuss office issues and client cases. Kelsey asks Kathryn to meet for lunch at a crowded sandwich shop in the office building where she works to discuss a recent office issue. Kathryn can see that something is troubling her friend. After getting a seat at the lunch counter they order lunch and Kelsey begins to confide in Kathryn.

Kelsey regularly does freelance work for two lawyers— one who specializes in intellectual-property issues and one who does mostly personal injury work. Both are working on the same case and both have asked Kelsey to work on the file. One lawyer represents the plaintiff, a close family friend, and the other lawyer represents the defendant. Both lawyers want Kelsey to interview the clients, witnesses, and generally handle the file. Kelsey is wondering if she should be working "both sides of the fence." Kelsey describes to Kathryn the clients and the case in detail while they wait for their lunch to be served.

Kelsey explains that she often does most of the work on the plaintiff lawyer's cases not related to intellectual property, including settling the cases with insurance company adjusters or the lawyers representing the defendants. Kelsey knows the adjuster on this case and he has revealed to her that the insurance company for the defendant wants to settle the case quickly and avoid a trial. Kelsey asks Kathryn for advice.

Consider the issues involved in this scenario as you read the chapter.

INTRODUCTION TO ETHICS AND PROFESSIONAL RESPONSIBILITY

Professions such as law and medicine are regulated for the protection of the public. It may be by licensing or other regulation. Every profession develops a set of guidelines for those in the profession to follow. These may be codes of conduct or **ethical guidelines**, such as the **ABA Model Rules of Professional Conduct** for lawyers. With only a few exceptions, most states have adopted some form of the current or former version of the American Bar Association's Model Rules of Professional Conduct. This provides a high degree of consistency in the ethical guidelines for the legal profession across the country.

Members of national paralegal associations, such as NALA, the National Association of Legal Assistants, and NFPA, the National Federation of Paralegal Associations, have ethics guidelines. These organizations require members to conduct themselves in accordance with these guidelines, observance of which by its members is a condition of continued membership in the organization.

These codes typically set forth the minimum in ethical behavior—the very least each professional should do. In the field of law, these rules are referred to as "the rules of ethics" or "the rules of professional responsibility." Each state controls the right to practice law and, therefore, each state has adopted its own "rules of ethics." The supreme court or legislature of each state has a committee or board that is authorized to enforce state rules of professional responsibility. States typically use a "bar association" to receive and investigate complaints against lawyers.

Regulation of the Practice of Law

Just as the practice of medicine and other professions is regulated, the practice of law is regulated by state government and court rule in an attempt to protect the public from incompetent and unscrupulous practitioners. To protect the public, certain occupations and professions, such as law, require obtaining a license as a method of regulating and monitoring those who offer services to the public. Obtaining a license may be as simple as completing a form and providing proof that the required education and or experience requirements have been satisfied. The profession of law, in most cases, requires taking a qualifying examination after proving that the required educational background has been obtained. This has not always been the case. In the past, admission was possible by satisfying the court that one had studied or, as it was called, "read" the law and had worked under the supervision of a lawyer.

In some states, prior admission for a required period of time allowed admission to the new jurisdiction without taking the examination. Today's rules generally have eliminated these alternative methods of admission to the practice of law. Even seasoned attorneys seeking admission to other states such as California and Florida must retake the examination for that state as a condition for admission.

This examination is generally called the "bar exam." The term "bar" in bar exam has been attributed to the custom of separating the public by a bar from those allowed to pass the bar and approach the judge or court. Most modern courtrooms continue the tradition with a barrier separating the area where spectators sit from where the lawyers, judges, and juries sit. The bar examination tests the applicant's basic legal knowledge and attempts to assure a minimum standard of competency.

Passing the bar exam is the first step in "getting admitted to practice." Admission usually is a ceremonial swearing-in by the court to which the person is "admitted to practice" upon the recommendation of the state or local bar examiners and

---

Ethical guidelines Rules of minimally acceptable professional conduct.

ABA Model Rules of Professional Conduct
A recommended set of ethics and professional conduct guidelines for lawyers, prepared by American Bar Association, originally released in 1983; prior release was Model Code of Professional Conduct.

Web Exploration

Check the latest version of the ABA Model Rules of Professional Conduct at http://www.abanet .org/cpr/mrpc/model_rules.htm.

Web Exploration

The American Bar Association (ABA) Center for Professional Responsibilty website with links to other national, state, and international ethics resources are available online. One of the resources available online is its report on the status of individual state review of Professional Conduct Rules. The full report may be viewed at http://www .abanet.org/cpr/jclr/ethics_ 2000_status_chart.pdf.

the introduction and motion for admission by an existing member of the bar of that court.

Admission to practice before one court does not automatically authorize practice before other courts. Each state has its own rules and standards. Generally, admission to the highest court of the state confers admission to all of the other state and municipal and minor judiciary courts of that state. The right to practice before the various federal courts requires separate application and admission to practice. Admission to federal court is generally granted upon motion of an existing member of the court bar upon submission of proof of admission to practice before the highest court of the state of admission and proof of good character.

For the lawyer, the rules that must be followed in the practice of law are found in the individual code of professional responsibility or canons of ethics, such as the Model Rules of Professional Conduct of the American Bar Association, as adopted by the individual state's highest court. The rules of conduct or ethics are enforced by disciplinary committees and their recommendation to the court for sanctions against offending attorneys. Complaints about breaches of ethical behavior normally are referred to a committee for investigation. In some states, minor infractions can subject the lawyer to private reprimand, public reprimand or censure, or in serious cases, temporary or permanent loss of the license to practice law, usually called disbarment.

Breaches of unauthorized practice of law complaint generally are referred to the state attorney or local prosecutor for criminal prosecution as a violation of statute and not a breach of the court rules of ethical behavior. It should be noted that some ethical breaches also may be violations of statute. Attorneys who breach a client's trust by taking the client's fund are guilty of violating an ethical rule and a criminal act of theft.

An appreciation for the system of admission and monitoring of those who seek to practice law can be found in the Preamble to the Illinois Supreme Court Rules of Professional Conduct:

> The practice of law is a public trust. Lawyers are the trustees of the system by which citizens resolve disputes among themselves, punish and deter crime, and determine their relative rights and responsibilities toward each other and their government. Lawyers therefore are responsible for the character, competence and integrity of the persons whom they assist in joining their profession; for assuring access to that system through the availability of competent legal counsel; for maintaining public confidence in the system of justice by acting competently and with loyalty to the best interests of their clients; by working to improve that system to meet the challenges of a rapidly changing society; and by defending the integrity of the judicial system against those who would corrupt, abuse or defraud it.
>
> To achieve these ends, the practice of law is regulated by the following rules. Violation of these rules is grounds for discipline. No set of prohibitions, however, can adequately articulate the positive values or goals sought to be advanced by those prohibitions. This preamble therefore seeks to articulate those values in much the same way as did the former canons set forth in the Illinois Code of Professional Responsibility. Lawyers seeking to conform their conduct to the requirements of these rules should look to the values described in this preamble for guidance in interpreting the difficult issues which may arise under the rules.
>
> The policies which underlie the various rules may, under certain circumstances, be in some tension with each other. Wherever feasible, the rules themselves seek to resolve such conflicts with clear statements of duty. For example, a lawyer must disclose, even in breach of a client confidence, a client's intent to commit a crime involving a serious risk of bodily harm. In other cases, lawyers must carefully weigh conflicting values, and make decisions, at the peril of violating one or more of the following rules. Lawyers are trained to make just such decisions, however, and should not shrink from the task. To reach correct ethical decisions, lawyers must be sensitive to the duties imposed by these rules and, whenever practical, should discuss particularly difficult issues with their peers.

The Paralegal and Licensing

There are, with a few exceptions, no state licensing requirements for one to work as a paralegal—unlike the procedures that lawyers must follow to practice law. Some states, such as California, Maine, and North Carolina, have enacted legislation establishing licensure to perform certain functions frequently performed by paralegals. Generally, these are attempting to regulate the unsupervised performance by freelance or independent paralegals, such as document-completion services.

At best, these laws carve out a small part of the practice of law that can be performed by nonlawyers without risking the performance of acts that constitute the unlawful practice of law. But none allow anyone other than a lawyer properly admitted to practice in the jurisdiction to give legal advice or opinions. Even the selection of the correct form is considered a lawyer's function. (See the California Business Code on the next page.) The client must select the forms.

There is a fine line between lawful activity and unlawful practice of law. Recommending or selecting a form that may impact on a person's legal rights is more likely than not to be treated as practicing law and therefore subject the unlicensed person to a charge of UPL. The dilemma for the paralegal is knowing when giving advice or helping someone fill in blank forms is the **Unauthorized Practice of Law (UPL)**.

Unauthorized Practice of Law (UPL) Giving legal advice, if legal rights may be affected, by anyone not licensed to practice law.

Although each state is free to define the practice of law differently, the statutes have certain elements in common. Typical of the various states' definitions of the Practice of Law is that of *Rule 31, Rules of the Supreme Court of Arizona.*

A. "Practice of law" means providing legal advice or services to or for another by:

(1) preparing any document in any medium intended to affect or secure legal rights for a specific person or entity;
(2) preparing or expressing legal opinions;
(3) representing another in a judicial, quasi-judicial, or administrative proceeding, or other formal dispute resolution process such as arbitration and mediation;
(4) preparing any document through any medium for filing in any court, administrative agency or tribunal for a specific person or entity; or
(5) negotiating legal rights or responsibilities for a specific person or entity . . .

Penalties for the Unauthorized Practice of Law

States such as Pennsylvania have specifically addressed the issue of unauthorized practice of law by paralegals and legal assistants. The Pennsylvania statute on the unauthorized practice of law makes it a misdemeanor for "any person, including, but not limited to, a paralegal or legal assistant who within this Commonwealth, shall practice law . . . " 42 Pa. C.S.A. § 2524.

The Pennsylvania statute seems to address concerns that the general public will misinterpret the title of paralegal or legal assistant as denoting a person admitted to practice law in the commonwealth. An unresolved issue in Pennsylvania, and in other states, is to define what specific conduct the courts will hold to be the practice of law. Because the interpretation will vary from state to state, the paralegal must be aware of the local requirements and limitations that define the unauthorized practice of law within that jurisdiction.

In those states that have enacted legislation regulating paralegal activity some guidance is offered by the defined activity that is permitted. For example, California has included within its Business and Professional Code, licensing of persons as "Unlawful Detainer Assistant" and "Legal Document Assistant" and defining the activity permitted.

Chapter 5.5. Legal Document Assistants and Unlawful Detainer Assistants

Article 1. General Provisions

6400(a) "Unlawful detainer assistant" means any individual who for compensation renders assistance or advice in the prosecution or defense of an unlawful detainer claim or action, including any bankruptcy petition that may affect the unlawful detainer claim or action.

(b) "Unlawful detainer claim" means a proceeding, filing, or action affecting rights or liabilities of any person that arises under Chapter 4 (commencing with Section 1159) of Title 3 of Part 3 of the Code of Civil Procedure and that contemplates an adjudication by a court.

(c) "Legal document assistant" means:

(1) Any person who is not exempted under Section 6401 and who provides, or assists in providing, or offers to provide, or offers to assist in providing, for compensation, any self-help service to a member of the public who is representing himself or herself in a legal matter, or who holds himself or herself out as someone who offers that service or has that authority. This paragraph does not apply to any individual whose assistance consists merely of secretarial or receptionist services.

Avoiding UPL: Holding Oneself Out

With so much uncertainty in what constitutes the unauthorized practice of law the question for every paralegal must be "How Do I Avoid UPL?" Some general guidelines should be followed. A common thread in the law of UPL is the prohibition of holding oneself out as a lawyer when not admitted to practice law. The Florida statute was amended recently to read:

> Any person not licensed or otherwise authorized to practice law in this state who practices law in this state or holds himself or herself out to the public as qualified to practice law in this state, or who willfully pretends to be, or willfully takes or uses any name, title, addition, or description implying that he or she is qualified, or recognized by law as qualified, to practice law in this state, commits a felony of the third degree. . . .
>
> Chapter *2004-287*, Senate Bill 1776.

California, in the Business and Professional Code mentioned above, reinforces the concept of not misleading the public into thinking one is a lawyer when he/she provides limited service, by requiring the following statement to prospective clients:

> (4) The statement: "I am not an attorney" and, if the person offering legal document assistant or unlawful detainer assistant services is a partnership or a corporation, or uses a fictitious business name, "(name) is not a law firm. I/we cannot represent you in court, advise you about your legal rights or the law, or select legal forms for you."

For the paralegal, the first rule must be to inform the parties with whom they are dealing that they are not lawyers. Paralegals must not hold themselves out as being anything more than a paralegal. Parties with whom the paralegal has contact must know the limited role the person plays as a paralegal on the legal team. Other lawyers, members of the legal team, and courthouse staff are put on notice by being informed of the person's status as paralegal. This may be by oral comment, written statement, such as a letter signed using the title "paralegal," or presentment with a business card clearly showing the title of paralegal.

Advising clients, witnesses, and other members of the general public of the role of the paralegal is not as easy. Those who are not properly educated in the role of the paralegal may believe that a paralegal is someone with advanced training and knowledge who can perform some of the functions normally performed by lawyers, including giving legal advice and opinions. The safest course is to be certain the other party is not misled about the role of the paralegal. Use of the statement from the California Business Code above is a start: "I am not an attorney" . . . "I . . . cannot represent you in court, advise you about your legal rights or the law, or select legal forms for you."

Even this may have its peril when the individual is not aware of the differences in our legal system in the functions of members of the legal team. Some members of the community may come from backgrounds where the distinctions are not clear—for example, those coming from other countries where the legal systems are different and the roles of people in the system are different or where different terms are used for those who perform legal-type functions such as notaries.

For non-native English-speaking people, translation also may play a role in the misunderstanding. To some clients, the paralegal is the "face" or main contact with the law firms. The paralegal may be the first point of contact and the one through whom all documents and information is communicated by the lawyers in the firm.

Paralegals must make it clear that they are paralegals and not lawyers. In a first meeting with anyone—client, witness, opposing counsel, or court personnel—the wisest course of action is to advise them of your position as a paralegal. A short, "I am Miss Attorney's paralegal" may be sufficient to put the other party on notice. Business cards and letterhead, where permitted, should clearly state the title of paralegal. Correspondence always should include the title as part of the signature block.

Never allow the other party to think you are anything other than what you are—a professional who is a paralegal. For those who are not familiar with the role of the paralegal, you may have to clarify what the paralegal can and cannot do in your jurisdiction.

Avoiding UPL: Giving Advice

Every UPL statute or rule prohibits anyone other than a lawyer properly admitted to practice in the state or jurisdiction from preparing or expressing legal opinions. Clearly, then, a paralegal cannot give a legal opinion or give legal advice. It sounds easy, but the reality is that paralegals must be on guard constantly to avoid giving legal advice or rendering a legal opinion. Clients and those seeking "a little free advice" may not want to respect the limitations on the paralegal's role in the legal system.

Certain conduct required or requested by an attorney or client should, at the very least, cause the paralegal to pause. A client who asks you to prepare a power of attorney "without bothering the lawyer," or to "go with me to the support conference" should raise a caution flag in the paralegal's mind. Even in a social setting, you may have to repeat the statement, "I am not an attorney". . . "I/we cannot represent you in court, advise you about your legal rights or the law, or select legal forms for you."

When is giving advice an unauthorized practice of law? If legal rights may be affected, it probably is legal advice. The question of what advice is legal advice is not easy to answer. Consider the seemingly innocent question, "How should I sign my name?" In most circumstances the answer might be: "Just sign it the way you normally write your name." But when a person is signing a document in a representative capacity—for example as the officer of a corporation or on behalf of another person under a power of attorney—telling the client to "just sign your name" might be giving legal advice because the client's legal rights could be affected if he or she does not indicate representative capacity.

Avoiding UPL: Filling Out Forms

Filling out forms for clients also can be a source of trouble. In some jurisdictions, paralegals are permitted to assist clients in preparing certain documents. Other courts, however, view this assistance as rendering legal advice.

> As a general matter, other courts have held that the sale of self-help legal kits or printed legal forms does not constitute the unauthorized practice of law as long as the seller provides the buyer no advice regarding which forms to use or how the forms should be filled out.

Fifteenth Jud. Dis. v. Glasgow, M1996-00020-COA-R3-CV (Tenn.App. 12-10-1999)(FN4)

The Florida court addressed this issue in an unlawful practice of law case, holding the UPL consisted of

> . . . a nonlawyer who has direct contact with individuals in the nature of consultation, explanation, recommendations, advice, and assistance in the provision, selection, and completion of legal forms engages in the unlicensed practice of law; . . . [W]hile a nonlawyer may sell certain legal forms and type up instruments completed by clients, a nonlawyer "must not engage in personal legal assistance in conjunction with her business activities, including the correction of errors and omissions. . . ."

The Florida Bar, petitioner, versus **We The People Forms and Service Center of Sarasota, Inc., et al.**, No. SC02—1675

Avoiding UPL: Representing Clients

Knowing when someone may represent a client before a judicial or quasi-judicial board, such as an administrative agency, is a difficult question to answer. The difficulty is in knowing what the individual courts allow or will permit in individual circumstances. Some jurisdictions and administrative agencies do permit those who are not licensed or admitted to practice to appear in court or before administrative law judges or referees on behalf of clients. Typically, these are law students acting under the guidance and supervision of an attorney under limited circumstances, but they may include paralegals. Depending upon the jurisdiction, nature of the action, and level of the court, the paralegal might be permitted to appear with or on behalf of a client—for example, before a Social Security Administration Administrative Law Judge.

Who may represent clients is not a simple question for lawyers, or for paralegals. Representation of parties traditionally has been the role of lawyers. But even lawyers are not always permitted to represent parties. Appropriate admission to practice in the jurisdiction is typically a requirement. A lawyer admitted to practice in one state may not necessarily represent the same client in another state. Lawyers admitted to practice in one jurisdiction, however, may ask the court of another jurisdiction for permission to appear and try a specific case. This is a courtesy generally granted for a single case, and usually when the trial attorney has retained local counsel who will appear as well to advise on local rules and procedures. But the issue of out-of-state counsel is not without other issues. The complexity of the issue is raised in a portion of a report on the Unauthorized Practice of Law prepared by the Nevada Assistant Bar Counsel.

> The Bar has received complaints of out-of-state counsel participating in the pre-litigation mediation procedures. Writing notification letters, engaging in discovery, and appearing at pre-litigation mediations in a representative capacity is generally the practice of law. In Nevada there is no mechanism to obtain authority from the Supreme Court to appear in pre-litigation cases. Therefore, engaging in legal activities involving Nevada disputes and Nevada parties requires a licensed Nevada attorney. . . .

(Unauthorized Practice of Law, David A. Clark, Assistant Bar Counsel, September 20, 2001)

If the representation of clients is not clear for members of the bar, it certainly is not clear for members of the paralegal profession. Generally, only duly admitted lawyers in the jurisdiction may represent parties. But this rule has been modified to allow law students in some states to represent parties in certain situations, generally under appropriate supervision.

In some states a nonlawyer employee may represent a business in some proceeding before administrative agencies or before the minor judiciary, such as small claims courts. There is no uniformity of rules when nonlawyers may represent parties or before which agencies or courts. Any appearance before a court must be approached carefully. Even the presentation of a request for continuance of a case may be considered by some courts to be the practice of law.

Appearance on behalf of clients before federal and state administrative agencies is no less lacking in uniformity than appearances before courts. But it frequently is easier to determine the ability to appear as a paralegal representing a client. Some federal agencies specifically permit nonlawyers to appear. Most notable is the Social Security Administration, which allows representation by nonlawyers with few differences from representation by lawyers. The U.S. Patent Office also specifically permits nonlawyer practice. Some states, by specific legislation or administrative rule, also permit representation by nonlawyers.

Avoiding UPL: Guidelines

The National Association of Legal Assistants, Inc. Model Standards and Guidelines for the Utilization of Legal Assistants provides guidelines on conduct that may prevent UPL.

Guideline 1

Legal Assistants Should:

1. Disclose their status as legal assistants at the outset of any professional relationship with a client, other attorneys, a court or administrative agency or personnel thereof, or members of the general public.

Guideline 2

Legal Assistants Should Not:

1. Establish attorney–client relationships; set legal fees; give legal opinions or advice; or represent a client before a court, unless authorized to do so by said court; nor
2. Engage in, encourage, or contribute to any act that could constitute the unauthorized practice of law.

Guideline 3

Legal Assistants May Perform Services for an Attorney in the Representation of a Client, Provided:

1. The services performed by the legal assistant do not require the exercise of independent professional legal judgment;
2. The attorney maintains a direct relationship with the client and maintains control of all client matters;
3. The attorney supervises the legal assistant;
4. The attorney remains professionally responsible for all work on behalf of the client, including any actions taken or not taken by the legal assistant in connection therewith; and
5. The services performed supplement, merge with, and become the attorney's work product.

Ethical Obligations

Ethical behavior is expected and required of every member of the legal team, attorney, paralegal, litigation support, information technologist, and outside consultant. What is sometimes not clear in the minds of nonlawyer members of the legal team is what ethical obligations they have and how the ethics rules are to be followed and enforced.

Duty to Supervise

The attorney is ultimately responsible for the ethic conduct of everyone on the legal team. The supervising attorney is the one in charge of a case and those working on the case.

The duty of supervision is required of partners and lawyers with managerial authority in the firm to ensure other lawyers' conduct conforms to the ethical code. Rule 5.1. Direct supervising attorneys with authority over nonlawyers have an ethical obligation to ensure those persons' conduct is compatible with the obligations of the lawyer. Rule 5.3(b). What happens in the handling and processing of a case by the legal team is ultimately the responsibility of the supervising attorney. Any ethical breaches or lapses are ultimately the responsibility of the attorney under the ethical guidelines and under common law principles of agency law. (The principal is responsible for the acts of the agent when the agent is acting within the scope of their employment.) The attorney is the one to whom the client looks for professional advice and the outcome of the case. The attorney will suffer any sanctions that result from a failure to follow and enforce the ethical rules by members of the legal team. As noted in the *opinion of the magistrate judge in the Qualcomm v. Broadcom* case:

> . . . Producing 1.2 million pages of marginally relevant documents while hiding 46,000 critically important ones does not constitute good faith and does not satisfy either the client's or attorney's discovery obligations. Similarly, agreeing to produce certain categories of documents and then not producing all of the documents that fit within such a category is unacceptable. Qualcomm's conduct warrants sanctions.

> **C. Sanctions**

> The Court's review of Qualcomm's declarations, the attorneys' declarations, and Judge Brewster's orders leads this Court to the inevitable conclusion that Qualcomm intentionally withheld tens of thousands of decisive documents from its opponent in an effort to win this case and gain a strategic business advantage over Broadcom.

> Qualcomm could not have achieved this goal without some type of assistance or deliberate ignorance from its retained attorneys. Accordingly, the Court concludes it must sanction both Qualcomm and some of its retained attorneys . . .

QUALCOMM INCORPORATED, v. BROADCOM CORPORATION, and RELATED COUNTER-CLAIMS. Case No. 05cv1958-B (BLM)

Ethical obligations of lawyers are enforced by the court in the jurisdiction where the attorney is practicing or where the case is being tried. The supervising attorney of every legal team must follow the ethics rules and ensure the members of the legal team follow the same rules as the supervising attorney. The obligation to ensure ethical conduct is that of the **supervising attorney** under the ethical obligation to supervise all who work on the case for the attorney, under Rules 5.1 and 5.3.

These rules are as much a part of the administration of justice as the rules of civil or criminal procedure and the rules of evidence. The bigger issue is who has the responsibility to instruct the nonlawyer members of the legal or trial team and who is responsible for ensuring their compliance. While it is ultimately the responsibility of the lawyer to supervise the nonlawyers support staff, such as secretaries, investigators, litigation support staff, and technical consultants, in many cases this obligation falls to the paralegal or litigation manager on the legal team. Each person working for or supervised by the attorney is in fact the **agent** of the attorney. Under fundamentals of agency law, the agent and the **principal**—the attorney—have a **fiduciary relationship** to each other. The agent must obey the reasonable instructions of the principal and the principal is presumed to know everything the agent learns in the ordinary course of working for the attorney on the case. The attorney is ultimately responsible for the ethical conduct of the agent.

Supervising attorney The member of the legal team to whom all others on the team report and who has the ultimate responsibility for the actions of the legal team.

Agent A party who acts on behalf of another.

Principal A party who employs another person to act on his or her behalf.

Fiduciary relationship A relationship under which one party has a duty to act for the interest and benefit of another while acting within the scope of the relationship.

By definition, the paralegal works under the supervision of an attorney. As such, the paralegal is the agent of the attorney and therefore owes a duty to the supervising attorney similar to that of the traditional agent–servant relationship found in agency law—that of a fiduciary obligation. Among the fiduciary obligations of an agent are the duty to exercise reasonable care, skill, and diligence.

The agent also owes a duty of loyalty to the principal. This includes the obligation to act for the employer's benefit rather than for his or her own benefit or the benefit of another whose interest may be adverse to that of the employer.

Ethical Guidelines and Rules

Lawyers generally need to follow only one set of ethics guidelines. Although it may be a set enacted by the state legislature, it usually is one adopted by the supreme court of the state in which they practice.

The most widely adopted is the Model Rules of Professional Conduct, prepared by the American Bar Association and originally released in 1983. The prior release, the Model Code of Professional Conduct (Model Code), is still in use in some jurisdictions. Procedurally, each state reviews the Model Rules or Model Code and adopts the entire recommended set of Model Rules or the Model Code, or portions as it thinks appropriate for its jurisdiction.

Unlike the ABA for lawyers, no single source of ethical rules is set out for the legal assistant. Absent a single unified body of ethical rules, legal assistants must follow state statutes and conduct themselves in conformity with the rules of professional conduct applicable to attorneys and with the ethics opinions of their professional associations. The two major legal assistant organizations providing an ethical code for their members are the National Federation of Paralegal Associations (NFPA) and the National Association of Legal Assistants (NALA).

Although legal assistants are not governed directly by the American Bar Association ethical rules, there is an intertwined relationship between the lawyer, the client, and the paralegal. What the paralegal does or does not do can have a real impact on the lawyer's duty and obligation to the client. Under the Model Rules, the lawyer ultimately is responsible for the actions of the legal assistant.

Model Guidelines for the Utilization of Legal Assistant Services A set of guidelines by ABA policymaking body, the House of Delegates, intended to govern conduct of lawyers when utilizing paralegals or legal assistants.

ABA Model Guidelines for the Utilization of Paralegal Services

In 1991, the American Bar Association's policymaking body, the House of Delegates, initially adopted a set of guidelines intended to govern the conduct of lawyers when utilizing paralegals or legal assistants. These guidelines were updated in 2002 to reflect the legal and policy developments that had taken place since 1991.

Attorneys are bound by the ethical code adopted by the state in which they practice. The ethical guidelines for the paralegal are a combination of the ethical rules imposed on the supervising attorney and the paralegal professional association rules imposed on paralegals. As a general rule, whatever the ethical rules forbid the attorney from doing, they also forbid the paralegal from doing. Paralegals, therefore, can look to their state's adopted set of rules, or code, of professional responsibility for guidance in deciding what is appropriate or inappropriate from an ethical perspective.

By extension of the rule of agency, the paralegal, as a subagent of the supervising attorney, becomes an agent of the client. The attorney is an agent of the client, and the paralegal is a subagent. As an agent of the client, the same duties that are owed to the law firm as the employer are also owed to the client.

One of the questions that arise in firms engaged in corporate practice and in securities practice is whether the paralegal can purchase stock (securities) in a client corporation. Some firms have written policies prohibiting members of the firm, including

Paralegals *in* Practice

PARALEGAL PROFILE
Vicki Voisin

Vicki Voisin, an Advanced Certified Paralegal, is nationally recognized as an author and speaker on ethical issues related to the paralegal profession. She is the creator and presenter of EthicsBasics, a program designed to raise awareness of ethical concerns by legal professionals and corporate employees. She also publishes an e-magazine titled Strategies for Paralegals Seeking Excellence (www.paralegalmentor.com). Vicki is a past president of the National Association of Legal Assistants (NALA), and presently serves on NALA's Advanced Certification Board. She has over 20 years of paralegal experience and is currently employed by Running, Wise & Ford in Charlevoix, Michigan.

The most important paralegal skills needed in the law office where I work are a familiarity with court rules and ethical issues, the ability to communicate clearly with clients, excellent organizational skills, and an attentiveness to detail and accuracy.

I also believe that technology plays an important role in the legal profession. Although technology allows attorneys and paralegals to work faster, it does not necessarily guarantee that all of the work results are accurate. Paralegals should be aware of the potential ethical hazards that technology can introduce, especially in the areas of confidentiality and conflicts of interest. For example, unless done properly, redaction (editing) on electronically filed documents can be uncovered, resulting in the disclosure of confidential and/or privileged information to third parties.

All paralegals should be aware of their ethical obligations and those of an attorney. My advice is to familiarize yourself with the American Bar Association's *Model Rules of Professional Conduct*, as well as its *Guidelines for the Utilization of Paralegal Services*. Then, become acquainted with the related *Model Rules and Guidelines* for your particular state, if available. Also, join professional associations to keep abreast of trends, and attend continuing education programs as often as possible.

paralegals, from purchasing the securities (stock) of client corporations. At the forefront is the propriety of using the information leading to the purchase or the transaction in client securities. Among the issues is whether the purchase was made based upon material inside information, information not generally available to the public, the knowledge of which would cause a person to buy or sell a corporate security. Use of material inside information of publicly traded stocks is generally a violation of federal securities laws prohibiting insider transactions.

For the attorney, guidance is available from Model Rule 1.7 and the comments to the Model Rule and under the previous Model Code DR 5–101A, which provides that an attorney must refuse employment when personal interests, including financial interests, might sway professional judgment. To the extent that this rule applies to the attorney, good judgment would dictate that it applies to the paralegal as well.

Uniformity of Paralegal Ethics

The paralegal profession has no unified code of ethics. State regulations and ethics opinions are not uniform. National organizations such as the National Association of Legal Assistants and the National Federation of Paralegal Associations each provide a uniform code of ethical conduct for members.

Ethics Codes of Paralegal Associations

The two leading national paralegal membership organizations are the National Federation of Paralegal Associations and the National Association of Legal Assistants. Each of these groups has formulated a set of ethical guidelines for its respective membership, as well as for others looking for ethical guidance in regulating the paralegal profession.

 Web Exploration

The National Associations Ethics Codes and ethical guidelines can be reviewed at:

National Federation of Paralegal Associations
www.paralegals.org/display common.cfm?an=1&subarti clenbr=330

National Association of Legal Assistants
www.nala.org/

NALS. . . . the Association for Legal Professionals
http://www.nals.org

Association of Legal Administrators
www.alanet.org

National Federation of Paralegal Associations

The National Federation of Paralegal Associations, Inc. is a professional organization composed of paralegal associations and individual paralegals throughout the United States and Canada. Members of NFPA have varying backgrounds, experiences, education, and job responsibilities that reflect the diversity of the paralegal profession. NFPA promotes the growth, development, and recognition of the paralegal profession as an integral partner in the delivery of legal services.

In April 1997, NFPA adopted the Model Disciplinary Rules (Model Rules) to make possible the enforcement of the Canons and Ethical Considerations contained in the NFPA Model Code. At present, unlike a violation by an attorney of the state-adopted rules that can result in loss of the right to practice (disbarment), no such sanction exists for the paralegal breach of association rules except loss of membership.

National Association of Legal Assistants

The National Association of Legal Assistants, formed in 1975, is a leading professional association for legal assistants. NALA provides continuing professional education, development, and certification. It may best be known in the profession for its Certified Legal Assistant (CLA) examination. The ABA Standing Committee on Paralegals has recognized the CLA designation as a designation marking a high level of professional achievement.

A proper coverage of the ethical rules and guidelines is the subject for a course by itself. This overview highlights some key ethical issues that the paralegal must be aware of as a member of a legal team. As a part of the legal team, the paralegal is required to follow the same rules as the supervising attorney. In a majority of jurisdictions these ethical rules are based on the ABA Model Rules of Professional Conduct. Among the ethical obligations of the attorney, and the legal team acting as agent of the attorney, which will be discussed below, are those of:

- Competency, Model Rules of Professional Conduct Rule 1.1,
- Confidentiality, Model Rules of Professional Conduct Rule 1.6(A),
- Conflicts Of Interest, Model Rules of Professional Conduct Rule 1.7,
- Candor, Model Rules of Professional Conduct Rule 3.3,
- Fairness To Opposing Party And Counsel, Model Rules of Professional Conduct Rule 3.4, and
- Duty to Supervise, Model Rules of Professional Conduct Rules 5.1 and 5.3.

Related to the ethical obligation of confidentiality are the related rules of evidence that limit the obligation of the members of the legal team from having to testify under the attorney–client privilege and protect the work product of the legal team prepared for trial from disclosure (Federal Rules of Evidence 501). Paralegals and other nonlawyers also must be concerned with the ethical issues as discussed in the Advice from the Field by Betty Wells.

Competence

Competence/competent The minimum level of knowledge and skill required of a professional.

Rules of court A court's rules for the processing and presentation of cases.

ABA Model Rule of Professional Conduct 1.1 requires that lawyers provide competent representation to a client. **Competent** representation requires the legal knowledge, skill, thoroughness, and preparation reasonably necessary for the representation. Few ethics opinions have been written on the subject of competent representation required under Rule 1.1 as it relates to nonspecific legal issues of workload and legal knowledge. However, the minimum standards clearly require an understanding of the **rules of court**. These rules continue to grow in number and complexity including the adoption of rules regarding electronic discovery. New rules require a new level of knowledge to competently represent clients. Further, lawyers

Advice *from the* Field

Betty Wells, PP, PLS, TSC, is currently employed in the Austin, Texas, office of Cox Smith Matthews Incorporated, a San Antonio law firm. She joined NALS in 1994, is a NALS Life Member, and is serving as webmaster for her local chapter, Corresponding Secretary for her state association, Chair of the NALS Foundation, as well as a non-voting Board Member of NALS. She received the Member of the Year in 1997–98 and 2001–02 from her local chapter, the Legal Professional of the Year award in 1997–98 from her state association and the NALS Award of Excellence in 2003. In 2004–05 she received the Mentor of the Year award from her local chapter.

This article was originally published in the Winter 2002-3 issue of *@Law*, the NALS magazine for legal professionals. It is printed with the permission of *@Law* and NALS, the association for legal professionals. © NALS, Inc. Reprinted with permission. All rights reserved.

The American Bar Association and NALS . . . *the association for legal professionals* uses this definition for a legal assistant or paralegal: "A legal assistant or paralegal is a person, qualified by education, training or work experience who is employed or retained by a lawyer, law office, corporation, governmental agency or other entity and who performs specifically delegated substantive legal work for which a lawyer is responsible."

In simple language, a legal assistant is a non-lawyer who provides substantive legal services and is supervised by a lawyer. Legal services performed by non-lawyers differ from firm to firm but may include anything from answering the phone to complex research. Just as the description of legal tasks the non-lawyer may be asked to perform varies from firm to firm, so do non-lawyer classifications. In one firm, a legal secretary may simply answer the attorney's phone and revise documents, while in another firm a legal secretary may prepare complex wills and research case law. You may be "classed" as a legal secretary in your firm while you are actually asked to perform "legal assistant or paralegal" work while working under the supervision of an attorney.

Non-lawyers should be aware of how their conduct could affect not only themselves, but also the lawyer and firm for whom they work. Although legal assistants or paralegals are not directly subject to any rules of professional conduct promulgated by courts, legislatures, or government agencies, those non-lawyer personnel could loose [sic] their job for not following the rules of ethical conduct. In addition, the supervising lawyer could be reprimanded, suspended, or even disbarred, depending on the severity of the unethical conduct of the non-lawyer. Legal assistants or paralegals who are members of national and/or local paralegal associations are required to follow the ethical codes of those associations.

Possibly the biggest ethical situation a non-lawyer faces is the unauthorized practice of law ("UPL"). If you are "tenured," you may find you know more about a particular area of the law than some newly "sworn" lawyers. Because of your knowledge, you may get dangerously close to crossing or may have already crossed the UPL line. Tasks a non-lawyer may perform are limited by statutory or court authority, and the lawyer's determination of the non-lawyer's competency. As the legal profession has evolved so has the role of non-lawyers. Today a non-lawyer is well-educated and well-trained with a variety of backgrounds and experience. The practice of law includes accepting cases, setting fees, giving legal advice, preparing or signing legal documents, and appearing before a court or other judicial body in a representative capacity. The unauthorized practice of law occurs when a non-lawyer engages in activities which affect the legal rights and obligations of clients. The biggest risk for a non-lawyer is giving legal advice instead of general legal information especially when the request comes from a family member or friend. Family members are typically the hardest to convince that you cannot give them legal advice, and they can be relentless in their pursuit of advice. Be aware: Your willingness to dispense legal advice to the family member or friend could potentially result in your unemployment.

How can the non-lawyer avoid UPL? The best way is to always identify oneself as a legal secretary, legal assistant or paralegal who has posed the specific question to a supervising lawyer and as one who is relaying information gleaned from that lawyer. Make certain all legal documents and correspondence that could be considered legal opinion are reviewed, approved and signed by your supervising lawyer or another lawyer in the firm that is familiar with the matter. If you do not know what the UPL provisions are in your state, call your state bar and ask them for the guidelines non-lawyers must follow. Find out today before you are forced to explain what you have done, not only to your employer but to the bar association in your state.

Confidentiality is another area non-lawyers are faced with each and every day. It is important to a lawyer's practice that his clients are able to speak freely with the lawyer's support personnel and for the clients to know the information they are relaying through you will be held in the strictest of confidence. Did the firm where you are employed ask you to sign a confidentiality statement when you were hired? If they did, did they explain to you what client confidentiality meant? If they didn't, ask them for the form and ask them to explain client confidences.

If the firm doesn't have a confidentiality form for non-lawyers, ask them to create one—their malpractice insurance carrier will love you for it. In simple

(continued)

terms, protecting a client's confidence means you do not talk about clients or cases in your firm with anyone, anywhere, especially in public places—the ethics rules require the lawyer to exercise reasonable care to prevent his employees or associates from violating the obligation regarding client confidences or secrets. In other words, the non-lawyer must follow the same rules as the lawyer when it comes to protecting client confidentiality.

Have you ever interviewed for a position at a law firm only to find yourself conflicted out of employment? More and more often, law firms are asking support personnel to provide a list of clients they have worked with. On occasion a non-lawyer has not been hired due to a conflict of interest that cannot be resolved. Have you been hired by a firm, or found yourself doing temp work in a firm and realized you have knowledge from your past job that could change the outcome of the matter on which you are working? Did you immediately go to the supervising lawyer or HR department and tell them of the possibility of a conflict? You should never make the decision that the

information you have is inconsequential or take it for granted simply because you are "just a temp." Remember, it is important for you to inform your employer of the potential conflict to avoid potential problems as the matter progresses, not only for you but for the lawyer and their firm as well.

What about receiving legal fees? Can you "troll" for clients and be compensated when your firm is hired? Remember, you are not allowed to set fees, you must not practice law or give the appearance of practicing law, so therefore, you must not accept fees. The reasoning behind this is to protect the lawyer's professional independence of judgment. The obligations of the lawyer to the client do not change simply because you "brought" the client to the firm.

Your unethical behavior may cause you to loose [sic] your job *and* it may cost your employer his or her career. Stay current with ethical requirements in your profession by attending continuing legal education seminars offered by local and state bar associations, as well as through your local, state, and national association. You and your employer will be glad you did.

must be able to communicate with clients in the language of technology about methods of creation and sources of electronic documents and the methods for retrieving them and processing them for submission to opposing counsel and the court. Consider the need to use "interpreters of the language of technology" as similar to the use of language interpreters as explained in the Formal Opinion of the Association of the Bar of the City of New York in the following Ethical Perspective and the notes to the Wisconsin rules on competence when the lawyer is not knowledgeable about a particular issue.

Conflict of Interest

Conflict of interest The representation of one client being directly adverse to the interest of another client.

Web Exploration

The complete version of the Formal Opinion at: http://www.nycbar.org/Ethics/eth1995-12.htm.

A **conflict of interest** exists if the representation of one client will be adverse to the interest of another client. Conflict of interest may best be explained by the adage that no one can serve two masters. If the master is entitled to complete loyalty, any conflict in loyalties presents a conflict of interest in which neither master can be certain of the loyalty of his or her servant. It's easy to see the conflict that would arise in a lawyer's going to court representing both the plaintiff and the defendant.

Less obvious are situations in which the attorney represents two parties with a common interest, such as a husband and wife purchasing a new home. In most cases, the interests would be the same and no conflict would exist. When these clients are seeking counseling for marital problems, however, the conflict becomes more obvious as one of them seeks a greater share of the common property or other rights and the lawyer is called upon to give legal advice as to the right to the parties. Finally, lawyers clearly cannot represent both husband and wife in court in the marital dissolution trial.

The American Bar Association Model Rules of Professional Conduct provide a guideline in Rule 1.7, Conflict of Interest: General Rule, which provides in part that a lawyer shall not represent a client if the representation of that client will be directly adverse to another client, unless the lawyer reasonably believes the representation will not adversely affect the relationship with the other client; and each client consents after

ETHICAL PERSPECTIVE

The Association of the Bar of the City of New York Formal Opinion 1995-12
Committee on Professional and Judicial Ethics
July 6, 1995
Action: Formal Opinion

. . . DR 6-101(A)(2) mandates that "[a] lawyer shall not . . . [h]andle a legal matter without preparation adequate in the circumstances." Adequate preparation requires, not only that a lawyer conduct necessary legal research, but also that he or she gather information material to the claims or defenses of the client. See *Mason v. Balcom*, 531 F.2d 717, 724 (5th Cir. 1976). The lawyer's inability, because of a language barrier, to understand fully what the client is telling him or her may unnecessarily impede the lawyer's ability to gather the information from the client needed to familiarize the lawyer with the circumstances of the case. This makes communication via the interpreter vital since it may be the only practical way that a free-flowing dialogue can be maintained with the client, and the only means by which the lawyer can actually and substantially assist the client.

The duty to represent a client competently, embodied in DR 6-101(A)(1), requires a lawyer confronted with a legal matter calling for legal skills or knowledge outside the lawyer's experience or ability, to associate with lawyers with skills or knowledge necessary to handle the legal matter. When a lawyer is confronted with a legal matter requiring nonlegal skills or knowledge outside the lawyer's experience or ability and these skills or knowledge are necessary for the proper preparation of the legal matter, DR 6-101(A)(2) appears to require that the lawyer associate with professionals in other disciplines who possess the requisite skills or knowledge needed by the lawyer to prepare the legal matter. The interpreter appears to be the type of professional envisioned by EC 6-3's observation that "[p]roper preparation and representation may require the association by the lawyer of professionals in other disciplines." When the need for an interpreter is apparent or it is reasonable to conclude that an interpreter is required for effective communication, failure to take steps with the client to secure an interpreter may be a breach of the duty to represent the client competently.

The Association of the Bar of the City of New York, 42 W. 44th, New York, NY. 10036, (212) 382–6600

consultation. The essence of the rule is that of loyalty to the client. The 1981 version of the American Bar Association Model Code of Professional Responsibility provides in Canon 5:

> A lawyer should exercise independent professional judgment on behalf of a client.

The ethical considerations comment to Canon 5 states:

> EC–1 The professional judgment of a lawyer should be exercised, within the bounds of the law, solely for the benefit of his client and free of compromising influences and loyalties. Neither his personal interests, the interests of other clients, nor the desires of third persons should be permitted to dilute his loyalty to his client.

Clearly, a lawyer should not accept the employment if the lawyer's personal interests or desires will, or if there is a reasonable probability that they will, adversely affect the advice to be given or services to be rendered to the prospective client. The

WISCONSIN RULES OF PROFESSIONAL CONDUCT FOR ATTORNEYS

SIDEBAR

SCR 20:1.1 Competence
A lawyer shall provide competent representation to a client. Competent representation requires the legal knowledge, skill, thoroughness and preparation reasonably necessary for the representation. Contrast and compare the **Wisconsin Rules of Professional Conduct for Attorneys** at http://www.legis.state.wi.us/rsb/scr/5200.pdf2006, with the American Bar Association Model Rules of Professional Responsibility at http://www.abanet.org/cpr/mrpc/mrpc_toc.html, and the ethical rules in your jurisdiction.

information that may be considered to create a conflict of interest is not limited solely to that of the attorney representing a client. It also includes the information held by another member of the legal team, including the legal assistant.

The National Federation of Paralegal Associations Model Code of Ethics provides in Canon 8:

> A paralegal shall avoid conflicts of interest and shall disclose any possible conflict to the employer or client, as well as to their prospective employers or clients.

The ultimate obligation to determine the conflict of interest of the paralegal or legal assistant rests with the supervising attorney. Standard procedure in law firms is to check for conflicts of interest within the law firm before accepting a new client or undertaking a new matter for an existing client. Just as other attorneys are asked to review lists of new clients and new matters, so must paralegals check to be certain they do not have a conflict of interest.

Conflicts of interest may arise for paralegals when they change from one employer to another. If the previous employer represented a client or handled certain matters for a client during the period in which the paralegal was employed, a conflict of interest may exist. A more difficult concern for the paralegal is the conflict of interest that can arise from a law firm's representation of family members and personal friends. Paralegals frequently refer family and friends to the attorney or the law firm where they work. The mere relationship or friendship itself might not create conflict, but in some cases could give rise to a claim of undue influence wherein the paralegal may stand to benefit from the action of the law firm. Examples are the drafting of wills and trusts in which the paralegal may be named as a beneficiary or instances in which the paralegal may be named as the executor of the estate or as a trustee receiving compensation.

Ethical Wall

Ethical wall An environment in which an attorney or a paralegal is isolated from a particular case or client to avoid a conflict of interest or to protect a client's confidences and secrets.

Law firms use the term **"ethical wall"**—also called a Chinese wall (after the Great Wall of China)—to describe an environment in which an attorney or a paralegal is isolated from a particular case or client to avoid a conflict of interest or to protect a client's confidences and secrets. By creating this boundary or wall, any potential communications, whether written or oral, are prevented between members of the legal team handling a particular matter or client and the person with whom there may be a conflict of interest.

In an age of consolidation of law firms in many areas, the number of individual employers has diminished while the number of clients has increased. As a result, professionals today may find themselves in firms that were on the opposite side of cases in the past. Creating an ethical wall permits the professional to accept employment with the other firm. It also permits greater mobility by professionals, as they can go to a new firm in which there may have been a conflict.

Freelance or Independent Paralegal

Freelance or independent paralegals who work for more than one firm or attorney face the potential problem of conflict of interest. Special caution has to be taken to avoid accepting employment in cases where conflicts may exist. Freelance and independent paralegals are keenly aware of this and generally take precautions to prevent conflicts. The law firms and attorneys for whom they work usually are aware of the potential and also take special precautions to isolate potential conflict situations. Full-time paralegals who seek outside income should pay special attention to potential conflicts that may arise.

Not all of these conflicts are obvious. Consider the case of a paralegal working for a plaintiff's negligence firm handling cases against a major retail store. That

HISTORY: SUP. CT. ORDER NO. 04–07, 2007 WI 4, 293 WIS. 2D XV. ABA COMMENT: LEGAL KNOWLEDGE AND SKILL

1. In determining whether a lawyer employs the requisite knowledge and skill in a particular matter, relevant factors include the relative complexity and specialized nature of the matter, the lawyer's general experience, the lawyer's training and experience in the field in question, the preparation and study the lawyer is able to give the matter and whether it is feasible to refer the matter to, or associate or consult with, a lawyer of established competence in the field in question. In many instances, the required proficiency is that of a general practitioner. Expertise in a particular field of law may be required in some circumstances.

2. A lawyer need not necessarily have special training or prior experience to handle legal problems of a type with which the lawyer is unfamiliar. A newly admitted lawyer can be as competent as a practitioner with long experience. Some important legal skills, such as the analysis of precedent, the evaluation of evidence and legal drafting, are required in all legal problems. Perhaps the most fundamental legal skill consists of determining what kind of legal problems a situation may involve, a skill that necessarily transcends any particular specialized knowledge. A lawyer can provide adequate representation in a wholly novel field through necessary study. Competent representation can also be provided through the association of a lawyer of established competence in the field in question.

3. In an emergency a lawyer may give advice or assistance in a matter in which the lawyer does not have the skill ordinarily required where referral to or consultation or association with another lawyer would be impractical. Even in an emergency, however, assistance should be limited to that reasonably necessary in the circumstances, for ill-considered action under emergency conditions can jeopardize the client's interest.

4. A lawyer may accept representation where the requisite level of competence can be achieved by reasonable preparation. This applies as well to a lawyer who is appointed as counsel for an unrepresented person. See also Rule 6.2.

Thoroughness and Preparation

5. Competent handling of a particular matter includes inquiry into and analysis of the factual and legal elements of the problem, and use of methods and procedures meeting the standards of competent practitioners. It also includes adequate preparation. The required attention and preparation are determined in part by what is at stake; major litigation and complex transactions ordinarily require more extensive treatment than matters of lesser complexity and consequence. An agreement between the lawyer and the client regarding the scope of the representation may limit the matters for which the lawyer is responsible. See Rule 1.2(c).

Maintaining Competence

6. To maintain the requisite knowledge and skill, a lawyer should keep abreast of changes in the law and its practice, engage in continuing study and education and comply with all continuing legal education requirements to which the lawyer is subject.

SOURCE: http://www.legis.state.wi.us/rsb/scr/5200.pdf2006

paralegal's acceptance of employment at the retail store the firm is suing presents a conflict of interest. Knowledge of the strategy of the case would be of interest to the retail store employer. But divulging the information would breach the confidence of the law firm and the confidence of the law firm's client. Failing to disclose information to the retail store that directly affects its business breaches the duty of loyalty to that employer.

The Duty of Confidentiality, Attorney–Client Privilege, and Work–Product Doctrine

The three concepts—duty of confidentiality, attorney–client privilege, and work–product doctrine—have something in common: they are all connected to the legal profession's obligation to protect the secrets of the client so that the client can provide all the information necessary for the legal team to conduct an effective representation of the client.

ETHICAL PERSPECTIVE

Wyoming Rules of Professional Conduct for Attorneys at Law

RULE 1.6 CONFIDENTIALITY OF INFORMATION

(a) A lawyer shall not reveal confidential information relating to the representation of a client unless the client makes an informed decision, the disclosure is impliedly authorized in order to carry out the representation or the disclosure is permitted by paragraph (b).

(b) A lawyer may reveal such information to the extent the lawyer reasonably believes necessary:

(1) to prevent the client from committing a criminal act;

(2) to secure legal advice about the lawyer's compliance with these Rules;

(3) to establish a claim or defense on behalf of the lawyer in a controversy between the lawyer and the client, to establish a defense to a criminal charge or civil claim against the lawyer based upon conduct in which the client was involved, or to respond to allegations in any proceeding concerning the lawyer's representation of the client;

(4) to comply with other law or a court order; or

(5) to protect the best interests of an individual when the lawyer has been appointed to act as a guardian ad litem or as an attorney for the best interests of that individual.

Attorney–client privilege
A rule that says a client can tell his or her lawyer anything about the case without fear that the attorney will be called as a witness against the client.

Web Exploration

Review the most current version of Rule 1.6 on Confidentiality in your jurisdiction with the American Bar Association Model Rules of Professional Conduct at the American Bar Association website at www.abanet.org/cpr/mrcp/rule1.6.html.

Attorney–client privilege is founded on the belief that clients should be able to tell their attorneys everything about their case so the attorney can give proper legal advice to the client. For the attorney, the ABA Model Rules provide in Rule 1.6, Confidentiality of Information, that a lawyer shall not reveal information relating to representation of a client unless the client consents after consultation, except for disclosures that are impliedly authorized. What is confidential information is also defined in the ABA model rules: "all information, regardless of the source, gained in the representation of the client." Even information that may be published in the newspaper is confidential for the lawyer and paralegal working for the client and may not be discussed with others. The article may or may not be accurate and any discussion with others could result in discussion of items not in the newspaper story, therefore the lawyer or paralegal cannot confirm or deny anything.

As stated by the federal court in the case of Claus Von Bulow, the attorney–client privilege extends to those working on the case for the attorney representing the client.

The law is clear in this circuit the person claiming the attorney–client privilege has the burden of establishing all the essential elements thereof. The question is a simple one: Was Reynolds [a friend of Claus Von Bulow claiming that information given to her by the defendant was privileged] an agent of an attorney and has she presented sufficient evidence of this relationship? In other words, were communications made to her, in confidence, in her capacity as an agent of an attorney for the purpose of obtaining legal advice from that attorney? We think not.

The attorney–client privilege is founded on the assumption that encouraging clients to make the fullest disclosure to their attorneys enables the latter to act more effectively. We have recognized that an attorney's effectiveness depends upon his ability to rely on the assistance of various aides, be they secretaries, file clerks, telephone operators, messengers, clerks not yet admitted to the bar, and aides of other sorts. The privilege must include all the persons who act as the attorney's agents. *Von Bulow v. Von Bulow*, 811 F. 2d 136 (2d Cir. 1987)

In every case there are two sides, each represented by an attorney. The attorney for each party to a case has a competing interest, either to obtain information or to protect information from the other. Attorneys want to protect the information received from their clients, or developed in the process of preparing for litigation. The conflict over protecting or releasing information has intensified in recent years as private counsel and government counsel challenge the attorney's obligation to maintain in confidence information obtained directly and through use of agents such as paralegal, and public relations consultants in criminal and civil matters before commencement of litigation. Increased regulatory obligations have created additional obligations on businesses to conduct internal investigations, which has resulted in a new area of federal and state privilege—"the audit privilege."

Increased use of electronic communications tools, such as email and text messaging, has created the era of the instant message, and with it the instant inadvertent disclosure of potentially privileged material with the press of a key. Lawyers and paralegals must know what action the courts will require of the attorney or paralegal to preserve confidential and privileged information that is inadvertently disclosed and, when possible, prevent a loss of the confidentiality privilege that could result in a potential loss of the case and a possible malpractice claim against the law firm. Email has become a universal form of communication, not only for personal communication but also for business and between attorneys and client. Consider the frequent situation where an email is sent to the wrong party by accident. It may be necessary to avoid using electronic communications in jurisdictions that take a hard line that all disclosure, inadvertent or intentional, is a breach of confidentiality or privilege.

Confidentiality

The duty of **confidentiality** is just that for the legal team, a duty. It is a duty imposed on the attorney and each member of the legal team working under the supervision of the attorney to enable clients to obtain legal advice by allowing the client to freely and openly give the members of the legal team all the relevant facts without fear of disclosure of these facts except in limited situations, such as to prevent commission of a crime or to defend against a client's suit.

Attorneys, and the members of the legal team, have a duty to treat client information obtained in the course of representation of a client in confidence under ABA Rule 1.6.[i] Members of the legal team cannot tell anyone the client's information. The duty does not end when the case ends but continues forever and precludes discussing the information with friends, spouses, strangers, or anyone else who might inquire about the case.

The duty of confidentiality also extends to paralegals under ethical guidelines of the major national paralegal organizations such as NALA.[ii] Although these ethical rules are not mandatory on the paralegal, in most states the paralegal's position as an agent creates an obligation to the attorney and to the client.

In the modern practice of law, the attorney must rely on others, such as paralegals, legal secretaries, investigators, law clerks, and the like, to assist in vigorous representation of the client. These "agents" also must be covered by the attorney–client privilege. To do otherwise would require the attorney to guard every document,

Confidentiality A duty imposed on the attorney to enable clients to obtain legal advice by allowing the client to freely and openly give the attorney all the relevant facts.

---

[i] American Bar Association Model Rules of Professional Conduct Rule 1.6, Confidentiality of Information (a) A lawyer shall not reveal information relating to the representation of a client unless the client gives informed consent, the disclosure is impliedly authorized in order to carry out the representation or the disclosure is permitted by paragraph (b).

[ii] NALA Code of Ethics and Professional Responsibility *Canon* 7. A legal assistant must protect the confidences of a client and must not violate any rule or statute now in effect or hereafter enacted controlling the doctrine of privileged communications between a client and an attorney.

ETHICAL PERSPECTIVE

NALA Code of Ethics and Professional Responsibility Canon 7

A legal assistant must protect the confidences of a client and must not violate any rule or statute now in effect or hereafter enacted controlling the doctrine of privileged communications between a client and an attorney.

exhibit, and pretrial memorandum from the eyes of everyone on the legal team and perform every task personally from interviews of clients and witnesses, to the typing of reports and memorandum of law, to the conduct of fact and legal research to the preparation of trial exhibits and documents. This is clearly not desirable or cost effective for the client or the administration of justice.

Attorney–Client Privilege

The attorney–client privilege differs from the duty of confidentiality because it applies only to information obtained from the client—for example, the client's confession of commission of the crime. This privilege is found in the state or federal evidence code. It is a rule of evidence that applies in cases where the Rules of Evidence apply: a court of law, a deposition, or other places where a witness is under oath, such as interrogatories, responses to requests for documents, or grand jury hearings. The attorney–client privilege is a part of both state and federal law. The law of each jurisdiction must be consulted to determine the extent of the privilege. In the federal courts the rule determining which privilege rules are followed is governed under the Federal Rules of Evidence Rule 501.

> Except as otherwise required by the Constitution of the United States or provided by Act of Congress or in rules prescribed by the Supreme Court pursuant to statutory authority, the privilege of a witness, person, government, State, or political subdivision thereof shall be governed by the principles of the common law as they may be interpreted by the courts of the United States in the light of reason and experience. However, in civil actions and proceedings, with respect to an element of a claim or defense as to which State law supplies the rule of decision, the privilege of a witness, person, government, State, or political subdivision thereof shall be determined in accordance with State law. (Jan. 2, 1975, P.L. 93–595, § 1, 88 Stat. 1933)[iii]

For example, Pennsylvania is typical of many states in treating the privilege as part of the state common law tradition that has been incorporated in state law (*Commonwealth v. Noll*, 662 A.2d 1123, 1126 (Pa.Super. 1995), appeal denied, 543 Pa. 726, 673 A.2d 333 (1996)).

The "privilege" belongs to the client, not to the attorney. The client may waive the privilege and allow the attorney or paralegal to reveal the information; however, the

---

[iii] Rule 501 General Rule Except as otherwise required by the Constitution of the United States or provided by Act of Congress or in rules prescribed by the Supreme Court pursuant to statutory authority, the privilege of a witness, person, government, State, or political subdivision thereof shall be governed by the principles of the common law as they may be interpreted by the courts of the United States in the light of reason and experience. However, in civil actions and proceedings, with respect to an element of a claim or defense as to which State law supplies the rule of decision, the privilege of a witness, person, government, State, or political subdivision thereof shall be determined in accordance with State law. (Jan. 2, 1975, P.L. 93–595, §1, 88 Stat. 1933).

attorneys or paralegals may not of themselves waive the privilege when asked what the client has told them. In a court proceeding, an appropriate answer to the question of what the client said would be: "I declined to answer because of the attorney–client privilege." If the client had revealed or released the same information to someone else, the privilege is lost. Thus, the client must really keep the information secret for the privilege to apply.

The concept of privilege also extends to persons while acting within certain roles as discussed by the U.S. Supreme Court:

> The privileges between priest and penitent, attorney and client, and physician and patient limit protection to private communication. These privileges are rooted in the imperative need for confidence and trust. The priest-penitent privilege recognizes the human need to disclose to a spiritual counselor, in total and absolute confidence, what are believed to be flawed acts or thoughts and to receive priestly consolation and guidance in return. The lawyer-client privilege rests on the need for the advocate and counselor to know all that relates to the client's reasons for seeking representation if the professional mission is to be carried out. Similarly, the physician must know all that a patient can articulate in order to identify and to treat disease; barriers to full disclosure would impair diagnosis and treatment.

Trammell v. United States, 445 U.S. 40 (1980)

Additional relationships include:

1. Spouse[iv]
2. Psychotherapist–patient. *Jaffe v. Redmond*, 518 US 1[v]
3. Participants in settlement negotiations. *Federal Rules of Evidence* 408[vi]

Claim of Privilege

Privilege is not automatically invoked. The person claiming the privilege—usually the client—has the burden to establish the existence of the privilege.

Privilege A special legal right.

> To sustain a claim of privilege, the party invoking it must demonstrate that the information at issue was a communication between client and counsel or his employee, that it was intended to be and was in fact kept confidential, and that it was made in order to assist in obtaining or providing legal advice or services to the client[vii]

Extension of Attorney–Client Privilege to Others

It is now accepted that the efficient administration of justice requires lawyers to engage others, such as legal assistants, accountants, and other experts. This would not be possible if the privilege did not extend to these agents of the attorney including, most recently, public relations firms.

The U.S. District Court for the Southern District of New York summarized the law, stating:

> . . . the privilege in appropriate circumstances extends to otherwise privileged communications that involve persons assisting the lawyer in the rendition of legal services. This principle has been applied universally to cover office personnel, such as secretaries and law clerks, who assist lawyers in performing their tasks. But it has been

---

[iv] *Trammell v. U.S.* 445 U.S. 40 (1980).
[v] *Jaffe v. Redmond*, 518 US 1 (1996).
[vi] Rule 480 FRE: . . . evidence of conduct or statements made in compromise negotiation is . . . not admissible. Also see *The Goodyear Tire and Rubber Company v Chiles Power Supply, Inc, et al*, 2003 Fed App 0197P (6th Cir).
[vii] *SR International Bus. Ins. Co v. World Trade Center* Prop No 01 Civ 9291 (S.D.N.Y. 2002), quoting *Browne of New York City, Inc v. Ambase Corp.*

applied more broadly as well. For example, In *United States v Kovel*, the Second Circuit held that a client's communication with an accountant employed by his attorney were privileged where made for the purpose of enabling the attorney to understand the client situation in order to provide legal advice.

(IN RE Grand Jury Subpoenas dated March 24, 2003 directed to (A) Grand Jury Witness Firm and (B) Grand Jury Witness, M11-188 (USDC, S.D.N.Y.) (June 2, 2003)).

Common Interest Privilege

Common interest privilege To permit a client to share confidential information with the attorney for another who shares a common legal interest.

Another variation of privilege is the **common interest privilege**. "The purpose of the common interest privilege is to permit a client to share confidential information with the attorney for another who shares a common legal interest, such as the attorney for a co-defendant who has separate counsel.

The key consideration is that the nature of the interest be identical, *not similar* [emphasis added], and be legal, not solely commercial.[viii-ix]

Work–Product Doctrine

Work–product doctrine A qualified immunity from discovery for "work product of the lawyer" except on a substantial showing of "necessity or justification" of certain written statements and memoranda prepared by counsel in representation of a client, generally in preparation for trial.

The **work–product doctrine** is different from both the attorney–client privilege and the duty of confidentiality. The attorney–client privilege and the duty of confidentiality relate to the information provided by the clients regardless of whether they involve potential litigation. The U.S. Supreme Court recognized the work–product doctrine and its importance saying:

Proper preparation of a client's case demands that he assemble information, sift what he considers to be the relevant from the irrelevant facts, prepare his legal theories and plan his strategy without undue and needless interference. That is the historical and the necessary way in which lawyers act within the framework of our system of jurisprudence to promote justice and to protect their clients' interests.

This work is reflected, of course, in interviews, statements, memoranda, correspondence, briefs, mental impressions, personal beliefs, and countless other tangible and intangible ways—aptly though roughly termed by the Circuit Court of Appeals in this case as the "work product of the lawyer." Were such materials open to opposing counsel on mere demand, much of what is now put down in writing would remain unwritten.

An attorney's thoughts, heretofore inviolate, would not be his own. Inefficiency, unfairness and sharp practices would inevitably develop in the giving of legal advice and in the preparation of cases for trial. The effect on the legal profession would be demoralizing. And the interests of the clients and the cause of justice would be poorly served.

. . . where relevant and non-privileged facts remain hidden in an attorney's file and where production of those facts is essential to the preparation of one's case, discovery may be properly had.

Hickman v. Tayler, 329 U.S. 495 (1947) at page 511

The work–product doctrine provides a limited protection for material prepared by the attorney or those working for the attorney in anticipation of litigation or for trial, such as research on theories of law or defenses that may be raised in the trial or trial strategy for the order of presentations or methods of impeaching the credibility of witnesses for the other side.

[viii] *International Bus. Ins. Co. v. World Trade Center Prop* No 01 Civ 9291 (S.D.N.Y. 2002), quoting North River Insurance Co. v. Columbia Casualty Company No. 9 Civ 2518, 1995 WL 5792.

[ix] Also see the interesting article on the issue of providing privileged information to insurers. Guarding privileged documents poses challenge to "utmost good faith" doctrine, *National Underwriter; Eranger, April 28, 2003; Sally Agel; Felton Newell.*

The work–product doctrine is narrower than the attorney–client privilege in that it protects only materials prepared "in anticipation of litigation," Fed. R. Civ. P. 26(b)(3), whereas the attorney–client privilege protects confidential legal communications between an attorney and client regardless of whether they involve possible litigation.[x]

The work–product doctrine is codified in the Federal Rules of Civil Procedure Rule 26 (B) (3),[xi] and in Rule 16 (B) (2) of the Federal Rules of Criminal Procedure.[xii]

FRCP 26 (b) Discovery Scope and Limits

Unless otherwise limited by order of the court in accordance with these rules, the scope of discovery is as follows:

(1) In General. Parties may obtain discovery regarding any matter, not privileged, that is relevant to the claim or defense of any party, including the existence, description, nature, custody, condition, and location of any books, documents, or other tangible things and the identity and location of persons having knowledge of any discoverable matter. For good cause, the court may order discovery of any matter relevant to the subject matter involved in the action. Relevant information need not be admissible at the trial if the discovery appears reasonably calculated to lead to the discovery of admissible evidence. All discovery is subject to the limitations imposed by Rule 26(b)(2)(i),(ii), and (iii).

Exceptions and Limitations to the Work–Product Doctrine

The work–product doctrine has some exceptions. It does not cover documents prepared in the normal operation of the client's business, such as sales reports, data analysis, or summaries of business operations.

The work–product doctrine does not extend to documents in an attorney's possession that were prepared by a third-party in the ordinary course of business and that would have been created in essentially similar form irrespective of any litigation anticipated by counsel.[xiii]

In other words, the client cannot obtain protection for internal business documents by giving them to the attorney and thereby protect them from discovery by the other side because they are in the possession of the attorney.

Exception to the Third-Party Document Exception

The courts have made an exception to the exception in which a lawyer is trying to find out the other party's strategy by asking about documents already in his/her possession that would not be protected under the third-party exception. To protect the lawyer's trial strategy, the court may impose a privilege where it would not otherwise exist. We, too, have observed that

Where a request is made for documents already in the possession of requesting party, with precise goal of warning what the opposing attorney's thinking or strategy may be, even **third-party documents** may be protected. Id[xiv]

Third-party documents
Documents prepared by a third party in the ordinary course of business that would have been prepared in similar form if there was no litigation.

[x] *Electronic Data Systems Corporation v. Steingraber Case* 4:02 CV 225 USDC, E.D. Texas (2003).
[xi] FRCP 26 (b) Discovery Scope and Limits. Unless otherwise limited by order of the court in accordance with these rules, the scope of discovery is as follows:
(1) In General. Parties may obtain discovery regarding any matter, not privileged, that is relevant to the claim or defense of any party, including the existence, description, nature, custody, condition, and location of any books, documents, or other tangible things and the identity and location of persons having knowledge of any discoverable matter. For good cause, the court may order discovery of any matter relevant to the subject matter involved in the action. Relevant information need not be admissible at the trial if the discovery appears reasonably calculated to lead to the discovery of admissible evidence. All discovery is subject to the limitations imposed by Rule 26(b)(2)(i),(ii), and (iii).
[xii] Fed. R. Crim. P. 16.
[xiii] In Re Grand Jury Subpoenas, 318 F. 3d 379 (2nd Cir 2002) at page 385.
[xiv] Id page 385.

Governmental Attorney Exception

The attorney–client privilege does not extend to government attorneys. Individuals and corporations are both subject to criminal liability for their transgressions. Individuals will not talk and corporations will have no incentive to conduct or cooperate in internal investigations if they know that any information disclosed may be turned over to the authorities. . . . A state agency, however, cannot be held criminally liable. . . . A government attorney should have no privilege to shield relevant information from the public citizens to whom she owes ultimate allegiance, as represented by the grand jury.[xv]

Inadvertent Disclosure of Confidential Information

Inadvertent disclosure of confidential or privileged information does happen. It may be the slip of the finger in sending an email, an accidental pushing of the wrong number on the speed dial of a fax machine or the sending of a misaddressed envelope.

The admissibility of the inadvertently disclosed documents may hinge on the steps the firm takes before and after the disclosure. Having a proper screening policy in place and monitoring this policy may prevent a claim of negligence.[xvi]

The treatment will depend on the individual jurisdiction. The courts follow no single policy.

Judicial Views

There are three judicial views on handling the inadvertent disclosure under the attorney–client privilege: (1) Automatic waiver; (2) no waiver; (3) and balancing test.[xvii]

Automatic Waiver
These cases hold that once the confidentiality is breached, the privilege is therefore waived.

No Waiver
There can only be a waiver when a client makes a knowing voluntary waiver of the privilege. Therefore, the attorney's inadvertent disclosure does not constitute a waiver.

Balancing Test
The courts using the balancing test looked to the nature of the methods taken to protect the information, efforts made to correct the error, the extent of the disclosure and fairness. Remedies under this test range from unlimited use of the disclosed materials, to court-ordered return of documents, to disqualification of attorneys who have reviewed inadvertently disclosed privileged documents.

ABA Ethics Opinion

The American Bar Association has issued a formal opinion modifying the long-standing opinion 92-368, which advocated for confidentiality of privileged materials to protect the client, and imposing a burden upon receiving attorneys not to review privileged material and return it following instructions given to them by the disclosing attorney, issuing a clarifying formal opinion 05-437, which states:

A lawyer who receives a document from opposing parties or their lawyers and knows or reasonably should know that the document was inadvertently sent should promptly notify the sender in order to permit the sender to take protective measures. To the extent that Formal Opinion 92-368 opined otherwise, it is hereby withdrawn.

[xv] *In Re a Witness*, 288 F.3d 289 (7th Cir.2002) at pages 293–294.
[xvi] *VLT Inc. Lucent Technologies*, no 00–11049-PBS (D. Mass. 01/21/03).
[xvii] Inadvertent Disclosure: Approaches and Remedies, *The Practical Lawyer;* Philadelphia, April 2001, by Kevin M. McCarthy.

Internal Investigations and Evidentiary Privileges

Businesses, and particularly corporations with publicly traded stocks, are under state and federal requirement to take a proactive approach to determine wrongdoing and identify violations of statutes and regulations. These investigations and "audits" create a body of documents all, some, or none of which may be subject to evidentiary privilege.

Candor and Fairness in Litigation

Litigation is the practice of advocacy, advocating a legal position to the court or trying to persuade a **trier of facts** to accept the facts as presented. It is the duty of the advocate to avoid any conduct that undermines the integrity of the process. The duty to the client to persuasively present the case is a qualified duty, qualified by the ethical obligation (**candor**) to not mislead the court or opposing counsel with false statements of law or of facts which the lawyer knows to be false. Without mutual respect, honesty, and fairness the system cannot function properly. It may be a simple ethical duty to competently research and present the current case and statutory law, even when the most current version is not favorable to the position taken. In the technology age, this duty requires making a complete search for ALL the law, statutory enactments and case law, and not just the part that is favorable to the client's position. In an age of vast numbers of electronic cases, it is easy to lose a few or not run the search as professionally as possible. Not making the proper inquiry of the client's staff to find all of the law may lead to sanctions and potentially worse, disbarment.

Trier of facts The trier of facts decides what facts are to be accepted and used in making the decision. It is usually a jury, but may be a judge who hears a case without a jury and decides the facts and applies the law.

Candor A duty of honesty to the court.

Fairness to Opposing Party and Counsel

Fairness in the practice of law has been an issue probably as long as there has been an adversarial justice system. A number of states have established professionalism commissions and committees. Attorneys are advocates for their clients and occasionally forget that the purpose of the legal system is justice for all. The ethical rule of fairness to opposing counsel and parties is an attempt to set the guidelines to ensure justice is done even if one's client loses the case. Each side is expected to use its best skills and knowledge and present fairly their position in the form of evidence for the trier of fact to determine where the truth lies. Destroying, falsifying, or tampering with evidence destroys the fabric of the system. If people lose confidence in the system because of these unfair tactics society loses confidence in the system and it breaks down. Just consider the criminal cases where the prosecutor does not turn over, as required, **exculpatory evidence** that might show the defendant innocent.

The obligation of the supervising attorney to the court and to the other side may extend not only to the legal term but also in insuring that the client and the client's staff fully comply with the rules of court. Sanctions for failure to properly supervise can come from two sources: the court hearing the underlying action (as in the *Qualcomm*

Exculpatory evidence Evidence which tends to prove the innocence of the accused or prove the facts of the defendant's case.

ETHICAL PERSPECTIVE

One Last Word About Integrity

Model Rule 8.1 states that legal professionals should be persons of integrity. The more integrity each of us brings to the profession, the better the legal system will be. Regardless of a person's expertise or extraordinary gift for the law, the person still will be held to high standards of moral ethical conduct, as has been the case historically. (See also EC8-7)

Ethics: Ten Top Rules for Paralegals, by Deborah K. Orlik. © 2006, Pearson Education, Upper Saddle River, N.J. Reproduced by permission.

A list of commissions and committees may be seen at www .ABANET.org/cpr/professionals/ profcommissions.htm.

case above) and the attorney disciplinary agency. The court typically punishes this sort of misbehavior with monetary sanctions, the purpose of which is to recompense the other side for the time and effort they have expended or will expend because of the discovery abuse. The attorney disciplinary agency's punishment can include, in extreme cases, disbarment or suspension from practice before the court for a period of time, or in less extreme cases public or private censure. In addition, under some circumstances "unfair" litigation tactics may result in a suit for malpractice by the client against the attorney and the law firm.

Concept Review *and* Reinforcement

LEGAL TERMINOLOGY

ABA Model Rules of Professional Conduct   40
Agent   48
Attorney–client privilege   56
Candor   63
Common interest privilege   60
Competence/competent   52
Confidentiality   57
Conflict of interest   52

Ethical guidelines   40
Ethical wall   54
Exculpatory evidence   63
Fiduciary relationship   48
Model Guidelines for the Utilization of Legal Assistant Services   49
Principal   48
Privilege   59

Rules of court   52
Supervising attorney   48
Third-party documents   61
Trier of facts   63
Unauthorized Practice of Law (UPL)   43
Work–product doctrine   60

SUMMARY OF KEY CONCEPTS

Regulation of the Practice of Law

Purpose of Regulation	The practice of law is regulated by state government and court rule in an attempt to protect the public from incompetent and unscrupulous practitioners.
The Paralegal and Licensing	There are, with a few exceptions, no state licensing requirements for one to work as a paralegal—unlike the procedures that lawyers must follow to practice law.
Penalties for the Unauthorized Practice of Law	States such as Pennsylvania have specifically addressed the issue of unauthorized practice of law by paralegals and legal assistants. The Pennsylvania statute on the unauthorized practice of law makes it a misdemeanor for "any person, including, but not limited to, a paralegal or legal assistant who within this Commonwealth, shall practice law."

Avoiding UPL: Holding Oneself Out

Avoiding UPL: Holding Oneself Out	Parties with whom the paralegal has contact must know the limited role the paralegal plays on the legal team.
Avoiding UPL: Giving Advice	A paralegal cannot give a legal opinion or give legal advice. If legal rights may be affected, it is probably legal advice.
Avoiding UPL: Filling Out Forms	UPL may consist of a nonlawyer who explains, recommends, advises, and assists in the selection, completion, and corrections of errors and omissions of legal forms.

Avoiding UPL: Representing Clients	1. Some jurisdictions and administrative agencies do permit those who are not licensed or admitted to practice to appear in court or before administrative law judges or referees on behalf of clients.
	2. No uniformity of rules exists outlining when nonlawyers may represent parties or the specific agencies or courts before which nonlawyers can appear. Any appearance before a court must be approved carefully.
	3. The presentation of a request for continuance of a case may be considered by some courts to be the practice of law.
	4. Some federal agencies specifically permit nonlawyers to appear. Most notable are the Social Security Administration and the U.S. Patent Office.

Avoiding UPL: Guidelines	**Guideline 1**
	Legal assistants should:
	1. disclose their status as legal assistants at the outset of any professional relationship with a client, other attorneys, a court or administrative agency or personnel thereof, or members of the general public.
	Guideline 2
	Legal assistants should not:
	1. establish attorney–client relationships; set legal fees, give legal opinions or advice, or represent a client before a court, unless authorized to do so by said court; nor
	2. engage in, encourage, or contribute to any act that could constitute the unauthorized practice of law.
	Guideline 3
	Legal assistants may perform services for an attorney in the representation of a client, provided that
	1. the services performed by the legal assistant do not require the exercise of independent professional legal judgment;
	2. the attorney maintains a direct relationship with the client and maintains control of all client matters;
	3. the attorney supervises the legal assistant;
	4. the attorney remains professionally responsible for all work on behalf of the client, including any actions taken or not taken by the legal assistant in connection therewith.

Ethical Obligations

Expected Behavior	Ethical behavior is expected and required of every member of the legal team, attorney, paralegal, litigation support, information technologist, and outside consultant.
Duty to Supervise	The obligation to ensure ethical conduct is that of the supervising attorney under the ethical obligation to supervise all who work on the case for the attorney.
	Ethical behavior is expected and required of every member of the legal team, attorney, paralegal, litigation support, information technologist, and outside consultant.
	Ethical obligations of lawyers are enforced by the court in the jurisdiction where the attorney is practicing or where the case is being tried.

Ethical Guidelines and Rules

	Every profession develops a set of guidelines for those in the profession to follow. These may be codes of conduct or ethical guidelines. These codes typically set forth the minimum in ethical behavior—the very least each professional should do.

ABA Model Guidelines for the Utilization of Paralegal Services	A set of guidelines intended to govern the conduct of lawyers when utilizing paralegals or legal assistants.
Uniformity of Paralegal Ethics	No single source of ethical rules is set out for the paralegal. At present, unlike a violation by an attorney of the state-adopted rules that can result in loss of the right to practice (disbarment), no such sanction exists for the paralegal breach of association rules except loss of membership.
Ethics Codes of Paralegal Associations	1. National Federation of Paralegal Associations, Inc. 2. National Association of Legal Assistants
Competence	Competent representation requires the legal knowledge, skill, thoroughness, and preparation reasonably necessary for the representation.
Conflict of Interest	1. A conflict of interest exists if the representation of one client will be adverse to the interest of another client. 2. Conflicts of interest may arise for paralegals when they change from one employer to another if the previous employer represented a client or handled certain matters for a client during the period in which the paralegal was employed.
Ethical Wall	This is an environment in which an attorney or a paralegal is isolated from a particular case or client to avoid a conflict of interest or to protect a client's confidences and secrets.
Freelance or Independent Paralegal	Freelance or independent paralegals who work for more than one firm or attorney face the potential problem of conflict of interest.

The Duty of Confidentiality, Attorney–Client Privilege, and the Work–Product Doctrine

Attorney–Client Privilege	1. This privilege is found in the state or federal evidence code and is a rule of evidence that applies in cases where the Rules of Evidence apply: a court of law, a deposition, or other places where a witness is under oath: such as interrogatories, responses to requests for documents or grand jury hearings. 2. The "privilege" belongs to the client not to the attorney. 3. The person claiming the privilege, usually the client, has the burden to establish the existence of the privilege.
Confidentiality	This is a duty imposed on the attorney and each member of the legal team working under the supervision of the attorney to enable clients to obtain legal advice by allowing the client to freely and openly give the members of the legal team all the relevant facts without fear of disclosure of these facts except in limited situations, such as to prevent commission of a crime or to defend against a client's suit.
Claim of Privilege	The person claiming the privilege, usually the client, has the burden to establish the existence of the privilege.
Extension of Attorney–Client Privilege to Others	The efficient administration of justice requires the privilege to extend to agents of the attorney.
Work–Product Doctrine	1. The work–product doctrine provides a limited protection for material prepared by the attorney or those working for the attorney in anticipation of litigation or for trial. 2. The work–product doctrine is different from both the attorney–client privilege and the duty of confidentiality. The attorney–client privilege and the duty of confidentiality relate to the information provided by the clients regardless of whether they involve potential litigation.

Exceptions and Limitations to the Work–Product Doctrine	Does not cover documents prepared in the normal operation of the client's business, such as sales reports, data analyses, or summaries of business operations.
Exception to the Third-Party Document Exception	Courts have made an exception when a lawyer is trying to find out the other party's strategy by asking about documents already in his/her possession.
Governmental Attorney Exception	Government attorneys should have no privilege to shield relevant information from the public citizens to whom they owe ultimate allegiance, as represented by the grand jury.
Inadvertent Disclosure of Confidential Information	The treatment will depend on the individual jurisdiction. The courts follow no single policy.
Judicial Views	The three judicial views on handling the inadvertent disclosure under the attorney–client privilege are 1. automatic waiver 2. no waiver 3. balancing test
Internal Investigations and Evidentiary Privilege	Internal investigations and audits mandated by state and federal regulation create a body of documents, some or none of which may be subject to evidentiary privilege.

Candor and Fairness in Litigation

	It is the duty of the advocate to avoid any conduct that undermines the integrity of the process. The duty to the client to persuasively present the case is a qualified duty, qualified by the ethical obligation (candor) to not mislead the court or opposing counsel with false statements of law or of facts which the lawyer knows to be false.
Fairness to Opposing Party and Counsel	The ethical rule of fairness to opposing counsel and parties is an attempt to set the guidelines to ensure justice is done even if one's client loses the case.

WORKING THE WEB

1. Download the latest ethics opinions and guidelines from the NALA website at www.NALA.org.
2. Download any ethics updates from the NFPA website at www.paralegal.org.
3. Download a personal reference copy of the Model Rules of Professional Conduct from the ABA Center for Professional Responsibility at www.abanet.org.
4. Use a web browser or search engine to find the URL (web address) for your state or local bar association website that provides guidance or opinions on legal ethics. Three popular search engines are www.google.com, www.yahoo.com, or www.ask.com and www.bing.com.
5. Use the NFPA website to find the names of agencies that allow nonlawyer practice. www.paralegals.org/Development/Roles/allow.html

CRITICAL THINKING & WRITING QUESTIONS

1. What is the general theory for regulating the practice of law? How is this applied?
2. Why is "just giving advice" potentially the unauthorized practice of law?
3. How would regulation of the paralegal profession assure the public of quality legal services?
4. When may nonlawyers represent clients?
5. How can the paralegal avoid UPL?
6. How do unauthorized-practice-of-law statutes protect the public?
7. Why should the paralegal be familiar with the ABA Model Rules of Professional Conduct?

8. How do the ABA Model Guidelines for the Utilization of Legal Assistant Services define the role of the paralegal in the law office?
9. Does a paralegal's violation of the ethics rules of the national paralegal associations have the same impact as violating the ethical rules of attorneys on the right to practice?
10. Would a paralegal dating a client have a conflict of interest caused by compromising influences and loyalties?
11. What is the reason for creating privileged communications?
12. Under what circumstances might a paralegal have a conflict of interest in taking a new job in a law firm?
13. How does an ethical wall protect the client?
14. What is a "Chinese wall"?
15. What are the potential dangers in paralegal's moonlighting?
16. What is a conflict of interest under the Model Rules of Professional Conduct?

17. Does a client have an attorney–client privilege regarding information given to a paralegal during the preparation of a case?
18. What duty does a paralegal owe to the supervising attorney?
19. How is a paralegal an agent of the client?
20. In possible conflict of interest, with whom does the ultimate decision rest?
21. Under what circumstance must a lawyer or a paralegal refuse employment?
22. What is required to invoke the attorney–client privilege?
23. What is covered under the work–product doctrine?
24. Should a paralegal be considered an "other representative" under the Federal Rules of Civil Procedure, Rule 26? Why or why not?
25. What is the duty of the trier of fact?
26. What is exculpatory evidence?

Building Paralegal Skills

VIDEO CASE STUDIES

Disclosure of Status

A client is meeting with his new attorney and the attorney's paralegal. He expresses some concerns about confidentiality of information given to the paralegal.

After viewing the video case study at www.pearsonhighered.com/goldman answer the following:

1. Does the paralegal have a duty to reveal their status as a paralegal? Does the supervising attorney have the duty?
2. Is the paralegal bound by the same rules of confidentiality as the lawyer?
3. Is the paralegal covered under the attorney client privilege?

Confidentiality Issue: Family Exception?

Paralegal Judy meets with her mother in a public coffee shop and tells her mother details of the case she is working on that has her stressed out.

After viewing the video case study at www.pearsonhighered.com/goldman answer the following:

1. Does being stressed out change the rules of confidentiality?
2. Is there a privilege that permits discussing the facts of a case with a family member?
3. Can the facts be discussed if names are left out?

Confidentiality Issue: Public Information

A law firm has a case that has received coverage in the local newspaper. Two of the paralegals from the same law firm are having coffee in a public coffee shop. One of the paralegals who is not assigned to the case reads an article about the client and asks her friend who is working on the case about the accuracy of the article.

After viewing the video case study at www.pearson highered.com/goldman answer the following:

1. How does public disclosure of information about a client or a case change the paralegals responsibility to maintain confidentiality?
2. Are there any ethical issues in discussing cases in a public area?
3. Is the paralegal who was not working on the case under any duty of confidentiality?

ETHICS ANALYSIS & DISCUSSION QUESTIONS

1. Are paralegals held to the same standard as attorneys when there is no supervising attorney?
2. What is the paralegal's duty to the client when the paralegal's employer breaches its duty to the client?
3. Who is responsible for the quality of the legal work performed for a client—the attorney or the paralegal?
4. Assume you have graduated from a paralegal program at a local college. While you are looking for a job where your talents can be properly utilized, a friend asks you to help him fill out a set of bankruptcy forms using a computer program he purchased at the local office supply mega warehouse. The program is designed to pick out the exemptions after the requested information is plugged in. [*In Re Kaitangian*, Calif. 218 BR 102 (1998).] Is this the unauthorized practice of law?

Paralegal Ethics in Practice

5. Assume you are offered the opportunity to work with a local law firm providing living trust services to the public. Your responsibility would be to make a presentation to community groups and in other public meetings on the advantages of living trusts. After the general session, any interested person would meet with you and you would fill out the forms, collect the fee, and send the completed form and half the fee collected to the law firm for review and transmittal to the client. You would retain half the amount collected as your fee. [*Cincinnati Bar Assn. v. Kathman*, 92 Ohio St.3d 92 (2001).] What ethical issues are involved? Explain.

DEVELOPING YOUR COLLABORATION SKILLS

Working on your own or with a group of other students assigned by your instructor, review the scenario at the beginning of the chapter.

1. In a group or individually, identify all the potential ethical issues involved in this scenario.
2. Imagine that a local lawyer who knows both Kathryn and Kelsey was sitting next to them and overheard their conversation. The lawyer sends a letter to the local Ethics Board. Let one group represent the Ethics Board, one group represent Kathryn's employer, and another Kelsey's employers.
   a. How should the Ethics Board respond?
   b. How should the lawyers Kelsey works for respond?
3. Write or discuss a summary of the advice the group would give to Kathryn and Kelsey, and the law firms that employ them.

PARALEGAL PORTFOLIO EXERCISE

Prepare a memorandum of law for submission to a potential employer, outlining the existing regulations in your state for paralegals, and the application of any unauthorized practice of law statutes. Include complete citations to any cases, statutes or regulations, and the Internet address of any state or local ethics sites for lawyers and/or paralegals.

LEGAL ANALYSIS & WRITING CASES

In Re Estate of Devine 263 Ill. App.3d 799 (1994)

A paralegal working in a small office became friendly with a client of the attorney and assisted the client in personal matters outside of the office, including helping him to shop and handle personal finances. In that role, the paralegal was given power to sign checks for the client. After the client died, the paralegal withdrew $165,958 from the joint account with the deceased client. Is a lawyer responsible for the actions of a paralegal?

The court held both the paralegal and the attorney liable for breach of fiduciary duty, holding that if the attorney, who performed work including writing a will leaving a bequest to the attorney and the paralegal, was a fiduciary, so then was the paralegal as a matter of law. Further, the court noted that the law in a number of states holds the attorney liable for a paralegal's acts including the responsibility for unethical conduct by nonlawyer employees of the lawyer. The Illinois court quoted New York and New Jersey cases holding the employing attorney in violation of the Code of Professional Conduct for failing to properly supervise employed paralegals.

Questions

1. Does this case effectively extend the lawyer's ethical rules to the conduct of paralegals?
2. May a paralegal maintain a personal relationship with a client of the firm?
3. Should a paralegal be as familiar as the supervising (employing) attorney with the ABA Model Rules of Professional Conduct?

In the Matter of JOHN A. ARETAKIS, an Attorney, Respondent.   791 N.Y.S.2d 687
COMMITTEE ON PROFESSIONAL STANDARDS, Petitioner.

An attorney made certain statements public from a complaint filed against him with the state committee on disciplinary standards in violation of the rules on confidentiality of proceeding on complaints against attorneys.

The court stated . . . "The Court of Appeals has observed that Judiciary Law § 90 and its counterparts reflect a policy of keeping disciplinary proceedings involving licensed professionals confidential until they are finally determined. The policy serves the purpose of safeguarding information that a potential complainant may regard as private or confidential and thereby removes a possible disincentive to the filing of complaints of professional misconduct. The State's policy also evinces a sensitivity to the possibility of irreparable harm to a professional's reputation resulting from unfounded accusations—a possibility which is enhanced by the more relaxed nature of the [proceedings] . . . Indeed, . . . Professional reputation 'once lost, is not easily restored.'"

Questions

1. Can the reputation of a professional be tarnished by disclosure of unsubstantiated claims of ethical breaches?
2. Once tarnished can a professional reestablish his or her professional integrity?
3. Is the greater good to allow all complaints to be made public?

WORKING WITH THE LANGUAGE OF THE COURT CASE

Tegman v. Accident and Medical Investigations

30 P.3d 8 (Wash. Ct. App. 2001)
Court of Appeals of Washington, Division One

Read the following case excerpted from the Court of Appeals opinion. Review and brief the case. In your brief, answer the following questions.

1. How does this court define "the practice of law"?
2. What is the standard or duty of care that this court imposes on a paralegal who does not have a supervising attorney?
3. What action does this court suggest that a paralegal take when it becomes clear that there is no supervising attorney?
4. Why should a paralegal contact the supervising attorney immediately upon being given a case to handle?
5. Based on this case, should a paralegal advise the client that he or she is a paralegal? If so, when? Why?

Becker, Mary K., A.C.J.

Between 1989 and 1991, plaintiffs Maria Tegman, Linda Leszynski, and Daina Calixto were each injured in separate and unrelated automobile accidents. After their accidents, each plaintiff retained G. Richard McClellan and Accident & Medical Investigations, Inc.

(AMI) for legal counsel and assistance in handling their personal injury claims. . . . Each plaintiff signed a contingency fee agreement with AMI, believing that McClellan was an attorney and AMI a law firm. McClellan has never been an attorney in any jurisdiction. McClellan and AMI employed Camille Jescavage, . . . [a] licensed attorney. . . .

Jescavage . . . learned that McClellan entered into contingency fee agreements with AMI's clients and that McClellan was not an attorney. [Attorneys for AMI] settled a number of cases for AMI, and learned that McClellan processed settlements of AMI cases through his own bank account. . . .

In July 1991, McClellan hired Deloris Mullen as a paralegal. Mullen considered Jescavage to be her supervising attorney, though Jescavage provided little supervision. Jescavage resigned from AMI in the first week of September 1991. McClellan told Mullen that her new supervising attorney would be James Bailey. Mullen did not immediately contact Bailey to confirm that he was her supervising attorney. [He] later told Mullen he was not.

While at AMI, Mullen worked on approximately 50–60 cases, including those of [the] plaintiffs. . . . Mullen was aware of some of McClellan's questionable practices and knew that there were substantial improprieties involved with his operation. Mullen stopped working at AMI on December 6, 1991, when the situation became personally intolerable to her and she obtained direct knowledge that she was without a supervising attorney.

When she left, she did not advise any of the plaintiffs about the problems at AMI. After Mullen left, McClellan settled each plaintiff's case for various amounts without their knowledge or consent, and deposited the funds in his general account by forging their names on the settlement checks.

The "practice of law" clearly does not just mean appearing in court. In a larger sense, it includes "legal advice and counsel, and the preparation of legal instruments and contracts by which legal rights are secured." Mullen contends that her status as a paralegal precludes a finding that she was engaged in the practice of law. She argues that a paralegal is, by definition, someone who works under the supervision of an attorney, and that it is necessarily the attorney, not the paralegal, who is practicing law and owes a duty to the clients. Her argument assumes that she had a supervising attorney.

The trial court's determination that Mullen was negligent was dependent on the court's finding that Mullen knew, or should have known, that she did not have a supervising attorney over a period of several months while she was at AMI. . . . The label "paralegal" is not in itself a shield from liability. A factual evaluation is necessary to distinguish a paralegal who is working under an attorney's supervision from one who is actually practicing law. A finding that a paralegal is practicing law will not be supported merely by evidence of infrequent contact with the supervising attorney.

As long as the paralegal does in fact have a supervising attorney who is responsible for the case, any de-ficiency in the quality of the supervision or in the quality of the paralegal's work goes to the attorney's negligence, not the paralegal's.

In this case, Mullen testified that she believed James Bailey was her supervising attorney after Jescavage left. The court found Mullen was not justified in that belief. . . . Mullen testified that she had started to distrust McClellan before he informed her that Bailey would be her supervising attorney. Mullen also testified that she did not contact Bailey to confirm that he was supervising her. Bailey testified at a deposition that he did not share Mullen's clients and she did not consult him regarding any of her ongoing cases. He also said that one of the only conversations he remembers having with Mullen with respect to AMI is one where he told her that he was not her supervising attorney after she raised the issue with him. This testimony amply supports the trial court's finding that Mullen was unjustified in her belief that Bailey was her supervising attorney.

[Mullen] continued to send out demand and representation letters after Jescavage left AMI. Letters written by Mullen before Jescavage's departure identify Mullen as a paralegal after her signature, whereas letters she wrote after Jescavage's departure lacked such identification. Even after Mullen discovered, in late November 1991, that Bailey was not her supervising attorney, she wrote letters identifying "this office" as representing the plaintiffs, neglecting to mention that she was a paralegal and that no attorney was responsible for the case. This evidence substantially supports the finding that Mullen engaged in the practice of law.

Accordingly, we conclude the trial court did not err in following Bowers and holding Mullen to the duty of an attorney. The duty of care owed by an attorney is that degree of care, skill, diligence, and knowledge commonly possessed and exercised by a reasonable, careful, and prudent lawyer in the practice of law in Washington. . . .

The court found that the standard of care owed by an attorney, and therefore also by Mullen, required her to notify the plaintiffs of: (1) the serious problems concerning the accessibility of their files to persons who had no right to see them, (2) the fact that client settlements were not processed through an attorney's trust account but, rather, McClellan's own account, (3) the fact that McClellan and AMI, as nonlawyers, had no right to enter into contingent fee agreements with clients and receive contingent fees, (4) the fact that McClellan was, in fact, engaged in the unlawful practice of law, and that, generally, (5) the clients of McClellan and AMI were at substantial risk of financial harm as a result of their association with AMI. Mullen breached her duty to her clients in all of these particulars.

(continued)

We conclude the finding is supported by substantial evidence. Accordingly, the trial court did not err in concluding that Mullen was negligent. . . .

Although Mullen was a paralegal, she is held to an attorney's standard of care because she worked on the plaintiffs' cases during a period of several months when she had no supervising attorney. The fact that she did not render legal advice directly does not excuse her; in fact, her failure to advise the plaintiffs of the improper arrangements at AMI is the very omission that breached her duty. Under these circumstances it is not unjust to hold her accountable as a legal cause of the plaintiffs' injuries. As all the elements of negligence have been established, we affirm the judgment against Mullen.

Affirmed.

WE CONCUR: AGID, J., COLEMAN, J.

This case also was scheduled to be published in the Washington Appellate Reports, and if cited in the courts of Washington, would require that citation as well. This case has a Lexis number of 2001 Wash. App. LEXIS 1890.

Rubin v. Enns

23 S.W.3d 382 Tex. App.-Amarillo (7th Dist. 2000)

1. Does the court's "rebuttable presumption" test work? Would any other test work better?
2. Using the court's "rebuttable presumption" test, would there be some temptation on the part of the second law firm to obtain confidential information that the paralegal learned at the first law firm?
3. Do the ethics standards of the American Bar Association and paralegal associations adequately address ethical conflicts that paralegals face? Discuss.

FACTS

Inda Crawford was employed as a legal assistant by the law firm of Hicks, Thomas & Lilienstern (HTL) for a number of years prior to May 1999. During her employment with the HTL law firm, HTL represented Michael Rubin and other real estate agents in a lawsuit against Westgate Petroleum and other defendants. Crawford worked on this case as a legal assistant for HTL and billed 170 hours of work on the case.

In May 1999, Crawford left her employment at HTL and went to work for the law firm Templeton, Smithee, Hayes, Fields, Young & Heinrich (Templeton). Templeton represented Westgate Petroleum and the other defendants in the previously mentioned lawsuit. Rubin and the other real estate agents in this case filed a writ of mandamus with trial court judge the Honorable Ron Enns to have the Templeton firm disqualified as counsel for Westgate et al. because Crawford had now switched firms.

Rubin argued that because Crawford had previously worked on the case for the HTL firm, the opposing counsel she now worked for should be disqualified from representing the opposing side in the lawsuit. The trial court judge denied the petitioners' writ of mandamus. The petitioners appealed.

ISSUE

Should the writ of mandamus be approved disqualifying a law firm that represents one side of a lawsuit because a legal assistant who worked for the law firm that represented the other side of the lawsuit has now switched firms and works for the law firm sought to be disqualified?

Boyd, Chief Justice

In *Phoenix Founders, Inc. v. Marshall*, 887 S.W.2d 831, 835 (Tex. 1994), the court had occasion to discuss at some length circumstances such as the one before us in which a paralegal has changed employment from a law firm on one side of a case to a law firm on the other side of the case. In doing so, it recognized the countervailing interests involved and noted with approval the ABA suggestion that any restrictions on the nonlawyer's employment should be held to the minimum standard necessary to protect confidentiality of client information. In the course of its discussion, the court held that a paralegal or legal assistant who changes employment and who has worked on a case is subject to a conclusive presumption that confidences and secrets were imparted. While the presumption that a legal assistant obtained confidential information is not rebuttable, the presumption that the information was shared with a new employer is rebuttable.

Such distinction was created to ensure that a nonlawyer's mobility would not be unduly restricted.

However, the court emphasized that the only way the rebuttable presumption could be overcome would be (1) to instruct the legal assistant not to work on any matter on which the paralegal worked during the prior employment, or regarding which the paralegal had information relating to the former employer's representation; and (2) "to take other reasonable steps to ensure that the paralegal does not work in connection with the matters on which the paralegal worked during the prior employment, absent client consent."

The trial court also had before it copies of a May 17, 1999, memo from Joe Hayes, managing partner of the Templeton firm, addressed to all the lawyers and staff of the Templeton firm. In the memo, Hayes designated two cases (one of which underlies this proceeding) as those about which Crawford might possess confidential information. In the memo, the recipients were instructed that Texas Disciplinary Rules 1.05(b)(1) and 5.03(a) prohibited them, as Crawford's supervising employers, "from revealing any confidential information she might have regarding the cases." The memo also advised that to satisfy the requirements of the Disciplinary Rules, as well as those set forth by the supreme court in the *In Re American Home Products Corporation* case, the firm was implementing the following six policies and procedures, effective immediately:

1. Inda shall not perform any work or take any action in connection with the *Westgate* case or the *Seger* case [the second, unrelated, case].
2. Inda shall not discuss the *Westgate* case or the *Seger* case, or disclose any information she has concerning these cases, with anyone.
3. No lawyer or staff member shall discuss the *Westgate* case or the *Seger* case with Inda, or in her presence.
4. All computer information relating to the *Westgate* case and the *Seger* case shall be removed from the firm's computer system. No future information concerning either the *Westgate* case or the *Seger* case shall be stored in any electronic medium but, rather, kept solely in hard copy form with the files in the respective case.
5. The files in the *Westgate* case and the *Seger* case shall be kept in locked files under my supervision. No one shall have access to those files other than me, and

those to whom I have given specific authority to access these files. Inda shall not have access to these files or the area where the files are to be maintained. At the close of each business day, all documents relating to these cases shall be placed in their respective files, which shall be returned to their storage places, which shall then be locked.
6. Inda shall not be given access to any of the files pertaining to the *Westgate* case or the *Seger* case, or their contents. None of the documents pertaining to either of these cases shall be disclosed to Inda, discussed with her, or discussed in her presence.

Our review of the record before the trial court convinces us that we cannot say he abused his discretion in arriving at his decision to deny the motion to disqualify the Templeton law firm. Accordingly, relators' petition seeking mandamus relief must be, and is, denied.

DECISION AND REMEDY

The court of appeals affirmed the trial court's denial of the writ of mandamus, thus permitting Crawford to work for the second law firm, which had imposed sufficient safeguards to assure that confidential information obtained at the first law firm was not disclosed to the second law firm.

The court also may find that the lower court has made an error that can be corrected, by sending the case back to the lower court, and **remand** the case to the lower court, to take additional action or conduct further proceedings. For example, the lower court may be directed to hold further proceedings in which a jury hears testimony related to the issue of damages and makes an award of monetary damages.

An appellate court will reverse a lower court decision if it finds an *error of* law the record. An error of law occurs if the jury was improperly instructed by the trial court judge, prejudicial evidence was admitted at trial when it should have been excluded, prejudicial evidence was obtained through an unconstitutional search and seizure, and the like. An appellate court will not reverse a finding of fact unless such finding is unsupported by the evidence or is contradicted by the evidence.

The Paralegal Workplace

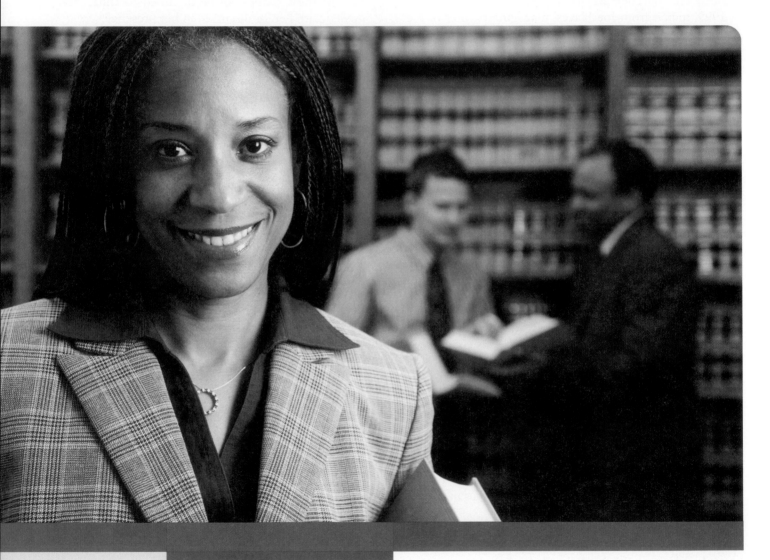

DIGITAL RESOURCES

Chapter 3 Digital Resources at *www.pearsonhighered.com/goldman*

- Video Case Studies:
  - Preparing for a Job Interview: Resume Advice
  - Preparing for a Job Interview: Interviewing Advice
  - Interviewing: The Good, the Bad, and the Ugly
- Chapter Summary • Web Links • Court Opinions • Glossary • Comprehension Quizzes
- Technology Resources

> " A lawyer's time and advice are his stock in trade. "

Abraham Lincoln

After studying this chapter, you should be able to:

1. Describe the different types of practice arrangements of lawyers and law firms.
2. Explain the organizational structure of law offices.
3. Describe the administrative procedures found in most law offices.
4. Understand the purpose and the importance of conflict checking in the law office.
5. Explain why knowledge of accounting is important in a law practice.
6. Describe the emerging fields in paralegal specialty practice.
7. Be able to prepare a traditional resume and an electronic resume.
8. Create an effective cover letter submitting your resume for employment.
9. Understand the planning needed for a successful job interview.

Paralegals at Work

Law Offices
Goldenberg, Craigie, and Luria

INTEROFFICE MEMO

TO: Natasha Weiser
FROM: Cary Moritz, Office Manager
SUBJECT: Mentoring for New Hires

All of us at Goldenberg, Craigie, and Luria welcome you to our firm. We know you had other job opportunities but believe you will be professionally satisfied and challenged by working here.

The paralegal profession has changed dramatically since I first started in this field, and the one thing we can count on is more change. Please know that you can call on me at any time for advice and guidance. No question is too big or too small.

After all these years I have seen a number of major changes in the profession. When I started out, we were hired based on our keyboarding skills and basically operated as secretaries. Today, more and more lawyers treat us as a part of the legal team and demand as much, if not more, of us than they do new law graduates.

In your new job as a paralegal for Goldenberg, Craigie, and Luria, you frequently will represent our firm as the client's first point of contact and be responsible for conducting initial interviews with clients. As you prepare your interview strategies, please use me as a sounding board. It is important to build rapport so clients will feel comfortable sharing sensitive and personal information with someone who is, at first, a complete stranger. As time goes on, clients often become most comfortable with the paralegal assigned to their case.

As a paralegal, you will be expected to follow a case and do much of the administrative work, such as keeping track of the time and costs associated with each case. Bookkeeping and accounting skills can be a real plus! When I first started, I did only litigation work. When the lawyers in my firm found out that I had been a bookkeeper and had taken accounting classes, I was asked not only to work in the estates area but also was given responsibility for some of the in-office accounting. This is something to think about as you look to develop your professional skill set. Getting a Bachelor's degree eventually led to my job as Office Manager. Additional education is always a plus!

Please know that you can count on me to help you succeed in the present and also to plan and prepare for future endeavors here at Goldenberg, Craigie, and Luria.

Consider the issues involved in this scenario as you read the chapter.

INTRODUCTION FOR THE PARALEGAL

As the paralegal profession has evolved, so, too, have the duties and roles of the paralegal within the legal system and elsewhere. The earliest legal assistant was probably a legal secretary who developed specialized skills while working for an attorney in one of the legal specialties. As the need for specialized skills became more obvious, legal assistant programs and paralegal programs were created to teach the requisite skills.

In the classic sense, a paralegal performs those tasks and activities that assist the supervising attorney in representing clients. In the broader view, the paralegal performs many of the same functions that attorneys perform, under the supervision of an attorney but limited by laws and regulations on the unauthorized practice of law (UPL). The paralegal's actual tasks and functions vary according to the type of practice, size of the firm or organization, and skill of the individual paralegal.

Arrangements and Organization of Law Offices and Firms

The classic image of the law firm was of the practitioner working alone in a small office in a small town. The more modern view portrayed in movies and on TV is that of a large national or global law firm. In between are small partnerships and other environments—corporations, insurance companies, government agencies, and consulting firms composed of accountants, lawyers, and management consultants. Exhibit 3.1 shows organization charts for four typical types of arrangements in which the paralegal may find work.

Solo Practice

Solo practice One lawyer practicing alone without the assistance of other attorneys.

Solo practice refers to one lawyer practicing alone without the assistance of other attorneys. The solo practitioner still exists, not only in small towns but in large metropolitan areas as well. The solo practitioner may well be the employer who most depends on the skills of the paralegal in running the office, working with clients, and assisting at trial. A solo practice offers perhaps the greatest challenge for the paralegal who wishes to be involved in every aspect of a law practice. Tasks that otherwise might be assigned to an associate will fall to the paralegal to perform.

In a litigation practice or a practice in which the attorney is frequently out of the office attending meetings, the paralegal becomes the main point of contact and coordination between clients and the supervising attorney. Jobs that might be done in larger firms by an accounting staff, such as preparation of payroll and maintenance of client escrow accounts, frequently are done by the paralegal in solo practices. Many solo practitioners consider their paralegal to be a key resource in the practice of law.

Small Offices

Small offices Small-office arrangements range from individual practitioners sharing space to partnerships.

Small-office arrangements range from individual practitioners sharing space to partnerships. For the small practitioner, the cost of maintaining an adequate law library,

Exhibit 3.1   Typical organization charts for various-sized firms

(continued)

conference room, office space, and office support services such as photocopy and fax machines is daunting. Therefore, practices frequently share these common services while separating client practices. The lawyers might have a similar type of practice, such as criminal law or family law, or dissimilar practices, such as family law and insurance defense work. Depending upon the arrangement, the practitioners might refer clients back and forth. The responsibility for the client and the client relationship is a personal one for the attorney.

Depending upon the arrangement, personnel, such as the receptionist, secretary, or paralegal, might be shared. In these situations the paralegal must be certain which of the attorneys is the supervising attorney with regard to each client. The paralegal who is working for more than one attorney in a sharing arrangement might be privy to confidential information that may not be shared with the other attorneys in the office unless they are working on the same case. In some respects this can be thought of as an "ethical wall" environment. At the very least, the paralegal and the attorneys must clearly understand the ethical issues involved.

Exhibit 3.1   Typical organization charts for various-sized firms *(continued)*

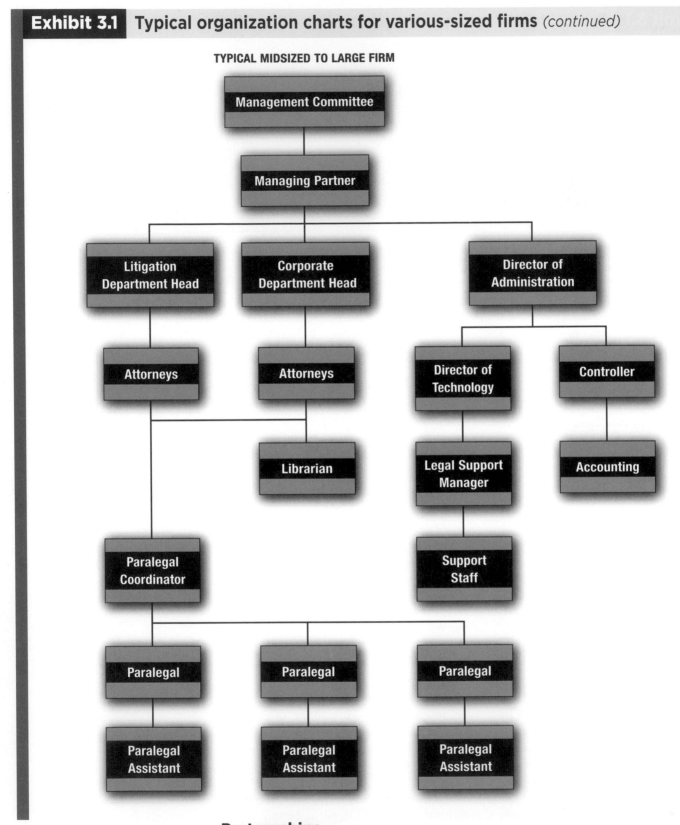

TYPICAL MIDSIZED TO LARGE FIRM

Management Committee

Managing Partner

Litigation Department Head — Corporate Department Head — Director of Administration

Attorneys — Attorneys — Director of Technology — Controller

Librarian — Legal Support Manager — Accounting

Support Staff

Paralegal Coordinator

Paralegal — Paralegal — Paralegal

Paralegal Assistant — Paralegal Assistant — Paralegal Assistant

Partnerships

Partnership Two or more natural (human) or artificial (corporation) persons who have joined together to share ownership and profit or loss.

In a **partnership** arrangement, two or more natural (human) or artificial (corporation) persons have joined together to share ownership and profit or loss. Partnerships in small-office arrangements may take the form of true partnerships, sharing all aspects of the practice, or may be partnerships in name only. In the latter case, the same ethical issues that the paralegal faces in the pure office-sharing arrangement must be considered.

Exhibit 3.1   **Typical organization charts for various-sized firms** (continued)

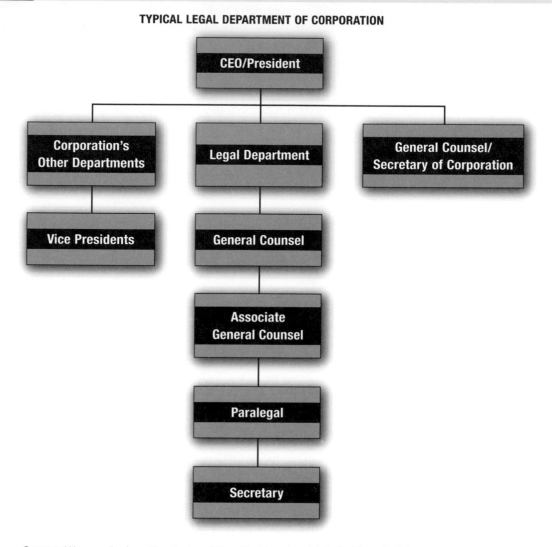

TYPICAL LEGAL DEPARTMENT OF CORPORATION

Source: *Wagner, Andrea, How to Land Your First Paralegal Job: Insiders, 3rd, © 2001. Electronically reproduced by permission of Pearson Education, Inc., Upper Saddle River, New Jersey.*

If all of the attorneys are partners with complete responsibility for each other and the practice, paralegals may find themselves working for more than one of the partners. In effect, the partners share the paralegal's services. This can give rise to certain issues for the paralegal when more than one of the partners demand something at the same time with the same sense of urgency. The fact that each of the partners will consider himself or herself to be "boss" can create a delicate situation for the paralegal.

A common solution in many offices is for one of the partners to be the primary supervising attorney for the paralegal, through whom the other partner (or partners) funnels work and requests. From an ethical point of view this solves the problem of who the supervising attorney is for the clients and files on which the paralegal is working and at the same time clarifies the lawyers' responsibilities under the lawyers' Rules of Professional Conduct.

Large Offices

Historically, what are now viewed as **large law offices** are an outgrowth of traditional law offices that have expanded over the years, adding partners and associates along the way. Initially, the larger law firms were regional, confined to major cities such as

Large law offices Large law offices are an outgrowth of traditional law offices that have expanded over the years, adding partners and associates along the way.

New York, Chicago, Philadelphia, and Los Angeles. With the growth of government at the national level, many firms found themselves establishing offices in the nation's capital to service clients appearing before federal agencies.

Continued growth of the national economy and business and corporate clients around the country resulted in many firms establishing offices in other large cities, giving them a presence on each of the coasts as well as central locations such as Chicago, with offices in Washington, D.C., and elsewhere. Growth of the global economy has taken us one step farther, with law firms establishing offices in foreign countries. As a result, the large law firm has taken on the characteristics of many corporations, with firms merging to bring specialty areas of law within one firm while expanding the global availability of legal services.

For the paralegal the large office can be an exciting and dynamic area of practice. Paralegals may be called upon to travel with other members of the legal team or on their own as part of the practice. Even when no travel is required, the paralegal might be called upon to work with clients who have diverse backgrounds, both domestically and internationally. One of the values of the large law firm for clients is the availability of a number of legal specialties within one legal services provider. For the paralegal this offers the opportunity to work in different areas of legal specialty.

Working in a large law firm also has some disadvantages. The larger the firm, the greater is the potential for fewer personal relationships and contacts with clients and other members of the legal team. In some firms, just as in any large organization, "playing politics" becomes very real. A paralegal's status, as well as some of the perks and benefits of the job, may depend on the status of the individual's supervising attorney. At the same time, the opportunities for advancement in a large firm might outweigh the disadvantages.

Large Firms

Unlike the small office, in which the paralegal also might be the bookkeeper, office manager, receptionist, and second chair in litigation, a department within a large firm typically hires support staff for each of these functions. The first contact for a paralegal with a large firm may be with the human resources department as part of the job-application process. Bookkeeping or accounting departments usually handle payroll, check requests, and other financial issues. In the larger firms, even the function of making copies takes place in a duplicating department, and the firm might have a mailroom for handling incoming and outgoing mail.

The large law firm has specialized components. In some ways this is similar to the structure of the English legal system, in which the solicitor deals directly with clients and the barrister litigates the cases. United States law firms frequently have litigation specialists who spend their time in the actual litigation of cases while other attorneys within the same firm rarely, if ever, go to court. The role of the latter is to work with clients and, when the need arises, prepare the materials for the litigation department.

Just as the law has become more complex, lawyers also have come to specialize in narrow areas of practice such as environmental law, intellectual-property law, health-care law, insurance law, tort law, and family law. This means that paralegals in large law firms also become specialists within their supervising attorney's primary field of law. Large-practice firms encourage clients to use the firm for all of their legal needs, so a lawyer within the firm frequently refers clients to other specialists in the firm while maintaining primary contact with the clients. Some firms have lawyers whose expertise is in getting new clients. These lawyers, often former politicians and government officials, frequently are referred to as the "rainmakers." They use their contacts to obtain clients and then refer the clients to the specialists within the firm.

Compensation for attorneys within large firms is generally based on how much new business the attorney has brought in, as well as how many billable hours the supervising attorneys have been able to bill for themselves and their paralegals. In this kind of environment, the paralegal who is able to maintain relationships with clients is an invaluable asset to the firm.

ETHICAL PERSPECTIVE

Lawyers Who Share Offices

It is "impermissible for unaffiliated attorneys to have unrestricted access to each other's electronic files (including email and word-processing documents) and other client records. If separate computer systems are not utilized, each attorney's confidential client information should be protected in a way that guards against unauthorized access and preserves client confidences and secrets."

Source: District of Columbia Ethics Opinion 303.

General Practice

A **general law practice** is one that handles all types of cases. This is what people usually think of as the small-town lawyer, the generalist to whom everyone in town comes for advice. The reality is that the same generalists practice in cities as well as small towns throughout the country. Their practices are as diverse as the law itself, handling everything from adoptions to zoning appeals. As general practitioners, they serve the same function in law as the general family practice doctor does in medicine.

Lawyers in this type of practice often work in several areas of law within the same day—attending a hearing in small-claims court in the morning, preparing a will before lunch, having a luncheon meeting with an opposing attorney to discuss settlement of an accident case, then helping someone who is forming a corporation, and finally appearing at a municipal government meeting in the evening to seek a zoning approval. For many, the general practice is the most exciting type of practice, with a continually changing clientele offering all sorts of legal challenges. The paralegal in this environment has the opportunity to work with different types of clients on different types of legal matters on a constant basis. The challenge in this type of practice is to stay current in each of the areas of law of the practice.

General law practice A general law practice is one that handles all types of cases.

Specialty Practice

A **specialty practice** is involved in one area of law. Lawyers with specialty backgrounds, such as engineering, might choose to work in patent law or intellectual-property law. Those coming into the legal profession with accounting backgrounds might specialize in tax matters. Others have special interests and passions such as working with senior

Specialty practice A specialty practice is involved in practice in one area of law.

Paralegals *in* Practice

PARALEGAL PROFILE
Ann W. Price

Ann W. Price, RP, has been a paralegal for over 25 years, working in different sized law firms in diverse practice areas. Ann is currently employed as a Litigation Paralegal Specialist in the U.S. Department of Justice's Environment and Natural Resources Division in Washington, D.C. She is a PACE™ Registered Paralegal which means she has passed the Paralegal Advanced Competency Exam, a certification test developed by the National Federation of Paralegal Associations (NFPA).

In my first few paralegal positions, I was either the only paralegal in the office, or one of two paralegals supporting several attorneys. Because these were small law firms, I was given a large degree of responsibility right from the start. I routinely prepared client correspondence, assisted with discovery (gathering and managing evidence), interviewed clients, and attended trials.

Next, I worked in larger law firms, specializing in food and drug law and environmental law. As a food and drug law paralegal, I researched congressional reports, the Federal Register, and other news and legal databases to summarize findings that might be of interest to the firm's clients. As an environ-

mental law paralegal, I worked on all phases of discovery, trial preparation, and arbitration proceedings in Superfund cases that mostly involved municipal landfill clean-ups.

My next two jobs were both related to paralegal management for large law firms with hundreds of attorneys. In one of these positions, I was an active paralegal in addition to my management duties. Eventually, I became a paralegal manager where my duties were entirely managerial. I currently work for the U.S. Department of Justice's Environment and Natural Resources Division where I provide litigation support to approximately 60 attorneys.

There are pros and cons in every type of legal work setting. Paralegals in large law firms are usually paid a larger salary, but the work they perform is often far less substantive than the work performed by paralegals in smaller firms. Large firms often give the most substantive work to the associate attorneys, particularly those right out of law school. In smaller firms, every person is expected to be able to meet any need the case requires. Also, in larger firms, there is often pressure to meet a specified number of client billable hours; many smaller law firms do not even set a minimum.

In my various jobs, the basic skills used and the work performed did not change significantly from practice area to practice area. However, the terminology and legal resources varied considerably. Continuing legal education opportunities are more prevalent in larger law firms than smaller ones. In smaller firms, education is generally limited to on-the-job training. Most law firms in the metro D.C. area, particularly the large ones, require a four-year degree, and many want a paralegal certificate as well. Individuals with two-year degrees are more likely to find employment at smaller firms, at least for their first paralegal job.

citizens in an elder law practice, or protecting the interests of children as child advocates, or practicing criminal law.

With the increasing complexity of the law, legal specialists frequently are receiving referrals from attorneys in other specialties or in general practice. The paralegal working for a specialist often acquires such a high level of knowledge in a specific area of law that it rivals that of many general practitioners. One of the dangers for the paralegal with this extent of specialty knowledge is that other attorneys could ask the paralegal questions to which the answers border on, or actually result in, the unauthorized practice of law.

Because the paralegal in a specialty law practice is dependent—as are the supervising attorney and the practice—on referrals from other attorneys, the natural tendency is to accommodate referral attorneys by trying to answer questions of a legal nature. To avoid a potential claim of UPL, the paralegal must diplomatically avoid giving legal advice even to an attorney from another firm.

Maintaining relationships with other law firms and their paralegals and secretaries becomes a primary job function for the paralegal in a specialty practice. The paralegal commonly obtains referrals for the supervising attorney and the firm as a result of relationships developed in professional associations with other paralegals who recommend their friend who works for a lawyer specializing in the area sought.

In many areas of specialty, the paralegal has become a vital team member. Paralegals with specialty skills in specific substantive areas perform services that allow the attorney to concentrate on other substantive issues of law. In addition, the paralegal handles office management tasks and functions. These encompass intraoffice support including coordination between members of the professional team and the client.

Legal Nurse Consultants and Nurse Paralegals

Nurse paralegals or **legal nurse consultants** Nurses who have gained medical work experience and combine it with paralegal skills.

Nurse paralegals or **legal nurse consultants** are nurses who have gained medical work experience and combine it with paralegal skills. Becoming a legal nurse consultant or a nurse paralegal is an ideal career opportunity for nurses with clinical nursing experience who want to work in the legal environment. Entry to most education programs requires a current license as a Registered Nurse and a minimum of 2,000 to 6,000 hours of clinical nursing experience, usually one to three years. Some programs are open to those with an associate degree in nursing, but usually a bachelor's degree in nursing is requested or desired.

Nurse paralegals draw upon their knowledge of medical terminology, medical procedures, and nursing practice to decipher medical records for the legal community. The most obvious advantage is their ability to analyze medical records from both medical and legal standpoints. Their experience also enables them to conduct more effective interviews with clients, fact witnesses, and expert witnesses in cases of medical malpractice and cases involving injury and damage investigation. Graduates of these programs often work as independent nurse consultants for law firms and insurance companies. Others find positions with insurance companies and law firms specializing in medical malpractice and personal injury.

Although the ABA considers the nurse paralegal and legal nurse consultant to be part of the paralegal profession, the American Association of Legal Nurse Consultants (AALNC) views this role as a subspecialty of nursing. In March 1998, the then named Standing Committee on Legal Assistants of the American Bar Association, now named the Standing Committee on Paralegals, decided that "legal nurses and legal nurse consultants fall squarely within the ABA definition of 'paralegal/legal assistant.'" By contrast, AALNC has defined the legal nurse consultant as a specialty practitioner of nursing whose education should be developed and presented as specialty nursing curricula by nurse educators in partnership with legal educators. The ethical code and regulations that must be followed may depend on which profession they are associated with.

Web Exploration

Further information on Legal Nurse Consulting can be obtained at www.Aalnc.org.

Real Estate

Paralegals with real estate experience in sales or from title insurance agencies can perform many of the tasks associated with a real estate practice, such as communicating between buyers and sellers, coordinating the documentation for settlement, and preparing documents for recording purposes. In most jurisdictions, becoming a licensed salesperson or a real estate broker requires completion of a course of study that provides a foundation in the practices and procedures of real estate practice and equips the paralegal with a terminology base that facilitates effective communication with the supervising attorney.

Complex Litigation

Complex litigation takes many forms, from class-action lawsuits to complex product-liability cases. Paralegals working in complex litigation typically oversee the requests for document production and maintain indexes, usually on computer databases, of the paperwork generated from litigation. In large cases the paralegal might supervise a staff of other paralegals or law students in summarizing discovery documents. At trial, these paralegals frequently coordinate the production of exhibits.

Complex litigation Cases involving many parties as in a class action or multiple or complex legal issues.

Environmental Law

Environmental law covers everything from toxic waste dumps to protection of wildlife and the environment. A challenge for the environmental paralegal is in locating and obtaining public records and other documents necessary to establish the areas of concern and claims, some of which predate computer records, such as toxic waste dumps created during World War II and the early 1950s.

Environmental law An area of the law dealing with the protection of the environment.

Intellectual Property

In a survey by The Affiliates, a company providing temporary and full-time legal personnel, 48 percent of the surveyed attorneys indicated **intellectual property** as the fastest growing field in law. The intellectual-property paralegal is concerned with the formalities of protecting intellectual-property interests including patent rights, trade secrets, and copyrights and trademarks. The two main areas are (a) prosecution, which involves establishing the priority of the claims that will result in granting of the patent or copyright, and (b) litigation, which protects those rights against claims by others, such as in patent-infringement cases.

Intellectual property Protection of intellectual-property interests like patents, trademarks, and copyrights.

Elder Law

With the aging of the population has come an increased need to protect the rights of the elderly and obtain all the benefits to which they are entitled. This includes simple tasks such as helping individuals to apply for Social Security, Medicare, or Medicaid benefits. It also entails working with the elderly to create estate plan documents, powers of attorney, and health-care directives. More and more, the paralegal or legal assistant is becoming an advocate for the elderly, in many cases working in a pro bono capacity or through social service agencies. **Elder law** has come to include the additional issues of helping the elderly work through the maze of health care and government benefits.

Elder law Advocacy for the elderly.

Paralegal Managers

As paralegal staffs have grown, even at some of the smaller firms, the position of **paralegal manager** has emerged. With higher turnover rates and increased specialization comes the associated need for someone to hire, supervise, train, and evaluate paralegals. In many firms this person is the interface between the paralegal and the attorneys.

Paralegal manager Someone who hires, supervises, trains, and evaluates paralegals.

As paralegals gain specialized knowledge in specific fields, they find themselves working for different attorneys in specialties, such as intellectual property, real estate, or securities law that require paralegals with specific expertise. Attorneys, for the most part, do not have the time to handle the nonlegal aspects of managers, such as acting as leader, mentor, employee advocate, supervisor, trainer, evaluator, problem solver, and resource manager.

The largest firms appoint a managing partner to handle the management tasks and human resources issues. In many smaller firms, these duties fall to the individual with the title of paralegal manager. This new specialty is well recognized and supported by its own organization, the International Paralegal Management Association.

Pro Bono Paralegals

Pro bono means working without compensation on behalf of individuals and organizations that otherwise could not afford legal assistance. Increasingly, the legal profession has taken on the role of working without compensation in legal aid offices and community legal service programs. As members of professional associations, paralegals participate in pro bono activities at varying levels and time commitments. For example, the Massachusetts Paralegal Association supports a number of pro bono projects. In one of these, the Family Law Project, paralegals partner with attorneys to help handle domestic violence cases without compensation. Pro bono work is seen as part of an ethical obligation of the legal profession.

Government Employment

Federal, state, and local governments are large employers of paralegals, and paralegals are expected to be utilized even further in **government employment** at every level in the future. Many of the federally employed paralegals are found in administrative agencies. A good example is the work of paralegals in the Social Security Administration as decision writers, case schedulers, and case specialists. Just as the private law firm has discovered the value of the paralegal on the legal team, so have government law offices such as the U.S. Attorney's Office and the Office of the Solicitor General. These offices are involved with both criminal prosecutions and civil litigation where the government is a party. Many other agencies that conduct administrative hearings utilize paralegals at all levels.

Legal Departments of Corporations

Many people think of a corporate legal department as a laid-back, conservative environment with little activity other than drafting minutes of meetings and filing corporate records with federal and state governments. The reality today is that, in the global economy, more and more corporations with in-house staffs are engaged in international trade. A whole body of law relates to compliance for imports and exports.

For example, the transfer and sale of certain high-tech equipment and technology must have prior government approval. Sales involving shipments to other countries require letters of credit and currency conversion. International trade creates a host of unique issues related to the laws of the countries with which the domestic corporation may be doing business.

The paralegal is in the middle of these transactions, juggling the requirements from both the legal perspective and the sales/marketing perspective. Paralegals with foreign language skills find themselves in even greater demand in handling communication issues. Those with cultural ties to, or background in, the countries with which the corporation is doing business will find their knowledge frequently tapped to avoid cultural mistakes resulting from miscommunication.

DuPont is one of the largest corporations in the United States. In an effort to reduce costs, DuPont changed the way it uses legal assistants—elevating the work, positions, and numbers of legal assistants. Legal assistants have been given more responsibility in handling documents, technology, and investigations. In doing so, DuPont reportedly reduced by almost 90 percent the number of outside law firms and services it formerly used.

Web Exploration

Check the latest IPMA News at the IPMA website www.ipma.org.

Pro bono Working without compensation on behalf of individuals and organizations that otherwise could not afford legal assistance.

Government employment Working for federal, state, and local government agencies and authorities.

As of 2000, the DuPont legal department had 51 paralegals working with 140 lawyers. In the DuPont model, the legal department acts as counsel to the other DuPont-owned companies and deals with them as clients much in the way that the outside law firms did in the past.[1]

Self-Employment

The paralegal has some opportunities to be self-employed, although state regulation may limit the opportunities or restrict paralegal **self-employment.** Where authorized by federal law, the paralegal may actively represent clients without the supervision of an attorney, such as before the U.S. Patent Office or Social Security Administration. Many paralegals work as freelancers for different attorneys, usually on a case-by-case basis. In addition to the normal ethical obligations regarding confidentiality and conflict of interest, the freelance paralegal must observe the ethical guidelines on advertising in the local jurisdiction and avoid creating the appearance of being available to render legal advice except where authorized.

Self-employment Working independently either as a freelance paralegal for different lawyers or, when authorized by state or federal law, performing services for the public.

Networking

Regardless of the size or type of working environment, **networking** is important for the individual. It establishes contact with others with whom questions and information are shared. Many paralegals develop a referral list of other paralegals they can call to get a quick answer in their own jurisdiction and in others. Most paralegals facing a deadline are not too proud to call their contacts—whether they are across the street, across the state, or across the country—to meet a deadline or get the necessary form. During interviews, hiring attorneys have been known to ask about the paralegal's networking activity.

For the paralegal, networking may also be the key to obtaining a job. As you've heard no doubt, it is not what you know but whom you know. Knowing the right person or a person who can refer you to the right person is a valuable asset.

Networking The establishment of contact with others with whom questions and information are shared.

Paralegal Tasks and Functions

The actual tasks and functions the paralegal performs vary according to the type of practice, size of the firm or organization, and skill of the individual paralegal. Some of the more generic tasks include

- conducting interviews
- maintaining written and verbal contacts with clients and counsel
- setting up, organizing, and maintaining client files
- preparing pleadings and documents
- reviewing, analyzing, summarizing, and indexing documents and transcripts
- assisting in preparing witnesses and clients for trial
- maintaining calendar and tickler systems
- conducting research, both factual and legal
- performing office administrative functions including maintaining time and billing records

Client Interviews

Many paralegals act as the first line of contact with clients. Although paralegals may not ethically or legally give legal advice or set legal fees, they frequently conduct the initial interview with the client. This might involve taking the initial client information

DOCUMENT SPECIALIST OR PARALEGAL?

Under the definition enacted by the Maine legislature, anyone calling himself or herself a paralegal or legal assistant must work under the supervision of an attorney. Independent paralegals no longer can use the title "paralegal" or "legal assistant." This has resulted in some of them changing the name of their freelance business to "document specialist" (*Bangor Daily News,* August 16, 1999).

The California legislature has a law prohibiting self-help legal document service providers from receiving compensation unless the legal document assistant is registered in the county where the service is provided and provides a bond of $25,000.

SIDEBAR

---

[1]"The DuPont Experience," from *Paralegals Are Part of DuPont's Legal Team*, by D. L. Hawley. As seen in the March 2000 issue of *Legal Assistant Today*. Copyright 2000 James Publishing, Inc. Reprinted courtesy of *Legal Assistant Today* magazine. For subscription information call (800) 394-2626, or visit www.legalassistanttoday.com.

and preparing the client data sheet (see Exhibit 3.2) or conducting a more in-depth interview to determine the facts of the matter for the attorney's review. Frequently, the paralegal continues to function as the contact point with the client and the supervising attorney or the law firm. Paralegals frequently establish rapport with clients and earn their confidence.

The paralegal always must be keenly aware of the ethical limitations in dealing with clients. This is especially true when the client develops a high level of confidence in dealing with the paralegal. Clients come to the attorney for advice. When they have confidence in a paralegal, they might tend to ask the paralegal for advice and recommendations instead of "bothering" the attorney. Providing such advice or recommendations may be in violation of UPL restrictions.

Exhibit 3.2 **Client data sheet**

CLIENT DATA SHEET

ACTION TAKEN/REQUIRED

1. Client Name:

2. Client/Matter Number:
3. Client Address:

4. Phone: Work:
    Home:
    Fax:
5. Email address:
6. Social Security No.:
7. Date of Birth:
8. Marital Status:
9. Client Contact:
10. Matter:

(a) Adverse Party:
(b) Date of Incident:
(c) Statute of Limitations Period:
(d) Statute of Limitations Date:
11. Opposing Counsel:

12. Opposing Counsel Address:

13. Opposing Counsel Phone:

For example, to the client, the question, "Should I make my son my power of attorney?" seems simple. But the answer is not so simple and involves many legal consequences, so it must be referred to the supervising attorney. Another UPL might be to help the client complete blank legal forms, such as bankruptcy forms or will forms purchased at a retail store.

Investigations

The paralegal may be asked to act as the direct representative of the supervising attorney in conducting an investigation into a pending case. A paralegal trained in the specific area of law understands the factual needs of a case and the sources of information available. A paralegal who has had the opportunity to observe or work with an attorney and has watched the presentation of evidence in a trial obtains a good sense of what will make good demonstrative evidence, such as models and photographs.

In the case of photos, an understanding of the kind of questions that might be asked in direct examination and cross-examination about the photographs offered as evidence enables the paralegal to be certain that the photographs are taken from the correct angles with the correct landmarks or measurements included. Interviews conducted by the paralegal in preparation for trial could qualify as privileged for the attorney–client privilege just as they do when conducted by attorneys. The paralegal must be aware of how interview material may be used and potentially obtained by opposing parties and act to protect clients' privileged communication with the paralegal as a representative of the supervising attorney.

Legal Writing

Paralegals frequently are called upon to maintain the written communications with clients, opposing attorneys, and the court. These may be in the form of correspondence, memos of law, or briefs for the court. Many paralegals become extremely adept at drafting complaints and supporting memoranda of law and briefs. Although the content is the ultimate responsibility of the supervising attorney, the paralegal with good writing skills is an invaluable asset. Well-written and well-reasoned documentation is easy to review for signature and transmittal and is a major time-saver for the attorney.

Legal Research

In the modern law office, legal research is conducted with hardcopy books and also with electronic media, including extensive use of the Internet. The ability to conduct research into case law, statutory enactments, and regulatory rules and procedures gives the paralegal a major advantage in getting the job in the first place and advancing in most firms. Legal research today requires the ability to use online legal services such as Lexis, Westlaw, VersusLaw, and Loislaw, as well as the ability to find information on government websites and private websites.

What Paralegals in Legal Specialties Do

In addition to the various generic tasks that most paralegals or legal assistants perform, paralegals working in specialty areas find themselves performing additional and more specialized tasks that frequently require special knowledge, education, or skill beyond the basic skills and knowledge required of all paralegals. Following are some of the tasks that paralegals in specialty practice perform.

General business practice:

- Draft lease agreements
- Draft partnership agreements
- Draft noncompetition agreements
- Prepare agreements of sale and attend real estate settlements

- Draft contracts for business arrangements and new ventures
- Draft employee agreements

Debtor rights and creditor remedies:

- Draft correspondence complying with state and federal regulations concerning debt collection
- Prepare documentation to support garnishment proceedings
- Arrange for execution and support judgments, including publication of notice of sales and levies on personal property
- Transfer judgments to other jurisdictions
- Prepare, file, and terminate Uniform Commercial Code financing statements
- Assist clients in filing bankruptcy petitions, including the preparation of schedules and proofs of claim
- Prepare Chapter 11 debtor's financial statements
- Attend Chapter 13 confirmation hearings

Corporate practice:

- Determine availability and reserve fictitious or corporate name
- Prepare and file fictitious name registrations
- Prepare articles of incorporation, minutes, and bylaws for corporation
- Prepare, issue, and transfer stock certificates
- Prepare shareholder agreements
- Prepare applications and file for employer identification numbers and tax registration numbers
- Prepare and file annual reports
- Prepare and file articles of dissolution
- Prepare and file securities registrations and required filings with state regulatory agencies and with the United States Securities & Exchange Commission

Environmental law:

- Track information with regard to Superfund sites
- Determine applicability of brown fields to client property
- Research history of properties to determine environmental activity
- Obtain the appropriate information about sites from state and federal environmental agencies
- Obtain documentation and assist in the preparation of environmental audits
- Organize and index documentation

Family law:

- Collect information from clients with regard to marital status and prior marital status
- Interview client and collect information with regard to child support (see Exhibit 3.3)
- Draft prenuptial agreements
- Draft divorce complaints and responsive pleadings
- Prepare motions for support
- Prepare motions for custody and visitation
- Prepare property settlement agreements
- Prepare protection-from-abuse petitions
- Prepare petitions for termination of parental rights
- Prepare adoption petitions

Exhibit 3.3 Child support data form

_____ v. _____ No. _____

THIS FORM MUST BE FILLED OUT

(If you are self-employed or if you are salaried by a business of which you are owner in whole or in part, you must also fill out the Supplemental Income Statement which appears on the last page of this Income and Expense Statement.)

INCOME AND EXPENSE STATEMENT OF

_____

I verify that the statements made in this Income and Expense Statement are true and correct. I understand that false statements herein are made subject to the penalties of 18 Pa.C.S. §4904 relating to unsworn falsification to authorities.

Date: _____ Plaintiff or Defendant: _____

INCOME

Employer: _____

Address: _____

Type of Work: _____

Payroll Number: _____

Pay Period (weekly, biweekly, etc.): _____

Gross Pay per Pay Period: $ _____

Itemized Payroll Deductions:	Federal Withholding	$ _____
	Social Security	_____
	Local Wage Tax	_____
	State Income Tax	_____
	Retirement	_____
	Savings Bonds	_____
	Credit Union	_____
	Life Insurance	_____
	Health Insurance	_____
	Other (specify)	_____
	_____	_____
	Net Pay per Pay Period	$_____

OTHER INCOME: (Fill in Appropriate Column)

	Weekly	_Monthly_	_Yearly_
Interest	$_____	$_____	$_____
Dividends	_____	_____	_____
Pension	_____	_____	_____
Annuity	_____	_____	_____
Social Security	_____	_____	_____
Rents	_____	_____	_____
Royalties	_____	_____	_____
Expense Account	_____	_____	_____
Gifts	_____	_____	_____
Unemployment Comp.	_____	_____	_____
Workmen's Comp.	_____	_____	_____
_____	_____	_____	_____
Total	_____	_____	_____
TOTAL INCOME			$_____

Immigration law:

- Prepare applications and petitions for filing with the Immigration and Naturalization Service (INS) (see Exhibit 3.4 for a sample)
- Coordinate translation of foreign documents
- Prepare immigration and nonimmigration visa applications
- Coordinate activities with clients in foreign jurisdictions seeking visa and entry into the United States

Exhibit 3.4   Sample immigration and naturalization service form

U.S. Department of Justice
Immigration and Naturalization Service

**Notice of Entry of Appearance
as Attorney or Representative**

Appearances - An appearance shall be filed on this form by the attorney or representative appearing in each case. Thereafter, substitution may be permitted upon the written withdrawal of the attorney or representative of record or upon notification of the new attorney or representative. When an appearance is made by a person acting in a representative capacity, his personal appearance or signature shall constitute a representation that under the provisions of this chapter he is authorized and qualified to represent. Further proof of authority to act in a representative capacity may be required. **Availability of Records** - During the time a case is pending, and except as otherwise provided in 8 CFR 103.2(b), a party to a proceeding or his attorney or representative shall be permitted to examine the record of proceeding in a Service office. He may, in conformity with 8 CFR 103.10, obtain copies of Service records or information therefrom and copies of documents or transcripts of evidence furnished by him. Upon request, he/she may, in addition, be loaned a copy of the testimony and exhibits contained in the record of proceeding upon giving his/her receipt for such copies and pledging that it will be surrendered upon final disposition of the case or upon demand. If extra copies of exhibits do not exist, they shall not be furnished free on loan; however, they shall be made available for copying or purchase of copies as provided in 8 CFR 103.10.

In re:

Lim Chi

Date: 09-15-2002

File No. A1357

I hereby enter my appearance as attorney for (or representative of), and at the request of the following named person(s):

Name:

Lim chi

☑ Petitioner   ☐ Applicant
☐ Beneficiary

Address: (Apt. No.)   (Number & Street)   (City)   (State)   (Zip Code)

275 Swamp Road   Newtown   Pa 18940

Name:

☐ Petitioner   ☐ Applicant
☐ Beneficiary

Address: (Apt. No.)   (Number & Street)   (City)   (State)   (Zip Code)

Check Applicable Item(s) below:

☑ 1. I am an attorney and a member in good standing of the bar of the Supreme Court of the United States or of the highest court of the following State, territory, insular possession, or District of Columbia

Pennsylvania   Supreme Court   and am not under a court or administrative agency
Name of Court
order suspending, enjoining, restraining, disbarring, or otherwise restricting me in practicing law.

☐ 2. I am an accredited representative of the following named religious, charitable, social service, or similar organization established in the United States and which is so recognized by the Board:

☐ 3. I am associated with
the attorney of record previously filed a notice of appearance in this case and my appearance is at his request. (*If you check this item, also check item 1 or 2 whichever is appropriate.*)

☐ 4. Others (Explain Fully.)

SIGNATURE

COMPLETE ADDRESS
138 North State Street
Newtown, pa 18940

NAME (Type or Print)
Thomas F. Goldman

TELEPHONE NUMBER
215 555 4321

PURSUANT TO THE PRIVACY ACT OF 1974, I HEREBY CONSENT TO THE DISCLOSURE TO THE FOLLOWING NAMED ATTORNEY OR REPRESENTATIVE OF ANY RECORD PERTAINING TO ME WHICH APPEARS IN ANY IMMIGRATION AND NATURALIZATION SERVICE SYSTEM OF RECORDS:
Thomas F. Goldman

(Name of Attorney or Representative)

THE ABOVE CONSENT TO DISCLOSURE IS IN CONNECTION WITH THE FOLLOWING MATTER:

Name of Person Consenting

Signature of Person Consenting

Date

(NOTE: Execution of this box is required under the Privacy Act of 1974 where the person being represented is a citizen of the United States or an alien lawfully admitted for permanent residence.)

This form may not be used to request records under the Freedom of Information Act or the Privacy Act. The manner of requesting such records is contained in 8CFR 103.10 and 103.20 Et.SEQ.

Form G-28 (09/26/00)Y

- Assist clients in obtaining work visa to work in foreign countries
- Assist clients in the preparation of documentation to prove claim of marital status for submission to INS

Intellectual property:

- Prepare patent search
- Prepare trademark search
- Prepare applications for patent, trademark, or copyright (Exhibit 3.5 is a sample)
- Assist in preparation of documentation in opposition, interference, infringement, and similar proceedings
- Coordinate activities and filings with foreign patent, trademark, and copyright attorneys and agents
- Work with engineers in preparation of applications and defense of patents and trade secrets
- Draft licensing agreements for intellectual property items

Exhibit 3.5   Copyright form

(continued)

Exhibit 3.5 Copyright form (continued)

EXAMINED BY	FORM TX
CHECKED BY	
☐ CORRESPONDENCE Yes	FOR COPYRIGHT OFFICE USE ONLY

DO NOT WRITE ABOVE THIS LINE. IF YOU NEED MORE SPACE, USE A SEPARATE CONTINUATION SHEET.

PREVIOUS REGISTRATION Has registration for this work, or for an earlier version of this work, already been made in the Copyright Office?   **5**
☐ Yes ☐ No If your answer is "Yes," why is another registration being sought? (Check appropriate box.) ▼
a. ☐ This is the first published edition of a work previously registered in unpublished form.
b. ☐ This is the first application submitted by this author as copyright claimant.
c. ☐ This is a changed version of the work, as shown by space 6 on this application.
If your answer is "Yes," give: **Previous Registration Number** ▶   **Year of Registration** ▶

DERIVATIVE WORK OR COMPILATION   a **6**
Preexisting Material Identify any preexisting work or works that this work is based on or incorporates. ▼

See instructions
before completing
this space.

Material Added to This Work Give a brief, general statement of the material that has been added to this work and in which copyright is claimed. ▼   b

DEPOSIT ACCOUNT If the registration fee is to be charged to a Deposit Account established in the Copyright Office, give name and number of Account.   a **7**
Name ▼   **Account Number** ▼

CORRESPONDENCE Give name and address to which correspondence about this application should be sent.   Name/Address/Apt/City/State/ZIP ▼   b

Area code and daytime telephone number ▶ 480-991-7881   Fax number ▶
Email ▶

CERTIFICATION* I, the undersigned, hereby certify that I am the   **8**
                              Check only one ▶   ☐ author
                                                 ☐ other copyright claimant
                                                 ☐ owner of exclusive right(s)
of the work identified in this application and that the statements made   ☑ authorized agent of _____
by me in this application are correct to the best of my knowledge.   Name of author or other copyright claimant, or owner of exclusive right(s) ▲

Typed or printed name and date ▼ If this application gives a date of publication in space 3, do not sign and submit it before that date.
_____   Date ▶ _____

Handwritten signature (X) ▼

☞   X _

		9
Certificate will be mailed in window envelope to this address:	Name ▼	**YOU MUST:** • Complete all necessary spaces • Sign your application in space 8
	Number/Street/Apt ▼	**SEND ALL 3 ELEMENTS IN THE SAME PACKAGE:** 1. Application form 2. Nonrefundable filing fee in check or money order payable to Register of Copyrights 3. Deposit material
	City/State/ZIP ▼	**MAIL TO:** Library of Congress Copyright Office 101 Independence Avenue, S.E. Washington, D.C. 20559-6000

As of
July 1,
1999,
the
filing
fee for
Form TX
is $30.

*17 U.S.C. § 506(e): Any person who knowingly makes a false representation of a material fact in the application for copyright registration provided for by section 409, or in any written statement filed in connection
with the application, shall be fined not more than $2,500.
June 1999—200,000   ♻ PRINTED ON RECYCLED PAPER   ☆U.S. GOVERNMENT PRINTING OFFICE: 1999-454-879/49
WEB REV: June 1999

Human resources law:

- Draft plan documents for tax-sheltered employee benefit plans
- Draft deferred compensation plans
- Prepare and file for Internal Revenue Service determination letters of plans
- Prepare and file annual reports including 5500 series Internal Revenue Service forms
- Calculate employer and employee contribution levels and limitations
- Draft, review, and distribute summary plan descriptions

Litigation:

- Investigate factual allegations of case
- Help to locate witnesses and physical evidence
- Draft summons, complaint, answers, and other defenses and responsive pleadings

Exhibit 3.6 Subpoena

Commonwealth of Pennsylvania
County of Philadelphia

In the matter of:

COURT OF COMMON PLEAS

Henry Thomas
_____
(Plaintiff)   *(Demandante)*

October _____ Term, Yr. <u>2007</u>

vs.

No. <u>68-96874</u>

Thomas Cheese
_____
(Defendant)   *(Demandado)*

Subpoena

To: <u>Elizabeth Rhodes</u>

(Name of Witness)   *(Nombre del Testigo)*

1. YOU ARE ORDERED BY THE COURT TO COME TO *(El tribunal le ordena que venga a)*

<u>Court room 654</u> , AT PHILADELPHIA, PENNSYLVANIA ON *(en Filadelfia,*

Pennsylvania el) <u>November 4, 2007</u> , AT *(a las)* <u>10</u> O'CLOCK <u>A</u> .M., TO

TESTIFY ON BEHALF OF *(para atestiguar a favor de)* <u>Henry Thomas</u> IN THE ABOVE

CASE, AND TO REMAIN UNTIL EXCUSED *(en el caso arriba mencionado y permanecer hasta que le autoricen irse).*

2. AND BRING WITH YOU THE FOLLOWING *(Y traer con usted lo siguiente):*

_____

_____

NOTICE	AVISO
If you fail to attend or to produce the documents or things required by this subpoena, you may be subject to the sanctions authorized by Rule 234.5 of the Pennsylvania Rules of Civil Procedure, including but not limited to costs, attorney fees and imprisonment.	**Si usted falla en comparecer o producir los documentos o cosas requeridas por esta cita, usted estara sujeto a las sanciones autorizadas por la regla 234.5 de las reglas de procedimiento civil de Pensilvania, incluyendo pero no limitado a los costos, remuneracion de abogados y encarcelamiento.**

INQUIRIES CONCERNING THIS SUBPOENA SHOULD BE ADDRESSED TO *(Las preguntas que tenga acerca de esta Citacion deben ser dirigidas a):*
ISSUED BY:

<u>Edith Hannah</u>
       (Attorney)   *(Abogado/Abogada)*

ADDRESS *(Direccion)* <u>8 North Broad Street, Philadelphia, PA</u>

TELEPHONE NO. *(No. de Telefono)* <u>215 555 9999</u>

ATTORNEY *(Abogado ID #)* <u>A5B6</u>

BY THE COURT *(Por El Tribunal)*
JOSEPH H. EVERS
PROTHONOTARY *(Protonotario)*

PRO_____
       (Clerk)   *(Escribano)*

10-200 (Rev. 7/99)   Completed Subpoena must be signed and sealed by the Prothonotary (Room 266 City Hall) before service.

- Organize and maintain litigation files
- Assist in the preparation of trial notebooks
- Gather, review, summarize, and index documents for use at trial
- Locate and arrange for interviews with expert witnesses
- Prepare written interrogatories

- Assist in preparing and conducting oral depositions, including videotape depositions
- Prepare or obtain subpoenas (see sample in Exhibit 3.6) and arrange for service upon witnesses
- Coordinate, assist, and arrange for trial exhibits
- Obtain jury-pool information, and assist in the selection of appropriate jury members
- Attend trial and assist in the handling of witnesses, exhibits, and evidence
- Prepare contemporaneous summaries of witness statements during trial

Administrative Procedures in Law Offices and Firms

Certain administrative procedures, such as conflict checking and time keeping, are common to most, if not all, law offices. Depending on the size of the law firm and the nature of the practice, a paralegal also may be called upon to perform what might be thought to be accounting or financial activities, such as preparing invoices, maintaining client escrow accounts, maintaining trust accounts, preparing payroll records, preparing court required accounting, and completing real estate settlement forms.

Conflict Checking

Conflict checking Verifying that the attorneys in the firm do not have a personal conflict and have not previously represented and are not currently representing any party with an adverse interest or conflict with the potential client.

Conflict checking is necessary to verify that current and prior representations of parties and matters handled will not present a conflict of interest for the firm in accepting a new client or legal matter. Checking for conflicts of interest is an essential function designed to avoid the ethical violations of representing competing interests. Many offices use computer database software for conflict checking. Names of clients, opposing parties, counsel, and law firms can be quickly searched electronically. Some firms still rely on a manual check of paper lists and file-card indexes containing the names of clients, opposing parties, and opposing attorneys in cases. To determine conflicts where there has been only indirect representation is difficult.

Attorneys and paralegals who change firms may have to do a preliminary conflict check before they accept or start employment. The conflict comes when the former firm and the new firm are, or were, on opposite sides of a case. It may be a conflict for someone who has had access to information about a case to switch to the firm representing the opposing party. Confidential disclosure for the limited purpose of checking for a conflict before starting employment could prevent a serious or perceived ethical breach in the form of a breach of confidentiality or conflict of interest. In some cases, the conflict of interest may result from a financial interest such as stock ownership or investments. Making full disclosure of these potential conflict situations to the supervising attorney or to the appropriate conflict checker with the firm is important.

In many cases, the conflict can be resolved by isolating the individual from information about the case—sometimes called building an ethical wall. An ethical wall, also known as a Chinese wall, is an attempt to shield a paralegal or lawyer from access to information about a case when there is the possibility of a conflict of interest. Most courts permit the establishment of an ethical wall to protect the parties from the conflict of interest or breach of confidentiality. As commented by a Connecticut trial court in an unpublished opinion:

> . . . The court does not subscribe to the argument that, as a matter of law, screening would be ineffective when a nonlawyer switches employment to 'the other side.' The ABA opinions indicate that a law firm can set up appropriate screening and administrative procedures to prevent nonlawyers from working on the other side of those common cases and disclosing confidential information. . . .
>
> **Source:** Devine v. Beinfield, *1997 Ct. Sup. 7674, 1997 Conn Super Lexis 1966, No. CV93 0121721 S (Jul. 1, 1997).*

The Nevada Supreme Court specifically addresses the issue of paralegals in the *Leibowitz* case.

IN THE WORDS OF THE COURT

LEIBOWITZ V. DIST. CT., 119 NEV. ADV. OP. NO. 57, 39683 (2003) 78 P.3D 515

The Nevada Supreme Court in overturning a 1994 ethics opinion [*Ciaffone v. District Court*, 113 Nev. 1165 (1997), 945 P.2d 950] that prohibited paralegals from working for a firm that represents any client that had an adversarial relationship to any client of the former employer law firm, summarized the rationale for the ethical wall and provided an instructive guide . . .

. . . As pointed out by the amici's brief, the majority of professional legal ethics commentators, ethics tribunals, and courts have concluded that nonlawyer screening is a permissible method to protect confidences held by nonlawyer employees who change employment. Nevada is in a minority of jurisdictions that do not allow screening for nonlawyers moving from private firm to private firm.

Imputed disqualification is considered a harsh remedy that "should be invoked if, and only if, the [c]ourt is satisfied that real harm is likely to result from failing to invoke it."

This stringent standard is based on a client's right to counsel of the client's choosing and the likelihood of prejudice and economic harm to the client when severance of the attorney–client relationship is ordered. It is for this reason that the ABA opined in 1988 that screening is permitted for nonlawyer employees, while conversely concluding, through the Model Rules of Professional Conduct, that screening is not permitted for lawyers. The ABA explained that "additional considerations" exist justifying application of screening to nonlawyer employees (*i.e.,* mobility in employment opportunities which function to serve both legal clients and the legal profession) versus the Model Rule's proscription against screening where lawyers move from private firm to private firm. In essence, a lawyer may always practice his or her profession regardless of an affiliation to a law firm. Paralegals, legal secretaries, and other employees of attorneys do not have that option.

We are persuaded that *Ciaffone* misapprehended the state of the law regarding nonlawyer imputed disqualification. We therefore overrule *Ciaffone* to the extent it prohibits screening of nonlawyer employees.

When a law firm hires a nonlawyer employee, the firm has an affirmative duty to determine whether the employee previously had access to adversarial client files. If the hiring law firm determines that the employee had such access, the hiring law firm has an absolute duty to screen the nonlawyer employee from the adversarial cases irrespective of the nonlawyer employee's actual knowledge of privileged or confidential information.

Although we decline to mandate an exhaustive list of screening requirements, the following provides an instructive minimum:

(1) *"The newly hired nonlawyer [employee] must be cautioned not to disclose any information relating to the representation of a client of the former employer."*

(2) *"The nonlawyer [employee] must be instructed not to work on any matter on which [he or] she worked during the prior employment, or regarding which [he or] she has information relating to the former employer's representation."*

(3) *"The new firm should take . . . reasonable steps to ensure that the nonlawyer [employee] does not work in connection with matters on which [he or] she worked during the prior employment, absent client consent [i.e., unconditional waiver] after consultation."*

In addition, the hiring law firm must inform the adversarial party, or their counsel, regarding the hiring of the nonlawyer employee and the screening mechanisms utilized. The adversarial party may then: (1) make a conditional waiver (*i.e.,* agree to the screening mechanisms); (2) make an unconditional waiver (eliminate the screening mechanisms); or (3) file a motion to disqualify counsel.

(continued)

However, even if the new employer uses a screening process, disqualification will always be required—absent unconditional waiver by the affected client—under the following circumstances:

(1) *"[W]hen information relating to the representation of an adverse client has in fact been disclosed [to the new employer]"; or, in the absence of disclosure to the new employer,*

(2) *"[W]hen screening would be ineffective or the nonlawyer [employee] necessarily would be required to work on the other side of a matter that is the same as or substantially related to a matter on which the nonlawyer [employee] has previously worked."*

Once a district court determines that a nonlawyer employee acquired confidential information about a former client, the district court should grant a motion for disqualification unless the district court determines that the screening is sufficient to safeguard the former client from disclosure of the confidential information. The district court is faced with the delicate task of balancing competing interests, including: (1) "the individual right to be represented by counsel of one's choice," (2) "each party's right to be free from the risk of even inadvertent disclosure of confidential information," (3) "the public's interest in the scrupulous administration of justice," and (4) "the prejudices that will inure to the parties as a result of the [district court's] decision."

Time Keeping and Billing

Keeping track of billable time is a critical function to ensure that the law firm will be compensated properly for its advice and efforts on behalf of clients. Tracking time extends beyond just the efforts of attorneys to paralegals and, in some cases, secretaries and clerks.

Billing is the most important function in a law firm. Without billings there is no revenue to pay expenses and salaries. As important as it is, in many offices billing is not treated with enough importance. Time records are the basis for most law firm billings. Without accurate time records, billings cannot be made.

The propriety of fees is addressed in Rule 1.5 of the Model Rules of Professional Conduct.

The Utah Rules of Professional Conduct provide:

Rule 1.5. Fees.

(a) A lawyer shall not make an agreement for, charge or collect an unreasonable fee or an unreasonable amount for expenses. The factors to be considered in determining the reasonableness of a fee include the following:

(a)(1) the time and labor required, the novelty and difficulty of the questions involved and the skill requisite to perform the legal service properly;

(a)(2) the likelihood, if apparent to the client, that the acceptance of the particular employment will preclude other employment by the lawyer;

(a)(3) the fee customarily charged in the locality for similar legal services;

(a)(4) the amount involved and the results obtained;

(a)(5) the time limitations imposed by the client or by the circumstances;

(a)(6) the nature and length of the professional relationship with the client;

(a)(7) the experience, reputation and ability of the lawyer or lawyers performing the services; and

(a)(8) whether the fee is fixed or contingent.

(b) The scope of the representation and the basis or rate of the fee and expenses for which the client will be responsible shall be communicated to the client, preferably in writing, before or within a reasonable time after commencing the representation, except when the lawyer will charge a regularly represented client on the same basis or rate. Any changes in the basis or rate of the fee or expenses shall also be communicated to the client.

(c) A fee may be contingent on the outcome of the matter for which the service is rendered, except in a matter in which a contingent fee is prohibited by paragraph (d) or other law. A contingent fee agreement shall be in a writing signed by the client and shall state the method by which the fee is to be determined, including the percentage or percentages that shall accrue to the lawyer in the event of settlement, trial or appeal; litigation and other expenses to be deducted from the recovery; and whether such expenses are to be deducted before or after the contingent fee is calculated. The agreement must clearly notify the client of any expenses for which the client will be liable whether or not the client is the prevailing party. Upon conclusion of a contingent fee matter, the lawyer shall provide the client with a written statement stating the outcome of the matter and, if there is a recovery, showing the remittance to the client and the method of its determination.

(d) A lawyer shall not enter into an arrangement for, charge or collect:

   (d)(1) any fee in a domestic relations matter, the payment or amount of which is contingent upon the securing of a divorce or upon the amount of alimony or support, or property settlement in lieu thereof; or

   (d)(2) a contingent fee for representing a defendant in a criminal case.

(e) A division of a fee between lawyers who are not in the same firm may be made only if:

   (e)(1) the division is in proportion to the services performed by each lawyer or each lawyer assumes joint responsibility for the representation;

   (e)(2) the client agrees to the arrangement, including the share each lawyer will receive, and the agreement is confirmed in writing; and

   (e)(3) the total fee is reasonable.

Web Exploration

View the comments to the Utah rules at http://www.utcourts .gov/resources/rules/ucja/ ch13/1_5.htm.

The billing of clients is not limited to the time of lawyers but may include that of paralegals as the 11th Circuit Court of Appeals has stated:

> We have held that paralegal time is recoverable as part of a prevailing party's award for attorney's fees and expenses, [but] only to the extent that the paralegal performs work traditionally done by an attorney." Quoting from *Allen v. United States Steel Corp.*, 665 F.2d 689, 697 (5th Cir. 1982): "To hold otherwise would be counterproductive because excluding reimbursement for such work might encourage attorneys to handle entire cases themselves, thereby achieving the same results at a higher overall cost.
>
> *Jean v. Nelson*, 863 F. 2d 759 (11th Cir. 1988).

Client expense records, by contrast, are usually well maintained because a check is usually written, which provides a documented record for billing purposes. But the time record must come from the recording of time spent by the attorney, paralegal, or legal team member. This information frequently is maintained manually on pieces of paper called time slips or time records. Client bills are prepared manually from these records.

More frequently, the client billing is prepared using a computer time and billing program, such as the popular AbacusLaw program. Most of these programs allow for random entry of the individual time record information and then automatically sort by client and project or case. These programs also allow for the entry and inclusion in the final billing report or printout of the costs expended in the current period and the costs and fees received from previous billing periods and the application of retainers.

Accounting in the Law Office

In the law office working environment, your ability to understand basic financial issues makes you a more valuable member of the law office team. A law firm is a business that, as Abraham Lincoln said, deals in time and advice, unlike retail, wholesale, or manufacturing businesses that trade in goods or commodities.

A major function of the legal support staff is to keep track of the time the lawyers and support staff spend on a case and then bill the client for the time expended. Financial account records must be kept accurately both for internal office activities and for matters related to specific clients. Expenses may be associated with specific clients or part of the overall cost of running the office. If accurate records are not kept for the law office operation, it may fail or close.

When the funds involved belong to clients, errors can result in malpractice claims for improperly prepared documentation and the filing of inaccurate court documents and tax returns. At worst, errors may result in a loss or misappropriation of client funds, which can lead to sanctions, including disbarment or even criminal prosecution.

In addition to understanding the internal operations accounting needs of a law firm is the need to understand the accounting and financial affairs of clients. Understanding accounting and financial reports and documents is essential in many areas of law today.

Family Law

Every domestic relations case has concerns related to property settlement, support, and alimony. In today's marital climate, there is an increasing demand for full financial disclosure in prenuptial agreements. A basic understanding of the nature and the sources of the family financial information will enable you to prepare the necessary documents. As an example, Exhibit 3.7 shows selected pages from the New Jersey Family Part Case Information.

Commercial Litigation

Commercial litigation typically involves actions resulting from claims of breach of contract or interpretations of provisions of a contract stating the obligations of the parties. It has become more complex—in no small matter because of the financial implications of contract breaches and remedies. The tasks of finding, analyzing, and presenting financial matters increasingly fall on litigation paralegals.

Litigation

Even in the simplest of litigation matters, a measure of damages has to be computed. Calculations of wages lost, projection of future losses, and the current or present value may have to be computed or reviewed for accuracy.

Maintaining Law Firm Financial Information

Law firms, like any other business, have numerous forms of financial obligations. Utility bills and employees have to be paid on a regular basis. Accurate records have to be maintained to determine which costs are chargeable to individual clients. Office operations frequently involve record keeping for client funds in the form of escrow accounts.

Records of the various receipts and disbursements are used to prepare the firm's tax returns, including quarterly and annual employee withholding and employer tax returns, income tax returns, and informational tax returns, such as reports for nonemployee compensation and independent contractors such as freelance paralegals, or reporters and investigators.

Regular use of a systematic system simplifies the completion of financial reports. By using a standard system of accounting, lawyers, bookkeepers, paralegals, and secretarial personnel can easily communicate, contributing information of charges and revenues that are usable for all concerned including the outside accountants and auditors.

Reconstructing the financial information is a common task in many law offices. In many cases, clients deliver piles of financial documents and expect the law office personnel to sort, classify, and organize seemingly unrelated pieces of paper into tax returns, estate tax returns, and documents with which settlements and major decisions will be made. Knowing how to attack the piles of paper can save time, stress, and frustration.

Safekeeping of client property and segregation of client funds from those of the law firm is an ethical obligation imposed under Rule 1.15 of the Model Rules of Professional Conduct of which that of South Dakota provides in part:

Rule 1.15. Safekeeping Property.

(a) A lawyer shall hold property of clients or third persons that is in a lawyer's possession in connection with a representation separate from the lawyer's own property.

Exhibit 3.7 New Jersey family case information

PART D - MONTHLY EXPENSES (computed at 4.3 wks/mo.)

Joint Marital Life Style should reflect standard of living established during marriage. Current expenses should reflect the current life style. Do not repeat those income deductions listed in Part C–3.

	Joint Marital Life Style Family, including _____ children	Current Life Style Yours and _____ children
SCHEDULE A: SHELTER		
If Tenant:		
Rent	$_____	$_____
Heat (if not furnished)	$_____	$_____
Electric & Gas (if not furnished)	$_____	$_____
Renter's Insurance	$_____	$_____
Parking (at Apartment)	$_____	$_____
Other Charges (Itemize)	$_____	$_____
If Homeowner:		
Mortgage	$_____	$_____
Real Estate Taxes (if not included w/mortgage payment)	$_____	$_____
Homeowners Ins. (if not included w/mortgage payment)	$_____	$_____
Other Mortgages or Home Equity Loans	$_____	$_____
Heat (unless Electric or Gas)	$_____	$_____
Electric & Gas	$_____	$_____
Water & Sewer	$_____	$_____
Garbage Removal	$_____	$_____
Snow Removal	$_____	$_____
Lawn Care	$_____	$_____
Maintenance	$_____	$_____
Repairs	$_____	$_____
Other Charges (Itemize)	$_____	$_____
Tenant or Homeowner:		
Telephone	$_____	$_____
Mobile/Cellular Telephone	$_____	$_____
Service Contracts on Equipment	$_____	$_____
Cable TV	$_____	$_____
Plumber/Electrician	$_____	$_____
Equipment & Furnishings	$_____	$_____
Internet Charges	$_____	$_____
Other (Itemize)	$_____	$_____
TOTAL	$_____	$_____
SCHEDULE B: TRANSPORTATION		
Auto Payment	$_____	$_____
Auto Insurance (number of vehicles)	$_____	$_____
Registration, License	$_____	$_____
Maintenance	$_____	$_____
Fuel and Oil	$_____	$_____
Commuting Expenses	$_____	$_____
Other Charges (Itemize)	$_____	$_____
TOTAL	$_____	$_____

(continued)

Exhibit 3.7 New Jersey family case information *(continued)*

PART E - BALANCE SHEET OF ALL FAMILY ASSETS AND LIABILITIES STATEMENT OF ASSETS

Description	Title to Property (H, W, J)	Date of purchase/acquisition. If claim that asset is exempt, state reason and value of what is claimed to be exempt	Value $ Put * after exempt	Date of Evaluation Mo./Day/Yr.
1. Real Property				
2. Bank Accounts, CDs				
3. Vehicles				
4. Tangible Personal Property				
5. Stocks and Bonds				
6. Pension, Profit Sharing, Retirement Plan(s) 401(k)s, etc. [list each employer]				
7. IRAs				
8. Businesses, Partnerships, Professional Practices				
9. Life Insurance (cash surrender value)				
10. Loans Receivable				
11. Other (specify)				

TOTAL GROSS ASSETS: $_____
TOTAL SUBJECT TO EQUITABLE DISTRIBUTION: $_____
TOTAL NOT SUBJECT TO EQUITABLE DISTRIBUTION: $_____

Funds shall be kept in a separate account maintained in the state where the lawyer's office is situated, or elsewhere with the consent of the client or third person. Other property shall be identified as such and appropriately safeguarded. Complete records of such account funds and other property shall be kept by the lawyer and shall be preserved for a period of five years after termination of the representation. A lawyer may deposit the lawyer's own funds in a client trust account for the sole purpose of paying bank service charges on that account, but only in an amount necessary for that purpose. A lawyer shall deposit into a client trust account legal fees and expenses that have been paid in advance, to be withdrawn by the lawyer only as fees are earned or expenses incurred.

(b) Upon receiving funds or other property in which a client or third person has an interest, a lawyer shall promptly notify the client or third person. Except as stated in this Rule or otherwise permitted by law or by agreement with the client, a lawyer shall promptly deliver to the client or third person any funds or other property that the client or third person is entitled to receive and, upon request by the client or third person, shall promptly render a full accounting regarding such property.

(c) When in the course of representation a lawyer is in possession of property in which two or more persons (one of whom may be the lawyer) claim interests, the property shall be kept separate by the lawyer until the dispute is resolved. The lawyer shall promptly distribute all portions of the property as to which the interests are not in dispute.

(d) Preserving Identity of Funds and Property of Client.

　(1) All funds of clients paid to a lawyer or law firm, including advances for costs and expenses, shall be deposited in one or more identifiable bank accounts maintained in the state in which the law office is situated and no funds belonging to the lawyer or law firm shall be deposited therein except as follows:

　　(i) Funds reasonably sufficient to pay bank charges may be deposited therein.

　　(ii) Funds belonging in part to a client and in part presently or potentially to the lawyer or law firm must be deposited therein, but the portion belonging to the lawyer or law firm may be withdrawn when due unless the right of the lawyer or law firm to receive it is disputed by the client, in which event the disputed portion shall not be withdrawn until the dispute is finally resolved.

　(2) A lawyer shall:

　　(i) Promptly notify a client of the receipt of his funds, securities, or other properties.

　　(ii) Identify and label securities and properties of a client promptly upon receipt and place them in a safe deposit box or other place of safekeeping as soon as practicable.

　　(iii) Maintain complete records of all funds, securities, and other properties of a client coming into the possession of the lawyer and render appropriate accountings to his client regarding them.

　　(iv) Promptly pay or deliver to the client as requested by a client the funds, securities, or other properties in the possession of the lawyer which the client is entitled to receive. . . .

 Web Exploration

The complete rule may be viewed at http://www.sdbar.org/Rules/Rules/PC_Rules.htm.

Accounting for Client Retainers and Costs

Law firms frequently request a **retainer**—a payment at the beginning of handling a new matter for a client. This amount may be used to offset the fees for services rendered or costs advanced on behalf of the client. Unless there is some other arrangement, agreed upon in conformity with applicable court rules and ABA guidelines, these funds belong to the law firm only when they have been earned by rendering of the service or actual cost expenditure. Unused amounts may have to be returned to the client and those expended accounted for to the client.

Increasingly, under the rules of professional conduct, many states also require a written fee agreement in contingent-fee cases, whereas in other types of cases, it is preferred but not required.

A new approach to providing legal services is sometimes called "unbundled" legal services or discrete task representation. The term refers to a broad range of discrete tasks that an attorney might undertake, such as advice, negotiation, document review, document preparation, and limited representation. A sample retainer agreement under Maine Bar Rule 3.4(I) is shown in Exhibit 3.8.

Retainer A payment at the beginning of the handling of a new matter for a client. This amount may be used to offset the fees for services rendered or costs advanced on behalf of the client.

Exhibit 3.8   Limited representation agreement

Date:_____, 20_____
1. The client, _____, retains the attorney, _____, to perform limited legal services in the following matter:
_____ v. _____.

2. The client seeks the following services from the attorney (indicate by writing "yes" or "no"):

a. _____ Legal advice: office visits, telephone calls, fax, mail, e-mail;
b. _____ Advice about availability of alternative means to resolving
   the dispute, including mediation and arbitration;
c. _____ Evaluation of client self-diagnosis of the case and advising
   client about legal rights and responsibilities;
d. _____ Guidance and procedural information for filing or serving
   documents;
e. _____ Review pleadings and other documents prepared by client;
f. _____ Suggest documents to be prepared;
g. _____ Draft pleadings, motions, and other documents;
h. _____ Factual investigation: contacting witnesses, public record
   searches, in-depth interview of client;
i. _____ Assistance with computer support programs;
j. _____ Legal research and analysis;
k. _____ Evaluate settlement options;
l. _____ Discovery: interrogatories, depositions, requests for
   document production;
m. _____ Planning for negotiations;
n. _____ Planning for court appearances;
o. _____ Standby telephone assistance during negotiations or
   settlement conferences;
p. _____ Referring client to expert witnesses, special masters, or
   other counsel;
q. _____ Counseling client about an appeal;
r. _____ Procedural assistance with an appeal and assisting with
   substantive legal argument in an appeal;
s. _____ Provide preventive planning and/or schedule legal checkups:
t. _____ Other:

_____

_____

3. The client shall pay the attorney for those limited services as follows:
a. Hourly Fee:

The current hourly fee charged by the attorney or the attorney's law firm for services under this agreement are as follows:
 i. Attorney: $_____
 ii. Associate: $_____
 iii. Paralegal: $_____
 iv. Law Clerk: $_____

Unless a different fee arrangement is established in clause b. of this paragraph, the hourly fee shall be payable at the time of the service. Time will be charged in increments of one-tenth of an hour, rounded off for each particular activity to the nearest one-tenth of an hour.

b. Payment from Deposit:

For a continuing consulting role, client will pay to attorney a deposit of $_____, to be received by attorney on or before _____, and to be applied against attorney fees and costs incurred by client. This amount will be deposited by attorney in attorney trust account. Client authorizes attorney to withdraw funds from the trust account to pay attorney fees and costs as they are incurred by client. The deposit is refundable. If, at the termination of services under this agreement, the total amount incurred by client for attorney fees and costs is less than the amount of the deposit, the difference will be refunded to client. Any balance due shall be paid within thirty days of the termination of services.

Exhibit 3.8 **Limited representation agreement** *(continued)*

c. Costs:

Client shall pay attorney out-of-pocket costs incurred in connection with this agreement, including long distance telephone and fax costs, photocopy expense and postage. All costs payable to third parties in connection with client case, including filing fees, investigation fees, deposition fees, and the like shall be paid directly by client. Attorney shall not advance costs to third parties on client behalf.

4. The client understands that the attorney will exercise his or her best judgment while performing the limited legal services set out above, but also recognizes:

a. the attorney is not promising any particular outcome,
b. the attorney has not made any independent investigation of the facts and is relying entirely on the client limited disclosure of the facts given the duration of the limited services provided, and
c. the attorney has no further obligation to the client after completing the above described limited legal services unless and until both attorney and client enter into another written representation agreement.

5. If any dispute between client and attorney arises under this agreement concerning the payment of fees, the client and attorney shall submit the dispute for fee arbitration in accordance with Rule 9(e)-(k) of the Maine Bar Rules. This arbitration shall be binding upon both parties to this agreement.

WE HAVE EACH READ THE ABOVE AGREEMENT BEFORE SIGNING IT.
Signature of client _____
Signature of attorney _____

A lawyer may request a nonrefundable retainer. This is a common practice when the client does not want the law firm to be able to represent the opposing party in a pending legal action. This is seen most commonly in family law or divorce actions. Legal ethics prohibit taking on a client where there is a conflict of interest. In cases of nonrefundable retainers, a statement of application of the funds may or should be made as a matter of the financial accounting practice.

Costs Advanced

Law firms typically pay directly to the court any fees for filing documents for the client. In some cases, the cost of stenographers, expert witnesses, and duplication of records, travel, phone, and copying also will be advanced. The firm must keep proper accounting for these items to be able to bill a client properly or charge the amounts expended against prepaid costs or retainers. Good practice is to include in the initial client fee letter the nature and amount of costs that will be charged for these various items.

Civil Practice: Fee and Cost Billing

In a civil litigation practice, fees may be calculated on an hourly rate, a contingent fee, or a combination of the two. The time records for each member of the firm must be obtained, either from the hard copies of time records or the computer printout of hours spent working on the case. The actual time may be reported to the client chronologically, with all activity by each person who worked on the file integrated with all the others, but may be listed separately by the individual.

The difficulty is in calculating the correct amount for each person at his/her respected hourly rate. It is not unusual to have a senior partner bill at one rate, a junior partner at another rate, and a paralegal at a third rate. It is good practice to calculate the total for each billable person separately, and then collectively. The totals of the individuals, of course, must equal the grand total. Therefore, the comparison acts as a check on mathematical accuracy.

Client bills can be prepared manually from paper copies of time records or other office records. More frequently, the client billing is prepared using a computer program. Most of these programs allow input of the individual time record in a random order that can be sorted automatically by client and project. In addition to the time billing, these programs allow for entry and inclusion in the final billing of costs expended in the current billing period and costs and payments received from previous billing periods and retainers.

Timely Disbursements

As part of the settlement of a case for a client, the opposing side may pay the amount of the cash settlement to the lawyer. These funds must be disbursed to the client and until disbursed, retained in a separate escrow account and not commingled with the lawyer's own funds. Records of the receipt and disbursement of these funds must be maintained properly to avoid charges of misuse of client funds.

A lawyer is not required to make disbursements until the draft or check has cleared. A check or draft is deemed cleared when the funds are available for disbursement. But, lawyers cannot retain the amount for an unreasonable time. The client is entitled to earn the potential interest on the amount to be dispersed. The lawyer is not entitled to keep the amount and earn interest for his/her own account.

Trust Accounts

Trust account The funds of the client.

A **trust account** or fiduciary account contains the client's funds and should never be commingled with those of the firm or the individual attorney. A clear record of all trust transactions must be maintained. In many cases, such as trusts, estates, or cases involving children, detailed reports must be filed with the court following the court-imposed rules as shown in Exhibit 3.9 for the Probate Courts of the State of New Hampshire. When a checking account has been established, the check register is a primary source for creating any required or desired reports. With some larger accounts, checking accounts may not have been set up. Many trust and estate accounts are invested in money market funds, stocks, bonds, and mutual funds.

Keeping a clear record is made more difficult by the potential for periodic increases and decreases in value that are not actually realized—referred to as paper gains and losses. They exist on paper but have not been realized by the actual sale or transfer of the asset. For the attorney, the client or state law must authorize any investments of assets held in trust. Separate records should be maintained showing the activity in each of the trust accounts, including all deposits, interest earned, and disbursements, including bank charges.

Exhibit 3.9 **Selected provisions of the rules of practice and procedure in the probate courts of the state of New Hampshire**

RULE 108. FIDUCIARY ACCOUNTING STANDARDS

The following standards shall be applicable to all interim and final accountings of Administrators, trustees, guardians and conservators, required or permitted to be filed with the Court.

A. Accounts shall be stated in a manner that is understandable by Persons who are not familiar with practices and terminology peculiar to the administration of estates, trusts, guardianships and conservatorships. . . .

B. A Fiduciary account shall begin with a concise summary of its purpose and content. The account shall begin with a brief statement identifying the Fiduciary, the subject matter, the relationship of Parties interested in the account to the account, and, if applicable, appropriate notice of any limitations on or requirements for action by Parties interested in the account. . . .

C. A Fiduciary account shall contain sufficient information to put parties interested in the account on notice as to all significant transactions affecting administration during the accounting period. . . .

IOLTA Accounts

Many states, by court rule, impose an obligation to deposit client funds, when the amount is too small to earn interest, into a special interest-bearing account, the **IOLTA account** (Interest on Lawyers Trust Accounts). Interest generated from these small accounts is paid to the court-designated agency, usually the local legal aid agency, to fund their activities. Because the cost of setting up individual small accounts is greater than the interest earned, or the amount deposited is so small that no interest would accrue to the client, everyone wins by having these funds generate some income for the public good. Reconciliation of this account is simpler because no accounting for the interest to the client has to be made.

IOLTA account Where the amount is too small to earn interest, court rules require the funds be deposited into a special interest-bearing account, and the interest generally paid to support legal aid projects (Interest on Lawyers Trust Accounts).

Interest-Bearing Escrow Accounts

Lawyers frequently are asked to act as escrow agents or to retain client funds for future disbursements. In some cases the amounts may be significant. Prudent handling of the client's monies dictates that the fiduciary treat them in the same manner as would any prudent investor. If the amount is sufficient to earn interest, the amount earned belongs to the client, not to the attorney, and must be accounted for, to the client.

If earning interest, it is good practice and expected to open up separate accounts for each client. In opening these accounts, the client's Social Security number or other employer identification number should be used. If the law firm maintains the account under its tax identification number, it will have to report interest annually to the client and to the federal and state government.

A significant body of law has emerged to avoid money-laundering. In a law firm this may require reporting when significant amounts of cash are received. The problem is balancing the money-laundering rules and the attorney–client privilege. When amounts in excess of $10,000 are received in cash from a client, current legislation and regulation must be consulted.

To open an account with a financial institution requires a federal identification number. This identification number may be that of the client, the trust, the estate, or other legal entity having a current identification number. In some cases the financial institution may require copies of any documentation that created the client entity, such as the trust documents, death certificate, or decedent's will. The concern of the financial institution is to properly comply with existing regulations on federal withholding and money-laundering or large-deposit reporting obligations. A state requirement is to complete the federal form W-9.

Court Accounting

In addition to the preparation of filing federal and state estate tax returns, the fiduciary often has to file an accounting with the local court that administers or supervises trust and estate matters. These **court accounting** reports are designed to show that the fiduciary has administered the estate or trust properly.

Court accounting An accounting with the local court that administers or supervises trust and estate matters. These reports are designed to show that the fiduciary has properly administered the estate or trust.

Reports to the court also are required in many jurisdictions in civil cases involving minors. Approval of tort actions involving a minor may be negotiated between the lawyers for the insurance company or defendant and the minor's parent or guardian, subject to the approval of the court. This usually requires submitting a brief accounting of the expenses, including counsel fees, and the proposed disbursements to compensate for out-of-pocket expenses and proposed investments of the proceeds until the minor reaches a set age or by other order of court.

All of the parties are considered as acting as fiduciaries in the best interest of the minor. Local practice and court rules will furthermore dictate the form and methods of fiduciary accounting. The uniform system of accounts has been accepted by some jurisdictions without formal court rule and others by inclusion in the local court rules.

The basic objective of the uniform system of accounts is to present the financial information in a consistent manner that is understandable to the court and all the interested parties. The parties are entitled to full disclosure, clarity, and, when appropriate, supplemental information. Exhibit 3.10 is a sample of a model executor's account template using the uniform system of accounts.

Exhibit 3.10	Model executor's account template sample—Pennsylvania Orphan's Court

ORPHANS' COURT RULES

MODEL EXECUTOR'S ACCOUNT

First and Final Account

FIRST AND FINAL ACCOUNT OF

William C. Doe, Executor

For

ESTATE OF John Doe, Deceased

Date of Death: November 14, 1978
Date of Executor's Appointment: November 24, 1978
Accounting for the Period: November 24, 1978 to November 30, 1979

Purpose of Account: William C. Doe, Executor, offers this account to acquaint interested parties with the transactions that have occurred during his administration.

The account also indicates the proposed distribution of the estate.[1]
It is important that the account be carefully examined. Requests for additional information or questions or objections can be discussed with:

[Name of Executor, Counsel or other appropriate person]
[address and telephone number]

[*Note:* See discussion under Fiduciary Accounting Principle II with respect to presentation of collateral material needed by beneficiaries.]

Note

In Pennsylvania the date of first advertisement of the grant of letters should be shown after the date of the personal representative's appointment.

[1] Optional—for use if applicable.

SUMMARY OF ACCOUNT

	Page	Current Value	Fiduciary Acquisition Value
Proposed Distribution to Beneficiaries[1]	645	$102,974.56	$ 90,813.96
Principal			
Receipts	636		$160,488.76
			2,662.00
Net Gain (or Loss) on Sales or Other Disposition	638		$163,150.76
Less Disbursements:			
Debts of Decedent	639	$ 485.82	
Funeral Expenses	639	1,375.00	
Administration Expenses	639	194.25	
Federal and State Taxes	639	5,962.09	
Fees and Commissions	639	11,689.64	19,706.80
Balance before Distributions			$143,443.96

Exhibit 3.10 | **Model executor's account template sample—Pennsylvania Orphan's Court** (continued)

FIDUCIARY ACCOUNTING STANDARDS

Distributions to Beneficiaries	641	52,630.00
Principal Balance on Hand	641	$ 90,813.96
For Information:		
Investments Made	642	
Changes in Investment Holdings	642	
Income		
Receipts	643	$ 2,513.40
Less Disbursements	643	178.67
Balance Before Distributions		$ 2,334.73
Distributions to Beneficiaries	644	2,334.73
Income Balance on Hand		-0-
Combined Balance on Hand		$ 90,813.96

[1]Optional—for use if applicable.

RECEIPTS OF PRINCIPAL

Assets Listed in Inventory (Valued as of Date of Death)			Fiduciary Acquisition Value
Cash:			
First National Bank—checking account		$ 516.93	
Prudent Saving Fund Society—savings account		2,518.16	
Cash in possession of decedent		42.54	$ 3,077.63
Tangible Personal Property:			
Jewelry—			
1 pearl necklace			515.00
Furniture—			
1 antique highboy		$ 2,000.00	
1 antique side table		60.00	
1 antique chair		55.00	2,115.00
Stocks:			
200 shs.	Home Telephone & Telegraph Co., common	$ 25,000.00	
50 shs.	Best Oil Co., common	5,000.00	
1,000 shs.	Central Trust Co., capital	50,850.00	
151 shs.	Electric Data Corp., common	1,887.50	
50 shs.	Fabulous Mutual Fund	1,833.33	
200 shs.	XYZ Corporation, common	6,000.00	90,570.83
Realty:			
Residence—	86 Norwood Road West Hartford, CT		$ 50,000.00
	Total Inventory		$146,278.46

Receipts Subsequent to Inventory (Valued When Received)

2/22/79	Proceeds of Sale—Best Oil Co., rights to subscribe received 2/15/79	$ 50.00[1]	
3/12/79	Fabulous Mutual Fund, capital gains dividend received in cash	32.50	
5/11/79	Refund of overpayment of 1978 U.S. individual income tax	127.80	
9/25/79	From Richard Roe, Ancillary Administrator, net proceeds on sale of oil and gas leases in Jefferson Parish, Louisiana	10,000.00	$ 10,210.30

[1]Proceeds of sale of rights may be treated as an additional receipt, as illustrated here, or may be applied in reduction of carrying value as illustrated on page 646 of the Model Trustee's Account. Either method, consistently applied, is acceptable.

Preparing Your Resume

Getting a job requires presenting your credentials including education and experience; a well-prepared resume is usually the first impression you will make on a prospective employer.

Resume A short description of a person's education, a summary of work experience, and other related and supporting information that potential employers use in evaluating a person's qualifications for a position in a firm or an organization.

A **resume** is a short description of a person's education, a summary of work experience, and other related and supporting information that potential employers use in evaluating a person's qualifications for a position in a firm or an organization. Exhibits 3.11 and 3.12 provide examples. You should prepare a resume as you see yourself today. Look at your resume from the perspective of a future employer. What areas do you need to strengthen to demonstrate your ability to perform the type of job you would like to have?

You should look at your resume as being a continuing work in progress. Constantly update your resume to include any new job responsibilities, part-time employment skills and qualifications, and special achievements. Add meaningful items to your resume in the form of courses, skills, and outside interests that will land you that first paralegal job after you complete your training.

After you have gathered all of the necessary information, put it into a proper resume form, then review it. Does the resume reflect the information you want to communicate to a prospective employer? Try to look at it with an open, objective mind.

Exhibit 3.11	**Sample functional resume**

SARA MARKS

2222 Market Way
Brooklyn, NY 11223
(212) 555-8634 (Home)
(212) 555-9234 (Office)

EDUCATION
Reading College, Brooklyn, NY, 2008
    Associate of Science degree, GPA 4.0
        Paralegal Major—ABA-approved program
    Dean's List, Vice President of the Honor Society

EMPLOYMENT HISTORY
Paralegal field work, Brooklyn, NY, 2006 to 2008
    Advisor, Small Claims Court and the Brooklyn Department of
Consumer Affairs
- Assisted claimants with small claim forms
- Counseled individuals on consumer affairs issues

Registration and admissions clerk, Brooklyn, NY, 2004 to 2006
    Reading College
- Registered incoming and returning students
- In charge of organizing the filing system, creating more efficiency in the office

Cosmetologist and Barber, Brooklyn, NY, 2000 to 2004
- Self-employed
- Handled all phases of business, including purchasing, bookkeeping, and payroll

SPECIAL SKILLS
- WordPerfect, Microsoft Office Suite
- Excellent ability to communicate with general public

PROFESSIONAL AFFILIATIONS
Manhattan Paralegal Association

Excellent references available upon request

Exhibit 3.12 Sample chronological resume

MICHAEL C. SMITH

2345 Oregon Street, #A
Portland, OR 98765
(363) 282-7890

EDUCATION

Paralegal Certificate, General Litigation, 2008
University of Portland (ABA approved)
Curriculum included:

Family Law	Paralegal Practices and Procedures
Criminal Law	Legal Research and Writing
Civil Litigation	Estates, Trusts, and Wills

Bachelor of Science Degree,
    Transportation and Distribution Management
    Golden Gate University, San Francisco, CA

EXPERIENCE

Paralegal Practice

- Drafted memos to clients
- Prepared notice of summons
- Conducted research for misdemeanor appeal cases
- Prepared points and authorities for motions
- Observed bankruptcy and family law court proceedings
- Completed necessary documents for probate
- Wrote legal memorandum

Administration and Management

- Participated in new division startup
- Dispatched and routed for the transportation of 80 to 120 special education students daily
- Supervised between 20 and 25 drivers
- Designed and implemented daily operation logs
- Liaison between drivers and school officials or parents
- Evaluated various conditions when assigning routes and equipment

EMPLOYMENT HISTORY

Susan Hildebrand, Attorney, Portland, OR Paralegal Intern	2008
Laidlaw Transit, Inc., San Francisco, CA Dispatch Manager	2002 to 2008
Hayward Unified School District Teaching Assistant	2001 to 2002
San Mateo Union High School District Office Clerk	2000 to 2001

Employers are looking for individuals who demonstrate a good work ethic, willingness to accept responsibility and take direction, and the skills necessary for the job for which they are applying.

Set your roadmap for the job you wish to obtain. What additional educational skills are required? This will determine your future course of study. Work–study programs in your field and cooperative education are good ways of demonstrating on-the-job training. Depending upon your goals, resources, and timeframe, a specialized certificate such as a paralegal certificate, an associate's degree in paralegal studies, or a bachelor's degree in paralegal studies will certainly demonstrate your level of interest and ability to achieve the minimum level of education for the job.

Resume Formats

Many formats may be used in preparing a resume: functional, chronological, reverse chronological, combination, technical, and electronic.

The **chronological resume format** presents education and job history in a time sequence with the most recent experience listed first. An alternative format is the reverse chronological resume format, with the latest job listed last. The **functional resume format** usually gives a summary of the individual's qualifications and current experience and education without emphasizing dates of employment. The combination resume format combines the chronological and functional resume formats.

There are no hard and fast rules for choosing a proper resume format, except perhaps to put your name and contact information at the top. Some suggest that the chronological resume is the form used most commonly in the legal field. Always remember that the main purpose of the resume is to get a job interview and, you hope, employment.

If responding to an ad in the paper, tailor your resume to the job description or to the job listing of the individual employer. You may have to develop resumes in more than one format if the employment opportunities presented require different skill sets. For example, the resume sent to an employer looking for someone with specific computer skills should show that functional skill first. A job description looking for depth of experience probably should use the chronological approach.

Common elements of most resumes include:

- Heading, with your name and contact information
- Career objective, concise and to the point, geared to the job description of the position you seek
- Education, generally at the beginning of the resume if you are a recent graduate, including specific academic honors and awards if applicable to the job
- Experience, including paid and unpaid activities showing the employer the skills you have to offer
- Activities, a brief listing unless directly related to the job description, including professional organizations and educational and volunteer activities

Cover Letters

Always include a **cover letter** with your resume. This applies to email applications, too. The cover letter creates the first impression. Brief though it is, it represents a sample of your writing skills and ability to communicate in writing. Take the time to be sure it properly reflects who you are and your skills. The cover letter should be brief, as your qualifications will be covered in the accompanying resume.

The cover letter should describe the job you are seeking, summarize your qualifications, request an interview, and express a desire for the job. If possible, address the cover letter directly to the person who is responsible for the hiring decision. Be sure to spell the person's name correctly and include the correct job title.

Just as you may need different resumes for different jobs, you should personalize each letter for each job application.

References

References may be requested in responses to advertisements or you may wish to add them to your resume. Select your references carefully, they are frequently called or contacted for comment as part of the hiring process. Those you select must be contacted before you use their names and their permission secured. Faculty members and former employers are frequently asked to be used as references. In some schools and workplaces, there is a policy that limits the information that may be given out about dates or work or attendance. An employer following up on one of these references may take a negative inference from the limited information given. Keep in touch with those who do agree to give a reference and who will say good things about you to a potential

---

Chronological resume format Presents education and job history in chronological order with the most recent experience listed first.

Functional resume format Lists a summary of the individual's qualifications with current experience and education without any emphasis on dates of employment.

Cover letter A brief letter sent with a document identifying the intended recipient and the purpose of the attachment.

employer. Keep them informed on your latest work and other extracurricular activities like charity or pro bono work so they may speak knowledgeably about you if contacted.

Creating an Electronic Resume

A growing number of employers are using computers to search the Internet for job applicants and to sort electronically through the resumes they receive. Human resources managers search through resumes received online or through Internet sites by entering a few words or phrases that describe the required skills and qualifications for the position they are trying to fill. Only the resumes in the computer system that match these electronic sorting terms and phrases are considered for the job offered. To have your resume considered, you will need an electronic resume in addition to the traditional printed resume.

Computer programs that are used to search resumes generally look for certain descriptive words in the resume, these are called key words, like the key words used to conduct legal or actual research. For example, to highlight your initiative use words like initiated, started, created, introduced; for leadership skills, use words like directed, guided, organized; to attract interest to problem-solving skills, uses words like evaluated, reorganized, simplified, solved, eliminated. Be sure to use these types of key words in your electronic resume where appropriate to make your accomplishments stand out from the other resumes. A starting point is to gather all the information as shown in the Resume Checklist.

Converting a Traditional Resume into an Electronic Resume

If you plan to send your resume as an attachment to an email, the only way you can be sure the person you are sending it to can read it is if you send it as an ASCII file or in a universally usable format such as Rich text file RTF. If you already have created a resume using a word-processing program, open the file containing your resume and save it as a plain ASCII text file or RTF file. You will want to change the name of the new text file to distinguish it from the file name used for the traditional printed version.

Text-only files cannot accommodate type formatting and special characters, so be sure that your electronic resume appears in one simple font and one font size. You also

CHECKLIST Resume

PERSONAL INFORMATION
- ☐ Name
- ☐ Address

EDUCATION
- ☐ High school
  - ☐ Year of graduation
- ☐ College
  - ☐ Year of graduation
  - ☐ Degree
  - ☐ Grade point average or class rank

WORK EXPERIENCE
- ☐ Current or last employer
  - ☐ Position(s) held
- ☐ Prior employer
  - ☐ Position held and dates

SPECIFIC SKILLS
- ☐ Office skills
- ☐ Computer skills
- ☐ Language skills
- ☐ Other job-related skills

OTHER
- ☐ Organizational memberships
- ☐ Licenses/certifications

must remove line justification, tables, rules (lines), and columns. Align all text at the left to avoid indentation problems. Exhibit 3.13 is an example of an electronic resume.

The first line of your resume should contain only your full name. Type your street address, phone and fax numbers, and email address on separate lines below your name.

Because many human resource managers search by key words, you'll want to include a key word section near the top of your resume. List nouns that describe your job-related skills and abilities. If you have work experience with specific job titles such as "paralegal," list these key words as well. Also include language proficiency or other specialty qualifications such as "nurse–paralegal" or "fluent in Spanish."

Exhibit 3.13   Sample electronic resume

JANE DOE
1234 N. Maple Street
Anytown, USA 90000
Home: (213) 555-1111 * Work: (213) 555-3333
Jane.doe@att.net

LITIGATION PARALEGAL

Education
University of Paralegal Studies, Fremont, CA
Paralegal Specialist Certificate, 2002, Honors graduate
Approved by ABA
Course of study: Legal Research and Writing, Contracts, Torts, Ethics, Litigation Specialization

University of California at Berkeley
Bachelor of Arts Degree in History, 2001
Graduated Cum Laude

Skills and Abilities
• Ability to analyze documents, digest depositions, draft discovery, and prepare cases for trial
• Knowledge of torts and contract law, legal research techniques, and basic civil procedure
• Fluent in French, both written and spoken
• Proficient in Word for Windows, WordPerfect 6.0, and Excel

Legal Internship
Jones, Smith, Smythe and Smooth, Los Angeles, 2001–2002
• Digested depositions for complex litigation case
• Organized multiple documents using several software programs

Work Experience
Los Angeles Unified School District, 1998–1999
Secondary School Teacher
• Arranged classroom materials
• Supervised student teachers
• Chaired English Department
• Created curricula for advanced students

Professional Associations
Los Angeles Paralegal Association
University of Paralegal Studies Alumni Association

References and writing samples available upon request.

Source: *Wagner, Andrea,* How to Land Your First Paralegal Job: Insiders, *3rd, © 2001. Electronically reproduced by permission of Pearson Education, Inc., Upper Saddle River, New Jersey.*

After you have created your resume, save it again as an ASCII plain text file. Email the resume to yourself or to a friend to see how it looks when sent over the Internet.

Think of getting a job as a process that starts with the resume and continues through the interview and the follow-up to the interview as shown in the Checklist for Interview Strategies.

CHECKLIST Interview Strategies

GETTING READY
- ☐ Write resume.
- ☐ Make contacts.
- ☐ Network.
- ☐ Make appointments from mass mailings, telephone solicitations, and network contacts.

BEFORE THE INTERVIEW
- ☐ Know your resume.
- ☐ Be familiar with a typical application form.
- ☐ Know something about the company or firm. Check the Martindale-Hubbell or Standard and Poor's directories.
- ☐ Have a list of good questions to ask the interviewer, and know when to ask them.
- ☐ Rehearse your answers to possible interview questions, then rehearse again.
- ☐ Plan a "thumbnail" sketch of yourself.
- ☐ Know the location of the interview site and where to park, or become familiar with the public transportation schedule.
- ☐ Be at least 10 minutes early.
- ☐ Go alone.
- ☐ Bring copies of your resume, list of references, and writing samples in a briefcase or portfolio.
- ☐ Check local salary ranges for the position.
- ☐ Be prepared to answer questions regarding your salary expectations.
- ☐ Try to anticipate problem areas, such as inexperience or gaps in your work history.
- ☐ Be prepared to handle difficult questions, and know how to overcome objections.

THE INTRODUCTION
- ☐ Dress the part.
- ☐ Do not smoke, eat, chew gum, or drink coffee prior to or during the interview.

- ☐ Maintain good eye contact and good posture.
- ☐ Shake hands firmly.
- ☐ Establish rapport and be cordial without being overly familiar.
- ☐ Be positive—convert negatives to positives.
- ☐ Keep in mind that the first impressions are lasting impressions.

THE INTERVIEW
- ☐ Provide all important information about yourself.
- ☐ Sell yourself—no one else will.
- ☐ Use correct grammar.
- ☐ Do not be afraid to say, "I don't know."
- ☐ Ask questions of the interviewer.
- ☐ Do not answer questions about age, religion, marital status, or children unless you wish to. Try to address the perceived concern.
- ☐ Find out about the next interview or contact.
- ☐ Find out when a decision will be made.
- ☐ Shake hands at the end of the interview.

AFTER THE INTERVIEW
- ☐ Immediately document the interview in your placement file.
- ☐ Send personalized thank-you letters to each person who interviewed you.
- ☐ Call to follow up.

Source: Andrea Wagner, *How to Land Your First Paralegal Job* (Upper Saddle River, NJ: Prentice Hall, 2001), pp. 163–164.

Advice *from the* Field

THE PARALEGAL'S PORTFOLIO

Kathryn Myers, Coordinator, Paralegal Studies, Saint Mary-of-the-Woods College, Paralegal Studies Program

INTERVIEW

Q: How did the practice of assembling a portfolio come about?

A: This portfolio is actually based on the old concept of the "artist's portfolio." Anyone who is involved in a "hands-on" profession has utilized this concept for years.

Q: Instead of pictures, what do you mean when you speak of a portfolio for paralegal students?

A: A portfolio for paralegal students consists of two parts. One part is for my use in the program. The students have growth papers for each class, plus a series of other papers. I look at the collection of work to determine whether the paralegal program is doing what it says it will and whether it needs to be changed. I have modified a number of classes based on the material in this portfolio.

The other part is a professional portfolio. The students pull material from the above portfolio and create their own professional portfolio to take on interviews. This contains a copy or copies of their resume, transcripts, selected writing samples, projects, or any other document they believe would be useful at the interview. Employers have been very impressed with this presentation.

Q: Do potential employers ever balk at seeing something that bulky? If so, how would you suggest handling it?

A: This has not been a problem for my students. As indicated earlier, we "create" two portfolios—one program-related and the other for professional purposes. I think this eliminates any problems at the interview.

Q: What is the most important thing about a portfolio?

A: The most important thing in the professional portfolio appears to be that the employer has another tool to assess the quality of the potential employee. Grades do not mean that much anymore. An "A" at [our college] may well come from a more demanding curriculum than an "A" at another institution. There is no basis for comparison unless the employer knows the grading scales/demands of the different programs. However, having a portfolio of material allows the employer to see what an interviewee can do.

Q: With that in mind, what should a paralegal student keep in mind when putting together the portfolio?

A: How a student puts a portfolio together says a lot about the student. I encourage students to incorporate both good and "not so good" work. That shows the employer that the interviewee can learn and can improve. Students collect material as they go through the program rather than waiting until the end.

Students should highlight their growth, their abilities, and their determination. They need to provide documentation that can show abilities that counter any poor grades that might appear on the transcript. This shows potential employers that test-taking is not necessarily the be-all, end-all to grades.

Most of all, the students need to let themselves shine through within the portfolio materials. Each student is unique and each has different talents to highlight. That is the value of the portfolio.

Kathryn Myers is Coordinator, Paralegal Studies, Saint Mary-of-the-Woods College, Paralegal Studies Program. Used by permission.

Interviewing for a Job

Most students today work at part-time or full-time jobs while pursuing their education. These might be summer jobs, holiday fill-in positions, or full-time jobs. The interview for a part-time, summer, or holiday position, or the interview for a new full-time position provides an opportunity to perfect your interviewing skills. Interviewing for a job can be highly stressful but careful preparation can reduce the stress and help you put your best foot forward so you can get that dream job you want.

After the interview, you should review what happened and the results of the interview as a way of learning how to improve your interviewing skills. Even if you obtain the job, you'll want to learn what you did correctly that helped you to get the job, as well as what you could have done better, to prepare for future interviews.

The Interview

An interview for a job need not be intimidating. With a little preparation and research you can appear confident and make a good impression. The starting point is careful reading of the job description and the employer's requested qualifications. Be sure that you can answer questions related to these qualifications, such as your experience in the particular area of law or special training in the use of specialty legal software. Research the firm by finding articles about the firm or lawyers online and by looking at its website. Prepare a list of questions that you want to ask that shows your interest in the firm and the particular job as shown in the Checklist of Interview Questions. After you leave the interview analyze how you did in the interview by reviewing the Checklist below. Then, prepare and send the thank-you note to the person with whom you interviewed to make a positive, lasting impression.

CHECKLIST Questions to Ask at the Interview

- ☐ How does the firm evaluate paralegals?
- ☐ What is the growth potential for a paralegal in the firm?
- ☐ Why did the prior paralegal leave?
- ☐ How is work assigned?
- ☐ What support services are available to paralegals?
- ☐ What consideration is given for membership in paralegal associations?
- ☐ Does the firm provide any assistance for continuing education for paralegals?

CHECKLIST Analyzing How I Handled the Interview

- ☐ I arrived early for the interview.
- ☐ I greeted the interviewer warmly, with a smile and a firm handshake.
- ☐ I maintained good posture.
- ☐ I did not smoke or chew gum during the interview.
- ☐ I spoke clearly, using good grammar.
- ☐ I demonstrated enthusiasm and interest.
- ☐ I was able to answer questions asked of me.
- ☐ I sent a thank-you note within 24 hours after the interview.

Concept Review *and* Reinforcement

LEGAL TERMINOLOGY

Chronological resume format   110
Complex litigation   83
Conflict checking   94
Court accounting   105
Cover letter   110
Elder law   83
Environmental law   83
Functional resume format   110
General law practice   81

Government employment   84
Intellectual property   83
IOLTA account   105
Large law offices   79
Networking   85
Nurse paralegals or legal nurse consultants   82
Paralegal manager   83
Partnership   78

Pro bono   84
Resume   108
Retainer   101
Self-employment   85
Small offices   76
Solo practice   76
Specialty practice   81
Trust account   104

SUMMARY OF KEY CONCEPTS

Arrangements and Organization of Law Offices and Firms

Solo Practice	One lawyer practicing alone without the assistance of other attorneys.
Small Offices	Range from individual practitioners sharing space to partnerships.
Partnerships	Two or more natural (human) or artificial (corporation) persons who have joined together to share ownership and profit or loss.
Large Offices	An outgrowth of traditional law offices that have expanded over the years, adding partners and associates along the way.
General Practice	Handles all types of cases.

Specialty Practice

Legal Nurse Consultants and Nurse Paralegals	Nurses who have gained medical work experience and combine it with paralegal skills.
Real Estate	Paralegals with real estate experience in sales or from title insurance agencies.
Complex Litigation	Requires document production and maintaining indexes, usually on computer databases, of the paperwork generated from litigation.
Environmental Law	Covers everything from toxic waste dumps to protection of wildlife and the environment.
Intellectual Property	Concerned with the formalities of protecting intellectual-property interests including patent rights, trade secrets, and copyrights and trademarks.
Elder Law	Protecting the rights of the elderly and obtaining all the benefits to which they are entitled.
Paralegal Managers	Hire, supervise, train, and evaluate paralegals.
Pro Bono Paralegals	Work without compensation on behalf of individuals and organizations that otherwise could not afford legal assistance.
Government Employment	Paralegals are found in administrative agencies and federal offices involved with both criminal prosecutions and civil litigation.
Legal Departments of Corporations	Paralegals handle documents, technology, and investigations juggling legal, sales, and marketing perspectives.
Self-Employment	State regulation may limit the opportunities or restrict paralegal self-employment. Where authorized by federal law, the paralegal may actively represent clients without the supervision of an attorney.
Networking	Establishing contact with others to exchange questions and information.

Paralegal Tasks and Functions

1. Conducting interviews
2. Maintaining written and verbal contacts with clients and counsel
3. Setting up, organizing, and maintaining client files
4. Preparing pleadings and documents
5. Reviewing, analyzing, summarizing, and indexing documents and transcripts
6. Assisting in preparing witnesses and clients for trial
7. Maintaining calendar and tickler systems
8. Conducting research, both factual and legal
9. Performing office administrative functions including maintaining time and billing records

Administrative Procedures in Law Offices and Firms

Conflict Checking	To verify that current and prior representations of parties and matters handled will not present a conflict of interest for the firm in accepting a new client or legal matter.
Time Keeping and Billing	Keeping track of billable time.

Accounting in the Law Office

Maintaining Law Firm Financial Information	A paralegal needs to understand the internal accounting needs of the firm and to understand and prepare client financial information.
Accounting for Client Retainers and Costs Advanced	A payment at the beginning of the handling of a new matter for a client. This amount may be used to offset the fees for services rendered or costs advanced on behalf of the client.
Civil Practice: Fee and Cost Billing	May be calculated on an hourly rate, a contingent fee, or a combination of the two.
Timely Disbursements	Lawyers cannot retain settlement funds for an unreasonable time.
Trust Accounts	The client's funds.
IOLTA Accounts	Where the amount is too small to earn interest, court rules require that the funds be deposited into a special interest-bearing account, and the interest generally paid to support legal aid projects (Interest on Lawyers Trust Accounts).
Interest-Bearing Escrow Accounts	If the amount held for a client is sufficient to earn substantial interest it should be deposited in an interest-bearing account for the benefit of the client.
Court Accounting	An accounting with the local court that administers or supervises trust and estate matters; these reports are designed to show that the fiduciary has properly administered the estate or trust.

Preparing Your Resume

Resume Formats	Brief description of a person's education, a summary of work experience, and other related and supporting information that potential employers use in evaluating a person's qualifications for a position in a firm or an organization. Chronological Resume Format 1. Presents education and job history in chronological order with the most recent experience listed first. Functional Resume Format 2. Gives a summary of the individual's qualifications with current experience and education without emphasizing dates of employment.
Cover Letters	The cover letter creates the first impression, and is a sample of your writing skills and ability to communicate in writing.
Creating an Electronic Resume	A growing number of employers use computers to search the Internet for job applicants, sorting resumes electronically.
Converting a Traditional Resume into an Electronic Resume	Traditional word-processing documents may not be readable in electronic form and need to be converted to a readable format.

Interviewing for a Job

The Interview	Careful interview preparation can help to eliminate some of the stress and help you put your best foot forward.

WORKING THE WEB

1. Download the Tips for Networking Success from the NALS website at http://www.nals.org/students/reading/networkingsuccess.html.
2. Review some of the job opportunities posted on the American Alliance of Paralegals. What are the common qualifications? http://aapipara.org/Jobbank.htm
3. Check and download from the websites of the various paralegal professional associations information on paralegal occupational opportunities:
   a. National Association of Legal Assistants at www.nala.org
   b. National Federation of Paralegal Associations at www.paralegals.org
   c. Legal Assistant Management Association at www.lamanet.org
   d. American Association of Legal Nurse Consultants at www.aalnc.org
   e. The American Association of Nurse Attorneys at www.taana.org
   f. American Corporate Legal Assistants Association at www.aclaa.org
4. What paralegal opportunities are posted at www.monster.com?
5. What online resources are available to help in creating resumes?
   a. Purdue University at www.owl.English.purdue.edu
   b. College of William and Mary at www.wm.edu/csrv/career/stualum/resmdir
6. What online career sources are available at:
   a. Career Resource Library at www.labor.state.ny.us
   b. America's Job Bank at www.ajb.dni.us/index.html
   c. Wall Street Journal at www.careers.wsj.com
   d. CareerWEB at www.employmentguide.com
7. What law firms in your area have a website that offers employment opportunities? Use the Martindale-Hubbell Legal Directory to find the law firms.

CRITICAL THINKING & WRITING QUESTIONS

1. What are the different forms of practice arrangements that lawyers use?
2. What are the advantages and disadvantages of working for a lawyer in solo practice?
3. What are the advantages and disadvantages of working in a small multi-lawyer office or partnership?
4. What are the advantages and disadvantages of working in large law offices or firms?
5. Would working in a specialty practice be less stressful than working in a general practice?
6. What are the advantages and disadvantages of working in a corporate legal department?
7. Why would a law firm want to hire nurse paralegals?
8. What additional costs might a paralegal incur in working in a large-city practice in contrast to a small-town office?
9. Why would a paralegal who specializes in one legal field be at greater risk for unauthorized practice of law?
10. Other than revealing potential employment opportunities, what advantages does networking have for a paralegal?
11. Are interviews conducted by paralegals privileged?
12. Why is doing a conflict check important?
13. Is it necessary to do a conflict check before starting employment at a new law firm? Why?
14. When is an ethical wall required?
15. What steps should be taken to ensure that a proper ethical screen is in place?
16. Why is accurate time keeping important to the paralegal and the law firm?
17. What is a retainer?
18. What is an IOLTA account, and what is the reason behind maintaining IOLTA?
19. What is the purpose of filing a court accounting?
20. What is the objective of the Uniform System of Accounts?
21. Prepare the resume you would like to have five years from now. How would this resume help you in selecting courses, extracurricular activities, and interim employment?
22. Prepare your current resume in print form. What format did you use? Why?
23. Convert a print resume to an electronic resume. Email a copy to your instructor if requested.
24. How does assessing your interests and skills help in preparing your personal resume?

Building Paralegal Skills

VIDEO CASE STUDIES

Preparing for a Job Interview: Resume Advice

Paralegal student Reed meets with a college counselor for advice about preparing his resume and obtains some suggestions for enhancing his resume and preparing a cover letter.

After viewing the video case study at www.pearsonhighered.com/goldman answer the following:

1. Prepare an outline of your resume with the appropriate sections, and save it as a template for future use.
2. Complete the resume using the template by adding your current qualifications and experience.
3. Prepare and print out a copy of the resume using the paper you would use for submitting a resume to a potential employer.
4. Prepare the resume for electronic submission with an email. Prepare and send the email to yourself as if you were the potential employer.

Preparing for a Job Interview: Interviewing Advice

Paralegal student Reed meets with his college counselor to obtain advice about interviewing for a job. His counselor helps him with some of the questions he may be asked that trouble him.

After viewing the video case study at www.pearson highered.com/goldman answer the following:

1. Pair up with another student and role-play with one of you acting as the human resource director and the other the applicant.
2. Make a list of questions you would ask as the interviewer.
3. Make a list of questions you would ask as the applicant.
4. Conduct the interview in front of the class or another person who can offer comments and critiques of the interview.
5. Prepare a follow-up note to the interviewer.
6. What are questions that cannot be asked? If they are asked how will you answer them.

Interviewing: The Good, The Bad, and the Ugly

Three paralegals are applying for a job at a prestigious law firm. Each presents themselves in a different manner and with a distinctive style.

After viewing the video case study at www.pearsonhighered.com/goldman answer the following:

1. Make a list of suggestions for each of the three applicants on what they should have done or can do in their next interview to make the most positive impression.
2. What interviewing rules did each applicant make?
3. How important is the way you dress for an interview, why?

ETHICS ANALYSIS & DISCUSSION QUESTIONS

1. In changing jobs from one firm to another, how does the paralegal avoid a conflict of interest?
2. What ethical and UPL problems do freelance paralegals face that those working in a single firm do not?
3. What ethical issues might arise in determining the paralegal's supervising attorney when the paralegal is working in a small firm of three attorneys?
4. Say you are working as a paralegal in a small law office, shared by three attorneys, each of whom is a solo practitioner. To save money, they share a law library and a fax machine, and they use a common computer network with separate workstations but with a common file server to save files because it has an automatic backup system. You

work for each of the lawyers as the need arises, answering phones and generally performing paralegal services. [District of Columbia Ethics Opinion 303.] What issues of confidentiality should be considered? As the office paralegal, do you have any conflict of interest problems?

Paralegal Ethics in Practice

5. You hold a bachelor's degree in paralegal studies from a prestigious college. You want to work as an independent paralegal. May you advertise in the local newspaper and put a sign on the door of your office that uses the term "paralegal," according to your state law?

DEVELOPING YOUR COLLABORATION SKILLS

Working on your own or with a group of other students assigned by your instructor, review the scenario at the beginning of the chapter discussing the changes and the opportunities in the paralegal profession.

1. Dividing the class into groups of three, one person will play the role of Cary Moritz and another the role of Natasha Weiser; the third person will act as recorder and presenter.
2. Role-play Natasha's first day on the job. She receives the memo from Cary and goes to her office to offer her thanks.

a. What additional questions could Natasha ask Cary?
b. What additional advice could Cary offer?

3. The recorder keeps detailed notes of the conversation.
4. Once the role-play is completed, the group summarizes the expectations that Natasha and Cary would have of the other in their working relationship.
5. Now it is Natasha's turn to prepare a memo thanking Cary and summarizing their conversation.

PARALEGAL PORTFOLIO EXERCISE

Develop your resume, using the functional format to prepare the resume you would like to have when you finish your education as a paralegal. List the skills you expect to develop or learn before you apply for your desired paralegal position.

LEGAL ANALYSIS & WRITING CASES

Jean v. Nelson   863 F.2d 759 (11th Cir. 1988)

Reimbursement for Paralegal Time under Federal Statute

The district court awarded, and the 11th Circuit Court of Appeals upheld, reimbursement for time spent by paralegals and law clerks where the work normally was done by an attorney. The hourly rate awarded was $40, the rate at which the law firm whose paralegals and clerks were involved bills its clients.

The government challenges the rate awarded, and contends that paralegal time is compensational only at the actual cost to the plaintiff's counsel. In the context of a Title VII case, [the court] held that paralegal time is recoverable as "part of a prevailing party's award for attorney's fees and expenses, [but]

only to the extent that the paralegal performs work traditionally done by an attorney. To hold otherwise would be counterproductive because excluding reimbursement for such work might encourage attorneys to handle entire cases themselves, thereby achieving the same results at a higher overall cost."

Questions

1. Does this rationale encourage lawyers to use paralegals?
2. Does this decision facilitate the availability of lower-cost quality legal services?
3. Should an attorney be allowed to charge more than out-of-pocket costs for paralegal services?

In Re Busy Beaver Bldg. Centers, Inc.   19 F.3d 833 (3rd Cir. 1994)

Paralegal Fees Based on Skill Level

In deciding the propriety of awarding paralegal fees in bankruptcy cases, the court held:

As is true with recently graduated attorneys, entry-level paralegals perform the more mundane tasks in the paralegal work spectrum, some of which may resemble those tasks generally deemed "clerical" in nature. Yet, even with these

tasks, paralegals may have to bring their training or experience to bear, thereby relieving attorneys of the burden of extensive supervision and ensuring the proper completion of tasks involving the exercise, or potential exercise, of some paraprofessional judgment. Of course, the appropriate rate the attorney will command for paralegal services will ordinarily parallel the paralegal's credentials and the degree of experience, knowledge, and skill the task at hand calls for. . . . [P]urely clerical or secretarial tasks should not be billed at a paralegal rate, regardless of who performs them.

The short of it is that the market-driven approach of the [bankruptcy act] § 330 permits compensation for relatively low-level paralegal services if and only if analogous non-bankruptcy clients agree to pay for the same, and then only at that rate. [T]hose services not requiring the exercise of professional legal judgment . . . must be included in "overhead."

We cannot agree that in all cases the general ability of a legal secretary to perform some particular task determines whether a paralegal or a legal secretary is the appropriate, most efficient, employee to perform it at any given instant.

At times temporal constraints may foreclose the delegation option. At other times a paralegal—or, for that matter, an attorney—can more productively complete a clerical task, such as photocopying documents, than can a legal secretary.

Questions

1. How can the attorney prove the skill level of paralegals when seeking compensation for paralegal services?
2. Will this kind of reasoning by the court force attorneys to hire more skilled paralegals?
3. Would the existence of a certificate or degree in paralegal studies be useful in proving that the person who worked on a case was a paralegal?

WORKING WITH THE LANGUAGE OF THE COURT CASE

Phoenix Founders Inc. v. Marshall

887 S.W.2d 831 (Tex. 1994)
Supreme Court of Texas

Read the following case, excerpted from the state supreme court's opinion. Review and brief the case. In your brief, answer the following questions.

1. What is the danger in hiring a paralegal who has worked at a competing law firm when handling a case on appeal?
2. What is the supervising attorney's responsibility in hiring a paralegal who has worked at another law firm?
3. What steps must be taken when hiring a paralegal who worked at another law firm that represents an opposing party?
4. What instructions should the paralegal who worked at another firm be given when hired?
5. Under what general circumstances will a law firm be disqualified after hiring a paralegal?

Spector, Justice, delivered the opinion of the Court, in which Hillips, Chief Justice, and Gonzalez, Hightower, Hecht, Doggett, Cornyn, and Gammage, Justices join.

In this original proceeding, we consider whether a law firm must be disqualified from ongoing litigation because it rehired a legal assistant who had worked for opposing counsel for three weeks. We hold that disqualification is not required if the rehiring firm is able to establish that it has effectively screened the paralegal from any contact with the underlying suit. Because this standard had not been adopted in Texas prior to the trial court's disqualification order, we deny mandamus relief without prejudice to allow the trial court to reconsider its ruling in light of today's opinion.

The present dispute arises from a suit brought by Phoenix Founders, Inc. and others ("Phoenix") to collect a federal-court judgment against Ronald and Jane Beneke and others. The law firm of Thompson & Knight represented Phoenix in the original federal-court suit, which began in 1990 and ended in 1991, and has also represented them in the collection suit since its commencement in 1992. The Benekes have been represented in the latter suit by the firm of David & Goodman.

In July of 1993, Denise Hargrove, a legal assistant at Thompson & Knight, left her position at that firm to begin working for David & Goodman as a paralegal. While at David & Goodman, Hargrove billed six-tenths of an hour on the collection suit for locating a pleading. She also discussed the case generally with

(continued)

Mark Goodman, the Benekes' lead counsel. After three weeks at David & Goodman, Hargrove returned to Thompson & Knight to resume work as a paralegal. At the time of the rehiring, Thompson & Knight made no effort to question Hargrove in regard to potential conflicts of interest resulting from her employment at David & Goodman.

Three weeks after Hargrove had returned, counsel for the Benekes wrote to Thompson & Knight asserting that its renewed employment of Hargrove created a conflict of interest. The letter demanded that the firm withdraw from its representation of Phoenix. Hargrove resigned from Thompson & Knight the next week, after having been given the option of either resigning with severance pay or being terminated. The firm itself, however, refused to withdraw from the case. The Benekes then filed a motion to disqualify.

This Court has not previously addressed the standards governing a disqualification motion based on the hiring of a nonlawyer employee. With respect to lawyers, however, this Court has adopted a standard requiring disqualification whenever counsel undertakes representation of an interest that is adverse to that of a former client, as long as the matters embraced in the pending suit are "substantially related" to the factual matters involved in the previous suit. This strict rule is based on a conclusive presumption that confidences and secrets were imparted to the attorney during the prior representation [Coker, 765 S.W.2d at 400].

We agree that a paralegal who has actually worked on a case must be subject to the presumption set out in Coker; that is, a conclusive presumption that confidences and secrets were imparted during the course of the paralegal's work on the case. We disagree, however, with the argument that paralegals should be conclusively presumed to share confidential information with members of their firms. The Disciplinary Rules require a lawyer having direct supervisory authority over a nonlawyer to make reasonable efforts to ensure that the nonlawyer's conduct is compatible with the professional obligations of the lawyer.

The Texas Committee on Professional Ethics has considered the application of these rules in the context of a "right hand" legal secretary or legal assistant leaving one small firm and joining another that represents an adverse party. The Committee concluded that the Rules do not require disqualification of the new law firm, provided that the supervising lawyer at that firm complies with the Rules so as to ensure that the nonlawyer's conduct is compatible with the professional obligations of a lawyer. This view is consistent with the weight of authority in other jurisdictions.

The American Bar Association's Committee on Professional Ethics, after surveying case law and ethics opinions from a number of jurisdictions, concluded that the new firm need not be disqualified, as long as the firm and the paralegal strictly adhere to the screening process set forth in the opinion, and as long as the paralegal does not reveal any information relating to the former employer's clients to any person in the employing firm. A number of courts have since relied on the ABA's opinion to allow continued representation under similar conditions.

Underlying these decisions is a concern regarding the mobility of paralegals and other nonlawyers. A potential employer might well be reluctant to hire a particular nonlawyer if doing so would automatically disqualify the entire firm from ongoing litigation. This problem would be especially acute in the context of massive firms and extensive, complex litigation. Recognizing this danger, the ABA concluded "any restrictions on the nonlawyer's employment should be held to the minimum necessary to protect confidentiality of client information" [ABA Op. 1526].

We share the concerns expressed by the ABA, and agree that client confidences may be adequately safeguarded if a firm hiring a paralegal from another firm takes appropriate steps in compliance with the Disciplinary Rules. Specifically, the newly hired paralegal should be cautioned not to disclose any information relating to the representation of a client of the former employer. The paralegal should also be instructed not to work on any matter on which the paralegal worked during the prior employment, or regarding which the paralegal has information relating to the former employer's representation. Additionally, the firm should take other reasonable steps to ensure that the paralegal does not work in connection with matters on which the paralegal worked during the prior employment, absent client consent after consultation. Each of these precautions would tend to reduce the danger that the paralegal might share confidential information with members of the new firm. Thus, while a court must ordinarily presume that some sharing will take place, the challenged firm may rebut this presumption by showing that sufficient precautions have been taken to guard against any disclosure of confidences.

Absent consent of the former employer's client, disqualification will always be required under some circumstances, such as (1) when information relating to the representation of an adverse client has in fact been disclosed, or (2) when screening would be ineffective or the nonlawyer necessarily would be required to work on the other side of a matter that is the same as or substantially related to a matter on which the nonlawyer has previously worked. Ordinarily, however, disqualification is not required as long as "the practical effect of formal screening has been achieved."

In reconsidering the disqualification motion, the trial court should examine the circumstances of Hargrove's employment at Thompson & Knight to determine whether the practical effect of formal screening has been achieved. The factors bearing on such a determination will generally include the substantiality of the relationship between the former and current matters; the time elapsing between the matters; the size of the firm; the number of individuals presumed to have confidential information; the nature of their involvement in the former matter; and the timing and features of any measures taken to reduce the danger of disclosure. The fact that the present case involves representation of adverse parties in the same proceeding, rather than two separate proceedings, increases the danger that some improper disclosure may have occurred. Evidence regarding the other factors, however, may tend to rebut the presumption of shared confidences.

The ultimate question in weighing these factors is whether Thompson & Knight has taken measures sufficient to reduce the potential for misuse of confidences to an acceptable level. Because we have modified the controlling legal standard, the writ of mandamus is denied without prejudice to allow the trial court to reconsider the disqualification motion in light of today's opinion. The stay order previously issued by this Court remains in effect only so long as necessary to allow the trial court to act.

Ramirez v. Plough, Inc.

12 Cal. Rptr. 2d 423 (Cal. Ct. App. 1992)*
Court of Appeal of California

Read, and if assigned, brief this case. Prepare a written answer to each of the following questions. Note the words of the California Supreme Court on appeal.

1. How does this case illustrate clients' cultural differences?
2. Are the views and conduct of the parent in this case the same as you have and would have taken?
3. What ethical obligation does the paralegal have to be sure the client who does not speak the same language understands the advice given? Does it matter if it is medical directions, as in this case, or legal advice?
4. Does a law firm have a higher duty to a non-English-speaking client than a drug company, such as the defendant in this case, does in selling a product?
5. Does the law firm have a duty to explain cultural differences in the American legal system and its procedures to non-English-speaking, non-native born clients?

Thaxter, Judge

Jorge Ramirez, a minor, by his guardian ad litem Rosa Rivera, appeals from a summary judgment in favor of Plough, Inc. Appellant sued Plough alleging negligence, product liability, and fraud. The action sought damages for injuries sustained in March of 1986 when Jorge, who was then four months old, contracted Reye's Syndrome after ingesting St. Joseph Aspirin for Children (SJAC). Plough marketed and distributed SJAC.

Reye's Syndrome is a serious disease of unknown cause characterized by severe vomiting, lethargy, or irritability, which may progress to delirium or coma.

In December 1985, the Food and Drug Administration (FDA) requested that aspirin manufacturers voluntarily place a label on aspirin products warning consumers of the possible association between aspirin and Reye's Syndrome. Plough voluntarily complied and began including a warning and insert in SJAC packaging. On June 5, 1986, the Reye's Syndrome warning became mandatory.

In March 1986, SJAC labeling bore the following warning: "Warning: Reye's Syndrome is a rare but serious disease which can follow flu or chicken pox in children and teenagers. While the cause of Reye's Syndrome is unknown, some reports claim aspirin may increase the risk of developing this disease. Consult a doctor before use in children or teenagers with flu or chicken pox." In addition, the SJAC package insert included the following statement: "The symptoms of Reye's Syndrome can include persistent vomiting,

*If citing in a California court, add "15 Cal. App. 4th 1110" after the case name and before the citation from the California Reporter, set off by commas. Ramirez v. Plough, Inc., 15 Cal. App. 4th 1110, 12 Cal. Rptr. 2d 423 (1992)

(continued)

sleepiness and lethargy, violent headaches, unusual behavior, including disorientation, combativeness, and delirium. If any of these symptoms occur, especially following chicken pox or flu, call your doctor immediately, even if your child has not taken any medication. Reye's Syndrome is serious, so early detection and treatment are vital."

Rosa Rivera purchased SJAC on March 12, 1986, and administered it to appellant, who was suffering from what appeared to be a cold or upper respiratory infection. She gave appellant the aspirin without reading the directions or warnings appearing on the SJAC packaging. The packaging was in English and Ms. Rivera can speak and understand only Spanish. She did not seek to have the directions or warnings translated from English to Spanish, even though members of her household spoke English.

The trial court granted Plough's motion for summary judgment on the grounds that "there is no duty to warn in a foreign language and there is no causal relationship between plaintiff's injury and defendant's activities."

It is undisputed that SJAC was marketed and intended for the treatment of minor aches and pains associated with colds, flu, and minor viral illnesses. The SJAC box promised "fast, effective relief of fever and minor aches and pains of colds." . . . In March 1986, federal regulations requiring a Reye's Syndrome warning had been promulgated and were final, although not yet effective. . . . The scientific community had already confirmed and documented the relationship between Reye's Syndrome and the use of aspirin after a viral illness. There is no doubt Plough had a duty to warn of the Reye's Syndrome risk.

The question thus is whether the warning given only in English was adequate under the circumstances. Respondent argues that, as a matter of law, it has no duty to place foreign-language warnings on products manufactured to be sold in the United States and that holding manufacturers liable for failing to do so would violate public policy.

While the constitutional, statutory, regulatory, and judicial authorities relied on by respondent may reflect a public policy recognizing the status of English as an official language, nothing compels the conclusion that a manufacturer of a dangerous or defective product is immunized from liability when an English-only warning does not adequately inform non-English literate persons likely to use the product.

Plough's evidence showed that over 148 foreign languages are spoken in the United States and over 23 million Americans speak a language other than English in their homes. That evidence plainly does not prove that Plough used reasonable care in giving an English-only warning. Plough, then, resorts to arguing that the burden on manufacturers and society of requiring additional warnings is so "staggering" that the courts should preclude liability as a matter of law. We are not persuaded.

Certainly the burden and costs of giving foreign-language warnings is one factor for consideration in determining whether a manufacturer acted reasonably in using only English. The importance of that factor may vary from case to case depending upon other circumstances, such as the nature of the product, marketing efforts directed to segments of the population unlikely to be English-literate, and the actual and relative size of the consumer market which could reasonably be expected to speak or read only a certain foreign language. Plough presented no evidence from which we can gauge the extent of the burden under the facts of this case.

Ramirez submitted evidence that Plough knew Hispanics were an important part of the market for SJAC and that Hispanics often maintain their first language rather than learn English. SJAC was advertised in the Spanish media, both radio and television. That evidence raises material questions of fact concerning the foreseeability of purchase by a Hispanic not literate in English and the reasonableness of not giving a Spanish-language warning. If Plough has evidence conclusively showing that it would have been unreasonable to give its label warning in Spanish because of the burden, it did not present that evidence below.

. . . [I]f we accepted Plough's arguments in this case, in effect we would be holding that failure to warn in a foreign language is not negligence, regardless of the circumstances. Such a sweeping grant of immunity should come from the legislative branch of government, not the judicial. In deciding that Plough did not establish its right to judgment as a matter of law, we do not hold that manufacturers are required to warn in languages other than English simply because it may be foreseeable that non-English-literate persons are likely to use their products. Our decision merely recognizes that under some circumstances the standard of due care may require such warning.

Because the evidence shows triable issues of material fact and because Plough did not establish its immunity from liability as a matter of law, its motion for summary judgment should have been denied.

California Supreme Court on Appeal—Ramirez v. Plough, Inc.

6 Cal.4th 539 (1993), 863 P.2d 167, 25, Cal.Rptr.2d 97

Opinion

Kennard, J.

IV

. . . We recognize that if a Spanish language warning had accompanied defendant's product, and if plaintiff's mother had read and heeded the warning, the tragic blighting of a young and innocent life that occurred in this case might not have occurred. Yet, as one court has aptly commented, "The extent to which special consideration should be given to persons who have difficulty with the English language is a matter of public policy for consideration by the appropriate legislative bodies and not by the Courts." (*Carmona* v. *Sheffield* (N.D.Cal. 1971) 325 F. Supp. 1341, 1342, affd. *per curiam* (9th Cir. 1973) 475 F.2d 738.) (**4b**) We hold only that, given the inherent limitations of the judicial process, manufacturers of nonprescription drugs have no presently existing legal duty, within the tort law system, to include foreign-language warnings with their packaging materials. . . .

Mosk, J.

I concur. I write separately to emphasize the majority's caveat that "We do not . . . foreclose the possibility of tort liability premised upon the *content* of foreign-language advertising. For example, we do not decide whether a manufacturer would be liable to a consumer who detrimentally relied upon foreign-language advertising that was materially misleading as to product risks and who was unable to read English language package warnings that accurately described the risks. No such issue is presented here. . . ."

. . . Evidence of the content, timing, duration, and scope of distribution of foreign-language advertising bears substantially on the question whether a non-English-literate consumer has been materially misled about product risks, and a trial court must consider that evidence if properly presented.

The majority do not define "materially misleading as to product risks," leaving that issue for another day— a day likely to arrive soon, given the high probability that foreign-language media will continue to expand in California.

Technology and the Paralegal

Chapter 4 Digital Resources at *www.pearsonhighered.com/goldman*

- Video Case Studies:
  - Attorney Meet and Confer
  - Remote Videoconference Taking Witness Video Deposition
  - Privilege Issue: Misdirected E-mail
- Chapter Summary • Web Links • Court Opinions • Glossary • Comprehension Quizzes
- Technology Resources

> " Laws too gentle are seldom obeyed; too severe, seldom executed. "

Benjamin Franklin,
Poor Richard's Almanack (1756)

Paralegals at Work

Edith Hannah and Alice Hart, Attorneys at Law, have decided to combine their practices to create the Hannah Hart Law Office. Miss Hannah has had a thriving practice for 35 years, and Miss Hart has been in practice for only 5 years. Both attorneys rely heavily on their paralegal staff to run their businesses. Elma Quinn has worked for Miss Hannah for 25 years, and Cary Moritz has been with Miss Hart for only 3 years. The Hannah law firm was located across the street from the county courthouse and the Hart office a block from the federal courthouse and government complex in a neighboring city 20 miles away.

When Elma first visited the Hart office, she was surprised to see how small the Hart library was compared to Miss Hannah's library. She also noticed that the Hart office had many fewer filing cabinets and boxes and no large ledger books.

Elma sat down next to Cary's workstation and asked: "Where do you store all of your files? We have at least a dozen heavy fireproof file cabinets and a rented warehouse room full of boxes of closed files. I've heard of the paperless office, but you must have records somewhere and how do you do legal research without a decent law library?" Cary explained how they were able to access almost everything needed to research cases online and use the Internet and online research subscriptions to find all of the latest cases, statutes, and regulations. And, that all the client files and records were also kept on the computer system.

Elma expressed her real concern to Cary: "I come from the old school, we use paper files and ledger books. How much will I have to learn if they decide to use your computer system? It takes an hour to get between the offices; I don't want to have to be the one to travel between the offices to exchange documents.

The attorneys spend most of their time in court; I just don't see how they will be able to find the time to work together."

When they combine their offices, do you think they will have any problems combining files, clients, and office procedures? Consider the issues involved in this scenario as you read this chapter.

INTRODUCTION FOR THE PARALEGAL

The increased use of technology and computers in the law office, the court system, and the courtroom has changed the way many traditional procedures are performed. The computer and the Internet are increasingly used, not just for traditional document preparation, but also for maintaining client databases, keeping office and client accounting records, engaging in electronic communications, research and filing documents with the court, and trial presentation as shown in Exhibit 4.1.

Computer technology is used in the following ways in the law office:

Word processing—Prepare documents

Electronic spreadsheets—Perform financial calculations and financial presentations

Time and billing programs—Record accurate client time and billing

Accounting programs—Manage firm financial records, payroll, and client escrow accounts

Calendaring—Track deadlines, appointments, and hearing dates

Graphic presentation software—Prepare persuasive presentations

Trial presentation software—Organize trial presentations

Internet search engines—Search for accurate and current legal information and factual information to support a case

Databases—Maintain records and documents

Document scanning—Convert documents to electronic format

Document search features—Locate relevant material in documents and exhibits

Email and document delivery—Communicate electronically

Web Exploration

Compare the results of the latest survey information with the data listed to the right. The full survey may be viewed at the International Paralegal Management Association website at http://www.paralegalmanagement.org/ipma/.

Exhibit 4.1 IPMA survey results

Technology Most Often Used by Paralegals

In a survey by the International Paralegal Management Association (IPMA), the most frequently used programs as reported by respondents were:

General

Microsoft Word	99%
Document management programs	83%
General Internet research	74%
Spreadsheets	57%
Databases	57%
Billing applications	53%

Litigation

Litigation support	75%
Electronic court filing	42%
Online docket programs	33%
Trial preparation	25%

Source: 2005 Utilization Survey IPMA.

Paralegals *in* Practice

PARALEGAL PROFILE
Vanessa A. Lozzi

Vanessa A. Lozzi specializes in litigation, or law suit proceedings, in the areas of securities, class actions, appellate law, and labor and employment law. Her current position is Litigation Technology Specialist for Butzel Long, a law firm in Detroit, Michigan with about 250 attorneys.

As the Litigation Technology Specialist for my firm, I am responsible for understanding, supporting, and training firm employees to use litigation software; assisting with technology aspects of trials and arbitration; project management for document intensive cases; and staying up-to-date on the best and most cost-effective technology products and tools available.

Technology is a significant part of paralegal work. In litigation, probably 75% of the job involves some sort of technology. For example, at my firm:

- All time and billing is done electronically through a software application.
- The paralegals and secretaries work together to complete e-filings, the electronic filing of court documents.
- Paralegals are involved with electronic discovery, or e-discovery. This is the process of collecting, reviewing, managing, producing, and exchanging electronic data as evidence in a legal case.
- Paralegals are often asked to conduct legal research and locate other information. Since books are hardly used, they often use LexisNexis® and Westlaw®, online legal and factual research tools. Both offer a host of databases.
- Case-related information is managed electronically in many ways, including an internal electronic filing system for the firm's records; electronic calendars; and software used to manage document productions, transcripts, and trial presentations.

In the future, I believe that paralegals will be expected more and more to be technology experts. Since many paralegal educational programs have difficulty keeping up with technology's rapid changes, you can help educate yourself by participating in your local or state bar associations, subscribing to technology newsletters and magazines, and participating in Webinars (online seminars) and software demonstrations.

Online collaboration—Use the Internet to work collaboratively

Online electronic document repositories—Use for remote storage and access to documents

Need for Computer Skills

Computers are being used with greater frequency to share information in **digital format** between remote offices, courthouses, government agencies, and clients. Computer files are shared today more and more by the use of the Internet as well as in the form of CDs, DVDs, and as **attachments** to emails. In the past, paper had to be physically copied and sent, frequently by costly messenger service or express mail service. Today large files can be quickly, almost instantaneously, exchanged electronically, anywhere in the world, without any paper **(hardcopy).** Whereas formerly the physical safety of the delivery of paper documents was a concern, today the security and confidentiality of documents sent in electronic format are increasing concerns.

The legal team is increasingly using the Web and the Internet for more than just pure legal research. Access to most government information is obtained online through Internet websites. Finding businesses and individuals through private service providers, such as the yellow pages and white pages, is now handled most efficiently through Web search engines such as Google and Yahoo!. Though legal firms are increasingly developing and using websites for their own businesses as shown in Exhibit 4.2, only the best of these sites are created in a way that effectively helps to retain clients and attract new clients.

The implementation of new federal court rules on electronic discovery, the use of electronically stored documents in litigation, and emerging electronic discovery case law is creating increased demand for skills and knowledge in the use of technology in civil litigation. Increasingly the legal team must be able to interface with technology professionals in maximizing the efficiency of internal computer usage, and in obtaining and handling client and trial data electronically. Everyone on the legal team must now

Digital format A computerized format utilizing a series of 0's and 1's.

Attachment A popular method of transmitting text files and graphic images by attaching the file to an email.

Hardcopy Paper copies of documents.

Exhibit 4.2 **A typical law firm website, the new yellow pages**

Source: Reprinted with permission from Mellon, Webster, & Shelly Law Offices.

have a working familiarity with computers and the types of computer programs used in the law office. Not too many years ago, the average law office had a typewriter, an adding machine, and a duplicating machine of some type. Paper was king, with every document typed, edited, retyped—and frequently retyped again. In each instance, a paper copy was produced and delivered to the supervising attorney for review and additional changes. It then was returned for retyping and eventually sent to the client, to the opposing counsel, or filed with the court. File cabinets abounded in the law office, and the storage of paper files created back rooms, warehouses, and other storage locations filled with box after box of paper. The trend is toward eliminating paper in the law office through the use of computer technology and software.

Members of the legal team frequently find themselves working from locations outside the traditional office. In some cases, the legal team members are located in different offices of the firm or are from different firms located in different parts of the country or world. Each member of the team may need access to the case data or electronic files. One solution is to have all of the files stored electronically in an **electronic repository** on a secure, protected file server to which everyone authorized has access over the Internet.

Members of the team may use the Internet to work collaboratively using **online collaboration** software that allows each person to see the documents and, in some cases, each other, and make on-screen notes and comments. A number of companies provide services and software for converting case documents to electronic format and storing of the documents on a secure server. Collaboration software is provided for the individual members of the legal or litigation team. Exhibit 4.3 shows a typical, secure remote litigation network.

Electronic repository An off-site computer used to store records that may be accessed over secure Internet connections.

Online collaboration Using the internet to conduct meetings and share documents.

Exhibit 4.3 Secure remote access for the legal profession

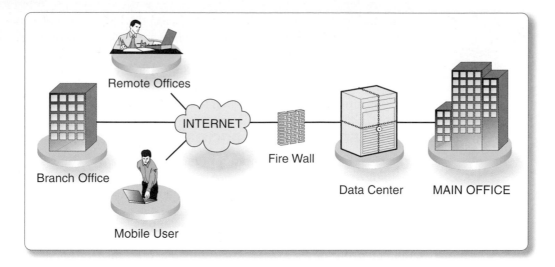

Technology Usage in the Law

The role of technology in the law has evolved in a very few years from a minor function, such as the stand-alone word processor, to a ubiquitous element in the management of law offices of all sizes. Computers are now being used for everything from word processing to computerized timekeeping, payroll productions, and tax return preparation. In some offices computerized telephone systems even use a computerized attendant to answer the phone without human intervention. The use of technology in litigation was once limited to large law firms working on large cases for wealthy clients who could pay the cost of the technology. Today even the smallest law firm and litigator must use technology. Some courts are demanding computerized filing. Records previously available in paper form, such as medical records in litigation cases, are now provided electronically. The result is that offices of all sizes need to have computer or technology support, in some cases with dedicated technologists or support of the computerized infrastructure and others dedicated to providing litigation support.

Outsourcing

Outsourcing has become a buzzword for shipping work out of the office or overseas to save money. Some of the services that can be performed in-house may, in fact, be better outsourced. For years, many law firms have outsourced the payroll function instead of preparing payroll checks and tax returns in-house. The confidentiality of information about salaries may dictate that an outside firm handle the payroll process so that only a few people in the office have access to the critical payroll information. In a similar vein, the accounting functions may be outsourced to an outside bookkeeping or accounting firm. Using an outside computer consultant to help with support for the hardware and software of the office is a form of outsourcing and may involve a help desk located in a foreign location to answer questions.

Outsourcing Use of persons or services outside of the immediate office staff.

How Much Do I Really Need To Know

No one can be an expert in everything. What is important is to know enough to know what you do not know and be able to find someone who does. The need is to understand the basic concepts and be able to communicate with those who are the experts. Having a basic understanding of the different programs used in the legal environment is a starting point. Know the functions of the programs used in daily support of the legal team, such as word processing, spreadsheet, database, and the like. Understand the differences in the software and computer tools used by the litigation specialist from those used by the in-house legal support team. Most important is the ability to communicate with the legal side and the technology side of a firm. Learn the language of the other, what some refer to as "geek talk." Keep current by reading the professional journals and legal papers for new tools and services being offered to make the job of legal and litigation teams more efficient. Attend the local, regional, and national technology shows for the legal industry to see the products and services and ask questions to learn enough to make the suggestions for updating and changing the tools of your profession.

Understanding the Language of Technology

An understanding of the terminology of technology is a prerequisite to understanding the technology found in the law office, the courthouse, and the clients' business. Law has developed its own lexicon of terms that enables those in the legal community to communicate effectively and with precision. The technology world also has developed its own lexicon. The legal team and the technology support team must learn one another's language to communicate their needs and solutions. Each group thinks it is communicating, but the same word sometimes has different meanings. For example, the word *protocol*. To the legal team, *protocol* is defined as "A summary of a document or treaty; or, a treaty amending another treaty, or the rules of diplomatic etiquette" (*Black's Law Dictionary*—West Group). To the technology specialist, *protocol* is defined as "A set of formal rules describing how to transmit data, especially across a network. Low level protocols define the electrical and physical standards to be observed, bit- and byte-ordering and the transmission and error detection and correction of the bit stream. High level protocols deal with the data formatting, including the syntax of messages, the terminal to computer dialogue, character sets, sequencing of messages etc." (Free On-Line Dictionary of Computing [http://foldoc.org/]).

Another example is the word *cell*. To the criminal lawyer, a cell is a place where clients are held in jail. To the computer support staff, it is a space on a spreadsheet where a piece of data is displayed. Lawyers, paralegals, and other members of the legal team, and the members of the technology support team must learn one another's language in order to effectively meet the needs of clients and work together productively.

Computer Hardware

Computer hardware is the term used to describe the tangible or physical parts of a computer system; a **computer system** includes at least one input device, a computer processor, and at least one output device. A system may be as small and portable as a digital watch or as large as a **mainframe** computer requiring a large room to house it.

Older models of computers, many of which are still found in many law offices, are large, ugly metal boxes connected to large, bulky, and heavy desktop monitors, sometimes taking up half of a desktop. Newer models are smaller and less obtrusive. In some offices the computer system consists of a portable laptop computer, weighing as little as three to four pounds, the size of a large book, used at the user's desk with a docking station to connect it to a flat-screen monitor, external keyboard and mouse, Internet connection, and network.

With the reduction in size have come increased speed and functionality. On older models, opening more than one document uses most of the computer system resources, slowing them down or even "freezing" or stopping the processing of data. The newer models typically run well while allowing the display of multiple documents from multiple applications all running at the same time—Word files, Excel spreadsheets, calendaring programs, and timekeeping applications. Exhibit 4.4 shows a monitor display of four programs running at the same time.

Computer hardware Hardware is the term that encompasses all of the tangible or physical items including computers, monitors, printers, fax machines, duplicators, and similar items that usually have either an electrical connection or use batteries as a power source.

Computer system A combination of an input device, a processor, and an output device.

Mainframe A large computer system used primarily for bulk processing of data and financial information.

Exhibit 4.4 · 4-page display in Microsoft Office suite

Source: Microsoft product box shot reprinted with permission from Microsoft Corporation.

The ability to perform multiple functions simultaneously is in part the result of the increase in processing speed permitted by newer **central processing units (CPUs)**, also called processors, and the availability of inexpensive dynamic or volatile computer memory, **random access memory (RAM)**. A CPU is the computer "chip" that interprets computer instructions and processes data, and RAM is the temporary computer memory that stores work in progress.

Hardware of all sizes requires software instructions to run and perform desired functions. **Operating system** software provides the basic instructions for starting up the computer and processing the basic input and output activity. The processing of data requires additional applications software such as that used for word processing and financial data processing.

All computer components must have a power source (electrical outlet or battery) to operate, including the basic CPU, the dynamic memory modules used for temporary storage of data (RAM), and output devices like the computer monitor and printer. Just as an automobile depends on fuel to continue to operate, so is the computer dependent on a power source to operate. Computers cannot remember data or information that appears on the computer screen (work in process) after the power is turned off—unless it has been saved to a permanent memory device. The transfer of the information in the

Central processing unit (CPU) The computer chip and memory module that perform the basic computer functions.

Random access memory (RAM) Temporary computer memory that stores work in processs.

Operating system The operating system is a basic set of instructions to the computer on how to handle basic functions—how to process input from "input devices" such as the keyboard and mouse, the order in which to process information, and what to show on the computer monitor.

form of electrical signals also requires power to write the information on devices such as magnetic tape, floppy disks, or hard disk drives, or to portable memory devices like USB memory devices, or removable memory cards such as the popular secure digital (SD) cards, CDs, or DVDs. These permanent memory devices do not require power to retain data—only to write or read the data to or from a computer.

Uninterruptible power supply (UPS) battery backup systems for the computer are used frequently to guard against loss of the "work-in-process" files when there is a short-term power loss or long-term outage. A UPS is a battery system that can supply power to a computer or computer peripheral for a short period of time. The length of time the computer will continue to work after loss of its permanent power supply depends on the size of the battery in the UPS, and may be as short as a few minutes or as long as an hour or more. The UPS is designed to allow time to save the current work-in-process files and shut down the computer normally in the event of a major power outage.

Uninterruptable power supply (UPS) A battery system that can supply power to a computer or computer peripheral for a short period of time.

Operating Systems

The two most popular computer systems are the PC, or personal computer, and the Apple. The original designs of these two systems were built around different central processor system chips manufactured by different companies—Intel in the case of the PC, and Motorola in the case of Apple. Each computer system requires its own unique operating system.

Although both computer systems have advocates, the PC has a dominant position in the legal and business communities where the main use is text and mathematical computations in the form of word processing and spreadsheets. The Apple system achieved the dominant position in the graphic and artistic communities, and to some extent among computer game players. New models of both systems have **software** that permits the other computer system software to run on the competitive machine.

Software Refers to programs containing sets of instructions that tell the computer and the other computer-based electronic devices what to do and how to do it.

In 2006, Apple started to utilize the same CPU manufacturer as the PC manufacturers use, allowing the new Apple computers to use software for both systems on its computers without any additional software to interpret the software instruction of the other system.

Microsoft Windows™ is the most commonly used computer operating system for the personal computer. A number of different versions of the Windows operating system are found in the workplace with the latest versions, such as Windows XP, Vista, and Windows 7, designed to take advantage of increased computer operating speeds and to better display screen graphics. The original PC operating systems did not provide for the **graphic user interface (GUI)**, which everyone has now come to expect. Exhibit 4.5 shows a command line interface and a graphic user interface.

Graphic user interface (GUI) A set of screen presentations and metaphors that utilize graphic elements such as icons in an attempt to make an operating system easier to operate.

Among the newer computer systems gaining followers is the Linux opperative system. It is offered as an alternative to Microsoft operating systems and provided without a license or royalty fee with the agreement that any improvements will be made available without a fee to anyone using the system.

Applications Software

Applications software programs are those that perform specific tasks, such as prepare documents, sort information, perform computations, and create and present graphic displays. These are the software programs used in the management of the law office and the management of client cases.

Applications software Applications programs are software that perform generic tasks such as word processing.

Word Processing

Written communication and document preparation are at the heart of every law office. It may be preparation of letters to clients, other counsel or the court, or contracts and agreements, or pleadings. To achieve written clarity and accuracy frequently

Exhibit 4.5 A Windows screen showing the command line within a GUI interface

Source: *Microsoft product box shot reprinted with permission from Microsoft Corporation.*

means writing, rewriting, and correcting the same document, sometimes multiple times and by a number of different members of the legal team. The ability to easily make even minor changes in language has a direct impact on the willingness of those reviewing the document to suggest changes and make them in the final document. Computerized word processing makes this possible. Word processing files are sent electronically to the appropriate members of the legal team for review. Changes or revisions are frequently made to the electronic file copy by the reviewer. Where multiple parties may be working on a document, changes made to the original document by each person on the legal team may be monitored by using built-in features such as MS Word's **"Track Changes"** tool. This feature shows the original text, the deleted text, and the new text by a series of lines that show as a strike through the deleted text and by margin notes on the document. When the final document is completed it may be sent by email, fax (frequently directly from the computer without any intermediate paper), and in some jurisdictions filed electronically with the court. Exhibit 4.6 shows the original word file, the changes inserted and old text with a strike through it, and the final version with the changes still showing in the margin of the document.

Today the most commonly used software program in the law office is the word processor. Although many different word processing programs are available, the legal community most commonly uses either WordPerfect™ or Microsoft Word™. In addition to the usual typing functions, these programs have built-in software tools that check spelling and grammar and allow customized formatting using a variety of

Track Changes Track Changes, as found in MS Word, shows the original text, the deleted text, and the new text as well as a strike through for deleted text, underlining or highlighting of new text, as well as margin notes on the document.

Exhibit 4.6 Microsoft Word track changes

Source: Microsoft product box shot reprinted with permission from Microsoft Corporation.

ETHICAL PERSPECTIVE

Document Comparison Software

When using Track Changes or similar comparison programs, be sure to remove the history of the changes and other information from the document before sending it to the opposing counsel, the client, or the court. The history of changes and other document information is called *metadata*.

The history of the changes may offer the reader insight into the strategy of the case—for example, showing the final price the client is willing to pay, which appeared in the original draft and not the first offer that appeared in the final version sent to the opposing party. Word Help offers instructions on how to remove this information. WordPerfect X4 allows documents to be saved without the metadata, using a file save option—**Save without Metadata**—making it easy to quickly remove private or sensitive data that can be hidden in, but easily extracted from, office productivity documents.

type sizes and font styles in the same document—functions that have not been possible with a typewriter. Some offices even use different programs, each with its own file format.

Most word processing programs allow the opening and saving of files in the file formats of other word processing programs. When a file is saved, a **file extension** (a period followed by characters) is added to the end of the filename that identifies the program or format in which the file has been saved.

For example:

the file name NAME	the extension EXT
Microsoft Word 2003	filename.doc
Microsoft Word 2007	filename.docx
WordPerfect	filename.wpd
Microsoft Works	filename.wps
Web documents	filename.htm
Generic (rich text file) word processing format	filename.rtf
Generic (text file) word processing format	filename.txt

File extension When a file is saved, a file extension (a period followed by three characters) is added to the end of the filename to identify the program or format in which the file has been saved.

The newer versions of WordPerfect even permit simulation of the Microsoft Word workspace. Word processor files are saved with the document properties such as type font and type size, and document formatting details. The saved files also include instructions to the computer on how to display the document, security features, and hidden information such as the "Track Changes information."

Spreadsheet Programs

Many areas of legal practice involve the calculation and presentation of financial information. For example, in family law practice, the preparation of family and personal balance sheets and income and expense reports are routinely prepared for support and equitable distribution hearings; estate lawyers must submit an "accounting" to the court for approval, showing details of how the fiduciary handled the financial affairs of the estate or trust; and litigation firms must prepare documentation showing the receipts and disbursements of cases, sometime for court approval.

Spreadsheet programs Programs that permit the calculation and presentation of financial information in a grid format of rows and columns.

As shown in Exhibit 4.7, in an estate, the calculation involved may be as simple as multiplying the number of shares owned by a decedent by the value on the date of death (D of D), then calculating the profit or loss when the stock was sold. Without a computerized spreadsheet, all of the calculations would have to be done manually,

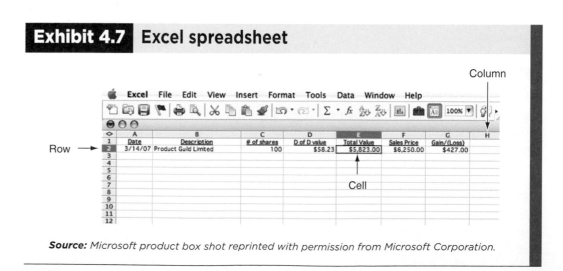

Exhibit 4.7 Excel spreadsheet

Source: Microsoft product box shot reprinted with permission from Microsoft Corporation.

using a multicolumn form known as a spreadsheet or accountant's working papers. The information then has to be typed in a report format for submission to the court, the beneficiaries, or the taxing authorities.

Using a computerized spreadsheet such as Microsoft Excel or Corel Quattro Pro, the numbers are entered in cells, as identified in Exhibit 4.7, and a formula assigned to the cell in which the result is to be displayed, such as "multiply column c by column d," and the result displayed in column e. The computerized spreadsheet, when laid out in the format acceptable to the court, can be printed without reentering the data, or copied into word documents using a simple "Cut and Paste" operation.

The use of computer spreadsheets reduces the errors associated with manual mathematical calculations and errors in retyping the information. Caution must be taken to make sure that the formula is accurate and performs the desired calculation. Even expert spreadsheet users use a set of sample numbers to test the formulas, knowing what the result should be, based on prior use or calculations.

Many offices save spreadsheet templates in the same way that sample forms are saved in word processing. For example, a real estate settlement spreadsheet with formulas and headings may be saved without numbers. Because the formulas do not change and the form has proven accurate, it may be used as a template for other clients' real estate settlements.

Database Programs

Database program A database program is an electronic repository of information of all types that can be sorted and presented in a meaningful manner.

A **database program** is a repository of information of all types that can be sorted and presented in a desired meaningful manner. Some offices use a manual card system to keep track of the names of clients and opposing parties, these cards are searched to determine possible conflicts of interest in representing new clients. For the small office this system works. But for the larger office with multiple attorneys and possibly multiple offices, timely entry and searching of large amounts of information is not realistic. Computerized database software, such as Microsoft Access and Corel DB, will facilitate timely, accurate access to information by every authorized member of the legal team. For example, information may be stored on the law firm's server in an information database that includes the names, addresses, contact information, personal data such as birthdates of every client, every opposing party, every fact witness and expert witness, and every opposing counsel with whom any member of the firm has ever had contact in litigation, contract negotiations, or counseling session, or met in any business or legal setting. With a few keystrokes, a list can be prepared for manually checking for conflicts of interest, or a computer search can be performed with a printout of any matter or litigation where a name appears.

In addition to the obvious use in avoiding accepting a client with a potential conflict of interest, the information frequently is used in maintaining client relations. Many firms use the information to send birthday and anniversary greetings and updates on specific changes in the law for which the client has consulted the firm previously.

Presentation Graphics Programs

It has been said that a picture is worth a thousand words. Presentation graphics software programs, such as WordPerfect Presentation X4 (see Exhibit 4.8) and Microsoft PowerPoint, are being used to create high-quality slide shows and drawings. These graphic presentations can include text, data charts, and graphic objects.

One of the advantages of these programs is their flexibility. They can be used to prepare and present the graphic presentation electronically, using a computer, with or without a projector, and to print out paper copies for distribution. Presentation programs typically provide stock templates of graphics, artwork, and layout as a sample that the user can easily modify. More advanced users can add sound clips to the presentation, include still photos, and incorporate custom graphics from other programs, as well as video clips.

Exhibit 4.8	WordPerfect presentation X4

Source: WordPerfect screen shot reprinted with permission of Corel. All rights reserved.

Office Software Suites

Office software suites are sets of commonly used office software programs that manage data and database programs; manipulate financial or numeric information, spreadsheet programs; or display images and presentation graphics programs. Some of the tools in the two most common program suites, Microsoft Office and Corel WordPerfect, are:

	Microsoft Office	Corel WordPerfect Office X4
Word processor	Word	WordPerfect
Spreadsheet	Excel	Quattro Pro X4
Database	Access	Paradox
Presentation graphics	PowerPoint	Presentation X4
Graphics	Visio	Presentation Graphics X4

The software suites usually are delivered on one CD, enabling all the programs to be loaded at one time, which simplifies and saves installation time. With common features and appearance, it is easier to switch between programs and copy information between the programs, like copying part of a spreadsheet into a word processing document.

Specialty Application Programs

Every year, computers become more powerful, operating faster with more operating and storage memory. Software programs are getting more powerful and capable of performing more complex functions on more data. Whereas older models of computers can perform only basic word processing and data management, newer, more powerful computers can perform complex functions seamlessly, thereby permitting management of law office functions and management of cases and litigation.

Specialty application programs combine many of the basic functions found in software suites, word processing, database management, spreadsheets, and graphic presentations to perform law office case and litigation management. They simplify the operation with the use of customized input screens and preset report generators.

Office software suites This software consists of commonly used office software programs that manage data and database programs; manipulate financial or numeric information, spreadsheet programs; or display images and presentation graphics programs.

Specialty applicaton programs Specialty programs combine many of the basic functions found in software suites, word processing, database management, spreadsheets, and graphic presentations to perform law office, case, and litigation management.

Web Exploration

For a self-running video demo of Tabs 3, go to http://www.tabs3.com/products/video.html.

Web Exploration

Information on the features of Abacuslaw may be found at http://www.abacuslaw.com.

Web Exploration

Details and additional sample screen graphics about PCLaw are available at http://www.pclaw.com/.

Case and litigation management software Case and litigation management programs are used to manage documents and the facts and issues of cases.

Legal specialty software programs fall generally into the following categories:

Office management

Case management

Litigation support

Transcript management

Trial presentation

Of the office management specialty application programs, the most basic are the time and billing programs. These provide a standard input screen to record the time spent on a client's case, store the information and, with a request for an invoice for a given client, automatically sort the data, apply the billing rates, and print out an invoice.

Among the popular programs in this group are:

Tabs 3 from Software Technology, Inc.

Abacuslaw from Abacus Data Systems Inc.

ProLaw from Thomson Elite

PCLaw from LexisNexis

Timeslips from Sage

Exhibit 4.9 is an example of an application input screen.

Early versions of time reporting software are limited to timekeeping. With faster computers and greater memory capacity, most of these programs have other features integrated into them, such as accounting functions to track costs and expenses, and practice management functions such as calendar and contact management.

Exhibit 4.10 shows the multiple functions integrated in Abacuslaw Accounting.

Case and Litigation Management Software

Paper has long been the bane of the litigation attorney. Even simple cases can involve hundreds of pages of documents. Complex litigation may involve millions of documents and hundreds of witnesses and, in the case of class-action litigation, potentially millions of clients. Keeping track of all of the documentation and parties is an overwhelming task even with a large staff of assistants and endless rows of organized file cabinets and file boxes.

Before the availability of fast computers with inexpensive memory-running case and litigation management software, most case management work was done manually, usually by a team of paralegals and junior associate attorneys. In two of the most notable cases—the IBM antitrust suit and the Ford Pinto negligence suit—teams of law students were hired, some for multiyear positions, to read through and identify the documents, manually index them, and look for a document that would make the case, sometimes referred to as the "smoking gun" document. In the Ford Pinto case, in a serendipitous discovery just such a smoking gun document was found, which detailed the engineering cost savings and the inherent risk by eliminating a specific part that led to the fire that engulfed the Pinto when it was struck by another car from the rear.

The use of computers for email and document storage by business and government has caused a massive increase in the number of potential documents that may have to be reviewed, tracked, and made available to opposing counsel in a case. Managing cases and litigation with the massive amount of data has become increasingly difficult. As the number of documents has increased and cases have become more complex, the number of members of the legal team working on a given case also has increased. These factors have led to greater use of the computer to manage the case files and the litigation process.

In pre-computer days, attorneys frequently concentrated on one case, personally working on all of the documentation, pleadings, and discovery, and learning every detail of the case in anticipation of trying the case with little backup support except in the largest cases in the larger firms. The legal-team approach to case management and

Exhibit 4.9 Tabs3 time and billing screens

litigation has allowed, in some ways, for specialization within the legal team. Some members of the litigation team may specialize in discovery of documents. Others may be concerned with locating, interviewing, and preparing witnesses. Still others concentrate on investigative matters and legal research.

Effective case management, therefore, requires some central repository of the information gathered by each of the team members, as well as the ability of each to access the case information input by others. Computer systems today even permit members of the legal team to access the same information from remote locations across town, across the country, and sometimes around the world.

A typical case file contains documentation of the:

Interview of the client

Interviews of fact and expert witnesses

Investigation reports

Expert reports

Exhibit 4.10 Abacus Accounting input screens

Source: *Reprinted with permission from Abacus Data Systems.*

Research memoranda

Pleadings

Trial preparation material

The trial team frequently has to quickly find a document or information on a specific issue from among potentially thousands of pages of documents. With a computer and the proper specialty software program, this is possible. Some of the litigation and case management specialty software programs found in the law office are discussed below.

CaseMap

CaseMap™ from LexisNexis® CaseSoft is a case management and analysis software tool that acts as a central repository for critical case knowledge. As facts are gathered, parties identified, and documents and research assembled, they may be entered into the program, allowing for easy organization and exploration of the facts, the cast of characters, and the issues by any member of the legal team.

Typical of integrated software applications, CaseMap allows seamless transfer of data to other programs such as TimeMap™, a timeline graphic program, and word processor programs. It also allows for creating specialty reports and documents including trial notebook information. Exhibit 4.11 shows the flow of information in a typical case, using CaseMap as a case management tool.

Web Exploration

Demonstration versions of CaseSoft products and Webinar tutorials on their use can be found at http://www.casesoft.com/student.asp.

CaseMap–The Focal Point for Case Analysis

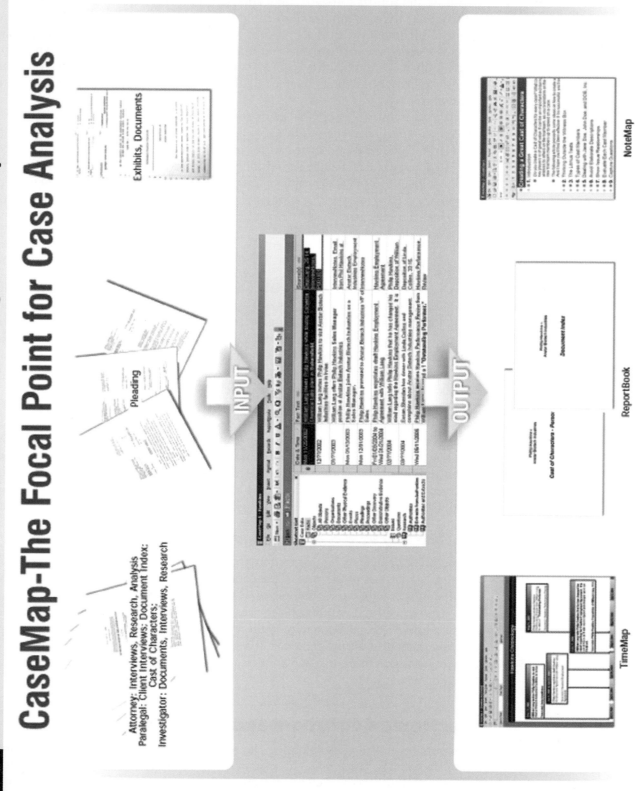

Summation

Web Exploration

View an online demo of Summation®LG at http://info.summation.com/demo/modules.htm.

The Summation family of products, from CT Summation, Inc. (a Wolters Kluwer business) and similar software applications programs are classified as litigation support systems. As the number of documents increases in a case, the ability to locate relevant documents in a timely fashion becomes more and more critical. Managing the documents is critical to successful litigation outcomes. In cases involving potentially millions of documents, it is essential to be able to find the relevant information quickly, sometimes in the middle of the direct or cross-examination of a witness.

Summation-type programs allow for easy search and retrieval of all of the evidence, whether documents, testimony, photographs, or electronic files, with a single command. Documents associated with a case are stored on the computer in electronic folders. These folders may be set up to include transcripts, pleadings, text files (from OCR or otherwise), casts of characters, and core databases. Some versions of these programs are designed to work on stand-alone systems such as a laptop carried into court. Others permit concurrent use by many users over a network, and some permit remote access over the Internet.

Concordance

Web Exploration

Learn more about Concordance at http://www.dataflight.com.

LexisNexis Concordance is a litigation support system program that provides document management. Early versions of Concordance were limited to storing and handling 4 gigabytes of data, or approximately 280,000 documents. The newer version allows the management of 128 times that amount, or more than 35 million documents. Like other document support tools, Concordance has a powerful search engine that allows searches by word, phrase, date, email address, or document type, as well as Boolean, using the fuzzy and wildcard searches.

A Boolean search uses connectors between words such as AND, OR, or NOT to narrow the search. A fuzzy or fuzzy string search is the name for a search that looks for strings or letters or characters that approximately match some given pattern. A wildcard search allows the use of a "wild" character such as the symbol * to replace a letter in the search word that allows you to search for plurals or variations of words using a wildcard character. It also is a good way to search if you do not know the spelling of a word. For example: Book* finds Booking and Books.

Sanction II by Verdict Systems and TrialDirector by inData

Web Exploration

An interactive demo of TrialDirector showing how trial presentation software can be used in litigation at http://www.indatacorp.com/flash/tdstutorial.swf.

These multifaceted trial presentation programs offer a comprehensive approach to presenting all types of exhibits in the courtroom, including documents, photographs, graphic images, video presentations, and recorded depositions.

Unlike PowerPoint, which requires the creation of individual slides, these programs allow existing documents and files to be presented without any more effort than copying them into the program data file and making a selection for presentation. Trial presentation programs, like Sanction, are databases of the documents in either a case file or on a computer.

Electronic Courtroom and Paperless Office

Computer technology is changing the way that law offices and court systems perform traditional functions. The ease of creating documents, including traditional letters and contracts and electronic communications in the form of emails, has resulted in a document explosion. At the same time, cases are coming to trial faster because of the demand for "quicker justice," which allows less time to prepare and present a case in court. The result has been growth in the use of electronic documentation and computerized case management and the use of computers in litigation.

The Electronic Courtroom

Increasingly, judges are embracing the use of electronics and computer-based systems in the courts. The initial reluctance to allow the "newfangled" technology is giving way to acceptance of tools that enhance the speedy administration of justice. One of the earliest uses of technology in the courtroom was the playing of videotaped depositions of expert witnesses on TV monitors in court.

To get experts to testify is difficult when the schedule for their testimony is uncertain because of uncertain trial schedules. Many experts, such as noted surgeons and medical forensics experts, have active lucrative practices and demand compensation that can range in the thousands of dollars per hour for time lost waiting to testify. The average litigant can rarely afford this litigation cost. A videotape, or electronic recording, of a deposition can be used in trial as a cost-effective method of presenting expert witnesses or for witnesses who for reasons of health or distance, could not otherwise be available to testify personally at a trial.

As judicial budgets allow, courtrooms are being outfitted with computers and audiovisual presentation systems. Exhibit 4.12 shows the U.S. Tax Court's electronic courtroom in Virginia. Computerized courtrooms can be seen frequently on Court TV televised trials, in which computer terminals are present at each lawyer's table, the judge's bench, for each of the court support personnel, and monitors for the jury.

Litigation support software is used in trial to display documentary evidence, graphic presentations, and simulations of accident cases. Relevant portions of documents can be displayed for everyone to see at the same time without passing paper copies to everyone, as the witness testifies and identifies the document. Lawyers can rapidly search depositions and documents, sometimes in the tens of thousands of pages, on their laptop computer to find pertinent material for examination or cross-examination of the witness.

The electronic courtroom also is used in many jurisdictions in criminal cases for preliminary matters in which the judge is located at a central location, and the defendants at various lock-up facilities with video cameras and monitors recording and displaying the parties to each other.

Exhibit 4.12 | **U.S. Tax Court's electronic courtroom**

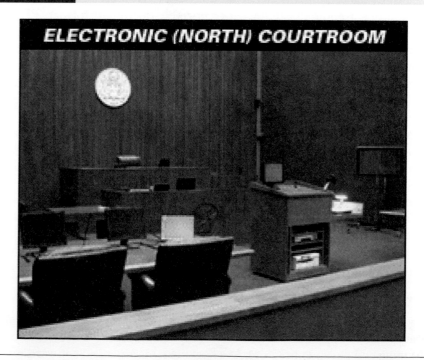

The Paperless Office

To some people, the ideal office is one that has no paper documents, or hardcopy, as they are sometimes referred to. The office where documents are created and stored electronically is sometimes referred to as the "**paperless office**," or "electronic office." Difficult as it may seem for some who have grown up in the paper world, the paperless office is rapidly approaching reality. In the traditional office, documents are created electronically with word processing software, or received by fax or email and then printed. In the paperless office, documents are created using computer-based word processor programs such as Microsoft Word or Corel WordPerfect. These electronic files then are sent electronically to the attorney for review.

The reviewer frequently makes changes or revisions to the electronic file copy and when multiple parties are working on a document; changes made to the original document by each person on the legal team may be monitored by using built-in features such as Track Changes in MS Word. This feature shows the original text, the deleted text, and the new text by a strike through the deleted text, underlining of new text, and by margin notes on the document. When the final document is completed, it may be sent by email, fax (frequently directly from the computer without any intermediate paper) and, in some jurisdictions, filed electronically with the court.

Electronic portability requires inexpensive portable computer memory, a computer to store and transport the documents, and small, lightweight computers to display them. Conversion of existing paper documents requires the availability of scanners and software that converts the documents to an acceptable format that cannot be easily changed.

The paperless law office indeed is becoming the norm with the advent of modern scanning technology, secured methods for transmission of documents, accepted protocols for use of electronic replacements for paper documents, and rules of court permitting electronic submission of documents.

Portable Document Format (PDF)

The ability to save documents in a format that cannot be easily changed through use of the computer is one of the basic requirements of a system that allows for electronic documentation. Anyone who has received a word processing document file knows that they may change it, save it, and present it as an original. Now, documents may be saved in a graphic image format or portable document format (PDF), developed by Adobe Systems. The recipient cannot easily or readily change these graphic images.

Although creating documents in PDF format requires specialty software such as Adobe Acrobat, everyone can download a free Adobe Reader to view these documents. With the acceptance of this format has come a willingness to scan and store documents electronically in this format, eliminating or returning to the client the original paper copies. Companies such as Adobe Systems frequently provide free, limited versions of their programs, downloadable from their website, that allow the opening and reading of files created using their proprietary software formats, such as Adobe's PDF file format.

Many websites that provide programs using these proprietary formats, such as the Internal Revenue Service forms website, contain links to these programs. They are limited in that they allow the user to open and read the files but do not allow changes or the creation of new document files, which requires the full version of the program.

Scanning

Scanning and storing of paper documents has become easier with the development of software such as PaperPort by Nuance. This software provides easy-to-use, high-speed scanning and document capture. As a document management software application, it allows for organizing, finding, and sharing paper and digital documents, which permits the elimination of paper documents.

The original scanning hardware was costly and frequently unreliable. Modern scanners provide double-sided (front and back) scanning of documents with a high degree of accuracy at a relatively low cost. Scanning today has become a common feature in office printers and copy machines. Double-sided scanning is found today in multifunction devices featuring printing, scanning, copying, and faxing, at prices under $100. These devices, when coupled with application software such as PaperPort, allow virtually anyone to create electronic documents.

OCR

Obviously, at times, documents have to be converted from a graphic image to a format that allows for editing or other use in an office suite of applications. These software applications have come to be referred to as OCR, or optical character recognition. Products such as OmniPage, by Nuance, provide document-conversion solutions by permitting any scanned page, PDF file, or other image or document file to be converted quickly and accurately into one of a number of different editable formats including Microsoft Word or Corel WordPerfect.

Networks

The first computers in law offices, as we said, generally consisted of a computer, a monitor, and a printer. In the contemporary law office this is called a **workstation**. A **computer network** is a group of workstations connected together. This may be as little as two workstations, or in large law firms, hundreds of workstations and other peripheral devices such as shared printers and fax machines all connected through a network file server. Exhibit 4.13 is a typical computer network system in a law office.

A **network file server** is generally a separate computer that acts as the traffic cop of the system, controlling the flow of information between workstations and the file server and other peripheral devices and requests to use the resources of the system or access data stored on the system.

Like the computer that requires an operating system to run, the server requires network operating software that tells it how to communicate with the connected workstations and peripheral devices. These computers and devices are referred to as "connections."

Workstation A computer connected to a network that is used for access consisting of a monitor, input device, and computer.

Computer network A set of workstations connected together.

Network file server A separate computer in a network that acts as the traffic cop of the system controlling the flow of data.

Exhibit 4.13 **Typical network system**

Network System

copier   scanner   printer

File server

Workstation   Workstation   Workstation

Network Rights and Privileges

Network rights and privileges Rights or privileges determine who has access to the server, the data stored on the server, and the flow of information between connections.

Network software programs have security protocols that limit access to the file server, peripherals such as printers, or other workstations. These rights to access the server and the other devices are sometimes called "**network rights and privileges.**" The rights or privileges determine who has access to the server, the data stored on the server, and the flow of information between connections.

Network Administrator

Network administrator The network administrator usually is the person with the highest-level access to the network file server.

Generally the person with the highest level access is called the **network administrator.** Law offices that use network servers generally use these servers as the central repository for all electronic files. Although an individual workstation can store documents or data on the workstation, it is usually stored centrally. This offers a level of protection by limiting access to those who have the proper authorization, most often requiring a password for access. It also makes backing up data easier.

The ability to limit access to files on a file server is one method to ensure confidentiality in a large office. File access can be limited by password-protecting files and granting password access only to those with a need to access and work on those specific files. Because each file or set of files, called folders, can be password-protected separately, ethical walls can be established by restricting access to just those on the legal team who are working on a case.

Advice *from the* Field

TECHNOLOGY IS A TOOL, NOT A CASE STRATEGY IN THE COURTROOM
Michael E. Cobo

The latest legal technology products such as animations and courtroom presentation systems can be very alluring to lawyers. After learning about these products, you may be anxious to use them. But you should keep in mind that technology products are only tools to implement a solution and are not solutions in themselves. The key issue is: What is your case strategy and what do you need to present?

An expensive, ill-planned use of technology may result in losses at trial. These losses, or even an uncomfortable implementation of a technology product, may ultimately cause some to feel the experiment was unsuccessful and abandon future use of courtroom technology.

On the other hand, such potentially devastating results can be avoided by carefully planning a case strategy with the same care as you would plan a general trial strategy. The pitfalls will be avoided and you will present a more effective case to the trier of fact.

The trial team must remember that it is the message, not the medium, that wins at trial. Take this opportunity to vary the presentation media and develop some exhibit boards or utilize an overhead. Certain exhibits are displayed best as foamcore boards. Timelines or chronologies generally lend themselves to a board, as do other exhibits that need to be larger and hold more visual or textual information. Strategically, some exhibits need to be used in conjunction with others or need to be in the view of the jury more often than not.

ASSESS YOURSELF

Before you spend a dime to develop the visual strategy, create a presentation or invest in any technology, make a critical self-assessment. Will you be comfortable with the strategy and the technological tools that will be developed for the trial? The most effective visual communication strategy will never be effective if it is never implemented or is delivered without conviction because you are not comfortable using the tools.

The effective use of technology involves (1) creating an inventory of the visual requirements, (2) selecting the proper technologies, medium and tools, and (3) being prepared to properly use the products to implement your case strategy.

Backing Up Data

With everything on one file server, the **backup of data** can be automated to make copies of everyone's files and not just the files on workstations of those who remember to back up their computer. Backing up data regularly is an essential function to prevent loss of critical files and office data in the event of a disaster such as a flood, fire, earthquake, or tornado.

Good backup policy is to back up the file server daily and store the duplicate copy in a safe location away from the server location, such as a fireproof safe or a bank safe deposit box. Imagine trying to reconstruct files, court-filed documents, and other essential information after a devastating hurricane and resultant flood that destroys a law firm's and courthouse paper records, as occurred in New Orleans in 2005 as a result of Hurricane Katrina!

Backup of data Making a copy of critical files and programs in case of a loss of the original computer files.

Wide Area and Wireless Networks

Time can be saved by electronically sharing information instead of by personal delivery or by having a courier deliver paper copies of documents, whether on a different floor, building, or city. Many firms—some as small as two people—maintain multiple office sites, such as a center-city and a suburban office location, or a main office and a satellite office across from the courthouse. Each of these offices may have a separate computer network.

With high-speed communications lines, these separate networks may be connected to form a "network of networks." Access to a workstation on one of the networks allows access to the other networks in the system and the peripherals attached to the network, including network printers. This allows a person in one office to print documents on a printer in another office. Files may be shared among all the members of the legal team regardless of the office in which they are physically located.

Wide area network A wide area network is a network of networks. Each network is treated as if it were a connection on the network.

Wireless network A wireless network uses wireless technology instead of wires for connecting to the network.

The Internet

In its most basic form, the **Internet** or the World Wide Web may be thought of as nothing more than a group of computers linked together with the added ability to search all the connections for information. If you work in an office in which all of the computers are networked together, you have a small version of the Internet. Each person's computer is connected to other people's computers, generally with a main computer on which resides the frequently shared data files and the software (network operating system) that controls the connections and how the requests from each computer are handled and directed. This main control computer usually is referred to as the file server (see Exhibit 4.14).

Internet The Internet or the World Wide Web is a group of computers linked together with the added ability to search all the connections for information.

Exhibit 4.14 Network system

Local area network (LAN)
A network of computers at one location.

Internet service provider (ISP) The company providing the connection between the user and the Internet.

Modem A device to translate electrical signals to allow computers to communicate with each other.

The **local area, or office, network (LAN)** search tool is usually a program such as Microsoft Windows Explorer—not to be confused with the Internet browser Internet Explorer—which permits files to be found on the local computer or the other computers with shared access, by location or other characteristics. Exhibit 4.15 shows the Explorer screen, and Exhibit 4.16 shows search companion. **Internet service providers (ISPs)** provide local or toll-free access numbers that most people use to connect to their service. Larger offices and companies may have a direct connection (hardwired, or by dedicated telephone line) that eliminates the need to dial up the ISP. A device called a **modem** is used to translate the electrical signals for transmission over these connections so the computers can "talk" to each other. The modem converts (modulates) the information from the keyboard and computer into a form that can be transferred electronically over telephone lines, cable connections, and radio waves.

At the receiving end of the signal is another modem that reconverts (demodulates) the signal into a form usable by the computer. Depending on the modem and the ISP service, speeds of transmission vary widely. The slower the connection provided by the modem and the service, the longer it takes to transmit and receive information. As with most services, the higher the speed, the higher is the cost. It is easy to see that a multipage document will take longer to transmit or receive than a single-page document. The reasonableness of the cost of a high-speed connection depends upon the volume of pages regularly sent or received.

Perhaps less obvious is the size of the files and those that are in graphic format. Most government forms are available in a graphic form rather than a text form. A single one-page form in graphic format may be the equivalent of a 10-page text document. Again depending upon the frequency of downloads of forms, it might be advisable to upgrade to a high-speed line.

Online Computer Resources

The number of online or Internet resources increases daily. Finding the desired information is easy when you know the specific source and piece of information. In these cases, you can enter the computer address of the specific page or document and obtain

Exhibit 4.15 Explorer screen

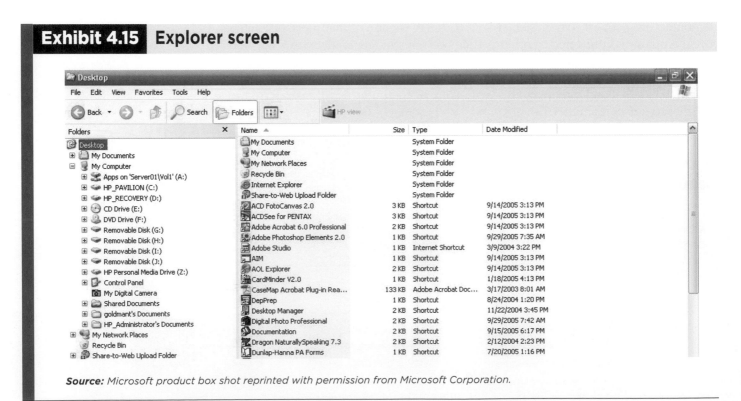

Source: *Microsoft product box shot reprinted with permission from Microsoft Corporation.*

Exhibit 4.16 Search companion

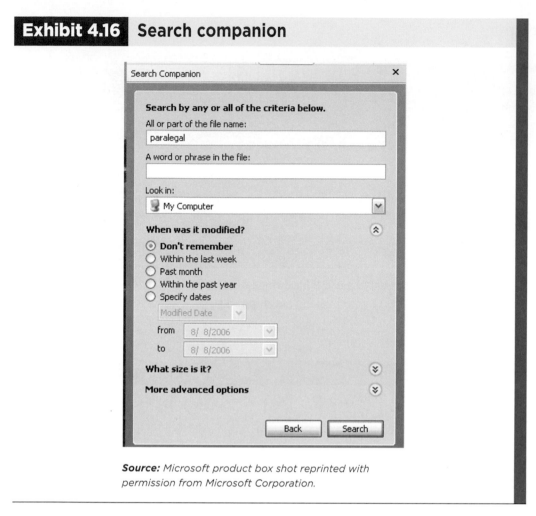

Source: *Microsoft product box shot reprinted with permission from Microsoft Corporation.*

your result almost instantly. More frequently, you will have to locate information about a specific item without knowing where to find it.

Internet Browsers

The solution is found in **Internet (Web) browsers** such as AOL and Internet Explorer. These browsers provide a search feature, usually referred to as a search engine, that allows a search of available Web resources. These searches require only inputting into the search engine a word or phrase to obtain a listing of potentially relevant information. Also useful are specialized search engines such as Google and Yahoo!, which use highly developed algorithms to search for relevant information and return a listing in order of relevancy with amazing accuracy.

An Internet or Web browser is a software program that allows a person to use a computer to access the Internet. Unless you have a direct connection to a computer database, you will be working with a software program known as a Web browser. The two most popular Web browsers are Microsoft Internet Explorer and AOL, both of which provide content. These browsers typically are used with Internet service providers that do not themselves provide any content but, rather, act as an intermediary between the user and the World Wide Web. Some services, such as America OnLine (AOL) and MSN, provide content, such as news and weather and specialty sections for sharing information, along with providing the traditional Internet connections and email.

All of the browsers basically provide two main screens—one to display email (see Exhibit 4.17) and to display content and Internet search results (see Exhibit 4.18.)

Internet (Web) browsers An Internet or Web browser is a software program that allows a person to use a computer to access the Internet. The two most popular Web browsers are Microsoft Internet Explorer and AOL.

 Web Exploration

Obtain a copy of the current AOL browser at www.daol.aol.com/software.

Exhibit 4.17 **Email display**

Exhibit 4.18 **AOL Internet browser**

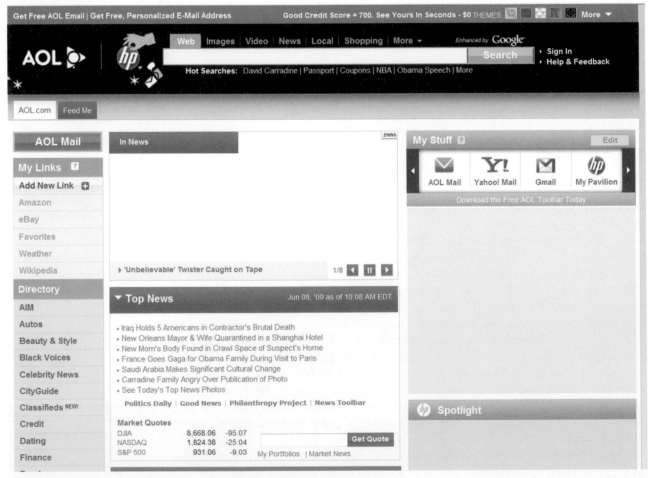

Search Engines

An **Internet search engine** is a program designed to take a word or set of words and search websites on the Internet. Of the available Internet search engines, each searches in a different fashion. The same search request may generate totally different results on different search engines. The number of search engines is expanding constantly. Some search engines are more suitable than others for legal searches. Many search engines are designed for use by children and families, so they may not return the results needed in the professional areas.

It is useful to create a search query and run the query through a number of different search engines, then compare the results. For example, you may wish to search the topic "regulation of paralegals." Each of the search engines shown below may be accessed by entering its **URL (uniform resource locator)** in your Web browser:

AltaVista	www.altavista.com
Ask.com	www.ask.com
Dogpile	www.dogpile.com
Excite	www.excite.com
Google	www.google.com
MetaCrawler	www.metacrawler.com
Yahoo!	www.yahoo.com

Some of the information is shown on the screen and will not require any more searching. The data—such as a phone number, address, or other limited information—will appear and may be copied manually or printed out to capture the displayed page. Other information may be in the form of large text or graphic files. These may be many pages long or involve use of graphic display programs such as the popular Adobe. Typical of the graphic images are the tax forms available from the Internal Revenue Service.

A word of caution: Addresses of websites tend to change frequently. It is a good idea to keep a list of frequently used websites handy and update it regularly.

Addresses and Locations

Obviously, finding something requires knowing where it resides. We find people by looking for their home or business address or by their telephone number. The modern equivalent of a telephone number is the **computer address and location**. Web pages also have addresses, known as uniform resource locators, or URLs.

The URL is made up of three parts:

Protocol://Computer/Path

The **protocol** is usually http (hypertext transfer protocol). The computer is the Internet computer name, such as **www.bucks.edu.** And the path is the directory or subdirectory on the computer where the information can be found.

The URL may be thought of as a file cabinet, in which the protocol is the name of the file cabinet, the computer is the drawer in the file cabinet, and the path is the file folder in the drawer. Not all URLs have a path as part of the address.

Part of the naming protocol is a domain nomenclature, with extensions such as the "edu" in www.bucks.edu. Common extensions are:

.org	organizations
.edu	educational institutions
.com	commercial operations
.gov	government agencies
.bus	business
.mil	military

In addition, there are extensions such as

.jp	Japan
.fr	France
.uk	United Kingdom

Internet search engine An Internet search engine is a program designed to take a word or set of words and locate websites on the Internet.

Uniform resource locator (URL) The address of a site on the Internet.

Web Exploration

Internal Revenue Service: Obtain copies of tax forms at www.irs.gov.

Computer address and location The modern equivalent of a person's telephone number is the email address. Pages on the Internet also have addresses known as the Uniform Resource Locator (URL), made up of three parts: protocol, computer, and path.

Protocol In a URL the required format of the Web address.

These designations refer to the country where the computer is located.

Many people save information on websites for future use, which may be in hard-copy, on cards, or in a database. The Website Profile Checklist below provides suggested headings.

CHECKLIST Website Profile

☐ Address (URL):   ☐ Secondary subject:

☐ Name of organization or site: ☐ Cost:

☐ Key subject: ☐ Comments:

In determining the authenticity of information found on the Internet, knowing if the computer is a commercial site (.com or .bus) or a government site (.gov) is sometimes useful. Some websites may appear to be official government websites or may appear to contain official information but actually are private sites.

For example, the official URL for the Internal Revenue Service is **www.irs.gov.** This is not to be confused with the unofficial private website www.irs.com. To obtain the official Internal Revenue Service forms and information, you must use the official site, **www.irs.gov.**

Potentially, one of the biggest time-savers for the paralegal is the ready availability of information, forms, and files on the Internet or World Wide Web. Public information that would have required a trip to the courthouse or other government office is instantly available without leaving the office. This information may come from public or private sources. Government information typically is available without cost or at minimum cost. Private information may be free to all, or at a cost per use, per page, or per time period (such as a month).

Legal Research

Web Exploration

Check the free resources of the Cornell Law School website at http://www.law.cornell.edu/.

A major use of the Internet in the law office is to perform research, both factual and legal. Using powerful search engines such as Google, Yahoo!, and Ask can help the paralegal locate almost any information that is available on the Internet. More and more legal research is being conducted on the Internet as law offices reduce the size of paper-based law libraries in favor of online resources. A number of companies provide access to case law, statutory material, and other secondary legal sources for a fee. Among the most widely used of these are Westlaw, LexisNexis, Loislaw, and Versus-Law. Although some websites offer information without charge, most do not have the depth of available resources that the for-fee sites offer. The Cornell University Law school site is among the most popular of the no-fee sites.

Formats of Available Information

Most of the items that are displayed can be printed to a printer attached to a computer. At the top of most Web browsers is a printer icon or a Print command in the FILE icon at the top of the page. Clicking on the icon or word PRINT in the FILE pull-down menu will initiate the print process. Patience may be necessary, as the computer may have to take some time to access the original source of the information. Clicking several times will not speed up the process and actually may result in several copies of the same information being printed.

File Attachments

A popular method for transmitting text files and graphic images is by **attachment** of the file to an email. This is much easier than it sounds. Today, almost everyone has an email address, whether at home or at work, or both. To send or receive emails requires the use of an Internet service provider and a browser such as Internet Explorer, Netscape, or one of the other specialty email programs. In the traditional email, text is entered on the keyboard and transmitted to the email account of a recipient, who reads it online. Virtually any file can be attached (linked) and sent with an email. The receiver needs only to click the mouse on the attachment, which may appear as an icon. In most cases, the file will open using the same program from which it was created, such as Microsoft Word, Corel WordPerfect, or Adobe Acrobat. Occasionally a file may be transmitted in a format that the receiver does not have the software to open. This is particularly true with regard to graphic images, pictures, and drawings.

File attachment The attachment is a popular method for transmitting text files, and occasionally graphic images, by attaching the file to an email.

Receiving and Downloading Files and Attachments

The method for downloading files and attachments is the same. Users first should determine the directory (folder) into which they will be downloading these files. In Windows this usually is a folder called My Download Files or My Files. If there is no existing folder, Windows Explorer can be used to create a file with a name such as Download. Windows Explorer is a program in the Start directory under Programs. (This is not the same as Windows Internet Explorer, which is an Internet browser.)

CHECKLIST To Retrieve and Download a Form

☐ Select a file format.

☐ Select the file(s) you wish to receive. To select multiple items, hold the Control button down while selecting.

☐ Click the Review Selected Files button. A Results page will be displayed with links to the file(s) you requested.

☐ Select the file title to retrieve.

Most of the files attached as part of email will be document files created and saved as either Microsoft Word documents or WordPerfect documents. The user may want to save these files directly into the Word or WordPerfect directory. Saving them in the computer download is one option, as is opening the file on the screen immediately instead of saving it for later use. Alternative file formats may be offered, such as MS Word or WordPerfect or PDF, so be sure you have the appropriate program on your computer that can open and view the file.

Normally, text files and graphic images are static files; that is, by themselves they do not perform any function but are merely data-usable within another program such as a word processor or graphic image viewer. It has become common, however, to send, as attachments, files that have within them miniprograms such as macros that perform functions when activated, such as those used to calculate sums in spreadsheets. Others are self-contained software programs such as screensavers containing animation and animated cartoons.

Some program files have an extension of either ".exe" or ".com." Files with these extensions may run automatically after downloading. Therefore, greater caution must be taken in downloading any file, particularly files with these or other unknown file extensions, which may contain macros (mini files), such as Excel files, which may contain formulas that run automatically and may contain computer viruses, as discussed below. Remember that it is not enough to rely on the sender being a reliable source, as even the most reliable source can have a security breach that allows a virus to be attached to a file, or the source may be forwarding files from other, less reliable sources without checking the files before sending them to you.

Sending Files

Some Internet Service Providers (ISPs) limit the amount of information that may be sent at one time, depending on the speed of the connection and how busy the system is at different times of the day. This may limit the number of pages that may be sent at one time. With increased transmission speed, also referred to as bandwidth, comes the ability to transmit much larger files and more pages in the same time.

Increasingly, large-size graphics files and images such as photographs are sent or attached to emails. The larger files being transmitted require more bandwidth (the pipeline) to avoid slowing down the system. Bandwidth may be thought of as the amount of data that can be sent in a given timeframe. For example:

Telephone dial-up service	24–56 kilobits (amount of data) per second (kps)
Digital Subscriber Line (DSL)	up to 750 kps
Fiber Optic Service (FIOS)	up to 15 megabits

As with any pipeline, only a limited amount of product can be transmitted at any one time. To more equitably share the limited pipeline resource, ISPs and network operators permanently—or temporarily during peak usage times—limit the number of files or the size of files that one user may transmit. In some offices, the same limitations may be imposed to overcome the size limitation; files may be transmitted in a compressed format, frequently referred to as zip files. Large files are run through a program that compresses them before being sent. The recipient of the compressed file then must uncompress the file before being able to read it.

A number of programs are available to compress and decompress files. Some of these require several steps, and other programs perform the task automatically. For occasional use, the manual method is acceptable, but with the increasing number of compressed files, it may be more time-efficient to purchase one of the automatic programs. Limited time-trial versions of some of these decompression programs may be downloaded without charge over the Internet from software companies who are encouraging users to buy the full version after the trial period expires.

Electronic Filing

A number of courts have established procedures for the electronic filing of pleadings. Each court is free to set up its own rules and procedures and must be consulted before attempting to use this service. The Internal Revenue Service and some states have combined in a joint effort to allow electronic filing of both the federal and state individual income tax returns in one step. The local or state tax authority retrieves the information from the Internal Revenue Service. A feature of this service, known as IRS e-file, is the return receipt when the federal and state governments receive the form.

Types of Image Formats

With increasing frequency, the Internet is being used to obtain needed forms. These may be government agency forms, tax forms, or court forms. Even the best-equipped office will require one form or another that is not in the office supply room for completing a case. This may be an unusual federal tax form or a form from your state or another state.

The most popular format for the federal government forms is PDF form, and many state agencies also use the PDF format for document delivery. Other options may be presented for selection.

Computer and Network Security

Security has become a critical issue as law offices, courts, and clients become more dependent upon the use of the computer and the Internet. With only a single computer, the security concern is limited to introducing a program that does not work properly. With computer networks, the potential is introduced to adversely impact every workstation on the network and the network file server itself. On a network, any workstation is a potential input source of problems in the form of software programs that could corrupt the system or the files stored on the system. Though not common, there are instances of employees introducing annoying or potentially harmful programs as a method of getting even with an employer. Part of the solution to these kinds of issues is to limit access to the network, including limiting the ability to access the file server from workstations and limiting the ability or right to make changes to operating systems and limit other activity to saving of documents.

Use of the Internet from workstations has introduced the security concern about unauthorized parties gaining access to the computer network—referred to informally as "**hacking**." In some instances, the unauthorized party wants to gain access to information in files stored on the network. In other cases, it is to undermine the integrity of the system by causing files and programs to be modified or to introduce computer viruses that can cause minor inconvenience or even destroy entire systems by deleting files, programs, and operating systems.

Hacking Unauthorized access to a computer or computer network.

Firewalls

A **firewall** is a program designed to limit access to a computer or to a computer network system. Depending upon the complexity of the program, it may restrict total access without proper validation in the form of passwords, or limit all access to the system for certain kinds of programs or sources not deemed to be acceptable to the network or system administrator. For example, many parents use a form of a firewall designed to limit children's access to certain kinds of programs and certain sites on the Internet that are deemed to be unacceptable.

A firewall can be a two-edged sword for the paralegal: It prevents unauthorized access to the network, and it may prevent the paralegal working at an offsite location such as a courthouse, client's office, or opposing counsel's offices from accessing files on the firm's computer or other Internet connection. It is important to check a connection to be sure it will allow data to be accessed from a remote location and sent as

Firewalls Programs designed to limit access to authorized users and applications.

planned before it is needed for trial, depositions, or presentation. With enough time, any issue may be resolved with the local system administrator.

Encryption Technology

Encryption technology permits a computer user to basically put a lock around its computer information to protect it from being discovered by others. Encryption technology is like a lock on a house. Without the lock in place, unwanted persons can easily enter the house and steal its contents; with the lock in place, it is more difficult to enter and take the house's contents. Encryption software serves a similar function in that it lets computer users scramble information so only those who have the encryption code can enter the database and discover the information.

Encryption

Confidential or privileged information sent over the Internet is frequently encrypted by the sender and unencrypted by the receiver because of the concerns that it will be intercepted when transmitted over the Internet. Encryption programs use algorithms (mathematical formulas) to scramble documents. Without the proper password or encryption key, unauthorized persons are not able to read the files and determine their content.

To understand the levels of protection offered by the different encryption programs, think of the protection offered by a combination lock. The least security is provided by a two-number combination lock frequently found with inexpensive luggage. As the numbers required for opening the lock increase to two, three, four or more numbers, the security also increases. It is not hard to see how the two-digit combination lock can be quickly opened while the four-digit lock requires more time and effort. For an amateur computer hacker with a simple encryption-breaking program, a basic encryption program might be thought to be the equivalent of a two- or three-number combination lock. The higher-level program with tougher algorithms designed to thwart a professional code-breaker would require the four or more number combinations. As computers become faster, more sophisticated methods will be required.

> **ETHICAL PERSPECTIVE**
> ## *Interception of Electronic Communications*
>
> Interception or monitoring of email communications for purposes other than assuring quality of service or maintenance is illegal under the Electronic Communications Privacy Act of 1986, as amended in 1994. [18 U.S.C. B2511(2)(a)(i)]

Computer Viruses

Unfortunately, some computer-knowledgeable people take sadistic pleasure in developing and disseminating programs that attack and destroy computer programs, internal computer-operating systems, and occasionally even the hard disk drives of computers. These programs are known as **computer viruses**. Viruses range from those that create minor inconvenience to those that can destroy data and cause computer shutdowns.

Some simple precautions can prevent disaster. A virus-protection program, such as those sold by Norton, McAfee, and others, is as important to have on your computer as the computer operating system itself. This should be the first program loaded on a new computer.

Encryption Encryption is technology that allows computer users to put a "lock" around information to prevent discovery by others.

Computer viruses Viruses are programs that attack and destroy computer programs, internal computer operating systems, and occasionally the hard disk drives of computers.

Anti-virus programs scan the computer to identify the presence of viruses, and the better programs eliminate the virus. Every disk should be scanned with a virus program before being used. Files that are downloaded from other computers or over the Internet also should be checked. As good as these programs are, they quickly go out of date as new viruses are created and unleashed. Therefore, these virus checking programs should be updated regularly.

Future Trends in Law Office Technology

The pressure is on law offices to be more productive. The increased cost of operating law offices is a major factor in law office managers looking for new ways to use technology to increase productivity. Clients and the courts are not willing to approve fees and costs where more cost-effective methods are available. The demand for speedy justice in the courts has resulted in less time to prepare and present cases, requiring the legal team to use technology to become faster and more productive with less time in which to do it. Advances in computer technology are providing solutions to the productivity and cost issues.

Looking ahead to what's on the technological horizon is imperative to the smooth and profitable functioning of the law office. Anticipating change and incorporating it requires IT knowledge and savvy, whether it comes in the form of in-house staff or external technology consultants. Corporate law firms might have a chief information officer or chief technology officer whose role includes anticipating change and planning for it in concrete as well as visionary ways. Those responsible for IT at smaller firms, as well, have the responsibility to be well-informed of technology trends in order to assess when a new tool should be added to their technology repertoire—and when it should be avoided.

The legal team is an increasingly mobile workforce. Working out of the office is a fact of life for trial attorneys and their support staff. The litigation team may spend much of their time in courthouses and outside the office taking depositions as close as across the street or across the country and around the globe. Increasingly, the support staff is also located or working outside the traditional law office.

In some cases it is because of outsourcing of activity to other firms or companies in remote locations, such as the legal support firms in India. It is also lawyers, paralegals, and litigation support members of the legal team who, for various reasons, work from home. With advances in technology it is possible to connect with the traditional office and access all the needed files and electronic resources on a computer at home; these workers are sometimes referred to as **teleworkers**. The following sections describe emerging technology that is available now and in use at some law firms and technology that is available but not fully deployed. The list is not exhaustive but rather illuminative of what businesses might expect in the near and distant future. How soon is a matter of conjecture, but we know from recent technology trends that it will be sooner than we could have expected even a few years ago.

As Raymond Kurzweil writes in his essay, "The Law of Accelerating Returns" (2001), "An analysis of the history of technology shows that technological change is exponential, contrary to the common-sense "intuitive linear" view. So we won't experience 100 years of progress in the 21st century—it will be more like 20,000 years of progress (at today's rate). The "returns," such as chip speed and cost-effectiveness, also increase exponentially. There's even exponential growth in the rate of exponential growth."

Teleworker People who work from remote locations, typically home.

Videoconferencing

Videoconferencing is the use generally of the Internet, or in some cases telephone lines or special satellite systems, to transmit and receive video and audio signals in real time to allow parties to see and hear each other. It is defined in the Wisconsin court rules (subchapter III of Wis. Stat. chapter 885) as; *Videoconferencing*, as defined in section 885.52(3) of the new rule, means an interactive technology that sends video, voice, and data signals over a transmission circuit so that two or more individuals or groups

Videoconferencing Conferencing from multiple locations using high speed Internet connections to transmit sound and images.

can communicate with each other simultaneously using video monitors. It is a live, real-time, interactive form of communication and does not include the presentation of prerecorded video testimony pursuant to subchapter II of Wis. Stat. chapter 885. The definition is intended to encompass emerging technologies such as Web-based solutions, as they appear, so long as the functional requirements of the definition are met.

The Wisconsin Supreme Court adopted a rule effective July 1, 2008, entitled "Use of Videoconferencing in the Circuit Courts," one of the most advanced rules on the use of this technology in the country. Videoconferencing has been used in many courts for criminal proceedings at various stages of the process, usually at the beginning of the process. The Wisconsin rule advances the use to all aspects of criminal and civil litigation.

Many law firms and their clients use videoconferencing on a regular basis as a method of "face-to-face" communication when parties are at remote sites. With Wisconsin leading the way it can be expected to be an important new tool in the litigation practice.

VoIP

VoIP Voice over internet protocol is a computer internet replacement for traditional telephone connections.

Voice over Internet Protocol **(VoIP)** is a protocol for using the Internet as a method of communication instead of traditional telephone company services. A computer with a microphone and headset or speaker is used to complete a call to another computer or telephone over the Internet. It may be a voice connection or voice and image.

Software is installed on the computer that facilitates the desired activity. An example of a popular service for VoIP is Yahoo Messenger, which has provisions for traditional telephone calling and short message service to cell phone and other portable devices. The initial limitation of VoIP was the inability to call a traditional phone or receive a call. Services like Yahoo Messenger provide options that permit calling traditional phones at a very nominal rate, sometimes as low as one cent per minute.

The relative ease of use of these services and the low cost make conferencing, including videoconferencing, a reality. The days of going to a special location and paying substantial fees to conduct a videoconference are gone. Anyone with an Internet connection, a laptop with built-in microphone and speakers, and an inexpensive video camera can set up a videoconference from almost anywhere there is an Internet connection.

Voice Recognition

Voice recognition Computer programs for converting speech into text or commands without the use of other in/out devices such as keyboards.

Voice recognition software has been around for a number of years. Many will remember trying out an earlier version of a speech recognition program as a possible alternative to typing. More computer technology has brought this software to the point of accuracy approaching, and in some cases exceeding, the accuracy of typing.

Speech-enabled devices include cell phones, personal digital assistants (PDAs), and other handheld devices. It is now possible with programs like Dragon Naturally Speaking Legal Version to dictate working drafts of legal documents directly into almost any program, including word processors, spreadsheets, and databases, without touching a computer keyboard, and send the document to another member of the legal team electronically over a network or by email, as shown in Exhibit 4.19. So advanced have the systems become, portable dictation devices can be used out of the office and then connected to the office computer, on which the speech recognition program has been installed, and the documents transcribed without the intervention of a typist. At up to 160 words a minute for speech input, for the average typist on the legal team the savings are significant. The underlying technology that enables voice technology to perform is now being used in automated response systems, like automatic call attendants that replace operators and receptionists in some firms. It is also a technology that permits those with physical disabilities that prevent using a keyboard, such as carpal tunnel syndrome, to remain or become productive in a world of word processors.

Miniaturization and Portability

The trend in computers and related computer devices has been toward miniaturization and portability. Smaller devices are becoming more powerful than some of the older

Exhibit 4.19 | **Dictation using theBoom noise reduction microphone with Dragon NaturallySpeaking legal software**

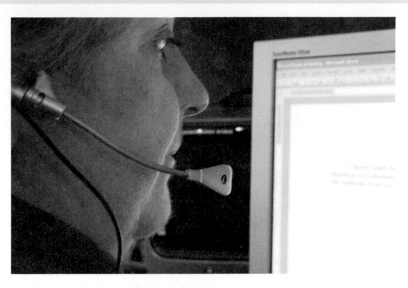

theBoom is a registered trademark of UmeVoice Inc. Dragon NaturallySpeaking is a registered trademark of Nuance Communications.

desktop systems and laptops. Even the telephone has been reduced to a pocket-sized wireless communication device that is also capable of taking and displaying photo images, video, documents, and emails and accessing the Internet—many functions that formerly were reserved to large hardwired computer devices.

The Apple iPhone is an example of a device that can perform many functions formerly requiring a computer. Laptops have been reduced in size, with some weighing less than three pounds. They include all of the features previously mentioned together with built-in Web camera for videoconferencing and have built-in and removable memory greater than many file servers in some small offices.

Wireless Technology

Hardware in many offices today includes the wireless telephone and the laptop computer with built-in wireless Internet capability. The worldwide availability of inexpensive high-speed Internet connections has expanded the availability and use of new technologies. These tools allow constant communication and enable work to be performed virtually anywhere—home, courthouse, airport lounge, or coffee shop. The connection to the office may be by wireless network using the cell phone, or by a wireless connection with built-in wireless network hardware on the computer, or using an adapter card plugged into the computer that uses a wireless Internet connection.

Unlike a few years ago, wires are not necessary to access networks or to set up network connections. Today they may be set up using wireless technology in a wireless network. Just as the cell phone has enabled communications without wires, so has wireless technology allowed networks to be set up where workstations, servers, and peripherals connect over a wireless connection. Remote access is also possible by the use of wireless Internet connection using laptops and other personal computing devices including cell phones with built-in Web or Internet access.

Remote Access

Remote access allows members of the legal team working on cases out of the office to connect with the office file server to retrieve documents, work on them, and send them to other members of the team anywhere in the world. If hardcopy is needed, documents may be printed on any printer accessible over the Internet, including printers in remote office locations, public access points in airports, clients' offices, and courthouses.

Remote Collaboration

Remote collaboration Working on a common document utilizing remote access by two or more parties.

Remote collaboration means that members of the team can work collaboratively from multiple locations as if in the same physical location. This is possible through software conferencing programs that allow the sharing of files while communicating and seeing each other on the same screen using small desktop cameras or cameras built into laptop computers. The same remote access technology allows for the taking of witness statements from remote locations while the parties can see each other or view exhibits on the computer screen.

With higher-speed Internet connections the reality of true real-time videoconferencing has become a reality. Formerly, limited-speed connections restricted how much information could be transmitted. In the simplest form, slower speed increased the time to send a document. If not fast enough it prevented full-motion, full-screen video. With the introduction of fiber optic and cable Internet services in offices and in homes, videoconferencing from multiple locations, which requires a high-speed Internet connection to simultaneously transmit both the sound and the images, is now available on-site at many offices.

Wireless Computer Networks

Wireless computer networks A wireless network uses wireless technology in place of wires for connecting to the network.

Wireless computer networks are like cell phone networks in that both use radio waves to transmit signals to a receiver. Cell phone systems use cell towers located at strategic points all over the world to receive the signals from the cell phone subscriber's cellular device. The wireless network uses wireless access points, which are essentially receivers of radio signals that convert them so they can be transmitted over a connecting wire to a computer or other connection to the Internet.

Unlike cell phone towers, these access points are more limited. With the exception of a few cities that have access points over a large portion of the city these access points are local, often with a range limited to a few hundred feet. Many of these access points are provided in coffee shops, airport lounges, hotels, libraries, and bookstores without charge or at a nominal fee to encourage customers to use the facility instead of a competitor's.

Hot spot A wireless access point, generally in a public area.

With the growth of wireless **"hot spot"** locations, the wire connection has been cut. Lawyers and their paralegals may be connected anywhere in the world and send documents electronically back and forth with the same ease as sending them within the same building. With the growth of Internet connections to portable devices over cell phone connections, computers with built-in devices or with the use of plug-in devices can access the Internet over wide areas not previously possible.

Wireless Laptop Connections

Laptops may be used wirelessly to connect to the Internet without the limitation of use of a "hot spot" by using plug-in devices such as the AT&T Laptop Connect Card, Sierra Wireless Air Card, and a subscription to the service provided by most major providers like AT&T, Verizon, and Sprint. These services essentially provide service virtually anywhere there is a cellular connection. The popularity of these wireless services has resulted in many newer-generation laptops having the feature built in, eliminating the need for the external cards.

Thin Client

Thin client A computer system where programs and files are maintained on a centralized server.

A trend called **"thin client"** or cloud computing is emerging where programs and files are maintained on a centralized server and each user has access through a dumb terminal (one without programs or data). The thin client model offers some additional level of control and prevents loss of information through the loss of a computer. This general concept also includes Software as a Service (SaaS) and Web 2.0. It can be expected that the increased usage of the smaller, lighter computers, commonly called netbooks, designed for accessing the Internet will increase the demand for software and data repositories to minimize the need to support software and large data devices on these very portable computers.

ETHICAL PERSPECTIVE
Unauthorized Eavesdropping

With the increased freedom of communication comes an increased risk of eavesdropping by unauthorized parties accessing the wireless signals. Security measures, such as encryption and access restricted by password, are essential to prevent ethical breaches in confidentiality. Use of public access points, such as the coffee shop with wireless access, the airport lounge, or other public location, invites the curious to eavesdrop and look over the shoulder at the screen of the laptop user. With the growing availability of Internet access on airplanes, the eyes of the adjoining seatmate may be those of a member of the opposing team traveling to the same destination on the same case.

Concept Review *and* Reinforcement

LEGAL TERMINOLOGY

Applications software   134
Attachment   129
Backup of data   149
Case and litigation management software   140
Central processing unit (CPU)   133
Computer addresses and locations   153
Computer hardware   132
Computer network   147
Computer system   132
Computer viruses   158
Database program   138
Digital format   129
Electronic repository   130
Encryption   158
File attachment   155
File extension   137
Firewalls   157
Graphic user interface (GUI)   134

Hacking   157
Hardcopy   129
Hot spot   162
Internet   149
Internet (Web) browsers   151
Internet search engine   153
Internet service provider (ISP)   150
Local area network (LAN)   150
Mainframe   132
Modem   150
Network administrator   148
Network file server   147
Network rights and privileges   148
Office software suites   139
Online collaboration   130
Operating system   133
Outsourcing   131
Paperless office   146
Protocol   153
Random access memory (RAM)   133

Remote collaboration   162
Software   134
Specialty application programs   139
Spreadsheet programs   137
Teleworker   159
Thin client   162
Track Changes   135
Uniform resource locator (URL)   153
Uninterruptible power supply (UPS)   134
Videoconferencing   159
Voice recognition   160
VoIP   160
Wide area network   149
Wireless computer networks   162
Wireless network   149
Workstation   147

SUMMARY OF KEY CONCEPTS

Need for Computer Skills

The Need	Computers are being used with greater frequency to share information in digital format between remote offices, courthouses, government agencies, and clients.
Technology Usage in the Law	Computers are now being used for everything from word processing to computerized timekeeping, payroll productions, and tax return preparation. Today even the smallest law firm and litigator must use technology. Some courts are demanding computerized filing.
Outsourcing	Outsourcing has become a buzzword for shipping work out of the office or overseas to save money. Using an outside computer consultant to help with support for the hardware and software of the office is a form of outsourcing and may involve a help desk located in a foreign location to answer questions.
How Much Do I Really Need to Know	No one can be an expert in everything. What is important is to know enough to know what you do not know and be able to find someone who does.

Understanding the Language of Technology

Why	An understanding of the terminology of technology is a prerequisite to understanding the technology found in the law office, the courthouse, and the clients' business.

Computer Hardware

Computer Hardware	Hardware is the term that encompasses all of the tangible or physical items including computers, monitors, printers, fax machines, duplicators, and similar items that usually have either an electrical connection or use batteries as a power source.

Operating Systems

	The operating system is a basic set of instructions to the computer on how to handle basic functions—how to process input from "input devices" such as the keyboard and mouse, the order in which to process information, and what to show on the computer monitor.

Applications Software

Applications Software Programs	Applications programs are software that perform generic tasks such as word processing.
Word Processing Programs	Programs for creating written documents in electronic format.
Track Changes	Track Changes, as found in MS word, shows the original text, the deleted text, and the new text as well as a strike through for deleted text, underlining or highlighting of new text, as well as margin notes on the document.
File Extensions	When a file is saved, a file extension (a period followed by three characters) is added to the end of the filename to identify the program or format in which the file has been saved.
Spreadsheet Programs	Programs that permit the calculation and presentation of financial information in a grid format of rows and columns.
Database Programs	A database program is an electronic repository of information of all types that can be sorted and presented in a meaningful manner.

Presentation Graphic Programs

	Software programs used to create high quality slide shows and drawings.

Specialty Application Programs

	Specialty applications programs combine many of the basic functions found in software suites, word processing, database management, spreadsheets, and graphic presentations to perform law office, case, and litigation management.
Case and Litigation Management Software	Case and litigation management programs are used to manage documents and the facts and issues of cases.

The Electronic Courtroom and Paperless Office

Electronic Courtroom	The use of electronics and computer-based systems are used in the electronic courtroom.
Paperless Office	The paperless office is one in which documents are created and stored electronically.

Networks

Workstation	A workstation generally consists of a computer, a monitor, and a printer.
Computer Network	A network is a set of workstations connected together.
Network Server	The network file server generally is a separate computer that acts as the traffic cop of the system controlling the flow of information; it requests to use the resources of the system or data, between the connected workstations and other peripherals that are part of the network. These servers usually are the central repository for all electronic files.
Network Rights and Privileges	Rights or privileges determine who has access to the server, the data stored on the server, and the flow of information between connections.
Network Administrator	The network administrator usually is the person with the highest-level access to the network file server.
Backup of Data	Backing up data—making copies of files—regularly is an essential function to prevent loss of critical files and office data in the event of a disaster.
Wide Area Network	A wide area network is a network of networks. Each network is treated as if it were a connection on the network.
Wireless Network	A wireless network uses wireless technology instead of wires for connecting to the network.

The Internet

What Is It?	The Internet or the World Wide Web is a group of computers linked together with the added ability to search all the connections for information.

Online Computer Resources

Internet Browsers	An Internet or Web browser is a software program that allows a person to use a computer to access the Internet. The two most popular Web browsers are Microsoft Internet Explorer and AOL.
Search Engines	An Internet search engine is a program designed to take a word or set of words and locate websites on the Internet.

Addresses and Locations	The modern equivalent of a person's telephone number is the email address. Pages on the Internet also have addresses known as the Uniform Resource Locator (URL), made up of three parts: protocol, computer, and path.

Formats of Available Information

File Attachments	The attachment is a popular method for transmitting text files, and occasionally graphic images, by attaching the file to an email.
Receiving and Downloading Files and Attachments	The method for downloading files and attachments is the same. They are downloaded into a directory (a folder), which in Windows usually is called My Download Files or My Files. If there is no existing folder, Windows Explorer can be used to create a file with a name, such as Download.

Electronic Filing

Courts	Many courts have established procedures for the electronic filing of pleadings. Each court is free to set up its own rules and procedures and must be consulted before attempting to use this service.
IRS	The Internal Revenue Service and some states have combined in a joint effort to allow the filing of both the federal and state individual income tax returns.
Types of Image Formats	The most popular format for computerized forms is PDF.

Computer and Network Security

Security	Security is a critical issue in law offices and for the court as they become more and more dependant on computers and the Internet.
Firewalls	A firewall is a software program designed to limit access to a computer network system.
Encryption	Encryption is technology that allows computer users to put a "lock" around information to prevent discovery by others.
Computer Viruses	Viruses are programs that attack and destroy computer programs, internal computer operating systems, and occasionally the hard disk drives of computers.
Precautions	Virus-protection programs such as Norton or McAfee should be updated regularly.

Future Trends in Law Office Technology

	Looking ahead to what's on the technological horizon is imperative to the smooth and profitable functioning of the law office. Anticipating change and incorporating it requires IT knowledge and savvy, whether it comes in the form of in-house staff or external technology consultants.
Videoconferencing	Use, generally, of the Internet, or in some cases telephone lines or special satellite systems, to transmit and receive video and audio signals in real time to allow parties to see and hear each other.
VoIP	Voice over Internet Protocol (VoIP) is a protocol for using the Internet as a method of communication instead of traditional telephone company services. A computer with a microphone and headset or speaker is used to complete a call to another computer or telephone over the Internet. It may be a voice connection or voice and image.
Voice Recognition	More computer technology has brought this software to the point of accuracy, approaching, and in some cases exceeding, the accuracy of typing.

Miniaturization and Portability	Smaller devices are becoming more powerful than some of the older desktop systems and laptops. Even the telephone has been reduced to a pocket-sized wireless communication device.
Wireless Technology	Hardware in many offices today includes the wireless telephone and the laptop computer with built-in wireless Internet capability. The worldwide availability of inexpensive high-speed Internet connections has expanded the availability and use of new technologies.
Remote Access	Remote access allows members of the legal team working on cases while out of the office to connect with the office file server to retrieve documents, work on them, and send them to other members of the team anywhere in the world.
Remote Collaboration	Remote collaboration means that members of the team can work collaboratively from multiple locations as if in the same physical location. This is possible through software conferencing programs that allow the sharing of files while communicating and seeing each other on the same screen.
Wireless Computer Networks	Like cell phone networks that use radio waves to transmit signals to a receiver.
Wireless Laptop Connections	Laptops may be used wirelessly by using plug-in devices to connect to the Internet without the limitation or use of a "hot spot."
Thin Client	A trend called "thin client" or cloud computing is emerging where programs and files are maintained on a centralized server and each user has access through a dumb terminal (one without programs or data).

WORKING THE WEB

1. Download the latest 1040 tax form and instructions from the Internal Revenue Service website at www.irs.gov.
2. Use one of the search engines listed below to find information on your school or local government:
   a. AltaVista: http://www.altavista.com
   b. Ask.com: http://www.ask.com
   c. Dogpile: http://www.dogpile.com
   d. Excite: http://www.excite.com
   e. Google: http://www.google.com
   f. MetaCrawler: http://www.metacrawler.com
   g. Netscape: http://www.netscape.com
   h. Yahoo!: www.yahoo.com
3. Use the Google search engine to find information on how firewalls work, and print out the first page of the results. Using one of the results, print out a copy of the information that is most responsive to the search, and write a short summary describing what a firewall does. http://www.google.com
4. Use a search engine of your choice to run a search for legal research resources. Print a copy of the first 10 results.

Mark each result you think will be useful in the future as a paralegal and state why.

5. Prepare a step-by-step list of how to find the Code of Federal Regulations on the Government Printing Office website. http://www.access.gpo.gov
6. Prepare a list of the legislative information available from the Library of Congress online. http://www.LOC.gov
7. Use any search engine or browser search tool to find the document "How Our Laws Are Made," as revised and updated by Charles W. Johnson-Parliamentarian, on a federal government website. Hint: use quotation marks around the names. Print out the specific query you used and the URL of the source where the document was found.
8. Print out a copy of the results of the search for "firewall" using Yahoo!, and compare the results to the result from Google. How many of the first 20 listings are the same?

CRITICAL THINKING & WRITING QUESTIONS

1. How can the computer and the Internet increase a paralegal's productivity?
2. What is meant by the term "computer hardware"?
3. What is the danger in using the word processing feature "Track Changes"?
4. What are applications software programs? Give an example.
5. What are the advantages of using office suite programs?
6. How can database programs be used to avoid ethical issues?
7. How can legal office management programs help prevent malpractice?
8. What is meant by the "paperless office"? What changes in law office administration have encouraged this?
9. What is the function of a network server?
10. Why is making a backup essential in a law office?
11. What is the advantage to the legal team in having a wide area network or wireless network?
12. How has the availability of the high-speed Internet impacted the use of the Internet in the law office?
13. What is an Internet browser? How is this different from Windows Explorer?
14. How reliable are forms and documents obtained over the Internet?
15. What advantages does knowing how to use the Internet provide the paralegal in the law office?
16. What are the limitations of using a website to attract new clients to your state?
17. Do cross-jurisdictional boundary websites present any problems for the law firm using the Internet? If so, why?
18. What are some of the ways in which using an Internet browser can assist the paralegal working on a file or a case? How are URLs used in conducting Internet searches?
19. What copyright issues must a paralegal consider in using the Internet to prepare written documents and reports?
20. How can authenticity of information obtained on the Internet be validated? Explain the issues in downloading information.
21. What is the purpose of a firewall? What are the implications to the law office of not having a firewall?
22. What is a computer virus, and what should a paralegal do to protect the firm against computer viruses?
23. Should encryption software be used regularly in transmitting files electronically? Why?
24. Why would the legal team want to use encryption when transmitting a document?
25. What is a wireless access point? How could this be used in a law firm?
26. What ethical issues arise in the use of "hot spots" or public access points?

Building Paralegal Skills

VIDEO CASE STUDIES

Attorney Meet and Confer

Opposing counsel are meeting as required under the Federal Rules of Civil Procedure to discuss discovery issues in the case. Defense counsel has recently taken over the file and is not familiar with its contents and asks for additional time to complete discovery.

After viewing the video case study at www.pearsonhighered .com/goldman answer the following:

1. What is the purpose of the meet and confer under the Federal Rules of Civil Procedure.
2. If the lawyers are not familiar with some of the electronic discovery issues, do they have an ethical obligation to have someone there who is more knowledgeable?
3. How important is it for the lawyers and paralegals to be aware of the issues in the electronic discovery?

Remote Videoconference Taking Witness Video Deposition

The parent of an accident victim is not available locally for deposition. To save time and costs his deposition is being taken by videoconferencing.

After viewing the video case study at www.pearsonhighered.com/goldman answer the following:

1. What arrangements must be made to take a deposition using video conferencing?
2. What are the advantages and disadvantages of using video conferencing for taking depositions of fact witnesses?
3. What is the role of the court reporter in a video conference deposition?

Privilege Issue: Misdirected E-mail

 The paralegal working on a confidential memo for a client has accidentally sent it to opposing counsel. The supervising attorney, visibly upset, gives instructions on how to handle the situation.

After viewing the video case study at www.pearsonhighered .com/goldman answer the following:

1. What is the potential of fact of the e-mail and confidential information to the opposing party?
2. What steps should be taken in your jurisdiction when e-mail is inadvertently sent to the wrong party?
3. Who is ultimately responsible and what are the penalties for inadvertent disclosure of confidential information by e-mail?

ETHICS ANALYSIS & DISCUSSION QUESTIONS

1. What are the ethical issues related to a law firm website that is available around the world when the firm is licensed to practice only in one jurisdiction?
2. Explain the ethical implication of the following: "In today's society, with the advent of the information superhighway, federal and state legislation and regulations, as well as information regarding industry trends, are easily accessed."
3. What are the ethical issues of erroneously sending or receiving by email or fax a confidential trial strategy memorandum?
4. What ethical issues arise for the law firm when it does not maintain an off-premises copy of files and client records? Does a major catastrophe, such as the flooding caused by Hurricane Katrina in New Orleans in 2005, excuse not having backup files and records?
5. What role do security protocols have in ethical compliance?
6. What ethical issues are involved in combining law practices as discussed in the opening scenario? What specific steps should be taken? Explain how these steps will prevent ethical breaches.
7. You are working in a sophisticated law firm that has the latest computers and software. You have not been trained in the use of the firm's computer encryption software for transmitting email and other electronic documents to clients and other offices of the firm. You live a few blocks from the office and consent to stay late on Friday night before a major holiday weekend when everyone has left early to avoid the rush hour traffic.

   A client calls and asks for a copy of the trial strategy memorandum for a major case to take with him for review over the weekend. He advises that he is getting ready to get on a plane but has a computer with him that has reverse encryption software the firm gave him and tells you he wants to read the memo while he is on the plane for the next 14 hours on his way to Tokyo. He hangs up and you do not have his cell phone number. You send the email without using the encryption software. [*U.S. v. Thomas*, 74 F.3d. 701 (1996), ABA Ethics Opinion, Utah Ethics Opinion 00-01.] Have you breached any rules on client confidentiality by sending unencrypted email containing confidential client information?

DEVELOPING YOUR COLLABORATION SKILLS

Working on your own or with a group of other students assigned by your instructor, review the scenario at the beginning of the chapter that deals with combining a paper-based office and an electronic office.

1. Divide into two teams, one team playing the role of the junior paralegal and the other the senior paralegal. Put yourself in that person's place, and make a list of the benefits of the type of office system (electronic or paper) that they are accustomed to working in.
2. Share your list with the other team. As a group, decide what systems/practices you think will be most efficient

and effective to use in the combined office to perform the following activities:
- Manage conflicts of interest
- Perform legal research
- Manage cases
- Handle client files
- Communicate with clients
- Manage financial accounts
3. As a group, identify areas of ethical concern in a merger, and discuss how best to handle these issues.

PARALEGAL PORTFOLIO EXERCISE

Prepare a memo for a potential law office manager, outlining the advantages and disadvantages of the paperless office. What security and confidentiality issues must be considered? What potential solutions or office procedures should be put in place? Reference and cite any applicable ethical rules or opinions from your local or state court or bar association.

LEGAL ANALYSIS & WRITING CASES

Issue: Are Images Displayed on the Internet as a Result of a Search Protected by Copyright?

Defendant operates a "visual search engine" on the Internet that allows a user to obtain a list of related Web content in response to a search query entered by the user. Unlike other Internet search engines, defendant's search engine, the "Ditto" crawler, retrieves images instead of descriptive text. It produces a list of reduced, "thumbnail" pictures related to the user's query. By clicking on the desired thumbnail, a user could view the "image attributes" window displaying the full-size version of the image, a description of its dimensions, and an address for the website where it originated. By clicking on the address, the user could link to the originating website for the image. The search engine works by maintaining an indexed database of approximately two million thumbnail images obtained through a "crawler"—a computer program that travels the Web in search of images to be converted into thumbnails and added to the index.

Plaintiff Kelly is a photographer specializing in photographs of California Gold Rush country and photographs related to the works of Laura Ingalls Wilder. He does not sell the photographs independently, but his photographs have appeared in several books. Plaintiff also maintains two websites, one of which (www.goldrush1849.com) provides a "virtual tour" of California's Gold Rush country and promotes plaintiff's book on the subject. The other (www.showmethegold.com) markets corporate retreats in California's Gold Rush country.

Thirty-five of plaintiff's images were indexed by the Ditto crawler and put in defendant's image database. As a result, these images were made available in thumbnail form to users of defendant's visual search engine. After being notified of plaintiff's objections, Ditto removed the images from its database.

Plaintiff filed a copyright-infringement action. One of the questions of first impression is whether the display of copyrighted images by a "visual search engine" on the Internet constitutes fair use under the Copyright Act. The court found that defendant never held out plaintiff's work as its own, or even engaged in conduct specifically directed at plaintiff's work. Plaintiff's images were swept up along with two million others available on the Internet, as part of defendant's efforts to provide its users with a better way to find images on the Internet. Defendant's purposes were and are inherently transformative, even if its realization of those purposes was at times imperfect. Where, as here, a new use and new technology are evolving, the broad transformative purpose of the use weighs more heavily than the inevitable flaws in its early stages of development.

Questions

1. As the use of the Internet matures, will courts view use of information from the Web differently?

2. What are the implications in taking material off the Internet and including it in reports, memos, and briefs?

3. Would the decision have been different if the items were copyrighted legal forms also located by a "crawler" and displayed as a visual image such as a PDF file?

WORKING WITH THE LANGUAGE OF THE COURT CASE

CoStar Group Inc. v. LoopNet, Inc.

164 F. Supp. 2d 688 (D.C. Md. 2001)
United States District Court, Maryland

Read, and if assigned, brief this case. In your brief, include answers to the following questions.

1. What is a "contributory infringer" under the Digital Millennium Copyright Act?

2. Who is an online service provider as defined by the Digital Millennium Copyright Act (DMCA)?

3. When does a service provider lose its immunity under the DMCA?

4. What is a "safe harbor" under the DMCA?

5. What conduct takes a service provider out of the safe harbor?

Deborah K. Chasanow

I. BACKGROUND

Plaintiffs CoStar Group, Inc. and CoStar Realty Information, Inc. (collectively CoStar) filed suit against LoopNet, Inc. (LoopNet) alleging copyright infringement. CoStar is a national provider of commercial real estate information services . . . which includes photographs. . . .

LoopNet is an Internet-based company offering a service through which a user . . . may post a listing of commercial real estate available for lease. . . . To include a photograph, . . . it is uploaded into a separate "folder,". . . where it is reviewed by a LoopNet employee to determine that it is . . . a photograph of commercial property and that there is no obvious . . . violation of LoopNet's terms and conditions. If the photograph meets LoopNet's criteria . . . it is automatically posted. . . . CoStar claims that over 300 of its copyrighted photographs have appeared on LoopNet's site (the number has increased over time). . . .

Application of copyright law in cyberspace is elusive and perplexing. The World Wide Web has progressed far faster than the law and, as a result, courts are struggling to catch up. Legislatures and courts endeavor in this growing area to maintain the free flow of information over the Internet while still protecting intellectual property rights. . . .

Contributory Copyright Infringement

1. OVERVIEW

It is, today, a given that: one who, with knowledge of the infringing activity, induces, causes, or materially contributes to the infringing conduct of another, may be held liable as a "contributory" infringer. . . . Put differently, liability exists if the defendant engages in "personal conduct that encourages or assists the infringement.". . .

CoStar does not claim that LoopNet had knowledge of its users' infringements prior to its giving notice. . . . Given the nature of the infringements in this case, it was impossible for LoopNet to have knowledge of the alleged infringement before receiving notice from CoStar. CoStar does not attach a copyright notice to its photos and even CoStar's own expert could not identify a CoStar photo simply by reviewing it. . . . Thus, LoopNet cannot be charged with . . . knowledge before receiving claims of infringement from CoStar. . . . CoStar does not claim that LoopNet had knowledge of infringement prior to receiving notice from CoStar. [T]here remain . . . disputes about [its] knowledge . . . after receiving the claims of infringement. CoStar alleges that once it gave LoopNet notice that its photographs were being infringed, LoopNet can be charged with knowledge of continuing infringements. . . .

The DMCA was enacted both to preserve copyright enforcement in the Internet and to provide immunity to service providers from copyright infringement liability for "passive," "automatic" actions in which a service provider's system engages through a technological process initiated by another without the knowledge of the service provider. . . . The DMCA's protection of an innocent service provider disappears at the moment the service provider loses its innocence, i.e., at the moment it becomes aware that a third party is using its system to infringe. At that point, the Act shifts responsibility to the service provider to disable the infringing matter, "preserving the strong incentives for service providers and copyright owners to cooperate to detect and deal with copyright infringements that take place in the digital networked environment."

The DMCA seeks to strike a balance by shielding online service providers from liability in damages as long as they remove or prevent access to infringing material. . . . The initial inquiry is whether LoopNet can be considered a service provider for the purposes of the DMCA.

a. Service Provider

In order to qualify for the safe harbor in the DMCA, LoopNet must meet the definition of "online service provider." Under § 512 (k)(1)(A), a service provider is "an entity offering the transmission, routing, or providing of connections for digital online communications, between

(continued)

or among points specified by a user, of material of the user's choosing, without modification to the content of the material as sent or received." 17 U.S.C. § 512(k)(1)(A)(1998). . . . For the other safe harbor provisions, including (c), which is at issue here, the definition is broader: "a provider of online services or network access, or the operator of facilities therefore.". . .

"Online services" is surely broad enough to encompass the type of service provided by LoopNet that is at issue here. The term is, of course, only a threshold to the protections of the Act. Even if LoopNet qualifies as a service provider, it must meet the other criteria.

b. Stored at the Instance of the User

A service provider is only protected from liability by the DMCA, "for infringement of copyright by reason of its storage at the direction of user of material." 17 U.S.C. § 512(c)(1) . . . [The photographs at issue] are uploaded at the volition of the user and are subject . . . to a mere screening to assess whether they are commercial property and to catch any obvious infringements. . . . Although humans are involved rather than mere technology, they serve only as a gateway and are not involved in a selection process . . . Therefore, this threshold requirement is met and LoopNet is not disqualified from the safe harbor on these grounds.

c. Knowledge

The safe harbor protects service providers from liability unless they have knowledge of copyright infringement. There are three types of knowledge of infringement that can take a service provider out of the safe harbor: (1) the service provider can have actual knowledge of infringement; (2) it can be aware of facts which raise a "red flag" that its users are infringing; or (3) the copyright owner can notify the service provider in a manner "substantially" conforming with § 512 (c)(3) that its works are being infringed. . . . The service provider does not automatically lose its liability shield upon receiving notice, but "the Act shifts responsibility to the service provider to disable the infringing matter. . . ."

. . . LoopNet received notification of claimed infringement . . . so the adequacy of LoopNet's removal policy must be assessed to determine whether LoopNet is protected by the safe harbor.

d. Adequacy of Termination and "Take Down" Policy

Once a service provider has received notification of a claimed infringement as described in [the Act] . . . the service provider can remain in the safe harbor if it "responds expeditiously to remove, or disable access to, the material that is claimed to be infringing or to be the subject of infringing activity." 17 U.S.C. § 512 (c)(1)(C) (1998). . . .

There are several material factual disputes remaining as to whether the removal of allegedly infringing photographs was satisfactorily expeditious and whether LoopNet's termination policy was reasonable and effective. CoStar's infringement claims are based on the posting of specific photographs. Additionally, LoopNet's knowledge of the alleged infringements and its "take down" and termination policies have changed over time in fairly significant ways. In order to resolve this issue, the factfinder will have to focus on each photo and the policy in effect prior to the posting of each photo. Hence, neither party is entitled to summary judgment on this issue. . . .

3. LIABILITY FOR CONTRIBUTORY INFRINGEMENT

With regard to the photographs that were infringed before the safe harbor applied . . . and in case LoopNet's termination policy and take down of infringing photographs is found to be inadequate so as to remove it from the safe harbor, the analysis shifts from the DMCA back to contributory infringement. The determination of contributory infringement liability turns on a different issue of knowledge than the standard used to determine LoopNet's eligibility for the safe harbor. Here, the question is whether CoStar's notice of claimed infringement was sufficient to satisfy the knowledge prong of the test for contributory infringement either by providing actual knowledge, a "red flag" that infringement was occurring, or constructive knowledge.

. . . [T]he fact finder must determine along a continuum the adequacy of the policy in place prior to the posting of each specific photograph. Therefore, neither party is entitled to summary judgment on this issue.

e. Preemption of Non-Copyright Claims

. . . The Copyright Act preempts state law that is "equivalent to any of the exclusive rights within the general scope of copyright as specified by section 106." 17 U.S.C. § 301(a) (1996) . . . "To determine whether a state claim is preempted by the Act, courts must make a two-part inquiry: (1) the work must be within the scope of the subject matter of copyright, and (2) the state law rights must be equivalent to any exclusive rights within the scope of federal copyright." *Fischer v. Viacom Intern Corp.*, 115 F. Supp. 2d 535. 540 (D.Md. 2000). . . . The critical question, then, is whether CoStar's unfair competition claim contains an additional element or whether it is based solely on the alleged copying.

. . . Essentially, CoStar's claim is that LoopNet is exhibiting as its own photographs on its website that CoStar has an exclusive right to exhibit or license for exhibition. This type of reverse passing off is, in effect, a "disguised copyright infringement claim.". . . Therefore, this claim does not satisfy the "extra-element" test and so is equivalent to CoStar's claim under the Copyright Act. Accordingly, it is preempted. . . .

V. CONCLUSION

For the foregoing reasons; by separate order, both motions concerning the safe harbor defense of the DMCA will be denied, . . . both motions concerning contributory infringement will be denied, . . . summary judgment will be granted in favor of LoopNet on the . . . preemption of the state law claims.

Introduction to Law

The aspiring paralegal professional must become familiar with American legal heritage, including how the law developed in this country over the centuries. This includes learning the historical and current sources of law of federal and state law. In addition, a professional paralegal should have knowledge of the Constitution of the United States of America and how it created the federal government, delegating powers to the federal government, reserving powers to the states, and protecting us from unwelcomed government intrusion into our lives. A paralegal professional must have knowledge of the American court system and the process of judicial and non-judicial dispute resolution. A working knowledge of the civil litigation process, criminal litigation and procedure, and administrative law is a necessary part of a paralegal professional's education. Part II "Introduction to Law" provides the paralegal professional student with this knowledge.

American Legal Heritage and Constitutional Law

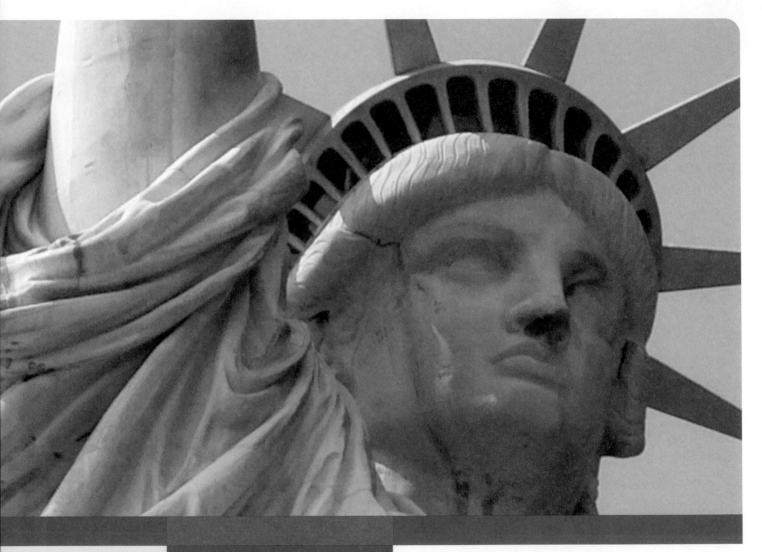

> "We the People of the United States, in Order to form a more perfect Union, establish Justice, insure domestic Tranquility, provide for the common defense, promote the general Welfare, and secure the Blessings of Liberty to ourselves and our Posterity, do ordain and establish this Constitution for the United States of America."
>
> **Preamble to the Constitution of the United States of America**

After studying this chapter, you should be able to:

1. Recognize the professional opportunities for paralegals in the constitutional law area.
2. Define *law* and describe the functions of law.
3. Describe the fairness and flexibility of the law.
4. List and describe the sources of law in the United States.
5. Describe and apply important clauses of the U.S. Constitution.
6. Describe and apply the protections of the Bill of Rights and other amendments to the U.S. Constitution.
7. Explain a paralegal's duty to avoid conflicts of interest.

Paralegals at Work

As a paralegal, you are working for a large law firm that specializes in handling constitutional law issues for clients. You work for Vivian Kang, a senior partner of the law firm. One day Ms. Kang calls you into her office and tells you that a new client, Mr. Hayward Storm, has retained the law firm. Ms. Kang asks you to sit in with her during an interview with Mr. Storm. Mr. Storm arrives on the day of the interview, and Ms. Kang, Mr. Storm, and you go into the conference room.

Mr. Storm tells the following story: For more than twenty years he has been on radio and television, primarily as a disc jockey and talk show host. Mr. Storm most recently hosted television shows where he did outlandish things such as using vulgar language, having guests appear on the show nude, telling disgusting jokes, and doing other things that offend many people. Mr. Storm also hosted a radio show in which he used profanity and offensive language. The Federal Communications Commission (FCC), a federal government agency, is responsible for regulating radio and television. Mr. Storm tells you that the FCC has fined him and his employer for his engaging in such conduct over the television and radio airwaves.

In addition, Mr. Storm explains that he will be leaving regular radio and television, which is regulated by the FCC, and has been hired to be a disc jockey for satellite radio broadcasts. He is making this change because satellite radio currently is not regulated by the FCC. Mr. Storm plans to continue his usual offensive programming on satellite radio and says he will expand his extreme language and conduct because satellite radio is not regulated by the FCC but is concerned that Congress will enact a federal statute granting the FCC power to regulate satellite radio.

Consider the issues involved in this scenario as you read the chapter.

INTRODUCTION FOR THE PARALEGAL

A paralegal must have a foundation in the basic sources of the law of the United States. Our society makes and enforces laws that govern the conduct of the individuals, businesses, and other organizations that function within it. In the words of Judge Learned Hand, "Without law we cannot live; only with it can we insure the future which by right is ours. The best of men's hopes are enmeshed in its success" (*The Spirit of Liberty*, 1960).

Although U.S. law is based primarily on English common law, other legal systems, such as Spanish and French civil law, also influenced it. The sources of law in this country are the U.S. Constitution, state constitutions, federal and state statutes, ordinances, administrative agency rules and regulations, executive orders, and judicial decisions by federal and state courts.

Paralegals should be renaissance men and women, who have an understanding of this country's founding, its constitutional protections, and the current debates concerning the application of the constitutional language in these modern times. This chapter covers the nature and definition of law, the history and sources of law, and the U.S. Constitution.

The following section discusses the career opportunities for paralegal professionals in the constitutional law area.

Web Exploration

Go to www.nps.gov/archive/stli/prod02.htm to read a history of the Statute of Liberty. Visit the World Heritage website describing the Statute of Liberty at www.unesco.org/en/list/307.

CAREER OPPORTUNITIES FOR PARALEGALS IN CONSTITUTIONAL LAW

Some members of the paralegal profession will work on cases that involve constitutional law issues. The Constitution of the United States of America is one of the most important documents ever drafted. The U.S. Constitution created a new country, one that was not ruled by kings, queens, monarchs, or dictators. The country was created as the world's first democracy—a crucial change in the history of the world.

The Constitution has been continually implemented since its ratification more than two centuries ago. The Constitution is considered a "living document" that has been interpreted by the United States Supreme Court and other courts to apply to an ever-changing society.

Paralegals who work in the constitutional law field will be called upon to conduct legal research relating to provisions and amendments to the U.S. Constitution, find relevant cases that interpret constitutional language, and assist lawyers who present cases to the courts regarding constitutional law issues. This is an exciting field of law to participate in as a paralegal professional. Some members of the paralegal profession will be fortunate to work on cases that will be heard and decided by the U.S. Supreme Court.

Several of the major provisions and protections of the U.S. Constitution and its amendments that paralegals should know, and which are covered in this chapter, are:

- Supremacy Clause
- Commerce Clause
- Freedom of speech
- Freedom of religion
- Due Process Clause
- Equal Protection Clause

The U.S. Constitution has many other important provisions as well. Paralegals should be fully informed citizens, and because of their position, understand how the Constitution created the federal government, built in checks and balances, granted powers to the federal government, and established protections for us against unconstitutional intrusions into our lives by the government. The Constitution of the United States of America is set forth in its entirety in Appendix F to this book.

What Is Law?

The first question a paralegal studying American legal heritage must answer is "What is law?" The law consists of rules that regulate the conduct of individuals, businesses, and other organizations within society. Laws are intended to protect persons and their property from unwanted interference from others and forbid persons from engaging in certain undesirable activities.

The concept of **law** is broad. Although it is difficult to state a precise definition, *Black's Law Dictionary*, 5th edition, gives one that is sufficient for this text:

> Law, in its generic sense, is a body of rules of action or conduct prescribed by controlling authority, and having binding legal force. That which must be obeyed and followed by citizens subject to sanctions or legal consequences is a law.

Law That which must be obeyed and followed by citizens subject to sanctions or legal consequences; a body of rules of action or conduct prescribed by controlling authority, and having binding legal force.

Fairness of the Law

On the whole, the American legal system is one of the most comprehensive, fair, and democratic systems of law ever developed and enforced. Nevertheless, some misuses and oversights of our legal system—including abuses of discretion and mistakes by judges and juries, unequal applications of the law, and procedural mishaps—allow some guilty parties to go unpunished.

In *Standefer v. United States* [447 U.S.10, 100 S.Ct.1999 (1980)] the Supreme Court *affirmed* (let stand) the criminal conviction of a Gulf Oil Corporation executive for aiding and abetting the bribery of an Internal Revenue Service agent. The agent had been acquitted in a separate trial. In writing the opinion of the Court, Chief Justice Warren Burger stated, "This case does no more than manifest the simple, if discomforting, reality that different juries may reach different results under any criminal statute. That is one of the consequences we accept under our jury system."

Flexibility of the Law

An important fact for a paralegal professional to learn is that American law is flexible. The law is generally responsive to cultural, technological, economic, and social changes.

Example Laws which are no longer viable—such as those that restricted the property rights of women—are often repealed.

Laws cannot be written in advance to anticipate every dispute that could arise in the future. Therefore, *general principles* are developed to be applied by courts and juries to individual disputes. This flexibility in the law leads to some uncertainty in predicting

FUNCTIONS OF THE LAW

The law is often described by the functions it serves within a society. The primary functions served by U.S. law are:

1. Keeping the peace (e.g., making certain activities crimes).
2. Shaping moral standards (e.g., enacting laws that discourage drug and alcohol abuse).
3. Promoting social justice (e.g., enacting statutes that prohibit discrimination in employment).
4. Maintaining the status quo (e.g., passing laws that prevent the forceful overthrow of government).
5. Facilitating orderly change (e.g., passing statutes only after considerable study, debate, and public input).
6. Facilitating planning (e.g., designing commercial laws to allow businesses to plan their activities, allocate their productive resources, and assess the risks they take).
7. Providing a basis for compromise (approximately 90 percent of all lawsuits are settled prior to trial).
8. Maximizing individual freedom (e.g., the rights of freedom of speech, religion, and association granted by the First Amendment to the U.S. Constitution).

results of lawsuits. The following quote by Judge Jerome Frank addresses the value of the adaptability of law (*Law and the Modern Mind*, 1930):

> The law always has been, is now, and will ever continue to be, largely vague and variable. And how could this be otherwise? The law deals with human relations in their most complicated aspects. The whole confused, shifting helter-skelter of life parades before it—more confused than ever, in our kaleidoscopic age.
>
> Men have never been able to construct a comprehensive, eternalized set of rules anticipating all possible legal disputes and formulating in advance the rules which would apply to them. Situations are bound to occur which were never contemplated when the original rules were made. How much less is such a frozen legal system possible in modern times?
>
> The constant development of unprecedented problems requires a legal system capable of fluidity and pliancy. Our society would be straightjacketed were not the courts, with the able assistance of the lawyers, constantly overhauling the law and adapting it to the realities of ever-changing social, industrial, and political conditions; although changes cannot be made lightly, yet rules of law must be more or less impermanent, experimental and therefore not nicely calculable.
>
> Much of the uncertainty of law is not an unfortunate accident; it is of immense social value.

Sometimes it takes years before the law reflects the norms of society. Other times, society is led by the law.

Schools of Jurisprudential Thought

The philosophy or science of the law is referred to as **jurisprudence**. Several different philosophies have been advanced about how the law developed, ranging from the classical natural theory to modern theories of law and economics and critical legal studies. Legal philosophers can be grouped into the following major categories.

- The **natural law school of jurisprudence** postulates that the law is based on what is "correct." Natural law philosophers emphasize a *moral theory of law*—that is, law should be based on morality and ethics. People "discover" natural law through reasoning and choosing between good and evil. Documents such as the U.S. Constitution, the Magna Carta, and the United Nations Charter reflect this theory.
- The **historical school of jurisprudence** believes that the law is an aggregate of social traditions and customs that have developed over the centuries. Changes in the norms of society will be reflected gradually in the law. The law is an evolutionary process. Thus, historical legal scholars look to past legal decisions (precedent) to solve contemporary problems.
- The **analytical school of jurisprudence** maintains that the law is shaped by logic. Analytical philosophers believe that results are reached by applying principles of logic to the specific facts of the case. The emphasis is on the logic of the result rather than how the result is reached.
- The **sociological school of jurisprudence** asserts that the law is a means of achieving and advancing certain sociological goals. Followers of this philosophy, known as *realists*, believe that the purpose of law is to shape social behavior. Sociological philosophers are unlikely to adhere to past law as precedent.
- The philosophers of the **command school of jurisprudence** believe that the law is a set of rules developed, communicated, and enforced by the ruling party rather than reflecting the society's morality, history, logic, or sociology. This school maintains that the law changes when the ruling class changes.
- The **critical legal studies school of jurisprudence** proposes that legal rules are unnecessary and are used as an obstacle by the powerful to

maintain the status quo. Critical legal theorists (the *"Crits"*) argue that legal disputes should be solved by applying arbitrary rules based on broad notions of what is "fair" in each circumstance. Under this theory, subjective decision making by judges would be permitted.

■ The **law and economics school** proposes that promoting market and economic efficiency should be the central goal of legal decision making. This school is called the "Chicago School" of jurisprudence because it had its roots at the University of Chicago. This school proposes, for example, that free-market principles, cost–benefit analysis, and supply-and-demand theories should be used to determine the passage of legislation and the outcome of lawsuits.

History of American Law

Paralegals need to know the history of the law in the United States and how the law developed to be what it is today. Every person in the United States, and paralegals in particular, should have knowledge of this country's legal history.

When the American colonies were first settled, the English system of common law was generally adopted as the system of jurisprudence. English common law became the source of much of the law of the American colonies and eventually of the United States of America. This was the foundation from which American judges developed a common law in the United States.

English Common Law

English **common law** was law developed by judges who issued their opinions when deciding a case. The principles announced in these cases became precedent for later judges deciding similar cases. The English common law can be divided into cases decided by the following courts:

■ **Law courts.** After 1066, William the Conqueror and his successors to the throne of England replaced various local laws with one uniform system of law. The king or queen appointed loyal followers as judges in all local areas. These judges were charged with administering the law in a uniform manner in what were called **law courts.** Law at this time tended to emphasize form (legal procedure) over the substance (merit) of the case. The only relief available in law courts was a monetary award for damages.

■ **Chancery (equity) courts.** Because of the sometimes unfair results and the limited remedy available in the law courts, a second set of courts— the **Court of Chancery** (or **equity court**)—was established, under the authority of the Lord Chancellor. Those who believed that the decision of the law court was unfair or that the law court could not grant an appropriate remedy could seek relief in the Court of Chancery. The Chancery Court inquired into the merits of the case rather than emphasize legal procedure. The Chancellor's remedies were called *equitable remedies* because they were shaped to fit each situation. Equitable orders and remedies of the Court of Chancery took precedence over the legal decisions and remedies of the law courts.

■ **Merchant courts.** As trade developed in the Middle Ages, the merchants who traveled around England and Europe developed certain rules to solve their commercial disputes. These rules, known as the "law of merchants" or the *law merchant*, were based upon common trade practices and usage. Eventually, a separate set of courts, called the **merchant court,** was established to administer these rules. In the early 1900s, the merchant court was absorbed into the regular law court system of England.

Web Exploration

Read the opinion of Chief Justice Warren of the U.S. Supreme Court in *Brown v. Board of Education* at http://www .nationalcenter.org/brown.html.

Common law Developed by judges who issue their opinions when deciding cases. The principles announced in these cases became precedent for later judges deciding similar cases.

Adoption of the English Common Law in America

All the states of the United States of America (except Louisiana) base their legal systems primarily on the English *common law*. In the United States, the law, equity, and merchant courts have been merged. Thus, most U.S. courts permit the aggrieved party to seek both law and equitable orders and remedies.

The importance of common law to the American legal system is described in the following excerpt from Justice William Douglas's opinion in the 1841 case of *Penny v. Little* [4 Ill. 301, 1841 Ill. Lexis 98 (Ill. 1841)]:

> The common law is a beautiful system, containing the wisdom and experiences of ages. Like the people it ruled and protected, it was simple and crude in its infancy, and became enlarged, improved, and polished as the nation advanced in civilization, virtue, and intelligence. Adapting itself to the conditions and circumstances of the people and relying upon them for its administration, it necessarily improved as the condition of the people was elevated. The inhabitants of this country always claimed the common law as their birthright, and at an early period established it as the basis of their jurisprudence.

Civil Law System

In addition to the Anglo-American common law system, one of the other major legal systems that has developed in the world is the Romano-Germanic **civil law system**. This legal system, commonly called the *civil law*, dates to 450 B.C., when Rome adopted a code of laws applicable to the Romans. A compilation of Roman law, called the *Corpus Juris Civilis* (the Body of Civil Law), was completed in A.D. 534. Later, two national codes—the French Civil Code of 1804 (the Napoleonic Code) and the German Civil Code of 1896—became models for countries that adopted civil codes.

In contrast to the Anglo-American common law, in which laws are created by the judicial system as well as by congressional legislation, the Civil Code and parliamentary statutes that expand and interpret it are the sole sources of the law in most civil law countries. Thus, the adjudication of a case is simply the application of the Code or the statutes to a specific set of facts. In some civil law countries, court decisions do not have the force of law.

Some states in America, particularly states that have a French or Spanish heritage, such as Louisiana and states of the southwestern United States, have incorporated civil law into their legal systems.

U.S. Congress, Washington, DC. The U.S. Congress, which is a bicameral system made up of the U.S. Senate and the U.S. House of Representatives, creates federal law by enacting statutes. Each state has two senators and is allocated a certain number of representatives, based on population.

Sources of Law in the United States

In more than 230 years since the founding of this country and adoption of the English common law, U.S. lawmakers have developed a substantial body of law. The laws of the United States are extremely complex.

Paralegals must have knowledge of the source of the laws that govern their work assignments. Paralegals often are called upon to conduct legal research to find relevant laws and judicial decisions that affect the cases or projects to which they are assigned. This chapter provides a detailed discussion of the sources of law in this country.

The sources of modern law in the United States are discussed in the following sections.

Constitutions

The **Constitution of the United States of America** is the *supreme law of the land*. This means that any law—federal, state, or local—that conflicts with the U.S. Constitution is unconstitutional and, therefore, unenforceable.

The principles enumerated in the Constitution are extremely broad, because the founding fathers intended them to be applied to evolving social, technological, and economic conditions. The U.S. Constitution often is referred to as a "living document" because it is so adaptable.

States also have their own constitutions, often patterned after the U.S. Constitution, though many are more detailed. Provisions of state constitutions are valid unless they conflict with the U.S. Constitution or any valid federal law.

> **Constitution of the United States of America** The supreme law of the United States. The Constitution of the United States of America establishes the structure of the federal government, delegates powers to the federal government, and guarantees certain fundamental rights.

Treaties

The U.S. Constitution provides that the President, with the advice and consent of the U.S. Senate, may enter into **treaties** with foreign governments. Treaties become part of the supreme law of the land. With increasing international economic relations among nations, treaties will become an even more important source of law affecting business in the future.

> **Treaty** A compact made between two or more nations.

Codified Law

Statutes are written laws that establish certain courses of conduct to which the covered parties must adhere. The U.S. Congress is empowered by the Commerce Clause and other provisions of the U.S. Constitution to enact **federal statutes** to regulate foreign and interstate commerce.

> **Statute** Written law enacted by the legislative branch of the federal and state governments that establishes certain courses of conduct that the covered parties must adhere to.

Examples Federal antitrust laws, securities laws, bankruptcy laws, labor laws, equal employment opportunity laws, environmental protection laws, consumer protection laws, and such.

State legislatures also enact **state statutes**.

Examples State corporation laws, partnership laws, workers' compensation laws, and the Uniform Commercial Code.

The statutes enacted by the legislative branches of the federal and state governments are organized by topic into code books, often called **codified law**. Paralegals are often called upon to conduct research to find appropriate codified law for cases that they are assigned to.

State legislatures often delegate lawmaking authority to local government bodies, including cities and municipalities, counties, school districts, water districts, and so on. These governmental units are empowered to adopt **ordinances**.

Examples Traffic laws, local building codes, and zoning laws. Ordinances are also codified.

Administrative Agencies

The legislative and executive branches of federal and state governments are empowered to establish **administrative agencies** to enforce and interpret statutes enacted by Congress and state legislatures. Many of these agencies regulate business.

> **Example** Congress has created the Securities and Exchange Commission (SEC) and the Federal Trade Commission (FTC), among others.

The U.S. Congress or the state legislatures usually empower these agencies to adopt administrative rules and regulations to interpret the statutes that the agency is authorized to enforce. These rules and regulations have the force of law. Administrative agencies usually have the power to hear and decide disputes. Their decisions are called *orders*. Because of their power, administrative agencies often are informally called the "fourth branch" of government.

Executive Orders

The executive branch of government, which consists of the President of the United States and state governors, is empowered to issue executive orders.

This power is derived from express delegation from the legislative branch and is implied from the U.S. Constitution and state constitutions.

> **Example** On October 8, 2001, President George W. Bush by Executive Order established within the Executive Office of the President an Office of Homeland Security to be headed by the Assistant to the President for Homeland Security.

Judicial Decisions

Judicial decision A ruling about an individual lawsuit issued by federal and state courts.

When deciding individual lawsuits, federal and state courts issue **judicial decisions**. In these written opinions, the judge or justice usually explains the legal reasoning used to decide the case. These opinions often include interpretations of statutes, ordinances, administrative regulations, and the announcement of legal principles used to decide the case. Many court decisions are printed (reported) in books available in law libraries.

ETHICAL PERSPECTIVE

Paralegal's Duty to Perform an Assignment

Mr. Harrington, a paralegal, works for attorney Ms. Zhou. Ms. Zhou represents a client who has been charged with insider trading in violation of federal securities laws. Ms. Zhou assigns Mr. Harrington the responsibility of conducting research and finding any relevant court decisions that would apply to the case and any administrative agency rules of the Securities and Exchange Commission (SEC) that might apply to the case as well. Mr. Harrington is to prepare a memorandum summarizing his findings for Ms. Zhou.

Mr. Harrington conducts computer research using Lexis and finds the U.S. Supreme Court and U.S. Court of Appeals decisions that are relevant to the case. But because researching of administrative agency rules is more difficult to conduct, Mr. Harrington fails to check these sources. Mr. Harrington reports his findings of relevant case law to Ms. Zhou, but reports that he has found no relevant SEC administrative rules relevant to the case.

Here, Mr. Harrington has been derelict in his duties in not performing the task he has been given. He has also engaged in deceit by reporting to Ms. Zhou, his supervising attorney, that he has found no relevant SEC agency rules when in fact he has not conducted such research at all. And finally, Mr. Harrington may cause damage to the client who may suffer a loss in court because the supervising attorney Ms. Zhou does not have all of the relevant information to properly prepare her defense for her client.

Priority of Law in the United States

Again, the U.S. Constitution and treaties take precedence over all other laws. Federal statutes take precedence over federal regulations, and valid federal law takes precedence over any conflicting state or local law. State constitutions rank as the highest state law, and state statutes take precedence over state regulations. Valid state law takes precedence over local laws.

The following feature discusses a paralegal's ethical duty to perform lawful duties that are assigned to him or her.

The Doctrine of *Stare Decisis*

Based on the common law tradition, past court decisions become precedent for deciding future cases. Lower courts must follow the precedent established by higher courts. That is why all federal and state courts in the United States must follow the precedents established by U.S. Supreme Court decisions.

The courts of one jurisdiction are not bound by the precedent established by the courts of another jurisdiction, although they may look to each other for guidance. Thus, state courts of one state are not required to follow the legal precedent established by the courts of another state.

Adherence to precedent is called ***stare decisis*** ("to stand by the decision"). The doctrine of *stare decisis* promotes uniformity of law within a jurisdiction, makes the court system more efficient, and makes the law more predictable for individuals and businesses. A court may change or reverse its legal reasoning later if a new case is presented to it and change is warranted.

Stare decisis Latin: "to stand by the decision." Adherence to precedent.

The doctrine of *stare decisis* is discussed in the following excerpt from Justice Musmanno's decision in *Flagiello v. Pennsylvania* [208 A.2d 193, 1965 Pa. Lexis 442 (Pa.1965)].

> Without *stare decisis*, there would be no stability in our system of jurisprudence. Stare decisis channels the law. It erects lighthouses and flies the signals of safety. The ships of jurisprudence must follow that well-defined channel which, over the years, has been proved to be secure and worthy.

Constitution of the United States of America

Prior to the American Revolution, each of the thirteen original colonies operated as a separate sovereignty under the rule of England. In September 1774, representatives of the colonies met as a Continental Congress. In 1776, the colonies declared their independence from England, and the American Revolution ensued.

The Constitutional Convention was convened in Philadelphia in May 1787, with the primary purpose of strengthening the federal government. After substantial debate, the delegates agreed to a new U.S. Constitution, reported to Congress in September 1787. State ratification of the Constitution was completed in 1788. Since that time, many amendments, including the Bill of Rights, have been added to the Constitution.

The U.S. Constitution serves several major functions:

1. It creates the three branches of the federal government (executive, legislative, and judicial) and allocates powers to these branches.
2. It grants the federal government certain authority to enact laws and enforce those laws.
3. It protects individual rights by limiting the government's ability to restrict those rights.

The Constitution itself provides that it may be amended to address social and economic changes. The first page of the Constitution of the United States of America is provided in Exhibit 5.1.

Exhibit 5.1 The Constitution of the United States

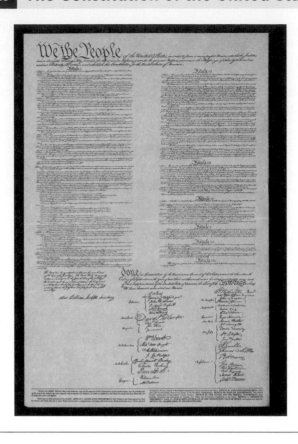

Federalism and Delegated Powers

The U.S. form of government is referred to as **federalism,** which means that the federal government and the 50 state governments share powers. When the states ratified the Constitution, they *delegated* certain powers to the federal government. These **delegated powers,** also called **enumerated powers,** authorize the federal government to deal with national and international affairs. State governments have powers that are not specifically delegated to the federal government by the Constitution and are empowered to deal with local affairs.

Doctrine of Separation of Powers

The first three Articles of the Constitution divide the federal government into three branches:

1. **Article I** of the Constitution establishes the **legislative branch** of government, which is bicameral—consisting of the Senate and the House of Representatives—collectively referred to as *Congress*. Each state is allocated two senators. The number of representatives to the House of Representatives is determined by the population of each state. The current number of representatives is determined from the 2000 census.
2. **Article II** of the Constitution establishes the **executive branch** of government by providing for the election of the President and Vice President. The President is not elected by popular vote but, instead, by the *electoral college*, whose representatives are appointed by state delegations.
3. **Article III** establishes the **judicial branch** of the government in the Supreme Court and provides for the creation of other federal courts by Congress.

Web Exploration

Read the article, "The Power of the Courts—*Marbury v. Madison*, 1803." At the top of the page shown, click on the sixth icon from the left, at http://archives .gov/national-archives-experience/ charters/charters.htm. What was the decision in this case?

Web Exploration

Read the section "How It Works" and answer the following question: "If no candidate for President receives an absolute electoral majority, how is the President of the United States elected?" at http://en.wikipedia.org/wiki/u.s. _electoral_college.

Checks and Balances

Certain **checks and balances** are built into the Constitution to ensure that no one branch of the federal government becomes too powerful. Some of the checks and balances in our system of government are as follows:

1. The judicial branch has authority to examine the acts of the other two branches of government and determine whether these acts are constitutional.
2. The executive branch can enter into treaties with foreign governments only with the advice and consent of the Senate.
3. The legislative branch is authorized to create federal courts and determine their jurisdiction and to enact statutes that change judicially made law.
4. The President has veto power over bills passed by Congress. The bill goes back to Congress, where a vote of two-thirds of each the Senate and the House of Representatives is required to override the President's veto.
5. The President nominates persons to be U.S. Supreme Court justices, and many other federal judges, but the U.S. Senate must confirm the candidate before he or she becomes a judge.
6. The House of Representatives has the power to impeach the President for certain activities, such as treason, bribery, and other crimes. The Senate has the power to try the impeachment case, which requires a two-thirds vote of the Senate to impeach the President.

Supremacy Clause

The **Supremacy Clause** establishes that the federal Constitution, treaties, federal laws, and federal regulations are the supreme law of the land [Article VI, Section 2]. State and local laws that conflict with valid federal law are unconstitutional. The concept of federal law taking precedence over state or local law is called the **preemption doctrine**.

Supremacy Clause A clause of the U.S. Constitution that establishes that the federal Constitution, treaties, federal laws, and federal regulations are the supreme law of the land.

Congress may expressly provide that a specific federal statute *exclusively* regulates a specific area or activity. No state or local law regulating the area or activity is valid if there is such a statute. More often, though, federal statutes do not expressly provide for exclusive jurisdiction. In these instances, state and local governments have *concurrent jurisdiction* to regulate the area or activity. But any state or local law that "directly and substantially" conflicts with valid federal law is preempted under the Supremacy Clause.

> **Example** The United States government entered into treaties with other countries that established the size and length of oil tanker ships. Thus, oil tankers can transport oil between different countries using the same oil tankers. The state of Washington enacted a law that only permitted smaller oil tankers to enter its Puget Sound watercourse, which flows from waters of the Pacific Ocean. Oil tanker companies sued the state of Washington, arguing that the state law was unconstitutional. The U.S. Supreme Court held that the state law conflicted with federal law and was therefore preempted by the Supremacy Clause.

Commerce Clause

The **Commerce Clause** of the U.S. Constitution grants Congress the power "to regulate commerce with foreign nations, and among the several states, and with Indian tribes" [Article I, Section 8, Clause 3]. Because this clause authorizes the federal government to regulate commerce, it has a greater impact on business than any other provision in the Constitution. Among other things, this clause is intended to foster the development of a national market and free trade among the states.

Commerce Clause A clause of the U.S. Constitution that grants Congress the power "to regulate commerce with foreign nations, and among the several states, and with Indian tribes."

The U.S. Constitution grants the federal government the power to regulate three types of commerce. These are:

1. Commerce with Indian tribes
2. Commerce with foreign nations
3. Interstate commerce

Native Americans

Web Exploration

Visit the website of the National Museum of the American Indian at www.nmai .si.edu. Go to http://www.youtube .com/watch?v=Gve7avdld78& feature=related and view the video about the "Trail of Tears." When did this occur?

Before Europeans arrived in the "New World," the land had been occupied for thousands of years by who we now refer to as Native Americans. When the United States was first founded over two centuries ago, it consisted of the original thirteen colonies, all located in the east, primarily on the Atlantic Ocean. At that time, these colonies (states), in the U.S. Constitution, delegated to the federal government the authority to regulate commerce with the Indian tribes. This included the original thirteen states as well as the territory that was to eventually become the United States of America.

Example The federal government enacted the Indian Gaming Regulatory Act[1] wherein the federal government authorized Native American tribes to operate gaming facilities. This act sets the terms of casino gambling and other gaming activities on tribal land. Today, casinos operated by Native Americans can be found in many states. Profits from the casinos have become an important source of income for members of certain tribes.

Foreign Commerce

The Commerce Clause gives the federal government the exclusive power to regulate commerce with foreign nations. Direct or indirect regulation of foreign commerce by state or local governments violates the Commerce Clause and is therefore unconstitutional.

Example Suppose the state of Michigan imposes a 20 percent sales tax on foreign automobiles sold in Michigan but only 6 percent tax on domestic automobiles sold in Michigan. This state act violates the Commerce Clause because Michigan has regulated foreign commerce differently than state commerce. If Michigan placed a 20 percent sales tax on all automobiles sold in Michigan, this would not violate the Commerce Clause. Under its Foreign Commerce Clause power, the federal government could enact a federal law that places a 20 percent tax on foreign automobiles sold in the United States.

Interstate Commerce

The Commerce Clause gives the federal government the authority to regulate **interstate commerce**. Originally, the courts interpreted this clause to mean that the federal government could regulate only commerce that moved *in* interstate commerce. The modern rule, however, allows the federal government to regulate activities that *affect* interstate commerce.

Web Exploration

Go to www.uscis.gov/portal/site/ uscis. Find information on this website that shows how to become a citizen of the United States of America.

Under the *effects on interstate commerce test*, the regulated activity does not itself have to be in interstate commerce. Thus, any **intrastate** (local) **commerce** that has an effect on interstate commerce is subject to federal regulation. Theoretically, this test subjects a substantial amount of business activity in the United States to federal regulation.

Example In the famous case of *Wickard, Secretary of Agriculture v. Filburn* [317 U.S. 111, 63 S.Ct. 82, 87 L.Ed. 122, 1942 U.S. Lexis 1046 (U.S.)] a federal statute limited the amount of wheat a farmer could plant and harvest for home consumption. Filburn, a farmer, violated the law. The U.S. Supreme Court

[1] 25 U.S.C. Sections 2701–2721.

upheld the statute on the grounds that it prevented nationwide surpluses and shortages of wheat. The Court reasoned that wheat grown for home consumption would affect the supply of wheat available in interstate commerce.

State Police Power

The states did not delegate all power to regulate business to the federal government. They retained the power to regulate intrastate and much interstate business activity that occurs within their borders. This is commonly referred to as states' **police power**.

Police power permits states (and, by delegation, local governments) to enact laws to protect or promote the *public health, safety, morals, and general welfare.* This includes the authority to enact laws that regulate the conduct of business.

Examples   State environmental laws, corporation and partnership laws, property laws, and local zoning ordinances and building codes are enacted under this power.

Bill of Rights and Other Amendments

In 1791, the states approved the 10 amendments commonly referred to as the **Bill of Rights,** and they became part of the U.S. Constitution (see Exhibit 5.2). The Bill of Rights guarantees certain fundamental rights to natural persons and protects these rights from intrusive government action. Most of these rights, or "freedoms," also have been found applicable to so-called artificial persons (i.e., corporations).

The First Amendment to the Constitution guarantees the rights of free speech, assembly, and religion. In addition to the Bill of Rights, seventeen amendments have been added to the Constitution. Two important clauses from these amendments are the Due Process Clause and the Equal Protection Clause. Because these amendments are continually litigated and are frequent subjects of U.S. Supreme Court opinions, they are singled out for discussion in the following paragraphs.

Bill of Rights The first 10 amendments to the Constitution. They were added to the U.S. Constitution in 1791.

Web Exploration

Go to http://www.youtube.com/ watch?v=ENiBuwkScEA to listen to a reading of the Bill of Rights.

Exhibit 5.2   Bill of Rights

Freedom of Speech

One of the most honored freedoms guaranteed by the Bill of Rights is the **freedom of speech** of the First Amendment. Many other constitutional freedoms would be meaningless without it. The First Amendment's Freedom of Speech Clause protects speech only, not conduct. The U.S. Supreme Court places speech into three categories: (1) fully protected, (2) limited protected, and (3) unprotected speech.

Fully Protected Speech

Fully protected speech is speech that the government cannot prohibit or regulate. Political speech is an example of such speech.

> **Example** The government could not enact a law that forbids citizens from criticizing the current President.

> The First Amendment protects oral, written, and symbolic speech.

> **Example** If a person burns the American flag in protest of a current government policy, this is symbolic speech that is protected by the First Amendment.

Limited Protected Speech

The Supreme Court has held that certain types of speech are only **limited protected speech** under the First Amendment. Although the government cannot forbid this type of speech, it can subject this speech to restrictions of time, place, and manner. The following types of speech are accorded limited protection:

- **Offensive speech** is speech that offends many members of society. (It is not the same as obscene speech, however.) The Supreme Court has held that offensive speech may be restricted by the government under time, place, and manner restrictions.

  > **Example** The Federal Communications Commission (FCC) can regulate the use of offensive language on television by limiting such language to times when children would be unlikely to be watching (e.g., late at night).

- **Commercial speech** is speech such as advertising and business solicitation. The Supreme Court has held that commercial speech is subject to proper time, place, and manner restrictions.

  > **Example** A city could prohibit billboards along its highways for safety and aesthetic reasons as long as other forms of advertising (e.g., print media) are available to the commercial advertiser.

Unprotected Speech

There are certain types of speech that the U.S. Supreme Court has held has no protection under the Freedom of Speech Clause. These types of speech may be entirely prohibited by the government. The Supreme Court has held that the following types of speech are **unprotected speech** under the First Amendment and may be totally forbidden by the government:

- Dangerous speech (including such things as yelling "fire" in a crowded theater when there is no fire)
- Fighting words that are likely to provoke a hostile or violent response from an average person
- Speech that incites the violent or revolutionary overthrowing of the government; the mere abstract teaching of the morality and consequences of such action is protected
- Defamatory language
- Child pornography
- Obscene speech

Definition of Obscene Speech

The definition of **obscene speech** is quite subjective. One Supreme Court justice stated, "I know it when I see it" [Justice Stewart in *Facobellis v. Ohio*, 378 U.S. 184, 84 S.Ct. 1676 12 L.Ed.2d 793, 1964 U.S. Lexis 822 (U.S.)]. In *Miller v. California*, the Supreme Court determined that speech is obscene under the following circumstances.

1. The average person, applying contemporary community standards, would find that the work, taken as a whole, appeals to the prurient interest.
2. The work depicts or describes, in a patently offensive way, sexual conduct specifically defined by the applicable state law.
3. The work, taken as a whole, lacks serious literary, artistic, political, or scientific value. [413 U.S. 15, 93 S.Ct. 2607, 37 L.Ed.2d 419, 1973 U.S. Lexis 149 (U.S.)]

States are free to define what constitutes obscene speech. Movie theaters, magazine publishers, Web operators, and so on are often subject to challenges that the materials they display or sell are obscene and, therefore, not protected by the First Amendment.

Free Speech in Cyberspace

Paralegals are at the forefront of witnessing development and application of traditional laws to the digital age. This is nowhere more relevant than the application of constitutional provisions—drafted centuries ago—to the modern age. Once or twice a century a new medium seems to come along that presents new problems in applying freedom-of-speech rights. This time it is the Internet. The following is a U.S. Supreme Court case that addressed free speech in cyberspace.

The U.S. Congress enacted the *Computer Decency Act* to regulate the Internet. This statute made it a felony to knowingly make "indecent" or "patently offensive" materials available on computer systems, including the Internet, to persons under 18 years of age. The Act provided for fines, prison terms, and loss of licenses for anyone convicted of violating its terms.

Immediately, cyberspace providers and users filed lawsuits challenging these provisions of the Act as violating their free speech rights granted under the First Amendment to the Constitution. Proponents of the Act countered that these provisions were necessary to protect children from indecent materials.

The U.S. Supreme Court decided to hear this issue. The Supreme Court came down on the plaintiff's side, overturning the challenged provisions of the Computer Decency Act. The Court found that the terms "indecent" and "patently offensive" were too vague to define and criminally enforce. The Supreme Court reasoned that limiting the content on the Internet to what is suitable for a child resulted in unconstitutional limiting of adult speech. The Court stated that parents can regulate their children's access to the Internet and can install blocking and filtering software programs to protect their children from seeing adult materials.

The Supreme Court declared emphatically that the Internet must be given the highest possible level of First Amendment free-speech protection. The Supreme Court stated,

> As the most participatory form of mass speech yet developed, the Internet deserves the highest protection from government intrusion.

The Court also reasoned that because the Internet is a global medium, there would be no way to prevent indecent material from flowing over the Internet from abroad.[2]

---

[2]*Reno v. American Civil Liberties Union*, 521 U.S. 844, 117 S.Ct. 2329, 138 L.Ed.2d 874, **Web** 1997 U.S. Lexis 4037 (Supreme Court of the United States).

Protest, Los Angeles, California. The Freedom of Speech Clause of the First Amendment to the U.S. Constitution protects the right to engage in political speech. Freedom of speech is one of Americans' most highly prized rights.

Freedom of Religion

The U.S. Constitution requires federal, state, and local governments to be neutral toward religion. The First Amendment actually contains two separate religion clauses:

Establishment Clause A clause to the First Amendment that prohibits the government from either establishing a state religion or promoting one religion over another.

1. The **Establishment Clause** prohibits the government from either establishing a state religion or promoting one religion over another. Thus, it guarantees that there will be no state-sponsored religion.

   Example The U.S. Supreme Court ruled that an Alabama statute that authorized a one-minute period of silence in school for "meditation or voluntary prayer" was invalid.[3] The Court held that the statute endorsed religion.

   Example The U.S. Supreme Court held that copies of the Ten Commandments that were prominently displayed in large, gold-frames, and hung alone in the McCreary County courthouse and the Pulaski County courthouse in Kentucky, so that visitors could see them, violated the Establishment Clause.[4]

Free Exercise Clause A clause to the First Amendment that prohibits the government from interfering with the free exercise of religion in the United States.

2. The **Free Exercise Clause** prohibits the government from interfering with the free exercise of religion in the United States. Generally, this clause prevents the government from enacting laws that either prohibit or inhibit individuals from participating in or practicing their chosen religion.

   Example The federal, state, or local governments could not enact a law that prohibited all religions or that prohibited churches, synagogues, mosques, or temples. The government could not prohibit religious practitioners from celebrating their major holidays and high holy days. Of course, this right to be free from government intervention in the practice of religion is not absolute.

   Example Human sacrifices are unlawful and are not protected by the First Amendment.

---

[3]*Wallace v. Jaffree*, 472 U.S. 38, 105 S.Ct. 2479, 86 L.Ed.2d 29, **Web** 1985 U.S. Lexis 91 (Supreme Court of the United States).

[4]*McCreary County, Kentucky v. American Civil Liberties Union*, 545 U.S. 844, 125 S.Ct. 2722, 162 L.Ed.2d 729, **Web** 2005 U.S. Lexis 5211 (Supreme Court of the United States).

Paralegals *in* Practice

PARALEGAL PROFILE
Charlotte A. Sheraden-Baker

Charlotte A. Sheraden-Baker started her legal career as a legal secretary after graduating from high school. After taking time out to raise a family, she resumed work as a legal secretary while attending night school to obtain her paralegal degree. In 2000, she graduated as Paralegal of the Year with an Associate of Applied Science degree, the oldest person in her class. After convincing her firm they needed another paralegal, Charlotte was promoted and continued evening classes to obtain her Bachelor of Arts degree. She currently works for the law firm of Warner, Smith & Harris in Fort Smith, Arkansas, where she has been employed for the last 14 years.

I work for a general practice that has 13 partners and three associates. I recently assisted in a constitutional law case that was appealed to the Arkansas Supreme Court over a First Amendment issue. Our client was a party to a lawsuit between two groups of a local temple. Both thought they were entitled to make governing rules for the temple, and maintain its original assets and location. Since the matter could not be resolved between the opposing parties, the state court judge was asked to do so, and determined that an election should be held, whereby the temple members would decide.

In the process, my firm's attorneys contended that the judge overstepped his duties by overriding the already-established governing documents of the temple and assigning a different definition as to who was a member of the congregation and entitled to vote. It was argued that the judge had prohibited the free exercise of religion, as guaranteed by the First Amendment of both the federal and state constitutions. Our case was lost on appeal because it was determined the judge did not intrude into anyone's religious rights. Nonetheless, the case was a great learning experience in my legal career.

At the state court level, some of my pretrial duties included preparing, gathering, and duplicating exhibits; copying and keeping up-to-date on important documents; making lists of witnesses and exhibits; and more. At trial, my primary job was to ensure that the judge, court clerk, and court reporter had all the necessary documents; monitor exhibits offered, admitted, or rejected; organize witnesses and keep track of their appearances and testimony; and take notes of testimony to help with the attorney's upcoming examinations.

My duties at the state Supreme Court level were slightly different. For any case that is appealed, each party gets to prepare a brief, and respond to the other party's brief within a short time. Then, the case is set for oral argument before the state Supreme Court. Preparation of appellate briefs is complicated and precise, as the Supreme Courts require specific style, format, and contents. I was asked to monitor filing deadlines, obtain the local trial transcripts and submit them to the Supreme Court, prepare an extensive summary of the pertinent trial testimony for the appeal brief, and verify or "Shepardize" all cases cited in the brief itself.

Due Process Clause

The **Due Process Clause** provides that no person shall be deprived of "life, liberty, or property" without due process of the law. It is contained in both the Fifth and the Fourteenth Amendments. The Due Process Clause of the Fifth Amendment applies to federal government action; that of the Fourteenth Amendment applies to state and local government action. The government is not prohibited from taking a person's life, liberty, or property, but the government must follow due process to do so. There are two categories of due process: *substantive* and *procedural*.

Due Process Clause A clause that provides that no person shall be deprived of "life, liberty, or property" without due process of the law.

Substantive Due Process

Substantive due process requires that government statutes, ordinances, regulations, or other laws be clear on their face and not overly broad in scope. The test of whether substantive due process is met is whether a "reasonable person" could understand the law to be able to comply with it. Laws that do not meet this test are declared *void for vagueness*.

> **Example** A city ordinance that makes it illegal for persons to wear "clothes of the opposite sex" would be held unconstitutional as void for vagueness because a reasonable person could not clearly determine whether his or her conduct violates the law.

Procedural Due Process

Web Exploration

How does Louisiana law differ from the other 49 states? Go to: http://www.la-legal.com/history_louisiana_law.htm.

Procedural due process requires that the government give a person proper *notice* and *hearing* of the legal action before that person is deprived of his or her life, liberty, or property. The government action must be fair.

Example If the federal government or a state government brings a criminal lawsuit against a defendant for the alleged commission of a crime, the government must notify the person of its intent (by charging the defendant with a crime) and provide the defendant with a proper hearing (a trial).

Example If the government wants to take a person's home by eminent domain to build a highway, the government must (1) give the homeowner sufficient notice of its intention, and (2) provide a hearing. Under the **Just Compensation Clause** of the Fifth Amendment, the government must pay the owner just compensation for taking the property.

Equal Protection Clause

Equal Protection Clause

A clause that provides that state, local, and federal governments cannot deny to any person the "equal protection of the laws."

The **Equal Protection Clause** of the Fourteenth Amendment to the Constitution, as interpreted by the U.S. Supreme Court, provides that state, local, and federal governments cannot deny to any person the "equal protection of the laws." The clause prohibits governments from enacting laws that classify and treat similarly situated persons differently. The clause is designed to prohibit invidious government discrimination. Natural persons and businesses are protected.

The Equal Protection Clause has not been interpreted literally by the U.S. Supreme Court. The Supreme Court has held that some government laws that treat people or businesses differently are constitutional. The Supreme Court has adopted three different standards for determining whether a government action that treats some persons or businesses differently than others is lawful:

1. *Strict scrutiny test.* Any government activity or regulation that classifies persons based on a *suspect class* (i.e., race) is reviewed for lawfulness using a strict scrutiny test. Under this standard, most government classifications of persons based on race are found to be unconstitutional.

   Example A government rule that permitted persons of one race, but not of another race, to receive government benefits such as Medicaid, would violate this test. But affirmative action programs that give racial minorities a "plus factor" when considered for public university admission is lawful, as long as it does not constitute a quota system.

2. *Intermediate scrutiny test.* The lawfulness of government classifications based on *protected classes* other than race (such as sex or age) is examined using an intermediate scrutiny test. Under this standard, the courts determine whether the government classification is "reasonably related" to a legitimate government purpose.

   Example A rule prohibiting persons over a certain age from military combat would be lawful, but a rule prohibiting persons over a certain age from acting as government engineers would not be. With regard to a person's gender, the U.S. Supreme Court has held that the federal government can require males, but not females, to register with the military for a possible draft.

3. ***Rational basis test***. The lawfulness of all government classifications that do not involve suspect or protected classes is examined using a rational basis test. Under this test, the courts will uphold government regulation as long as there is a justifiable reason for the law. This standard permits much of the government regulation of business.

Example Providing government subsidies to farmers but not to those in other occupations is permissible.

The ethical duty and social responsibility of a paralegal professional to avoid conflicts of interest is discussed in the following feature.

ETHICAL PERSPECTIVE

Paralegal's Duty to Avoid Conflicts of Interest

Ms. Jennifer Adams is hired as a paralegal at a law firm with expertise in real estate development law. She recently left a paralegal position at another law firm to take the new paralegal position with the current law firm.

At the new firm, Ms. Adams is assigned to work as the paralegal for Mr. Humberto Cruz, a senior partner of the law firm. Mr. Cruz is an expert in complex real estate transactions representing clients in the purchase, development, and leasing of large shopping malls. One client whom Mr. Cruz represents is Modern Properties L.P., a limited partnership that constructs and operates retail shopping malls across the country.

One day Mr. Cruz asks Ms. Adams to attend a meeting with himself and the president of Modern Properties L.P. At the meeting, the president of Modern Properties L.P. discloses a dispute that the partnership has with a tenant, Third National Bank, concerning the lease of a building by Third National Bank at a mall constructed and operated by Modern Properties L.P. The president explains that Third National Bank has filed a lawsuit against Modern Properties L.P. concerning this dispute. The president further explains that the partnership wants Mr. Cruz to represent the partnership in this lawsuit.

Ms. Adams realizes that her prior law firm represented Third National Bank in many lawsuits, and that she had worked as the paralegal on several of the cases involving Third National Bank. During the course of this work, she became privy to confidential information about Third National Bank, including its financial condition, operations, and legal strategy.

Does Ms. Adams have a conflict of interest? If so, what should she do?

Model and state paralegal Code of Ethics and Professional Responsibility provide that a paralegal is under a duty to avoid conflicts of interest. Thus, a paralegal cannot conduct work on any matter where there would be a conflict of interest with a present or past employer or with a client.

PARALEGAL'S ETHICAL DECISION

Thus, Ms. Adams must immediately disclose the fact that she previously worked on cases involving Third National Bank at the prior law firm where she was employed, and that because of that employment she possesses confidential information about Third National Bank. Because of this conflict of interest, Ms. Adams must excuse herself from working on the *Third National Bank v. Modern Properties L.P.* case.

Concept Review *and* Reinforcement

LEGAL TERMINOLOGY

Administrative agencies 184

Analytical school
   of jurisprudence 180

Bill of Rights 189

Court of Chancery
   (or equity court) 181

Checks and balances 187

Civil law system 182

Codified law 183

Command school of
   jurisprudence 180

Commerce Clause 187

Commercial speech 190

Common law 181

Constitution of the United States
   of America 183

Critical legal studies school
   of jurisprudence 180

Delegated powers 186

Due Process Clause 193

Enumerated powers 186

Equal Protection Clause 194

Establishment Clause 192

Executive branch 186

Federal statutes 183

Federalism 186

Free Exercise Clause 192

Freedom of speech 190

Fully protected speech 190

Historical school
   of jurisprudence 180

Intermediate scrutiny test 194

Interstate commerce 188

Intrastate commerce 188

Judicial branch 186

Judicial decision 184

Jurisprudence 180

Just Compensation Clause 194

Law 179

Law and economics school 181

Law courts 181

Legislative branch 186

Limited protected speech 190

Merchant court 181

Natural law school of
   jurisprudence 180

Obscene speech 191

Offensive speech 190

Ordinances 183

Police power 189

Preemption doctrine 187

Procedural due process 194

Rational basis test 195

Separation of powers 186

Sociological school of
   jurisprudence 180

Stare decisis 185

State statutes 183

Statutes 183

Strict scrutiny test 194

Substantive due process 193

Supremacy Clause 187

Treaty 183

Unprotected speech 190

SUMMARY OF KEY CONCEPTS

What Is Law?

Definition	Law consists of a body of rules of action or conduct prescribed by controlling authority and having binding legal force.
Functions of Law	1. Keep the peace 2. Shape moral standards 3. Promote social justice 4. Maintain the status quo 5. Facilitate orderly change 6. Facilitate planning 7. Provide a basis for compromise 8. Maximize individual freedom
Fairness	Although the American legal system is one of the fairest and most democratic systems of law, abuses and mistakes in the application of the law still occur.
Flexibility	The law must be flexible to meet social, technological, and economic changes.

Schools of Jurisprudential Thought

Natural Law	Postulates that law is based on what is "correct"; it emphasizes a moral theory of law—that is, law should be based on morality and ethics.
Historical	Believes that law is an aggregate of social traditions and customs.
Analytical	Maintains that law is shaped by logic.
Sociological	Asserts that the law is a means of achieving and advancing certain sociological goals.
Command	Believes that the law is a set of rules developed, communicated, and enforced by the ruling party.
Critical Legal Studies	Maintains that legal rules are unnecessary and that legal disputes should be solved by applying arbitrary rules based on fairness.
Law and Economics	Believes that promoting market efficiency should be the central concern of legal decision making.

History of American Law

English Common Law	English common law (judge-made law) forms the basis of the legal systems of most states in this country. Louisiana bases its law on the French civil code.

Sources of Law in the United States

Constitutions	The U.S. Constitution establishes the federal government and enumerates its powers. Powers not given to the federal government are reserved to the states. State constitutions establish state governments and enumerate their powers.
Treaties	The President, with the advice and consent of the Senate, may enter into treaties with foreign countries.
Codified Law	1. *Statutes* are enacted by Congress and state legislatures. 2. *Ordinances* and statutes are passed by municipalities and local government bodies to establish courses of conduct that must be followed by covered parties.
Administrative Agencies	Administrative agencies are created by the legislative and executive branches of government; they may adopt rules and regulations that govern the conduct of covered parties.
Executive Orders	Executive orders, issued by the President and governors of states, regulate the conduct of covered parties.
Judicial Decisions	Courts decide controversies by issuing decisions that state the holding of each case and the rationale the court used to reach that decision.

Doctrine of Stare Decisis

Definition	*Stare decisis* means "to stand by the decision." This doctrine provides for adherence to precedent.

Constitution of the United States of America

Scope	The Constitution consists of seven articles and 27 amendments. It establishes the three branches of the federal government, enumerates their powers, and provides important guarantees of individual freedom. The Constitution was ratified by the states in 1788.

Basic Constitutional Concepts	1. *Federalism:* The Constitution created the federal government, which shares power with the state governments.
	2. *Delegated powers:* When the states ratified the Constitution, they delegated certain powers, called *enumerated powers*, to the federal government.
	3. *Reserved powers:* Those powers not granted to the federal government by the Constitution are reserved to the states.
	4. *Separation of powers:* Each branch of the federal government has separate powers.
	  a. Legislative branch—power to make the law
	  b. Executive branch—power to enforce the law
	  c. Judicial branch—power to interpret the law
	5. *Checks and balances:* Certain checks and balances are built into the Constitution to ensure that no one branch of the federal government becomes too powerful.

Supremacy Clause

The Supremacy Clause stipulates that the U.S. Constitution, treaties, and federal law (statutes and regulations) are the *supreme law of the land*. State or local laws that conflict with valid federal law are unconstitutional. This is called the *preemption doctrine*.

Commerce Clause

1. *Commerce Clause:* Authorizes the federal government to regulate commerce with foreign nations, among the states, and with Indian tribes.
2. *Interstate commerce:* Under the broad *effects test*, the federal government may regulate any activity (even intrastate commerce) that *affects* interstate commerce.
3. *Police Powers:* Power reserved to the states to regulate commerce.

Bill of Rights and Other Amendments

1. *Bill of Rights:* The Bill of Rights consists of the first 10 amendments to the Constitution. They establish basic individual rights. The Bill of Rights was ratified in 1791.
2. *Other amendments:* In addition to the 10 amendments of the Bill of Rights, there are seventeen other amendments to the U.S. Constitution.

Freedom of Speech

Freedom of Speech Clause of the First Amendment guarantees that the government shall not infringe on a person's right to speak. Protects oral, written, and symbolic speech. This right is not absolute—that is, some speech is not protected and other speech is granted only limited protection. The U.S. Supreme Court has placed speech in the following three categories:

1. *Fully protected speech:* Speech that cannot be prohibited or regulated by the government
2. *Limited protected speech:* Types of speech that are granted only limited protection under the Freedom of Speech Clause—that is, they are subject to governmental *time, place, and manner restrictions:*
   a. Offensive speech
   b. Commercial speech
3. *Unprotected speech:* Speech that is not protected by the Freedom of Speech Clause:
   a. Dangerous speech
   b. Fighting words
   c. Speech that advocates the violent overthrow of the government
   d. Defamatory language
   e. Child pornography
   f. Obscene speech

Freedom of Religion

There are two religion clauses in the First Amendment. They are:
1. *Establishment Clause.* Prohibits the government from establishing a state religion or promoting religion
2. *Free Exercise Clause.* Prohibits the government from interfering with the free exercise of religion. This right is not absolute: for example, human sacrifices are forbidden.

Due Process Clause

Due Process Clause provides that no person shall be deprived of "life, liberty, or property" without due process. There are two categories of due process:
1. *Substantive due process:* Requires that laws be clear on their face and not overly broad in scope. Laws that do not meet this test are *void for vagueness*.
2. *Procedural due process:* Requires that the government give a person proper *notice* and *hearing* before that person is deprived of his or her life, liberty, or property. An owner must be paid *just compensation* if the government takes his or her property.

Equal Protection Clause

Equal Protection Clause prohibits the government from enacting laws that classify and treat "similarly situated" persons differently. This standard is not absolute and the government can treat persons differently in certain situations. The U.S. Supreme Court has applied the following tests to determine if the Equal Protection Clause has been violated:
1. *Strict scrutiny test.* Applies to *suspect classes* (e.g., race, national origin)
2. *Intermediate scrutiny test.* Applies to other *protected classes* (e.g., sex, age)
3. *Rational basis test.* Applies to government classifications that do not involve a suspect or protected class

WORKING THE WEB

1. Go to the website http://www.usconstitution.net/const.html. Scroll down to "Amendment 7." When was this amendment ratified? What does this amendment provide? Explain.
2. Visit the website http://www.archives.gov/exhibits/charters/charters.html. A page entitled "The Charters of Freedom—A New World is at Hand" will appear on your computer screen. Do the following exercises:
   a. On the page shown, click on the third icon from the left. Read the article entitled, "The Spirit of the Revolution—The Declaration of Independence." What did the Declaration of Independence do? Explain.
   b. On the page shown, click on the sixth icon from the left. Read the article "The Constitutional Convention—Creation of the Constitution." How many states were required to ratify the Constitution for it to be enacted?
   c. At the top of the page shown, click on the second-to-the-last icon from the right. Read the article "Expansion of Rights and Liberties—The Right of Suffrage." What amendment to the U.S. Constitution gave women the right to vote? What year was this amendment ratified?
3. Visit the website http://www.senate.gov/. Click on the word "Senators." Who are the two senators who represent your state in the U.S. Senate? Go to each senator's website and email the senator, expressing your view on a legal issue in which you are interested.
4. Visit the website http://www.house.gov/. Who is the person who represents your home district? Go to that representative's website and read about his or her position on a current legal issue. What is the issue, and what is your representative's view on it?
5. Go to http://google.com. Choose a country in which you are interested and search for a treaty of this country (e.g., "China treaty"). Briefly describe this treaty.

CRITICAL THINKING & WRITING QUESTIONS

1. Define the "law." Is this an easy concept to define? Why?
2. What functions does the law serve? Which of these functions do you think is the most important?
3. Is the law always fair? Give an example of where you think the law was applied unfairly.
4. Should the language of the U.S. Constitution be applied in its original meaning, or should it be applied in a more expansive sense? Explain.
5. What is the power of the legislative branch of government? What is a statute?
6. Do you think that the U.S. Supreme Court makes law when it interprets the U.S. Constitution? Explain.
7. What is the doctrine of *stare decisis*? Why is this doctrine important?
8. What does the doctrine of federalism provide?
9. What does the doctrine of separation of powers provide? Can you give any examples where the separation of the powers of the three branches of government is blurred?
10. What does the doctrine of checks and balances provide? Can you give any examples where one branch of the government checks the power of another branch of the government?
11. What does the Supremacy Clause provide? What would be the consequences if the Supremacy Clause did not exist? Explain.
12. What does the Commerce Clause of the U.S. Constitution do? Explain.
13. The First Amendment to the U.S. Constitution contains the Freedom of Speech Clause. Explain the difference between fully protected speech, partially protected speech, and unprotected speech.
14. The U.S. Constitution guarantees freedom of religion. Explain the difference between the Establishment Clause and the Free Exercise Clause. Can you give an example of a legitimate government restriction of a possible religious practice?
15. What is the difference between substantive due process and procedural due process? Explain.
16. What does the Equal Protection Clause provide? Explain the differences between the (a) strict scrutiny test, (b) intermediate scrutiny test, and (c) rational basis test.

Building Paralegal Skills

VIDEO CASE STUDIES

Difference Between a Criminal and a Civil Trial

An interview with Judge Kenney, a trial court judge, who discusses the difference between a civil and a criminal trial.

After viewing the video case study at www.pearsonhighered.com/goldman answer the following:

1. What are the differences in the burden of proof between a criminal and civil matter?
2. What protections does the U.S. Constitution afford those accused of criminal acts?

A School Principal Reacts: Student Rights Versus School's Duty

As the result of an altercation in a school bus, and a claim that the student involved had a contraband knife on his person, the principal has ordered that he be searched for the knife.

After viewing the video case study at www.pearsonhighered .com/goldman answer the following:

1. Does a student have a constitutional right of privacy?
2. Does the school have a right to search a student?
3. Is the school district and those working for it immune from suit for the actions taken?

Confidentiality Issue: Attorney–Client Privilege

Paralegal Alicia Jackson meets with a client to review answers to documents that must be sent to opposing counsel. While reviewing the answers he tells her about a potentially fraudulent claim.

After viewing the video case study at www.pearsonhighered .com/goldman answer the following:

1. Does the attorney–client privilege apply to information given to a paralegal?
2. To whom does the privilege belong?
3. How is the attorney–client privilege different from the duty of confidentiality?

ETHICS ANALYSIS & DISCUSSION QUESTIONS

1. Are there any ethical issues in allowing one's personal feelings to be expressed in working on a case? What if you have strong feelings against the client's position?

2. Does the American system of law depend on the legal team to put aside its personal beliefs and work diligently on unpopular cases or issues? How does this ensure equal justice and allow for change in the system?

3. You are working in a law firm for an attorney who has had a series of strokes that have caused a permanent reading disability and memory impairment. Do you have any ethical obligation to the attorney's clients? Do you have any ethical obligation to the firm and to the attorney? [Philadelphia Ethics Opinion 2002-12 (2000); also, see Texas Ethics Opinion 522 (1997)].

DEVELOPING YOUR COLLABORATION SKILLS

With a group of other students, selected by you or as assigned by your instructor, review the facts of the following case. As a group, discuss the following questions.

1. What does the federal Driver's Privacy Protection Act mandate?

2. Was the federal Driver's Privacy Protection Act (DPPA) properly enacted by the U.S. Congress pursuant to the Commerce Clause power granted to the federal government by the U.S. Constitution?

3. Did the sale of drivers' personal information by the states violate a driver's right to privacy?

Reno, Attorney General of the United States v. Condon, Attorney General of South Carolina

State Departments of Motor Vehicles (DMVs) register automobiles and issue driver's licenses. State DMVs require automobile owners and drivers to provide personal information, which includes a person's name, address, telephone number, vehicle description, Social Security number, medical information, and a photograph, as a condition for registering an automobile or obtaining a driver's license.

Many states' DMVs sold this personal information to individuals, advertisers, and businesses which then used this information to solicit business from the registered automobile owners and drivers. Sales of automobile owners' and drivers' personal information generated significant revenues for the states.

After receiving thousands of complaints from individuals whose personal information had been sold, the Congress of the United States enacted the **Driver's Privacy Protection Act of 1994 (DPPA)**. This federal statute prohibits a state from selling the personal information of a person unless the state obtains that person's affirmative consent to do so. South Carolina sued the United States, alleging that the federal government did not have power under the Commerce Clause of the U.S. Constitution to adopt the federal DPPA that prohibits the state from selling personal information of its registered automobile owners and drivers.

Source: *Reno, Attorney General of the United States v. Condon, Attorney General of South Carolina*, 528 U.S. 141, 120 S.Ct. 666, 145 L.Ed.2d 587, **Web** 2000 U.S. Lexis 503 (Supreme Court of the United States, 2000)

PARALEGAL PORTFOLIO EXERCISE

Research and find an article that discusses a Federal Communications Commission (FCC) clash with a radio, cable, or television station regarding the subject matter that it may broadcast. Write a memorandum, no longer than two pages, that discusses this dispute and the outcome of the case.

LEGAL ANALYSIS & WRITING CASES

Youngstown Co. v. Sawyer, Secretary of Commerce
343 U.S. 579, 72 S.Ct. 863, 96 L.Ed.2d 1153, Web 1952 U.S. Lexis 2625

Supreme Court of the United States

In 1951, a dispute arose between steel companies and their employees about the terms and conditions that should be included in a new labor contract. At the time, the United States was engaged in a military conflict in Korea that required substantial steel resources from which to make weapons and other military goods.

On April 4, 1952, the steelworkers' union gave notice of a nationwide strike called to begin at 12:01 A.M. on April 9. The indispensability of steel as a component in weapons and other war materials led President Dwight D. Eisenhower to believe that the proposed strike would jeopardize the national defense and that governmental seizure of the steel mills was necessary to ensure the continued availability of steel. Therefore, a few hours before the strike was to begin, the President issued Executive Order 10340, which directed the Secretary of Commerce to take possession of most of the steel mills and keep them running. The steel companies obeyed the order under protest, and brought proceedings against the President.

Question

1. Was the seizure of the steel mills constitutional?

Bonito Boats, Inc. v. Thunder Craft Boats, Inc.
489 U.S. 141, 109 S.Ct. 971, 103 L.Ed.2d 118, Web 1989 U.S. Lexis 629

Supreme Court of the United States

Article 1, Section 8, Clause 8 of the U.S. Constitution grants Congress the power to enact laws to give inventors the exclusive right to their discoveries. Pursuant to this power, Congress enacted federal patent laws that establish the requirements to obtain a patent. Once a patent is granted, the patent holder has exclusive rights to use the patent.

Bonito Boats, Inc. developed a hull design for a fiberglass recreational boat that it marketed under the trade name Bonito Boats Model 5VBR. The manufacturing process involved creating a hardwood model that was sprayed with fiberglass to create a mold. The mold then served to produce the finished fiberglass boats for sale. Bonito did not file a patent application to protect the utilitarian or design aspects of the hull or the manufacturing process.

After the Bonito 5VBR was on the market for six years, the Florida legislature enacted a statute prohibiting the use of a direct molding process to duplicate unpatented boat hulls and forbade the knowing sale of hulls so duplicated. The protection afforded under the state statute was broader than that provided for under the federal patent statute.

Subsequently, Thunder Craft Boats, Inc. produced and sold boats made by the direct molding process. Bonito sued Thunder Craft under Florida law.

Question

1. Is the Florida statute valid?

Rostker, Director of the Selective Service v. Goldberg
453 U.S. 57, 101 S.Ct. 2646, 69 L.Ed.2d 478, 69 L.Ed.2d 478, Web 1981 U.S. Lexis 126

Supreme Court of the United States

In 1975, after the war in Vietnam, the U.S. government discontinued draft registration for men in this country. In 1980, after the Soviet Union invaded Afghanistan, President Jimmy Carter asked Congress for funds to reactivate draft registration. President Carter suggested that males and females alike be required to register. Congress allocated funds only for the registration of males. Several men who were subject to draft registration brought a lawsuit that challenged the law as being unconstitutional in violation of the Equal Protection Clause of the U.S. Constitution. The U.S. Supreme Court upheld the constitutionality of the draft registration law, reasoning as follows:

The question of registering women for the draft not only received considerable national attention and was the subject of wide-ranging public debate, but also was extensively considered by Congress in hearings, floor debate, and in committee. The foregoing clearly establishes that the decision to exempt women from registration was not the "accidental by-producer of a traditional way of thinking about women."

This is not a case of Congress arbitrarily choosing to burden one of two similarly situated groups, such as would be the case with an all-black or all-white, or an all-Catholic or all-Lutheran, or an all-Republican or all-Democratic registration. Men and women are simply not similarly situated for purposes of a draft or registration for a draft.

Justice Marshall dissented, stating that "The Court today places its imprimatur on one of the most potent remaining public expressions of 'ancient canards about the proper role of women.' It upholds a statute that requires males but not females to register for the draft, and which thereby categorically excludes women from a fundamental civic obligation. I dissent."

Question

1. Was the decision fair? Was the law a "progressive science" in this case? Was it ethical for males, but not females, to have to register for the draft?

Van Orden v. Perry, Governor of Texas

125 S.Ct. 2854 162 L.Ed.2d 607, Web 2005 U.S. Lexis 5215

Supreme Court of the United States

The 22 acres surrounding the Texas State Capital contains seventeen monuments and twenty-one historical markers. The monuments and markers commemorate the people and historical events of Texas. Some of the monuments are: Heroes of the Alamo, confederate Soldiers, a Texas Cowboy, Texas Pioneer Women, Disabled Veterans, and Texas Police Officers. One monument is a 6-feet high and 3-feet wide monument on which is carved an eagle grasping an American flag, an eye inside a pyramid, Stars of David, Greek letters, and the Ten Commandments. This monument has been on the grounds for more than 40 years.

Thomas Van Orden, a native Texan and resident of Austin, Texas, where the Texas State Capitol is located,

sued to have the Ten Commandments' monument removed, alleging that the monument violated the Establishment Clause of the U.S. Constitution. The U.S. District Court held that the monument did not violate the Establishment Clause, finding that the monument had a secular purpose. The U.S. Court of Appeals affirmed. Van Orden appealed to the U.S. Supreme Court.

Question

1. Does the monument containing the Ten Commandments, which is located with other monuments on the grounds of the Texas State Capitol, violate the Establishment Clause?

Grutter v. Bollinger, Dean of the University of Michigan Law School

539 U.S. 306, 123 S.Ct. 2325, 156 L.Ed.2d 304, Web 2003 U.S. Lexis 4800

Supreme Court of the United States

Barbara Grutter, a Caucasian resident of the state of Michigan, applied to the Law School of the University of Michigan, a state government–supported institution. She had a 3.8 undergraduate grade point average and a 161 LSAT score. The Law School rejected her application. The Law School received 3,500 applications for a class of 350 students. The Law School used race as one of the factors in considering applicants for admission to law school. The race of minority applicants, defined as Blacks, Hispanics, and Native Americans, was considered as a "plus factor" in considering their applications to law school. Caucasians and Asians were not given such a plus factor. The Law School stated that it used race as a plus factor to obtain a critical mass of underrepresented minority students, to create diversity at the school.

Grutter brought a class action lawsuit against the Law School of the University of Michigan, alleging that its use of a minority's race as a plus factor in admissions violated the Equal Protection Clause of the Fourteenth Amendment to the U.S. Constitution. The District Court held that the Law School's use of race as a factor in admissions violated the Equal Protection Clause. The Court of Appeals reversed. The U.S. Supreme Court granted certiorari to hear the appeal.

Question

1. Does the University of Michigan Law School's use of race as a plus factor in accepting minority applicants for admission to the Law School violate the Equal Protection Clause of the Fourteenth Amendment to the U.S. Constitution?

WORKING WITH THE LANGUAGE OF THE COURT CASE

Lee v. Weisman

505 U.S. 577, 112 S.Ct. 2649 120 L.Ed.2d. 467, Web 1992 U.S. Lexis 4364
Supreme Court of the United States

Read the following case, excerpted from the U.S. Supreme Court's opinion. Review and brief the case. In your brief, answer the following questions.

1. Who are the plaintiff and defendant?
2. What does the Establishment Clause provide?
3. What test did the court use to determine if the practice violates the Establishment Clause?
4. Was the fact that the prayer was nonsectarian important to the Supreme Court's decision?
5. Is nonsectarian prayer permitted under the Establishment Clause?
6. How close was the vote by the justices in this case?

(continued)

Kennedy, Justice (joined by Blackmun, Stevens, O'Connor, and Souter)

Deborah Weisman graduated from Nathan Bishop Middle School, a public school in Providence, Rhode Island, at a formal ceremony in June 1989. She was about 14 years old. For many years it has been the policy of the Providence school committee and the Superintendent of Schools to permit principals to invite members of the clergy to give invocations and benedictions at middle school and high school graduations. Many, but not all, of the principals elected to include prayers as part of the graduation ceremonies. Acting for himself and his daughter, Deborah's father, Daniel Weisman, objected to any prayers at Deborah's middle school graduation, but to no avail. The school principal, petitioner Robert E. Lee, invited a rabbi to deliver prayers at the graduation exercises for Deborah's class. Rabbi Leslie Gutterman, of the Temple Beth El in Providence, accepted.

It also has been the custom of Providence school officials to provide invited clergy with a pamphlet entitled "Guidelines for Civic Occasions," prepared by the National Conference of Christians and Jews. The Guidelines recommended that public prayers at nonsectarian civic ceremonies be composed with "inclusiveness and sensitivity," though they acknowledge that "prayer of any kind may be inappropriate on some civic occasions." The principal gave Rabbi Gutterman the pamphlet before the graduation and advised him that the invocation and benediction should be nonsectarian.

Deborah's graduation was held on the premises of Nathan Bishop Middle School on June 29, 1989. Four days before the ceremony, Daniel Weisman, in his individual capacity as a Providence taxpayer and as next friend of Deborah, sought a temporary restraining order in the United States District Court for the District of Rhode Island to prohibit school officials from including an invocation or a benediction in the graduation ceremony. The court denied the motion for lack of adequate time to consider it. Deborah and her family attended the graduation, where the prayers were recited.

In July 1989, Daniel Weisman filed an amended complaint seeking a permanent injunction barring petitioners, various officials of the Providence public schools, from inviting the clergy to deliver invocations and benedictions at future graduations.

The case was submitted on stipulated facts. The District Court held that petitioners' practice of including invocations and benedictions in public school graduations violated the Establishment Clause of the First Amendment, and it enjoined petitioners from continuing the practice. The court applied the three-part Establishment Clause test. Under that test, to satisfy the Establishment Clause a governmental practice must (1) reflect a clearly secular purpose, (2) have a primary effect that neither advances nor inhibits religion, and (3) avoid excessive government entanglement with religion. On appeal, the United States Court of Appeals for the First Circuit affirmed.

These dominant facts mark and control the confines of our decision: State officials direct the performance of a formal religious exercise at promotional and graduation ceremonies for secondary schools. Even for those students who object to the religious exercise, their attendance and participation in the state-sponsored religious activity are in a fair and real sense obligatory, though the school district does not require attendance as a condition for receipt of the diploma.

The controlling precedents as they relate to prayer and religious exercise in primary and secondary public schools compel the holding here that the policy of the city of Providence is an unconstitutional one. It is beyond dispute that, at a minimum, the Constitution guarantees that government may not coerce anyone to support or participate in religion or its exercise, or otherwise act in a way which "establishes a state religion or religious faith, or tends to do so."

We are asked to recognize the existence of a practice of nonsectarian prayer within the embrace of what is known as the Judeo-Christian tradition, prayer which is more acceptable than one which, for example, makes explicit references to the God of Israel, or to Jesus Christ, or to a patron saint. If common ground can be defined which permits once conflicting faiths to express the shared conviction that there is an ethic and a morality which transcend human invention, the sense of community and purpose sought by all decent societies might be advanced. But though the First Amendment does not allow the government to stifle prayers which aspire to these ends, neither does it permit the government to undertake that task for itself.

The sole question presented is whether a religious exercise may be conducted at a graduation ceremony in circumstances where, as we have found, young graduates who object are induced to conform. No holding by this Court suggests that a school can persuade or compel a student to participate in a religious exercise. That is being done here, and it is forbidden by the Establishment Clause of the First Amendment.

For the reasons we have stated, the judgment of the Court of Appeals is affirmed.

The Court System and Alternative Dispute Resolution

DIGITAL RESOURCES

Chapter 6 Digital Resources at *www.pearsonhighered.com/goldman*

- Video Case Studies:
  - Meet the Courthouse Team
  - Jury Selection: Potential Juror Challenged for Cause
  - Settlement Conference with Judge
- Chapter Summary • Web Links • Court Opinions • Glossary • Comprehension Quizzes
- Technology Resources

> I was never ruined but twice; once when I lost a lawsuit, and once when I won one. "

Voltaire

Paralegals at Work

You have applied for a position as a paralegal at a law firm that specializes in litigation. Most of the law firm's practice is in the area of tort litigation, particularly representing plaintiffs in negligence cases. The firm has scheduled an interview with you. On the day you arrive for the interview, you are called into the office of Ms. Harriet Green, a senior partner in the firm. Ms. Green wants to determine your knowledge of judicial and nonjudicial dispute resolution. Ms. Green informs you that she will tell you the facts of a case and will ask you several questions about the case.

Ms. Green explains that Ms. Heather Andersen has retained the law firm as the plaintiff to represent her in an accident case. Ms. Green explains that Ms. Andersen was driving her automobile on the main road of your city when Mr. Joseph Burton, driving another automobile, ran a red street light and hit Ms. Andersen's vehicle, causing her severe physical injuries, as well as pain and suffering. The law firm plans to file a lawsuit for the tort of negligence on behalf of Ms. Andersen, the plaintiff, against Mr. Burton, the defendant. Ms. Andersen is a resident of your state. Mr. Burton is a resident of another state who was visiting your state when the accident occurred.

Ms. Green asks you the following questions: "What is a complaint?" "In what court or courts can our law firm file the complaint on behalf of Ms. Andersen?" "If we lose the case at trial, to what court can our law firm, on behalf of Ms. Andersen, appeal the trial court's decision?" "After the case is filed in the court, is there any way of resolving the case in favor of Ms. Andersen before the case goes to trial?"

Consider the issues involved in this scenario as you read the chapter.

INTRODUCTION FOR THE PARALEGAL

A paralegal often assists attorneys who represent clients in the courts of this country. The court systems and the procedure to bring and defend a lawsuit are complicated, and a paralegal should be knowledgeable of court systems and how a lawsuit proceeds to trial and is decided in court.

Also, some parties to a dispute will choose to settle a case, or have the case reviewed or determined by a private party rather than by the courts. Thus, a paralegal should be knowledgeable of the manner and procedures for having disputes resolved outside of the court system.

The two major court systems in the United States are: (1) the federal court system, and (2) the court systems of the 50 states and the District of Columbia. Each of these systems has jurisdiction to hear different types of lawsuits. The process of bringing, maintaining, and defending a lawsuit is called **litigation**. Litigation is a difficult, time-consuming, and costly process that must comply with complex procedural rules. Although it is not required, most parties employ a lawyer to represent them when they are involved in a lawsuit.

Several forms of *nonjudicial* dispute resolution have developed in response to the expense and difficulty of bringing a lawsuit. These methods, collectively called alternative dispute resolution (ADR), are being used more and more often to resolve commercial disputes.

Paralegals are especially valuable in providing support to lawyers who are engaged in litigation and alternative dispute resolution. Paralegals interview clients, prepare documents submitted to courts, conduct legal research, and assist lawyers during trial and alternative dispute resolution.

This chapter focuses on the various court systems, the jurisdiction of courts to hear and decide cases, the litigation process, and alternative dispute resolution.

The following feature discusses the career opportunities for paralegal professionals in courts and litigation.

State Court Systems

Paralegal professionals should be familiar with the **state court system** in which he or she could be involved in assisting attorneys who practice before one of these state

---

CAREER OPPORTUNITIES FOR PARALEGALS IN COURTS AND LITIGATION

Paralegals are an extremely fortunate group of individuals because many of them get to work in a special environment—the court system. Paralegals are often hired by state and federal courts to assist judges in the preparation of trial. Paralegals often assist a judge or justice by conducting research, briefing arguments, preparing documents, and such.

In addition to working for the courts directly, many more paralegals are employed by attorneys who represent clients who are involved in litigation in the courts. These paralegals may work for plaintiffs' attorneys and defendants' attorneys in civil litigation lawsuits such as breach of contract, negligence and product liability, business litigation, and other civil lawsuits. These civil lawsuits may be either in state courts or federal courts.

Paralegals are also hired to work for prosecuting attorneys and defense attorneys in the criminal law area. Paralegals assist prosecuting and defense attorneys to prepare for trial and assist the attorney during trial. Criminal law cases are brought both in state and federal courts, depending on the jurisdiction of the court.

A paralegal who works for the courts or litigation attorneys must have a detailed knowledge of the court systems that serve the relevant jurisdiction that he or she works in. Paralegals who work in positions that are not directly involved in supporting lawsuits in court should still have knowledge of the court systems in this country and the jurisdiction of such court systems.

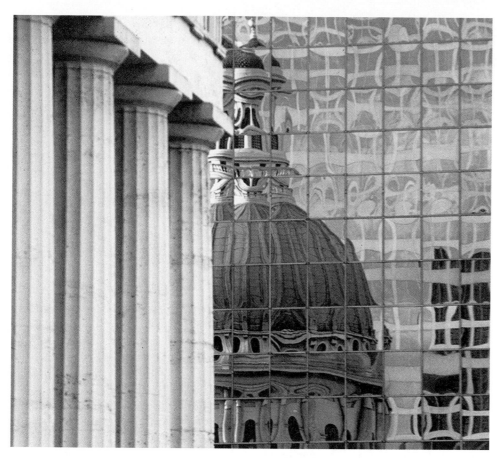

Courthouse, St. Louis, Missouri. State courts hear and decide the majority of cases in the United States.

courts. Each state and the District of Columbia have separate court systems. Most state court systems include:

- Limited-jurisdiction trial courts
- General-jurisdiction trial courts
- Intermediate appellate courts
- Supreme court (or highest state court)

Limited-Jurisdiction Trial Court

State **limited-jurisdiction trial courts**, which sometimes are referred to as *inferior trial courts*, hear matters of a specialized or limited nature.

Examples Traffic courts, juvenile courts, justice-of-the-peace courts, probate courts, family law courts, and courts that hear misdemeanor criminal law cases and civil cases involving lawsuits of less than a certain dollar amount. Because these courts are trial courts, evidence can be introduced and testimony given. Most limited-jurisdiction courts keep a record of their proceedings. Their decisions usually can be appealed to a general-jurisdiction court or an appellate court.

Many states also have created **small-claims courts** to hear civil cases involving small dollar amounts (e.g., $5,000 or less). Generally, the parties must appear individually and cannot have a lawyer represent them. The decisions of small-claims courts are often appealable to general-jurisdiction trial courts or appellate courts.

General-Jurisdiction Trial Court

Every state has a **general-jurisdiction trial court**. These courts often are called **courts of record** because the testimony and evidence at trial are recorded and stored for future reference. These courts hear cases that are not within the jurisdiction of

Web Exploration

Use www.google.com and find out if your state has a small-claims court. If so, what is the dollar limit for cases to qualify to be heard by the small-claims court?

General-jurisdiction trial court (courts of record) A court that hears cases of a general nature that are not within the jurisdiction of limited-jurisdiction trial courts.

limited-jurisdiction trial courts, such as felonies, civil cases above a certain dollar amount, and so on. Some states divide their general-jurisdiction courts into two divisions, one for criminal cases and another for civil cases.

General-jurisdiction trial courts hear evidence and testimony. The decisions these courts hand down are appealable to an intermediate appellate court or the state supreme court, depending on the circumstances.

Intermediate Appellate Court

Intermediate appellate court An intermediate court that hears appeals from trial courts.

In many states, **intermediate appellate courts** (also called *appellate courts* or *courts of appeal*) hear appeals from trial courts. These courts review the trial court record to determine any errors at trial that would require reversal or modification of the trial court's decision. Thus, the appellate court reviews either pertinent parts or the entire trial court record from the lower court. No new evidence or testimony is permitted. The parties usually file legal briefs with the appellate court, stating the law and facts that support their positions. Appellate courts usually grant a short oral hearing to the parties.

Appellate court decisions are appealable to the state's highest court. In less populated states that do not have an intermediate appellate court, trial court decisions can be appealed directly to the state's highest court.

Highest State Court

Highest state court The top court in a state court system; it hears appeals from intermediate state courts and certain trial courts.

Each state has a **highest state court** in its court system. Most states call this highest court *supreme court*. The function of a state supreme court is to hear appeals from intermediate state courts and certain trial courts. The highest court hears no new evidence or testimony. The parties usually submit pertinent parts of or the entire lower court record for review. The parties also submit legal briefs to the court and typically are granted a brief oral hearing. Decisions of state supreme courts are final, unless a question of law is involved that is appealable to the U.S. Supreme Court.

Exhibit 6.1 portrays a typical state court system. Exhibit 6.2 lists the websites for the court systems of 50 states and jurisdictions associated with the United States.

Web Exploration

Go to Exhibit 6.2. Find the website for your state or district or territory and go to this website. What is the name of the highest court? In what city is the highest court located?

Federal Court System

Paralegal professionals are sometimes involved in assisting attorneys who practice before one of the many federal courts. Article III of the U.S. Constitution provides that the federal government's judicial power is vested in one "supreme court." This court is the U.S. Supreme Court. The Constitution also authorizes Congress to establish "inferior" federal courts in the **federal court system**. Pursuant to this power, Congress has established special federal courts, the U.S. district courts, and the U.S. courts of appeal. Federal judges are appointed for life by the President with the advice and consent of the Senate (except bankruptcy court judges, who are appointed for 14-year terms, and U.S. Magistrate Judges, who are appointed for an 8-year term).

Special Federal Courts

Web Exploration

Go to http://www.uscourts.gov/courtlinks/. Choose and click on "Bankruptcy Court." Place the cursor on your state and click. What is the location of the Bankruptcy Court closest to you?

The **special federal courts** established by Congress have limited jurisdiction. They include:

- **U.S. Tax Court**: Hears cases involving federal tax laws
- **U.S. Court of Federal Claims**: Hears cases brought against the United States
- **U.S. Court of International Trade**: Hears cases involving tariffs and international commercial disputes
- **U.S. Bankruptcy Court**: Hears cases involving federal bankruptcy laws

Exhibit 6.1 Typical state court system

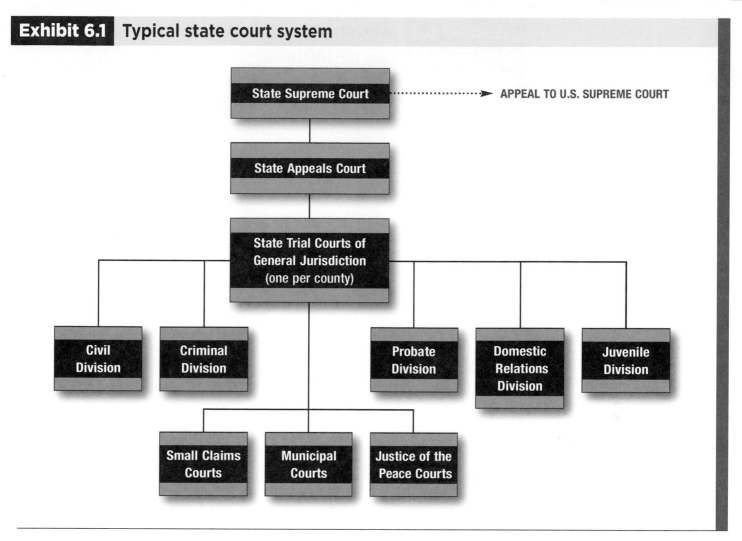

U.S. District Courts

The **U.S. District Courts** are the federal court system's trial courts of general jurisdiction. The District of Columbia and each state have at least one federal district court; the more populated states have more than one. The geographical area that each court serves is referred to as a *district*. At present there are 94 federal district courts. The federal district courts are empowered to impanel juries, receive evidence, hear testimony, and decide cases. Most federal cases originate in federal district courts.

U.S. Courts of Appeals

The **U.S. Courts of Appeals** are the federal court system's intermediate appellate courts. The federal court system has 13 circuits. **Circuit** refers to the geographical area served by a court. Eleven are designated by a number, such as the "First Circuit," "Second Circuit," and so on. The Twelfth Circuit court is located in Washington, D.C., and is called the District of Columbia Circuit.

As appellate courts, these circuit courts hear appeals from the district courts located in their circuit, as well as from certain special courts and federal administrative agencies. The courts review the record of the lower court or administrative agency proceedings to determine if any error would warrant reversal or modification of the lower court decision. No new evidence or testimony is heard. The parties file legal briefs with the court and are given a short oral hearing. Appeals usually are heard by a three-judge panel. After the panel renders a decision, a petitioner can request a review *en banc* by the full court.

U.S. District Courts The federal court system's trial courts of general jurisdiction.

 Web Exploration

Go to http://www.uscourts.gov/courtlinks/. Choose and click on "District Court." Place the cursor on your state and click. What is the location of the U.S. District Court closest to you?

U.S. Courts of Appeals The federal court system's intermediate appellate courts.

 Web Exploration

Visit the website of the U.S. Court for the Federal Circuit at www.fedcir.gov/.

Exhibit 6.2 Websites for state court systems and jurisdictions

State	Website
Alabama	www.judicial.state.al.us
Alaska	www.state.ak.us/courts
Arizona	www.supreme.state.az.us
Arkansas	www.courts.state.ar.us
California	www.courtinfo.ca.gov/courts
Colorado	www.courts.state.co.us
Connecticut	www.jud.state.ct.us
Delaware	www.courts.state.de.us
District of Columbia	www.dccourts.gov
Florida	www.flcourts.org
Georgia	georgiacourts.org
Guam	www.guamsupremecourt.com
Hawaii	www.courts.state.hi.us
Idaho	www.isc.idaho.gov
Illinois	www.state.il.us/court
Indiana	www.in.gov/judiciary
Iowa	www.judicial.state.ia.us
Kansas	www.kscourts.org
Kentucky	www.courts.ky.gov
Louisiana	www.lasc.org
Maine	www.courts.state.me.us
Maryland	www.courts.state.md.us
Massachusetts	www.mass.gov/courts
Michigan	www.courts.michigan.gov
Minnesota	www.courts.state.mn.us
Mississippi	www.mssc.state.ms.us
Missouri	www.courts.mo.gov
Montana	www.montanacourts.org
Nebraska	court.nol.org
Nevada	www.nvsupremecourt.us
New Hampshire	www.courts.state.nh.us
New Jersey	www.judiciary.state.nj.us
New Mexico	www.nmcourts.com
New York	www.courts.state.ny.us
North Carolina	www.nccourts.org
North Dakota	www.ndcourts.com
Ohio	www.sconet.state.oh.us
Oklahoma	www.oscn.net/oscn/schome
Oregon	www.ojd.state.or.us
Pennsylvania	www.courts.state.pa.us

Exhibit 6.2   Websites for state court systems and jurisdictions *(continued)*

State	Website
Puerto Rico	www.tribunalpr.org
Rhode Island	www.courts.state.ri.us
South Carolina	www.judicial.state.sc.us
South Dakota	www.sdjudicial.com
Tennessee	www.tsc.state.tn.us
Texas	www.courts.state.tx.us
Utah	www.utcourts.gov
Vermont	www.vermontjudiciary.org
Virginia	www.courts.state.va.us
Virgin Islands	www.visuperiorcourt.org
Washington	www.courts.wa.gov
West Virginia	www.wv.gov
Wisconsin	www.wicourts.gov
Wyoming	www.courts.state.wy.us

Exhibit 6.3   Map of the federal circuit courts

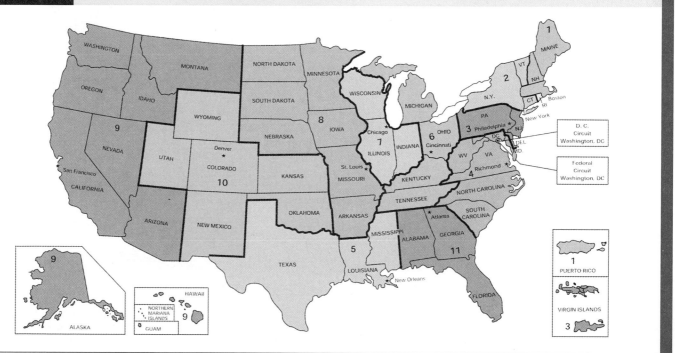

The Thirteenth Circuit court of appeals was created by Congress in 1982. Called the **Court of Appeals for the Federal Circuit** and located in Washington, D.C., this court has special appellate jurisdiction to review the decisions of the Court of Federal Claims, the Patent and Trademark Office, and the Court of International Trade. This court of appeals was created to provide uniformity in the application of federal law in certain areas, particularly patent law.

The map in Exhibit 6.3 shows the 13 federal circuit courts of appeals. Exhibit 6.4 lists the websites of the 13 U.S. courts of appeals.

Web Exploration

Go to http://www.uscourts.gov/courtlinks/. Choose and click on "Court of Appeals." Place the cursor on your state and click. What is the location of the U.S. Court of Appeals closest to you?

Exhibit 6.4 Websites for federal courts of appeals

United States Court of Appeals	Main Office	Website
First Circuit	Boston, Massachusetts	www.ca1.uscourts.gov
Second Circuit	New York, New York	www.ca2.uscourts.gov
Third Circuit	Philadelphia, Pennsylvania	www.ca3.uscourts.gov
Fourth Circuit	Richmond, Virginia	www.ca4.uscourts.gov
Fifth Circuit	Houston, Texas	www.ca5.uscourts.gov
Sixth Circuit	Cincinnati, Ohio	www.ca6.uscourts.gov
Seventh Circuit	Chicago, Illinois	www.ca7.uscourts.gov
Eighth Circuit	St. Paul, Minnesota	www.ca8.uscourts.gov
Ninth Circuit	San Francisco, California	www.ca9.uscourts.gov
Tenth Circuit	Denver, Colorado	www.ca10.uscourts.gov
Eleventh Circuit	Atlanta, Georgia	www.ca11.uscourts.gov
District of Columbia	Washington, DC	www.dcd.uscourts.gov
Court of Appeals for the Federal Circuit	Washington, DC	www.cafc.uscourts.gov

Supreme Court of the United States, Washington, DC. The highest court in the land is the Supreme Court of the United States, located in Washington, DC. The U.S. Supreme Court decides the most important constitutional law cases and other important issues it deems ripe for review and decision. The Supreme Court's unanimous and majority decisions are precedent for all the other courts in the country.

Supreme Court of the United States

Paralegals should be familiar with Supreme Court of the United States, its jurisdiction, the types of cases it hears, how cases are determined to be heard by the Supreme Court, and the voting of the Supreme Court justices. The highest court in the land is the **Supreme Court of the United States** located in Washington, D.C. This court is composed of nine justices who are nominated by the President and confirmed by the

Exhibit 6.5   Federal court system

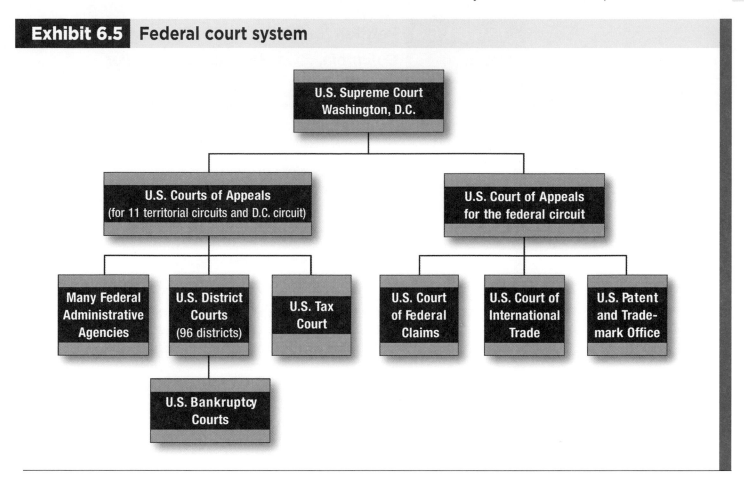

Senate. The President appoints one justice as **chief justice**, responsible for the administration of the Supreme Court. The other eight justices are **associate justices**.

The **U.S. Supreme Court**, which is an appellate court, hears appeals from federal circuit courts of appeals and, under certain circumstances, from federal district courts, special federal courts, and the highest state courts. The Supreme Court hears no evidence or testimony. As with other appellate courts, the lower court record is reviewed to determine whether an error has been committed that warrants a reversal or modification of the decision. Legal briefs are filed, and the parties are granted a brief oral hearing. The Supreme Court's decision is final.

Exhibit 6.5 illustrates the federal court system.

U.S. Supreme Court The Supreme Court was created by Article III of the U.S. Constitution. The Supreme Court is the highest court in the land. It is located in Washington, DC.

Petition for *Certiorari*

A petitioner must file a **petition for *certiorari*** asking the Supreme Court to hear the case. If the Court decides to review a case, it will issue a ***writ of certiorari.*** Because the Court issues only about 100 opinions each year, *writs* usually are granted only in cases involving constitutional and other important issues.

The justices meet once a week to discuss what cases merit review. The votes of four justices are necessary to grant an appeal and schedule an oral argument before the Court ("rule of four"). Written opinions by the justices usually are issued many months later.

The U.S. Constitution gives Congress the authority to establish rules for the appellate review of cases by the Supreme Court, except in the rare case where mandatory review is required. Congress has given the Supreme Court discretion to decide what cases it will hear.

Exhibit 6.6 shows a petition for certiorari to the U.S. Supreme Court.

Petition for *certiorari* A petition asking the Supreme Court to hear one's case.

Writ of certiorari An official notice that the Supreme Court will review one's case.

Exhibit 6.6   Petition for certiorari for the case *District of Columbia, . . . v. Dick Anthony Heller*

No. 07-

IN THE

𝔖𝔲𝔭𝔯𝔢𝔪𝔢 𝔠𝔬𝔲𝔯𝔱 𝔬𝔣 𝔱𝔥𝔢 𝔘𝔫𝔦𝔱𝔢𝔡 𝔖𝔱𝔞𝔱𝔢𝔰

DISTRICT OF COLUMBIA AND
ADRIAN M. FENTY, MAYOR OF THE DISTRICT OF COLUMBIA,

Petitioners,

v.

DICK ANTHONY HELLER,

Respondent.

**On Petition for a Writ of Certiorari to the
United States Court of Appeals for the
District of Columbia Circuit**

PETITION FOR A WRIT OF CERTIORARI

THOMAS C. GOLDSTEIN	LINDA SINGER
CHRISTOPHER M. EGLESON	*Attorney General*
Akin Gump Strauss Hauer	ALAN B. MORRISON
& Feld LLP	*Special Counsel to the*
1333 New Hampshire	*Attorney General*
Avenue, NW	TODD S. KIM
Washington, DC 20036	*Solicitor General*
	Counsel of Record
WALTER DELLINGER	EDWARD E. SCHWAB
MATTHEW M. SHORS	*Deputy Solicitor General*
MARK S. DAVIES	DONNA M. MURASKY
GEOFFREY M. WYATT	LUTZ ALEXANDER PRAGER
O'Melveny & Myers LLP	Office of the Attorney General
1625 Eye Street, NW	for the District of Columbia
Washington, DC 20006	441 Fourth Street, NW
	Washington, DC 20001
	(202) 724-6609

Attorneys for Petitioners

QUESTION PRESENTED

Whether the Second Amendment forbids the District of Columbia from banning private possession of handguns while allowing possession of rifles and shotguns.

ii

PARTIES TO THE PROCEEDING

Petitioners District of Columbia and Mayor Adrian M. Fenty were defendants-appellees below. Mayor Fenty was substituted automatically for the previous Mayor, Anthony A. Williams, under Federal Rule of Appellate Procedure 43(b)(2).

Exhibit 6.6 Petition for certiorari for the case *District of Columbia, . . . v. Dick Anthony Heller* (continued)

Respondent Dick Anthony Heller was the only plaintiff-appellant below held by the court of appeals to have standing. The other plaintiffs-appellants were Shelly Parker, Tom G. Palmer, Gillian St. Lawrence, Tracey Ambeau, and George Lyon.

iii

TABLE OF CONTENTS

Page(s)

Vote of the U.S. Supreme Court

Each justice of the Supreme Court, including the chief justice, has an equal vote. The Supreme Court can issue the following types of decisions:

- **Unanimous decision**. If all of the justices voting agree as to the outcome and reasoning used to decide the case, it is a unanimous opinion. Unanimous decisions are precedent for later cases.

  Example Suppose all nine justices hear a case, and all nine agree to the outcome (the petitioner wins) and the reason why (the Equal Protection Clause of the U.S. Constitution had been violated); this is a unanimous decision.

- **Majority decision**. If a majority of the justices agree to the outcome and reasoning used to decide the case, it is a majority opinion. Majority decisions are precedent for later cases.

  Example If all nine justices hear a case, and five of them agree as to the outcome (the petitioner wins) and all of these five justices agree to the same reason why (the Equal Protection Clause of the U.S. Constitution has been violated), it is a majority opinion.

- **Plurality decision**. If a majority of the justices agree to the outcome of the case, but not to the reasoning for reaching the outcome, it is a plurality opinion. A plurality decision settles the case but is not precedent for later cases.

  Example If all nine justices hear a case, and five of them agree as to the outcome (the petitioner wins), but not all of these five agree to the reason why (suppose that three base their vote on a violation of the Equal Protection Clause and two base their vote on a violation of the Freedom of Speech Clause of the U.S. Constitution), this is a plurality decision. Five justices have agreed to the same outcome, but those five have not agreed for the same reason. The petitioner wins his or her case, but the decision is not precedent for later cases.

- **Tie decision**. Sometimes the Supreme Court sits without all nine justices present because of illness or conflict of interest, or because a justice has not been confirmed to fill a vacant seat on the court. In the case of a tie vote, the lower court decision is affirmed. These votes are not precedent for later cases.

  Example A petitioner won her case at the court of appeals. At the U.S. Supreme Court, only eight justices hear the case. Four justices vote for the petitioner, and four justices vote for the respondent. This is a tie vote. The petitioner remains the winner because she won at the court of appeals. The decision of the Supreme Court sets no precedent for later cases.

A justice who agrees with the outcome of a case but not the reason proffered by other justices can issue a **concurring opinion**, setting forth his or her reasons for deciding the case. A justice who does not agree with a decision can file a **dissenting opinion** that sets forth the reasons for his or her dissent.

Jurisdiction of Federal and State Courts

Subject-matter jurisdiction
Jurisdiction over the subject matter of a lawsuit.

A federal or state court must have **subject-matter jurisdiction** to hear a case. Article III, Section 2, of the U.S. Constitution sets forth the jurisdiction of federal courts. Federal courts have *limited jurisdiction* to hear cases involving federal questions and cases involving diversity of citizenship. State courts have jurisdiction to hear certain types of cases. Jurisdiction of federal and state courts to hear cases is discussed in the following paragraphs.

Web Exploration

Go to the website of the U.S. Supreme Court at www .supremecourtus.gov. Who are the nine justices of the U.S. Supreme Court? Who is the Chief Justice? What President appointed each justice and what political party (e.g., Democrat, Republican) did that President belong to?

Subject-Matter Jurisdiction of Federal Courts

Federal courts have jurisdiction to hear cases based on the subject matter of the case. The federal courts have jurisdiction to hear cases involving "federal questions." **Federal question** cases are cases arising under the U.S. Constitution, treaties, and federal statutes and regulations. There is no dollar-amount limit on federal question cases that can be brought in federal court.

> **Example**   A lawsuit involving federal securities law concerns a federal question (a federal statute) and will be heard by a U.S. district court.

Federal question A case arising under the U.S. Constitution, treaties, or federal statutes and regulations.

Subject-Matter Jurisdiction of State Courts

State courts have jurisdiction to hear cases involving subject matters that federal courts do not have jurisdiction to hear. These usually involve state laws.

> **Examples**   Real estate law, corporation law, partnership law, limited liability company law, contract law, sales and lease contracts, and negotiable instruments are state law subject matters.

Diversity of Citizenship

A case involving a state court subject matter may be brought in federal court if there is **diversity of citizenship**. Diversity of citizenship occurs if the lawsuit involves (a) citizens of different states, (b) a citizen of a state and a citizen or subject of a foreign country, and (c) a citizen of a state and a foreign country is the plaintiff. A corporation is considered to be a citizen of the state in which it is incorporated and in which it has its principal place of business. The reason for providing diversity of citizenship jurisdiction was to prevent state court bias against nonresidents. The federal court must apply the appropriate state's law in deciding the case. The dollar amount of the controversy must exceed $75,000 to be brought in federal court. If this requirement is not met, the action must be brought in the appropriate state court.

Diversity of citizenship A case between (1) citizens of different states, (2) a citizen of a state and a citizen or subject of a foreign country, and (3) a citizen of a state and a foreign country where a foreign country is the plaintiff.

> **Example**   Henry, a resident of the state of Idaho, is driving his automobile in the state of Idaho when he negligently hits Mary, a pedestrian. Mary is a resident of the state of New York. There is no federal question involved in this case; it is an automobile accident that involves state negligence law. However, there is diversity of citizenship in this case: Henry is from the state of Idaho, while Mary is from another state, the state of New York. Usually the case must be brought in the state in which the automobile accident occurred because this is where most of the witnesses and evidence will be from. In this case, Mary, the plaintiff, may bring her lawsuit in federal court in Idaho, and if she does so the case will remain in federal court. If Mary brings the case in Idaho state court it will remain in Idaho state court if Henry agrees; however, Henry can move the case to federal court.

Exclusive and Concurrent Jurisdiction

Federal courts have **exclusive jurisdiction** to hear cases involving federal crimes, antitrust, bankruptcy, patent and copyright cases, suits against the United States, and most admiralty cases. State courts cannot hear these cases.

State and federal courts have **concurrent jurisdiction** to hear cases involving diversity of citizenship and federal questions over which federal courts do not have exclusive jurisdiction (e.g., cases involving federal securities laws). If a plaintiff brings a case involving concurrent jurisdiction in state court, the defendant can remove the case to federal court. If a case does not qualify to be brought in federal court, it must be brought in the appropriate state court.

The following feature discusses a paralegal's duty to investigate in what court a particular action should be brought.

ETHICAL PERSPECTIVE

Duty of a Paralegal to Investigate What Court in Which to Bring a Lawsuit

Mya is driving her automobile in St. Ignace, Michigan, when her car is rear-ended by another automobile driven by Pierre. Mya is injured in the accident. The accident was caused by Pierre's negligence in driving above the speed limit and not paying attention to the road. Mya comes to attorney Paula Johnson's office to consult about suing Pierre to recover monetary damages for her physical injuries and also to recover damages for the pain and suffering.

You work as the paralegal for Attorney Johnson. Attorney Johnson asks you to investigate the facts and determine in what court the case could be brought. You correctly determine that the subject matter of the case—negligence in causing an automobile accident—belongs in state court. And because the accident occurred in Michigan you automatically assume that the case should be brought in Michigan state court. However, you fail to determine what states the plaintiff and defendant are residents of.

You report to Attorney Johnson that the case should be brought in Michigan state court. Here, you have failed to conduct the proper investigation necessary to determine the proper court for the case to be brought in. You have failed to find out what states the parties are residents of, or if one of the parties is a resident of a foreign country. If the parties are from different states, or one of the parties is from a foreign country, the case qualifies to be brought in federal court because of diversity of citizenship. By failing to conduct a proper investigation you have been negligent and have breached your ethical duty as a paralegal that you owe to your supervising attorney. By failing to discover whether the case involves diversity of citizenship, the case may end up being brought in Michigan state court when in fact the case qualifies to be brought in federal court as well. Without this information, Attorney Johnson is lacking sufficient information to decide the benefits of bringing the case in either state or federal court.

Personal Jurisdiction and Other Issues

Not every court has the authority to hear all types of cases. First, to bring a lawsuit in a court, the plaintiff must have *standing to sue*. In addition, the court must have *jurisdiction* to hear the case, and the case must be brought in the proper *venue*. These topics are discussed in the following paragraphs.

Standing to Sue

To bring a lawsuit, a plaintiff must have **standing to sue**. This means the plaintiff must have some stake in the outcome of the lawsuit.

> **Example**   Linda's friend Jon is injured in an accident caused by Emily. Jon refuses to sue. Linda cannot sue Emily on Jon's behalf because she does not have an interest in the result of the case.

In Personam Jurisdiction

In personam **(personal) jurisdiction** Jurisdiction over the parties to a lawsuit.

Jurisdiction over a person is called *in personam* **jurisdiction**, or **personal jurisdiction**. A *plaintiff*, by filing a lawsuit with a court, gives the court *in personam* jurisdiction over himself or herself. The court must also have *in personam* jurisdiction over the *defendant*, which is usually obtained by having a summons served to that person within the territorial boundaries of the state (i.e., **service of process**). Service of process is usually accomplished by personal service of the summons and complaint on the defendant.

If personal service is not possible, alternative forms of notice, such as mailing of the summons or publication of a notice in a newspaper, may be permitted. A corporation is subject to personal jurisdiction in the state in which it is incorporated, has its principal office, and is doing business.

A party who disputes the jurisdiction of a court can make a *special appearance* in that court to argue against imposition of jurisdiction. Service of process is not permitted during such an appearance.

In Rem Jurisdiction

A court may have jurisdiction to hear and decide a case because it has jurisdiction over the property of the lawsuit: This is called *in rem* **jurisdiction** ("jurisdiction over the thing").

> **Example**   A state court would have jurisdiction to hear a dispute over the ownership of a piece of real estate located within the state. This is so even if one or more of the disputing parties lives in another state or states.

In rem **jurisdiction** Jurisdiction to hear a case because of jurisdiction over the property of the lawsuit.

Quasi in Rem Jurisdiction

Sometimes a plaintiff who obtains a judgment against a defendant in one state will try to collect the judgment by attaching property of the defendant that is located in another state. This is permitted under *quasi in rem* **jurisdiction**, or **attachment jurisdiction**.

> **Example**   If a plaintiff wins a monetary judgment against a defendant in a Florida state court, but the defendant's only property to satisfy the judgment is located in Idaho, the Idaho state court has *quasi in rem* jurisdiction to order the attachment of the defendant's property in Idaho to satisfy the Florida court judgment.

Quasi in rem **(attachment) jurisdiction** Jurisdiction allowed a plaintiff who obtains a judgment in one state to try to collect the judgment by attaching property of the defendant located in another state.

Long-Arm Statutes

In most states, a state court can obtain jurisdiction over persons and businesses located in another state or country through the state's **long-arm statute**. These statutes extend a state's jurisdiction to nonresidents who were not served a summons within the state. The nonresident must have had some *minimum contact* with the state [*International Shoe Co. v. Washington*, 326 U.S. 310, 66 S.Ct. 154, 90 L.Ed. 95, 1945 U.S. Lexis 1447 (1945)]. In addition, maintenance of the suit must uphold the traditional notions of fair play and substantial justice.

Long-arm statute A statute that extends a state's jurisdiction to nonresidents who were not served a summons within the state.

The exercise of long-arm jurisdiction is generally permitted over nonresidents who have (1) committed torts within the state (e.g., caused an automobile accident in the state), (2) entered into a contract either in the state or that affects the state (and allegedly breached the contract), or (3) transacted other business in the state that allegedly caused injury to another person.

Venue

Venue requires lawsuits to be heard by the court with jurisdiction nearest the location in which the incident occurred or where the parties reside.

> **Example**   Harry, a Georgia resident, commits a felony crime in Los Angeles County, California. The California Superior Court, located in Los Angeles, is the proper venue because the crime was committed in Los Angeles County and the witnesses are probably from the area, and so on.

Venue A concept that requires lawsuits to be heard by the court with jurisdiction that is nearest the location in which the incident occurred or where the parties reside.

Occasionally, pretrial publicity may prejudice jurors located in the proper venue. In these cases, a **change of venue** may be requested so a more impartial jury can be found. The courts generally frown upon *forum shopping* (i.e., looking for a favorable court without a valid reason).

Forum-Selection and Choice-of-Law Clauses

Parties sometimes agree in their contract as to what state's courts, federal courts, or country's court will have jurisdiction to hear a legal dispute should one arise. Such clauses in contracts are called **forum-selection clauses**.

In addition to agreeing to a forum, the parties also often agree in contracts as to what state's law or country's law will apply in resolving a dispute. These clauses are called **choice-of-law clauses**.

Alternative Dispute Resolution (ADR)

Alternative dispute resolution (ADR) Methods of resolving disputes other than litigation.

The use of the court system to resolve business and other disputes can take years and cost thousands, if not millions, of dollars in legal fees and expenses. In commercial litigation, the normal business operations of the parties are often disrupted. To avoid or lessen these problems, businesses are increasingly turning to methods of **alternative dispute resolution (ADR)** and other aids to resolving disputes. The most common form of ADR is *arbitration*. Other forms of ADR are *negotiation, mediation, conciliation, minitrial, fact-finding*, and using a *judicial referee*.

The following feature discusses the career opportunities for paralegal professionals in alternative dispute resolution.

Negotiation

Negotiation A procedure in which the parties to a dispute engage in negotiations to try to reach a voluntary settlement of their dispute.

The simplest form of alternative dispute resolution is engaging in negotiation between the parties to try to settle a dispute. **Negotiation** is a procedure whereby the parties to a dispute engage in discussions to try to reach a voluntary settlement of their dispute. Negotiation may take place either before a lawsuit is filed, after a lawsuit is filed, or before other forms of alternative dispute resolution are engaged in.

In a negotiation, the parties, who often are represented by attorneys, negotiate with each other to try to reach an agreeable solution to their dispute. During

CAREER OPPORTUNITIES FOR PARALEGALS IN ALTERNATIVE DISPUTE RESOLUTION

The growth in using alternative dispute resolution to solve disputes has been phenomenal. Alternative dispute resolution is just that—an alternative to using the litigation process and court systems to resolve disputes.

The major form of alternative dispute resolution is arbitration. The United States Supreme Court has upheld the use of arbitration in many types of disputes. Arbitration is used particularly in contract disputes, because many contracts contain arbitration clauses—that is, the parties to the contract have agreed in their contract not to use the court systems to solve their disputes. Instead, they have expressly agreed that an arbitrator, and not a jury, will resolve their dispute.

Most major companies have placed arbitration agreements in their contracts.

Examples Arbitration clauses appear in contracts to purchase goods, to lease automobiles, to employ services, and in other types of contracts. Also, arbitration clauses are included by employers in many employment contracts. Thus, if an employee has a dispute with his or her employer, the dispute goes to arbitration for resolution because the employee has given up his or her right to use the court system by agreeing to the arbitration clause.

Mediation also has become an indispensable method of helping to solve disputes. In mediation, the mediator does not act as a decision-maker but, instead, acts as a facilitator to try to help the disputing parties reach a settlement of their dispute. Mediation often is used in family law matters, particularly in helping reach a settlement in divorce cases.

Paralegals who work for lawyers in business law-related matters, contract disputes, and family law matters should have a thorough understanding of alternative dispute resolution. Paralegals often are called upon to help attorneys prepare for arbitration, mediation, and other forms of alternative dispute resolution. This chapter addresses the major forms of alternative dispute resolution.

negotiation proceedings, the parties usually make offers and counteroffers to one another. The parties or their attorneys also may provide information to the other side that would assist the other side in reaching an amicable settlement.

Many courts require that the parties to a lawsuit engage in settlement discussions prior to trial to try to negotiate a settlement of the case. The judge must be assured that a settlement of the case is not possible before he or she permits the case to go to trial. Judges often convince the parties to engage in further negotiations if the judge determines that the parties are not too far apart in the negotiations of a settlement.

If a settlement of the dispute is reached through negotiation, a settlement agreement is drafted that contains the terms of the agreement. A **settlement agreement** is an agreement that is voluntarily entered into by the parties to a dispute that settles the dispute. Each side must sign the settlement agreement for it to be effective. The settlement agreement usually is submitted to the court, and the case will be dismissed based on execution of the settlement agreement.

Settlement agreement An agreement voluntarily entered into by the parties to a dispute that settles the dispute.

Arbitration

Paralegals working in many areas of the law—litigation, contract law, business law, and such—will encounter arbitration clauses in some of the cases that they are working on. In **arbitration**, the parties choose an impartial third party to hear and decide the dispute. This neutral party is called the **arbitrator**. Arbitrators usually are selected from members of the American Arbitration Association (AAA) or another arbitration association.

Arbitration A form of ADR in which the parties choose an impartial third party to hear and decide the dispute.

Labor union agreements, franchise agreements, leases, and other commercial contracts often contain **arbitration clauses** that require disputes arising out of the contract to be submitted to arbitration. If there is no arbitration clause, the parties can enter into a **submission agreement**, whereby they agree to submit a dispute to arbitration after the dispute arises.

The benefits of arbitration are that it is less expensive than litigation, is completed faster than a lawsuit, and is decided by a person who is knowledgeable in the area of law that is in dispute. Some consumers and employees who are subject to arbitration agreements argue that arbitration unfairly favors businesses and employers over them.

In the past, some courts were reluctant to permit arbitration of a dispute or found that arbitration agreements were illegal. However, in a series of cases the U.S. Supreme Court upheld the validity of many types of arbitration clauses or agreements.

Exhibit 6.7 is the form for a Demand for Arbitration.

Federal Arbitration Act

The **Federal Arbitration Act (FAA)** was originally enacted by Congress in 1925 to reverse the longstanding judicial hostility to arbitration agreements that had existed as English common law and had been adopted by American courts [9 U.S.C. Sections 1 et. seq.]. The Act provides that arbitration agreements involving commerce are valid, irrevocable, and enforceable contracts, unless some grounds exist at law or equity (e.g., fraud, duress) to revoke them. The FAA permits one party to obtain a court order to compel arbitration if the other party has failed, neglected, or refused to comply with an arbitration agreement.

About half of the states have adopted the **Uniform Arbitration Act**, which promotes the arbitration of disputes at the state level. Many federal and state courts have instituted programs to refer legal disputes to arbitration or another form of alternative dispute resolution.

ADR Providers

ADR services usually are provided by private organizations or individuals who qualify to hear and decide certain disputes. For example, the **American Arbitration Association (AAA)** is the largest private provider of ADR services. The AAA employs persons

Exhibit 6.7 Demand for arbitration

American Arbitration Association
Dispute Resolution Services Worldwide

_____**ARBITRATION RULES**
(ENTER THE NAME OF THE APPLICABLE RULES)
Demand for Arbitration

MEDIATION: *If you would like the AAA to contact the other parties and attempt to arrange mediation, please check this box.* ☐ *There is no additional administrative fee for this service.*	
Name of Respondent	Name of Representative (if known)
Address:	Name of Firm (if applicable):
	Representative's Address

City	State	Zip Code	City	State	Zip Code
Phone No.	Fax No.		Phone No.	Fax No.	
Email Address:			Email Address:		

The named claimant, a party to an arbitration agreement dated _____, which provides for arbitration under the
_____Arbitration Rules of the American Arbitration Association, hereby demands arbitration.

THE NATURE OF THE DISPUTE

Dollar Amount of Claim $	Other Relief Sought: ☐ Attorneys Fees ☐ Interest ☐ Arbitration Costs ☐ Punitive/ Exemplary ☐ Other _____

AMOUNT OF FILING FEE ENCLOSED WITH THIS DEMAND (please refer to the fee schedule in the rules for the appropriate fee) $

PLEASE DESCRIBE APPROPRIATE QUALIFICATIONS FOR ARBITRATOR(S) TO BE APPOINTED TO HEAR THIS DISPUTE:

Hearing locale_____ (check one) ☐ Requested by Claimant   ☐ Locale provision included in the contract

Estimated time needed for hearings overall: _____hours or _____days	Type of Business: Claimant _____ Respondent_____

Is this a dispute between a business and a consumer?   ☐Yes ☐ No
Does this dispute arise out of an employment relationship? ☐Yes ☐ No

If this dispute arises out of an employment relationship, what was/is the employee's annual wage range? Note: This question is required by California law. ☐Less than $100,000 ☐ $100,000 - $250,000 ☐ Over $250,000

You are hereby notified that copies of our arbitration agreement and this demand are being filed with the American Arbitration Association's Case Management Center, located in (check one) ☐ Atlanta, GA ☐ Dallas, TX   ☐ East Providence, RI ☐ Fresno, CA ☐ International Centre, NY, with a request that it commence administration of the arbitration. Under the rules, you may file an answering statement within the timeframe specified in the rules, after notice from the AAA.

Signature (may be signed by a representative) Date:	Name of Representative
Name of Claimant	Name of Firm (if applicable)
Address (to be used in connection with this case):	Representative's Address:

City	State	Zip Code	City	State	Zip Code
Phone No.	Fax No.		Phone No.	Fax No.	
Email Address:			Email Address:		

To begin proceedings, please send two copies of this Demand and the Arbitration Agreement, along with the filing fee as provided for in the Rules, to the AAA. Send the original Demand to the Respondent.

Please visit our website at www.adr.org if you would like to file this case online. AAA Customer Service can be reached at 800-778-7879

Source: Reprinted with permission of American Arbitration Association

Web Exploration

Go to the website of the American Arbitration Association (AAA) at http://www.adr.org/sp.asp?id= 28749 and read the article entitled "Arbitration and Mediation."

who are qualified in special areas of the law to provide mediation and arbitration services in those areas. These persons are called **neutrals**.

For example, if parties have a contract dispute involving an employment contract, a construction contract, an Internet contract, or other commercial contract or business dispute, the AAA has a special group of neutrals that can hear and decide these cases. Other mediation and arbitration associations are located throughout the United States and internationally.

ADR Procedure

An arbitration agreement often describes the specific procedures that must be followed for a case to proceed to and through arbitration. If one party seeks to enforce an arbitration clause, that party must give notice to the other party. The parties then select an arbitration association or arbitrator as provided in the agreement. The parties usually agree on the date, time, and place of the arbitration. This can be at the arbitrator's offices, at a law office, or at any other agreed-upon location.

At the arbitration, the parties can call witnesses to give testimony, and introduce evidence to support their case and refute the other side's case. Rules similar to those followed by federal courts usually are adhered to at the arbitration. Often, each party pays a filing fee and other fees for the arbitration. Sometimes the agreement provides that one party will pay all of the costs of the arbitration. Arbitrators are paid by the hour or day, or other agreed-upon method of compensation.

Decision and Award

After the hearing is complete, the arbitrator reaches a decision and issues an **award**. The parties often agree in advance to be bound by an arbitrator's decision and remedy. This is called **binding arbitration**. In this situation, the decision and award of the arbitrator cannot be appealed to the courts. If the arbitration is not binding, the decision and award of the arbitrator can be appealed to the courts. This is called **non-binding arbitration**. Courts usually give great deference to an arbitrator's decision and award.

If a decision and award has been rendered by an arbitrator but a party refuses to abide by the arbitrator's decision, the other party may file an action in court to have the arbitrator's decision enforced.

> **Example**   Assume that there has been a contract dispute between NorthWest Corporation and SouthEast Corporation that goes to binding arbitration. The arbitrator issues a decision that awards SouthEast Corporation $5 million against NorthWest Corporation. If NorthWest Corporation fails to pay the award, SouthEast Corporation can file an action in court to have the award enforced by the court.

Other Forms of ADR

As mentioned, in addition to arbitration and negotiation, the other forms of ADR are *mediation*, *conciliation*, *minitrial*, *fact-finding*, and using a *judicial referee*. These forms of ADR are discussed in the following paragraphs.

Mediation

Mediation is a form of negotiation in which a neutral third party assists the disputing parties in reaching a settlement of their dispute. The neutral third party is called a **mediator**. The mediator usually is a person who is an expert in the area of the dispute, or a lawyer or retired judge. The mediator is selected by the parties as provided in their agreement, or as otherwise selected by the parties. Unlike an arbitrator, however, a mediator does not make a decision or an award.

A mediator's role is to assist the parties in reaching a settlement. The mediator usually acts as an intermediary between the parties. In many cases the mediator will meet with the two parties at an agreed-upon location, often the mediator's office or one of the offices of the parties. The mediator then will meet with both parties, usually separately, to discuss their side of the case.

After discussing the facts of the case with both sides, the mediator will encourage settlement of the dispute and will transmit settlement offers from one side to the other. In doing so, the mediator points out the strengths and weaknesses of each party's case and gives his or her opinion to each side why they should decrease or increase their settlement offers. The mediator's job is to facilitate settlement of the case.

Mediation A form of negotiation in which a neutral third party assists the disputing parties in reaching a settlement of their dispute.

Mediator A neutral third party who assists the disputing parties in reaching a settlement of their dispute. The mediator cannot make a decision or an award.

Paralegals *in* Practice

Kathleen A. Stradley is a Certified Arbitrator and Certified Mediator with 26 years of paralegal experience. She also is an Advanced Certified Paralegal and Civil Litigation Specialist. Since 1998, Kathleen has worked as an independent contractor of litigation support and consulting services in North Dakota and Minnesota. She assists trial attorneys and corporations with case management and trial preparation. She also serves as a private arbitrator and mediator in legal disputes.

Becoming involved in alternative dispute resolution (ADR) has been an interesting process. Before starting my own business, I worked for several law firms and a corporation in Ohio and North Dakota. During that time, I was aware that ADR could save a lot of time and money. However, I did not know much about putting ADR into practice. So, I enrolled in an intense course that allowed me to obtain my mediator certification after 40 hours of training.

A short time later, I trained for a new binding arbitration program for the North Dakota Workers' Compensation Bureau. This program provided employees and employers with the option of binding arbitration rather than a formal administrative hearing or judicial solution. Instead, a hearing was held in front of three arbitrators, one from each of three societal areas: labor, industry, and the public. For about a year, I served as a public sector arbitrator and chairperson for the panel. After the panel was reduced to one person, I continued to serve as an arbitrator for Workers' Compensation hearings.

Later, I served as an arbitrator and mediator through the American Arbitration Association (AAA) for family, commercial, personal injury, employment/workplace, and construction industry claims. In 1997, after a terrible flood destroyed my hometown of Grand Forks, North Dakota, I mediated in many disaster-related commercial and construction disputes, as well as family law cases. In more recent years, I spoke with a number of disaster victims who experienced an ADR process. Most of them agreed that ADR was a valuable course of action that helped them rebuild their homes and lives.

Due to mandatory arbitration provisions in most contracts, and the trend of court ordered dispute resolution proceedings, I think there will be fewer trials in the future. Instead, I believe more and more lawsuits will be resolved with alternative methods. Cases using ADR proceedings typically involve fewer documents. However, these documents need to be prepared much earlier, and in greater detail than cases that are tried in court with a jury. In mediation, each party submits their statement of the case and its value to the mediator in advance of the mediation. In arbitration, the evidence is submitted to the arbitrator in advance of the arbitration. ADR proceedings usually occur after discovery is completed and well in advance of the scheduled trial.

Source: Stradley, Kathleen A., "ADR: Changing Ground." *Facts & Findings, the Journal for Legal Assistants* XXXI.4 (January 2005): 16–17. Career Chronicle Edition 2004, NALA.

The mediator gives his or her opinion to the parties as to what he or she believes to be a reasonable settlement of the case, and usually proposes settlement of the dispute. The parties are free to accept or reject such proposal. If the parties agree to a settlement, a settlement agreement is drafted that expresses their agreement. Execution of the settlement agreement ends the dispute. The parties, of course, must perform their duties under the settlement agreement.

Example   Parties to a divorce action often use mediation to try to help resolve the issues involved in the divorce, including property settlement, payment of alimony and child support, custody of children, visitation rights, and other issues.

Exhibit 6.8 is the form for a Request for Mediation.

Conciliation A form of dispute resolution in which a conciliator transmits offers and counteroffers between the disputing parties in helping to reach a settlement of their dispute.

Conciliation

Conciliation is another form of alternative dispute resolution. In conciliation, a party named a **conciliator** helps the parties to try to reach a resolution of their dispute. Conciliation often is used when the parties refuse to face each other in an adversarial setting. The conciliator schedules meetings and appointments during which information can be transferred between the parties. A conciliator usually carries offers and counteroffers for a settlement back and forth between the disputing parties. A conciliator cannot make a decision or an award.

Conciliator A third party in a conciliation proceeding who assists the disputing parties in reaching a settlement of their dispute. The conciliator cannot make a decision or an award.

Although the role of a conciliator is not to propose a settlement of the case, many often do. In many cases, conciliators are neutral third parties, although in some

Exhibit 6.8 **Request for mediation**

American Arbitration Association
Dispute Resolution Services Worldwide

REQUEST FOR MEDIATION

Name of Responding Party	Name of Representative (if known)		
Address:	Name of Firm (if applicable)		
	Representative's Address:		

City	State	Zip Code	City	State	Zip Code
Phone No.		Fax No.	Phone No.		Fax No.
Email Address:			Email Address:		

The undersigned party to an agreement contained in a written contract dated _____, providing for mediation under the
_____ Mediation Procedures of the American Arbitration Association, hereby requests mediation

THE NATURE OF THE DISPUTE

CLAIM OR RELIEF SOUGHT (amount, if any):

AMOUNT OF FILING FEE ENCLOSED WITH THIS REQUEST: $

Mediation locale_____ (check one) ☐ Requested by Filing Party ☐ Locale provision included in the contract

Type of Business: Filing Party _____   Responding Party_____

You are hereby notified that copies of our mediation agreement and this request are being filed with the American Arbitration Association's Case Management Center, located in (check one) ☐ Atlanta, GA ☐ Dallas, TX ☐ East Providence, RI ☐ Fresno, CA ☐ International Centre, NY, with a request that it commence administration of this mediation.

Signature (may be signed by a representative) Date:	Name of Representative		
Name of Filling Party	Name of Firm (if applicable)		
Address (to be used in connection with this case):	Representative's Address:		

City	State	Zip Code	City	State	Zip Code
Phone No.		Fax No.	Phone No.		Fax No.
Email Address:			Email Address:		

To begin proceedings, please send two copies of this Request and the Mediation Agreement, along with the filing fee as provided for in the Rules, to the AAA. Send the original Request to the responding party.

Please visit our website at www.adr.org if you would like to file this case online. AAA Customer Service can be reached at 800-778-7879

Source: Reprinted with permission of American Arbitration Association.

circumstances the parties may select an interested third party to act as the conciliator. If the parties reach a settlement of their dispute through the use of conciliation, a settlement agreement is drafted and executed by the parties.

Minitrial

A **minitrial** is a voluntary private proceeding in which the lawyers for each side present a shortened version of their case to the representatives of the other side. The representatives of each side who attend the minitrial have the authority to settle the

Minitrial A voluntary private proceeding in which the lawyers for each side present a shortened version of their case to representatives of the other side, and usually to a neutral third party, in an attempt to reach a settlement of the dispute.

dispute. In many cases, the parties also hire a neutral third party, often someone who is an expert in the field concerning the disputed matter or a legal expert, who presides over the minitrial. After hearing the case, the neutral third party often is called upon to render an opinion as to how the court would most likely decide the case.

During a minitrial, the parties get to see the strengths and weaknesses of their own position and that of the opposing side. Once the strengths and weaknesses of both sides are exposed, the parties to a minitrial often settle the case. The parties also often settle a minitrial based on the opinion rendered by the neutral third party. If the parties settle their dispute after a minitrial, they will enter into a settlement agreement setting forth their agreement.

Minitrials serve a useful purpose in that they act as a substitute for the real trial, but they are much briefer and not as complex and expensive to prepare for. By exposing the strengths and weaknesses of both sides' cases, the parties usually are more realistic regarding their own position and the merits of settling the case prior to an expensive, and often more risky, trial.

Fact-Finding

In some situations, called fact-finding, the parties to a dispute will employ a neutral third party to act as a fact-finder to investigate the dispute. The fact-finder is authorized to investigate the dispute, gather evidence, prepare demonstrative evidence, and prepare reports of his or her findings.

A fact-finder is not authorized to make a decision or award. In some cases, a fact-finder will recommend settlement of the case. The fact-finder presents the evidence and findings to the parties, who then may use such information in negotiating a settlement if they wish.

Judicial Referee

If the parties agree, the court may appoint a **judicial referee** to conduct a private trial and render a judgment. Referees, who often are retired judges, have most of the powers of a trial judge, and their decisions stand as a judgment of the court. The parties usually reserve their right to appeal.

Online ADR

Web Exploration

Go to the website of the American Arbitration Association (AAA) at http://www.adr.com. Does the AAA provide online dispute resolution?

Several services now offer **online arbitration**. Most of these services allow a party to a dispute to register the dispute with the service and then notify the other party by email of the registration of the dispute. Most online arbitration requires the registering party to submit an amount that the party is willing to accept or pay to the other party in the online arbitration. The other party is afforded the opportunity to accept the offer. If that party accepts the offer, a settlement has been reached. The other party, however, may return a **counteroffer**. The process continues until a settlement is reached or one or both of the parties remove themselves from the online ADR process.

Also, several websites offer **online mediation** services. In an online mediation, the parties sit before their computers and sign onto the site. Two chat rooms are assigned to each party. One chat room is used for private conversations with the online mediator, and the other chat room is for conversations with both parties and the mediator.

Online arbitration and mediation services charge fees for their services. The fees are reasonable. In an online arbitration or mediation, a settlement can be reached rather quickly without paying lawyers' fees and court costs. The parties also are acting through a more objective online process than meeting face-to-face or negotiating over the telephone, either of which could conclude with verbal arguments.

The ethical duty and social responsibility of a paralegal professional to provide *pro bono* services to the public is discussed in the following feature.

ETHICAL PERSPECTIVE

A Paralegal's Duty to Provide Pro Bono *Services to the Public*

Mr. Alvarez is a paralegal in a law firm and works directly with Ms. Dawson, a partner in the law firm. In addition to her law practice with the law firm, Ms. Dawson volunteers to work one evening per week at a domestic abuse center that serves women and children.

At the center, Ms. Dawson interviews domestic abuse victims and pursues whatever legal actions that can be taken to assist the victims and their families. This often includes doing the legal work for obtaining restraining orders, government assistance, and spousal and child support. All of Ms. Dawson's services at the domestic abuse center are provided *pro bono*, that is, for free.

One day Ms. Dawson asks her paralegal, Mr. Alvarez, if he would be interested in volunteering to help her one night each month at the domestic abuse shelter. Ms. Dawson explains that she could use Mr. Alvarez's assistance as a paralegal to help conduct interviews, prepare documents, and obtain government and other assistance for the domestic abuse victims and their families. Mr. Alvarez would be under the supervision of Ms. Dawson while working at the center.

Does a paralegal owe an ethical duty to provide *pro bono* services to the public?

Model and state paralegal Code of Ethics and Professional Responsibility provide that a paralegal has an ethical duty to provide *pro bono* services. Thus, a paralegal should strive to provide *pro bono* services under the authority of an attorney or as authorized by a court. It is best if these services are provided to assist the poor, persons with limited education, charitable programs, or protect civil rights.

PARALEGAL'S ETHICAL DECISION

Because a paralegal owes an ethical duty to provide *pro bono* services to the public, Mr. Alvarez should agree to assist Ms. Dawson at the domestic abuse shelter one evening each month in order to fulfill his duty to the public. This would be an excellent way for Mr. Alvarez to satisfy his ethical duty as a paralegal professional.

Concept Review *and* Reinforcement

LEGAL TERMINOLOGY

SUMMARY OF KEY CONCEPTS

State Court Systems

Limited-Jurisdiction Trial Court	This state court hears matters of a specialized or limited nature (e.g., misdemeanor criminal matters, traffic tickets, civil matters under a certain dollar amount). Many states have created small-claims courts that hear small-dollar-amount civil cases (e.g., under $5,000) in which parties cannot be represented by lawyers.
General-Jurisdiction Trial Court	This is a state court that hears cases of a general nature that are not within the jurisdiction of limited-jurisdiction trial courts.
Intermediate Appellate Court	This state court hears appeals from state trial courts. The appellate court reviews the trial court record in making its decision; no new evidence is introduced at this level.
Highest State Court	Each state has a highest court in its court system. This court hears appeals from appellate courts and, where appropriate, trial courts. This court reviews the record in making its decision; no new evidence is introduced at this level. Most states call this court the *supreme court.*

Federal Court System

Special Federal Courts	Federal courts that have specialized or limited jurisdiction. They include: 1. *U.S. Tax Court:* hears cases involving federal tax laws 2. *U.S. Court of Federal Claims:* hears cases brought against the United States 3. *U.S. Court of International Trade:* hears cases involving tariffs and international commercial disputes 4. *U.S. Bankruptcy Court:* hear cases involving federal bankruptcy law
U.S. District Courts	Federal trial courts of general jurisdiction that hear cases that are not within the jurisdiction of specialized courts. Each state has at least one U.S. district court; more populated states have several district courts. The area served by one of these courts is called a *district.*

U.S. Courts of Appeals	Intermediate federal appellate courts that hear appeals from district courts located in their circuit, and in certain instances from special federal courts and federal administrative agencies. There are 12 geographical *circuits* in the United States. Eleven serve areas composed of several states, and another is located in Washington, DC. A thirteenth circuit court—the *Court of Appeals for the Federal Circuit*—is located in Washington, DC, and reviews patent, trademark, and international trade cases.

Supreme Court of the United States

U.S. Supreme Court	Highest court of the federal court system; hears appeals from the circuit courts and, in some instances, from special courts and U.S. district courts. The Court, located in Washington, DC, comprises nine justices, one of whom is named Chief Justice.
Decisions by U.S. Supreme Court	*Petition of certiorari and writ of certiorari:* To have a case heard by the U.S. Supreme Court, a petitioner must file a *petition for certiorari* with the Court. If the Court decides to hear the case, it will issue a *writ of certiorari.*
Voting by the U.S. Supreme Court	1. *Unanimous decision:* All of the justices agree as to the outcome and reasoning used to decide the case; the decision becomes precedent. 2. *Majority decision:* A majority of justices agrees as to the outcome and reasoning used to decide the case; the decision becomes precedent. 3. *Plurality decision:* A majority of the justices agrees to the outcome but not to the reasoning; the decision is not precedent. 4. *Tie decision:* If there is a tie vote, the lower court's decision stands; the decision is not precedent. 5. *Concurring opinion:* A justice who agrees as to the outcome of the case but not the reasoning used by other justices may write a concurring opinion setting forth his or her reasoning. 6. *Dissenting opinion:* A justice who disagrees with the outcome of a case may write a dissenting opinion setting forth his or her reasoning.

Jurisdiction of Federal and State Courts

Subject-Matter Jurisdiction	The court must have jurisdiction over the subject matter of the lawsuit; each court has limited jurisdiction to hear only certain types of cases.
Limited Jurisdiction of Federal Courts	Federal courts have jurisdiction to hear the following types of cases: 1. *Federal question:* cases arising under the U.S. Constitution, treaties, and federal statutes and regulations; no dollar-amount limit. 2. *Diversity of citizenship:* cases between (a) citizens of different states, (b) a citizen of a state and a citizen or subject of a foreign country; and (c) a citizen of a state and a foreign country where the foreign country is the plaintiff. The controversy must exceed $75,000 for the federal court to hear the case.
Jurisdiction of State Courts	State courts have jurisdiction to hear cases that federal courts do not have jurisdiction to hear.
Exclusive Jurisdiction	Federal courts have exclusive jurisdiction to hear cases involving federal crimes, antitrust, and bankruptcy; patent and copyright cases; suits against the United States; and most admiralty cases. State courts may not hear these matters.
Concurrent Jurisdiction	State courts hear some cases that may be heard by federal courts. State courts have concurrent jurisdiction to hear cases involving diversity of citizenship cases and federal question cases over which the federal courts do not have exclusive jurisdiction. The defendant may have the case removed to federal court.

Personal Jurisdiction and Other Issues

Standing to Sue	To bring a lawsuit, the plaintiff must have some stake in the outcome of the lawsuit.
In Personam Jurisdiction (or Personal Jurisdiction)	The court must have jurisdiction over the parties to a lawsuit. The plaintiff submits to the jurisdiction of the court by filing the lawsuit there. Personal jurisdiction is obtained over the defendant by serving that person *service of process*.
In Rem Jurisdiction	A court may have jurisdiction to hear and decide a case because it has jurisdiction over the property at issue in the lawsuit (e.g., real property located in the state).
Quasi In Rem Jurisdiction (or Attachment Jurisdiction)	A plaintiff who obtains a judgment against a defendant in one state may utilize the court system of another state to attach property of the defendant's located in the second state.
Long-Arm Statutes	These statutes permit a state to obtain personal jurisdiction over an out-of-state defendant as long as the defendant had the requisite minimum contact with the state. The out-of-state defendant may be served process outside the state in which the lawsuit has been brought.
Venue	A case must be heard by the court that has jurisdiction nearest to where the incident at issue occurred or where the parties reside. A *change of venue* will be granted if prejudice would occur because of pretrial publicity or another reason.
Forum-Selection Clause	This clause in a contract designates the court that will hear any dispute that arises out of the contract.
Choice-of-Law Clause	This clause in a contract designates what state's law or country's law will apply in resolving a dispute.

Alternative Dispute Resolution (ADR)

ADR	ADR consists of *nonjudicial* means of solving legal disputes. ADR usually saves time and money required by litigation.

Negotiation

Negotiation	A procedure whereby the parties to a dispute engage in discussions to try to reach a voluntary settlement of their dispute.

Arbitration

Arbitration	Arbitration is a form of ADR where an impartial third party, called the arbitrator, hears and decides the dispute. The arbitrator makes an award. The award is appealable to a court if the parties have not given up this right. Arbitration is designated by the parties pursuant to: 1. *Arbitration clause:* Agreement contained in a contract stipulating that any dispute arising out of the contract will be arbitrated. 2. *Submission agreement:* Agreement to submit a dispute to arbitration after the dispute arises.
Federal Arbitration Act (FAA)	Federal statute that provides that arbitration agreements involving commerce are valid, irrevocable, and enforceable contracts, unless some grounds exist at law or equity (e.g., fraud, duress) to revoke them.

Other Forms of ADR

Mediation	In mediation, a neutral third party, called a *mediator*, assists the parties in trying to reach a settlement of their dispute. The mediator does not make an award.
Conciliation	In conciliation, an interested third party, called a *conciliator*, assists the parties in trying to reach a settlement of their dispute. The conciliator does not make an award.
Minitrial	A minitrial is in a short session, the lawyers for each side present their case to representatives of each party who has the authority to settle the dispute.

Fact-Finding	In fact-finding, the parties hire a neutral third person, called a *fact-finder*, to investigate the dispute and report his or her findings to the adversaries.
Judicial Referee	With the consent of the parties, the court can appoint a judicial referee (usually a retired judge or lawyer) to conduct a private trial and render a judgment. The judgment stands as the judgment of the court and may be appealed to the appropriate appellate court.

Online ADR

Online ADR	A form of alternative dispute resolution where the parties use an online provider of ADR services. This could be online arbitration, online mediation, and other forms of online ADR.

WORKING THE WEB

1. Visit the website http://www.clickNsettle.com. What services are offered by this website? What are the costs of using this site's services?
2. Visit the website http://www.internetneutral.com. What services are offered by this site? What are the costs of these services?
3. Visit the website http://www.abanet.org/published/preview/briefs/home.html. Select one of the case names. Find the "Petitioner's Brief" for the selected case and either print out or write down the "Question Presented" for that case.
4. Visit the website http://www.law.cornell.edu/supct/index.html. Find the most recent decision of the U.S. Supreme Court. Read the case heading and the summary of the case. Who are the parties? What issue was presented to the Supreme Court? What was the decision of the Supreme Court?
5. Go to the website http://www.adr.org.overview. Read "A Brief Overview of the American Arbitration Association." Define a "neutral."
6. Find the homepage for the courts in your state. What are the names of the courts in your state? Draw a diagram of the courts of your state. Include limited-jurisdiction courts, general-jurisdiction trial courts, appellate courts, and the highest state court.

CRITICAL THINKING & WRITING QUESTIONS

1. Describe the difference between state limited-jurisdiction courts and general-jurisdiction courts.
2. What are the functions of the state intermediate courts and the highest state courts? Explain.
3. List the special federal courts, and describe the types of cases that each of these courts can hear.
4. What is the function of U.S. District Courts? How many are there?
5. What is the function of U.S. Courts of Appeals? How many U.S. Courts of Appeals are there? How does the Court of Appeals for the Federal Circuit differ from the other U.S. Courts of Appeals?
6. What is the function of the U.S. Supreme Court? How many justices does the Supreme Court have? How does the Chief Justice differ from Associate Justices?
7. Explain the difference between the following types of decisions by the U.S. Supreme Court: (1) unanimous decision, (2) majority decision, (3) plurality decision, and (4) tie decision. Which types of decision or decisions establish precedent? What are concurring opinions and dissenting opinions?
8. Explain the difference between a federal court's jurisdiction to hear a case based on (1) federal question jurisdiction and (2) diversity of citizenship jurisdiction.
9. Explain the difference between subject-matter jurisdiction and *in personam* jurisdiction. Explain the difference between *in rem* jurisdiction and *quasi in rem* jurisdiction.
10. What is a long-arm statute? What is the purpose of a long-arm statute?
11. What is venue? When can a change of venue be granted?
12. What is the difference between judicial dispute resolution and nonjudicial alternative dispute resolution? Why would one be preferred over the other, and who would have a preference?
13. Define arbitration. Describe how the process of arbitration works. What is an award?
14. Describe the difference between mediation and conciliation. How do these differ from arbitration?
15. Describe minitrial and fact-finding.

Building Paralegal Skills

Meet the Courthouse Team

An interview with Judge Kenney, a trial judge, who introduces members of the courthouse and the roles they serve as members of the courtroom team.

After viewing the video case study at www.pearsonhighered .com/goldman answer the following:
1. What type of relationship should the paralegal develop with the courthouse team?
2. In addition to the courtroom team, what other members of the courthouse should the paralegal know about?

Jury Selection: Potential Juror Challenged for Cause

Trial counsel for a case, which is going to be tried before a jury, are interviewing the individual potential jurors to select an appropriate jury member.

After viewing the video case study at www.pearsonhighered .com/goldman answer the following:
1. What is the role of the jury in the justice system?
2. Why are the attorneys allowed to request that certain individuals not be allowed to serve on a jury?
3. Is everyone guaranteed a right to a jury trial and the American system of justice?

Settlement Conference with Judge

Opposing counsel are meeting with Judge Lee prior to the start of the trial. The trial judge is presenting the strengths and weaknesses of each side in an attempt to get the parties to settle the case.

After viewing the video case study at www.pearsonhighered .com/goldman answer the following:
1. How is a settlement conference with a judge before trial like an alternative method of dispute resolution?
2. Is the judge in the settlement conference being unfair to one side or the other?
3. Why is the judge trying to settle the case before trial?

1. May a paralegal represent a client in court?
2. Are a paralegal's time records or calendar subject to the attorney–client privilege?
3. You have been appointed as a trustee of a client's children's educational trust. You need to petition the court for a release of the funds for noneducational purposes—paying the taxes on the trust income. [*Ziegler v. Harrison Nickel*, 64 Cal. App. 4th 545; 1998 Lexis 500.] May you appear alone as the trustee and represent the trust in the court proceedings? Would a nonlawyer, nonparalegal be permitted to appear?

With a group of other students, selected by you or as assigned by your instructor, review the facts of the following case. As a group, discuss the following questions.
1. What is a forum-selection clause?
2. Is putting a forum-selection clause (or choice-of-law clause) in a contract good practice?
3. If there had not been a forum-selection clause in the contract, would the state of Washington have jurisdiction over Carnival Cruise Lines to make it answer the Shute's lawsuit in Washington?

Carnival Cruise Lines, Inc. v. Shute

Mr. and Mrs. Shute, residents of the State of Washington, purchased passage for a seven-day cruise on the *Tropicale*, a cruise ship operated by Carnival Cruise Lines. Inc. (Carnival). They paid the fare to the travel agent, who forwarded the payment to Carnival's headquarters in Miami, Florida. Carnival prepared the tickets and sent them to the Shutes. Each ticket consisted of five pages, including contract terms. The ticket contained a forum-selection clause that designated the State of Florida as the forum for any lawsuits arising under or in connection with the ticket and cruise. The Shutes boarded the *Tropicale* in Los Angeles, which set sail for Puerto Vallarta, Mexico. While the ship was on its return voyage and in international waters off the coast of Mexico, Mrs. Shute was injured when she slipped on a deck mat during a guided tour of the ship's galley. Upon return to the State of Washington, she filed a negligence lawsuit against Carnival in U.S. district court in Washington, seeking damages. Carnival defended, arguing that the lawsuit could only be brought in a court located in the State of Florida pursuant to the forum-selection clause contained in its ticket.

The U.S. Supreme Court held that the forum-selection clause contained in Carnival Cruise Lines' ticket was enforceable against Mrs. Shute. The Supreme Court stated that including a reasonable forum clause in a form contract is permissible for several reasons. First, a cruise line has a special interest in limiting the number of jurisdictions in which it potentially could be subject to a lawsuit. Because a cruise ship typically carries passengers from many locales, it is likely that a mishap on a cruise could subject the cruise line to litigation in several different jurisdictions. Secondly, a clause establishing the forum for dispute resolution dispels any confusion as to where lawsuits arising from the contract must be brought and defended, sparing litigants the time and expense of pretrial motions to determine the correct forum, and conserving judicial resources needed to decide such issues. Finally, passengers who purchase tickets containing a forum-selection clause benefit in reduced fares reflecting the savings that the cruise line enjoys by limiting the forum in which it may be sued.

The Supreme Court held that the forum-selection clause in Carnival Cruise Lines' ticket was fair and reasonable, and therefore enforceable against Mrs. Shute. If Mrs. Shute wished to sue Carnival Cruise Lines, she must do so in a court in the State of Florida, not in a court in the State of Washington.

Source: *Carnival Cruise Lines, Inc. v. Shute*, 499 U.S. 585, 111 S.Ct. 1522, 113 L.Ed.2d 622, **Web** 1991 U.S. Lexis 2221 (Supreme Court of the United States)

PARALEGAL PORTFOLIO EXERCISE

Based on the facts of the case described in the Opening Scenario, prepare and complete the following documents as well as you can from the facts of the scenario.

1. A complaint to file the case on behalf of the plaintiff against the defendant in the appropriate trial court of your state.
2. The defendant's answer to the complaint.

LEGAL ANALYSIS & WRITING CASES

Ashcroft, Attorney General v. The Free Speech Coalition

535 U.S. 234, 122 S.Ct. 1389, 152 L.Ed.2d 403, Web 2002 U.S. Lexis 2789

Supreme Court of the United States

Congress enacted the Child Pornography Prevention Act (CPPA). Section 2256(8)(B) of the act prohibits "any visual depiction, including any photograph, film, video, picture, or computer-generated image or picture" that "is, or appears to be, of a minor engaging in sexually explicit conduct." This section includes computer-generated images known as "virtual child pornography." A first-time offender may be imprisoned for 15 years; repeat offenders face prison sentences up to 30 years. The Free Speech Coalition, a trade association for the adult-entertainment industry, sued the United States, alleging that Section 2256(8)(B) violated their constitutional free speech rights. The District Court granted summary judgment to the United States government, but the court of appeals reversed. The U.S. Supreme Court granted certiorari.

Question

1. Does Section 2256(8)(B), which criminalizes virtual child pornography, violate the Freedom of Speech Clause of the First Amendment to the U.S. Constitution?

Carnival Cruise Lines, Inc. v. Shute

499 U.S. 585, 111 S.Ct. 1522, 113 L.Ed.2d 622, Web 1991 U.S. Lexis 2221

Supreme Court of the United States

Mr. and Mrs. Shute, residents of the state of Washington, purchased passage for a seven-day cruise on the *Tropicale*, a cruise ship operated by the Carnival Cruise Lines, Inc. (Carnival). They paid the fare to the travel agent, who forwarded the payment to Carnival's headquarters in Miami, Florida. Carnival prepared the tickets and sent them to the Shutes. Each ticket consisted of five pages, including contract terms. The ticket contained a forum-selection clause that designated the state of Florida as the forum for any lawsuits arising under or in connection with the ticket and cruise.

The Shutes boarded the *Tropicale* in Los Angeles, which set sail for Puerto Vallarta, Mexico. While the ship was on its return voyage and in international waters off the Mexican coast, Mrs. Shute was injured when she slipped on a deck mat during a guided tour of the ship's galley. Upon return to Washington, she filed a negligence lawsuit against Carnival in U.S. district court in Washington, seeking damages. Carnival filed a motion for summary judgment contending that the suit could be brought only in a court located in the state of Florida. The District Court granted Carnival's motion. The court of appeals reversed, holding that Mrs. Shute could sue Carnival in Washington. Carnival appealed to the U.S. Supreme Court.

Question

1. Is the forum-selection clause in Carnival Cruise Lines' ticket enforceable?

Allison v. ITE Imperial Corporation

729 F.Supp. 45, Web 1990 U.S. Dist. Lexis 607

United States District Court for the Southern District of Mississippi

James Clayton Allison, a resident of Mississippi, was employed by the Tru-Amp Corporation as a circuit breaker tester. As part of his employment, Allison was sent to inspect, clean, and test a switch gear located at the South Central Bell Telephone Facility in Brentwood, Tennessee. One day he attempted to remove a circuit breaker manufactured by ITE Corporation (ITE) from a bank of breakers when a portion of the breaker fell off. The broken piece fell behind a switching bank and, according to Allison, caused an electrical fire and explosion. Allison was severely burned in the accident. Allison brought suit against ITE in Mississippi state court, claiming damages.

Question

1. Can this suit be removed to federal court?

AMF Inc. v. Brunswick Corporation

621 F.Supp. 456, Web 1985 U.S. Dist. Lexis 14205

United States District Court for the Eastern District of New York

AMF Incorporated and Brunswick Corporation both manufacture electric and automatic bowling center equipment. The two companies became involved in a dispute over whether Brunswick had advertised certain automatic scoring devices in a false and deceptive manner. The two parties settled the dispute by signing an agreement that any future problems between them involving advertising claims would be submitted to the National Advertising Council for arbitration. Two years later Brunswick advertised a new product, Armor Plate 3000, a synthetic laminated material used to make bowling lanes. Armor Plate 3000 competed with wooden lanes produced by AMF. Brunswick's advertisements claimed that bowling centers could save up to $500 per lane per year in maintenance and repair costs if they would switch to Armor Plate 3000 from wooden lanes. AMF disputed this claim and requested arbitration.

Question

1. Is the arbitration agreement enforceable?

Calder v. Jones

465 U.S. 783, 104 S.Ct. 1482, 79 L.Ed.2d 804, Web 1984 U.S. Lexis 41

Supreme Court of the United States

The National Enquirer, Inc., a Florida corporation, has its principal place of business in Florida. It publishes the *National Enquirer*, a national weekly newspaper with a circulation of more than 5 million copies. About 600,000 copies, almost twice the level of the next highest state, are sold in California. The *Enquirer* published an article about Shirley Jones, an entertainer. Jones, a California resident, filed a lawsuit in California state court against the *Enquirer* and its president, a resident of Florida. The suit sought damages for alleged defamation, invasion of privacy, and intentional infliction of emotional distress.

Question

1. Are the defendants subject to suit in California?

Burnham v. Superior Court of California — **495 U.S. 604, 110 S.Ct. 2105, 109 LEd.2d 631, Web 1990 U.S. Lexis 2700**

Supreme Court of the United States

Dennis and Francis Burnham were married and lived in New Jersey, where their two children were born. Ten years later the Burnhams decided to separate. Mrs. Burnham, who intended to move to California, was to have custody of the children. Mr. Burnham agreed to file for divorce on grounds of "irreconcilable differences." Mr. Burnham threatened to file for divorce in New Jersey on grounds of "desertion." After unsuccessfully demanding that Mr. Burnham adhere to the prior agreement, Mrs. Burnham brought suit for divorce in California state court. One month later Mr. Burnham visited California on a business trip. He then visited his children in the San Francisco Bay area, where his wife resided. He took the older child to San Francisco for the weekend. Upon returning the child to Mrs. Burnham's home, he was served with a California court summons and a copy of Mrs. Burnham's divorce petition. He then returned to New Jersey. Mr. Burnham made a special appearance in the California court and moved to quash the service of process.

Question

1. Did Mr. Burnham act ethically in trying to quash the service of process? Did Mrs. Burnham act ethically in having Mr. Burnham served on his visit to California? Is the service of process good?

WORKING WITH THE LANGUAGE OF THE COURT CASE

Adler v. Duval County School Board

112 F.3d 1475, Web 1997 U.S. App. Lexis 10000
United States Court of Appeals for the Eleventh Circuit

Read the following case, excerpted from the court of appeals opinion. Review and brief the case. In your brief, answer the following questions.

1. What is the doctrine of mootness?
2. What was the action the plaintiffs complained of?
3. When would the plaintiffs have had to file and have their case heard for the court to rule on their claim?
4. How would bringing the cases as a class action have allowed the court to hear the case under the Case or Controversy requirement?
5. How does this case differ from the case of *Lee v. Weisman* in Chapter 5?

Tjoflat, Circuit Judge

Appellants are four former high school students in the Duval County, Florida, school system who brought this action under 42 U.S.C. § 1983 (1994), alleging that a Duval County school policy permitting student-initiated prayer at high school graduation ceremonies (the "policy") violated their rights under the First and Fourteenth Amendments.

On June 7, 1993, three of the appellants graduated from Mandarin, one of the schools in the Duval County system. A fourth appellant graduated in June 1994. Because all four appellants have graduated, we find that to the extent they seek declaratory and injunctive relief, their case is moot. The only justiciable controversy in this case is the appellants' claim for money damages. We affirm the District Court's grant of summary judgment for the appellees on this claim, but we do so without reviewing the merits of the District Court's constitutional analysis. We begin by noting that appellants' claims for declaratory and injunctive relief are moot. All appellants have graduated, and none is threatened with harm from possible prayers in future Duval County graduation ceremonies. . . .

Article III of the Constitution limits the jurisdiction of the federal courts to the consideration of certain "Cases" and "Controversies.". . . The doctrine of mootness is derived from this limitation because an action that is moot cannot be characterized as an active case or controversy. "[A] case is moot when the issues presented are no longer 'live' or the parties lack a legally cognizable interest in the outcome." Any decision on the merits of a moot case would be an impermissible advisory opinion.

To apply the doctrine of mootness to this case, we must distinguish the appellants' claims for equitable relief from their claim for money damages. . . .

(continued)

Equitable relief is a prospective remedy, intended to prevent future injuries. In contrast, a claim for money damages looks back in time and is intended to redress a past injury. The plaintiff requests money damages to redress injuries caused by the defendant's past conduct and seeks equitable relief to prevent the defendant's future conduct from causing future injury. When the threat of future harm dissipates, the plaintiff's claims for equitable relief become moot because the plaintiff no longer needs protection from future injury. This is precisely what happened in this case.

Appellants argue that, despite their graduation from high school, their claims for declaratory and injunctive relief are not moot because the original injury is "capable of repetition, yet evading review." This exception to the mootness doctrine is narrow. In the absence of a class action, the "capable of repetition, yet evading review" doctrine is limited to the situation where two elements combine: (1) the challenged action [is] in its duration too short to be fully litigated prior to its cessation or expiration, and (2) there is a reasonable expectation that the same complaining party will be subjected to the same action again. This case does not satisfy the second element. Because the complaining students have graduated from high school, there is no reasonable expectation that they will be subjected to the same injury again.

Having disposed of the appellants' claims for equitable relief, we are left with their claim for money damages, which we now address. Because the appellants' claim for money damages does not depend on any threat of future harm, this claim remains a live controversy. We accordingly turn our focus to the basis for the appellants' claim for damages. The complaint alleges that a "senior class chaplain" delivered a prayer at the June 7, 1993, Mandarin graduation ceremony at which appellants Adler, Jaffa, and Zion graduated. The only past injury for which the appellants could seek redress is being subjected to this prayer at their graduation ceremony. To prove that the appellees caused this injury, the appellants alleged in their complaint that the prayer was "a direct consequence" of the school's policy. In their answer, the appellees admitted that a student said the prayer, but denied that the prayer was a consequence of the policy.

The only issue the appellants raise on appeal is whether the District Court erred in holding the policy constitutional. While the constitutionality of the policy may have been central to the now moot issue of whether equitable relief is warranted to prevent the policy from being implemented at future graduations, it does not dispose of the issue of whether the appellants should be awarded money damages for being subjected to the prayer at their graduation. In other words, any claim for damages does not depend on the constitutionality of the policy in the abstract or as applied in other Duval County schools.

Even if the policy is unconstitutional, the defendants might not be liable if, for example, they did not implement the policy at the ceremony in question or if the prayer would have been delivered without the policy. On the other hand, if the District Court was correct in finding the policy constitutional, defendant Epting, Mandarin's principal, might nonetheless be liable if he implemented the policy in an unconstitutional manner.

The constitutionality of the policy, therefore, has little independent relevance to the appellants' damages claim. Whether they are entitled to damages depends entirely on the circumstances under which the prayer was delivered at their graduation ceremony. In order to prevail, the appellants must have some theory connecting the individual defendants to the prayer. For these reasons, even if we were to find fault with the district court's constitutional analysis of the policy, this conclusion by itself would not answer the question of whether the court erred in granting the appellees summary judgment on the damages claim. The appellants offer no other grounds in their briefs for finding trial court error.

After considering the appellants' briefs and oral argument, we are convinced that they either fail to understand the basis for their damages claim or do not seriously seek damages. They have offered us no connection between the prayer and their damages claim; their briefs offer no indication as to any of the circumstances surrounding the Mandarin graduation prayer. They failed to argue that the prayer was a "direct consequence" of the policy, or any other theory connecting the defendants' actions to the Mandarin prayer. Their briefs do not even include the allegation made in their complaint that a prayer was delivered at Mandarin.

For all these reasons, we hold that they have waived their damages claim on appeal. We therefore affirm the District Court's order to the extent it denied the appellants' motion for summary judgment and granted the appellees' motions for summary judgment on the appellants' damages claim. For the foregoing reasons, we vacate the district court's order granting the appellees summary judgment on the appellants' claims for declaratory and injunctive relief and remand the case with instructions that the District Court dismiss those claims. We affirm the District Court's denial of the appellants' motion for summary judgment and its grant of summary judgment for the appellees on the appellants' damages claim. It is so ordered.

UPDATE TO CASE

After a rehearing en banc the court, upon a majority vote of the judges of the court, issued a subsequent opinion on June 3, 1999, and on March 15, 2000, on further proceeding the Court ruled that the policy on prayer did not violate the Establishment Clause. On June 19, 2000, the Supreme Court rendered a decision in *Santa Fe Independent School District v. Doe*, 530 U.S. 290, which invalidated a Texas school board's policy permitting students to vote on a prayer subject to officials' approval at home football games. The Duval Court proceeded to rehear the case based on the *Santa Fe* decision and ruled again in favor of the Duval School Board because the prayer there was not subject to official approval or input [*Adler v. Duval County School Board*, 250 F.3d 1330, 2001 U.S. App. Lexis 8880 (United States Court of Appeals for the Eleventh Circuit)].

Civil Litigation

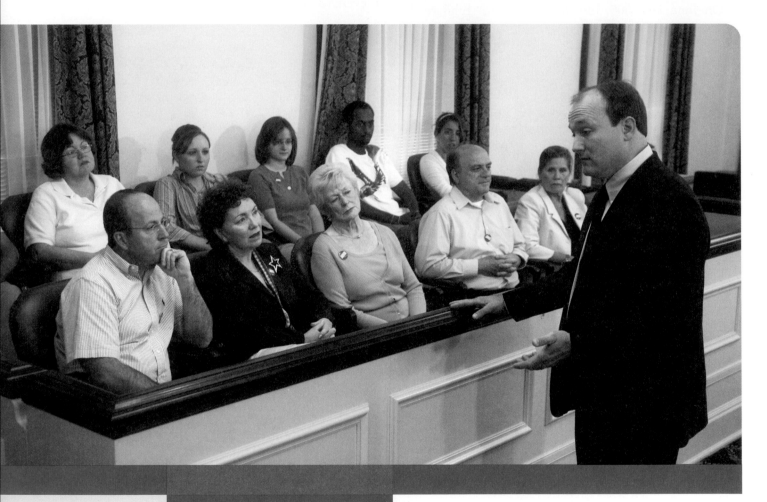

DIGITAL RESOURCES

Chapter 7 Digital Resources at *www.pearsonhighered.com/goldman*

- Video Case Studies:
  - Videotaped Deposition: Deposing an Expert Witness for Use at Trial
  - Trial: Direct and Cross-examination of a Witness
  - Preparing for Trial: Preparing a Fact Witness
- Chapter Summary • Web Links • Court Opinions • Glossary • Comprehension Quizzes
- Technology Resources

> " Discourage litigation. Persuade your neighbors to compromise whenever you can. Point out to them how the nominal winner is often a real loser—in fees, and expenses, and waste of time. As a peacemaker, the lawyer has a superior opportunity of being a good man. There will still be business enough. "
>
> *Abraham Lincoln,*
> *Notes on the Practice of Law (1850)*

After studying this chapter, you should be able to:

1. Complete a set of basic documents used in civil litigation.
2. Describe the discover process and its purposes.
3. Explain the purposes of pretrial motions.
4. Explain what happens in a settlement conference.
5. Describe the steps in a trial.
6. Explain how verdicts and judgments are rendered at trial.
7. Describe how a case is appealed and what decisions can be rendered by an appellate court.

Paralegals at Work

Rowan, a middle school student, and his sister Isis, a high school student, were passengers on the last school bus of the day on their way home after Rowan's basketball practice and his sister's choir practice. The bus had made its regular stops and was on a public highway when it was struck by a large commercial truck. Rowan's injuries were severe enough to prevent him from playing basketball for the rest of the season on his school team and local club team that was in the championship. Isis had been practicing and eagerly looking forward to traveling with the school choir on an invitational European tour.

Their parents have retained your law firm, on a contingent fee basis, to pursue a claim for their children's injuries and their out-of-pocket expenses. A review of the medical bills shows expenses in excess of $75,000 for each child. Because of the nature of the accident it was investigated by the National Transportation Safety Board, which issued a report indicating the probable cause of the accident was the failure of the brakes on the truck. The truck driver in his initial police statement indicated that he had had no problems with the vehicle before the accident and that he relied upon the mechanics in the maintenance facility to maintain the vehicle, and especially the brakes. The trucking company has denied any liability. No initial reports or documentation were provided by the trucking company to the police because all of the truck and maintenance records were kept in electronic format at the company's corporate headquarters in another state. The first decision is deciding in which court to commence suit.

Consider the issues involved in this scenario as you read the chapter.

INTRODUCTION FOR THE PARALEGAL

Litigation The process of bringing, maintaining, and defending a lawsuit.

Paralegals often work for lawyers who specialize in civil litigation, seeking monetary damages or other remedies, or in the prosecution or defense of criminal cases. The bringing, maintaining, and defense of a lawsuit comprise the litigation process, or **litigation**.

Civil litigation is an area in which a paralegal's talents can shine. The paralegal's analytical ability, expertise in legal research, ability to draft pleadings and documents, and other skills are truly put to the test. Paralegals who choose to work in the litigation field must have excellent knowledge of the various facets of the litigation process, the rules of evidence, and court procedure.

A paralegal's first introduction to a new lawsuit will be when a client employs the law firm for whom the paralegal works to represent the client in a civil lawsuit. The client may be either the plaintiff or the defendant. Many times the paralegal's first work assignment is to sit in on conferences between the attorney and the client, and to take notes of pending issues.

Then the paralegal usually is notified to "start a file" for the lawsuit. This means obtaining available evidence, documents, and other items relevant to the case. Each attorney has his or her own system for preparing a case for trial (or settlement), and the paralegal has his or her own way of preparing the file as well.

The paralegal often is assigned to help draft the pleadings for the case. In addition, the paralegal may interview the client, contact the client for information, draft documents to obtain production of documents and other evidence, and assist in the preparation of depositions to be taken or attended by his or her supervising attorney.

At this stage, the paralegal is involved in the case as much as his or her supervising attorney. Because of their knowledge of a case, paralegals can be indispensable in the proper preparation for lawyer–client meetings, discovery, depositions, and settlement conferences.

If the case is to go to trial, the paralegal usually is called upon to help conduct the legal research that will be placed in the brief of the case to be submitted to the court. The paralegal's responsibility is to help organize the case for trial, and to use all available technology to prepare the case for trial. At trial, the paralegal becomes indispensable in assisting the attorney to present his or her case on behalf of the client.

Civil Litigation

Civil litigation involves legal action to resolve disputes between parties, as contrasted with criminal litigation, which is brought by the government against a party accused of violating the law. The parties to civil litigation may be individuals, businesses, or in some cases, government agencies. Although the fundamental process is the same, the court and the procedure may vary.

Many lawyers specialize in civil litigation, in which a plaintiff sues a defendant to recover money damages or other remedy for the alleged harm the defendant causes the plaintiff. This may be an automobile accident case, a suit alleging a breach of a contract, a claim of patent infringement, or any of a myriad of other civil wrongs.

In a civil case, either party can appeal the trial court's decision once a final judgment is entered. In a criminal case, only the defendant can appeal. The appeal is made to the appropriate appellate court. This chapter discusses civil litigation and the appellate process; the criminal process is covered in Chapter 8.

Pleadings

Pleadings The paperwork that is filed with the court to initiate and respond to a lawsuit.

The paperwork that is filed with the court to initiate and respond to a lawsuit is referred to as the **pleadings**. The major pleadings are the complaint, or petition in some states, the answer, the cross-complaint, and the reply.

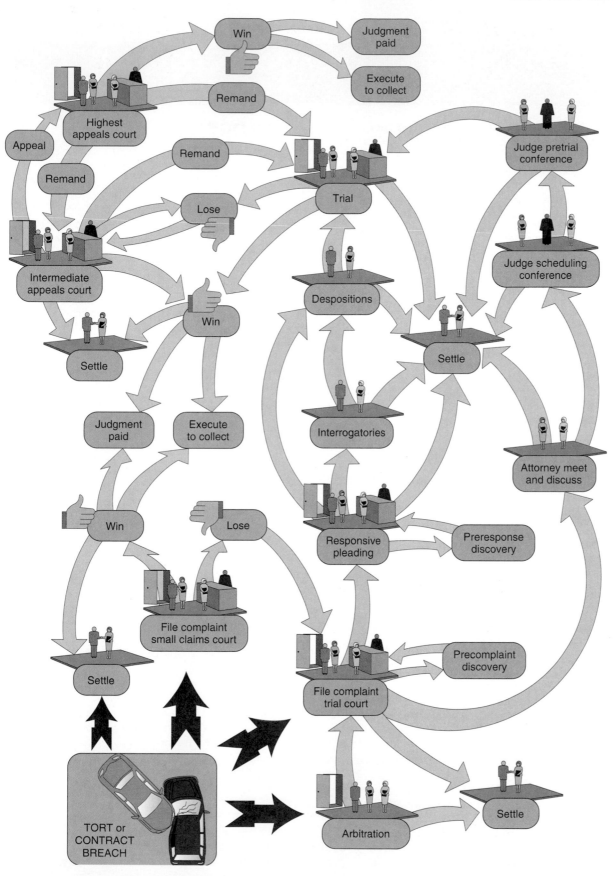

Advice *from the* Field

From your first conversation with a prospective client, you're learning about the dispute that led the individual or corporation to seek counsel. There are many benefits to taking a systematic approach to analyzing this knowledge. Not least of these is the favorable impression you'll make on those who retain you.

The following article presents a method for organizing and evaluating the facts about any case. And it illustrates how the early results of this dispute analysis process can be used to great effect in an initial case analysis session with your client.

When you take this approach to case analysis, you'll gain a thorough understanding of the dispute and clarify your thinking about it. And, as you sort out what you do know about the case, you'll find it easy to Identify what you don't know and need to find out.

The process focuses on creating four analysis reports: a Cast of Characters, a Chronology, an Issue List, and a Question List. These reports provide a framework for organizing and evaluating critical case knowledge. If multiple people are involved in the analysis process, the reports provide a way to divide responsibility and share results. Moreover, once you standardize the analysis work product, it's easy to compare the findings in one matter to the analysis results from other similar disputes.

You should create your case analysis reports using database software, not a word-processor. Database software makes the knowledge you're organizing far easier to explore and evaluate. For example, using database software, it's easy to filter your Chronology so it displays only facts that have been evaluated as being particularly troublesome.

CAST OF CHARACTERS

Create a Cast of Characters that lists the individuals and organizations you know are involved in the dispute. This report should also catalog key documents and other important pieces of physical evidence. Capture each player's name and a description of the role the person, organization, or document plays in the case.

Also include a column in which you can indicate your evaluation of cast members. Even if you don't evaluate every player, it's essential to note the people and documents that are particularly worrisome, as well as the basis for your concerns. If you follow my recommendation that you build your dispute analysis reports using database software, you will find it easy to filter the entire cast list down to the problem players you've identified.

CHRONOLOGY

A chronology of key facts is a critical tool for analyzing any dispute. As you create the chronology, important factual disputes and areas of strength and weakness become obvious.

Begin by listing the fact and the date on which it occurred. As you enter each fact, be sure to make the important details about the fact explicit. For example, rather than simply stating "Gayle phoned David," write "Gayle phoned David, and asked him to shred the Fritz Memo." Remember that your chronology should be a memory replacement, not a memory jogger.

Since you're analyzing the case within weeks of being retained, there will be many facts for which you have only partial date information. For example, you may know that Gayle called David about the Fritz Memo sometime in June of 1993, but be unsure as to the day within June. When you run into this problem, a simple solution is to substitute a question mark for the portion of the date that's undetermined, e.g., 6/?/99.

In addition to capturing the fact and the date, be sure to list a source or sources for each fact. Now, in the early days of a case, it's likely that the sources of many of the facts you are entering in your chronology are not of a type that will pass muster come trial. However, by capturing a source such as "David Smith Interview Notes," you know to whom or what you will need to turn to develop a court-acceptable source.

The mission in early dispute analysis is to take a broad look at the potential evidence. Therefore, your chronology should be more than a list of undisputed facts. Be sure to include disputed facts and even prospective facts (i.e., facts that you suspect may turn up as the case proceeds toward trial). You'll want to distinguish the facts that are undisputed from those that are disputed or merely prospective. Include in your chronology a column that you use for this purpose.

Finally, include a column that you use to separate the critical facts from others of lesser importance. A simple solution is to have a column titled "Key" that you set up as a checkbox (checked means the fact is key, unchecked means its not). If you're using database software, filtering the chronology down to the key items should take you about 2 seconds.

ISSUE LIST

Build a list of case issues including both legal claims and critical factual disputes. If the case has yet to be filed, list the claims and counter-claims or cross-claims you anticipate. Rather than listing just the top-level issues, consider breaking each claim down to its component parts. For example, rather than listing Fraud, list Fraud: Intent, Fraud: Reliance, and so on as separate dimensions.

In addition to listing a name for each issue, create a more detailed description of it. The description might include a brief summary of each party's position on the issue and, if it's a legal issue, the potential language of the judge's instruction.

As your case proceeds to trial, your Issue List will increase in importance. You'll use the Issue List to return to the Cast of Characters and Chronology and establish relationships between each fact, each witness, each document, and the issue or issues to which it relates. Once you've made these links, it will be easy to focus on the evidence that's being developed regarding each issue and to make decisions about case strategy based on this analysis.

QUESTION LIST

When you start case analysis early, your knowledge of the dispute is sure to be incomplete. But as you map out what is known about the case, what is unknown and must be determined becomes clear.

Each time you come up with a question about the case that you can't readily answer, get it into your Question List. You'll want your report to include a column for the question and another column where you can capture notes regarding the answer. Also include a column for evaluating the criticality of each question. Use a simple A (extremely critical), B, C, and D scale to make your assessment. Other columns to consider for your Question List are "Assigned To" and "Due Date."

The analysis reports you've begun are "living" ones. As you head toward trial, keep working on your Cast of Characters, your Chronology, your Issue List, and your Question List. These analysis reports will do far more than help you think about your case. They'll serve a myriad of concrete purposes. They'll help you keep your client up-to-date, plan for discovery, prepare to take and defend depositions, create motions for summary judgment, and make your case at settlement conferences and at trial.

Copyright DecisionQuest 1994, 2006. Michael E. Cobo is a founding member of DecisionQuest, the nation's leading trial consulting firm. The principals of DecisionQuest have retained on over 12,500 high-stakes, high-risk litigation cases spanning a wide range of industries. Discover more at www.decisionquest.com.

Complaint

The party who is suing—the **plaintiff**—must file a **complaint**, also called a plaintiff's original petition or summons in some jurisdictions, with the proper court. The content and form of the complaint will vary depending on local courts' procedural rules. Many courts follow the federal practice of "notice pleading." Other state courts follow the traditional form requiring detailed allegations of the basis for the action.

A complaint must name the parties to the lawsuit, allege the ultimate facts and law violated, and state the remedy desired and the "prayer for relief" to be awarded by the court. The complaint can be as long as necessary, depending on the case's complexity. Exhibit 7.1 is a sample state trial court complaint filed in Pennsylvania. Exhibit 7.2 is a federal complaint. Exhibit 7.3 is a bilingual notice to plead a complaint.

In some jurisdictions, after a complaint has been filed with the court, the court issues a **summons**, a court order directing the **defendant** to appear in court and answer the complaint. A fundamental requirement is that notice be given to the defendant. A sheriff, another government official, or a private process server may serve the complaint and, where required, the summons on the defendant. In some cases, the defendant may be served by other means, such as by publication when the defendant cannot otherwise be found to be served personally.

Plaintiff The party who files the complaint.

Complaint The document the plaintiff files with the court and serves on the defendant to initiate a lawsuit.

 Web Exploration

Go to www.eff.org/IP/digitalradio/XM_complaint.pdf to view a copy of a complaint filed in U.S. district court.

Summons A court order directing the defendant to appear in court and answer the complaint.

Defendant The party who files the answer.

Fact and Notice Pleading

In the federal courts and in some state courts, the complaint need only provide a general allegation of the wrongful conduct alleged, this is called **notice pleading**. The sample complaint in Exhibit 7.2 is an example of a notice pleading in federal court. In other states, the plaintiff must plead specific facts alleged to have been committed that constitute the wrong complained of, this is known as **fact pleading**. The sample state complaint in Exhibit 7.1 is an example of a fact pleading.

Court rules require an attorney to sign the documents filed unless a person is filing on his or her own behalf, called a *pro se* filing. In federal court, Rule 11 governs the attorney's obligations and the potential penalties, as discussed in the following case.

IN THE WORDS OF THE COURT

Notice Pleading

CONLEY V. GIBSON, 355 U.S. 41, 47-48 (1957) 78 S.CT. 99

. . . The respondents also argue that the complaint failed to set forth specific facts to support its general allegations of discrimination and that its dismissal is therefore proper. The decisive answer to this is that the Federal Rules of Civil Procedure do not require a claimant to set out in detail the facts upon which he bases his claim. To the contrary, all the Rules require is "a short and plain statement of the claim" that will give the defendant fair notice of what the plaintiff's claim is and the grounds upon which it rests. The illustrative forms appended to the Rules plainly demonstrate this. Such simplified "notice pleading" is made possible by the liberal opportunity for discovery and the other pretrial procedures established by the Rules to disclose more precisely the basis of both claim and defense and to define more narrowly the disputed facts and issues. Following the simple guide of Rule 8(f) that "all pleadings shall be so construed as to do substantial justice," we have no doubt that petitioners' complaint adequately set forth a claim and gave the respondents fair notice of its basis. The Federal Rules reject the approach that pleading is a game of skill in which one misstep by counsel may be decisive to the outcome and accept the principle that the purpose of pleading is to facilitate a proper decision on the merits. Cf. *Maty v. Grasselli Chemical Co., 303 U.S. 197* . . .

IN THE WORDS OF THE COURT

Federal Rule 11

LEAHY V. EDMONDS SCHOOL DISTRICT (W.D.WASH. 3-2-2009)

. . . C. Rule 11 Sanctions

Defendants also argue that Plaintiff's counsel should personally be liable for attorney's fees under Rule 11. Rule 11 generally provides guidelines for attorneys to follow when submitting a pleading to the court. The rule "imposes a duty on attorneys to certify that they have conducted a reasonable inquiry and have determined that any papers filed with the court are well grounded in fact, legally tenable, and not interposed for any improper purpose." *Cooter & Gell v. Hartmarx Corp.*, 496 U.S. 384, 393 (1990). "The central purpose of Rule 11 is to deter baseless filing in district court[.]" *Id.* (internal quotations omitted). Additionally, "[s]anctions must be imposed on the signer of a paper if the paper is 'frivolous.'" *In re Keegan Mgmt. Co., 78 F.3d 431, 434* (9th Cir. 1996). Although the word "frivolous" does not appear in the text of the rule, it is well-established that it denotes "a filing that is *both* baseless *and* made without a reasonable and competent inquiry." *Id.* (citation omitted) (emphasis in original). The Ninth Circuit has explained that "there are basically three types of submitted papers which warrant sanctions: factually frivolous (not 'well grounded in fact'); legally frivolous (not 'warranted by existing law or a good faith argument for the extension, modification, or reversal of existing law'); and papers 'interposed for an improper purpose.'" *Business Guides, Inc. v. Chromatic Commc'ns Enterprises, Inc., 892 F.2d 802, 808* (9th Cir. 1989) (quoting FRCP *11*). . . .

Exhibit 7.1 Sample state

IN THE COURT OF COMMON PLEAS OF BUCKS COUNTY, PA.
CIVIL ACTION-LAW

COUNTY LINE FENCE CO., INC.   :   NO.
2051 W. County Line Road
Warrington, PA 18976   :

     V.   ATTORNEY I.D. #12204

WAYNE YARNELL   :
5707 Dunbar Court
Bensalem, PA 19020   :

COMPLAINT

1. Plaintiff is County Line Fence Company, Inc., a Pennsylvania corporation duly authorized to do business in Pennsylvania, with a place of business at 2051 W. County Line Road, Warrington, Bucks County, Pennsylvania.

2. Defendant, WAYNE YARNELL, is an adult individual residing at 5707 Dunbar Court, Bensalem, Pennsylvania.

3. On or about April 30, 2002, Defendant entered into a contract with the Plaintiff for a 140 ft. Bufftech fence to be installed on Defendant's property at 5707 Dunbar Court, Bensalem, PA 19020. (See Exhibit "A")

4. Plaintiff properly and adequately installed the fencing per the contract.

5. Defendant agreed to pay a total of $5,300.00 for the fence.

6. Demand was made upon the Defendant by Plaintiff for payment of the amount due for fencing and installation.

7. In spite of the demand for payment, Defendant has failed and refused, and continues to fail and refuse to pay Plaintiff the balance due.

WHEREFORE, Plaintiff demands judgment in the amount of $5,300.00, together with attorneys fees, costs of suit and any additional amounts as the court deems proper.
THOMAS F. GOLDMAN & ASSOCIATES

Thomas F. Goldman

Thomas F. Goldman, Esquire
Attorney for Plaintiff

Exhibit 7.2 **Complaint filed in federal court**

UNITED STATES DISTRICT COURT
FOR THE DISTRICT OF COLUMBIA

UNITED STATES OF AMERICA	) CASE NUMBER 1:01CV01660
	) JUDGE: Ricardo M. Urbina
	) DECK TYPE: General Civil
Plaintiff,	) DATE STAMP: 08/01/2002
	)
v.	)
	) Civ. No.
	) COMPLAINT FOR CIVIL
ENHANCED SERVICES BILLING, INC.	) PENALTIES, PERMANENT
BILLING CONCEPTS, INC.,	) INJUNCTION, CONSUMER
Delaware Corporations,	) REDRESS AND OTHER
both with their principal place of business at	) EQUITABLE RELIEF
7411 John Smith Drive, Suite 200	)
San Antonio, Texas 78229,	)
	)
NEW CENTURY EQUITY HOLDINGS CORP.	)
A Delaware Corporation,	)
10101 Reunion Place, Suite 450	)
San Antonio, Texas 78216	)
	)
	)
Defendants.	)

Plaintiff, the United States of America, acting upon notification and authorization to the Attorney General by the Federal Trade Commission ("FTC" or "Commission"), for its complaint alleges that:

1. Plaintiff brings this action under Sections 5(a)(1), 5(m)(1)(A), 9, 13(b), 16(a) and 19 of the Federal Trade Commission Act, 15 U.S.C. §§45(a)(1),

Exhibit 7.2   **Complaint filed in federal court** *(continued)*

45(m)(1)(A), 49, 53(b), 56(a) and 57b, and the Telephone Disclosure and Dispute Resolution Act of 1992 ("TDDRA"), 15 U.S.C. §§ 5701 *et. seq.*, to obtain injunctive relief and consumer redress for violations of Section 5(a)(1) of the Federal Trade Commission Act, 15 U.S.C. § 45(a)(1), and to obtain monetary civil penalties, consumer redress and injunctive and other relief for Defendants' violations of the Commission's Trade Regulation Rule Pursuant to the Telephone Disclosure and Dispute Resolution Act of 1992 ("900-Number Rule"), 16 C.F.R. Part 308.

JURISDICTION AND VENUE

2. This court has jurisdiction over this matter under 28 U.S.C. §§ 1331, 1337(a), 1345 and 1355 and under 15 U.S.C. §§ 45(m)(1)(A), 49, 53(b), 56(a), 57b, 5721 and 5723. This action arises under 15 U.S.C. § 45(a)(1).

3. Venue in the District of Columbia is proper under 15 U.S.C. § 53(b) and 28 U.S.C. §§ 1391(b) and (c) and 1395(a).

DEFENDANTS

4. Defendant Enhanced Services Billing, Inc. is a Delaware corporation with its principal place of business at 7411 John Smith Drive, Suite 200, San Antonio, Texas 78229. Enhanced Services Billing, Inc. provides or provided billing and collection services for vendors who market Internet Web sites, psychic memberships, voice mail and hospital telephone and television rental, and other enhanced services. Enhanced Services Billing, Inc. was incorporated on March 17, 1994. Enhanced Services Billing, Inc. transacts or has transacted business in this district.

5. Defendant Billing Concepts, Inc. is a Delaware corporation with its principal place of business at 7411 John Smith Drive, Suite 200, San Antonio, Texas 78229. Billing Concepts, Inc. provides or provided billing and collection services for vendors who market . . .

Exhibit 7.3 **Bilingual notice to plead a complaint**

IN THE COURT OF COMMON PLEAS
OF PHILADELPHIA COUNTY, PENNSYLVANIA
CIVIL ACTION LAW

KATHRYN KELSEY   : NO.

    vs.   : ATTORNEY I.D. NO.

KATHRYN CARROLL   : COMPLAINT IN EQUITY

COMPLAINT – CIVIL ACTION

NOTICE	AVISO
You have been sued in court. If you wish to defend against the claims set forth in the following pages, you must take action within twenty (20) days after this complaint and notice are served, by entering a written appearance personally or by attorney and filing in writing with the court your defenses or objections to the claims set forth against you. You are warned that if you fail to do so the case may proceed without you and a judgment may be entered against you by the court without further notice for any money claimed in the complaint or for any other claims or relief requested by the plaintiff. You may lose money or property or other rights important to you.	Le han demandado a usted en la corte. Si usted quiere defenderse de estas demandas expuestas en las paginas siguientes, usted tiene veinte (20) dias de plazo al partir de la fecha de la demanda y la notificacion. Hace falta asentar una compancia escrita o en persona o con un abogado y entregar a la corte en forma escrita sus defensas o sus objeciones a las demandas en contra de su persona. Sea avisado que si usted no se defiende, la corta tomara medidas y puede continuar la demanda en contra suya sin previo aviso o notificacion. Ademas, la corte puede decidir a favor del demandante y requiere que usted cumpla con todas las provisiones de esta demanda. Usted puede perer dinero o sus propiedades u oetros derechos importantes para usted.
You should take this paper to your lawyer at once. If you do not have a lawyer or cannot afford one, go to or telephone the office set forth below to find out where you can get legal help.	*Lieva esta demanda a un abogado immediatamente. Si no tiene abogado o si no tiene el dinero suficiente de pagartal servicio, vaya en persona o llame por telefono a la oficina cuya direccion se encuentra escrita abajo para averiguar donde se puede conseguir asistencia legal.*
Philadelphia Bar Association Lawyer Referral and Information Service One Reading Center Philadelphia, Pennsylvania 19107 215-238-1701	Asociacion de Licenciados de Filadelfia Servicio de Referencia e Informacion Legal One Reading Center Filadelfia, Pennsylvania 19107 215-238-1701

Pleading Deadlines

After filing the complaint and having the summons issued, the plaintiff must serve the defendant, in federal court within 120 days, state courts vary but typically 30 to 60 days after the initial filing. Failure to serve the complaint within the time limit can result in the complaint being dismissed. Alternatively, the plaintiff may file a motion seeking the court's permission to reinstate the complaint and reissue the summons. The time for the defendant to file a responsive pleading begins to run when the complaint is served, not on the last day the complaint could have been served. If served with the traditional means—in federal cases by U.S. Marshall, or in state courts by the sheriff, private process server, or other authorized person—the defendant has a time limit within which to respond to the complaint, for example in federal court it is 20 days or if served by notice and waiver, 60 days. Failure to respond in a timely fashion permits the plaintiff to obtain a default judgment against the defendant. Default is not an automatic procedure but a right the plaintiff may enforce. Calculating for the due date is important for the plaintiff as well as the defendant. The defendant also must know the rule and properly calculate the due date to avoid a **default judgment** for nonaction. All pleadings after the initial complaint and answer have a response time. This includes the plaintiff's response to counterclaims or affirmative defenses asserted by the defendant and the response to any motion.

Default judgment Judgment obtained by the plaintiff against the defendant where the defendant has failed to respond in a timely fashion to the complaint.

Responsive Pleadings

Upon receipt of the complaint, petition, or summons, the defendant, the responding party, and counsel have some critical decisions to make. In many instances, defendants know that a lawsuit may be filed against them. Being served with a complaint may not be a surprise, but the quickly approaching deadlines can be intimidating for the legal defense team, if it is not promptly advised by the client. If served personally, the defendant has a limited time in which to file a responsive pleading, in federal court, if the defendant was personally served it is 20 days, which is probably insufficient time to thoroughly investigate and respond. Just as plaintiffs frequently wait until the last date before the statute of limitations is filed, defendants frequently wait to meet with an attorney until the date the response is due to be filed in court. The first step may be to request an **extension of time to respond** from opposing counsel. If that request is granted, the team, if in federal court and some state courts, must prepare and file a stipulation with the court, if refused, a motion to extend the time asks the court to grant an extension of time to respond.

Answer

The defendant is required to respond to the allegations contained in the plaintiff's complaint. This is done by preparing, filing, and serving an **answer** to the complaint. Like a complaint, an answer is made up of the same sections, whether in federal or state court: caption, numbered paragraphs, prayer for relief, and alternative defenses.

When responding to the averments of the complaint, there are two basic choices:

1. **Admitted**—the facts of the averment in the complaint are true, or
2. **Denied**—the facts of the averment in the complaint are not true.

In some jurisdictions, simply denying averments of the complaint is not sufficient. In those jurisdictions, the word "Denied" with nothing more is a **general denial** and the averment of the complaint is treated as if it were "Admitted." In those jurisdictions where the reason for the denial is crucial to any defense, the reasons for the denial must be listed and include:

1. Denied as the facts are not as stated and set forth specifically the alternate facts.
2. Denied as after reasonable investigation the defendant lacks adequate knowledge to determine whether the information is true.
3. Denied as the averment represents a conclusion of law to which no response is required.

RECOGNIZING A FRIVOLOUS LAWSUIT

Although paralegals are not lawyers, they should still have some concept of whether a lawsuit has merit or not. Consider the following case. The Chungs are Korean residents who came to the United States. The Chungs opened a dry cleaning store and eventually owned three dry cleaning stores in the Washington, D.C. (D.C.) area. Roy L. Pearson was a District of Columbia administrative judge who was a customer at one of the Chungs' dry cleaning stores. Pearson walked to the Chungs' store because he did not have a car.

The Chungs had signs in the window of their store that stated "Satisfaction Guaranteed" and "Same Day Service." Pearson claimed that the Chungs lost a pair of his pants. He sued the Chungs $67 million in damages alleging that they violated the D.C. consumer protection act. Pearson later reduced his demand to $54 million. Pearson demanded $3 million for violation of the "Satisfaction Guaranteed" sign, $2 million for mental suffering and inconvenience, $500,000 in legal fees for representing himself, $6 million for ten years of rental car fees to drive to another cleaners, and $51 million to help similarly dissatisfied D.C. customers. Pearson stated that he had no choice but to take on "the awesome responsibility" for suing the Chungs on behalf of every D.C. resident. A website was set up to accept donations for the Chungs' legal fees of $83,000, which was eventually paid by donations.

Do you think plaintiff Pearson had a legitimate legal case, or was this a frivolous lawsuit?

In some instances, particularly when there are multiple defendants to whom the complaint is directed, there may be paragraphs to the complaint that do not require an answer. In that event, the appropriate response would be:

No answer is required as the averments are addressed to another defendant.

Cross-Complaint and Reply

A defendant who believes that he or she has been injured by the plaintiff can file a **cross-complaint**, or counter petition as it is called in some jurisdictions, against the plaintiff in addition to an answer. In the cross-complaint, the defendant (now the **cross-complainant**) sues the plaintiff (now the **cross-defendant**) for damages or some other remedy. The original plaintiff must file a **reply**, or answer to the cross-complaint. Exhibit 7.4 is a sample state answer. The reply—which can include affirmative defenses—must be filed with the court and served on the original defendant.

Exhibit 7.5 illustrates the pleadings process.

Intervention and Consolidation

If other persons have an interest in a lawsuit, they may step in and become parties to the lawsuit—called an **intervention**. For instance, a bank that has made a secured loan on a piece of real estate can intervene in a lawsuit between parties who are litigating ownership of the property.

If several plaintiffs have filed separate lawsuits stemming from the same fact situation against the same defendant, the court can initiate a **consolidation** of the cases into one case if it would not cause undue prejudice to the parties. Suppose, for example, that a commercial airplane crashes, killing and injuring many people. The court could consolidate all of the lawsuits against the defendant airplane company.

Statute of Limitations

Some crimes, such as murder, have no limitation on the time in which a defendant can be charged. In civil actions, however, the plaintiff must bring suit within a certain period of time after the action that gives rise to the complaint or lose the right to use the courts to enforce the civil right and remedy. This period is called the **statute of limitations**.

If a lawsuit is not filed in keeping with the statute of limitations, the plaintiff loses his or her right to sue. A statute of limitations usually begins to "run" at the time the plaintiff first has the right to sue the defendant (e.g., when the accident happens, or when the breach of contract occurs). Depending on state law, it also may begin to run when the plaintiff knows or should have known of the defendant's wrongful action that gives rise to a cause of action. In the case of minors, the statute may not begin to run—regardless of the time of discovery of the accrual of the cause of action—until the minor reaches the age of majority.

Federal and state governments have established statutes of limitations for each type of lawsuit. Most are from one to four years, depending on the type of lawsuit. A one-year statute of limitations is common for some ordinary negligence actions. For example, if on July 1, 2010, Otis negligently causes an automobile accident in which Cha-Yen is injured, Cha-Yen has until July 1, 2012, to bring a negligence lawsuit against Otis. If she waits longer than that, she loses her right to sue him.

Procedural time limits in the rules of court are similar to the statute of limitations for filing a cause of action. Each court may establish the times within which actions must be taken, such as the number of days within which a plaintiff must serve the complaint and/or summons on the defendant, or the time limit for the defendant to file a responsive pleading, such as an answer. Software, such as AbacusLaw, use rules-based calendaring programs to calculate these deadlines. Deadlines on Demand™ is an internet based program that calculates the various time deadlines based on the different state and federal rules as shown in the sample for a school-bus accident case in Exhibit 7.6.

Exhibit 7.4   **Sample state answer**

DATZ and GOLDBERG

BY: MARC C. BENDO, ESQUIRE

IDENTIFICATION NO.   80075   ATTORNEY FOR   DEFENDANT

1311 SPRUCE STREET

PHILADELPHIA, PENNSYLVANIA 19107

(215) 545-7960

COUNTY LINE FENCE CO., INC.   *COURT OF COMMON PLEAS*
2051 W. County Line Road
Warrington, PA 18976
                                         BUCKS COUNTY DIVISION
vs.
                                         TERM

WAYNE YARNALL
5707 Dunbar Court
Bensalem, PA 19020   NO. 99004879-23-1

<u>ANSWER OF DEFENDANT, WAYNE YARNALL, TO PLAINTIFF'S CIVIL ACTION WITH
NEW MATTER</u>

1. Denied. Plaintiff is without knowledge or information sufficient to form a belief as to the truth or falsity of this averment. Accordingly, same is denied with strict proof demanded at time of Trial.

2. Admitted. By way of further answer, however, Plaintiff's Civil Action has misspelled Defendant's proper name, which is Wayne Yarnall.

3. Denied. These allegations constitute conclusions of law to which no response is required pursuant to the applicable Pennsylvania Rules of Civil Procedure . . .

Exhibit 7.5 — Pleadings process

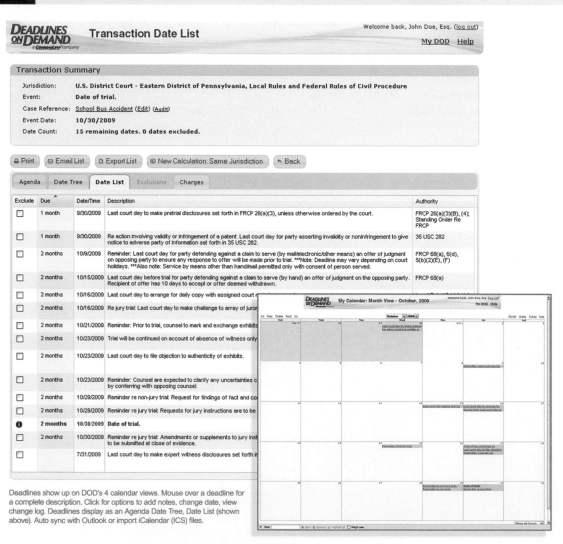

Plaintiff → complaint → Defendant
Plaintiff ← answer ← Defendant

Plaintiff (cross-defendant) ← cross-complaint ← Defendant (cross-complainant)
Plaintiff (cross-defendant) → reply → Defendant (cross-complainant)

Exhibit 7.6 — Sample time deadlines using Deadlines On Demand™

DEADLINES ON DEMAND — Transaction Date List

Welcome back, John Doe, Esq. (log out) My DOD Help

Transaction Summary

Jurisdiction: U.S. District Court - Eastern District of Pennsylvania, Local Rules and Federal Rules of Civil Procedure
Event: Date of trial.
Case Reference: School Bus Accident (Edit) (Audit)
Event Date: 10/30/2009
Date Count: 15 remaining dates. 0 dates excluded.

Print | Email List | Export List | New Calculation: Same Jurisdiction | Back

Agenda | Date Tree | Date List | Exclusions | Charges

Exclude	Due	Date/Time	Description	Authority
☐	1 month	9/30/2009	Last court day to make pretrial disclosures set forth in FRCP 26(a)(3), unless otherwise ordered by the court.	FRCP 26(a)(3)(B), (4); Standing Order Re FRCP
☐	1 month	9/30/2009	Re action involving validity or infringement of a patent: Last court day for party asserting invalidity or noninfringement to give notice to adverse party of information set forth in 35 USC 282.	35 USC 282
☐	2 months	10/9/2009	Reminder: Last court day for party defending against a claim to serve (by mail/electronic/other means) an offer of judgment on opposing party to ensure any response to offer will be made prior to trial. ***Note: Deadline may vary depending on court holidays. ***Also note: Service by means other than hand/mail permitted only with consent of person served.	FRCP 68(a), 6(d), 5(b)(2)(E), (F)
☐	2 months	10/15/2009	Last court day before trial for party defending against a claim to serve (by hand) an offer of judgment on the opposing party. Recipient of offer has 10 days to accept or offer deemed withdrawn.	FRCP 68(a)
☐	2 months	10/16/2009	Last court day to arrange for daily copy with assigned court r...	
☐	2 months	10/16/2009	Re jury trial: Last court day to make challenge to array of juror...	
☐	2 months	10/21/2009	Reminder: Prior to trial, counsel to mark and exchange exhibits...	
☐	2 months	10/23/2009	Trial will be continued on account of absence of witness only ...	
☐	2 months	10/23/2009	Last court day to file objection to authenticity of exhibits.	
☐	2 months	10/23/2009	Reminder: Counsel are expected to clarify any uncertainties c... by conferring with opposing counsel.	
☐	2 months	10/29/2009	Reminder re non-jury trial: Request for findings of fact and co...	
☐	2 months	10/29/2009	Reminder re jury trial: Requests for jury instructions are to be ...	
ⓘ	2 months	10/30/2009	Date of trial.	
☐	2 months	10/30/2009	Reminder re jury trial: Amendments or supplements to jury inst... to be submitted at close of evidence.	
☐		7/31/2009	Last court day to make expert witness disclosures set forth in ...	

Deadlines show up on DOD's 4 calendar views. Mouse over a deadline for a complete description. Click for options to add notes, change date, view change log. Deadlines display as an Agenda Date Tree, Date List (shown above). Auto sync with Outlook or import iCalendar (ICS) files.

These sample deadlines are provided as examples for instructional purposes only and are not to be relied upon in the practice of law. Any use other than that which is described herein is strictly prohibited. Neither CompuLaw nor Deadlines On Demand will be liable for any use or misuse of this information, regardless of the circumstances. Copyright © 2009 CompuLaw LLC®. All Rights Reserved. CompuLaw is a Registered Trademark of CompuLaw LLC.Copyright © 2009 Deadlines On Demand™. All Rights Reserved. Deadlines On Demand is a Trademark of Deadlines On Demand LLC. U.S. Patents 7,171,416 and 7,302,433 and International Patent 2002330911. Other U.S. and foreign patents pending.

E-Filings in Court

When litigation ensues, the clients, lawyers, and judges involved in the case usually are buried in paper—pleadings, interrogatories, documents, motions to the court, briefs, and memoranda; the list goes on and on. By the time a case is over, reams of paper are stored in dozens, if not hundreds, of boxes. Further, court appearances, no matter how small the matter, must be made in person. For example, lawyers often wait hours for a 10-minute scheduling or other conference with the judge. Additional time is required to drive to and from court, which in an urban area may amount to hours.

Paralegals are at the forefront of e-litigation where many of the documents filed in court are done electronically. The technology currently is available for implementing electronic filing—**e-filing**—of pleadings, briefs, and other documents related to a lawsuit. E-filing would include using CD-ROMs for briefs, scanning evidence and documents into a computer for storage and retrieval, and emailing correspondence and documents to the court and the opposing counsel. Scheduling and other conferences with the judge or opposing counsel could be held via telephone conferences and email.

Some courts have instituted e-filing already. For example, in the Manhattan bankruptcy court, e-filing is now mandatory. Other courts around the world are doing the same. Companies such as Microsoft and LexisNexis have developed systems to manage e-filings of court documents. Some forward-thinking judges and lawyers envision a day when the paperwork and hassle are reduced or eliminated in a "virtual courthouse."

Discovery

Discovery is a step in the litigation process where the plaintiff and the defendant share information relevant to their dispute. The discovery process can be a time-consuming and sometimes frustrating phase in litigation. Successful discovery requires familiarity with the rules of court that apply to discovery and an organized approach. Increasingly important are the rules relating to discovery of electronic files that may be the source of information needed in the litigation process. The methods used to locate, preserve, and produce these cyber documents require a new set of skills for the legal team and the paralegal. Paralegals on the litigation team are often charged with coordinating discovery requests and responses from clients and opposing parties and working with information technology experts.

Discovery serves a number of purposes: understanding and evaluating the client's case, focusing the legal team on the strengths and weaknesses of its case; understanding and evaluating the strengths and weaknesses of the opponent's case; preserving testimony; potentially facilitating settlement; and learning information that may be used to impeach a witness, such as showing inconsistencies in testimony.

Case Evaluation

By answering each other's questions, the parties share information about the facts, documents, and statements of fact and expert witnesses related to the legal dispute. By openly sharing information that may be used at trial, each side is forced to evaluate its case and the opponent's case and determine the ability to meet its burdens of proof. With each side fully aware of the potential evidence that can be presented, including potential damages, the legal team can, based on prior experience or reported similar cases, put a potential value on a trial outcome. In many cases the decision to try a case or settle a case is a business decision.

Is the cost of a trial outweighed by the potential recovery? With two well-prepared legal teams, the evaluation is surprisingly close and settlement is more likely than not.

Preparing for Trial

Properly completed discovery eliminates the potential for surprises in evidence presented at trial. In fact, many of the "surprises" one sees on television trial dramas are not possible under rules that are designed to prevent the introduction of surprise witnesses and evidence.

Cross-complaint Filed by the defendant against the plaintiff to seek damages or some other remedy.

Reply Filed by the original plaintiff to answer the defendant's cross-complaint.

 Web Exploration

Locate the U.S. District Court that serves the county or parish in which you live. Go to that court's website and find and review the "Court Forms" for that court. http://uscourts.gov/.

Statute of limitations A law that establishes the period during which a plaintiff must bring a lawsuit against a defendant.

 Web Exploration

Go to http://www.statutes-of-limitations.com/state/Alabama. On the right-hand side of the page there is a list of states. Click on your state to find out what the statute of limitations is for filing a negligence action in your state.

E-filing The electronic filing of pleadings, briefs, and other documents related to a lawsuit with the court.

 Web Exploration

Visit www.abanet.org/tech/ltrc/research/efiling/ for a discussion of e-filings and the use of electronic documents in federal courts.

Discovery A legal process during which both parties engage in various activities to elicit facts of the case from the other party and witnesses prior to trial.

Advice *from the* Field

THE ELECTRONIC PARALEGAL

William Mulkeen, Past President, American Association for Paralegal Education

COULD THIS BE THE FIRST DAY OF EMPLOYMENT FOR A RECENT PARALEGAL PROGRAM GRADUATE?

Maria was up before the alarm went off, ready to begin her new job and her new career. The newest paralegal at one of California's most prestigious law firms was ready to go to work. She still was amazed at how easily she had completed the interviews and had proceeded through the hiring process of the past few weeks. To be hired by such a prominent law firm was beyond her wildest dreams. She knew that her good grades, her excellent work samples and her technology skills would help her look for a position but never thought she would be so successful so quickly. The knowledge and sophisticated skill set she had acquired in her paralegal studies had paid immediate dividends.

Clutching a small portfolio embossed with her paralegal school's logo, she took the elevator to the thirty-fifth floor, got off and went through the big glass doors. Maria's legal degree and her newly acquired Certificate in Legal Information Management were about to be tested.

She knew that this potent combination of legal content and legal information management had been her key to success yet she was still very apprehensive about this new venture. Little did Maria know, but her new employers were as apprehensive as she was on her first day at the office. They had created the title of Paralegal Information Manager and that sign on the door was the first thing that caught Maria's eyes as she was showed her new office.

Maria remembered the interview a few weeks ago when she was led through a large conference room full of file boxes that she thought contained the information on the major cases she would be working on at the firm. She had asked, "Is that the Magnate case materials?" And the answer was "No, they will be accessed through the computer workstation in your new office." She remembered the senior partner telling her that the judge in the Magnate case had ordered the case to be handled electronically as much as possible. All of the documents had either been imaged or produced in native file format and a basic index of all documents had been created. The firm had chosen to optically character recognize the imaged documents for full text search capability. The trial exhibit list had to be filed electronically and the pre-trial order directed that the attorneys use all the technology available in the electronic courtroom to locate and display every document for the judge and jury.

Here she was, the Paralegal Information Manager, the gatekeeper of the management and the flow of information, the one who was primarily responsible for getting the information processed and presented. She felt overwhelmed but was ready to begin. Maria sat down and turned on the computer. She had taken the first step.

Can this happen to a paralegal school graduate? Will this happen in the near future? How can paralegal students be prepared best? What are the implications for paralegals? And what paralegal school courses and programs should the paralegal take to be prepared?

This scenario is already occurring in small ways throughout the country. Paralegals must start thinking about the training and skills necessary to work on the electronic civil litigation team emerging in the present, for many the future is here now. The process of electronic discovery; the gathering and acquisition of electronic records; the filing and preparation of this discovery; and the presentation of it in electronic courtrooms is already upon us. Demand for advanced litigation skills including an understanding of the role of electronic databases and the management of electronic documents is becoming commonplace. Paralegals must understand the technology and the ethical considerations and implications of these technological advances.

Preserving Oral Testimony

Discovery is also a method for preserving oral testimony. There are times when witnesses may not be available to attend trial to testify. Examples include witnesses who are gravely ill and not expected to live until trial, those who are elderly or incapacitated and physically unable to come to the courthouse, and those who are outside the geographical jurisdiction of the court. Under limited circumstances, the deposition testimony of these unavailable witnesses may be presented at trial. The deposition of witnesses is given the same treatment as if the witness was in court testifying in person.

IN THE WORDS OF THE COURT

United States District Court, S.D. New York

**SECURITIES AND EXCHANGE COMMISSION, PLAINTIFF,
V. COLLINS & AIKMAN CORP., ET AL., DEFENDANTS
NO. 07 CIV. 2419(SAS). JAN. 13, 2009**

II. The Discovery Disputes

This opinion addresses four distinct but related discovery disputes. Stockman served a document request pursuant to Rule 34, asking the SEC to "produce for inspection and copying the documents and things identified" in fifty-four separate categories.[FN4] In response, the SEC produced 1.7 million documents (10.6 million pages) maintained in thirty-six separate Concordance databases-many of which use different metadata protocols.[FN5] Stockman raises the following objections. *First,* the SEC failed to identify documents responsive to requests for documents supporting particular factual allegations in the Complaint, preferring instead to "dump" 1.7 million potentially responsive documents on Stockman and then suggesting that he is capable of searching them to locate those that are relevant. *Second,* the SEC failed to perform a reasonable search for documents relating to accounting principles governing supplier rebates-both in general and with respect to the automobile industry. Instead, the SEC unilaterally limited its search to three of its divisions-and only if those divisions possessed "centralized compilations of non-privileged documents dealing specifically with rebates or accounting for rebates in the automobile industry."[FN6] *Third,* the SEC improperly asserted the deliberative process privilege with regard to certain documents. *Fourth,* the SEC failed to search its own e-mails, attachments thereto, and other records created and maintained solely in an electronic format that related to either "(i) the investigation and litigation of this matter or (ii) the handling of several large cases unrelated to C & A and the Commission's regulatory role in matters relating to rebates and rebate accounting."[FN7] The objections were raised in a series of letters rather than by formal motion.[FN8]

1. Attorney Work Product Protection Applied to Selection and Compilation

The Second Circuit has recognized that the selection and compilation of documents may fall within the protection accorded to attorney work product, despite the general availability of documents from both parties and non-parties during discovery.[FN18] However, it has labeled this protection a "narrow exception"[FN19] aimed at preventing requests with "the precise goal of learning what the opposing attorney's thinking or strategy may be."[FN20] Moreover, equity favors rejection of work product protection to a compilation of documents that are otherwise unavailable or "beyond reasonable access."[FN21] The Circuit has suggested that a court may permit *ex parte* communication of the strategy the withholding party wishes to conceal and *in camera* review of documents, so that the court may make an educated assessment whether production of the compilation will reveal a party's litigation strategy.[FN22]

C. Discussion

1. Work Product Protection

It is first necessary to determine the level of protection afforded to the *selection* of documents by an attorney to support factual allegations in a complaint. Such documents are not "core" work product. Core work product constitutes legal documents drafted by an attorney-her mental impressions, conclusions, opinions, and legal theories. This highest level of protection applies to a compilation only if it is organized by legal theory or strategy. The SEC's theory-that every document or word reviewed by an attorney is "core" attorney work product-leaves nothing to surround the core.[FN35] The first step in responding to any document request is an attorney's assessment of relevance with regard to potentially responsive documents. It would make no sense to then claim that an attorney's determination of relevance shields the selection of responsive documents from production.

(continued)

With few exceptions, *Rule 26(f)* requires the parties to hold a conference and prepare a discovery plan. The Rule specifically requires that the discovery plan state the parties' views and proposals with respect to "the subject on which discovery may be needed . . . and whether discovery should be conducted in phases or be limited to or focused on particular issues"[FN66] and "any issues about disclosure or discovery of electronically stored information. . . ."[FN67] Had this been accomplished, the Court might not now be required to intervene in this particular dispute. I also draw the parties' attention to the recently issued Sedona Conference Cooperation Proclamation, which urges parties to work in a cooperative rather than an adversarial manner to resolve discovery issues in order to stem the "rising monetary costs" of discovery disputes.[FN68] The Proclamation notes that courts see the discovery rules "as a mandate for counsel to act cooperatively."[FN69] Accordingly, counsel are directly to meet and confer forthwith and develop a workable search protocol that would reveal *at least some* of the information defendant seeks. If the parties cannot craft an agreement, the Court will consider the appointment of a Special Master to assist in this effort. . . . The logic of *Rule 34* supports this limitation. When records do not result from "routine and repetitive" activity, there is no incentive to organize them in a predictable system. The purpose of the Rule is to facilitate production of records in a useful manner and to minimize discovery costs; thus it is reasonable to require litigants who do not create and/or maintain records in a "routine and repetitive" manner to organize the records in a usable[FN55] fashion prior to producing them.

. . . By rough analogy to *Rule 803(6)*, the option of producing documents "as they are kept in the usual course of business" under *Rule 34* requires the producing party to meet either of two tests. *First,* this option is available to commercial enterprises or entities that function in the manner of commercial enterprises. *Second,* this option may also apply to records resulting from "regularly conducted activity."[FN53] Where a producing party's activities are not "routine and repetitive" such as to require a well-organized record-keeping system-in other words when the records do not result from an "ordinary course of business"-the party must produce documents according to the sole remaining option under *Rule 34*: "organize[d] and label[ed] . . . to correspond to the categories in the request."[FN54]

B. Applicable Law

"A district court has wide latitude to determine the scope of discovery."[FN62] The general scope of discovery in civil litigation is defined by *Rule 26(b)(1)*.

FN62. In re Agent Orange Product Liab. Litig., 517 F.3d 76, 103 (2d Cir.2008).

Parties may obtain discovery regarding any nonprivileged matter that is relevant to any party's claim or defense.. . . For good cause, the court may order discovery of any matter relevant to the subject matter involved in the action. Relevant information need not be admissible at the trial if the discovery appears reasonably calculated to lead to the discovery of admissible evidence.

. . . A court must limit the "frequency or extent of discovery" if one of three conditions in *Rule 26(b)(2)(C)* is present. The third limits production when "the burden or expense of the proposed discovery outweighs its likely benefit, considering the needs of the case, the amount in controversy, the parties' resources, the importance of the issues at stake in the action, and the importance of the discovery in resolving the issues."[FN63] The burden or expense may be defined in terms of time, expense, or even the "adverse consequences of the disclosure of sensitive, albeit unprivileged material."[FN64] . . .

VII. Conclusion

When a government agency initiates litigation, it must be prepared to follow the same discovery rules that govern private parties (albeit with the benefit of additional privileges such as deliberative process and state secrets). For the reasons set forth above, the SEC is ordered to produce or identify documents organized in response to Stockman's requests; to negotiate an appropriate search protocol to locate documents responsive to requests described above in Part IV; to submit materials allegedly covered by the deliberative process privilege to the Court for *in camera* review, together with a supporting memorandum within twenty days of the date of this Order;

and to negotiate an appropriately limited search protocol with respect to agency e-mail. While the SEC has raised legitimate concerns about the burdens imposed by particular requests, it cannot unilaterally determine that those burdens outweigh defendants' need for discovery. At the very least, the SEC must engage in a good faith effort to negotiate with its adversaries and craft a search protocol designed to retrieve responsive information without incurring an unduly burdensome expense disproportionate to the size and needs of the case. The parties are therefore directed to engage in a cooperative effort to resolve the scope and design of a search with respect to the rebate issues and a search of e-mail created and maintained by the SEC. A conference is scheduled for February 13, at 5:00 pm, by which date the parties should have completed the meet and confer process in the hope of establishing an acceptable discovery program. If the parties remain at an impasse, the Court will be prepared to resolve further disputes and will consider the appointment of a Special Master to supervise the remaining discovery in this case.

SO ORDERED.

Federal Rules of Civil Procedure—Rule 26(a) Disclosure Requirements

Rule 26(a) makes mandatory the disclosure of certain information that for years was available only after a formal written discovery request was issued. For many cases, no action was taken on a file until one side moved the case forward with a formal discovery request. Under current rules, everything the legal team intends to rely upon to prove its claims must be disclosed early in the litigation. Insufficient time to investigate the claim is not a valid excuse for failure to comply. The benefits of mandatory disclosure are twofold: 1. It provides for the early evaluation and settlement of claims; and 2. it reduces the amount, nature, and time necessary to conduct formal discovery. From a practical standpoint, the plaintiff's legal team must be prepared for disclosure at or shortly after filing the complaint. While the new rules contemplate a specific time frame for disclosure, they do permit the attorneys to agree to some other time frame for the disclosure. Although the attorneys may agree to extend that time, the judge at the scheduling conference may encourage them to conclude the disclosure at a faster pace. The investigation that might have occurred under prior rules must now be completed before filing suit. For the defense team, the time to investigate and comply is very short. There is no time for procrastination in investigating and establishing the grounds to defend the claims.

Information Subject to Mandatory Disclosure

Almost anything relied upon in developing the claim, regardless of whether it is admissible at trial, must be disclosed. This disclosure includes the identity of witnesses, copies of documents, a computation of damages, and a copy of any insurance policy that may be used to satisfy a judgment obtained in the litigation.

In the past, information used to compute damages represented the plaintiff attorney's thought process and was typically not released as part of discovery under the work–product privilege. Under the current rule, the attorney's value on the case is made known within months of the complaint being filed.

From the defense standpoint, the disclosure of insurance coverage, which is not admissible at trial, is a significant change from traditional discovery. A key element in settling most cases is the existence of and limitations on insurance coverage. With both the plaintiff's calculation of damages and the defendant's ability to pay based upon disclosure of insurance coverage known within months of filing the lawsuit, the chances for fruitful settlement discussions are enhanced.

Experts and Witnesses

Expert witnesses expected to be called at trial must also be identified, accompanied by a copy of the expert's qualifications as an expert including a list of publications for which the witness has written from the preceding 10 years, a statement of compensation, and a list of other cases in which the expert has testified. The most critical element to be shared is the written report of the expert's opinion. The report represents what the expert is expected to say at trial. The written report must include the opinion of the expert, the basis of that opinion including the information relied upon, and any assumptions made. The disclosure of the expert and his or her report must be made at least 90 days prior to trial. Some courts require the disclosure of the expert at the time of the initial disclosure or within 30 days of receipt of the expert's report. Many lawsuits become a battle of the experts. The early disclosure of the expert and his or her opinion often leads to early resolution of the case.

Depositions

Deposition Oral testimony given by a party or witness prior to trial. The testimony is given under oath and is transcribed.

A **deposition** is the oral testimony given, under oath, by a party or witness prior to trial. The person giving the deposition is called the **deponent**. The *parties* to the lawsuit must give their depositions, if the other party calls them to do so. The deposition of a **witness** can be given voluntarily or pursuant to a **subpoena** (court order). The deponent can be required to bring documents to the deposition.

Depositions are used to preserve evidence (e.g., if the deponent is deceased, ill, or otherwise not available at trial) and to impeach testimony given by witnesses at trial. Most depositions are taken at the office of one of the attorneys. The deponent is placed under oath and then asked oral questions by the attorneys for one or both parties to the lawsuit. The questions and answers are recorded in written form by a court reporter. Depositions also can be videotaped. The deponent is given an opportunity to correct his or her answers prior to signing the deposition, depending on local practice or rules.

Interrogatories

Interrogatories Written questions submitted by one party to another party. The questions must be answered in writing within a stipulated time.

Interrogatories are written questions submitted by one party to a lawsuit to another party. The questions can be highly detailed, as illustrated by the sample interrogatory in Exhibit 7.7. In addition, in some jurisdictions certain documents have to be attached to the answers. A party is required to answer the interrogatories in writing within a specified time period (e.g., 60 to 90 days). An attorney usually helps with preparation of the answers. The answers are signed under oath.

Production of Documents

Production of documents Request by one party to another party to produce all documents relevant to the case prior to the trial.

Often, particularly in complex business cases, a substantial portion of the lawsuit is based on information contained in documents (e.g., memoranda, correspondence, company records). One party to a lawsuit may request that the other party produce all documents that are relevant to the case prior to trial. This is called **production of documents**. If the documents sought are too voluminous to be moved or are in permanent storage, or if moving the documents would disrupt the ongoing business of the party who is to produce them, the requesting party may be required to examine the documents at the other party's premises. Exhibit 7.8 is an example of a request for production of documents.

Physical and Mental Examination

Physical and mental examinations (in some jurisdictions called an **Independent Medical Examination** or **IME**) of the parties to the lawsuit are permitted where the physical or mental condition of one of the parties is an element of the cause of action. In a personal injury action, the physical injuries suffered and the damages that result from those injuries are elements of the cause of action for negligence. Thus, the defense

Exhibit 7.7 Sample interrogatory

THOMAS F. GOLDMAN & ASSOCIATES
138 N. State Street
Newtown, PA 18940
(123) 555-1234

KATHRYN KELSEY	:	COURT OF COMMON PLEAS
	:	PHILADELPHIA COUNTY
	:	
vs.	:	APRIL TERM, 2011
KATHRYN CARROLL	:	NO. 1234

INTERROGATORIES ADDRESSED TO KATHRYN KELSEY

You are to answer the following interrogatories under oath or verification pursuant to the Pa. R.C.P. 4005 and 4006 within thirty days from the service hereof. The answering party is under a duty to supplement responses to any questions with information discovered after these answers were given.

Also, a party or expert witness must amend prior responses if he/she obtains information upon the basis of which:

(a) he/she knows the response was incorrect when made; or

(b) he/she knows that the response, though correct when made, is no longer true.

The words "your vehicle" as used in the following interrogatories are defined as the motor vehicle you were operating at the time of the accident.

When a Standard Interrogatory uses the word: "identify", the party served with the Interrogatory must identify all documents, things and persons known to that party or to that party's attorney, and the address of all persons identified MUST be set forth.

Where a Standard Interrogatory is marked with an asterisk (*), a Request for Production may accompany the Interrogatory.

**STANDARD INTERROGATORIES PURSUANT TO
PHILADELPHIA RULE OF CIVIL PROCEDURE *4005**

INJURIES AND DISEASES ALLEGED

1. State in detail the injuries or diseases that you allege that you suffered as a result of the accident referred to in the Complaint.

MEDICAL TREATMENT & REPORTS*

2. If you received medical treatment or examinations (including x-rays) because of injuries or diseases you suffered as a result of the accident, identify:

   (a) Each hospital at which you were treated or examined;

   (b) The dates on which each such treatment or examination at a hospital was rendered and the charges by the hospital for each;

   (c) Each doctor or practitioner by whom you were treated or examined;

   (d) The dates on which each such treatment or examination by a doctor or practitioner was rendered and the charges for each;

   (e) All reports regarding any medical treatment or examinations, setting forth the author and date of such reports.

* This document can be viewed in its entirety on the companion website.

Exhibit 7.8 Sample request for production of documents

THOMAS F. GOLDMAN & ASSOCIATES
138 N. State Street
Newtown, PA 18940
(123) 555-1234

KATHRYN KELSEY	: COURT OF COMMON PLEAS
	: PHILADELPHIA COUNTY
vs.	: APRIL TERM, 2011
KATHRYN CARROLL	: NO. 1259

REQUEST TO PRODUCE UNDER PA R.C.P. 4033 and 4009
DIRECTED TO PLAINTIFFS

Within thirty (30) days of service, please produce for inspection and copying at the office of THOMAS F. GOLDMAN & ASSOCIATES, 138 North State Street, Newtown, Pennsylvania 18940, the following:

1. All photographs and/or diagrams of the area involved in this accident or occurrence, the locale or surrounding area of the site of this accident or occurrence, or any other matter or things involved in this accident or occurrence.
2. All property damage estimates rendered for any object belonging to the Plaintiffs which was involved in this accident or occurrence.
3. All property damage estimates rendered for any object belonging to the Defendant which was involved in this accident or occurrence.
4. All statements concerning this action or its subject matter previously made by any party or witness. The statements referred to here are defined by Pa. R.C.P. 4003.4.
5. All transcriptions and summaries of all interviews conducted by anyone acting on behalf of the Plaintiff or Plaintiff's insurance carrier of any potential witness and/or person(s) who has any knowledge of the accident or its surrounding circumstances.
6. All inter-office memorandum between representative of Plaintiffs' insurance carrier or memorandum to Plaintiffs' insurance carrier's file concerning the manner in which the accident occurred.
7. All inter-office memorandum between representative of Plaintiffs' insurance carrier or memorandum to Plaintiffs' insurance carrier's file concerning the injuries sustained by the Plaintiffs.
8. A copy of any written accident report concerning this accident or occurrence signed by or prepared by Plaintiff for Plaintiffs' insurance carrier or Plaintiff's employers.
9. A copy of the face sheet of any policy of insurance providing coverage to Plaintiffs for the claim being asserted by Plaintiff in this action.
10. All bills, reports, and records from any and all physicians, hospitals, or other health care providers concerning the injuries sustained by the Defendants from this accident or occurrence.
11. All photographs and/or motion pictures of any and all surveillance of Defendant performed by anyone acting on behalf of Plaintiff, Plaintiffs' insurer and/or Plaintiffs' attorney.
12. All photographs taken of Plaintiffs' motor vehicle which depict any damage to said vehicle which was sustained as a result of this accident.
13. All photographs taken of defendant's motor vehicle which depict any damage to said vehicle which was sustained as a result of this accident.
14. Any and all reports, writings, memorandum, Xeroxed cards and/or other writings, lists or compilations of the Defendant and others with similar names as indexed by the Metropolitan Index Bureau, Central Index Bureau or other Index Bureau in possession of the Plaintiffs or the Plaintiffs' insurance carrier.

team may obtain a physical examination of the plaintiff from a doctor of its choosing. In a guardianship proceeding, the plaintiff seeks to be appointed guardian over someone who lacks mental capacity to handle financial and other matters. The cause of action is dependent on the mental state of the individual. Therefore, a mental examination would be appropriate.

Requests for Admission

Requests for admission are written requests issued by one party to the lawsuit to the other asking that certain facts or legal issues be admitted as true. Properly used, requests for admission can narrow the focus of trial and streamline the testimony. Some facts are generally not in controversy, such as names, addresses, and other personal information.

Locations of accidents, time of day, and related facts may also be admitted without calling witnesses. Who was speeding, not observant, or otherwise negligent are facts rarely admitted because they represent an admission of liability. However, if liability is admitted the only issue left is damages. Where the damages are minimal, parties may admit to the facts of liability to avoid the time and cost of trial to obtain a finding of fact of something obvious.

The remaining issue of how much monetary value is assigned to the wrong may be agreed upon between the parties or determined by the trier of fact in very short order at little time or expense.

> **Example:** If the defendant admits as true his liability for the automobile accident, then that issue is no longer in dispute. No evidence as to the cause of the accident will be required at trial. The trial will be limited to determining damages only, making a more focused and streamlined case.

E-Discovery

The use of email, electronic retention of records, establishment of websites, selling goods and services online, and other digital technologies has exploded in conducting business. This technology is used extensively in conducting personal affairs as well. Therefore, in many lawsuits, much of the evidence is in digital form. The winning or losing of lawsuits may lie in the ability of a party to conduct **electronic discovery**, or **e-discovery**.

e-discovery The discovery of emails, electronically stored data, e-contracts, and other electronically stored records.

Modern discovery practices permit the electronic discovery of evidence. Most federal and state courts have adopted rules that permit the e-discovery of emails, electronically stored data, e-contracts, and other electronic records. E-discovery is fast becoming a burgeoning part of the preparation of a case for trial or settlement.

The lawyer and the paralegal must have a sound understanding of permissible e-discovery. Courts have resoundingly permitted the discovery of emails and electronic databases where relevant to a court case. A party seeking e-discovery must prepare the proper requests for such discovery as required by court rules.

In addition to discovery of email and electronic information, courts permit the use of electronic interrogatories to be proffered to the other side, as well as the electronic response to such e-interrogatories. Some courts also permit the taking of depositions electronically. This requires that the questions by the lawyers and answers of the deponent be communicated electronically by email.

Federal and state courts have established rules of evidence that require the parties to a lawsuit not to destroy or delete documents or other evidence that is relevant to the pending lawsuit. This prohibition is particularly important when the documents and evidence are digital. The destruction or deletion of e-evidence may subject the violating party to civil and criminal penalties.

In the case where digital evidence has been destroyed or deleted from electronic files, it may be possible to reconstruct the evidence. The use of computer experts will be necessary to find the missing evidence and digitally reconstruct it.

Paralegals *in* Practice

Emily A. Ewald is a graduate of Xavier University with a Bachelor of Science degree. She also has a Paralegal Certificate from Davenport University. Emily currently works in the area of civil/commercial and appellate litigation at the large law firm of Dickinson Wright in Grand Rapids, Michigan.

Although I have been a paralegal for six years, the first three were spent focused on one enormous case. During that period, I reviewed, organized, and managed over 450,000 documents, 1,650 deposition exhibits, a 98-page trial exhibit list, deposition designations from over 70 depositions, and other numerous assignments to assist attorneys preparing for discovery and trial. In this case, our client, the defendant, was being sued for $74 mil-lion. However, three weeks before the scheduled trial date, the case was settled for a much lower amount.

My current work duties include drafting interrogatories, interrogatory responses, motions and briefs, witness lists, juror questionnaires, and verdict forms. I also help prepare for and attend depositions, hearings, mediations, arbitrations, and trials. Additionally, I go to client meetings, expert witness meetings, and deposition preparation sessions.

More and more legal documents are being digitally produced and exchanged. For instance, we are required by all federal courts to file everything electronically through an online program called PACER (Public Access to Court Electronic Records). For e-discovery purposes, we use Summation®, a software program used to summarize case documents and search them for specific data. TrialDirector® software is used to load case exhibits, videos, and other documents onto a laptop computer, which can later be projected onto a courtroom screen for judge and jurors to see.

My main advice to new paralegals is to be flexible. You should expect to be asked to go back and forth between different case assignments, at a moment's notice. You are also likely to get some assignments in which you have little or no interest. However, always do them to the best of your ability because you will gain from the experience.

E-discovery will continue to increase as an important feature in many lawsuits. The recovery of emails, mining of electronic databases, and reconstructing thought-to-be destroyed electronic evidence will play an ever more important part of discovery in current and future lawsuits. E-discovery is clearly an important part of the digital law office and the virtual courtroom.

Pretrial Motions

Pretrial motion A motion a party can make to try to dispose of all or part of a lawsuit prior to trial.

Paralegals employed in the civil litigation field are often called upon to prepare **pretrial motions** to try to dispose of all or part of a lawsuit prior to trial. The three major pretrial motions are the motion to dismiss, the motion for judgment on the pleadings, and the motion for summary judgment.

Motion to Dismiss

Motion to dismiss A motion that alleges that the plaintiff's complaint fails to state a claim for which relief can be granted. Also called a *demurrer*.

A defendant can file a **motion to dismiss** the plaintiff's complaint for failure to state a claim for which relief can be granted. A motion to dismiss is sometimes called a *demurrer*. A motion to dismiss a case alleges that even if the facts as presented in the plaintiff's complaint are true, there is no reason to continue the lawsuit. For example, a motion to dismiss would be granted if the plaintiff alleges that the defendant was negligent but the facts as alleged do not support a claim of negligence.

A motion to dismiss can be filed with the court prior to the defendant's having filed an answer in the case. If the motion to dismiss is denied, the defendant is given further time to answer. If the court grants the motion to dismiss, the defendant does not have to file an answer. The plaintiff usually is given time to file an amended complaint. If the plaintiff fails to file an amended complaint, judgment will be entered against the plaintiff. If the plaintiff files an amended complaint, the defendant must answer the complaint or file a new motion to dismiss.

Motion for Judgment on the Pleadings

Once the pleadings are complete, either party can make a **motion for judgment on the pleadings**. This motion alleges that if all of the facts presented in the pleadings are true, the party making the motion would win the lawsuit when the proper law is applied to these facts. In deciding this motion, the judge cannot consider any facts outside the pleadings.

Motion for Summary Judgment

The trier of the fact (i.e., the jury, or, if no jury, the judge) determines *factual issues*. A **motion for summary judgment** asserts that there are no factual disputes to be decided by the jury and that the judge should apply the relevant law to the undisputed facts to decide the case. Motions for summary judgment, which can be made by either party, are supported by evidence outside the pleadings. Affidavits from the parties and witnesses, documents (e.g., a written contract between the parties), depositions, and such are common forms of evidence.

If, after examining the evidence, the court finds no factual dispute, it can decide the issue or issues raised in the summary judgment motion. This may dispense with the entire case or with part of the case. If the judge finds that a factual dispute exists, the motion will be denied and the case will go to trial.

Settlement Conference

Federal court rules and most state court rules permit the court to direct the attorneys or parties to appear before the court for a **pretrial hearing**, or **settlement conference**. One of the major purposes of these hearings is to facilitate settlement of the case. Pretrial conferences often are held informally in the judge's chambers. If no settlement is reached, the pretrial hearing is used to identify the major trial issues and other relevant factors.

More than 90 percent of all cases are settled before they go to trial. In cases that do proceed to trial, the trial judge may advise the attorneys of the rules or timetable of the individual judge. The judges also will advise the attorneys of any deadlines for discovery and the deadline for submitting any final motions with regard to what may be offered at the trial, called *motions in limine*.

In a number of jurisdictions, cases are referred to arbitration or other forms of alternative dispute resolution. Depending on the amount of money in controversy, some cases are required to be submitted before court-approved panels of attorneys sitting as arbitrators of the dispute. In other courts, the litigants may elect to have the case heard before an arbitration panel. Appeal rights from arbitration panel decisions vary, but cases typically may be appealed *de novo* to the trial court as if no arbitration had occurred, except possibly the payment of an appeal fee to cover part of the cost of the arbitration.

Exhibit 7.9 shows the sequence of key events before trial.

Trial

Pursuant to the Seventh Amendment to the U.S. Constitution, a party to an action at law is guaranteed the right to a **jury trial** in cases in federal court. Most state constitutions contain a similar guarantee for state court actions. If either party requests a jury, the trial will be by jury. If both parties waive their right to a jury, the trial will be without a jury. In non-jury trials, the judge sits as the **trier of fact**. These trials also are called *waiver trials* or **bench trials.** At the time of trial, the parties usually submit to the judge **trial briefs** containing legal support for their side of the case.

Trials usually are divided into the following phases:

- Jury selection
- Opening statements
- Plaintiff's case
- Defendant's case
- Rebuttal and rejoinder

Motion for judgment on the pleadings A motion that alleges that if all the facts presented in the pleadings are taken as true, the party making the motion would win the lawsuit when the proper law is applied to these asserted facts.

Motion for summary judgment A motion that asserts that there are no factual disputes to be decided by the jury and that the judge can apply the proper law to the undisputed facts and decide the case without a jury. These motions are supported by affidavits, documents, and deposition testimony.

Web Exploration

Go to http://www.legalzoom.com/legal-articles//article11331.html and read the article "Top Ten Frivolous Lawsuits."

Trier of fact The jury in a jury trial; the judge where there is not a jury trial.

Exhibit 7.9 **Key events before trial**

Discovery
Mar 2002 - Sep 2002

Crandall deposition
Apr 15, 2002

Brainstorming session—Settle/Try Decision
Oct 2002

Lang deposition
Apr 30, 2002

Mandatory settlement conference
Nov 2002

Remetz deposition
May 15, 2002

Final pretrial conference
Jan 2003

Hawkins deposition
Jun 1, 2002

Trial
Feb–Mar 2003

Connors deposition
Jun 15, 2002

Feb | Mar | Apr | May | Jun | Jul | Aug | Sep | Oct | Nov | Dec | Jan | Feb | Mar
2002 | 2003

- Closing arguments
- Jury instructions
- Jury deliberation
- Entry of judgment

Jury Selection

In **jury selection**, the pool of the potential jurors usually is selected from voter or automobile registration lists. Potential jurors are asked to fill out a questionnaire such as that shown in Exhibit 7.10. Individuals are selected to hear specific cases through the process called *voir dire* ("to speak the truth"). Lawyers for each party and the judge can ask questions of prospective jurors to determine if they would be biased in their decision. Jurors can be "stricken for cause" if the court believes that the potential juror is too biased to render a fair verdict. Lawyers may also use preemptory challenges to exclude a juror from sitting on a particular case without giving any reason for the dismissal. Once the appropriate number of jurors is selected (usually six to twelve jurors), they are impaneled to hear the case and are sworn in. The trial is ready to begin. In cases in which the Court is concerned for the safety of the jury, such as a high-profile murder case, it can **sequester,** or separate it from the outside world. Jurors are paid minimum

Voir dire Process whereby prospective jurors are asked questions by the judge and attorneys to determine if they would be biased in their decision.

Exhibit 7.10   Sample jury questionnaire

JURY QUESTIONNAIRE
(Please Print)

NAME _____   JUROR NO. _____

      (Last)   *(First)*   *(Middle initial)*

SECTION OF CITY _____

      (Currently)   *(Other sections of city lived in within past ten years)*

Marital Status ☐ Married   ☐ Single   ☐ Divorced   ☐ Separated   ☐ Widowed

Occupation _____

      (Currently)   *(Other occupations within past ten years)*

Occupation of ☐ Spouse *(or deceased spouse)*   ☐ Other

_____

      (Currently)   *(Other occupations within past ten years)*

No. of Male Children _____ Ages _____

No. of Female Children _____ Ages _____

Your Level of Schooling Completed _____

Race   ☐ White   ☐ Hispanic   ☐ Black   ☐ Other

STOP HERE
Writing below this line is prohibited until the juror video is shown

---

QUESTIONS TO BE ANSWERED IN THE JURY ASSEMBLY ROOM

1. Do you have any physical or psychological disability or are you presently taking any medication?   ☐ YES   ☐ NO

2. (a) Have you ever been a juror before?   ☐ YES   ☐ NO

    (b) If so, were you ever on a hung jury?   ☐ YES   ☐ NO

Questions 3 through 15 apply to criminal cases only

3. Do you have any religious, moral or ethical beliefs that would prevent you from sitting in judgment in a criminal case and rendering a fair verdict?   ☐ YES   ☐ NO

4. Have you or anyone close to you ever been a victim of a crime?   ☐ YES   ☐ NO

5. Have you or anyone close to you ever been charged with or arrested for a crime, other than a traffic violation?   ☐ YES   ☐ NO

6. Have you or anyone close to you ever been an eyewitness to a crime, whether or not it ever came to Court?   ☐ YES   ☐ NO

(continued)

Exhibit 7.10 | **Sample jury questionnaire** *(continued)*

7. Have you, or has anyone close to you, ever worked as a police officer or in other law enforcement jobs? This includes prosecutors, public defenders, private criminal defense lawyers, detectives, and security or prison guards. ❏ YES ❏ NO

8. Would you be more likely to believe the testimony of a police officer or any other law enforcement officer just because of his job? ❏ YES ❏ NO

9. Would you be less likely to believe the testimony of a police officer or any other law enforcement officer just because of his job? ❏ YES ❏ NO

10. Would you have any problem following the Court's instruction that the defendant in a criminal case is presumed to be innocent until proven guilty beyond a reasonable doubt? ❏ YES ❏ NO

11. Would you have any problem following the Court's instruction that the defendant in a criminal case does not have to take the stand or present evidence, and it cannot be held against the defendant if he or she elects to remain silent? ❏ YES ❏ NO

12. Would you have any problem following the Court's instruction in a criminal case that just because someone is arrested, it does not mean that the person is guilty of anything? ❏ YES ❏ NO

13. In general, would you have any problem following and applying the judge's instructions on the law? ❏ YES ❏ NO

14. Would you have any problem during jury deliberations in a criminal case discussing the case fully but still making up your own mind? ❏ YES ❏ NO

15. Is there any other reason you could not be a fair juror in a criminal case? ❏ YES ❏ NO

Questions 16 through 24 apply to civil cases only

16. Have you or anyone close to you ever sued someone, been sued, or been a witness? ❏ YES ❏ NO

17. Have you or anyone close to you been employed as a lawyer or in a law-related job? ❏ YES ❏ NO

18. Have you or anyone close to you been employed as a doctor or nurse or in a medical-related job? ❏ YES ❏ NO

19. In a civil case, would you have any problem following the Court's instruction that the plaintiff has the burden or proof, but unlike in a criminal case, the test is not beyond a reasonable doubt but "more likely than not"? ❏ YES ❏ NO

20. In a civil case, would you have any problem putting aside sympathy for the plaintiff and deciding the case solely on the evidence? ❏ YES ❏ NO

21. In a civil case, would you have any problem following the Court's instruction to award money for damages for things like pain and suffering, loss of life's pleasures, etc., although it is difficult to put a dollar figure on them? ❏ YES ❏ NO

22. Would you have any problem during jury deliberations in a civil case discussing the case fully but still making up your own mind? ❏ YES ❏ NO

23. Is there any reason in a civil case that you cannot follow the Court's instructions on the law? ❏ YES ❏ NO

24. Is there any reason in a civil case that you cannot otherwise be a fair juror? ❏ YES ❏ NO

fees for their service. Courts can hold people in contempt and fine or jail them for will-ful refusal to serve as a juror.

Opening Statements

Each party's attorney is allowed to make an **opening statement** to the jury. In open-ing statements, attorneys usually summarize the main factual and legal issues of the case and describe why they believe their client's position is valid. The information given in this statement is not considered as evidence. It is the attorney's opportunity to tell the trier of fact what he or she intends to tell the jury through witnesses and evidence.

Plaintiff's Case

Plaintiffs bear the **burden of proof** to persuade the trier of fact of the merits of their case. This is called the **plaintiff's case**. The plaintiff's attorney calls witnesses to give testimony. After a witness has been sworn in, the plaintiff's attorney examines (ques-tions) the witness. This is called **direct examination**. Documents and other evidence can be introduced through each witness.

After the plaintiff's attorney has completed his or her questions, the defendant's attorney can question the witness in **cross-examination**. The defendant's attorney can ask questions only about the subjects that were brought up during the direct examina-tion. After the defendant's attorney completes his or her questions, the plaintiff's attor-ney can ask questions of the witness in **redirect examination**. The defendant's attorney then can ask questions of the witness again. This is called **recross examination**. Exhibit 7.11 illustrates this sequence for examining witnesses.

Defendant's Case

After the plaintiff has concluded his or her case, the **defendant's case** proceeds. The defendant's case must

1. rebut the plaintiff's evidence.
2. prove any affirmative defenses asserted by the defendant.
3. prove any allegations contained in the defendant's cross-complaint.

The defendant's witnesses are examined by the defendant's attorney. The plain-tiff's attorney can cross-examine each witness. This is followed by redirect examination by the defendant and recross examination of witnesses by the plaintiff.

Rebuttal and Rejoinder

After the defendant's attorney has completed calling witnesses, the plaintiff's attorney can call witnesses and put forth evidence to rebut the defendant's case. This is called a **rebuttal.** The defendant's attorney can call additional witnesses and introduce other evidence to counter the rebuttal. This is called the **rejoinder**.

Closing Arguments

At the conclusion of the evidence, each party's attorney is allowed to make a **closing argument** to the jury. Each attorney tries to convince the jury to render a verdict for his or her clients by pointing out the strengths in the client's case and the weaknesses in the other side's case.

Information given by the attorneys in their closing statements is not evidence. It is a chance for the attorneys to tell the jury what they said they would tell the jury through witnesses and evidence in the opening statements and how they had done that during the trial.

Jury Instructions

Once the closing arguments are completed, the judge reads **jury instructions**, or **charges** to the jury. These instructions inform the jury about what law to apply in deciding the case

Plaintiff's case Process by which the plaintiff calls witnesses and introduces evidence to prove the allegations contained in his or her complaint.

CONDUCTING A COST-BENEFIT ANALYSIS OF A LAWSUIT

A paralegal should have knowledge of how expensive and time-consuming a lawsuit is both for the client and for the lawyer and law office. Therefore, the choice of whether to bring or defend a lawsuit should be analyzed like any other business decision. This includes performing a **cost-benefit analysis** of the lawsuit. For the plaintiff, it may be wise not to sue. For the defendant, or the plaintiff, it may be wise to settle.

The following factors should be considered in deciding whether to bring or settle a lawsuit:

- The probability of winning or losing
- The amount of money to be won or lost
- Lawyers' fees and other costs of litigation
- Loss of time by managers and other personnel
- The long-term effects on the relationship and reputation of the parties
- The amount of prejudgment interest provided by law
- The aggravation and psychological costs associated with a lawsuit
- The unpredictability of the legal system and the possibility of error
- Other factors peculiar to the parties and lawsuit

Exhibit 7.11   Sequence for examining witnesses

Defendant's case Process by which the defendant calls witnesses and introduces evidence to (1) rebut the plaintiff's evidence, (2) prove affirmative defenses, and (3) prove allegations made in a cross-complaint.

Jury instructions (charges) Instructions given by the judge to the jury that informs them of the law to be applied in the case.

Verdict Decision reached by the jury.

Judgment The official decision of the court.

(see Exhibit 7.12). For example, in a criminal trial the judge will read the jury the statutory definition of the crime charged. In an accident case, the judge will read the jury the legal definition of *negligence*.

Jury Deliberation and Verdict

The jury then goes into the jury room to deliberate its findings. **Jury deliberation** can take from a few minutes to many weeks. After deliberation, the jury announces its **verdict**. In civil cases, the jury also assesses damages. In criminal cases, the judge assesses penalties.

Entry of Judgment

After the jury has returned its verdict, in most cases the judge enters **judgment** to the successful party, based on the verdict. This is the official decision of the court. But the court may overturn the verdict if it finds bias or jury misconduct. This is called a **judgment notwithstanding the verdict**, or **judgment n.o.v.**, or **j.n.o.v.**, for the Latin *judgment non obstante verdicto*.

In a civil case, the judge may reduce the amount of monetary damages awarded by the jury if he or she finds the jury to have been biased, emotional, or inflamed. This is called **remittitur**. The trial court usually issues a **written memorandum** setting forth the reasons for the judgment. This memorandum, together with the trial transcript and evidence introduced at trial, constitutes the permanent *record* of the trial court proceeding.

Appeal The act of asking an appellate court to overturn a decision after the trial court's final judgment has been entered.

Appellant The appealing party in an appeal. Also known as *petitioner*.

Appellee The responding party in an appeal. Also known as *respondent*.

Briefs Documents submitted by the parties' attorneys to the judge that contain legal support for their side of the case.

Appeal

In a civil case, either party can **appeal** the trial court's decision once a final judgment is entered. In a criminal case, only the defendant can appeal. The appeal is made to the appropriate **appellate court** (see Exhibit 7.13). A notice of appeal must be filed within a prescribed time after judgment is entered (usually within 60 or 90 days). The appealing party is called the **appellant**, or **petitioner**. The responding party is called the **appellee**, or **respondent**. The appellant often is required to post an **appeal bond** (e.g., one-and-one-half times the judgment) on appeal.

Briefs and Oral Argument

The parties may designate all or relevant portions of the trial record to be submitted to the appellate court for review. The appellant's attorney may file an **opening brief** with the court, setting forth legal research and other information to support his or her

Exhibit 7.12 **Sample jury instructions**

6.01J (Civ) PROPERTY DAMAGE

The plaintiff is entitled to be compensated for the harm done to his (her) property. If you find that the property was a total loss, damages are to be measured by either its market value or its special value to plaintiff, whichever is greater. If the property was not a total loss, damages are measured by (the difference in value before and after the harm) (the reasonable cost of repairs) and you may consider such evidence produced by defendant by way of defense to plaintiff's claim. In addition, plaintiff is entitled to be reimbursed for incidental costs or losses reasonably incurred because of the damage to the property, such as (rental of a replacement vehicle during repairs), (towing charges), (loss of use of the property), (etc.).

SUBCOMMITTEE NOTE

Damage to property is covered generally by Restatement of Torts, §§ 927 and 928. Section 927 provides for damages to be measured by the "market value" or "damages based upon its special value to [plaintiff] if that is greater than its market value." Restatement of Torts, § 927, Comment c (1934). Section 928 provides, in the case of damages not amounting to total destruction, damages measured by "the difference between the value of the chattel before the harm and the value after the harm or, at plaintiff's election, the reasonable cost of repair or restoration." This accounts for the parenthesized phrases (the difference in value before and after the harm) and (the reasonable cost of repairs).

Incidental costs will depend on the nature of the property damage. Rental of a substitute vehicle has long been recognized as one such compensable item. *Bauer v. Armour & Co.*, 84 Pa.Super. 174 (1924). Compensation for loss of use is specifically authorized by Restatement of Torts, § 928(b), in the case of less than total loss. The Subcommittee can see no logical reason why such damages should not be awarded under Section 927 in the case of total loss. *Nelson v. Johnson*, 55 D. & C. 2d 21 (Somerset C.P. 1970). Any further expense, proximately resulting from the loss or damage is recoverable under general provisions of tort law. *Nelson v. Johnson, supra*, at 33-34.

In the case of damage to automobiles, however, the appellate courts have adhered to the ancient rule requiring testimony of the one who supervised or made the repairs, prior to admission of damage estimates. *Mackiw v. Pennsylvania Threshermen & Farmers Mut. Cas. Ins. Co.*, 201 Pa.Super. 626, 193 A.2d 745 (1963). This rule has been criticized as time-consuming and "technical" by the very courts adhering to it. *Mackiw, supra*, 193 A.2d at 745. It further creates an intolerable burden on the courts, in a period when backlog has led to "compulsory" arbitration in many counties of cases valued below $10,000. E.g., *Loughery v. Barnes*, 181 Pa.Super. 352, 124 A.2d 120 (1956) (appeal after verdict of $341.30 for property damage); *Wilk v. Borough of Mt. Oliver*, 152 Pa.Super. 539, 33 A.2d 73 (1943) (new trial ordered after verdict of $175). The Subcommittee therefore adopts a rule requiring only the submission of a repair bill or estimate in proof of damages to automobiles (such bill being submitted prior to trial to defense counsel); should defendant wish to challenge such an estimate, he may do so through cross-examination and through the introduction of evidence in his own case. See *Watsontown Brick Co. v. Hercules Powder Co.*, 265 F.Supp. 268, 275 (M.D.Pa.), *aff'd*, 387 F.2d 99 (3rd Cir. 1967) (after introduction of damage evidence, burden shifts to defendant to show reduction).

Absent stipulation, the issue of reasonable compensation remains a jury issue.

6.01F (Civ) FUTURE PAIN AND SUFFERING

The plaintiff is entitled to be fairly and adequately compensated for such physical pain, mental anguish, discomfort, inconvenience and distress as you believe he (she) will endure in the future as a result of his (her) injuries. [. . .]

| **Exhibit 7.13** | **Form 1 of appellate rules** |

United States District Court for the _Eastern_ _____

District of _Pennsylvania_ _____

File Number _US3CA 01234_ _____

Ethan Marshall

           v.   )   Notice of Appeal

Sara Elliott

Notice is hereby given that _Ethan Marshall_ _____ (plaintiffs) in the above named case,* hereby appeal to the United States Court of Appeals for the _Third_ _____ Circuit _from the final judgment_ _____ entered in this action on the _06_ day of _February_ , _2011_ .

(s) _[signature]_

Thomas F. Goldman

_____
(Address)

Attorney for _Plaintiff_ _____

Address: _138 North State Street_
Newtown, Pa, 18940

* See Rule 3(c) for permissible ways of identifying appellants.

contentions on appeal. The appellee can file a **responding brief** answering the appellant's contentions.

In some appeals, the attorneys submit their case on "brief" only and ask the court to make a decision based upon the written submission. In other cases, the attorneys on their own or at the request of the court make oral arguments to support their position and clarify what they believe to be the appropriate law. Appellate courts usually permit a brief oral argument at which each party's attorney is heard.

Not every appellate court permits or allows oral argument in every case. Many cases are decided on the brief submitted. In some courts, it is necessary, at the time of filing, to make any desired request for oral argument or indicate a willingness to have the matter decided on the briefs alone. In some cases, the oral argument is allowed automatically, and in other cases a reason for the desired oral argument must be stated.

In the federal court of appeals, oral argument is allowed unless a panel of three judges unanimously agrees, after reviewing the briefs, that the oral argument is unnecessary because the appeal is frivolous, the dispositive issues have been authoritatively decided, or the facts and argument are presented adequately in the briefs and record and the decisional process would not be aided by oral argument [F.R.A.P. 344].

Typically, oral arguments are made before the court without the presence of clients or witnesses. Because no additional fact-finding is permitted, it is merely a matter of making appropriate legal arguments to attempt to persuade the court to rule in favor of the legal position being argued. Many appellate courts establish a time limit for each side. In some courts, the time limit is enforced by a flashing light when the time has expired, and in other courts by a warning light when the time has almost been used. This is done to allow for final statements.

The judges may waive the time limits, particularly when they use up the attorneys' allotted time by asking questions. Local practice, however, is what determines how the court will treat the time limit.

Actions by the Appellate Courts

After review of the briefs, the record in the form of the trial court transcript, and oral arguments by the attorneys, an appellate court may affirm, reverse, or remand the case to the lower court.

If the appellate court believes there had been no errors in application of the procedural law or the substantive law, it will **affirm** the decision of lower court and the lower court decision will stand. If the appellate court rules that the lower court has made a substantial error, either in the procedural law or the substantive law of the case, it may **reverse** the decision of lower court. In other cases when the court finds a reversible error, the court may **reverse and remand** the case. This means that the appellate court feels that based on the correction of the error of law that the case needs to be retried. The retrial will take place in front of a new judge and a new jury.

In the federal court of appeals, oral argument is allowed unless a panel of three judges unanimously agrees, after reviewing the briefs, that the oral argument is unnecessary because the appeal is frivolous, the dispositive issues have been authoritatively decided, or the facts and argument are presented adequately in the briefs and record and the decisional process would not be aided by oral argument [F.R.A.P. 344].

Typically, oral arguments are made before the court without the presence of clients or witnesses. Because no additional fact-finding is permitted, it is merely a matter of making appropriate legal arguments to attempt to persuade the court to rule in favor of the legal position being argued. Many appellate courts establish a time limit for each side. In some courts, the time limit is enforced by a flashing light when the time has expired, and in other courts by a warning light when the time has almost been used. This is done to allow for final statements.

The judges may waive the time limits, particularly when they use up the attorneys' allotted time by asking questions. Local practice, however, is what determines how the court will treat the time limit.

The court also may find that the lower court has made an error that can be corrected, and **remand** the case to the lower court to take additional action or conduct further proceedings. This is called reverse and remand. For example, the lower court may be directed to hold further proceedings in which a jury hears testimony related to the issue of damages and makes an award of monetary damages.

An appellate court will reverse a lower court decision if it finds an **error of law** in the record. An error of law occurs if the jury was improperly instructed by the trial court judge, prejudicial evidence was admitted at trial when it should have been excluded, prejudicial evidence was obtained through an unconstitutional search and seizure, and the like. An appellate court will not reverse a finding of fact unless such finding is unsupported by the evidence or is contradicted by the evidence.

Web Exploration

Check the "Court Rules" of the U.S. Supreme Court, Rule 129, at http://supremecourtus.gov/.

Concept Review *and* Reinforcement

LEGAL TERMINOLOGY

SUMMARY OF KEY CONCEPTS

Civil Litigation

Description	The legal process for resolving disputes between parties. In civil litigation, the plaintiff sues a defendant to recover monetary damages or other remedy for the alleged harm the defendant caused the plaintiff.

Pleadings

Description	Pleadings consist of paperwork that initiates and responds to a lawsuit.
Complaint	A complaint (petition) is filed by the plaintiff with the court and served, in some states, with a summons on the defendant. It sets forth the basis of the lawsuit.

Fact and Notice Pleading	Depending on the jurisdiction, the complaint must either provide a general allegation of the wrongful conduct alleged, called notice pleading; or plead specific facts alleged, called fact pleading.
Pleading Deadlines	Individual court rules provide a time within which the initial complaint or petition must be served, and responsive pleading must be filed to avoid dismissal of the action or a default judgment.
Responsive Pleadings	The responding party (defendant) must file a responsive pleading within the time limit allowed by rule of court, or request an extension of time to respond from the opposing attorney or from the court.
Answer	An answer is filed by the defendant with the court and served on the plaintiff. It usually denies most allegations of the complaint.
Cross-Complaint	A cross-complaint is filed and served by the defendant if he or she countersues the plaintiff. The defendant is the cross-complainant and the plaintiff is the cross-defendant. The cross-defendant must file and serve a reply (answer).
Intervention	In an intervention, a person who has an interest in a lawsuit becomes a party to the lawsuit.
Consolidation	Consolidation means that the court combines separate cases against the same defendant arising from the same incident into one case if it will not cause prejudice to the parties.
Statute of Limitations	A statute of limitations establishes the period during which a plaintiff must bring a lawsuit against a defendant. If a lawsuit is not filed within this time period, the plaintiff loses his or her right to sue.

Discovery

Description	Discovery is the pretrial litigation process for eliciting facts of the case from the other party and witnesses, for purposes of understanding and evaluating the client's case, focusing the legal team on the strengths and weaknesses of its case; understanding and evaluating the strengths and weaknesses of the opponent's case; preserving testimony; potentially facilitating settlement; and learning information that may be used to impeach a witness.
Depositions	Depositions are oral testimony given by *deponents*, either a party or witness, and transcribed.
Interrogatories	Interrogatories are written questions submitted by one party to the other party. These questions must be answered within a specified period of time.
Production of Documents	A party to a lawsuit may obtain copies of all relevant documents from the other party called a production of documents.
Physical and Mental Examination	Physical and mental examinations of a party are permitted upon order of the court where injuries are alleged that could be verified or disputed by such examination.
Requests for Admission	Written requests issued by one party to the lawsuit to the other asking that certain facts or legal issues be admitted as true.
E-Discovery	In many lawsuits, much of the evidence is in digital form. The winning or losing of lawsuits may lie in the ability of a party to conduct electronic discovery. The lawyer and the paralegal must have a sound understanding of permissible e-discovery.

Pretrial Motions

Motion to Dismiss	A motion to dismiss alleges that even if the facts as presented in the plaintiff's complaint are true, there is no reason to continue the lawsuit. Also called a *demurrer*.

Motion for Judgment on the Pleadings	A motion for judgment on the pleadings alleges that if all facts as pleaded are true, the moving party would win the lawsuit. No facts outside the pleadings may be considered.
Motion for Summary Judgment	A motion for summary judgment alleges that there are no factual disputes, so the judge may apply the law and decide the case without a jury. Evidence outside the pleadings, however, may be considered (e.g., affidavits, documents, depositions).

Settlement Conference

Description	A settlement conference is held prior to trial between the parties in front of the judge to facilitate settlement of the case. Also called *pretrial hearing*. If a settlement is not reached, the case proceeds to trial.

Trial

Jury Selection	Jury selection is done through a process called *voir dire*. Biased jurors are dismissed and replaced.
Opening Statements	The parties' lawyers make opening statements. These do not constitute evidence.
Plaintiff's Case	The plaintiff bears the burden of proof. The plaintiff calls witnesses and introduces evidence to try to prove his or her case.
Defendant's Case	The defendant calls witnesses and introduces evidence to rebut the plaintiff's case and to prove affirmative defenses and cross-complaints.
Rebuttal and Rejoinder	In rebuttal and rejoinder, the plaintiff and defendant may call additional witnesses and introduce additional evidence.
Closing Arguments	Closing arguments are made by the parties' lawyers. Their statements are not evidence.
Jury Instructions	The judge reads instructions to the jury as to what law the jurors are to apply to the case.
Jury Deliberation	The jury retires to the jury room and deliberates until it reaches a *verdict*.
Entry of Judgment	The judge may: a. enter the verdict reached by the jury as the court's *judgment*. b. grant a motion of *judgment* n.o.v. if the judge finds that the jury was biased. This means that the jury's verdict does not stand. c. order *remittitur* (reduction) of any damages awarded if the judge finds the jury to have been biased or emotional.

Appeal

Appellate Court	1. Unlike the trial court, whose main function is to make findings of facts, the appellate court's main function is to make findings of law. 2. In a civil case, unlike a criminal case, either party can appeal the trial court's decision once a final judgment is entered. In a criminal case, only the defendant can appeal. The appeal is made to the appropriate appellate court.
Briefs	In some appeals, the attorneys submit their case on "brief" only, and ask the court to make a decision based upon the written submission.
Oral Arguments	In other cases, the attorneys, on their own or at the request of the court, make an oral argument to support their position and clarify what they believe to be the appropriate law. Not every appellate court permits or allows oral argument in every case.

Actions by the Appellate Courts

Affirm	The appellate court believes there have been no errors in the application of the procedural law or the substantive law and allows the prior decision to stand.
Reverse	The appellate court rules that the lower court has made a substantial error in either the procedural or the substantive law of the case.
Remand	The court finds that the lower court has made an error that can be corrected by sending the case back to the lower court.

WORKING THE WEB

1. Locate the website for your local state trial court that serves your city, if that website is available. If the website is not available, visit the local state trial court. Locate the local rules for filing complaints, answers, and other documents with the court. Are these rules complicated? Explain.

2. Visit the website http://uscourts.gov/. Locate the U.S. District Court that serves the county or parish in which you live. Go to that court's website. Does the court permit electronic filing of documents? If so, review the "user manual" on how to make electronic filings with the court.

3. Visit the website http://supremecourt.us.gov/. Click on "Paid Cases Brief Chart" and review the types of forms that can be filed with the U.S. Supreme Court. How much detail does a paralegal need to know when assisting an attorney to file documents with the U.S. Supreme Court? Explain.

4. Visit the website http://www.lexisone.com/. Click on the feature "Deadlines on Demand." Read about the services available. Are these useful services?

5. Visit the website http://www.lexisone.com/. Click on "Register" and register for the free service to obtain court forms. Find a state form for the state court that serves the county or parish where you live. Find a federal form for the U.S. District Court that serves the county or parish where you live.

CRITICAL THINKING & WRITING QUESTIONS

1. Define "plaintiff." Define "defendant."
2. What is civil litigation? What remedy or remedies are sought by the plaintiff in civil litigation?
3. What are pleadings? Describe the following pleadings: (a) complaint, (b) answer, (c) cross-complaint, and (d) reply.
4. What is a summons? Describe service of process.
5. What is intervention? What is consolidation?
6. Explain statutes of limitations. What purpose do they serve?
7. What is the process of discovery? What purposes does discovery serve? Explain.
8. Describe the following types of discovery: (a) deposition, (b) interrogatories, (c) production of documents, and (d) physical and mental examination.
9. Describe the differences between the following pretrial motions: (a) motion to dismiss, (b) motion for judgment on the pleadings, and (c) motion for summary judgment.
10. What is a settlement conference? What is its purpose?
11. How is a jury selected for a case? What is *voir dire*? What does trier of fact mean?
12. Describe the following phases of a trial: (a) opening statements, (b) plaintiff's case, (c) defendant's case, (d) rebuttal and rejoinder, and (e) closing arguments.
13. What are jury instructions? Explain. What is a verdict? What is a judgment?
14. What is an appeal? Define appellant (petitioner) and appellee (respondent).
15. Describe the following possible decisions by an appellate court: (a) affirm, (b) reverse, and (c) reverse and remand.

Building Paralegal Skills

Videotaped Deposition: Deposing an Expert Witness for Use at Trial

 An expert witness whose testimony is critical to the issue of negligence may not be available at time of trial. The parties have agreed to the videotaping of the expert's deposition using a real-time reporting system that provides standard word processing documents simultaneously for the parties.

After viewing the video case study at www.pearsonhighered .com/goldman answer the following:

1. What are the pros and cons to taking a video deposition of an expert witness?
2. Are there any special preparations that need to be made in taking videotaped depositions?
3. How much credibility would you as a juror give to videotaped deposition of an expert witness?

Trial: Direct and Cross-examination of a Witness

 The attorneys in a trial ask questions of a fact witness in direct and then in cross-examination to develop the facts of a case.

After viewing the video case study at www.pearsonhighered .com/goldman answer the following:

1. What is the purpose of direct examination?
2. What is the purpose of cross-examination?
3. Why would the attorney ask if it was acceptable to approach the witness?

Preparing for Trial: Preparing a Fact Witness

 A paralegal is preparing a witness for deposition and trial and attempts to put the witness at ease by answering the witness's questions and explaining the procedures.

After viewing the video case study at www.pearsonhighered .com/goldman answer the following:

1. Why is it necessary to prepare a person for deposition or for trial?
2. What is the most important advice the paralegal gives the witness?
3. Is preparing a witness the unauthorized practice of law?

1. Is there an ethical obligation not to file certain lawsuits?
2. What is meant by frivolous lawsuit? Are there sanctions for filing frivolous lawsuits? Explain.
3. Should email between lawyers and paralegals be treated as confidential and not subject to use as evidence in a case? Why or why not?
4. A former client of the firm where you work sees you on the street at a local lunch stand and shows you a copy of a judgment rendered against him in a small-claims court. He tells you he is out of work and cannot afford to hire a lawyer. [Pennsylvania comments to Ethics Rule 5.5.] Can you help the client proceed *pro se* (on his own, acting as his own lawyer)? Can you help him prepare the paperwork to appeal the judgment? Does any of this constitute the unauthorized practice of law?
5. You have been advised in your orientation of the ethical rule prohibiting communication with an opponent who is represented by counsel. While surfing the Web, you decide to see if the opposing party has a website. You locate it and check it carefully for any information that might help the investigation of the case assigned to you. You send a request to the site and receive information related to the lawsuit. [Oregon State Bar Op2001–164.] Have you violated the ethical prohibition barring communications with a represented party?

DEVELOPING YOUR COLLABORATION SKILLS

With a group of other students, selected by you or as assigned by your instructor, review the Paralegals at Work at the beginning of the chapter. As a group, discuss the following questions.

1. Identify what document or documents your law firm should prepare on behalf of Rowan, Isis, and their parents to start the lawsuit. Identify what document the trucking company will file with the court to defend the lawsuit.
2. What are the time limits for filing and responding to a complaint? Are there any other local requirements to commence and respond to the lawsuit?
3. Why would the state or federal court be more preferable?

PARALEGAL & PORTFOLIO EXERCISE

Refer to the Paralegals at Work opening scenario. Find online if possible, or if not found online, find in the law library or the federal U.S. District Court, the proper form for filing a complaint for personal injuries in the federal U.S. district court that serves your city. Prepare as best as possible, from the facts of the Paralegals at Work, the complaint and answer in the case presented. If insufficient facts are provided to complete the complaint or answer, make up the missing information and complete these documents.

LEGAL ANALYSIS & WRITING CASES

Swierkiewicz v. Sorema N.A.
534 U.S. 506, 122 S.Ct. 992, 152 L.Ed. 1 2002 U.S. Lexis 1374 (U.S.)

In April 1989, Akos Swierkiewicz, a native of Hungary, began working for Sorema N.A., a reinsurance company headquartered in New York. Swierkiewicz initially was employed as senior vice president and chief underwriting officer. Nearly six years later, the chief executive officer of the company demoted Swierkiewicz to a marketing position, and he was removed from his underwriting responsibilities. Swierkiewicz's underwriting responsibilities were transferred to a 32-year-old employee with less than 1 year of underwriting experience. Swierkiewicz, who was 53 years old at the time and had 26 years of experience in the insurance industry, was dismissed by Sorema.

Swierkiewicz sued Sorema to recover monetary damages for alleged age and national-origin discrimination in violation of federal antidiscrimination laws. Sorema moved to have Swierkiewicz's complaint dismissed. The District Court dismissed Swierkiewicz's complaint for not being specific enough, and the Court of Appeals affirmed. Swierkiewicz appealed to the U.S. Supreme Court.

Question
1. Under the notice pleading system, was plaintiff Swierkiewicz's complaint sufficiently stated to permit the case to go to trial?

Norgart v. The Upjohn Company
21 Cal.4th 383, 87 Cal.Rptr.2nd 453 1999 Cal. Lexis 5308 (Cal.)

Kristi Norgart McBride lived with her husband in Santa Rosa, California. Kristi suffered from manic-depressive mental illness (now called bipolar disorder). In this disease, the person cycles between manic (ultrahappy, expansive, extrovert) episodes to depressive episodes. The disease is often treated with prescription drugs. In April 1984, Kristi attempted suicide. A psychiatrist prescribed an antianxiety drug. In May 1985, Kristi attempted suicide again by overdosing on drugs. The doctor prescribed Halcion, a hypnotic drug, and added Darvocet-N, a mild narcotic analgesic. On October 16, 1985, after descending into a severe depression, Kristi committed suicide by overdosing on Halcion and Darvocet-N.

On October 16, 1991, exactly six years after Kristi's death, Leo and Phyllis Norgart, Kristi's parents, filed a lawsuit against the Upjohn Company, the maker of Halcion, for wrongful death based on Upjohn's alleged failure to warn of the unreasonable dangers of taking Halcion. The trial court granted Upjohn's motion for summary judgment based on the fact that the one-year statute of limitations for wrongful death actions had run. The Court of Appeals reversed, and Upjohn appealed to the Supreme Court of California.

Question
1. Is the plaintiff's action for wrongful death barred by the one-year statute of limitations?

Engler v. Winfrey   201 F.3d 680 2000 U.S. App. Lexis 1723 (5th Cir.)

In early 1996, a disease called Mad Cow Disease was diagnosed in Britain. The disease triggers a deadly brain condition in cattle, which in turn causes degeneration and fatal brain disease in humans who eat beef from infected cattle. Oprah Winfrey hosts a popular television show in the United States, which is produced by Harpo Productions, Inc., a company wholly owned by Winfrey. Producers, editors, and other employees of the Oprah Winfrey Show researched the Mad Cow Disease topic as part of a "Dangerous Foods" episode of the Oprah Winfrey Show. Guests on the show included Dr. Gary Weber, who holds a Ph.D. in animal science and represented the National Cattlemen's Beef Association; Dr. Will Hueston from the U.S. Department of Agriculture and a leading expert on Mad Cow Disease; Dr. James Miller, a physician with experience in treating individuals inflicted with the disease; and Howard Lyman, a former cattle rancher turned vegetarian and an activist for the Humane Society.

On the show, which was aired April 16, 1996, Lyman made several statements regarding the threat that Mad Cow Disease posed to people in the United States. The experts on the show countered that no case of Mad Cow Disease had been reported in the United States and explained the extensive animal testing and oversight employed by the U.S. Department of Agriculture and cattle producers to prevent Mad Cow Disease in the United States.

Following the broadcast of Oprah Winfrey's "Dangerous Foods" show, the cattle market in Texas dropped drastically.

In the week before the show aired, finished cattle sold for approximately $61.90 per hundredweight; after the show, the price dropped to the mid-$50s. The live cattle futures market on the Chicago Mercantile Exchange dropped within an hour of the airing of the Oprah Winfrey Show. The depressed market for finished cattle continued its slump for approximately three months after the show.

Plaintiffs Paul Engler and Cattle Feeders, Inc. filed a lawsuit against defendants Oprah Winfrey and Harpo Productions, Inc., alleging that the defendants had engaged in the intentional tort of business disparagement of the product cattle. After testimony was heard from both sides, the trial court judge submitted the following question to the jury: "Did a named defendant publish a false, disparaging statement that was of and concerning the cattle of a plaintiff?" The trial court jury returned the answer "no" to this question, and the trial court judge entered judgment in favor of the defendants Oprah Winfrey and Harpo Productions, Inc. The plaintiffs appealed this decision to the U.S. Court of Appeals, arguing that the trial court judge's business disparagement instruction was in error.

Question

1. Was the trial court judge's business disparagement instruction to the jury an error that requires the case to be reversed on this issue on appeal?

Ferlito v. Johnson & Johnson Products, Inc.   771 F.Supp. 196 1991 U.S. Dist. Lexis 11747 (E.D.Mich.)

Susan and Frank Ferlito were invited to a Halloween party. They decided to attend as Mary (Mrs. Ferlito) and her little lamb (Mr. Ferlito). Mrs. Ferlito constructed a lamb costume for her husband by gluing cotton batting manufactured by Johnson & Johnson Products, Inc. (JJP), to a suit of long underwear. She used the same cotton batting to fashion a headpiece, complete with ears. The costume covered Mr. Ferlito from his head to his ankles, except for his face and hands, which were blackened with paint. At the party, Mr. Ferlito attempted to light a cigarette with a butane lighter. The flame passed close to his left arm, and the cotton batting ignited. He suffered burns over one-third of his body. The Ferlitos sued JJP to recover damages, alleging that JJP failed to warn them of the ignitability of cotton batting. The jury returned a verdict for Mr. Ferlito in the amount of $555,000 and for Mrs. Ferlito in the amount of $70,000. JJP filed a motion for judgment notwithstanding the verdict (j.n.o.v.).

Question

1. Should defendant JJP's motion for j.n.o.v. be granted?

Pizza Hut, Inc. v. Papa John's International, Inc.   227 F.3d 489 2000 U.S. App. Lexis 23444 (5th Cir.)

Pizza Hut, Inc., the largest pizza chain in the United States, operates more than 7,000 restaurants. Papa John's International, Inc., is the third-largest pizza chain in the United States, with more than 2,050 locations. In May 1995, Papa John's adopted a new slogan, "Better Ingredients. Better Pizza," and applied for and received a federal trademark for this slogan. Papa John's spent more than $300 million building customer recognition and goodwill for this slogan. The slogan has appeared on millions of signs, shirts, menus, pizza boxes, napkins, and other items and has regularly appeared as the tag line at the end of Papa John's radio and television advertisements.

On May 1, 1997, Pizza Hut launched a new advertising campaign in which it declared "war" on poor-quality pizza. The advertisements touted the "better taste" of Pizza Hut's pizza and "dared" anyone to find a better pizza. A few weeks later, Papa John's launched a comparative advertising campaign that touted the superiority of Papa John's pizza over Pizza Hut's pizza. Papa John's claimed it had sauce and dough superior to Pizza Hut's. Many of these advertisements were accompanied by Papa John's slogan, "Better Ingredients. Better Pizza."

In 1998, Pizza Hut filed a civil action in federal District Court, charging Papa John's with false advertising in violation of Section 43(a) of the federal Lanham Act. The District Court found that Papa John's slogan "Better Ingredients. Better Pizza," standing alone, was mere puffery and did not constitute false advertising. The District Court found, however, that Papa John's claims of superior sauce and dough were misleading and that Papa John's slogan "Better Ingredients. Better Pizza" became tainted because it was associated with these misleading statements. The District Court enjoined Papa John's from using the slogan "Better Ingredients. Better Pizza." Papa John's appealed.

Question

1. Should the U.S. District Court's opinion in favor of Pizza Hut, Inc. be reversed?

Conrad v. Delta Airlines, Inc.   494 F.2d 914 1974 U.S. App. Lexis 9186 (7th Cir.)

Captain Conrad was a pilot for Delta Airlines. In 1970, the airline forced Conrad to resign. He sued, alleging that he was discharged because of his pro-union activities and not because of poor job performance, as claimed by Delta.

During discovery, a report written by a Delta flight operations manager was produced, stating: "More than a few crew members claimed that Conrad professed to being a leftist-activist. His overactivity with the local pilots' union, coupled with inquiries regarding company files to our secretary, led to the conclusion that potential trouble will be avoided by acceptance of his resignation."

Conrad claims that the report is evidence of the anti-union motivation for his discharge. Delta made a summary judgment motion to the Trial Court.

Question

1. Should its summary judgment motion be granted?

Haviland & Co. v. Montgomery Ward & Co.   31 F.R.D. 578 1962 U.S. Dist. Lexis 5964 (S.D.N.Y.)

Haviland & Company filed suit against Montgomery Ward & Company in U.S. District Court, claiming that Ward used the trademark "Haviland" on millions of dollars worth of merchandise. As the owner of the mark, Haviland & Company sought compensation from Ward. Ward served notice to take the deposition of Haviland & Company's president, William D. Haviland. The attorneys for Haviland told the court that Haviland was 80 years old, lived in Limoges, France, and was too ill to travel to the United States for the deposition. Haviland's physician submitted an affidavit confirming these facts.

Question

1. Must Haviland give his deposition?
2. What other alternative way to take the testimony may be used?

Simblest v. Maynard   427 F.2d1 1970 U.S. App. Lexis 9265 (2nd Cir.)

On November 9, 1965, Mr. Simblest was driving a car that collided with a fire engine at an intersection in Burlington, Vermont. The accident occurred on the night on which a power blackout left most of the state without lights. Mr. Simblest, who was injured in the accident, sued the driver of the fire truck for damages.

During the trial, Simblest testified that when he entered the intersection, the traffic light was green in his favor. All of the other witnesses testified that the traffic light had gone dark at least 10 minutes before the accident. Simblest testified that the accident was caused by the fire truck's failure to use any warning lights or sirens. Simblest's testimony was contradicted by four witnesses who testified that the fire truck had used both its lights and sirens. The jury found that the driver of the fire truck had been negligent and rendered a verdict for Simblest. The defense made a motion for judgment n.o.v.

Question

1. Who wins?

IN RE M.C., 09-08-00465-CV (Tex.App.-Beaumont [9th Dist.] 3-5-2009)

On January 9, 2009, the court notified the parties that the appeal would be dismissed for want of prosecution unless arrangements were made for filing the record or the appellant explained why additional time was needed to file the record. It also notified the parties that the appeal would be dismissed unless the appellant remitted the filing fee for the appeal. The appellant, Blanca Carrillo, did not respond to the Court's notices. The appellant did not file an affidavit of indigence and is not entitled to proceed without payment of costs. There was no satisfactory explanation for the failure to file the record, and no reasonable explanation for the

failure to pay the filing fee for the appeal. The court dismissed the appeal for want of prosecution.

Question

1. Why would a court dismiss a case for failure to meet a time deadline?
2. Why would a court dismiss a case for not paying the filing fees?
3. Is justice served by the court enforcing these time limits and filing requirements?

WORKING WITH THE LANGUAGE OF THE COURT CASE

Gnazzo v. G.D. Searle & Co.

973 F.2d 136 1992
U.S. App. Lexis 19453 United States Court of Appeals, Second Circuit

Read the following case, excerpted from the Court of Appeals opinion. Review and brief the case. In your brief, answer the following questions.

1. What is a statute of limitations? What purposes does such a statute serve?
2. What was the Connecticut statute of limitations for the injury alleged by the plaintiff?
3. What is summary judgment? When will it be granted?
4. What was the decision of the trial court? Of the Court of Appeals?

Pierce, Circuit Judge

On November 11, 1974, Gnazzo had a CU-7 intrauterine device (IUD) inserted in her uterus for contraceptive purposes. The IUD was developed, marketed, and sold by G.D. Searle & Co. (Searle). When Gnazzo's deposition was taken, she stated that her doctor had informed her that "the insertion would hurt, but not for long," and that she "would have uncomfortable and probably painful periods for the first three to four months." On October 11, 1975, Gnazzo found it necessary to return to her physician due to excessive pain and cramping. During this visit she was informed by her doctor that he thought she had pelvic inflammatory disease (PID). She recalled that he stated that the infection was possibly caused by venereal disease or the use of the IUD. The PID was treated with antibiotics and cleared up shortly thereafter. Less than one year later, Gnazzo was again treated for an IUD-associated infection. This infection was also treated with antibiotics. Gnazzo continued using the IUD until it was finally removed in December of 1977.

Following a laparoscopy in March of 1989, Gnazzo was informed by a fertility specialist that she was infertile because of PID-induced adhesions resulting from her prior IUD use. Subsequent to this determination, and at the request of her then-attorneys, Gnazzo completed a questionnaire dated May 11, 1989. In response to the following question, "When and why did you first suspect that your IUD had caused you any harm?" Gnazzo responded "sometime in 1981" and explained: "I was married in April 1981, so I stopped using birth control so I could get pregnant—nothing ever happened (of course), then I started hearing and reading about how damaging IUDs could be. I figured that was the problem; however, my marriage started to crumble, so I never pursued the issue."

On May 4, 1990, Gnazzo initiated the underlying action against Searle. In an amended complaint, she alleged that she had suffered injuries as a result of her use of the IUD developed by Searle. Searle moved for summary judgment on the ground that Gnazzo's claim was time-barred by Connecticut's three-year statute of limitations for product liability actions. Searle argued, inter alia, that Gnazzo knew in 1981 that she had suffered harm caused by her IUD. Gnazzo contended that her cause of action against Searle accrued only when she learned from the fertility specialist that the IUD had caused her PID and subsequent infertility.

In a ruling dated September 18, 1991, the district court granted Searle's motion for summary judgment on the ground that Gnazzo's claim was time-barred by the applicable statute of limitations. In reaching this result, the court determined that Connecticut law provided no support for Gnazzo's contention that she should not have been expected to file her action until she was told of her infertility and the IUD's causal connection. This appeal followed.

On appeal, Gnazzo contends that the district court improperly granted Searle's motion for summary judgment because a genuine issue of material fact exists as to when she discovered, or reasonably should have discovered, her injuries and their causal connection to the defendant's alleged wrongful conduct. Summary judgment is appropriate when there is no genuine issue as to any material fact and the moving party is entitled to judgment as a matter of law. We consider the record in the light most favorable to the non-movant. However, the non-movant "may not rest upon the mere allegations of denials of her pleading, but must set forth specific facts showing that there is a genuine issue for trial."

Under Connecticut law, a product liability claim must be brought within "three years from the date when the injury is first sustained or discovered or in the exercise of reasonable care should have been discovered." In Connecticut, a cause of action accrues when a plaintiff suffers actionable harm. Actionable harm occurs when the plaintiff discovers or should discover, through the exercise of reasonable care, that he or she has been injured and that the defendant's conduct caused such injury.

Gnazzo contends that "the mere occurrence of a pelvic infection or difficulty in becoming pregnant does not necessarily result in notice to the plaintiff of a cause of action." Thus, she maintains that her cause of action did not accrue until 1989 when the fertility specialist informed her both that she was infertile and that this condition resulted from her previous use of the IUD.

Under Connecticut law, however, "the statute of limitations begins to run when the plaintiff discovers some form of actionable harm, not the fullest manifestation thereof." Therefore, as Gnazzo's responses to the questionnaire indicate she suspected "sometime in 1981" that the IUD had caused her harm because she had been experiencing trouble becoming pregnant and had "started hearing and reading about how damaging IUDs could be and had figured that was the problem."

Thus, by her own admission, Gnazzo had recognized, or should have recognized, the critical link between her injury and the defendant's causal connection to it. In other words, she had "discovered, or should have discovered through the exercise of reasonable care, that she had been injured and that Searle's conduct caused such injury." However, as Gnazzo acknowledged in the questionnaire, she did not pursue the "issue" at the time because of her marital problems. Thus, even when viewed in the light most favorable to Gnazzo, the non-moving party, we are constrained to find that she knew by 1981 that she had "some form of actionable harm." Consequently, by the time she commenced her action in 1990, Gnazzo was time-barred by the Connecticut statute of limitations.

Since we have determined that Gnazzo's cause of action commenced in 1981, we need not address Searle's additional contention that Gnazzo's awareness in 1975 of her PID and her purported knowledge of its causal connection to the IUD commenced the running of the Connecticut statute of limitations at that time.

We are sympathetic to Gnazzo's situation and mindful that the unavoidable result we reach in this case is harsh. Nevertheless, we are equally aware that "it is within the Connecticut General Assembly's constitutional authority to decide when claims for injury are to be brought. Where a plaintiff has failed to comply with this requirement, a court may not entertain the suit." The judgment of the district court is affirmed.

Criminal Procedure and Administrative Law

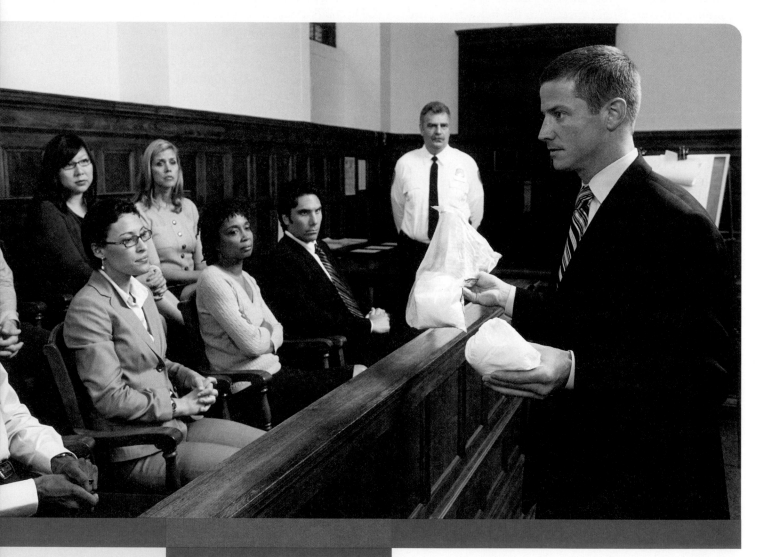

Sir William Blackstone, Commentaries
on the Laws of England (1809)

Paralegals at Work

You are a paralegal at a law firm that does criminal defense work. The law firm specializes in defending executives in white-collar criminal law matters. You work for Ms. Heather Josephson, a renowned attorney in the area of white-collar criminal defense. Ms. Josephson informs you that the law firm has been retained to represent Mr. Keith Day, an executive now facing criminal charges for alleged white-collar crimes. Ms. Josephson informs you that you will assist her in preparing the defense of Mr. Day.

Ms. Josephson explains the following facts and issues to you: Mr. Day was the founder and Chief Executive Officer (CEO) of the E-Run Corporation. The E-Run Corporation was one of the largest companies in the United States and operated an energy business. Mr. Day has been served a complaint, *United States v. Day*, wherein Mr. Day has been charged by the federal government with various crimes, including financial fraud.

Ms. Josephson explains that immediately after being served with the complaint that the federal government agents asked Mr. Day many questions concerning his business affairs as they pertained to his employment at E-Run Corporation and his involvement in the financial affairs of the company. Mr. Day explained to the federal agents how the fraud worked and his involvement in this situation. Ms. Josephson asks Mr. Day if the federal agents read him any rights before they questioned him and Mr. Day answered that they had not. Mr. Day is now concerned that the information he told the federal agents "may come back to haunt him."

The complaint alleges that Mr. Day, as well as Mr. Don Scott, E-Run Corporation's Chief Financial Officer (CFO), and other corporate officers agreed with each other to "cook the books" of the corporation to make the corporation seem like it was making huge profits when it was not. The complaint alleges that the executives failed to report on its financial statements large debts incurred by the corporation causing the corporation to show a large financial profit when in fact the corporation was losing money. When the alleged misdeeds were discovered, the E-Run Corporation failed and had to declare bankruptcy. Shareholders lost their entire investment, and the creditors of the corporation were not paid.

In addition, the complaint alleges that Mr. Day, Mr. Scott, and other corporate officers stole money directly from the corporation and diverted corporate cash and other property to their own personal bank accounts. Mr. Day is alleged to have used the mail, telephones, and computers to implement and operate the entire scheme. The complaint also alleges that Mr. Day had purchased a restaurant and used the restaurant to hide and move the stolen money through it to make it seem that he had another business that generated the stolen property for him.

Ms. Josephson explains to you that the federal government had engaged in a wiretap of Mr. Day's telephones for twelve months but had failed to obtain a warrant to conduct the wiretap on Mr. Day's telephone. Ms. Josephson also explains that Mr. Day had said that his spouse "knows everything" and that she is willing to be a witness against him at trial. Also, the federal government has reached a plea bargain with Mr. Scott that grants Mr. Scott immunity from prosecution in return for his testimony against Mr. Day at trial.

INTRODUCTION FOR THE PARALEGAL

Paralegals often work for criminal lawyers, and therefore require knowledge of the criminal legal process. Some private lawyers specialize in representing clients accused of criminal wrongdoing. Other lawyers work for the government, either for the prosecution team that represents the government in the criminal lawsuit against the defendant, or for a government-appointed defense counsel representing defendants who cannot afford a private attorney to represent them.

For members of society to coexist peacefully and commerce to flourish, people and their property must be protected from injury by other members of society. Federal, state, and local governments' **criminal laws** are intended to accomplish this by providing an incentive for persons to act reasonably in society and imposing penalties on persons who violate them.

A person charged with a crime in the United States is *presumed innocent until proven guilty*. The **burden of proof** is on the government to prove that the accused is guilty of the crime charged. The accused must be found guilty **"beyond a reasonable doubt."** Conviction requires a unanimous jury vote.

Paralegals who work in the criminal law field must have a thorough understanding of the protections in the U.S. Constitution that protect a person charged with a crime in the United States. These include the protections against unreasonable search and seizure, against self-incrimination, against double jeopardy, against cruel and unusual punishment, and the right to a public jury trial.

Many paralegal professionals work in the area of administrative law. This may consist of working for federal administrative agencies such as the Securities and Exchange

Commission (SEC), the Federal Trade Commission (FTC), and other federal agencies. Paralegals also often work for state administrative agencies. These include state environmental protection agencies, corporations departments, and other such agencies.

In the administrative law field paralegals may also work for attorneys who represent clients who are regulated by administrative agencies. For example, if a client has proceedings brought against him or her for violation of federal securities laws by the SEC, an attorney will represent the client at the proceeding. Other attorneys will represent clients who are seeking licenses to conduct business from an administrative agency. For example, clients who wish to form a national bank must obtain permission from the Office of the Comptroller of the Currency. Paralegals often assist attorneys in preparing for administrative agency matters.

This chapter covers criminal litigation and procedure and administrative law.

The following feature discusses the career opportunities for paralegal professionals in criminal law.

CAREER OPPORTUNITIES FOR PARALEGALS IN CRIMINAL LAW AND PROCEDURE

The area of criminal law provides abundant opportunities for jobs for paralegals. The criminal law system in this country is extremely large and requires the services of thousands of lawyers and, thus, thousands of paralegals. The job opportunities for paralegals are quite varied in this area of law.

Most of the crimes prosecuted in the United States involve violations of state laws. These include many physical crimes, such as assault, battery, robbery, rape, and such. In addition, many crimes involve illegal drug sales, fraud, and other violations of criminal law.

In each case when a defendant is charged with a state-law crime, the state brings the lawsuit against the alleged criminal. The lawsuits are brought by prosecutors of the local jurisdiction where the crime has been alleged to have been committed. The prosecutors are lawyers who are state government employees. The prosecutor is responsible for investigating the alleged crime and for assembling the government's case against the defendant. Paralegals have opportunities to work for state government assisting prosecuting attorneys in bringing and pursuing criminal charges.

Paralegals have opportunities to work for the state government or other defense attorneys assisting in the defense of criminally-charged defendants. Many defendants in criminal cases cannot afford their own attorneys, so the government provides defense attorneys to represent the defendant in the criminal case. The defense attorneys frequently are government employees as well. These lawyers often are referred to as public defenders. In this case, paralegals can work as state government employees assisting in the defense in a criminal case. Sometimes the court will appoint an attorney in private practice to represent a defendant. The government, of course, pays the private attorney's fees.

Paralegals who work for the prosecutor's office or for the defense attorneys typically are relied on heavily to conduct investigations, prepare documents that will be filed with the court, conduct legal research, and assist attorneys at criminal trials. Thus, substantial job opportunities are available for paralegals in this criminal law area.

In addition, some defendants—individuals, corporations, and other businesses—are charged with committing white-collar crimes, including criminal fraud, securities fraud, money laundering, racketeering, and such. White-collar criminal defendants can be charged with violating either state or federal criminal laws, depending on the crimes they are alleged to have committed.

In white-collar criminal law cases, whether in state or federal court, the government employs lawyers to represent the government in its case against the accused. In state criminal law cases, the lawyers are state employees. In federal criminal law cases the lawyers are federal employees. There are excellent opportunities for paralegals to become federal government employees and assist attorneys in the prosecution of federal crimes.

On the other side, white-collar defendants often have sufficient funds to employ private attorneys to represent them in white-collar criminal law cases. This could be the case of either wealthy individuals or corporations and businesses. Paralegals can work for the law firms who represent white-collar criminals and businesses or for the legal department of a corporation if it is the defendant in a white-collar criminal case.

White-collar criminal cases are often complex. These cases require substantial investigation, as well as preparation for trial. Paralegals are indispensable in preparing for these complex white-collar criminal cases.

There will always be criminals; therefore, there will always be a need for attorneys to represent the government on one side of the case and the defendant on the other side of the case. In a parallel fashion, there will always be a need for paralegals on the government prosecutor's side of the case, as well as the defendant's side of the case. The area of criminal law will remain an important source of employment for paralegals.

Parties and Attorneys of a Criminal Action

In a criminal lawsuit, the government (not a private party) is the **plaintiff**. The government prosecuting a case can either be the federal government or a state or territory government. The government is represented by a **prosecuting attorney**. The lawyer who prosecutes criminal cases on behalf of a state is called the **district attorney (DA)**. The lawyer who prosecutes federal criminal cases is called the **United States Attorney** (see Exhibit 8.1).

The accused, which is usually an individual or a business, is the **defendant**. The accused is represented by a **defense attorney**. Sometimes the accused will hire a private attorney to represent him or her if he can afford to do so. If the accused cannot afford a private defense lawyer, the government will provide one free of charge. This government defense attorney is often called a **public defender** (see Exhibit 8.1).

Criminal Procedure

The court procedure for initiating and maintaining a criminal action is quite detailed. It encompasses both pretrial procedures and the actual trial. Pretrial criminal procedure consists of several distinct stages: *arrest*, *indictment* or *information*, *arraignment*, and possible *plea bargaining*.

Federal Rules of Criminal Procedure govern all criminal proceedings in the courts of the United States (federal courts) [F.R.C.P. Rule 1]. Each state has its own rules of criminal procedure that govern criminal proceedings in state courts.

Criminal Complaint

In criminal cases the government must file a **criminal complaint** charging the accused with the alleged crimes he or she, or the corporation or other business, is accused of committing. F.R.C.I Rule 3 (Complaint) states "The complaint is a written statement of the essential facts constituting the offense charged. It must be made under oath before a magistrate judge or, if none is reasonably available, before a state or local judicial officer." States have their own requirements for the information to be contained in a criminal complaint

A complaint is usually filed after the government has obtained sufficient evidence to charge the accused with the crime. This government investigation may consist of watching the accused's activities, wiretaps, obtaining information from informants or

---

Exhibit 8.1 Parties and attorneys involved in a criminal case

PARTIES TO A CRIMINAL LAWSUIT

Government	Person or Business
(plaintiff)	(defendant)

ATTORNEYS REPRESENTING THE PARTIES

Prosecutor	Defense Attorney
(government attorney)	(private attorney or public defender)

witnesses, and through other means of obtaining sufficient evidence for filing the complaint.

A copy of a criminal complaint filed by the United States government appears as Exhibit 8.2.

Arrest

Before the police can arrest a person for committing a crime, they often must obtain an **arrest warrant** based upon a showing of **probable cause**—the substantial likelihood that the person either committed or is about to commit a crime.

> **Example** The police are tipped off by a source that a person has been involved in selling illegal drugs. If the judge finds that the information is reliable, and that it constitutes probable cause, the judge will issue an arrest warrant.

If the police do not have time to obtain a warrant the police still may arrest the suspect. **Warrantless arrests**, too, are judged by the probable-cause standard. A warrantless arrest can be made by the police if they arrive during the commission of a crime, when a person is fleeing from the scene of a crime, or when it is likely that evidence will be destroyed.

After a person is arrested, he or she is taken to the police station for *booking*—the administrative proceeding for recording the arrest, fingerprinting, and so on.

Arrest warrant A document for a person's detainment based upon a showing of probable cause that the person committed the crime.

Bail

When a person is arrested, a **bail** amount is usually set. If the arrested person "posts" bail, he or she can be released from prison until the date of the trial. The bail can be posted by the arrested person, or a bail bonds person is paid to post the bond. Bail will not be set if the crime is substantial (e.g., murder) or if the arrestee is a flight risk who might not later show up for trial.

Most arrestees (or a relative or friend) pay a professional bail bonds person who operates a bail bonds business to post the **bail bond**. Bail bonds persons usually require payment of 10 percent of the bail in order to post bond. If the bail is set at $100,000, then the amount for payment of the bail bond is $10,000. The bail bonds person keeps this $10,000 payment. The bail bonds person guarantees the court that he or she will pay the court $100,000 if the arrestee does not show up for trial. If this happens, the bail bonds person will attempt the amount of the bond from the arrestee. Bail bonds persons often require collateral (e.g., title to an automobile, second mortgage on a house and such) before they issue a bail bond.

> **Examples** Susan is arrested for possession of an illegal narcotic. The court sets a bail of $100,000. Susan can pay $100,000 to the court and get out of jail until the time of her trial. At the time of her trial she will be paid back the $100,000. If Susan cannot post bail herself, she can pay a bail bonds person $10,000 to post bail.

Indictment or Information

Accused persons must be formally charged with a crime before they can be brought to trial. This usually is done by the issuance of a **grand jury indictment** or a **magistrate's (judge's) information**. Evidence of serious crimes, such as murder, is usually presented to a **grand jury**.

F.R.C.P. Rule 6 (The Grand Jury) states that a federal grand jury shall consist of between 6 and 23 citizens who are charged with evaluating the evidence presented by the government. State grand juries provide for a varying number of grand jurors. Grand jurors sit for a fixed time, such as one year.

Exhibit 8.2 Complaint filed by the United States government in *United States of America v. Bernard L. Madoff*

Mar 08 MAG 2735 COPY

Approved: _____
MARC LITT
Assistant United States Attorney

Before: HONORABLE DOUGLAS F. EATON
           United States Magistrate Judge
           Southern District of New York

--x

UNITED STATES OF AMERICA   :   **COMPLAINT**

        - v. -   :   Violation of
                                                     15 U.S.C. §§ 78-j(b),
BERNARD L. MADOFF,   :   78ff; 17 C.F.R. §
                                                     240.10b-5
        Defendant.   :

                                            :   COUNTY OF OFFENSE:
                                                     NEW YORK

--x

SOUTHERN DISTRICT OF NEW YORK, ss.:

        THEODORE CACIOPPI, being duly sworn, deposes and says
that he is a Special Agent with the Federal Bureau of
Investigation, and charges as follows:

COUNT ONE
(Securities Fraud)

        1. From at least in or about December 2008 through the
present, in the Southern District of New York and elsewhere,
BERNARD L. MADOFF, the defendant, unlawfully, wilfully and
knowingly, by the use of the means and instrumentalities of
interstate commerce and of the mails, directly and indirectly, in
connection with the purchase and sale of securities, would and
did use and employ manipulative and deceptive devices and
contrivances in violation of Title 17, Code of Federal
Regulations, Section 240.10b-5, by (a) employing devices,
schemes, and artifices to defraud; (b) making untrue statements
of material facts and omitting to state material facts necessary
in order to make the statements made, in the light of the
circumstances under which they were made, not misleading, and (c)
engaging in acts, practices, and courses of business which
operated and would operate as a fraud and deceit upon persons, to
wit, MADOFF deceived investors by operating a securities business
in which he traded and lost investor money, and then paid certain

investors purported returns on investment with the principal received from other, different investors, which resulted in losses of approximately billions of dollars.

(Title 15, United States Code, Sections 78j(b) & 78ff; Title 17, Code of Federal Regulations, Section 240.10b-5; and Title 18, United States Code, Section 2.)

The bases for my knowledge and the foregoing charges are, in part, as follows:

2.   I have been a Special Agent with the Federal Bureau of Investigation ("FBI") for approximately six and one-half years, and I have been personally involved in the investigation of this matter. The information contained in this Complaint is based upon my personal knowledge, as well as information obtained from other sources, including: a) statements made or reported by various witnesses with knowledge of relevant facts; and b) my review of publicly available information relating to BERNARD L. MADOFF, the defendant. Because this Complaint is being submitted for the limited purpose of establishing probable cause, it does not include every fact that I have learned during the course of the investigation. Where the contents of documents and the actions, statements and conversations of others are reported herein, they are reported in substance and in part, except where otherwise indicated.

3.   I have reviewed the publicly available web site of a securities broker dealer named Bernard L. Madoff Investment Securities LLC, from which I have learned the following: (a) BERNARD L. MADOFF, the defendant, is the founder of Bernard L. Madoff Investment Securities LLC; (b) Bernard L. Madoff Investment Securities LLC is a securities broker dealer with its principal office in New York, New York; (c) Bernard L. Madoff Investment Securities LLC "is a leading international market maker. The firm has been providing quality executions for broker-dealers, banks and financial institutions since its inception in 1960;" (d) "[w]ith more than $700 million in firm capital, Madoff currently ranks among the top 1% of US Securities firms; (e) BERNARD L. MADOFF, the defendant, is a former Chairman of the board of directors of the NASDAQ stock market; and (f) "Clients know that Bernard Madoff has a personal interest in maintaining an unblemished record of value, fair-dealing, and high ethical standards that has always been the firm's hallmark."

4.   I have interviewed two senior employees of Bernard L. Madoff Investment Securities LLC ("Senior Employee No. 1", and "Senior Employee No. 2", collectively the "Senior Employees").

(continued)

Exhibit 8.2 Complaint filed by the United States government in *United States of America v. Bernard L. Madoff* *(continued)*

The Senior Employees informed me, in substance, of the following:

a. The Senior Employees are employed by Bernard L. Madoff Investment Securities LLC, in a proprietary trading, and market making capacity. According to the Senior Employees, BERNARD L. MADOFF, the defendant, conducts certain investment advisory business for clients that is separate from the firm's proprietary trading and market making activities. According to the Senior Employees, MADOFF ran his investment adviser business from a separate floor in the New York offices of Bernard L. Madoff Investment Securities LLC. According to Senior Employee No. 1, MADOFF kept the financial statements for the firm under lock and key, and stated that MADOFF was "cryptic" about the firm's investment advisory business.

b. In or about the first week of December, BERNARD L. MADOFF, the defendant, told Senior Employee No. 2 that there had been requests from clients for approximately $7 billion in redemptions, that he was struggling to obtain the liquidity necessary to meet those obligations, but that he thought that he would be able to do so. According to the Senior Employees, they had previously understood that the investment advisory business had assets under management on the order of between approximately $8-15 billion. According to a Form ADV filed by MADOFF on behalf of Bernard L. Madoff Investment Securities LLC with the SEC on or about January 7, 2008, MADOFF's investment advisory business served between 11 and 25 clients and had a total of approximately $17.1 billion in assets under management.

c. On or about December 9, 2008, MADOFF informed Senior Employee No. 1 that he wanted to pay bonuses to employees of the firm in December, which was earlier than employee bonuses are usually paid. Accordingly to the Senior Employees, bonuses traditionally have been paid in February of each year. On or about December 10, 2008, the Senior Employees visited MADOFF at the offices of Bernard L. Madoff Investment Securities LLC to discuss the situation further, particularly because it MADOFF had appeared to the Senior Employees to have been under great stress in the prior weeks. At that time, MADOFF informed the Senior Employees that he had recently made profits through business operations, and that now was a good time to distribute it. When the Senior Employees challenged his explanation, MADOFF said that he did not want to talk to them at the office, and arranged a meeting at MADOFF's apartment in Manhattan. According to Senior Employee No. 2, MADOFF stated, in substance, that he "wasn't sure he would be able to hold it together" if they continued to discuss the issue at the office.

Exhibit 8.2 Complaint filed by the United States government in *United States of America v. Bernard L. Madoff* (continued)

          d.   At MADOFF's Manhattan apartment, MADOFF informed the Senior Employees, in substance, that his investment advisory business was a fraud. MADOFF stated that he was "finished," that he had "absolutely nothing," that "it's all just one big lie," and that it was "basically, a giant Ponzi scheme." The Senior Employees understood MADOFF to be saying, in substance, that he had for years been paying returns to certain investors out of the principal received from other, different, investors. MADOFF stated that the business was insolvent, and that it had been for years. MADOFF also stated that he estimated the losses from this fraud to be at least approximately $50 billion. One of the Senior Employees has a personal account at Bernard L. Madoff Investment Securities LLC in which several million had been invested under the management of MADOFF.

          e.   At MADOFF's Manhattan apartment, MADOFF further informed the Senior Employees that, in approximately one week, he planned to surrender to authorities, but before he did that, he had approximately $200-300 million left, and he planned to use that money to make payments to certain selected employees, family, and friends.

          f.   At MADOFF's Manhattan apartment, MADOFF further informed the Senior Employees that he had also recently informed a third senior employee ("Senior Employee No. 3"), of the facts that MADOFF had just told the Senior Employees.

          5.   On December 11, 2008, I spoke to BERNARD L. MADOFF, the defendant. After identifying myself, MADOFF invited me, and the FBI agent who accompanied me, into his apartment. He acknowledged knowing why we were there. After I stated, "we're here to find out if there's an innocent explanation." MADOFF stated, "There is no innocent explanation." MADOFF stated, in substance, that he had personally traded and lost money for institutional clients, and that it was all his fault. MADOFF further stated, in substance, that he "paid investors with money that wasn't there." MADOFF also said that he was "broke" and "insolvent" and that he had decided that "it could not go on," and that he expected to go to jail. MADOFF also stated that he had recently admitted what he had done to Senior Employee Nos. 1, 2, and 3.

(continued)

Exhibit 8.2 **Complaint filed by the United States government in *United States of America v. Bernard L. Madoff*** (continued)

WHEREFORE, deponent prays that BERNARD L. MADOFF, the defendant, be imprisoned, or bailed, as the case may be.

DEC 1 1 2008

THEODORE CACIOPPI
Special Agent
Federal Bureau of Investigation

Sworn to before me this
_____ day of December, 2008

HONORABLE DOUGLAS F. EATON
UNITED STATES MAGISTRATE JUDGE
SOUTHERN DISTRICT OF NEW YORK

Indictment The charge of having committed a crime (usually a felony), based on the judgment of a grand jury.

If the grand jury determines that there is sufficient evidence to hold the accused for trial, it issues an **indictment**. Note that the grand jury does not determine guilt. If an indictment is issued, the accused will be held for later trial.

Example Dominick is arrested and accused of the crime of first-degree murder. Usually, in this type of crime, Dominick will not be granted bail and remains in prison. Usually several months later, the government prosecutors will present to the Grand Jury evidence concerning Dominick's alleged crime. Dominick's lawyer will also introduce evidence claiming that Dominick did not commit the crime. After hearing this evidence, the Grand Jury issues an indictment. The indictment means that the Grand Jury found enough evidence to hold Dominick for trial for first-degree murder. The Grand Jury has made no decision whether Dominick is guilty, but has just decided there is enough evidence to hold him for a future trial for the crime of murder. In this case, Dominick will probably be denied bail and will remain in prison until the trial.

Information The charge of having committed a crime (usually a misdemeanor), based on the judgment of a judge (magistrate).

For lesser crimes (burglary, shoplifting and such), the accused will be brought before a **magistrate (judge)**. A magistrate who finds that there is enough evidence to hold the accused for trial will issue **information**. The case against the accused is dismissed if neither an indictment nor information is issued.

Excerpts of a federal grand jury indictment appear as Exhibit 8.3.

Arraignment

Arraignment A hearing during which the accused is brought before a court and is (1) informed of the charges against him or her and (2) asked to enter a plea.

If an indictment or information is issued, the accused is brought before a court for an **arraignment** proceeding during which the accused is (1) informed of the charges against him or her and (2) asked to enter a *plea*. The accused may plead ***guilty***, ***not guilty***, or *nolo contendere*.

Exhibit 8.3 **Grand jury indictment of the Court of Common Pleas, County of Summit, Ohio**

COPY

DANIEL M. HORRIGAN

2008 APR -9 PM 1:28

SUMMIT COUNTY
CLERK OF COURTS

IN THE COURT OF COMMON PLEAS
COUNTY OF SUMMIT, OHIO

INDICTMENT TYPE: BINDOVER

CASE NO. 2008-03-0968

INDICTMENT FOR: MURDER (1) 2903.02(B) SF; FELONIOUS ASSAULT (1) 2903.11(A)(1) F-2; ENDANGERING CHILDREN (1) 2919.22(B)(1) F-2; ENDANGERING CHILDREN (1) 2919.22(A) F-3

In the Common Pleas Court of Summit County, Ohio, of the term of MARCH in the year of our Lord, Two Thousand and Eight.

The Jurors of the Grand Jury of the State of Ohio, within and for the body of the County aforesaid, being duly impaneled and sworn and charged to inquire of and present all offenses whatever committed within the limits of said County, on their oaths, IN THE NAME AND BY THE AUTHORITY OF THE STATE OF OHIO,

COUNT ONE

DO FIND AND PRESENT That **CRAIG R. WILSON** on or about the 12th day of March, 2008, in the County of Summit and State of Ohio, aforesaid, did commit the crime of **MURDER** in that he did cause the death of C.W. (DOB: 1/1/2008) as a proximate result of **CRAIG R. WILSON** committing or attempting to commit Endangering Children and/or Felonious Assault, an offense of violence that is a felony of the first or second degree, in violation of Section 2903.02(B) of the Ohio Revised Code, A SPECIAL FELONY, contrary to the form of the statute in such case made and provided and against the peace and dignity of the State of Ohio.

COUNT TWO

And the Grand Jurors of the State of Ohio, within and for the body of the County of Summit aforesaid, on their oaths in the name and by the authority of the State of Ohio, DO FURTHER FIND AND PRESENT, that **CRAIG R. WILSON** on or about the 12th day of March, 2008, in the County of Summit aforesaid, did commit the crime of **FELONIOUS ASSAULT** in that he did knowingly cause serious physical harm to C.W. (DOB: 1/1/2008), in violation of Section 2903.11(A)(1) of the Ohio Revised Code, A FELONY OF THE SECOND DEGREE, contrary to the form of the statute in such case made and provided and against the peace and dignity of the State of Ohio.

(continued)

Exhibit 8.3   **Grand jury indictment of the Court of Common Pleas, County of Summit, Ohio** (continued)

COPY

Criminal Indictment
Case No. 2008-03-0968
Page Two of Three

COUNT THREE

And the Grand Jurors of the State of Ohio, within and for the body of the County of Summit aforesaid, on their oaths in the name and by the authority of the State of Ohio, DO FURTHER FIND AND PRESENT, that **CRAIG R. WILSON** on or about the 12th day of March, 2008, in the County of Summit aforesaid, did commit the crime of **ENDANGERING CHILDREN** in that he did recklessly abuse C.W., 2 months, a child under eighteen years of age (DOB: 1/1/2008), resulting in serious physical harm to said child, in violation of Section 2919.22(B)(1) of the Ohio Revised Code, A FELONY OF THE SECOND DEGREE, contrary to the form of the statute in such case made and provided and against the peace and dignity of the State of Ohio.

COUNT FOUR

And the Grand Jurors of the State of Ohio, within and for the body of the County of Summit aforesaid, on their oaths in the name and by the authority of the State of Ohio, DO FURTHER FIND AND PRESENT, that **CRAIG R. WILSON** on or about the 1st day of January, 2008 to the 12th day of March, 2008, in the County of Summit aforesaid, did commit the crime of **ENDANGERING CHILDREN** in that he did being a parent, guardian, custody, person having custody or control, or person in loco parentis of C.W., 2 months, a child under eighteen years of age (DOB: 1/1/2008), did recklessly create a substantial risk to the health or safety of the child by violating a duty of care, protection or support resulting in serious physical harm to said child, in violation of Section 2919.22(A) of the Ohio Revised Code, A FELONY OF THE THIRD DEGREE, contrary to the form of the statute in such case made and provided and against the peace and dignity of the State of Ohio.

Sherri Bevan Walsh/mk
SHERRI BEVAN WALSH, Prosecutor/pw

Prosecutor, County of Summit, by

Margaret Kawelli
Date: 4-8-08

A TRUE BILL

_____
Grand Jury foreperson/Deputy Foreperson

COPY

Case No. 2008-03-0968
Page Three of Three

ORDER

TO: DREW ALEXANDER, Sheriff
County of Summit, Ohio

CRAIG R. WILSON

THAT he has been indicted by the Grand Jury of the County of Summit and that the person named in the indictment is hereby ordered to personally appear for the purpose of arraignment at 8 a.m. on the **11th** day of **April, 2008** before the Honorable Magistrate John H. Shoemaker, Judge of the Court of Common Pleas in the County of Summit Courthouse at 209 South High Street, Akron, Ohio, and THAT FAILURE TO APPEAR WILL RESULT IN A WARRANT FOR ARREST, FORFEITURE OF BOND, IF ANY, OR ADDITIONAL CRIMINAL CHARGES FOR FAILURE TO APPEAR UNDER O.R.C. SECTION 2937.99.

I certify that this is a true copy of the original indictment on file in this office.

DANIEL HORRIGAN, Clerk
Court of Common Pleas

By_____
Deputy

A plea of *nolo contendere* means that the accused agrees to the imposition of a penalty but does not admit guilt. A *nolo contendere* plea cannot be used as evidence of liability against the accused at a subsequent civil trial. Corporate defendants often enter this plea. The government has the option of accepting a *nolo contendere* plea or requiring the defendant to plead guilty or not guilty. Depending on the nature of the crime, the accused may be released upon posting bail.

Example The U.S. government sues a company for criminally violating federal pollution control laws. The company pleads *nolo contendere* and the government accepts the plea. The government and the company agree that the company must pay $100,000 in criminal fines but the company does not admit guilt.

Plea Bargaining

> **Plea bargain agreement** An agreement in which the accused admits to a lesser crime than charged. In return, the government agrees to impose a lesser sentence than might have been obtained had the case gone to trial.

Sometimes the accused and the government enter into a **plea bargain agreement**. The government engages in plea bargaining to save costs, avoid the risks of a trial, and prevent further overcrowding of the prisons. This arrangement allows the accused to admit to a lesser crime than charged. In return, the government agrees to impose a lesser penalty or sentence than might have been obtained had the case gone to trial. In the federal system, more than 90 percent plead guilty rather than go to trial.

Example Harold is arrested for the crime of felony burglary, which carries a typical penalty of three years in jail if he is found guilty. The government and Harold reach a plea bargain where he will plead guilty to misdemeanor burglary and agrees to a sentence of six months in jail and three years' probation.

Exhibit 8.4 compares the major features of criminal law and civil law.

Criminal Trial

> **Trier of fact** The jury is the trier of fact.

The **criminal trial** and the civil action trial have many similarities. The functions of the judge and jury are the same. The jury acts as the **trier of fact.** In cases in which the defendant exercises the right to proceed without a jury, also known as a **bench trial**, or **waiver trial**, the judge acts as the trier of fact. The judge also acts as the arbiter of procedural rules covering the conduct of the trial, and the judge ultimately is the one who applies the law to findings of fact, and guilt or innocence of the charges and who determines the sentence, fine, or other permitted forfeiture in cases of guilt. In some cases, such as murder trials, the jury also decides the sentence.

Exhibit 8.4 Civil and criminal law compared

Issue	Civil Law	Criminal Law
Party who brings the action	The plaintiff	The government
Trial by jury	Yes, except actions for equity	Yes
Burden of proof	Preponderance of the evidence	Beyond a reasonable doubt
Jury vote	Judgment for plaintiff requires specific jury vote (e.g., 9 of 12 jurors)	Conviction requires unanimous jury vote
Sanctions and penalties	Monetary damages and equitable remedies (e.g., injunction, specific performance)	Imprisonment, capital punishment, fine, probation

The order and presentation of evidence also are similar. The prosecution goes first and puts on its case, followed by the defense's presentation of its evidence. Motions for dismissal at the close of the prosecution's case also are similar to those in the civil action.

A significant difference is the concern in many cases to protect the record (the trial transcript). The defense counsel tends to be concerned especially with making appropriate objections on the record that can be used as the basis for an appeal. Prosecutors, too, are concerned that they not say anything on the record that the defendant can use as a basis for appeal in the event of a conviction.

Web Exploration

Go to http://www.thelaborers
.net/indictments/bellomo/
indictment_criminal_genovese_
family-2006-2-23.htm and read
a grand jury indictment of the
Genovese Organized Crime
Family.

Pretrial Discovery

A limited amount of **pretrial discovery** is permitted, with substantial restrictions to protect the identity of government informants and to prevent intimidation of witnesses. Defense attorneys often file motions to suppress evidence, which ask the court to exclude evidence from trial that the defendant believes the government obtained in violation of the defendant's constitutional rights, statute, or procedural rule. The government is under an obligation to provide **exculpatory evidence** to the defense attorney.

Under the Federal Rules of Criminal Procedure Rule 16, upon the defendant's request, the government must disclose and make available for inspection, copying, or photographing any relevant written or recorded statements made by defendant within the possession, custody, or control of the government, the existence of which is known, or where the exercise of due diligence may become known to the attorney for the government.

Determination of Guilt

At a criminal trial, unlike a civil-action trial, all jurors must agree *unanimously* before the accused is found guilty of the crime charged. If even one juror disagrees (i.e., has reasonable doubt) about the guilt of the accused, the accused is not guilty of the crime charged. If all of the jurors agree that the accused did not commit the crime, the accused is **innocent** of the crime charged.

After trial, the following rules apply:

- If the defendant is found guilty, he or she may appeal.
- If the defendant is found innocent, the government cannot appeal.
- If the jury cannot come to a unanimous decision about the defendant's guilt, the jury is considered a **hung jury**. The government may choose to retry the case before a new judge and jury.

Hung jury A jury that does not come to a unanimous decision about the defendant's guilt. The government may choose to retry the case.

Constitutional Safeguards

When our forefathers drafted the U.S. Constitution, they included provisions that protect persons from unreasonable government intrusion and provide safeguards for those accused of crimes. Although these safeguards originally applied only to federal cases, the Fourteenth Amendment's Due Process Clause made them applicable to state criminal law cases as well. The most important constitutional safeguards and privileges are discussed in the following paragraphs.

Fourth Amendment Protection Against Unreasonable Searches and Seizures

The **Fourth Amendment** to the U.S. Constitution protects persons and corporations from overzealous investigative activities by the government. It protects the rights of the people from **unreasonable search and seizure** by the government and permits people to be secure in their persons, houses, papers, and effects.

Unreasonable search and seizure Any search and seizure by the government that violates the Fourth Amendment.

Search Warrants

"Reasonable" search and seizure by the government is lawful. **Search warrants** based on probable cause are necessary in most cases. These warrants specifically state the place and scope of the authorized search. General searches beyond the specified area are forbidden.

> **Example** If the police receive a tip from a reasonable source that someone is engaged in criminal activity the police can present this information to a judge who will issue a search warrant if he or she finds probable cause. A copy of a search warrant appears as Exhibit 8.5.

Warrantless Searches

Warrantless searches generally are permitted only (1) incident to arrest, (2) where evidence is in "plain view," or (3) where evidence likely will be destroyed. Warrantless searches also are judged by the probable-cause standard.

> **Example** The police are notified that a person of a certain description has committed a crime in a specific location. The police arrive on the scene and nearby they find a suspect who meets the description. The police may conduct a warrantless search of the individual in order to protect the police from danger.

Search of Business Premises

Generally, the government does not have the right to search business premises without a search warrant on probable cause or pursuant to a warrantless search based on probable cause. However, businesses in certain hazardous and regulated industries are subject to warrantless searches if proper statutory procedures are met.

> **Examples** Sellers of firearms and liquor, coal mines, vehicle dismantling and automobile junkyards, and the like are subject to warrantless searches.

A business also may give consent to search the premises, including employee desks and computers, because of the lack of privacy in those items.

Exclusionary Rule

Exclusionary rule A rule that says evidence obtained from an unreasonable search and seizure can generally be prohibited from introduction at a trial or administrative proceeding against the person searched.

Evidence obtained from an unreasonable search and seizure is considered tainted evidence ("fruit of a poisonous tree"). Under the **exclusionary rule**, such evidence can be prohibited from introduction at a trial or administrative proceeding against the person searched. This evidence, however, is freely admissible against other persons. The U.S. Supreme Court created a *good-faith exception* to the exclusionary rule. This exception allows evidence otherwise obtained illegally to be introduced as evidence against the accused if the police officers who conducted the unreasonable search reasonably believed they were acting pursuant to a lawful search warrant.

Fifth Amendment Privilege Against Self-Incrimination

Self-incrimination The Fifth Amendment states that no person shall be compelled in any criminal case to be a witness against him- or herself.

The **Fifth Amendment** to the U.S. Constitution provides that no person "shall be compelled in any criminal case to be a witness against himself." Thus, a person cannot be compelled to give testimony against himself or herself. A person who asserts this right is described as having "taken the Fifth." This protection applies to federal cases and is extended to state and local criminal cases through the Due Process Clause of the Fourteenth Amendment.

The privilege against **self-incrimination** applies only to natural persons who are accused of crimes. Therefore, artificial persons (such as corporations and partnerships)

Exhibit 8.5 **Search warrant of the federal U.S. district court**

AO 93 (Rev. 01/09) Search and Seizure Warrant

UNITED STATES DISTRICT COURT
for the

In the Matter of the Search of	)
(Briefly describe the property to be searched	)
or identify the person by name and address)	) Case No.
	)
	)
	)

SEARCH AND SEIZURE WARRANT

To: Any authorized law enforcement officer

An application by a federal law enforcement officer or an attorney for the government requests the search of the following person or property located in the _____ District of _____
(identify the person or describe the property to be searched and give its location):

The person or property to be searched, described above, is believed to conceal *(identify the person or describe the property to be seized)*:

I find that the affidavit(s), or any recorded testimony, establish probable cause to search and seize the person or property.

YOU ARE COMMANDED to execute this warrant on or before _____
(not to exceed 10 days)

❏ in the daytime 6:00 a.m. to 10 p.m.   ❏ at any time in the day or night as I find reasonable cause has been
established.

Unless delayed notice is authorized below, you must give a copy of the warrant and a receipt for the property taken to the person from whom, or from whose premises, the property was taken, or leave the copy and receipt at the place where the property was taken.

The officer executing this warrant, or an officer present during the execution of the warrant, must prepare an inventory as required by law and promptly return this warrant and inventory to United States Magistrate Judge

_____ .
(name)

❏ I find that immediate notification may have an adverse result listed in 18 U.S.C. § 2705 (except for delay of trial), and authorize the officer executing this warrant to delay notice to the person who, or whose property, will be searched or seized *(check the appropriate box)* ❏ for _____ days *(not to exceed 30)*.
                                                    ❏ until, the facts justifying, the later specific date of _____ .

Date and time issued: _____   _____

                                                          Judge's signature

City and state: _____   _____

                                                          Printed name and title

(continued)

Exhibit 8.5 Search warrant of the federal U.S. district court *(continued)*

AO 93 (Rev. 01/09) Search and Seizure Warrant (Page 2)

Return		
Case No.:	Date and time warrant executed:	Copy of warrant and inventory left with:
Inventory made in the presence of :		
Inventory of the property taken and name of any person(s) seized:		

Certification

     I declare under penalty of perjury that this inventory is correct and was returned along with the original warrant to the designated judge.

Date: _____

_____
Executing officer's signature

_____
Printed name and title

cannot raise this protection against incriminating testimony. Thus, business records of corporations and partnerships are not protected from disclosure, even if they incriminate individuals who work for the business. But certain "private papers" of businesspersons (such as personal diaries) are protected from disclosure.

It is improper for a jury to infer guilt from the defendant's exercise of his or her constitutional right to remain silent.

Nontestimonial evidence may be required without violating the Fifth Amendment.

Examples Fingerprints, body fluids, and the like.

Miranda Rights

Most people have not read and memorized the provisions of the U.S. Constitution. The U.S. Supreme Court recognized this fact when it decided the landmark case *Miranda v. Arizona* in 1966 [384 U.S. 436, 86 S.Ct. 1602, 16 L.Ed.2d 694, 1966 U.S. Lexis 2817]. In that case, the Supreme Court held that the Fifth Amendment privilege against self-incrimination is not useful unless a criminal suspect has knowledge of this right. Therefore, the Supreme Court required that the following warning—colloquially called the *Miranda* **rights**—be read to a criminal suspect before he or she is interrogated by the police or other government officials:

- You have the right to remain silent.
- Anything you say can and will be used against you.
- You have the right to consult a lawyer and to have a lawyer present with you during interrogation.
- If you cannot afford a lawyer, a lawyer will be appointed free of charge to represent you.

Many police departments read a more detailed version of the *Miranda* rights, which is designed to cover all issues that a detainee might encounter while in police custody. A detainee may be asked to sign a statement acknowledging that the *Miranda* rights have been read to him or her. A copy of the *Miranda* rights appears as Exhibit 8.6.

Miranda **rights** Rights that a suspect must be informed of before being interrogated, so that the suspect will not unwittingly give up his or her Fifth Amendment right.

Exhibit 8.6 *Miranda* rights form

MIRANDA RIGHTS

- You have the right to remain silent and refuse to answer questions. Do you understand?

- Anything you do say may be used against you in a court of law. Do you understand?

- You have the right to consult an attorney before speaking to the police and to have an attorney present during questioning now or in the future. Do you understand?

- If you cannot afford an attorney, one will be appointed for you before any questioning if you wish. Do you understand?

- If you decide to answer questions now without an attorney present you will still have the right to stop answering at any time until you talk to an attorney. Do you understand?

- Knowing and understanding your rights as I have explained them to you, are you willing to answer my questions without an attorney present?

Excluded Admissions

Any statements or confessions obtained from a suspect prior to being read his or her *Miranda* rights can be excluded from evidence at trial. In 2000, the U.S. Supreme Court upheld *Miranda* in *Dickerson v. United States* [530 U.S. 428, 120 S.Ct. 2326, 147 L.Ed.2d 405, 2000 U.S. Lexis 4305]. The Supreme Court stated, "We do not think there is justification for overruling *Miranda*. *Miranda* has become embedded in routine police practice to the point where the warnings have become part of our national culture."

Example Margaret is arrested by the police for suspicion of using and distributing illegal narcotics. The police start asking her questions about these issues before reading Margaret her *Miranda* rights. During this questioning Margaret admits to the offenses. Margaret's statements are inadmissible at court because she had not been read her *Miranda* rights.

The Ethical Perspective discusses a paralegal's ethical duty to conduct careful research in a criminal case.

ETHICAL PERSPECTIVE

Duty to Conduct Careful Research in a Criminal Case

Ms. Smith is a newly hired paralegal who works for attorney Ms. Gutierrez. Ms. Gutierrez represents Mr. Granville, a client who has been charged by the state with dealing in illegal narcotics. Ms. Gutierrez requests that Ms. Smith sit in on her discussions with Mr. Granville when Ms. Gutierrez asks Mr. Granville questions concerning the case.

At the meeting, Mr. Granville discloses that yes he had been dealing and selling illegal narcotics. He explains that the police arrested him as he left his home one evening. The police searched Mr. Granville's person, and found illegal narcotics on his body. The police then questioned Mr. Granville and he admitted that the drugs were his and that he was a distributor of illegal narcotics. Pursuant to this admission, the police also searched Mr. Granville's automobile, where they found illegal narcotics. In addition, the police obtained a search warrant and searched Mr. Granville's home where they also discovered more illegal narcotics.

If all of this evidence is introduced against Mr. Granville at trial, he is most likely to be convicted of the crime of selling narcotics. Ms. Gutierrez gives Ms. Smith the assignment to conduct electronic legal research and find recent case law that affects the possible exclusion of evidence at Mr. Granville's criminal trial. Ms. Gutierrez also informs Ms. Smith that she will be using this research when she conducts settlement talks with the government regarding Mr. Granville's case.

Ms. Smith, who is not that sympathetic to Mr. Granville's situation anyhow, conducts minimal research and reports back to Ms. Gutierrez that she has found no relevant case law that would allow for the suppression of the evidence against Mr. Granville. However, if Ms. Smith had conducted a more thorough research she would have discovered an important case where the court had made a decision that would have been favorable to suppressing much of the evidence against Mr. Granville because of failure of the police to read him the *Miranda* rights before obtaining his confession, and that the further evidence discovered against Mr. Granville would also be inadmissible because of the excludable admission that led to the evidence being discovered.

Here, Ms. Smith has been derelict and negligent in the conduct of her duties as a paralegal. She failed to carry out an important assignment and therefore has jeopardized a case against a client of the lawyer for whom she works. Because of Ms. Smith's negligence, her supervising attorney Ms. Gutierrez may not have all of the relevant information to properly prepare for her settlement conference with the government or to prepare the trial defense for her client.

Immunity from Prosecution

On occasion, the government wants to obtain information from a suspect who has asserted his or her Fifth Amendment privilege against self-incrimination. The government can try to achieve this by offering the suspect **immunity from prosecution**, in which the government agrees not to use any evidence given by a person who has been granted immunity against that person. Once immunity is granted, the suspect loses the right to assert his or her Fifth Amendment privilege.

Grants of immunity often are given when the government wants the suspect to give information that will lead to the prosecution of other, more important criminal suspects. Partial grants of immunity also are available. For example, a suspect may be granted immunity from prosecution for a serious crime but not a lesser crime, in exchange for information. Some persons who are granted immunity are placed in witness protection programs in which they are given a new identity, relocated, and found a job.

Attorney–Client Privilege

To obtain a proper defense, the accused person must be able to tell his or her attorney facts about the case without fear that the attorney will be called as a witness against the accused. The **attorney–client privilege** is protected by the Fifth Amendment. Either the client or the attorney can raise this privilege. For the privilege to apply, the information must be told to the attorney in his or her capacity as an attorney, and not as a friend or neighbor or other such relationship.

> **Attorney–client privilege** A rule that says a client can tell his or her lawyer anything about the case without fear that the attorney will be called as a witness against the client.

> **Example** Cedric is accused of murder. He employs Hillary, a renowned criminal attorney, to represent him. During the course of their discussions Cedric confesses to the murder. Hillary cannot be a witness against Cedric at his criminal trial. Cedric is permitted to tell his lawyer the truth so that the lawyer can prepare the best defense she can for him.

Other Privileges

The following privileges have also been recognized under the Fifth Amendment where the accused may keep the following individuals from being a witness against him or her. The reasons are stated in parentheses.

- **Psychiatrist/psychologist–patient privilege** (so that the accused may tell the truth in order to seek help for his or her condition)
- **Priest/rabbi/minister/imam–penitent privilege** (so that the accused may tell the truth in order to repent, to obtain help, and seek forgiveness for his or her deed)
- **Spouse–spouse privilege** (so that the family will remain together)
- **Parent–child privilege** (so that the family will remain together)

A spouse or child who is injured by a spouse or parent (e.g., domestic abuse) may testify against the accused. In addition, if the accused discloses that he or she is planning to commit a crime in the future (e.g., murder), then the accused's lawyer, psychiatrist, or psychologist, and priest, rabbi, minister, or imam is required to report this to the police or other relevant authorities.

The U.S. Supreme Court has held that there is no accountant–client privilege under federal law. Thus, an accountant could be called as a witness in cases involving federal securities laws, federal mail or wire fraud, or other federal crimes. Nevertheless, approximately 20 states have enacted special statutes that create an **accountant–client privilege**. An accountant cannot be called as a witness against a client in a court action in a state where these statutes are in effect. Federal courts do not recognize these laws, however.

Fifth Amendment Protection Against Double Jeopardy

Double Jeopardy Clause A clause of the Fifth Amendment that protects persons from being tried twice for the same crime.

The **Double Jeopardy Clause** of the Fifth Amendment protects persons from being tried twice for the same crime. For example, if the state tries a suspect for the crime of murder and the suspect is found innocent, the state cannot bring another trial against the accused for the same crime. But if the same criminal act involves several different crimes, the accused may be tried for each of the crimes without violating the Double Jeopardy Clause. Suppose the accused kills two people during a robbery. The accused may be tried for two murders and for the robbery.

If the same act violates the laws of two or more jurisdictions, each jurisdiction may try the accused. For instance, if an accused person kidnaps a person in one state and brings the victim across a state border into another state, the act violates the laws of two states and the federal government. Thus, three jurisdictions can prosecute the accused without violating the Double Jeopardy Clause.

If an accused is tried once and the jury reaches a hung jury—that is, the verdict is not unanimous for either guilty or not guilty—then the government can retry the case against the accused without violating the Double Jeopardy Clause.

> **Example** Suppose the government tries a defendant for the crime of murder and the jury reaches a 10 to 2 verdict, that is, 10 jurors vote for guilty and two jurors vote for not guilty. This is a hung jury. Since no decision has been reached, the government may, if it wants, retry the case against the accused. This does not violate the Double Jeopardy Clause.

Sixth Amendment Right to a Public Trial

The **Sixth Amendment** guarantees that criminal defendants have these rights:

1. The right to be tried by an impartial jury of the state or district in which the alleged crime was committed.
2. The right to confront (cross-examine) the witnesses against the accused.
3. The right to have the assistance of a lawyer.
4. The right to have a speedy trial.

The federal **Speedy Trial Act** requires that a criminal defendant be brought to trial within 70 days after indictment [18 U.S.C. Section 3161(c)(1)]. States have similar acts that require speedy trials for criminal defendants. The court may grant continuances to serve the "ends of justice."

Eighth Amendment Protection Against Cruel and Unusual Punishment

The **Eighth Amendment** protects criminal defendants from **cruel and unusual punishment**.

> **Example** It prohibits the torture of criminals. This clause, however, does not prohibit capital punishment, but does limit the form of capital punishment that is allowed. The U.S. Supreme Court has held that injection by lethal dosage of drugs generally is permitted as a means of capital punishment.

Administrative Law and Agencies

Administrative law Substantive and procedural law that governs the operation of administrative agencies.

Federal and state governments enact laws that regulate business. The legislative and executive branches of government have created numerous administrative agencies to assist in implementing and enforcing these laws. The operation of these administrative agencies is governed by a body of **administrative law**. Because of their importance, administrative agencies are informally referred to as the "fourth branch of government."

The following feature discusses the career opportunities for paralegal professionals in administrative law.

CAREER OPPORTUNITIES FOR PARALEGALS IN ADMINISTRATIVE LAW

Lawyers increasingly employ paralegals in areas of law that involve practice before administrative agencies. Administrative law has become extremely important for businesses and individuals alike. Administrative agencies govern many aspects of general business operations, specific industries, and our personal lives as well.

The number of administrative agencies in this country is staggering. The federal government alone has dozens of administrative agencies. These range from agencies whose powers apply to the country and economy in general, to agencies that regulate specific industries. Some of the major federal administrative agencies are:

- Environmental Protection Agency (EPA): regulates air, water, hazardous waste, and other types of pollution.
- Equal Employment Opportunity Commission (EEOC): enforces many antidiscrimination laws that affect businesses, employees, disabled persons, and others.
- Federal Trade Commission (FTC): enforces many consumer protection laws.
- Food and Drug Administration (FDA): regulates the safety of foods, drugs, cosmetics, and medicinal devices.
- Federal Communications Commission (FCC): regulates radio, television, cable, and other broadcast media.
- National Labor Relations Board (NLRB): regulates labor union formation, elections, bargaining with employers, and other labor issues.
- Securities Exchange Commission (SEC): regulates the issuance, sale, and purchase of securities, including stocks and bonds.
- Department of Homeland Security (DHS): responsible for coordinating certain federal agencies in protecting the country against terrorism and other threats.

In addition to federal administrative agencies, there are thousands of state and local administrative agencies. These include state administrative agencies that regulate corporations, agencies that license and regulate financial institutions, state environmental protection agencies, and other state administrative agencies. At the local level, cities and municipalities have administrative agencies that regulate construction, set building codes, establish zoning regulations, issue water permits, and so forth.

Paralegals often work for lawyers who specialize in making appearances before specific federal, state, and local administrative agencies. For example, lawyers must prepare applications for submission to the Federal Communications Commission (FCC) to obtain a license for a client to operate a radio, television, or cable company. Lawyers must prepare applications for submission to the Federal Food and Drug Administration (FDA) to obtain approval for a client to market a new drug. Lawyers must prepare applications to be submitted to a state banking commission to obtain a license for a client to operate a new commercial bank.

The federal government has enacted the Administrative Procedure Act (APA), which establishes rules for legal practice before federal administrative agencies. The state has similar administrative procedures acts at the state level. In addition, each administrative agency has its own rules and regulations for submitting applications and appearing at hearings before the administrative agency.

Paralegals who work for lawyers specializing in certain administrative law practices must become familiar with that agency's rules and procedures. Paralegals often are called upon to assist in drafting documents that will be submitted to administrative agencies and preparing cases that will be heard and decided by these agencies. Thus, paralegals often become experts in areas of administrative law and, therefore, can be indispensable to lawyers who practice before administrative agencies.

Administrative Agencies

Administrative agencies are created by federal, state, and local governments. They range from large, complex federal agencies, such as the federal Department of Health and Human Services, to city zoning boards. At the federal government level, the legislative branch (Congress) and the executive branch (the president) have created more than 100 administrative agencies. Thousands of other administrative agencies have been created by state and local governments.

When Congress enacts a statute, it often creates an administrative agency to administer and enforce the statute (see Exhibit 8.7). When Congress enacts some statutes, it authorizes an existing administrative agency to administer and enforce the new statute.

Example When Congress enacted the Securities Act of 1933 and the Securities Exchange Act of 1934, it created the Securities and Exchange Commission (SEC), a federal administrative agency, to administer and enforce those statutes.

Exhibit 8.7 **Administrative agency**

Legislature
(Enacts a
statute)

Legislature enacts a
statute and creates an
administrative agency to
administer and enforce
the statute.

ADMINISTRATIVE
AGENCY
(Administers
the statute)

Administrative agencies are established with the overall goal of creating a body of professionals who are experts in a specific field. These experts have delegated authority to regulate an individual industry or a specific area of commerce.

Federal Administrative Agencies

Federal administrative agencies
Agencies established by legislative and executive branches of federal and state governments.

Federal administrative agencies can be created by either the *legislative* or the *executive* branch of the federal government.

Congress has established many federal administrative agencies. These agencies have broad regulatory powers over key areas of the national economy.

Examples The Securities and Exchange Commission (SEC), which regulates the issuance of and trading in securities, and the Commodity Futures Trading Commission (CFTC), which regulates trading in commodities futures contracts.

Other federal administrative agencies are created by the president of the United States to operate the federal government.

Examples The U.S. Department of Justice and the Commerce Department.

State Administrative Agencies

State administrative agencies
Administrative agencies that states create to enforce and interpret state law.

All states have created administrative agencies to enforce and interpret state law. **State administrative agencies** have a profound effect on business. State administrative agencies are empowered to enforce state statutes. They have the power to adopt rules and regulations to interpret the statutes they are empowered to administer.

Example Most states have a Corporations Department to enforce state corporation law and regulate the issuance of securities, a Banking Department to license and regulate the operation of banks, Fish and Game Departments to regulate fishing and hunting within the state's boundaries, Worker's Compensation Boards to decide workers' compensation claims for injuries that occur on the job, Environment Protection Departments to regulate the land, waterways and other environmental issues, and such.

Local governments and municipalities create administrative agencies to administer local law.

Examples Counties have numerous administrative boards to regulate county activities. Cities and towns have school boards, zoning commissions, and other administrative bodies to regulate city and town matters.

Government Regulation

Many administrative agencies, and the laws they enforce, regulate businesses and industries collectively. This is called **general government regulation**. That is, most of the industries and businesses in the United States are subject to these laws.

> **General government regulation** Government regulation that applies to many industries collectively.

Example The federal National Labor Relations Board (NLRB) is empowered to regulate the formation and operation of labor unions in most industries and businesses in the United States.

Some administrative agencies, and the laws they enforce, are created to regulate specific industries. That is, an industry is subject to administrative laws that are specifically adopted to regulate that industry. This is called **specific government regulation** of business. Administrative agencies, which are industry specific, are created to administer these specific laws.

> **Specific government regulation** Government regulation that applies to individual industries.

Example The Federal Communications Commission (FCC) issues licenses and regulates the operation of television and radio stations.

Administrative Procedure

Administrative law is a combination of *substantive* and *procedural law*. **Substantive law** is the law that has been created that the administrative agency enforces—the federal statute enacted by Congress or the state statute enacted by a state legislature. **Procedural law** establishes the procedures that must be followed by an administrative agency while enforcing substantive administrative laws.

Example The federal Environmental Protection Agency (EPA) has been created by Congress to enforce federal environmental laws that protect the environment. This is an example of substantive law—the laws to protect the environment. In enforcing these laws, the EPA must follow certain established procedural rules (e.g., notice, hearing). These are examples of procedural law.

Administrative Procedure Act (APA)

In 1946, Congress enacted the **Administrative Procedure Act (APA)** [5 U.S.C. Sections 551–706]. This act is very important because it establishes procedures that federal administrative agencies must follow in conducting their affairs. The APA establishes notice requirements of actions the federal agency plans on taking. It requires hearings to be held in most cases and certain procedural safeguards and protocol to be followed at these proceedings.

> **Administrative Procedure Act (APA)** An act that establishes certain administrative procedures that federal administrative agencies must follow in conducting their affairs.

The APA establishes how rules and regulations can be adopted by federal administrative agencies. This includes notice of proposed rule making, granting a time period for receiving comments from the public regarding proposed rule making, and holding hearings to take evidence. The APA provides a procedure for receiving evidence and hearing requests for the granting of federal licenses (e.g., to operate a national bank). The APA also establishes notice and hearing requirements and rules for conducting agency adjudicative actions, such as actions to take away certain parties' licenses (e.g., a securities broker's licenses).

Most states have enacted administrative procedural acts that govern state administrative procedures.

Administrative Law Judge

Administrative law judges (ALJs) preside over administrative proceedings. They decide questions of law and fact concerning a case. There is no jury. An ALJ is an employee of the administrative agency. Both the administrative agency and the respondent may be represented by counsel. Witnesses may be examined and cross-examined, evidence may be introduced, objections may be made, and such.

An ALJ's decision is issued in the form of an **order**. The order must state the reasons for the ALJ's decision. The order becomes final if it is not appealed. An appeal consists of a review by the agency. Further appeal can be made to the appropriate federal court (in federal agency actions) or state court (in state agency actions).

Exhibit 8.8 is an application form for an administrative hearing regarding a Social Security matter.

Powers of Administrative Agencies

When an administrative agency is created, it is delegated certain powers. The agency has only the legislative, judicial, and executive powers that are delegated to it. This is called the **delegation doctrine**. The courts have upheld this combined power of administrative agencies as being constitutional. If an administrative agency acts outside the scope of its delegated powers, it is an unconstitutional act.

The powers of administrative agencies are discussed in the following paragraphs.

Rule Making

Many federal statutes expressly authorize an administrative agency to issue **substantive rules**. A substantive regulation is much like a statute: It has the force of law and must be adhered to by covered persons and businesses. Violators may be held civilly or criminally liable, depending on the rule. The agency must give public notice of a proposed rule and consider public comments before adopting a substantive rule.

Example The Securities and Exchange Commission (SEC) is authorized to prohibit fraud in the purchase and sale of securities. The SEC therefore has the power to adopt rules that define what fraudulent conduct is prohibited by the federal securities laws.

Administrative agencies can issue an **interpretive rule** that interprets existing statutory language. Such rules do not establish new laws. Administrative agencies may also issue a **statement of policy** that announces a proposed course of action that an agency intends to follow in the future. Interpretive rules and statements of policy do not have the force of law and public notice and participation are not required.

Licensing Power

Statutes often require the issuance of a government **license** before a person can enter certain types of industries (e.g., the operation of banks, television and radio stations, and commercial airlines) or professions (e.g., doctors, lawyers, dentists, certified public accountants, and contractors). The administrative agency that regulates the specific area involved is granted the power to determine whether to grant a license to an applicant.

Applicants must usually submit detailed applications to the appropriate administrative agency. In addition, the agency usually accepts written comments from interested parties and holds hearings on the matter. Courts generally defer to the expertise of administrative agencies in licensing matters.

Example A group of persons wants to start a new national bank. To start a new national bank, the applicants must obtain approval from the Office of the

Exhibit 8.8 **Application for social security administrative hearing**

SOCIAL SECURITY ADMINISTRATION
OFFICE OF HEARINGS AND APPEALS

Form Approved
OMB No. 0960-0269

REQUEST FOR HEARING BY ADMINISTRATIVE LAW JUDGE
[Take or mail original and all copies to your local Social Security Office]

PRIVACY ACT NOTICE
ON REVERSE SIDE OF FORM.

1. CLAIMANT	2. WAGE EARNER, IF DIFFERENT	3. SOC. SEC. CLAIM NUMBER	4. SPOUSE's CLAIM NUMBER

5. I REQUEST A HEARING BEFORE AN ADMINISTRATIVE LAW JUDGE. I disagree with the determination made on my claim because:

An Administrative Law Judge of the Office of Hearings and Appeals will be appointed to conduct the hearing or other proceedings in your case. You will receive notice of the time and place of a hearing at least 20 days before the date set for a hearing.

6. If you have additional evidence to submit check the following block and complete the statement: ☐

I have additional evidence to submit from (name and address of source): _____

(Please submit it to the Social Security Office within 10 days. Attach an additional sheet if you need more space.)

7. Check one of the blocks:

☐ I wish to appear at a hearing.

☐ I do not wish to appear and I request that a decision be made based on the evidence in my case.
(Complete Waiver Form HA-4608)

You have a right to be represented at the hearing. If you are not represented but would like to be, your Social Security Office will give you a list of legal referral and service organizations. (If you are represented and have not done so previously, complete and submit form SSA-1696 (Appointment of Representative).)

[You should complete No. 8 and your representative (if any) should complete No. 9. If you are represented and your representative is not available to complete this form, you should also print his or her name, address, etc. in No. 9.]

8. (CLAIMANT'S SIGNATURE)	9. (REPRESENTATIVE'S SIGNATURE/NAME)
ADDRESS	(ADDRESS) ☐ ATTORNEY; ☐ NON ATTORNEY;
CITY STATE ZIP CODE	CITY STATE ZIP CODE
DATE AREA CODE AND TELEPHONE NUMBER	DATE AREA CODE AND TELEPHONE NUMBER

TO BE COMPLETED BY SOCIAL SECURITY ADMINISTRATION-ACKNOWLEDGMENT OF REQUEST FOR HEARING

10.
Request for Hearing RECEIVED for the Social Security Administration on _____ by: _____

(TITLE) _____ ADDRESS _____

11. Was the request for hearing received within 65 days of the reconsidered determination?
☐ YES ☐ NO

If no is checked, attach claimant's explanation for delay; and attach copy of appointment notice, letter, or other pertinent material or information in the Social Security Office.

12. Claimant not represented -
☐ list of legal referral and service organizations provided

13. Interpreter needed -
☐ enter language (including sign language): _____

14.
Check one: ☐ Initial Entitlement Case
☐ Disability Cessation Case
☐ Other Postentitlement Case

15.
Check claim type(s):

☐ RSI only --(RSI)
☐ Title II Disability-worker or child----------------(DIWC)
☐ Title II Disability-widow(er) only-----------------(DIWW)
☐ SSI Aged only--(SSIA)
☐ SSI Blind only--(SSIB)
☐ SSI Disability only ----------------------------------(SSID)
☐ SSI Aged/Title II ------------------------------------(SSAC)
☐ SSI Blind/Title II ------------------------------------(SSBC)
☐ SSI Disability/Title II -------------------------------(SSDC)
☐ HI Entitlement --------------------------------------(HIE)
☐ Other-Specify: ( )

16.
HO COPY SENT TO: _____ HO on _____
☐ CF Attached: ☐ Title II; ☐ Title XVI; or
☐ Title II CF held in FO to establish CAPS ORBIT; or
☐ CF requested ☐ Title II; ☐ Title XVI
(Copy of teletype or phone report attached)

17.
CF COPY SENT TO: _____ HO on _____
☐ CF Attached: ☐ Title II; ☐ Title XVI
☐ Other Attached: _____

FORM HA-501-U5 (5-1996) EF (7-2000)
Issue old stock

CLAIMS FOLDER

Comptroller of Currency (OCC), a federal administrative agency that charters, supervises, and regulates national banks. The group will hire lawyers, economists, accountants, and other professionals needed to prepare the appropriate application. After considering the application, the OCC will either approve or reject the application.

Paralegals *in* Practice

PARALEGAL PROFILE

Melvin E. Irvin

Since 1996, Melvin E. Irvin has worked as a non-attorney Social Security Disability Appeals Representative in the San Jose, California area. He legally represents clients before the Social Security Administration (SSA) in appeals for Social Security disability benefits. In addition to being a Marine Corps veteran, Mel is a graduate from Santa Clara University Law School Institute for Paralegal Studies. He also earned the Certified Paralegal (C.P.) designation from the National Association of Legal Assistants.

As President of my own corporation, Melvin E. Irvin Disability Representative, Inc., I represent about 55–60 clients at any given time. The most important skills needed in my position are above-average communication skills and a good working knowledge of Social Security Law. There are no specific educational requirements to become a non-attorney

Disability Representative except that you cannot be a disbarred attorney, or disallowed by another government administration from practicing. Naturally, a college degree and a paralegal certificate are very helpful.

Over the past 20 years, successful representation has become more difficult as the SSA has significantly reduced its claim allowance rates. SSA representation fees are paid only on a contingency basis, whether you are an attorney or non-attorney. Since the SSA is backlogged on disability cases, currently more than 700,000 nationally, it may take two or more years before a new representative sees the first paycheck. This is due to the length of time it takes for a case to be resolved. Even so, my work is very rewarding because it allows me to help people who really need assistance.

I find that many people in the U.S. today still believe that paralegals can perform work directly for the public. According to Section 6450 of the California Business and Professions Code, those who call themselves paralegals must be attorney supervised, with few exceptions. One exception is legally representing the public in administrative law settings such as the SSA. As the current President of the California Alliance of Paralegal Associations, I help educate others about the paralegal profession. Part of my role is to encourage local paralegal associations to appoint Public Information Officers who can respond to questions from the legal community, the public, and the media.

Judicial Authority

Many administrative agencies have the judicial authority to adjudicate cases through an administrative proceeding. Such a proceeding is initiated when an agency serves a complaint on a party the agency believes has violated a statute or an administrative rule or order.

> **Example** The Occupational Safety and Health Administration (OSHA) is a federal administrative agency empowered to enforce worker safety rules. OSHA can bring an administrative proceeding against an employer for violating a federal worker safety rule. OSHA can make a decision that the employer violated the rule and order the violator to pay a monetary fine.

Procedural due process requires the respondent to be given (1) proper and timely notice of the allegations or charges against him or her and (2) an opportunity to present evidence on the matter.

Executive Power

Administrative agencies are usually granted **executive powers**, such as the power to investigate and prosecute possible violations of statutes, administrative rules, and administrative orders.

> **Example** The Antitrust Division of the United States Department of Justice suspects that three companies in the same line of commerce are engaged in illegal price fixing. The Department of Justice has the authority to investigate whether a criminal violation of the federal Sherman Antitrust Act has occurred. The Department of Justice can prosecute suspected criminal violators of criminal antitrust laws.

Exhibit 8.9   Appeal of a federal administrative agency rule, order, or decision

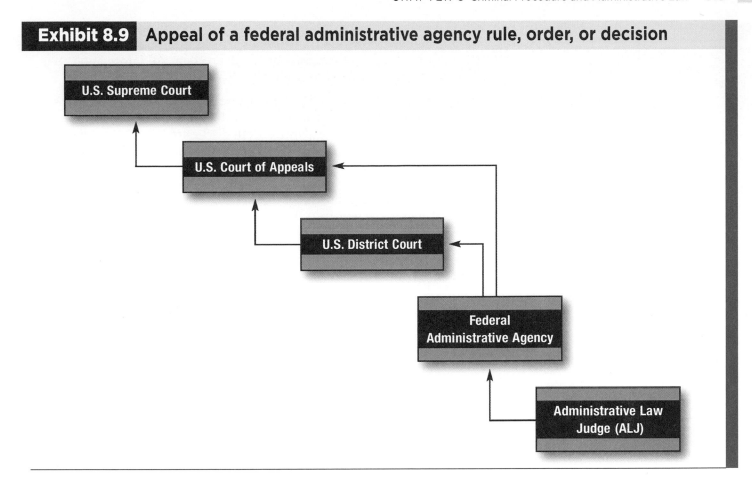

Judicial Review of Administrative Agency Actions

Many federal statutes expressly provide for judicial review of administrative agency actions. Where an enabling statute does not provide for review, the Administrative Procedure Act (APA) authorizes judicial review of federal administrative agency actions. The party appealing the decision of an administrative agency is called the **petitioner**.

Decisions of federal administrative agencies are appealed to the appropriate federal court. Decisions of state administrative agencies may be appealed to the proper state court. The federal appeal process is illustrated in Exhibit 8.9.

Disclosure of Administrative Agency Actions

Public concern over possible secrecy of administrative agency actions led Congress to enact several statutes that promote public disclosure of federal administrative agency actions and protect parties from overly obtrusive agency actions. These statutes are discussed in the paragraphs that follow.

Freedom of Information Act

The **Freedom of Information Act** (FOIA) was enacted to give the public access to most documents in the possession of federal administrative agencies. The act requires federal administrative agencies to publish agency procedures, rules, regulations, interpretations, and other such information in the *Federal Register*. The act also requires agencies to publish quarterly indexes of certain documents. In addition, the act specifies time limits for agencies to respond to requests for information, sets limits on copying charges, and provides for disciplinary action against agency employees who refuse to honor proper requests for information.

Freedom of Information Act
A law that was enacted to give the public access to most documents in the possession of federal administrative agencies.

Web Exploration

Go to http://www.rcfp.org/foiact/ which discusses the Freedom of Information Act. Go to "A brief overview of how the act works." Read it.

Example If a person suspects that he or she, or someone else, was subject to the Federal Bureau of Investigation (FBI) inquiry during the anti-communist McCarthy hearings, that person can submit a Freedom of Information Act request to obtain copies of any information on this subject from the FBI.

For purposes of privacy, the following documents are exempt from disclosure: (1) documents classified by the president to be in the interests of national security; (2) documents that are statutorily prohibited from disclosure; (3) records whose disclosure would interfere with law enforcement proceedings; (4) medical, personnel, and similar files; and (5) documents containing trade secrets or other confidential or privileged information.

Decisions by federal administrative agencies not to publicly disclose documents requested under the act are subject to judicial review in the proper U.S. district court.

Government in the Sunshine Act

Government in the Sunshine Act An act that was enacted to open certain federal administrative agency meetings to the public.

The **Government in the Sunshine Act** was enacted to open most federal administrative agency meetings to the public. There are some exceptions to this rule. These include meetings (1) where a person is accused of a crime, (2) concerning an agency's issuance of a subpoena, (3) where attendance of the public would significantly frustrate the implementation of a proposed agency action, and (4) concerning day-to-day operations. Decisions by federal administrative agencies to close meetings to the public are subject to judicial review in the proper U.S. district courts.

Example The Federal Communications Commission (FCC) is debating whether to grant an applicant permission to purchase a television station license. This meeting is not protected by any of the exceptions to the Government in the Sunshine Act. The FCC must publish a public notice of place, date, and time of the meeting so that persons may appear at the meeting.

Equal Access to Justice Act

Congress enacted the **Equal Access to Justice Act** to protect persons from harassment by federal administrative agencies. Under this act, a private party who is the subject of an unjustified federal administrative agency action can sue to recover attorneys' fees and other costs. The courts have generally held that the agency's conduct must be extremely outrageous before an award will be made under the act. A number of states have similar statutes.

Privacy Act

The federal **Privacy Act** concerns individual privacy. It stipulates that federal administrative agencies can maintain only information about an individual that is relevant and necessary to accomplish a legitimate agency purpose. The act affords individuals the right to have access to agency records concerning themselves and to correct these records. Many states have enacted similar privacy acts.

The Ethical Perspective discusses a paralegal's ethical and legal duty not to assist criminal activity.

Web Exploration

Find out the threat advisory for the risk of terrorist attacks today at http://dhs.gov/dhspublic/.

ETHICAL PERSPECTIVE
Duty Not to Assist Criminal Activity

Mr. Bush is a paralegal who works at a white-collar criminal defense law firm. Mr. Bush works directly for Ms. Swanson, a partner at the law firm.

One day Ms. Swanson requests that Mr. Bush sit in on a meeting with her with a client of the firm. The client, Mr. John White, owns White Enterprises Inc. Mr. White explains that he and White Enterprises Inc. are under investigation by the federal government for engaging in criminal fraud, wire fraud, mail fraud, and racketeering. Mr. White has hired Ms. Swanson to represent him and the company during the federal investigation and criminal lawsuit. At the meeting, Mr. White discloses that he wants "to get the cash out of White Enterprises and put it in a safe place" before the federal government goes any further with its investigation.

Ms. Swanson, who is an expert in white-collar criminal matters, tells Mr. White he can accomplish this if he starts another business that is secretly owned by Mr. White through a front, transfers the cash from White Enterprises to this new business, and then transfers the cash to a bank located in the Cayman Islands in a bank account in Mr. White's name. Ms. Swanson explains that the Cayman Islands has bank secrecy laws that prevent any party, including the United States government, from discovering the owner of and the amount of money in bank accounts that are located in the Cayman Islands.

Mr. White asks Ms. Swanson if she will help him do this, and Ms. Swanson agrees. The actions that Mr. White proposes, and Ms. Swanson has agreed to help accomplish, would constitute criminal conspiracy, criminal fraud, money laundering, racketeering, and other federal and state crimes. Ms. Swanson asks Mr. Bush, the paralegal, to assist her in accomplishing the illegal activities.

What should Mr. Bush do?

A paralegal is under a duty to not knowingly assist in the commission of a criminal act. Model and state paralegal Code of Ethics and Professional Responsibility provide that a paralegal is under an ethical duty to avoid engaging in criminal activity while performing paralegal responsibilities. A paralegal owes an ethical duty not to knowingly engage in criminal conduct. In addition, state and federal laws prohibit a paralegal from engaging in criminal acts.

PARALEGAL'S ETHICAL DECISION

The knowing participation of a paralegal in criminal activity on the job violates the law and the ethical duty of a paralegal. Mr. Bush cannot obey Ms. Swanson's direction to help assist Mr. White in engaging in criminal fraud, money laundering, racketeering, and other federal and state crimes. To do so would violate Mr. Bush's ethical duty as a paralegal. If Mr. Bush participates in the scheme, he would also be guilty of criminal conspiracy and other crimes.

Concept Review *and* Reinforcement

LEGAL TERMINOLOGY

SUMMARY OF KEY CONCEPTS

Parties and Attorneys of a Criminal Action

Parties to a Criminal Lawsuit	1. *Plaintiff:* the government. 2. *Defendant:* the person or business accused of the crime.

Attorneys in a Criminal Lawsuit	1. *Prosecuting attorney:* the attorney who represents the government. These can be:
	  a. District attorney (DA), who prosecutes criminal cases on behalf of the state.
	  b. United States Attorney, who prosecutes criminal cases on behalf of the federal government.
	2. *Defense attorney:* the attorney who represents the person or party accused of the crime. These can be:
	  a. Public defender, a government attorney who represents the accused.
	  b. Private attorney, a nongovernment attorney who the accused hires to represent him or her.

Criminal Procedure

Pretrial Criminal Procedure	1. *Arrest:* The person is arrested pursuant to an *arrest warrant* based upon a showing of *probable cause*, or, where permitted, by a *warrentless* arrest. 2. *Indictment or information:* Grand juries issue *indictments*; magistrates (judges) issue *informations*. These formally charge the accused with specific crimes. 3. *Arraignment:* The accused is informed of the charges against him or her and enters a *plea* in court. The plea may be *not guilty, guilty,* or *nolo contendere.* 4. *Plea bargaining:* The government and the accused may negotiate a settlement agreement wherein the accused agrees to admit to a lesser crime than charged.

Criminal Trial

Outcomes	1. *Conviction:* requires unanimous vote of jury
	2. *Innocent:* requires unanimous vote of jury
	3. *Hung jury:* nonunanimous vote of the jury; the government may prosecute the case again
Appeal	1. *Defendant:* may appeal his or her conviction
	2. *Plaintiff (government):* may not appeal a verdict of innocent

Constitutional Safeguards

Constitutional Safeguards	The U.S. Constitution includes provisions that protect persons from unreasonable government intrusion and provide safeguards for those accused of crimes.

Fourth Amendment Protection Against Unreasonable Searches and Seizures

Fourth Amendment Protection Against Unreasonable Searches and Seizures	The Fourth Amendment protects persons and corporations from *unreasonable searches and seizures.*
	1. *Reasonable searches and seizures:* based on *probable cause* are lawful:
	a. Search warrant: stipulates the place and scope of the search
	b. Warrantless search: permitted only:
	i. incident to an arrest
	ii. where evidence is in plain view
	iii. where it is likely that evidence will be destroyed
	2. *Exclusionary rule:* states that evidence obtained from an unreasonable search and seizure is *tainted evidence* that may not be introduced at a government proceeding against the person searched.
	3. *Business premises:* protected by the Fourth Amendment, except that certain *regulated industries* may be subject to warrantless searches authorized by statute.

Fifth Amendment Privilege Against Self-Incrimination

Fifth Amendment Privilege Against Self-Incrimination	The Fifth Amendment provides that no person "shall be compelled in any criminal case to be a witness against himself." A person asserting this privilege is said to have "taken the Fifth."
	1. *Nontestimonial evidence:* evidence (e.g., fingerprints, body fluids, etc.) that is not protected.
	2. *Businesses:* a privilege that applies only to natural persons; business cannot assert the privilege.
	3. *Miranda rights:* a right of a criminal suspect to be informed of his or her Fifth Amendment rights before the suspect can be interrogated by the police or government officials.
	4. *Immunity from prosecution:* granted by the government to obtain otherwise privileged evidence; the government agrees not to use the evidence given against the person who gave it.
	5. *Attorney–client privilege:* An accused's lawyer cannot be called as a witness against the accused.
	6. *Other privileges:* The following privileges have been recognized, with some limitations:
	a. psychiatrist/psychologist–patient
	b. priest/rabbi/minister/imam–penitent
	c. spouse–spouse
	d. parent–child
	7. *Accountant–client privilege:* None recognized at the federal level. Some states recognize this privilege in state law actions.

Fifth Amendment Protection Against Double Jeopardy

Fifth Amendment Protection Against Double Jeopardy	The Fifth Amendment protects persons from being tried twice by the same jurisdiction for the same crime. If the act violates the laws of two or more jurisdictions, each jurisdiction may try the accused.

Sixth Amendment Right to a Public Trial

Sixth Amendment Right to a Public Trial	The Sixth Amendment guarantees criminal defendants the following rights: 1. to be tried by an impartial jury 2. to confront the witness 3. to have the assistance of a lawyer 4. to have a speedy trial (Speedy Trial Law)

Eighth Amendment Protection Against Cruel and Unusual Punishment

Eighth Amendment Protection Against Cruel and Unusual Punishment	The Eighth Amendment protects criminal defendants from cruel and unusual punishment. Capital punishment is permitted.

Administrative Law and Agencies

Administrative Agencies	Created by federal and state legislative and executive branches; consist of professionals having expertise in a certain area of commerce, who interpret and apply designated statutes.
General Government Regulation	The government enacts laws that regulate businesses and industries collectively.
Specific Government Regulation	The government also enacts laws that regulate certain industries only.

Administrative Procedure

Administrative Procedure Act (APA)	The APA establishes procedures (e.g., notice, hearing) for federal agencies to follow in conducting their affairs. States have enacted their own procedural acts to govern state agencies.
Administrative Law Judge (ALJ)	The ALJ is an employee of the administrative agency who presides over the administrative proceeding; decides questions of law and fact, issues a decision in the form of an order.
Substantive Rule Making	Administrative agencies have the power to adopt substantive rules that have the force of law and must be adhered to by covered persons and businesses.
Licensing Power	Administrative agencies are authorized to issue licenses before a person or business can enter certain types of industries.

Disclosure of Administrative Agency Actions

Freedom of Information Act	The FOIA is a federal law that gives the public access to most documents in the possession of federal administrative agencies. It also requires federal administrative agencies to publish agency procedures, rules, regulations, interpretations, and other information in the *Federal Register*.
Government in the Sunshine Act	This federal law opens certain federal administrative agency meetings to the public.
Equal Access to Justice Act	This federal law protects persons from harassment by federal administrative agencies and provides certain penalties for its violation.
Privacy Act	The Privacy Act (a) restricts information a federal administrative agency can maintain about an individual, and (b) gives individuals the right to access agency records concerning themselves.

WORKING THE WEB

1. Go to the website of Crime Stoppers USA at http://www.crimestopusa.com/AboutUs.asp#. Read about what the organization does.
2. Go to http://www.thelaborers.net/indictments/bellomo/indictment_criminal_genovese_family-2006-2-23.htm and read a grand jury indictment of the Genovese Organized Crime Family.
3. Go to http://www.fbi.gov/wanted/topten/fugitives/fugitives.htm and find the persons on the most recent FBI's "Ten Most Wanted" criminals list. Pick out two of these individuals and read about the crimes they are wanted for.
4. Go to http:www.dailybreeze.com/ci_9009312 and read the ruling regarding searches of computers at the borders of the United States.
5. Go to http://www.youtube.com/watch?v=Y0oLsEVWwWM to see a video clip of an offer for a reward for reporting a criminal suspect.
6. Go to the website http://www.fda.gov/. This is the website for the Federal Food and Drug Administration (FDA). Click on one of the "Hot Topic" subject matters that interests you and write a one-page report on that information.
7. Using the Food and Drug Administration (FDA) website http://www.fda.gov/, click on the word "Forms." Choose a "Subject" and locate an FDA form. Print the form and write a brief description of what the form is used for.
8. Go to the website http://www.cpsc.gov/. This is the website for the federal Consumer Product Safety Commission (CPSC). Click on "Recent Recalls" for the most current month. Find a recall of a product that interests you and write a half-page report describing the product and its recall.

CRITICAL THINKING & WRITING QUESTIONS

1. Who are the parties to a criminal action?
2. What lawyers are involved in a criminal action?
3. Describe the function of a criminal complaint.
4. Explain the process of arrest. What is a search warrant? When are warrantless arrests permitted?
5. What is bail? What is a bail bond?
6. Describe a grand jury. What is the function of a grand jury? What is an indictment?
7. What is a magistrate judge? What is an information?
8. Describe the process of arraignment.
9. What is a plea? Describe the plea of *nolo contendere*.
10. Describe the process of plea bargaining. Why would an accused agree to a plea bargain agreement? Why would the government agree to a plea bargain agreement?
11. What is a trier of fact? What is its function in a criminal trial?
12. Describe the difference between a finding of *guilty* or *innocent* at a criminal trial.
13. What does the Fourth Amendment's protection against unreasonable search and seizure provide? What is a search warrant?
14. What is required for there to be a reasonable search and seizure? What is *probable cause*?
15. What is unreasonable search and seizure? Explain the exclusionary rule.
16. What does the Fifth Amendment privilege against self-incrimination provide? Describe the *Miranda* rights.
17. Describe the attorney–client privilege. What other privileges are there?
18. Explain the Fifth Amendment's protection against double jeopardy. What is a hung jury? Can the government retry the accused where there has been a hung jury in a criminal trial?
19. Explain the Sixth Amendment's right to a public jury trial.
20. Explain the Eighth Amendment's protection against cruel and unusual punishment.
21. What is an administrative agency? Who creates administrative agencies?
22. What is the purpose of an administrative agency? Explain.
23. Describe the difference between general government regulation and specific government regulation. Give an example of each.
24. What is an administrative law judge (ALJ)? What does an ALJ do?
25. Describe what the following federal statutes provide: (1) Freedom of Information Act, (2) Government in the Sunshine Act, (3) Equal Access to Justice Act, and (4) Privacy Act.

Building Paralegal Skills

Administrative Agency Hearing: The Role of the Paralegal

A school bus driver has been injured in what he claims to be a work-related injury. His employer—the school district—has raised objections requiring a Workers' Compensation hearing. A paralegal appears before the Workers' Compensation hearing officer representing the school bus driver.

After viewing the video case study at www.pearsonhighered .com/goldman answer the following:

1. Why are matters of this type heard before administrative hearing officers instead of going directly to court?
2. Is the paralegal committing the unauthorized practice of law in representing the school bus driver in this matter?
3. Are paralegals in your jurisdiction permitted to represent clients before administrative agencies?

1. Is the information given to a paralegal by a criminal client covered under the Fifth Amendment when he or she interviews a criminal?
2. What obligation does a paralegal have to make available exculpatory evidence discovered during the investigation of a case?
3. You are working at a firm with a large client base that does not speak English. You are fluent in three languages, and you are asked to translate for a firm attorney during an interview of a client in a criminal case. You take notes as you translate to be sure you are translating what is said properly [*Von Bulow by Auersperg v. Von Bulow*, 811 F. 2nd 136 1987 U.S. App. Lexis 2048 (2nd Cir. 1987).] Are the notes covered under the work–product doctrine? Does the attorney–client privilege apply to what you heard?
4. What ethical guidelines apply to the representation of parties before administrative agencies by a paralegal?
5. May paralegals advertise their availability to appear before administrative agencies? Explain.
6. As a recent graduate of a four-year degree program, you wish to get started in your career. You purchase a copy of Quicken Family Lawyer at your local computer store. You invite a group of friends and relatives to your place and offer to use the program to prepare powers of attorney and living wills (advance medical directives) for them. [*Unauthorized Practice of Law v. Parsons Tech.*, 179 F.3d 956 (5th Cir. 1999).] Are there any UPL issues? Explain.

With a group of other students, selected by you or as assigned by your instructor, review the facts of the following case. As a group, discuss the following questions.

1. What does the Fourth Amendment provide regarding searches and seizures of evidence?
2. Was the use of the GPS system in this case a search?
3. If it is not a search can the evidence discovered be used against the defendant at his criminal trial?

Prepare a memorandum, no longer than three pages, that discusses the general powers of a federal administrative agency and the specific powers of the Federal Food and Drug Administration (FDA).

United States of America v. Garcia

Bernardo Garcia had served time in jail for methamphetamine (meth) offenses. Upon release from prison, a person reported to the police that Garcia had brought meth to her and used it with her. Another person told police that Garcia bragged that he could manufacture meth in front of a police station without being caught. A store's security video system recorded Garcia buying ingredients used in making meth. From someone else the police learned that Garcia was driving a Ford Tempo.

The police found the car parked on the street near where Garcia was staying. The police placed a GPS (global positioning system) tracking device underneath the rear bumper of the car. The device receives and stores satellite signals that indicate the device's location. Using the device, the police learned that Garcia had been visiting a large tract of land. With permission of the owner of the land, the police conducted a search and discovered equipment and materials to manufacture meth. When the police were there, Garcia arrived in his car.

The police had not obtained a search warrant authorizing them to place the GPS tracker on Garcia's car. At Garcia's criminal trial in U.S. district court, the evidence the police obtained using the GPS system was introduced at court. Based upon this evidence, Garcia was found guilty of crimes related to the manufacture of meth. Garcia appealed to the U.S. court of appeals, arguing that the use of the GPS tracking system by the police was an unreasonable search in violation of the Fourth Amendment to the Constitution.

Source: *United States of America v. Garcia*, 474 F.3d 994, **Web** 2007 U.S. App. Lexis 2272 (United States Court of Appeals for the Seventh Circuit, 2007)

LEGAL ANALYSIS & WRITING CASES

Center Art Galleries–Hawaii, Inc. v. United States   875 F.2d 747, Web 1989 U.S. App. Lexis 6983

United States Court of Appeals for the Ninth Circuit
The Center Art Galleries–Hawaii sells artwork. Approximately 20 percent of its business involves art by Salvador Dalí. The federal government, which suspected the center of fraudulently selling forged Dalí artwork, obtained identical search warrants for six locations controlled by the center. The warrants commanded the executing officer to seize items that were "evidence of

violations of federal criminal law." The warrants did not describe the specific crimes suspected and did not stipulate that only items pertaining to the sale of Dalí's work could be seized. There was no evidence of any criminal activity unrelated to that artist.

Question
1. Is the search warrant valid?

United States v. John Doe   465 U.S. 605, 104 S.Ct. 1237, 79 L.Ed.2d 552, Web 1984 U.S. Lexis 169

Supreme Court of the United States
John Doe is the owner of several sole-proprietorship businesses. During the course of an investigation of corruption in awarding county and municipal contracts, a federal grand jury served several subpoenas on John Doe, demanding the production of certain business records. The subpoenas demanded the production of the following records: (1) general ledgers and journals, (2) invoices, (3) bank statements and canceled checks, (4) financial

statements, (5) telephone-company records, (6) safe-deposit box records, and (7) copies of tax returns. John Doe filed a motion in federal court, seeking to quash the subpoenas, alleging that producing these business records would violate his Fifth Amendment privilege of not testifying against himself.

Question
1. Do the records have to be disclosed?

People v. Paulson   216 Cal.App.3d 1480, 265 Cal. Rptr. 579, Web 1990 Cal.App. Lexis 10

Court of Appeal of California
Lee Stuart Paulson owned the liquor license for My House, a bar in San Francisco. The California Department of Alcoholic Beverage Control is the administrative agency that regulates bars in that state. The California Business and Professions Code, which the department administers, prohibit "any kind of illegal activity on licensed premises." An anonymous informer tipped the department that narcotics sales were occurring on the premises of My House and that the narcotics were kept in a safe behind the bar on the premises. A special department investigator

entered the bar during its hours of operation, identified himself, and informed Paulson that he was conducting an inspection. The investigator, who did not have a search warrant, opened the safe without seeking Paulson's consent. Twenty-two bundles of cocaine, totaling 5.5 grams, were found in the safe. Paulson was arrested. At his criminal trial, Paulson challenged the lawfulness of the search.

Question
1. Was the warrantless search of the safe a lawful search?

City of Indianapolis v. Edmond

531 U.S. 32, 121 S.Ct. 447, 148 L.Ed.2d 333, Web 2000 U.S. Lexis 8084 (2000)

Supreme Court of the United States

The police of the city of Indianapolis, Indiana, began to operate vehicle roadblock checkpoints on Indianapolis roads in an effort to interdict unlawful drugs. Once a car had been stopped, police questioned the driver and passengers and conducted an open-view examination of the vehicle from the outside. A narcotics-detection dog walked around outside each vehicle. The police conducted a search and seizure of the occupants and vehicle only if particular suspicion developed from the initial investigation. The overall "hit rate" of the program was approximately 9 percent.

James Edmond and Joel Palmer, each attorneys who had been stopped at one of Indianapolis's checkpoints, filed a lawsuit on behalf of themselves and the class of all motorists who had been stopped or were subject to being stopped at such checkpoints. They claimed that the roadblocks violated the Fourth Amendment to the Constitution. The district court found for Indianapolis, but the court of appeals reversed. The U.S. Supreme Court granted certiorari to hear the appeal.

Question

1. Does Indianapolis's highway checkpoint program violate the Fourth Amendment to the U.S. Constitution?

Donovan, Secretary of Labor v. Dewey

452 U.S. 594, 101 S.Ct. 2534, 69 L.Ed.2d 262, Web 1980 U.S. Lexis 58

Supreme Court of the United States

The Federal Mine Safety and Health Act of 1977 requires the Secretary of Labor to develop detailed mandatory health and safety standards to govern the operation of the nation's mines. The Act provides that federal mine inspectors are to inspect underground mines at least four times a year and surface mines at least twice a year to ensure compliance with these standards and to make the following inspections to determine whether previously discovered violations have been corrected. The Act also grants mine inspectors "a right of entry to, upon or through any coal or other mine" and states that "no advance notice of an inspection shall be provided to any person."

In July 1978, a federal mine inspector attempted to inspect quarries owned by Waukesha Lime and Stone Company (Waukesha) to determine whether all 25 safety and health violations uncovered during a prior inspection had been corrected. Douglas Dewey, Waukesha's president, refused to allow the inspector to inspect the premises without first obtaining a search warrant.

Question

1. Are the warrantless searches of stone quarries authorized by the Mine Safety and Health Act constitutional? Did Dewey act ethically in refusing to allow the inspections?

WORKING WITH THE LANGUAGE OF THE COURT CASE

Department of Justice v. Landano

508 U.S. 165, 113 S.Ct. 2014, 124 L.Ed.2d 84, 1993 U.S. Lexis 3727 (1993)
Supreme Court of the United States

Read the following case, excerpted from the U.S. Supreme Court's opinion. Review and brief the case. In your brief, answer the following questions:

1. Under what circumstances may a defendant obtain information under the Freedom of Information Act (FOIA)?
2. When may the government in a criminal case refuse to divulge information under the FOIA?
3. Is all information provided to the Federal Bureau of Investigation confidential and therefore not available under the FOIA?
4. Who has the burden of proof in FOIA cases?

O'Connor, J., delivered the opinion for a unanimous Court

Exemption 7(D) of the Freedom of Information Act, 5 U.S.C. Section 552 (FOIA), exempts from disclosure agency records "compiled for law enforcement purposes by criminal law enforcement authority in the course of a criminal investigation" if release of those records "could reasonably be expected to disclose" the identity of or information provided by a "confidential source" [Section 552(b)(7)(D)]. This case concerns the evidentiary showing that the Government must make to establish that a source is "confidential" within the meaning of Exemption 7(D). We are asked to decide whether the Government is entitled to a presumption that all sources supplying information to the Federal Bureau of Investigation (FBI or Bureau) in the course of a criminal investigation are confidential sources.

Respondent Vincent Landano was convicted in New Jersey state court for murdering Newark, New Jersey, police officer John Snow in the course of a robbery. The crime received considerable media attention. Evidence at trial showed that the robbery had been orchestrated by Victor Forni and a motorcycle gang known as "the Breed." There was testimony that Landano, though not a Breed member, had been recruited for the job. Landano always has maintained that he did not participate in the robbery, and that Forni, not he, killed Officer Snow. He contends that the prosecution withheld material exculpatory evidence in violation of Brady v. Maryland, 373 U.S. 83 (1963).

Landano apparently is currently pursuing a Brady claim in the state courts. Seeking evidence to support that claim, Landano filed FOIA requests with the FBI for information that the Bureau had compiled in the course of its involvement in the investigation of Officer Snow's murder. Landano sought release of the Bureau's files on both Officer Snow and Forni. The FBI released several hundred pages of documents. The Bureau redacted some of these, however, and withheld several hundred other pages altogether.

The information withheld under Exemption 7(D) included information provided by five types of sources: regular FBI informants; individual witnesses who were not regular informants; state and local law enforcement agencies; other local agencies; and private financial and commercial institutions. In the Government's view, all such sources should be presumed confidential. The deleted portions of the files were coded to indicate which type of source each involved.

Relying on legislative history, the court stated that a source is confidential within the meaning of Exemption 7(D) if the source received an explicit assurance of confidentiality or if there are circumstances "from which such an assurance could reasonably be inferred." An "assurance of confidentiality," the court said, is not a promise of absolute anonymity or secrecy, but "an assurance that the FBI would not directly or indirectly disclose the cooperation of the interviewee with the investigation unless such a disclosure is determined by the FBI to be important to the success of its law enforcement objective."

Exemption 7(D) permits the Government to withhold "records or information compiled for law enforcement purposes, but only to the extent that the production of such law enforcement records or information . . . could reasonably be expected to disclose the identity of a confidential source, including a state, local, or foreign agency or authority or any private institution which furnished information on a confidential basis, and, in the case of a record or information compiled by criminal law enforcement authority in the course of a criminal investigation, information furnished by a confidential source" [§ 552(b)(7)(D)]. The Government bears the burden of establishing that the exemption applies.

When FOIA was enacted in 1966, Exemption 7 broadly protected "'investigatory files compiled for law enforcement purposes except to the extent available by law to a private party.'" Congress adopted the current version of Exemption 7(D) in 1986. The 1986 amendment expanded "records" to "records or information," replaced the word "would" with the phrase "could reasonably be expected to," deleted the word "only" from before "confidential source," and clarified that a confidential source could be a state, local, or foreign agency or a private institution.

Under Exemption 7(D), the question is not whether the requested document is of the type that the agency usually treats as confidential, but whether the particular source spoke with an understanding that the communication would remain confidential. According to the Conference Report on the 1974 amendment, a source is confidential within the meaning of Exemption 7(D) if the source provided information under an express assurance of confidentiality or in circumstances from which such an assurance could be reasonably inferred. In this case, the Government has not attempted to demonstrate that the FBI made explicit promises of confidentiality to particular sources. That sort of proof apparently often is not possible: The FBI does not have a policy of discussing confidentiality with every source, and when such discussions do occur, agents do not always document them.

The precise question before us, then, is how the Government can meet its burden of showing that a source provided information on an implied assurance of confidentiality. The parties dispute two issues: the meaning of the word "confidential," and whether, absent specific evidence to the contrary, an implied assurance of confidentiality always can be inferred from the fact that a source cooperated with the FBI during a criminal investigation.

FOIA does not define the word "confidential." In common usage, confidentiality is not limited to complete anonymity or secrecy. A statement can be made "in confidence" even if the speaker knows the communication will be shared with limited others, as long as the speaker expects that the information will not be

(continued)

published indiscriminately. A promise of complete secrecy would mean that the FBI agent receiving the source's information could not share it even with other FBI personnel. Such information, of course, would be of little use to the Bureau.

We assume that Congress was aware of the Government's disclosure obligations under Brady and applicable procedural rules when it adopted Exemption 7(D). Congress also must have realized that some FBI witnesses would testify at trial. We therefore agree with the Court of Appeals that the word "confidential," as used in Exemption 7(D), refers to a degree of confidentiality less than total secrecy. A source should be deemed confidential if the source furnished information with the understanding that the FBI would not divulge the communication except to the extent the Bureau thought necessary for law enforcement purposes.

Considerations of "fairness" also counsel against the Government's rule. The Government acknowledges that its proposed presumption, though rebuttable in theory, is in practice all but irrebuttable. Once the FBI asserts that information was provided by a confidential source during a criminal investigation, the requester—who has no knowledge about the particular source or the information being withheld—very rarely will be in a position to offer persuasive evidence that the source in fact had no interest in confidentiality.

We agree with the Government that, when certain circumstances characteristically support an inference of confidentiality, the Government similarly should be able to claim exemption under Exemption 7(D) without detailing the circumstances surrounding a particular interview. Neither the language of Exemption 7(D) nor Reporters Committee, Page 178, however, supports the proposition that the category of all FBI criminal investigative sources is exempt.

But Congress did not expressly create a blanket exemption for the FBI; the language that it adopted requires every agency to establish that a confidential source furnished the information sought to be withheld under Exemption 7(D). In short, the Government offers no persuasive evidence that Congress intended for the Bureau to be able to satisfy its burden in every instance simply by asserting that a source communicated with the Bureau during the course of a criminal investigation. Had Congress meant to create such a rule, it could have done so much more clearly.

The Government has argued forcefully that its ability to maintain the confidentiality of all of its sources is vital to effective law enforcement. A prophylactic rule protecting the identities of all FBI criminal investigative sources undoubtedly would serve the Government's objectives, and would be simple for the Bureau and the courts to administer. But we are not free to engraft that policy choice onto the statute that Congress passed. For the reasons we have discussed, and consistent with our obligation to construe FOIA exemptions narrowly in favor of disclosure, we hold that the Government is not entitled to a presumption that a source is confidential within the meaning of Exemption 7(D) whenever the source provides information to the FBI in the course of a criminal investigation.

More narrowly defined circumstances, however, can provide a basis for inferring confidentiality. For example, when circumstances such as the nature of the crime investigated and the witness' relation to it support an inference of confidentiality, the Government is entitled to a presumption. In this case, the Court of Appeals incorrectly concluded that it lacked discretion to rely on such circumstances. Accordingly, we vacate the judgment of the Court of Appeals and remand the case for further proceedings consistent with this opinion. It is so ordered.

Paralegal Skills

The aspiring paralegal professional must develop a set of skills to allow them to understand and work in a supporting role as part of the legal team in the law office, the court, the administrative agency, and in the alternative dispute resolution working environment. Excellent verbal and written skills are crucial for paralegals who will be interviewing clients and witnesses and the general public. Paralegals must develop an ability to think critically and analytically when performing legal research and in writing briefs, memorandums of the law, and general correspondence. Today's paralegal must be familiar with the use of technology to conduct legal and factual research using a digital library and Internet research services, as well as how to use traditional print sources of information. Part III covers the basic skills needed for a paralegal professional to be successful in the job.

Interviewing and Investigation Skills

It is the spirit and not the form of law that keeps justice alive.

Earl Warren

LEARNING OBJECTIVES

After studying this chapter, you should be able to:

1. Explain the potential issues involved in a screening interview.
2. Describe the issues in preparing for and conducting an interview.
3. Explain the steps and process of conducting an investigation.
4. List and describe sources for obtaining information.
5. Explain the function of the trial notebook and its relationship to case management.

Paralegals at Work

Sara had been working for only a few weeks as a paralegal intern for a small, boutique litigation law firm. Mrs. Weiser, one of the two paralegals supporting the two trial attorneys, told Sara about her long-planned Alaskan cruise that she would be taking with her husband for their 25th anniversary. The reality of the situation started to set in when Sara was advised that the cruise would start from Anchorage the next day and Mrs. Weiser was scheduled to leave within the hour to catch a plane. Sara's concerns heightened when she and Mrs. Weiser reviewed the office calendar and it became obvious that Sara would be alone in the office. The attorneys and the other full-time paralegal were involved in a major medical malpractice case in another state for at least the next two weeks. Clearly, Sara would be in charge of the office, answering the phone and taking care of anyone who came in. Somewhat troubling would be the lack of any contact with Mrs. Weiser for the duration of the cruise, or contact with the other paralegal or attorneys during the trial day.

The instructions left no doubt that Sara would be busy when she was told: "Now remember—we advertise on TV, and Mr. Elliott expects us to screen potential clients without bothering him with loser cases. I've left a couple of files for you to work on while I'm gone. The Morales case just came in. It's an accident case that happened a few years ago, and you need to get her in for an initial interview—get all the necessary facts and see what else we have to do to move it along and either settle it or start suit. Oh, by the way, you do speak Spanish, don't you? Mrs. Morales is from Puerto Rico.

"The LaCorte case is on the trial list for next month. We don't have an expert yet who can substantiate our theory of the case. See what you can find. Oh, and you'd better get that case organized so they can start trial immediately in case the current trial lasts longer than the expected three weeks. All the material is in piles or in boxes in Mr. Martin's office. Prepare a trial notebook, or you can try that new case management software program we just got that is supposed to make life easier. I'm sure, with your computer skills, that you can get it up and running and use it to get the case ready for trial."

Consider the issues involved in this scenario as you read the chapter.

INTRODUCTION FOR THE PARALEGAL

Communication skills are at the heart of paralegals' ability to conduct successful interviews and investigations. The paralegal must be prepared to be the first point of contact with the client. In some practices, clients are interviewed first by the supervising attorney and then referred to the paralegal for a detailed factual interview. In other practices, the paralegal is the first one to meet with the client and conduct the initial interview before referring the client to the supervising attorney.

The paralegal must be able to interview clients, fact witnesses, expert witnesses, investigators, and others, including public records custodians who may have access to information necessary for the preparation of a case. The skill of the interviewer or investigator can determine the accuracy and completeness of the information obtained—and ultimately the outcome of the case. The impressions created and the relationship developed with a new client may be the deciding factor in whether the client stays with the firm or seeks other counsel. Professional relationships developed with public officials, public custodians of records, hospital records librarians, police investigators, and similar independent investigators can make the paralegal's job much easier and ultimately benefit the client.

Interviews

Screening interview Limited first contact with a prospective new client.

Any contact that a paralegal has with a client, or prospective client, constitutes an interview. It may involve limited contact, such as a **screening interview**, or an in-depth initial fact-gathering interview. In each case, the paralegal usually is the first point of contact with the client for the firm. The impression the paralegal makes is the impression the firm makes. As someone once said, we have only one opportunity to make a good first impression.

The initial contact with a client is what is sometimes called a screening interview. This usually begins with an initial telephone call to the firm, although a person may appear at the reception desk, looking for an attorney and wanting to determine if the firm is interested in taking the case, and usually what it will cost.

Also, paralegals frequently make the initial contact with potential witnesses. Again this may be a telephone call to set up a meeting or a telephone interview. The initial meeting with potential witnesses may be in the office or in the field at the witness's home or place of business. The initial contact with a potential witness, just as with a potential client, may set the tone for the interview and the willingness of the person to cooperate.

Screening Interview

Many clients come to a law firm or lawyer from a referral source, such as a current or former client. This source of clients acts as a potential screening. The individual probably has been told by the referral source something about the nature of the practice, the kind of work being done for the referring person, and the perceived reputation or ability of the lawyer or firm. Other potential clients find the firm's name and phone number in the telephone book, on a website listing of attorneys, or from another law firm advertisement or promotional piece.

Finally, some people simply appear at the office door and ask for an appointment or basic information about the firm's ability or interest in taking a case. In smaller offices the paralegal is the one who often takes these calls, doubling as receptionist–phone operator.

The initial contact is filled with potential landmines. If the paralegal solicits too much information or the prospective client volunteers too much information, an **implied attorney–client relationship** may be created. If too little information is obtained, the attorney will not have enough information to decide if he or she wants to talk to the potential client. Therefore, the paralegal or receptionist has to decide how much information to take and how much information to give.

First Meeting

At the very least, it is prudent for the paralegal to advise the potential client that paralegals are not lawyers, and that only a lawyer can give legal advice. Also, anything said to the paralegal may not be subject to the **attorney–client privilege**.

The prospective client may want a quick answer to the question, "Do I have a case?" The answer requires a legal analysis that only the attorney can make. The attorney–employer probably does not want to be bothered with most such early contacts but also does not want to lose a good case. Should the paralegal give advice or have this person speak with a lawyer? Most of these potential problems can be avoided by having a policy or strategy in place. Most offices have a policy on the fee for an initial interview. Many offer a no-cost initial interview to determine the validity of a case and any potential conflict of interests that might require the office to decline a case. In some cases, a nominal fee is charged. This may be a flat rate or an hourly rate. In many jurisdictions, referrals from the local lawyer referral office or legal aid office are charged at a token fee, sometimes as little as $5, or in indigent cases, no fee as part of the local pro bono program. The paralegal must ask the firm's policy before attempting to give and receive information from potential clients.

Implied Attorney–Client Relationship

If too much information is taken, the potential client may think he or she now has a lawyer. The courts have ruled on the side of the prospective client, holding that an implied attorney–client relationship exists. In this "implied" relationship, the client is entitled to expect the same degree of confidentiality under the attorney–client privilege. In this situation, a **conflict of interest** may result if the firm is already representing another party in the same matter, which would result in disqualification of the attorney or the establishment of an **ethical wall** to prevent access to information by members of the legal team with a conflict.

One of the biggest potential areas of potential malpractice is to miss a **statute of limitations** on a client's case. The statute of limitations is a time period within which a case must be filed with the court or the right to use the court for resolution of the case is lost. The statute of limitations is based on statute, and each jurisdiction has the power to set its own statute of limitations for each type of case. For example, in many states the time limit for filing a tort action arising out of an automobile action is two years, and a contract action six years, but in some states the suit must be filed in as little as 30 days. To a client seeking a new lawyer for an appeal, the timeframe may not be important. But to the lawyer, it is potentially critical to prevent malpractice, especially

Implied attorney—client relationship Implied attorney–client relationship may result when a prospective client divulges confidential information during a consultation with an attorney for the purpose of retaining the attorney, even if actual employment does not result.

Attorney–client privilege A client's right to have anything told to a lawyer while seeking legal advice, kept confidential in most instances.

Conflict of interest Representation of another with conflicting rights.

Ethical wall A artificial barrier preventing anyone not authorized who may have a conflict of interest from accessing client information.

Statute of limitations A time limit within which a case must be brought or lose the right to seek redress in court.

Web Exploration

Contrast and compare the Missouri Rule 4-1.18 at http://www.courts.mo.gov/courts/ClerkHandbooks P2RulesOnly.nsf with the ABA Rule 1.18 at www.abanet.org/cpr and the rule in your jurisdiction.

SIDEBAR

IMPLIED ATTORNEY–CLIENT RELATIONSHIP

Implied attorney–client relationship may result when a prospective client divulges confidential information during a consultation with an attorney for the purpose of retaining the attorney, even if actual employment does not result.

Pro-Hand Servs. Trust v. Monthei, 49 P.3d 56, 59 (Mont.2002).

The attorney–client privilege applies to all confidential communications made to an attorney during preliminary discussions of the prospective professional employment, as well as those made during the course of any professional relationship resulting from such discussions.

Hooser v. Superior Court, 101 Cal. Rptr. 2d 341, 346 (Ct. App. 2000).

ETHICAL PERSPECTIVE

Missouri Bar—Rules of Professional Conduct

RULE 4-1.18: DUTIES TO PROSPECTIVE CLIENT

(a) A person who discusses with a lawyer the possibility of forming a client–lawyer relationship with respect to a matter is a prospective client.

(b) Even when no client–lawyer relationship ensues, a lawyer who has had discussions with a prospective client shall not use or reveal information learned in the consultation, except as Rule 4-1.9 would permit with respect to information of a former client.

(c) A lawyer subject to Rule 4-1.18(b) shall not represent a client with interests materially adverse to those of a prospective client in the same or a substantially related matter if the lawyer received information from the prospective client that could be significantly harmful to that person in the matter, except as provided in Rule 4-1.18(d). If a lawyer is disqualified from representation under Rule 4-1.18(c), no lawyer in a firm with which that lawyer is associated may knowingly undertake or continue representation in such a matter, except as provided in Rule 4-1.18(d).

(d) When the lawyer has received disqualifying information as defined in Rule 4-1.18(c), representation is permissible if:

  (1) both the affected client and the prospective client have given informed consent, confirmed in writing, or:

  (2) the lawyer who received the information took reasonable measures to avoid exposure to more disqualifying information than was reasonably necessary to determine whether to represent the prospective client and the disqualified lawyer is timely screened from any participation in the matter.

---

when the timeframe is short, such as when the court has allowed a time limit for an appeal of 10 to 45 days, after which time the court order is not appealable barring special relief by the court.

The timing of the statute of limitations deadline always must be considered when taking the initial call or during the first contact with the potential client. If a court holds that an implied attorney–client relationship exists after the statute of limitations has run out (expired), the failure of the attorney to have taken action may be held to be malpractice and subject the lawyer to pay what would have been recovered if the case had gone forward and a recovery obtained. As the first point of potential client contact, the paralegal must be prepared to take appropriate action and refer the matter to the supervising attorney.

Some calls are not from potential clients but, rather, from those attempting to get information about the representation of other clients. This is not unusual. Particularly in family law cases, a party may call as if seeking representation but in reality is trying to find out if the other party has retained the firm.

Preparing for the Interview

The first step in preparing for an interview or conducting an investigation is to understand the outcome desired. One of the desired outcomes in an initial interview with a new client is to instill confidence in the firm and its personnel. The fundamentally desired outcome of any interview is to obtain all of the relevant facts for the case that has been assigned. Understanding the goals of the interview or investigation, the background or cultural issues of the individual, and the nature of the situation will help in structuring a successful interview.

Occasionally an interview has to be conducted without time for preparation, such as when the paralegal is asked to fill in for someone else at the last moment.

IN THE WORDS OF THE COURT

Identity of Clients

HOOSER V. SUPERIOR COURT OF SAN DIEGO COUNTY
84 CAL.APP.4TH 997 (2000) 101 CAL.RPTR.2D 341.

. . . the identity of an attorney's clients is sensitive personal information that implicates the clients' rights of privacy. "[E]very person [has the right] to freely confer with and confide in his attorney in an atmosphere of trust and serenity. . . ." (Willis v. Superior Court (1980) 112 Cal.App.3d 277, 293.)

Clients routinely exercise their right to consult with counsel, seeking to obtain advice on a host of matters that they reasonably expect to remain private. A spouse who consults a divorce attorney may not want his or her spouse or other family members to know that he or she is considering divorce.

Similarly, an employee who is concerned about conduct in his workplace, an entrepreneur planning a new business endeavor, an individual with questions about the criminal or tax consequences of his or her acts, or a family member who desires to rewrite a will may consult an attorney with the expectation that the consultation itself, as well as the matters discussed therein, will remain confidential until such time as the consultation is disclosed to third parties, through the filing of a lawsuit, the open representation of the client in dealing with third parties or in some other manner.

Upon such public disclosure of the attorney-client relationship, the client's privacy concerns regarding the fact of the consultation evaporate and there is no longer a basis for preventing the attorney from identifying the client. (See Satterlee v. Bliss (1869) 36 Cal. 489, 501.) However, until such a public disclosure occurs, the client's identity is itself a matter of privacy, subject to the protection against involuntary disclosure through compelled discovery against the attorney.

Investigation Checklists

The investigation checklist (Exhibit 9.1) should not be viewed as a static document. The checklist should start with a listing of all of the parties involved who should be interviewed, including initial fact witnesses. As additional parties and witnesses are interviewed, more people may have to be added to the list. Exhibit 9.2 is a witness information form. Investigation of locations and physical evidence may result in the need to examine other locations and evidence. Initial interviews also may result in the need to add one or more expert witnesses to the investigation checklist.

A checklist can be a valuable tool to be certain that all the information required for a certain type of case or other legal matter is obtained during the initial interview. The same checklist offers a good foundation for developing a more detailed interview plan when there is time for preparation.

Physical surroundings, clothing, and appearance are important in preparing for interviews and investigations. They merit your attention.

Physical Surroundings

The physical surroundings in the interview location can set the tone for the interview. Depending upon the purpose of the interview and the person being interviewed, the paralegal may wish to create either a formal or an informal environment. You probably can remember a situation in which someone interviewed you from across a desk. Didn't you feel a certain formality and possibly subservience to the interviewer? Contrast that situation with sitting in an informal setting with a low coffee table and living room-style chairs. This setting gives the meeting a more personal tone.

Putting a client at ease may be easier in the informal setting, whereas dealing with opposing counsel might be better handled in the formal, "across the desk" meeting.

Exhibit 9.1 Investigation checklist for auto accident

INVESTIGATION CHECKLIST

Client name _____

Phone (hm) _____ (wk) _____ (cell) _____

Current address _____

Prior address(es) _____

Date of birth _____ Place of birth _____

Social Security No. _____

VEHICLE CLIENT OPERATING/PASSENGER

Owner and type of motor vehicle _____

Insurance Co. _____ Policy number _____

Insurance company contact _____ Phone _____

Date of incident _____ Time of day _____ Weather conditions _____

Location of incident _____

City, State _____ County _____ Municipality _____

Opposing party _____

Address _____

Phone (hm) _____ (wk) _____ (cell) _____

Owner and type of motor vehicle _____

Insurance Co. _____ Policy number _____

FACT WITNESSES

Name _____ Address _____

Name _____ Address _____

Name _____ Address _____

Name of ambulance _____

Name of hospital _____

Police report issued _____ Copy ordered _____

Photographs of scene taken _____

Name of treating physicians _____

EXPERT WITNESSES

Name _____ Address _____

Name _____ Address _____

Summary of cause of action _____

Attach detailed accident/incident description, accident reports and diagrams.

In most cases, the paralegal will want to create the impression of a competent professional, although in some situations, creating a more casual and less professional impression may be beneficial. Some witnesses are more cooperative and helpful when they feel as if they are the ones in charge and are helping the paraprofessional.

Dress and Appearance

Remember the old saying, "First impressions count"? The impression a paralegal makes when walking into the room for the initial interview may set the stage for the entire relationship with the client or witness.

Exhibit 9.2 Witness information form

Witness Information

CLIENT PERSONAL DATA

Client Name		Case No.	File No.

Address	City, State, Zip	Phone

CASE DATA

File Label	Case issue	Date

Responsible Attorney(s)

WITNESS DATA

Witness Name

Aliases, if any		US Citizen ☐ Yes ☐ No

Current Address	City, State, Zip	Phone

Past Address(es)

Date & Place of Birth	Sex	Race	Age	Current Marital Status ☐ Single ☐ Divorced

Name of Spouse	Number/Former Marriages	Number/Children	☐ Married ☐ Widowed ☐ Separated

Name of Children (natural & adopted)	Age	Name	Age

Current Employer

Address	City, State, Zip	Phone

Job Title	Supervisor	From	To

Previous Employer

Address	City, State, Zip	Phone

Job Title	Supervisor	From	To

Education/Name of School	City/State	From	To	Degree
High School				
College				
Technical/Other				

Witness for ☐ Plaintiff ☐ Defendant	Type of Witness ☐ Expert ☐ Character ☐ Eye Witness	Have you ever been a party or witness in a court suit? ☐ No ☐ Yes

If yes, where & when

OTHER PERTINENT DATA

Form 9567 - 9/96 SYCOM Madison, WI Printed in U.S.A.

Clothing, posture, and manner of greeting create the first impression. Clothing sends a nonverbal message about the person and the firm or business. The impression a person makes upon walking into the room can enhance or destroy credibility. In the practice of law, or in a corporate law department, the unexpected can become the norm. Many attorneys, male and female alike, keep a "going-to-court suit" in the office just in case they need to have a more professional appearance at a moment's notice. When the new client comes in, they can change quickly while the receptionist or secretary buys them time to change to the "power" outfit.

A client may be offended by a paralegal's "casual Friday" appearance, believing that the paralegal is not taking the matter seriously. The working paralegal, however, usually doesn't have time to change when the unexpected arises, often being the one to "buy time" for the attorney. Therefore, paralegals always must be prepared to make a good impression and tailor their appearance appropriately as the situation warrants. In the case of field interviews, a casual appearance may be preferred to put the potential witness at ease. In the office, suits with jackets are appropriate for men and women. In the field, removing the jacket may give the impression of less formality.

Communication Skills in a Multicultural Society*

Those with whom paralegals communicate can be addressed in many ways. Clients, witnesses, and others with whom the paralegal comes in contact should never be stereotyped. At the same time, paralegals should be aware of the gender, religious, and ethic sensitivities of people. Paralegals' skills as interviewers depend on their ability to appreciate the differences in how and why individuals act and react differently. They must not assume that everyone in each category believes and acts the same and have to be sensitive to issues that may cause a person not to communicate as might have been anticipated from first impressions of them. We will point out some general differences in the way men and women communicate, followed by some cultural background considerations.

Gender Differences

A man, in comparison to a woman, is more likely to:

- have been socialized to perform more aggressively and boast of his successes;
- have learned from childhood games that winning is desirable;
- be motivated by competition;
- view conflict as impersonal, a necessary part of working relationships;
- be impressed by power, ability, and achievement;
- hear only the literal words and miss the underlying emotion;
- not express his true feelings through facial expressions;
- have a more direct communication style.

A woman is more likely to:

- have been socialized to work cooperatively and to be modest about her success;
- have learned from childhood games to compromise and collaborate, and continue to be motivated by affiliation;
- compete primarily with herself—with her own expectations of what she should be able to accomplish;
- take conflict personally;
- be impressed by personal disclosure and professional courage;
- have the ability to focus on several projects at the same time;
- be proficient at decoding nonverbal meanings and likely to display her feelings through facial expression and body language;
- have an indirect style, except with other women of equal rank.

Web Exploration

Check religious holiday dates at http://www.interfaithcalendar.org/.

Considering the receiver's attitudes about the paralegal:

- Man-to-man: He may afford the paralegal instant credibility based on the same gender.
- Woman-to-woman: She may expect the paralegal to be friendly, nurturing, and concerned and may afford the paralegal instant credibility based on same-gender assumptions.
- Paralegal man-to-woman. She may expect that the paralegal will not really listen to her.
- Paralegal woman-to-man: He may expect the paralegal to be friendly and nurturing, even passive-dependent. Any aggressive behavior or deviation from his expectation could cause him discomfort and confusion, or produce negative responses. He may simply disregard the female paralegal.

Cultural Sensitivity

The culturally sensitive person is aware of the reasons for differences in the way people behave, based on religious and ethnic background and belief system. As the cultural makeup of the United States has become more diverse, the need for cultural awareness and sensitivity in the legal and paralegal professions has grown. Just as men and women are said to be different in some ways, so are Europeans, Asians, Latinos, and Africans who have not fully assimilated into the culture of the country.

Interviewing a Latino male, for example, may require a different approach than interviewing an Asian female. Even subtleties of eye contact can affect an interview. Whereas Americans view eye contact as a sign of sincerity, some Asian cultures view this as aggressive. In developing communication skills, paralegals must become sensitive to how they are perceived and learn to fashion their approach to maximize accuracy of communication.

The effectiveness of paralegals also is influenced by how well they "read" the cultural backgrounds of those with whom they interact. This involves manner of speaking, dressing, and acting, and whether one is a man or a woman in that culture. What is heard may not be what was intended. What is perceived may not be what the other person perceives, because of cultural differences that affect the interpretation of words and body language. We will briefly highlight some general characteristics of four cultural groups.

European background. Generally, the countries of Western Europe, including Scandinavia, comprise the group of European background. This group is extraordinarily large and complex, which limits attempts to make cultural generalities. In terms of gender differences, men and women with roots in the European culture may have different initial reactions to the paralegal and attitudes about the topic. Male and female listeners alike tend to perceive men as having more credibility than women of equal rank, experience, and training. Men tend to be more credible to other men, and women may be more credible to other women.

Now consider the cultural implications of graphic pictures of physical injuries from car crashes. These photos are acceptable in the United States, but Germans tend to dislike the sight of blood and the British are likely to be offended by violence.

According to Kenton and Valentine, if the paralegal appears to be European–American, receivers of communication may be concerned that the paralegal will:

- reject their opinions;
- take advantage of them or hold them back;
- consider them different in a negative way;
- deny them equal opportunities.

Latino background. Collectively, Latin America encompasses 51 countries generally considered to be those south of the U.S. border: Mexico and the countries of Central America, South America, and the Caribbean islands. With so vast an area, many differences can be expected from country to country and even from city to city. The languages, too, are not the same. Portuguese is spoken in Brazil, and the Spanish that is spoken in South America differs from the Spanish spoken in Puerto Rico. The Latino–American population has moved closer to becoming the largest minority group in the United States. According to Kenton and Valentine, individuals with roots in the Latino culture tend to:

- value family and loyalty to family;
- honor nationalism;
- exhibit a strong sense of honor;
- have a fatalistic view of the world;
- express passion in speech, manner, and deed.

Asian background. More than 30 countries can be considered Asian—among them, China, Malaysia, Japan, the Philippines, India, and Korea. They, too, demonstrate vast differences from culture to culture. Some generalizations may be made, however. Asian cultures generally consider that being direct and to the point is rude, and relationships are considered top priority. The Japanese, for example, tend to prefer an indirect style of communication. In communicating with people who have an Asian background, then, it might be best to begin with pleasantries about the weather, sports, or inquire about the well-being of the individual and his or her family.

Roots in the African culture. African Americans represent the largest ethnic group in the United States. A distinction should be made between African Americans of recent immigration with stronger cultural ties to the African culture and African Americans with long family ties within the United States whose cultural roots are American. According to Kenton and Valentine, some of the African core beliefs and cultural values that may influence attitudes and behavior are:

- a holistic worldview;
- emotion and expressiveness;
- a keen sense of justice or fairness.

Conducting the Interview

In the first meeting, the paralegal must make clear that he or she is a paralegal and not an attorney. During the first few minutes of the interview, paralegals must build a relationship with the interviewees, explain the reason for the interview, and eliminate any barriers that would prevent obtaining the necessary information. Sometimes the interviewees seem to be fully cooperative when in fact they are not cooperating. Or the subject matter may be embarrassing, or they may have a fear of authority figures, or they might be uncomfortable using certain terms necessary to describe the situation.

Effective interviewers learn the verbal and nonverbal cues that help them understand the reasons for interviewees' reluctance to answer questions. In some situations the solution is first to ask easy questions, such as the person's name and address. Once interviewees start speaking, they have less trouble answering well thought-out questions that build logically on the previous information.

This is not always the case, though. In times of great stress, clients have been known to read the name from a nameplate in the office and state it as their own name! The interviewer must be careful to avoid embarrassing the interviewee and have prepared questions that can be answered easily and thereby help the person gain composure, such as, "My records show that you live at 123 South Main Street. Is that correct?" Or "How do you spell your name?"

Listening Skills

A good interviewer must master the skill of listening. Most of us hear the words being said but may not be listening to *what* is being said. Instead of concentrating on what is being said, listeners may be more concerned with the next question they want to

CHECKLIST Listening Skills

- ☐ Empathize with the person, and try to put yourself in his or her place to help you see the point.
- ☐ Don't interrupt; allow time for the person to say what he or she is trying to say.
- ☐ Leave your emotions behind, and control your anger. Emotions will prevent you from listening well.
- ☐ Get rid of distractions.
- ☐ Don't argue mentally.

- ☐ Don't antagonize the speaker. This could cause someone to conceal important ideas, emotions, and attitudes.
- ☐ Avoid jumping to conclusions. This can get you into trouble. For example, don't assume that the speaker is using the words in the same way that you are interpreting them. If you are unsure, ask for clarification.

© Student Counseling Service, Texas A&M University.

ask, or emotionally influenced by the speaker's message, or distracted by the speaker's physical behavior.

Interviewing clients and witnesses requires listening to what is being said in the context of the speaker's cultural makeup. It also requires an understanding of the type of witness—friendly, hostile, or expert—and the witnesses' bias toward the client or the type of case for which they are being interviewed. Fact witnesses may not want to get involved, or be hostile witnesses, saying what they either think you want to hear or what will move their agenda along. Fact witnesses in criminal matters involving members of different races or religions may not be as concerned for the truth as they are for "someone paying" for committing the crime. Bias and cultural identity may influence what is said.

The professional interviewer must listen to what is really being said in a nonjudgmental impartial manner.

When listening, the paralegal must focus on what is said and not how it is said. Some people are not articulate, and the facts may be lost if a person doesn't listen carefully. Others may try to shock or put off the paralegal by buzz words designed to get a reaction. In sports, this is referred to as "trash talk"—saying things to get the listener to react emotionally and lose concentration.

Good listeners avoid distractions. They do not allow themselves to lose focus because of environmental distractions such as noise or activity in the area of the interview, or a speaker's annoying physical habits, such as tapping the fingers or legs, or speech impediments, such as stuttering. Think about how hard it is to concentrate on what is being said in a large classroom. Good listeners focus on the message and block out distractions.

Further, good interviewers do not make assumptions about the facts of the case. They listen with an open mind. Making assumptions about people or facts can lead to attempts to make the facts fit the interviewer's preconceived notions. Sometimes the facts are not what they first seem to be. Look at the number of people released from jail after DNA evidence proves they did not do the crime everyone assumed they committed. Fact witnesses may have been interviewed and been given a version of the incident that the DNA does not prove to be correct, and the person is innocent.

Leading Questions

Leading questions are those that suggest the desired answer. In conducting a cross-examination, lawyers in trial frequently use leading questions to force the witness to answer in a desired manner. An obvious example is, "Have you stopped kicking your dog?"

On direct examination, an attorney might ask a more direct and neutral question: "Have you ever kicked your dog?"

Leading questions do not lead to open-ended answers but are directed toward a desired answer: "You ran the red light, didn't you?"

Web Exploration

For more information on listening skills see the Texas A&M Website at http://www.scs.tamu.edu/selfhelp/elibrary/listening_skills.asp.

Leading question A question which suggests the answer.

Open-Ended Questions

Open-ended questions are designed to give interviewees an opportunity to tell their story without the limitation of yes-or-no answers. Open-ended questions create a **narrative opportunity** for the witness. For example: "Tell me about your life"; "Tell me about your life since the accident."

In fact interviews, the witness should receive the opportunity for open-ended narrative answers. Asking a question to solicit an answer that you desire may cut off information that is essential to your case. For example, you may want to know whether your client was at the scene of an accident, and therefore you ask the witness, "Did you see my client at the scene of the accident?" The answer to this question may be "yes" or "no." A better question would be, "Who was present at the scene of the accident?" This kind of question may lead to additional information on additional witnesses you may want to interview.

Similarly, the question, "How fast were the cars going prior to the impact?" is much better than, "Were the cars speeding before the impact?" In this context, the term "speeding" may be interpreted as exceeding the speed limit instead of going too fast for the conditions.

With the witness's statements from the interview in hand at the time of trial, the trial attorney might appropriately ask a leading question such as, "My client wasn't present at the scene of the accident, was she?" Or, "Isn't it true that the defendant was speeding before the impact?" With knowledge of the prior statement, there should be no surprise in the answer at trial. If there is, the prior statement can be used to impeach the credibility of the witness, if desired, as part of the trial strategy.

At times, the interviewer may want to focus clients or witnesses by asking questions that give them a perspective of time or place, such as, "What did you observe at noon on Saturday?" or, "Tell me what happened on September 11, 2001." The tragedy of that day will haunt the memories of Americans and most of the rest of the world, so little stimulus will be needed to elicit where they were and what they observed. This is true of most traumatic events in people's lives—the loss of a loved one, the birth of a child, or a serious accident in which they were injured. Other days and times tend to blur and have to be brought to the consciousness of the witness by questions such as, "Let's think back to August 19, 2001" and, "What happened to you that day?"

Discovery Limitations

Discovery is the more formal term for the pretrial process of learning everything relevant about the case. This includes the investigation phase where basic information is gathered without the formality of statements signed under oath, such as written interrogatories, or before a court reporter authorized to administer oaths such as in a formal deposition.

The scope of the inquiry is only limited generally to that which is relevant. Evidence is relevant if the fact is logically connected and tends to prove or disprove a fact in issue. Under the federal rules of evidence:

Rule 26 (b)

Discovery Scope and Limits.
(1) Scope in General.
Unless otherwise limited by court order, the scope of discovery is as follows: Parties may obtain discovery regarding any nonprivileged matter that is relevant to any party's claim or defense—including the existence, description, nature, custody, condition, and location of any documents or other tangible things and the identity and location of persons who know of any discoverable matter. For good cause, the court may order discovery of any matter relevant to the subject matter involved in the action. Relevant information need not be admissible at the trial if the discovery appears reasonably calculated to lead to the discovery of admissible evidence. All discovery is subject to the limitations imposed by Rule 26(b)(2)(C).

For the investigator or interviewer, the rule then is: Information may be sought, even if it is not admissible, as long as it is relevant and may lead to relevant information that will be admissible at trial. This includes information that may be used in trial to show bias, lack of credibility, and challenges to the qualifications of an expert.

Moral Versus Ethical Considerations

At times in the investigation of a case, it is necessary to consider the difference between a moral consideration and an ethical consideration. A **moral obligation** is one based on one's own conscience or a person's perceived rules of correct conduct, generally in the person's own community. Some communities, for instance, may consider it to be morally improper to ask someone to give information about another person. An **ethical obligation**, for members of the legal team including those acting on behalf of a supervising attorney, are the responsibilities of the legal profession under the ABA Model Rules of Professional Conduct, including thoroughness in representing a client.

Moral obligation An obligation based on one's own conscience.

Ethical obligation A minimum standard of conduct usually within one's profession.

Is it ethically improper to ask someone to tell the truth surrounding the facts of a case that may lead to a neighbor, relative, or friend being subjected to liability for his or her actions? For the paralegal and the legal team, the primary ethical obligation is the duty to the client. Some members of the legal team, for example, may be offended to ask a mother to testify against a child. This is a moral issue for the mother, in which the results may cause financial hardship or ruin upon awarding a verdict for causing injury as the result of negligent conduct, but ethics may require this course of conduct for the paralegal.

Privileged Communication

Certain forms of communication are considered privileged and not usable at trial unless the privilege is waived. Forms of **privileged communication** are:

Privileged communication A communication that the person has a right to be kept confidential based on the relationship with the other part such as attorney and client.

1. Attorney–client communications
2. Doctor–patient communications
3. Priest–penitent communications
4. Spousal communications during marriage

Each of these privileges can be waived but the waiver must come from the client, the patient, the penitent, or the spouse making the statement with the belief that it is privileged. Changes in some of the rules of ethics, and by statute, may permit certain otherwise privileged communications to be revealed to prevent harm or injury to another. The spouse, the priest, or the doctor may have a moral issue in revealing what was communicated.

When the paralegal is acting on behalf of the attorney, communications between a client and the paralegal have the same privilege as those between the client and the attorney. Information gathered from the client as part of representation of

---

ETHICAL PERSPECTIVE

New Hampshire Rules of Professional Conduct

RULE 1.6. CONFIDENTIALITY OF INFORMATION

(a) A lawyer shall not reveal information relating to the representation of a client unless the client gives informed consent. The disclosure is impliedly authorized in order to carry out the representation or the disclosure is permitted by paragraph (B).

 Web Exploration

Contrast and compare the New Hampshire Rule at http://www .courts.state.NH.US/supreme/ orders/20072507.pdf with the ABA Model Rules at www.abanet.org/cpr and the rule in your jurisdiction.

the client and necessary for rendering competent legal advice is privileged. The paralegal, therefore, is in the same position as the attorney, the doctor, the priest, or the spouse to whom the confidential information has been communicated. Each must carefully guard the confidential information and not inadvertently or intentionally reveal the information. In some cases, such as when another person's life may be in danger, these people may be compelled by a court to testify even when they believe it is a violation of their moral duty to another person from whom they have received information.

Expert Witnesses

Expert witness A person qualified by education or experience to render an opinion based on a set of facts.

Expert witnesses are individuals whose background, education, and experience are such that courts recognize them as qualified to give opinions based on a set of facts. The expert witness may be a doctor certified by a board of medical experts or a scientist or engineer specializing in an area of science such as flammability of fabrics. The report of these experts may be advice based on the facts of a potential case to determine whether there is sufficient evidence to believe that a wrong has occurred or malpractice committed. Without this report, the lawyers may be obligated to advise clients that they have no actionable cause of action.

There is no clear rule on whether what is revealed to an expert in the preparation of a case is protected as part of the attorney–client privilege in the same manner as that revealed to a member of the trial team, including other attorneys, paralegals, and secretarial staff working on the case with the primary trial attorney. Almost certainly, anything revealed to an expert who is listed as an expert witness on the list of witnesses to be called at trial is discoverable.

Some law firms retain an expert to advise them but do not use that expert to testify. The advice and information provided by these experts to help in the preparation

---

IN THE WORDS OF THE COURT

Federal Rules of Civil Procedure 26 F.R.C.P. 26(b)(4)

(4) Trial Preparation: Experts

(A) A party may depose any person who has been identified as an expert whose opinions may be presented at trial. If a report from the expert is required under subdivision (a)(2)(B), the deposition shall not be conducted until after the report is provided.

(B) A party may, through interrogatories or by deposition, discover facts known or opinions held by an expert who has been retained or specially employed by another party in anticipation of litigation or preparation for trial and who is not expected to be called as a witness at trial, only as provided in Rule 35(b) or upon a showing of exceptional circumstances under which it is impracticable for the party seeking discovery to obtain facts or opinions on the same subject by other means.

(C) Unless manifest injustice would result, (i) the court shall require that the party seeking discovery pay the expert a reasonable fee for time spent in responding to discovery under this subdivision; and (ii) with respect to discovery obtained under subdivision (b)(4)(B) of this rule the court shall require the party seeking discovery to pay the other party a fair portion of the fees and expenses reasonably incurred by the latter party in obtaining facts and opinions from the expert.

for trial may come under the privilege. Although the privilege is the client's, the paralegal and others on the legal team must be careful not to divulge privileged or confidential material without authorization.

The expert retained for background trial advice must have as much confidence in the legal team as the legal team has in the expert's advice and integrity. Some experts fear that the legal team will give them only selected information. With the limited information provided, they might give an expert opinion that is not what they would have given if they had received the complete set of facts.

Exhibit 9.3 indicates factors to be considered in arranging for an expert witness.

Investigating Claims

The legal team must gather all of the relevant information about a cause of action before making a recommendation to a client to file a lawsuit or respond to a claim of wrongdoing. In most cases, before the first interview with the client is conducted, the paralegal has some indication of the area of law or the nature of the claim. It may be from a telephone interview when the client calls for an appointment, or from the referral from the supervising attorney to the paralegal to conduct the interview and investigation. If paralegals specialize in certain areas of law, they are likely to understand the underlying elements of the claims or rights the client wishes to assert. Those in general practice and those entering a new area have to understand the rules of law as they apply to that issue.

For example, in a product liability case, understanding traditional, or common-law, of negligence is not enough. One also must understand the law of **strict liability** for product defect cases as found in the **Restatement of the Law Third, Torts**: Product Liability. Where negligence requires a breach of duty, strict liability is without fault in cases where the doctrine applies. An interview conducted strictly considering negligence as the basis for a legal action could improperly result in the client's being advised that he or she does not have a claim when, under the no-fault strict liability concept for defective products, an action might exist.

The first step is to determine the legal basis of a client's claim. With an understanding of the legal basis of the claim and the applicable law, an investigative plan can be prepared to obtain the necessary witness statements, locate physical evidence, and obtain photographs, reports, and other evidence for use in preparation for and at trial. Where a claim of negligence is to be made, photographic evidence may be essential in demonstrating the nature of the hazard.

For example, when a client has injured himself or herself as the result of a fall in a store, photographs showing the hazardous condition should be obtained as quickly as possible. In the case of strict liability involving a product defect that caused injury or loss, preservation of the defective product or photographic documentation of the defect becomes essential as a matter of proof. Knowing what elements of the action must be proven dictates what evidence must be located in the form of witnesses, photographs, and physical evidence. Knowing the elements of the claim will ensure that the proper questions are asked in the interview, which then will dictate the necessary investigation steps.

One of the most useful tools in the gathering of information about a case is the digital camera. Digital photographs may be shared on computer networks or by Internet transfer to other members of the legal team, clients, and possible witnesses. It also is useful to take pictures of potential witnesses so other members of the legal team may recognize them later at the time of depositions and trial. If the photographs are going to be used at trial, it should be kept in mind that the photographer may be called to authenticate them.

Web Exploration

For more information in the changes in the revised Restatement of the Law Third, visit the American Law Institute http://www.ali.org/ ali/promo6081.htm.

Strict liability Liability without fault.

Restatement of the Law Third, Torts A legal treatise with suggested rules of laws relating to torts.

Exhibit 9.3   Expert witness form

EXPERT WITNESS CHECKLIST

BACKGROUND

Full name _____   Date of birth _____

Business address _____

Business telephone number _____   Business fax number _____

Business email address _____   Business website _____

Locations of prior offices _____

Home address _____

Home telephone number _____

EDUCATION

Schools attended _____   Dates of attendance _____

Degrees or honors awarded _____

Continuing education courses _____

WORK HISTORY

Place of employment _____   Dates of employment _____

Job description _____

Reasons for leaving _____

Specific area of expertise _____

Published articles and books _____

Professional affiliations _____

Professional magazines subscribed to _____

Licenses and jurisdictions _____

Litigations or disciplinary action _____

PRIOR LEGAL EXPERIENCE

Ratio of plaintiff/defense cases _____

Prior clients including date (plaintiff or defendant) _____

Types of investigations with dates _____

Deposition testimony given with dates _____

Court testimony with dates _____

Legal references _____

AVAILABILITY

Vacation plans and dates _____   Potential meeting dates _____

In the deposition, verify the accuracy and currency of the expert's professional information, including all resume and curriculum vitae items. Verify the opinions are those of the expert and, if based on the work of others, who these others are and what other experts' writings were consulted. It is important to have on the record the assumptions upon which the expert has formed the opinion and the steps followed in reaching the opinion.

A Defense Perspective

Most people quite naturally think of a lawsuit from the plaintiff's perspective. Most people think in terms of the violation of rights and resulting injury. In a perfect world, only legitimate actions would be filed and the law would provide a perfect remedy for all wrongs. But not every plaintiff is in the right, and some have been known to file frivolous or even fraudulent lawsuits.

The balance in the American legal system is achieved by a vigorous defense on behalf of the defendant. A plaintiff may claim, for example, that she slipped and was injured as a result of the negligence of a storeowner. The defendant storeowner might be innocent of any wrongdoing or breach of any duty. It is well to remember that for every plaintiff there is a defendant, and for each party there is a law firm, an attorney, and a paralegal.

Obtaining Official Reports

Most incidents giving rise to litigation have associated official reports. In the negligence action, it may be a police accident or incident report, emergency medical services report, fire department call report, or incident reports of safety violations by federal, state, or local authorities. These reports are filed in a central depository as public records. A useful starting point is to obtain any official reports associated with the case. These reports frequently indicate time, place, and the names of fact witnesses. In some cases, detailed diagrams or photographs may accompany the reports. Exhibit 9.4 is an example of a police accident report form.

Fact Analysis

Analyzing the facts starts with interviewing the clients and their recitation of the time, place, circumstances, and other people involved as participants or witnesses. Exhibit 9.5 is a sample client interview form. A complete analysis usually requires further field investigation of the location, the object involved, such as an automobile, and interviews of the parties and witnesses. One person's perception may not be reality. A client's recollection and description of the physical surroundings may not be proven by the investigator's visit to the location. What one person describes as a narrow, congested walkway may actually be a standard-width open sidewalk.

The ultimate trier of fact will be the jury, a panel of arbitrators, or a judge acting as the trier of fact. Therefore, analysis of the facts must be sufficient to justify the position taken and the presentation made in pursuing a client's claim or its defense in **arbitration** or in trial.

Arbitration A form of ADR in which the parties choose an impartial third party to hear and decide the dispute.

Locations

Careful analysis of a claim includes verification of the physical aspects of the actual location where the cause of action occurred. Ask any group of people to describe a location, and you're likely to get as many different descriptions as there are people in the group. How the person viewed the location, from the south, from the north, east, or west, may influence their description. Or the driver's view from behind the wheel of a large tractor-trailer might be different from the view from behind the wheel of a small sports car.

Investigation of a case should involve a trip to the location where the incident occurred. The trier of fact will be relying upon the plaintiff's and defendant's counsels to describe in their presentation the characteristics of the physical location. They also will be looking at the location from an impartial, neutral point of view, usually without prior familiarity with the location. The diagrams usually presented at trial are those of an aerial view with its sterile, one-dimensional presentation. Photographs from the points of view of all the participants can make the difference in understanding the duties and responsibilities of the litigants. Unlike diagrams of the location, these photographs more typically will be from the point of view of the plaintiff, defendant, or witness at ground level, or from behind the wheel of a vehicle, or looking out of a building window.

Exhibit 9.4 Sample police accident report form

COMMONWEALTH OF PENNSYLVANIA
POLICE ACCIDENT REPORT

(XX.) REFER TO OVERLAY SHEETS   REPORTABLE ☐   NON - REPORTABLE ☐   PENNDOT USE ONLY

POLICE INFORMATION	ACCIDENT LOCATION
1. INCIDENT NUMBER	20. COUNTY — CODE
2. AGENCY NAME	21. MUNICIPALITY — CODE
3. STATION/ PRECINCT — 4. PATROL ZONE	*PRINCIPAL ROADWAY INFORMATION*
5. INVESTIGATOR — BADGE NUMBER	22. ROUTE NO. OR STREET NAME
6. APPROVED BY — BADGE NUMBER	23. SPEED LIMIT — (24.) TYPE HIGHWAY — (25.) ACCESS CONTROL
7. INVESTIGATION DATE — 8. ARRIVAL TIME	*INTERSECTING ROAD:*

ACCIDENT INFORMATION	26. ROUTE NO. OR STREET NAME
9. ACCIDENT DATE — 10. DAY OF WEEK	27. SPEED LIMIT — (28.) TYPE HIGHWAY — (29.) ACCESS CONTROL
11. TIME OF DAY — 12. NUMBER OF UNITS	*IF NOT AT INTERSECTION:*
13. # KILLED — 14. # INJURED — 15. PRIV. PROP. ACCIDENT Y ☐ N ☐	30. CROSS STREET OR SEGMENT MARKER
16. DID VEHICLE HAVE TO BE REMOVED FROM THE SCENE? UNIT 1 — UNIT 2 — Y ☐ N ☐ Y ☐ N ☐ — 17. VEHICLE DAMAGE 0 - NONE UNIT 1 ☐ 1 - LIGHT 2 - MODERATE 3 - SEVERE UNIT 2 ☐	31. DIRECTION FROM SITE N S E W — 32. DISTANCE FROM SITE FT. MI. — 33. DISTANCE WAS MEASURED ☐ ESTIMATED ☐
18. HAZARDOUS MATERIALS Y ☐ N ☐ — 19. PENNDOT PROPERTY Y ☐ N ☐	(34.) CONSTRUCTION ZONE ☐ — (35.) TRAFFIC CONTROL DEVICE — PRINCIPAL ☐ INTERSECTING ☐

UNIT # 1	UNIT # 2
36. LEGALLY PARKED? Y☐ N☐ — 37. REG. PLATE — 38. STATE	36. LEGALLY PARKED? Y☐ N☐ — 37. REG. PLATE — 38. STATE
39. PA TITLE OR OUT-OF-STATE VIN	39. PA TITLE OR OUT-OF-STATE VIN
40. OWNER	40. OWNER
41. OWNER ADDRESS	41. OWNER ADDRESS
42. CITY, STATE & ZIPCODE	42. CITY, STATE & ZIPCODE
43. YEAR — 44. MAKE	43. YEAR — 44. MAKE
45. MODEL - (NOT BODY TYPE) — 46. INS. Y ☐ N ☐ UNK ☐	45. MODEL - (NOT BODY TYPE) — 46. INS. Y ☐ N ☐ UNK ☐
(47.) BODY TYPE — (48.) SPECIAL USAGE — (49.) VEHICLE OWNERSHIP	(47.) BODY TYPE — (48.) SPECIAL USAGE — (49.) VEHICLE OWNERSHIP
(50.) INITIAL IMPACT POINT — (51.) VEHICLE STATUS — (52.) TRAVEL SPEED	(50.) INITIAL IMPACT POINT — (51.) VEHICLE STATUS — (52.) TRAVEL SPEED
(53.) VEHICLE GRADIENT — (54.) DRIVER PRESENCE — (55.) DRIVER CONDITION	(53.) VEHICLE GRADIENT — (54.) DRIVER PRESENCE — (55.) DRIVER CONDITION
56. DRIVER NUMBER — 57. STATE	56. DRIVER NUMBER — 57. STATE
58. DRIVER NAME	58. DRIVER NAME
59. DRIVER ADDRESS	59. DRIVER ADDRESS
60. CITY, STATE & ZIPCODE	60. CITY, STATE & ZIPCODE
61. SEX — 62. DATE OF BIRTH — 63. PHONE	61. SEX — 62. DATE OF BIRTH — 63. PHONE
64. COMM. VEH. Y ☐ N ☐ — 65. DRIVER CLASS — 66. DRIVER SS #	64. COMM. VEH. Y ☐ N ☐ — 65. DRIVER CLASS — 66. DRIVER SS #
67. CARRIER	67. CARRIER
68. CARRIER ADDRESS	68. CARRIER ADDRESS
69. CITY, STATE & ZIPCODE	69. CITY, STATE & ZIPCODE
70. USDOT # — ICC # — PUC #	70. USDOT # — ICC # — PUC #
(72.) VEH. CONFIG. — (73.) CARGO BODY TYPE — 74. GVWR	(72.) VEH. CONFIG. — (73.) CARGO BODY TYPE — 74. GVWR
75. NO. OF AXLES — (76.) HAZARDOUS MATERIALS — 77. RELEASE OF HAZ MAT Y ☐ N ☐ UNK ☐	75. NO. OF AXLES — (76.) HAZARDOUS MATERIALS — 77. RELEASE OF HAZ MAT Y ☐ N ☐ UNK ☐

AA-45 (1/92)   PAGE·   CENTER FOR HIGHWAY SAFETY

Exhibit 9.4 **Sample police accident report form** (continued)

78. RESPONDING EMS AGENCY	INCIDENT #:
79. MEDICAL FACILITY	ACCIDENT DATE:

80. PEOPLE INFORMATION

A	B	C	D	E	F	G	NAME	ADDRESS	H	I	J	K	L	M

81. ILLUMINATION   82. WEATHER

83. ROAD SURFACE

84. PENNSYLVANIA SCHOOL DISTRICT (IF APPLICABLE)

85. DESCRIPTION OF DAMAGED PROPERTY

OWNER

ADDRESS

PHONE

86. DIAGRAM

87. NARRATIVE - IDENTIFY PRECIPITATING EVENTS, CAUSATION FACTORS, SEQUENCE OF EVENTS, WITNESS STATEMENTS, AND PROVIDE ADDITIONAL DETAILS. LIKE INSURANCE INFORMATION AND LOCATION OF TOWED VEHILCES, IF KNOWN.

INSURANCE INFORMATION	COMPANY		INSURANCE INFORMATION	COMPANY
UNIT 1	POLICY NO		UNIT 2	POLICY NO

88. WINTESSES

	NAME	ADDRESS	PHONE
	NAME	ADDRESS	PHONE

	89. VIOLATIONS INDICATED	90. SECTION NUMBERS (ONLY IF CHARGED)	TC NTC
UNIT 1			☐ ☐
UNIT 2			☐ ☐

	91. PROBABLE USE	92. TYPE TEST	93. RESULTS			91. PROBABLE USE	92. TYPE TEST	93. RESULTS		94. INVESTIGATION COMPLETE ?
UNIT 1			0.___%	☐ NO TEST ☐ REFUSE ☐ UNK	UNIT 2			0.___%	☐ NO TEST ☐ REFUSE ☐ UNK	YES ☐ NO ☐

AA-45 (1/92)   PAGE: **CENTER FOR HIGHWAY SAFETY**

Source: Pennsylvania Department of Transporatation, Bureau of Highway Safety and Traffic Engineering. Used with permission.

Exhibit 9.5	Initial client interview form

CLIENT INTERVIEW CHECKLIST

CLIENT PERSONAL INFORMATION

Name

Address

City _____ State _____ Zip

Phone (hm) _____ (wk) _____ (cell)

How long at this address

Date of birth _____ Place of birth

Social Security No.

Prior address

City _____ State _____ Zip

Dates at this address

Employer:

Job description

Marital status _____ Maiden name

Spouse's name _____ Date of birth

Child's name _____ Date of birth

Child's name _____ Date of birth

Child's name _____ Date of birth

CASE INFORMATION

Case referred by

Case type:
☐ Appeal ☐ Business ☐ Corporate ☐ Estate ☐ Litigation
☐ Municipal ☐ Real Estate ☐ Tax ☐ Trust ☐ Other

Opposing party(ies)

Opposing party

Address

Opposing attorney

Address

Date of incident _____ Statute of limitation date

Summary of facts

_____

_____

_____

_____

Web Exploration

Find your home on Google Earth at http://earth.google.com.

Satellite photos are available of locations around the world. Earth Google™ offers a Web access to images that may be modified to add desired descriptions such as street names, points of interest, including lodgings, restaurants, schools, churches, and many others by the click of the computer mouse. Images from before a loss such as Hurricane Katrina combined with images taken after the devastation may be helpful in submitting claims for damages.

Tangible Evidence

Tangible evidence consists of the physical objects that may have caused the injury. These may include items as small as a giveaway toy from a fast-food restaurant swallowed by a

2-year-old, to a bottle that exploded, to a large automobile whose brakes failed or whose seatbelts snapped. In some cases, the tangible evidence is essential to proving negligence or an element of strict liability in tort.

Much has been written about the effects of the plaintiffs' and defendants' failure to preserve critical evidence of this type. In some cases, failure to preserve the evidence has resulted in loss of the case by the plaintiff, and in other cases by the defendant.

It is important to understand the local rules with regard to **spoliation of evidence** and its effect on a cause of action. In determining the proper penalty for spoliation of evidence, courts are most likely to consider [*Schroeder v. Department of Transportation*, 551 Pa. 243, 710 A.2d 23, 26 (1998)]:

Spoliation of evidence
Destruction of evidence.

1. The degree of fault of the party who altered or destroyed the evidence.
2. The degree of prejudice suffered by the opposing party.
3. The availability of a lesser sanction that will protect the opposing party's rights and deter future similar conduct.

Following a Timeline

Causes of action should be viewed from the events leading up to the incident to the events and occurrences following the incident. (See Exhibit 9.6 for a comparison of conflicting accounts.) Few things in life that give rise to a potential claim occur in a vacuum. Usually some facts lead up to the incident and others follow the incident. The question may be, "Given the time in which the parties allege this happened, could this really have happened?" For example, could the parties have driven the 30 miles in

---

Exhibit 9.6 **Sample timeline using LexisNexis CaseSoft TimeMap**

Timeline created using TimeMap, from Decision Quest, CaseSoft (www.casesoft.com). Copyright LexisNexis® CaseSoft.

Web Exploration

The CPSC FOIA Request form can be completed online at http://xapps.cpsc.gov/FOIA/pages/requestentry.jsp.

Freedom of Information Act
A federal statute permitting access to federal agency records.

Web Exploration

Obtain a copy of the latest CPSC FOIA report at http:// www.cpsc.gov/LIBRARY/FOIA/foia.html.

Web Exploration

For information or making an FOIA request to the Department of Justice is available at www.usdoj.gov/04foia/.

20 minutes through crowded rush-hour traffic on city streets? In a food-poisoning case, could ingestion of the food at noon have caused the reaction claimed by 1:00 P.M. The claimant might have been negligent, or the first perceived wrongdoer perhaps was not the correct person, as most food-poisoning cases require 6 to 12 hours from ingestion of the tainted food until onset of symptoms of the illness.

The starting point is the time of the alleged injury. Also important, from a fault standpoint or defense standpoint, is what happened that led up to the incident. From the damages standpoint, what happened after the incident, including treatment and subsequent changes in the person's life or lifestyle, is important.

Freedom of Information Act (FOIA)

The **Freedom of Information Act** is a federal statute designed to open to the public the information possessed by the federal government and its agencies. President Obama issued a memorandum for the heads of executive departments and agencies highlighting the importance of openness of government that resulted in additional information being made available to the public under the FOIA. See Exhibit 9.7.

Many federal agencies do not require a formal FOIA request. Some federal agencies, such as the National Transportation Agency, make information available online (Exhibit 9.8). Other agencies, such as the Consumer Product Safety Commission (CPSC), permit requests to be made on the CPSC website (see Exhibit 9.9). The CPSC site also is helpful in finding information about defective products that may be a cause of a client's injuries. Limitations are placed on the information that an agency may disclose under applicable federal law. See examples in the CPSC limitations shown in the **sidebar** and the NTSB limitations shown in Exhibit 9.10.

Locating Witnesses

Most witnesses can be located by use of directories. The Web has also become a valuable tool for locating witnesses.

Exhibit 9.7 Freedom of Information Act

The federal government is a good source of information. Many of the documents required to be filed are available through the government, and frequently online, such as corporate filings with the Securities and Exchange Commission. Other information may be available by request, under the provisions of the Freedom of Information Act (FOIA), 5 U.S.C. § 552. Some limitations apply to the information available. The general exceptions, as found in the statute, are:

1. Classified documents concerning national defense and foreign policy.

2. Internal personnel rules and practices.

3. Exemptions under other laws that require information to be withheld, such as patent applications and income-tax returns.

4. Confidential business information and trade secrets.

5. Intra-agency and inter-agency internal communications not available by law to a party in litigation.

6. Protection of privacy of personnel and medical files and private lives of individuals.

7. Law-enforcement investigatory files.

8. Examination, operation, or condition reports of agencies responsible for the regulation and supervision of financial institutions.

9. Geological and geophysical information and data including maps concerning wells.

Exhibit 9.8	**Simplified online FOIA form to request information not already available from National Transporation Safety Board (NTSB)**

Freedom of Information Act (FOIA) Request

Be sure to read what's available under FOIA before making a request.

Please specify as much detail as possible about the item(s) you are requesting. Depending on the complexity of your request, turnaround could range from 3 weeks to 1 year or more. For assistance, please contact the Records Management Division at (800) 877-6799 or (202) 314-6551.

First Name: [   ]   Email Addr: [   ]
Last Name: [   ]   Phone No: [   ]
Street: [   ]
City: [   ]   Business/Affiliation: [   ]
State: [∨]   Zip: [   ]   Country: [   ]
Transportation: [- Select Mode - ∨]

Please describe your request or comment below - be specific about dates, locations, etc., where applicable:

[   ]

Directories

Investigators usually keep a collection of telephone books of the areas in which they work. Rarely today does a person not have a telephone of some sort, even if it is an unlisted number. In addition to the standard-issue telephone directories, the cross-reference directory (also known as a "criss-cross directory") is a standard tool; these list phone numbers by address or by phone number instead of by name. Therefore, an address may be checked for a corresponding phone number—for example, determining the phone number located at 123 Main Street, or using the phone numbers listed at an address to determine the physical location or billing address of the phone.

Telephone directories are not limited to just the United States but typically are published in most parts of the world in one form or another. Companies and businesses also can be located by use of commercial or industrial telephone directories, both domestically and internationally.

In addition to telephone directories, directories are published by trade organizations, professional groups, and educational institutions. These directories may be limited to membership but can be useful in cases where the name and the association are known, but not the city, state, or country where the person can be found.

The Web

As paper is replaced by electronic media, directories are being placed online. Search engines can help locate individuals, businesses, and organizations on the Internet. Communications companies and other private firms offer a number of online white pages for individuals and yellow pages for businesses. Many organizations and publishers of professional directories now offer their print directories online. An example is the Web version of Martindale–Hubbell for attorneys. These services may change or cancel their Web address and others may be added, so the list of websites has to be kept up to date.

 Web Exploration

Check frequently requested information at the NTSB website http://www.ntsb.gov/info/foia.htm.

Web Exploration

Experts can be located using the Lexis Nexis/Martindale–Hubbell free website at http://resources.martindale.com/mhes/index.jsp.

CPSC LIMITATIONS OF FOIA DISCLOSURE

SIDEBAR

15 U.S.C. § 2055. Public disclosure of information release date: 2005-08-01

(a) Disclosure requirements for manufacturers or private labelers; procedures applicable

(1) Nothing contained in this Act shall be construed to require the release of any information described by subsection (b) of section 552 of title 5 or which is otherwise protected by law from disclosure to the public.

(2) All information reported to or otherwise obtained by the Commission or its representative under this Act which information contains or relates to a trade secret or other matter referred to in section 1905 of title 18 or subject to section 552 (b)(4) of title 5 shall be considered confidential and shall not be disclosed.

(3) The Commission shall, prior to the disclosure of any information which will permit the public to ascertain readily the identity of a manufacturer or private labeler of a consumer product, offer such manufacturer or private labeler an opportunity to mark such information as confidential and therefore barred from disclosure under paragraph (2).

(4) All information that a manufacturer or private labeler has marked to be confidential and barred from disclosure under paragraph (2), either at the time of submission or pursuant to paragraph (3), shall not be disclosed, except in accordance with the procedures established in paragraphs (5) and (6). . . .

Exhibit 9.9 Online Freedom of Information request form for USPSC

US Consumer Product Safety Commission

▸ Consumer Safety ▸ About CPSC ▸ Library - FOIA ▸ Business

New FOIA Request Form

Requestor Information

Name Prefix:

* Last Name:

* First Name:

Phone No:

* Email Address:

If you represent a company or firm, enter it below, otherwise enter personal information.

Company Name:

Website:

* Mailing Address:

* City:

* State:

* ZIP Code:

* Country: United States

Request Detail

* Range of Search Request: 2002 * To 2005

* Subject:

* Request Type:

* Type of Requestor:

Product Description:

Brand/Model:

* Remarks:

* Some requests will include fees. Please check if you accept any fees associated with this request.

Submit   Clear

* Indicates Required Field

Questions on submitting a FOIA request should be directed to aheggs@cpsc.gov

The Web is also a good source of information about individuals, both expert and lay witnesses. Social networking sites such as Facebook offer information on millions of people who otherwise would not be in a directory. A search of Facebook, the video website YouTube, blogs, and other similar websites may produce information useful for finding people and learning about them, both good and questionable behavior that might demonstrate a credibility issue. For example, the posting of a Web camera image of a high-profile person like Michael Phelps at a party that resulted in a loss of endorsement contract with a cereal company because of questions of improper conduct. Public postings by the potential parties and witnesses may indicate a potential bias, hostility, or in the case of a potential juror, a predisposition or judgment. In some cases, jurors posting to their websites, Facebook, or other social networking sites may show a violation of jury deliberation secrecy that might result in a new trial.

Interviews, Investigations, and Trials

It is never too soon to start preparing for trial. Trial preparation starts with the first client contact and gathering the first document. Good preparation for trial includes an

Exhibit 9.10 Limitations on disclosure by the NTSB

NTSB EXEMPTIONS

The four most common exemptions under which the NTSB withholds information are:

(1) 5 USC 552 (b)(5), draft reports and staff analyses (see 49 CFR 801.54);

(2) 5 USC 552 (b)(6), personal information, where a personal interest in privacy outweighs a public interest in release; this includes graphic photographs of injuries in accidents and autopsy reports (see 49 CFR 801.55);

(3) 5 USC 552 (b)(4), Trade Secrets and/or confidential financial/commercial information submitted by private persons or corporations to the NTSB in the course of an investigation (see 49 CFR 801.59); and

(4) 5 USC 552 (b)(3), information protected from release by another statute (see 49 CFR 801.53). This includes information such as:

- Cockpit Voice Recorder (CVR) tapes. Release of the tapes is prohibited by 49 USC 1114(c). However, the Board will release a CVR transcript [edited or unedited], the timing of such release is also controlled by statute – 49 USC 1114(c)(B);

- Voluntarily provided safety-related information. 49 USC 1114(b)(3) prohibits the release of such information if it is not related to the exercise of the Board's accident or incident investigation authority and if the Board finds that the disclosure would inhibit the voluntary provision of that type of information; and

- Records or information relating to the NTSB's participation in foreign aircraft accident investigations. 49 USC 1114(e) prohibits the release of this information before the country conducting the investigation releases its report or 2 years following the accident, whichever occurs first.

assessment of how well clients and witnesses will react in depositions or in court under the pressure of cross-examination and how they will be perceived by opposing counsel, the judge, or the jury. Will they come across sympathetically as being truthful and likeable? Or will they appear sneaky, unpleasant, and trying to hide the truth? These observational notes may be of great interest when the legal team must decide whether to settle or try the case.

A practical consideration in deciding whether to try a case before a jury is how the parties will appear to the jury. If the client appears to be sympathetic and deserving and the opposing party unsympathetic and having adequate financial resources, a jury may try to reward the client with a finding unsupported by the facts or evidence.

Effectively managing a case may involve reviewing, sorting, and marking for identification hundreds or even thousands of documents, photographs, and other graphics. Careful tracking and handling should start at the beginning of the case management process. Good case management requires a thoughtful process for storing, handling, examining, evaluating, and indexing every page. In the computer age, case management includes making decisions on the appropriateness and potential use of electronic display technologies, as well as the fallback on traditional paper exhibit preparation. Demonstrative evidence, physical items, such as defective products in a strict liability action or an automobile in a motor vehicle accident, may have to be obtained and preserved for examination by expert witnesses or for use at trial.

There are almost as many different approaches to setting up case files and managing cases as there are legal teams. One of the traditional approaches includes the case notebook or case **trial notebook**. Summary information about the case is maintained in a notebook with tabs for each major activity, party, expert, or element of proof needed. A sample of the sections is shown in Exhibit 9.11. With the use of a trial notebook comes the responsibility to maintain the case file and file boxes or file cabinets into which the hardcopies of documents, exhibits, and physical evidence are maintained. If only one trial or case notebook is kept for the team, someone working on the case must take responsibility to be certain that there is no duplication of effort and that the most

Trial notebook A summary of the case tabbed for each major activity, witness, or element of proof.

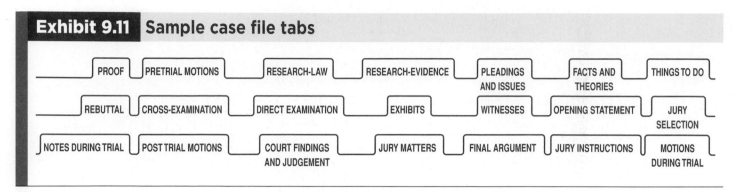

Exhibit 9.11 Sample case file tabs

PROOF	PRETRIAL MOTIONS	RESEARCH-LAW	RESEARCH-EVIDENCE	PLEADINGS AND ISSUES	FACTS AND THEORIES	THINGS TO DO
REBUTTAL	CROSS-EXAMINATION	DIRECT EXAMINATION	EXHIBITS	WITNESSES	OPENING STATEMENT	JURY SELECTION
NOTES DURING TRIAL	POST TRIAL MOTIONS	COURT FINDINGS AND JUDGEMENT	JURY MATTERS	FINAL ARGUMENT	JURY INSTRUCTIONS	MOTIONS DURING TRIAL

current activities are entered. When multiple copies are used, each trial notebook must be updated regularly, again to be sure that there is no duplication of effort and that current activity information is made available for all members of the legal team.

Case and Practice Management Software

The legal team may work on a number of cases at the same time, and each case may be in a different stage of preparation for trial. With the team approach to handling cases, each member of the team must be able to access case information and know what the other members of the team have done and what still needs to be done. In the traditional paper file case management approach, the physical file is the repository of everything from interview notes, to pleadings and exhibits. To work on the case, the physical file has to be located and the needed folder removed. In the **"paperless" office**, everything, in theory, is available on the computer screen. Documents are scanned into an electronic format and saved on the computer, pleadings and notes are saved as word-processor files, and transcripts of depositions and court hearings are stored in electronic

Paperless office An office with electronic documents.

Paralegals *in* Practice

PARALEGAL PROFILE
Kevin D. Gasiewski

Kevin D. Gasiewski is a Certified Legal Assistant Specialist in Intellectual Property. After a career in law enforcement, he obtained his first paralegal job in the City Attorney's Office of Ann Arbor, Michigan. Later, he worked for Ford Global Technologies, LLC, and is now employed by Brooks Kushman P.C. Kevin is an active member of the Legal Assistants Section of the State Bar of Michigan, of which he is a past chairperson and a recipient of its 2003 Mentor Award.

My work focuses mainly on trademark prosecution, maintenance, and protection. During the initial interview with a client interested in registering a trademark, it is important to fully identify all team members, vendors, and third-party manufacturers connected to the proposed mark. I also ask questions regarding the mark itself and who designed it, as well as the goods, services, and countries for which it is intended. This data will be needed if the trademark is challenged, and for future maintenance or protection requirements.

My job also includes protecting trademarks from illegal use. When customs officials notify us that they are detaining suspected counterfeit goods, I initiate an investigation. I examine the subject trademark, determine the origin of the goods, and ascertain the final destination of the goods. The investigation results help me confirm whether or not the suspect goods are genuine.

Interview and investigation data are stored electronically, including contacts' information, specimen images showing use of the trademark, evidence showing the fame of the mark, and documents filed in support of the mark. The databases I use also contain a field for listing key phrases, words, and acronyms to make data searches easier and more efficient.

Although formal education is a definite plus in my field, it is equally important to stress your skills when applying for a paralegal position. Not only were my police investigation and interview skills attractive to employers, these abilities also provided me with the confidence to complete the wide variety of assignments typically encountered as a trademark paralegal.

form. For the case with voluminous paperwork and days or weeks of deposition transcripts, only by use of computer file software can relevant documents or appropriate deposition notes be accessed quickly and efficiently.

A number of software programs can be used to manage the law office and the cases within the office. They generally provide what is sometimes referred to as case management, or practice management. Practice management programs have evolved out of the early programs that tracked time spent on cases, sometimes with a calendar component that could be used to track deadlines such as the statute of limitations for a case. Modern programs may include practice management functions such as time and cost tracking, calendaring, conflict checking, scheduling, and contact management. Others allow for management of the individual cases, tracking of documents, parties, issues, and events.

Software

Case management software is evolving constantly as the various vendors try to meet the demands and needs of their respective customers. Some nonlegal-specific software has case or practice management-type functions. Microsoft Outlook provides a combination contact manager, calendar–scheduler, task "to do" list, and email function. More sophisticated programs such as Practice Manager from Tabs3 provide the same functions, as well as outlining, billing, integrated research management, timelines, and other functions. LexisNexis CaseSoft provides individual programs that can share data, including CaseMap, TimeMap, TextMap, and NoteMap. One of the features of CaseMap is the ability to organize a case by facts, objects or parties, chronology, as shown in Exhibit 9.12, and then seamlessly create timelines from the chronological information by using the TimeMap program (see Exhibit 9.13). Summation's litigation support software allows transcripts, documents, issues, and events to be managed using computer technology.

Web Exploration

The complete set of General Guidelines for Judge Bruce Kauffman may be viewed at www.paed.uscourts.gov/documents/procedures/kaupol.pdf.

Exhibit 9.12 CaseMap features

Main	Date & Time	Fact Text	Source(s)	Key	Status +	Linked Issues	Eval by CA	Eval
	06/??/1999	William Lang makes decision to reduce size of staff.	Deposition of William Lang, 43:19	☐	Undisputed	Age Discrim Against Hawkins	↘	
	07/??/1999	Susan Sheridan is terminated.	Deposition of Philip Hawkins	☐	Undisputed	Pattern & Practice	↓	
	Sun 07/04/1999	Philip Hawkins allegedly makes derogatory remarks about Linda Collins to Karen Thomas during Anstar Biotech Industries Fourth of	Interview Notes	☑	Disputed by:	Hawkins Deserved Termination	↗	
	Mon 07/12/1999	Anstar Biotech Industries second quarter sales announced. Sales have dropped by 8%.		☐	Undisputed	Demotion, Hawkins Deserved Termination	→	
	Fri 07/30/1999	Philip Hawkins demoted to sales manager.	Deposition of Philip Hawkins, p. 24, I15.	☐	Undisputed	Demotion	↘	
	Thu 08/05/1999 #1	Philip Hawkins and William Lang meet.	????	☐	Undisputed	Age Discrim Against Hawkins	→	
	Thu 08/05/1999 #2	Philip Hawkins alleges that William Lang tells him "The old wood must be trimmed back hard."	Complaint, p. 8; Deposition of Philip...	☑	Disputed by: Us	Pattern & Practice, Demotion	↓	
	Mon 08/09/1999	Philip Hawkins transferred to Anstar Biotech Industries office in Fresno.	Deposition of Philip Hawkins, p.43, I18.	☐	Undisputed	Transfer, Hawkins Deserved Termination	↘	
	09/23/1999	Philip Hawkins writes letter to William Lang complaining about the way he's being treated and alleging plan to eliminate older staff	Hawkins Letter of 9/23/99	☐	Undisputed	Wrongful Termination, Age Discrim Against Hawkins	↘	
	Fri 11/12/1999	Reduction in force takes place. 55 Anstar Biotech Industries employees are let go including Philip Hawkins.		☑	Undisputed	Wrongful Termination, Age Discrim Against Hawkins	↓	
	Mon 11/22/1999	Philip Hawkins files suit.	Complaint	☐	Undisputed		→	
	Tue 12/14/1999	Philip Hawkins turns down job offer from Converse Chemical Labs.	Rumor William Lang heard	☐	Prospective	Failure to Mitigate	↗	
	01/??/2000	Philip Hawkins meets with Susan Sheridan.	Rumor William Lang heard	☐	Prospective		?	
	01/??/2000	Philip Hawkins is diagnosed as suffering Post Traumatic Stress Disorder.		☐		Mental Anguish	↗	

Source: Copyright LexisNexis® CaseMap.

Exhibit 9.13 **TimeMap features**

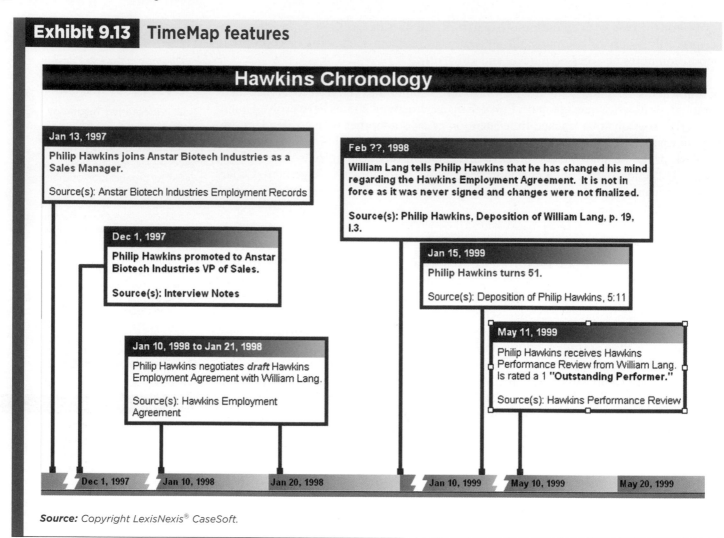

Source: *Copyright LexisNexis® CaseSoft.*

Advice *from the* Field

THE 10 AREAS OF INFORMATION YOU SHOULD ALWAYS HAVE AT YOUR FINGERTIPS

Neal R. Bevans

The ultimate paralegal resource guide is the place you save every important piece of information you have gathered in your daily work as a paralegal. This resource should contain telephone numbers, e-mails, important dates, notes about attorneys and judges and much more. The couple of hours you spend creating it will save you hundreds of hours throughout your career, give you a competitive edge and make you an invaluable member of your legal team. In fact, having all of this information at your fingertips will make you seem almost superhuman.

If putting together your own paralegal resource guide sounds unusual, it isn't. Legal professionals have been creating their own handy references for decades. When I first started out as a lawyer, a senior partner at my firm had a ragged manila file folder on his credenza containing copies of complaints he previously used in a wide variety of cases. When he needed a new complaint, he would pull out some of those old pleadings and reuse them. Your system might be a similar large file folder on your desk. Perhaps you keep everything stored in a database on your laptop, or in a network folder. Whatever method you currently use to hang on to your important information, you need to pull it all together and put it in one place. Let these 10 categories be your guide to organizing your resources and making your job easier.

1. COMPLETE CONTACT INFORMATION

Although there are a lot of telephone database programs available, including some basic software programs that came with most computers, many people find simple solutions are better.

A telephone reference is easy to create in any word processing program. The nice thing, about using Corel WordPerfect or Microsoft Word to create these tables is these programs already are running on your computer, you can keep the files open while you work on other materials, you can constantly update your entries and alphabetizing them is a breeze. For instance, Janice Johnson, a paralegal for attorney Russ Becker in Morganton N.C., said she uses a client list she originally created using WordPerfect. Her basic client list includes a chart consisting of the client's name, phone numbers, postal and e-mail addresses and notes.

Johnson said she encourages clients to contact her via e-mail. "I can check on e-mail in an extremely timely manner without having an interruption while a client is in my office," she said. "I also can respond back without getting caught on a call that ends up going entirely too long, Also, I have a word-for-word record of what information was given to the client through the e-mail contacts."

BlackBerry wireless devices are another great way to store contact information and have become very popular among law firms. Dana Martin, a paralegal at Greenbaum, Doll & McDonald, with offices in Ohio, Kentucky, Tennessee and the District of Columbia, likes the fact that with her BlackBerry, she can retrieve her e-mail anywhere, anytime. "We have Microsoft Outlook and [the BlackBerry] gives wireless access to that and my address book." She said she takes the BlackBerry with her wherever she goes.

The notes category is where your telephone reference really shines. You might not think having a notes section is important, but little details about your contacts really can help.

Denise Cunningham, a paralegal for attorney M. Lynne Osterholt in Louisville, Ky., said she lists personal information for many of her contacts. "Along with the addresses, I also put in other information, like birthdays and anniversaries."

Little, personal details, such as remembering a client's birthday or the names of a client or contact's children, can help build personal relationships and provide you with substantial help when you need it most. For instance, one client might be able to help you locate another client who is missing or unavailable. Personal relationships with courthouse personnel will put you on the inside track when it comes to things as simple as when to schedule a hearing or earn you a warning phone call when your firm forgets to file appropriate paperwork in a case.

2. ONE CENTRAL CALENDAR

Everyone knows having a calendar isn't a luxury, it's an absolute necessity. With so much to do and so little time to do it, your calendar must be accurate, easy to access and contain enough information so you can understand what you need to do. "Experts all agree you should have one calendar, not different calendars for work, for play and for the holidays. You should have one calendar for everything," said Cunningham, who has been a paralegal for almost 25 years.

Cunningham said the calendar feature on her Palm is the most used feature and it often comes in handy in court, especially when scheduling court dates. "We write in our appointments or when pleadings are due. We depend on the Palm now, although we also keep a regular calendar. I like the Palm. It's wonderful and I take it everywhere."

Martin has her BlackBerry synced to her office calendar. "If I have an event on my [office] calendar that would notify me that I had an event coming up, I would get the same notification on my BlackBerry."

Whether you use a book-sized calendar, software or the latest handheld device, the important thing is to have one central calendar that is easy to access and update.

3. COURTHOUSE CONTACTS

Whether you decide to go high-tech or stick with low-tech methods to create your paralegal resource, it should contain additional information beyond just telephone contacts and important dates. It should contain plenty of information about the courthouse, including a list of the types of information that can be found in

(continued)

each office, as well as the names of your contact people in those offices. When you find a friendly face at the courthouse, put that person's name in your courthouse reference in as many different places as possible. The next time you call that office, ask for that person.

4. ATTORNEY PECULIARITIES

No ultimate reference would be complete without an "attorney peculiarities" section. This is a section to remind you about the various idiosyncrasies of the people with whom you must interact everyday. If the attorney has a hang up about the way pleadings are prepared (such as never staple, always use paper clips) then make a running list of these preferences. These notes can save you a lot of time, effort and frustration later. If you get new employees in the firm, you also can provide this list to them.

5. JUDGE PECULIARITIES

The basic premise about keeping track of attorney peculiarities applies to judges even more. Every judge with whom I have ever worked has had a different approach to court proceedings, pleadings, drafting orders and even when and where the attorneys should stand in the courtroom. Some judges like to be referred to as "Your Honor" in every context. Some judges have a habit of leaving work everyday at 3 p.m.

Other judges think nothing of making you wait for hours outside their offices before they will sign an order. All of these characteristics should be written down for future reference. Attorneys have been doing this for years. When an attorney has a case pending before an unknown judge, he or she always will call a friend and ask about that judge's characteristics. Then the attorney adapts to that judge's approach. You should do the same thing.

One prosecutor, who preferred to remain anonymous, had a judge who would routinely appear for calendar calls in December wearing a Santa Claus cap. He would then give probation or suspended sentences to nearly every case pending. This is an important piece of information, not only for prosecutors who never wanted to have cases pending before that judge near Christmas, but also for defense attorneys who did.

6. ESSENTIAL FORMS

One of the primary reasons to create an ultimate paralegal resource is for the forms. Forms are the dirty little secret in the legal profession. Every time you come across a good form, put a copy into your paralegal reference guide. Copy the file over to your CD, store it on your flash memory card and put it someplace where you can access it again. There is another reason your forms should be stored in digital format: These days, many federal courts are requiring pleadings to be filed electronically.

"Federal courts are requiring briefs to be filed in Adobe Acrobat," Martin added. With a complete file of forms and pleadings, you will be ready to go in no time.

7. BRIEF AND MEMO BANKS

Your resource also should contain copies of briefs and memoranda used in other cases. We have all had the experience of realizing our current assignment is exactly like a brief we had to prepare last year in another case. Being able to pull up that previous brief can be a huge timesaver and be a real feather in your cap.

Although law firms often have firm-wide brief banks, keeping one of your own always is a good idea. The one time you need access to the law firm's brief bank probably will be the one time the system is down. Having your own brief bank also helps when you have to work at home and have no direct access to the firm's computer system. Your personal brief bank should contain all of the generic appellate briefs and memos you use on a daily basis. For anything more specialized than that, you always can pull it off the main network later.

8. FREQUENTLY ASKED QUESTIONS

If clients ask you the same questions repeatedly, it's time to digitize the answer and keep it available to print at a moment's notice. You might have clients who always ask how to get to the courthouse or what they should wear to court. Give them the answer in written form. It's easier for you and gives them something tangible they can review later.

Lisa Mazzonetto, a paralegal at the McDonald Law Offices in Asheville, N.C., handles domestic cases exclusively. She often gets questions about how long it takes to complete a case, what the basic rules about child visitation are, and what a client should do if he or she wishes to have a Temporary Restraining Order taken out against an unruly spouse. Mazzonetto has this information ready in writing, which frees up her time and gives clients a handy reference if they ever need it.

9. PRIVATE COMPUTER INFORMATION

In these days of Internet legal research and databases, it's important to have a handy reference containing all URLs, passwords and notes about how to access specific sites.

"There is an incredible amount of information out there that is key to day-to-day work in a law office. In my field of work, online tax records and register of deeds, [Department of Motor Vehicles] records, postal addresses, Web sites and people locator sites are very important," Mazzonetto said.

To keep all of your passwords confidential, yet easy to access, you can keep the list in a Word table and update it regularly. You also can password-protect the file to keep the wrong people from accessing it.

10. VENDOR AND SUPPLIER RECORDS

Your ultimate resource should contain information about all your office hardware and software, including vendor names, toll-free support numbers, license numbers and any other information you will need to get help if you have software or hardware problems. Keeping this information in your resource guide can save you a lot of time, especially when a service representative asks you for information contained on the computer or program that isn't currently working.

CREATING A DIGITIZED RESOURCE GUIDE

Now that you know the most important areas to include in your resource guide, you must decide in what format you will keep the information accessible. People have different preferences as to the format that suits them best. Some like to keep a binder with all the information printed out, while others prefer to keep a fully digitized version. Still others prefer a combination of both print and digital records for their resource guides.

There are a lot of different legal software programs available with which you can create a digital paralegal resource guide. They range from simple databases to complete law firm packages containing billing and accounting software, calendar features and complex databases. In high-tech offices, the calendar and case management system is available firm-wide and can be accessed by anyone on the network. However, not all law offices have taken this step into the 21st century. In situations where the office is filled with standalone systems, you will keep this information on your computer and on a backup CD.

David Moyer uses database programs to create lists of clients and documents in his freelance paralegal practice in Cuyahoga, Ohio. "I use database programs, such as Microsoft Access and Excel. I use the databases for client conflict of interest checks, to name just one example."

Use programs that have been tried and tested in the real world or in firms similar in size and structure to your firm. Mazzonetto's firm uses Time & Chaos (www.chaossoftware.com). "It acts as our daily, weekly and monthly calendar; client address book and To-Do lists. It's very inexpensive, but an incredible asset."

Johnson's North Carolina firm uses Abacus Data Systems AbacusLaw (www.abacuslaw.com), which has been around for years and functions as a client database, calendar and docketing system. "We use Abacus as a database and tracking system here at our office," Johnson said. "I don't know how we survived as well as we did before we went to this system. Today, not to have some type of program for client information and management, along with a deadline system is like living in the dark ages and asking for a malpractice suit."

Martin's firm has a separate Information Technology division. "We have a very complex piece of software that keeps track of client information, accounting, billing and case management. Our whole office is really tied together. We are a regional firm and everybody can get to the same documents."

For many firms, tailor-made programs are the best way to go. Norma Schvaneveldt, a paralegal in Chattanooga, Tenn., said her former firm, Eric Buchanan & Associates, relied on software created for the firm's specialty area of law. "We kept track of client information on the computer through a case management software program especially configured to handle Social Security cases. We also used it for our long-term disability cases. If you were out of town and needed to review a file, as long as you had Internet access, you could review any file."

THE POWER OF YOUR RESOURCE GUIDE

The smartest thing you can do with your ultimate paralegal resource is to organize it and keep it all in one place. Let everyone in the firm think you are superhuman, with an incredible memory for names, dates, telephone numbers and the myriad of other information law firms need on a daily basis. Your ultimate paralegal resource can be your secret weapon.

"Ultimate Resource Guide" by Neal R. Bevans, January/February 2005. As seen in the January/February 2005 issue of Legal Assistant Today. *Copyright 2005 James Publishing Inc. Reprinted courtesy of* Legal Assistant Today *magazine. For subscription information call (800) 394-2626, or visit www.legalassistanttoday.com.*

CHECKLIST Investigation Information Sources

Information Source	Web Address	Physical Location	Comments
Police Records–Local	www.		
Police Records–State	www.		
Birth Records	www.		
Death Records	www.		
Drivers License	www.		
Vehicle Registration	www.		
Corporate Records	www.		
Real Estate–Recorder	www.		
Real Estate–Tax	www.		
Real Estate–Land Mapping	www.		
Register of Wills	www.		
Trial Court	www.		
Federal District Court's Office	www.	Room Federal Court House	
Federal Bankruptcy Court	www.		
Occupational License	www.		
Weather Reports	www.		

Personalize this list by adding the local or regional office Web addresses, mailing addresses, and room numbers for personal visits, and comments, with any applicable contact people, costs, or hours of operation.

Concept Review *and* Reinforcement

LEGAL TERMINOLOGY

Arbitration   343
Attorney–client privilege   329
Conflict of interest   329
Ethical obligation   339
Ethical wall   329
Expert witnesses   340
Freedom of Information Act (FOIA)   348

Implied attorney–client relationship   329
Leading questions   337
Moral obligation   339
Narrative opportunity   338
Open-ended questions   338
Privileged communication   339

Restatement of the Law Third, Torts   342
Screening interview   328
Spoliation of evidence   347
Strict liability   342
Statute of limitations   329
Trial notebook   352

SUMMARY OF KEY CONCEPTS

Interviews/Interviewing

Interview	Any contact you have with a client, or prospective client is an interview.
Screening Interview	The typical first contact with a client usually is a telephone call, but some people just appear at the office door, asking for an appointment or basic information about the firm's ability or interest in taking a case.

First Meeting	1. The paralegal must be careful to make clear that he or she is a paralegal and not an attorney. 2. The paralegal must build a relationship with the individual, let him or her understand the purpose of the interview, and eliminate any barriers that would prevent obtaining the necessary information.
Implied Attorney–Client Relationship	If too much information is taken, the potential client will think he or she now has a lawyer. The courts have ruled on the side of the potential client holding that an implied attorney–client relationship exists.
Cultural Sensitivity	The culturally sensitive person is aware of the reasons for differences in the way people behave, based on religious and ethnic background and belief system.

Preparing for the Interview

Outcomes	1. The first step is to understand the outcomes desired, one of which is to instill confidence in the firm and its personnel. 2. The desired outcome of any interview is to obtain all needed, relevant facts for the case.
Physical Surroundings	Depending upon purpose of interview and the person being interviewed, a formal or an informal environment may be desired.
Dress and Appearance	Clothing worn in an interview sends a nonverbal message about the paralegal and the firm or business, and the initial impression can enhance or destroy credibility.
Communication Skills in a Multicultural Society	Interviewers must appreciate the difference of how and why individuals act and react differently.
Listening Skills	Learning to listen to "What" is being said and not just the words.
Leading Questions	Questions that suggest the desired answer. Lawyers in conducting a cross-examination in trial frequently use leading questions to force the witness to answer in a desired manner.
Open-Ended Questions	Questions designed to create a narrative opportunity for the witness.

Moral Versus Ethical Considerations

Moral Obligations	Based on one's own conscience or perceived rules of correct conduct, generally in the person's own community.
Ethical Obligations	Obligations of legal profession under ABA Model Rules of Professional Conduct, including thoroughness in representing a client.

Privileged Communications

Forms of Privileged Communications	Attorney–client communications Doctor–patient communications Priest–penitent communications Spousal communications during marriage
Waivers	Privileges can be waived, but the waiver must come from the client, the patient, the penitent, or the spouse making the statement with the belief that it is privileged.

Investigating Claims

Expert Witnesses

Definition	Expert witnesses are individuals whose background, education, and experience are such that courts will recognize them as qualified to give opinions based on a set of facts.

Freedom of Information Act (FOIA)

Definition	FOIA is a federal statute designed to open to the public the information in the possession of the federal government and its agencies.

Locating Witnesses

Directories	1. Phone books 2. Cross-reference directories 3. Membership directories
The Web	Search engines can help locate individuals, businesses, and organizations on the Internet. It is also a source of information about individuals from public sources and social networking sites.

Interviews, Investigations, and Trials

Trial Preparation	Trial preparation starts with the first client contact and the gathering of the first document. Good preparation for trial includes an assessment of how well clients and witnesses will react in depositions or in court under the pressure of cross-examination and how they will be perceived by opposing counsel, the judge, or the jury.
Case Management	Good case management requires a thoughtful process for storing, handling, examining, evaluating, and indexing every page. In the computer age, case management involves decisions on the appropriateness and potential use of electronic display technologies, as well as the fallback on traditional paper exhibit preparation.
Traditional Case Management	Traditional approaches includes the case notebook or case trial notebook.
Case and Practice Management Software	A number of software programs can be used to manage the law office and the cases within the office, in what is sometimes referred to as case management or practice management.

WORKING THE WEB

1. Use MapQuest to print out a map of the local area around your school. www.Mapquest.com
2. Use the MapQuest directions feature to obtain driving directions from your home to your school's main entrance. Don't worry if you live a long distance from your school. Print out the directions and related maps anyway.
3. Repeat items 1 and 2 using Yahoo! Maps. http://maps.yahoo.com and Mapblast from MSN www.mapblast.com. Which gives you the most information?
4. Obtain a satellite image of your school from Google Earth. http://earth.google.com. How might this be more helpful in investigating a case than the other maps available on the Internet?
5. Use Findlaw to locate an accounting expert in your state. www.findlaw.com. Print out a list of experts listed.
6. Use the LexisNexis Martindale–Hubbell website to locate an expert witness for a patent intellectual property case involving electronics. Print out a copy of the contact information you find.
7. Using the search function of your computer browser, find and print out a copy of Rule 26 of the Federal Rules of Civil Procedure.
8. Download a trial copy of TimeMap from LexisNexis on the Technology Resources Website—www.prenhall.com/goldman.
9. Prepare a timeline of the assignments and exams for the courses you currently are taking. Print a copy of the timeline.
10. Assume you have been asked to work on the case of a pedestrian struck by a car going north on the west side of the Flat Iron Building in Manhattan (New York City). Print out a satellite image of the location showing the building and the traffic flow using Earth Google at www.earth.google.com. Note that you will have to download the Earth Google viewer. Check with your instructor before downloading on a school computer. What is the proper direction of the vehicle traffic? Was the crosswalk visible? Were any other potential images available? Prepare a short report memorandum about your findings.

CRITICAL THINKING & WRITING QUESTIONS

1. What are the legal and ethical issues involved for the paralegal when the potential client says he or she just wants a quick answer to the question, "Do I have a case?" Explain fully, including references to your state statute.
2. What is a screening interview? What potential ethical and malpractice issues are involved?
3. How is the implied attorney–client relationship created? What are the critical issues for the law firm when this relationship is established?
4. Does the attorney have a duty to keep the names of clients confidential? Explain the ethical rules that apply.
5. What are the ethical and or legal implications of not advising a party that you are a paralegal and not a lawyer?
6. What is the difference between listening and hearing? Explain.
7. How can stereotypes prevent hearing what is said in interviews?
8. What effect do cultural issues play in the interview process? Explain.
9. What are the strategic reasons for using leading questions and using open-ended questions? Give an example of when each would be better used than the other type.
10. In representing a client, is it acceptable or required to ignore an ethical or moral consideration? Explain, giving an example and reason for breaching each.
11. Explain fully the ultimate reason for conducting a thorough investigation of a case. What ethical issues dictate how an investigation is to be conducted?
12. How can the Internet be used to effectively conduct an investigation of a case? Explain, using examples of traditional methods that also could be used.
13. Using the Facts in the *Palsgraf* case in Appendix A, prepare a list of witnesses who might be called in that case. Prepare an interview checklist for each of the witnesses.
14. Using the Facts in the *Palsgraf* case in Appendix A, prepare an investigative checklist, including a list of the evidence that should be gathered in the case, including a list and description of any photographs needed.
15. In conducting an interview, when would it be appropriate to dress in "Friday casual" attire?
16. Why is it important to visit the site of the accident in a motor-vehicle case being prepared for trial?
17. Under what circumstances might it be advisable for someone other than you in the firm to handle an interview with a client or witness?
18. Why would someone feel a moral obligation not to answer questions in an interview?
19. Why would a law firm hire an expert witness and not call that person as a witness at trial?
20. How useful is the Freedom of Information Act in obtaining state or local government documents? Explain.
21. Can a client restrict the use of information obtained as part of the investigation in preparation for trial even if doing so will have adverse consequences in the opinion of the attorney? Why or why not?
22. What are the issues and potential problems in using a trial notebook?
23. How does the use of case management software improve the effectiveness of the legal team? Who has the ultimate responsibility for managing the case file when using case management software?

Building Paralegal Skills

VIDEO CASE STUDIES

UPL Issue: Interviewing a Client

A lawyer is meeting with a new client when he is called away, leaving his paralegal to complete the interview.

After viewing the video case study at www.pearsonhighered.com/goldman answer the following:

1. Should the paralegal clarify his or her role as a paralegal when meeting a new client?
2. Can a paralegal give a client an opinion of whether a case exists?
3. What kind of questions should be asked in interviewing a new client?

UPL Issue: Working with a Witness

A paralegal investigating an accident case in the field creates the impression that he is acting in an official capacity requesting a fact witness to appear to give a formal statement. When the fact witness appears for the statement, he is offered compensation for his time.

After viewing the video case study at www.pearsonhighered .com/goldman answer the following:

1. Does the paralegal have a duty to divulge his role as a paralegal when interviewing potential witnesses?
2. Is it appropriate to offer compensation to a fact witness?
3. Should the same rules of ethics apply to investigators as well as to paralegals?

Zealous Representation Issue: When You Are Asked to Lie

 A paralegal has been instructed by his supervising attorney to do whatever is necessary to obtain information needed in a particular case.

After viewing the video case study at www.pearsonhighered .com/goldman answer the following:

1. What is pretexting?
2. Is it ethical to lie to obtain needed information?
3. Is a paralegal bound by ethical rules when acting as an investigator?

ETHICS ANALYSIS & DISCUSSION QUESTIONS

1. Review the opening scenario of this chapter. What are the ethical issues involved? Prepare a suggested policy, referencing the specific ethics code sections, to present to the supervising attorney of the firm. Address the issues of how to answer the phone and what should and should not be said. Your instructor may provide you with specifics, such as the fee for an initial consultation.

DEVELOPING YOUR COLLABORATION SKILLS

Working on your own or with a group of other students assigned by your instructor, review the scenario at the beginning of the chapter and the discussion that takes place between Sara and Mrs. Weiser.

1. a. Prepare a list of questions Sara should prepare before starting work. Discuss who should be asked and what action she should or should not take.
   b. What are the ethical issues facing Sara?
   c. What are the potential malpractice issues facing the firm?
2. Write a summary of the advice the group would give to Sara.

3. Form groups of three. Designate one person who will act as Sara, one as a potential client, and the third as a supervising paralegal.
   a. As the paralegal interviewer for the client who has just walked in the door of the office after being injured in an accident, use the facts of the *Palsgraf* case in the Appendix or one assigned by your instructor.
   b. As the client, you want to be sure that you have a case and that the fee is acceptable.
   c. As the supervising paralegal, comment on the interview, what issues were raised, and what you would have done differently.

PARALEGAL PORTFOLIO EXERCISE

Using the current information for your area or jurisdiction, complete the Investigation Information Source Checklist. Print out a copy for your portfolio.

LEGAL ANALYSIS & WRITING CASES

Limitations on Obtaining Information in Criminal Cases Under the FOIA

The FOIA can be a good source of information in criminal cases as well as civil litigation. As with discovery-limitation exemptions in civil cases, additional exemptions exist under the Act in criminal cases. Landano was convicted in New Jersey state court for murdering a police officer during what may have been a gang-related robbery. In an effort to support his claim in subsequent state court proceedings that his rights were violated by withholding material exculpatory evidence, he filed Freedom of Information Act requests with the Federal Bureau of Investigation (FBI) for information it had compiled in connection with the murder investigation.

When the FBI redacted some documents and withheld others, Landano filed an action, seeking disclosure of the contents of the requested files. The court held that the government is not entitled to a presumption that all sources supplying information to the FBI in the course of a criminal investigation are confidential sources within the meaning of Exemption 7(D). Further, a source should be deemed "confidential" if the source furnished information with the understanding that the FBI would not divulge the communication except to the extent it thought necessary for law-enforcement purposes.

Questions

1. Does this unfairly subject an informant to potential harassment?
2. Does limiting information unfairly prevent the defendant from receiving a fair trial?
3. Does the limitation effectively limit any usefulness in making a request under the FOIA?

Department of Justice v. Landano   508 U.S. 165 (1993)

Spoliation of Evidence In Re Daimlerchrysler Ag Securities Litigation (Usdc Del. 2003), Civil Action No. 00-993-JJF

Defendants requested relief in the form of sanctions against the plaintiff for the spoliation of evidence contending that a personal assistant to one of the Plaintiffs, Jaclyn Thode, had destroyed documents that she used to prepare a list of meetings and/or conversations prepared at the request of general counsel, who had failed to instruct her to preserve the documents used in making the list. The court in ruling on the defendant's motion concluded that sanctions were not warranted as a result of the alleged spoliation of evidence. The un-rebutted deposition testimony and affidavit of Ms. Thode establish that she discarded her handwritten notes after converting them into typewritten form, consistent with her practice in the past. Ms. Thode had no information or understanding about the substance of the litigation and no information as to the purpose of counsels' request, and thus she had no reason to alter or omit any information from the documents and that she acted unintentionally when she discarded the steno pads and pink message notes. The Court also found the Defendants did not suffer any prejudice, because they had a complete and accurate chronology of the contents of the documents that were discarded. The court cited *Son, Inc. v. Louis & Nashville R.R. Co.*, 695 F.2d 253, 259 (7th Cir.1982) (finding that destruction of evidence was not intentional where handwritten notes were discarded after being typed and person handling evidence had no reason to omit or alter necessary information).

Questions

1. Should the investigation of a case where documents include transcription include inquiry to the source of transcripted notes? Why or why not?
2. Why would not knowing the purpose of creating the notes matter in determining the potential spoliation of evidence?
3. What advice would you give to someone who has the responsibility of transcribing or keeping minutes of meetings?

WORKING WITH THE LANGUAGE OF THE COURT CASE

Department of the Interior v. Klamath Water Users Protective Association

532 U.S. 1 (2001)
Supreme Court of the United States

Read, and if assigned, brief this case. In your brief, answer the following questions.

1. What are the two conditions under which a document qualifies for exemption under the Freedom of Information Act, Exemption 5?
2. How is "agency" defined under the FOIA?
3. What is the "deliberative process" privilege? Does non-governmental litigation have an equivalent privilege?
4. What is the purpose of the deliberative process privilege?
5. What is the "general philosophy" behind the FOIA?

(continued)

Justice Souter delivered the opinion of the Court. Documents in issue here, passing between Indian Tribes and the Department of the Interior, addressed tribal interests subject to state and federal proceedings to determine water allocations. The question is whether the documents are exempt from the disclosure requirements of the Freedom of Information Act, as "intra-agency memorandums or letters" that would normally be privileged in civil discovery [5 U.S.C. § 552(b)(5)]. We hold they are not.

I

. . . [T]he Department's Bureau of Indian Affairs (Bureau) filed claims on behalf of the Klamath Tribe alone in an Oregon state-court adjudication intended to allocate water rights. Since the Bureau is responsible for administering land and water held in trust for Indian tribes . . . it consulted with the Klamath Tribe, and the two exchanged written memorandums on the appropriate scope of the claims ultimately submitted. . . . The Bureau does not, however, act as counsel for the Tribe, which has its own lawyers and has independently submitted claims on its own behalf.[1]

. . . [T]he Klamath Water Users Protective Association is a nonprofit association of water users in the Klamath River Basin, most of whom receive water from the Klamath Project, and whose interests are adverse to the tribal interests owing to scarcity of water. The Association filed a series of requests with the Bureau under the Freedom of Information Act (FOIA) [5 U.S.C. § 552] seeking access to communications between the Bureau and the Basin Tribes during the relevant time period. The Bureau turned over several documents but withheld others as exempt under the attorney work-product and deliberative process privileges. These privileges are said to be incorporated in FOIA Exemption 5, which exempts from disclosure "inter-agency or intra-agency memorandums or letters which would not be available by law to a party other than an agency in litigation with the agency" [§ 552(b)(5)]. The Association then sued the Bureau under FOIA to compel release of the documents. . . .

---

[1] The Government is "not technically acting as [the Tribes'] attorney. That is, the Tribes have their own attorneys, but the United States acts as trustee" [Tr. of Oral Arg. 5]. "The United States has also filed claims on behalf of the Project and on behalf of other Federal interests" in the Oregon adjudication [Id. At 6]. The Hoopa Valley, Karuk, and Yurok Tribes are not parties to the adjudication. [Brief for Respondent 7]

Upon request, FOIA mandates disclosure of records held by a federal agency, see 5 U.S.C. § 552, unless the documents fall within enumerated exemptions. . . .

A

Exemption 5 protects from disclosure "inter-agency or intra-agency memorandums or letters which would not be available by law to a party other than an agency in litigation with the agency" [5 U.S.C. § 552(b)(5)]. To qualify, a document must thus satisfy two conditions: Its source must be a Government agency, and it must fall within the ambit of a privilege against discovery under judicial standards that would govern litigation against the agency that holds it.

Our prior cases on Exemption 5 have addressed the second condition, incorporating civil discovery privileges. . . . So far as they might matter here, those privileges include the privilege for attorney work-product and what is sometimes called the "deliberative process" privilege. Work-product protects "mental processes of the attorney" while deliberative process covers "documents reflecting advisory opinions, recommendations and deliberations comprising part of a process by which governmental decisions and policies are formulated." The deliberative process privilege rests on the obvious realization that officials will not communicate candidly among themselves if each remark is a potential item of discovery and front-page news, and its object is to enhance "the quality of agency decisions," . . . by protecting open and frank discussion among those who make them within the Government. . . .

The point is not to protect Government secrecy pure and simple, however, and the first condition of Exemption 5 is no less important than the second; the communication must be "inter-agency or intra-agency" [5 U.S.C. § 552(b)(5)] . . . With exceptions not relevant here, "agency" means "each authority of the Government of the United States," and "includes any executive department, military department, Government corporation, Government- controlled corporation, or other establishment in the executive branch of the Government . . . , or any independent regulatory agency.". . .

Although neither the terms of the exemption nor the statutory definitions say anything about communications with outsiders, some Courts of Appeals have held that in some circumstances a document prepared outside the Government may . . . qualify . . . under Exemption 5. . . .

It is . . . possible . . . to regard as an intra-agency memorandum one that has been received by an agency, to assist it in the performance of its own functions, from a person acting in a governmentally conferred capacity other than on behalf of another agency—e.g., in a capacity as . . . consultant to the agency.

Typically, courts taking the latter view have held that the exemption extends to communications between Government agencies and outside consultants hired by them. . . . In such cases, the records submitted by outside consultants played essentially the same part in an agency's process of deliberation as documents prepared by agency personnel might have done. . . . [T]he fact about the consultant that is constant . . . is that the consultant does not represent an interest of its own, or the interest of any other client, when it advises the agency that hires it. Its only obligations are to truth and its sense of what good judgment calls for, and in those respects the consultant functions just as an employee would be expected to do.

B

. . . The Tribes, on the contrary, necessarily communicate with the Bureau with their own, albeit entirely legitimate, interests in mind. While this fact alone distinguishes tribal communications from the consultants' examples recognized by several Courts of Appeals, the distinction is even sharper, in that the Tribes are self-advocates at the expense of others seeking benefits inadequate to satisfy everyone.

. . . All of this boils down to requesting that we read an "Indian trust" exemption into the statute, a reading that is out of the question for reasons already explored. There is simply no support for the exemption in the statutory text, which we have elsewhere insisted be read strictly in order to serve FOIA's mandate of broad disclosure, which was obviously expected and intended to affect Government operations. In FOIA, after all, a new conception of Government conduct was enacted into law, "a general philosophy of full agency disclosure." Congress had to realize that not every secret under the old law would be secret under the new.

The judgment of the Court of Appeals is affirmed. *It is so ordered.*

The differences among the various circuits on the use of unpublished opinions was clarified by the Amendment to the Federal Rules of Appellate Procedure approved by the United States Supreme Court on April 12, 2006, when it approved the citation of unpublished opinions.

The proposed new Rule 32.1 as submitted for comment to Congress provided;

Proposed new Rule 32.1 permits the citation in briefs of opinions, orders, or other judicial dispositions that have been designated as "not for publication," "non-precedential," or the like and supersedes limitations imposed on such citation by circuit rules. New Rule 32.1 takes no position on whether unpublished opinions should have any precedential value, leaving that issue for the circuits to decide. The Judicial Conference amended the proposed rule so as to apply prospectively to unpublished opinions filed on or after January 1, 2007. A court may, by local rule, continue to permit or restrict citation to unpublished opinions filed before that date.

Traditional and Computerized Legal Research

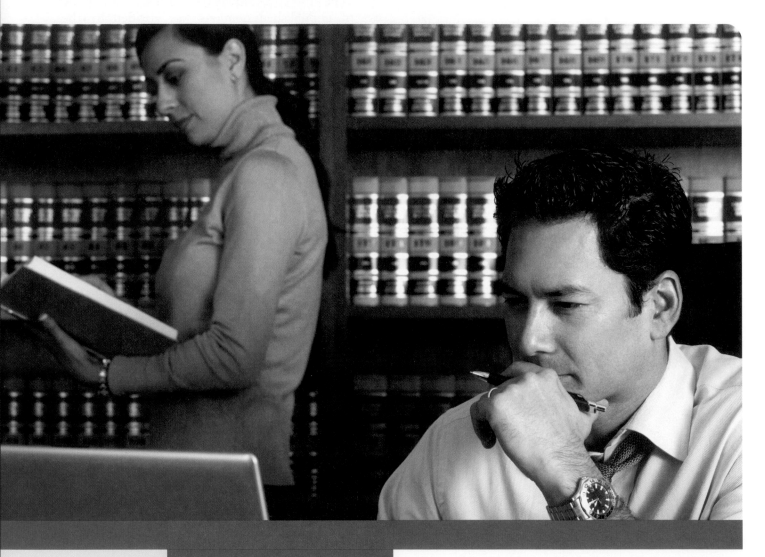

Chapter 10 Digital Resources at *www.pearsonhighered.com/goldman*

- Video Case Studies:
  - Legal Research: Are Books Obsolete?
  - Fees and Billing Issue: Using Time Effectively
  - Fees and Billing Issue: Contemporaneous Timekeeping
- Chapter Summary • Web Links • Court Opinions • Glossary • Comprehension Quizzes
- Technology Resources

> " This trial is a travesty; it's a travesty of a mockery of a sham of a mockery of a travesty of two mockeries of a sham. I move for a mistrial. "
>
> *Woody Allen, Bananas*

LEARNING OBJECTIVES

After studying this chapter, you should be able to:

1. Systematically analyze a research assignment.
2. Create a legal research plan.
3. Explain the differences between conducting legal research using a traditional paper law library and computer-based law resources.
4. Use publisher-specific and generalized legal terminology to create search queries using the computerized resources and traditional book resources.
5. Explain the differences between primary resources, secondary resources, and finding tools.
6. Explain the need for, and the methods of, updating legal research.
7. Read and use legal citations.

Paralegals at Work

As the managing partner of a large multinational law firm, Mr. Mulkeen was preparing for an executive committee meeting with the senior partners from the firm offices around the world. As with all law firms, cost saving was high on the agenda. The diverse group of partners ranged from young partners on the fast track to senior partners concerned more with developing client contacts than working on cases directly. Some firm's newer offices specialize in specific areas of law, such as the five-person health care group in a distant city to the 500-lawyer office in a major metropolitan area.

One of the major cost items on the firm's income statement was designated for the law library. Some partners wanted to expand the library, and others wanted to cut it. Mr. Mulkeen wanted to try to gain a consensus and keep as many members of the firm and support staff happy and have the necessary input from a cross-section of the firm. He invited a cross-section of the firm to a meeting to discuss the issue and get feedback. At the meeting, he indicated that the firm was at something of a crossroads in making a decision about the direction of the firm's law library, what to keep, what to get rid of, and to what to commit resources to. The cost of the space for the library, in the rental cost per square foot, was a major issue for the firm, as well as the increasing cost of law reporters and upkeep services.

Mr. Hains, a senior partner with the firm more than 25 years, reminded everyone that when he started with the firm, it didn't have as many resources as it had currently and that the law book collection was a point of pride he frequently pointed to with new clients. He said the firm could research case law in most jurisdictions where it had offices back to the first volume of the case reporters and the firm had all of the volumes of the state and federal statutes and codes. He indicated that research could be done on weekends if necessary, and pages copied out of the books. He said he didn't feel comfortable eliminating any of the hardbound volumes, and that there is something to be said for thumbing through the pages to find something even if you are not sure what you are looking for.

As one of the senior paralegals, Kathryn indicated that she didn't use the library that much, that it was mostly a place for her to spread things out. She said that she and her supervising attorney did most of their research at their desks, using computers to access the Internet and online research services. She felt limited, she said, in using the hourly-fee research services for research because the cost could not always be billed to the client and the bookkeeping people were critical about not passing on the fees. Kathryn's final point was that the litigation team was always in court or trying cases out of town, so the in-house library didn't really do the litigation team much good anyway.

Kevin, one of the long-term secretaries, expressed concern with eliminating the current library. He explained that in working for one of the general-practice attorneys, many times it was necessary to get up to speed on a new area of law and he had to browse through some of the encyclopedias and treatises just to understand the basic issues and terminology. He said he couldn't do this using the computer—at least until the issues and terminology were understood.

Consider the issues involved in this scenario as you read the chapter.

INTRODUCTION TO RESEARCH FOR THE PARALEGAL

One of the most important skills a paralegal can develop is the ability to find current relevant legal and factual information in a timely manner. Knowing where to look is just as important as knowing what to look for. Clients expect their legal counsel to use the latest law in advising them. The paralegal is expected to be able to understand the relevant facts and find the current statutory law and case law. The frequent changes in court decisions and statutory enactments present a challenge to the legal profession. Traditional law libraries consisting of printed text may not have available the latest case, statute, or regulation for days or weeks because of the time required to assemble, print, and send out updates. Internet and computer technology allows for more rapid access to the latest information. Many courts now issue the electronic version of court opinions at the same time as they distribute printed version. Instant availability is certainly a benefit if the paralegal is working on a similar case and the ethical duty of candor to the court may require the most current decision be used even before the printed version is available.

Although the ability to obtain current case law is important, in many cases an older common law case may still be precedent. The problem is that some electronic or online services, such as VersusLaw, may not have included the older cases in their database of available cases. For example, VersusLaw only includes state appellate court cases from Illinois, Pennsylvania, and Texas from 1950 and the California Court of Appeals from 1944. For that reason, being able to find the case the old-fashioned way by checking through the books is a valuable skill. When using an electronic case service such as VersusLaw, the dates of the available cases should be checked to be certain that they cover the time period needed for the search.

Legal Research

Legal research is a process for finding the answer to a legal question. In practice, the desired answer is usually the answer to a legal question involving a specific set of facts. The answer may include federal, state, and local statutory law, administrative agency regulation, and case law. Before starting, you have to have a clear picture of the legal question and what the person giving you the research assignment needs. With this in mind, proceeding in a systematic way will save time and ensure that all research avenues have been considered. A systematic approach begins with planning the research and knowing what issues must be addressed and covered.

Legal research The process for finding the answer to a legal question.

Creating a Research Plan

The first step in legal research is setting up a research plan. The research plan helps to focus on the issues, sources, and methods for finding the answer and controlling law. A few basic questions should be considered in setting up the research plan.

1. What is the issue or legal question?
    a statute or regulation, or
    a legal question involving a set of facts

Paralegals *in* Practice

PARALEGAL PROFILE
Ann G. Hill

Returning to school after spending over ten years as a legal secretary, Ann G. Hill earned a paralegal certificate at Illinois State University in 2000. She also earned the Insurance Institute of America Certificate in General Insurance in 2003, and obtained her paralegal certification through the National Association of Legal Assistants in 2004. Ann is currently a legal assistant for a major insurance company in Bloomington, Illinois. In her spare time, she serves as a pro bono paralegal providing legal assistance to Social Security clients of the local legal aid society.

I currently specialize in records/information management, legal research, and project management. Legal research is often similar to putting together a massive jigsaw puzzle. When researching a specific issue, I initially review applicable statutes and case law. Then, I look for agency rules, since agencies often have statutory authority to enact rules

that carry the force of law. When researching contracts issues, I examine project funding since funds are often tied to federal and state grant programs with many stipulations. I also look at professional organizations' Web sites for legal information relevant to their particular field.

A good research paralegal must be able to "step back," view the issue from different perspectives, and analyze the data. I try to identify factors that could impact the outcome of the legal opinion. I then ask the client more questions. Since clients are not always aware of relevant factors and potential issues, you must be able to "think outside the box" in order to know what questions will prove most helpful to the case.

During the research process, I take advantage of credible research already completed. I use a variety of online search services including Westlaw®, Lexis®, and PACER. Law journal and legal news articles posted on the Internet often contain information about specific laws, regulations, and cases relevant to a particular issue. No matter what research methods are used, I always "shepardize" case law, use annotated statutes when possible, and strive to be thorough.

To be truly successful in the paralegal profession, continue to pursue a variety of learning opportunities. For example, consider helping to fill the need for legal services among low income families and senior citizens who cannot afford private attorneys. By partnering with a legal aid society, you can gain valuable experience while serving your community.

2. What is the appropriate search terminology?
   words
   phrases
   legal terms
   popular names of statutes or cases
3. What type of research material is available?
   traditional
   computer
4. What jurisdiction or jurisdictions are involved?
   federal
   state
   local
5. What is the controlling law?
   statutory
   regulatory
   case law
6. What are the types of resources to be used?
   primary
   secondary
   finding tools
7. Where is the needed research material located?
   in-house traditional materials
   fee-based legal services
   free Web-based remote libraries

Using checklists for each search, such as the Research Plan: Words and Phrases, and Research Sources checklists shown later in the chapter, is a good way to be sure all appropriate terms and sources have been used and a record of the results prepared for follow-up by oneself or a colleague who takes over the research.

What Is the Issue or Legal Question?

Legal research is like a puzzle to be solved. Understanding the question is essential. A lot of time may be wasted if the paralegal takes the wrong research path, because the framer of the question has not been clear or the researcher is not clear on the information needed. At times the question is framed with some specificity:

Find the statute . . .
Get me the case of . . .

More often, however, the question is:

Based on these facts, what is the law about . . . ?

Researchers first must understand the facts that apply to the case they are asked to research. Unlike the cases in textbooks and court opinions, the **relevant facts** and the specific area of substantive or procedural law in real life usually are not so clear. The initial interview information may have focused on what the client or the interviewer thought was the applicable law. Further research may indicate other areas of law that must be considered.

For example, what may seem to be a simple rear-end automobile accident caused by negligent driving may be in actuality a case of product liability caused by a manufacturing defect by the automobile manufacturer or the supplier of a defectively manufactured part, such as the tires. To analyze a case properly, the researcher must know the factual elements of a negligence case and of a product liability case. The researcher must understand the facts of the case at hand. Some facts are crucial to the case; others may or may not be important or have no legal significance.

Relevant facts Facts crucial to the case and having legal significance.

What Is the Appropriate Search Terminology?

Knowing the legal terminology used in the indexes of the research materials is critical. Publishers of legal materials do not always use the same words or legal terms to index the same rules of law. For example, one publisher uses the term "infant" to identify people under the age of majority that another publisher indexes under "minor." Consider the legal question: "What are the contract rights of a person under the age of majority?" Using "minor" will not produce the desired results in some published materials where the information is listed under "infant." Print research materials require finding material based on a printed index of individual words as selected by the editors of the service.

Computer research is not as dependent on an index of terms and may require a completely different set of words or legal terms. Most computer research allows for searches of words found in the documents using a text search of requested words in the **search query**, in which the computer looks through the entire document for every instance of the desired words.

Search query Specific words used in a computerized search.

It is important to keep in mind the differences in terminology used in legal and factual research. Finding cases and statutes requires the use of the legal terminology used by the courts, legal professionals, and authors of legal treatises. These words and phrases may not be the most useful in finding factual information on the Internet. For example, it was noted above that some legal sources use the terms "infant" or "minor" when discussing people under the age of majority. Searches for information on under-age drinking by those under the age of majority may require different terms as used in newspaper articles. Or, statutes may use the terms "driving under the influence" while newspaper accounts and laypersons would probably use the terms "drunk driving" or "driving while intoxicated."

What Type of Research Material Is Available?

Traditionally, the law library has consisted of books in paper form, case reporters, legal encyclopedias, legal dictionaries, and a host of finding tools including paper card indexes and digests. Some modern law libraries are completely electronic, using online computer services such as Westlaw, Lexis, and Loislaw. Other libraries combine traditional paper-based materials and electronic materials.

Paralegal students who grew up in the era of the ever-available online research sources provided by some high schools and colleges frequently ask why they need to learn how to use a traditional "paper" law library. In the working world, not every office has access to all the latest computer resources, or the same ones. Ask anyone who has tried a case out of town or in a different courthouse and had to check an unexpected case or resource about the availability of resources or lack of them.

At times, paralegals accompany the lawyer to court. During the trial, they may be asked to slip out of the courtroom and conduct a quick bit of legal research. They may not be able to use a computer for legal research. In some courthouses, computers cannot be connected to outgoing phone lines for security reasons, and even cell phones are retained at the security desk. Other courthouses do not have a public computer terminal available in the law library. In these situations, the paralegal must conduct the research quickly and accurately using traditional book methods. In short, the paralegal must be able to find the information needed when the familiar resources are not available.

Computer research requires the use of appropriate search words to complete a successful search. As with any profession, the legal profession has its own vocabulary. These include words defined by the courts over the years to have specific meaning when used in a legal sense. For example, the legal definition of the term "holder" is "a person to whom a negotiable instrument has been properly negotiated." To the layperson, it may mean people holding something in their hands—not necessarily a negotiable instrument, or with any legal formality. Other words have a different meaning for a number of different groups. For example, to the medical community, the word "head" means the top of a person's body; to the sailor it means a bathroom; and to a bartender it means the top of a beer.

People in all areas of life develop words and phrases that help them understand their fields of interest. In creating laws, legislatures use language in special ways that may not be clear to laypersons or even legal researchers who are not accustomed to the terminology of the lawmakers. The people who create indexes to legal references, such as the professional indexers from the Library of Congress and the indexers of the numerous private legal publications, each have their own vocabulary and method of indexing material. For example, West Publishing Company editors index material using the 450 West Digest Topics (see Exhibit 10.1).

Unless the paralegal understands what items are included under each index classification, it is difficult to find the items even with a fast computer search engine. The word "holder," for example, is listed in the *West Digest* index as being under "Statutes," but the word "holder" as defined above, is actually found under the West Digest Topic "Bills and Notes." *Black's Law Dictionary* defines the same word in the language of the negotiable instrument law. Using the West Topic heading "Bills and Notes" and "holder" in a computer search will not return cases of negotiable instrument holders. But using the terms "negotiable instrument" and "holder" as the search words in a computer search will yield the desired result. Because paralegals cannot be sure whether the research will be done using a traditional paper library or a computer search, they must understand how each resource files the information.

Knowing how to use both traditional and computer methods, and recognizing the strengths and weaknesses of each system, is important in conducting searches. Traditional research may be better when general background research is needed and the paralegal isn't familiar with an area of law. Indexing systems are grouped by concept, and once paralegals get into the right area of law they can browse easily. The ability to flip pages back and forth when they are generally in the right area is particularly helpful in statutory research, as many of the computer-based systems perform that task slowly, if at all—and assuming the paralegal can figure out how the index has been developed to create the computer search term. In contrast, for a narrow, fact-based question, or if the research already has a citation or case name to work from, computer-based research usually is the best approach. Success in research depends on recognizing the best tools for a specific problem and using them efficiently.

What Jurisdiction or Jurisdictions Are Involved?

Research may involve federal, state, or local law. Some questions point to a certain jurisdiction—for example, "What is the age of majority in Florida?" Others are not as clear, "What law controls the situation of an unruly passenger on a flight from Los Angeles to Philadelphia?" Here the paralegal must consider jurisdictional issues related to California, Pennsylvania, and federal statutes. Or consider the case of the driver from Georgia who is driving a truck belonging to a South Carolina company and has an accident in Alabama. The legal team working on that case might want to know the law in each jurisdiction before deciding where to file suit. Focusing on a single jurisdiction or a minimum number of jurisdictions reduces the number of traditional volumes of books necessary and saves online computer search time.

What Is the Controlling Law?

The controlling law is found in primary sources of the law—statutes, regulations, and case law. Knowing which set of materials to use, the statutes of the jurisdiction, the regulation of a certain administrative agency, or the courts of a specific jurisdiction will save time in doing the research. Possibly, the controlling law is a local city, county, or parish ordinance, such as a zoning ordinance or a local plumbing code. Irrelevant sources can be eliminated from consideration and the source of the needed material located if not available onsite or online.

Exhibit 10.1 West Digest Topics and their numerical designations

1 Abandoned and Lost Property	59 Boundaries	103 Counterfeiting	160 Exchanges
2 Abatement and Revival	60 Bounties	104 Counties	161 Execution
4 Abortion and Birth Control	61 Breach of Marriage Promise	105 Court Commissioners	162 Executors and Administrators
5 Absentees	62 Breach of the Peace	106 Courts (see also Topic 170b Federal Courts)	163 Exemptions
6 Abstracts of Title	63 Bribery	107 Covenant, Action of	164 Explosives
7 Accession	64 Bridges	108 Covenants	165 Extortion and Threats
8 Accord and Satisfaction	65 Brokers	108a Credit Reporting Agencies	166 Extradition and Detainers
9 Account	66 Building and Loan Associations	110 Criminal Law	167 Factors
10 Account, Action on	67 Burglary	111 Crops	168 False Imprisonment
11 Account Stated	68 Canals	113 Customs and Usages	169 False Personation
11a Accountants	69 Cancellation of Instruments	114 Customs Duties	170 False Pretenses
12 Acknowledgment	70 Carriers	115 Damages	170a Federal Civil Procedure
13 Action	71 Cemeteries	116 Dead Bodies	170b Federal Courts
14 Action on the Case	72 Census	117 Death	171 Fences
15 Adjoining Landowners	73 Certiorari	117g Debt, Action of	172 Ferries
15a Administrative Law and Procedure	74 Champerty and Maintenance	117t Debtor and Creditor	174 Fines
16 Admiralty	75 Charities	118a Declaratory Judgment	175 Fires
17 Adoption	76 Chattel Mortgages	119 Dedication	176 Fish
18 Adulteration	76a Chemical Dependents	120 Deeds	177 Fixtures
19 Adultery	76h Children Out-of-Wedlock	122a Deposits and Escrows	178 Food
20 Adverse Possession	77 Citizens	123 Deposits in Court	179 Forcible Entry and Detainer
21 Affidavits	78 Civil Rights	124 Descent and Distribution	180 Forfeitures
23 Agriculture	79 Clerks of Courts	125 Detectives	181 Forgery
24 Aliens	80 Clubs	126 Detinue	183 Franchises
25 Alteration of Instruments	81 Colleges and Universities	129 Disorderly Conduct	184 Fraud
26 Ambassadors and Consuls	82 Collision	130 Disorderly House	185 Frauds, Statute of
27 Amicus Curiae	83 Commerce	131 District and Prosecuting Attorneys	186 Fraudulent Conveyances
28 Animals	83h Commodity Futures Trading Regulation	132 District of Columbia	187 Game
29 Annuities	84 Common Lands	133 Disturbance of Public Assemblage	188 Gaming
30 Appeal and Error	85 Common Law	134 Divorce	189 Garnishment
31 Appearance	88 Compounding Offenses	135 Domicile	190 Gas
33 Arbitration	89 Compromise and Settlement	135h Double Jeopardy	191 Gifts
34 Armed Services	89a Condominium	136 Dower and Curtesy	192 Good Will
35 Arrest	90 Confusion of Goods	137 Drains	193 Grand Jury
36 Arson	91 Conspiracy	138 Drugs and Narcotics	195 Guaranty
37 Assault and Battery	92 Constitutional Law	141 Easements	196 Guardian and Ward
38 Assignments	92b Consumer Credit	142 Ejectment	197 Habeas Corpus
40 Assistance, Writ of	92h Consumer Protection	143 Election of Remedies	198 Hawkers and Peddlers
41 Associations	93 Contempt	144 Elections	199 Health and Environment
42 Assumpsit, Action of	95 Contracts	145 Electricity	200 Highways
43 Asylums	96 Contribution	146 Embezzlement	201 Holidays
44 Attachment	97 Conversion	148 Eminent Domain	202 Homestead
45 Attorney and Client	98 Convicts	148a Employers' Liability	203 Homicide
46 Attorney General	99 Copyrights and Intellectual Property	149 Entry, Writ of	204 Hospitals
47 Auctions and Auctioneers	100 Coroners	150 Equity	205 Husband and Wife
48 Audita Querela	101 Corporations	151 Escape	205h Implied and Constructive Contracts
48a Automobiles	102 Costs	152 Escheat	206 Improvements
48b Aviation		154 Estates in Property	207 Incest
49 Bail		156 Estoppel	208 Indemnity
50 Bailment		157 Evidence	209 Indians
51 Bankruptcy		158 Exceptions, Bill of	
52 Banks and Banking		159 Exchange of Property	
54 Beneficial Associations			
55 Bigamy			
56 Bills and Notes			
58 Bonds			

(continued)

Exhibit 10.1   West Digest Topics and their numerical designations (continued)

210	Indictment and Information	269	Names	320	Railroads	369	Sunday
211	Infants	270	Navigable Waters	321	Rape	370	Supersedeas
212	Injunction	271	Ne Exeat	322	Real Actions	371	Taxation
213	Innkeepers	272	Negligence	323	Receivers	372	Telecommunications
216	Inspection	273	Neutrality Laws	324	Receiving Stolen Goods	373	Tenancy in Common
217	Insurance	274	Newspapers			374	Tender
218	Insurrection and Sedition	275	New Trial	325	Recognizances	375	Territories
		276	Notaries	326	Records	376	Theaters and Shows
219	Interest	277	Notice	327	Reference	378	Time
220	Internal Revenue	278	Novation	328	Reformation of Instruments	379	Torts
221	International Law	279	Nuisance			380	Towage
222	Interpleader	280	Oath	330	Registers of Deeds	381	Towns
223	Intoxicating Liquors	281	Obscenity	331	Release	382	Trade Regulation
224	Joint Adventures	282	Obstructing Justice	332	Religious Societies	384	Treason
225	Joint-Stock Companies and Business Trusts	283	Officers and Public Employees	333	Remainders	385	Treaties
				334	Removal of Cases	386	Trespass
		284	Pardon and Parole	335	Replevin	387	Trespass to Try Title
226	Joint Tenancy	285	Parent and Child	336	Reports	388	Trial
227	Judges	286	Parliamentary Law	337	Rescue	389	Trover and Conversion
228	Judgment	287	Parties	338	Reversions	390	Trusts
229	Judicial Sales	288	Partition	339	Review	391	Turnpikes and Toll Roads
230	Jury	289	Partnership	340	Rewards		
231	Justices of the Peace	290	Party Walls	341	Riot	392	Undertakings
232	Kidnapping	291	Patents	342	Robbery	393	United States
232a	Labor Relations	292	Paupers	343	Sales	394	United States Magistrates
233	Landlord and Tenant	294	Payment	344	Salvage		
234	Larceny	295	Penalties	345	Schools	395	United States Marshals
235	Levees and Flood Control	296	Pensions	346	Scire Facias		
		297	Perjury	347	Seals	396	Unlawful Assembly
236	Lewdness	298	Perpetuities	348	Seamen	396a	Urban Railroads
237	Libel and Slander	299	Physicians and Surgeons	349	Searches and Seizures	398	Usury
238	Licenses					399	Vagrancy
239	Liens	300	Pilots	349a	Secured Transactions	400	Vendor and Purchaser
240	Life Estates	302	Pleading	349b	Securities Regulation		
241	Limitation of Actions	303	Pledges	350	Seduction	401	Venue
242	Lis Pendens	304	Poisons	351	Sequestration	402	War and National Emergency
245	Logs and Logging	305	Possessory Warrant	352	Set-Off and Counterclaim		
246	Lost Instruments	306	Postal Service			403	Warehousemen
247	Lotteries	307	Powers	353	Sheriffs and Constables	404	Waste
248	Malicious Mischief	307a	Pretrial Procedure	354	Shipping	405	Waters and Water Courses
249	Malicious Prosecution	308	Principal and Agent	355	Signatures		
250	Mandamus	309	Principal and Surety	356	Slaves	406	Weapons
251	Manufactures	310	Prisons	356a	Social Security and Public Welfare	407	Weights and Measures
252	Maritime Liens	311	Private Roads				
253	Marriage	313	Process	357	Sodomy	408	Wharves
255	Master and Servant	313a	Products Liability	358	Specific Performance	409	Wills
256	Mayhem	314	Prohibition	359	Spendthrifts	410	Witnesses
257	Mechanics' Liens	315	Property	360	States	411	Woods and Forests
257a	Mental Health	316	Prostitution	361	Statutes	413	Workers' Compensation
258a	Military Justice	316a	Public Contracts	362	Steam		
259	Militia	317	Public Lands	363	Stipulations	414	Zoning and Planning
260	Mines and Minerals	317a	Public Utilities	365	Submission of Controversy	450	Merit Systems Protection (Merit Systems Protection Board Reporter)
265	Monopolies	318	Quieting Title				
266	Mortgages	319	Quo Warranto	366	Subrogation		
267	Motions	319h	Racketeer Influenced and Corrupt Organizations	367	Subscriptions		
268	Municipal Corporations			368	Suicide		

What Are the Types of Resources to Use?

Law libraries usually have primary and secondary sources of the law. A **primary source** is the actual law itself, which includes the statutes and the case law. The cases you have been briefing in this text are primary sources. **Secondary sources** are not the laws themselves but, instead, are writings about the law, such as legal encyclopedias and digests. This textbook is a secondary source. A third set of resources is referred to as finding tools—publications, such as digests or the *Index to Legal Periodicals*, used to find primary and secondary sources. Frequently, sources contain both secondary sources and **finding tools** in one publication, such as the *American Law Reports*. Some services combine all three into one service or publication. Exhibit 10.2 delineates primary and secondary sources and finding tools.

Ultimately, the primary sources of law are the ones that will be used in preparing the legal memo or brief. Secondary sources are useful, efficient ways to get an overview of an area of law or learn the terminology used in a certain field of law of which you are not familiar. The torts specialist suddenly asked to research an issue related to a different area of law, such as negotiable instruments, may be lost trying to remember the terminology and rules applicable from courses taken long ago.

Secondary sources such as encyclopedias can supply a quick review and point the research to the appropriate primary sources such as the *Uniform Commercial Code* as adopted by the state in question. Legal dictionaries frequently list cases that have defined the words in legal terms that can be a starting point for case research.

Primary source of law The actual law itself.

Secondary source of law Writings about the law.

Finding tools Publications used to find primary and secondary sources.

Where Is the Needed Research Material Located?

It would be nice to have a complete law school level print and electronic library available onsite to use for legal research. The reality is that law libraries are costly to acquire and maintain. The cost of the materials can run into the hundreds of dollars per volume, and the annual upkeep services not much less for pocket parts, supplemental volumes, and new case reporters. Space in office complexes is another factor. Office space is expensive, and as a library grows, more of the expensive floor space must be used for books instead of people. Finally the cost of filing the updates and keeping the space orderly must be considered. If the collection is large enough, a full-time librarian may be needed. In smaller offices these tasks take the time of paralegals that could be spent performing billable services for clients.

These cost and availability issues have spurred the adoption of electronic libraries such as the fee-based online services provided by Loislaw, Lexis, Westlaw, and VersusLaw, and the free online services provided by some colleges and universities such as the Cornell School of Law. Virtually all primary material is available online. Some certain proprietary secondary materials, such as encyclopedias, are available from some sources and not others. Depending on the resources needed to complete an assignment, the paralegal may have to locate the needed material at a remote library such as a bar association library or a law school library.

Exhibit 10.2	Research materials	
Primary Sources	**Secondary Sources**	**Finding Tools**
Constitutions	Legal dictionaries	Digests
Statutes	Legal encyclopedias	Citators
Court decisions	Treatises	Indexes
Common-law cases	Law reviews	
Administrative regulations	Textbooks	
Ordinances	Legal periodicals	
Court rules		

Creating a List of Research Terms

The paralegal should create a list of words for online searches and a separate list for traditional print sources. The list should be updated as the paralegal performs research, adding or deleting words and phrases and annotating the list with citations for future research. The word list should be developed from the facts of the question, the parties, locations, case-specific goods and services, and status and relationships between them.

Consider the case of the off-duty police officer who has just come from a doctor's visit and has been given a medication to reduce his blood pressure. He is involved in a rear-end collision with a van of school children returning from a fundraiser selling candy. The driver is one of the mothers, who is also a teacher in the school. A skateboarder darts in front of one of the vehicles. Using a Research Plan: Words and Phrases checklist is a good way to put together a list of the words and phrases to be searched.

What are some of the words and terms with which to start researching the issue of liability? As with most cases, each person has multiple roles or status that must be considered: teacher, parent, driver, police officer, student, child, principal, agent of school, agent of other parents, patient.

Further, the situation may have been caused by any of a number of factors, road conditions, and weather issues, time of day, speed, medical issues, carelessness, and distracted

CHECKLIST Research Plan: Words and Phrases

Concepts and Issues	Generic Words and Phrases	Text-Based Research Terms	Computer-Based Research Terms
Persons			
Status			
Relationship			
Occupation			
Group			
Class			
Item(s) Involved			
Location(s)			
Subject Matter			
Jurisdiction			
Federal			
State			
City			
Locality			
Cause of Action			
Tort			
Contract			
Family Law			
Commercial			
Relief Sought			
Injunction			
Damages			
Compensatory			
Punitive			
Mandamus			
Defenses			

driver. And what about the vehicles' braking ability, recalls of vehicles, and airbag deployment issues? Obviously not every issue relates in every case. Before starting the research, the researcher must identify the relevant terms that apply to the case being researched. The time spent creating the list will save time chasing dead ends or irrelevant issues. In creating the word list, the researcher should think of words, legal terms, and phrases and consider alternatives to those words—synonyms, antonyms, and related terms. Appropriate language may be found using secondary sources and finding tools such as legal dictionaries and legal encyclopedias and treatises.

Executing the Research Plan

Having laid out a plan of action based on answers to the preliminary questions, the research plan now can be executed. As with the execution of any plan, detours can be expected. The law is in a constant evolutionary state as new statutes are enacted and new case interpretations are handed down. During the research process, the researcher must look for changes and potential changes from pending legislation and cases on appeal. Word lists and citation must be updated and new search paths followed.

The time spent creating the list of terms, phrases, and search terms will save time when the research plan is executed. In looking for a statute, knowing the subject matter of the desired law, such as "blood alcohol level for driving," or the popular name of the law, such as "Sarbanes-Oxley," will save time by focusing the search on a specific statutory index or popular name index.

Not every search term will result in a successful search; some may lead to other search terms. The research plan should be executed in a systematic way using a checklist of the terms and research materials. The search is updated with citations, both successful and unsuccessful. When the inevitable circular search brings the researcher back to a previous result, this indicates a dead end, so the researcher can proceed on a more fruitful path.

When the time comes to finalize the research in a written document, the researcher will have the citation references and will not have to go back and find the material again. In the event of additional, similar research assignments, the researcher will have a ready reference to pick up the search and proceed quickly, using relevant terms and citations.

Finding the Law

Finding "the law" should be an easy thing to accomplish. We go to the original source and look at it. But what is the original source, and how is it located in a modern law library? The law is found in the statutes and regulations passed by the **legislative branch** and the case law in court decisions of the **judicial branch**. In the United States, laws are created at the federal, state, and local levels. At the federal legislative level laws are passed by the United States Congress, which is a **bicameral** legislative body—meaning that there are two legislative houses, the House of Representatives and the Senate. At the state government level, all of the state legislatures are bicameral except Nebraska. Local governing bodies include cities, towns, and boroughs. At the judicial level, both federal and state courts create case law through their issuing of court decisions. The law also is found in the regulations enacted by administrative agencies as a result of the authority granted to them by the legislative branch of government, whether federal, state, or local.

Generally, the assignment is to find the current controlling law. Occasionally the research assignment is to find the law that was in control at a point in the past, such as what the blood alcohol limit was last year when the client was cited for driving under the influence. In this case, we might start by asking:

Is there a statute?

Are there administrative regulations?

Is there case law on point?

Legislative branch The part of the government that consists of Congress (the Senate and the House of Representatives).

Judicial branch The court system.

Bicameral In the American system a legislature of a house of representatives and a senate.

CHECKLIST Research

Primary Sources	Secondary Sources
Case ☐ Name ☐ Citation	Encyclopedia—National ☐ Name ☐ Key or descriptive word
Federal statute ☐ Federal citation ☐ Popular name	Encyclopedia—State ☐ Name ☐ Key or descriptive word
State (name) ☐ State citation ☐ Popular name	Treatises ☐ Name ☐ Citation
Local jurisdiction name ☐ Local citation ☐ Popular name	Restatement of law ☐ Name ☐ Citation
Administrative regulations ☐ Federal agency name ☐ Citation	Periodicals ☐ Citation
State agency name ☐ Citation	Practice Books ☐ Name ☐ Citation
Local agency name ☐ Citation	Dictionary ☐ Name
Constitution ☐ Federal citation ☐ State citation	Digest ☐ Name ☐ Citation

If there is a statute in the applicable jurisdiction, it will be controlling. Regulations enacted to enforce the statute also will be controlling subject to compliance with the statutory authority under which they are enacted. Case law may exist to clarify and explain the law under the facts of the cases decided by the courts.

Primary Sources and Authority

Primary sources are the law. Primary sources include constitutions, both federal and state. Primary law includes statutes enacted by the legislative branch of government pursuant to the constitutional limitations and the regulations of the administrative agencies established by the legislature to carry out the statutory enactments. Court rules and court decisions are sources of primary law from the judicial branch of government. Exhibit 10.3 lists the primary sources at the federal level.

Mandatory and Persuasive Authority

Mandatory authority Court decisions that are binding on all lower courts.

Start with primary sources that are **mandatory authority**. Primary authority is the law itself. It is the constitution, the enactments of the legislative branch of government, and the case law decisions of the judicial branch of government. Mandatory authority is legal authority that the courts must follow. In addition to statutes and administrative regulations and ordinances, it includes case law from higher courts. The highest court in the United States is the United States Supreme Court. The decisions of the Supreme Court are mandatory on all lesser federal and state courts. The decisions of the highest appellate court of a state are mandatory authority for all lesser courts of that state.

Persuasive authority Court decisions the court is not required to follow but are well reasoned and from a respected court.

If mandatory authority cannot be found, the researcher should search for **persuasive authority**, authority the courts are not required to follow but is from a respected source and well reasoned. Decisions of some state courts traditionally have

WHEN ARE COURT DECISIONS PRECEDENTS?

Courts may issue published or unpublished opinions. A **published opinion** is a court's written explanation of its decision on a case intended to be relied upon as a statement of the law based on the facts of the case. In some cases, the court will issue an informal statement of its ruling, an **unpublished opinion**, which is intended to apply only to the parties before the court and to the very narrow issue of the particular case based on the specific facts before the court. Unlike published opinions, the courts generally do not intend that unpublished opinions be used as precedent in other cases. It should be made clear that unpublished opinions are not secret opinions, many are available online and others are available from the clerk's office.

There is a controversy with regard to the use of unpublished opinions in other court proceedings. In reviewing the issue, the Court in Anastasoff made the following observations:

Before concluding, we wish to indicate what this case is not about. It is not about whether opinions should be published, whether that means printed in a book or available in some other accessible form to the public in general. Courts may decide, for one reason or another, that some of their cases are not important enough to take up pages in a printed report. Such decisions may be eminently practical and defensible, but in our view they have nothing to do with the authoritative effect of any court decision.

The question presented here is not whether opinions ought to be published, but whether they ought to have precedential effect, whether published or not. We point out, in addition, that "unpublished" in this context has never meant "secret." So far as we are aware, every opinion and every order of any court in this country, at least of any appellate court, is available to the public. You may have to walk into a clerk's office and pay a per-page fee, but you can get the opinion if you want it. Indeed, most appellate courts now make their opinions, whether labeled "published" or not, available to anyone on line. Anastasoff v. U.S. *223 F. 3d 898 (8th cir. 2000)*

Following the publication of the initial opinion, the Anastasoff court declared the issues in the case, about recovery of tax payments, as moot since the taxpayer received her refund, Stating

. . . Here, the case having become moot, the appropriate and customary treatment is to vacate our previous opinion and judgment, remand to the District Court, and direct that Court to vacate its judgment as moot. We now take exactly that action. The constitutionality of that portion of Rule 28A(i) which says that unpublished opinions have no precedential effect remains an open question in this Circuit. . . . Anastasoff v. U.S. No. 99-3917EM, (Dec. 18, 2000)

The controversy has centered on the right of lawyers to use the unpublished opinions in argument to the court. The matter has been resolved with the passage of Rule 32.1 Citing Judicial Dispositions, which permits the inclusion of those published after January 1, 2007.

---

been looked at as being so well reasoned that other courts in other states have been persuaded to follow the legal reasoning in deciding cases for which their own state did not have any previously decided cases or statutes on point.

A good example of a persuasive opinion is that of Justice Cardozo in the New York Court of Appeals case of *Palsgraf* v. *Long Island Railroad Company*, 248 N.Y. 339 (1928) (see Appendix A, How To Brief a Case). Many courts, even today, find the logic and reasoning of Justice Cardozo persuasive and he is frequently quoted by courts in other states.

Constitutions

The United States Constitution is the ultimate primary law that sets the guidelines, limits, and authority of the federal government and the state governments. The individual state constitutions are the ultimate law for the individual state, and set the guidelines, the limits, and the authority of the state government and the local governing bodies of the state. The constitutions are primary sources, the original writing or primary source of law. Finding the United States Constitution is probably the easiest task in legal research. It is reproduced in many publications, including many textbooks, is available in virtually every public library, and is easily available on the Internet from many sources including the National Archives. Finding the Constitution for individual states however, is not as easy. Although some are posted on general-interest websites, most require access to specialty legal research websites, or to the paper version, generally found in the bound volumes of the state statutes.

Published opinion A court's written explanation of its decision on a case intended to be relied upon as a statement of the law based on the facts of the case.

Unpublished opinions Cases which the court does not feel have precedential effect and are limited to a specific set of facts.

 Web Exploration

View a high-resolution version of the original copy of the U.S. Constitution at www.archives.gov.

Exhibit 10.3 Federal primary sources

Source	Jurisdiction	Location	URL
Constitution	United States Constitution	U.S. Const. art 1, § 10,cl.3	http://www.gpoaccess.gov/constitution/index.html
Statutes	United States Code	19 U.S.C. § 2411 (2004)	http://www.gpoaccess.gov/uscode/index.html
Administrative Regulations	Code of Federal Regulations	31 C.F.R. § 515.329 (2002)	http://www.gpoaccess.gov/cfr/index.html
Highest Appellate Court	US Supreme Court	*Brown v. Bd. Of Educ.,* 349 U.S. 294 (1955)	http://www.supremecourtus.gov/opinions/opinions.html
Intermediate Appellate Court	US Court of Appeals	*McHenry v. Fla. Bar,* 21 F.3d 1038 (11th Cir. 1994)	http://www.uscourts.gov/courtlinks/
Trial Court	US District Court	*U.S. v. Chairse,* 18 F. Supp. 2d 1021 (D. Minn. 1998)	http://www.uscourts.gov/courtlinks/
Federal Rules of Civil Procedure		Fed. R. Civ. P. 26	http://www.law.cornell.edu/rules/frcp/
Federal Rules of Criminal Procedure		Fed. R. Crim. P. 21(a)	http://www.law.cornell.edu/rules/frcrmp/

Source: Citations in ALWD Citation format. Copyright © ALWD. Reprinted with permission.

Web Exploration

Read the latest U.S. Supreme Court opinion at http://www .supremecourtus.gov. Visit the homepage of the Legal Information Institute at Cornell University Law School to see the information provided. www.cornell .lii.edu.

Bench opinion The initial version of a decision issued from the bench of the court.

Slip opinion A copy of the opinion sent to the printer.

Case syllabus In a court opinion a headnote for the convenience of the reader.

Headnotes The syllabus or summary of the points of law prepared by the editorial staff of a publisher.

Statutes

Statutes enacted by the legislative branch of government are primary sources of the law. The statute of the United States—the United States Code—is available online from a number of free sources including the U.S. Government Printing Office. Many states currently make available their state statutes online through an official state website. Until a few years ago, this free-access source was generally limited to state legislators. Caution should still be the rule in using Web-based resources. Some unofficial sites have posted websites that appear to be an official primary source of the law but in reality are not complete or up-to-date.

Court Decisions

Court decisions also are primary authority. The U.S. Supreme Court and some federal courts provide their current opinions and decisions online. Notably, the Legal Information Institute at Cornell University provides free access to the U.S. Supreme Court opinions, as well as many others. Other court decisions generally are not available from free Web sources and require the use of a paid subscription or fee-based services such as Lexis, Westlaw, Loislaw, and VersusLaw. Exhibit 10.4 shows the homepage of U.S. Courts with judiciary links.

Courts such as the U.S. Supreme Court issue opinions from the "bench" called **bench opinions** and a **slip opinion** that is sent for printing. This second version may contain corrections in the bench opinion. See the U.S. Supreme Court comments on the difference in Exhibit 10.5.

The actual court language is a primary source of the law. The **case syllabus**, summaries, interpretations, or abstracts of the points of law presented by the editorial staff of the publishers of the case law, usually called **headnotes**, are not the primary source of law; rather they are explanations, interpretations, or comments that help the reader understand the legal concepts. As such, they are secondary sources. Note the cautionary

Exhibit 10.4	U.S. Courts website

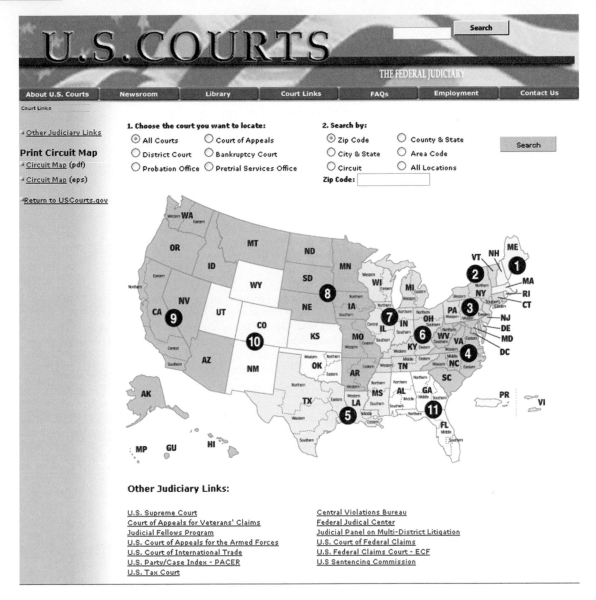

Source: *Administrative Office of the U.S. Courts, Washington, D.C.*

comment in the syllabus of the Supreme Court case in Exhibit 10.6. Contrast the syllabus of the case with the opinion of the court in Exhibit 10.7.

Legal dictionaries and encyclopedias use headnotes—short, single-concept definitions and summaries, to provide basic information. When doing research, it should be kept in mind that these short "snippets" are taken out of the context of the case in which they were presented. None of the factual or procedural background is presented that caused the statement to be made.

Taking court statements out of the context in which the case was presented and relying on headnotes or summaries can present many problems for the researcher—the most obvious of which is accuracy. Was the headnote or summary copied correctly from the final version of the opinion? Judges have been known to correct errors in the language of opinions. Did the editor writing the note use the final version of the opinion? More important—does this statement accurately reflect the majority view, or does

 Web Exploration

Search and view full text of Supreme Court decisions issued between 1937 and 1975 at www.fedworld.gov/supcourt.

Exhibit 10.5 Supreme Court explanation on differences between bench and slip opinions

Supreme Court of the United States

| HOME | ABOUT THE COURT | DOCKET | ORAL ARGUMENTS | MERITS BRIEFS | BAR ADMISSIONS | COURT RULES |
| CASE HANDLING GUIDES | OPINIONS | ORDERS | VISITING THE COURT | PUBLIC INFORMATION | JOBS | LINKS |

2005 TERM OPINIONS OF THE COURT

Slip Opinions, *Per Curiams* (PC), and Original Case Decrees (D)

The "slip" opinion is the second version of an opinion. It is sent to the printer later in the day on which the "bench" opinion is released by the Court. Each slip opinion has the same elements as the bench opinion--majority or plurality opinion, concurrences or dissents, and a prefatory syllabus--but may contain corrections not appearing in the bench opinion. The slip opinions collected here are those issued during October Term 2005 (October 3, 2005, through October 1, 2006). These opinions are posted on this Website within hours after the bench opinions are issued and will remain posted until the opinions are published in a bound volume of the United States Reports. For further information, see Column Header Definitions and the file entitled Information About Opinions.

Caution: These electronic opinions may contain computer-generated errors or other deviations from the official printed slip opinion pamphlets. Moreover, a slip opinion is replaced within a few months by a paginated version of the case in the preliminary print, and--one year after the issuance of that print--by the final version of the case in a U. S. Reports bound volume. In case of discrepancies between the print and electronic versions of a slip opinion, the print version controls. In case of discrepancies between the slip opinion and any later official version of the opinion, the later version controls.

Source: Supreme Court of the United States.

Exhibit 10.6 Sample of U.S. Supreme Court syllabus

Syllabus

NOTE: Where it is feasible, a syllabus (headnote) will be released, as is being done in connection with this case, at the time the opinion is issued.
The syllabus constitutes no part of the opinion of the Court but has been prepared by the Reporter of Decisions for the convenience of the reader.
See United States v. Detroit Timber & Lumber Co., 200 U.S. 321, 337.

SUPREME COURT OF THE UNITED STATES

ROPER, SUPERINTENDENT, POTOSI CORRECTIONAL CENTER v. SIMMONS

CERTIORARI TO THE SUPREME COURT OF MISSOURI

No. 03—633. Argued October 13, 2004-Decided March 1, 2005

At age 17, respondent Simmons planned and committed a capital murder. After he had turned 18, he was sentenced to death. His direct appeal and subsequent petitions for state and federal postconviction relief were rejected. This Court then held, in *Atkins* v. *Virginia*, 536 U.S. 304, that the Eighth Amendment, applicable to the States through the Fourteenth Amendment, prohibits the execution of a mentally retarded person. Simmons filed a new petition for state postconviction relief, arguing that *Atkins'* reasoning established that the Constitution prohibits the execution of a juvenile who was under 18 when he committed his crime. The Missouri Supreme Court agreed and set aside Simmons' death sentence in favor of life imprisonment without eligibility for release. It held that, although *Stanford* v. *Kentucky*, 492 U.S. 361, rejected the proposition that the Constitution bars capital punishment for juvenile offenders younger than 18, a national consensus has developed against the execution of those offenders since *Stanford*.

Held: The Eighth and Fourteenth Amendments forbid imposition of the death penalty on offenders who were under the age of 18 when their crimes were committed. Pp. 6–25.

(a) The Eighth Amendment's prohibition against "cruel and unusual punishments" must be interpreted according to its text, by considering history,

Source: Supreme Court of the United States

Exhibit 10.7 Sample opinion of the U.S. Supreme Court

Opinion of the Court

NOTICE: This opinion is subject to formal revision before publication in the preliminary print of the United States Reports. Readers are requested to notify the Reporter of Decisions, Supreme Court of the United States, Washington, D. C. 20543, of any typographical or other formal errors, in order that corrections may be made before the preliminary print goes to press.

SUPREME COURT OF THE UNITED STATES

No. 03—633

DONALD P. ROPER, SUPERINTENDENT, POTOSI CORRECTIONAL CENTER, PETITIONER v. CHRISTOPHER SIMMONS

ON WRIT OF CERTIORARI TO THE SUPREME COURT OF MISSOURI

[March 1, 2005]

Justice Kennedy delivered the opinion of the Court.

This case requires us to address, for the second time in a decade and a half, whether it is permissible under the Eighth and <u>Fourteenth Amendment</u>s to the Constitution of the United States to execute a juvenile offender who was older than 15 but younger than 18 when he committed a capital crime. In *Stanford* v. *Kentucky*, <u>492 U.S. 361</u> (1989), a divided Court rejected the proposition that the Constitution bars capital punishment for juvenile offenders in this age group. We reconsider the question.

I

At the age of 17, when he was still a junior in high school, Christopher Simmons, the respondent here, committed murder. About nine months later, after he had turned 18, he was tried and sentenced to death. There is little doubt that Simmons was the instigator of the crime. Before its commission Simmons said he wanted to murder someone. In chilling, callous terms he talked about his plan, discussing it for the most part with two friends, Charles Benjamin and John Tessmer, then aged 15 and 16 respectively. Simmons proposed to commit burglary and murder by breaking and entering, tying up a

Source: Supreme Court of the United States

it reflect a minority or dissenting view? Was it the actual decision on the point of law before the court and, therefore, the "**holding**" of the court having precedential weight, or merely comments having no precedential authority because they are not related directly to the court decision and, therefore, are what are referred to as **dicta**. Contrast the headnote and the full court opinion in the case in Exhibit 10.8.

Doing legal research requires finding the most current and accurate statement of the legislative enactments and of the court. Presenting editorial headnotes, judges' dicta, or a dissenting opinion as accurate current legal authority is a potential career-ending course of action. The members of your legal team may rely on the potentially erroneous information and prepare the case, its prosecution or defense strategy, on the inaccurate information. Notwithstanding the potential effect on the trial of the case, at best it may result in a severe reprimand or dismissal from employment. Presenting the erroneous information to the court is an ethical violation of the duty of candor toward the tribunal under Rule 3.3 of the Model Rules of Professional Conduct.

It does not matter to the court that it was prepared by someone other than the attorney presenting the case, the brief, or the oral argument. It is a breach of the duty of candor to the court by the attorney.

Holding The actual decision on the specific point of law the court was asked to decide.

Dicta Court comments on issues not directly related to the holding and therefore not having precedential effect.

Exhibit 10.8 Regional reporter sample page

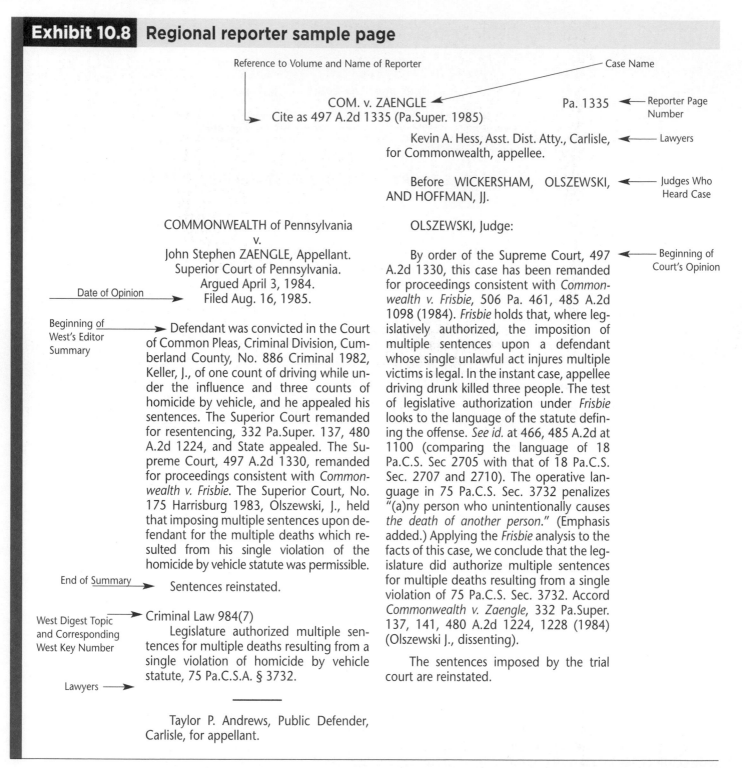

Reference to Volume and Name of Reporter

Case Name

COM. v. ZAENGLE

Cite as 497 A.2d 1335 (Pa.Super. 1985)

Pa. 1335

Reporter Page Number

Kevin A. Hess, Asst. Dist. Atty., Carlisle, for Commonwealth, appellee.

Lawyers

Before WICKERSHAM, OLSZEWSKI, AND HOFFMAN, JJ.

Judges Who Heard Case

COMMONWEALTH of Pennsylvania
v.
John Stephen ZAENGLE, Appellant.
Superior Court of Pennsylvania.
Argued April 3, 1984.
Filed Aug. 16, 1985.

Date of Opinion

OLSZEWSKI, Judge:

Beginning of West's Editor Summary

Defendant was convicted in the Court of Common Pleas, Criminal Division, Cumberland County, No. 886 Criminal 1982, Keller, J., of one count of driving while under the influence and three counts of homicide by vehicle, and he appealed his sentences. The Superior Court remanded for resentencing, 332 Pa.Super. 137, 480 A.2d 1224, and State appealed. The Supreme Court, 497 A.2d 1330, remanded for proceedings consistent with *Commonwealth v. Frisbie*. The Superior Court, No. 175 Harrisburg 1983, Olszewski, J., held that imposing multiple sentences upon defendant for the multiple deaths which resulted from his single violation of the homicide by vehicle statute was permissible.

End of Summary

Sentences reinstated.

West Digest Topic and Corresponding West Key Number

Criminal Law 984(7)

Legislature authorized multiple sentences for multiple deaths resulting from a single violation of homicide by vehicle statute, 75 Pa.C.S.A. § 3732.

Lawyers

Taylor P. Andrews, Public Defender, Carlisle, for appellant.

Beginning of Court's Opinion

By order of the Supreme Court, 497 A.2d 1330, this case has been remanded for proceedings consistent with *Commonwealth v. Frisbie*, 506 Pa. 461, 485 A.2d 1098 (1984). *Frisbie* holds that, where legislatively authorized, the imposition of multiple sentences upon a defendant whose single unlawful act injures multiple victims is legal. In the instant case, appellee driving drunk killed three people. The test of legislative authorization under *Frisbie* looks to the language of the statute defining the offense. *See id.* at 466, 485 A.2d at 1100 (comparing the language of 18 Pa.C.S. Sec 2705 with that of 18 Pa.C.S. Sec. 2707 and 2710). The operative language in 75 Pa.C.S. Sec. 3732 penalizes "(a)ny person who unintentionally causes *the death of another person.*" (Emphasis added.) Applying the *Frisbie* analysis to the facts of this case, we conclude that the legislature did authorize multiple sentences for multiple deaths resulting from a single violation of 75 Pa.C.S. Sec. 3732. Accord *Commonwealth v. Zaengle*, 332 Pa.Super. 137, 141, 480 A.2d 1224, 1228 (1984) (Olszewski J., dissenting).

The sentences imposed by the trial court are reinstated.

This is not to say that dissenting opinions and dicta may not be presented or argued to the court. Many of the finest jurists have issued dissenting views that became the law in future cases. And dicta in another case may well be a valid argument in a current case. The researcher's duty is to make clear the source of the information, whether from a primary or a secondary source. Sometimes it is not clear what is an enactment of the court as stated by one court:

What exactly constitutes "dicta" is hotly contested and judges often disagree about what is or is not dicta in a particular case. See *United States v. Johnson*, 256 F.3d 895, 914–16

(9th Cir. 2001) (en banc) (Kozinski, J., concurring). In Johnson, Judge Kozinski explained that, "where a panel confronts an issue germane to the eventual resolution of the case, and resolves it after reasoned consideration in a published opinion, that ruling becomes the law of the circuit, regardless of whether doing so is necessary in some strict logical sense." Id. at 914; accord *Cetacean Cmty. v. Bush*, 386 F.3d 1169,1173 (9th Cir. 2004) (quoting Johnson); *Miranda B. v. Kitzhaber*, 328 F.3d 1181, 1186 (9th Cir. 2003) (per curiam) (same).

Only "[w]here it is clear that a statement is made casually and without analysis, where the statement is uttered in passing without due consideration of the alternatives, or where it is merely a prelude to another legal issue that commands the panel's full attention, it may be appropriate to re-visit the issue in a later case." Johnson, 256 F.3d at 915. Nevertheless, "any such reconsideration should be done cautiously and rarely—only where the later panel is convinced that the earlier panel did not make a deliberate decision to adopt the rule of law it announced." Id. If, however, "it is clear that a majority of the panel has focused on the legal issue presented by the case before it and made a deliberate decision to resolve the issue, that ruling becomes the law of the circuit and can only be overturned by an en banc court or by the Supreme Court." Id. at 916; see also Cetacean Cmty., 386 F.3d at 1173; Miranda B., 328 F.3d at 1186.

This understanding of binding circuit authority was further articulated in *Barapind v. Enomoto*, 400 F.3d 744 (9th Cir. 2005) (en banc) (per curiam), where we said that when a panel has "addressed [an] issue and decided it in an opinion joined in relevant part by a majority of the panel," the panel's decision becomes "law of the circuit." Id. at 750-51 (footnote omitted). PADILLA v. LEVER, 03-56259 (9TH CIR. 2005)

Secondary Sources

Secondary sources explain the law. Trying to understand a new area of law can be difficult. Secondary sources are useful sources of information to learn about the history of an area of law, the issues involved, and in some situations the direction the law may be taking. A secondary source may be the editorial headnotes of a case or an in-depth scholarly interpretation, such as a treatise, a law review, or an article in a scholarly journal or other periodical.

Legal Dictionaries

Legal dictionaries, as opposed to general English or other specialized dictionaries, define words and phrases as used in the law. The "law," as with most professions, trades, and occupations, has developed its own specialized vocabulary. Each specialized area of law further develops a specialized terminology. Lawyers in specialty fields, such as antitrust law, use terms that have developed specialized meaning through case decisions such as the antitrust law term "tying arrangement," used to describe the situation in which one product can be purchased only with another product. This term comes from the 1947 antitrust case of *International Salt v. United States*, which held that a patent is presumed to give the patent holder "market power" (another legal term), making it illegal to "tie the sale of the patented product to the sale of another." Without an understanding of the basic terminology and legal concepts, it is hard to conduct proper legal search using either traditional books or computer-based services. Exhibit 10.9 is a sample page from *Black's Law Dictionary*, illustrating the term "tying."

Secondary Sources–Legal Encyclopedias

Legal encyclopedias, like legal dictionaries, can provide the needed background to understand an area enough to start the research. They can provide an overview of the concepts and history of an area of law, the legal issues involved, and the terminology. The annotations (lists of case citations) can provide a starting point for case law research. National encyclopedias such as *Corpus Juris Secundum* (CJS) and *American*

Exhibit 10.9 *Black's Law Dictionary,* sample page

confesses in open court. U.S. Const. Art. IV, § 2, cl. 2.

tying, *adj. Antitrust.* Of or relating to an arrangement whereby a seller sells a product to a buyer only if the buyer purchases another product from the seller <tying agreement>.

tying arrangement. *Antitrust.* **1.** A seller's agreement to sell one product or service only if the buyer also buys a different product or service. The product or service that the buyer wants to buy is known as the *tying product* or *tying service*; the different product or service that the seller insists on selling is known as the *tied product* or *tied service.* Tying arrangements may be illegal under the Sherman or Clayton Act if their effect is too anticompetitive. **2.** A seller's refusal to sell one product or

service unless the buyer also buys a different product or service. — Also termed *tying agreement; tie-in; tie-in arrangement.* Cf. RECIPROCAL DEALING.

tying product. See TYING ARRANGEMENT (1).

tyranny, *n.* Arbitrary or despotic government; the severe and autocratic exercise of sovereign power, whether vested constitutionally in one ruler or usurped by that ruler by breaking down the division and distribution of governmental powers. — **tyrannical, tyrannous**, *adj.*

tyrant, *n.* A sovereign or ruler, legitimate or not, who wields power unjustly and arbitrarily to oppress the citizenry; a despot.

Source: Black's Law Dictionary, *7e, 1995. Reprinted with permission of Thomson/West Publishing.*

Jurisprudence (AM JUR) provide cases from all jurisdictions for reference and research. Exhibit 10.10 is a sample page from *American Jurisprudence.*

State-specific encyclopedias generally limit case references or citations to that jurisdiction. Where the research is on a new area of law for the jurisdiction, the national coverage may provide information on persuasive authority from other jurisdictions. Exhibit 10.11 is a sample page from a secondary source, *Corpus Juris Secundum,* a national legal encyclopedia.

Treatises, Law Reviews, and Legal Periodicals

Some secondary sources are authoritative or of sufficient scholarly value to be persuasive to the court. For example, the treatise on Torts by Prosser is frequently used in argument as persuasive and accepted as such by most courts. In new areas of the law, such as cyber law, or emerging and changing areas such as privacy rights, courts frequently welcome a well-reasoned scholarly article from a law review or other legal journal that makes a clear and convincing argument with well-researched and reasoned thought. In some instances, these articles are like the *amicus curia* briefs submitted to the court by interested parties that have no actual standing as a party but have a clear interest in the outcome. Examples are Planned Parenthood and a national right-to-life organization in abortion-rights cases.

Amicus curia Briefs submitted by interested parties, as a "friend of the court," who do not have standing in the action.

Finding Tools

Finding tools help to "find" the law. Finding the right case, statute, or regulation can be difficult, particularly if the correct term or phrase is not used to conduct the search. As mentioned previously, West Publishing might use the phrase "Bills and Notes" and another publisher might use the term "holder" to refer to the same cases and material on negotiable instruments.

Indexes and Digests

Indexes and digests offer a way of finding the material.

Citator An index of cases.

1. Indexes and citators. Among the more useful sets of indexes and **citators** are those that cross-reference material. Some indexes use the commonly used or popular name of a case or statute to provide the citation or

Exhibit 10.10 *American Jurisprudence,* **sample page**

is infected with a contagious disease[90] or has been dangerously exposed to such a disease.[91]

§ 317. —Children infected with the AIDS virus

Acquired Immune Deficiency Syndrome (AIDS) disables victims of the disease by collapsing their immune systems, making them unable to fight infection.[92] State education authorities, rather than local school authorities, are the appropriate parties to promulgate regulations concerning the right of AIDS-infected children to attend public school, since the state's power to regulate on the issue, inferable from its broad grant of authority to supervise the schools, pre-empts any rights of local authorities under their statutory discretion to exclude children from school to prevent the spread of contagious disease.[93]

◆ *Caution:* State statutes and local health regulations concerning contagious diseases in general, which make no specific reference to AIDS, do not apply to the decision whether AIDS-infected students should be allowed to attend public school.[94]

Procedures for determining whether AIDS-infected children should be excluded from a public school have withstood a due process challenge, one court having upheld the constitutionality of a plan which provided for an impartial decision by a medical panel, proper notice, and the opportunity to call and cross-examine witnesses.[95] However, distinguishing between students known to be infected with AIDS and students who were unidentified carriers of AIDS-related complex or asymptomatic carriers is constitutionally unacceptable since the proposed exclusion from public school of only the known AIDS-infected children constitutes an equal protection violation.[96]

◆ *Practice Guide:* Numerous organizations, both medical and educational, have formulated guidelines on when AIDS carriers should be segregated from the rest of the population. In cases concerning the right of a student with AIDS to attend school, courts have received evidence of the guidelines

90. Kenney v. Gurley, 208 Ala. 623, 95 So. 34, 26 A.L.R. 813 (1923); Nutt v. Board of Education of City of Goodland, Sherman County, 128 Kan. 507, 278 P. 1065 (1929).

As to the right to public education, generally, see §§ 242 et seq.

Forms: Answer—Defense—School district providing home teaching to student with contagious or infectious disease pending determination whether student's attendance at school would be danger to others. 22 Am Jur Pl & Pr Forms (Rev), Schools, Form 182.

91. Bright v. Beard, 132 Minn. 375, 157 N.W. 501 (1916).

92. Board of Educ. of City of Plainfield, Union County v. Cooperman, 105 N.J. 587, 523 A.2d 655, 38 Ed. Law Rep. 607, 60 A.L.R.4th 1 (1987).

Law Reviews: AIDS in public schools: Resolved issues and continuing controversy, 24 J Law and Educ 1:69 (1995).

Students with AIDS: Protecting an infected child's right to a classroom education and

developing a school's AIDS policy, 40 S Dakota LR 1:72 (1995).

93. Board of Educ. of City of Plainfield, Union County v. Cooperman, 105 N.J. 587, 523 A.2d 655, 38 Ed. Law Rep. 607, 60 A.L.R.4th 1 (1987).

94. District 27 Community School Bd. by Granirer v. Board of Educ. of City of New York, 130 Misc. 2d 398, 502 N.Y.S.2d 325, 32 Ed. Law Rep. 740 (Sup. Ct. 1986).

95. Board of Educ. of City of Plainfield, Union County v. Cooperman, 105 N.J. 587, 523 A.2d 655, 38 Ed. Law Rep. 607, 60 A.L.R.4th 1 (1987).

Forms: Complaint, petition, or declaration—To enjoin expulsion of student who tested positive for AIDS virus—By guardian. 22 Am Jur Pl & Pr Forms (Rev), Schools, Form 177.

96. District 27 Community School Bd. by Granirer v. Board of Educ. of City of New York, 130 Misc. 2d 398, 502 N.Y.S.2d 325, 32 Ed. Law Rep. 740 (Sup. Ct. 1986).

537

Source: American Jurisprudence, 2e, 2000. Reprinted with permission of Thomson/West Publishing.

Exhibit 10.11 **Page from *Corpus Juris Secundum,* a legal encyclopedia**

§§ 58–59　SOCIAL SECURITY　　　　　81 C.J.S.

individual who died fully insured,[65] and have physical or mental impairments which, under regulations promulgated for the purpose, are deemed to be of such severity as to preclude engaging in any gainful activity.[66] The requirements for obtaining disability benefits by such persons are more restrictive than requirements for the insured individual himself.[67] The physical impairment necessary to a finding of disability is placed on a level of severity to be determined administratively,[68] and the regulations adopted to carry out the statutory provisions have been upheld.[69]

A claim for disability is judged solely by medical criteria,[70] without regard to non-medical factors[71] such as age, education, and work experience,[72] in contrast to the considerations given to an insured individual's age, education, and work experience, in determining his ability to engage in substantial gainful activity, as discussed supra § 56. An individual cannot qualify for disability insurance benefits unless suffering from an impairment listed in the appendix to the regulations applicable to disabilities, or from one or more unlisted impairments that singly or in combination are the medical equivalent of a listed impairment.[73] The benefits are to be paid only for a disabling medical impairment,[74] and not simply for the inability to obtain employment.[75]

§ 59.　Benefits of Disabled Child

A disabled child of an insured individual who is, or would have been, eligible for social security benefits, may be entitled to disability insurance benefits.

Research Note

Status as child eligible for benefits under statute generally is discussed supra § 41.

Library References

Social Security and Public Welfare ⬤123, 140.5.

Under the provisions of the Social Security Act,[76] disabled children of retired or disabled insured individuals, and of insured individuals who have died, may be paid benefits if they have been disabled since before they reached twenty-two years of age, and if they meet the other conditions of eligibility.[77] The purpose of the provision is to provide a measure of income and security to those who have lost a wage-earner on whom they depended,[78] or to provide support for the dependents of a disabled wage earner,[79] and not to replace only that support enjoyed by the child prior to the onset of disability.[80] The liberal perspective of the Act applies to the award of children's disability benefits.[81]

In order to be entitled to recover benefits under this provision, the child must have been disabled,[82] as defined elsewhere in the Act,[83] prior to attaining a specified age,[84] and must be un-

65. U.S.—Sullivan v. Weinberger, C.A. Ga., 493 F.2d 855, certiorari denied 95 S.Ct. 1958, 421 U.S. 967, 44 L.Ed.2d 455.

66. U.S.—Wokojance v. Weinberger, C.A.Ohio, 513 F.2d 210, certiorari denied 96 S.Ct. 106, 423 U.S. 856, 46 L.Ed.2d 82.

Hendrix v. Finch, D.C.S.C., 310 F. Supp. 513.

Baby sitting; domestic work
U.S.—Dixon v. Weinberger, C.A.Ga., 495 F.2d 202.

Time impairment manifest
U.S.—Sullivan v. Weinberger, C.A.Ga., 493 F.2d 855, certiorari denied 95 S.Ct. 1958, 421 U.S. 967, 44 L.Ed.2d 455.

67. U.S.—Wokojance v. Weinberger, C.A.Ohio, 513 F.2d 210, certiorari denied 96 S.Ct. 106, 423 U.S. 856, 46 L.Ed.2d 82.

Solis v. U. S. Secretary of Health, Ed. and Welfare, D.C.Puerto Rico, 372 F.Supp. 1223—Truss v. Richardson, D. C.Mich., 338 F.Supp. 741—Nickles v. Richardson, D.C.S.C., 326 F.Supp. 777.

68. U.S.—Gillock v. Richardson, D.C. Kan., 322 F.Supp. 354.

69. U.S.—Sullivan v. Weinberger, C.A. Ga., 493 F.2d 855, certiorari denied 95 S.Ct. 1958, 421 U.S. 967, 44 L.Ed.2d 455.

Gunter v. Richardson, D.C.Ark., 335 F.Supp. 907—Zanoviak v. Finch, D.C. Pa., 314 F.Supp. 1152—Frasier v. Finch, D.C.Ala., 313 F.Supp. 160, affirmed, C. A., 434 F.2d 597.

70. U.S.—Wokojance v. Weinberger, C. A.Ohio, 513 F.2d 210, certiorari denied 96 S.Ct. 106, 423 U.S. 856, 46 L.Ed.2d 82.

71. U.S.—Sullivan v. Weinberger, C.A. Ga., 493 F.2d 855, certiorari denied 95 S.Ct. 1958, 421 U.S. 967, 44 L.Ed.2d 455.

72. U.S.—Gillock v. Richardson, D.C. Kan., 322 F.Supp. 354.

73. U.S.—Wokojance v. Weinberger, C. A.Ohio, 513 F.2d 210, certiorari denied 96 S.Ct. 106, 423 U.S. 856, 46 L.Ed.2d 82.

Gillock v. Richardson, D.C.Kan., 322 F.Supp. 354—Hendrix v. Finch, D.C.S. C., 310 F.Supp. 513.

74. U.S.—Sullivan v. Weinberger, C.A. Ga., 493 F.2d 855, certiorari denied 95 S.Ct. 1958, 421 U.S. 967, 44 L.Ed.2d 455.

75. U.S.—Sullivan v. Weinberger, C.A. Ga., 493 F.2d 855, certiorari denied 95 S.Ct. 1958, 421 U.S. 967, 44 L.Ed.2d 455.

76. 42 U.S.C.A. § 402(d).

77. U.S.—Lowe v. Finch, D.C.Va., 297 F.Supp. 667—Blevins v. Fleming, D.C. Ark., 180 F.Supp. 287.

78. U.S.—Ziskin v. Weinberger, D.C. Ohio, 379 F.Supp. 124.

79. U.S.—Jimenez v. Weinberger, Ill., 94 S.Ct. 2496, 417 U.S. 628, 41 L.Ed.2d 363, appeal after remand, C.A., 523 F.2d 689, certiorari denied 96 S.Ct. 3200.

80. U.S.—Jimenez v. Weinberger, Ill., 94 S.Ct. 2496, 417 U.S. 628, 41 L.Ed.2d 363, appeal after remand, C.A., 523 F.2d 689, certiorari denied 96 S.Ct. 3200.

81. U.S.—Ziskin v. Weinberger, D.C. Ohio, 379 F.Supp. 124.

82. U.S.—Ziskin v. Weinberger, D.C. Ohio, 379 F.Supp. 124.

83. 42 U.S.C.A. § 423.

84. U.S.—Ziskin v. Weinberger, D.C. Ohio, 379 F.Supp. 124—Moon v. Richardson, D.C.Va., 345 F.Supp. 1182.

Source: From Corpus Juris Secundum, © The West Group, a Thomson Company. Reproduced with permission.

reference to the original source. For example, the commonly used or popular name for the statement of rights read to criminal defendants when arrested is "Miranda Rights." Using a popular name index provides the citation to the case in which the U.S. Supreme Court made mandatory the reading of these rights to defendants—*Miranda v Arizona* 384 US 436 (1966).

2. Legal digests provide lists of cases in subject topic format, with cases generally in chronological order from the earliest to the latest. Digests do not offer the detailed analysis found in encyclopedias. Exhibit 10.12 is a sample page from *West's Digest*.

Personal Research Strategy

Over time, each paralegal develops a personal search strategy based on the nature of the problem or issue to be researched and the resources available. When a legal issue is well defined and a specific case or statute is in question, it may be possible to start with the original primary source. More likely, though, the research assignment will be less defined and may be just a set of facts describing a situation. A possible area of relevant law may be suggested. This could be a specific area of law such as "driving too fast for conditions," or a general area of law such as "personal injury from an automobile accident."

The facts will determine the area of law. If the paralegal is unfamiliar with the area of law, the relevant facts may not be obvious. Secondary sources provide a good reference source to acquire a general understanding about an area of law. As the paralegal learns more about the specifics of the area of law and the essential elements of causes of actions, the relevant facts should become clearer. One of the advantages of using the traditional book form of research is the ability to flip pages back and forth and scan many items that can lead to a specific point of law. This is sometimes referred to as "the serendipity of research."

Computer search engines can lead to specific case law and statutes. The challenge is in how to construct the search query or question. If you do not know the relevant facts to include, the resulting report may not be accurate. Computers, for the most part, are limited to finding only the things the search query specifically asks for. Learning the relevant facts to create the proper question may involve using the print resources first to determine the relevant facts or the proper terminology. For example, in a fair-use doctrine case of alleged copyright violation, is the status of the alleged violator as a nonprofit organization relevant?

Always verify that the law and cases cited in the research and memo of law is current law or current authority. Look for pending cases and legislation that might change the answer to the legal question. Look in legal journals, periodicals, and legal newspapers, as well as newspapers of general circulation, for cases that are on appeal that involve the same legal issues. Check the legislative services for pending legislation that may have an impact on the case. Research that is concerned with giving clients advice on future actions may depend on knowing the changes that may occur that will change the basic parameters of the law. For example, can I have a smoking section in my new restaurant? Are the tax rates for estate planning going to change next year?

A Final Word on Executing the Legal Research Plan

We emphasize this final piece of advice: Know when to ask for help. Everyone on the legal team who has done legal research has at one time or another hit a research dead end. Sometimes taking a few minutes to ask a question will yield the "magic" word, term, or phrase that will result in the answer you seek.

Exhibit 10.12 *West's Federal Digest*, sample page

CRIMINAL LAW

SUBJECTS INCLUDED

Acts and omissions in violation of law punishable as offenses against the public

Nature and elements of crime in general

Capacity to commit crime, nature and extent of responsibility therefore in general, and responsibility of principals, accessories, etc.

Jurisdiction over and place of prosecution of crimes

Limitation of time for prosecution

Preliminary complaints, warrants, examination and commitment

Arraignment and pleas

Evidence in criminal proceedings

Trial, and acquittal or conviction

Motions in arrest of judgment and for new trial

Judgment or sentence and final commitment

Review on appeal, writ of error or certiorari

Prosecution and punishment of successive offenses or of habitual criminals

Modes of punishment and prevention of crime in general

SUBJECTS EXCLUDED AND COVERED BY OTHER TOPICS

Arrest, see ARREST

Bail, see BAIL

Constitutional rights and privileges of accused not peculiar to matters within scope of this topic, see CONSTITUTIONAL LAW, INDICTMENT AND INFORMATION, JURY, SEARCHES AND SEIZURES, WITNESSES and other specific topics

Convicts, disabilities and regulation, see CONVICTS

Costs in criminal prosecutions, see COSTS

Extradition of fugitives, see EXTRADITION AND DETAINERS

Fines in general, see FINES

Grand juries and inquisitions by them, see GRAND JURY

Habeas corpus to obtain discharge from imprisonment, see HABEAS CORPUS

Included offenses, conviction under indictment for broader offense, see INDICTMENT AND INFORMATION

Indictments or other accusations, see INDICTMENT AND INFORMATION and specific topics relating to particular offenses

Injunction against commission of crime, see INJUNCTION

Judgment of acquittal, conviction or sentence, effect as adjudication, see JUDGMENT

Jury trial, right to and waiver, and qualifications and selection of jurors, see JURY

Juvenile offenders, special rules and proceedings, see INFANTS

Source: *Federal Digest,* West's Federal Digest, *4e. Reprinted with permission of Thomson/West Publishing.*

Using Printed Legal Reference Works

Most legal references have a set of common features. They generally have a section, usually in the introduction, that explains the coverage and how to use the specific book or service. This usually includes the abbreviations used throughout the work (see Exhibit 10.13), and the method of pagination—for example, standard page numbering or use of section numbers. A table of contents at the beginning of the work (see Exhibit 10.14) provides a general list of major topics. The index at the end of the work provides the detailed coverage. Multivolume sets might have a separate set of volumes containing the index. Each volume also might contain an index for the specific volume.

Most legal words also contain a table of cases that are mentioned in the text. This is a useful feature when a case seems to be on point or relevant and the paralegal wants to research the area of law and other cases on the same issue. A table of statutes also may be included, to help the researcher find cases or discussions of a statute.

Rule 32.1. Citing Judicial Dispositions

(a) Citation Permitted. A court may not prohibit or restrict the citation of federal judicial opinions, orders, judgments, or other written dispositions that have been:
   (i) designated as "unpublished," "not for publication," "non-precedential," "not precedent," or the like; and
   (ii) issued on or after January 1, 2007.
(b) Copies Required. If a party cites a federal judicial opinion, order, judgment, or other written disposition that is not available in a publicly accessible electronic database, the party must file and serve a copy of that opinion, order, judgment, or disposition with the brief or other paper in which it is cited.

Updates

Print material is updated in a number of ways. One of the most frequent is the use of **pocket parts**, so called because they are slipped into a pocket in the back of the print volume. Usually these are annual updates, but they may be produced more or less frequently depending on the publisher and the need for updates. Also used are supplemental

Pocket parts An update to a book that is a separate document that slips into a pocket in the back of the main volume.

Exhibit 10.13 Sample list of abbreviations

A.	Atlantic Reporter	**Binns' Just.**	Binns' Justice
A.2d	Atlantic Reporter, Second Series	**Biss.**	Bissell's Reports, U.S.
Abb.	Abbott's Circuit Court Reports, U.S.	**Black**	Black's United States Supreme Court Reports
Abb.Adm.	Abbott's Admiralty Reports, U.S.	**Blair**	Blair County Law Reports
Adams L.J.	Adams County Legal Journal	**Blatchf.C.C.**	Blatchford's Reports, U.S.
Add.	Addison's Reports	**Bond**	Bond's Reports, U.S.
Am.Dec.	American Decisions	**B.R.**	Bankruptcy reports
Am.L.J., N.S.	American Law Journal, New Series	**Bright.E.C.**	Brightly's Election Cases
Am.L.J.,O.S.	American Law Journal, Hall's	**Bright.N.P.**	Brightly's Nisi Prius Reports
Am.L.Reg., N.S.	American Law Register, New Series	**Browne**	P.A. Browne's reports
Am.L.Reg., O.S.	American Law Register, Old Series	**Brock.**	Brockenbrough's Reports, U.S.
Am.Rep.	American Reports	**Bucks**	Bucks County Law Reporter
Am.St.Rep.	American State Reports	**C.A.**	United States Court of Appeals
Ann.Cas.	American & English Annotated Cases	**C.C.A.**	United States Circuit Court of Appeals
Ashm.	Ashmead's Reports	**Cambria**	Cambria County Legal Journal
Baldw.	Baldwin's Reports, U.S.	**Cambria C.R.**	Cambria County Reports
Beaver	Beaver County Legal Journal	**Camp.**	Campbell's Legal Gazette Reports
Ben.	Benedict's Reports, U.S.	**Cent.**	Central Reporter
Berks	Berks County Legal Journal	**C.C.**	(see Pa.C.C.) County Court Reports
Binn.	Binney's Reports	**Chest.**	Chester County Reports

Source: From Purdon's Pennsylvania Statutes Annotated, © 1994 by West Group, a Thomson Company. Reproduced with permission.

Exhibit 10.14 | **Sample table of contents**

Source: *From* Pennsylvania Estate Planning and Drafting, *2/E, by Robert J. Weinberg. © George T. Bisel Company, Inc., Reproduced by permission.*

pamphlets, usually paperbacks, to supplement the annual updates. Some are issued monthly, and others quarterly or semi-annually.

It is essential that the pocket part or supplement be consulted. In statutory research, the main volumes may be many years old and sections of the law repealed. The pocket parts or other supplements, not the main volume, contain the latest information. For this reason, some researchers look at the pocket part first, before consulting the main volume. More and more frequently, additional updates are provided online. The paralegal must learn how each resource is updated and the frequency of the updates. Exhibit 10.15 is a sample pocket part supplement.

Constructing a Computer Search Query

Constructing a search query requires one to select a computer search index, then to create the query.

Creating a Computer Search

The three primary full-service online providers of computer research services—Lexis, Loislaw, and Westlaw—provide a broad range of legal materials including cases, statutes, and regulations. In addition, a limited-service search provider, VersusLaw, specializes in providing cases and limited access to additional items, such as the *Code of Federal Regulations*.

In using a limited-service provider, it is important to check the coverage dates and content. In some cases the same information is available at other sources, such as the *United States Code* and the *Code of Federal Regulations*, which are available online through the GPO Access website. In all cases, researchers must be certain that they have checked all the latest update sources.

Search Method and Query

Each of the online providers uses words to find and retrieve documents. As part of the publication process, indexes are prepared of every word in the document, the words are tabulated for frequency, and a word index is prepared. The search you create searches this index. VersusLaw uses a full-text retrieval method that searches every word except "stop words"—words that are used too commonly in documents to be used in a search, such as "the," "not," "of," and "and."

Creating the Query

When you conduct a search, you are asking the search engine to find the indexed words you have chosen. These may be legal specialty words or common English words. Single words may be in any of the Internet or legal search engines. Frequently you will be looking for more detailed information. Using combinations of words in the search can narrow the search results. Usually, the most productive search contains a combination of words, which may consist of terms such as "strict liability," "legal malpractice," "automobile accident," or "reckless indifference," for example.

Using Connectors

Connectors are instructions to the search engine to look for documents containing combinations of words. Connectors may be thought of as instructions to the search engine: Find me documents in which the words "strict" AND "liability" appear. The word AND is a connector that instructs the search not to return the documents in which only one of the words is found. Exhibit 10.16 shows a Loislaw search with the AND connector.

Connectors Instructions in a search query on how to treat the words in the query.

Exhibit 10.15 Sample pocket part supplement

13 Pa.C.S.A. § 1105   COMMERCIAL CODE

DIVISION 1
GENERAL PROVISIONS

CHAPTER 11

SHORT TITLE, CONSTRUCTION, APPLICATION
AND SUBJECT MATTER OF TITLE

§ 1105.   Territorial application of title; power of parties to choose applicable law

Notes of Decisions

Bankruptcy 6

1. In general
In re Eagle Enterprises, Inc., Bkrtcy.E.D.Pa. 1998, 223 B.R. 290, [main volume] affirmed 237 B.R. 269.

2. Law governing
When parties agree to apply foreign law, pursuant to which their contract to "lease" goods kept in Pennsylvania will be deemed a true "lease," despite fact that contract does not permit lessor to terminate agreement but affords him an option to purchase goods for nominal consideration, Pennsylvania law will not give effect to that choice. In re Eagle Enterprises, Inc., E.D.Pa.1999, 237 B.R. 269.

4. Third parties
In re Eagle Enterprises, Inc., Bkrtcy.E.D.Pa. 1998, 223 B.R. 290, [main volume] affirmed 237 B.R. 269.

6. Bankruptcy
While Chapter 7 debtor and equipment lessor were generally free, under Pennsylvania statute, to agree what law would govern their rights and duties, debtor and equipment lessor could not impose their choice of law on Chapter 7 trustee, as party who never agreed to choice-of-law provision, in order to prevent trustee from challenging parties' characterization, as equipment "lease," of agreement which required debtor to pay alleged rent throughout full term of lease, and which then allowed debtor to acquire equipment at end of lease for nominal consideration of one dollar, merely because lease would allegedly have been recognized as true lease under law of foreign country that parties chose to govern their agreement. In re Eagle Enterprises, Inc., E.D.Pa.1999, 237 B.R. 269.

CHAPTER 12

GENERAL DEFINITIONS AND PRINCIPLES OF INTERPRETATION

§ 1201. General definitions

Notes of Decisions

11. Lease or lease intended as security
Under Pennsylvania law, "lease" transaction in which "lessee" cannot terminate "lease" during its term, but may thereafter become owner of "leased" goods for no additional or nominal additional consideration, does not create lease, but rather a security interest. In re Eagle Enterprises, Inc., E.D.Pa.1999, 237 B.R. 269.

When parties agree to apply foreign law, pursuant to which their contract to "lease" goods kept in Pennsylvania will be deemed a true "lease," despite fact that contract does not permit lessor to terminate agreement but affords him an option to purchase goods for nominal consideration, Pennsylvania law will not give effect to that choice. In re Eagle Enterprises, Inc., E.D.Pa.1999, 237 B.R. 269.

13. Security interest
Revised Pennsylvania statute defining term "security interest" seeks to correct shortcomings

of its predecessor by focusing inquiry of lease/security interest analysis on economics of the transaction, rather than on intent of the parties. In re Kim, Bkrtcy.E.D.Pa.1999, 232 B.R. 324.

Whether, under Pennsylvania law, lease or security interest is created by a particular transaction is no longer within exclusive control of the parties and subject to possible manipulation through artful document drafting; rather, issue is to be determined by reference to uniform criteria set forth in revised statute defining term "security interest." In re Kim, Bkrtcy.E.D.Pa.1999, 232 B.R. 324.

In determining whether debtor's lease was a disguised security interest or a true lease under Pennsylvania law, bankruptcy court was required to consider entire "transaction" and was not constrained to look solely to documents signed by the parties which were designated "lease" or which made use of terms commonly found in leases, but could examine both parol and extrin-

4

Exhibit 10.16 Loislaw search with AND connector

Source: Reproduced with permission of Aspen Publishers, Loislaw screen shot.

The connector OR instructs the search engine to find either term—the word "strict" OR the word "liability"—and retrieve the documents. Exhibit 10.17 depicts a Lexis search with the OR connector. The NOT connector instructs the search to eliminate certain words. For example, you may wish to review documents in which the word "malpractice" is found but *not* those with the word "medical."

In some cases it might be assumed that there will be other words between the desired terms, such as in the phrase "Paralegals are bound by the ethics of their profession." The NEAR connector helps to locate documents where the terms are near each other; for example: find "paralegal" NEAR "ethics." The NEAR connector allows the paralegal to search for words near each other by specifying the number of words apart that is acceptable.

Exhibit 10.18 gives a comparison of these concepts, by VersusLaw, and Exhibit 10.19 gives a guide to connectors from Westlaw.

Updating Legal Research

The legal team always must use the most current statutory and case law in advising clients and arguing cases to the court. One of the features of the American legal system is its constant change. Courts attempt to meet the needs of a changing society by reviewing prior case law and, when appropriate, overruling or modifying it as the contemporary American view of justice dictates. The American legal system concept of *stare decisis* provides that we use prior case law as **precedent** but change the law as American society changes. Occasionally, existing case law may be held unconstitutional, such as happened with the landmark case of *Roe v. Wade.*

Stare decisis The legal principle that prior case law should apply unless there is a substantial change in society necessitating a change in the case law.

Precedent Prior case law that is controlling.

Exhibit 10.17	Lexis search with OR connector

LexisNexis

Home | Sources | How Do I? | Site Map | What's New | Help

Academic Search Forms

> Quick Info
> News
> Business
> Legal Research
> Medical
> Reference

Basic | Guided Search

State Case Law: Illinois   Tips

Keyword and Additional Terms search the full text of cases. Only cases that match all the criteria you enter will be found.

Search terms: `Paralegal or Ethics`
Entry Required *e.g. professional negligence*

Narrow search with additional terms: [   ]
e.g. accountant OR CPA

Court: `Illinois All Courts` ▼ Source List

Date: ⦿ `Previous six months` ▼
○ From: [   ] To: [   ] Examples

[Search] [Clear Form]

Source: Copyright 2009 Lexis Nexis, a division of Reed Elsevier Inc. All Rights Reserved. LexisNexis and the Knowledge Burst logo are registered trademarks of Reed Elsevier Properties Inc. and are used with the permission of LexisNexis.

Exhibit 10.18	Comparison grid from VersusLaw

VersusLaw	LEXIS	Westlaw
Connectors		
and	and	and, &
or	or	or, *space*
not	and not	but not, %
Proximity operators		
w/n	w/n	w/n, /n
w/n	pre/n	pre/n, +n
Exact phrase match		
unlawful entry	unlawful entry	"unlawful entry"
Wild Cards - end of root words		
*	!	!
Wild Cards - single character		
?	*	*
Order of operators		
proximity operators, not, and, or	or, proximity operators, and, and not	or, proximity operators, and, but not

Source: © Copyright 2009 VersusLaw, Inc. Redmond, WA, USA. All rights reserved. www.versuslaw.com

Knowing if the case law being used in a legal argument is the current case law is a vital part of the lawyer's obligation to the client and to the court. Up to the moment before the arguments are made to the court or the brief is submitted, a case that the attorney or the opponent is using as a basis for a legal argument may be overturned. The ethical obligation of candor, shown below in the Ethical Perspective, to the court and of professional competency requires the use of current case law.

Exhibit 10.19   Westlaw guide to connectors

USING CONNECTORS

Connector	You type	Westlaw retrieves documents
AND	&	containing both search terms: **work-place & safety**
OR	a space	containing either search term or both search terms: **landlord lessor**
Grammatical Connectors	/p	containing search terms in the same paragraph: **warrant! /p habitat!**
	/s	containing search terms in the same sentence: **danger! /s defect!**
	+s	in which the first term precedes the second within the same sentence: **capital 1 s gain**
Numerical Connectors	/n (where *n* is a number)	containing search terms with *n* terms of each other: **issues /5 fact**
	+n (where *n* is a number)	in which the first term precedes the second by *n* terms: **20 1 5 1080**
BUT NOT	%	not containing the term or terms following the percent symbol (%): **tax taxation % tax taxation/3 income**

Source: Reproduced with permission from West Group.

ETHICAL PERSPECTIVE

Idaho Rules of Professional Conduct

RULE 3.3 CANDOR TOWARD THE TRIBUNAL

(a) A lawyer shall not knowingly:
  (1) make a false statement of fact or law to a tribunal or fail to correct a false statement of material fact or law previously made to the tribunal by the lawyer;
  (2) fail to disclose to the tribunal legal authority in the controlling jurisdiction known to the lawyer to be directly adverse to the position of the client and not disclosed by opposing counsel; or
  (3) offer evidence that the lawyer knows to be false. If a lawyer, the lawyer's client, or a witness called by the lawyer, has offered material evidence and the lawyer comes to know of its falsity, the lawyer shall take reasonable remedial measures, including, if necessary, disclosure to the tribunal. A lawyer may refuse to offer evidence, other than the testimony of a defendant in a criminal matter, that the lawyer reasonably believes is false.
(b) A lawyer who represents a client in an adjudicative proceeding and who knows that a person intends to engage, is engaging or has engaged in criminal or fraudulent conduct related to the proceeding shall take reasonable remedial measures, including, if necessary, disclosure to the tribunal.
(c) The duties stated in paragraphs (a) and (b) continue to the conclusion of the proceeding, and apply even if compliance requires disclosure of information otherwise protected by Rule 1.6.
(d) In an ex parte proceeding, a lawyer shall inform the tribunal of all material facts known to the lawyer that will enable the tribunal to make an informed decision, whether or not the facts are adverse.

 Web Exploration

Contrast and compare the Rhode Island rule at http://www.courts.ri.gov/supreme/pdf-files/Rules_Of_Professional_Conduct.pdf with the ABA Model Rules of Professional Conduct at www.abanet.org/cpr and the rule in your jurisdiction.

Thus, an essential part of legal research for paralegals is to verify that they have the latest case or statute. The process is complicated by the method by which changes in statutes or case law are released to the public. Ultimately, new statutes and new case law are reported in a published form, both in paper and electronically, but not all publications are able to disseminate the information daily. Paper versions take time to print and distribute. Not all electronic versions are posted immediately. Therefore, it becomes important to know how quickly the reporting or electronic services of the law firm or practice distribute post-statutory changes and new cases. More and more courts have their own websites and release case opinions electronically along with the print versions to the public and publishing companies. For example, you can check decisions of the U.S. Supreme Court daily.

What is difficult is knowing if the new cases or new statutes affect the case being researched. When the court specifically mentions a case being cited in a memo of law or a court brief, the paralegal has to know if the new case follows the older case law, reverses it, or in some way differs from the older case.

As soon as a case is entered into an electronic case law database, such as Westlaw, Lexis, Loislaw, or VersusLaw, a general search can be made for references to the case name or citation. Before it is entered, the same search will not show the newest reference. Even a reference to the case will not tell whether the case law has changed, only that another case has referred to it. Someone must actually read the case to see how the court has used it or referred to it in the opinion.

Shepard's

Long a standard tool of legal research in law libraries, *Shepard's Citations* is a multi-volume set of books listing cases and statutes by their respective citations and giving the citation of every other case in which the listed case was mentioned. The listings originally were compiled by editors who physically read through every case reported to find citations. These then were reported by case citation, with every other mention of the case reported by its citation in chronological fashion, with notations indicating if the opinion was reversed, affirmed, followed, overruled, and so on. The process of using *Shepard's* to check legal citations came to be called "Shepardizing"— a term that many legal assistants still use, even when using other citation-checking services such as Westlaw's KeyCite. An advantage to the *Shepard's Citator* is the editorial symbol system used to indicate how the new case affects the case being checked, as shown in Exhibit 10.20.

The problem with the traditional paper form of *Shepard's* is the lag in time for the print version to be prepared and sent out to subscribers. *Shepard's* now provides the same service online through the Lexis service; subscribers can obtain the latest case information, to the day, by calling a toll-free number. One of the difficulties in using the print version of *Shepard's* is the number of hardbound volumes and paperback updates required to be consulted, and finding the latest update pamphlet if someone has misfiled it in the law library. Exhibit 10.21 is an example of the print version case presentation in *Shepard's*.

Many educational institutions and public libraries subscribe to the Web-based LexisNexis Academic Universe. *Shepard's* citation service (**see** Exhibit 10.22) usually is available for the U.S. Supreme Court as part of the service, but other federal and state *Shepard's* citation services may not be included because of the cost of the additional license fees involved.

GlobalCite™

GlobalCite Loislaw's tool for searching cases containing references to another case.

Loislaw's **GlobalCite** provides a reverse chronological list of the case law, the statutes in the order of the highest number of citation occurrences, the regulations listed in

Exhibit 10.20 *Shepard's* symbols showing effects of new cases

Source: Copyright 2009 LexisNexis, a division of Reed Elsevier Inc. All Rights Reserved. LexisNexis and the Knowledge Burst logo are registered trademarks of Reed Elsevier Properties Inc. and are used with the permission of LexisNexis.

relevancy order, and reference to other databases in the Loislaw library. Exhibit 10.23 shows a GlobalCite screen.

KeyCite™

KeyCite is the Westlaw online citation update service. The Westlaw KeyCite is a combination citator and case finder. Unlike other similar services, KeyCite uses the West Key number system and West Headnotes.

KeyCite Westlaw's tool for searching cases containing references to another case.

V. Cite™

V. Cite, VersusLaw's citation tool, will produce a list of all cases within the selected jurisdictions that have cited the case being searched. The list that a V. Cite search produces will include cases that have cited the initial case, which most likely will discuss similar issues. Using the added V. Cite feature allows the appending of a specific term to the search request. For example, including the word "damages" in the "additional query information" section of the V. Cite form will restrict the search to cases that cite the searched case and also discuss "damages."

V. Cite VersusLaw's tool for searching cases containing references to another case.

Exhibit 10.21	**Example of print version case presentation in *Shepard's***

—157—	—558—	—558—
Oregon v Plowman 1992	**Oregon v Plowman 1992**	**Oregon v Plowman 1992**
(838P2d558)	(314Ore157)	(314Ore157)
s 107OrA782	s 813P2d1114	s 813P2d1114
cc 314Ore170	cc 813P2d1115	cc 813P2d1115
e 315Ore375	cc 838P2d566	cc 838P2d566
315Ore380	840P2d1324	840P2d1324
317Ore^{4}258	e 840P2d1325	e 840P2d1325
317Ore451	841P2d650	841P2d650
f 317Ore452	e 845P2d1285	e 845P2d1285
j 317Ore472	845P2d1289	845P2d1289
f 318Ore488	j 851P2d1147	j 851P2d1147
318Ore492	j 852P2d888	j 852P2d888
d 318Ore497	854P2d959	854P2d959
116OrA189	855P2d^{4}625	855P2d^{4}625
e 116OrA192	857P2d107	Calif
h 116OrA265	f 857P2d108	17CaR2d296
j 119OrA303	j 857P2d119	e 19CaR2d448
j 120OrA333	f 871P2d458	e 19CaR2d449
121OrA384	871P2d461	Iowa
j 128OrA14	d 871P2d463	500N W 42
71OLR689	j 874P2d1348	
22A5268n		

| Shepard's Oregon Citations, *Oregon Reports division,* shows citations from:

• state reports
• Oregon Law Review
• annotations (ALR® 5th) | Shepard's Oregon Citations, *Oregon Cases division, shows citations from Oregon as published in the Pacific Reporter.* | Shepard's Pacific Reporter Citations, *P.2d division, shows citations from all cases published in a West regional reporter.* |

Source: Copyright 2009 LexisNexis, a division of Reed Elsevier Inc. All Rights Reserved. LexisNexis and the Knowledge Burst logo are registered trademarks of Reed Elsevier Properties Inc. and are used with the permission of LexisNexis.

Parallel Citations

Parallel citation The citation to the same case in a different publication.

Most cases are reported in more than one service or set of books. A **parallel citation** is a cite to the same material, usually a case, in another source. Frequently a state has an official publication, such as the court's own publication, and a private publication, such as the *West Reporter*. In some cases, *West* was and is the official reporter, and there may not be a parallel print source. One of the many uses of *Shepard's* is to find the parallel citation to other locations for the same case.

Shepard's also provides update information on statutory citations. Amendments and repeals of statutory information are listed in *Shepard's*. Citations to any cases in which the statute has been cited also are listed, with information on how the case law considered the statute.

Exhibit 10.22 LexisNexis Total *Shepard's*® Table of Authorities

Source: *Copyright 2009 LexisNexis, a division of Reed Elsevier Inc. All Rights Reserved. LexisNexis and the Knowledge Burst logo are registered trademarks of Reed Elsevier Properties, Inc. and are used with the permission of LexisNexis.*

Exhibit 10.23 GlobalCite screen

GlobalCite Results List

Florida Case Law
THE FLORIDA BAR v. BARRETT, 897 So.2d 1269 (Fla. 2005)

2 found (1 - 2 shown)

Highlighted Case Treatment Terms

All Documents/Cases Reverse Chronological Order — 2	Treatises Only — 0
Cases Only -- Chronological Order — 2	Other Documents — 0
Statutes Only — 0	

#1
Florida Case Law
FLORIDA BAR v. COHEN, SC04-1019 (Fla. 2005)
No. SC04-1019.
November 23, 2005.

Fla. Bar v. Barrett, 897 So. 2d 1269, 1275-76 (Fla. 2005) (quoting Fla. Bar v. Lord, 433 So. 2d 983, 986 (Fla. 1983)).

#2
Florida Case Law
IN RE HENSON, SC04-1 (Fla. 2005)
No. SC04-1.
October 12, 2005.

Source: *Reprinted with permission of Aspen Publishers, from GlobalCite screen shot.*

CHECKLIST Research Search Items

☐ Client: ☐ Search combinations used:

☐ Issue: ☐ Date:

☐ Search terms and phrases:

CHECKLIST Research Sources Checked

Checked Source	Citation	Pocket Part Checked	√	Web Location
Primary Sources				
	State statute			www.
	USC			www.
	USCA			www.
	CFR			www.
	Local ordinance			www.
				www.
Secondary Sources				
	State digest			www.
	Federal digest			www.
	ALR			www.
				www.
	Encyclopedia			www.
	State			www.
	C.J.S.			www.
	Periodicals			www.
	Treatises			www.

Concept Review *and* Reinforcement

LEGAL TERMINOLOGY

Amicus curia 386
Bench opinion 380
Bicameral 377
Case syllabus 380
Citator 386
Connectors 393
Dicta 383
Finding tools 375
GlobalCite 398
Headnotes 380

Holding 383
Judicial branch 377
KeyCite 399
Legal research 369
Legislative branch 377
Mandatory authority 378
Parallel citation 400
Persuasive authority 378
Pocket parts 391
Precedent 395

Primary source of law 375
Published opinion 379
Relevant facts 370
Search query 371
Secondary source of law 375
Slip opinion 380
Stare decisis 395
Unpublished opinions 379
V. Cite 399

SUMMARY OF KEY CONCEPTS

Legal Research

Definition	Legal research is a process for finding the answer to a legal question.

Creating a Research Plan

	The research plan helps to focus on the issues, sources, and methods for finding the answer and controlling law.
What Is the Issue or Legal Question?	What are the relevant facts or statutory materials?
What Is the Appropriate Search Terminology?	Print research materials require finding material based on a printed index of individual words as selected by editors of the service. Computer research allows for searches of words found in the documents using a text search of requested words in the search query.
What Type of Research Material Is Available?	The paralegal must be able to find the information needed when the familiar resources are not available. Paralegals cannot be sure whether the research will be done using a traditional paper library or a computer search; they must understand how each resource files the information.
What Jurisdiction or Jurisdictions Are Involved?	Focusing on a single jurisdiction or a minimum number of jurisdictions reduces the numbers of traditional volumes of books necessary and saves online computer search time.
What Is the Controlling Law?	Knowing which set of materials to use, the statutes of the jurisdiction, the regulation of a given administrative agency, or the courts of a given jurisdiction will save time in doing the research.
What Are the Types of Resources to Use?	1. Primary sources of law are used in preparing the legal memo or brief. 2. Secondary sources are useful, efficient ways to get an overview of an area of law or learn the terminology of a particular field of law in which the paralegal is not familiar. 3. Finding tools are publications containing tools for finding both primary and secondary sources.
Where Is the Needed Research Material Located?	The needed material may have to be located at a remote library such as a bar association library or a law school library.
Creating a List of Research Terms	Separate lists should be created for online searches and traditional print sources.
Executing the Research Plan	As with the execution of any plan, detours can be expected, as the law is in a constant evolutionary state. New statutes are enacted, and new case interpretations are handed down. During the research process, the researcher must look for changes and potential changes from pending legislation and cases on appeal.

Finding the Law

The Controlling Law	The controlling law may be found at federal, state, or local legislative or judicial levels.
Primary Sources and Authority	Primary sources include the law, constitutions, statutes, regulations, court rules, and case decisions.
Mandatory and Persuasive Authority	1. Mandatory authority is legal authority that the courts must follow. 2. Persuasive authority is legal authority the courts are not required to follow but is from a respected source and well reasoned.

Constitutions	Constitutions are primary sources that set the guidelines, limits, and authority of the federal government and the state governments.
Statutes	Statutes are enacted by the legislative branch of government.
Court Decisions	The actual court language is a primary source of the law. The syllabus, summaries, interpretations, or abstracts of the points of law presented by the editorial staffs of the publishers of the case law—usually called headnotes—are not the primary source of law.
Secondary Sources	Secondary sources explain the law. 1. Legal dictionaries, as opposed to general English or other specialized dictionaries, define words and phrases as used in the law. 2. Legal encyclopedias provide the background to understand the area enough to start the research. They provide an overview of the concepts and history of an area of law, the legal issues involved, and the terminology. 3. Treatises, Law Reviews, and Legal Periodicals are authoritative or of sufficient scholarly value to be persuasive to the court.
Finding Tools	Finding tools help to "find" the law. 1. Digests provide lists of cases in a subject topic format, with cases generally in chronological order. 2. Indexes and citators cross-reference material, such as by the commonly used or popular name of a case or statute.

Personal Research Strategy

Over time, each paralegal develops a personal search strategy based on the nature of the problem or issue to be researched and the resources available.

Methods of verifying that the law and cases cited in your research and memo of law is current law or current authority, and methods for looking for pending cases and legislation that might change the answer to the legal question.

A Final Word on Executing the Legal Research Plan

Know when to ask for help.

Using Printed Legal Reference Works

Common Features	Table of abbreviations Table of contents in the front Index of terms in the back Table of cases and citations
Updates	Print material is frequently updated with pocket parts, usually issued annually, slipped into the back of the volume in a pocket. Paperback supplements are issued annually, quarterly, or monthly. Online updates from the publishers are increasingly available for some materials.

Constructing a Computer Search Query

Creating a Computer Search	A combination of words, phrases, and connectors used to search for a desired answer.
Search Method and Query	Each online provider uses words to find and retrieve documents. As part of the publication process, indexes are prepared of every word in the document, the words are tabulated for frequency, and a word index is prepared. The search created searches this index.
Creating the Query	The search engine is used to find the indexed words the paralegal has chosen; they may be legal specialty words or common English words. Using combinations of words in the search can narrow the search results.

Using Connectors	AND instructs the search not to return documents in which only one of the words is found. OR instructs the search engine to find either term. NEAR may be used to find the occurrence of desired words within a set number of words of each other.

Updating Legal Research

	1. *Shepard's:* A multivolume set of books listing cases and statutes by their respective citations and giving the citation of every other case in which the listed case was mentioned; checking citations is often called "Shepardizing." 2. GlobalCite (Loislaw): Provides a reverse chronological list of the case law, a list of statutes in the order of the highest number of citation occurrences, regulations in relevancy order, and reference to other databases in Loislaw library. 3. KeyCite (Westlaw): Online citation update service. 4. V. Cite (VersusLaw) Online citation tool.

Parallel Citation

	A citation to the same material, usually a case, in another source.
Statutory Law Updates	*Shepard's* provides updated information on amendments and repeals of statutory information. Citations to any cases in which the statute has been cited are also listed, with information on how the case law considered the statute.

WORKING THE WEB

1. Use the Government Printing Office website to find and print out the summary purpose of 21 CFR 404, or any other section assigned by your instructor. www.gpoaccess.gov

2. Make a list of the available federal primary sources available on the Government Printing Office website.

3. From the sitemap of the VersusLaw website, print out for your future computer searches the printable version of the *Versuslaw Research Manual.* http://www.versuslaw.com/features/sitemap.htm

4. Use the Legal Information Institute at the Cornell University website to find title 44 C.F.R. 201 and print out the list of key responsibilities of FEMA and state and local/tribal governments. http://lii.law.cornell.edu/. Does this site provide direct access or a link to another source? Explain. What primary federal sources does this site offer?

5. Conduct a search for information on paralegal ethics using two different search engines, and print out a copy of the first page of each result. Are they the same? What is the difference in results and order of presentation? Possible search engines include: Google, www.google.com; Yahoo, www.yahoo.com; www.ask.com; Findlaw, www.findlaw.com.

6. If you have access to Loislaw, NexisLexis, Westlaw, or VersusLaw, conduct a search for paralegal ethics cases for your jurisdiction. Prepare a list of authorities cited in the search.

7. Print out the current list of opinions of the U.S. Supreme Court at http://www.supremecourt.us.gov.

8. Print out the complete version of Rule 3.3, Candor Toward the Tribunal, of the *ABA Model Rules of Professional Conduct* at http://www.abanet.org/cpr/mrpc/mrpc_toc.html.

9. Under the theory of *stare decisis,* on which courts would the decisions of a court have a binding effect? Would a decision in a case be binding on future cases if the decision were available only in the clerk's office?

10. Would your answer be the same if the decision were available in the clerk's office at first but then available in printed form or online at a later date? When would the decision become effective as precedent?

11. Where is the "law" found?

12. Who makes the "law" under the United States system?

13. What is meant by a "bicameral" legislature?

14. In legal research, what is meant by "primary source?"

15. What is a "treatise?" Is it a primary source? Explain.

16. What is a headnote in legal research? Is it a primary source? Explain.

17. What is dicta? What is its effect on other courts? Explain.

18. Of what weight do courts give secondary sources? Explain fully.

19. Why are finding tools important to the legal researcher? Give an example of how a finding tool might be used.

20. Do unpublished opinions have precedential effect? Explain.

CRITICAL THINKING & WRITING QUESTIONS

1. Using the facts in the *Palsgraf* case in Appendix A, prepare a search query using connectors to locate the law or a similar case in your jurisdiction. Run the search using an online legal research service, if available.
2. Why does a paralegal have to be familiar with both traditional and electronic research tools and methods?
3. Why does the paralegal have to know how quickly changes in statutory and case law are updated by online and traditional primary and secondary sources?
4. Why is knowledge of the underlying law in an area important in constructing a question for online research?
5. How can a researcher be certain that a case that seems to be on point is still the current case law?

6. Why should secondary sources not be relied upon in citing binding authority?
7. Why would a researcher use a traditional paper resource before using an online research tool?
8. How does the use of connectors help in conducting online research? Give an example.
9. Why might an identical search query return different results?
10. Why must researchers clearly understand the question they are being asked to research? How can they be certain they do?

Building Paralegal Skills

VIDEO CASE STUDIES

Legal Research: Are Books Obsolete?

In the middle of a trial, a trial attorney sends his paralegal to the courthouse law library to find a case that has been cited as precedent by opposing counsel in oral argument. Without a valid password, the paralegal is advised to use traditional research methods.

After viewing the video case study at www.pearsonhighered.com/goldman answer the following:

1. What are the differences between using books and electronic legal research?
2. Are traditional paper-based reference materials as current as electronic reference sources?
3. Are there any differences in using the different legal research services such as Lexis, Westlaw, Loislaw, or VersusLaw?

Fees and Billing Issue: Using Time Effectively

A paralegal has responded to the request of her supervising attorney for information on a question of law. After spending considerable time, she is helped by another paralegal who quickly provides surety information she is looking for only to find out that her supervising attorney was merely curious and there was no client against which to bill the research time.

After viewing the video case study at www.pearsonhighered.com/goldman answer the following:

1. What questions should a paralegal ask before commencing to do research?
2. At what point should the paralegal ask for help and from whom should the help be sought?
3. Is there any value in doing legal research when there is no specific client or case to which it will apply?

Fees and Billing Issue: Contemporaneous Timekeeping

A paralegal is trying to reconstruct his time records for the day. Unable to remember everything that he did he arbitrarily assigns time to certain cases.

After viewing the video case study at www.pearsonhighered.com/goldman answer the following:

1. How can well-kept time records document the thoroughness of the research completed on a case?
2. Can time records be used to document the specific citations used in preparing legal research?
3. Is the misapplication of time spent to other clients and cases acceptable behavior for a paralegal?

ETHICS ANALYSIS & DISCUSSION QUESTIONS

1. Is there an ethical obligation under the Model Rules to perform legal research competently? Explain.

2. What is the ethical obligation under the Model Rules to provide the court with legal authority that is not favorable to your client's legal position?

3. What is the ethical obligation to "Shepardize" cases and statutes before submitting a brief or memo of law to the court?

For answers, look at American Bar Association Rule 3.3, Candor Toward the Tribunal, and Rule 1.1, Competence (ABA *Model Rules of Professional Conduct*, 2002).

Confidentiality

There are few certainties in the area of ethics, for paralegals or in any profession. What qualifies as ethical conduct is in most cases based on state law and court interpretation applied to a set of facts. The citation listed below represents one legal opinion and is provided as a research starting point. Do not assume that the same rule applies in your jurisdiction. For the following:

• Prepare a written statement based on your state law.
• Use your state bar association website as a starting point.

You are waiting for a fax needed for a case on which you are working. While you are standing by the fax machine, a fax comes in from an attorney at an opposing firm containing a letter about settlement that was clearly intended for the attorney's client and not for opposing counsel. It was sent by your best friend, the paralegal who is working on that case at the opposing firm. She is stressed out by the case and made the mistake of dialing your fax number rather than the client's. From your reading of the letter it appears the information would greatly help your law office win the case. [*ABA Formal Ethics Opinion, State Compensation Insurance Fund v. The WPS, Inc.*, 70 CA 4644; 82 C.R.2 799 (1999)] Do you quietly return the fax to your friend and say nothing to anyone? Do you read it carefully to be sure of the contents? Do you return it to opposing counsel? Do you tell your supervising attorney about the letter? The contents?

DEVELOPING YOUR COLLABORATION SKILLS

Working on your own or with a group of other students assigned by your instructor, review the scenario at the beginning of the chapter and discuss the different views on law libraries, including traditional versus computer legal research.

1. Write a summary of the potential advantages and disadvantages of each point of view.
2. Prepare a report to the executive committee, considering the different views of members of the firm with a solution that might satisfy most users of the firm's library.
3. The group is divided into two teams. One team will conduct a research assignment using traditional methods and the other will use computer research tools.

a. Each team is to complete the Research Sources Checked checklist and prepare a copy for the members of the other team and your instructor.
b. After you have completed the research, prepare a short memorandum of law to submit to your instructor.
4. Complete a second research project with each team now using the other approach to research. The traditional methods team now will use computer tools, and the computer tools team will conduct the research using traditional tools. Prepare a short memorandum and complete the Research Sources Checked checklist.
5. Based on your experience doing traditional and computer research, what recommendations would you make to the managing partner in the opening scenario?

PARALEGAL PORTFOLIO EXERCISE

Complete the "Web Location" section portion of the Research Sources Checked checklist. When preparing the list, include alternative sources where available. Print a copy for your portfolio for future use and a copy for your instructor.

LEGAL ANALYSIS & WRITING CASES

American Geophysical Union v. Texaco Inc.   37 F.3d 881 (2d Cir. 1994)

COPYING OF MATERIAL FOR FUTURE RESEARCH AND LAW LIBRARY ARCHIVES FROM COPYRIGHTED MAGAZINES AND JOURNALS

Most researchers understand that misuse of copyright material may subject them to liability under the copyright laws. The case of *American Geophysical Union v. Texaco* illustrates the

potential liability in regularly copying copyrighted articles for personal archives. Researchers of Texaco regularly made copies of articles for future reference from the works of the plaintiff and 82 other publishers of scientific and technical journals. Texaco raised the defense of "fair use" as permitted under the copyright law.

Fair use as a defense depends on four tests: (1) the purpose and character of the use—including whether for nonprofit educational purposes or commercial use; (2) the nature of copyright work—the law generally recognizes a greater need to disseminate factual works than works of fiction or fantasy; (3) amount and substantiality of portion used—was the quantity used reasonable in relation to the purpose of the copying? (4) effect on potential market or value—will the copying have an impact on the sale of the works, and is there an efficient mechanism for the licensing of the works?

Questions

1. How does copyright law apply to a student copying copyrighted materials while doing research for a class project?
2. Would the answer be the same if the student were doing the research as part of an assignment while working in a law office?
3. Does it matter if the work copied is a court case or an article by an expert in automobile airbags liability? Why?

WORKING WITH THE LANGUAGE OF THE COURT CASE

Hart v. Massanari

266 F.3d 1155 (2001)
United States Court of Appeals, Ninth Circuit

Read, and if assigned, brief this case. In your brief, answer the following questions.

1. Why are unpublished dispositions (opinion) of courts not valid as precedent in future cases?
2. What is the difference between controlling authority and persuasive authority?
3. How might an unpublished opinion be used in this case?
4. Has the adoption of Rule 32.1 changed the effect of this case?
5. Why does this court believe it is important, in writing an opinion of the court, to recite all the relevant facts?
6. What is the effect of binding precedent on other courts?

Kozinski, Circuit Judge

Appellant's . . . brief cites . . . an unpublished disposition, not reported in the *Federal Reporter*. . . . The full text . . . is marked with the following notice: "This disposition is not appropriate for publication and may not be cited to or by the courts of this circuit. . . ." Unpublished dispositions and orders of this Court are not binding precedent . . . [and generally] may not be cited to or by the courts of this circuit." . . . [9th Cir.R.36-3.]

We ordered counsel to show cause as to why he should not be disciplined for violating Ninth Circuit Rule 36-3. Counsel responds by arguing that Rule 36-3 may be unconstitutional. . . [relying] . . . on the Eighth Circuit's opinion in *Anastasoff v. United States*, [which] while vacated, continues to have persuasive force. . .

A. Anastasoff held that Eighth Circuit Rule 28A(i), . . . that unpublished dispositions are not precedential* . . .

Our rule operates . . . differently from . . . the Eighth Circuit . . . Rule 28A(i) [that] says that "[u]npublished decisions are not precedent." [W]e say that unpublished dispositions are "not binding precedent." . . . Our rule . . . prohibits citation of an unpublished disposition to any of the courts of our circuit. The Eighth Circuit's rule allows citation . . ., but provides that the authority is persuasive rather than binding.

violates Article III of the Constitution. . . . We believe that Anastasoff overstates the case. . . .

Anastasoff focused on one aspect of the way federal courts do business—the way they issue opinions—and held that they are subject to a constitutional limitation derived from the [constitutional] framers' conception of what it means to exercise the judicial power. . . . We question whether the "judicial power" clause contains any limitation at all, separate from the specific limitations of Article III and other parts of the Constitution. . . . The term "judicial power" in Article III is more likely descriptive than prescriptive. . . .

B. Modern federal courts are the successors of the English courts that developed the common law. . . . Common law judges did not make law as we understand that concept; rather, they "found" the law with the help of earlier cases that had considered similar matters. An opinion was evidence of what the law is, but it was not an independent source of law. . . . The idea that judges declared rather than made the law remained firmly entrenched in English jurisprudence until the early nineteenth century. . . . For centuries, the most important sources of law were not judicial opinions themselves, but treatises that restated the law. . . .

The modern concept of binding precedent... came about only gradually over the nineteenth and early twentieth centuries. Lawyers began to believe that judges made, not found, the law. This coincided with monumental improvements in the collection and reporting of case authorities ... and [as] a more comprehensive reporting system began to take hold, it became possible for judicial decisions to serve as binding authority....

II

Federal courts today do follow some common law traditions. When ruling on a novel issue of law, they will generally consider how other courts have ruled on the same issue.... Law on point is the law. If a court must decide an issue governed by a prior opinion that constitutes binding authority, the later court is bound to reach the same result, even if it considers the rule unwise or incorrect. Binding authority must be followed unless and until overruled by a body competent to do so.

In determining whether it is bound by an earlier decision, a court considers not merely the "reason and spirit of cases" but also "the letter of particular precedents.".... This includes not only the rule announced, but also the facts giving rise to the dispute, other rules considered and rejected, and the views expressed in response to any dissent or concurrence. Thus, when crafting binding authority, the precise language employed is often crucial to the contours and scope of the rule announced.

... A decision of the Supreme Court will control that corner of the law unless and until the Supreme Court itself overrules or modifies it.... Thus, the first panel to consider an issue sets the law not only for all the inferior courts in the circuit, but also future panels of the court of appeals. Once a panel resolves an issue in a precedential opinion, the matter is deemed resolved, unless overruled by the court itself sitting en banc, or by the Supreme Court....

Controlling authority has much in common with persuasive authority. Using the techniques developed at common law, a court confronted with apparently controlling authority must parse the precedent in light of the facts presented and the rule announced. Insofar as there may be factual differences between the current case and the earlier one, the court must determine whether those differences are material to the application of the rule or allow the precedent to be distinguished on a principled basis.... But there are also very important differences between controlling and persuasive authority.... [I]f a controlling precedent is determined to be on point, it must be followed.... Thus, an opinion of our court is binding within our circuit, not elsewhere....

III

While we agree with Anastasoff that the principle of precedent was well established in the common law courts by the time Article III of the Constitution was written, we do not agree that it was known and applied in the strict sense in which we apply binding authority today....

In writing an opinion, the court must be careful to recite all facts that are relevant to its ruling, while omitting facts that it considers irrelevant. Omitting relevant facts will make the ruling unintelligible to those not already familiar with the case; including inconsequential facts can provide a spurious basis for distinguishing the case in the future....

While federal courts of appeals generally lack discretionary review authority, they use their authority to decide cases by unpublished—and nonprecedential—dispositions to achieve the same end.... That a case is decided without a precedential opinion does not mean it is not fully considered.... The disposition is not written in a way that makes it suitable for governing future cases.... An unpublished disposition is, more or less, a letter from the court to parties familiar with the facts, announcing the result and the essential rationale of the court's decision....

IV

We conclude that Rule 36-3 is constitutional. We also find that counsel violated the rule. Nevertheless, we are aware that Anastasoff may have cast doubt on our rule's constitutional validity. Our rules are obviously not meant to punish attorneys who, in good faith, seek to test a rule's constitutionality. We therefore conclude that the violation was not willful and exercise our discretion not to impose sanctions.

The order to show cause is DISCHARGED.

In a footnote in the case of *Cogan v. Barnhart*, USDC Mass, 03-12421-WGY, the court commented:

"Citation to unpublished opinions has been an issue of considerable debate, which continues until today. The Eighth and Ninth Circuits are on extreme ends of the debate. *Anastasoff v. US*, 223 F. 3d 898... (holding that unpublished opinions have precedential effect); *Hart v. Massanari*,... (upholding its local rule prohibiting the citation of unpublished decisions as constitutional)....

Legal Writing and Critical Legal Thinking

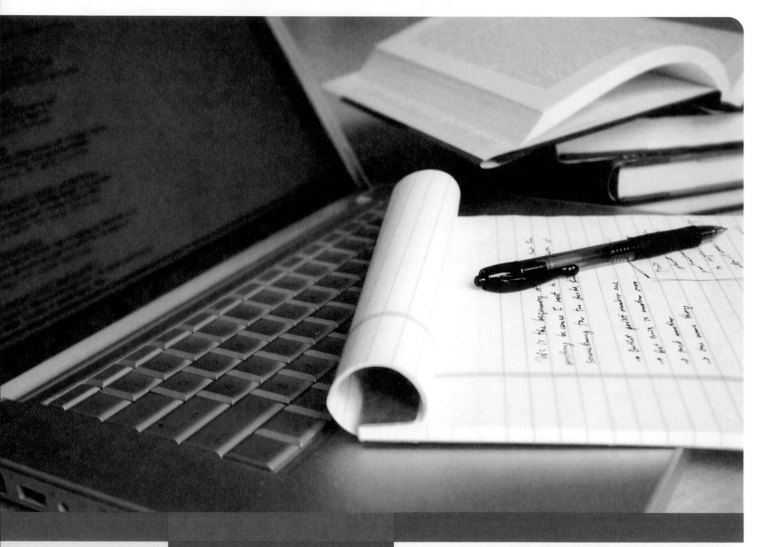

Justice is the end of government. It is the end of civil society. It ever has been, and ever will be pursued, until it be obtained, or until liberty be lost in the pursuit. "

James Madison

After studying this chapter, you should be able to:

1. Explain the process of critical legal thinking.
2. Explain the ethical duty of candor toward the tribunal.
3. Describe the similarities and differences between a memorandum of law and a court brief.
4. Explain the reasons for the various citation format rules.
5. Explain and describe the need for, and how to use, proper citation format.

Paralegals at Work

Amanda Chen had worked for the law firm of Douglas and Myers only a few weeks when the senior partner, who specialized in mergers and acquisitions, asked her to sit in on the initial meeting of a long-term client and the client's daughter. One of the more senior paralegals on staff told Amanda that her role was to take notes. The partner never took notes. He conducted the interview, asked the questions, and didn't want anyone else to interfere.

After escorting the client and the client's daughter, Bill and Tonya Johnson, from the reception area to the partner's office, Amanda was asked to take a seat in the corner and record the meeting notes. Bill Johnson made it clear that he was paying the bill and that he expected his attorney to get the charges of driving under the influence against Tonya dropped. Tonya acknowledged that she had been drinking at a country western bar and knew she was well over the legal drinking limit. She had tested her alcohol level on a breath analyzer that the bar made available to its patrons.

Upon leaving the bar, Tonya went out to her car, got in, started it, and then fell asleep at the wheel. A police officer found her in this condition, woke her, and took her to the hospital for a blood alcohol test. The officer cited her for operating a vehicle while under the influence of alcohol, based on her .09% blood alcohol reading.

After the clients left, the partner told Amanda to prepare a memorandum of law that he could use to get the charges against the client's daughter dismissed.

After doing a little research, Amanda realized that the law was against the client's getting the charges dismissed.

Furthermore, in the meeting with her father and the partner, Tonya had admitted to being intoxicated. Based on the advice from the other paralegals, Amanda was concerned about putting anything negative into the memo and decided to write a memo presenting a case for dismissal.

Consider the issues involved in this scenario as you read the chapter.

INTRODUCTION FOR THE PARALEGAL

Legal writing and critical legal thinking are intertwined. Legal writing can take a number of forms, memos, letters, opinions, memoranda of law for internal purposes, and briefs for the court. The differences in presentation are determined by the intended audience. The similarities are in the need for clarity and accuracy. Preparation of these documents starts with an understanding of the material facts of a case and identifying the legal issues. Critical legal thinking is used to identify what is material, what law applies, and then to apply the law to the facts and come to a conclusion that answers the issue or issues presented.

Critical Legal Thinking

Critical legal thinking The process of identifying the issue, the material facts, and the applicable law and applying the law to come to a conclusion.

Issue The legal matter in dispute.

Critical legal thinking is the process of identifying the **issue**—the legal matter in dispute—presented by a case, identifying the material (also called key or relevant) facts in the case and the applicable law, and then applying the law to the facts to come to a conclusion that answers the issue or issues presented. Critical legal thinking is the thought process that puts the pieces of the legal puzzle together. The critical thinking process starts with a clear understanding of the facts of the client's case and identifying the legal issues in that case.

Before starting the research, one must have a clear picture of all the material facts. Part of the interview with the client is to determine all the facts. Some of what the client thinks are important facts may in fact not be relevant in deciding the legal issue. And some of the facts that seemed unimportant to the client may in fact be relevant and on which the outcome may depend. For example, it may not seem important that the client was struck by a driver going north. It may be a material fact when it is determined that the street was a one-way street going south.

Consider the timeline on a contract case. Assume that a client signed an employee noncompetition contract three months after starting employment. State law may deny the enforceability of the covenant not to compete unless entered into before commencing employment or unless contemporary, full and adequate consideration is given for signing the agreement after commencing employment.

Understanding the relevant facts enables a review of the court cases and the statutory law to determine applicability to the client case. A difference of one fact may make all the difference in the world in the outcome of the case. Consider the case of the client charged with killing King Kong. The facts indicate that King Kong is not a human being. The murder statute of the jurisdiction defines murder as the taking of the life of a human being by another human being; therefore, the statute has not been violated. Other statutes may have been violated, but not the murder statute. The client may be guilty of hunting out of season, hunting without a license, or killing an endangered species, but not murder.

For these issues, additional facts, immaterial in the murder prosecution, may become material. The material facts also would be different in the civil action by the owner of the animal in a suit for damages for loss of an irreplaceable item. What is relevant as a fact depends on the type of case—civil or criminal—and the wrong committed or the right violated.

IN THE WORDS OF THE COURT

Alaska Case Law

WHITING V. STATE, A-8755 (ALASKA APP. 10-12-2005)

MANNHEIMER, Judge.

Michael T. Whiting appeals his conviction for felony driving under the influence, . . . the facts . . . : Whiting and his girlfriend and his girlfriend's six-year-old son decided to go fishing in Gastineau Channel. Whiting piloted a skiff into the channel and then turned the motor off. The three occupants of the skiff fished while the skiff drifted in the channel; Whiting sat in the rear of the skiff near the motor. While Whiting was fishing, he was also drinking alcoholic beverages.

A Coast Guard vessel approached the skiff . . ., discovered that he was under the influence. Whiting claimed that he had been sober when he piloted the boat into the channel, and that he did not become intoxicated until after he stopped the motor and the fishing began.

. . . Whiting's argument hinges on his assertion that the statutory definition of driving under the influence, AS 28.35.030(a) does not include the situation where an intoxicated person is in control of a watercraft whose engine is not running. Whiting's assertion is incorrect. . . . this Court held that "operating" a watercraft includes being in control of the watercraft, even if its engine is not running.

We addressed essentially the same argument in *Kingsley v. State*, 11 p. 3d 1001 (Alaska App. 2000). The defendant in *Kingsley* drove his car into a snow berm, where it became stuck. Kingsley turned the engine off and decided to remain in the car. According to Kingsley, it was only then that he consumed a bottle of whiskey and became intoxicated.

Kingsley argued that, under these circumstances, he was not intoxicated when he was operating the vehicle, and he was never in "control" of the vehicle after he became intoxicated. We rejected this narrow definition of "control".

As Kingsley acknowledges in his brief to this court, a person who engages the engine of a vehicle and allows it to run is not merely exercising physical control over the vehicle but is also "operating" it. Thus, if the engine of Kingsley's vehicle had been running when the police arrived, the State might have proved that Kingsley was operating the vehicle while intoxicated. But the State had to prove only that Kingsley was in actual physical control of the vehicle while intoxicated.

. . . A person's attempt to operate a vehicle may furnish convincing proof that the person is in actual physical control of the vehicle, but a person may exercise actual physical control over a vehicle without making active attempts to operate it.

Whiting was the one who had piloted the skiff into the channel, and Whiting remained primarily in the rear of the skiff, nearest the motor, while his girlfriend and her son sat in the front of the skiff. Under these facts, as a matter of law, Whiting was in physical control of the skiff, and he was therefore operating the skiff for purposes of the DUI statute.

The American justice system is based on the statutory law and case law. Just as in the criminal law issues discussed above, factual analysis requires determining the elements of the crime, looking at the statute, and applying the facts. It may be necessary to look at case law for precedent on the definition of an operative fact. For example, all states have laws prohibiting driving under the influence of alcohol. Some of these statutes also use the terms "vehicle" and "operating." One of the material facts for the researcher to determine is what is defined as a vehicle and what conduct is defined as "operating."

Defense counsel must look carefully to try to differentiate the client's fact pattern from decided cases. Slight variations in facts can be important in successfully arguing a case, or at least make a compelling argument.

Facts Information or details.

Facts are pieces of information or details that in actuality or reality exist, or have occurred, as opposed to someone's theory, supposition, or conjecture. Facts, in the law, are the circumstances of an event, motion, occurrence, or state of affairs, rather than interpretations of its significance. The car was going south on State Street at 55 miles per hour as shown on the radar unit. This <u>is a</u> fact. Supposition, conjecture, or theory, and not fact is the statement of the witness that everyone speeds down the street in front of their house, that the defendant has done it before, that they heard the car driven by the defendant while they were in the house watching TV facing away from the street, and that they heard the car going south at 55 mph.

Material facts A fact significant or essential to the issue.

Immaterial facts A fact not essential to the matter or issue at hand.

Facts may be divided into **material** (relevant) **facts** and **immaterial** (irrelevant) **facts**. A material fact is a fact that is significant or essential to the issue or matter at hand. An immaterial fact is one that is not essential to the matter at issue. Some facts, while not material, may lead to material facts. Consider the case of the person coming from the doctor's office, driving within the speed limit, who strikes another car in the rear at a red stoplight. Is the fact that he was coming from a doctor's office a material fact in the accident? It may be if he were given medication that caused blurred vision or drowsiness and if the doctor told him not to drive or operate any machinery. Certainly knowing this fact leads to the discovery of other relevant facts.

Legal Writing

There are as many writing styles as there are writers. Writers of novels have a style of writing that may devote pages to setting a stage for the characters and more pages developing the characters. Readers probably come to expect this and look forward to long paragraphs building the scene and setting the stage for the plot.

Writers of short stories are more like skilled legal writers. They must quickly and accurately set the stage in few words and tell the story in a short space. Skilled legal

Paralegals *in* Practice

PARALEGAL PROFILE
Ann L. Atkinson

Ann L. Atkinson is a graduate of the University of Nebraska with a Bachelor of Science Degree in Education. She is also an Advanced Certified Paralegal with over 27 years of legal experience. Her professional memberships include the Nebraska Paralegal Association, the National Association of Legal Assistants, and the National Association of Bond Lawyers. Ann is currently employed by the law firm of Kutak Rock LLP in their Omaha, Nebraska office.

I specialize in public finance law, which generally is transactional in nature—preparing, reviewing, and revising contracts or negotiated "deals" between parties. Specifically, I assist the attorneys as they work with state housing agencies or municipalities when they issue bonds for public purposes. The bonds represent a "loan" of money from bondholders. The attorneys with whom I work often act as bond counsel (where we are counsel for the bond issue itself), or we may also serve as underwriter's counsel (in which we are counsel to the underwriter of the bonds).

Since our department focuses primarily on single-family housing, we prepare all the documents that enable an issuer to issue bonds. These bonds then provide proceeds from which the issuer can offer single-family homes to first-time homebuyers at a "below market" interest rate. Our department also handles transactions for multi-family housing such as apartment buildings being constructed, acquired, and/or rehabilitated.

In my position, I coordinate all the things that need to be done in order for a bond issue to close. In order to do so, I rely heavily on writing and critical thinking skills. Tasks include preparing initial drafts of bond documents, researching statutes, proofing and reviewing offering documents and third-party opinions, and assisting with bond closings including the preparation of closing transcripts. Thus, a knowledge of correct grammar, spelling, and punctuation is essential. Critical thinking skills are very useful when preparing documents because they help you follow document processes—the flow of funds, the timing requirements for notices, and knowing when and how to obtain amendment approvals.

writers are those that can explain, persuade, and state facts for the record accurately, concisely, and clearly. The purpose of writing is to communicate. If the writing does not communicate the subject to the reader, it has not served its purpose. Unlike the novelist or poet, the legal writer must follow a set of guidelines dictated by ethical concerns for honesty and candor, while at the same time clearly present the answer to clients that they may not want to hear, or persuade the court to the advocated point of view.

Writing Styles

Both the brief and the memorandum may be on the exact same set of facts, legal issue, and applicable law, but the writing style is totally different. The **memorandum** is a working document for the legal team to be used in the preparation and presentation of a case. As a result, it has to be an objective analysis of the case, including factual subtleties and analysis of the applicable law with any alternate interpretations. For example, as stated by the Ninth Circuit Court of Appeals in *U.S. v. CASTRILLON*, 716 F.2d 1279 in determining whether consent was voluntary,

Memorandum A working legal document for the legal team for use in preparation and presentation of a case.

> . . . Fed.R.Crim.P. 12(e) states that "[w]here factual issues are involved in determining a [pretrial] motion, the court shall state its essential findings on the record." Such a record is necessary to our review. . . . Compliance with the rule 12(e) requirement is particularly important in a case such as this, where we examine "all the surrounding circumstances" . . . Factual subtleties may well affect a determination of voluntariness under this test. . .

The brief written for the court is designed to provide written advocacy of the client's position and must be written to convince the court to adopt a position favorable to the client. The **opinion letter** to a client requires a different style. The opinion letter must explain to a client, who is generally untrained in the law, what legal options the client has and what can and cannot be done based on a set of facts provided by the client. In some ways it is an educational document, it must be informative and detail the options sufficiently to allow the client to act in an appropriate manner. For example, you have asked us to advise you on whether you may set off a cannon at high noon each day, based on the law in . . .

Opinion letter A formal statement of advice based on the lawyers expert knowledge.

A WORD OF CAUTION

The ready availability and ease of use of email has created a new writing style that uses shorthand terminology such as LOL for "laugh out loud." Those in the legal profession must remember that every email is a potential piece of evidence in an electronic discovery request. Emails are frequently forwarded to others. Shortcuts should not be taken in writing emails. The same formality and care that goes into a hardcopy letter on legal stationery should be used in writing the email. Even greater care should be used when the email may contain privileged or confidential information that may accidentally get into the hands of those not covered by the ethical obligation to keep it confidential and may in some cases, such as accidentally sending it to opposing counsel, result in a breach of the attorney-client or work-product privilege.

CHECKLIST Memorandum of Law Template

☐ To:

☐ From:

☐ Date:

☐ Subject:

☐ Facts

☐ Issue(s)

☐ Discussion

☐ Conclusion

Duty of candor Honesty to the court.

Duty of Candor

The ethical obligation to be honest with the court is called the **duty of candor**, Rule 3.3 in the Model Rules of Professional Conduct. In some jurisdictions, such as Indiana, the ethical rule is titled. Conduct Toward the Tribunal.

Rule 3.3. Candor Toward the Tribunal

(a) A lawyer shall not knowingly:
  (1) make a false statement of fact or law to a tribunal or fail to correct a false statement of material fact or law previously made to the tribunal by the lawyer;
  (2) fail to disclose to the tribunal legal authority in the controlling jurisdiction known to the lawyer to be directly adverse to the position of the client and not disclosed by opposing counsel; or
  (3) offer evidence that the lawyer knows to be false. If a lawyer, the lawyer's client, or a witness called by the lawyer, has offered material evidence and the lawyer comes to know of its falsity, the lawyer shall take reasonable remedial measures, including, if necessary, disclosure to the tribunal. A lawyer may refuse to offer evidence, other than the testimony of a defendant in a criminal matter, that the lawyer reasonably believes is false.

(b) A lawyer who represents a client in an adjudicative proceeding and who knows that a person intends to engage, is engaging or has engaged in criminal or fraudulent conduct related to the proceeding shall take reasonable remedial measures, including, if necessary, disclosure to the tribunal.

(c) The duties stated in paragraphs (a) and (b) continue to the conclusion of the proceeding, and apply even if compliance requires disclosure of information otherwise protected by Rule 1.6.

(d) In an ex parte proceeding, a lawyer shall inform the tribunal of all material facts known to the lawyer which will enable the tribunal to make an informed decision, whether or not the facts are adverse.

Amended Sep. 30, 2004, effective Jan. 1, 2005.

Source: West Digest Topics. Reprinted with permission of Thomson/West Publishing.

Web Exploration

Contrast and compare the Indiana rule at http://www.state.in.us/judiciary/rules/prof_conduct/index.html#_Rule_3.3._Candor_Toward_the_Tribunal with the ABA Model Rules of Professional Conduct at www.abanet.org/cpr and the rule in your jurisdiction.

The legal team has an ethical obligation not to mislead the court. Just one brief that intentionally distorts or hides the truth or intentionally misleads the court can destroy a legal career. Even if it doesn't result in sanctions, suspension, or disbarment, judges talk with their colleagues, and a bad reputation for integrity to the court is hard to correct. At the least, the court always will remember that the attorney did shoddy work and may give more credibility to the opposing side in the future, even if later cases by the offending attorney are better prepared and more accurately on point.

Preparing Office Memorandums

In doing research and preparing the memorandum of law, the legal assistant must be careful to include all the relevant applicable statutes and case law. Some paralegals are intimidated by the gruff and even downright nasty attitude of certain lawyers, particularly trial counsel in the middle of a stressful case. The paralegals are afraid the lawyer will "shoot the messenger." The reality is that the attorney *must* know the weaknesses in the case along with the strengths. Nothing is more upsetting to the attorney, whether in court or in a meeting with a client or opposing counsel, than to be surprised by a case, facts, or law that has not been covered in the office memorandum of law.

Office memoranda are frequently indexed by subject and filed in the office for future reference. If the same or a similar fact pattern requires research, these provide a good starting point and can be a major time-saver. So that a memorandum may be indexed properly, the facts upon which the conclusion is based must be clearly stated. All statutes, regulations, and cases must be cited properly so anyone reading the memorandum in the future can look them up. Listing relevant websites used in the preparation also is helpful.

Starting Point

The starting point for the legal researcher is to understand the specific assignment. What is it that the researcher has been asked to research? For the memorandum of law, it usually is to answer a question:

What is the current law on . . . ?

What happens if . . . ?

What is the procedure for . . . ?

Before starting an assignment, the paralegal must be certain what is really being asked. Any questions should be resolved by asking the person for whom this is being prepared: "What does the attorney expect?" Where the paralegal's knowledge of the subject area is sufficient, he or she may know that certain facts may change the outcome—such as the requirement in some states that a subscribing witness to a decedent's will cannot be a beneficiary. Before starting, paralegals must be sure to have all the relevant facts, then restate what they believe they are being asked to research in the form of a statement of the question. For example: "You have asked for the law on the rights of individuals to . . . ."

Part of the skill in legal writing is using analytical skills to find the similarities and differences in cases that can be used as persuasive argument for the position being presented for the client. This is the critical legal thinking aspect of the legal writing process. And writing is a process. It requires research, analysis, organization, writing, editing, and proofreading. Sometimes it requires starting over when the final document when viewed from the position of the ultimate reader does not communicate the necessary information or tell the story.

In the legal working environment, time to rethink, re-research, and rewrite is a luxury. The pressure is on developing good skills to minimize the time necessary to produce an acceptable document, whether it is a letter, an office memorandum, or a court brief.

Memorandum of Law Format

A memo is frequently prepared by the supervising attorney with a request for research and an office memorandum of a specific subject or case. A sample of an assignment memo is shown in Exhibit 11.1. Frequently, the assignment is given in a face-to-face meeting. When the assignment is made orally, it is a good idea to confirm the specific assignment if there is any question of the details required.

Exhibit 11.1   **Assignment memo**

MEMORANDUM

To: Edith Hannah
From: Glenn Hains
Date: January 23, 2006
File   Number: GH 06-1002
Re: Commonwealth of Pennsylvania vs. Kevin Dones

Our client was stopped by a police officer at the bottom of the hill on route 332 in Northhampton Township, at 3:30 on Sunday afternoon, January 15, 2006. He was riding a bicycle south on route 332 and was given a citation for speeding. The police used a radar unit and claimed a speed of 35 mph in a 25 mph zone. He administered a field sobriety test, which gave a reading over the legal limit, and client was given a citation for driving under the influence. He tells me he was riding a bike because his license was suspended for a previous DUI.

Please prepare a brief memorandum of law, with citations and cases.

Exhibit 11.2 Word search function

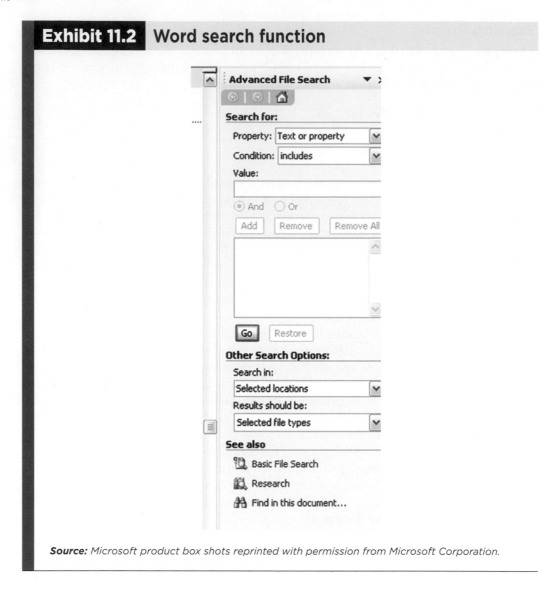

Source: Microsoft product box shots reprinted with permission from Microsoft Corporation.

The format or template for office memoranda is fairly standard, as shown in the Memorandum of Law Template. Some offices may add, for identification purposes, headings such as office file numbers or client identifiers. Some offices that maintain a paper format include subject matter legal terms or areas of law so they can be filed and retrieved if future cases require a memorandum on the same subject. Copies of memorandum are increasingly stored electronically as word processor files. These electronic files can be searched using a search function such as the file search function in Microsoft Word shown in Exhibit 11.2.

When taking an assignment to do research and write a memorandum, a few basics have to be remembered. The attorney, in all probability, will not redo the research or do much more than refer to the material submitted with the memorandum. The memorandum must be an unbiased presentation of the law as it exists, clearly presented. If the content of the memorandum is not accurate and complete, the attorney relying on the analysis and discussion may be, at the least, embarrassed by the opposing counsel or, at the worst, by the court.

Points to remember in preparing a memorandum of law are:

- **Never** rely on case law headnotes. Headnotes are not a primary source of the law.
- **Always** check the language of the court cases. It is the primary authority.

- **Check** the dates of the cases and of the statutes. Be sure they are current law.
- **Shepardize** (GlobalCite, KeyCite, V.Cite) the cases you used and relied on to be certain they have not been overruled by a later case or law.
- **Don't** be afraid to show the cases and law against your client's position.
- **Cite all** sources used. Never plagiarize.
- **Analyze** opposing case law for any differences that may give the attorney a chance to argue that the negative cases are different in some factual or legal way.
- **Ask**, if you don't understand the issues or question involved. It is better to admit that you are having a problem with the research than to give the attorney wrong, incomplete, or unintelligible information.

The format of the memorandum of law is determined by the nature of the assignment, the number of issues, and the ultimate use that will be made of the memorandum, as well as personal preferences of the person making the assignment.

The components of a memorandum of law and the components of a court opinion (case) are similar. Exhibit 11.3 presents a comparison.

Some case opinions have a brief summary or syllabus of the case that is prepared by an editor, such as the West editors or Supreme Court editors, which is not an official part of the case but is provided for reader convenience. Some attorneys prefer to have a Brief Answer under the Statement of the Assignment in a Memorandum of Law. The brief answer is generally a shortened version of the main points of the conclusion.

Samples of a traditional memorandum of law and one prepared for internal government use are shown in Exhibits 11.4 and 11.5.

If you have ever "briefed" a case you will notice the similarity to the list of items shown in the comparison above. A sample of a case and a case brief is provided in Appendix A: How to Brief a Case.

Facts

Paralegals, of course, must have a clear statement of the facts from which to work. The facts relied upon in writing the memo must be part of the ultimate final memorandum. Other people may read the memorandum. They need to understand the specific facts upon which the analysis is based, particularly if they read it at a time when the

Exhibit 11.3 Components of court opinions and memorandums of law

COURT OPINIONS	MEMORANDUMS OF LAW
Caption: Parties, citation, relevant dates	**Heading:** Assigning party, client, file number
Judicial history: Prior proceeding (how the case got to this court)	**Statement of the assignment:** History of what happened and why the client sought representation
Issue: Legal question before the court	**Issue:** Legal issues of clients raised in statement of assignment
Facts: Relevant facts used to decide case	**Statement of facts:** Relevant facts
Analysis and discussion: Discussion of the facts, rules of law, issues, judicial reasons for decision	**Analysis and discussion:** Discussion of each issue, how the applicable law applies, what relevant facts impact the decision
Conclusion: Holding of the Court	**Conclusion:** Restatement of the conclusion to each issue analyzed and discussed above, summarizing the main points

Exhibit 11.4 Sample memorandum of law prepared by leading legal research provider

MEMORANDUM OF LAW

TO: Ellen Holroyd, Esq.

FROM: ███████████████████

DATE: January 29, 2004

RE: SEC Definitions of Terms Under the Sarbanes-Oxley Act of 2002

QUESTION PRESENTED

With regard to its regulations promulgated pursuant to the Sarbanes-Oxley Act of 2002, how does the Security and Exchange Commission define the concepts "material violation", "credible evidence", and "reasonable behavior" by an attorney?

DISCUSSION

Section 307 of the Sarbanes-Oxley Act of 2002 ("Sarbanes-Oxley") requires the Securities and Exchange Commission ("SEC") to "prescribe minimum standards of professional conduct for attorneys appearing and practicing before the Commission in any way in the representation of issuers." Implementation of Standards of Professional Conduct for Attorneys, Securities Act Release No. 33,8185, 68 Fed. Reg. 6,296 (Feb. 6, 2003.) According to the SEC, these standards "must include a rule requiring an attorney to report evidence of a material violation of securities laws or breach of fiduciary duty or similar violation by the issuer." Id., at 6,296. This memorandum discusses the definitions embraced by the SEC for "material violation," "credible evidence," and "reasonable behavior" by an attorney, three concepts found in the regulations adopted by the SEC pertaining to Sarbanes-Oxley.

Page 4 of 27

Exhibit 11.4 **Sample memorandum of law prepared by leading legal research provider** (continued)

III. Definition of "Reasonable Behavior" By An Attorney

Such a definition necessarily brings up next the question of what the SEC deems to be "reasonable behavior" for attorneys with regard to their duty to report actual or suspected Sarbanes-Oxley violations. In its formulation of what constitutes "reasonable behavior" on the part of an attorney under the Sarbanes-Oxley regulations, the SEC points out that it is not a "bright line" test, and that it is dependent on the circumstances surrounding not just the alleged violation, but also the attorney involved:

> This formulation, while intended to adopt an objective standard, also recognizes that there is a range of conduct in which an attorney may engage without being unreasonable. The "circumstances" are the circumstances at the time the attorney decides whether he or she is obligated to report the information. These circumstances may include, among others, the attorney's professional skills, background and experience, the time constraints under which the attorney is acting, the attorney's previous experience and familiarity with the client, and the availability of other lawyers with whom the lawyer may consult.

Implementation of Standards of Professional Conduct for Attorneys, Securities Act Release No. 33,8185, 68 Fed. Reg. 6,296, 6,302 (Feb. 6, 2003.) Thus, what is deemed reasonable behavior for one attorney could differ significantly from that for another attorney, depending on the various factors laid out by the SEC.

CONCLUSION

While the SEC provided guidance as to the meanings of all three concepts discussed in this memo, it is clear that it intended there to be no "bright line", "one size fits all" definitions for these phrases. That said, a "material violation" for purposes of the SEC's Sarbanes-Oxley rules would appear to be a violation of such consequence that a reasonable and prudent investor would consider it important to know about when determining whether to buy, sell, or hold a particular security. "Credible evidence" would appear to be evidence of a material violation substantial enough that a prudent

U.S. Department of Justice
Immigration and Naturalization Service

HQADN 70/23

Office of the Executive Associate Commissioner

425 1 Street NW
Washington, DC 20536

May 24, 2001

MEMORANDUM FOR   Michael A. Pearson
Executive Associate Commissioner
Office of Field Operations

FROM: Michael D. Cronin /s/
Acting Executive Associate Commissioner
Office of Programs

SUBJECT: Public Law 106-378, adjustment of status of certain Syrian nationals.

This memorandum provides eligibility information and adjudication policy guidance for the implementation of Public Law 106-378, which pertains to the adjustment of certain Syrian nationals who were granted asylum after arriving in the United States after December 31, 1991.

ELIGIBILITY

Public Law 106-378 provides for the adjustment of status of a principal alien as well as an alien who is the spouse, child, or unmarried son or daughter of a principal alien.

Principal alien. In order to be eligible for adjustment under this law, the principal alien must:
1. Be a Jewish national of Syria;
2. Have arrived in the United States after December 31, 1991, after being permitted by the Syrian government to depart from Syria;
3. Be physically present in the United States at the time of filing the application to adjust status;
4. Apply for adjustment of status under Public Law 106-378 no later than October 26, 2001, or, have applied for adjustment of status under another provision of law prior to October 27, 2000, and request to have the basis of that application changed to Public Law 106-378;
5. Have been physically present in the United States for at least one year after being granted asylum;
6. Not be firmly resettled in any foreign country; and Memorandum: Public Law 106-378, adjustment of status of certain Syrian nationals.

REQUIRED FIELD OFFICE ACTION

Field offices are to identify all potentially eligible Syrian asylee adjustment applications and forward them and the related A-files to NSC within 30-days of this memorandum. The appropriate code, "SY6, 7 or 8" and reference to Public Law 106-378 must be noted. A-files are to be routed to the NSC in separate batches, with individual cover sheets attached to the outside face of each file reflecting "**SYRIAN ASYLEE P. L. 106-378**". If, for whatever reason, a field office cannot accomplish this goal, they are to provide a report to their respective region identifying each case,
explaining the reason(s), and advising the anticipated date of completion of the A-file transfer. Regions are requested to review the report and take appropriate action.

SERVICE CENTER ACTION ON APPROVED ASYLEE APPLICATIONS

The NSC must review all asylum adjustment cases received via Direct Mail as well as all cases forwarded to them from the field to cull out those Syrian nationals whose applications contain evidence of Syrian nationality, arrival in the United States

| **Exhibit 11.5** | **Sample memorandum of law prepared by the U.S. Department of Justice** *(continued)* |

after December 31, 1991, and a grant of asylum or asylee dependent status. The NSC must also retrieve A-files belonging to qualifying Syrian applicants inappropriately coded as "AS" adjustments, and take corrective action. A list containing the names of Syrian asylees has already been provided to the NSC to help in this regard. The NSC will also track the total number of cases approved. After the NSC approves 2,000 principal beneficiaries under this law, the NSC will stop adjudicating applications, and will notify HQ ISD and HQ ADN that the numerical limitation has been reached.

SUPPLEMENTAL FILING INSTRUCTIONS

The Form I-485 supplemental filing instructions are being modified to instruct qualified applicants to identify themselves by writing **"SYRIAN ASYLEE P. L. 106-378"** in Part 2, Block 2. Since many qualified Syrian asylees may be unaware of their special classification or the correct way to claim it, the NSC should review all newly submitted asylee adjustment applications, and, when appropriate, endorse the Form I-485 as described above. When an applicant's eligibility to adjust under Public Law 106-378 has been verified, the adjudicator will check the "other" block in the "Section of Law" portion of the FOR INS USE ONLY Section of Form I-485 and will enter the notation, **"Public Law 106-378."**

CONCLUSION

Segregating the Syrian asylum adjustments for proper adjudication is essential to preserve the use of the 10,000 visa numbers authorized annually for other asylees who are eligible to adjust their status. If you have questions regarding the adjudication of Syrian-processed asylum adjustments, please contact your center or regional representative. If needed, service center. . . .

Source: *United States Department of Justice.*

paralegal is not available to answer questions, such as in the middle of a case, when out ill, on vacation, or if the paralegal has left the firm. It also is frequently necessary to recite other facts not relied upon and the reason for not considering them—that the result would be different. An example is a notation that this fact pattern is based upon the participants' all being over the age of majority for contracting, or over the age to purchase and consume alcoholic beverages.

Analysis

A memorandum must present both sides of the issue and, in that respect, be a neutral, unbiased, objective presentation of applicable laws as they apply to the facts of the case. Issues that the opposing attorney or the judge may raise should be considered and presented. A good analysis will include a discussion of how the fact pattern may differ in cases that are not on point but may be used by opposing counsel.

The memorandum the paralegal prepares may be the basis for the court brief that the attorney or someone else will prepare. To be able to meet the ethical obligation to the court, the person who presents a persuasive argument favoring the client must know all the relevant statutory and case law.

Editing and Rewriting

The written word is a reflection of the writer. Everyone who reads the memorandum will measure the researcher's reputation and skill level. Each person who reads the memorandum will measure the writer's communication skills. The paralegal, however, may be writing for a certain audience, and someone other than that might read the memorandum unaware of the intended reader.

Certain elements of writing style transcend the audience. For example:

- Is it clear?
- Are the words used properly?

- Is the spelling correct?
- Is it written using proper English grammar?
- If it is being written for an audience for whom English is a second language, is that made clear?
- Where there are variations in translation of foreign language terms, have these been clarified? For example, were the facts translated from words spoken by someone from Spain or someone from Puerto Rico, from someone who speaks Northern High German or Bavarian Southern German or Swiss German?

Preparing Court Briefs

Amicus curia Briefs submitted by interested parties, as a "friend of the court," who do not have standing in the action.

Each court has court rules on the requirements for briefs submitted by the parties and by "friends of the court—*amicus curia*." The format and required sections of a brief prepared for the court is determined by these rules, and in some cases the personal preferences of the judge or justices. Before undertaking the task the preparer should always obtain a current copy of the court rules and as a practice pointer, contact the judge's law clerk for any additional limitations or requirements.

At times the court is unable to thoroughly read the brief before oral argument. In these situations the preliminary statement becomes an important part of focusing the court on the issues presented for your side of the case. Being able to state your side of the case briefly is not easy, but it is worth the effort. It requires clear, concise, and careful choice of words that will be remembered as the hearing progresses, and later when the court is making its analysis and decision.

The table of contents, partial table of authorities, summary of the argument, and conclusion of an amicus curia brief submitted in a case to the United States Supreme Court is shown in Exhibit 11.6.

Citations

Citation A reference to the source of the information.

A legal **citation** is a reference to the source of the information that allows someone else to find the case or other material mentioned in a document. The form of the citation must allow others to find the material. The format must be one that others in the legal community generally accept and use. If a person in California submits a brief to a court, a person in New York or in Florida must be able to use the citation to locate the items referred to in the document in a traditional legal library or electronic law source such as Loislaw, VersusLaw, Lexis, or Westlaw.

Primary authority The actual law itself.

Secondary authority Writings that explain the law.

All legal authorities can be divided into two groups—primary authority and secondary authority. **Primary authority** includes constitutions, statutes, cases, and administrative regulations. Everything else is a **secondary authority** explaining the primary authority or a finding tool providing a method of locating primary authority. With a consistent citation format, the reader can determine the source of the authority mentioned and find the applicable primary source (constitution, statute, regulation, or case) or secondary source or finding tool (treatise, encyclopedia, digest, or dictionary).

Judges and lawyers in some states are abandoning the longstanding tradition of putting citations in the body of a document and now are putting the citations at the bottom of the document in the footnotes. They claim it makes reading legal opinions easier by eliminating the interference of the citations with the flow of words.

Traditional Sources (Print)

The traditional method for publishing primary and secondary authority is the paper form, including books, collections of books, and series of books. Where a case, statute, or regulation is available in more than one series of books, such as the official reporter of the state and a private publication such as those published by West Publishing, the citation to both locations—known as parallel citations—is required. The citation form is basically the same:

Volume	Book or Series	Page
232	Atlantic 2d	44

In this example, written as 232 A.2d 44, 232 refers to the volume in the Atlantic 2d series reporter service of West Publishing Company, and 44 refers to the page on which the authority may be found.

Bluebook

The most commonly used guide to citation form is the publication *The Bluebook: A Uniform System of Citation*. This is the generally accepted authority for proper citation form unless the rules of a particular court dictate a different citation format.

Exhibit 11.6 *Amicus curia* brief filed with the U.S. Supreme Court

No. 08-479

In The
Supreme Court of the United States

Safford Unified School District #1, *et al.*,
Petitioners,

v.

April Redding,
LEGAL GUARDIAN OF MINOR CHILD,
Respondent.

On Writ of Certiorari to the
United States Court of Appeals
for the Ninth Circuit

**BRIEF OF *AMICI CURIAE*
THE RUTHERFORD INSTITUTE,
GOLDWATER INSTITUTE
AND CATO INSTITUTE
IN SUPPORT OF RESPONDENT**

John W. Whitehead
Counsel of Record
Douglas R. McKusick
The Rutherford Institute
1440 Sachem Place
Charlottesville, VA 22911
(434) 978-3888

Timothy Lynch
Ilya Shapiro
Cato Institute
1000 Massachusetts Ave., NW
Washington, DC 20001
(202) 218-4600

Clint Bolick
Nicholas C. Dranias
Goldwater Institute
Scharf-Norton Center
For Constitutional
Litigation
500 E. Coronado Road
Phoenix, AZ 85004
(602) 462-5000

TABLE OF AUTHORITIES

Cases

Bell v. Wolfish, 441 U.S. 520 (1979)........................7, 9

C.B. by and through Breeding v. Driscoll, 82 F.3d 383 (11th Cir. 1996)................................13

Calabretta v. Floyd, 189 F.3d 808 (9th Cir. 1991).......5

Camara v. Municipal Court, 387 U.S. 523 (1967)..6, 7

Cornfield by Lewis v. Consol. High Sch. Dist. No. 230, 991 F.2d 1316 (7th Cir. 1993) 8, 11, 17

Doe v. Renfrow, 631 F.2d 91 (7th Cir.), *reh'g denied*, 635 F.2d 582 (7th Cir. 1980), *cert. denied*, 451 U.S. 1022 (1981) 5

Edwards v. Aguillard, 482 U.S. 578 (1987)..............19

Illinois v. Gates, 462 U.S. 213 (1983)......................16

Leatherman v. Tarrant County Narcotics, Intelligence & Coordination Unit, 507 U.S. 163 (1993) 22

Lilly v. Virginia, 527 U.S. 116 (1999) 12

Mary Beth G. v. City of Chicago, 723 F.2d 1263 (7th Cir. 1983)..5

Maryland v. Garrison, 480 U.S. 79 (1987) 15

New Jersey v. T.L.O., 469 U.S. 325 (1985) ....passim

O'Connor v. Ortega, 480 U.S. 709 (1987)..................6

Pearson v. Callahan, 129 S.Ct. 808 (2009).........21, 22

Phaneuf v.Fraikin, 448 F.3d 591 (2d Cir. 2006)   5, 8, 11

(continued)

Exhibit 11.6 *Amicus curia* brief filed with the U.S. Supreme Court *(continued)*

SUMMARY OF THE ARGUMENT

In *New Jersey v. T.L.O.*, 469 U.S. 325 (1985), this Court accommodated the interests of public school educators and administrators in maintaining order and discipline in public schools by easing the restrictions on searches normally imposed upon state actors by the Fourth Amendment. In ruling that in-school searches of students in the school setting need not be supported by probable cause, however, the *T.L.O.* decision made clear that the "reasonableness" of a school search largely depends on whether the search is "excessively intrusive in light of the age and sex of the student and nature of the infraction." *Id.* at 342. This Court clearly signaled that the severity of the privacy invasion must be considered when deciding whether school officials have violated a student's Fourth Amendment rights.

In light of *T.L.O.*'s direction to consider the intrusiveness of a search, the *en banc* Ninth Circuit correctly understood here that a strip search of a student will be reasonable only when school officials have clear evidence to justify it. Strip searches are unquestionably privacy invasions of a different order and higher degree than "ordinary" searches and should be undertaken rarely. Only when school officials have highly credible evidence showing (1) the student is in possession of objects posing a significant danger to the school and (2) that the student has secreted the objects in a place only a strip search will uncover is such a search reasonable.

CONCLUSION

Throughout their merits brief, Petitioners decry a regrettable consequence of the decision below: educators must now "school themselves" in Fourth Amendment jurisprudence and allows courts to second-guess their judgment. But, given the seriousness of the intrusion effected by strip searches, this consequence is unavoidable.

School officials must realize that they may conduct strip searches only in extremely limited circumstances, and only on the basis of compelling evidence. The alternative implicit in the Petitioners' suggested resolution of this case is an unblinking deference to school officials that places students' privacy and security in grave jeopardy.

For the above reasons, the Ninth Circuit properly found that the strip search of Savana Redding was not reasonable and therefore violated the Fourth Amendment. That decision should be affirmed as guidance to school officials, and to ensure that the practice of strip-searching students remains appropriately rare.

For example, the executive administrator of the Superior Court of Pennsylvania issued this notice:

> Pennsylvania Superior Court will be issuing opinions containing a Universal Citation. This citation will be as follows:
>
> Jones v. Smith, 1999 PA Super, 1.
>
> The second number is a Court-issued number on the opinion. Each opinion will also have numbered paragraphs, to be used for pinpoint citation, e.g., Jones v. Smith, 1999 PA Super, 1, 15. Citation to opinions that have not yet been issued an Atlantic 2d citation are to be in the Universal Citation number. After the official citation has been issued, citation is to be only the official citation, and not the Universal Citation.

Effectively, the old citation format, citing to the book, is still to be used.

ALWD Citation Format

Association of Legal Writing Directors (ALWD) A society for professors who coordinate legal writing instruction.

A citation format, written by the **Association of Legal Writing Directors (ALWD)**, is provided in the *ALWD Citation Manual, A Professional System of Citation*. The ALWD is a society for professors who coordinate legal writing instruction in legal education.

One of the attributes of the manual, as set out in the preface, is that it is "a set of rules that reflects a consensus in the legal profession about how citations should function." The *ALWD Manual* includes, in addition to the general citation rules, an appendix containing court citation rules for the individual states. Exhibit 11.7 shows the comparison between the Bluebook and the ALWD rules for citation format.

Universal Citation Format

The *Universal Citation Guide* represents an attempt by the American Association of Law Libraries (AALL), Committee on Citation Formats, to create a set of universal citation rules for American law that are vendor (publisher) neutral and medium (print and electronic) neutral.

The various formats of electronic distribution require a system of citation that can be applied consistently to allow researchers to find the referenced authority regardless of the research tool used. Whereas the traditional, paper or book-based, citation uses information based on internal page numbers, the **Universal Citation Format** relies upon the courts to use numbered paragraphs in its opinions. Any publisher of the case law then can preserve the information provided by the court including the citation references to the case and paragraph.

Anyone who has read and compared a case in a book with a case online is aware that the page size and the display are different. Unless the online computer display is in a photo-image format, such as Adobe PDF, locating a specific page or reference can be difficult. Librarians and courts are recognizing the need for pinpoint citations for the on-screen user.

The Universal Citation Format represents an attempt to solve this problem. The difficulty with some courts is the requirement that the Universal Citation Format be used only until the hardcopy is published, at which time the traditional citation must be used. As a result, you may see the following citation format within documents:

Jones v. Smith, 1999 Pennsylvania Superior 1, ___Pa Super___, ___A2d___(1999) in which the blank spaces are provided to insert the ultimate volume and page number in the print version when it is available. Appendix D lists court name abbreviations.

Other Citation Formats

Many states, including Pennsylvania, have adopted as their official citation format one that originally was created by publishers such as West Publishing Company. These sometimes are referred to as **vendor-specific citation formats**. The West Publishing Company format is based on the West Regional Reporter system and its publications of federal material.

New methods of electronic information technology, in the form of databases, CD-ROMs, and the Internet, have created a number of problems with the traditional citation format. Some of the vendors have claimed copyright protection for their pagination systems.

In 1985, West Publishing Company, in a case against Mead Data Central, argued successfully that the wholesale use of its *pagination* by a competing online publisher infringed upon West's copyright interest in the arrangement of cases in its court reports. And in a 1998 case involving Matthew Bender & Company and West Publishing Company, the Second Circuit held that West's pagination was not protected by copyright. Obviously, all claims to a pagination system or citation system that is vendor-specific will result in some action to protect the corporate claim for copyright, trademark, or potential patent for some electronic methodology.

Table of Authorities

A **table of authorities** is a listing of the citations or other references in a document and the page numbers where they are located. A Table of Authorities creation tool is included in the two most popular word processor programs used in the law office, WordPerfect and Microsoft Word. Each desired authority is first identified and marked by opening the Table of Authorities menu (pressing ALT+ SHIFT+ I) and organized by category, as shown in Exhibit 11.8. Each authority is marked and an identifier inserted in the document called a TA or Table of Authority Entry in MS Word. These marks are visible when the Hidden Marks button is selected, as shown in Exhibit 11.9.

Web Exploration

Check the ALWD website for the latest updates at www.alwd.org.

Universal Citation Format A system for citation relying on the courts to number the paragraphs in their opinions.

Web Exploration

Download A Draft User Guide to the AALL universal case citation at http://www.allnet.org/committee/citation/case.html.

Vendor-specific citation format Citation format of a legal publisher adopted by a court.

Web Exploration

For a discussion on the use of citations in the traditional format or as footnotes, see the *New York Times* article "Legal Citations on Trial In Innovation v. Tradition" by William Glaberson at http://www.nytimes.com/2001/07/08/us/legal-citations-on-trial-in-innovation-v-traditional.html.

Table of authorities A listing of the citations or other references in a document and the page numbers where they are located.

Exhibit 11.7 Comparison of selected ALWD third edition rules and *The Bluebook* 18th edition rules

RULE	ALWD CITATION	BLUEBOOK CITATION	DIFFERENCES
Typeface **ALWD:** Rule 1 **BB:** B13 & Rule 2.0	Ordinary type and *italics* (or <u>underlining</u>). No distinctions based on type of document (law review v. court document) or placement of citation within the paper. Rule 1.1 in the third edition indicates that some journals and book publishers that do not follow ALWD require the use of large and small capital letters; Sidebar 23.2 provides examples of how to use large and small capital letters in various circumstances.	Ordinary type, *italics* (or <u>underlining</u>), and SMALL CAPS. Different fonts required depending on type of document and where source is cited within the paper.	ALWD has one set of conventions, not two. ALWD does not use small caps as a typeface.
Abbreviations and Spacing **ALWD:** Rule 2 **BB:** B5.1.1(v), B10.1, & Rule 6.1	F. Supp. F.3d Corp. Govt. Intl. Petr. In citations, ALWD gives the writer the flexibility to abbreviate words found in the appendices.	F. Supp. F.3d Corp. Gov't Int'l Pet'r In citations, the Bluebook requires that words in a case citation (as opposed to a case name used in a textual sentence) be abbreviated if the words appear in the Tables.	No substantial differences on spacing. ALWD abbreviations end with periods; some Bluebook abbreviations include apostrophes. ALWD provides flexibility regarding use of abbreviations.
Capitalization **ALWD:** Rule 3 **BB:** B10.6 & Rule 8	*Federal Civil Procedure before Trial*	*Federal Civil Procedure Before Trial*	ALWD eliminates the "and prepositions of four or fewer letters" part of the Bluebook, which brings legal citation closer to non-legal style.
Numbers **ALWD:** Rule 4 **BB:** Rule 6.2	Indicates that the convention in law is to use words for zero through ninety-nine in all text and notes. However, ALWD provides flexibility on whether to designate numbers with words or numerals. Ordinal contractions are presented as follows: 1st, 2d, 3d, 4th, etc.	Use words for zero through ninety-nine in all text and notes. Ordinal contractions are presented as follows: 1st, 2d, 3d, 4th, etc.	No substantial differences, other than ALWD allows for more flexibility. However, ALWD inserts a comma in some four-digit numerals: 3,000.
Page spans **ALWD:** Rule 5 **BB:** Rule 3.2(a)	125–126 **or** 125–26	125–26	ALWD gives a choice on how to present a page span; you may retain all digits or drop repetitive digits and retain two digits on the right-hand side of the span, as in Bluebook 3.2(a).

Exhibit 11.7	Comparison of selected ALWD third edition rules and *The Bluebook* 18th edition rules *(continued)*		

RULE	ALWD CITATION	BLUEBOOK CITATION	DIFFERENCES
Footnotes and endnotes **ALWD:** Rule 7 **BB:** Rule 3.2(b)–(c)	n. 7 nn. 12–13	n. 7 nn. 12–13	ALWD requires a space after n. or nn. abbreviation.
Supra* and *infra **ALWD:** Rule 10 **BB:** Rule 3.5	*Supra* n. 45.	*Supra* note 45.	Under ALWD, abbreviate note as "n." and place a space after the period.
Id. **ALWD:** Rule 11.3 **BB:** B5.2, Rules 4.1, 10.9 & 12.9	*Id.* at 500.	*Id.* at 500.	Basically similar rules. ALWD eliminates the "5 *id.* in a row" rule found in Bluebook Rule 10.9. In the ALWD Manual, *id.* cannot be used with Practitioner and Court documents. Rule 29.6.
Cases **ALWD:** Rule 12 **BB:** B5 & Rule 10	*Brown v. Bd. of Educ.,* 349 U.S. 294, 297 (1955). *MBNA Am. Bank, N.A. v. Cardoso,* 707 N.E.2d 189 (Ill. App. 1st Dist. 1998). [required inclusion of district court information]	*Brown v. Bd. of Educ.,* 349 U.S. 294, 297 (1955). *MBNA Am. Bank, N.A. v. Cardoso,* 707 N.E.2d 189 (Ill. App. Ct. 1st Dist. 1998). [permissive inclusion of district information]	Under ALWD, case names are always italicized or underlined. Under ALWD, you do not have to abbreviate words in case names. For those who want to abbreviate, Appendix 3 provides a longer list of words that are abbreviated. ALWD requires division and district information for state appellate courts, and eliminates "Ct." from most court abbreviations. For cases cited from Westlaw or LexisNexis, ALWD does not require the docket number of the case. ALWD also requires two asterisks to identify multiple pages of a pinpoint cite.
Constitutions **ALWD:** Rule 13 **BB:** B7 & Rule 11	U.S. Const. amend. V.	U.S. Const. amend. V.	No substantial differences.
Statutes **ALWD:** Rule 14	18 U.S.C. § 1965 (2000).	18 U.S.C § 1965 (2000).	No substantial differences.

Exhibit 11.7 **Comparison of selected ALWD third edition rules and *The Bluebook* 18th edition rules** *(continued)*

RULE	ALWD CITATION	BLUEBOOK CITATION	DIFFERENCES
BB: B6.1.1, B6.1.2 & Rule 12			
Legislative Materials **ALWD:** Rules 15 & 16 **BB:** B6.1.6 & Rule 13	Sen. Res. 146, 109th Cong. (2005).	S. Res. 146, 109th Cong. (2005).	ALWD abbreviates Senate as "Sen." instead of "S." to avoid confusion with other abbreviations. Most forms are relatively consistent.
Court Rules **ALWD**: Rule 17 **BB:** B6.1.3 & Rule 12.8	Fed. R. Civ. P. 11.	Fed. R. Civ. P. 11.	No substantial differences.
Administrative Materials **ALWD:** Rules 19 and 20 **BB:** B6.1.4 & Rule 14.2	34 C.F.R. § 607.1 (2006). 70 Fed. Reg. 10868 (Mar. 5, 2005).	34 C.F.R. § 607.1 (2006). 70 Fed. Reg. 10868 (Mar. 5, 2005).	C.F.R. citation is the same. Both require an exact date for Fed. Reg. citations. ALWD includes guidance about how to cite C.F.R. references found on unofficial electronic databases, such as Westlaw and LexisNexis. Rule 19.1(d).
Books and Treatises **ALWD**: Rule 22 **BB:** B8 & Rule 15	Charles Alan Wright, Arthur R. Miller & Mary Kay Kane, *Federal Practice and Procedure* vol. 7A, § 1751, 10–17 (3d ed., West 2005). OR Charles Alan Wright et al., *Federal Practice and Procedure* vol. 7A, § 1751, 10–17 (3d ed., West 2005).	7A Charles Alan Wright, Arthur R. Miller & Mary Kay Kane, *Federal Practice and Procedure* § 1751, at 10–17 (3d ed. 2005). OR 7A Charles Alan Wright et al., *Federal Practice and Procedure* § 1751, at 10–17 (3d ed. 2005).	ALWD places volume information after the title, just like any other subdivisions. ALWD separates subdivisions separated with a comma, but no "at." ALWD requires that the publisher be included, no matter what type of document. ALWD uses et al. for three authors or more, compared with the Bluebook which uses et al. for two authors or more.
Legal Periodicals **ALWD**: Rule 23	Geoffrey P. Miller, *Bad Judges*, 83 Tex. L. Rev. 431 (2004). Margaret Graham Tebo, *Duty Calls*, 91 ABA J. 35 (Apr. 2005).	Geoffrey P. Miller, *Bad Judges*, 83 Tex. L. Rev. 431 (2004). Margaret Graham Tebo, *Duty Calls*, A.B.A. J., Apr. 2005, at 35.	ALWD eliminates most distinctions between Consecutively and non-consecutively paginated articles. Include longer date for non-consecutively paginated journals, but do so within the parenthetical.

Exhibit 11.7	Comparison of selected ALWD third edition rules and *The Bluebook* 18th edition rules *(continued)*		

RULE	ALWD CITATION	BLUEBOOK CITATION	DIFFERENCES
BB: B9 & Rule 16	Carrie Ann Wozniak, Student Author, *Difficult Problems Call for New Solutions: Are Guardians Proper for Viable Fetuses of Mentally Incompetent Mothers in State Custody?* 34 Stetson L. Rev. 193 (2004). Jodi Wilgoren, *Prosecution Lays out Case for Harsh Sentencing of B.T.K. Killer in Gory Detail*, 154 N.Y. Times A14 (Aug. 18, 2005).	Carrie Ann Wozniak, Comment, *Difficult Problems Call for New Solutions: Are Guardians Proper for Viable Fetuses of Mentally Incompetent Mothers in State Custody?* 34 Stetson L. Rev. 193 (2004). Jodi Wilgoren, *Prosecution Lays out Case for Harsh Sentencing of B.T.K. Killer in Gory Detail*, N.Y. Times, Aug. 18, 2005, at A14.	ALWD uses the term "Student Author" to replace Note, Comment, Recent Development, etc.
A.L.R. Annotations **ALWD:** Rule 24 **BB:** Rule 16.6.6	Carolyn Kelly MacWilliam, *Individual and Corporate Liability for Libel and Slander in Electronic Communications, Including E-mail, Internet and Websites*, 3 A.L.R.6th 153 (2005).	Carolyn Kelly MacWilliam, Annotation, *Individual and Corporate Liability for Libel and Slander in Electronic Communications, Including E-mail, Internet and Websites*, 3 A.L.R.6th 153 (2005).	ALWD eliminates the "Annotation" reference.
Legal Dictionaries **ALWD:** Rule 25 **BB:** Rule 15.8	*Black's Law Dictionary* 87 (Bryan A. Garner ed., 8th ed., West 2004).	*Black's Law Dictionary* 87 (8th ed. 2004).	ALWD treats dictionaries like books.
Legal Encyclopedias **ALWD:** Rule 26 **BB:** Rule 15.8	98 C.J.S. *Witnesses* § 397 (2002). 68 Am. Jur. 2d *Schools* §§ 20–24 (2000 & Supp. 2005).	98 C.J.S. *Witnesses* § 397 (2002). 68 Am. Jur. 2d *Schools* §§ 20–24 (2000 & Supp. 2005).	No substantial differences; however, ALWD provides expanded coverage and includes a list of many abbreviations for state encyclopedias.
Internet **ALWD:** Rule 40 **BB:** Rule 18.2.3	Fed. Jud. Ctr., *History of the Federal Judiciary*, http://www.fjc.http://www.fjc.gov/history/home.nsf (accessed Aug. 18, 2005).	Federal Judicial Center, *History of the Federal Judiciary* (visited Aug. 18, 2005), at http://www.fjc.gov/history/home.nsf.	ALWD permits the abbreviation of an organizational author's name, to save space. ALWD uses "accessed" instead of "visited" to be consistent with non-legal citation guides. The Bluebook contains different formats for material that appears only on the Web and for material that appears on the Web and in other medium. The position of the date parenthetical moves depending on the type of information cited.

(continued)

Exhibit 11.7   **Comparison of selected ALWD third edition rules and *The Bluebook* 18th edition rules** *(continued)*

RULE	ALWD CITATION	BLUEBOOK CITATION	DIFFERENCES
Signals **ALWD**: Rule 44 **BB**: B4 & Rule 1.2	Signals are *e.g., accord, see, see also, cf., contra, compare . . . with, but see, but cf.,* and *see generally.*	Signals are *e.g., accord, see, see also, cf., contra, compare . . . with, but see, but cf.,* and *see generally.*	Under ALWD, all signals may be separated with semicolons. Under the Bluebook, a new citation sentence must start when there is a new type of signal. (Signals are categorized by type in the Bluebook—supportive, comparative, contradictory, or background—whereas in ALWD, the signals are ordered individually.) ALWD does not use any punctuation after a signal.
Order of Cited Authority **ALWD**: Rule 45 **BB**: B4.5 & Rule 1.4	ALWD lists federal, state, and foreign court cases first by jurisdiction, then in reverse chronological order.	Federal (appellate and trial) court cases are ordered in reverse chronological order. State court cases are first, alphabetized by state, and then ranked within each state.	Minor differences in the order when looking at the list of specific sources: (1) Under ALWD, statutes (federal and state) come before rules of evidence and procedure, whereas in the Bluebook, federal statutes and rules of evidence and procedure come before state statutes and rules of evidence and procedure. (2) Under the ALWD, the student-authored articles are classified with all other material in law reviews, law journals, and other periodicals, whereas in the Bluebook, the student-authored articles are separate, and cited after the non-student-authored articles.
Quotations **ALWD**: Rule 47 **BB**: B12 & Rule 5	ALWD says to block indent passages if they contain at least fifty words OR if they exceed four lines of typed text.	The *Bluebook* says to block indent passages if they contain at least 50 words.	ALWD does not require you to count the exact number of words in long quotations.

Source: Copyright © 2005, Darby Dickenson. Reprinted with permission.

Exhibit 11.8 Table of Authorities selection menus

Exhibit 11.9 Table of Authorities hidden characters

The table of authorities may be inserted using the Insert Table of Authorities selection in the Reference tab, as shown in Exhibit 11.10.

Cite Checking

Cite checking is the process of verifying that the proper citation format has been used in a document. The term also means checking the referenced case or statute to determine that it is valid and that it has not been repealed or overturned. The strictness with which the citation rules must be applied, as well as the method—*Bluebook*, *ALWD Citation Manual*, or Universal Citation Format—depends on the wishes and demands of the attorney for whom the document is prepared or the court or judge to

Cite checking The process of verifying proper citation format in a document.

Exhibit 11.10 Table of Authorities options menu

whom it is submitted. Some courts view the presentation of improper citation format with a jaundiced eye, just as they view improper punctuation, improper spelling, and bad grammar. Others are upset if the citation to the paper references or online legal research service available to them is not used.

Bluebook and *ALWD* Compared

Which citation format is used depends on the local custom and courts in which the firm or supervising attorney practices (and the wishes of your instructors!). The two forms used most commonly—the *Bluebook* and the *ALWD Manual*—have a number of similarities. Both of these documents are divided into parts and rules—the *Bluebook* into three parts and the *ALWD Manual* into seven parts.

The parts are further divided into rules. The *Bluebook* has 20 basic rules, and the *ALWD* 50 rules. Most of the rules have a common pattern, and some are the same, such as *Bluebook* Rule 12–Statutes, and *ALWD* Rule 14 on the method of citing the United States Code: 18 U.S.C. § 1965 (1994). Others are minor variations in presentation, such as *Bluebook* Rule 10.2.2, which provides, "Do not abbreviate 'United States,'" and *ALWD* Rule 12.2(g) "United States as party: Cite as U.S. Omit 'America.'"

Sample *Bluebook* citation formats:

Rule 11 Constitutions:	U.S.Const.art.I, § 9, cl.2.
Rule 10 Cases:	United States v Shaffer Equip. Co., 11 F.3d 450 (4th Cir. 1993)
Rule 12 Statutes:	42 U.S.C. § 1983 (1994)

Sample *ALWD* citation formats:

Rule 13 Constitutions:	U.S. Const.art. IV, § 5(b)
Rule 12 Cases:	Brown v. Bd. Of Educ., 349 U.S. 294
	U.S. v. Chairse, 18 F.Supp. 2d 1021
	(D. Minn. 1998)
Rule 14 Statutory Codes:	18 U.S.C. § 1965 (1994)
Session Laws, SlipLaws:	

Advice *from the* Field

PROFESSIONAL COMMUNICATION

by Kathryn L. Myers, Associate Professor and Coordinator of Paralegal Studies at Saint Mary-of-the-Woods College in Saint Mary-of-the-Woods, IN

There are countless misunderstandings, conflicts, and disagreements in every organization in the United States. Effective listening skills are almost extinct in many firms, and gossip among colleagues has become commonplace. The result is lost productivity, hurt feelings, hidden agendas, loss of innovative ideas, and mistrust among coworkers.

The importance of professional communication skills in dealing with these problems cannot be overstressed. *The Wall Street Journal* recently reported a study involving more than one hundred Fortune 500 executives who ranked interpersonal communication first, across the board, as the most valuable skill they considered in hiring or promotion decisions. Lack of interpersonal communication skills impedes professional effectiveness in influencing persuading, and negotiating, all of which are crucial to success.

Professional communication may take the form of written communication, active listening, or nonverbal communication, all of which require interpersonal communication skills. All three skills work together to define professional communication, but this article focuses specifically on written communication.

Writing intimidates many people, but there are times when writing is the best way to communicate and often is the only way to get a message across. Good writers must have access to at least one quality writing guide. Some good choices are: *The Elements of Style*, by William Strunk, Jr., and E.B. White for lawyers, paralegals, and others engaged in formal writing; *The Bedford Handbook*, by Diana T. Hacker; *How 10: A Handbook for Office Professionals*, by James L. and Lyn R. Clark; and *The Associated Press Stylebook* for traditional journalists is the professional bible.

The following tips are offered as examples of what careful writers must consider.

BE CAUTIOUS

Written communication is more concrete than verbal communication and is less forgiving of errors. Once something is written and sent, it cannot be taken back; and it cannot be nuanced or explained away as readily as can be done with the spoken word.

Communicators in writing must meet the challenges of spelling, grammar, punctuation, and style in addition to the actual wording (rhetoric). Modern technology superficially makes writing seem easier by providing grammar and spelling checks, but these tools are not failsafe. They may actually contribute to egregious errors if the writer is not carefully involved with the writing and proofreading the material for sense.

REMEMBER THE ABC'S OF WRITING

Accuracy—Proof and reproof

Brevity—Keep sentences short

Clarity—Use active voice for clear meaning

BEWARE OF COMMON ERRORS

Commas—Use commas after each part of full dates (*e.g.*, "Wednesday, July 13, 2005," or "July 13, 2005," unless the year falls at the end of the sentence. No comma is used with a calendar date expressed alone (*e.g.*, "February 14.") Do not use commas where the year stands by itself (*e.g.*, "the year 2005 was special.")

Restrictive words, phrases, or clauses modify the main idea and are essential to its meaning. These are not set off by commas. Nonrestrictive words, phrases, or clauses, however, do not significantly change the meaning of the sentence and are set off by commas. Place commas inside quotation marks and parentheses.

Semicolons—Use semicolons when there are two or more independent clauses that do not have coordinating conjunctions, or when the clauses are joined by a transitional expression such as "however." Also use them to separate clauses in a series which have internal commas. Place semicolons outside quotation marks and parentheses.

Colons—Use colons after independent clauses that introduce a formal list or enumeration of items, but not if a verb of being precedes the list. Use a colon after a business salutation and to introduce formal quotations (*e.g.*, the court held: "no offense was proven . . .")

Dashes—Use dashes instead of commas to achieve greater pause and emphasis to what follows. Also use them in place of commas with parenthetical expressions or appositives that contain internal commas.

Ellipsis—An ellipsis is a series of three periods to indicate one or more words are missing from the middle of a sentence in the quoted text. If the missing text is at the end of a sentence, this fact is indicated with a fourth period—the sentence period—at the end of the series.

Quotation Marks—Quotation marks are used to show directly quoted speech or text as well as the titles of published articles. Quotations of 50 words or more do not use quotation marks but, rather, are written as separate paragraph(s), single spaced, and indented on the right and left margins greater than the normal text.

Apostrophe—The apostrophe is used to indicate a missing letter in a contraction (*e.g.*, "it's" for "it is" or "don't" for "do not") or to denote singular possession

(continued)

(*e.g.*, "Mary's"), or plural possession (*e.g.*, "the companies' policies.") "Its" is the correct (albeit counterintuitive) possessive form of "it." No apostrophe is used. All possessive case pronouns (my, your, yours, their, its, whose, theirs, ours) are written without apostrophes.

When there is joint ownership, the apostrophe attaches to the last noun (*e.g.*, "it was Dick and Jane's home"). With individual possession where there are two or more nouns, each noun shows ownership (*e.g.*, "it was either Dick's or Jane's").

WATCH YOUR GRAMMAR

Active Voice—Using action verbs and active voice provides clear and readable sentences.

Noun/Pronoun Agreement—A singular noun (legal assistant) must have a singular pronoun (his/her). Plural nouns (legal assistants) must have plural pronouns (their). Avoid confusion by writing in the plural form when possible.

Subjective Case—Use the subjective case of a pronoun (I, he, she, you, we, they, who, it, whoever) for the subject, for the complement of a "being" verb, and after the infinitive "to be" when this verb does not have a subject directly preceding it.

Objective Case—Use the objective case of a pronoun (me, him, her, you, us, them, whom, it, whomever) as the direct or indirect object of a verb, the object of a preposition, the subject of any infinitive, the object of the infinitive "to be" when it has a subject directly preceding it, and the object of any other infinitive.

Noun/Verb Agreement—Singular nouns take singular verbs. Know the difference among present, past, and future tenses. Do not switch verb tenses in documents unless the material requires the switch.

Identifiers (Modifiers)—Place identifiers (modifiers) (*e.g.*, adjectives and adverbs) as close as possible to the words they identify (modify).

Proper Pairs—Certain words (correlative conjunctions) must be used in pairs (*e.g.*, either/or, neither/nor, not only/but also).

Clichés, Slang, and Jargon—Avoid clichés: use them only when there is a sound reason to believe that a particular cliché will strengthen your rhetoric. Use slang and "legalese" only when it would be awkward for the reader not to do so, and only if you are sure the reader will understand the reference. A judge, for example, expects to read some amount of legalese. He or she likely would be disappointed to see none at all in a trial brief.

Spelling—Use your spelling checker, but proofread to make sure you do not have correct spelling of the wrong word (*e.g.*, "she was soaking in the tube.") Great care should be taken to spell the names of people and companies correctly.

Acronyms and Abbreviations—Except for acronyms and abbreviations in common usage and which are self-explanatory in context (*e.g.*, "the Hon. James Parker" or "she is an interpreter with NATO"), give full titles and names when the acronym or abbreviation first is mentioned. Err on the side of spelling it out if there is any doubt.

Numbers—In general, single-digit numbers should be written as words; double digit, as numerals in written materials unless the number is used to begin a sentence (*e.g.*, "I had only 10 reference books when I began five years ago.")

Source Acknowledgement—The source of borrowed material of any kind must be attributed with quotation marks if directly quoted, or by attribution if not directly quoted (*e.g.*, "I shall return," Gen. MacArthur promised, or, "General Douglas MacArthur promised he would be back"). In formal research and in legal writing, complete citations must be provided according to the legal convention or the style prescribed by the particular publication.

LETTERS

Correspondence is a primary form of communication between the law firm and the world. It is vital that correspondence be crafted well to properly reflect both the reputation of the law office and your own professionalism. Correspondence must be free of grammar and spelling errors, and the research and analysis must be absolutely correct.

There are different types of letters for different purposes: informational letters, opinion letters, and demand letters, to name a few. Although paralegals would not sign their names to opinion or demand letters, it is quite common for them to draft substantial portions of this correspondence.

There are certain parts to a letter that are necessary for successful correspondence.

Format—There are three primary formats: 1) full block, 2) modified block with blocked paragraphs, and 3) modified block with indented paragraphs.

Letterhead—Preprinted letterhead needs no additional information; but subsequent pages need to contain an identification of the letter, or a header including the name of the addressee, the date, and the page number.

Date—The full date appears below the letterhead at the left or right margin depending on the format used.

Method of Delivery—This appears at the left margin below the date if delivery other than U.S. Postal Service is used.

Recipient's Address Block—The inside address is placed at the left margin and should include:

The recipient

The recipient's title (if any)

The name of the business (if appropriate)

The address

Reference Line—Usually introduced with "Re:" the reference line identifies the subject of the letter. Depending upon office requirements, it may contain case identification.

Salutation—Legal correspondence generally is formal; and the salutation is followed with a colon, such as "Dear Ms. Myers:" You can use the first name if you know the person well, although it is a safer practice to remain formal. It is best to address the letter to a named individual. This may mean calling the recipient business and identifying a person to whom the letter should be addressed.

Body—The body of the letter should have three components:

1. Introduction: For normal business letters, your letter should start with an overall summary, showing in the first paragraph why the letter is relevant to the reader. Don't make reader go past the first paragraph to find out why the letter was sent.
2. Main section: The body of the letter needs to explain the reason for the correspondence, including any relevant background and current information. Make sure the information flows logically to make your points effectively.
3. Requests/instructions: The closing of the letter is the final impression you leave with the reader. End with an action point such as, "I will call you later this week to discuss the matter."

Closing—Following the body of the letter, the closing consists of a standard statement and/or an action item.

Signature and Title—Clearly identify the writer by name and title.

Initials of Drafter—This is a reference to the author (KLM) and the typist (sbk).

Enclosure Notation—"Enc." or "Encs." notations are used to identify one or more enclosures.

Copies to Others—The traditional "cc" notation, formerly meaning "carbon copy," now means "courtesy copy" and is used universally. Some writers, however, will use only "c" or "copy to," along with the name(s), to identify others receiving copies of the document.

PROOFREADING

Even when you believe your draft is exactly what you want, read it one more time. This rule is for everything you write whether it is a memorandum, letter, proposal, or some other document. It is true no matter how many drafts you have written.

Use both the grammar and spelling checker on your computer, paying very close attention to every word highlighted. Do not place total faith in your computer. Instead, have both a printed dictionary and a thesaurus nearby to double-check everything your computer's editing tools highlight, because the computer tools are not always reliable.

Make sure your document is clear and concise. Is there anything that could be misinterpreted? Does it raise questions or fail to make the point you need to make? Can you reduce the number of words or unnecessarily long words? Do not use a long word when a short one works as well; do not use two words when one will do; and do not waste the reader's time with unnecessary words or phrases.

Is your written communication well organized? Does each idea proceed logically from one paragraph to the next? Make sure written communications are easy to read, contain the necessary information, use facts where needed, and avoid information that is not relevant. Be sure to specify the course of action you expect, such as a return call or an order.

Close appropriately, whether formally or informally, according to the nature of the communication. This may seem obvious, but it is sometimes overlooked and can make written communications look amateurish. This diminishes your chances of meeting your written communication's goals.

Communication is vital to the success of any workplace; and in the legal arena, professionals live or die by the communicated word. Well-crafted documents are a positive step toward being a successful professional.

Reprinted with permission of the National Association of Legal Assistants and Kathryn L. Myers. The article originally appeared in the May 2005 issue of FACTS & FINDINGS, the quarterly journal for legal assistants. The article is reprinted here in its entirety. For further information, contact NALA at www.nala.org or phone 918-587-6828.

Concept Review *and* Reinforcement

LEGAL TERMINOLOGY

Critical Legal Thinking: Definitions

Critical Legal Thinking	The process of identifying legal issues, determining the relevant facts, and applying the applicable law to come to a conclusion that answers the legal question the issues present. The paralegal must understand the audience for whom the document is being prepared: the client, the supervising attorney and other members of the legal team, or the court.
Facts	Facts are pieces of information or details that in actuality or reality exist, or have occurred, as opposed to someone's theory, supposition, or conjecture. A fact is, in the law, the circumstances of an event, motion, occurrence, or state of affairs, rather than an interpretation of its significance.
Material (Relevant) Fact	A material fact is a fact that is significant or essential to the issue or matter at hand.
Immaterial (Irrelevant) Fact	An immaterial fact is one that is not essential to the matter at issue.

Legal Writing

Standards	1. The language used must be clear to the intended reader. 2. The writer must make an honest presentation of the facts and argument. 3. Arguments advocating a new interpretation to the existing law, as well as the current law, must be clearly stated. 4. The ethical obligation to the court must be obeyed, including the presentation of adverse authority in the jurisdiction. 5. Factual variation must be presented, and the sources used clearly identified by proper citation in a format acceptable to the reader.
Duty of Candor	There is an obligation to be honest with the court and not to mislead the court.

Preparing Office Memorandums

Purpose	1. The memorandum is a working document for the legal team to be used in preparation and presentation of a case. 2. The paralegal must understand the specific assignment. For the memorandum of law, it usually is the answer to a question. 3. Office memoranda are frequently indexed by subject and filed in the office for future reference; if the same or a similar fact pattern requires research, it is a good starting point and can be a major time-saver. 4. The facts relied upon in writing the memo must be a part of the final memorandum; other people who read the memorandum need to understand the specific facts. 5. A memorandum must present both sides of the issue, and in that respect be a neutral, unbiased, objective presentation of applicable laws as they apply to the facts of the case. Issues that the opposing attorney or the judge may raise should be considered and presented. A good analysis includes a discussion of how the fact pattern may differ in cases that are not on point.

Preparing Court Briefs

	Written for the court, the brief provides written advocacy of the client's position and must be written to convince the court to adopt a position favorable to the client.

Citations

Purpose	A citation should allow someone else to find the case or other material mentioned in a document, and the form of citation must do this. The format must be generally accepted and used by others in the legal community.

Traditional Sources (Print) Citation Format	The basic paper or traditional citation form is: Volume • Book or Series • Page e.g., 232 Atlantic 2d 44 232 refers to the volume in the Atlantic 2d series reporter service of West Publishing Company, and 44 refers to the page on which the authority may be found.
Bluebook Citation Format	*Bluebook* has been the generally accepted authority for proper citation form unless the rules of a particular court dictated a different citation format.
ALWD Citation Format	This citation format authority was written by Association of Legal Writing Directors.
Universal Citation Format	Traditionally, paper or book-based citation used information based on internal page numbers. Universal Citation Format relies upon the courts to provide numbered paragraphs in their opinions.
Table of Authorities	A table of authorities is a listing of the citations or other references in a document and the page numbers where they are located.
Cite Checking	Documents must be checked to verify that they use the proper citation format and that the referenced cases and statutes are valid and the cases have not been repealed or overturned. The strictness with which the citation rules must be applied, as well as the method—*Bluebook*, *ALWD*, or Universal Citation Format—depends on the wishes and demands of the attorney for whom the document is being prepared, or the court or judge to whom it is submitted.

WORKING THE WEB

1. Summarize in a memo the requirements for briefs submitted to the United States Supreme Court, and the citation to the applicable rule. http://www.supremecourt.us.gov/ctrules/rulesofthecourt.pdf or http://www.law.cornell.edu/rules/supct/overview.html
2. Use the Internet to find the information to prepare an internal office memorandum on the requirements for filing briefs in your jurisdiction's highest court. For example, in California at http://www.courtinfo.ca.gov/rules/titleone/title1-1-59.htm, or Kansas at http://www.kscourts.org/ctruls/ctrul610.htm.

3. The Legal Law Institute at Cornell Law School offers a number of sources for the legal writer, including citation information. Use the LII website to download the section from Introduction to Basic Legal Citation by Peter W. Martin—"Who Sets Citation Norms"—at http://www.law.cornell.edu/citation/1-600.htm.
4. Use the homepage link from the Web page in question 3, and download your personal copy of the reference document.
5. If you are using the ALWD manual for citation rules, download a copy of the latest updates at www.alwd.org.

CRITICAL THINKING & WRITING QUESTIONS

1. What is critical legal thinking? Explain and give an example.
2. Why is it important to have all the material facts before beginning the research to prepare a memorandum of law?
3. What is meant by "material facts?" Give an example of a material fact.
4. What is meant by an "immaterial fact?" Give an example.
5. What is the goal of legal writing?
6. Why should headnotes not be used in legal writing?
7. How important is it to Shepardize the cases in a memorandum of law or brief? When should this be done? Why?
8. How are the memorandum of law and the court brief similar, and different? Explain fully.
9. Contrast and compare the fact situation in the opening scenario and the Alaskan case of *Whiting v. State* in the chapter. What are the similarities, and what are the points that could be used to argue that the law does not apply?
10. How does the general duty to inform the court preserve the integrity of the judicial process? (*Hazel-Atlas Glass Co. v. Hartford-Empire Co.*, 322 U.S. 238)
11. Are sanctions against attorneys for failing to observe a duty of candor to the court an appropriate remedy? [*Beam v. IPCO Corp.*, 838 F.2d 242 (7th Cir. 1998)]
12. What are the relevant facts in the *Palsgraf v. LIRR* case found in Appendix A? What facts are interesting but not relevant facts? Create a computer search query using the facts in the *Palsgraf* case, and search the case law of your jurisdiction using these relevant facts. Prepare a short brief of the latest case you find, including proper *Bluebook* and *ALWD* citation format.

13. What questions should a paralegal ask before preparing a memo of law or a brief?
14. Why should both sides of a case be presented in an office memo of law?
15. Why would an attorney request that all parallel citations be listed for each case listed in a memo of law?

16. How would knowing the intended audience influence the writing of a memo of law or a legal brief?
17. What level of confidentiality should be attached to the preparation and handling of a memo of law? Why?

Building Paralegal Skills

VIDEO CASE STUDIES

Zealous Representation Issue: Candor to the Court

The supervising attorney is due in another courtroom and asks the paralegal to appear for him and submit a brief, which the paralegal has prepared. The lawyer does not read the petition and accepts the paralegal's statement that it is the current law on the subject.

After viewing the video case study at www.pearsonhighered .com/goldman answer the following:

1. What is the duty of the legal team to present up-to-date information to the court when seeking relief?
2. Can legal research from a prior case be used in an argument to the court?
3. Who is responsible for misleading the court on the currency of the information, the paralegal or the attorney?

Zealous Representation Issue: Signing Documents

Court rules require that pleadings be signed by the attorney. With the court about to close and the statute of limitations running out that day, the paralegal signs the attorney's name and files the paperwork.

After viewing the video case study at www.pearsonhighered .com/goldman answer the following:

1. What is the purpose of having the attorney sign all pleadings?
2. Would electronic filing have avoided this problem?
3. What are the dangers in relying upon electronic filing of documents?

ETHICS ANALYSIS & DISCUSSION QUESTIONS

1. What are the ethical issues in failing to properly cite authorities used in a document?
2. What are the ethical obligations in arguing to the court for a change in the law and not following the current law?
3. What are the ethical obligations to the client when analysis of the law indicates there is no valid claim?
4. Assume you have been working for a legal specialist in estate law for a number of years and have taken a number of advanced courses in the field. You are highly regarded in the paralegal community as the person to call for help in the field. Your supervising attorney decides to take a three-week bicycle trip through the Swiss Alps and leaves you in charge of the office.

   During his absence, you give a talk to a local senior citizens group on the advantages of preparing a will. You meet with most of the people in the audience after the talk and tell them a simple will can be prepared for $25 (your office's standard fee) and proceed to take the information from them for a will. You prepare the individual wills and send copies marked DRAFT to each person, along with an invoice for the $25 fee with a note to return the fee if they wish to have the will completed. Everyone accepts and sends in the fee.

   Upon his return, the attorney looks over the wills, tells you they are "letter perfect" and says "It's just what I would have done." [*Cincinnati Bar v. Kathman*, 92 Ohio St. 92 (2001) quoting *People v. Cassidy*, 884 P.2d 309 (Colo. 1994).] What are the legal and ethical issues?

5. It is the week between Christmas and New Year's Day. You are the only one covering the office while all of the lawyers and support personnel are on vacation. A client who is traveling in Asia calls and asks you to fax to his hotel a copy of an opinion letter prepared by your supervising attorney. You helped prepare the opinion letter and know that it contains a summary of the facts, including details about the opposing parties, case strategy, and potential violations of law. May you send it? What are the ethical issues, if any?

6. You are working for the local prosecutor as a paralegal. The District Attorney asks you to prepare an office

memorandum of law on the question: Is there any duty to advise the court of any changes in the law or facts after the case has been presented.

7. You prepared a memorandum of law for the firm's trial attorney, and a brief for the court that was used in the case that started today. Closing arguments will be made tomorrow. You now discover that there is case law that is favorable to the other side that effectively overturns the case law you used in the memo of law and brief. What do you do? Are there any ethical issues? Explain fully.

DEVELOPING YOUR COLLABORATION SKILLS

Working on your own or with a group of other students assigned by your instructor, review the scenario at the beginning of the chapter.

1. Divide the group into two teams.
   a. One team is to prepare a memo for the court in the form of a brief.
   b. One team is to prepare a memo of law for the partner.
   c. After the memos are finished, each group should compare and write a report on the differences between the memos.

2. As a group, prepare a memo that Amanda might prepare for the supervising paralegal or other attorney on the handling of the interview and any concerns or recommendations.

3. Discuss any ethical concerns that Amanda might have, based on the interview and the potential handling of the case.

PARALEGAL PORTFOLIO EXERCISE

Prepare a memorandum of law for the supervising attorney using the information in the memorandum assignment below. Use the statutory and case law of your local jurisdiction.

Memorandum Assignment

To: Edith Hannah
From: Glenn Hains
Date: January 23, 2006
File   Number: GH 06-1002
Re: State of (your state) v. Kevin Dones

Our client was stopped by a police officer at the bottom of a 1-mile-long 10% grade hill on state Route 332 in Northhampton Township, at 3:30 p.m. on Sunday afternoon, January 15, 2006. He was riding a bicycle south on State Route 332. He was given a motor vehicle citation for speeding. They used a radar unit and claim a speed of 35 mph in a 25 mph zone. He also was administered a field sobriety test, which gave a reading over the legal limit and was given a citation for driving under the influence. He tells me he was riding a bike because his license was suspended for having two previous DUIs.

Please prepare a brief memorandum of law, with citations and cases.

LEGAL ANALYSIS & WRITING CASES

United States v. Shaffer Equipt. Co.   *11 F.3d 450 (4th Cir. 1993)*

Issue: Continuing Duty to Inform Court of Changes in the Law

Government counsel learned that its expert witness had lied about his credentials and that the witness had lied in other litigation. The attorney did not immediately notify the court or opposing counsel. In finding against the government, the court extended the duty of candor to include a continuing duty to inform the court of any development that may conceivably affect the outcome of litigation.

Questions

1. Is preserving the integrity of the judicial process more important than the duty to vigorously pursue a client's case?

2. Is there a duty to inform the court when an attorney suspects that a client may have committed perjury?

3. What additional burden is placed on the paralegal in preparing material for a case in light of this decision?

WORKING WITH THE LANGUAGE OF THE COURT CASE

Golden Eagle Distributing Corp. v. Burroughs

801 F.2d. 1531 (9th Cir. 1986)
United States Court of Appeals, Ninth Circuit

Read, and if assigned, brief this case. In your brief, answer the following questions.

1. What is the intent of Federal Rules of Civil Procedure Rule 11?
2. What test does the court use to determine if sanctions should be imposed under FRCP Rule 11?
3. What is meant by the "ethical duty of candor"?
4. Is there a conflict between the attorney's ethical obligations under the ABA Model Rules and the requirements of FRCP 11?
5. Do attorneys have any duty to cite cases adverse to their case? Explain.

Schroeder, Circuit Judge

This is an appeal from the imposition of sanctions under Rule 11 of the Federal Rules of Civil Procedure as amended in 1983. The appellant, a major national law firm, raises significant questions of first impression.

The relevant portions of the amended Rule provide: Every pleading, motion, and other paper of a party represented by an attorney shall be signed by at least one attorney.... The signature of an attorney ... constitutes a certificate by him that he has read the pleading, motion, or other paper; that to the best of his knowledge, information, and belief formed after reasonable inquiry, it is well grounded in fact and is warranted by existing law or a good faith argument for the extension, modification, or reversal of existing law.... If a pleading, motion, or other paper is signed in violation of this rule, the court, upon motion or upon its own initiative, shall impose upon the person who signed it, a represented party, or both, an appropriate sanction....

In this appeal, we must decide whether the district court correctly interpreted Rule 11.

... Golden Eagle Distributing Corporation filed the underlying action in Minnesota state court for fraud, negligence, and breach of contract against Burroughs, because of an allegedly defective computer system. Burroughs removed the action to the federal district court in Minnesota. Burroughs then moved pursuant to 28 U.S.C. § 1404(a) to transfer the action to the Northern District of California.... Burroughs next filed the motion for summary judgment, which gave rise to the sanctions at issue here. It argued that the California, rather than the Minnesota, statute of limitations applied and that all of Golden Eagle's claims were time-barred under California law. It also contended that Golden Eagle's claim for economic loss arising from negligent manufacture lacked merit under California law. Golden Eagle filed a response, arguing that Minnesota law governed the statute of limitations question and that Burroughs had misinterpreted California law regarding economic loss....

After a hearing, the district judge denied Burroughs' motion and directed the Kirkland & Ellis attorney who had been responsible for the summary judgment motion to submit a memorandum explaining why sanctions should not be imposed under Rule 11.... Proper understanding of this appeal requires some comprehension of the nature of Burroughs' arguments and the faults which the district court found with them....

Kirkland & Ellis's opening memorandum argued that Golden Eagle's claims were barred by California's three-year statute of limitations. The question was whether the change of venue from Minnesota to California affected which law applied.... In imposing sanctions, the district court held that Kirkland & Ellis's argument was "misleading" because it suggested that there already exists a *forum non conveniens* exception to the general rule that the transferor's law applies.... [The case cited] raised the issue but did not decide it.... Kirkland & Ellis's corollary argument, that a Minnesota court would have dismissed the case on *forum non conveniens* grounds, was found to be "misleading" because it failed to note that one prerequisite to such a dismissal is that an alternative forum be available....

Kirkland & Ellis also argued that Golden Eagle's claim for negligent manufacture lacked merit because Golden Eagle sought damages for economic loss, and such damages are not recoverable under California law [as demonstrated in the *Seely* case].... The district court sanctioned Kirkland & Ellis for not citing three cases whose holdings it concluded were adverse to *Seely*: ... The district court held that these omissions violated counsel's duty to disclose adverse authority, embodied in Model Rule 3.3, Model Rules of Professional Conduct Rule 3.3 (1983), which the court viewed as a "necessary corollary to Rule 11."

. . . The district court's application of Rule 11 in this case strikes a chord not otherwise heard in discussion of this Rule. The district court did not focus on whether a sound basis in law and in fact existed for the defendant's motion for summary judgment. Indeed it indicated that the motion itself was nonfrivolous. . . . Rather, the district court looked to the manner in which the motion was presented. The district court in this case held that Rule 11 imposes upon counsel an ethical "duty of candor." . . . It said:

The duty of candor is a necessary corollary of the certification required by Rule 11. A court has a right to expect that counsel will state the controlling law fairly and fully; indeed, unless that is done the court cannot perform its task properly. A lawyer must not misstate the law, fail to disclose adverse authority (not disclosed by his opponent), or omit facts critical to the application of the rule of law relied on. . . .

With the district court's salutary admonitions against misstatements of the law, failure to disclose directly adverse authority, or omission of critical facts, we have no quarrel. It is, however, with Rule 11 that we must deal. The district court's interpretation of Rule 11 requires district courts to judge the ethical propriety of lawyers' conduct with respect to every piece of paper filed in federal court. This gives us considerable pause. . . .

The district court's invocation of Rule 11 has two aspects. The first, which we term "argument identification," is the holding that counsel should differentiate between an argument "warranted by existing law" and an argument for the "extension, modification, or reversal of existing law." The second is the conclusion that Rule 11 is violated when counsel fails to cite what the district court views to be directly contrary authority.

. . . The text of the Rule . . . does not require that counsel differentiate between a position which is supported by existing law and one that would extend it. The Rule on its face requires that the motion be either one or the other. . . . The district court's ruling appears to go even beyond the principle of Rule 3.3 of the ABA Model Rules, which proscribes "knowing" false statements of material fact or law. The district court made no finding of a knowing misstatement, and, given the well-established objective nature of the Rule 11 standard, such a requirement would be inappropriate. Both the earnest advocate exaggerating the state of the current law without knowingly misrepresenting it, and the unscrupulous lawyer knowingly deceiving the court, are within the scope of the district court's interpretation.

This gives rise to serious concerns about the effect of such a rule on advocacy. It is not always easy to decide whether an argument is based on established law or is an argument for the extension of existing law.

Whether the case being litigated is . . . materially the same as earlier precedent is frequently the very issue which prompted the litigation in the first place. Such questions can be close.

Sanctions under Rule 11 are mandatory. . . . In even a close case, we think it extremely unlikely that a judge, who has already decided that the law is not as a lawyer argued it, will also decide that the loser's position was warranted by existing law. Attorneys who adopt an aggressive posture risk more than the loss of the motion if the district court decides that their argument is for an extension of the law which it declines to make. What is at stake is often not merely the monetary sanction but the lawyer's reputation.

The "argument identification" requirement adopted by the district court therefore tends to create a conflict between the lawyer's duty zealously to represent his client, Model Code of Professional Responsibility Canon 7, and the lawyer's own interest in avoiding rebuke. The concern on the part of the bar that this type of requirement will chill advocacy is understandable. . . .

. . . Were the scope of the rule to be expanded as the district court suggests, mandatory sanctions would ride on close decisions concerning whether or not one case is or is not the same as another. We think Rule 11 should not impose the risk of sanctions in the event that the court later decides that the lawyer was wrong. The burdens of research and briefing by a diligent lawyer anxious to avoid any possible rebuke would be great. And the burdens would not be merely on the lawyer. If the mandatory provisions of the Rule are to be interpreted literally, the court would have a duty to research authority beyond that provided by the parties to make sure that they have not omitted something.

The burden is illustrated in this case, where the district court based its imposition of sanctions in part upon Kirkland & Ellis's failure to cite authorities which the court concluded were directly adverse to a case it did cite. The district court charged the appellant with constructive notice of these authorities because they were identified in Shepard's as "distinguishing" the case Kirkland & Ellis relied on.

. . . Amended Rule 11 of the Federal Rules of Civil Procedure does not impose upon the district courts the burden of evaluating under ethical standards the accuracy of all lawyers' arguments. Rather, Rule 11 is intended to reduce the burden on district courts by sanctioning, and hence deterring, attorneys who submit motions or pleadings which cannot reasonably be supported in law or in fact. We therefore reverse the district court's imposition of sanctions for conduct which it felt fell short of the ethical responsibilities of the attorney. Reversed.

Legal Subjects

Part IV presents an overview of the basic rules of law in the most common areas of law in which paralegals may work. The principles discussed in each area are generally applicable in all jurisdictions, however, there are variations in state law and local laws and paralegals must check for variations in state and local law in the jurisdiction in which they work. By studying these areas of law you will begin to learn the terminology of the law. Read each of the substantive law chapters with a view toward identifying those areas that stimulate an interest in taking more advanced courses or as a possible area of specialization as a paralegal.

Torts and Product Liability

DIGITAL RESOURCES

Chapter 12 Digital Resources at *www.pearsonhighered.com/goldman*

- Video Case Studies:
  - A Salesman's Courtroom Testimony: Fact or Misrepresentation?
  - Solicitation in the ER: Ethical Duties of the Profession
  - The Judge Instructs the Jury before Deliberation
- Chapter Summary • Web Links • Court Opinions • Glossary • Comprehension Quizzes
- Technology Resources

> **Negligence is not actionable unless it involves the invasion of a legally protected interest, the violation of a right. Proof of negligence in the air, so to speak, will not do.**

C. J. Cardozo,
Palsgraf v. Long Island Railroad Co. (1928)

Paralegals at Work

As a paralegal, you work for a law firm that represents clients in tort actions against automobile insurance companies and other defendants. Most of the law firm's business comes from automobile accident cases. Your firm specializes in representing the injured plaintiffs in these negligence and product liability lawsuits.

You work for Mr. Joshua Berk, senior litigator for the firm. One day Mr. Berk invites you in to his office. He explains that the firm has just been retained by a plaintiff, Mrs. Helen Sheen, to represent her and her daughter Jessica in a lawsuit. Mr. Berk explains that you will be assisting him in preparation of the case.

Mr. Berk explains the following facts of the case: Two months ago Mrs. Helen Sheen and her husband, Mr. Patrick Sheen, were driving on the Interstate 10 freeway to Las Vegas in their one-year old SUV (sports utility vehicle) manufactured by Chrysler. When Mrs. Sheen was driving the SUV, Mr. Sheen was in the passenger's seat, and their 4-year-old daughter Jessica was in the back seat of the car. Mrs. Sheen, Mr. Sheen, and Jessica were wearing their seat belts.

While in the State of Nevada, and about 20 miles from Las Vegas, Mrs. Sheen heard the steering wheel of the SUV rattle and then felt it loosen in her hands. Mrs. Sheen lost control of the vehicle and the vehicle flipped over several times before coming to a stop upside down and 40-feet from the freeway. Mr. Sheen died in the accident.

Jessica suffered severe back injuries from the accident that will require at least $100,000 of surgeries over the next year. Her future injuries from the accident are unknown at this time. Mrs. Sheen was not physically injured in the accident, but suffers severe emotional distress caused by the accident.

Investigators of the accident scene have determined that Mrs. Sheen was driving at the legal speed limit of 70 miles per hour. Investigation also has shown that one of the bolts holding the steering wheel in place had broken off, causing the steering wheel to become loose and unmanageable at the time of the accident. The steering wheel and steering wheel column for the SUV was manufactured by the sub-manufacturer Steering Columns Corporation and installed in the Chrysler SUVs.

Consider the issues involved in this scenario as you read this chapter.

INTRODUCTION FOR THE PARALEGAL

Many paralegals work for lawyers who represent clients involved in intentional tort, negligence, and product liability cases. These are civil lawsuits in which the plaintiff is usually seeking to recover monetary damages from the defendant or the defendant's insurance company. In this type of case, the paralegal may be working for the plaintiff's lawyer, the defendant's lawyer, or lawyers at the defendant's insurance company.

Tort A wrong. There are three categories of torts: (1) intentional torts, (2) unintentional torts (negligence), and (3) strict liability.

Tort is the French word for a "wrong." Tort law protects a variety of injuries and provides remedies for them. Under tort law, an injured party can bring a civil lawsuit to seek compensation for a wrong done to the party or to the party's property. Many torts originate in common law. The courts and legislatures have extended tort law to reflect changes in modern society.

Tort damages are monetary damages sought from the offending party, intended to compensate the injured party for the injury suffered. These may consist of past and future medical expenses, loss of wages, pain and suffering, mental distress, and other damages caused by the defendant's tortious conduct. If the victim of a tort dies, his or her beneficiaries can bring a **wrongful death action** to recover damages from the defendant.

A special type of tort—strict liability—is available primarily in product liability cases. Under strict liability a party can be held liable even if that party was not negligent or at fault for causing the plaintiff's injuries. Manufacturers, sellers, and other parties in the chain of distribution of a defective product can be held strictly liable. Punitive damages, which are awarded to punish the defendant, are often recoverable in strict liability cases.

Tort and product liability lawsuits make up a substantial portion of the civil lawsuits in the United States. Therefore, a paralegal should have knowledge of the major tort principles and the elements of each tort.

This chapter covers various tort laws, including intentional torts, negligence, and strict liability.

Intentional Torts Against Persons

Intentional torts A category of torts that requires that the defendant possessed the intent to do the act that caused the plaintiff's injuries.

The law protects a person from unauthorized touching, restraint, or other contact. In addition, the law protects a person's reputation and privacy. Violations of these rights are actionable as **intentional torts**. Intentional torts against persons are discussed in the paragraphs that follow.

CAREER OPPORTUNITIES FOR PARALEGAL PROFESSIONALS IN TORT AND PRODUCT LIABILITY LAW

A substantial number of lawsuits in the United States involve torts. Therefore, a substantial number of paralegals work for lawyers who practice in this area of the law. A tort occurs when one party violates a duty owed to another party and injures that party. The injured party often brings a civil lawsuit to recover monetary damages and other remedies.

The most familiar form of a tort is negligence. And the most common form of negligence occurs in automobile accidents. Attorneys representing clients who have been injured in automobile accidents usually have a volume practice—that is, the lawyer handles a large number of cases. The defense law firms who represent the insurance companies also have large caseloads of negligence automobile lawsuits.

Paralegals who work for either the plaintiff lawyers or the defense lawyers in automobile injury cases are responsible for handling a large caseload. Paralegals who work for plaintiff lawyers are typically called upon to draft complaints, requests for discovery, and other documents associated with the case. Paralegals who work for defense law firms have parallel duties of drafting answers, requests for discovery, and other documents associated with the cases. Paralegals who work on automobile tort cases become experts and often do much of the work on these cases, under the supervision of the attorney, of course.

Because 90 percent of these cases settle, there is usually not much opportunity to conduct legal research concerning these cases. More complex cases, and those that do go to trial, however, may require legal research by the paralegal to help the attorney prepare the brief for the case.

Among the many other types of torts are professional malpractice (e.g., medical malpractice by doctors), defamation of character, intentional infliction of emotional distress, invasion of privacy, misappropriation of the right to publicity, malicious prosecution, negligent infliction of emotional distress, liability of landowners, and other forms of intentional and unintentional torts.

A special area of tort law is product liability law. These cases involve lawsuits by injured plaintiffs against companies who manufacture and sell products to consumers. A special tort doctrine called strict liability often applies to these types of cases. These tort cases usually are more complex and, therefore, require more expertise of the paralegals who work for the plaintiff and defense lawyers who represent clients in these cases. In product liability cases paralegals are called upon to interview persons, conduct investigations, conduct research, and draft documents associated with these more complex cases.

The area of torts will remain an important area for the employment of paralegals. Therefore, paralegals should have knowledge of the various types of intentional torts, unintentional torts, and product liability.

Assault

Assault is (1) the threat of immediate harm or offensive contact, or (2) any action that arouses reasonable apprehension of imminent harm. Actual physical contact is unnecessary.

Example Suppose a 6-foot 5-inch, 250-pound male makes a fist and threatens to punch a 5-foot, 100-pound woman. If the woman is afraid that the man will physically harm her, she can sue him for assault. If she is a black-belt karate champion and laughs at the threat, there is no assault because the threat does not cause any apprehension.

Battery

Battery is unauthorized and harmful or offensive physical contact with another person. Basically, the interest protected here is each person's reasonable sense of dignity and safety.

Example Intentionally hitting someone is considered battery because it is harmful.

Example If an injury results, throwing a rock, shooting an arrow or a bullet, knocking off a hat, pulling a chair out from under someone, and poisoning a drink are all instances of actionable battery. The victim need not be aware of the harmful or offensive contact (e.g., it may take place while the victim is asleep). Assault and battery often occur together, although they do not have to (e.g., the perpetrator hits the victim on the back of the head without any warning).

Sometimes a person acts with the intent to injure one person but actually injures another. The **doctrine of transferred intent** applies to these situations. Under this doctrine, the law transfers the perpetrator's intent from the target to the actual victim of the act. The victim then can sue the defendant.

> **Example** Peter shoots a gun toward Mable with the intent of killing her but instead the bullet strikes Mildred, a bystander, who is injured. Mildred can recover damages from Peter for her injuries.

False Imprisonment

The intentional confinement or restraint of another person without authority or justification and without that person's consent constitutes **false imprisonment**. The victim may be restrained or confined by physical force, barriers, threats of physical harm, or the perpetrator's false assertion of legal authority (i.e., *false arrest*). A threat of future harm or moral pressure is not considered false imprisonment. The false imprisonment must be complete.

> **Example** Merely locking one door to a building when other exits are not locked is not false imprisonment. A person is not obliged to risk danger or an affront to his or her dignity by attempting to escape.

Shoplifting causes substantial losses to merchants each year. Almost all states have enacted **merchant protection statutes**, also known as the **shopkeeper's privilege**. These statutes allow merchants to stop, detain, and investigate suspected shoplifters without being held liable for false imprisonment if:

1. There are reasonable grounds for the suspicion,
2. Suspects are detained for only a reasonable time, and
3. Investigations are conducted in a reasonable manner.

Defamation of Character

A person's reputation is a valuable asset. Therefore, every person is protected during his or her lifetime from false statements by others. This protection ends upon a person's death. The tort of **defamation of character** requires a plaintiff to prove that (1) the defendant made an *untrue statement of fact* about the plaintiff, and (2) the statement was intentionally or accidentally *published* to a third party. In this context, publication simply means that a third person heard or saw the untrue statement. It does not just mean appearance in newspapers, magazines, or books.

The term for an oral defamatory statement is **slander**.

> **Example** If a radio host makes an untrue statement of fact about a person over the radio waves, it would be slander. A false statement that appears in writing or other fixed medium is **libel**.

> **Examples** False statements that appear in a letter, newspaper, magazine, book, photograph, movies, video, and the like would be libel.

Publishing an untrue statement of fact is not the same as publishing an opinion. The publication of opinions is usually not actionable.

> **Examples** The statement "My lawyer is lousy" is an opinion and is not defamation. The statement "My lawyer has been disbarred from the practice of law," when she has not been disbarred, is an untrue statement of fact and is actionable as defamation.

Web Exploration

Go to http://www.supreme.courts
.state.tx.us/historical/1998/feb/
970558.pdf and read the case
Wal-Mart Stores v. Resendez. What
issue was involved in this case?
Was Wal-Mart found liable in this
case? Why or why not?

Merchant protection statute
A state statute that allows merchants to stop, detain, and investigate suspected shoplifters without being held liable for false imprisonment if (1) there are reasonable grounds for the suspicion, (2) suspects are detained for only a reasonable time, and (3) investigations are conducted in a reasonable manner.

Slander Oral defamation of character.

Libel A false statement that appears in a letter, newspaper, magazine, book, photograph, movie, video, or other media.

In *New York Times Co. v. Sullivan* [376 U.S. 254, 84 S.Ct. 710 (1964)], the U.S. Supreme Court held that *public officials* cannot recover for defamation unless they can prove that the defendant acted with "actual malice." Actual malice means that the defendant made the false statement knowingly or with reckless disregard of its falsity. This requirement has since been extended to *public figure* plaintiffs such as movie stars, sports personalities, and other celebrities.

Disparagement or Trade Libel

Business firms rely on their reputation and the quality of their products and services to attract and keep customers. State unfair-competition laws protect businesses from disparaging statements made by competitors or others. A disparaging statement is an untrue statement made by one person or business about the products, services, property, or reputation of another business.

Example   If a competitor of Dell Computers told a prospective customer that "Dell Computers always break down," when in fact they rarely break down, that would be product disparagement. **Disparagement** is also called **trade libel** and **product disparagement**.

Misappropriation of the Right to Publicity

Each person has the exclusive legal right to control and profit from the commercial use of his or her name and personality during his or her lifetime. This is a valuable right, particularly to well-known persons such as sports figures and movie stars. Any attempt by another person to appropriate a living person's name or identity for commercial purposes is actionable. The wrongdoer is liable for the tort of **misappropriation of the right to publicity** (also called the *tort of appropriation*).

> **Misappropriation of the right to publicity** A tort in which one party appropriates a person's name or identity for commercial purposes.

Example   If an advertising agency places likeness of a famous actor on a billboard advertising a product without the actor's permission, it has engaged in the tort of misappropriation of the right to publicity.

In such cases, the plaintiff can (1) recover the unauthorized profits made by the offending party, and (2) obtain an injunction against further unauthorized use of his or her name or identity. Many states provide that the right to publicity survives a person's death and may be enforced by the deceased's heirs.

Invasion of the Right to Privacy

The law recognizes each person's right to live his or her life without being subjected to unwarranted and undesired publicity. Violation of this right constitutes the tort of **invasion of the right to privacy**. Examples of this tort are reading someone else's mail, wiretapping, and such. In contrast to defamation, the fact does not have to be untrue. Therefore, truth is not a defense to a charge of invasion of privacy. If the fact is public information, there is no claim to privacy. But a fact that was once public (e.g., the commission of a crime) may become private after the passage of time.

> **Invasion of the right to privacy** A tort that constitutes the violation of a person's right to live his or her life without being subjected to unwarranted and undesired publicity.

Examples   Secretly taking photos of another person with a cell phone camera in a men's or women's locker room would constitute invasion of the right to privacy. Reading someone else's mail, wiretapping someone's telephone, and reading someone else's e-mail without authorization to do so are also examples of invasion of the right to privacy.

Placing someone in a "false light" constitutes an invasion of privacy.

Example   Sending an objectionable telegram to a third party and signing another's name would place the purported sender in a false light in the eyes of the receiver. Falsely attributing beliefs or acts to another also can form the basis of a lawsuit.

Intentional Infliction of Emotional Distress

In some situations a victim suffers mental or emotional distress without first being physically harmed. The Restatement (Second) of Torts provides that a person whose *extreme and outrageous conduct* intentionally or recklessly causes severe emotional distress to another is liable for that emotional distress. This is called the tort of **intentional infliction of emotional distress**, or the *tort of outrage*. The plaintiff must prove that the defendant's conduct was "so outrageous in character and so extreme in degree as to go beyond all possible bounds of decency, and to be regarded as atrocious and utterly intolerable in a civilized society." An indignity, an annoyance, rough language, or an occasional inconsiderate or unkind act does not constitute outrageous behavior. However, repeated annoyances or harassment coupled with threats are considered "outrageous."

The tort does not require any publication to a third party or physical contact between the plaintiff and defendant.

> **Example**   A credit collection agency making harassing telephone calls to a debtor every morning between 1:00 and 5:00 A.M. is outrageous conduct.

The mental distress suffered by the plaintiff must be severe. Many states require that this mental distress be manifested by some form of physical injury, discomfort, or illness, such as nausea, ulcers, headaches, or miscarriage. This requirement is intended to prevent false claims. Some states have abandoned this requirement. The courts have held that shame, humiliation, embarrassment, anger, fear, and worry constitute severe mental distress.

Malicious Prosecution

Businesses and individuals often believe they have a reason to sue someone to recover damages or other remedies. If the plaintiff has a legitimate reason to bring the lawsuit and does so, but the plaintiff does not win the lawsuit, he or she does not have to worry about being sued by the person whom he or she sued. But a losing plaintiff does have to worry about being sued by the defendant in a second lawsuit for **malicious prosecution** if certain elements are met. In a lawsuit for malicious prosecution, the original defendant sues the original plaintiff. In this second lawsuit, which is a *civil* action for damages, the original defendant is the plaintiff and the original plaintiff is the defendant. To succeed in a malicious prosecution lawsuit, the courts require the plaintiff to prove all of the following:

1. The plaintiff in the original lawsuit (now the defendant) instituted or was responsible for instituting the original lawsuit.
2. There was no *probable cause* for the first lawsuit (that is, it was a frivolous lawsuit).
3. The plaintiff in the original action brought it with *malice*. (Caution: This is a very difficult element to prove.)
4. The original lawsuit was terminated in favor of the original defendant (now the plaintiff).
5. The current plaintiff suffered injury as a result of the original lawsuit.

> **Example**   A customer purchases a dress at a retail women's clothing store. A button falls off the dress, so the customer brings a civil lawsuit against the store to recover $1 million for negligence and intentional infliction of emotional distress. The store spends $30,000 for legal fees in defending the lawsuit. The jury does not hold for the customer. The store can now bring a case against the customer for malicious prosecution. The store has a very good chance of proving the elements of malicious prosecution and recovering damages against the customer.

Intentional infliction of emotional distress A tort that occurs when a person's extreme and outrageous conduct intentionally or recklessly causes severe emotional distress to another person. Also known as the *tort of outrage.*

Malicious prosecution A lawsuit in which the original defendant sues the original plaintiff for bringing a lawsuit without probable cause and with malice.

Civil Fraud

Contracting parties must be careful not to be taken by **fraud**. Basically if a deal sounds "too good to be true," it is a signal that the situation might be fraudulent. Other frauds are difficult to detect. If there is fraud, the innocent party can get out of the contract and recover his or her losses. To prove fraud, the following elements must be shown:

1. *The wrongdoer made a false representation of material fact.* To be actionable as fraud, the misrepresentation must be of a past or existing material fact. Statements of opinion or predictions about the future generally do not form the basis for fraud.
2. *The wrongdoer intended to deceive the innocent party.* Thus, the person making the misrepresentation must either have had knowledge that the representation was false or made it without sufficient knowledge of the truth. This is called **scienter** ("guilty mind").
3. *The innocent party justifiably relied on the misrepresentation.* A misrepresentation is not actionable unless the innocent party to whom the misrepresentation was directed acted upon it.
4. *The innocent party was injured.* To recover damages, the innocent party must prove that the fraud caused economic injury. The measure of damages is the difference between the value of the property as represented and the actual value of the property.

Where fraud has occurred, the victim of the fraud can sue the fraudulent party for fraud. The plaintiff may recover damages from the defendant. However, in many cases of fraud the perpetrator of the fraud has spent the money or possibly has hidden the money so that it cannot be recovered. In this case, the victim loses the money or property.

Intentional Torts Against Property

There are two general categories of property: real property and personal property. *Real property* consists of land and anything permanently attached to that land. *Personal property* consists of things that are movable, such as automobiles, books, clothes, pets, and such. The law recognizes certain torts against real and personal property. These torts are discussed in the paragraphs that follow.

Trespass to Land

Interference with an owner's right to exclusive possession of land constitutes the tort of **trespass to land**. There does not have to be any interference with the owner's use or enjoyment of the land; the ownership itself is what counts. Thus, unauthorized use of another person's land is trespass even if the owner is not using it. Actual harm to the property is not necessary.

Examples Trespass to land includes entering another person's land without permission, remaining on the land of another after permission to do so has expired (e.g., a guest refuses to leave), or causing something or someone to enter another's land (e.g., one person builds a dam that causes another person's land to flood). A person who is pushed onto another's land or enters that land with good reason is not liable for trespass. A person may enter another person's land to save a child or a pet from harm.

Trespass to and Conversion of Personal Property

The tort of **trespass to personal property** occurs whenever one person injures another person's personal property or interferes with that person's enjoyment of his or her personal property. The injured party can sue for damages.

Example Breaking another's car window is trespass to personal property.

Depriving a true owner of the use and enjoyment of his or her personal property by taking over such property and exercising ownership rights over it constitutes the tort of **conversion of personal property**. Conversion also occurs when someone who originally is given possession of personal property fails to return it (e.g., fails to return a borrowed car). The rightful owner can sue to recover the property. If the property was lost or destroyed, the owner can sue to recover its value.

Unintentional Torts—Negligence

Unintentional tort/negligence
A doctrine that says a person is liable for harm that is the foreseeable consequence of his or her actions.

Under the doctrine of **unintentional tort**, commonly referred to as **negligence**, a person is liable for harm that is the *foreseeable consequence* of his or her actions. Negligence is defined as "the omission to do something which a reasonable man would do, or doing something which a prudent and reasonable man would not do" [*Blyth v. Birmingham Waterworks Co.*, 11 Exch. 781, 784 (1856)].

Example A driver who causes an automobile accident because he or she fell asleep at the wheel is liable for any resulting injuries caused by his or her negligence.

To be successful in a negligence lawsuit, the plaintiff must prove that (1) the defendant owed a *duty of care* to the plaintiff, (2) the defendant *breached* this duty of care, (3) the plaintiff suffered *injury*, and (4) the defendant's negligent act *caused* the plaintiff's injury. Each of these elements is discussed in the paragraphs that follow.

Duty of Care

Duty of care The obligation we all owe each other not to cause any unreasonable harm or risk of harm.

To determine whether a defendant is liable for negligence, it first must be ascertained whether the defendant owed a **duty of care** to the plaintiff. Duty of care refers to the obligation we all owe each other—the duty not to cause any unreasonable harm or risk of harm.

Examples Each person owes a duty to drive his or her car carefully, not to push or shove on escalators, not to leave skateboards on the sidewalk, and the like. Businesses owe a duty to make safe products, not to cause accidents, and so on.

The courts decide whether a duty of care is owed in specific cases by applying a **reasonable person standard**. Under this test, the courts attempt to determine how an *objective, careful, and conscientious person would have acted in the same circumstances*, and then measure the defendant's conduct against this standard. The defendant's subjective intent ("I didn't mean to do it") is immaterial in asserting liability. Certain impairments do not affect the reasonable person standard.

Example There is no reasonable alcoholic standard.

Defendants with specific expertise or competence are measured against a **reasonable professional standard**. This standard is applied in much the same way as the reasonable person standard.

Example A brain surgeon is measured against a reasonable brain surgeon standard rather than a lower reasonable doctor standard. Children are generally required to act as a *reasonable child* of similar age and experience would act.

Breach of Duty

Breach of the duty of care
Failure to exercise care or to act as a reasonable person would act.

Once a court finds that the defendant actually owed the plaintiff a duty of care, it must determine whether the defendant breached that duty. A **breach of the duty of care** is the failure to exercise care. In other words, it is the failure to act as a reasonable person would act. A breach of this duty may consist of an action.

Example Throwing a lit match on the ground in the forest and causing a fire is a breach of a duty of care. A breach of duty may also consist of a failure to act when there is a duty to act.

Example   A firefighter who refuses to put out a fire when her safety is not at stake is a breach of a duty of care for failing to act when she has a duty to act. Generally, passersby are not expected to rescue others gratuitously to save them from harm.

Injury to Plaintiff

Even though a defendant's act might have breached a duty of care owed to the plaintiff, this breach is not actionable unless the plaintiff suffers **injury**.

Example   A business's negligence causes an explosion and fire at its factory at night but no one is injured and there is no damage to the neighbor's property. The negligence is not actionable.

The damages recoverable depend on the effect of the injury on the plaintiff's life or profession.

Examples   Suppose two men injure their hands when a train door malfunctions. The first man is a professional basketball player. The second is a college professor. The first man can recover greater damages.

Causation

A person who commits a negligent act is not liable unless this act was the *cause* of the plaintiff's injuries. Courts have divided **causation** into two categories—causation in fact and proximate cause—and require each to be shown before the plaintiff may recover damages.

Causation The two types of causation that must be proven are (1) causation in fact (actual cause) and (2) proximate cause (legal cause).

1. *Causation in fact.* The defendant's negligent act must be the **causation in fact** (or **actual cause**) of the plaintiff's injuries.

    Examples   Suppose a corporation negligently pollutes the plaintiff's drinking water. The plaintiff dies of a heart attack unrelated to the polluted water. Although the corporation has acted negligently, it is not liable for the plaintiff's death. There was a negligent act and an injury, but there was no *cause-and-effect* relationship between them. If, instead, the plaintiff had died from the pollution, there would have been causation in fact and the polluting corporation would have been liable.

2. *Proximate cause.* Under the law, a negligent party is not necessarily liable for all damages set in motion by his or her negligent act. Based on public policy, the law establishes a point along the damage chain after which the negligent party is no longer responsible for the consequences of his or her actions. This limitation on liability is referred to as **proximate cause**, or **legal cause**. The general test of proximate cause is *foreseeability*. A negligent party who is found to be the actual cause—but not the proximate cause—of the plaintiff's injuries is not liable to the plaintiff. Situations are examined on a case-by-case basis.

Example   The landmark case establishing the doctrine of proximate cause is *Palsgraf v. Long Island Railroad Company* [248 N.Y. 339, 162 N.E. 99, 1928 N.Y. Lexis 1269 (1928)]. Helen Palsgraf was standing on a platform waiting for a passenger train. The Long Island Railroad Company owned and operated the trains and employed the station guards. As a man carrying a package wrapped in a newspaper tried to board the moving train, railroad guards tried to help him. As they did so, the package was dislodged from the man's arm, fell to the railroad tracks, and exploded. The package contained hidden fireworks. The explosion shook the railroad platform, causing a scale on the platform to fall on Palsgraf, injuring her. She sued the railroad for negligence. Justice Cardozo denied her recovery, finding that the railroad was not the proximate cause of her injuries.

A complaint alleging negligence appears as Exhibit 12.1.

Exhibit 12.1 Complaint for negligence

Percival R. Cheeseman
Clarence K. Fields
Cheeseman & Fields, LLP
100 Main Street
Los Angeles, CA 90089
213-750-1234

Attorney for Plaintiff

SUPERIOR COURT OF THE STATE OF CALIFORNIA
COUNTY OF LOS ANGELES

	)
	)
	)
Edith A. Rhodes,	) CASE NO: 62-2009-0009428
Plaintiff	)
v.	) COMPLAINT FOR
Retail Corporation	) NEGLIGENCE
Defendant	)
	)
	)
	)
	)
	)

Plaintiff complains and for causes of action alleges as follows:

1. Plaintiff, Edith A. Rhodes, is an individual and is now, and at all times mentioned in this complaint was, a resident of Los Angeles County, California.

2. Defendant Retail Corporation is now, and at all times mentioned in this complaint was, a corporation organized and existing under the laws of the State of California, with its place of business in Los Angeles County, California.

3. At all times mentioned in this complaint, defendant Retail Corporation operated a clothing store known as On the Edge Clothing Store located at 500 Exposition Boulevard, Los Angeles, County of Los Angeles, California.

4. Defendant Retail Corporation invited the general public, including plaintiff, to enter the premises of defendant's clothing store and purchase various clothing and other items from the defendant.

5. On February 1, 2011, at approximately 4:30 p.m. plaintiff was on the premises of defendants' clothing store for the purpose of shopping and possibly to purchase clothing. Upon entering the defendant's store, plaintiff proceeded to a location in the store when plaintiff suddenly and without warning slipped on a clothes hanger on the floor and fell to the floor, causing plaintiff to sustain the serious injuries and damages described below.

6. Defendant, as owner and operator of the clothing store negligently:

    a. Failed to maintain the floor of the clothing store in a reasonably safe condition;

    b. Allowed a clothes hanger to come into contact with and remain on the floor of the clothing store when defendant knew, or in the exercise of reasonable care should have known, that the clothes hanger created an unreasonable risk of harm to customers in the store;

    c. Failed to warn plaintiff of the danger presented by the presence of the clothes hanger on the floor;

    d. Failed to otherwise exercise due care with respect to the matters alleged in this complaint.

7. As a direct and proximate result of the negligence of defendant as set forth above plaintiff slipped and fell while in the clothing store.

8. As a further direct and proximate result of the negligence of the defendant, plaintiff sustained the following serious injuries and damages: cost of a hip replacement operation and other medical expenses, lost wages, physical injuries, and pain and suffering.

Exhibit 12.1 **Complaint for negligence** *(continued)*

WHEREFORE, plaintiff demands judgment against the defendant for the following:

1. General damages according to proof;

2. Damages for medical expenses according to proof;

3. Damages for loss of earnings according to proof;

4. Pain and suffering according to proof;

5. Interest according to law;

6. Costs of this action;

7. Expert fees; and

8. Any other and further relief that the court considers proper.

DEMAND FOR JURY TRIAL: Plaintiff hereby demands trial by jury for each and every claim for which the plaintiff has a right to jury trial.

DATED: February 28, 2011

By: Percival R. Cheeseman

Attorney for Plaintiff

Cheeseman & Fields, LLP
Percival R. Cheeseman
Clarence K. Fields

VERIFICATION

I, Edith A. Rhodes, am the plaintiff in the above-entitled action. I have read the foregoing *Complaint for Negligence* and know the contents thereof. The same is true of my own knowledge, except as to those matters which are therein alleged on information and belief, and as to those matters, I believe it to be true.

I declare under penalty of perjury that the foregoing is true and correct and that this declaration was executed at Los Angeles, Los Angeles County, California.

DATED: February 28, 2011.

Edith A. Rhodes

(Signature)

Special Negligence Doctrines

The courts have developed many *special negligence doctrines*. The most important of these are discussed in the paragraphs that follow.

Professional Malpractice

Professionals, including doctors, lawyers, architects, accountants, and others, owe a duty of ordinary care in providing their services. This duty is known as the *reasonable professional standard*. A professional who breaches this duty of care is liable for the injury that his or her negligence causes. This liability is commonly referred to as **professional malpractice.**

Professional malpractice The liability of a professional who breaches his or her duty of ordinary care.

Examples A doctor who amputates a wrong leg is liable for *medical malpractice*. A lawyer who fails to file a document with the court on time causing the client's case to be dismissed is liable for *legal malpractice*. An accountant who fails to use reasonable care, knowledge, skill, and judgment when providing auditing and other accounting services to a client is liable for *accounting malpractice*.

Negligent Infliction of Emotional Distress

Negligent infliction of emotional distress A tort that permits a person to recover for emotional distress caused by the defendant's negligent conduct.

Some jurisdictions have extended the tort of emotional distress to include the **negligent infliction of emotional distress**. The most common example of this tort involves bystanders who witness the injury or death of a loved one that is caused by another's negligent conduct. Under this tort, the bystander, even though not personally physically injured, can sue the negligent party for his or her own mental suffering.

Generally, to be successful in this type of case, the plaintiff must prove that (1) a relative was killed or injured by the defendant, (2) the plaintiff suffered severe emotional distress, and (3) the plaintiff's mental distress resulted from a sensory and contemporaneous observance of the accident. Some states require that the plaintiff's mental distress be manifested by some physical injury; other states have eliminated this requirement.

Example A father is driving his young daughter to school in his automobile when another driver negligently runs a red light and hits their automobile. Suppose that the young daughter dies from her injuries, and the father is uninjured. If the father suffers severe emotional distress by seeing his daughter die (and if he manifests this by a physical injury if required by state law), the father can recover damages for negligent infliction of emotional distress.

ETHICAL PERSPECTIVE

Paralegal's Duty Not to Commit Professional Malpractice

Paralegals work in a profession that requires them to be careful and to act reasonably while performing the assignments of their profession. As professionals, they are subject to malpractice lawsuits if they are negligent in the performance of their work. In determining whether a paralegal has been negligent, the court will examine what a reasonable paralegal would have done in like and similar circumstances.

Therefore, while performing the tasks assigned to them by supervising attorneys, a paralegal must be constantly vigilant to perform at the highest level of competence. Paralegal professionals are therefore required to be conscientious when conducting legal research to make sure that all avenues of research have been explored. When drafting documents, paralegals must draft the documents carefully, and spend the time to proofread the documents so that there are no errors.

Paralegals must perform their assignments carefully. If a paralegal does not meet the reasonable professional standard of the paralegal profession, then the paralegal can be found to be negligent. Such negligence could cause a loss to a client and possible loss to the law firm that employs him or her and to the insurance company who provides liability insurance to the law firm. As the tortfeasor, a paralegal who has committed professional malpractice could also be held personally liable for the damages caused by his or her negligence.

It is a paralegal's ethical duty to perform the tasks assigned to him or her with competence, diligence, and with reasonable care. A paralegal who violates this ethical duty and causes malpractice could cause a negligent lawsuit to be brought against the paralegal and the law firm he or she works for and possibly a client whom the law firm represents.

Negligence *Per Se*

Statutes often establish duties that one person owes to another. Violating a statute that proximately causes an injury is **negligence *per se***. The plaintiff in such an action must prove that (1) a statute existed, (2) the statute was enacted to prevent the type of injury suffered, and (3) the plaintiff was within a class of persons the statute meant to protect.

> **Negligence *per se*** Tort where the violation of a statute or ordinance constitutes the breach of the duty of care.

Example Most cities have an ordinance that places the responsibility for fixing public sidewalks in residential areas on the homeowners whose homes front the sidewalk. A homeowner is liable if he or she fails to repair a damaged sidewalk in front of his or her home and a pedestrian falls and is injured because of the damage. The injured party does not have to prove that the homeowner owed the duty because the statute establishes that.

Res Ipsa Loquitur

If a defendant is in control of a situation in which a plaintiff has been injured and has superior knowledge of the circumstances surrounding the injury, the plaintiff might have difficulty proving the defendant's negligence. In such a situation, the law applies the doctrine of *res ipsa loquitur* (Latin for "the thing speaks for itself"). This doctrine raises a presumption of negligence and switches the burden to the defendant to prove that he or she was *not* negligent. *Res ipsa loquitur* applies in cases where the following elements are met:

> ***Res ipsa loquitur*** Tort where the presumption of negligence arises because (1) the defendant was in exclusive control of the situation, and (2) the plaintiff would not have suffered injury but for someone's negligence. The burden switches to the defendant(s) to prove they were not negligent.

1. The defendant had exclusive control of the instrumentality or situation that caused the plaintiff's injury.
2. The injury ordinarily would not have occurred "but for" someone's negligence.

Example Haeran goes in for major surgery and is given anesthesia to put her to sleep during the operation. Sometime after the operation, it is discovered that a surgical instrument has been left in Haeran during the operation. She suffers severe injury because of the left-in instrument. Haeran would be hard-pressed to identify which doctor or nurse had been careless and left the instrument in her body. Haeran could bring a negligence lawsuit and name the doctor, the nurse, any other medical personnel who assisted in the operation, and the hospital as defendants. In this case, the court can apply the doctrine of *res ipsa loquitur* and place the presumption of negligence on the defendants. Any defendant who can prove that he or she did not leave the instrument in Haeran escapes liability; any defendant who does not disprove his or her negligence is liable. Other typical *res ipsa loquitur* cases involve commercial airplane crashes, falling elevators, and the like.

Good Samaritan Law

In the past, exposure to liability made many doctors, nurses, and other medical professionals reluctant to stop and render aid to victims in emergency situations, such as highway accidents. Almost all states have enacted a **Good Samaritan law** that relieves medical professionals from liability for injury caused by their ordinary negligence in such circumstances.

> **Good Samaritan law** A state statute that relieves medical professionals from liability for ordinary negligence when they stop and render aid to victims in emergency situations.

Good Samaritan laws protect medical professionals only from liability for their *ordinary negligence*, not for injuries caused by their gross negligence or reckless or intentional conduct. Most Good Samaritan laws protect licensed doctors and nurses and laypersons who have been certified in CPR. Good Samaritan statutes generally do not protect laypersons who are not trained in CPR—that is, they are liable for injuries caused by their ordinary negligence in rendering aid.

Example A driver is injured in an automobile accident and is unconscious in his car. A medical doctor who is driving by the scene of the accident stops, pulls the injured driver from the car, and administers first-aid. In doing so, the doctor negligently breaks the person's shoulder. If the doctor's negligence is ordinary negligence, she is not liable to the injured party because the Good Samaritan law protects her from liability. If the doctor was grossly negligent or reckless in administering aid, she is liable for the injuries she caused.

Dram Shop Act

Many states have enacted a **Dram Shop Act** that makes a tavern and bartender civilly liable for injuries caused to or by patrons who are served too much alcohol. The alcohol must be either served in sufficient quantity to make the patron intoxicated or served to an already intoxicated person. Both the tavern and the bartender are liable to third persons injured by the patron and for injuries the patron suffered. They also are liable for injuries caused by or to minors served by the tavern, regardless of whether the minor is intoxicated.

Liability of Landowners

Owners and renters of real property owe certain duties to protect visitors from injury while on the property. A landowner's and tenant's liability generally depends on the visitor's status. Visitors fall into the following two categories:

1. *Invitees and licensees.* An **invitee** is a person who has been expressly or impliedly invited onto the owner's premises for the *mutual benefit* of both parties (e.g., guests invited for dinner, the mail carrier, and customers of a business). A **licensee** is a person who, *for his or her own benefit*, enters the premises with the express or implied consent of the owner (e.g., Avon representative, encyclopedia salesperson, Jehovah's Witnesses). An owner owes a **duty of ordinary care** to invitees and licensees. An owner is liable if he or she negligently causes injury to an invitee or licensee.

   Duty of ordinary care The duty an owner or renter of real property owes an invitee or a licensee to prevent injury or harm when the invitee or licensee steps on the owner's premises.

   Example A homeowner is liable if she leaves a garden hose across the walkway on which an invitee or a licensee trips and is injured.

2. *Trespassers.* A **trespasser** is a person who has no invitation, permission, or right to be on another's property. Burglars are a common type of trespasser. Generally, an owner does not owe a duty of ordinary care to a trespasser.

   Duty not to willfully or wantonly injure The duty an owner or renter of real property owes a trespasser to prevent intentional injury or harm to the trespasser when the trespasser is on his or her premises.

   Example If a trespasser trips and injures himself on a bicycle the owner negligently left out, the owner is not liable. An owner, however, does owe a **duty not to willfully or wantonly injure** a trespasser. Thus, an owner cannot set traps to injure trespassers.

A few states have eliminated the invitee–licensee–trespasser distinction. These states hold that owners and renters owe a duty of ordinary care to all persons who enter the property.

Liability of Common Carriers and Innkeepers

The common law holds common carriers and innkeepers to a higher standard of care than most other businesses. **Common carriers** and **innkeepers** owe a **duty of utmost care**—rather than a duty of ordinary care—to their passengers and guests.

Example Innkeepers must provide security for their guests. If a large hotel does not provide security measures and a third party poses as a "waiter" delivering room service and injures a guest, the hotel could be held liable to the injured guest. Obviously, a large hotel must provide greater security to guests than a "mom-and-pop" motel has to provide. Some states and cities have adopted specific statutes and ordinances relating to this duty.

Defenses to Negligence

A defendant in a negligence lawsuit may raise several defenses to the imposition of liability. These defenses are discussed in the following paragraphs.

Superseding or Intervening Event

Under negligence, a person is liable only for foreseeable events. Therefore, an original negligent party can raise a **superseding (or intervening) event** as a defense to liability.

> **Example**   Assume that an avid golfer negligently hits a spectator with a golf ball, knocking the spectator unconscious. While lying on the ground waiting for an ambulance to come, the spectator is struck by a bolt of lightning and killed. The golfer is liable for the injuries caused by the golf ball. He is not liable for the death of the spectator, however, because the lightning bolt was an unforeseen intervening event.

Assumption of the Risk

If a plaintiff knows of and voluntarily enters into or participates in a risky activity that results in injury, the law recognizes that the plaintiff assumed, or took on, the risk involved. Thus, the defendant can raise the defense of **assumption of the risk** against the plaintiff. This defense assumes that the plaintiff (1) had knowledge of the specific risk, and (2) voluntarily assumed that risk.

> **Example**   Under this theory, a race car driver assumes the risk of being injured or killed in a crash.

Assumption of the risk A defense a defendant can use against a plaintiff who knowingly and voluntarily enters into or participates in a risky activity that results in injury.

Contributory Negligence

Under the common law doctrine of **contributory negligence**, a plaintiff who is partially at fault for his or her own injury cannot recover against the negligent defendant.

> **Example**   Suppose a driver who is driving faster than the speed limit negligently hits and injures a pedestrian who is jaywalking. The jury finds that the driver is 80 percent responsible for the accident and the jaywalker is 20 percent responsible. The pedestrian suffered $100,000 in injuries. Under the doctrine of contributory negligence, the pedestrian cannot recover any damages from the driver.

The doctrine of contributory negligence has one major exception: The defendant has a duty under the law to avoid the accident if at all possible. This rule is known as the *last clear chance rule*.

> **Example**   A driver who sees a pedestrian walking across the street against a "Don't Walk" sign must avoid hitting him or her if possible. When deciding cases involving this rule, the courts consider the attentiveness of the parties and the amount of time each had to respond to the situation.

Comparative Negligence

As seen, application of the doctrine of contributory negligence could reach an unfair result where a party only slightly at fault for his or her injuries could not recover from an otherwise negligent defendant. Many states have replaced the doctrine of contributory negligence with the doctrine of **comparative negligence**. Under this doctrine, damages are apportioned according to fault.

Comparative negligence A doctrine under which damages are apportioned according to fault.

> **Example**   When the comparative negligence rule is applied to the previous example, the result is much fairer. The plaintiff–pedestrian can recover 80 percent of his or her damages (or $80,000) from the defendant–driver. This is an example of *pure comparative negligence*. Several states have adopted *partial comparative negligence*, which provides that a plaintiff must be less than 50 percent responsible for causing his or her own injuries to recover under comparative negligence; otherwise, contributory negligence applies.

Paralegals *in* Practice

PARALEGAL PROFILE
Ruth S. Conley

Ruth S. Conley's legal specialty is personal injury and product liability litigation. A paralegal for over 20 years, she is currently employed by the law firm of Andrews Kurth LLP in Houston, Texas. Ruth has a Bachelor of Science degree in Communications, and obtained the Certified Paralegal designation from the National Association of Legal Assistants (NALA). Previously elected as the first President of the Houston Paralegal Association, Ruth currently serves on NALA's Continuing Education Council. She also serves on the Paralegal Advisory Committee at San Jacinto College's North Campus in Houston.

I feel that the ability to manage time well is the most important skill a litigation paralegal must master. You may have the ability to prepare an excellent trial notebook, and to color-code and cross-reference trial exhibits with fact and expert witness testimony. But, if you cannot prepare these items in a timely manner, then your work product serves no benefit to your attorney, your client, or the progression of your case.

Personal injury and product liability litigation is a "trendy" area of law. Many subjects in news headlines eventually end up in a courtroom, such as Firestone tires, Phen-Fen, and Vioxx. These products were, and continue to be, the source of massive personal injury and product liability litigation across the country. Therefore, as a litigation paralegal, it is important to daily read your newspaper and watch national news television shows. In addition, join a paralegal association and attend its continuing legal education events. Knowledge gained from these resources will help keep you informed.

With the growth of technology and the acceptability of paperless files, many law firms are becoming open to the idea of flexible working hours and work-at-home options for paralegals. As little as ten years ago, this practice would never have been extended to non-attorney staff. However, these options are generally offered only to trusted and experienced paralegals. As a novice paralegal, you must first prove your reliability, work ethic, and profitability to your employer.

Product Liability and Strict Liability

Where a product causes injury or death to a person, a lawsuit may be brought by the injured person or the heirs of the deceased person against the manufacturer or seller of the product for negligence. In order to prove negligence, the elements of negligence must be proven.

In the landmark case *Greenmun v. Yuba Power Products, Inc.* [59 Cal.2d 57, 27 Cal.Rptr. 697, 377 P.2d 897, 1963 Cal. Lexis 140 (1963)], the California Supreme Court adopted the **doctrine of strict liability in tort** as a basis for **products liability** actions. Most states now have adopted this doctrine as a basis for product liability actions. The doctrine of strict liability removes many of the difficulties for the plaintiff associated with proving a case based on negligence. In this section of this chapter, we will examine the scope of the strict liability doctrine.

> **Products liability** The liability of manufacturers, sellers, and others for the injuries caused by defective products.

Liability without Fault

Unlike negligence, strict liability does not require the injured person to prove that the defendant breached a duty of care. **Strict liability** *is imposed irrespective of fault*. A seller can be found strictly liable even though he or she has exercised all possible care in the preparation and sale of his or her product.

The doctrine of strict liability applies to sellers and lessors of products who are engaged in the business of selling and leasing products. Casual sales and transactions by nonmerchants are not covered. Thus, a person who sells a defective product to a neighbor in a casual sale is not strictly liable if the product causes injury.

Strict liability applies only to products, not services. In hybrid transactions involving both services and products, the dominant element of the transaction dictates whether strict liability applies.

> **Strict liability** A tort doctrine that makes manufacturers, distributors, wholesalers, retailers, and others in the chain of distribution of a defective product liable for the damages caused by the defect *irrespective of fault*.

Example In a medical operation that requires a blood transfusion, the operation would be the dominant element and strict liability would not apply. Strict liability may not be disclaimed.

All in the Chain of Distribution Are Liable

All parties in the **chain of distribution** of a defective product are strictly liable for the injuries caused by that product. Thus, all manufacturers, distributors, wholesalers, retailers, lessors, and subcomponent manufacturers may be sued under this doctrine. This view is based on public policy. Lawmakers presume that sellers and lessors will insure against the risk of a strict liability lawsuit and spread the cost to their consumers by raising the price of products.

> **Chain of distribution** All manufacturers, distributors, wholesalers, retailers, lessors, and subcomponent manufacturers involved in a transaction.

Example Suppose a subcomponent manufacturer produces a defective tire and sells it to a truck manufacturer. The truck manufacturer places the defective tire on one of its new-model trucks. The truck is distributed by a distributor to a retail dealer. Ultimately, the retail dealer sells the truck to a buyer. The defective tire causes an accident in which the buyer is injured. All of the parties in the tire's chain of distribution can be sued by the injured party. In this case, the liable parties are the subcomponent manufacturer, the truck manufacturer, the distributor, and the retailer.

A defendant who has not been negligent but who is made to pay a strict liability judgment can bring a separate action against the negligent party in the chain of distribution to recover its losses. In the preceding example, the retailer could sue the manufacturer to recover the strict liability judgment assessed against it. Exhibit 12.2 compares the doctrines of negligence and strict liability.

Parties Who Can Recover for Strict Liability

Because strict liability is a tort doctrine, privity of contract between the plaintiff and the defendant is not required. The doctrine applies even if the injured party had no contractual relations with the defendant. Under strict liability, sellers and lessors are liable to the ultimate user or consumer. Users include the purchaser or lessee, family members, guests, employees, customers, and persons who passively enjoy the benefits of the product (e.g., passengers in automobiles).

Most jurisdictions have judicially or statutorily extended the protection of strict liability to bystanders. The courts have stated that bystanders should be entitled to even greater protection than a consumer or user. This is because consumers and users have the chance to inspect for defects and to limit their purchases to articles manufactured by reputable manufacturers and sold by reputable retailers, whereas bystanders do not have the same opportunity.

Example Fred purchases an automobile manufactured by Motors Corporation. The automobile has a defect in it that causes Fred to get into an automobile accident with an automobile driven by Sarah. Both Fred and Sarah are severely injured. Motors Corporation is liable to Fred, the owner and user of the automobile, and to Sarah, a bystander.

Damages Recoverable for Strict Liability

The damages recoverable in a strict liability action vary by jurisdiction. Damages for personal injuries are recoverable in all jurisdictions that have adopted the doctrine of strict liability, although some jurisdictions limit the dollar amount of the award. Property damage is recoverable in most jurisdictions, but economic loss (e.g., lost income) is recoverable in only a few jurisdictions. **Punitive damages** are generally allowed if the plaintiff can prove that the defendant either intentionally injured him or her or acted with reckless disregard for his or her safety.

A court can award punitive damages against a defendant in a product liability lawsuit if it finds that the defendant's conduct was committed with intent or reckless disregard for human life. Punitive damages are meant to punish the defendant and to send

| Exhibit 12.2 | Doctrines of negligence and strict liability compared |

Defendant → **Manufacturer negligent** ← Defendant

DEFECTIVE | PRODUCT

Distributor ← Defendant

Negligent party is liable

All in the chain of distribution are liable

Retailer ← Defendant

Negligence lawsuit   **Consumer**   Strict liability lawsuit

DEFECTIVE PRODUCT CAUSES INJURY

a message to the defendant that such behavior will not be tolerated. Large punitive damage awards usually make the headlines.

Concept of Defect

Defect Something wrong, inadequate, or improper in manufacture, design, packaging, warning, or safety measures of a product.

To recover for strict liability, the injured party must show that the product that caused the injury had a **defect.** (Remember that the injured party does not have to prove who caused the product to become defective.) A product can be found to be defective in many ways. The most common types of defects are *defects in manufacture*, *failure to warn*, *defects in design*, and *defects in packaging*. These defects are discussed in the following paragraphs.

Defect in Manufacture

Web Exploration

Go to http://www
.productliabilitylawblog.com/
2008/03/general_motors_settles_
defecti.html and read the article
about General Motors settling a
product liability lawsuit.

A **defect in manufacture** occurs when the manufacturer fails to (1) properly assemble a product, (2) properly test a product, or (3) adequately check the quality of the product.

> **Example**   If a manufacturer of ladders fails to bolt one step to the ladder side and the step breaks off while being used and the user is injured, the manufacturer would be strictly liable for a defect in manufacture.

Failure to Warn

Certain products are inherently dangerous and cannot be made any safer and still accomplish the task for which they are designed. Manufacturers and sellers of such products are under a *duty to warn* users about the product's dangerous propensities. A proper and conspicuous warning placed on the product insulates the manufacturer and others in the chain of distribution from strict liability. **Failure to warn** of these dangerous propensities is a defect that will support a strict liability action.

> **Example**   Certain prescription drugs cause side effects, allergies, and other injuries to some users. If a manufacturer or seller of prescription drugs fails to warn about these side effects and dangers, it can be held liable to anyone injured because of the failure to warn.

Defect in Design

A **defect in design** can support a strict liability action. A design defect is where an entire product line is defectively designed. In evaluating the adequacy of a product's design, the courts apply a risk–utility analysis and consider the gravity of the danger posed by the design, the likelihood that injury will occur, the availability and cost of producing a safer alternative design, the social utility of the product, and other factors.

> **Defect in design** A flaw that occurs when a product is improperly designed.

> **Examples**   Design defects that have supported strict liability awards include toys that are designed with removable parts that could be swallowed by children, machines and appliances designed without proper safeguards, and trucks and other vehicles designed without warning devices to let people know that the vehicle is backing up.

Defect in Packaging

Manufacturers owe a duty to design and provide safe packages for their products. A manufacturer's failure to meet this duty subjects that manufacturer and others in the chain of distribution of the product to strict liability for **defect in packaging**.

Web Exploration

Go to http://www.core77.com/ blog/object_culture/ antitamper_bottle_cap_5086 .asp to see a version of a tamperproof cap for beverage bottles.

> **Examples**   This duty requires manufacturers to provide packages and containers that are tamperproof or that clearly indicate if they have been tampered with. Certain manufacturers, such as drug manufacturers, owe a duty to place their products in containers that cannot be opened by children.

Other Product Defects

Other product defects can prove the basis for a strict liability action.

> **Example**   **Failure to provide adequate instructions** for either the safe assembly or safe use of a product is a defect that subjects the manufacturer and others in the chain of distribution to strict liability. Other defects include inadequate testing of products, inadequate selection of component parts of materials, and improper certification of the safety of a product. The concept of defect is an expanding area of the law.

A complaint alleging product liability appears as Exhibit 12.3.

Defenses to Product Liability

Defendant manufacturers and sellers in strict liability or negligence actions may raise the following defenses to the imposition of liability:

1. *Generally known danger.* Certain products are inherently dangerous and are known to the general population to be so. Manufacturers and sellers are not strictly liable for failing to warn of generally known dangers.

   > **Example**   Because it is a known fact that guns shoot bullets, manufacturers and sellers of guns do not have to place a warning on the barrel of a gun warning of this generally known danger.

2. *Government contractor defense.* Defense and other contractors that manufacture products to government specifications are not usually liable if the product causes injury.

Exhibit 12.3 Complaint for product liability

UNITED STATES DISTRICT COURT
WESTERN DISTRICT OF KENTUCKY
LOUISVILLE DIVISION

CASE NO. 3:08-CV-349

---X
ALISON COX PREGLIASCO, mother and natural
guardian of A.P., an infant, and ALISON
COX PREGLIASCO, Individually,

                Plaintiffs,

        -against-   **AMENDED COMPLAINT**

                                              Plaintiff Demands
CROCS, INC.,   Trial by Jury
A Colorado Corporation

                         Defendant.
---X

Plaintiffs, ALISON COX PREGLIASCO, mother and natural guardian of A.P., an infant,

and ALSION COX PREGLIASCO, Individually, by their attorneys, WATERS LAW GROUP,

PLLC and ROBINSON & YABLON, P.C., complaining of the defendant, sets forth as follows:

1.   This is an action pursuant to Kentucky products liability law. Jurisdiction of the

Court is predicated upon diversity of citizenship pursuant to 28 U.S.C. §1332 (a) (1) because the

dispute involves the plaintiffs, who are citizens of Kentucky, and defendant, a Colorado

corporation, and because the amount in controversy is greater than $100,000.00.

FIRST CAUSE OF ACTION

PRODUCT LIABILITY

Exhibit 12.3 Complaint for product liability *(continued)*

2.   At all times hereinafter mentioned, Plaintiff A.P., an infant under the age of fourteen, and her mother and natural guardian, ALISON COX PREGLIASCO, were residents of Kentucky, residing in the City of Louisville. At all times hereinafter mentioned, defendant, CROCS, INC. ("CROCS") was and still is a foreign corporation transacting business in the state of New York.

3.   At all times hereinafter mentioned, CROCS was and is a foreign corporation, duly authorized to do business in the state of Kentucky.

4.   At all times hereinafter mentioned, CROCS was a Colorado corporation.

5.   At all times hereinafter mentioned, CROCS had its principal place of business in Niwot, Colorado.

6.   At all times hereinafter mentioned, CROCS contracted to supply goods in the state of Kentucky.

7.   At all times hereinafter mentioned, CROCS regularly did and solicited business and/or engaged in other persistent courses of conduct and/or derived financial revenue from the goods supplied in the state of Kentucky.

8.   At all times hereinafter mentioned, CROCS expected, or reasonably should have expected acts done by it to have consequences in the state of Kentucky.

(continued)

Exhibit 12.3 **Complaint for product liability** *(continued)*

9.   At all times hereinafter mentioned, CROCS was engaged in the business of manufacturing, selling and/or distributing footwear, and, in particular, colored footwear comprised of closed-cell resin.

10.   In or about 2002, CROCS began to manufacture, sell and distribute a line of closed-cell resin footwear.

11.   In or about 2002, CROCS promoted, advertised and marketed its footwear as a slip-resistant outdoor shoe for boating and other outdoor use.

12.   In or about 2005, CROCS did commence promotion, marketing and advertising its footwear as an all-purpose shoe for children in small sizes for children.

13.   In furtherance of the promotion, marketing, and advertising geared toward the child marketplace, CROCS did commence the selling of footwear in small sizes for children, in child-friendly colors, made use of Disney characters, and promotion of Jibbitz, all in an effort to generate revenue from the sale of CROCS to parents of small children.

14.   CROCS did engage in this course of promotion, marketing and sales, directly and through its distributors in the state of Kentucky.

15.   In 2005, CROCS did become aware of reports of children being injured while wearing CROCS' shoes when said shoes were sucked into moving escalators.

Exhibit 12.3 **Complaint for product liability** *(continued)*

16. In 2005, the issue of CROCS' shoes being sucked into escalators causing injuries to children was featured on ABC's Good Morning America.

17. In 2005, in response to reports of CROCS' shoes being sucked into escalators causing injuries to children, CROCS did issue statements to media that its shoes were safe and that the reported escalator incidents were the fault not of CROCS but rather the parents of the injured children and/or those responsible for maintenance and repair of escalators. CROCS further stated that it was looking into the happening of such incidents and that it was concerned about escalator safety.

18. The statements issued by CROCS and its employees and/or agents, as referenced in ¶17, *supra*, were patently false.

19. CROCS recklessly and knowingly issued the aforementioned false statements in an effort to deflect blame and so as to maximize its corporate profits.

20. In 2006, CROCS did become aware of multiple further reports of children being injured while wearing CROCS' shoes when said shoes were sucked into moving escalators.

21. In 2006, in response to reports of CROCS' shoes being sucked into escalators causing injuries to children, CROCS did issue statements to media that its shoes were safe and that the reported escalator incidents were the fault not of CROCS but rather the parents of the injured children and/or those responsible for maintenance and repair of escalators. CROCS further stated that it was looking into the happening of such incidents and that it was concerned about escalator safety.

(continued)

Exhibit 12.3 **Complaint for product liability** *(continued)*

22. The statements issued by CROCS and its employees and/or agents, as referenced in 21, *supra*, were patently false.

23. CROCS knowingly issued the aforementioned false statements in an effort to deflect blame and so as to maximize its corporate profits.

24. On or about March 21, 2008, Plaintiff, ALISON COX PREGLIASCO did purchase a pair of children's CROCS for her daughter, the infant plaintiff, in the state of Kentucky.

25. At the time of the manufacture, distribution, and sale of said pair of CROCS footwear, the footwear contained no safety design features, safety guards and/or warnings of any kind.

26. At the time of the manufacture, distribution and sale of said pair of CROCS, defendant knew, or had reason to know that, despite its promotion, marketing and advertising, CROCS were not suitable and were unsafe as "all purpose shoes for comfort and fashion."

27. At the time of the manufacture, distribution and sale of said pair of CROCS, defendant knew, or had reason to know, of multiple prior reported incidents where young children wearing CROCS were injured when their CROCS were caught in escalators. Defendant further knew that said prior reported incidents all involved claims of similar serious foot injuries to young children.

Exhibit 12.3 **Complaint for product liability** *(continued)*

28.　　On or about June 4, 2008, infant plaintiff A.P., while wearing CROCS, was severely and permanently injured when one of her CROC shoes was caught in an escalator at Hartsfield Airport in Atlanta, Georgia, causing her right foot to be seriously injured as depicted in the two (2) color photographs annexed as Exhibit "1".

29.　　The aforesaid occurrence and the injuries resulting therefrom and suffered by the plaintiffs were caused solely by reason of the recklessness, negligence and carelessness of the defendant in its design, manufacturing, testing, inspection, production, assembly, distribution, and sale of its CROCS footwear including the aforesaid pair of CROCS footwear worn by infant plaintiff.

30.　　By reason of the foregoing, plaintiffs have been damaged and are entitled to compensatory damages in the amount of ONE MILLION DOLLARS ($1,000,000.00).

SECOND CAUSE OF ACTION
BREACH OF EXPRESS & IMPLIED WARRANTY

31.　　Plaintiffs, repeat, restate and reallege each and every allegation contained in paragraphs "1" through "30" with the same force and effect as if fully set forth herein.

32.　　CROCS in connection with its business activities aforementioned herein, made both express and implied warranties with regard to the aforesaid product; warranting that it was fit, safe, capable and suitable for the use and purpose intended, and that it was not unsafe or defective.

(continued)

Exhibit 12.3 **Complaint for product liability** *(continued)*

33.   The aforesaid warranties and representations were false, misleading and inaccurate in that the aforesaid CROCS footwear was unsafe, dangerous and defective.

34.   Both express and implied warranties were breached by CROCS.

35.   Solely as a result of the aforesaid breaches of warranty, plaintiffs suffered severe injuries and damages while using CROCS footwear for their warranted use and purpose.

36.   By reason of the foregoing, plaintiffs have been damaged in a sum in the amount of ONE MILLION DOLLARS ($1,000,000.00).

THIRD CAUSE OF ACTION

FAILURE TO WARN OF KNOWN DEFECT

37.   Plaintiffs, repeat, restate and reallege each and every allegation contained in paragraphs "1" through "36" with the same force and effect as if fully set forth herein.

38.   At all times herein mentioned, defendant CROCS was aware of problems with regard to the safety and suitability of its footwear as manufactured, sold and marketed.

39.   Defendant, notwithstanding said knowledge, failed to design its footwear with adequate safety features and failed to notify and warn purchasers and users of its dangerous product, including plaintiffs herein.

Exhibit 12.3 **Complaint for product liability** *(continued)*

40.   As a result of said failure to warn, CROCS is liable to plaintiffs for the injuries and damages they suffered.

41.   By reason of the foregoing, plaintiffs have been damaged in the sum of ONE MILLION DOLLARS ($1,000,000.00).

FOURTH CAUSE OF ACTION

LOSS OF SERVICES

42.   Plaintiffs, repeat, restate and reallege each and every allegation contained in paragraphs "1" through "41" with the same force and effect as if fully set forth herein.

43.   That the Plaintiff, ALISON COX PREGLIASCO, individually, is the mother and natural guardian of the infant-plaintiff, A.P.

44.   That by reason of the foregoing incident, Plaintiff, ALSION COX PREGLIASCO was caused to sustain pecuniary losses due to the injuries suffered by her daughter, infant plaintiff, A.P.

45.   That by reason of the foregoing incident, Plaintiff, ALSION COX PREGLASCO was deprived her daughter's services stemming from the serious nature and severity of infant plaintiff, A.P.'s injuries, incurred substantial expenses and was forced to provide services on her behalf.

(continued)

Exhibit 12.3 **Complaint for product liability** *(continued)*

46. By reason of the foregoing, plaintiffs have been damaged in the sum of ONE MILLION DOLLARS ($1,000,000.00).

<u>**FIFTH CAUSE OF ACTION**</u>

PUNITIVE DAMAGES

47. Plaintiffs, repeat, restate and reallege each and every allegation contained in paragraphs "1" through "46" with the same force and effect as if fully set forth herein.

48. The acts and omissions of CROCS, demonstrate a reckless and willful pattern of wanton and depraved indifference to the likelihood of harm to children as a result of product defects in CROCS' footwear.

49. At every crucial juncture, when the onus was upon CROCS to modify its footwear and its marketing so as to warn consumers of dangers known to CROCS, CROCS instead recklessly and knowingly made misleading statement in an effort to maximize its corporate profits at the expense of injuries to young and innocent children.

50. When confronted with incident upon incident of children being injured due to product defects in its footwear, rather than act to protect children and inform their parents and consumers of known dangers, CROCS, instead issued false statements, baselessly attempting to blame persons and entities who were wholly free from fault.

Exhibit 12.3   **Complaint for product liability** *(continued)*

51.   The acts and omissions of CROCS, as detailed, *supra*, demonstrate a high degree of moral turpitude warranting the imposition of punitive and/or exemplary damages in the amount of ONE MILLION DOLLARS ($1,000,000.00)

WHEREFORE, Plaintiffs, ALISON COX PREGLIASCO, mother and natural guardian of A.P., an infant and ALISON COX PREGLIASCO, individually demand judgment against the defendant along with such other and further relief as may be granted by the Court, including but not limited to the costs and disbursements of this action.

Dated: July 1, 2008   Respectfully submitted,

s/ Benjamin S. Shively
WATERS LAW GROUP, PLLC
Robert R. Waters, Esq.
rrwaters@waterslawoffice.com
Benjamin S. Shively, Esq.
bsshively@waterslawoffice.com
Enrico A. Mazzoli, Esq.
eamazzoli@waterslawoffice.com
714 Lyndon Lane, Suite 6
Louisville, KY 40222
T: 502-425-2424
F: 502-425-9724

-   and –

ROBINSON & YABLON, P.C.
Andrew M. Laskin, Esq. (AL9379)
ALaskin@robyablaw.com
232 Madison Avenue, Suite 1200
New York, New York 10016
(212) 725-8566

Attorneys for Plaintiffs

Exhibit 12.3 **Complaint for product liability** *(continued)*

CERTIFICATE OF SERVICE

I hereby declare that on this 1st day of July, 2008, I electronically filed a true and accurate copy of the foregoing document through the ECF system, which will send a notice of electronic filing to Andrew Laskin of Robinson & Yablon, P.C., and on this 1st day of July, 2008, I mailed a true and accurate copy of the foregoing document, postage prepaid, via United States Certified Mail, return receipt requested, to the following:

CROCS, INC.   Certified Mail #: 7004 2890 0001 7826 8480
6328 Monarch Park Place
Niwot, CO 80503

(Principal Office / Street Address for Defendant)

- and -

The Corporation Company   Certified Mail #: 7004 2890 0001 7826 8473
1675 Broadway, Suite 1200
Denver, CO 80202

(Registered Agent for Defendant)

s/ Benjamin S. Shively, Esq

Example A manufacturer that produces a weapon to U.S. Army specifications is not liable if the weapon is defective and causes injury.

3. *Misuse of the product.* A manufacturer or seller is relieved of product liability if the plaintiff has *abnormally misused* the product.

   Example A manufacturer or seller of a power lawn mower is not liable if a consumer lifts a power lawn mower on its side to cut the hedge which causes the lawn mower to fall, cutting the consumer.

4. *Supervening event.* The manufacturer or seller is not liable if the product is materially altered or modified after it leaves the seller's possession and the alteration or modification causes an injury.

   Example A seller is not liable if a consumer purchases a truck and then replaces the tires with large off-road tires which cause the truck to rollover, injuring the driver or passenger.

Some states have enacted **statutes of repose** which limit a manufacturer's and seller's liability to a certain number of years from the date when the product was first sold. The period of repose varies from state to state.

Example Assume that a state statute of repose is seven years. If a consumer purchases a product on May 1, 2011, the statute of repose expires on May 1, 2018. If the product is defective but does not cause injury until after that date, the manufacturer and seller are not liable.

ETHICAL PERSPECTIVE

Duty to Disclose Information That Could Result in Bodily Harm

Ms. Phan is a paralegal who works for a large law firm that represents major corporate clients. One of the clients that the law firm represents is the Wheels Corporation, which manufactures and sells automobile tires. Wheels Corporation is a major supplier of automobile tires to automobile manufacturers who then install tires on their automobiles, SUVs, trucks, and other vehicles that they sell to the public.

Wheels Corporation designed and manufactured a new automobile tire it calls SafeTrack. Wheels Corporation advertises the tires as having new technology that makes vehicles ride safer, as well as being longer-lasting than tires made by other tire manufacturers. Millions of SafeTrack tires are purchased by vehicle manufacturers and placed on new and used vehicles that are sold around the world.

After one year, Wheels Corporation has received thousands of complaints from vehicle owners who allege that their SafeTrack tires easily shred and explode, causing accidents in which drivers and passengers have been injured or killed. Many lawsuits have been filed against Wheels Corporation, alleging product defects in the SafeTrack tires.

Wheels Corporation determines, after a secret internal investigation, that the SafeTrack tires most likely shred and explode when the temperature rises above 85 degrees Fahrenheit. Therefore, most of the accidents involving SafeTrack tires have occurred in areas of the United States and the world that have warmer climates. Wheels Corporation does not make this information available to the public.

Ms. Phan is assigned by her defense law firm to work on many of the product liability lawsuits that Wheels Corporation now faces concerning the defect in its SafeTrack tires. At one of the meetings with the lawyers of the law firm and the executives of Wheels Corporation that Ms. Phan attends, the executives of the Wheels Corporation disclose a cost-benefit analysis they have prepared showing that it will be cheaper for the corporation to let the existing SafeTrack tires remain on vehicles without a recall and pay monetary damages to injured victims and the heirs of deceased victims than to recall and replace the defective tires. The lawyers and the executives agree to this strategy and decide not to recall any of the defective tires and not to inform government authorities of the cost–benefit analysis.

Does Ms. Phan, who has heard this strategy, have any ethical duty to disclose this confidential information to government authorities?

A paralegal professional is ordinarily under a duty not to voluntarily disclose information about a client to a government regulatory authority. However, model and state paralegal codes of conduct and social responsibility provide that a paralegal is under an ethical duty to disclose information about a client or the client's conduct that could cause serious bodily harm or death to consumers or others.

PARALEGAL'S ETHICAL DECISION

In this case, although the information revealed at the meeting is normally confidential, Ms. Phan owes an ethical duty to disclose this information to the appropriate government authority because it is necessary to prevent the client, Wheels Corporation, from committing an act that will result in bodily injury and deaths to consumers driving vehicles equipped with the SafeTrack tires, passengers, drivers of other vehicles, pedestrians, and others. Ms. Phan must disclose these confidential facts to the appropriate government authorities.

Concept Review *and* Reinforcement

SUMMARY OF KEY CONCEPTS

Intentional Torts Against Persons

Assault	Assault is the threat of immediate harm or offensive contact, or any action that arouses reasonable apprehension of imminent harm.
Battery	Battery is the unauthorized and harmful or offensive physical contact with another person. *Transferred intent doctrine:* If a person intends to injure one person but actually harms another person, the law transfers the perpetrator's intent from the target to the actual victim.
False Imprisonment	Intentional confinement or restraint of another person without authority or justification and without that person's consent

Merchant Protection	Merchant protection statutes permit businesses to stop, detain, and investigate suspected shoplifters (and not be held liable for false imprisonment) if the following requirements are met. 1. There are reasonable grounds for the suspicion. 2. Suspects are detained for only a reasonable time. 3. Investigations are conducted in a reasonable manner.
Defamation of Character	When the defendant makes an untrue statement of fact about the plaintiff that is published to a third party, it is defamation of character. Truth is an absolute defense. Types of defamation: 1. *Slander:* Oral defamation 2. *Libel:* Written defamation Public-figure plaintiffs must prove the additional element of *malice*. *Disparagement.* An untrue statement made by a person or business about the products, services, property, or reputation of another business.
Misappropriation of the Right to Publicity	Also called *tort of appropriation*, this tort means appropriating another person's name or identity for commercial purposes without that person's consent.
Invasion of the Right to Privacy	Unwarranted and undesired publicity of a private fact about a person is invasion of privacy. The fact does not have to be untrue. Truth is not a defense.
Intentional Infliction of Emotional Distress	Also known as *tort of outrage*, this is extreme and outrageous conduct intentionally or recklessly done that causes severe emotional distress. Some states require that the mental distress be manifested by physical injury.
Malicious Prosecution	A successful defendant in a prior lawsuit can sue the plaintiff if the first lawsuit was frivolous.
Civil Fraud	Civil fraud occurs where one party fraudulently deceives another party and steals his or her money or property. To prove fraud, the following elements must be shown: 1. The wrongdoer made a false representation of material fact. 2. The wrongdoer intended to deceive the innocent party. 3. The innocent party justifiably relied on the misrepresentation. 4. The innocent party was injured.

Intentional Torts Against Property

Trespass to Land	In this form of trespass, a person interferes with an owner's right to exclusive possession of land.
Trespass to Personal Property	In this form of trespass, a person injures another person's personal property or interferes with that person's enjoyment of his or her property.
Conversion of Personal Property	Conversion of personal property means taking over another person's personal property and depriving him or her of the use and enjoyment of the property.

Unintentional Torts—Negligence

Definition	Negligence is defined as the omission to do something that a reasonable person would do, or doing something that a prudent and reasonable person would not do.

Elements of Negligence	To establish negligence, the plaintiff must prove:
	1. The defendant owed *a duty of care* to the plaintiff.
	2. The defendant *breached this duty*.
	3. The plaintiff suffered *injury*.
	4. The defendant's negligent act *caused* the plaintiff's injury. Two types of causation must be shown:
	  a. *Causation in fact* (or actual cause): The defendant's negligent act was the actual cause of the plaintiff's injury.
	  b. *Proximate cause* (or legal cause): The defendant is liable only for the *foreseeable* consequences of his or her negligent act.

Special Negligence Doctrines

Professional Malpractice	Doctors, lawyers, architects, accountants, and other professionals owe a duty of ordinary care in providing their services. They are judged by a *reasonable professional standard*. Professionals who breach this duty are liable to clients and some third parties for *professional malpractice*.
Negligent Infliction of Emotional Distress	A person who witnesses a close relative's injury or death may sue the negligent party who caused the accident, to recover damages for any emotional distress the bystander suffered. To recover for *negligent infliction of emotional distress*, the plaintiff must prove: 1. A relative was killed or injured by the defendant. 2. The plaintiff suffered severe emotional distress. 3. The plaintiff's mental distress resulted from a sensory and contemporaneous observance of the accident. Some states require that the mental distress be manifested by physical injury.
Negligence *Per Se*	A statute or ordinance establishes the duty of care. A violation of the statute or ordinance constitutes a breach of this duty of care.
Res Ipsa Loquitur	A presumption of negligence is established if the defendant had exclusive control of the instrumentality or situation that caused the plaintiff's injury and the injury would not have ordinarily occurred but for someone's negligence. The defendants may rebut this presumption.
Good Samaritan Law	Good Samaritan laws relieve doctors and other medical professionals from liability for ordinary negligence when they render medical aid in emergency situations.
Dram Shop Act	A Dram Shop Act is a state statute that makes taverns and bartenders liable for injuries caused to or by patrons who are served too much alcohol and cause injury to themselves or others.
Liability of Landowners	Landowners (and tenants) owe the following duties to persons who come upon their property: 1. *Invitees:* Duty of ordinary care 2. *Licensees:* Duty of ordinary care 3. *Trespassers:* Duty not to willfully and wantonly injure trespassers
Liability of Common Carriers and Innkeepers	Common carriers and innkeepers owe a *duty of utmost care*, rather than the duty of ordinary care, to protect their passengers and patrons from injury.

Defenses to Negligence

Superseding or Intervening Event	An intervening activity by another person that caused the plaintiff's injuries, which relieves the defendant from liability.
Assumption of the Risk	A defendant is not liable for the plaintiff's injuries if the plaintiff had knowledge of a specific risk and voluntarily assumed that risk.
Contributory and Comparative Negligence	States have adopted one of the following two rules that affect a defendant's liability if the plaintiff had been partially at fault for causing his or her own injuries: 1. *Contributory negligence:* A plaintiff cannot recover anything from the defendant. 2. *Comparative negligence:* Damages are apportioned according to the parties' fault. Also called *comparative fault*.

Product Liability and Strict Liability

Products Liability	Products liability is the liability of manufacturers, sellers, and others for the injuries caused by defective products.

Strict Liability	A manufacturer or seller who sells a defective product is liable to the ultimate user who is injured thereby. All in the chain of distribution are liable irrespective of fault.
Defect	To recover for strict liability, the injured party must show that the product that caused the injury was defective. The most common types of defects are: 1. Defect in manufacture 2. Failure to warn 3. Defect in design 4. Defect in packaging 5. Failure to provide adequate instructions

WORKING THE WEB

1. Visit the website http://en.wikipedia.org/wiki/negligence .html. On the right side of the screen, pick a negligence issue that interests you and click on this subject. Read the material that is available and write a half-page report about this negligence issue.
2. Visit the website http://www.atra.org.html. Click on "State and Federal Reform," then click on your state. Write a one-page report describing recent tort reforms in your state.
3. Go to the website http://www.google.com/html or similar Internet search engine. Using an Internet search, find your state's Good Samaritan law. Print out this law or write a half-page brief of this law.

4. Go to the website http://stellaawards.com/html. Subscribe to receive True Stella Awards case write-ups free. Many of these case write-ups are about tort cases. For the next tort case that you receive from this site, write a half-page report describing this case.
5. Visit the website http://en.wikipedia.org/wiki/intentional_ torts.html. On the right side of the screen, pick an intentional tort issue that interests you and click on this subject. Read the material that is available and write a half-page report about this negligence issue.

CRITICAL THINKING & WRITING QUESTIONS

1. Define the word *tort*.
2. What is an *intentional* tort?
3. Define and differentiate assault and battery.
4. Define false imprisonment. What do merchant protection statutes provide? What requirements must be met to be protected by a merchant protection statute?
5. Describe the following intentional torts: (a) defamation of character, (b) misappropriation of the right to publicity, (c) invasion of the right to privacy, and (d) intentional infliction of emotional distress.
6. What is negligence? What elements must be proven to find negligence? Describe duty of care and breach of duty of care.
7. For a plaintiff to win a tort lawsuit, must the plaintiff have suffered injury? Explain.
8. What is the difference between causation in fact (actual cause) and proximate cause (legal cause)?
9. Describe the following special negligence doctrines: (a) professional malpractice, (b) negligence *per se*, (c) *res*

ipsa loquitur, and (d) negligent infliction of emotional distress.
10. Describe Good Samaritan laws. What public policy do these laws serve?
11. Define the following parties: (a) invitees, (b) licensees, and (c) trespassers. Describe the liability of landowners and tenants to each of these persons.
12. Describe the following two defenses to negligence: (a) superseding event, and (b) assumption of the risk.
13. Describe the difference between contributory negligence and comparative negligence. Give an example of each.
14. Describe the doctrine of strict liability. To what type of lawsuit does this doctrine apply? Describe how strict liability differs from negligence.
15. Describe the following types of product defects and give an example of each: (a) defect in manufacture, (b) failure to warn, (c) defect in design, and (d) defect in packaging.

Building Paralegal Skills

A Salesman's Courtroom Testimony: Fact or Misrepresentation?

The salesman for a company that sells truck brake parts admits in trial testimony that the part sold may not have been appropriate for the required use.

After viewing the video case study at www.pearsonhighered .com/goldman answer the following:

1. What are the elements necessary to make a case for fraudulent misrepresentation?
2. Is the salesman's employer bound by the conduct in making the sale and therefore liable for any harm caused from the sale of the inappropriate products?
3. If a product is shipped in a defective condition, which makes it inherently dangerous, do the representations of the salesman matter?

Solicitation in the ER: Ethical Duties of the Profession

The parents of a child injured in an accident are approached by a clerk in the emergency room who offers them the opportunity of hiring a lawyer to handle their case and shares their information with a paralegal who was in the emergency room.

After viewing the video case study at www.pearsonhighered .com/goldman answer the following:

1. Are the clerk and the paralegal guilty of solicitation?
2. Has the parents' and the child's information been improperly divulged?
3. Is the claim that the bus driver appeared woozy and was drunk actionable defamation?

The Judge Instructs the Jury before Deliberation

The trial judge gives a jury instructions on how the trial will proceed and then at the end of the trial charges the jury with specific instructions that relate to questions of law upon which they must deliberate.

After viewing the video case study at www.pearsonhighered .com/goldman answer the following:

1. What is the purpose of giving the jury preliminary instructions at the beginning of the trial?
2. What is the purpose of the jury charge on a specific point of law?
3. Is the jury bound by the instructions given to them by the judge?

1. What ethical obligation does the legal team have to inform clients, even when the client does not ask for advice, of actions they should take to avoid liability?
2. What is the "reasonable professional standard" for a paralegal?
3. As a recent graduate with school loans to pay, you also work at a local food market at night. You are working on a slow Tuesday evening and instead of walking the aisle of the store, you take a coffee break in the back of the store. A customer slips on a small bunch of grapes, which are in the aisle, breaking a bone in the leg. The injured customer is also a long-time client of the law firm where you work. Is there any conflict of interest? How can the conflict be resolved?

With a group of other students, selected by you or assigned by your instructor, review the "Paralegals at Work" Scenario at the beginning of the chapter. As a group, discuss the following questions.

1. Who are the plaintiffs in this case? Who are the defendants in this case?
2. Should the plaintiffs sue the defendants for negligence? What is negligence? What elements must be established to prove negligence?
3. What are the elements to establish negligent infliction of emotional distress? Can Mrs. Sheen recover for her emotional distress under this tort?
4. What is the doctrine of strict liability and how does this differ from negligence? Does the doctrine of strict liability apply to this case?
5. What damages, if any, can be recovered in this case?

PARALEGAL PORTFOLIO EXERCISE

Prepare a memorandum, no longer than three pages, that discusses the doctrine of strict liability as used in product liability cases, the different types of defects that can be asserted in a strict liability case, and the types of damages that can be awarded in strict liability cases.

LEGAL ANALYSIS & WRITING CASES

James v. Meow Media, Inc.   300 F.3d 683, Web 2002 U.S. App. Lexis 16185

United States Court of Appeals for the Sixth Circuit
Michael Carneal was a 14-year-old freshman student at Heath High School in Paducah, Kentucky. Carneal regularly played the violent interactive video and computer games *Doom, Quake, Castle Wolfenstein, Rampage, Nightmare Creatures, Mech Warrior, Resident Evil,* and *Final Fantasy.* These games involved the player shooting virtual opponents with computer guns and other weapons. Carneal also watched videotaped movies, including one called *The Basketball Diaries,* in which a high-school student protagonist dreams of killing his teacher and several of his fellow classmates. Carneal brought a .22-caliber pistol and five shotguns to the lobby of Heath High School and shot several of his fellow students, killing three and wounding many others. The three students killed were Jessica James, Kayce Steger, and Nicole Hadley.

The parents of the three dead children ("James") sued the producers and distributors of the violent video games and movies that Carneal had watched previous to the shooting. The parents sued to recover damages for wrongful death, alleging that the defendants were negligent in producing and distributing such games and movies to Carneal. The U.S. district court applied Kentucky law and held that the defendants did not owe or breach a duty to the plaintiffs and therefore were not liable for negligence. The plaintiffs appealed.

Question
1. Did the defendant video and movie producers and distributors owe a duty of care to the plaintiffs by selling and licensing violent video games and movies to Carneal, who killed the three students?

Cheong v. Antablin   16 Cal. 4th 1063, 68 Cal.Rptr.2d 859, 946 P.2d 817, Web 1997 Cal. Lexis 7662

Supreme Court of California
Wilkie Cheong and Drew R. Antablin, long-time friends and experienced skiers, skied together at Alpine Meadows, a resort near Tahoe City, California. While skiing, Antablin accidentally collided with Cheong, causing injury to him. Cheong sued Antablin to recover damages for negligent skiing. The trial court granted Antablin's motion for summary judgment,

holding that the doctrine of assumption of risk barred Cheong's claim and dismissed the lawsuit. The court of appeals affirmed. Cheong appealed to the California Supreme Court.

Question
1. Does the doctrine of assumption of risk bar recovery?

Lakin v. Senco Products, Inc.   925 P.2d 107, Web 1996 Ore. App. Lexis 1466

Court of Appeals of Oregon
Senco Products, Inc. (Senco) manufactures and markets a variety of pneumatic nail guns, including the SN325 nail gun, which discharges 3.25-inch nails. The SN325 uses special nails designed and sold by Senco. The SN325 will discharge a nail only if two trigger mechanisms are activated; that is, the user must both squeeze the nail gun's finger trigger and press the nail gun's muzzle against a surface, activating the bottom trigger for safety. The SN325 can fire

up to nine nails per second if the trigger is continuously depressed and the gun is bounced along the work surface, constantly reactivating the muzzle safety/trigger.

John Lakin was using a Senco SN325 nail gun to help build a new home. When attempting to nail 2×4s under the eaves of the garage, Lakin stood on tiptoe and raised a 2×4 over his head. As he held the board in position with his left hand and the nail gun in his right hand, he pressed the nose of the SN325 up against the board, depressed the safety, and pulled the finger trigger to fire the nail into the board. The gun fired the first nail and then, in a phenomenon known as "double firing," immediately discharged an unintended second nail that struck the first nail. The gun recoiled violently backward toward Lakin and, with Lakin's finger still on the trigger, came into contact with his cheek. That contact activated the safety/trigger, causing the nail gun to fire a third nail. This third nail went through Lakin's cheekbone and into his brain.

The nail penetrated the frontal lobe of the right hemisphere of Lakin's brain, blocked a major artery, and caused extensive tissue damage. Lakin was unconscious for several days and ultimately underwent multiple surgeries. He suffers permanent brain damage and is unable to perceive information from the left hemisphere of the brain. He also suffers partial paralysis of the left side of his body. Lakin has undergone a radical personality change and is prone to violent outbursts. He is unable to obtain employment. Lakin's previously warm and loving relationship with his wife and four children has been permanently altered. He can no longer live with his family and instead resides in a supervised group home for brain-injured persons.

Lakin and his wife sued Senco for strict liability based on design defect. The trial court found Senco liable and awarded $3.6 million to Lakin, $457,000 to his wife, and $4 million in punitive damages against Senco. Senco appealed.

Question

1. Is Senco liable to Lakin for strict liability based on a design defect in the SN325 that allowed it to double-fire?

Johnson v. Kmart Enterprises, Inc.   297 N.W.2d 74, Web 1980 Wisc. App. Lexis 3197

Court of Appeals of Wisconsin

At about 7:30 P.M. one evening Deborah A. Johnson entered a Kmart store located in Madison, Wisconsin, to purchase some diapers and several cans of motor oil. She took her young child along to enable her to purchase the correct-size diapers, carrying the child in an infant seat that the mother had purchased at Kmart two or three weeks previously. A large Kmart price tag was still attached to the infant seat. Johnson purchased the diapers and oil and some children's clothes. She was in a hurry to leave because it was 8:00 P.M., her child's feeding time, and she hurried through the checkout lane. She paid for the diapers, the oil, and the clothing.

Just after leaving the store, she heard someone ask her to stop. She turned around and saw a Kmart security officer. He showed her a badge and asked her to come back into the store, which she did. The man stated, "I have reason to believe that you have stolen this car seat." Johnson explained that she had purchased the seat previously. She demanded to see the manager, who was called to the scene. When Johnson pointed out that the seat had cat hairs, food crumbs, and milk stains on it, the man said, "I'm really sorry. There's been a terrible mistake. You can go." Johnson looked at the clock when she left, which read 8:20 P.M. Johnson sued Kmart for false imprisonment.

Question

1. Is Kmart liable?

Karns v. Emerson Electric Co.   817 F.2d 1452, Web 1987 U.S. App. Lexis 5608

United States Court of Appeals for the Tenth Circuit

The Emerson Electric Co. manufactures and sells a product called the Weed Eater Model XR-90. The Weed Eater is a multipurpose weed-trimming and brush-cutting device. It consists of a handheld gasoline-powered engine connected to a long drive shaft, at the end of which can be attached various tools for cutting weeds and brush. One such attachment is a 10-inch circular sawblade capable of cutting through growth up to 2 inches in diameter. When this sawblade is attached to the Weed Eater, approximately 270 degrees of blade edge are exposed when in use.

The owner's manual contained the following warning: "Keep children away. All people and pets should be kept at a safe distance from the work area, at least 30 feet, especially when using the blade."

Donald Pearce, a 13-year-old boy, was helping his uncle clear an overgrown yard. The uncle was operating a Weed Eater XR-90 with the circular sawblade attachment. When Pearce stooped to pick up something off the ground about 6 to 10 feet behind and slightly to the left of where his uncle was operating the Weed Eater, the sawblade on the Weed Eater struck something near the ground. The Weed Eater kicked back to the left and cut off Pearce's right arm to the elbow. Pearce, through his mother, Charlotte Karns, sued Emerson to recover damages under strict liability.

Question

1. Is Emerson liable?

Braun v. Soldier of Fortune Magazine, Inc.

968 F.2d 1110 1992 U.S. App. Lexis 18556
United States Court of Appeals for the Eleventh Circuit

Read the following case, excerpted from the Court of Appeals opinion. Review and brief the case. In your brief answer the following questions:

1. Who are the plaintiffs? What are they suing for?
2. When does a magazine owe a duty to refrain from publishing an advertisement?
3. Was the advertisement the proximate cause of the plaintiff's injuries?
4. Should the award of punitive damages have been reduced?

Anderson, Circuit Judge

In January 1985, Michael Savage submitted a personal service advertisement to Soldier of Fortune (SOF). After several conversations between Savage and SOF's advertising manager, Joan Steel, the following advertisement ran in the June 1985 through March 1986 issues of SOF:

> GUN FOR HIRE: 37-year-old professional mercenary desires jobs. Vietnam Veteran. Discrete [sic] and very private. Body guard, courier, and other special skills. All jobs considered. Phone (615) 436-9785 (days) or (615) 436-4335 (nights), or write: Rt. 2, Box 682 Village Loop Road, Gatlinburg, TN 37738.

Savage testified that, when he placed the ad, he had no intention of obtaining anything but legitimate jobs. Nonetheless, Savage stated that the overwhelming majority of the 30 to 40 phone calls a week he received in response to his ad sought his participation in criminal activity such as murder, assault, and kidnapping. The ad also generated at least one legitimate job as a bodyguard, which Savage accepted.

In late 1984 or early 1985, Bruce Gastwirth began seeking to murder his business partner, Richard Braun. Gastwirth enlisted the aid of another business associate, John Horton Moore, and together they arranged for at least three attempts on Braun's life, all of which were unsuccessful. Responding to Savage's SOF ad, Gastwirth and Moore contacted him in August 1985 to discuss plans to murder Braun.

On August 26, 1985, Savage, Moore, and another individual, Sean Trevor Doutre, went to Braun's suburban Atlanta home. As Braun and his 16-year-old son Michael were driving down the driveway, Doutre stepped in front of Braun's car and fired several shots into the car with a MAC 11 automatic pistol. The shots hit Michael in the thigh and wounded Braun as well. Braun managed to roll out of the car, but Doutre walked over to Braun and killed him by firing two more shots into the back of his head as Braun lay on the ground.

On March 31, 1988, appellees Michael and Ian Braun filed this diversity action against appellants in the United States District Court for the Middle District of Alabama, seeking damages for the wrongful death of their father. Michael Braun also filed a separate action seeking recovery for the personal injuries he received at the time of his father's death. The district court consolidated these related matters.

Trial began on December 3, 1990. Appellees contended that, under Georgia law, SOF was liable for their injuries because SOF negligently published a personal service advertisement that created an unreasonable risk of the solicitation and commission of violent criminal activity, including murder. To show that SOF knew of the likelihood that criminal activity would result from placing an ad like Savage's, appellees introduced evidence of newspaper and magazine articles published prior to Braun's murder which described links between SOF and personal service ads and a number of criminal convictions including murder, kidnapping, assault, extortion, and attempts thereof. Appellees also presented evidence that, prior to SOF's acceptance of Savage's ad, law enforcement officials had contacted SOF staffers on two separate occasions in connection with investigations of crimes.

In his trial testimony, SOF president Robert K. Brown denied having any knowledge of criminal activity associated with SOF's personal service ads at any time prior to Braun's murder in August 1985. Both Jim Graves, a former managing editor of SOF, and Joan

(continued)

Steel, the advertising manager who accepted Savage's advertisement, similarly testified that they were not aware of other crimes connected with SOF ads prior to running Savage's ad. Steel further testified that she had understood the term "Gun for Hire" in Savage's ad to refer to a "bodyguard or protection service-type thing" rather than to any illegal activity.

The jury returned a verdict in favor of appellee and awarded compensatory damages on the wrongful death claim in the amount of $2,000,000. The jury also awarded appellee Michael Braun $375,000 in compensatory damages and $10,000,000 in punitive damages for his personal injury claim.

To prevail in an action for negligence in Georgia, a party must establish the following elements:

1. A legal duty to conform to a standard of conduct raised by the law for the protection of others against unreasonable risks of harm,
2. a breach of this standard,
3. a legally attributable causal connection between the conduct and the resulting injury, and
4. some loss or damage flowing to the plaintiff's legally protected interest as a result of the alleged breach of the legal duty.

To the extent that SOF denies that a publisher owes any duty to the public when it publishes personal service ads, its position is clearly inconsistent with Georgia law. We believe, however, that the crux of SOF's argument is not that it had no duty to the public but that, as a matter of law, there is a risk to the public when a publisher prints an "unreasonable" advertisement only if the ad openly solicits criminal activity.

SOF further argues that imposing liability on publishers for the advertisements they print indirectly threatens core, noncommercial speech to which the Constitution accords its full protection. Supreme Court cases discussing the limitations the First Amendment places on state defamation law indicate that there is no constitutional infirmity in Georgia law holding publishers liable under a negligence standard with respect to the commercial advertisements they print. Past Supreme Court decisions indicate, however, that the negligence standard the First Amendment permits is a "modified" negligence stan-

dard. The Court's decisions suggest that Georgia law may impose tort liability on publishers for injury caused by the advertisements they print only if the ad on its face, without the need to investigate, makes it apparent that there is a substantial danger of harm to the public.

We conclude that the First Amendment permits a state to impose upon a publisher liability for compensatory damages for negligently publishing a commercial advertisement where the ad on its face, and without the need for investigation, makes it apparent that there is a substantial danger of harm to the public. The absence of a duty requiring publishers to investigate the advertisements they print and the requirement that the substance of the ad itself must warn the publisher of a substantial danger of harm to the public guarantee that the burden placed on publishers will not impermissibly chill protected commercial speech.

Our review of the language of Savage's ad persuades us that SOF had a legal duty to refrain from publishing it. Savage's advertisement (1) emphasized the term "Gun for Hire," (2) described Savage as a "professional mercenary," (3) stressed Savage's willingness to keep his assignments confidential and "very private," (4) listed legitimate jobs involving the use of a gun—bodyguard and courier—followed by a reference to Savage's "other special skills," and (5) concluded by stating that Savage would consider "all jobs."

The ad's combination of sinister terms makes it apparent that there was a substantial danger of harm to the public. The ad expressly solicits all jobs requiring the use of a gun. When the list of legitimate jobs—i.e., bodyguard and courier—is followed by "other special skills" and "all jobs considered," the implication is clear that the advertiser would consider illegal jobs. We agree with the district court that "the language of this advertisement is such that, even though couched in terms not explicitly offering criminal services, the publisher could recognize the offer of criminal activity as readily as its readers obviously did." We find that the jury had ample grounds for finding that SOF's publication of Savage's ad was the proximate cause of Braun's injuries.

For the foregoing reasons, we affirm the District Court's judgment.

Contracts and E-Commerce

The movement of the progressive societies has hitherto been a movement from status to contract."

Sir Henry Maine, Ancient Law

LEARNING OBJECTIVES

After studying this chapter, you should be able to:

1. Recognize the professional opportunities for paralegals in contract and e-commerce law.
2. List the elements necessary to form a valid contract.
3. Define an offer and an acceptance.
4. Define consideration and analyze whether contracts are lacking in consideration.
5. Identify illegal contracts that are contrary to statutes and that violate public policy.
6. List and describe the contracts that must be in writing under the Statute of Frauds.
7. Describe compensatory, consequential, and liquidated damages.
8. Define sales contracts governed by Article 2 of the UCC and lease contracts governed by Article 2A of the UCC.
9. Describe the writing, signature, and other special requirements for Internet contracts.
10. Describe e-commerce.
11. Define *e-contract* and describe the formation and enforcement of e-contracts.
12. Explain a paralegal's duty not to engage in fraudulent billing practices.

Paralegals at Work

You are a paralegal who works for Mr. Andrew Copan, a lawyer who represents small businesses. A significant part of Mr. Copan's practice is the drafting of contracts for the business clients when they are dealing with individuals and other businesses. Mr. Copan also engages in civil litigation and represents his clients bringing or defending contract-related cases in court.

One of Mr. Copan's clients is Jewelry Associates Corporation (JAC), a small corporation that is in the retail jewelry business. The business has three owners. The business buys jewels in overseas markets and sells the jewels in a retail store serving customers.

One day, the three owners of Jewelry Associates Corporation make an appointment to see Mr. Copan to discuss several business matters. As his paralegal, Mr. Copan asks you to sit in on the meeting, which you do. At the meeting, the three owners explain that they have found a new source of jewels, Overseas Mines Inc., which is a foreign company located in the country of Sri Lanka. The owners ask Mr. Copan to draft a contract that will be used between JAC and Overseas Mines. JAC will be the buyer, and the foreign company will be the seller of jewels. The owners ask Mr. Copan to research the law applicable to the situation and prepare a contract for this transaction.

The owners further explain that they have obtained the Web address jewelryjewelry.com and that they want to begin selling jewelry through e-commerce. They disclose that they are having a website designed, and that they need an online contract drafted for the sale of jewelry online. They ask Mr. Copan to draft the necessary online contract that will be placed on the website.

In addition, the owners of Jewelry Associates Corporation disclose that the business currently leases its retail store space from an owner of the building housing their retail store, but that their lease will be over in nine months. The owners disclose that their corporation entered into a contract with Real Estate Developers Inc. to purchase a building and land to which they will transfer their retail business. The clients disclose, however, that Real Estate Developers Inc. now has refused to go through with the contract and has refused to sell JAC the building and land. The owners ask Mr. Copan what course of action to take to obtain the building.

After the clients have left, Mr. Copan asks you, as his paralegal, to assist him in conducting the legal research necessary for these matters, and to prepare first drafts of the contracts discussed at the meeting.

Consider the issues involved in this scenario as you read this chapter.

INTRODUCTION FOR THE PARALEGAL

Many paralegal professionals work in the field of contract law. The law of contracts makes up a substantial portion of many lawyers' practices. Lawyers rely heavily on the help of paralegals in drafting and reviewing contracts. Lawyers are called upon to prepare and review all sorts of contracts, including contracts for the sale of personal property and real property, commercial sales and lease contracts, licenses, and other contracts.

Contracts are the basis of many of our daily activities. They provide the means for individuals and businesses to sell and otherwise transfer property, services, and other rights. The purchase of goods is based on sales contracts; the hiring of employees is based on service contracts; and the lease of apartments is based on rental contracts. In addition, electronic contracts—e-contracts—are formed using email and the Internet. The list is almost endless. Without enforceable contracts, commerce would collapse.

Contracts are voluntarily entered into by parties. The terms of the contract become *private law* between the parties. The courts are obliged to give legal effect to such contracts according to the true interests of the parties.

This chapter covers the study of traditional contract law, e-contracts, and e-commerce.

Sources of Contract Law

There are several sources of contract law. These include the common law of contracts, the Uniform Commercial Code (UCC), and electronic commerce law. Each of these is described following.

The Common Law of Contracts

A major source of contract law is the **common law of contracts**. The common law of contracts developed from early court decisions that became precedent for later decisions. A limited federal common law of contracts applies to contracts made by the federal government. The larger and more prevalent body of common law has been

Common law of contracts Contract law developed primarily by state courts.

CAREER OPPORTUNITIES FOR PARALEGALS IN CONTRACT LAW

There is probably no area of substantive law in which paralegals are more involved in than contract law. Contracts make the world go round. The list of contracts in an individual's life and those of businesses are staggering.

Contracts are used to support most commercial transactions. Business contracts consist of those for the sale and lease of goods and the provision of services. Lawyers who practice in the area of business law are consistently called upon to draft contracts for their clients. And business contracts may be those for smaller businesses, such as sole proprietorships and general partnerships, to those between Fortune 500 companies such as Microsoft Corporation and Intel Corporation.

Contracts are needed for the sale, transfer, and lease of real property. Lawyers involved in the practice of real estate law must draft contracts for these transfers of interests in real estate. These include short contracts for simple matters such as an apartment lease, to long, detailed contracts for construction of shopping malls, the building of skyscrapers, and other real estate matters.

Other contracts are needed to sell, lease, or transfer ownership of any property. Contracts are required for the settlement of divorce cases, agreements between owners of businesses, the creation of franchises, the licensing of intellectual property (e.g., patents, copyrights), the mergers of large corporations, and so on. In addition, the provision of services, such as that of architects, lawyers, doctors, consultants, and other professionals, require contracts between the client and the professional.

Paralegals are indispensable in assisting lawyers in drafting and reviewing contracts for individuals and businesses that are clients of the law firm that the paralegal works for. A paralegal must be familiar with general contract law principles. In addition, paralegals also must become familiar with specific types of contracts that the lawyer they work for practices in. So, a paralegal who works for a lawyer who practices in the real estate field must be familiar with real estate contracts. A paralegal who works for a lawyer who practices family law must be familiar with the specifics of divorce settlement agreements. And so on.

Many lawsuits are brought concerning contracts. For example, a client of the law firm the paralegal works for may have reason to bring a lawsuit against the other contracting party for breach of contract. On the other hand, a client of the law firm may find itself being sued for an alleged breach of a contract. This is where a paralegal's skill in conducting interviews, uncovering evidence, preparing the file for trial, and conducting contract law research is needed. Paralegals with an expertise in contract law are called upon to support lawyers who litigate contract disputes.

Paralegals who are familiar with contract law, drafting contracts, and researching contract law are in substantial demand. This demand will continue as the number and complexity of contracts increase in importance to individuals and businesses.

developed from state court decisions. Thus, although the general principles remain the same throughout the country, there is some variation from state to state.

Uniform Commercial Code (UCC)

Another major source of contract law is the **Uniform Commercial Code (UCC)**. The UCC, which was first drafted by the National Conference of Commissioners on Uniform State Laws in 1952, has been amended several times. Its goal is to create a uniform system of commercial law among the 50 states. Provisions of the UCC normally take precedence over the common law of contracts.

Uniform Commercial Code (UCC) A comprehensive statutory scheme that includes laws covering aspects of commercial transactions.

The UCC is divided into nine main articles. Every state has adopted at least part of the UCC. In the area of contract law, two of the major provisions of the UCC are:

1. *Article 2 (Sales).* This article prescribes a set of uniform rules for the creation and enforcement of contracts for the sale of goods. These contracts are often referred to as **sales contracts**. For example, the sale of equipment is a sales contract subject to Article 2 of the UCC.
2. *Article 2A (Leases).* This article prescribes a set of uniform rules for the creation and enforcement of contracts for the lease of goods. These contracts are referred to as **lease** contracts. For example, the lease of an automobile is a lease subject to Article 2A of the UCC.

E-Contract Law

As we entered the twenty-first century, a new economic shift brought the United States and the rest of the world into the Information Age. Computer technology and the use of the Internet increased dramatically. A new form of commerce—**electronic commerce**, or **e-commerce**—is flourishing. All sorts of goods and services are now sold by **e-contract** over the Internet. You can purchase automobiles and children's toys, participate in auctions, purchase airline tickets, make hotel reservations, and purchase other goods and services over the Internet.

Much of the new cyberspace economy is based on electronic contracts and the licensing of computer information. E-commerce created problems for forming contracts over the Internet, enforcing e-commerce contracts, and providing consumer protection. To address these problems, the National Conference of Commissioners on Uniform State Laws (a group of lawyers, judges, and legal scholars) drafted the Uniform Computer Information Transactions Act (UCITA).

The UCITA establishes uniform legal rules for the formation and enforcement of electronic contracts and licenses. The UCITA addresses most of the legal issues that are encountered while conducting e-commerce over the Internet. The UCITA is a model act that does not become law until a state legislature adopts it as a statute for the state. Since its promulgation in July 1999, many states have adopted the UCITA in whole or part. Because of the need for uniformity of e-commerce rules, the UCITA is becoming the basis for the creation and enforcement of cyberspace contracts and licenses.

Formation of a Contract

A **contract** is an agreement that is enforceable by a court of law or equity. A simple and widely recognized definition is:

> A contract is a promise or a set of promises for the breach of which the law gives a remedy or the performance of which the law in some way recognizes a duty. [Restatement (Second) of Contracts, Section 1].

Most contracts are performed without the aid of the court system. This usually is because the parties feel a moral duty to perform as promised. Although some contracts, such as illegal contracts, are not enforceable, most are **legally enforceable**. This means that if a party fails to perform a contract, the other party may call upon the courts to enforce the contract.

Elements of a Contract

To be an enforceable contract, the following four basic requirements must be met:

1. *Agreement.* To have an enforceable contract, there must be an agreement between the parties.
2. *Consideration.* The promise must be supported by a bargained-for consideration that is legally sufficient.
3. *Contractual capacity.* The parties to a contract must have the capacity to contract.
4. *Lawful object.* The object of the contract must be lawful, or legal.

The text of this chapter discusses these requirements in greater detail.

Every contract involves at least two parties. The **offeror** is the party who makes an offer to enter into a contract. The **offeree** is the party to whom the offer is made (see Exhibit 13.1). In making an offer, the offeror promises to do—or to refrain from doing—something. The offeree then has the power to create a contract by accepting the offeror's offer. A contract is created if the offer is accepted. No contract is created if the offer is not accepted.

E-commerce The sale of goods and services by computer over the Internet.

E-contract A contract that is entered into by email and over the World Wide Web.

Legally enforceable A contract in which if one party fails to perform as promised, the other party can use the court system to enforce the contract and recover damages or other remedy.

Offeror The party who makes an offer to enter into a contract.

Offeree The party to whom an offer to enter into a contract is made.

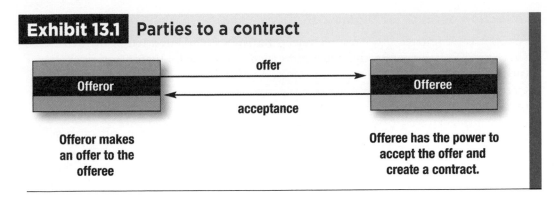

Exhibit 13.1 Parties to a contract

offer
Offeror → Offeree
acceptance

Offeror makes an offer to the offeree

Offeree has the power to accept the offer and create a contract.

Agreement

Agreement is the manifestation by two or more persons of the substance of a contract. It requires an *offer* and *acceptance*. The process of reaching an agreement usually proceeds as follows: Prior to entering into a contract, the parties may engage in preliminary negotiations about price, time of performance, and such. At some point during these negotiations, one party makes an **offer**. The person who makes the offer is called the offeror and the person to whom the offer is made is called the offeree. The offer sets forth the terms under which the offeror is willing to enter into the contract. The offeree has the power to create an agreement by accepting the offer.

Agreement The manifestation by two or more persons of the substance of a contract.

Offer

Section 24 of the Restatement (Second) of Contracts defines an offer as:

> The manifestation of willingness to enter into a bargain, so made as to justify another person in understanding that his assent to that bargain is invited and will conclude it.

To be effective, (1) the offeror must *objectively intend* to be bound by the offer; (2) the terms of the offer must be definite or reasonably *certain*; and (3) the offer must be *communicated* to the offeree.

The offer must be unequivocal.

Offer The manifestation of willingness to enter into a bargain, so made as to justify another person in understanding that his assent to that bargain is invited and will conclude it.

Example A question such as "Are you interested in selling your building for $2 million?" is not an offer. It is an invitation to make an offer or an invitation to negotiate. But the statement "I will buy your building for $2 million" is a valid offer because it indicates the offeror's present intent to contract.

An offer may be terminated by several means. The termination of an offer is discussed in the following paragraphs.

Revocation of an Offer by the Offeror

Under the common law, an offeror may revoke (i.e., withdraw) an offer any time prior to its acceptance by the offeree. Generally, an offer can be so revoked even if the offeror promised to keep the offer open for a longer time. The **revocation** may be communicated to the offeree by the offeror or by a third party and made by (1) the offeror's express statement (e.g., "I hereby withdraw my offer") or (2) an act of the offeror that is inconsistent with the offer (e.g., selling the goods to another party). Most states provide that a revocation is not effective until it is actually received by the offeree or the offeree's agent.

Revocation Withdrawal of an offer by the offeror which terminates the offer.

Offers made to the public may be revoked by communicating the revocation by the same means used to make the offer.

Example If a reward offer for a lost watch was published in two local newspapers each week for four weeks, notice of revocation must be published in the same newspapers for the same length of time. The revocation is effective against all offerees, even those who saw the reward offer but not the notice of revocation.

Rejection of an Offer by the Offeree

An offer is terminated if the offeree rejects it. Any subsequent attempt by the offeree to accept the offer is ineffective and is construed as a new offer that the original offeror (now the offeree) is free to accept or reject. A **rejection** may be evidenced by the offeree's express words (oral or written) or conduct. Generally, a rejection is not effective until it is actually received by the offeror.

> **Example** Harriet Jackson, sales manager of IBM Corporation, offers to sell 1,000 computers to Ted Green, purchasing manager of General Motors Corporation, for $250,000. The offer is made on August 1. Green telephones Jackson to say that he is not interested. This rejection terminates the offer. If Green later decides that he wants to purchase the computers, an entirely new contract must be formed.

Counteroffer by the Offeree

A **counteroffer** by the offeree simultaneously terminates the offeror's offer and creates a new offer.

> **Example** Suppose that Fei Jia says to Harold Brown, "I will sell you my house for $700,000." Brown says, "I think $700,000 is too high; I will pay you $600,000." Brown has made a counteroffer. The original offer is terminated, and the counteroffer is a new offer that Jia is free to accept or reject.

Option contracts

An offeree can prevent the offeror from revoking his or her offer by paying the offeror compensation to keep the offer open for an agreed-upon period of time. This is called an **option contract**, in which the offeror agrees not to sell the property to anyone but the offeree during the option period. The death or incompetency of either party does not terminate an option contract unless it is for the performance of a personal service.

> **Example** Anne Mason offers to sell a piece of real estate to Harold Greenberg for $1 million. Mr. Greenberg wants time to make a decision, so he pays Ms. Mason $20,000 to keep her offer open to him for 6 months. At any time during the option period, Mr. Greenberg may exercise his option and pay Ms. Mason the $1 million purchase price. If he lets the option expire, however, Ms. Mason may keep the $20,000 and sell the property to someone else.

Acceptance

Acceptance is a manifestation of assent by the offeree to the terms of the offer in a manner invited or required by the offer as measured by the objective theory of contracts. Recall that generally (1) unilateral contracts can be accepted only by the offeree's performance of the required act, and (2) a bilateral contract can be accepted by an offeree who promises to perform (or, where permitted, by performance of) the requested act.

Only the offeree has the legal power to accept an offer and create a contract. Third persons usually do not have the power to accept an offer. If an offer is made individually to two or more persons, each has the power to accept the offer. Once an offeree accepts the offer, though, it terminates as to the other offerees. An offer that is made to two or more persons jointly must be accepted jointly.

The offeree's acceptance must be unequivocal. For an acceptance to exist, the offeree must accept the terms as stated in the offer. This is called the **mirror image rule**. Generally, a "grumbling acceptance" is a legal acceptance.

Rejection Express words or conduct by the offeree that rejects an offer. Rejection terminates the offer.

Counteroffer A response by an offeree that contains terms and conditions different from or in addition to those of the offer. A counteroffer terminates an offer.

SIDEBAR

TERMINATION OF AN OFFER

Action	Description
Revocation	The offeror *revokes* (withdraws) the offer any time prior to its acceptance by the offeree.
Rejection	The offeree rejects the offer by his or her words or conduct.
Counteroffer	A counteroffer by the offeree creates a new offer and terminates the offeror's offer.

Acceptance A manifestation of assent by the offeree to the terms of the offer in a manner invited or required by the offer as measured by the objective theory of contracts.

Mirror image rule A rule that states that for an acceptance to exist, the offeree must accept the terms as stated in the offer.

Example   A response such as "Okay, I'll take the car, but I sure wish you would make me a better deal" creates an enforceable contract. An acceptance is equivocal if certain conditions are added to the acceptance.

Example   If the offeree responds, "I accept, but only if you repaint the car red." There is no acceptance in this case.

Express and Implied Contracts

An actual contract (as distinguished from a quasi-contract, discussed later in this chapter) may be either *express* or *implied-in-fact*.

1. **Express contracts** are stated in oral or written words. Examples of such contracts include an oral agreement to purchase a neighbor's bicycle and a written agreement to buy an automobile from a dealership.
2. **Implied-in-fact contracts** are implied from the conduct of the parties. Implied-in-fact contracts leave more room for questions. The following elements must be established to create an implied-in-fact contract:
   a. The plaintiff provided property or services to the defendant.
   b. The plaintiff expected to be paid by the defendant for the property or services and did not provide the property or services gratuitously.
   c. The defendant was given an opportunity to reject the property or services provided by the plaintiff but failed to do so.

> **Express contract** An agreement that is expressed in written or oral words.
>
> **Implied-in-fact contract** A contract in which agreement between parties has been inferred from their conduct.

Consideration

Consideration is a necessary element for a contract to exist. Consideration is defined as something of legal value given in exchange for a promise. Consideration can come in many forms.

> **Consideration** Something of legal value given in exchange for a promise.

Examples   The most common types consist of either a tangible payment (e.g., money, property) or the performance of an act (e.g., providing legal services). Less usual forms of consideration include the forbearance of a legal right (e.g., accepting an out-of-court settlement in exchange for dropping a lawsuit) and noneconomic forms of consideration (e.g., refraining from using alcohol).

Written contracts are presumed to be supported by consideration. This is a rebuttable presumption that may be overcome by sufficient evidence. A few states provide that contracts made under seal cannot be challenged for lack of consideration.

Gift Promise

Gift promises, also called **gratuitous promises**, are unenforceable because they lack consideration. To change a gift promise into an enforceable promise, the promisee must offer to do something in exchange—that is, consideration—for the promise.

> **Gift promise** A promise that is unenforceable because it lacks consideration.

Examples   Suppose Mrs. Colby promised to give her son $10,000 and then rescinded the promise. The son would have no recourse to recover the $10,000 because it was a gift promise that lacked consideration. If, however, Mrs. Colby promised her son $10,000 for getting an "A" in his "Introduction to Paralegal" course and the son performed as required, the contract would be enforceable. A completed gift promise cannot be rescinded for lack of consideration.

Capacity to Contract

Generally, the law presumes that the parties to a contract have the requisite **capacity to contract** to enter into the contract. Certain persons, however, do not have this capacity. They include minors, mentally incompetent persons, and intoxicated persons.

The common law of contracts and many state statutes protect persons who lack **contractual capacity** from having contracts enforced against them. The party asserting incapacity or his or her guardian, conservator, or other legal representative bears the burden of proof.

Minors

Minors do not always have the maturity, experience, or sophistication needed to enter into contracts with adults. States have enacted statutes that specify the *age of majority*. The most prevalent age of majority is 18 years for males and females alike. Any age below the statutory age of majority is called the *period of minority*.

To protect minors, the law recognizes the **infancy doctrine**, which allows minors to **disaffirm** (or cancel) most contracts they have entered into with adults. A minor's right to disaffirm a contract is based on public policy, with the reasoning that minors should be protected from unscrupulous behavior of adults.

Under the infancy doctrine, a minor has the option of choosing whether to enforce the contract (i.e., the contract is *voidable* by a minor). The adult party is bound to the minor's decision. If both parties to the contract are minors, both parties have the right to disaffirm the contract.

A minor can expressly disaffirm a contract orally, in writing, or by the minor's conduct. No special formalities are required. The minor may disaffirm the contract at any time prior to reaching the age of majority plus a "reasonable time." The designation of a reasonable time is determined on a case-by-case basis.

Minors are obligated to pay for the **necessaries of life** that they contract for. Otherwise, many adults would refuse to sell these items to them. There is no standard definition of what is a *necessary of life*, but items such as food, clothing, shelter, medical services, and the like are generally understood to fit this category. Goods and services such as automobiles, tools of trade, education, and vocational training also have been found to be necessaries of life in some situations. The minor's age, lifestyle, and status in life influence what is considered necessary.

Mentally Incompetent Persons

Mental incapacity may arise because of mental illness, brain damage, mental retardation, senility, and the like. The law protects **mentally incompetent persons** from enforcement of contracts against them because these persons may not understand the consequences of their actions in entering into a contract.

Intoxicated Persons

Most states provide that contracts entered into by certain **intoxicated persons** are voidable by that person. The intoxication may occur because of alcohol or drug use. The contract is not voidable by the other party if that party had contractual capacity. Under the majority rule, the contract is voidable only if the person was so intoxicated when the contract was entered into that he or she was incapable of understanding or comprehending the nature of the transaction. In most states, this rule holds even if the intoxication was self-induced. A contract disaffirmed based on intoxication generally must be returned to the status quo.

Lawful Object

As an essential element for the formation of a contract, the object of the contract must be *lawful*. A contract to perform an illegal act is called an **illegal contract**. Illegal contracts are void; they cannot be enforced by either party to the contract. Because illegal contracts are void, the parties cannot sue for nonperformance. Further, if an illegal contract is executed, the court will generally leave the parties where it finds them. Most contracts are presumed to be lawful. The burden of proving that a contract is unlawful rests on the party who asserts its illegality.

Infancy doctrine A doctrine that allows minors to disaffirm (cancel) most contracts they have entered into with adults.

Illegal contract A contract to perform an illegal act; cannot be enforced by either party to the contract.

Illegality—Contracts Contrary to Statutes

Federal and state legislatures alike have enacted statutes prohibiting certain **contracts contrary to statutes**. Contracts to perform an activity that is prohibited by statute are illegal contracts. These contracts include gambling contracts, contracts that provide for usurious rates of interest, and contracts that violate Sabbath laws and licensing statutes.

> **Example** An agreement between two companies to engage in price fixing in violation of federal antitrust statutes is illegal and therefore void. Thus, neither company to this illegal contract can enforce the contract against the other company.

Illegality—Contracts Contrary to Public Policy

Certain contracts are illegal because they are **contracts contrary to public policy**. Although *public policy* eludes a precise definition, the courts have held contracts to be contrary to public policy if they have a negative impact on society or interfere with the public's safety and welfare.

> **Example** Assume a husband purchases a life insurance policy on his wife and names himself beneficiary of his wife's life insurance policy. If the husband kills his wife he cannot recover on the life insurance policy because it would violate public policy to allow him to recover for his murderous deed.

Unconscionable Contract

The general rule of freedom of contract holds that if (1) the object of a contract is lawful and (2) the other elements for the formation of a contract are met, the courts will enforce a contract according to its terms. Although it is generally presumed that parties are capable of protecting their own interests when contracting, it is a fact of life that dominant parties sometimes take advantage of weaker parties. As a result, some lawful contracts are so oppressive or manifestly unfair that they are unjust.

To prevent the enforcement of such contracts, the courts developed the equitable doctrine of unconscionability, which is based on public policy. A contract found to be unconscionable under this doctrine is called an **unconscionable contract**, or a *contract of adhesion*.

The courts are given substantial discretion in determining whether a contract or contract clause is unconscionable. There is no single definition of *unconscionability*. The doctrine may not be used merely to save a contracting party from a bad bargain.

The following elements must be shown to prove that a contract or clause in a contract is unconscionable:

- The parties possessed severely unequal bargaining power.
- The dominant party unreasonably used its unequal bargaining power to obtain oppressive or manifestly unfair contract terms.
- The adhering party had no reasonable alternative.

If the court finds that a contract or contract clause is unconscionable, it may (1) refuse to enforce the contract, (2) refuse to enforce the unconscionable clause but enforce the remainder of the contract, or (3) limit the applicability of any unconscionable clause so as to avoid any unconscionable result. The appropriate remedy depends on the facts and circumstances of each case. Note that because unconscionability is a matter of law, the judge may opt to decide the case without a jury trial.

> **Example** Suppose a door-to-door salesperson sells a poor family a freezer full of meat and other foods for $3,000, with monthly payments for 60 months at 20 percent interest. If the actual cost of the freezer and the food is $1,000, this

contract could be found to be unconscionable. The court could either find the entire contract unenforceable, or the court could rewrite the contract to have reasonable terms.

Statute of Frauds—Writing Requirement

Statute of Frauds A state statute that requires certain types of contracts to be in writing.

All states have enacted a **Statute of Frauds** that requires certain types of contracts to be in *writing*. This statute is intended to ensure that the terms of important contracts are not forgotten, misunderstood, or fabricated.

Generally, an **executory contract** that is not in writing even though the Statute of Frauds requires it to be is unenforceable by either party. (If the contract is valid in all other respects, however, it may be voluntarily performed by the parties.) The Statute of Frauds usually is raised by one party as a defense to enforcement of the contract by the other party.

However, if an oral contract that should have been in writing under the Statute of Frauds is already executed (fully performed), neither party can seek to rescind the contract on the ground of noncompliance with the Statute of Frauds. Contracts that are required to be in writing under the Statute of Frauds are discussed in the following paragraphs.

Contracts Involving Interests in Real Property

Any contract that transfers an ownership interest in real property must be in writing to be enforceable under the Statute of Frauds. Real property includes the land itself, buildings, trees, soil, minerals, timber, plants, crops, fixtures, and things permanently affixed to the land or buildings. Certain personal property that is permanently affixed to the real property—for example, built-in cabinets in a house—are *fixtures* that become part of the real property.

Other contracts that transfer an ownership interest in land must be in writing under the Statute of Frauds.

> **Example** Borrowers often give a lender an interest in real property as security for the repayment of a loan. This must be done through a written *mortgage* or *deed of trust*. A lease is the transfer of the right to use real property for a specified period of time. Most Statutes of Frauds require leases for a term of more than one year to be in writing.

One-Year Rule

According to the Statute of Frauds, an executory contract that cannot be performed by its own terms within one year of its formation must be in writing. This **one-year rule** is intended to prevent disputes about contract terms that otherwise may occur toward the end of a long-term contract. If performance of the contract is possible within the one-year period, the contract may be oral.

> **Examples** An employer hires a person as an employee for 6 months. This contract may be oral. If the employment contract was for 13 months, it would have to be in writing to be enforceable.

Formality of the Writing

Many written commercial contracts are long, detailed documents that have been negotiated by the parties and drafted and reviewed by their lawyers. Other written contracts are preprinted forms that are prepared in advance to be used in recurring situations.

To be legally binding, a written contract does not have to be either drafted by a lawyer or formally typed. Regarding the **formality of the writing**, the law generally requires only a writing containing the essential terms of the parties' agreement. Under this rule, any writing—letters, telegrams, invoices, sales receipts, handwritten agreements written on scraps of paper, and such—can be an enforceable contract.

Required Signature

The Statute of Frauds and the UCC require the written contract, whatever its form, to be signed *by the party against whom the enforcement is sought*. The signature of the person who is enforcing the contract is not necessary. Thus, a written contract may be enforceable against one party but not the other party.

Generally, the signature may appear anywhere on the writing. In addition, it does not have to be a person's full legal name. The person's last name, first name, nickname, initials, seal, stamp, engraving, or other symbol or mark (e.g., an X) that indicates the person's intent can be binding. The signature may be affixed by an authorized agent.

ETHICAL PERSPECTIVE

Paralegal Loses $900,000 for Failing to Get a Contract in Writing

Paralegals are sometimes themselves involved in contract disputes. Consider the following case. Barbara Lucinda Sawyer worked as a paralegal for Melbourne Mills, Jr., an attorney at a law firm. Ms. Sawyer proposed that Mr. Mills and the law firm become engaged in class-action lawsuits. Mr. Mills agreed to pay Ms. Sawyer an unspecified bonus when "the ship comes in." After Ms. Sawyer's assistance and persistence, the law firm became involved in class-action litigation—primarily the Fen-Phen class-action litigation. After the law firm received millions of dollars in fees from the Fen-Phen class-action lawsuits, Ms. Sawyer and her husband Steve met with Mills to discuss Ms. Sawyer's bonus. Mr. Mills orally agreed to pay Ms. Sawyer $1,065,000 as a bonus to be paid in monthly installments over 167 months. Ms. Sawyer secretly tape-recorded the conversation. Mr. Mills later refused to sign a written contract conveying the terms of the oral agreement.

After Mr. Mills had paid $165,000, he quit making further payments. Ms. Sawyer sued Mr. Mills to collect the remaining $900,000. Mr. Mills defended, arguing that the oral contract exceeded one year and was therefore unenforceable because it was not in writing as required by the Statute of Frauds. The jury ruled in favor of Ms. Sawyer. Mr. Mills made a motion to the trial court judge to refuse to enforce the oral contract against him. The trial court heard and decided the motion. The trial court ruled in favor of Mr. Mills, finding that the oral contract was for over one year and was not in writing as required by the Statute of Frauds. The court stated:

Sawyer produced no writing signed by Mills consistent with the oral discussions of the parties. Sawyer argues that the "writing" requirement of the Statute of Frauds has been satisfied in this case because of the cassette tape which was played to the jury and which surreptitiously recorded. . . . [T]he cassette tape recording is not a "writing signed by the party to be charged" as required by the Statute of Frauds. The Court is aware of the apparent harshness of this ruling. The trial jury found, and the Court heard Mills state on the tape recording, that he agreed to make monthly payments to Sawyer which would eventually total over one million dollars. Honoring that oral agreement would be the "moral" and "right" thing for Mills to do. However, this Court is obligated by Oath of Office and Kentucky law, to consider cases based on the facts presented and the applicable law. The end result may not seem "fair" to Sawyer. The Statute of Frauds, by its own terms, can be considered "harsh" in that it will bar oral agreements between parties under certain conditions. This is simply the nature of the beast.

The Court of Appeals of Kentucky affirmed the trial court's decision.

In this case, the lawyer acted unethically. The Statute of Frauds protected the attorney from legally having to perform an oral contract to pay his paralegal the remaining $900,000 due on their oral contract. The paralegal Ms. Sawyer should have gotten the contract in writing with the attorney Mr. Mills and therefore have avoided the unfair result reached by the application of the Statute of Frauds.

Source: *Sawyer v. Mills*, Web 2007 Ky. App. Lexis (Court of Appeals of Kentucky, 2007).

Performance and Breach

Paralegal professionals who work in the area of contract law must know the legal rules regarding the performance and breach of contracts. They must also know the remedies that may be awarded where a breach of contract has been found. Many paralegals work for law firms that litigate breach of contract cases.

In contracts, parties make certain promises to each other. These promises may be classified as *covenants* or *conditions*. Performance may be classified as complete performance, substantial performance (minor breach), or inferior performance (material breach). A **breach of contract** occurs when a contracting party fails to perform an absolute duty owed under the contract. These topics are covered in the following paragraphs.

Covenant

A **covenant** is an unconditional promise to perform. Nonperformance of a covenant is a breach of contract that gives the other party the right to sue.

> **Example** If Medcliff Corporation borrows $100,000 from a bank and signs a promissory note to repay this amount plus 10 percent interest in one year, this promise is a covenant. It is an unconditional promise to perform.

Condition Precedent

If the contract requires the occurrence (or nonoccurrence) of an event before a party is obligated to perform a contractual duty, there is a **condition precedent**. The happening (or nonhappening) of the event triggers the contract or duty of performance. If the event does not occur, no duty to perform arises, because there is a failure of condition.

> **Example** Suppose X Company offers Joan Andrews a job as an industrial engineer upon her graduation from college. If Ms. Andrews graduates, the condition has been met. If the employer refuses to hire Ms. Andrews at that time, she can sue the employer for breach of contract. But if Ms. Andrews does not graduate, X company is not obligated to hire her, because there has been a failure of condition.

Complete Performance

Most contracts are discharged by the **complete performance** of the contracting parties. Complete performance occurs when a party to a contract renders performance exactly as required by the contract. A fully performed contract is called an **executed contract**.

Tender of performance also discharges a party's contractual obligations. Tender is an unconditional and absolute offer by a contracting party to perform his or her obligations under the contract.

> **Example** Suppose Ashley's Dress Shops, Inc., contracts to purchase dresses from a dress manufacturer for $25,000. Ashley's has performed its obligation under the contract once it tenders the $25,000 to the manufacturer. If the manufacturer fails to deliver the dresses, Ashley's can sue it for breach of contract.

Substantial Performance (Minor Breach)

Substantial performance occurs when there has been a **minor breach** of contract. It occurs when a party to a contract renders performance that deviates only slightly from complete performance. The nonbreaching party may (1) convince the breaching party to elevate his or her performance to complete performance, or (2) deduct the cost to

---

Breach of contract A contracting party's failure to perform an absolute duty owed under a contract.

Covenant An unconditional promise to perform.

Condition precedent A condition that requires the occurrence of an event before a party is obligated to perform a duty under a contract.

Complete performance A situation in which a party to a contract renders performance exactly as required by the contract. Complete performance discharges that party's obligations under the contract.

Substantial performance Performance by a contracting party that deviates only slightly from complete performance.

Minor breach A breach that occurs when a party renders substantial performance of his or her contractual duties.

repair the defect from the contract price and remit the balance to the breaching party, or (3) sue the breaching party to recover the cost to repair the defect if the breaching party has already been paid.

Example   Suppose Donald Trump contracts with Big Apple Construction Co. to have Big Apple construct an office building for $50 million. The architectural plans call for installation of three-ply windows in the building. Big Apple constructs the building exactly to plan except that it installs two-ply windows. There has been substantial performance. It would cost $300,000 to install the correct windows. If Big Apple agrees to replace the windows, its performance is elevated to complete performance and Trump must remit the entire contract price. But if Trump has to hire someone else to replace the windows, he may deduct this cost of repair from the contract price and remit the difference to Big Apple.

Inferior Performance (Material Breach)

Inferior performance occurs when there has been a **material breach** of a contract. A material breach results when a party fails to perform certain express or implied obligations that impair or destroy the essence of the contract. Because there is no clear line between a minor breach and a material breach, determination is made on a case-by-case basis. Where there has been a material breach of a contract, the nonbreaching party has two choices:

1. The nonbreaching party may *rescind* the contract, seek restitution of any compensation paid under the contract to the breaching party, and be discharged from any further performance under the contract.
2. The nonbreaching party may treat the contract as being in effect and sue the breaching party to recover *damages*.

Example   Suppose a university contracts with a general contractor to build a new three-story building with classroom space for 1,000 students. But the completed building can support the weight of only 500 students because the contractor used inferior materials. The defect cannot be repaired without rebuilding the entire structure. Because this is a material breach, the university may rescind the contract and require removal of the building. The university is discharged of any obligations under the contract and is free to employ another contractor to rebuild the building. Alternatively, the university could accept the building and deduct from the contract price the damages caused by the defect.

Monetary Damages

If a breach of contract has been found, the nonbreaching party is awarded a **remedy** for the breach. The most common remedy for a breach of contract is an award of **monetary damages**. This is often called the "law remedy." Monetary damages are discussed in the following paragraphs.

Compensatory Damages

Compensatory damages are intended to compensate a nonbreaching party for the loss of the bargain. They place the nonbreaching party in the same position as if the contract has been fully performed by restoring the "benefit of the bargain."

Example   Suppose Lederle Laboratories enters into a written contract to employ a manager for three years at a salary of $6,000 per month. Before work is to start, the manager is informed that he will not be needed. This is a material breach of contract.

SIDEBAR

TYPES OF PERFORMANCE

Type of Performance	Legal Consequence
Complete performance	The contract is discharged.
Substantial performance (minor breach)	The nonbreaching party may recover damages caused by the breach.
Inferior performance (material breach)	The nonbreaching party may either (1) rescind the contract and recover restitution or (2) affirm the contract and recover damages.

Inferior performance A situation in which a party fails to perform express or implied contractual obligations and impairs or destroys the essence of the contract.

Material breach A breach that occurs when a party renders inferior performance of his or her contractual duties.

Monetary damages An award of money.

Compensatory damages An award of money intended to compensate a nonbreaching party for loss of the bargain. Compensatory damages place the nonbreaching party in the same position as if the contract had been fully performed by restoring the "benefit of the bargain."

Consequential damages
Foreseeable damages that arise from circumstances outside the contract. To be liable for these damages, the breaching party must know or have reason to know that the breach will cause special damages to the other party.

SIDEBAR

TYPES OF MONETARY DAMAGES

Type of Damage	Description
Compensatory	Damages that compensate a nonbreaching party for the loss of a bargain. It places the nonbreaching party in the same position as if the contract had been fully performed.
Consequential	Damages that compensate a nonbreaching party for foreseeable special damages. The breaching party must have known or should have known that these damages would result from the breach.
Liquidated	An agreement by the parties in advance that sets the amount of damages recoverable in case of breach. These damages are lawful if they do not cause a penalty.

Liquidated damages Damages to which parties to a contract agree in advance should be paid if the contract is breached.

Mitigation of damages A nonbreaching party's legal duty to avoid or reduce damages caused by a breach of contract.

Example Assume that the manager finds another job, but it pays only $5,000 a month. The manager may recover $1,000 per month for 36 months (total $36,000) from Lederle Laboratories as compensatory damages. These damages place the manager in the same situation as if the contract with Lederle had been performed.

Consequential Damages

A nonbreaching party sometimes can recover *special* or **consequential damages** from the breaching party. Consequential damages are *foreseeable* damages that arise from circumstances outside the contract. To be liable for consequential damages, the breaching party must know or have reason to know that the breach will cause special damages to the other party.

Example Suppose Soan-Allen Co., a wholesaler, enters into a contract to purchase 1,000 men's suits for $150 each from the Fabric Manufacturing Co., a manufacturer. Prior to contracting, the wholesaler tells the manufacturer that the suits will be resold to retailers for $225. The manufacturer breaches the contract by failing to manufacture the suits. The wholesaler cannot get the suits manufactured by anyone else in time to meet his contracts. He can recover $75,000 of lost profits on the resale contracts (1,000 suits × $75 profit) as consequential damages from the manufacturer because the manufacturer knew of this special damage to Soan-Allen Co. if it were to breach the contract.

Liquidated Damages

Under certain circumstances, the parties to a contract may agree in advance to the amount of damages payable upon a breach of contract. These are called **liquidated damages**. To be lawful, the actual damages must be difficult or impracticable to determine, and the liquidated amount must be reasonable in the circumstances. An enforceable liquidated damage clause is an exclusive remedy even if actual damages are later determined to be different.

Example A buyer enters into a contract to purchase a condominium for $5 million in a high-rise cooperative building to be built in New York City by a real estate developer. The contract requires the buyer to pay a nonrefundable deposit of 10 percent of the purchase price at the time of contracting that may be retained by the real estate developer if the buyer refuses to complete the purchase once the building is completed. This is a reasonable liquidated damage clause.

A liquidated damage clause is considered a *penalty* if actual damages are clearly determinable in advance or the liquidated damages are excessive or unconscionable. If a liquidated damage clause is found to be a penalty, it is unenforceable. The nonbreaching party then may recover actual damages.

Mitigation of Damages

If a contract has been breached, the law places a duty on the innocent nonbreaching party to take reasonable efforts to mitigate (i.e., avoid and reduce) the resulting damages. The extent of **mitigation of damages** required depends on the type of contract involved.

Example If an employer breaches an employment contract, the employee owes a duty to mitigate damages by trying to find substitute employment. The employee is required only to accept comparable employment. In determining the comparability of jobs, the courts consider factors such as compensation, rank, status, job description, and geographical location.

Equitable Remedies

If a monetary award does not provide adequate relief the court may order any one of several nonmonetary remedies—**equitable remedies**—including specific performance, injunction, reformation, and quasi-contract. Equitable remedies are based on the concept of fairness. These remedies are discussed in the following paragraphs.

Specific Performance

An award of **specific performance** orders the breaching party to *perform* the acts promised in the contract. The courts have the discretion to award this remedy if the subject matter of the contract is unique. Works of art, antiques, item of sentimental value, rare coins, stamps, heirlooms, and such also fit the requirement for uniqueness. Most other personal property does not.

This remedy is available to enforce land contracts because every piece of real property is considered unique.

> **Example** If a buyer has entered into a contract to purchase a house from a seller but the seller refuses to sell the house when the time for sale arrives, the buyer can bring an action of specific performance and obtain a judgment that orders the seller to sell the house to the buyer.

Specific performance of personal-service contracts is not granted because the courts would find it difficult or impracticable to supervise or monitor performance of the contract.

> **Example** If a professional basketball player has a three-year contract to play for a professional team but quits before his contract is completed, the professional team cannot obtain an order of specific performance that would make the athlete play for the team. In this case, the team's remedy is to sue the athlete for damages caused by his breach.

Injunction

An **injunction** is a court order that prohibits a person from doing a certain act. To obtain an injunction, the requesting party must show that he or she will suffer irreparable injury unless the injunction is issued.

> **Example** Suppose a professional football team enters into a five-year employment contract with a star quarterback. The quarterback breaches the contract and enters into a contract to play for a competing team. Here, the first team can seek an injunction to prevent the quarterback from playing for the other team.

Reformation

Reformation is an equitable doctrine that permits the court to *rewrite* a contract to express the parties' true intentions.

> **Example** Suppose a clerical error is made during the typing of the contract and both parties sign the contract without discovering the error. If a dispute later arises, the court can reform the contract to correct the clerical error to read what the parties originally intended.

Quasi-Contract

A **quasi-contract** (also called an *implied-in-law contract*) is an equitable doctrine that permits the recovery of compensation even though no enforceable contract exists between the parties because of lack of consideration, the Statute of Frauds has

---

SIDEBAR

TYPES OF EQUITABLE REMEDIES

Type of Equitable Remedy	Description
Specific performance	A court orders the breaching party to perform the acts promised in the contract. The subject matter of the contract must be unique.
Reformation	A court rewrites a contract to express the parties' true intentions. It is usually used to correct clerical errors.
Injunction	A court prohibits a party from doing a certain act. Injunctions are available in contract actions only in limited circumstances.
Quasi-contract	A court awards monetary damages to a plaintiff for providing work or services to a defendant even though no actual contract existed in order to prevent unjust enrichment to the defendant.

Specific performance A remedy that orders the breaching party to perform the acts promised in the contract. Specific performance usually is awarded in cases where the subject matter is unique, such as in contracts involving land, heirlooms, and paintings.

Injunction A court order that prohibits a person from doing a certain act.

Reformation An equitable doctrine that permits the court to rewrite a contract to express the parties' true intentions.

Quasi-contract An equitable doctrine whereby a court may award monetary damages to a plaintiff for providing work or services to a defendant even though no actual contract existed.

Paralegals *in* Practice

PARALEGAL PROFILE
Annette R. Brown

Annette R. Brown, ACP has been employed by the Rocky Mountain Elk Foundation, Inc. virtually since the creation of its in-house legal department in 1995. The Elk Foundation is a charitable non-profit corporation in Missoula, Montana, with a mission to protect habitat for elk and other wildlife. In addition to her paralegal degree, Annette also has Advanced Paralegal Certifications in Real Estate, Trademarks, and Contracts Administration/ Contracts Management from the National Association of Legal Assistants (NALA). She is currently serving as NALA's Region VIII Director which includes the states of Alaska, Idaho, Montana, Oregon, and Washington.

My practice is mainly centered on real estate and other transactions. This includes drafting and reviewing purchase and sale contracts, deeds and closing documents, title review, water rights, and other due diligence elements. I also work with other types of contracts such as independent contractor, convention center, fundraising, entertainment, trademark licensing, sponsorship, and many more.

Our corporation owns a 100,000-acre working ranch in New Mexico that is managed for habitat conservation, and land managers work alongside educators, biologists, and government agencies to test new land-management practices. I've handled employment contracts, water rights, hunting contracts, easements, and state grazing applications for this project.

When working in a busy corporate legal department, you need the ability to move from one project to another without losing track of your priorities. In addition to legal knowledge, my position requires proficiency in contract drafting, research skills, organizational skills, proofreading, and editing.

Technology advancements have streamlined many processes. When negotiating and drafting contracts, we work across the country with landowners, government agencies, title companies, appraisers, and attorneys. The word processing tracking feature allows for documents' data to be edited by various sources while maintaining an information "trail." Some of our contracts allow the parties to digitally scan and e-mail the signed document to confirm execution. We can also scan and save incoming documents relevant to our projects for easier data retrieval.

Web Exploration

Go to http://www.oscn.net/applications/oscn/Deliver Document.asp?CiteID=74212 to read a jury instruction on the issue of quasi-contract.

run out, or the like. Such contracts are imposed by law to prevent unjust enrichment. Under quasi-contract, a party can recover the reasonable value of the services or materials provided.

> **Example** A physician who stops to render aid to an unconscious victim of an automobile accident may recover the reasonable value of his services from that person.

Equity

Equity A doctrine that permits judges to make decisions based on fairness, equality, moral rights, and natural law.

Although the courts usually interpret a valid contract as a solemn promise to perform, this view of the sanctity of a contract can cause an unjust result, however. Therefore, a judge may apply the doctrine of **equity** and save a contracting party from the strict enforcement of a contract or contract terms. Equity is based on the concepts of fairness, equality, and moral rights.

Uniform Commercial Code (UCC)

Paralegal professionals who work in the contract law field often must know how UCC rules differ from traditional contract law. This difference arose because one of the major frustrations of businesspersons conducting interstate business was that they were subject to the laws of each of the states in which they operate. To address this problem, in 1949 the National Conference of Commissioners on Uniform State Laws promulgated the Uniform Commercial Code (UCC).

The UCC is a model act that contains uniform rules that govern commercial transactions. To create this uniformity, individual states had to enact the UCC as their commercial law statute. In fact, they did. Every state (except Louisiana, which has adopted only parts of the UCC) enacted the UCC as a commercial statute. The UCC is being revised continually to reflect changes in modern commercial practices and technology.

The UCC is divided into articles, with each article establishing uniform rules for a specific facet of commerce in the United States. The articles of the UCC are:

Article 1	General provisions
Article 2	Sales
Article 2A Revised	Leases
Article 3	Negotiable instruments
Article 4	Bank deposits and collections
Article 4A	Wire transfers
Article 5	Letters of credit
Article 6	Bulk transfers
Article 7	Documents of title
Article 8	Investment securities
Article 9	Secured transactions

Paralegal professionals who work in the area of contract law should be familiar with the major provisions of the Uniform Commercial Code.

Article 2 (Sales) of the UCC

Article 2 (Sales) of the UCC applies to *transactions in goods*—that is, the sale of goods [UCC 2-102]. All states except Louisiana have adopted some version of Article 2 of the UCC. A sale consists of the passing of title from a seller to a buyer for a price [UCC 2-106(1)].

> **Example** The purchase of a plasma television is a sale subject to Article 2. This is so whether the television was paid for by cash, check, credit card, or another form of consideration.

Article 2 establishes a uniform law covering the formation, performance, and default of sales contracts.

Goods are defined as tangible things that are movable at the time of their identification to the contract [UCC 2-105(1)]. Examples of goods are specially manufactured goods and the unborn young of animals. Money and intangible items, such as stocks, bonds, and patents, are not tangible goods. Therefore, they are not subject to Article 2.

Real estate is not subject to Article 2 either, because it is not movable [UCC 2-105(1)]. Minerals, structures, growing crops, and other things that are severable from real estate may be classified as goods subject to Article 2, however.

> **Examples** The sale and removal of a chandelier in a house is a sale of goods subject to Article 2 because its removal would not materially harm the realty. But the sale and removal of the furnace would be a sale of real property because its removal would cause material harm [UCC 2-107(2)].

Contracts for the provision of services—including legal services, medical services, dental services, and such—are not covered by Article 2. Sometimes, however, a sale involves the provision of both a service and a good in the same transaction. This is referred to as a *mixed sale*. Article 2 applies to mixed sales only if the goods are the predominant part of the transaction. The UCC provides no guidance for deciding cases based on mixed sales. Therefore, the courts decide these issues on a case-by-case basis.

Article 2 (Sales) of the UCC An article of the UCC that governs the sale of goods.

Article 2A (Leases) of the UCC

Article 2A (Leases) of the UCC An article of the UCC that governs the lease of goods.

Personal property leases are a billion-dollar industry. Consumer rentals of automobiles and equipment, and commercial leases of such items as aircraft and industrial machinery, fall into this category.

Article 2A (Leases) of the UCC was promulgated in 1987. This article, cited as the Uniform Commercial Code—Leases, directly addresses personal property leases [UCC 2A-101]. It establishes a comprehensive, uniform law covering the formation, performance, and default of leases in goods [UCC 2A-102, 2A-103(h)].

Article 2A is similar to Article 2. In fact, many Article 2 provisions were changed to reflect leasing terminology and practices and carried over to Article 2A. Many states have adopted Article 2A, and many more are expected to do so in the future.

A lease is a transfer of the right to the possession and use of the named goods for a set term in return for certain consideration [UCC 2A-103(1)(i)(x)]. The leased goods can be anything from a hand tool leased to an individual for a few hours to a complex line of industrial equipment leased to a multinational corporation for a number of years.

In an ordinary lease, the **lessor** is the person who transfers the right of possession and use of goods under the lease [UCC 2A-103(1)(p)]. The **lessee** is the person who acquires the right to possession and use of goods under a lease [UCC 2A-103(1)(n)].

UCC Firm Offer Rule

Recall that the common law of contracts allows the offeror to revoke an offer any time prior to its acceptance. The only exception allowed by the common law is an *option contract* (i.e., where the offeree pays the offeror consideration to keep the offer open).

The UCC recognizes another exception, which is called the **firm offer rule**. This rule states that a merchant who (1) offers to buy, sell, or lease goods and (2) gives a written and signed assurance on a separate form that the offer will be held open cannot revoke the offer for the time stated or, if no time is stated, for a reasonable time. The maximum amount of time permitted under this rule is three months [UCC 2-205, 2A-205].

> **Example** On June 1, a merchant–seller offers to sell a Mercedes-Benz to a buyer for $50,000. The merchant–seller signs a written assurance to keep that offer open until August 30. On July 1, the merchant–seller sells the car to another buyer. On August 21, the original offeree tenders $50,000 for the car. The merchant–seller is liable to the original offeree for breach of contract.

UCC Statute of Frauds

The UCC includes Statute of Frauds provisions that apply to all sales and lease contracts. All contracts for the sale of goods costing $500 or more (the 2003 amendments to the UCC changes this amount to $5,000 or more) and lease contracts involving payments of $1,000 or more must be in writing [UCC 2-201(1), 2A-201(1)]. The writing must be sufficient to indicate that a contract has been made between the parties. The writing must be signed by the party against whom enforcement is sought or by his or her authorized agent or broker. If a contract falling within these parameters is not written, it is unenforceable.

> **Example** A seller orally agrees to sell her computer to a buyer for $550. When the buyer tenders the purchase price, the seller asserts the Statute of Frauds and refuses to sell the computer to him. The seller is correct. The contract must be in writing to be enforceable because the contract price for the computer exceeds $499.99.

E-Commerce and E-Contracts

Use of the Internet and the World Wide Web to sell goods and services through e-commerce is commonplace today. E-commerce also is referred to as **online commerce**. Businesses and individuals sell goods and services over the Internet through websites and registered domain names. Consumers and businesses can purchase or sell almost any good or service they want over the Internet, using their own sites or sites such as Amazon.com, eBay, and others. In addition, software and information may be licensed either by physically purchasing the software or information and installing it on a computer or by merely downloading the software or information directly into the computer.

E-Contracts

Email and the Web have exploded as a means of personal and business communication. In the business environment, email and the Web are sometimes the methods used to negotiate and agree on contract terms and to send and agree to a final contract. Are email and Web contracts enforceable? Assuming that all the elements to establish a contract are present, an email or **Web contract** is valid and enforceable. These are typically called e-contracts. The main problem in a lawsuit seeking to enforce an e-contract is evidence, but this problem, which exists in almost all lawsuits, can be overcome by printing out the e-contract and its prior email or Web negotiations, if necessary.

E-Writing

One of the main features of the E-SIGN Act is that it recognizes electronic contracts as meeting the *writing requirement* of the Statute of Frauds for most contracts. Statutes of Frauds are state laws that require certain types of contracts to be in writing. The E-SIGN Act provides that electronically signed contracts cannot be denied effect

E-license A contract that transfers limited rights in intellectual property and informational rights.

CAREER OPPORTUNITIES FOR PARALEGALS IN E-COMMERCE

As a paralegal, you have witnessed the explosive growth of electronic commerce, or e-commerce, around the world. You can find almost anything being sold over the Internet through Web pages. Large companies and small companies alike, as well as individuals, are selling and buying over the Internet.

When someone sells and purchases something over the Internet, they usually enter into an e-contract, also called a Web contract or online contract. Originally, state contract law solely regulated the formation and performance of e-contracts. This led to an often nonuniform application of law to e-contracts.

Some of the common law of contracts and provisions of the Uniform Commercial Code (UCC) did not directly apply to e-contracts. To alleviate this problem, the UCC has been updated to apply to sales and leases made over the Internet. Modern changes to the UCC have helped considerably in bringing uniform contract rules to electronic commerce. A uniform law for e-contracts also has been promulgated and is being adopted in whole or part by state legislatures.

A special kind of contracting that is especially suited for online commerce is licensing. Many companies transfer software, data, information technology, and other forms of intellectual property over the Internet

through the use of licenses. Special rules of licensing apply to these **e-licenses.** A model act, called the Uniform Computer Information Transactions Act (UCITA), has been promulgated to apply to e-licenses. Many states have adopted this act or provisions similar to this act that create more uniform contract law for e-licenses.

In addition, the federal government has stepped in and enacted federal statutes to bring uniformity to e-commerce transactions. The major law in this area is the Electronic Signature in Global and National Commerce Act. This federal act establishes special rules that recognize electronic contracts, or e-contracts, and signatures. The federal government is expected to continue to adopt laws as is necessary to bring more uniform law to the area of e-commerce.

Paralegals have a unique opportunity to become experts in this relatively new area of the law. E-contracts and e-licenses face special rules in their formation, performance, and enforcement. In addition, many lawsuits involving e-contracts and e-licenses will be litigated in the courts. Paralegals will be needed to assist lawyers in drafting e-contracts and e-licenses, as well as assisting in the litigation of disputes involving e-commerce.

ELECTRONIC SIGNATURE IN GLOBAL AND NATIONAL COMMERCE ACT (E-SIGN ACT)

In 2000, the federal government enacted the **Electronic Signature in Global and National Commerce Act.** This is a federal statute enacted by Congress and, therefore, has national reach. The act is designed to place the world of electronic commerce on a par with the world of paper contracts in the United States.

Electronic Signature in Global and National Commerce Act (E-SIGN Act) A federal statute that recognizes that electronic contracts, or e-contracts, meet the writing requirement of the Statute of Frauds and gives electronic signatures, or e-signatures, the same force and effect as pen-inscribed signatures on paper.

because they are in electronic form or delivered electronically. The act also provides that record retention requirements are satisfied if the records are stored electronically.

The federal law was passed with several provisions to protect consumers.

1. Consumers must consent to receiving electronic records and contracts.
2. To receive electronic records, consumers must be able to demonstrate that they have access to the electronic records.
3. Businesses must tell consumers that they have the right to receive hard-copy documents of their transaction.

In the past, signatures have been hand-applied by the person signing the document. No more. In the electronic commerce world, it is now, "What is your mother's maiden name?" "Slide your smart card in the sensor," or "Look into the iris scanner."

E-Signature

Another main feature of the E-SIGN Act is that it recognizes an *electronic signature* or **e-signature**. The act gives an e-signature the same force and effect as a pen-inscribed signature on paper. The act is technology neutral, however, in that the law does not define or decide which technologies should be used to create a legally binding signature in cyberspace.

Loosely defined, a **digital signature** is some electronic method that identifies an individual. The challenge is to make sure that someone who uses a digital signature is the person he or she claims to be. The act provides that a digital signature basically can be verified in one of three ways:

1. By something the signatory knows; such as a secret password, pet's name, and so forth
2. By something a person has, such as a "smart card," which looks like a credit card and stores personal information
3. By biometrics, which uses a device that digitally recognizes fingerprints or the retina or iris of the eye

The verification of electronic signatures is creating a need for scanners and methods for verifying personal information.

E-License

Licensor An owner of intellectual property or informational rights who transfers rights in the property or information to the licensee.

Licensee A party who is granted limited rights in or access to intellectual property or informational rights owned by a licensor.

Intellectual property and information rights are extremely important assets of many individuals and companies. Software programs, data, copyrights, and such constitute valuable intellectual property and information rights.

The owners of intellectual property and information rights often wish to transfer limited rights in the property or information to parties for specified purposes and limited duration. The agreement that is used to transfer such limited rights is called a **license**. The parties to a license are the licensor and the license. The **licensor** is the party who owns the intellectual property or information rights and obligates himself or herself to transfer rights in the property or information to the licensee. The **licensee** is the party who is granted limited rights in or access to the intellectual property of information rights. A licensing arrangement is illustrated in Exhibit 13.2.

Exhibit 13.2	Parties to a license

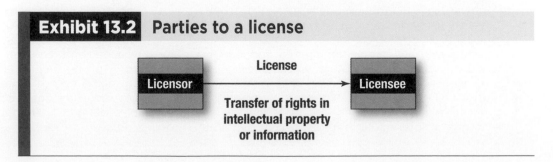

Uniform Computer Information Transactions Act (UCITA)

In 1999 the National Conference of Commissioners on Uniform State Laws (a group of lawyers, judges, and legal scholars) drafted the **Uniform Computer Information Transactions Act (UCITA)**. This model act establishes a uniform and comprehensive set of rules that govern the creation, performance, and enforcement of computer information transactions. A computer information transaction is an agreement to create, transfer, or license computer information or information rights [UCITA Section 102(a)(11)].

The UCITA does not become law until a state's legislature enacts it as a state statute. States have adopted the UCITA or laws similar to the UCITA as their law for computer transactions and the licensing of informational rights.

Uniform Computer Information Transactions Act (UCITA) A model state law that creates contract law for the licensing of information technology rights.

Licensing Agreement

A licensor and a licensee usually enter into a written **licensing agreement** that expressly states the terms of their agreement. Licensing agreements tend to be very detailed and comprehensive contracts. This is primarily because of the nature of the subject matter and the limited uses granted in the intellectual property or informational rights.

The parties to a contract for the licensing of information owe a duty to perform the obligations stated in the contract. If a party fails to perform as required, there is a breach of the contract. Breach of contract by one party to a licensing agreement gives the nonbreaching party the right to recover damages or other remedies.

Licensing agreement
A detailed and comprehensive written agreement between a licensor and a licensee that sets forth the express terms of their agreement.

 Web Exploration

Go to http://www.microsoft.com/about/legal/useterms. Find the licensing agreement for a Microsoft software product. Do you have any ability to negotiate the terms of this licensing agreement?

ETHICAL PERSPECTIVE

Duty Not to Engage in Fraudulent Billing Practices

Ms. Pease works as a paralegal for a large law firm with more than 100 attorneys. The law firm has established annual billing goals for both attorneys and paralegals. When making decisions for promotions, payment of bonuses, and keeping one's employment at the firm, the law firm considers meeting this billing-hour goal. At her level, Ms. Pease is responsible for billing 1,600 hours per year.

Although intending to reach the 1,600 hours of billing time, during the first 10 months of the current year, Ms. Pease has not billed enough hours to reasonably reach her goal of 1,600 billable hours. Ms. Pease is therefore tempted to "book" additional time in November and December on some of the files she has been working on but without actually doing the work. By doing so she could reach the goal of billing the 1,600 hours.

What decision should Ms. Pease reach?

Many model and state paralegal professional codes of ethics and responsibility require that a paralegal professional honestly and thoroughly keep billing records and only bill for the time that he or she has actually worked on a case. A paralegal cannot inflate the hours that are billed to a client or his or her employer.

PARALEGAL'S ETHICAL DECISION

Thus, Ms. Pease owes an ethical duty not to inflate her hours but to honestly and thoroughly report the hours that she has worked. If by the end of the year she does not reach the 1,600 billable-hours goal set by the firm, she should discuss this matter with her supervising attorney and determine whether the 1,600 billable-hours goal is reasonable, and if so, how she may better reach that goal in the coming year.

Concept Review *and* Reinforcement

LEGAL TERMINOLOGY

Acceptance 494

Agreement 493

Article 2 (Sales) of the Uniform Commercial Code (UCC) 505

Article 2A (Leases) of the Uniform Commercial Code (UCC) 506

Breach of contract 500

Capacity to contract 495

Common law of contracts 490

Compensatory damages 501

Complete performance 500

Condition precedent 500

Consequential damages 502

Consideration 495

Contract 492

Contracts contrary to public policy 497

Contracts contrary to statutes 497

Contractual capacity 496

Counteroffer 494

Covenant 500

Digital signature 508

Disaffirm 496

E-commerce 492

E-contract 492

E-licenses 507

E-signatures 508

Electronic Commerce 492

Electronic Signature in Global and National Commerce Act (E-SIGN Act) 508

Equitable remedies 503

Equity 504

Executed contract 500

Executory contract 498

Express contract 495

Firm offer rule 506

Formality of the writing 498

Gift promise (gratuitous promise) 495

Goods 505

Illegal contract 496

Implied-in-fact contract 495

Infancy doctrine 496

Inferior performance 501

Injunction 503

Intellectual property and information rights 508

Intoxicated persons 496

Lawful object 496

Lease 491

Legally enforceable 492

Lessee 506

Lessor 506

License 508

Licensee 508

Licensing agreement 509

Licensor 508

Liquidated damages 502

Material breach 501

Mental incapacity 496

Mentally incompetent persons 496

Minor breach 500

Minors 496

Mirror image rule 494

Mitigation of damages 502

Monetary damages 501

Necessaries of life 496

Offer 493

Offeree 492

Offeror 492

One-year rule 498

Online commerce 507

Option contract 494

Quasi-contract (implied-in-law contract) 503

Reformation 503

Rejection (of an offer) 494

Remedy 501

Required signature 499

Revocation (of an offer) 493

Sales contract 491

Specific performance 503

Statute of Frauds 498

Substantial performance 500

Tender of performance 500

UCC firm offer rule 506

UCC Statute of Frauds 506

Unconscionable contract 497

Uniform Commercial Code (UCC) 491

Uniform Computer Information Transactions Act (UCITA) 509

United Nations Convention on Contracts for the International Sale of Goods (CISG) 506

Web contract 507

SUMMARY OF KEY CONCEPTS

Sources of Contract Law

Sources of Contract Law	1. Common law of contracts (law) 2. Uniform Commercial Code (law) 3. Restatement (Second) of Contracts (advisory only, not law)

Formation of a Contract

Definition	A contract is a promise or set of promises for the breach of which the law gives a remedy or the performance of which the law in some way recognizes a duty.
Parties to a Contract	1. *Offeror:* Party who makes an offer to enter into a contract. 2. *Offeree:* Party to whom the offer is made.
Elements of a Contract	1. Agreement 2. Consideration 3. Contractual capacity 4. Lawful object

Agreement

	An agreement is the manifestation by two or more persons of the substance of a contract. It requires an *offer* and *acceptance*.
Offer	1. *Offer:* Manifestation by one party of a willingness to enter into a contract. 2. *Offeror:* Party who makes an offer. 3. *Offeree:* Party to whom an offer is made. This party has the power to create an agreement by accepting the terms of the offer.
Termination of an Offer by Action of the Parties	1. *Revocation:* The offeror may *revoke* (withdraw) an offer any time prior to its acceptance by the offeree. 2. *Rejection:* An offer is terminated if the offeree rejects the offer by his or her words or conduct. 3. *Counteroffer:* An offer by the offeree that terminates the offeror's offer and creates a new offer.
Option Contract	A contract that is created if an offeree pays the offeror compensation to keep an offer open for an agreed-upon period of time. The offeror cannot sell the property to anyone else during the *option period*.
Acceptance	Manifestation of assent by the offeree to the terms of the offer. Acceptance of the offer by the offeree creates a contract.
Express and Implied Contracts	1. *Express contract:* A contract expressed in oral or written words. 2. *Implied-in-fact contract:* A contract implied from the conduct of the parties.

Consideration

Consideration	Thing of value given in exchange for a promise. May be tangible or intangible property, performance of a service, forbearance of a legal right, or another thing of value.
Gift Promise	Promises to make gifts that are unenforceable because they lack consideration. Also called *gratuitous promise*.

Capacity to Contract

Capacity to Contract	1. *Minors:* Under the *infancy doctrine* minors under the age of majority may *disaffirm* (cancel) most contracts they have entered into with adults. The contract is *voidable* by the minor but not by the adult.
	2. *Mental incompetence:* Contracts by persons who are insane are *voidable* by the insane person but not by the competent party to the contract.
	3. *Intoxicated persons:* Contracts by *intoxicated* persons are *voidable* by the intoxicated person but not by the competent party to the contract.

Lawful Object

Lawful Object	The object of the contract must be *lawful* for the contract to be enforceable.
Illegal Contract	An illegal contract is *void*. Therefore, the parties cannot sue for nonperformance. If the contract has been executed, the court will *leave the parties where it finds them*.
	1. Contracts that violate statutes are illegal, void, and unenforceable.
	2. Contracts that violate public policy are illegal, void, and unenforceable.

Unconscionable Contract

	Unconscionable contracts are oppressively unfair or unjust. Also called *contracts of adhesion.*
	Elements: The elements of an unconscionable contract are:
	1. The parties possessed severely unequal bargaining power.
	2. The dominant party unreasonably used its power to obtain oppressive or manifestly unfair contract terms.
	3. The adhering party had no reasonable alternative.
	Remedies: Where a contract or contract clause is found to be unconscionable, the court may do one of the following:
	1. Refuse to enforce the contract.
	2. Refuse to enforce the unconscionable clause but enforce the remainder of the contract.
	3. Limit the applicability of any unconscionable clause so as to avoid any unconscionable result.

Statute of Frauds—Writing Requirement

Writing Requirement	A state statute requires the following contracts to be in writing:
	1. *Contracts involving the transfer of interests in real property:* Includes contracts for the sale of land, buildings, and items attached to land, mortgages, leases for a term of more than one year, and express easements.
	2. Contracts that cannot be performed within one year of their formation (*one-year rule*).
	3. *Contracts for the sale of goods* costing $500 or more (UCC 201). (The 2003 amendments to the UCC change this contract to $5,000 or more).
Sufficiency of the Writing	1. *Formality of the writing:* A written contract does not have to be formal or drafted by a lawyer to be enforceable. Informal contracts, such as handwritten notes, letters, invoices, and the like, are enforceable contracts.
	2. *Required signature:* The party against whom enforcement of the contract is sought must have signed the contract. The signature may be the person's full legal name, last name, first name, nickname, initials, or other symbol.

Performance and Breach

Covenant	A covenant is an unconditional promise to perform. Nonperformance of a covenant is a breach of contract that gives the other party the right to sue.

Condition Precedent	A condition precedent requires the occurrence or nonoccurrence of an event before a party is obligated to perform.
Levels of Performance	1. *Complete performance:* A party renders performance exactly as the contract requires. That party's contractual duties are discharged. 2. *Substantial performance:* A party renders performance that deviates only slightly from complete performance. There is a *minor breach*. The nonbreaching party may recover damages caused by the breach. 3. *Inferior performance:* A party fails to perform express or implied contractual duties that impair or destroy the essence of the contract. There is a *material breach*. The nonbreaching party may either (1) rescind the contract and recover restitution or (2) affirm the contract and recover damages.

Monetary Damages

Types of Monetary Damages	1. *Compensatory damages:* Damages that compensate a nonbreaching party for loss of the contract. Restore the "benefit of the bargain" to the nonbreaching party as if the contract had been fully performed. 2. *Consequential damages:* Foreseeable damages that arise from circumstances outside the contract and of which the breaching party either knew or had reason to know. Also called *special damages*. 3. *Liquidated damages:* Damages payable upon breach of contract that are agreed on in advance by the contracting parties. Liquidated damages substitute for actual damages.
Mitigation of Damages	The duty the law places on a nonbreaching party to take reasonable efforts to avoid or reduce the resulting damages from a breach of contract. To mitigate a breach of an employment contract, the nonbreaching party must only accept "comparable" employment.

Equitable Remedies

Specific Performance	Specific performance is a court order that requires the breaching party to perform his or her contractual duties. It is available only if the subject matter of the contract is *unique*.
Injunction	An injunction is a court order that prohibits a person from doing a certain act. The requesting party must show that he or she will suffer irreparable injury if the injunction is not granted.
Reformation	Reformation permits the court to rewrite a contract to express the parties true intention. Available to correct clerical and mathematical errors.
Quasi-Contract	A quasi-contract permits the court to order recovery of compensation even though no enforceable contract exists between the parties. It is used to prevent unjust enrichment. Also called an *implied-in-law contract* or *quantum meruit*.
Equity	Equity is a doctrine that permits judges to make decisions based on fairness, equality, moral rights, and natural law.

Uniform Commercial Code (UCC)

Definition	The UCC is a comprehensive statutory scheme that includes laws covering most aspects of sales and lease contracts of goods.
Article 2 (Sales)	Article 2 of the UCC applies to sales transactions in goods.
Article 2A (Leases)	Article 2A of the UCC applies to personal property leases of goods.

UCC Firm Offer Rule	The UCC firm offer rule says that a merchant who (1) makes an offer to buy, sell, or lease goods and (2) assures the other party in a separate writing that the offer will be held open cannot revoke the offer for the time stated, or if no time is stated, for a reasonable time.
UCC Statute of Frauds	The UCC Statute of Frauds requires contracts for the sale of goods costing $500 or more and lease contracts involving payments of $1,000 or more to be in writing.
Convention on Contracts for the International Sale of Goods (CISG)	The CISG establishes uniform rules for the formation and enforcement of contracts involving the international sale of goods. The parties to any international contract can agree that the CISG controls their contract.

E-Commerce and E-Contracts

Definition	Electronic commerce, or e-commerce, is the use of the Internet and the World Wide Web to sell goods and services. Also called *online commerce*.
E-Contract	An electronic contract is entered into by email or only the Internet for the sale or lease of goods, other property, or services.
Electronic Signature in Global and National Commerce Act (E-SIGN Act)	This federal act applies to e-commerce and does the following: 1. *E-writing:* The federal act recognizes that e-contracts meet the writing requirements of the Statutes of Fraud. 2. *E-signature:* The federal act gives electronic signatures the same force and effect as pen-inscribed signatures on paper.

E-License

E-License	The electronic license is a contract that is entered into by email or over the Internet that transfers limited rights in intellectual property and informational rights. 1. *Licensor:* An owner of intellectual property or informational rights who transfers rights in the property or information to the licensee. 2. *Licensee:* A party who is granted limited rights in or access to intellectual property or information rights owned by a licensor.
Uniform Computer Information Transactions Act (UCITA)	The UCITA is a model act issued by the National Conference of Commissioners on Uniform State Laws that establishes a uniform and comprehensive set of rules that govern the creation, performance, and enforcement of computer information transactions.
Licensing Agreement	A licensing agreement is a detailed and comprehensive written agreement between a licensor and a licensee that sets forth the express terms of their agreement.

WORKING THE WEB

1. Visit the website http://www.lectlaw.com/formb/html. Click on the words "Contract, Sale of Goods." Print this form and review the form.
2. Using the website http://www.google.com/html or other Internet search engine, locate an article about a Microsoft software licensing agreement. Write a one-page report on the specifics of the licensing agreement.
3. Visit the website http://cisg.law.pace.edu/html, which is the website for the Institute of International Commercial Law. Click on "CISG-AC Opinion no 1."

Write a one-page report about what Sections 11.1, 13.1, and 13.2 provide.
4. Visit the website http://lectlaw.com/forma/html. Click on the words "Fee Agreement—Contingent." Read this form in its entirety. What type of form contract is this?
5. Using the website http://www.google.com/html or other Internet search engine, locate an article about a recent contract dispute. Write a one-page report on the specifics of this contract dispute.

CRITICAL THINKING & WRITING QUESTIONS

1. Define a contract.
2. Define an offer. Who is the offeror? Who is the offeree?
3. What are the four elements necessary for an enforceable contract?
4. Describe the common law of contracts. Describe the Uniform Commercial Code (UCC).
5. Explain the following: (a) revocation of an offer, (b) rejection of an offer, and (c) counteroffer. What is the effect of each?
6. What is an acceptance? Explain the mirror image rule.
7. Describe the following: (a) express contract, and (b) implied-in-fact contract. Give an example of each.
8. Define an option contract. When would one be used?
9. What is consideration? Give an example.
10. Define a gift promise. Give an example. Is it enforceable? Explain.
11. Define capacity to contract. Explain the enforceability of contracts made by (a) minors (the infancy doctrine), (b) mentally incompetent persons, and (c) intoxicated persons.
12. Define lawful object. What is an illegal contract? What is the effect of an illegal contract?
13. Explain the difference between the illegality of (a) contracts contrary to statutes and (b) contracts contrary to public policy. Give an example of each.
14. What is the Statute of Frauds. What is the effect if the Statute of Frauds is not met?
15. What types of contracts does the Statute of Frauds cover? Give examples. What does the UCC Statute of Frauds provide?
16. What is contract fraud? What are the elements to prove fraud? What is the legal effect of contract fraud?
17. Describe the difference between: (a) covenant and (b) condition precedent.
18. Define complete performance? What is the effect of complete performance? Give an example. Define tender of performance.
19. Describe substantial performance. Is there a breach of the contract? Give an example.
20. Define inferior performance. Is this a breach of contract? Give an example.
21. Explain the following types of monetary damages: (a) compensatory damages and (b) consequential damages. Give an example of each.
22. Define liquidated damages. Give an example.
23. What does mitigation of damages require? Give an example.
24. Describe the following types of equitable remedies: (a) specific performance, (b) injunction, and (c) reformation. Give an example of each.
25. Define quasi-contract (implied-in-law contract). Give an example.
26. Define an unconscionable contract. Give an example. If the court finds a contract to be unconscionable, what remedies may the court order?
27. What is Article 2 (Sales) of the Uniform Commercial Code? What type of contracts does it cover? Give an example.
28. What is Article 2A (Leases) of the Uniform Commercial Code? What type of contracts does it cover? Give an example.
29. What is e-commerce? Explain (a) e-contract and (b) e-license.
30. What is the Electronic Signature in Global and National Commerce Act? Explain how this statute (a) affects the Statute of Frauds for e-contracts, and (b) gives effect to e-signatures.
31. What is the Uniform Computer Information Transactions Act (UCITA)?
32. Describe the United Nations Convention on Contracts for the International Sale of Goods (CISG).

Building Paralegal Skills

VIDEO CASE STUDIES

Parent and Child Consult the Legal Team: Confidentiality Issues

A family is meeting with the attorney provided for them by their insurance company. Issues of what is and what is not covered by the insurance contract are discussed and a question arises as to who the client really is.

After viewing the video case study at www.pearsonhighered .com/goldman answer the following:

1. How are the rights of the parties determined by the insurance contract?
2. If the attorney is being paid by the insurance company, who is the client to whom the lawyer has a loyalty and duty?
3. Is there a conflict of interest between representing the parents and representing the child?

ETHICS ANALYSIS & DISCUSSION QUESTIONS

1. Is it ethical to copy into your word processor, and use as your own, a standard-form real estate contract that contains a copyright notice from the state association of realtors?

2. You have been asked to witness the signature of a client's spouse who is not present. Are there any ethical issues?

3. You are a paralegal not otherwise licensed to practice law. Because of your substantial expertise, you are requested to prepare a complex set of legal documents for a former client. You enter into a fee agreement and are paid upon completion of the work. The "clients" then seek return of the funds paid, claiming they did not understand the significance of the UPL law in the state. [*Vista Designs v. Silverman*, 774 So.2d 884 (Fla.App. 4 Dist. 2001).] Can you be compelled to return the fee paid? Has the client breached its contract?

DEVELOPING YOUR COLLABORATION SKILLS

With a group of other students, selected by you or assigned by your instructor, review the "Paralegals at Work" scenario at the beginning of the chapter. As a group, discuss the following questions.

1. What contract terms would you consider placing in the JAC-Overseas Mines contract that would protect JAC's rights?

2. What contract terms would you include in JAC's Web contract with Internet customers?

3. Does JAC have a breach of remedy claim against Real Estate Developers Inc.?

PARALEGAL PORTFOLIO EXERCISE

Find a sample buy–sell agreement between owners of a business where the owners agree that if one of them leaves the business or dies, the remaining owners will purchase his or her shares, either by paying the leaving partner or by paying the beneficiaries or heirs of a deceased owner. Using this sample agreement, draft the buy–sell agreement for the three owners of Jewelry Associates Corporation (JAC) referred to in the Opening Scenario. The owners are Maxine Armstrong, ViVi Wei, and Jose Ramirez.

LEGAL ANALYSIS & WRITING CASES

Cooper v. Smith 800 N.E.2d 372, Web 2003 Ohio App. Lexis 5446

Court of Appeals of Ohio

Lester Cooper suffered serious injuries that caused him to be hospitalized for an extended time. While he was hospitalized, Julie Smith, whom Cooper had met the year before, and Janet Smith, Julie's mother, made numerous trips to visit him. Although Julie was married to another man at the time, a romantic relationship developed between Cooper and Julie. While in the hospital, Cooper proposed marriage to Julie, and she accepted. Julie obtained a divorce from her husband. Cooper ultimately received an $180,000 settlement for his injuries.

After being released from the hospital, Cooper moved into Janet's house and lived with Janet and Julie. Over the next couple of months, Cooper purchased a number of items for Julie, including a diamond engagement ring, a car, a computer, a tanning bed, and horses. On Julie's request, Cooper paid off Janet's car. Cooper also paid for various improvements to Janet's house, such as having a new furnace installed and having wood flooring laid in the kitchen.

Two months after moving in with Julie, Cooper's settlement money had run out and Julie had not yet married Cooper. Six months later Julie and Cooper had a disagreement and Cooper moved out of the house. Julie returned the engagement ring to Cooper. Cooper sued Julie and Janet to recover the gifts or the value of the gifts he gave them. The magistrate who heard the case dismissed Cooper's case, and the Trial Court affirmed the dismissal of the case. Cooper appealed.

Question

1. Can Cooper recover the gifts or the value of the gifts he gave to Julie and Janet Smith?

Flood v. Fidelity & Guaranty Life Insurance Co.

394 So.2d 1311, Web 1981 La. App. Lexis 3538

Court of Appeal of Louisiana

Ellen and Richard Alvin Flood, who were married, lived in a home in Louisiana. Richard worked as a maintenance man, and Ellen was employed at an insurance agency. Evidence at trial showed that Ellen was unhappy with her marriage. Ellen took out a life insurance policy on the life of her husband and named herself as beneficiary. The policy was issued by Fidelity & Guaranty Life Insurance Company (Fidelity).

Seven years after they were married Richard became unexpectedly ill. He was taken to the hospital, where his condition improved. After a visit at the hospital from his wife, however, Richard died. Ellen was criminally charged with the murder of her husband by poisoning. Evidence showed that six medicine bottles at the couple's home, including Tylenol and paregoric bottles, contained arsenic. The court found that Ellen had fed Richard ice cubes laced with arsenic at the hospital.

Ellen was tried and convicted of the murder of her husband. Ellen, as beneficiary of Richard's life insurance policy, requested Fidelity to pay her the benefits. Fidelity refused to pay the benefits and returned all premiums paid on the policy. This suit followed. The District Court held in favor of Ellen Flood and awarded her the benefits of the life insurance policy. Fidelity appealed.

Question

1. Was the life insurance policy an illegal contract that is void?

Wilson v. Western National Life Insurance Co.

235 Cal.App.3d 981, 1 Cal.Rptr.2d 157, Web 1991 Cal. App. Lexis 1249

California Court of Appeals

Daniel and Doris Wilson were husband and wife: One day Daniel fainted from a narcotics overdose and was rushed, unconscious, to the hospital. Doris accompanied him. Daniel responded to medication used to counteract a narcotics overdose and recovered. The emergency room physician noted that Daniel probably had incurred a heroin overdose and that Daniel had multiple puncture sites on his arms.

Two months later an agent for Western National Life Insurance Company (Western) met with the Wilsons in their home for the purpose of taking their application for life insurance. The agent asked questions and recorded the Wilsons' responses on a written application form. Daniel answered the following questions:

	Yes	No
13. In the past 10 years, have you been treated or joined an organization for alcoholism or drug addiction? If "Yes," explain on the reverse side.		X
17. In the past 5 years, have you consulted or been treated or examined by any physician or practitioner?		X

Both of the Wilsons signed the application form and paid the agent the first month's premium. Under insurance law and the application form, the life insurance policy took effect immediately. Daniel Wilson died from a drug overdose two days later. Western rescinded the policy and rejected Doris Wilson's claim to recover the policy's $50,000 death benefit for Daniel's death, alleging failure to disclose Daniel's drug overdose incident. Doris sued to recover the death benefits. The Trial Court granted summary judgment for Western. Doris appealed.

Question

1. Was there concealment of a material fact that justified Western's rescission of the life insurance policy?

Walgreen Co. v. Sara Creek Property Co.

966 F.2d 273, Web 1992 U.S. App. Lexis 14847

United States Court of Appeals for the Seventh Circuit

Walgreen Company operated a pharmacy in the Southgate Mall in Milwaukee for years. Its lease contained an exclusivity clause in which the landlord, Sara Creek Property Company, promised not to lease space in the mall to anyone else who wants to operate a pharmacy or a store containing a pharmacy.

With ten years left on the lease, Sara Creek informed Walgreen that it intended to lease the anchor tenant space to Phar-Mor Corporation. Phar-Mor, a "deep discount" chain, would occupy 100,000 square feet, of which 12,000 square feet would be occupied by a pharmacy the same size as Walgreen's. The entrances to the two stores would be within a few hundred feet of each other. Walgreen sued Sara Creek for breach of contract and sought a permanent injunction against Sara Creek's leasing the anchor premises to Phar-Mor.

Question

1. Do the facts of this case justify issuing a permanent injunction? Did Sara Creek act ethically in not living up to the contract?

WORKING WITH THE LANGUAGE OF THE COURT CASE

Carnival Leisure Industries Ltd. v. Aubin

938 F.2d 624, Web 1991 U.S. App. 18704
United States Court of Appeals for the Fifth Circuit

Read the following case, excerpted from the Court of Appeals opinion. Review and brief the case. In your brief, answer the following questions.

1. What were the plaintiff's contentions on appeal?
2. What law was applied by the court in this case, Bahamian law or Texas law? Why was that law applied?
3. What is the consequence of finding an illegal contract? Apply this rule to the facts of this case.

4. Did Aubin act ethically in avoiding an obligation that he knowingly made? Do you think he would have given back the money if he had won at gambling?

Garwood, Circuit Judge

During a January 1987 visit to the Bahamas, George J. Aubin, a Texas resident, visited Cable Beach Hotel and Casino (the Casino), which was owned and operated by Carnival Leisure Industries, Ltd. (Carnival Leisure). While gambling at the Casino, Aubin received markers or chips from the Casino and the Casino received drafts drawn on Aubin's bank accounts in Texas. Aubin spent all of the markers provided on gambling, although he also could have spent them on food, beverages, souvenirs, or lodging at the Casino. Aubin ultimately gambled and lost $25,000, leaving the Casino with the same amount in bank drafts.

Carnival Leisure was unable to cash the bank drafts because Aubin had subsequently directed his bank to stop payment. Carnival Leisure sued Aubin in the United States District Court for the Southern District of Texas to enforce the debt. The district court granted Carnival Leisure's motion for summary judgment against Aubin in the amount of $25,000 and attorney's fees and costs. Carnival Leisure claimed that the debt was enforceable under Texas law because public policy had changed and now favored enforcement of gambling debts. The district court agreed. Aubin raises on appeal only the issue of whether public policy in Texas continues to prevent the enforcement of gambling debts.

Carnival Leisure claims, however, that since 1973 the public policy of Texas toward gambling and the legality of gambling debts has changed. Although gambling is generally proscribed in Texas, there has been an exception for the "social" gambler since 1973. The Texas legislature enacted the Bingo Enabling Act in 1981, the Texas Racing Act in 1986, and the Charitable Raffle Enabling Act in 1989. Provisions were added to

the Texas Penal Code excepting these three activities from its general proscription against gambling.

The enactment of statutes legalizing some forms of gambling admittedly evidences some dissipation or narrowing of public disapproval of gambling. However, such statutes hardly introduce a judicially cognizable change in public policy with respect to gambling generally. The social gambling permitted is confined to private places where no one receives any benefit other than his personal winnings and all participants are subject to the same risks, a categorically vastly different kind of activity from the sort involved here. The racing, bingo, and raffling exceptions are narrow, strictly regulated exceptions to a broad public policy in Texas against most forms of gambling. Further, the kind of gambling engaged in here is not of the sort permitted by any of these exceptions.

Even if gambling legislation in Texas were evidence sufficient to warrant judicial notice of a shift in public policy with respect to legalized gambling, such a shift would not be inconsistent with a continued public policy disfavoring gambling on credit. Although Aubin could have used the loaned markers for nongambling purposes at the Casino, it is undisputed that they were in fact used exclusively for gambling. Aubin's gambling debt therefore fits squarely within the terms of the public policy of Texas prohibiting the enforcement of gambling debts owed to gambling participants incurred for the purpose of gambling.

We hold that the public policy in Texas against gambling on credit prevents enforcement of the debt incurred for the purpose of gambling and provided by a participant in the gambling activity. The district court's grant of summary judgment in favor of Carnival Leisure is accordingly reversed and this case is remanded to the district court for further proceedings consistent with this opinion.

DIGITAL RESOURCES

Chapter 14 Digital Resources at *www.pearsonhighered.com/goldman*

- Video Case Studies:
  - UPL Issue: Traditional Exceptions
- Chapter Summary • Web Links • Court Opinions • Glossary • Comprehension Quizzes
- Technology Resources

Property and law are born and must die together. "

Jeremy Bentham,
Principles of the Civil Code

LEARNING OBJECTIVES

After studying this chapter, you should be able to:

1. Recognize the professional opportunities for paralegals in the property law area.

2. Define *personal property* and describe the methods for acquiring ownership.

3. Explain bailments and the parties to a bailment.

4. List and describe the types of real property.

5. Identify the types of co-ownership.

6. Name and describe the types of freehold estates.

7. Identify and describe the various types of leaseholds and explain the landlord–tenant relationship.

8. Explain some features of land-use control, including zoning laws.

9. Explain a paralegal's duty not to engage in conduct that would exceed the paralegal professional's authority under the law.

Paralegals at Work

As a paralegal, you work for Mr. Nicholas Klapova, a lawyer who specializes in real estate law. As a paralegal in the area of real estate law, you often are assigned to conduct legal research on real estate law issues, and to draft documents and contracts that Mr. Klapova reviews. You also attend conferences with Mr. Klapova and his clients concerning property law issues.

One day Ms. Eve Trump, an existing client of the law firm, arrives at the law office for a meeting with Mr. Klapova. Mr. Klapova invites you to sit in on the initial meeting. At the meeting, Ms. Trump discloses the following information: She owns a 200-acre parcel of land that is beachfront property, with 3,000 front feet of beach at the property. Ms. Trump purchased the property 25 years ago for $250,000 when the property and the entire surrounding area was all vacant land. Ms. Trump has been approached by a real estate developer who wants to buy the property from her for $7,000,000. The developer wants to develop the property and build a resort hotel.

Ms. Trump states that she would like to sell the property. She continues to disclose the following facts: Her property currently is zoned for single-family residences. Many of the large vacant properties in the area have been sold and developed as individual housing tracts over the past 10 years. Ms. Trump explains that when she purchased the property 25 years ago, an old fence line separated her property and the 100-acre beachfront property owned by Mrs. Lorraine Gasper on the west side of Ms. Trump's property. Upon conducting a recent survey, it was determined that the fence line encroaches upon Ms. Trump's property by 120 feet. The proposed purchaser wants the 120 feet to be included in the purchase.

521

Ms. Trump also explains that about 10 years ago when the owner of the 150-acre parcel of beachfront property to the east of her property was purchased by Clive Jones, he asked if he could continue to use an existing dirt road over Ms. Trump's property to reach his property that the prior owner of his property had used for 20 years. The dirt road runs from the highway that is north of Ms. Trump's, Mrs. Gasper's, and Mr. Jones's properties. The south side of each of the three properties is the lake and beach. The dirt road runs from the highway beginning about one-third of the way from the east lot line with Mr. Jones, traverses across Ms. Trump's property, and arrives at the front of Mr. Jones's property at the beach on Mr. Jones's property about 20 feet across the lot line with Ms. Trump's property. The neighbor and Ms. Trump have no formal written agreement, however.

Ms. Trump asks Mr. Klapova to look into these matters for her and to advise her if she has any legal problems concerning the proposed sale of her property. Consider the issues involved in this scenario as you read the chapter.

INTRODUCTION FOR THE PARALEGAL

Private ownership of property forms the foundation of our economic system. As such, a comprehensive body of law has been developed to protect property rights. The law protects the right of property owners to use, sell, dispose of, control, and prevent others from trespassing on their rights.

This chapter discusses the kinds of personal property, methods of acquiring ownership in personal property, and property rights in mislaid, lost, and abandoned property. Sometimes persons entrust their property to others for transport or safekeeping, a situation that could create a bailment. The law of bailment of personal property is covered in this chapter.

Property and ownership rights in real property play an important part in the U.S. society and economy. Individuals and families own houses, farmers and ranchers own farmland and ranches, and businesses own commercial and office buildings. The concept of real property is concerned with the legal rights to the property rather than the physical attributes of the tangible land. Other rights in real property, such as mineral and air rights, are also covered in this chapter.

Although the United States has the most advanced private property system in the world, the ownership and possession of real estate are not free from government regulation. Pursuant to constitutional authority, federal, state, and local governments have enacted myriad laws that regulate the ownership, possession, lease, and use of real property. These laws include zoning laws and other laws.

Individuals and families rent houses and apartments, professionals and businesses lease office space, small businesses rent stores, and businesses lease commercial and manufacturing facilities. In these situations, a landlord–tenant relationship is created. The party who owns or controls the leased space is called the lessor and the party who is renting the space is called the lessee. The contract between them is called a lease. The parties to a landlord–tenant relationship have certain legal rights and duties that are governed by a mixture of real estate and contract law.

The ownership and possession of real estate in the United States is commonly a private affair. However, the ownership and leasing of real property is not free from government regulation. For example, the government may also take private property for public use under its power of eminent domain, assuming that certain requirements are met and just compensation is paid to the owner.

CAREER OPPORTUNITIES FOR PARALEGALS IN PROPERTY LAW

Many paralegal professionals work in positions for lawyers who practice in the area of real estate law. Most real estate law is state law and, therefore, is state-specific. In addition to having general knowledge of real estate law, then, paralegals must have significant knowledge of the intricacies of the real estate law of the state in which they work.

A paralegal often is involved in drafting and completing documents for real estate transactions. This includes the purchase and sale of single-family houses, condominiums, cooperatives, and other housing units. Although the buyer and the seller usually use real estate brokers to represent them, lawyers often are involved in representing clients in these transactions. The paralegal must know the specific documents required in these transactions.

Lawyers, and therefore their paralegals, often are involved in the purchase, sale, or transfer of vacant real property. This might involve a single buyer or multiple buyers. In these transactions, paralegals usually are called upon to prepare documents and otherwise assist the lawyers on both the seller's and the buyer's side in completing the transaction.

Paralegals frequently are called upon to use their expertise in complex real estate transactions. These include transactions where a developer is going to develop an entire housing tract, shopping mall, office building, or commercial building. Each of these types of development requires substantial work by lawyers representing clients on both sides of the transaction. These real estate transactions require paralegals to also have knowledge of the complex real estate law.

Another facet of real estate law in which paralegals assist lawyers is the area of leasing. Some leases are simple—for example, the lease of an apartment. The lawyer for the owner of the property usually drafts the lease for the landowner. Other leases are extremely complex. For example, leases on large office building space and commercial properties are negotiated individually by both sides, usually using their lawyers. The lawyers then draft the leases and other documents necessary to complete an agreed-upon lease transaction. Paralegals often assist lawyers in representing clients in these complicated lease transactions.

Paralegals who work in the real estate area often acquire expertise in specific types of real estate transactions. Many paralegals learn the intricate procedures, documents, and law that are necessary to complete real estate transactions handled by the lawyers for whom they work.

Many lawyers practice in the area of real estate law. A paralegal often is called upon to assist an attorney in preparing the necessary documents for the sale of real property and for the recording of transfers of real property.

This chapter covers the topics of personal property, real property, landlord–tenant relationships, and land-use regulation.

Personal Property

The two kinds of property are real property and personal property.

1. Real property includes land and property that is permanently attached to it.

   Examples Minerals, crops, timber, and buildings that are attached to land are generally considered real property.

2. **Personal property** (sometimes referred to as *goods* or *chattels*) consists of everything that is not real property.

> **Personal property** Tangible property such as automobiles, furniture, and equipment, and intangible property such as securities, patents, and copyrights.

Personal property can be either tangible or intangible. **Tangible property** includes physically defined property, such as goods, animals, and minerals. **Intangible property** represents rights that cannot be reduced to physical form, such as stock certificates, certificates of deposit, bonds, and copyrights.

Personal property that is permanently affixed to land or buildings is called a *fixture*. Such property, which includes things such as heating systems and storm windows, is categorized as real property. Unless otherwise agreed, fixtures remain with a building when it is sold. Personal property (e.g., furniture, pictures, and other easily portable household items) may be removed by the seller prior to sale. Real property can become personal property if it is removed from the land.

Example   A tree that is part of a forest is real property; a tree that is cut down is personal property.

Purchase or Production

The most common method of acquiring title to personal property is by *purchasing* the property from its owner.

Example   Urban Concrete Corporation owns a large piece of equipment. City Builders, Inc., purchases the equipment from Urban Concrete for $50,000. Urban Concrete signs the title to the equipment to City Builders. City Builders is now the owner of the equipment.

Production is another common method of acquiring ownership in personal property. Thus, a manufacturer that purchases raw materials and produces a finished product owns that product.

Gift

Gift A voluntary transfer of title to property without payment of consideration by the donee. To be a valid gift, three elements must be shown: (1) *donative intent,* (2) *delivery,* and (3) *acceptance.*

Donor A person who gives a gift.

Donee A person who receives a gift.

A **gift** is a voluntary transfer of property without consideration. The lack of consideration is what distinguishes a gift from a purchase. The person making a gift is called the **donor**. The person who receives the gift is called the **donee**. The three elements of a valid gift are:

1. *Donative Intent.* For a gift to be effective, the donor must have intended to make a gift. Donative intent can be inferred from the circumstances or language used by the donor. The courts also consider factors such as relationship of the parties, size of the gift, and mental capacity of the donor.
2. *Delivery.* Delivery must occur for there to be a valid gift. Although *physical delivery* is the usual method of transferring personal property, it sometimes is impracticable. In such circumstances, *constructive delivery* (or *symbolic delivery*) is sufficient.

   Example   If the property being gifted is kept in a safe-deposit box, physically giving the key to the donee is enough to signal the gift. Most intangible property is transferred by written conveyance (e.g., conveying a stock certificate represents a transfer of ownership in a corporation).

3. *Acceptance.* Acceptance usually is not a problem because most donees readily accept gifts. In fact, the courts presume acceptance unless there is proof that the gift was refused. Nevertheless, a person cannot be forced to accept an unwanted gift.

A gift made during a person's lifetime that is an irrevocable present transfer of ownership is a **gift *inter vivos***. A **gift *causa mortis*** is a gift made in contemplation of death. A gift *causa mortis* is established when (1) the donor makes a gift in anticipation of approaching death from some existing sickness or peril and (2) the donor dies from such sickness or peril without having revoked the gift. A gift *causa mortis* can be revoked by the donor up until the time he or she dies. A gift *causa mortis* takes precedence over a prior conflicting will.

Example   Suppose Sandy is a patient in the hospital. She is to have a major operation from which she may not recover. Prior to going into surgery, Sandy removes her diamond ring and gives it to her friend Pamela, stating, "In the event of my death, I want you to have this." This gift is a gift *causa mortis*. If Sandy dies from the operation, the gift is effective and Pamela owns the ring. If Sandy lives, the requisite condition for the gift (her death) has not occurred; therefore, the gift is not effective, and Sandy can recover the ring from Pamela.

Uniform Gift to Minors Act

All states have adopted in whole or part the **Uniform Gift to Minors Act** or the **Revised Uniform Gift to Minors Act**. These laws establish procedures for adults to make irrevocable gifts of money and securities to minors. Gifts of money can be made by depositing the money in an account in a financial institution with the donor or another trustee (such as another adult or bank) as custodian for the minor. Gifts of securities can be made by registering the securities in the name of a trustee as custodian for the minor. The laws give custodians broad discretionary powers to invest the money or securities for the benefit of the minor.

Uniform Gift to Minors Act or **Revised Uniform Gift to Minors Act** Acts that establish procedures for adults to make gifts of money and securities to minors.

Will or Inheritance

Title to personal property is frequently acquired by **will** or **inheritance**. If the person who dies has a valid will, the property is distributed to the **beneficiaries** pursuant to the provisions of that will. Otherwise the property is distributed to the **heirs**, as provided in the relevant state's inheritance statute.

Mislaid Property

Property is called **mislaid property** when its owner voluntarily places the property somewhere and then inadvertently forgets it. It is likely that the owner will return for the property upon realizing that it was misplaced.

The owner of the premises where the property is mislaid is entitled to take possession of the property against all except the rightful owner. This right is superior to the rights of the person who finds it. Such possession does not involve a change of title. Instead, the owner of the premises becomes an involuntary bailee of the property (bailments are discussed later in this chapter) and owes a duty to take reasonable care of the property until it is reclaimed by the owner.

Mislaid property Property that an owner voluntarily places somewhere and then inadvertently forgets.

> **Example** Suppose Felicity is on a business trip and stays in a hotel during her trip. Felicity accidentally leaves her diamond engagement ring in the hotel room she has stayed in and checks out of the hotel. The engagement ring is mislaid property, and the hotel has a duty to return it to Felicity, its rightful owner.

Lost Property

Property is considered **lost property** when its owner negligently, carelessly, or inadvertently leaves it somewhere. The finder obtains title to such property against the whole world except the true owner. The lost property must be returned to its rightful owner, whether he or she discovers the loser's identity or the loser finds him or her. A finder who refuses to return the property is liable for the tort of conversion and the crime of larceny. Many states require the finder to conduct a reasonable search (e.g., place advertisements in newspapers) to find the rightful owner.

Lost property Property that the owner leaves somewhere because of negligence, carelessness, or inadvertence.

> **Example** If a commuter finds a laptop computer on the floor of a subway station in New York City, the computer is considered lost property. The finder can claim title to the computer against the whole world except the true owner. If the true owner discovers that the finder has her computer, she may recover it from the finder. If there is identification of the owner on the computer (e.g., name, address, and telephone number), the finder owes a duty to contact the rightful owner and give back the computer.

Estray Statutes

Most states have enacted **estray statutes** that permit a finder of *mislaid* or *lost* property to clear title to the property if:

1. The finder reports the found property to the appropriate government agency and then turns over possession of the property to this agency,

Web Exploration

Use www.google.com to find the estray statute or other law in your state that applies to finding of personal property. If there is an estray statute, what requirements must be met and what is the waiting period?

2. Either the finder or the government agency posts notices and publishes advertisements describing the lost property, and

3. A specified time (usually a year or a number of years) has passed without the rightful owner's reclaiming the property.

Many state estray statutes require that the government receive a portion of the value of the property. Some statutes provide that title cannot be acquired in found property that is the result of illegal activity.

Example Title has been denied to finders of property and money deemed to have been used for illegal drug purchases.

Abandoned Property

Property is classified as **abandoned property** if (1) an owner discards the property with the intent to relinquish his or her rights in it or (2) an owner of mislaid or lost property gives up any further attempts to locate it. Anyone who finds abandoned property acquires title to it. The title is good against the whole world, including the original owner.

Example Property left at a garbage dump is abandoned property. It belongs to the first person who claims it.

Bailment

A **bailment** occurs when the owner of personal property delivers his or her property to another person to be held, stored, or delivered, or for some other purpose. In a bailment, the owner of the property is the **bailor** and the party to whom the property is delivered for safekeeping, storage, or delivery (e.g., warehouse or common carrier) is the **bailee** (see Exhibit 14.1).

A bailment is different from a sale or a gift because title to the goods does not transfer to the bailee. Instead, the bailee must follow the bailor's directions concerning the goods.

Example Suppose Hudson Corp. is relocating its offices and hires American Van Lines to move its office furniture and equipment to the new location. American Van Lines (the bailee) must follow Hudson's (the bailor) instructions regarding delivery. The law of bailments establishes the rights, duties, and liabilities of parties to a bailment.

Mutual Benefit Bailments

Mutual benefit bailments are bailments that *benefit both parties*. The bailee owes a **duty of reasonable care**, or **ordinary care**, to protect the bailed goods. This means that the bailee is liable for any goods that are lost, damaged, or destroyed because of his or her negligence.

SIDEBAR

MISLAID, LOST, AND ABANDONED PROPERTY

Type of Property	Ownership Rights
Mislaid property	The owner of the premises where property is mislaid is entitled to possession but does not acquire title. He or she holds the property as an involuntary bailor until the owner reclaims it.
Lost property	The finder acquires title to the property against the whole world except the true owner; the owner may reclaim his or her property from the finder.
Abandoned property	The finder acquires title to the property, even against its original owner.

Bailment A transaction in which an owner transfers his or her personal property to another to be held, stored, delivered, or for some other purpose. Title to the property does not transfer.

Bailor The owner of property in a bailment.

Bailee A holder of goods who is not a seller or a buyer (e.g., a warehouse or common carrier).

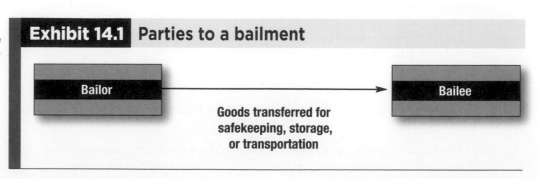

Exhibit 14.1 **Parties to a bailment**

Bailor → Bailee

Goods transferred for safekeeping, storage, or transportation

Example   Suppose ABC Garment Co. delivers goods to Lowell, Inc., a commercial warehouse, for storage. A fee is charged for this service. ABC Garment Co. receives the benefit of having its goods stored, and Lowell, Inc., receives the benefit of being paid compensation for storing the goods. In this example, Lowell, Inc. (the bailee) owes a duty of ordinary care to protect the goods.

Real property The land itself as well as buildings, trees, soil, minerals, timber, plants, and other things permanently affixed to the land.

Real Property

Property and ownership rights in real property play an important part in this country's society and economy. Individuals and families own or rent houses, farmers and ranchers own farmland and ranches, and businesses own or lease commercial and office buildings. **Real property** includes the following:

1. *Land and buildings.* **Land** is the most common form of real property. A landowner usually purchases the **surface rights** to the land—that is, the right to occupy the land. The owner may use, enjoy, and develop the property as he or she sees fit, subject to any applicable government regulations.

   Examples   **Buildings** constructed on land—such as houses, apartment buildings, manufacturing plants, and office buildings—are real property. Things such as radio towers, bridges, and the like are considered real property as well.

2. *Subsurface rights.* The owner of land possesses **subsurface rights** (or **mineral rights**), to the earth located beneath the surface of the land. These rights can be valuable.

   Examples   Gold, uranium, oil, or natural gas may lie beneath the surface of land. Theoretically, mineral rights extend to the center of the earth. In reality, mines and oil wells usually extend only several miles into the earth. Subsurface rights may be sold separately from surface rights.

3. *Plant life and vegetation.* **Plant life and vegetation** growing on the surface of land are considered real property. This includes natural plant life (e.g., trees) and cultivated plant life (e.g., crops). When land is sold, any plant life growing on the land is included unless the parties agree otherwise. Plant life that is severed from the land is considered personal property.

4. *Fixtures.* Certain personal property is associated so closely with real property that it becomes part of the realty. These items are called **fixtures**.

   Examples   Kitchen cabinets, carpeting, and doorknobs are fixtures, but throw rugs and furniture are personal property. Unless otherwise provided, if a building is sold, the fixtures are included in the sale. If the sale agreement is silent as to whether an item is a fixture, the courts make their determinations on the basis of whether the item can be removed without causing substantial damage to the realty.

AIR RIGHTS

SIDEBAR

Common law provided that the owners of real property owned that property from the center of the earth to the heavens. This rule has been eroded by modern legal restrictions such as land-use control laws, environmental protection laws, and air navigation requirements. Even today, however, the owners of land may sell or lease air space parcels above their land.

An **air-space parcel** is a three-dimensional cube of air above the surface of the earth. Air-space parcels are valuable property rights, particularly in densely populated metropolitan areas where building property is scarce.

Example   Many developments have been built in air-space parcels in New York City. The most notable are Madison Square Garden and Two Penn Plaza, which were built in air-space parcels above Penn Station.

Freehold Estates in Land

A person's ownership rights in real property are called an **estate in land**, or **estate**. An estate is defined as the bundle of *legal rights* that the owner has to possess, use, and enjoy the property. The type of estate that an owner possesses is determined from the deed, will, lease, or other document that transferred the ownership rights to him or her.

A **freehold estate** is one in which the owner has a *present possessory interest* in the real property; that is, the owner may use and enjoy the property as he or she sees fit, subject to any applicable government regulation or private restraint. The two types of freehold estates are *estates in fee* and *life estates*, which are discussed in the following paragraphs.

Fixtures Goods that are affixed to real estate so as to become part thereof.

Estate (estate in land) Ownership rights in real property; the bundle of legal rights of the owner to possess, use, and enjoy the property.

Freehold estate An estate in which the owner has a present possessory interest in the real property.

Fee simple absolute (fee simple) A type of ownership of real property that grants the owner the fullest bundle of legal rights that a person can hold in real property.

Fee simple defeasible (qualified fee) A type of ownership of real property that grants the owner all the incidents of a fee simple absolute except that it may be taken away if a specified condition occurs or does not occur.

Life estate An interest in land for a person's lifetime; upon that person's death, the interest will be transferred to another party.

FREEHOLD ESTATES

Estate	Description
Fee simple absolute	Is the highest form of ownership of real property. Ownership (1) is infinite in duration, (2) has no limitation on inheritability, and (3) does not end upon the occurrence or nonoccurrence of an event.
Fee simple defeasible	Grants the owner all the incidents of a fee simple absolute except that it may be taken away if a specified condition occurs or does not occur.
Life estate	Is an interest in property that lasts for the life of a specified person. A life estate terminates upon the death of the named person and reverts back to the grantor or his or her estate or other designated person.

Estates in Fee

A **fee simple absolute** (or **fee simple**) is the highest form of ownership of real property because it grants the owner the fullest bundle of legal rights that a person can hold in real property. This **estate in fee** is the type of ownership that most people connect with "owning" real property. A fee simple owner has the right to exclusively possess and use his or her property to the extent that the owner has not transferred any interest in the property (e.g., by lease).

A **fee simple defeasible**, or **qualified fee**, grants the owner all the incidents of a fee simple absolute except that it may be taken away if a specified *condition* occurs or does not occur.

Example A conveyance of property to a church "as long as the land is used as a church or for church purposes" creates a qualified fee. The church has all of the rights of an owner of a fee simple absolute except that its ownership rights are terminated if the property is no longer used for church purposes.

Life Estate

A **life estate** is an interest in real property that lasts for the life of a specified person, usually the grantee.

Example A conveyance of real property "to Anna for her life" creates a life estate. A life estate also may be measured by the life of a third party (e.g., "to Anna for the life of Benjamin"). This is called an **estate *pur autre vie***. A life estate may be defeasible (e.g., "to John for his life, but only if he continues to occupy this residence"). Upon the death of named person, the life estate terminates and the property reverts to the grantor or the grantor's estate or other designated person.

A life tenant is treated as the owner of the property during the duration of the life estate. He or she has the right to possess and use the property except to the extent that it would cause permanent *waste* of the property. A life tenant may sell, transfer, or mortgage his or her estate in the land. The mortgage, however, cannot exceed the duration of the life estate. A life tenant is obligated to keep the property in repair and to pay property taxes.

Future Interests

A person may be given the right to possess property in the *future* rather than in the present. This right is called a **future interest**. The two forms of future interests are *reversion* and *remainder* (see Exhibit 14.2).

1. *Reversion.* A **reversion** is a right of possession that returns to the *grantor* after the expiration of a limited or contingent estate. Reversions do not have to be stated expressly because they arise automatically by law.

   Example If a grantor conveys property "to M. R. Harrington for life," the grantor has retained a reversion in the property. That is, when Harrington dies, the property reverts to the grantor or, if he or she is not living, then to his or her estate.

2. *Remainder.* If the right of possession returns to a *third party* upon the expiration of a limited or contingent estate, it is called a **remainder**. The person who is entitled to the future interest is called a **remainderman**.

   Example A conveyance of property "to Joe for life, remainder to Meredith" is a vested remainder—the only contingency to Meredith's possessory interest is Joe's death.

Exhibit 14.2 Future interests

Concurrent Ownership

When two or more persons own a piece of real property, it is called **co-ownership** or **concurrent ownership**. The following forms of co-ownership are recognized: *joint tenancy, tenancy in common, tenancy by the entirety, community property.* These are each discussed in the following paragraphs.

Joint Tenancy

To create a **joint tenancy**, words that clearly show a person's intent to create a joint tenancy must be used. Language such as "Marsha Leest and James Leest, as joint tenants" is usually sufficient. The most distinguishing feature of a joint tenancy is the co-owners' **right of survivorship**. This means that upon the death of one of the co-owners or **joint tenants** the deceased person's interest in the property passes automatically to the surviving joint tenants. Any contrary provision in the deceased's will is ineffective.

> **Example** Jones, one of four people who own a piece of property in joint tenancy, executes a will leaving all of his property to a university. Jones dies. The surviving joint tenants—not the university—acquire his interest in the piece of property. Each joint tenant has a right to sell or transfer his or her interest in the property, but such conveyance terminates the joint tenancy. The parties then become tenants in common.

Tenancy in Common

In a **tenancy in common**, the interests of a surviving **tenant in common** pass to the deceased tenant's estate and not to the co-tenants. A tenancy in common may be created by express words, such as "Iran Cespedes and Joy Park, as tenants in common." Unless otherwise agreed, a tenant in common can sell, give, devise, or otherwise transfer his or her interest in the property without the consent of the other co-owners.

> **Example** Lopez, one of four tenants in common who own a piece of property, has a will that leaves all of his property to his granddaughter. When Lopez dies, the granddaughter receives his interest in the tenancy in common, and the granddaughter becomes a tenant in common with the three other owners.

A co-tenancy is presumed to be a tenancy in common if it is not clear that the co-tenancy is a joint tenancy.

Tenancy by the Entirety

Tenancy by the entirety is a form of co-ownership of real property that can be used only by married couples. This type of tenancy must be created by express words, such as "Harold Jones and Maude Jones, husband and wife, as tenants by the entireties." A surviving spouse has the right of survivorship.

Future interest The interest that the grantor retains for him- or herself or a third party.

Reversion A right of possession that returns to the grantor after the expiration of a limited or contingent estate.

Remainder (remainderman) A right of possession that returns to a third party upon the expiration of a limited or contingent estate.

FUTURE INTERESTS

Future Interest	Description
Reversion	Right to possession of real property returns to the grantor after the expiration of a limited or contingent estate.
Remainder	Right to possession of real property goes to a third person upon the expiration of a limited or contingent estate.

SIDEBAR

Co-ownership (concurrent ownership) A situation in which two or more persons own a piece of real property. Also called *concurrent ownership*.

Joint tenancy A form of co-ownership that includes the right of survivorship.

Tenancy in common A form of co-ownership in which the interest of a surviving tenant in common passes to the deceased tenant's estate and not to the co-tenants.

Tenancy by the entirety A form of co-ownership of real property that can be used only by married couples.

ETHICAL PERSPECTIVE

Paralegal's Duty to Act Carefully When Preparing Legal Documents

Ms. Webster is a paralegal professional who works for Mr. Anderson, an attorney who practices law in a small, rural town. Ms. Susan White and Mr. Mark Smith, who were recently married, come to Mr. Anderson's office to see him about having a new deed drawn up for a piece of real estate owned by Ms. White prior to marriage. They explain that Ms. White inherited the property prior to their marriage and that the real estate deed to the property is currently in her name only. Ms. White wants to place the name of Mr. Smith, her new husband, on the deed so as to make them joint tenant owners of the property with the right to survivorship. Mr. Anderson agrees to do so.

Mr. Anderson explains the situation to Ms. Webster and assigns Ms. Webster the task to prepare a new deed that accomplishes the intended result. Ms. Webster prepares the deed but when Mr. Anderson reviews the deed he discovers that the deed states, "Ms. Susan White and Mr. Mark Smith, co-tenants." Because this language is unclear that there is a joint tenancy, if it were signed by Ms. White it would create a tenancy in common with Mr. Smith instead of a joint tenancy. Mr. Anderson has Ms. Webster prepare a new deed that correctly states, "Ms. Susan White and Mr. Mark Smith, joint tenants."

A paralegal owes an ethical duty to be careful when he or she is preparing legal documents to make sure that they are completed properly. This example shows how important it is for a paralegal to carefully prepare documents and to proofread the documents to make sure that they are correct before giving them to the supervising attorney for review.

Tenancy by the entirety is distinguished from a joint tenancy in that neither spouse may sell or transfer his or her interest in the property without the other spouse's consent. Only about half of the states recognize a tenancy by the entirety.

Community Property

Nine states—Arizona, California, Idaho, Louisiana, Nevada, New Mexico, Texas, Washington, and Wisconsin—recognize a form of co-ownership known as **community property**. This method of co-ownership applies only to married couples and is based on the notion that a husband and wife should share equally in the fruits of the marital partnership.

Community property A form of ownership in which each spouse owns an equal one-half share of the income of both spouses and the assets acquired during the marriage.

Under these laws, each spouse owns an equal one-half share of the income of both spouses and the assets acquired during the marriage regardless of who earns the income. Property that is acquired through gift or inheritance either before or during marriage remains separate property.

When a spouse dies, the surviving spouse automatically receives one-half the community property. The other half passes to the heirs of the deceased spouse as directed by will or by state intestate statute if there is no will.

During the marriage, neither spouse can sell, transfer, or gift community property without the consent of the other spouse. Upon a divorce, each spouse has a right to one-half of the community property.

The location of the real property determines whether community property law applies. For example, if a married couple who lives in a non–community property state purchases real property located in a community property state, community property laws apply to that property.

Example A husband and wife have community property assets of $1.5 million and the wife dies with a will. The husband automatically has a right to receive $750,000 of the community property. The remaining $750,000 passes as directed by the wife's will. Any separate property owned by the wife, such as jewelry she inherited, also passes in accordance with her will. Her husband has no vested interest in that property.

Other Forms of Ownership

Condominium

The **condominium** is a common form of ownership in multiple-dwelling buildings. Purchasers of a condominium (1) have title to their individual units, and (2) own the common areas (e.g., hallways, elevators, parking areas, and recreational facilities) as tenants in common with the other owners. Owners may sell or mortgage their units without the permission of the other owners. Owners are assessed monthly fees for maintenance of common areas. In addition to dwelling units, the condominium form of ownership is offered for office buildings, boat docks, and such.

Cooperative

A **cooperative** is a form of co-ownership of a multiple-dwelling building in which a corporation owns the building and the residents own shares in the corporation. Each cooperative owner then leases a unit in the building from the corporation under a renewable, long-term, proprietary lease. Individual residents may not secure loans with the units they occupy. The corporation may borrow money on a blanket mortgage, and each shareholder is jointly and severally liable on the loan. Usually, cooperative owners may not sell their shares or sublease their units without the approval of the other owners.

Transfer of Ownership of Real Property

Ownership of real property may be transferred from one person to another. Title to real property may be transferred by sale, tax sale, gift, will, or inheritance. **Deeds** are used to convey real property by sale or gift. The seller or donor is called the **grantor**. The buyer or recipient is called the **grantee**. A deed may be used to transfer a fee simple absolute interest in real property or any lesser estate (e.g., life estate).

State laws recognize different types of deeds that provide differing degrees of protection to grantees. A **warranty deed** contains the greatest number of warranties and provides the most protection to grantees. A **quitclaim deed** provides the least amount of protection because the grantor conveys only whatever interest he or she has in the property.

Sale of Real Estate

A **sale** or conveyance is the most common method for transferring ownership rights in real property. An agreement for the sale of real property under the state Statute of Frauds must be in writing to be enforceable. Exhibit 14.3 shows the parties to a real estate sale. The seller delivers a deed to the buyer and the buyer pays the purchase price at the closing or settlement.

CONCURRENT OWNERSHIP

Form of Ownership	Right of Survivorship	Tenant May Unilaterally Transfer His or Her Interest
Joint tenancy	Yes, deceased tenant's interest automatically passes to co-tenants.	Yes, tenant may transfer his or her interest without the consent of co-tenants. Transfer severs joint tenancy.
Tenancy in common	No, deceased tenant's interest passes to his or her estate.	Yes, tenant may transfer his or her interest without the consent of co-tenants. Transfer does not sever tenancy in common.
Tenancy by the entirety	Yes, deceased tenant's interest passes to his or her estate.	No, neither spouse may transfer his or her interest without the other spouses's consent.
Community property	Yes, when a spouse dies, the surviving spouse automatically receives one-half of the community property. The other half passes to the heirs of the deceased spouse, as directed by a valid will or by state intestate statute if there is no will.	No, neither spouse may transfer his or her interest without the other spouse's consent.

Condominium A common form of ownership in a multiple-dwelling building in which the purchaser has title to the individual unit and owns the common areas as a tenant in common with the other condominium owners.

Cooperative A form of co-ownership of a multiple-dwelling building in which a corporation owns the building and the residents own shares in the corporation.

Deed A writing that describes a person's ownership interest in a piece of real property.

Grantor The party who transfers an ownership interest in real property.

Grantee The party to whom an interest in real property is transferred.

Sale The passing of title from a seller to a buyer for a price. Also called a *conveyance*.

Exhibit 14.3 Parties and documents in a real estate transaction

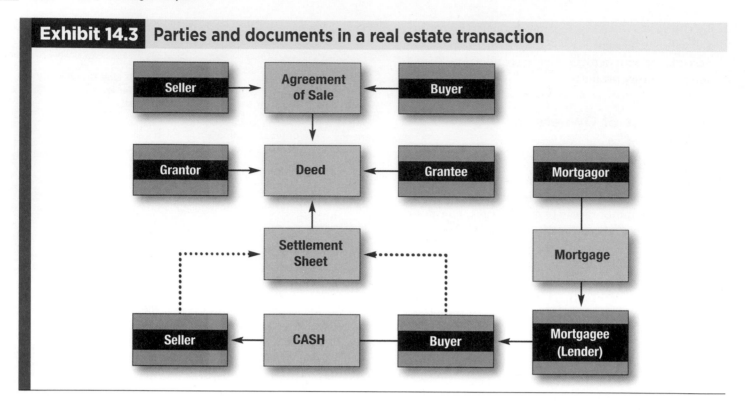

A copy of an agreement form for the sale of real estate is set forth in Exhibit 14.4. A **settlement statement** is shown in Exhibit 14.5.

Recording Statutes

Recording statute A state statute that requires a mortgage or deed of trust to be recorded in the county recorder's office of the county in which the real property is located.

Every state has a **recording statute** that provides that copies of deeds and other documents concerning interests in real property (e.g., mortgages, liens, easements) may be filed in a government office where they become public records open to viewing by the public. Recording statutes are intended to prevent fraud and to establish certainty in the ownership and transfer of property. Instruments usually are filed in the *county recorder's office* of the county in which the property is located. A fee is charged to record an instrument.

Persons interested in purchasing the property or lending on the property check these records to determine if the grantor or borrower actually owns the property and whether any other parties (e.g., lienholders, mortgages, easement holders) have an interest in the property. The recordation of a deed is not required to pass title from the grantor to the grantee. Recording the deed gives *constructive notice* to the world of the owner's interest in the property.

Quiet title action An action brought by a party seeking an order of the court declaring who has title to disputed property. By its decision, the court "quiets title."

A party who is concerned about his or her ownership rights in a parcel of real property can bring a **quiet title action** to have a court determine the extent of those rights. Public notice of the hearing must be given so that anyone claiming an interest in the property may appear and be heard. After the hearing, the judge declares who has title to the property—that is the court "quiets title" by its decision.

Registrar of Deeds

Records of all transfers of real estate, claims against real estate, and the form of mortgages and means are generally maintained in a separate office under the direction of the Registrar, or Recorder, of Deeds. The **Registrar of Deeds** may be an elected or appointed official and is responsible for recording documents related to the transfer of real estate, and documents related to claims against property in the form of mortgages and liens. These records may be hardcopy or electronic copies, or a combination.

Exhibit 14.4 Agreement for the sale of real property

STANDARD AGREEMENT FOR THE SALE OF REAL ESTATE   A/S-R

This form recommended and approved for, but not restricted to use by, the members of the Pennsylvania Association of REALTORS® (PAR).

SELLER'S BUSINESS RELATIONSHIP WITH PA LICENSED BROKER

BROKER (Company)_____ PHONE _____
ADDRESS_____ FAX _____
LICENSEE(S) _____ Designated Agent? ☐ Yes ☐ No
BROKER IS THE AGENT FOR SELLER.   OR (if checked below):
Broker is NOT the Agent for Seller and is a/an: ☐ AGENT FOR BUYER   ☐ TRANSACTION LICENSEE

BUYER'S BUSINESS RELATIONSHIP WITH PA LICENSED BROKER

BROKER (Company)_____ PHONE _____
ADDRESS_____ FAX _____
LICENSEE(S) _____ Designated Agent? ☐ Yes ☐ No
BROKER IS THE AGENT FOR BUYER.   OR (if checked below):
Broker is NOT the Agent for Buyer and is a/an: ☐ AGENT FOR SELLER ☐ SUBAGENT FOR SELLER ☐ TRANSACTION LICENSEE

When the same Broker is Agent for Seller and Agent for Buyer, Broker is a Dual Agent. All of Broker's licensees are also Dual Agents UNLESS there are separate Designated Agents for Buyer and Seller. If the same Licensee is designated for Seller and Buyer, the Licensee is a Dual Agent.

1. **This Agreement,** dated _____, is between

   SELLER(S): _____
   _____, called "Seller," and
   BUYER(S): _____
   _____, called "Buyer."

2. **PROPERTY (9-05)** Seller hereby agrees to sell and convey to Buyer, who hereby agrees to purchase:
   ALL THAT CERTAIN lot or piece of ground with buildings and improvements thereon erected, if any, known as:
   _____ in the _____ of _____
   County of _____ in the Commonwealth of Pennsylvania. Identification (e.g., Tax ID #; Parcel #;
   Lot, Block; Deed Book, Page, Recording Date): _____

3. **TERMS (9-05)**
   (A) Purchase Price _____
   _____ U.S. Dollars,
   which will be paid to Seller by Buyer as follows:
   1. Cash or check at signing this Agreement: $ _____
   2. Cash or check within ____ days of the execution of this Agreement: _____ $ _____
   3. _____ $ _____
   4. Cash or cashier's check at time of settlement: $ _____
   TOTAL $ _____
   (B) Deposits paid by Buyer within __50__ DAYS of settlement will be by cash or cashier's check. Deposits, regardless of the form of payment and the person designated as payee, will be paid in U.S. Dollars to Broker for Seller (unless otherwise stated here), _____, who will retain deposits in an escrow account until consummation or termination of this Agreement in conformity with all applicable laws and regulations. Any check tendered as deposit monies may be held uncashed pending the acceptance of this Agreement.
   (C) Seller's written approval to be on or before: _____
   (D) Settlement to be on _____, or before if Buyer and Seller agree.
   (E) Settlement will occur in the county where the Property is located or in an adjacent county, during normal business hours, unless Buyer and Seller agree otherwise.
   (F) Conveyance from Seller will be by fee simple deed of special warranty unless otherwise stated here: _____
   (G) Payment of transfer taxes will be divided equally between Buyer and Seller unless otherwise stated here: _____
   (H) At time of settlement, the following will be adjusted pro-rata on a daily basis between Buyer and Seller, reimbursing where applicable: current taxes (see Information Regarding Real Estate Taxes); rents; interest on mortgage assumptions; condominium fees and homeowner association fees; water and/or sewer fees, together with any other lienable municipal service. All charges will be pro-rated for the period(s) covered. Seller will pay up to and including the date of settlement and Buyer will pay for all days following settlement, unless otherwise stated here: _____

Buyer Initials: _____   A/S-R Page 1 of 10   Seller Initials: _____
Revised 9/05
COPYRIGHT PENNSYLVANIA ASSOCIATION OF REALTORS® 2005
9/05

Pennsylvania Association of REALTORS®

(continued)

Exhibit 14.4 Agreement for the sale of real property *(continued)*

4. FIXTURES & PERSONAL PROPERTY (9-05)

(A) INCLUDED in this sale are all existing items permanently installed in the Property, free of liens, including plumbing; heating; lighting fixtures (including chandeliers and ceiling fans); water treatment systems; pool and spa equipment; garage door openers and transmitters; television antennas; unpotted shrubbery, plantings and trees; any remaining heating and cooking fuels stored on the Property at the time of settlement; sump pumps; storage sheds; mailboxes; wall to wall carpeting; existing window screens, storm windows and screen/storm doors; window covering hardware, shades and blinds; awnings; built-in air conditioners; built-in appliances; and the range/oven unless otherwise stated. Also included: _____

(B) LEASED items (not owned by Seller): _____

_____

(C) EXCLUDED fixtures and items: _____

_____

5. DATES/TIME IS OF THE ESSENCE (9-05)

(A) The settlement date and all other dates and times referred to for the performance of any of the obligations of this Agreement are of the essence and are binding.

(B) For purposes of this Agreement, the number of days will be counted from the date of execution, excluding the day this Agreement was executed and including the last day of the time period. The Execution Date of this Agreement is the date when Buyer and Seller have indicated full acceptance of this Agreement by signing and/or initialing it. All changes to this Agreement should be initialed and dated.

(C) The settlement date is not extended by any other provision of this Agreement and may only be extended by mutual written agreement of the parties.

(D) Certain time periods are pre-printed in this Agreement as a convenience to the Buyer and Seller. All pre-printed time periods are negotiable and may be changed by striking out the pre-printed text and inserting a different time period acceptable to all parties.

6. MORTGAGE CONTINGENCY (9-05)

☐ WAIVED. This sale is NOT contingent on mortgage financing, although Buyer may still obtain mortgage financing.

☐ ELECTED.

(A) This sale is contingent upon Buyer obtaining mortgage financing as follows:

First Mortgage on the Property	**Second Mortgage on the Property**
Loan Amount $_____	Loan Amount $_____
Minimum Term _____ years	Minimum Term _____ years
Type of mortgage _____	Type of mortgage _____
Mortgage lender _____	Mortgage lender _____
Interest rate _____%; however, **Buyer agrees to accept the interest rate as may be committed by the mortgage lender,** not to exceed a maximum interest rate of _____%.	Interest rate _____%; however, **Buyer agrees to accept the interest rate as may be committed by the mortgage lender,** not to exceed a maximum interest rate of _____%.
Discount points, loan origination, loan placement and other fees charged by the lender as a percentage of the mortgage loan (excluding any mortgage insurance premiums or VA funding fee) not to exceed _____% (0% if not specified) of the mortgage loan.	Discount points, loan origination, loan placement and other fees charged by the lender as a percentage of the mortgage loan (excluding any mortgage insurance premiums or VA funding fee) not to exceed _____% (0% if not specified) of the mortgage loan.

The interest rate(s) and fee(s) provisions in paragraph 6 (A) are satisfied if the mortgage lender(s) gives Buyer the right to guarantee the interest rate(s) and fee(s) at or below the maximum levels stated. Buyer gives Seller the right, at Seller's sole option and as permitted by law and the mortgage lender(s), to contribute financially, without promise of reimbursement, to the Buyer and/or the mortgage lender(s) to make the above mortgage terms available to Buyer.

(B) Within _____ days (10 if not specified) from the Execution Date of this Agreement, Buyer will make a completed, written mortgage application for the mortgage terms stated above to the mortgage lender(s) identified in paragraph 6 (A), if any, otherwise to a responsible mortgage lender(s) of Buyer's choice. **Broker for Buyer, if any, otherwise Broker for Seller, is authorized to communicate with the mortgage lender(s) to assist in the mortgage loan process.**

(C) **Should Buyer furnish false or incomplete information to Seller, Broker(s), or the mortgage lender(s) concerning Buyer's legal or financial status, or fail to cooperate in good faith in processing the mortgage loan application, which results in the mortgage lender(s) refusing to approve a mortgage loan commitment, Buyer will be in default of this Agreement.**

(D) 1. **Mortgage commitment date:** _____. If Seller does not receive a copy of Buyer's mortgage commitment(s) by this date, **Buyer and Seller agree to extend the mortgage commitment date until Seller terminates this Agreement by written notice to Buyer.**

2. Upon receiving a mortgage commitment, Buyer will promptly deliver a copy of the commitment to Seller.

3. Seller may terminate this Agreement in writing after the mortgage commitment date, if the mortgage commitment(s):

   a. Is not valid until the date of settlement, OR

   b. Is conditioned upon the **sale and settlement of any other property,** OR

   c. Does not satisfy all the mortgage terms as stated in paragraph 6 (A), OR

   d. Contains any other condition not specified in this Agreement that is not satisfied and/or removed in writing by the mortgage lender(s) within __7__ DAYS after the **mortgage commitment date in paragraph 6 (D) (1),** other than those conditions that are customarily satisfied at or near settlement, such as obtaining insurance and confirming employment status.

4. If this Agreement is terminated pursuant to paragraphs 6 (D) (1) or (3), or the mortgage loan(s) is not obtained for settlement, all deposit monies will be returned to Buyer according to the terms of paragraph 30 and this Agreement will be VOID. Buyer will be responsible for any costs incurred by Buyer for any inspections or certifications obtained according to the terms of this Agreement, and any costs incurred by Buyer for: (1) Title search, title insurance and/or mechanics' lien insurance, or any fee for cancellation; (2) Flood insurance and/or fire insurance with extended coverage, mine subsidence insurance, or any fee for cancellation; (3) Appraisal fees and charges paid in advance to mortgage lender(s).

Buyer Initials: _____   A/S-R Page 2 of 10   Seller Initials: _____
Revised 9/05

Exhibit 14.5 Settlement statement

A. Settlement Statement

U.S. Department of Housing
and Urban Development

OMB Approval No. 2502-0265

B. Type of Loan

| 1. ☐ FHA 2. ☐ FmHA 3. ☐ Conv. Unins. | 6. File Number: | 7. Loan Number: | 8. Mortgage Insurance Case Number: |
| 4. ☐ VA 5. ☐ Conv. Ins. | | | |

C. Note: This form is furnished to give you a statement of actual settlement costs. Amounts paid to and by the settlement agent are shown. Items marked "(p.o.c.)" were paid outside the closing; they are shown here for informational purposes and are not included in the totals.

D. Name & Address of Borrower:	E. Name & Address of Seller:	F. Name & Address of Lender:
Ethan & Ariel Marshall 52 Moritz Way Anyplace, PA 55555	Sara and Natasha Elliot 138 Weisser Place Anyplace, PA 55555	4th National Bank OneSouth Main St. Newcity, PA 44444

G. Property Location:	H. Settlement Agent:	
1 Zollinger Way	Roberts	
	Place of Settlement: Newcity	I. Settlement Date: 08-19-2002

J. Summary of Borrower's Transaction		K. Summary of Seller's Transaction	
100. Gross Amount Due From Borrower		**400. Gross Amount Due To Seller**	
101. Contract sales price	150000	401. Contract sales price	150000
102. Personal property		402. Personal property	
103. Settlement charges to borrower (line 1400)	21000	403.	
104.		404.	
105.		405.	
Adjustments for items paid by seller in advance		**Adjustments for items paid by seller in advance**	
106. City/town taxes 08-19-2002 to 12-31-2002	650	406. City/town taxes 08-19-2002 to 12-31-2002	650
107. County taxes to		407. County taxes to	
108. Assessments to		408. Assessments to	
109.		409.	
110.		410.	
111.		411.	
112.		412.	
120. Gross Amount Due From Borrower	152750	**420. Gross Amount Due To Seller**	150650
200. Amounts Paid By Or In Behalf Of Borrower		**500. Reductions In Amount Due To Seller**	
201. Deposit or earnest money		501. Excess deposit (see instructions)	
202. Principal amount of new loan(s)		502. Settlement charges to seller (line 1400)	9000
203. Existing loan(s) taken subject to		503. Existing loan(s) taken subject to	
204.		504. Payoff of first mortgage loan	75000
205.		505. Payoff of second mortgage loan	
206.		506.	
207.		507.	
208.		508.	
209.		509.	
Adjustments for items unpaid by seller		**Adjustments for items unpaid by seller**	
210. City/town taxes to		510. City/town taxes to	
211. County taxes to		511. County taxes to	
212. Assessments to		512. Assessments to	
213.		513.	
214.		514.	
215.		515.	
216.		516.	
217.		517.	
218.		518.	
219.		519.	
220. Total Paid By/For Borrower	135000	**520. Total Reduction Amount Due Seller**	84000
300. Cash At Settlement From/To Borrower		**600. Cash At Settlement To/From Seller**	
301. Gross Amount due from borrower (line 120)	152750	601. Gross amount due to seller (line 420)	150650
302. Less amounts paid by/for borrower (line 220)	(135000)	602. Less reductions in amt. due seller (line 520)	(84000)
303. Cash ☑ From ☐ To Borrower	17750	**603. Cash** ☑ To ☐ From Seller	

Section 5 of the Real Estate Settlement Procedures Act (RESPA) requires the following: • HUD must develop a Special Information Booklet to help persons borrowing money to finance the purchase of residential real estate to better understand the nature and costs of real estate settlement services; • Each lender must provide the booklet to all applicants from whom it receives or for whom it prepares a written application to borrow money to finance the purchase of residential real estate; • Lenders must prepare and distribute with the Booklet a Good Faith Estimate of the settlement costs that the borrower is likely to incur in connection with the settlement. These disclosures are manadatory.

Section 4(a) of RESPA mandates that HUD develop and prescribe this standard form to be used at the time of loan settlement to provide full disclosure of all charges imposed upon the borrower and seller. These are third party disclosures that are designed to provide the borrower with pertinent information during the settlement process in order to be a better shopper.

The Public Reporting Burden for this collection of information is estimated to average one hour per response, including the time for reviewing instructions, searching existing data sources, gathering and maintaining the data needed, and completing and reviewing the collection of information.

This agency may not collect this information, and you are not required to complete this form, unless it displays a currently valid OMB control number.

The information requested does not lend itself to confidentiality.

Exhibit 14.6 Title insurance policy

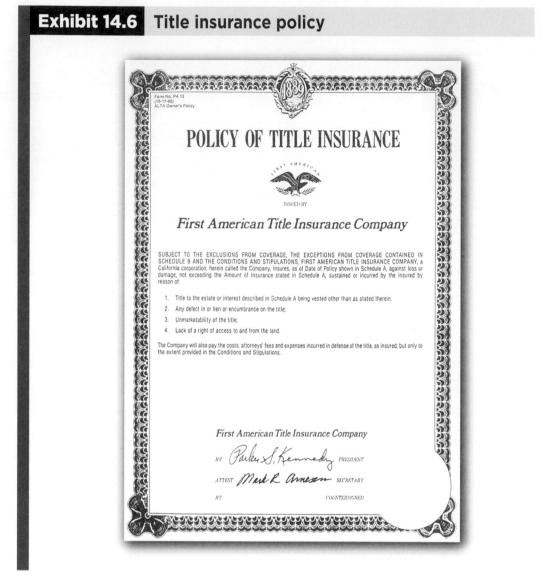

The Registrar of Deeds office is concerned with the authenticity of the deeds filed and proper authentication by way of notarization. In filing documents, it is necessary to determine the standards of the individual office with regard to the form of the notarization and any additional paperwork required before it will accept the document for recording.

This office also may collect the taxes as an agent for the taxing authority, whether local or state, and additional paperwork is required in this regard. The Registrar also generally charges a fee for filing documents, which may include additional charges when the pages exceed a certain number. It is always best to check with the office to determine the number and amounts of the checks, drafts, or other forms of payment required.

Marketable Title

Marketable title Title to real property that is free from any encumbrances or other defects that are not disclosed but would affect the value of the property. Also called *good title*.

Marketable title means that the title is free from any encumbrances, defects in title, or other defects that are not disclosed but would affect the value of the property. A buyer of real property can purchase **title insurance** from a title insurance company. The **title insurance policy** lists any defects in the title of the property, if any, and ensures against unlisted defects in title.

The title insurer must reimburse the insured for any losses caused by undiscovered defects in the title. Each time a property is transferred, a new title insurance policy must be obtained. Exhibit 14.6 shows the opening two pages of a title insurance policy.

Exhibit 14.6 Title insurance policy (continued)

FIRST AMERICAN TITLE INSURANCE COMPANY

OWNERS FORM

SCHEDULE A

Policy Number	Date of Policy	Amount of Insurance
00000000000	**January 1, 2002**	**$200,500.00**

File Number **ABC 12345**

1. Name of Insured on the Owner's Policy:

   Mary Jane Smith

2. The estate or interest in the land described in this Schedule and which is encumbered by the insured mortgage is Fee Simple.

3. The estate or interest referred to herein is at Date of Policy vested in the insured:

   The Insured by virtue of a Deed from Thomas Jones dated 12/31/2001 and recorded 1/1/2002 in Bucks County in Land Record Book 1111 page 111.

4. The land herein described is encumbered by the following mortgage or trust deed, and assignments:

   $150,500.00   Mary Jane Smith to Country Bank dated 12/31/2001 and recorded 1/1/2002 in Bucks County in land Record Book 1111 page 222. and the mortgage or trust deeds, if any, shown in Schedule B hereof.

5. The land referred to in this policy is situated in the State of Pennsylvania, County of Bucks and is described as follows:

   See attached Exhibit "A"
   Commonly known as:

   County Parcel Number 12-12-12-12-12
   123 Main Street
   Main Township
   Bucks County, Pennsylvania

PA-3

Adverse Possession

In most states, a person who wrongfully possesses someone else's real property obtains title to that property if certain statutory requirements are met. This is called **adverse possession**. Property owned by federal and state governments is not subject to adverse possession.

Under this doctrine, the transfer of the property is involuntary and does not require delivery of a deed. For a person to obtain title under adverse possession, the wrongful possession must be

- **For a statutorily prescribed period of time.** In most states, this period is between 10 and 20 years.
- **Open, visible, and notorious.** The adverse possessor must occupy the property so as to put the owner on notice of the possession.
- **Actual and exclusive.** The adverse possessor must physically occupy the premises. The planting of crops, grazing of animals, or building of a structure on the land constitutes physical occupancy.
- **Continuous and peaceful.** The occupancy must be uninterrupted for the required statutory period. Any break in normal occupancy terminates the adverse possession. This means that the adverse possessor may leave

Adverse possession A situation in which a person who wrongfully possesses someone else's real property obtains title to that property if certain statutory requirements are met.

Web Exploration

Use www.google.com and find the time for adverse possession in your state.

the property to go to work, to the store, on a vacation, and such. The adverse possessor cannot take the property by force from an owner.

- **Hostile and adverse.** The possessor must occupy the property without the express or implied permission of the owner. Thus, a lessee cannot claim title to property under adverse possession.

If the elements of adverse possession are met, the adverse possessor acquires clear title to the land. But title is acquired only as to the property actually possessed and occupied during the statutory period, and not the entire tract.

Example An adverse possessor who occupies one acre of a 200,000-acre ranch for the statutory period of time acquires title to only the one acre.

Easements

Easement A given or required right to make limited use of someone else's land without owning or leasing it.

An **easement** is an interest in land that gives the holder the right to make limited use of another's property without taking anything from it. Typical easements include common driveways, party walls, right-of-ways, and such.

Easements may be *expressly* created by (1) grant (in which an owner gives another party an easement across his or her property), called **easement by grant**, or (2) **reservation** (where an owner sells land he or she owns but reserves an easement on the land).

There also may be (3) **easements by implication** in which an owner subdivides a piece of property with a well, path, road, or other beneficial appurtenant that serves the entire parcel, or (4) **easements by necessity**; for example, "landlocked" property has an implied easement across surrounding property to enter and exit the landlocked property.

Easements also can be created by adverse possession.

Exhibit 14.7 shows a dominant and servient easement with a common driveway. Exhibit 14.8 shows a landlocked real property and easement by necessity.

Web Exploration

Go to http://www.nature.org/aboutus/howwework/conservationmethods/privatelands/conservationeasements/ and read about "Conservation Easements."

Landlord–Tenant Relationship

Landlord–tenant relationships are common in the United States because (1) more than half of the population rent their homes, and (2) many businesses lease office space, stores, manufacturing facilities, and other commercial property. The parties to the relationship have certain legal rights and duties governed by a mixture of real estate and contract law.

Exhibit 14.7 Dominant and servient easement

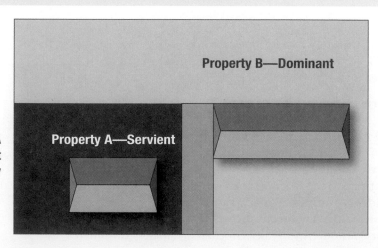

Property A grants easement to use driveway to Property B

Property A—Servient

Property B—Dominant

Property B with house on the property line

Exhibit 14.8 Easement by necessity

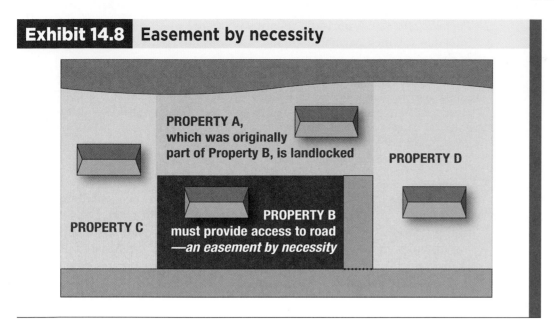

Exhibit 14.9 Parties to a lease

A landlord–tenant relationship is created when the owner of a freehold estate (i.e., an estate in fee or a life estate) transfers a right to exclusively and temporarily possess the owner's property. The tenant receives a **nonfreehold estate** in the property—that is, the tenant has a right to possession of the property but not title to the property.

Exhibit 14.9 shows the parties to a lease.

Types of Tenancy

The tenant's interest in the property is called a **leasehold estate**, or **leasehold**. The owner who transfers the leasehold estate is called the **landlord**, or **lessor**. The party to whom the leasehold estate is transferred is called the **tenant**, or **lessee**. *Tenancies* are of four types:

1. *Tenancy for years.* A **tenancy for years** is created when the landlord and the tenant agree on a specific duration for the lease. Any lease for a stated period—no matter how long or short—is called a tenancy for years.

   Examples   These arrangements range from office space leased in a high-rise office building on a 30-year lease to a cabin leased for the summer. A tenancy for years terminates automatically, without notice, upon expiration of the stated term.

Leasehold A tenant's interest in property.

Landlord An owner who transfers a leasehold.

Tenant The party to whom a leasehold is transferred.

Tenancy for years A tenancy created when the landlord and the tenant agree on a specific duration for a lease.

Periodic tenancy A tenancy created when a lease specifies intervals at which payments are due but does not specify the length of the lease.

Tenancy at will A tenancy created by a lease that may be terminated at any time by either party.

Tenancy at sufferance A tenancy created when a tenant retains possession of property after the expiration of another tenancy or a life estate without the owner's consent.

2. *Periodic tenancy.* A **periodic tenancy** is created when a lease specifies intervals at which payments are due but does not specify the duration of the lease.

   Example A lease that states, "Rent is due on the first day of the month" establishes a periodic tenancy. Many such leases are created by implication. A periodic tenancy may be terminated by either party at the end of any payment interval but adequate notice of the termination must be given. At common law, the notice period equaled the length of the payment period. Therefore, a month-to-month tenancy requires a one-month notice of termination.

3. *Tenancy at will.* A lease that may be terminated at any time by either party is termed a **tenancy at will**. A tenancy at will may be created expressly (e.g., "to tenant as long as landlord wishes") but more likely is to be created by implication. Most states have enacted statutes requiring minimum advance notice for the termination of a tenancy at will. The death of either party terminates a tenancy at will.

4. *Tenancy at sufferance.* A **tenancy at sufferance** is created when a tenant retains possession of the property after the expiration of another tenancy or a life estate without the owner's consent. That is, the owner suffers the *wrongful possession* of his or her property by the holdover tenant. This is not really a true tenancy but merely the possession of property without right. Technically, a tenant at sufferance is a trespasser. A tenant at sufferance is liable for the payment of rent during the period of sufferance. To evict a holdover tenant, most states require an owner to go through certain legal proceedings, called *eviction proceedings* or *unlawful detainer actions*. A few states allow owners to use self-help to evict a holdover tenant as long as force is not used.

TYPES OF TENANCIES

SIDEBAR

Types of Tenancy	Description
Tenancy for years	Continues for the duration of the lease and then terminates automatically without requiring notice. It does not terminate upon the death of either party.
Periodic tenancy	Continues from payment interval to payment interval. It may be terminated by either party with adequate notice. It does not terminate upon the death of either party.
Tenancy at will	Continues at the will of the parties and may be terminated by either party at any time with adequate notice. It terminates upon the death of either party.
Tenancy at sufferance	Arises when a tenant wrongfully occupies real property after the expiration of another tenancy or life estate. It continues until the owner either evicts the tenant or holds him or her over for another term. It terminates upon the death of the tenant.

The Lease

Lease A transfer of the right to the possession and use of real property for a set term in return for certain consideration; the rental agreement between a landlord and a tenant.

The rental agreement between the landlord and the tenant is called the **lease**. Leases generally can be either oral or written, except that most statutes of frauds require written leases for periods of time longer than one year. The lease must contain the essential terms of the parties' agreement. The lease frequently is a form contract prepared by the landlord and presented to the tenant. This is particularly true of residential leases. Other leases are negotiated between the parties.

   Example A bank's lease of a branch office would be negotiated with the owner of the building. Lease forms typically are considerably longer than two pages.

Implied Warranty of Habitability

Implied warranty of habitability A warranty that provides that leased premises must be fit, safe, and suitable for ordinary residential use.

The courts of many jurisdictions hold that an **implied warranty of habitability** applies to residential leases for their duration. This warranty provides that the leased premises must be fit, safe, and suitable for ordinary residential use. On the one hand, unchecked rodent infestation, leaking roofs, and unworkable bathroom facilities have been held to breach the implied warranty of habitability. On the other hand, a small crack in the wall or some paint peeling from a door does not breach this warranty.

Paralegals *in* Practice

PARALEGAL PROFILE
John M. Rizzini

John M. Rizzini is a Senior Real Estate Paralegal with over 22 years of paralegal experience. He is currently employed by the law firm of Edwards Angell Palmer & Dodge LLP in Providence, Rhode Island. John has a Bachelor of Arts Degree in Political Science and a Paralegal Studies Certificate from Roger Williams University. He is also a member of the Rhode Island Paralegal Association and the National Federation of Paralegal Associations.

Some of my daily duties include drafting and reviewing real estate documents such as deeds, promissory notes, mortgages, title affidavits, release documents, leases, and more. On some days, I may focus on a simple residential sale of real estate. On other days, I only work on matters related to zoning and subdivisions. I also address litigation and trust/estate issues that involve real estate.

One of the biggest trends in property law is the ability to search real estate titles online. For some states, you can search titles by city, town, or county on a registry Web site, as far back as the early 1950s. Another trend is the ability to electronically file real estate documents. We cannot do this in Rhode Island yet, so paralegals must go in person to the city or town hall to record original documents.

There is a lot of discussion within the legal community about regulating paralegals. I would not say that regulation would expand my paralegal role, but I do think that it would create a pool of paralegals who have met certain judicial or legislative requirements. In other words, regulation would eliminate the so-called "fly-by-night" paralegal programs.

My advice to new paralegals is: never "burn bridges." Working relationships developed at the beginning of your career are as important as contacts made in coming years. Also, find an experienced paralegal willing to give you career guidance and learn as much as possible from him or her. Having a mentor in this profession is priceless.

If the landlord's failure to maintain or repair the leased premises affects the tenant's use or enjoyment of the premises, state statutes and judicial decisions provide various remedies. Generally, the tenant may (1) withhold from his or her rent the amount by which the defect reduced the value of the premises to him or her, (2) repair the defect and deduct the cost of repairs from the rent due for the leased premises, (3) cancel the lease if the failure to repair constitutes constructive eviction, or (4) sue for damages for the amount the landlord's failure to repair the defect reduced the value of the leasehold.

Land-Use Control

Generally, the ownership of property entitles the owner to use his or her property as he or she wishes. Such use, however, is subject to limitations imposed by government regulation. These limitations are collectively referred to as **land-use control**, or **land-use regulation**. Several forms of land-use regulation are discussed in the following paragraphs.

> **Land-use control** or **land-use regulation** The collective term for the laws that regulate the possession, ownership, and use of real property.

Zoning

Most counties and municipalities have enacted **zoning ordinances** to regulate land use. Zoning ordinances generally (1) establish use districts within the municipality (i.e., areas are generally designated residential, commercial, or industrial); (2) restrict the height, size, and location of buildings on a building site; and (3) establish aesthetic requirements or limitations for the exterior of buildings.

A **zoning commission** usually formulates zoning ordinances, conducts public hearings, and makes recommendations to the city council, which must vote to enact an ordinance. Once a zoning ordinance is enacted, the zoning ordinance commission enforces it. If landowners believe that a zoning ordinance is illegal or that it has been applied unlawfully to them or their property, they may institute a court proceeding seeking judicial review of the ordinance or its application.

> **Zoning ordinances** Local laws that are adopted by municipalities and local governments to regulate land use within their boundaries.

An owner who wishes to use his or her property for a use different from that permitted under a current zoning ordinance may seek relief from the ordinance by obtaining a **variance**. To obtain a variance, the landowner must prove that the ordinance causes an undue hardship by preventing him or her from making a reasonable return on the land as zoned. Variances usually are difficult to obtain.

Rent Control

Web Exploration

Go to http://www.housingnyc.com/html/about/about.html and read the Mission Statement of the New York City Rent Guidelines Board.

Many local communities across the country have enacted **rent control ordinances** that set an amount of rent a landlord can charge for residential housing. Most of these ordinances fix the rent at a specific amount and provide for minor annual increases. Although many communities have adopted rent control ordinances, New York City is the most famous one.

Landlords, of course, oppose rent control, arguing that rent control ordinances are merely a "regulatory tax" that transfers wealth from landowners to tenants. Tenants and proponents of rent control say that it is necessary to create affordable housing, particularly in high-rent urban areas. The U.S. Supreme Court has upheld the use of rent control. *Yee v. City of Escondido, California*, 503 U.S. 519, 112 S.Ct. 1522, 118 L.Ed.2d 153, **Web** 1992 U.S. Lexis 2115 (Supreme Court of the United States).

Eminent Domain

Eminent domain The government's power to take private property for public use, provided that just compensation is paid to the private property holder.

The government may use its power of **eminent domain** to acquire private property for public purposes. However, the **Due Process Clause** of the Fifth Amendment to the U.S. Constitution (and state constitutions, where applicable) requires that the government only take property for "public use." The government must allow the owner of the property to make a case for keeping the property.

Just Compensation Clause A clause of the U.S. Constitution that requires the government to compensate the property owner, and possibly others, when the government takes property under its power of eminent domain.

The **Just Compensation Clause** of the Fifth Amendment to the U.S. Constitution requires the government to compensate the property owner (and possibly others, such as lessees) when it exercises the power of eminent domain. Anyone who is not satisfied with the compensation offered by the government can bring an action to have the court determine the compensation to be paid.

> **Example** Assume that Henry owns a large piece of vacant beachfront property with the intention of building his retirement house on the property at some future time. Now suppose the city government wants to build a new public boat dock on the property. The city government can use its power of eminent domain to acquire the needed property for this public use. There has been a "taking," so the government must pay Henry just compensation.

Civil Rights Acts

Federal and state laws guarantee **civil rights** in the purchase, sale, lease, and use of real property. Several major federal statutes that regulate real estate are:

Civil Rights Act A federal statute that prohibits racial discrimination in the transfer of real property.

1. **Civil Rights Act**. A federal statute that prohibits racial discrimination in the transfer of real property, including housing, commercial, and industrial property. The act prohibits private and public discrimination and permits lawsuits to recover damages and obtain injunctions against offending conduct [42 U.S.C. Section 1971 *et seq.*].

Fair Housing Act A federal statute that makes it unlawful for a party to refuse to rent or sell a dwelling to any person because of his or her race, color, national origin, sex, or religion.

2. **Fair Housing Act**. A federal statute that makes it unlawful for a party to refuse to rent or sell a dwelling to any person because of his or her race, color, national origin, sex, or religion. The act also prohibits discrimination by real estate brokers, mortgage lenders, and

THE *KELO* "TAKINGS" CASE

Obviously the government can "take" an owner's real property to use the property for a public use such as building a highway, school, fire station, and such. However, the extent of what qualifies as "public use" was tested in a recent major U.S. Supreme Court ruling. A discussion of the facts of the case and the Supreme Court's ruling follows.

The City of New London is located in southeastern Connecticut at the junction of the Thames River and Long Island Sound. The city has suffered decades of economic decline, including the closing of the federal military base in the Fort Trumbull area of the city. The city's unemployment rate was nearly double that of the state's unemployment rate and the city's population of 24,000 was the lowest since 1920.

To try to remedy the situation, state and local officials targeted the City of New London for economic revitalization. The government created the New London Development Corporation (NLDC) to assist the city in planning economic redevelopment. The NLDC finalized an integrated redevelopment plan for 90 acres in the Fort Trumbull area of the city. The redevelopment plan included a waterfront conference hotel, restaurants, stores, a marina, 80 new residences, and office buildings. Importantly, these projects were to be constructed and owned by private developers and parties selected by the city. The stated purposes were to make the city more attractive, create jobs, and increase tax revenue.

The only problem was that some of the property needed for the redevelopment was owned by individual homeowners. The city purchased most of the land needed for the redevelopment from private owners. However, Susette Kelo and several other homeowners in the redevelopment district (collectively Kelo) refused to sell their properties. Their properties were well kept and were not blighted.

A Connecticut state statute authorized the use of eminent domain to take property to promote economic development. Thus, The NLDC initiated eminent domain actions to take the properties. Kelo defended, arguing that the taking violated the "public use" requirement of the Fifth Amendment to the U.S. Constitution because the properties were being taken from one private party—Kelo and the other holdout homeowners—and were being transferred to other private owners, the developers. The state trial court held for Kelo. However, the Connecticut Supreme Court held that the taking of private property by the NLDC

was valid. Kelo appealed to the U.S. Supreme Court. The issue directed at the U.S. Supreme Court was: Does the City of New London's decision to take Kelo's property by eminent domain for the purpose of economic development satisfy the "public use" requirement of the Fifth Amendment?

The U.S. Supreme Court, in a 5-4 decision, held that the general benefits a community enjoys from economic growth qualifies as a permissible "public use" to support the taking of private property for such redevelopment plans under the Takings Clause of the Fifth Amendment. In the majority opinion, Justice Stevens wrote:

> The disposition of this case therefore turns on the question whether the City's development plan serves a "public purpose." Without exception, our cases have defined this concept broadly. The concept of the public welfare is broad and exclusive. The values it represents are spiritual as well as physical, aesthetic as well as monetary. It is within the power of the legislature to determine that the community should be beautiful as well as healthy, spacious as well as clean, well-balanced as well as carefully patrolled.

The U.S. Supreme Court upheld the State of Connecticut's statute that permitted the taking of private property for the purposes of economic development. Thus, Kelo's property could be taken by the redevelopment agency and transferred to another private party—the developers—who in turn would build and own commercial property where Kelo's house once stood. The Supreme Court opinion stated, "In affirming the City's authority to take petitioners' properties, we do not minimize the hardship that condemnations may entail, notwithstanding the payment of just compensation."

The response to the *Kelo* case was swift. The Supreme Court's decision was widely criticized by members of the public who believed the decision violated private property rights. State politicians were quick to respond, with over half of the states enacting state laws that make it more difficult for state and local governments to acquire private property by eminent domain than the standard permitted in the *Kelo* ruling.

SOURCE: *Kelo v. City of New London, Connecticut*, 545 U.S. 469, 125 S.Ct. 2655, 162 L.Ed.2d 439, **Web** 2005 U.S. Lexis 5011 (Supreme Court of the United States, 2005).

advertisers concerning the sale or rental of real property [42 U.S.C. Section 360 *et seq.*].

Title III of the Americans with Disabilities Act A federal statute that prohibits discrimination on the basis of disability in places of public accommodation by private entities.

3. **Title III of the Americans with Disabilities Act (ADA).** Title III of the ADA is a part of a federal statute that prohibits discrimination on the basis of disability in places of public accommodation operated by private entities. Title III applies to public accommodations and commercial facilities such as motels, hotels, restaurants, theaters, recreation facilities, colleges and universities, department stores, retail stores, and office buildings. It does not generally apply to residential facilities (single- and multifamily housing). The ADA provides for both private right of action and enforcement by the attorney general. Individuals may seek injunctive relief and monetary damages, while the attorney general may seek equitable relief and civil fines for any violation [42 UCC Section 1201 *et seq.*].

ETHICAL PERSPECTIVE

Duty Not to Engage in Conduct that Would Exceed a Paralegal Professional's Authority Under the Law

Mr. Fields is an attorney who practices law in the credit and bankruptcy area. Mr. Fields' clients are mainly individuals who file for bankruptcy. Ms. Harrington, an experienced paralegal in the bankruptcy law area, is hired by Mr. Fields as his paralegal.

Several months after Ms. Harrington's employment, Mr. Fields opens a second law office in another part of the city to attract additional clients. Mr. Fields spends Mondays, Wednesdays, and Fridays at his first office, and Tuesdays and Thursdays at the new second office. Both offices are successful in attracting clients.

Mr. Fields assigns Ms. Harrington to work at the office that he is not working at—that is, when he is working at the first office, Ms. Harrington is assigned to work at the second office. Mr. Fields directs Ms. Harrington to sign up as many clients as she can who come into the office she is covering.

Mr. Fields instructs Ms. Harrington to answer any questions that potential clients or clients may have regarding how unsecured credit, credit card debt, secured credit, and assets are handled under bankruptcy law, and to answer any other questions that they may have. Mr. Fields tell Ms. Harrington that because she is an expert in credit and bankruptcy law, she should give whatever advice she thinks is pertinent to a client's case.

The issue is whether Ms. Harrington would be engaged in the unauthorized practice of law.

Model and state paralegal professional codes of ethics and responsibility require that a paralegal professional comply with the applicable law that governs the unauthorized practice of law by a paralegal. Bankruptcy law permits a paralegal to complete the forms necessary for a bankruptcy filing. The law does not allow a paralegal to give legal advice, however.

PARALEGAL'S ETHICAL DECISION

Attorney Mr. Fields' instruction to Ms. Harrington to give legal advice to potential and actual clients violates his attorney ethical duties. In addition, model and state ethics codes prohibit professional paralegals from engaging in the unauthorized practice of law. Therefore, Ms. Harrington may perform the functions allowed by bankruptcy law, but must refuse to engage in the unlawful practice of law.

Concept Review *and* Reinforcement

Abandoned property   526
Adverse possession   537
Air-space parcel   527
Americans with Disabilities Act (ADA)   544
Bailee   526
Bailment   526
Bailor   526
Beneficiaries   525
Buildings   527
Civil Rights Act   542
Community property   530
Concurrent ownership (co-ownership)   529
Condominium   531
Cooperative   531
Deed   531
Donee   524
Donor   524
Due Process Clause   542
Duty of reasonable care or ordinary care   526
Easement   538
Easement by grant   538
Easement by implication   538
Easement by necessity   538
Easement by reservation   538
Eminent domain   542
Estate (estate in land)   527
Estate in fee   528
Estate *pur autre vie*   528
Estray statute   525
Fair Housing Act   542
Fee simple absolute (fee simple)   528

Fee simple defeasible (qualified fee)   528
Fixtures   527
Freehold estates   527
Future interest   528
Gift   524
Gift *causa mortis*   524
Gift *inter vivos*   524
Grantee   531
Grantor   531
Heirs   525
Implied warranty of habitability   540
Inheritance   525
Intangible property   523
Joint tenancy/Joint tenants   529
Just Compensation Clause   542
Land   527
Landlord/lessor   539
Landlord–tenant relationship   538
Land-use control or land-use regulation   541
Lease   540
Leasehold estate/leasehold   539
Lessee   539
Life estate   528
Lost property   525
Marketable title   536
Mineral rights (subsurface rights)   527
Mislaid property   525
Mutual benefit bailment   526
Nonfreehold estate   539
Periodic tenancy   540
Personal property   523
Plant life and vegetation   527

Quiet title   532
Quitclaim deed   531
Real property   527
Recording statute   532
Registrar of Deeds   532
Remainder/remainderman   528
Rent control   542
Reversion   528
Right of survivorship   529
Sale   531
Settlement statement   532
Subsurface rights (mineral rights)   527
Surface rights   527
Tangible property   523
Tenancy at sufferance   540
Tenancy at will   540
Tenancy by the entirety   529
Tenancy for years   539
Tenancy in common/tenant in common   529
Tenant   539
Title III of the Americans with Disabilities Act (ADA)   544
Title insurance   536
Title insurance policy   536
Uniform Gift to Minors Act or Revised Uniform Gift to Minors Act   525
Variance   542
Will   525
Warranty deed   531
Zoning commission   541
Zoning ordinance   541

SUMMARY OF KEY CONCEPTS

Personal Property

Definition	Personal property is everything that is not real property; sometimes referred to as *goods* or *chattels*.
Types of Personal Property	1. *Tangible property:* Physically defined property such as goods, animals, and minerals. 2. *Intangible property:* Rights that cannot be reduced to physical form, such as stock certificates, bonds, and copyrights.

Acquiring Ownership of Personal Property	Ownership to personal property may be acquired by the following means:
	1. *Purchase:* A person can purchase property from its rightful owner.
	2. *Production:* A person can produce a finished product from raw materials and supplies.
	3. *Gift:* A gift is a voluntary transfer of property by its owner to a donee without consideration. The three elements necessary to create a valid gift are:
	  a. Donative intent.
	  b. Delivery.
	  c. Acceptance.
	4. *Will or inheritance:* Gifts made to beneficiaries of a will, and inheritances stipulated in an inheritance statute.

Types of Gifts	1. *Gift inter vivos:* These gifts are made during a donor's lifetime. 2. *Gift causa mortis:* These gifts are made in anticipation of death.

Mislaid and Lost Personal Property	1. *Mislaid property:* Mislaid property is personal property that an owner voluntarily places somewhere and then inadvertently forgets. The owner of the premises where the property is mislaid does not acquire title to the property but has the right of possession against all except the rightful owner. The rightful owner can reclaim the property.
	2. *Lost property:* Lost property is personal property that an owner leaves somewhere because of negligence or carelessness. The finder obtains title to the property against the whole world except the true owner. The rightful owner can reclaim the property.
	3. *Abandoned property:* Abandoned property is property that an owner discards with the intent to relinquish his or her rights in it or property that an owner has mislaid or lost and who has given up any further attempts to locate it. Anyone who finds abandoned property acquires title to it.
	4. *Estray statutes:* These state statutes permit a finder of mislaid or lost property to obtain title to the property. To obtain clear title, the finder must:
	  a. Report the find to the appropriate government agency and turn over possession of the property to the agency.
	  b. Post and publish required notices.
	  c. Wait the statutorily required time (e.g., one year) without the rightful owner claiming the property.

Bailment

Description	Bailments occur when the owner of personal property delivers the property to another person to be held, stored, or delivered, or for some other purpose.
Parties	1. *Bailor:* Owner of the property 2. *Bailee:* Party to whom the property is delivered

Mutual Benefit Bailment	A mutual benefit bailment arises when both parties benefit from the bailment. This includes commercial bailments. The bailee owes a duty of *reasonable care* (or *ordinary care*) and is liable for *ordinary negligence*.

Real Property

Nature of Real Property	Real property is immovable; it includes land, buildings, subsurface rights, air rights, plant life, and fixtures.
Freehold Estates in Land	Estates where the owner has a present possessory interest in the real property.
Types of Fees	Estates in Fee 1. *Fee simple absolute (or fee simple):* Highest form of ownership 2. *Fee simple defeasible (or qualified fee):* Estate that ends if a specified condition occurs
Life Estate	A life estate is an interest in real property that lasts for the life of a specified person; called an *estate pur autre vie* if the time is measured by the life of a third person.
Future Interests	Future interest means the right to possess real property in the future rather than currently. Two types: 1. *Reversion:* Right to possession that returns to the grantor after the expiration of a limited or contingent estate. 2. *Remainder:* Right to possession that goes to a third person after the expiration of a limited or contingent estate; the third person is called a *remainderman*.
Concurrent Ownership	When two or more persons jointly own real property, it is called concurrent ownership. Types of concurrent ownership are: 1. *Joint tenancy:* Owners may transfer their interests without the consent of co-owners; transfer severs the joint tenancy. Under the *right of survivorship*, the interest of a deceased owner passes to his or her co-owners. 2. *Tenancy in common:* Owners may transfer their interests without the consent of co-owners; transfer does not sever the tenancy in common. Interest of a deceased owner passes to his or her estate. 3. *Tenancy by the entirety:* Form of co-ownership that can be used only by a married couple; neither spouse may transfer his or her interest without the other spouse's consent. A surviving spouse has the right of survivorship. 4. *Community property:* Form of co-ownership in certain states that applies only to a married couple; neither spouse may transfer his or her interest without the other spouse's consent. When a spouse dies, the surviving spouse automatically receives one-half of the community property.
Other Forms of Ownership	1. *Condominium:* Owners have title to their individual units and own the common areas as tenants in common; owners may transfer their interests without the consent of other owners. 2. *Cooperative:* A corporation owns the building, and the residents own shares of the corporation. Usually, owners may not transfer their shares without the approval of the other owners.

Transfer of Ownership of Real Property

Sale of Real Estate	An owner sells his or her property to another for consideration.
Recording Statutes	Recording statutes permit copies of deeds and other documents concerning interests in real property (e.g., mortgages, liens) to be filed in a government office, where they become public record. This puts third parties on notice of recorded interests.

Deed	A deed is an instrument used to convey real property by sale or gift. 1. *Warranty deed:* Provides the most protection to the grantee because the grantor makes warranties against defect in title. 2. *Quitclaim deed:* Provides least amount of protection to the grantee because the grantor transfers only the interest he or she has in the property.
Quiet Title Action	A lawsuit in which a court determines ownership rights to real property.
Marketable Title	A marketable title is a title free of encumbrances, defects in title, or other defects.
Adverse Possession	A person who occupies another's property acquires title to the property if the occupation has been: 1. for a statutory period of time (in many states, 10 to 20 years). 2. open, visible, and notorious. 3. actual and exclusive. 4. continuous and peaceful. 5. hostile and adverse.
Easement	An interest in land that gives the holder the right to make limited use of another's property without taking anything from it (e.g., driveways, party walls).

Landlord–Tenant Relationship

Definition	A landlord–tenant relationship is created when an owner of a freehold estate transfers a right to another to exclusively and temporarily possess the owner's property.
Types of Tenancy	1. *Tenancy for years:* Tenancy for a specified period of time 2. *Periodic tenancy:* Tenancy for a period of time determined by the payment interval 3. *Tenancy at will:* Tenancy that may be terminated at any time by either party 4. *Tenancy at sufferance:* Tenancy created by the wrongful possession of property
The Lease	The rental agreement between the landlord and the tenant that contains the essential terms of the parties' agreement.
Implied Warranty of Habitability	An implied warranty of habitability provides that leased premises must be fit, safe, and suitable for ordinary residential use.

Land-Use Control

Zoning	*Zoning ordinances* are laws adopted by local governments that restrict use of property, set building standards, and establish architectural requirements. *Variance:* Permits an owner to make a nonzoned use of his or her property; requires permission from a zoning board.
Rent Control	A law that that fixes the amount of rent a landlord can charge for residential housing. Most rent control laws provide for minor annual increases.
Eminent Domain	*Eminent domain*: Grants power to the government to acquire private property for public purposes. *Just Compensation Clause*: A clause of the U.S. Constitution that mandates that the government compensate the property owner and possibly others (e.g., renters) just compensation when the government exercises its power of eminent domain.

Civil Rights Acts

Federal and state laws guarantee civil rights in the purchase, sale, lease, and use of real property.

1. *Civil Rights Act:* A federal statute that prohibits racial discrimination in the transfer of real property, including housing, commercial, and industrial property.
2. *Fair Housing Act:* A federal statute that makes it unlawful for a party to refuse to rent or sell a dwelling to any person because of his or her race, color, national origin, sex, or religion.
3. *Title III of the Americans with Disabilities Act (ADA):* A part of a federal statute that prohibits discrimination on the basis of disability in places of public accommodation operated by private entities.

WORKING THE WEB

1. Using the website http://www.google.com/html or similar Internet search engine, or the Internet legal search services Westlaw or LexisNexis, find the estray statute for your state. What requirements must be met for a finder to obtain title to mislaid or lost property that he or she finds?
2. Using the website http://www.google.com/html or similar Internet search engine, find a listing of houses or property that is for sale in your area. Compare home prices. Are the prices higher or lower than you thought they would be?
3. Using the website http://www.google.com/html or similar Internet search engine, or the Internet legal search services Westlaw or LexisNexis, find information about a conservation easement in your state. Write a one-page report about this easement.
4. Using the website http://www.google.com/html or similar Internet search engine, or the Internet legal search services Westlaw or LexisNexis, find the law for your state for transferring property to minors. Write a one-page report on your state's requirements for transferring property to minors.
5. Visit the website http://nationalatlas.gov/printable/image/pdf/fedlands/id.pdf. The map will show the lands owned by the federal government in the state of Idaho. Substitute your state's two letter code (e.g., al for Alabama, ny for New York) where the "id" appears in the website, and find the map showing the lands that are owned by the federal government in your state. Does the federal government own land in your area? If so, what department or bureau of the federal government owns the land?

CRITICAL THINKING & WRITING QUESTIONS

1. Define personal property. What is the difference between tangible and intangible personal property? Give an example of each.
2. What is the difference between a gift *inter vivos* and a gift *causa mortis*?
3. What does the Uniform Gift to Minors Act and the Revised Uniform Gift to Minors Act provide? Explain.
4. What is the difference between mislaid property and lost property? Give an example of each.
5. Describe an estray statute. What is the purpose of an estray statute? Explain how an estray statute works.
6. Define a bailment. Who is the bailor? Who is the bailee?
7. Define real property. What is land? What are buildings? What are surface rights?
8. Describe subsurface rights (or mineral rights). Give an example.
9. What are fixtures? Give an example.
10. What is an estate in land (estate)? Define a freehold estate.
11. Define a fee simple absolute (or fee simple). Define a fee simple defeasible (or qualified fee).
12. What is a life estate? Give an example.
13. What is a future interest? What is the difference between a reversion and a remainder? Give an example of each.
14. What is concurrent ownership (co-ownership)?
15. Define joint tenancy. Define the right of survivorship.

16. Define tenancy in common. How does the real property of a deceased tenant in common pass upon her or his death?
17. Define tenancy by the entirety. Who can have a tenancy by the entirety?
18. Define community property. Give an example.
19. What is a condominium? What is a cooperative?
20. Define the following: (a) deed, (b) warranty deed, (c) quitclaim deed. Who are the grantor and the grantee?
21. Describe a recording statute. What does the Registrar of Deeds do? Explain.
22. Describe a quiet title action. What is its purpose?
23. What does the legal doctrine of adverse possession provide? What elements have to be met for adverse possession to occur? Give an example.
24. What is title insurance? What protection does title insurance provide?
25. What is an easement? Describe the difference between the following types of easements: (a) easement by grant, (b) easement by reservation, (c) easement by implication, and (d) easement by necessity.
26. Define *landlord*. Define *tenant*.
27. Describe the following types of tenancies: (a) tenancy for years, (b) periodic tenancy, (c) tenancy at will, and (d) tenancy at sufferance.
28. Define the implied warranty of habitability. Give an example of its breach.
29. What is land-use control?
30. Define zoning. What does a zoning ordinance do? Give an example of zoning.
31. What is a variance?
32. Define eminent domain. What is a "taking?" What does the Just Compensation Clause of the U.S. Constitution require?

Building Paralegal Skills

VIDEO CASE STUDIES

UPL Issue: Traditional Exceptions

 Sara has inherited a large sum of money and asks her friend Barbara, an investment counselor with a bank, for advice. She is given tax advice and some recommendations.

After viewing the video case study at www.pearsonhighered .com/goldman answer the following:

1. What are the incidental activities that a paralegal may perform or about which they may give advice without violating the UPL laws in your state?

2. Does a real estate salesperson give what would be considered legal advice to buyers and seller? Would it be UPL if the paralegal worked in a law firm that specialized in real estate?

3. Is giving tax advice by someone working in an accounting firm UPL? Would it be UPL if the paralegal worked in a law firm that specialized in taxation?

ETHICS ANALYSIS & DISCUSSION QUESTIONS

1. Does the preparation of a report for a client showing the history of the ownership of a property, as shown in public records, and claims against the property, as shown in public records, constitute the practice of law?

2. In your jurisdiction is priority given to real estate based upon the time of filing of deeds? Is the failure to promptly file a deed malpractice?

3. As an experienced paralegal, you have investigated many complex cases and developed a reputation for discovering little-known facts and obtaining information not normally obtained by investigators. A law firm proposes to have its client hire you to conduct the investigation of a complex and troublesome environmental case involving a major corporation that appears to be hiding information. [*Ethics Opinion 510, Texas Professional Ethics Committee Opinions.*] Can you accept the case with your compensation based on a contingent fee if paid directly from the client from his or her award, if any? From the firm? Can you accept a "substantial" bonus from the law firm?

DEVELOPING YOUR COLLABORATION SKILLS

With a group of other students, selected by you or assigned by your instructor, review the "Paralegals at Work" scenario at the beginning of the chapter. As a group, discuss the following questions.

1. From the facts of the case, make a drawing of the properties owned by Ms. Trump, Mrs. Gasper, and Mr. Jones. Draw the beach side and the highway side of the properties. Also draw Mrs. Gasper's fence line, and the dirt road that runs across Ms. Trump's property to reach Mr. Jones's property.
2. What is the zoning restriction on Ms. Trump's property? What would have to be obtained for this property for it to be able to be developed as a resort by the proposed purchaser?
3. What problem is caused by Mrs. Gasper's fence line? In a quiet title action *Trump v. Gasper*, who do you think would win? Why?
4. What problem is caused by the dirt road that traverses Ms. Trump's property to reach Mr. Jones's property? In a quiet title action *Trump v. Jones*, who do you think would win? Why?
5. For the proposed purchaser to be sure that the property has no other problems, what would you advise him to do? Explain.
6. If the proposed purchaser actually purchases the property from Ms. Trump, what should he purchase to protect him if other parties later come forward claiming ownership rights in the property?

PARALEGAL PORTFOLIO EXERCISE

Prepare a memorandum, no longer than three pages, that does the following two things: (1) describes the requirements for title to property to be obtained by the doctrine of adverse possession in your state; (2) finds two cases in your state where the doctrine of adverse possession has been asserted to try to obtain title to property, and discuss the results of the cases.

LEGAL ANALYSIS & WRITING CASES

Sisters of Charity of the Incarnate Word v. Meaux

122 S.W.3d 428, Web 2003 Tex. App. Lexis 10189

Court of Appeals of Texas

The Sisters of Charity of the Incarnate Word d/b/a St. Elizabeth Hospital of Beaumont, operates a health and wellness center. Phil Meaux was a paying member of the health center. The rules of the center, which Meaux had been given, state: "The Health & Wellness Center is not responsible for lost or stolen items." A sign stating "We cannot assure the safety of your valuables" was posted at the check-in desk. The wellness center furnished a lock and key to case members but had a master key to open lockers in case a member forgot or lost his or her key.

Meaux went to the wellness center, placed his clothes and an expensive Rolex watch and a money clip with $400 cash in the locker assigned him. Upon returning from swimming, Meaux discovered that his locker had been pried open, and his watch and money had been stolen by some unknown person. Meaux sued the Sisters of Charity, alleging that a bailment had been created between him and the Sisters and that the Sisters, as bailee, were negligent and therefore liable to him for the value of his stolen property.

The Trial Court held in favor of Meaux and awarded him $19,500 as the value of the stolen property, plus interest and attorneys' fees. The Sisters of Charity appealed.

Question

1. Was a bailment created between Meaux and the Sisters of Charity?

Cunningham v. Hastings   556 N.E.2d 12, Web 1990 Ind. App. Lexis 764

Court of Appeals of Indiana

Warren R. Hastings and Joan L. Cunningham, who were unmarried, purchased a house together. Hastings paid $45,000 down payment toward the purchase price out of his own funds. The deed referred to Hastings and Cunningham as "joint tenants with the right of survivorship." Hastings and Cunningham occupied the property jointly. After their relationship ended, Hastings took sole possession of the property. Cunningham filed a complaint seeking partition of the real estate. Based on its determination that the property could not be split, the trial court ordered it to be sold. The

Trial Court further ordered that $45,000 of the sale proceeds be paid of Hastings to reimburse him for his down payment and that the remainder of the proceeds be divided equally between Hastings and Cunningham. Cunningham appealed, alleging that Hastings should not have been given credit for the down payment.

Question

1. Is Cunningham entitled to an equal share of the proceeds of the sale of the real estate?

Naab v. Nolan   327 S.E.2d 151, Web 1985 W.Va. Lexis 476

Supreme Court of Appeals of West Virginia

Joseph and Helen Naab purchased a tract of land in a subdivision of Williamstown, West Virginia. At the time of purchase, the property had both a house and a small concrete garage. Evidence showed that the garage had been erected sometime prior to 1952 by one of the Naabs' predecessors in title. Two years later, Roger and Cynthia Nolan purchased a lot contiguous to that owned by the Naabs. The following year, the Nolans had their property surveyed. The survey indicated

that one corner of the Naabs' garage encroached 1.22 feet onto the Nolans' property and the other corner encroached 0.91 feet over the property line. The Nolans requested that the Naabs remove the garage from their property. When the Naabs refused, the lawsuit ensued.

Question

1. Who wins?

Love v. Monarch Apartments   771 P.2d 79, Web 1989 Kan. App. Lexis 219

Court of Appeals of Kansas

Sharon Love entered into a written lease agreement with Monarch Apartments for apartment 4 at 441 Winfield in Topeka, Kansas. Shortly after moving in, she experienced serious problems with termites. The walls swelled, clouds of dirt came out, and when she checked on her children one night, she saw termites flying around the room. She complained to Monarch, which arranged for the apartment to be fumigated.

When the termite problem persisted, Monarch moved Love and her children to apartment 2. Upon moving in, Love noticed that roaches crawled over the walls, ceilings, and floors of the apartment. She complained, and Monarch called an exterminator, who sprayed the apartment. When the roach problem persisted, Love vacated the premises.

Question

1. Did Love lawfully terminate the lease?

Souders v. Johnson   501 So.2d 745, Web 1987 Fla. App. Lexis 6579

Court of Appeal of Florida

When Dr. Arthur M. Edwards died, leaving a will disposing of his property, he left to his stepson, Ronald W. Souders, the villa-type condominium in which he lived, its "contents," and $10,000. Edwards left the residual of his estate to other named legatees. In administering the estate, certain stock certificates, passbook savings accounts, and other bank statements were found in Edwards' condominium. Souders claimed that these items belonged to him because they were "contents" of the condominium. The other legatees opposed Souders' claim,

alleging that the disputed property was intangible property and not part of the contents of the condominium. The value of the property was as follows: condominium, $138,000; furniture in condominium, $4,000; stocks, $377,000; and passbook and other bank accounts, $124,000.

Question

1. Who is entitled to the stocks and bank accounts? Do you think Souders acted ethically in this case?

WORKING WITH THE LANGUAGE OF THE COURT CASE

Walker v. Quillen

622 A.2d 1097, Web 1993 Del. Lexis 105
Supreme Court of Delaware

Read the following case, excerpted from the Court of Appeals opinion. Review and brief the case. In your brief answer the following questions:

1. Who were the plaintiffs (appellees)? Who was the defendant (appellant)?
2. Describe the tract of land owned by the plaintiffs and defendant.

3. What was the issue in this case? How did the court decide this issue?

Moore, Justice

Pursuant to Supreme Court Rule 25(a), appellees, Elizabeth Star Ayres and Clara Louise Quillen, have moved to affirm a judgment of the Court of Chancery granting an implied easement in favor of appellees' servient estate, as against the dominant estate of appellant, Irvin C. Walker ("Walker"). The appellees contend that sufficient evidence supports the findings of the Court of Chancery and that there was no abuse of discretion in granting the implied easement. We agree and affirm.

The appellees own in fee simple absolute a tract of land in Sussex County known as "Bluff Point." The tract is surrounded on three sides by Rehoboth Bay and is landlocked on the fourth side by Walker's land. At one time, the two tracts in question were held by a common owner. In 1878, Bluff Point was sold in fee simple absolute apart from the other holdings, thereby landlocking the parcel. A narrow dirt road, which traverses Walker's land, connects Bluff Point to a public road and is its only means of access.

Under the doctrine of implied easement or easement by necessity, the Court of Chancery found that the appellees were entitled to cross over a portion of Walker's land for access to Bluff Point. The court also found that water access, even if a reasonable substitute for land access, was not feasible because of the shallowness of the water surrounding Bluff Point. There is ample evidence in the record to support the finding that the two tracts originated from the unified holdings of one owner, and that an implied easement was created by the severance that landlocked Bluff Point. The record also sufficiently supports the finding that navigable access to Bluff Point was not feasible. Now, therefore, it is ordered that the judgment of the Court of Chancery be, and the same hereby is, affirmed.

CHAPTER
15

Estates and Elder Law

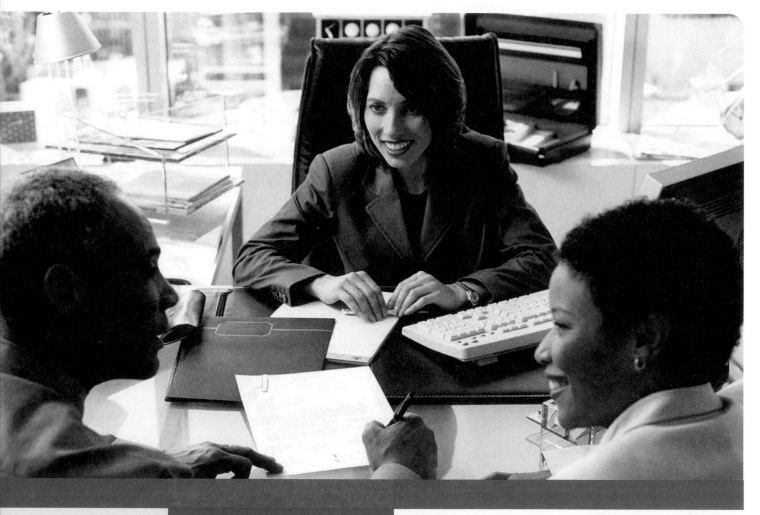

DIGITAL RESOURCES

Chapter 15 Digital Resources at *www.pearsonhighered.com/goldman*

- Video Case Studies:
  - A Senior Citizen Consults a New Lawyer: Conflict of Interest
- Chapter Summary • Web Links • Court Opinions • Glossary • Comprehension Quizzes
- Technology Resources

When you have told someone you have left him a legacy, the only decent thing to do is to die at once. "

Samuel Butler

LEARNING OBJECTIVES

After studying this chapter, you should be able to:

1. Recognize the professional opportunities for paralegals in wills, trusts, estates, and elder law.
2. List and describe the requirements for making a valid will.
3. Describe how a will can be changed and revoked.
4. Explain the effect of entering into a mutual will.
5. Identify how property is distributed under intestacy statutes if a person dies without a will.
6. Describe the process of probate.
7. Define *trust* and identify the parties to a trust.
8. Describe a living trust.
9. Explain what a living will and health care derivative are.
10. Describe elder law.
11. Explain a paralegal's duty to report dishonest or fraudulent acts pertaining to the handling of funds.

Paralegals at Work

You are a paralegal for Mr. Patrick O'Rourke, an expert in estate planning law. As the paralegal for Mr. O'Rourke, you conduct research, attend client conferences, and prepare estate planning documents for Mr. O'Rourke's review.

One day Mr. O'Rourke asks you to sit in on a client conference. The clients are Ms. Harriet Huntington and Mr. Theodore Huntington. At the meeting, the Huntingtons disclose the following information: Ms. Huntington is 45 years old, and Mr. Huntington is 50 years old. They have been married 15 years. Mr. Huntington owns his own business, a successful retail store. Ms. Huntington works as a manager at a large software company. Mr. Huntington earns about $150,000 per year, and Ms. Huntington earns about $250,000 per year. They have three children, ages 13, 10, and 7.

During the course of their marriage, the Huntingtons have accumulated the following assets: A home that is worth $1,000,000 with a $300,000 mortgage, securities of $500,000, and cash savings in bank accounts totaling $100,000. Ms. Huntington and Mr. Huntington each has a pension at work, and each has a life insurance policy for $1,000,000. Together they have accumulated two automobiles, furniture, and jewelry worth $50,000.

The Huntingtons explain that they currently do not have any wills or trusts. They explain that they would like to have Mr. O'Rourke advise them on matters of estate planning and prepare the necessary documents to effectuate the plans they agree to. The Huntingtons explain that they each want the other to receive all of their property if one of them should die. They explain further that they want to have control over their assets during their lifetime and receive all of the income from their property during their life. But they would like to avoid probate.

Both Mr. and Ms. Huntington explain their personal wish that certain life saving measures not be taken on their behalf should they become severely ill or injured. They also each want the other to make health care decisions for them if they are unable to do so.

The Huntingtons ask Mr. O'Rourke to develop an estate plan for them. As Mr. O'Rourke's paralegal, you will assist him in developing the estate plan for the Huntingtons and help him prepare the necessary documents to implement the estate plan.

Consider the issues involved in this scenario as you read this chapter.

INTRODUCTION FOR THE PARALEGAL

Many paralegals work for lawyers who represent clients in estate planning. Paralegals often assist lawyers in drafting wills, trusts, and other estate planning documents. Paralegals who work in this field also assist lawyers in the transfers of assets pursuant to trust and living trust arrangements, as well as assist in handling matters of probate. Clients also often want living trusts and health care proxies completed while they are living.

Wills transfer property upon a person's death. When that person dies, his or her property is distributed as provided in the will. If a person dies without a will, state law provides how the deceased person's property is distributed. A person may transfer property to a trust while he or she is living. Some trusts are living trusts—the trust is created for the benefit of the beneficiaries while they are living. Other trusts are established to go into effect when a person dies. In addition, many people sign a living will and health care *proxy* that states their wishes should an accident or illness disable them so they no longer can make decisions themselves and appoint someone else to make any necessary decisions for them.

A paralegal working in the estate planning field must have knowledge of wills, trusts, living trusts, living wills, health care proxies, probate, and other matters related to estate planning. This chapter covers all of the legal issues and documents associated with estate planning.

A growing specialty in law is the area of elder law. Many attorneys now represent older individuals in obtaining benefits that are due them, protecting elders against unscrupulous and fraudulent conduct, and otherwise enforcing the rights of elders. Paralegal professionals are now also specializing in this area of the law.

The following section discusses the career opportunities available to paralegal professionals in the area of wills, trusts, estates, and elder law.

Wills

Will A declaration of how a person wants his or her property to be distributed upon death.

A **will** is a declaration of how a person wants his or her property to be distributed upon his or her death. It is a *testamentary* deposition of property. The person who makes the will is called the **testator** (or **testatrix**). The persons designated in the will to receive the testator's property are called **beneficiaries**. Exhibit 15.1 shows the parties to a will.

Testator or **testatrix** The person who makes a will.

Requirements for Making a Will

Beneficiary A person or organization designated in the will that receives all or a portion of the testator's property at the time of the testator's death.

Every state has a **Statute of Wills** that establishes the requirements for making a valid will in that state. These requirements are:

Statute of Wills A state statute that establishes the requirements for making a valid will.

- **Testamentary capacity.** The testator must have been of legal age and "sound mind" when the will was made. The courts determine

CAREER OPPORTUNITIES FOR PARALEGALS IN ESTATES AND ELDER LAW

An important area of the law that paralegals can work in is the area of wills, trusts, and estates. Many lawyers and the paralegals who work for them specialize in this area of law.

"Estate law" is a composite of many areas of the law, including providing estate planning, giving tax advice, drafting wills and trusts, preparing living wills and health care proxies, representing clients in Medicaid, Social Security, and disability matters, and areas of the law affecting the elderly.

Many lawyers specialize in estate planning—that is, planning how the estate of a client will be distributed when the client dies. Estate planning requires detailed knowledge of state and federal inheritance laws and tax laws. Attorneys working in this field advise clients as to the best means of accomplishing their goals.

Paralegals assist lawyers in estate planning. This may consist of attending meetings, obtaining information from clients, and conducting legal research. Paralegals also assist lawyers in drafting wills, trust agreements, and other documents required to effectuate the client's estate plan.

In today's modern world, many individuals want to direct how their medical care will be handled if they are not able to make such decisions. Persons who do not want their life prolonged indefinitely by artificial means can sign a living will in advance, setting forth their wishes. In addition, people can sign a health care proxy naming individuals to make medical decisions if they are unable to do so. Paralegals assist lawyers in drafting living wills, health care proxies, and other related documents in this field of law.

A relatively new area of the law is the use of living trusts. Persons establish living trusts while they are alive. A living trust is a method of holding property during a person's lifetime and distributing the property upon a person's death. Living trusts have become a major form of estate planning. Paralegals assist lawyers in this area of the law and preparing the documents necessary to create the living trusts.

Elder law involves advising clients about their rights under government programs. Such programs include Social Security benefits, Medicaid benefits, and other government-sponsored benefits for the elderly. Paralegals often are called upon to assist lawyers in obtaining such benefits for elderly clients.

The specialized and complex area of elder law provides substantial employment opportunities for paralegals. Paralegals who work in this field must have detailed knowledge of the state and federal laws, regulations, procedures, forms, applications, and other documents necessary to carry forth the estate planning wishes and other goals of clients that are represented by the lawyer the paralegal works for.

Exhibit 15.1 **Parties to a will**

Testator or Testatrix

Will
A written document that names a beneficiary or beneficiaries to receive the testator's or testatrix's property upon the death of the testator or testatrix.

Beneficiary or Beneficiaries

Web Exploration

Go to http://www.abanet.org/soloseznet/threads/0511/storewills.html and read the article "Where is the Best Place to Store a Will."

testamentary capacity on a case-by-case basis. The legal age for executing a will is set by state statute.

- **Writing**. Wills must be in writing to be valid (except for dying declarations, discussed later in this chapter). The writing may be formal or informal. Although most wills are typewritten, they can be handwritten (see the discussion of holographic wills). The writing may be on legal paper, scratch paper, envelopes, napkins, or other paper. A will may incorporate additional documents by reference.
- **Testator's signature**. Wills must be signed.

Most jurisdictions require the testator's signature to appear at the end of the will. This is to prevent fraud that could occur if someone were to add provisions to the will below the testator's signature. Generally, courts have held that initials ("R.K.H."), a nickname ("Buffy"), title ("mother"), or even an "X" is a valid signature on a will if it can be proven that the testator intended it to be his or her signature.

Attestation by Witnesses

Attestation The action of a will being witnessed by the required number of competent people.

Wills must be attested to by mentally competent witnesses. Although state law varies, most states require two or three witnesses to **attestation**. The witnesses do not have to reside in the jurisdiction in which the testator is domiciled. Most jurisdictions stipulate that interested parties (e.g., a beneficiary under the will or the testator's attorney) cannot be witnesses. If an interested party has attested to a will, state law either voids any clauses that benefit such person or voids the entire will.

Witnesses usually sign the will following the signature of the testator. This is called the **attestation clause**. Most jurisdictions require that each witness attest to the will in the presence of the other witnesses.

A will that meets the requirements of the Statute of Wills is called a *formal will*. A sample will is shown as Exhibit 15.2.

Changing a Will

Codicil A separate document that must be executed to amend a will. It must be executed with the same formalities as a will.

A will cannot be amended by merely striking out existing provisions and adding new ones. **Codicils** are the legal way to change an existing will. A codicil is a separate document that must be executed with the same formalities as a will. In addition, it must incorporate by reference the will it is amending. The codicil and the will then are read as one instrument. A codicil is shown as Exhibit 15.3.

Revoking a Will

A will may be revoked by acts of the testator. A will is revoked if the testator intentionally burns, tears, obliterates, or otherwise destroys it. A properly executed **subsequent will** revokes a prior will if it specifically states that it is the testator's intention to do so. If the second will does not expressly revoke the prior will, the wills are read together. If any will provisions are inconsistent, the provisions in the second will controls.

Wills can be revoked by operation of law. For example, divorce or annulment revokes disposition of property to the former spouse under the will. The remainder of the will is valid. The birth of a child after a will has been executed does not revoke the will but does entitle the child to receive his or her share of the parents' estate as determined by state statute.

The following discusses the importance of the government officer—the Registrar of Wills—in the probate of an estate.

Special Types of Wills

The law recognizes some types of wills that do not meet all of the requirements discussed above. Two special types of wills admitted by the courts are holographic wills and noncupative wills.

Exhibit 15.2 Sample will

Last Will and Testament of Florence Winthorpe Blueblood

I, FLORENCE WINTHORPE BLUEBLOOD, presently residing at Boston, County of Suffolk, Massachusetts, being of sound and disposing mind and memory, hereby make, publish, and declare this to be my Last Will and Testament.

FIRST. I hereby revoke any and all Wills and Codicils previously made by me.

SECOND. I direct that my just debts and funeral expenses be paid out of my Estate as soon as practicable after my death.

THIRD. I am presently married to Theodore Hannah Blueblood III.

FOURTH. I hereby nominate and appoint my husband as the Personal Representative of this my Last Will and Testament. If he is unable to serve as Personal Representative, then I nominate and appoint Mildred Yardly Winthorpe as Personal Representative of this my Last Will and Testament. I direct that no bond or other security be required to be posted by my Personal Representative.

FIFTH. I hereby nominate and appoint my husband as Guardian of the person and property of my minor children. In the event that he is unable to serve as Guardian, then I nominate and appoint Mildred Yardly Winthorpe Guardian of the person and property of my minor children. I direct that no bond or other security be required to be posted by any Guardian herein.

SIXTH. I give my Personal Representative authority to exercise all the powers, rights, duties, and immunities conferred upon fiduciaries under law with full power to sell, mortgage, lease, invest, or reinvest all or any part of my Estate on such terms as he or she deems best.

SEVENTH. I hereby give, devise, and bequeath my entire estate to my husband, except for the following specific bequests:

I give my wedding ring to my daughter, Hillary Smythe Blueblood.

I give my baseball card collection to my son, Theodore Hannah Blueblood IV.

In the event that either my above-named daughter or son predeceases me, then and in that event, I give, devise, and bequeath my deceased daughter's or son's bequest to my husband.

EIGHTH. In the event that my husband shall predecease me, then and in that event, I give, devise and bequeath my entire estate, with the exception of the bequests in paragraph SEVENTH, to my beloved children or grandchildren surviving me, per stirpes.

NINTH. In the event I am not survived by my husband or any children or grandchildren, then and in that event, I give, devise, and bequeath my entire estate to Harvard University.

IN WITNESS WHEREOF, I Florence Winthorpe Blueblood, the Testatrix, sign my name to this Last Will and Testament this 3rd day of January, 2007.

_____
(Signature)

Signed, sealed, published and declared by the above-named Testatrix, as and for her Last Will and Testament, in the presence of us, who at her request, in her presence and in the presence of one another, have hereunto subscribed our names as attesting witnesses, the day and year last written above.

Witness   *Address*

_____   _____

_____   _____

_____   _____

Holographic Wills

Holographic wills are entirely handwritten and signed by the testator. The writing may be in ink, pencil, crayon, or some other writing instrument. Many states recognize the validity of such wills even though they are not witnessed.

Holographic will Will that is entirely handwritten and signed by the testator.

Exhibit 15.3 Sample codicil

SECOND CODICIL TO
THE LAST WILL AND TESTAMENT OF
SARA ELLIOTT

I, SARA ELLIOTT, of Scottsdale, Maricopa County, Arizona, declare this to be a Second Codicil to my Last Will and Testament dated March 13, 2000, and the Codicil to my Last Will and Testament dated June 22, 2002.

ARTICLE FIRST: I hereby revoke Article Third of my Will dated March 13, 2000, as amended by the Codicil of June 22, 2002, and substitute the following:

(a) I devise and bequeath all my jewelry to my daughter, Kaylee E. Sam, presently of Mesa, Arizona.

(b) I devise and bequeath the house and real property located at 1840 Norwood Place, Clearwater, Florida, to my daughter, Kaylee E. Sam, presently of Mesa, Arizona.

ARTICLE SECOND: I do hereby reaffirm all other provisions of my Last Will and Testament dated March 13, 2000, as amended by my First Codicil to my Last Will and Testament dated June 22, 2002.

IN WITNESS WHEREOF, I have hereunto set my hand this _____ day of _____ 2007.

_____

SARA ELLIOTT

The preceding instrument consisting of two typewritten pages, identified by the signature of the testatrix, was on the date thereof, signed, published and declared by SARA ELLIOTT in the presence of us who, in her presence and at her request and in the presence of each other, have subscribed our names as witnesses hereto.

_____ _____
(Name)   (Address)

_____ _____
(Name)   (Address)

_____ _____
(Name)   (Address)

Noncupative Wills

Deathbed will Oral will that is made dying declaration before a witness during the testator's last illness.

Noncupative wills are oral wills made before witnesses. These wills are usually valid only if they are made during the testator's last illness. They sometimes are called **deathbed wills** or **dying declarations**.

REGISTRAR OF WILLS

Initiation of the proceedings involving wills and the administration of estates may be delegated to the Registrar of Wills, who may be an elected official or one appointed to oversee the authentication of wills. The process, usually referred to as probate, starts with filing of the will and any codicils to the will with the court. Typically this involves presenting the will together with a death certificate to the court-designated officers.

The named executor or executrix—or administrator where no executor is available or named in the will—usually must appear at the same time and acknowledge his or her willingness to act as the executor or administrator. Depending upon the requirements of the local jurisdiction, the subscribing witnesses to the will also may be required to appear to authenticate their signatures and the will and the signature of the deceased.

Filing fees are part of the process, and appropriate checks for payment are generally required. Fees may vary depending upon the size of the probate estate. Additional forms may be required with regard to the assets and their values. In some jurisdictions, the Registrar of Wills or his or her agents may come to the attorney's office or to other locations as a convenience to the parties or where the parties, by virtue of age or disability, are unable to go to the courthouse.

Testamentary Gifts

In a will, a gift of real estate by will is called a **devise**. A gift of personal property by will is called a **bequest** or **legacy**. Gifts in wills can be specific, general, or residuary.

- **Specific gifts**: specifically named pieces of property, such as a ring, a boat, or a piece of real estate.
- **General gifts**: gifts that do not identify the specific property from which the gift is to be made, such as a cash amount that can come from any source in the decedent's estate.
- **Residuary gifts**: established by a **residuary clause** in the will. The clause might state, for example, "I give my daughter the rest, remainder, and residual of my estate." This means that any portion of the estate left after the debts, taxes, and specific and general gifts have been paid belongs to the decedent's daughter.

> **Specific gift** A gift of a specifically named piece of property.
>
> **General gift** A gift that does not identify the specific property from which the gift is to be made.
>
> **Residuary gift** A gift of the estate left after the debts, taxes, and specific and general gifts have been paid.

A person who inherits property under a will or an intestacy statute takes the property subject to all of the outstanding claims against it (e.g., liens, mortgages). A person can **renounce an inheritance**—and often does—when the liens or mortgages against the property exceed the value of the property.

Videotaped Wills

Many will contests involve written wills. The contesters allege things such as mental incapacity of the testator at the time the will was made, undue influence, fraud, or duress. Although the written will speaks for itself, the mental capacity of the testator and the voluntariness of his or her actions cannot be determined from the writing alone.

To prevent unwarranted will contests, a testator can use a **videotaped will** to supplement a written will. Videotaping a will that can withstand challenges by disgruntled relatives and alleged heirs involves a certain amount of planning.

The following procedure should be followed. A written will should be prepared to comply with the state's Statute of Wills. The video session should not begin until after the testator has become familiar with the document. The video should begin with the testator reciting the will verbatim. Next, the lawyer should ask the testator questions to demonstrate the testator's sound mind and understanding of the implications of his or her actions. The execution ceremony—the signing of the will by the testator and the attestation by the witnesses—should be the last segment on the film. The videotape then should be stored in a safe place.

With the testator's actions crystallized on videotape, a judge or jury will be able to determine the testator's mental capacity at the time the will was made and the

 Web Exploration

Go to http://www.cnn.com/WORLD/9803/04/diana.will/index.html to read the will of Princess Diana of England.

 Web Exploration

Go to http://www.ibiblio.org/elvis/elvwill.html to read the will of Elvis Presley "The King."

voluntariness of his or her testamentary gifts. In addition, fraudulent competing wills will fall in the face of such proof.

Simultaneous Deaths

Sometimes people who would inherit property from each other die simultaneously. If it is impossible to determine who died first, the question becomes one of inheritance. The **Uniform Simultaneous Death Act** provides that each deceased person's property is distributed as if he or she survived.

> **Example** Suppose a husband and wife make wills leaving their entire estate to each other. Assume that the husband and wife are killed simultaneously in an airplane crash. Here, the husband's property would go to his relatives and the wife's property would go to her relatives.

Joint and Mutual Wills

If two or more testators execute the same instrument as their will, the document is called a **joint will**. A joint will may be held invalid as to one testator but not the other(s).

Mutual or **reciprocal wills** are developed when two or more testators execute separate wills that make testamentary dispositions of their property to each other on the condition that the survivor leave the remaining property on his or her death as agreed by the testators. The wills usually are separate instruments with reciprocal terms. Because of their contractual nature, mutual wills cannot be revoked unilaterally after one of the parties has died.

Undue Influence

Undue influence Occurs where one person takes advantage of another person's mental, emotional, or physical weakness and unduly persuades that person to make a will; the persuasion by the wrongdoer must overcome the free will of the testator.

A will may be found to be invalid if it was made as a result of **undue influence** on the testator. Undue influence can be inferred from the facts and circumstances surrounding the making of the will. For example, if an 85-year-old woman leaves all of her property to the lawyer who drafted her will and ignores her blood relatives, the court is likely to presume undue influence.

Undue influence is difficult to prove by direct evidence, but it may be proved by circumstantial evidence. The elements that courts examine to find the presence of undue influence include the following:

- The benefactor and beneficiary are involved in a relationship of confidence and trust.
- The will contains substantial benefit to the beneficiary.
- The beneficiary caused or assisted in effecting execution of the will.
- There was an opportunity to exert influence.
- The will contains an unnatural disposition of the testator's property.
- The bequests constitute a change from a former will.
- The testator was highly susceptible to the undue influence.

Probate

Settlement of estate (probate) The process of a deceased's property being collected, debts and taxes being paid, and the remainder of the estate being distributed.

When a person dies, his or her property must be collected, debts and taxes paid, and the remainder of the estate distributed to the beneficiaries of the will or the heirs under the state intestacy statute. This process is called **settlement of the estate** or **probate**. The process and procedures for settling an estate are governed by state statute. A specialized state court, called the probate court, usually supervises the administration and settlement of an estate.

A *personal representative* must be appointed to administer the estate during its settlement phase. If the testator's will names the personal representative, that person is called an **executor** or **executrix**.

Paralegals *in* Practice

PARALEGAL PROFILE
Victoria M. Newman

Victoria M. Newman specializes in the legal areas of probate, trust administration, and estate planning. After working 28 years for Livingston, Stone & McGowan in San Francisco, California, she decided to become a contract paralegal. Vickie not only obtained the PACE™ Registered Paralegal® designation from the National Federation of Paralegal Associations (NFPA), she helps promote the PACE (Paralegal Advanced Competency Exam). As the current PACE Coordinator— Ambassadors, she develops guidelines and goals for the Ambassador Program, and assists PACE Ambassadors from NFPA member associations.

As a contract paralegal, I work mostly for solo legal practitioners and small law firms with less than ten attorneys. In addition to ethics, organizational skills, and efficient time management, some of the aptitudes most needed by someone in my position are:

- **People Skills.** In probate and trust administration, you work with people who are grieving and/or emotional. Thus, do not take behaviors personally, and gently remind clients of deadlines. In estate planning, you must frequently deal with procrastinators. Many clients avoid filling out the initial questionnaire, making it necessary to send out multiple reminders and/or call them.
- **Attentiveness to Details.** The probate process is very detailed oriented. Not all probate, trust administrations, or estate plans are alike, even though procedures are much the same. Preparing and regularly updating checklists will help you monitor case progress, avoid missing deadlines, and quickly locate information.
- **Strong Mathematical and Analytical Skills.** Numbers are an integral part of probate and trust administration. For example, you will need to prepare court accountings, calculate distributions, allocate assets between trusts, determine if taxes are owed, and sometimes pro-rate taxes among beneficiaries.

My advice to new paralegals is to always keep current. Forms, laws, and codes change often. Simply using an outdated form might get your paperwork rejected by the court. Also, build relationships with people who can help you in unfamiliar situations. For example, in some courts, the probate examiners are available to answer procedural questions.

The **Uniform Probate Code (UPC)** was promulgated to establish uniform rules for creating wills, administering estates, and resolving conflicts in estate settlements. These rules provide a speedy, efficient, and less expensive method than many existing state laws for settling estates. Only about one-third of the states have adopted all or part of the UPC.

Lineal Descendants

A testator's will may state that property is to be left to his or her **lineal descendants** (children, grandchildren, great-grandchildren, etc.) either *per stirpes* or *per capita*. The difference between these two methods is discussed in the following paragraphs.

> **Lineal descendants** The testator's children, grandchildren, great-grandchildren, and so on.

Per Stirpes Distribution

Pursuant to *per stirpes* **distribution**, the lineal descendants *inherit by representation of their parent*; that is, they split what their deceased parent would have received. If their parent is not deceased, they receive nothing.

> **Per stirpes distribution** A distribution of the estate that makes grandchildren and great-grandchildren of the deceased inherit by representation of their parent.

Example Suppose Anne dies without a surviving spouse and she had three children, Bart, Beth, and Bruce. Bart, who survives his mother, has no children. Beth has one child, Carla, and they both survive Anne. Bruce, who predeceased his mother, had two children, Clayton and Cathy; and Cathy, who predeceased Anne, had two children, Deborah and Dominic, both of whom survive Anne.

If Anne leaves her estate to her lineal descendants *per stirpes*, Bart and Beth each get one-third, Carla receives nothing because Beth is alive, Clayton gets one-sixth, and Deborah and Dominic each get one-twelfth. Exhibit 15.4 illustrates this example.

Exhibit 15.4 Example of *per stirpes* distribution

Per Capita Distribution

Per capita distribution A distribution of the estate that makes each grandchild and great-grandchild of the deceased inherit equally with the children of the deceased.

Pursuant to *per capita* distribution, the lineal descendants equally share the property of the estate. That is, children of the testator share equally with grandchildren, great-grandchildren, and so forth.

Example Suppose the facts are the same as in the previous example, except that Anne leaves her estate to her lineal descendants *per capita*. In this case, all of the surviving lineal descendants—Bart, Beth, Carla, Clayton, Deborah, and Dominic—share equally in the estate. That is, they each get one-sixth of Anne's estate. See Exhibit 15.5.

Ademption and Abatement

Ademption A principle that says if a testator leaves a specific devise of property to a beneficiary, but the property is no longer in the estate when the testator dies, the beneficiary receives nothing.

Abatement If the property the testator leaves is not sufficient to satisfy all the beneficiaries named in a will and there are both general and residuary bequests, the residuary bequest is abated first (i.e., paid last).

If a testator leaves a specific gift of property to a beneficiary, but the property is no longer in the estate of the testator when he or she dies, the beneficiary receives nothing. This doctrine is called the doctrine of **ademption**.

If the testator's estate is not large enough to pay all the devises and bequests, the doctrine of **abatement** applies. The doctrine works as follows:

- If a will provides for both general and residuary gifts, the residuary gifts are abated first.

  Example Suppose a testator executes a will when he owns $500,000 of property that leaves (1) $100,000 to the Red Cross, (2) $100,000 to a university, and (3) the residue to his niece. Suppose that when the testator dies, his estate is worth only $225,000. Here, the Red Cross and the university each receive $100,000 and the niece receives $25,000.

- If a will provides only for general gifts, the reductions are proportionate.

  Example Suppose a testator's will leaves $75,000 to two beneficiaries, but the estate is only $100,000. Each beneficiary would receive $50,000.

Exhibit 15.5 Example of *per capita* distribution

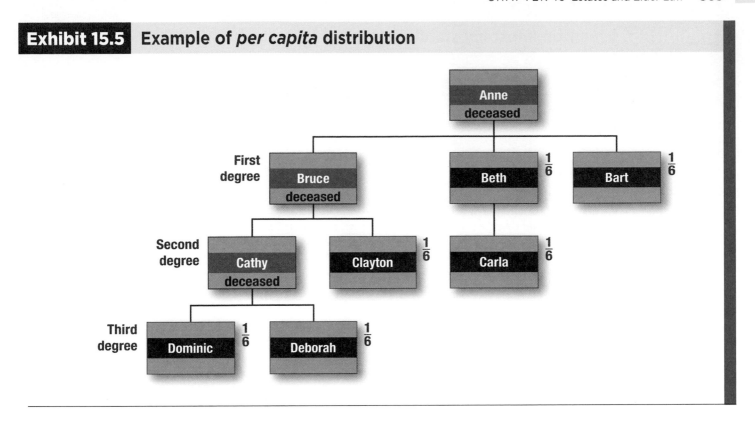

Intestate Succession

If a person dies without a will, or his or her will fails for some legal reason, that person dies **intestate**. In this case, the deceased person's property is distributed to his or her relatives pursuant to the state's **intestacy statute**.

Relatives who receive property under these statutes are called **heirs**. Although intestacy statutes differ from state to state, the general rule is that the deceased's real property is distributed according to the intestacy statute of the state where the real property is located and the deceased's personal property is distributed according to the intestacy statute of the state where the deceased had his or her permanent residence.

Intestacy statutes usually leave the deceased's property to his or her heirs in this order: spouse, children, lineal heirs (e.g., grandchildren, parents, brothers and sisters), collateral heirs (e.g., aunts, uncles, nieces, nephews), and other next of kin (e.g., cousins). If the deceased has no surviving relatives the deceased's property **escheats** (goes) to the state. In-laws do not inherit under most intestacy statutes. If a child dies before his or her parents, the child's spouse does not receive the inheritance.

To avoid the distribution of an estate as provided in an intestacy statute, a person should have a properly written, signed, and witnessed will that distributes the estate property as the testator wishes.

Exhibit 15.6 sets forth the Florida state intestacy statutes.

Living Will and Health Care Directive

Technological breakthroughs have greatly increased the life span of human beings. This same technology, however, permits life to be sustained long after a person is "brain dead." Some people say they have a right to refuse such treatment. Others argue that human life must be preserved at all costs. In 1990, the U.S. Supreme Court was called upon to decide the **right to die** issue. [*Cruzan v. Director, Missouri Department of Health*, 497 U.S. 261, 110 S.Ct. 2841, 111 L.Ed.2d 224, 1990 U.S. Lexis 3301 (1990)].

Intestate The state of having died without leaving a will.

Intestacy statute A state statute that specifies how a deceased's property will be distributed if he or she dies without a will or if the last will is declared void and there is no prior valid will.

COMPARISON OF DYING WITH AND WITHOUT A VALID WILL

Situation	Parties Who Receive Deceased's Property
Deceased dies with a valid will	*Beneficiaries* named in the will.
Deceased dies without a valid will	*Heirs* set forth in the applicable state intestacy statute. If no heirs, the deceased's property escheats to the state.

SIDEBAR

Exhibit 15.6 Florida intestacy statute

Intestate Estate

(1) Any part of the estate of a decedent not effectively disposed of by will passes to the decedent's heirs as prescribed in the following section of this code.

(2) The decedent's death is the event that vests the heirs' right to the decedent's intestate property. Florida Statutes, 732.101

Spouse's Share of Intestate Estate

The intestate share of the surviving spouse is:

(1) If there is no surviving descendant of the decedent, the entire intestate estate.

(2) If there are surviving descendants of the decedent, all of whom are also lineal descendants of the surviving spouse, the first $60,000 of the intestate estate, plus one-half of the balance of the intestate estate. Property allocated to the surviving spouse to satisfy the $60,000 shall be valued at the market value on the date of distribution.

(3) If there are surviving descendants, one or more of whom are not lineal descendants of the surviving spouse, one-half of the intestate estate. Florida Statutes, 732.102

Share of Other Heirs

The part of the intestate estate not passing to the surviving spouse under s. 732.102, or the entire intestate estate if there is no surviving spouse, descends as follows:

(1) To the descendants of the decedent.

(2) If there is no descendant, to the decedent's father and mother equally, or to the survivor of them.

(3) If there is none of the foregoing, to the decedent's brothers and sisters and the descendants of deceased brothers and sisters.

(4) If there is none of the foregoing, the estate shall be divided, one-half of which shall go to the decedent's paternal, and the other half to the decedent's maternal, kindred in the following order:

    (a) To the grandfather and grandmother equally, or to the survivor of them.

    (b) If there is no grandfather or grandmother, to uncles and aunts and descendants of deceased uncles and aunts of the decedent.

    (c) If there is either no paternal kindred or no maternal kindred, the estate shall go to the other kindred who survive, in the order stated above.

(5) If there is no kindred of either part, the whole of the property shall go to the kindred of the last deceased spouse of the decedent as if the deceased spouse had survived the decedent and then died intestate entitled to the estate.

(6) If none of the foregoing, and if any of the descendants of the decedent's great-grandparents were Holocaust victims as defined in s. 626.9543(3)(a), including such victims in countries cooperating with the discriminatory policies of Nazi Germany, then to the descendants of the great-grandparents. The court shall allow any such descendant to meet a reasonable, not unduly restrictive, standard of proof to substantiate his or her lineage. This subsection only applies to escheated property and shall cease to be effective for proceedings filed after December 31, 2004. Florida Statutes, 732.103

Inheritance Per Stirpes

Descent shall be per stirpes, whether to descendants or to collateral heirs. Florida Statutes, 732.104

Half Blood

When property descends to the collateral kindred of the intestate and part of the collateral kindred are of the whole blood to the intestate and the other part of the half blood, those of the half blood shall inherit only half as much as those of the whole blood; but if all are of the half blood they shall have whole parts. Florida Statutes. 732.105

Afterborn Heirs

Heirs of the decedent conceived before his or her death, but born thereafter, inherit intestate property as if they had been born in the decedent's lifetime. Florida Statutes, 732.106

Exhibit 15.6 **Florida intestacy statute** *(continued)*

Escheat

(1) When a person dies leaving an estate without being survived by any person entitled to a part of it, that part shall escheat to the state.

(2) Property that escheats shall be sold as provided in the Florida Probate Rules and the proceeds paid to the Chief Financial Officer of the state and deposited in the State School Fund.

(3) At any time within 10 years after the payment to the Chief Financial Officer, a person claiming to be entitled to the proceeds may reopen the administration to assert entitlement to the proceeds. If no claim is timely asserted, the state's rights to the proceeds shall become absolute.

(4) The Department of Legal Affairs shall represent the state in all proceedings concerning escheated estates. Florida Statutes, 732.107

Adopted Persons and Persons Born out of Wedlock

(1) For the purpose of intestate succession by or from an adopted person, the adopted person is a descendant of the adopting parent and is one of the natural kindred of all members of the adopting parent's family, and is not a descendant of his of her natural parents, nor is he or she one of the kindred of any member of the natural parent's family or any prior adoptive parent's family, except that:

    (a) Adoption of a child by the spouse of a natural parent has no effect on the relationship between the child and the natural parent or the natural parent's family.

    (b) Adoption of a child by a natural parent's spouse who married the natural parent after the death of the other natural parent has no effect on the relationship between the child and the family of the deceased natural parent.

    (c) Adoption of a child by a close relative, as defined in s. 63.172(2), has no effect on the relationship between the child and the families of the deceased natural parents.

(2) For the purpose of intestate succession in cases not covered by subsection (1), a person bore out of wedlock is a descendant of his or her mother and is one of the natural kindred of all members of the mother's family. The person is also a descendant of his or her father and is one of the natural kindred of all members of the father's family, if:

    (a) The natural parents participated in a marriage ceremony before or after the birth of the person born out of wedlock, even though the attempted marriage is void.

    (b) The paternity of the father is established by an adjudication before or after the death of the father.

    (c) The paternity of the father is acknowledged in writing by the father. Florida Statutes, 732.108

Aliens

Aliens shall have the same rights of inheritance as citizens. Florida Statutes, 32.1101.

In the *Cruzan* case, the U.S. Supreme Court acknowledged that the right to refuse medical treatment is a personal liberty protected by the due process clause of the U.S. Constitution. The Court stated that this interest must be expressed through clear and convincing proof that the patient did not want to be sustained by artificial means.

The clear message of the Supreme Court's opinion is that people who do not want their lives prolonged indefinitely by artificial means should sign a **living will** that stipulates their wishes before catastrophe strikes and they become unable to express it themselves because of an illness or an accident. The living will should state which life-saving measures the signor does and does not want. In addition, the signor can specify that he or she wants to have any such treatments withdrawn if doctors determine that there is no hope of a meaningful recovery. The living will provides clear and convincing proof of a patient's wishes with respect to medical treatment.

In a living will or in a separate document usually called a **health care directive** or **health care proxy**, the maker should name someone, such as a spouse or another relative or trusted party, to be his or her **health care agent** to make all health care decisions in accordance with his or her wishes in the living will. An alternative person also should be named in case the originally designated health care agent is unable or chooses not to serve in that capacity.

Living will A document that states which life-saving measures the signor does and does not want, and can specify that he or she wants such treatments withdrawn if doctors determine that there is no hope of a meaningful recovery.

Health care directive (health care proxy) A document in which the maker should name someone to be his or her health care agent to make all health care decisions in accordance with his or her wishes in the living will.

A well-known example of a person not having a living will and health care proxy was the Terri Shiavo case. In February 1990, Terri collapsed and was placed on life support systems. For 15 years, Terri remained in a vegetative state. Her husband wanted Terri to be taken off life support systems, but her parents did not. After years of legal battles that included more than fifty trial and appellate court hearings, in April 2005 the Florida Supreme Court ordered Terri to be taken off life support systems. Days later she died.

Much of the legal battle concerned what Terri's intention would have been about staying on, or being removed from, life support systems. If Terri would have had a living will and health care proxy, her intentions would have been clear. A living will and health care proxy is set forth in Exhibit 15.7.

Trusts

A **trust** is a legal arrangement under which one person—the **settlor, trustor,** or **transferor**—delivers and transfers legal title to property to another person, bank, or other entity called the **trustee** to be held and used for the benefit of a third person or entity (the **beneficiary of a trust**). The property and assets held in trust is called the **trust** *corpus* or **trust** *res*. The trust has legal title to the trust *corpus*, and the beneficiary has equitable title. Unlike wills, trusts are not public documents, so property can be transferred in privacy.

A trust can be created and become effective during a trustor's lifetime, or it can be created during a trustor's lifetime to become effective upon the trustor's death.

During the existence of the trust, the trustee collects money owed to the trust, pays taxes and necessary expenses of the trust, makes investment decisions, pays the income to the income beneficiary, and keeps necessary records of transactions.

Trusts often provide that any trust income is to be paid to a person or entity called the **income beneficiary**. The person or entity to receive the trust corpus upon the termination of the trust is called the **remainder beneficiary**. The income beneficiary and the remainder beneficiary can be the same person or different persons. The designated beneficiary can be any identifiable person, animal (such as a pet), charitable organization, or other institution or cause that the settlor chooses. There can be multiple income and remainder beneficiaries. An entire class of persons—for example, "my grandchildren"—can be named.

A trust can allow the trustee to invade (use) the trust *corpus* for certain purposes. These purposes can be named (e.g., "for the beneficiary's college education"). The trust agreement usually specifies how the receipts and expenses of the trust are to be divided between the income beneficiary and the remainder beneficiary.

Generally, the trustee has broad management powers over the trust property. Thus, the trustee can invest the trust property to preserve its capital and make it productive. The trustee must follow any restrictions on investments contained in the trust agreement or state statute.

Exhibit 15.8 shows the parties to a trust.

Express Trust

An **express trust** is created voluntarily by the settlor. It usually is written. The agreement is called a *trust instrument* or *trust agreement*. Express trusts fall into two categories:

1. *Inter vivos* **trust**, created while the settlor is alive. The settlor transfers legal title of property to a named trustee to hold, administer, and manage for the benefit of named beneficiaries.
2. **Testamentary trust**, created by will. The trust comes into existence when the settlor dies. If the will that establishes the trust is found to be invalid, the trust is also invalid.

Trust A legal arrangement established when one person transfers title to property to another person to be held and used for the benefit of a third person.

Settlor, trustor, or **transferor** Person who creates a trust.

Trustee Person or entity that holds legal title to the trust *corpus* and manages the trust for the benefit of the beneficiary or beneficiaries.

Trust *corpus* or **trust** *res* The property and assets held in trust.

Income beneficiary Person or entity to be paid income from the trust.

Remainder beneficiary Person or entity to receive the trust *corpus* upon termination of the trust.

Express trust A trust created voluntarily by the settlor.

Inter vivos **trust** A trust that is created while the settlor is alive.

Testamentary trust A trust created by will: the trust comes into existence when the settlor dies.

Exhibit 15.7 **Sample living will and health care proxy**

Living Will and Health Care Proxy

I. Living Will Including Statement Concerning Right to Die

Death is as much a reality as birth, growth, maturity and old age—it is the one certainty of life. If the time comes when I, John Doe, can no longer take part in decisions for my own future, let this statement stand as an expression of my wishes and directions to my Health Care Agent and others while I am still of sound mind. I intend, without otherwise limiting the absolute authority granted to my Health Care Agent in this instrument, that this instrument be binding upon my Health Care Agent.

If the situation should arise in which there is no reasonable expectation of my recovery from extreme physical or mental disability, including, but not limited to, a circumstance where there is no reasonable expectation that I will recover consciousness, commonly referred to as "brain dead," I direct that I be allowed to die and not be kept alive by medications, artificial means, including but not limited to artificial nutrition and hydration, or "heroic measures." Without limiting the generality of the foregoing, I hereby consent in such situation to an order not to attempt cardiopulmonary resuscitation. I do, however, ask that medication be mercifully administered to me to alleviate suffering even though this may shorten my remaining life and retard my consciousness.

II. Health Care Proxy

I hereby appoint my spouse, Jane Doe, to be my health care agent to make any and all health care decisions in accordance with my wishes and instructions as stated above and as otherwise known to her. In the event the person I appoint above is unable, unwilling or unavailable to act as my Health Care Agent, I hereby appoint my twin brother, Jack Doe, as my health care agent.

This health care proxy shall take effect in the event that I become unable to make my own health care decisions. I hereby revoke any prior health care proxy given by me to the extent it purports to confer the authority herein granted. I understand that, unless I revoke it, this health care proxy will remain in effect indefinitely.

Although I do not know today the exact circumstances that will exist when my Health Care Agent is called upon to make a decision or decisions on my behalf, I have selected my Health Care Agent with the confidence that such person understands my feelings in these matters and will make the decision I will want made considering the circumstances as they exist at the time. It is my intention, therefore, that the decision of my Health Care Agent be taken as a final and binding decision of mine, and will be the conclusive interpretation of the wishes I have made known in this document.

III. Waiver and Indemnity

To the extent permitted by law, I, for myself and for my heirs, executors, legal representatives and assigns, hereby release and discharge and agree to indemnify and hold harmless my Health Care Agent from and against any claim or liability whatsoever resulting from or arising out of my Health Care Agent's reliance on my wishes and directions as expressed herein. To induce any third party to act hereunder, I hereby agree that any third party receiving a duly executed copy or facsimile of this instrument may act hereunder, and that revocation or termination by me hereof shall be ineffective as to such third party unless and until actual notice or knowledge of such revocation shall have been received by such third party, and, to the extent permitted by law, I, for myself and for my heirs, executors, legal representatives and assigns, hereby release and discharge and agree to indemnify and hold harmless any such third party from and against any claims or liability whatsoever that may arise against such third party by reason of such third party having relied on the provisions of this instrument.

I understand the full import of this directive and I am emotionally and mentally competent to make this directive.

Signed _____

The declarant has been personally known to me and I believe him or her to be of sound mind.

Witness _____

Witness _____

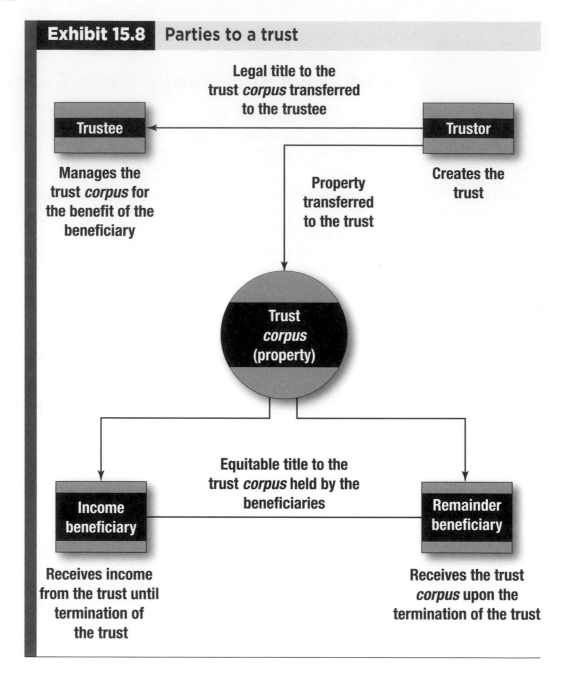

Exhibit 15.8 Parties to a trust

Legal title to the trust *corpus* transferred to the trustee

Trustee — Manages the trust *corpus* for the benefit of the beneficiary

Trustor — Creates the trust

Property transferred to the trust

Trust *corpus* (property)

Equitable title to the trust *corpus* held by the beneficiaries

Income beneficiary — Receives income from the trust until termination of the trust

Remainder beneficiary — Receives the trust *corpus* upon the termination of the trust

Example Suppose grandmother creates a trust and places assets in the trust that consist of stocks, bonds, bank accounts, and an apartment building. In the trust document, grandmother designates her daughter to receive the income from the trust (e.g., dividends, interest, and rental income) until the daughter dies, and upon the daughter's death the trust corpus is to be divided equally among grandmother's three granddaughters. Grandmother names Country Bank the trustee. This is a testamentary trust. Grandmother is the trustor, Country Bank is the trustee, the daughter is the income beneficiary, and the three granddaughters are the remainder beneficiaries.

Constructive Trust

Constructive trust An equitable trust that is implied by law to avoid fraud, unjust enrichment, and injustice.

A **constructive trust** is an equitable trust that is implied by law to avoid fraud, unjust enrichment, and injustice. In constructive trust arrangements, the holder of the actual title to property (i.e., the trustee) holds the property in trust for its rightful owner.

Example Suppose Thad and Kaye are partners. Assume Kaye embezzles partnership funds and uses the stolen funds to purchase a piece of real estate. In this case, the court can impose a constructive trust under which Kaye (who holds actual title to the land) is considered a trustee who is holding the property in trust for Thad, its rightful owner.

Resulting Trust

A **resulting trust** is implied from the conduct of the parties.

Resulting trust A trust that is implied from the conduct of the parties.

Example Suppose Henry is purchasing a piece of real estate but cannot attend the closing. He asks his brother, Gregory, to attend the closing and take title to the property until he can return. In this case, Gregory holds the title to the property as trustee for Henry until he returns.

Special Types of Trusts

Trusts may be created for special purposes. Three types of special trusts that are fairly common are:

1. **Charitable trusts**, created for the benefit of a segment of society or society in general. An example is a trust that is created for the construction and maintenance of a public park.
2. **Spendthrift trusts**, designed to prevent a beneficiary's personal creditors from reaching his or her trust interest. All control over the trust is removed from the beneficiary. Personal creditors still can go after trust income that is paid to the beneficiary, however.
3. **Totten trusts**, created when a person deposits money in a bank account in his or her own name and holds it as a trustee for the benefit of another person. A totten trust is a tentative trust because (a) the trustee can add or withdraw funds from the account, and (b) the trust can be revoked at any time prior to his or her death or prior to completing delivery of the funds to the beneficiary.

Termination of a Trust

A trust is irrevocable unless the settlor reserves the right to revoke it. Most trusts fall into the first category. Usually, a trust either contains a specific termination date or provides that it will terminate upon the happening of an event (e.g., when the remainder beneficiary reaches a certain age). Upon termination, the trust *corpus* is distributed as provided in the trust agreement.

The following Ethical Perspective feature discusses a paralegal's duty to act honestly and not to misappropriate trust funds.

Living Trusts

Living trusts have become a popular method for holding property during a person's lifetime and distributing the property upon that person's death. A living trust works as follows: During his or her life, a person establishes a living trust, which is a legal entity used for estate planning. A living trust also is referred to as a **grantor's trust** or a **revocable trust**. The person who creates the trust is called the **grantor**, or the **trustor**.

Living trust A method for holding property during a person's lifetime and distributing the property upon that person's death. Also called a *grantor's trust* and a *revocable trust*.

Grantor (trustor) The person who creates a living trust. Also called the *trustor*.

Benefits of a Living Trust

The primary purpose of using a living trust is to avoid probate associated with using a will. If a person dies with a will, the will must be probated so the deceased's assets can

ETHICAL PERSPECTIVE

Paralegal's Duty Not to Misappropriate Trust Funds

Ms. Nottingham, a paralegal, works for attorney Mr. Zachery who is a partner in a law firm. Mr. Zachery is an estate attorney. A client who is the executor of a will employs Mr. Zachery's law firm to handle the probate of the will. The assets of the estate consist of several pieces of real property, securities, bank accounts, and bearer bonds. The total value of the estate is $4 million. The beneficiaries of the will are the deceased's three children, who are to split the estate equally. Mr. Zachery assigns Ms. Nottingham to assist him in handling the estate.

Bearer bonds are bonds that are payable to the bearer, that is, to the person in possession of the bonds. The bearer bonds total $300,000. The bearer bonds are placed in the trust account of the law firm of which Mr. Zachery is a partner.

Ms. Nottingham, as the paralegal on the estate, has access to the bearer bonds. Ms. Nottingham, who is in financial difficulty because of the accumulation of too much credit card and other debt, faces the possibility of losing her house to foreclosure because of nonpayment of her mortgage. Ms. Nottingham sees no way out of losing her home and having to declare bankruptcy.

Ms. Nottingham realizes the significance of the bearer bonds: Whoever possesses them may cash them in and obtain payment from the issuer of the bonds. Ms. Nottingham steals the bearer bonds, delivers them to the issuer, and receives the $300,000 cash. She pays off her mortgagee and other debts.

Subsequently, the law firm discovers Ms. Nottingham's action. In this case, Ms. Nottingham has violated model and state codes of ethical conduct for paralegal professionals. As such, the state board that licenses paralegals could rescind her license to practice as a paralegal. In addition, the lawyers are under an ethical duty to report the defalcation to the client and to the law firm's insurance carrier. If there is no insurance carrier or the insurance does not cover such a loss, the law firm is responsible for paying the loss. In addition, Ms. Nottingham has violated the law by her action. She could face criminal charges by the state, and, if convicted, could be sentenced to jail.

---

be properly distributed according to the will. A probate judge is named to oversee the probate process, and all documents, including the will, are public record. By contrast, a living trust is private.

When the grantor dies, the assets are owned by the living trust and therefore are not subject to probate proceedings. In addition, if real property is owned in more than one state and a will is used, ancillary probate must be conducted in the other state. If a living trust is used, ancillary probate is avoided.

Living trusts often are promoted for claimed benefits that do not exist. The true facts are that a living trust:

- does not reduce estate taxes any more than a will does.
- does not reduce the grantor's income taxes. All the income earned by the trust is attributed to the grantor, who must pay income taxes on the earnings just as if the trust did not exist.
- does not avoid creditors. Thus, creditors can obtain liens against property in the trust.
- is subject to property division upon divorce.
- is usually not cheaper than a will. Both require payments to lawyers and usually to accountants and other professionals to draft and probate a will or draft and to manage a living trust.
- does not avoid controversies upon the grantor's death. Like wills, living trusts can be challenged for lack of capacity, undue influence, duress, and other legal grounds.

Funding and Operation of a Living Trust

To fund a living trust, the grantor transfers title to his or her property to the trust. This property is called the trust *corpus*. Bank accounts, stock certificates, real estate, personal property, intangible property, and other property owned by the grantor must be retitled to the trust's name.

For example, the grantor must execute deeds transferring title to real estate to the trust. Once property is transferred to the trust, the trust is considered funded. A living trust is revocable during the grantor's lifetime. Thus, a grantor can later change his or her mind and undo the trust and retake title of the property in his or her own name.

A living trust names a trustee who is responsible for maintaining, investing, buying, or selling trust assets. The trustee is usually the grantor. Thus, the grantor who establishes the trust does not lose control of the property placed in the trust and may manage and invest trust assets during his or her lifetime. The trust should name a *successor trustee* to replace the grantor–trustee if the grantor becomes incapacitated or too ill to manage the trust.

Beneficiaries

A living trust names a beneficiary or beneficiaries who are entitled to receive income from the living trust while it is in existence and to receive the property of the trust when the grantor dies. Usually the grantor is the income beneficiary, who receives the income from the trust during his or her lifetime. Upon the death of the grantor, assets of the trust are distributed to the remainder beneficiary or beneficiaries named in the trust. The designated trustee has the fiduciary duties of identifying assets, paying creditors, paying income and estate taxes, transferring assets to named beneficiaries, and rendering an accounting.

Pour-Over Will

A **pour-over will** is necessary to distribute any property acquired in the name of the grantor after the living trust is established or any property that was not transferred to the trust in the first place. The pour-over will transfers this property to the trust upon the grantor's death, and it then is distributed to the named beneficiaries of the trust. A pour-over will is subject to probate and is therefore public. A pour-over will usually is created at the same time that the living trust is established.

A living trust is a legitimate planning tool for many people. A person should seek professional advice from and have an attorney draft the living trust, pour-over will, and other necessary documents.

For a discussion of a paralegal's duty to report dishonest or fraudulent acts pertaining to the handling of funds or assets, see the following Ethical Perspective.

Pour-over will A will that, upon the grantor's death, distributes the grantor's property that is not in the living will.

Elder Law

Paralegals should be aware of a growing area of the law called **elder law**. This is a specialized area of the law that involves many subjects other than estates. Elders often employ lawyers who specialize in elder law to assist them in pursuing their rights and protecting them from unscrupulous and fraudulent behavior by others. Paralegals often assist elder law attorneys in these matters.

Some of the areas in which elderly people may need legal assistance are the following:

- Obtaining Social Security benefits and representing elders who have been defrauded out of their Social Security benefits.
- Obtaining and protecting rights to Medicare and Medicaid and other government health care related programs.
- Protecting elders from undue influence in executing wills, trusts, and contracts, and suing to have contracts and documents that were signed under undue influence rescinded.

ETHICAL PERSPECTIVE

Paralegal's Duty to Report Dishonest or Fraudulent Acts Pertaining to the Handling of Funds

Ms. Vivian Zhong works as a paralegal for a law firm that specializes in the area of wills, trusts, and estates. The lawyers of the firm engage in estate planning for clients, draft wills and trusts, and represent clients in other areas of elder law. As required by law, the law firm has established trust funds at banks where clients' funds are kept on deposit during the period that a will or trust is being administered by the law firm.

Mr. Richard Hawthorne is a partner of the law firm. Mr. Hawthorne currently is going through a divorce and has several children in college whom he helps support. Mr. Hawthorne, who needs money to support himself and his family, falsifies records at the law firm and misappropriates $200,000 from a trust fund being administered by the law firm.

Ms. Zhong, who is the paralegal assigned to assist in administering the trust fund, discovers Mr. Hawthorne's misappropriation of the funds from the trust. Ms. Zhong faces the dilemma of whether to report Mr. Hawthorne's misappropriation of the trust funds, and if so, to whom.

Does Ms. Zhong have a duty to report the dishonest and fraudulent act of attorney Mr. Hawthorne? If so, to whom?

Model and state paralegal codes of ethics and professional responsibility provide that a paralegal is under a duty to report knowledge of any dishonest or fraudulent acts by any person pertaining to the handling of the funds or assets of a client. Depending on the nature and circumstances of the misconduct, a paralegal owes a duty to report knowledge of a dishonest or fraudulent act to partners of the law firm, local prosecutors, bar associations, or other appropriate party. A paralegal's failure to report such knowledge violates model and state paralegal ethics codes.

PARALEGAL'S ETHICAL DECISION

Thus, Ms. Zhong owes a duty to report Mr. Hawthorne's dishonest and fraudulent conduct of stealing funds from a client's trust fund. At minimum, Ms. Zhong owes a duty to report Mr. Hawthorne's conduct to the ethics committee of the law firm, and if there is no such committee, then to the managing partners of the law firm. Under the circumstances of this case, Ms. Zhong would probably owe a duty to report Mr. Hawthorne's conduct to the appropriate government agency, such as the state's attorney general's office, as well as to the state bar association.

- Obtaining and enforcing contracts for the provision of long-term care insurance if an insurance carrier denies benefits for which elders have paid premiums for that insurance protection.
- Protecting elders from elder abuse and pursuing charges against those who have abused elders.
- Protecting elders from age discrimination and bringing lawsuits to enforce the antidiscrimination laws that protect elders from such discrimination.
- Helping elders to defend against charges of incompetency that may be unfairly brought against elders by relatives or others.

- Protecting elders from unscrupulous parties, including some relatives, who might take advantage of elders who suffer from diminished mental capacity to make informed decisions.
- Helping elders to have their wishes enforced that they have clearly delineated in living wills.
- Enforcing the wishes of elders to receive medical treatment in their homes rather than be moved to nursing homes.

The legal issues that elders may be involved in are numerous. Lawyers often are employed to help elders to address many of these issues. Paralegals who work in the field of elder law must become familiar with the many government programs, contract issues, and other legal issues involving representing elders and protecting them from fraud, undue influence, and other misconduct by others.

Exhibit 15.9 sets forth the excerpts of the standards that attorneys should follow when engaging in the practice of elder law.

Exhibit 15.9 Aspirational standards for the practice of elder law

Excerpts from National Academy of Law Attorneys

Preamble

In the past 20 years, Elder Law has developed as a separate specialty area because of the unique and complex issues faced by older persons. Elder Law includes helping such persons and their families with planning for incapacity and long-term care, Medicaid and Medicare, including coverage of nursing home and home care, health and long-term care insurance, and health care decision making. It also includes the drafting of special needs and other trusts, the selection of long-term care providers, home care and nursing home problem solving, retiree health and income benefits, retirement housing, and fiduciary services or representation.

In these and other areas, the Elder Law Attorney is often asked to advocate for clients with diminished capacity. Family members and persons with fiduciary responsibilities become involved. The traditional client–attorney relationship is not always clear. Issues such as substituted judgment, best interests, and "who is the client?" present problems not regularly faced by other lawyers.

In recognizing Elder Law as a specialty practice area to meet the legal needs of older persons and persons with disabilities and their families, the National Academy of Elder Law Attorneys (NAELA) was founded in 1987. The following Guidelines set out Aspirational Standards of professionalism and ethical behavior for Elder Law Attorneys. They are the product of study and deliberation by NAELA members and, specifically, NAELA's Professionalism and Ethics Committee.

Competent Legal Representation
The Elder Law Attorney:
(1) Recognizes the special range of client needs and professional skills unique to the practice of Elder Law and holds himself or herself out as an Elder Law Attorney only after ensuring his or her professional competence in handling elder law and disability related matters.
(2) Approaches client matters in a holistic manner, recognizing that legal representation of clients often is enhanced by the involvement of other professionals, support groups, and aging network resources.
(3) Regularly pursues continuing professional education and peer collaboration in Elder Law. Continuing education should include a broad range of Elder Law related subjects as well as an understanding of the physical, cognitive, and psychosocial challenges of aging and disability, and the skills needed to serve persons who are physically or mentally challenged.
(4) Ensures adequate training and supervision of legal and non-legal staff with a corresponding emphasis on the knowledge and skills needed to best serve persons facing the challenges of aging and disability.

Source: Copyright © The National Academy of Elder Law Attorneys (NAELA). Reprinted with permission.

Concept Review *and* Reinforcement

LEGAL TERMINOLOGY

SUMMARY OF KEY CONCEPTS

Wills

Definition	A will is a declaration of how a person wants his or her property to be distributed upon his or her death.
Parties to a Will	1. *Testator or testatrix:* The person who makes a will. 2. *Beneficiary:* The person designated in the will to receive the testator's property. There may be multiple beneficiaries. 3. *Executor or executrix:* The person named in a will to administer the testator's estate during settlement of the estate.

Requirements for Making a Will	1. *Statute of Wills:* A state statute that establishes the requirements for making a valid will.
	2. The normal requirements for making a will are:
	  a. *Testamentary capacity* (legal age and "sound mind")
	  b. *In writing*
	  c. *Testator's signature*
	  d. *Attestation by witnesses* (mentally competent and uninterested)

Changing a Will	1. *Codicil:* a legal way to change an existing will 2. Must be executed with the same formalities as a will

Special Types of Wills

Holographic Will	A holographic will is entirely handwritten and is signed by the testator. Most states recognize the validity of these wills even though they are not witnessed.
Noncupative Will	A noncupative will is an oral will made by dying persons before witnesses. Many states recognize these oral wills. Also called a *deathbed will* or a *dying declaration*.

Testamentary Gifts

Types of Gifts	1. *Specific gift:* Gift of a specifically mentioned piece of property (e.g., a ring) 2. *General gift:* Gift that does not identify the specific property from which the gift is to be made (e.g., gift of cash) 3. *Residuary gift:* Gift of the remainder of the testator's estate after the debts, taxes, and specific and general gifts have been paid
Simultaneous Deaths	Uniform Simultaneous Death Act provides that if people who would inherit property from each other die simultaneously, each deceased person's property is distributed as if he or she had survived.
Mutual or Reciprocal Will	Two or more testators execute separate wills that leave property in favor of the other on condition that the survivor leave the remaining property upon his or her death as agreed by the testators.
Undue Influence	A will may be found to be invalid if it was made under undue influence, in which one person takes advantage of another person's mental, emotional, or physical weakness and unduly persuades that person to make a will.

Probate

Definition	Legal process of settling a deceased person's estate.
Administrator or Administratrix	Person named to administer the estate of a deceased person who dies intestate. An administrator also is named if an executor is not named in a will or the executor cannot or does not serve.
Lineal Descendants	1. *Per stirpes distribution:* Lineal descendants inherit by representation of their parent; they split what their deceased parent would have received. 2. *Per capita distribution:* Lineal descendants equally share the property of the estate without regard to degree.
Ademption	If a testator leaves a specific gift but the property is no longer in the estate when the testator dies, the beneficiary of that gift receives nothing.
Abatement	If the testator's estate is insufficient to pay the stated gifts, the gifts are abated (reduced) in the following order: (1) residuary gifts, then (2) general gifts proportionately.

Intestate Succession

Intestate Succession	1. *Intestacy statute:* State statute that stipulates how a deceased's property will be distributed if he or she dies without leaving a will or if the will fails for some legal reason. 2. *Heirs:* Relatives who receive property under an intestacy statute. 3. *Escheat:* If no heirs, deceased's property goes to the state, under intestacy statutes.

Living Will and Health Care Directive

Right to Die	The right to die is a personal liberty protected by the U.S. Constitution.
Living Will	A living will is a document signed by a person that stipulates his or her wishes to not have his or her life prolonged by artificial means.
Health Care Directive	A health care proxy, or directive, is a document that names a person as a health care agent who has the authority to make health care decisions for the maker of the health care directive in accordance with the maker's wishes. Also called a *health care proxy*.

Trusts

Definition	A trust is a legal arrangement whereby one person delivers and transfers legal title to property to another person to be held and used for the benefit of a third person.
Trust Corpus	*Trust corpus* is the property that is held in trust, also called *trust res*.

Parties	1. *Settlor:* Person who establishes a trust; also called a *trustor* or *transferor*.
	2. *Trustee:* Person to whom *legal title* of the trust assets is transferred; responsible for managing the trust assets as established by the trust and law.
	3. *Beneficiary:* Person for whose benefit a trust is created; holds *equitable title* to the trust assets. There can be multiple beneficiaries, including:
	   a. *Income beneficiary:* person to whom trust income is to be paid
	   b. *Remainder beneficiary:* person who is entitled to receive the *trust corpus* upon termination of the trust

Express Trusts	Express trusts are voluntarily created by the settlor. Two types are: 1. *Inter vivos trust:* Created while the settlor is alive; also called a *living trust*. 2. *Testamentary trust:* Created by will and comes into existence when the settlor dies.
Constructive Trust	Constructive trusts are equitable trusts imposed by law to avoid fraud, unjust enrichment, and injustice.
Resulting Trust	Resulting trusts are created from the conduct of the parties.
Special Types of Trusts	1. *Charitable trust:* A trust created for the benefit of a segment of society or society in general. 2. *Spendthrift trust:* A trust whereby the creditors of the beneficiary cannot recover the trust's assets to satisfy debts owed to them by the beneficiary. 3. *Totten trust:* A trust created when a person deposits money in a bank account in his or her own name and holds it as a trust for the benefit of another person.

Living Trusts

Definition	A living trust is a legal entity used for estate planning. Also called a *grantor's trust*, *revocable trust*, or *inter vivos trust*.
Trust Corpus	The *trust corpus* is the property that is placed in a living trust to fund the trust.
Parties	1. *Grantor:* A person who establishes a living trust. 2. *Trustee:* A person who is responsible for maintaining, investing, buying, and selling trust assets. 3. *Income beneficiary:* A person who is entitled to receive income from a living trust. 4. *Remainder beneficiary:* A person who is entitled to receive the assets of a trust upon the death of the grantor.

Pour-Over Will	A pour-over will is necessary to distribute to the trust upon the grantor's death, any of the grantor's property not in the living trust at the time of the grantor's death.

Elder Law

Elder Law	Law that involves protecting the rights of elders, obtaining benefits due to elders, and otherwise representing elders in legal issues and cases that they are involved in.

WORKING THE WEB

1. Using Internet search engines such as http://www .google.com.html or Internet legal search services such as Westlaw or LexisNexis, find your state's will statute. What are the requirements for completing a valid will in your state? What are the attestation requirements? Write a one-page report on your findings. If you can, print out a sample will and attach it to your report.
2. Using Internet legal search services such as Westlaw or LexisNexis or Internet search engines such as http:// www.google.com.html, find your state's intestacy statute. Make a list, in descending order of heirs, of how the property of a deceased person will be distributed if he or she dies without a will. When does the property escheat to the state?
3. Using Internet search engines such as http://www .google.com.html or Internet legal search services such as Westlaw or LexisNexis, find your state's living trust statute. What are the requirements for completing a valid living trust in your state? Write a one-page report on your findings. If you can, print out a sample living trust and attach it to your report.
4. Using Internet legal search services such as Westlaw or LexisNexis or Internet search engines such as http:// www.google.com.html, find your state's living will statute. What are the requirements for completing a valid living will in your state? Also find your state's health care directive (health care proxy) statute. What are the requirements for completing a valid health care directive in your state? Write a one-page report on your findings. If you can, print out a sample living will and sample health care directive and attach these to your report.
5. Using the Internet search engine http://www.google. com.html or other Internet search engines, find articles that discuss Ms. Anna Nicole Smith's will challenge to her husband Howard Marshall's will. Write a one-page report on the case and the court decisions in the case.

CRITICAL THINKING & WRITING QUESTIONS

1. What is a will? What are the requirements for making a will?
2. Define a beneficiary of a will.
3. What is a codicil? What is a subsequent will?
4. Define holographic will and nuncupative will.
5. What is a devise (or legacy)? Describe the following types of devises: (a) specific gift, (b) general gift, and (c) residuary gift.
6. Define a lineal descendant. Explain the difference between *per capita* and *per stirpes* distribution of property to lineal descendants.
7. What is the difference between abatement and ademption?
8. What is a joint (or mutual) will?
9. Explain the doctrine of undue influence. Give an example.
10. What does it mean for a person to die intestate? Describe what an intestacy statute does? Who is an heir? What is escheat?
11. Describe a living will. What is a heath care directive (or proxy)?
12. What is a trust? Define settlor (trustor or transferor). What is *trust corpus* (*trust res*)? Define an income beneficiary and a remainder beneficiary.
13. Define the following types of trusts: (a) express trust, (b) constructive trust, (c) resulting trust, (d) charitable trust, (e) spendthrift trust, and (f) totten trust.
14. Describe a living will and what it accomplishes. Describe a health care directive (health care proxy) and what it accomplishes.
15. What is a living (grantor's or revocable) trust? Define the following parties: grantor (trustor), trustee, and beneficiary. What are the benefits of establishing a living trust?

Building Paralegal Skills

VIDEO CASE STUDY

A Senior Citizen Consults a New Lawyer: Conflict of Interest

 A client is meeting with his attorney to seek advice and about actions that he can take to protect himself from actions which he took based on the advice of another attorney.

After viewing the video case study at www.pearsonhighered.com/goldman answer the following:

1. What are the standards and the elements that must be proven to make a case of malpractice against a lawyer?

2. What is the obligation of the lawyer to determine the legal competency of his or her clients?

3. Would the manner in which the property was titled have changed the need for legal action after the death of the wife?

ETHICS ANALYSIS & DISCUSSION QUESTIONS

1. As a paralegal, what duty of honesty do you owe regarding the handling of funds held in trust by the law firm you work for in probate, estate, and trust administration matters?

2. What duty does a paralegal owe if he knows that a will he has been assigned to draft for a client of his supervising attorney has been obtained through undue influence? What if the supervising attorney has knowledge of the situation?

3. In working as a paralegal, a client of the law firm you work for dies intestate. No immediate relatives can be located. Your supervising attorney assigns you the task of locating persons who could take under the state's intestate statute. How hard must you look for distant relatives?

DEVELOPING YOUR COLLABORATION SKILLS

With a group of other students, selected by you or as assigned by your instructor, review the facts of the following case. As a group, discuss the following questions.

1. What types of devises were made by Ethel Ramchissel?
2. Are Anderson and Baker entitled to the cash in the two bank accounts?

Opperman v. Anderson

Ethel M. Ramchissel executed a will that made the following bequests: (1) one-half of the stock she owned in Pabst Brewing Company (Pabst) to Mary Lee Anderson, (2) all of the stock she owned in Houston Natural Gas Corporation (Houston Natural Gas) to Ethel Baker and others (Baker), and (3) the residual and remainder of her estate to Boysville, Inc.

Later, the following events happened. First, in response to an offer by G. Heilman Brewing Company to purchase Pabst, Ramchissel sold all of her Pabst stock and placed the cash proceeds in a bank account to which no other funds were added. Second, pursuant to a merger agreement between Internorth, Inc., and Houston Natural Gas, Ramchissel converted her Houston Natural Gas stock to cash and placed the cash in a bank account to which no other funds were added. When Ramchissel died about 3 1/2 years after making her will, her will was admitted into probate. Anderson and Baker argued that they were entitled to the cash in the two bank accounts, respectively.

Source: *Opperman v. Anderson*, 782 S.W.2d 8, Web 1989 Tex. App. Lexis 3175 (Court of Appeals of Texas)

PARALEGAL PORTFOLIO EXERCISE

Review the Paralegals at Work at the beginning of the chapter. Prepare a joint will for Mr. and Ms. Huntington that meets your state's will requirements. Have another person and you sign the will as if you were Mr. and Ms. Huntington, and have the proper attestation of the will as required in your state.

LEGAL ANALYSIS & WRITING CASES

In the Matter of the Estate of Jansa   670 S.W.2d 767, Web 1984 Tex. App. Lexis 5503

Court of Appeals of Texas

Martha Jansa executed a will naming her two sons as executors of her will and leaving all of her property to them. The will was properly signed and attested to by witnesses. Thereafter, Martha died. When Martha's safe deposit box at a bank was opened, the original of this will was discovered along with two other instruments that were dated after the will. One was a handwritten document that left her home to her grandson, with the remainder of her estate to her two sons; this document was not signed. The second document was a typed version of the handwritten one; this document was signed by Martha but was not attested to by witnesses.

Question

1. Which of the three documents should be admitted to probate?

In re Estate of Potter   469 So.2d 957, Web 1985 Fla. App. Lexis 14338

Court of Appeals of Florida

Mrs. Mildred D. Potter executed a will providing that, upon her death, her residence in Pompano Beach, Florida, was to go to her daughter and an equivalent amount of cash to her son. Evidence showed that Mrs. Potter's intent was to treat the daughter and son equally in the distribution of her estate. When she died, her will was admitted into probate. At the time, she still possessed her home in Pompano Beach. Unfortunately, assets were insufficient to pay Mrs. Potter's son the equivalent amount of cash.

Question

1. Can the son share in the value of the house so that his inheritance is equal to his sister's?

Jones v. Jones   718 S.W.2d 416, Web 1986 Tex.App. Lexis 8929

Court of Appeals of Texas

In 1967, Homer and Edna Jones, husband and wife, executed a joint will that provided: "We will and give to our survivor, whether it be Homer Jones or Edna Jones, all property and estate of which the first of us that dies may be seized and possessed. If we should both die in a common catastrophe, or upon the death of our survivor, we will and give all property and estate then remaining to our children, Leonida Jones Eschman, daughter, Sylvia Marie Jones, daughter, and Grady V. Jones, son, share and share alike."

When Homer dies 18 years later, Edna Jones received his entire estate under the will. Two years later Edna executed a new will that left a substantially larger portion of the estate to her daughter, Sylvia Marie Jones, than to the other two children. Edna died five years after making her will. Edna's daughter Sylvia introduced Edna's new will for probate. The other two children introduced the 1967 will for probate.

Question

1. Who wins?

In re the Estate of Danforth   705 S.W.2d 609, Web 1986 Mo. App. Lexis 3757

Court of Appeals of Missouri

Dr. Duncan R. Danforth, a 75-year-old man of substantial means, married 21-year-old Loretta Ollison. Immediately following the ceremony, the newlyweds went to a lawyer's office, where Danforth executed a newly prepared will naming Ollison a principal beneficiary of his estate. Four days later, Danforth was murdered by Michael Stith, Ollison's lover. In a criminal trial, Ollison was convicted of conspiracy to commit murder and was sentenced to 10 years in prison.

Question

1. Can Ollison recover under the will or take her elective share of the estate under the state's intestate statute?

WORKING WITH THE LANGUAGE OF THE COURT CASE

In re Estate of Vallerius

629 N.E.2d 118, Web 1994 Ill. App. Lexis 267 (1994)
Appellate Court of Illinois

Read the following case, excerpted from the Court of Appeals opinion. Review and brief the case. In your brief, answer the following questions.

1. Who was to inherit Adella Vallerius's property upon her death?
2. What criminal acts did Douglas and Craig White commit?
3. Who is Renie White? Whose property did she inherit, and why?
4. Who was to inherit Renie White's property upon her death?
5. Were Douglas or Craig White permitted to inherit either Adella's or Renie's property upon her death?

Lewis, Presiding Justice

On December 22, 1987, Douglas White murdered his grandmother, Adella G. Vallerius. On the same day, at the same time, and in the same house, Douglas' brother, Craig White, murdered his grandmother's friend, Carroll Pieper. Douglas was convicted of Mrs. Vallerius' murder. Craig entered a negotiated plea of guilty to, and was convicted of, the murder of Carroll Pieper. Craig testified for the State in Douglas' murder trial as part of his negotiated guilty plea.

Mrs. Vallerius died testate, naming Douglas and Craig as her sole beneficiaries. Mrs. Vallerius' only heir was her daughter, Renie White, Douglas and Craig's mother. On January 11, 1988, Mrs. Vallerius' will was admitted to probate. In compliance with the terms of the will, Douglas White and Dennis Johnson were appointed legal representatives of Mrs. Vallerius' estate. About 2½ months after Mrs. Vallerius was murdered, on March 7, 1988, Renie White died, intestate, of natural causes. She left as her only heirs her two sons, Douglas and Craig.

On March 12, 1990, the appellees, Peter M. Vallerius, Glenna F. Giacoletto, Lawrence Joe Davis, Helen L. Vallerius, Gail Kadavi, Iione V. Henry, Janis Murray, Terrie L. Illies, and Duffy Joe Vallerius, filed a petition to intervene and to consolidate the estates of Mrs. Vallerius and Renie White and an "Objection to Distribution" in the estate of Mrs. Vallerius, wherein they alleged that "Douglas Keith White and Craig Steven White, having intentionally and unjustifiably caused the death of Adella G. Vallerius, cannot lawfully receive any property, benefit or other interest" by reason of her death, through the estate of Mrs. Vallerius or through the estate of Renie White.

After an evidentiary hearing on the appellees' objection to distribution, the court entered an order granting the appellees' request. The trial court found that the issue in the case was whether Douglas and Craig could receive any property or interest by reason of the death of Mrs. Vallerius, whether through her estate or the estate of Renie White. The court determined that, under both statute and common law, the public policy of Illinois has long been to prevent wrongdoers from profiting from intentionally committed wrongful acts. The court further found that the petitioner-objectors (appellees herein) had sustained their burden of proof, by clear and convincing evidence, that Douglas and Craig intentionally caused the death of their grandmother, Mrs. Vallerius.

Appellants argue that the law does not preclude a murderer from inheriting property from a person other than the victim. The obvious intent of the law is that persons like Douglas and Craig White must not profit from their brutal murder of their grandmother. The fact that there is an intervening estate should not expurgate the wrong of the murderer.

The appellants argue that Craig cannot be held accountable for Douglas' murder of Mrs. Vallerius, since Craig did not actually swing the sledgehammer that killed Mrs. Vallerius but only killed Carroll Pieper after Douglas killed Mrs. Vallerius. Appellants argue that even though Craig "may have borne criminal responsibility for the actions of Douglas White under the criminal accountability statute," Craig cannot be denied his right of inheritance from his mother.

Craig White cannot be permitted to receive any benefit by reason of the death of Mrs. Vallerius, whether through her estate directly or indirectly through the estate of her daughter, Renie White. If we were to allow Craig White to receive any property, benefit, or interest from the estate of Renie White, our decision would directly contravene the state's unambiguous mandate that he not receive any property by reason of his grandmother's death in any capacity or by any circumstance.

The happiest moments of my life have been the few which I have passed at home in the bosom of my family. "

Thomas Jefferson,
Letter to Francis Willis, Jr., 1790

Paralegals at Work

As a paralegal, you work for Ms. Sara Khan, a lawyer who specializes in family law and domestic relations issues. Specializing in family law, you often are assigned to investigate and discover information pertinent to clients' cases, conduct legal research on family law issues, and draft documents for review by Ms. Khan before they are submitted to the family law court. You also attend meetings of Ms. Khan and her clients wherein the clients are interviewed to obtain relevant information about their family law matter.

One day Ms. Jennifer Aston, a new client, arrives at the law office. Ms. Khan invites you to sit in on the initial meeting with Ms. Aston. At the meeting, Ms. Aston discloses that she wants to obtain a divorce from her spouse, Mr. Breton. At the meeting, Ms. Aston tells the following facts about her marriage. Ms. Aston and Mr. Breton met after she graduated from medical school. They have been married 15 years. Ms. Aston is now 45 years old, and Mr. Breton is 42 years old. They have two children: Kayla, their 10-year-old daughter born to the spouses, and Jason, an adopted son who is 6 years old.

Ms. Aston discloses the following facts about her and her spouse's financial situation: Ms. Aston is a medical doctor who earns $500,000 per year. Mr. Breton is an actor/waiter who earns $50,000 per year. They have a joint bank account into which both of their earnings are deposited. During the course of their marriage, they have accumulated the following assets from their earnings: (1) the house where they live with their children, valued at $1,000,000 and with a $300,000 mortgage (loan) against it; (2) $800,000 of securities in the stock market; (3) a $200,000 savings account at a bank; (4) two automobiles, each valued at $25,000; and (5) personal property, including furniture, valued at $150,000.

Ms. Aston reveals these additional facts: During the course of the marriage, she inherited $1,000,000 of securities from her grandmother. Ms. Aston has kept these securities in her own name. The securities have increased to $1,600,000 in value at this time. Mr. Breton has no separate property.

Ms. Khan asks Ms. Aston if there is a prenuptial agreement, and Ms. Aston states that there is no such agreement. Ms. Aston explains that she wants to keep the house and retain custody of the two children.

Consider the issues involved in this scenario as you read the chapter.

INTRODUCTION FOR THE PARALEGAL

Family law and domestic relations is a broad area of the law, involving premarital issues, prenuptial agreements, marriage, dissolution of marriage, division of property upon dissolution of marriage, spousal and child support payments, child custody, and other family law issues.

Paralegals often work in the family law and domestic relations area. Those who work in this area of the law are called upon to interview clients, investigate and obtain relevant information, draft letters and documents to be sent to clients, and prepare legal forms that will be submitted to the family law or domestic relations court. The paralegal must report to and submit letters, documents, and forms to the supervising attorney for approval and often signature.

This chapter provides the paralegal with an introduction to the issues most commonly encountered in a family law legal practice.

Career opportunities for paralegal professionals in the family law area are discussed below.

Premarriage Issues

Prior to marriage, several legal issues may arise. These include promises to marry, engagement, and prenuptial agreements.

Promise to Marry

In the nineteenth century, many courts recognized an action for breach of a **promise to marry**. This usually would occur if a man proposed marriage, the woman accepted, and then the man backed out before the marriage took place. The lawsuit was based on a breach-of-contract theory.

Today, most courts do not recognize a breach of a promise-to-marry lawsuit. The denial of such lawsuits is based on current social norms. If, however, the potential groom backs out late, after many of the items for the pending marriage were purchased or contracted for (e.g., flowers, rental of a reception hall), he may be responsible for paying these costs.

Engagement

As a prelude to getting married, many couples go through a period of time known as **engagement**. The engagement usually begins when the male proposes marriage to the female, and if the female accepts, he gives her an engagement ring (usually a diamond ring). In these modern times, a female also may propose marriage to a male. During an engagement, the female is called the **fiancée** and the male is called the **fiancé**. The engagement period runs until the wedding is held or the engagement is

Web Exploration

Using www.google.com find out whether your state uses the fault rule or the objective rule in determining which party gets the engagement ring if an engagement is terminated.

CAREER OPPORTUNITIES FOR PARALEGALS IN FAMILY LAW

With the divorce rate in this country around 50 percent, a substantial number of lawyers and paralegals work in the family law area. A paralegal in the family law area usually is involved in a broad spectrum of legal issues.

A divorce case is a lawsuit. Therefore, the legal rules and procedures involving the court system apply. Paralegals must know these procedures for the state in which they work. For example, a divorce case usually involves investigating finances and other issues concerning the divorce, preparing notices for discovery of evidence, drafting interrogatories, and preparing other documents needed in the divorce case.

Most divorces are settled before they go to trial. This often requires negotiation between the parties and their lawyers to reach an acceptable settlement agreement. The paralegal frequently sits in on many of the meetings and negotiation sessions between the parties and their attorneys.

If a settlement is reached, the paralegal often is called upon to prepare a draft of the settlement agreement. This will require substantial knowledge of the law of the state, as well as of the facts of the individual divorce case. In addition, the paralegal may be assigned to prepare the documents associated with the settlement of a divorce case, such as deeds and documents to transfer real property, securities, bank accounts, and other property necessary to complete the divorce.

In many divorce cases, custody battles over children arise. The lawyers will represent the parties in these custody disputes, and their paralegals will assist the lawyers in preparing for these disputes. Other issues in divorce cases may include visitation rights, child support payments, and alimony, among others. Again, the paralegal must be familiar with these legal issues, and the procedures and documents associated with these issues.

In many instances, the parties sign a prenuptial agreement prior to marriage. These agreements establish the rights of parties should the parties separate. The paralegal often is responsible for preparing drafts of prenuptial agreements and other documents necessary to support the prenuptial agreement.

Other issues in the family law area concern the adoption of children, contracts for surrogate mothers, proceedings to determine the capacity of parents, spouses, and other loved ones, the appointment of conservators, and other family law matters. These areas usually require the expertise of family law lawyers and their paralegals.

One current area of the law pertains to the rights and duties of same-sex partners. These couples require legal representation in many family law issues. These may include the drafting of legal documents, adoption of children, separation of the partners, division of assets upon separation of partners, and other issues. In addition, lawyers are called upon to represent same-sex partners in cases to establish legal rights and duties, and to eliminate laws that treat same-sex partners different from heterosexual partners.

The family law area provides a wealth of opportunities for well-trained and knowledgeable paralegals.

---

broken off. If a couple gets married, they often exchange wedding band rings at the marriage ceremony.

Sometimes the engagement is broken off prior to the wedding. Then the issue becomes: Who gets the engagement ring if the engagement is broken off? Some states follow a **fault rule**, which works as follows:

- If the prospective groom breaks off the engagement, the prospective bride gets to keep the engagement ring.
- If the prospective bride breaks off the engagement, she must return the engagement ring to the prospective groom.

The fault rule is sometimes difficult to apply. Questions often arise as to who broke off the engagement, which then requires a trial to decide the issue.

The modern rule and trend is to abandon the fault rule and adopt an **objective rule**: If the engagement is broken off, the prospective bride must return the engagement ring, regardless of who broke off the engagement. This objective rule is clear and usually avoids litigation unless the female refuses to return the ring.

Prenuptial Agreements

In today's society, many spouses sign prenuptial agreements in advance of their marriage. **Prenuptial agreements**—also called **premarital agreements**—are contracts that specify how property will be distributed upon termination of the marriage or death of a spouse. To be enforced, a prenuptial agreement must be in writing.

Objective rule A rule stating that if an engagement is broken off, the prospective bride must return the engagement ring, regardless of which party broke off the engagement.

Prenuptial agreement A contract entered into prior to marriage that specifies how property will be distributed upon the termination of the marriage or death of a spouse.

Web Exploration

Go to http://www.people.com/people/archive/article/0,20186762,00.html and read the article about the divorce judgment in the Paul McCartney-Heather Mills divorce proceeding.

Prenuptial agreements often are used where both parties to a marriage have their own career and have accumulated assets prior to the marriage, or one of the spouses has significant assets prior to the marriage. Prenuptial agreements also are often used where there are children from a prior marriage and the agreement guarantees that these children will receive a certain share of the assets of the remarrying spouse if he or she dies or the marriage is terminated.

For a prenuptial agreement to be enforceable each party must make full disclosure of all his or her assets and liabilities and each party should be represented by his or her own attorney. Prenuptial agreements must be entered into voluntarily, without threats or undue pressure. They must provide for the fair distribution of assets and must not be unconscionable. Generally, courts will enforce a properly negotiated prenuptial agreement even if the agreement provides for an unequal distribution of assets and eliminates financial support of a spouse in case the marriage is terminated.

Courts will not enforce a prenuptial agreement in the following circumstances:

- One of the parties was not represented by an attorney.
- One of the parties failed to make full disclosure of his or her assets and liabilities.
- The agreement was entered into at the "last moment," immediately prior to the marriage.
- The terms of the agreement are unfair or unconscionable.
- The agreement violates public policy (for example, if a party is forced to live on government assistance if the agreement is enforced).

Issues Covered in a Prenuptial Agreement

Prenuptial agreements often include the following issues:

- **Separate Property.** A list of each party's separate property that the party is bringing into the marriage and a statement that the listed property shall remain separate property unless changed by writing during the course of the marriage.

  Example Miles and Nikki are getting married. Nikki has the following separate property: securities worth $1 million, pension worth $1 million, real estate worth $ 1 million, bank accounts of $1 million. Miles has $50,000 in the bank. The prenuptial agreement could state that Nikki's separate property is her separate property and will remain so during the course of the marriage unless Nikki otherwise transfers ownership to any of her separate property in writing to Miles. The prenuptial agreement could treat Miles's $50,000 separate property similarly.

- **Income.** An agreement as to how income will be treated during the marriage. For example, a high income earner may be awarded a certain percentage or dollar amount of his or her income as separate property.

  Example In the previous example, Nikki is a brain surgeon who makes $1 million per year in income. Miles makes $75,000 per year income. The prenuptial agreement can agree that a certain percent (e.g., 50 percent) or certain amount ($500,000) of Nikki's income is her separate property each year, and the remainder is joint property.

- **Alimony.** The prenuptial agreement can set forth the alimony that will be paid if the parties are divorced.

  Example In the previous example, the prenuptial agreement could set forth that Nikki, the high income earner, will pay Miles, the low income earner, a specified amount of alimony each month (e.g., $3,000 per month) for a specified period of time (e.g., five years) if the parties are divorced.

- **Child Custody.** The prenuptial agreement can provide for child custody and visitation rights.

Example   The prenuptial agreement could specify that Nikki is awarded custody of the children of the marriage and that Miles will have specified visitation rights (every other weekend and two weeks in the summer).

- **Marital Property.** The prenuptial agreement can handle the division of marital property upon divorce.

  Example   Nikki could be awarded the family residence in which to rear the children, possibly with a cash payment being made to Miles for his interest in the house. The parties can agree upon who gets what vehicles and personal property such as furniture, artwork, and such.

- **Other Issues.** The prenuptial agreement can handle the treatment of other issues that can arise in a marriage.

  Examples   These could be value, division, and use of second homes, division of vacant real property, division of pensions, the value and division of co-owned businesses, and any other issues important to the parties.

Sometimes the parties enter into an agreement during the marriage, setting forth the distribution of property upon death or termination of the marriage. This is called an **antenuptial agreement**. The courts apply the same standards for enforceability as in prenuptial agreements.

Marriage

Each state has marriage laws that recognize a legal union between a man and a woman. **Marriage** confers certain legal rights and duties upon the spouses, as well as upon the children born of the marriage. A couple wishing to marry must meet the legal requirements established by the state in which they are to be married. The following paragraphs discuss the legal rights and duties of spouses.

Marriage A legal union between spouses that confers certain legal rights and duties upon the spouses and upon the children born of the marriage.

Marriage Requirements

State law establishes certain **marriage requirements** that must be met before two people can be married. Most states require that the parties be a man and a woman. The parties must be of a certain age (usually 18 years of age). States will permit younger persons to be married if they have the consent of their parents or if they are emancipated from their parents. **Emancipation** means that the person is not supported by his or her parents and provides for himself or herself.

All states provide that persons under a certain age, such as 14 or 15 years of age, cannot be married. States also prohibit marriages between persons who are closely related, usually by blood. For example, a brother could not marry his sister or half-sister. Cousins may marry in some states. Another requirement of marriage is that neither party currently is married to someone else.

Web Exploration

Using www.google.com find out the marriage requirements in your state.

Marriage License

To be legally married, certain legal procedures must be followed. State law requires that the parties obtain a **marriage license** issued by the state. Marriage licenses usually are obtained at the county clerk's office. Some states require that the parties take a blood test prior to obtaining a license to determine if the parties have certain diseases, particularly sexually transmitted diseases.

Marriage license A legal document issued by a state certifying that two people are married.

Some states require that, in addition to a marriage license, there must be some sort of **marriage ceremony**. This ceremony usually is held in front of a justice of the peace or similar government officer, or at a church, temple, or synagogue, in front of a minister, priest, or rabbi. At the ceremony, the parties exchange wedding vows, in which they make a public statement that they will take each other as wife and husband.

After the wedding ceremony, the marriage license is recorded. Some states require a waiting period between the time the marriage license is obtained and when the wedding ceremony takes place.

Financial Support

Most states require a spouse to provide **financial support** to the other spouse and their children during their marriage. This includes providing for the necessities such as food, shelter, clothing, and medical care. A spouse is obligated only up to the level he or she is able to provide. In some states this duty exists even if the spouses are living apart. The spouses are free to agree on additional duties in separate contracts. Contracts to provide sex violate public policy and therefore are illegal.

Common-Law Marriage

Several states recognize a form of marriage called a **common-law marriage**. A common-law marriage is one in which the parties have not obtained a valid marriage license, nor have they participated in a legal marriage ceremony. Instead, a common-law marriage is recognized if the following requirements are met: (1) The parties are eligible to marry; (2) the parties voluntarily intend to be husband and wife; (3) the parties must live together; and (4) the parties hold themselves out as husband and wife.

Two misconceptions about common-law marriages are: (1) cohabitation is not sufficient in and of itself to establish a common-law marriage, and (2) the length of time the parties live together is not sufficient alone to establish a common-law marriage. For example, couples who immediately live together and intend a common-law marriage have one, whereas couples who live together a long time but do not intend a common-law marriage do not have one.

When a state recognizes a common-law marriage and the necessary requirements are met to establish one, the couple has a legal and formal marriage. All the rights and duties of a normal licensed marriage apply. As such, a court decree of divorce must be obtained to end a common-law marriage.

Same-Sex Marriage

Same-sex partners have been fighting for years to obtain the same rights as heterosexual couples to marry. In most states, same-sex couples do not have the same rights to marry as heterosexual couples. This is because most state marriage statutes are expressly drafted to permit only couples of different sexes to marry.

Same-sex partners have been lobbying their state legislatures and bringing lawsuits in the courts to change marriage statutes to permit them to marry. In these lawsuits, same-sex partners allege that the state statutes that permit heterosexual partners to marry but do not let same-sex partners marry cause discrimination that violates equal protection clauses of state constitutions and the U.S. Constitution.

The states of Massachusetts and Iowa permit same-sex partners to marry. Most other states have not done so, however. Several states, including Vermont, New Hampshire, and New Jersey, have enacted statutes that permit same-sex partners to join in a **civil union**. These civil union statutes grant same-sex partners most of the rights granted to heterosexual partners under marriage statutes.

Many employers provide the same health, pension, and other employment benefits to same-sex partners as they do to heterosexual married couples. The granting of same-sex partners such employment rights will continue to increase in the future.

In 1996, the federal government enacted the **Defense of Marriage Act (DOMA)** [28 U.S.C. Section 1738C], which bars same-sex couples from enjoying federal benefits (e.g., Social Security benefits, Veterans' benefits, and such) that otherwise would be accorded heterosexual married couples. Same-sex partners argue that this part of DOMA violates the Equal Protection Clause of the U.S. Constitution by treating same-sex partners differently than heterosexual married couples.

DOMA also provides that states cannot be forced to recognize same-sex marriages performed in other states. For example, if a same-sex couple gets lawfully married in Massachusetts and moves to another state that does not recognize same-sex marriages, this new state does not have to recognize the partners' same-sex marriage from Massachusetts.

The battle for recognizing **same-sex marriages** and the granting of rights to same-sex partners equal to heterosexual couples will continue to be waged in state and federal legislatures, as well as state and federal courts.

Parents and Children

In many instances, a major purpose of marriage is to have children. Couples who have children have certain legal rights and duties that develop from their parental status.

Parents' Rights and Duties

Parents have the obligation to provide food, shelter, clothing, medical care, and other necessities to their children until a child reaches the age of 18 or until emancipation. A child becomes emancipated if he or she leaves the parents and lives voluntarily on his or her own. The law imposes certain **parents' duties** as well. For example, a parent must see to it that the child attends school until 16 or 18 years of age, depending on the state, unless the child is home-schooled. Parents may be legally responsible for a child beyond the age of majority if the child has a disability.

Also, **parents' right** to control the behavior of a child is legally mandated. Parents have the right to select the schools for their children and the religion they will practice. Parents have the right to use corporal punishment (physical punishment) as long as it does not rise to the level of child abuse. For example, mild slapping or spanking is legally permitted.

Child neglect occurs when a parent fails to provide a child with the necessities of life or other basic needs. The state may remove a child, either temporarily or permanently, from situations of child neglect. A parent's refusal to obtain medical care for a child can be punished as a crime.

Paternity Actions

If there is any question as to whom the father of a child is, called **paternity**, a **paternity action** may be filed in court to determine the true identity of the father. Most of these actions are filed by a mother against a man whom the mother claims to be the father of the child. This often is done to seek financial assistance from the father for the child's upbringing.

Paternity lawsuits sometimes are brought by the government if the mother is receiving welfare payments. In these cases, the government seeks to recover the financial assistance payments made to the mother and to establish the father's financial responsibility in the future. Sometimes a paternity action is brought by a male to prove that he is not the father of a child.

At other times, a father will bring a paternity action to establish that he is the biological father of a child. This is usually done when the father seeks to obtain legal rights, such as custody or visitation rights, concerning the child. Most states have a **father's registry** in which a male may register as the father of a child. This requires that the father be notified of a planned adoption of the child so the father may appear and oppose the adoption.

In most states, the law presumes that the husband of a wife who bears a child is the legal father of the child. In about half of the states, a husband who believes that he is not the father can bring a lawsuit to prove that he is not the father. The other half of the states do not permit such actions.

A male can be proven to be or not to be the father of a child through DNA testing. Also, a male may prove that he is not the father of a child if he had no access to the mother at the time of pregnancy or if he is impotent or had a vasectomy prior to the pregnancy.

Paternity action A legal proceeding that determines the identity of the father of a child.

Parent's Liability for a Child's Wrongful Act

Generally, parents are not liable for their children's negligent acts. For example, if a child negligently injures another child while they are playing, the parents of the child who caused the injury are not liable. Parents are liable if their negligence caused their child's act. For example, if a parent lets a child who does not have a driver's license drive an automobile and the child-driver injures someone, the parents are liable.

About half of the states have enacted **child liability statutes** that make the parents financially liable for the intentional torts of their children. This liability usually is limited to a specified dollar amount, such as $5,000.

Adoption

Adoption A situation in which a person becomes the legal parent of a child who is not his or her biological child.

Adoption occurs when a person becomes the legal parent of a child who is not his or her biological child. Thus, a married couple can adopt a child together, a single parent can adopt a child, and a spouse can adopt the child of his or her new spouse.

The process for adoption is complicated and is regulated by state law. Basically, the procedure for adoption consists of the following requirements:

- All procedures of the state law for adoption are met.
- The biological parents' legal rights as parents are terminated by legal decree or death.
- A court formally approves the adoption.

The two main ways by which persons can become adoptive parents are *agency adoptions* and *independent adoptions*.

Agency Adoption

Agency adoption An adoption that occurs when a person adopts a child from a social service organization of a state.

An **agency adoption** occurs when a person adopts a child from a social service organization of a state. The state often obtains jurisdiction over children who are born out of wedlock and the biological parents give up the child for adoption by terminating their parental rights. The state also may obtain jurisdiction over a child if the child has been permanently removed from parents who are judged unsuitable to be parents, or where parents are deceased and no relative wants or qualifies to become the child's parents.

In the past, the identity of the biological parents of adopted children was kept confidential in an agency adoption. Currently, many states allow for disclosure of the identity of the biological parents in certain circumstances. Usually, the court will notify the other side—either the child or the biological parent—that the other wishes to meet with them. If both sides consent, the meeting will be arranged.

Open Adoption

In many cases today, **open adoption** procedures are being used. In these cases, the biological and **adoptive parents** are introduced prior to the adoption. The **biological parents** may screen the prospective adoptive parents to assure that the adoptive parents are suitable for the child. In many instances, the adoptive and biological parents remain in contact with each other, and the biological parents are given visitation rights to see the child.

Independent Adoption

Independent adoption An adoption in which there is a private arrangement between the biological parents and adoptive parents.

An **independent adoption** occurs when there is a private arrangement between the biological and adoptive parents. Often, an intermediary, such as a lawyer, doctor, or private adoption agency, introduces the two parties. The biological parents and the adoptive parents enter into a private arrangement for adoption of the child. Adoptive parents usually pay intermediaries a fee for their services, as well as paying the costs of the adoption.

Many divorced people who have children remarry. Often, a new stepparent formally adopts the child or children of his or her new spouse. To do so, the child's other biological parent must relinquish his or her legal rights concerning the child. This can be done voluntarily or by order of the court if it is deemed to be in the best interests of the child.

Court Approval of Adoption

In both agency adoptions and independent adoptions, the court must approve the adoption before it is legal. The court will consider the home environment, financial resources, and family stability of the adoptive parents, as well as their religious beliefs, ages, and other factors. The decision of the court will be based on the best interests of the child. Although preference usually is given to couples, single parents can adopt children. States vary as to whether they permit homosexual couples to adopt children.

Once the court approves an adoption, the adoptive couple is subject to a probation period which usually is six months or one year. During this time, government social workers investigate whether the adoptive parents are caring for the adopted child properly. If they are not, the court can remove the child from the adoptive parents.

The following feature describes and discusses the importance of family law judges.

Foster Care

A child may become the responsibility of the state under several circumstances. The first is if a child's parents or parent dies and there are no relatives to take the child or no other arrangements have been made for the care of the child. Another situation occurs if the state institutes a proceeding to remove a child from the parents' or parent's custody based upon the parent being unfit to care for the child or because the child is in danger (such as from child abuse).

Today, the primary means of caring for children under the state's jurisdiction is to place children in **foster care**. This is usually a temporary arrangement. The state pays the **foster family** for the care given to the **foster child**. This temporary arrangement will be terminated if the child is returned to his or her biological parents or if the child is legally adopted. Sometimes the **foster parents** will legally adopt a child who has been placed in their care.

Termination of Marriage

Once a state has recognized the marital status of a couple, only the state can terminate this marital status. This is so even if the couple separate and live apart from one another. As long as they are married, they continue to have certain legal rights and duties to one another. The law recognizes two methods for **marriage termination**: *annulment* and *divorce*.

FAMILY LAW JUDGES

Many states have specialized courts that handle family law matters. These courts most often are called Family Law Courts. Other states provide that family law matters be heard and decided by their courts of general jurisdiction. In these cases, the courts that hear family law matters typically are a separate division of the general court system.

Judges that hear family law matters usually are referred to as Family Law Judges. These judges are experts in family law issues. In the course of their work, these judges hear and decide matters of paternity, annulments, divorce, division of property upon divorce, child custody, child visitation rights, child support, conservatorship, and other family law cases.

Because of the number of family law issues that arise in society, family law judges hear and decide a significant number of cases. Family law judges will continue to be an integral part of each state's judicial system.

Annulment

An **annulment** is an order of the court declaring that a marriage did not exist. The order invalidates the marriage. Annulments are granted rarely now that most states recognize no-fault divorces.

Certain grounds must be asserted to obtain a legal annulment. One is that the parties lacked capacity to consent. Examples are:

1. One of the parties was a minor and had not obtained his or her parents' consent to marry.
2. One of the parties was mentally incapacitated at the time of marriage.
3. A party was intoxicated at the time of the marriage.
4. The marriage was never consummated.

Marriage also can be annulled if the parties are too closely related to one another or there was bigamy (one of the parties was already married). A marriage also can be annulled if there was duress or fraud leading to the marriage (e.g., one of the parties declared that he or she could conceive children when the person knew in fact that he or she could not).

Many annulments are sought because of a person's religion. For example, a Roman Catholic cannot be remarried in the church if he or she is divorced. An annulment would allow for a subsequent marriage in the church. A person also may be required to go through a procedure to seek an annulment from the church. A legal annulment and a religious annulment are two separate and distinct procedures.

The law considers children born of a marriage that is annulled to be legitimate. When a marriage is annulled, issues of child support, child custody, spousal support, and property settlement must be agreed upon by the couple or decided by the court.

Divorce

The most common option used by married partners to terminate their marriage is divorce. **Divorce** is a legal proceeding whereby the court issues a decree that legally orders a marriage terminated.

Traditionally, a married person who sought a divorce had to prove that the other person was *at fault* for causing a major problem with continuing the marriage. An **at-fault divorce** requires the petitioning party to allege grounds for seeking the divorce. Grounds for granting a divorce consisted of adultery, physical or emotional abuse, abandonment, substance or alcohol abuse, or insanity.

Beginning in the 1960s, states began to recognize **no-fault divorce**. A spouse wishing to obtain a divorce merely had to assert **irreconcilable differences** with his or her spouse. In a no-fault divorce, neither party is blamed for the divorce. Today, every state recognizes no-fault divorce. A spouse still may decide to assert that the other party was at fault for causing the divorce in those states that consider fault when deciding how to divide **marital assets** and award spousal support.

Divorce Proceedings

A divorce proceeding is commenced by a spouse filing a **petition for divorce** with the proper state court. The petition must contain required information, such as the names of the spouses, date and place of marriage, names of minor children, and reason for the divorce. The petition must be served on the other spouse. This spouse then has a certain period of time (usually 20 to 30 days) to file an answer to the petition.

If the spouses do not reach a settlement of the issues involved in the divorce—such as property division, custody of the children, and spousal and child support—the case will go to trial. The parties are permitted to conduct discovery, which includes taking depositions and obtaining the production of documents. If the case goes to trial, each side is permitted to call witnesses, including expert witnesses (e.g., financial experts), to testify on his or her behalf. Both parties also are allowed to introduce evidence that will support their claims.

Many states require a certain waiting period from the date a divorce petition is filed to the date the court grants a divorce. A typical waiting period is six months. The public policy for this waiting period is to give the parties time for reconciliation. After the waiting period has passed, a court will enter a **decree of divorce**, which is a court order terminating the marriage. The parties then are free to marry again. The decree of divorce may be granted even if the other issues concerning the divorce, such as division of property or support payments, have not yet been settled or tried.

Decree of divorce A court order that terminates a marriage.

If there is a showing that one partner is likely to injure the other spouse, a court may issue a **restraining order**. This places limitations on the ability of the dangerous partner to go near the innocent partner.

Exhibit 16.1 shows a petition for a divorce.

Pro Se Divorce

In a ***pro se* divorce**, the parties do not have to hire lawyers to represent them but may represent themselves in the divorce proceeding. Most states permit *pro se*—commonly called "do-it-yourself"—divorces. If substantial assets are at stake in the divorce, or if there are other complicated issues involving child custody, child support, or spousal support, the parties usually hire lawyers to represent them in the divorce proceeding.

Divorce Settlement

Approximately 90 percent of divorce cases are settled between the parties prior to trial. The parties often engage in negotiations to try to settle a divorce lawsuit in order to save the time and expense of a trial and to reach a **divorce settlement** that is acceptable to each side. These negotiations usually are conducted between the parties with the assistance of each of their attorneys.

Some divorcing parties use mediation to try to reach a settlement of the issues involved in terminating their marriage. Some states have mandatory mediation before divorcing couples can use the court to try the case. In **mediation**, a neutral third party—an attorney, a retired judge, or other party—acts as a **mediator** between the parties. A mediator is not empowered to make a decision but, instead, acts as a go-between and facilitator to try to help the parties reach an acceptable settlement of the issues. Mediation tends to be successful because it forces the parties to consider all facets of the case, even the position of the opposing side.

If a settlement is reached, a **settlement agreement** is drafted, usually by the attorneys. After being signed by the parties, the settlement agreement is presented to the court. The court will accept the terms of the settlement agreement if the judge believes the settlement is fair and that the rights of the parties and minor children are properly taken care of. If a case is not settled, the case will go to trial.

Settlement agreement A written document signed by divorcing parties that evidences their agreement settling property rights and other issues of their divorce.

The following Ethical Perspective feature discusses a paralegal's duty not to discuss confidential information learned while employed as a paralegal professional.

Division of Assets and Spousal Support

Upon termination of a marriage, the parties may own certain assets, including property owned prior to marriage, gifts and inheritances received during marriage, and assets purchased with income earned during marriage. In most cases, the parties reach a settlement as to how these assets are to be divided. If no settlement agreement is reached, the court will order the **division of assets**.

Separate Property

In most states, each spouse's separate property is awarded to the spouse who owns the separate property. **Separate property** includes property owned by a spouse prior to the marriage as well as inheritances and gifts received during the marriage. In most states, upon the termination of a marriage, each spouse is awarded his or her separate property.

Separate property Property owned by a spouse prior to marriage, as well as inheritances and gifts received by a spouse during the marriage.

But if separate property is commingled with marital property during the course of the marriage, or if the owner of the separate property changes title to the separate

Exhibit 16.1 Petition for divorce

IN THE CIRCUIT COURT OF THE _____ JUDICIAL CIRCUIT,
IN AND FOR _____ COUNTY, FLORIDA

Case No.: _____
Division: _____

_____,
Petitioner, and

Respondent. _____,

PETITION FOR DISSOLUTION OF MARRIAGE
WITH DEPENDENT OR MINOR CHILD(REN)

I, {**full legal name** _____, the [**one** only]
( ) Husband ( ) Wife, being sworn, certify that the following statements are true:

1. JURISDICTION/RESIDENCE
( ) Husband ( ) Wife ( ) Both has (have) lived in Florida for at least 6 months before the filing of this Petition for Dissolution of Marriage.

2. The husband [one only] ( ) is ( ) is not a member of the military service.
The wife [one only] ( ) is ( ) is not a member of the military service.

3. MARRIAGE HISTORY
Date of marriage: {*month, day, year*}_____
Place of marriage: {*city, state, country*} _____
Date of separation: {*month, day, year*} _____ (ffl if approximate)

4. DEPENDENT OR MINOR CHILD(REN)
[all that apply]

a. [____] The wife is pregnant. Baby is due on: {*date*} _____

b. [____]The minor (under 18) child(ren) common to both parties are:

Name	Place of Birth	Birth date	Sex
_____	_____	_____	_____
_____	_____	_____	_____
_____	_____	_____	_____
_____	_____	_____	_____
_____	_____	_____	_____
_____	_____	_____	_____

c. [____]The minor child(ren) born or conceived during the marriage who are not common to both parties are:

Name	Place of Birth	Birth date	Sex
_____	_____	_____	_____
_____	_____	_____	_____

The birth father(s) of the above minor child(ren) is (are) {*name and address*} _____

_____

d. [____]The child(ren) common to both parties who are 18 or older but who are dependent   upon the parties due to a mental or physical disability are:

Name	Place of Birth	Birth date	Sex
_____	_____	_____	_____
_____	_____	_____	_____
_____	_____	_____	_____

Exhibit 16.1 Petition for divorce *(continued)*

5. A completed Uniform Child Custody Jurisdiction and Enforcement Act (UCCJEA) Affidavit, Florida Supreme Court Approved Family Law Form 12.902(d), is filed with this petition. (You must complete and attach this form in a dissolution of marriage with minor child(ren)).

6. A completed Notice of Social Security Number, Florida Supreme Court Approved Family Law Form 12.902(j), is filed with this petition.

7. This petition for dissolution of marriage should be granted because:
   [**one** only]
   a. [___] The marriage is irretrievably broken.
   b. [___] One of the parties has been adjudged mentally incapacitated for a period of 3 years prior to the filing of this petition. A copy of the Judgment of Incapacity is attached.

SECTION I. MARITAL ASSETS AND LIABILITIES
[**one** only]
1. [___] There are no marital assets or liabilities.
2. [___] There are marital assets or liabilities. All marital and nonmarital assets and liabilities are (or will be) listed in the financial affidavits, Florida Family Law Rules of Procedure Form 12.902(b) or (c), to be filed in this case.
   [ffl all that apply]
   a. [___] All marital assets and liabilities have been divided by a written agreement between the parties, which is attached, to be incorporated into the final judgment of dissolution of marriage. (The parties may use Marital Settlement Agreement for Dissolution of Marriage with Dependent or Minor Child(ren), Florida Supreme Court Approved Family Law Form 12.902(f)(1).
   b. [___] The Court should determine how the assets and liabilities of this marriage are to be distributed, under section 61.075, Florida Statutes.
   c. [___] Petitioner should be awarded an interest in Respondent's property because:

   _____
   _____
   _____
   _____

SECTION II. SPOUSAL SUPPORT (ALIMONY)
[one only]
1. [___] Petitioner forever gives up his/her right to spousal support (alimony) from Respondent.
2. [___] Petitioner requests that the Court order Respondent to pay the following spousal support (alimony) and claims that he or she has a need for the support that he or she is requesting **and Respondent has the ability to pay that support.** Spousal support (alimony) is requested in the amount of $_____ every ( ) week ( ) other week ( ) month, beginning *{date}* _____ and continuing until *{date or event}* _____.
   Explain why the Court should order Respondent to pay and any specific request(s) for type of alimony (temporary, permanent, rehabilitative, and/or lump sum):

   _____
   _____
   _____
   _____
   _____

   [**if** applies] ( ) Petitioner requests life insurance on Respondent's life, provided by Respondent, to secure such support.

(continued)

Exhibit 16.1 **Petition for divorce** *(continued)*

SECTION III. PARENTING PLAN ESTABLISHING PARENTAL RESPONSIBILITY AND TIME-SHARING

1. The minor child(ren) currently reside(s) with ( ) Mother ( ) Father ( ) Other: *{explain}*

    _____

2. **Parental Responsibility.** It is in the child(ren)'s best interests that parental responsibility be:
    [one only]
    a. [____] shared by both Father and Mother.
    b. [____] awarded solely to ( ) Father ( ) Mother. Shared parental responsibility would be detrimental to the child(ren) because: _____

    _____

    _____

    _____

3. **Parenting Plan and Time-Sharing. It is in the best interests of the child(ren) that the family** be ordered to comply with a Parenting Plan that ( ) includes ( ) does not include parental time-sharing with the child(ren). The Petitioner states that it is in the best interests of the child(ren) that:
    (Choose only one)
    a. [____] The attached proposed Parenting Plan should be adopted by the court. The parties
    ( ) have ( ) have not agreed to the Parenting Plan.
    b. [____]The court should establish a Parenting Plan with the following provisions:
    [____]No time-sharing for the [____] Husband [____] Wife.
    [____] Limited time-sharing with the [____] Husband [____] Wife.
    [____] Supervised Time-Sharing for the [____] Husband [____] Wife.
    [____] Supervised or third-party exchange of the child(ren).
    [____]Time-Sharing Schedule as follows:

    _____

    _____

4. Explain why this request is in the best interests of the child(ren):

    _____

    _____

    _____

    _____

SECTION IV. CHILD SUPPORT
[**all** that apply]

1. [____] Petitioner requests that the Court award child support as determined by Florida's child support guide-lines, section 61.30, Florida Statutes. A completed Child Support Guidelines Worksheet,
    Florida Family Law Rules of Procedure Form 12.902(e), is, or will be filed. Such support should be ordered retroactive to:
    a. [____]the date of separation *{date}* _____ .
    b. [____] the date of the filing of this petition.
    c. [____] other *{date}* _____ *{explain}* _____.
2. [____] Petitioner requests that the Court award child support to be paid beyond the age of 18 years because:
    a. [____] the following child(ren) *{name(s)}* _____
    is (are) dependent because of a mental or physical incapacity which began before the age of 18. *{explain}*

    _____

    _____

Exhibit 16.1 Petition for divorce *(continued)*

    b. [____] the following child(ren) *{name(s)}* _____ is (are) dependent in fact and is (are) in high school while he/she (they) are between the ages of 18 and 19; said child(ren) is (are) performing in good faith with reasonable expectation of graduation before the age of 19.

3. [____] Petitioner requests that the Court award a child support amount that is more than or less than Florida's child support guidelines. Petitioner understands that Motion to Deviate from Child Support Guidelines, Florida Supreme Court Approved Family Law Form 12.943, **must** be filed before the court will consider this request.

4. [____] Petitioner requests that medical/dental insurance coverage for the minor child(ren) be provided by: [one only]
    a. [____] Father.
    b. [____] Mother.

5. [____] Petitioner requests that uninsured medical/dental expenses for the child(ren) be paid:
[**one** only]
    a. [____] by Father.
    b. [____] by Mother.
    c. [____] by Father and Mother [each pay one-half].
    d. [____] according to the percentages in the Child Support Guidelines Worksheet, Florida Family Law Rules of Procedure Form 12.902(e).
    e. [____] Other *{explain}:*

_____

_____

6. Petitioner requests that life insurance to secure child support be provided by:
    a. [____] Father.
    b. [____] Mother.
    c. [____] Both.

SECTION V. OTHER

1. [If Petitioner is also the Wife, please indicate by either ( ) yes ( ) or no whether Petitioner/Wife wants to be known by her former name, which was *{full legal name}*

_____

2. Other relief *{specify}:*

_____

_____

_____

_____

SECTION VI. PETITIONER'S REQUEST (This section summarizes what you are asking the Court to include in the final judgment of dissolution of marriage.)

Petitioner requests that the Court enter an order dissolving the marriage **and:**
[all that apply]

1. [____] distributing marital assets and liabilities as requested in Section I of this petition;
2. [____] awarding spousal support (alimony) as requested in Section II of this petition;
3. [____] adopt or establish a Parenting Plan containing provisions for parental responsibility and time sharing for the dependent or minor child(ren) common to both parties, as requested in Section III of this petition;
4. [____] establishing child support for the dependent or minor child(ren) common to both parties, as requested in Section IV of this petition;
5. [____] restoring Wife's former name as requested in Section V of this petition;
6. [____] awarding other relief as requested in Section V of this petition; and any other terms the Court deems necessary.

(continued)

Exhibit 16.1 **Petition for divorce** *(continued)*

I understand that I am swearing or affirming under oath to the truthfulness of the claims made in this petition and that the punishment for knowingly making a false statement includes fines and/or imprisonment.

Dated: _____ _____ Signature of Petitioner

Printed Name _____

Address: _____

City, State, Zip: _____

Telephone Number: _____

Fax Number: _____

STATE OF FLORIDA
COUNTY OF _____

Sworn to or affirmed and signed before me on _____ by _____.
_____ NOTARY PUBLIC or DEPUTY CLERK
_____ [Print, type, or stamp commissioned name of notary or deputy clerk.]
[_____] Personally known
[_____] Produced identification
    Type of identification produced _____

IF A NONLAWYER HELPED YOU FILL OUT THIS FORM, HE/SHE MUST FILL IN THE BLANKS BELOW: [fill in **all** blanks]
I, *{full legal name and trade name of nonlawyer}* _____, a
nonlawyer, located at *{street}* _____, *{city}* , _____
_____ *{state}* _____, *{phone}* _____, helped *{name}*
_____ who is the petitioner, fill out this form.

property by placing the other spouse's name on title to the property (e.g., real estate), the separate property is considered a marital asset.

Marital Property

Marital property Property acquired during the course of marriage using income earned during the marriage, and separate property that has been converted to marital property.

Marital property consists of property acquired during the course of the marriage, using income earned by the spouses during the marriage and separate property that has been converted to marital property.

Different states adhere to two major legal theories when dividing marital assets upon the termination of a marriage. These are the theories of *equitable distribution* and *community property*.

Equitable Distribution

Equitable distribution A law used by many states where the court orders a *fair distribution* of marital property to the divorcing spouses.

In states that follow the rule of **equitable distribution**, the court may order the **fair distribution** of property. The fair distribution of property does not necessarily mean the equal distribution of property. In determining the fair distribution of property, the court may consider factors such as:

- Length of the marriage
- Occupation of each spouse
- Standard of living during the marriage
- Wealth and income-earning ability of each spouse
- Which party is awarded custody of the children

- Health of the individuals
- Other factors relevant to the case

In most states, the house is awarded most often to the parent who is granted custody of the children. A court may order the house to be sold and the proceeds divided fairly between the individuals.

Community Property

Under the doctrine of **community property**, all property acquired during the marriage using income earned during the marriage is considered marital property. It does not matter which spouse earned the income or which spouse earned the higher income. Money placed in pension funds, stock options, the value of businesses, the value of professional licenses, and such, are considered community property.

In community-property states, marital property is divided *equally* between the individuals. An **equal division** of property does not necessarily mean that each piece of property is sold and the proceeds divided equally between the individuals. Typically, each asset of the marital asset is valued using appraisers and expert witnesses. The court then awards the property to the spouses. If one spouse is awarded the house, the other spouse is awarded other property of equal value.

Community property A law used by some states in which the court orders an *equal division* of marital property to the divorcing spouses.

Web Exploration

Using www.google.com find out whether your state is an equitable distribution or community property state.

Division of Debts

Upon termination of the marriage, individuals often have debts that must be divided. How these debts are divided depends on the type of debt and on state law. In most states, each spouse is personally liable for his or her own premarital debts and the other

SIDEBAR

DIVISION OF MARITAL PROPERTY

Law	Description
Equitable distribution	The marital property is distributed fairly. This does not necessarily mean the equal distribution of the property.
Community property	The marital property is divided *equally* between the parties.

Spousal support Payments made by one divorced spouse to the other divorced spouse. Also called *alimony*.

Child custody The awarding of legal custody of a child to a parent based on the best interests of the child. The parent awarded custody is called the *custodial parent*.

spouse is not liable for these debts. This is because the debt was incurred prior to the marriage. Student loans are a good example of this type of debt.

Debts that are incurred during the marriage for necessities and other joint needs including but not limited to shelter, clothing, automobiles, medical expenses, and such, are **joint marital debts** and are the joint responsibility of each spouse. The court may distribute these debts equally upon termination of the marriage. Spouses are jointly liable for taxes incurred during their marriage.

If a debt is not paid by the spouse to whom the court has distributed the debt, the third-party creditor may recover payment of the debt from the other spouse, however. This individual's only recourse is to recover the amount paid from his or her prior spouse.

Upon the termination of a marriage, it is wise for the individuals to notify prior creditors that they will no longer be responsible for the other's debts. This is particularly true if the individuals have joint credit cards.

Spousal Support

In some cases where a marriage is terminated, a court may award **spousal support**—also called **alimony**—to one of the divorced spouses. The other divorced spouse typically is ordered to pay the alimony in monthly payments. The parties may agree to the amount of alimony to be paid. If they do not reach an agreement, the court will determine whether the payment of alimony is warranted and, if so, the amount of alimony to be paid. In the past, alimony usually has been awarded to the female. Today, with the female often earning more than the male, the male has been awarded alimony in some cases.

Alimony is usually awarded for a specific period of time. This is called **temporary alimony** or **rehabilitation alimony**. This alimony is designed to provide the receiving individual with payment for a limited time during which the individual can obtain the necessary education or job skills necessary to enter the job force. Alimony also is awarded in cases where a parent, usually the female, is needed to care for a child with a disability and must remain home to care for the child. The amount of alimony is based on the needs of the individual who will receive the alimony and the income and ability of the other individual to pay.

Spousal support payments terminate if the former spouse dies, remarries, or otherwise becomes self-sufficient. Spousal support awards may be modified by the court if circumstances change. This occurs if the paying individual loses his or her job, or his or her income decreases, if the receiving individual's income increases, or similar circumstances. A party wishing to have a spousal support award changed must petition the court to *modify* the award of spousal support.

The award of **permanent alimony**—sometimes called **lifetime alimony**—is usually awarded only if the individual to receive the alimony is of an older age and if that individual has been a homemaker who has little opportunity to obtain job skills to enter the workplace. Permanent alimony must be paid until the individual receiving it dies or remarries.

Child Custody and Child Support

When a marriage is terminated, the custody of a child or children must be decided. In addition, child support may be awarded. These issues are discussed next.

Child Custody

When a couple terminates their marriage and they have children, the issue of who is legally and physically responsible for raising the children must be decided, either by settlement or by the court. The legal term **custody** is used to describe who has legal responsibility for raising a child. **Child custody** is one of the most litigated issues of a divorcing couple.

Paralegals *in* Practice

PARALEGAL PROFILE
Adam M. Johnston

Adam M. Johnston has been a paralegal for four years. He specializes in family law at the firm of Murphy, Murphy & Nugent in New Haven, Connecticut. Adam graduated from the University of Rhode Island and obtained his Paralegal Certificate from Branford Hall Career Institute.

I work most frequently on child custody cases. My supervising attorney is often appointed by the court as a guardian ad litem to represent the best interests of a child or children. The attorney meets with the parents and the child or children, and also speaks with collateral sources such as teachers, school psychologists, therapists, and healthcare workers. My job involves coordinating the communications between the attorney and all the individuals directly or indirectly involved in the dispute. This includes frequent contact with both parents as they present their respective positions and concerns throughout the case. Strict confidentiality must always be maintained by the paralegal.

The most challenging cases are the ones that involve a parent who has alienated the child or children from the other parent. In these situations, mental health professionals often play a significant role. Since these cases are typically complicated and emotionally charged, agreements can be difficult to reach. Thus, as a family law paralegal, it is important not to take anything personal, but instead to remember you are helping people through a very stressful and life-altering time in their lives.

Every divorce case I've worked on has settled prior to trial. Connecticut is a "no-fault" state and follows the equitable distribution doctrine for dividing marital property. However, many factors can influence the division of marital property, such as prenuptial agreements, the earning capacity of the parties, the length of the marriage, and custody issues. The recent downturn in the economy has resulted in more *pro se* divorce filings. Interacting with *pro se* parties can be difficult because they may be unaware of court proceedings, appropriate interaction between opposing sides, and the sequencing of events throughout the course of litigation.

Traditionally, the court almost always granted custody of a child to the mother. Today, with fathers taking a more active role in childrearing, and with many mothers working, this is not always the case.

In **child custody disputes,** where both parents want custody of a child, the courts will determine what is in the **best interests of the child** in awarding custody. Some of the factors that a court considers are:

- The ability of each parent to provide for the emotional needs of the child.
- The ability of each parent to provide for the needs of the child, such as education.
- The ability of each parent to provide a stable environment for the child.
- The ability of each parent to provide for the special needs of a child if the child has a disability or requires special care.
- The desire of each parent to provide for the needs of the child.
- The wishes of the child. This factor is given more weight the older the child is.
- The religion of each parent.
- Other factors the court deems relevant.

The awarding of custody to a **custodial parent** is not permanent. Custody may be altered by the court if circumstances change.

The parent who is awarded custody has **legal custody** of the child. This usually includes physical custody of the child. The custodial parent has the right to make day-to-day decisions and major decisions concerning the child's education, religion, and other such matters.

The court will not award custody to a parent, and sometimes not to either parent, if it is in the child's best interest not to be awarded to a parent, or if there has been **child abuse,** or because of other extenuating circumstances. In such cases, the court may award custody to other relatives, such as grandparents, or place the child in a foster home.

Joint Custody

Most states now permit joint custody of a child. **Joint custody** means that both parents are responsible for making major decisions concerning the child, such as his or her education, religion, and other major matters.

Parents sometimes are awarded **joint physical custody** of the child as well. This means that the child will spend a certain portion of time being raised by each parent. For example, the child may spend every other week with each parent, or the weekdays with one parent and the weekends with another parent. These arrangements are awarded only if the child's best interests are served—for example, the child remaining in the same school while in the physical custody of each parent.

Visitation Rights

If the parents do not have joint custody of a child, the noncustodial parent typically is awarded **visitation rights**. This means that the noncustodial parent is given the right to visit the child for limited periods of time, as determined by a settlement agreement or by the court.

If the court is concerned about the safety of a child, the court may grant only supervised visitation rights to a noncustodial parent. This means that a court-appointed person must be present during the noncustodial parent's visitation with the child. This usually is done if there has been a history of child abuse or there is a strong possibility that the noncustodial parent may kidnap the child.

Child Support

The noncustodial parent is obligated to contribute to the financial support of his or her natural and adopted children. This includes the child's costs for food, shelter, clothing, medical expenses, and other necessities of life. This payment is called **child support**. The custodial and noncustodial parents may agree to the amount of child support. If they do not, the court will determine the amount of child support to be paid.

In awarding child support, the court considers several factors, including the number of children, needs of the children, net income of the parents, standard of living of the children prior to termination of the marriage, any special medical or other needs of the children, and other factors that the court deems relevant. The duty to pay child support usually continues until a child reaches the age of majority or graduates from high school, or emancipates himself or herself by voluntarily choosing to live on his or her own.

To help in the determination of child support, about half of the states have adopted a formula for computing the amount of child support, based on a percentage of the noncustodial parent's income. A court is permitted to deviate from the formula if a child has special needs, such as if the child has a disability or requires special educational assistance.

An award of child support may be *modified* if conditions change. For example, an award of child support may be decreased if the noncustodial parent loses his or her job. Or the amount of child support may be modified if the child's needs change, such as if the child needs special care because of a disability. The parent wishing to obtain modification of child support must petition the court to change the award of child support.

Child support Payments made by the noncustodial parent to help pay for the financial support of his or her children.

Web Exploration

Go to www.google.com. Find a Legal Aid Society that serves your area for which you would like to volunteer to do *pro bono* work.

Family Support Act

In the past, many noncustodial parents failed to pay child support when due. This often required long and expensive legal procedures by the custodial parent to obtain child support payments. To remedy this situation, the federal government enacted the **Family Support Act**. This federal law, effective in 1994, provides that all original or modified child support orders require automatic wage withholding from a noncustodial parent's income. The Family Support Act was designed primarily to prevent noncustodial parents from failing to pay required support payments.

Assume that a court order requires a noncustodial parent to pay 25 percent of his or her gross monthly income for child support. In this case, the court will order that noncustodial parent's employer to deduct this amount from that parent's income and send a check in this amount to the custodial parent. The noncustodial parent receives a check for the remainder of his or her income.

The ethical duty and social responsibility of a paralegal professional to provide *pro bono* services to the public is discussed in the following Ethical Perspective.

ETHICAL PERSPECTIVE

Paralegal's Duty to Provide Pro Bono Services to the Public

Mr. Alvarez is a paralegal in a law firm and works directly for Ms. Dawson, a partner in the law firm. In addition to her law practice with the law firm, Ms. Dawson volunteers to work one evening per month at a domestic abuse center that serves females and their children.

At the center, Ms. Dawson interviews domestic abuse victims and pursues whatever legal actions can be taken to assist the victims and their families. This includes doing the legal work for obtaining restraining orders, government assistance, and spousal and child support. All of Ms. Dawson's services at the domestic abuse center are provided *pro bono*, that is, for free.

One day Ms. Dawson asks her paralegal, Mr. Alvarez, if he would be interested in volunteering to help her one night each month at the domestic abuse shelter. Ms. Dawson explains that she could use Mr. Alvarez's assistance as a paralegal to help conduct interviews, prepare documents, and obtain government and other assistance for the domestic abuse victims and their families. Mr. Alvarez would be under the supervision of Ms. Dawson while working at the center.

Does Mr. Alvarez, as a paralegal professional, owe an ethical duty to provide *pro bono* services to the public?

Model and state paralegal Code of Ethics and Professional Responsibility provide that a paralegal is under an ethical duty to provide *pro bono* services to the public. Paralegals should engage in the provision of *pro bono* services to improve access to justice and the law, particularly to assist persons of limited means who cannot afford to employ lawyers to assert their rights. Paralegal professionals can meet their responsibility for providing *pro bono* services by volunteering to work for charitable, civic, governmental, and other organizations that provide legal services to the poor and needy members of society.

PARALEGAL'S ETHICAL DECISION

Based upon his ethical duty to provide *pro bono* services to the public, Mr. Alvarez should agree to assist Ms. Dawson at the domestic abuse center one evening each month. This would be an excellent way for Mr. Alvarez to satisfy his ethical duty as a paralegal professional to provide *pro bono* services to the public.

Concept Review *and* Reinforcement

Adoption 592
Adoptive parents 592
Agency adoption 592
Alimony 602
Annulment 594
Antenuptial agreement 589
At-fault divorce 594
Best interests of the child 603
Biological parents 592
Child abuse 603
Child custody 602
Child custody disputes 603
Child liability statute 592
Child neglect 591
Child support 604
Civil union 590
Common-law marriage 590
Community property 601
Custodial parent 603
Custody 602
Decree of divorce 595
Defense of Marriage Act (DOMA) 590
Division of assets 595
Divorce 594
Divorce settlement 595
Emancipation 589

Engagement 586
Equal division 601
Equitable distribution 600
Fair distribution 600
Family Support Act 605
Father's registry 591
Fault rule 587
Fiancé 586
Fiancée 586
Financial support 590
Foster care 593
Foster child 593
Foster family 593
Foster parent 593
Independent adoption 592
Irreconcilable differences 594
Joint custody 604
Joint marital debts 602
Joint physical custody 604
Legal custody 603
Lifetime alimony 602
Marital assets 594
Marital property 600
Marriage 589
Marriage ceremony 589
Marriage license 589

Marriage requirements 589
Marriage termination 593
Mediation 595
Mediator 595
No-fault divorce 594
Objective rule 587
Open adoption 592
Parents 591
Parents' duties 591
Parents' right 591
Paternity 591
Paternity action 591
Permanent alimony 602
Petition for divorce 594
Premarital agreement 587
Prenuptial agreement 587
Promise to marry 586
Pro se divorce 595
Rehabilitation alimony 602
Restraining order 595
Same-sex marriage 591
Separate property 595
Settlement agreement 595
Spousal support 602
Temporary alimony 602
Visitation rights 604

Premarriage Issues

Promise to Marry	A promise by one person to marry is made to another person. The courts usually do not enforce such promises as contracts.
Engagement	The engagement is a period of time that begins when one person asks another person to marry him or her, and ends when the parties get married or terminate their engagement. The prospective bride is called the *fiancée*, and the prospective groom is called the *fiancé*. Most often, the male is the one who gives the female an engagement ring to signify their engagement. Females also may give males engagement rings.

Termination of an Engagement	If a party ends the engagement, states apply one of the following rules regarding return of the engagement ring. a. *Fault rule:* If the prospective groom breaks off the engagement, the prospective bride may keep the ring. If the prospective bride breaks off the engagement, the ring must be returned to the prospective groom. b. *Objective rule:* If the engagement is broken off, the prospective bride must return the ring to the prospective groom irrespective as to which party broke off the engagement.
Prenuptial Agreement	A prenuptial agreement is a contract entered into by prospective spouses prior to marriage, specifying how property will be distributed upon termination of the marriage or death of a spouse. Prenuptial agreements often include agreements regarding the following financial and family issues: 1. Separate property 2. Marital or community property 3. Income and debt of the spouses 4. Alimony 5. Child custody 6. Child support 7. Other financial and family issues
Antenuptial Agreement	An antenuptial agreement is a contract entered into by prospective spouses during marriage, specifying how property will be distributed upon termination of the marriage or death of a spouse.

Marriage

Marriage	Marriage has been defined as a legal union between a male and a female that confers certain duties and rights upon the spouses. Some states permit the marriage of spouses of the same sex.
Marriage License	A marriage license is a legal document issued by the state, certifying that two people are married.
Marriage Ceremony	A marriage ceremony is held before a designated government official, or at a church, temple, synagogue, mosque, or other place of worship before a minister, priest, rabbi, or mullah. At the ceremony, the parties exchange wedding vows.
Common-Law Marriage	A common-law marriage is a type of marriage recognized by several states, wherein two people who have not been officially married are considered married if certain requirements are met, such as living together for a specified period of time.
Same-Sex Marriage	Same-sex marriage is a marriage between two people of the same sex. Several states permit same-sex marriages. Some other states permit *civil unions* between persons of the same sex.

Parents and Children

Emancipation	Emancipation occurs if a child leaves the parents and voluntarily lives on his or her own. The child then is responsible for providing his or her own livelihood.
Paternity Action	A paternity action is a legal proceeding in which the court identifies the true identity of the father of a child.
Adoption	Adoption occurs when a person becomes the legal parent of a child who is not his or her biological child. 1. *Agency adoption:* A person adopts a child from a social organization of a state. 2. *Open adoption:* The biological mother is introduced to the adoptive parent or parents prior to the adoption. 3. *Independent adoption:* The biological mother or parents enter into a private arrangement with the adoptive parent or parents for the adoption of the child.

Foster Care	Foster care is an arrangement in which a child is placed temporarily with a foster family. The state government pays the foster family a fee for caring for the foster child.

Termination of Marriage

Annulment	An annulment is an order of the court declaring that a marriage did not exist.
Divorce	A divorce is an order of the court that terminates a marriage. A *decree of divorce* is issued by the court that terminates the divorce. 1. *At-fault divorce:* A divorce recognized by the law of a state that requires the petitioning party to allege and prove grounds for obtaining a divorce. 2. *No-fault divorce:* A divorce recognized by the law of a state where neither party is blamed for the divorce; the petitioning party merely has to assert irreconcilable differences.
Pro Se Divorce	*Pro se* denotes a divorce proceeding in which the parties do not hire an attorney but instead represent themselves in the divorce action.
Divorce Settlement	Prior to going to court, the parties sometimes settle their divorce voluntarily. The *settlement agreement* is the written document signed by the divorcing parties that evidences their agreement to settle property rights and other issues of their divorce.

Division of Assets and Spousal Support

Separate Property	Separate property is the property owned by a spouse prior to marriage, as well as inheritances and gifts received by the spouse during the marriage.
Marital Property	Marital property is the property acquired during the course of marriage using income earned during the marriage, plus property that has been converted into marital property. Two methods are: 1. A method used by some states where the court orders *equitable* (fair) *distribution* of marital property to the divorcing spouses. This does not necessarily mean the equal distribution of marital property. 2. A method used by some states where the court orders an *equal distribution* of marital property to the divorcing spouses.
Division of Debts	*Joint marital debts* incurred during the marriage are the joint responsibility of divorcing spouses. The court may distribute these debts to individual divorcing spouses, but if that spouse does not pay the debt, the creditor can seek payment from the other divorced spouse.
Spousal Support	Spousal support is an amount of money ordered by a court to be paid by one divorcing spouse to another divorcing spouse for a period of time during and after the divorce is final. Also called *alimony* of which there are two types: 1. *Temporary alimony:* An amount ordered by the court to be paid to one divorcing spouse to the other divorcing spouse for a limited period of time. Also called *rehabilitation alimony*. 2. *Permanent alimony:* An amount ordered by the court to be paid to one divorcing spouse to the other divorcing spouse until the receiving spouse dies or remarries. Sometimes called *lifetime alimony*.

Child Custody and Child Support

Child Custody	The awarding of child custody to a parent is based on the best interests of the child. The parent awarded custody is called the *custodial parent*. The other parent is called the *noncustodial parent*.
Joint Custody	Joint custody means that both divorcing parents are responsible for making major decisions concerning the child.

Joint Physical Custody	Joint physical custody means that the child of divorcing parents spends a certain amount of time being raised by each parent.
Visitation Rights	Visitation rights confer to the noncustodial parent the right to visit his or her child for limited periods of time.
Child Support	Child support consists of payments made by the noncustodial parent to help pay for the financial support of his or her children.
Family Support Act	The Family Support Act is a federal statute that provides for the automatic withholding of child support payments from a noncustodial parent's income.

WORKING THE WEB

1. Using http://google.com or similar Internet search engine, find the marriage requirements for your state. Write a one-page report describing the requirements for getting married in your state.
2. Go to the website http://en.wikipedia.org/wiki/cohabitation_agreement. What is a cohabitation agreement? When would such an agreement be used? Write a one-page report describing a cohabitation agreement, and the advantages and disadvantages of using one.
3. Using http://google.com or similar Internet search engine, find the law or an article about the law of dividing marital property upon divorce in your state. Does your state follow the equitable distribution rule or the community property rule for dividing marital property?
4. Go to the website http://www/fbi.gov/hq/cid/cac/recovery.htm. Read this page regarding the federal crimes associated with not paying child support. Write a one-page report discussing these federal crimes and the penalties for committing these crimes.
5. Choose a country, and using the website http://google.com or similar Internet search engine, find information about adopting a child from that country. Write a one-page report discussing the adoption services available and the requirements for adopting a child from that country.

CRITICAL THINKING & WRITING QUESTIONS

1. What is a promise to marry? Is such a promise enforceable?
2. What is engagement? Who gets the engagement ring if the engagement is broken off, under (a) the fault rule, and (b) the objective rule.
3. Describe a prenuptial agreement. Under what circumstances will prenuptial agreements not be enforced?
4. Define marriage. What are the legal requirements to be able to be married? Define a marriage license.
5. What is a common-law marriage?
6. What is same-sex marriage? In which states are same-sex marriages recognized?
7. Describe a parent's rights and duties toward his or her children?
8. What is a paternity action? What is a father's registry?
9. Describe the following: (a) agency adoption, (b) open adoption, and (c) independent adoption.
10. Define and describe foster care.
11. What is an annulment? What are the requirements for obtaining an annulment?
12. Define divorce. Describe the difference between (a) at-fault divorce, and (b) no-fault divorce.
13. Describe the following: (a) petition for divorce, (b) decree of divorce, and (c) *pro se* divorce.
14. Describe a divorce settlement. What is a settlement agreement?
15. Describe the difference between (a) separate property, and (b) marital property.
16. Describe the rule of equitable distribution. Describe the doctrine of separate property.
17. What is spousal support? Explain the difference between (a) temporary alimony or rehabilitation alimony, and (b) permanent alimony or lifetime alimony.
18. Describe (a) child custody, (b) joint custody, (c) joint physical custody, and (d) visitation rights.
19. What is child support?
20. What does the Family Support Act provide?

Building Paralegal Skills

Lillian Harris, Small Family Law Practice

Interview with Lillian Harris, Esq., a sole practitioner with a family law practice.

After viewing the video case study at www.pearsonhighered.com/goldman answer the following:

1. What are the soft skills necessary for working in a small office? How do these differ from paralegals working in a large firm?
2. How important are the functions performed by a paralegal in a small office?
3. What are the advantages of working in a small firm?

UPL Issue: Helping the Client without Practicing Law

Paralegal Michael Reed is asked questions by a client in an interview discussing custody issues and what the client should do.

After viewing the video case study at www.pearsonhighered.com/goldman answer the following:

1. Did the paralegal commit UPL by answering the client's questions?
2. Are clients in domestic cases different from those in other areas of practice?
3. What additional skills does the paralegal need in working in a family law practice?

1. What are the ethical obligations of a paralegal regarding discussing facts about a client's divorce with others? Explain.
2. As a paralegal, can you give any advice to clients of your law firm regarding the procedures for obtaining a divorce in your state? What are the limits of the information that you can tell a client about such procedures?
3. As a paralegal, the attorney you work for has requested that you research how to adopt a child from another country. You find out this information. The client calls to see if you have found out this information. As a paralegal, are you at liberty to share this information with the client? Explain.

With a group of other students, selected by you or as assigned by your instructor, review the facts of the following case. As a group, discuss the following questions.

1. What is the doctrine of equitable distribution?
2. What is alimony? How much alimony did the court award George Neville?
3. Should George Neville have been awarded part of the value of his ex-wife's medical license and practice?

Neville v. Neville

George Neville and Tina Neville were married. At the time, George was 31 years old and a practicing attorney; Tina was a 23-year-old medical student. After 7 years, Tina became a licensed physician. Soon after, George filed for divorce from Tina because she was having an adulterous affair with another doctor. At the time of the divorce, George was

earning $55,000 per year practicing law; Tina was earning $165,000 per year as a physician.

The divorce was filed in Mississippi, where the couple lived. Mississippi follows the doctrine of equitable distribution. George sought to have Tina's medical license and medical practice valued as an ongoing business, and he claimed a portion of the value. The court refused George's request and instead applied the doctrine of equitable distribution and awarded him rehabilitative alimony of $1,400 per month for 120 months. The aggregate amount of the alimony was $168,000. George appealed this award, alleging on appeal that Tina's medical license and practice should be valued and that he should receive a portion of this value.

Source: *Neville v. Neville*, 734 So.2d 352, **Web** 1999 Miss. App. Lexis 68 (Court of Appeals of Mississippi)

PARALEGAL PORTFOLIO EXERCISE

Refer to the Paralegals at Work scenario at the beginning of the chapter. Prepare a memorandum, no longer than three pages, that describes how the property of Ms. Aston and Mr. Breton would be distributed under (1) the rule of equitable distribution, and (2) the rule of community property. Make any assumptions you think are necessary, but be sure to list those assumptions in your memorandum.

LEGAL ANALYSIS & WRITING CASES

Johnston v. Johnston   38 Mass. App. Ct. 531, 649 N.E.2d 799, Web 1995 Miss. App. Lexis 68

Appeals Court of Massachusetts

Ronald R. and Edith Johnston were married and had three sons, who ranged in age from 12 to 16 when the parties separated. Edith filed for divorce the same year. The Johnstons owned a primary residence worth $186,000, with no mortgage on it. Ronald was a successful entrepreneur. He owned Depot Distributors, Inc., a business involved in selling and installing bathroom cabinets. He also owned several other businesses. In the four years leading up to the divorce, Ronald's income was $543,382, $820,439, $1,919,713, and $1,462,712. Ronald invested much of his income in commercial and residential real estate, which was held in his name only. At the time of the divorce trial, the real estate was valued at $11,790,000 and was subject to mortgages of $4,966,343.

After their separation, Ronald engaged in certain transfers of property and distributions of property, in violation of the court's order that obfuscated his income and net worth. The Trial Court judge therefore accepted Edith's appraisals of the value of the real estate. The trial court judge applied the equitable distribution doctrine of Massachusetts and awarded Edith real estate totaling $2,446,000, the family residence, and alimony of $1,200 per month. The trial court judge awarded Ronald real estate valued at $9,314,000 subject to mortgages of $4,966,343, for a net value of $4,347,657. The judge characterized this as a roughly 60-40 split of the real estate (i.e., 60 percent for Ronald and 40 percent for Edith). Ronald appealed the split of real estate and the award of alimony as violating the equitable distribution doctrine.

Question

1. Under the doctrine of equitable distribution, was the Trial Court's award fair, or should Ronald win on appeal?

Schweinberg v. Click   627 So.2d 548, Web 1993 Fla. App. Lexis 11660

Court of Appeal of Florida

Randolph J. Schweinberg and Sandra Faye Click were married. Thirteen years later, Sandra Click moved out of the couple's home, and the couple was divorced the same year. At the time of the divorce, the couple had two minor children, Randolph II and Russell. Randolph II had cerebral palsy and walked with difficulty. The children lived with Randolph after Sandra moved out. Randolph was a sergeant in the United States Air Force, stationed in South Carolina; however, he considered Florida as his permanent home.

In the divorce proceeding, the court awarded custody of the two minor children to Randolph. The two children were doing well in school, and the court found that Randolph II needed the emotional support provided by his brother Russell. Sandra was permitted visitation rights to see the children. Sandra later married a new husband, who previously had been convicted of lewd and lascivious behavior on a female child and was under court supervision for 15 years.

Sandra petitioned the court to modify the custody order to grant her custody of the two minor children. The trial court granted the petition and awarded custody to Sandra. Randolph appealed the trial court's decision.

Question

1. Under the best interests test, should Randolph or Sandra be awarded custody of the two minor children?

Chadwick v. Janecka, Prison Warden, Pennsylvania   312 F.3d 597, Web 2002 U.S. App. Lexis 25263

United States Court of Appeals, Third Circuit

Mrs. Barbara Chadwick filed for divorce in Pennsylvania from Mr. H. Beatty Chadwick. During an equitable distribution conference, Mr. Chadwick informed the divorce court that he had transferred more than $2.5 million of the marital estate to pay an alleged debt he owed to Maison Blanche, Ltd., a Gibraltar partnership. It later was discovered that the principals of Maison Blanche had transferred $995,726 to a bank account in Switzerland in Mr. Chadwick's name and had purchased $869,106 of insurance annuity contracts in Mr. Chadwick's name. Mr. Chadwick redeemed these annuity contracts and received the money. In addition, $550,000 in stock certificates in Mr. Chadwick's name had been "lost."

The divorce court ordered Mr. Chadwick to return the $2,502,000 to an account under the jurisdiction of the court. When Mr. Chadwick refused, the court held Mr. Chadwick in civil contempt of court and ordered him jailed. During a seven-year period of incarceration, Mr. Chadwick applied 14 times to be released from prison, and each request was denied. Mr. Chadwick filed another request to be released

from prison, alleging that he should be released because of the unlikelihood that he would comply with the divorce court's order to turn over the money and that therefore the civil contempt order has lost its coercive effect.

The District Court agreed and granted Mr. Chadwick's petition to be released from prison. The government appealed the case to the U.S. Court of Appeals.

Question

1. Did Mr. Chadwick act ethically in this case? Should Mr. Chadwick be released from prison?

WORKING WITH THE LANGUAGE OF THE COURT CASE

Troxel v. Granville

530 U.S. 57, 120 S.Ct. 2054, 147 L.Ed.2d 49
Supreme Court of the United States

Read the following case, excerpted from the U.S. Supreme Court opinion. Review and brief the case. In your brief, answer the following questions.

1. Who were the original plaintiffs?
2. What rights did the plaintiffs seek? What law did the plaintiffs assert that gave them this right?
3. Who is the defendant?
4. What rights did the original defendant seek? What law did the defendant assert that gave her this right?
5. What was the decision of the U.S. Supreme Court? What law did the Supreme Court apply in reaching its decision?

Section 26.10.160(3) of the Revised Code of Washington permits "any person" to petition a superior court for visitation rights "at any time," and authorizes that court to grant such visitation rights whenever "visitation may serve the best interest of the child." Petitioners Jenifer and Gary Troxel petitioned a Washington Superior Court for the right to visit their grandchildren, Isabelle and Natalie Troxel. Respondent Tommie Granville, the mother of Isabelle and Natalie, opposed the petition. The case ultimately reached the Washington Supreme Court, which held that Section 26.10.160(3) unconstitutionally interferes with the fundamental right of parents to rear their children.

Tommie Granville and Brad Troxel shared a relationship that ended in June 1991. The two never married, but they had two daughters, Isabelle and Natalie. Jenifer and Gary Troxel are Brad's parents, and thus the paternal grandparents of Isabelle and Natalie. After Tommie and Brad separated in 1991, Brad lived with his parents and regularly brought his daughters to his parents' home for weekend visitation. Brad committed suicide in May 1993. Although the Troxels at first continued to see Isabelle and Natalie on a regular basis after their son's death, Tommie Granville informed the

Troxels in October 1993 that she wished to limit their visitation with her daughters to one short visit per month.

In December 1993, the Troxels commenced the present action by filing, in the Washington Superior Court for Skagit County, a petition to obtain visitation rights with Isabelle and Natalie. The Troxels filed their petition under Washington statute Wash. Rev. Code Section 26.10.160(3) (1994). Section 26.10.160(3) provides: "Any person may petition the court for visitation rights at any time including, but not limited to, custody proceedings. The court may order visitation rights for any person when visitation may serve the best interest of the child."

At trial, the Troxels requested two weekends of overnight visitation per month and two weeks of visitation each summer. Granville did not oppose visitation altogether, but instead asked the court to order one day of visitation per month with no overnight stay. In 1995, the Superior Court issued an oral ruling and entered a visitation decree ordering visitation one weekend per month, one week during the summer, and four hours on both of the petitioning grandparents' birthdays.

Granville appealed, during which time she married Kelly Wynn. Before addressing the merits of Granville's appeal, the Washington Court of Appeals remanded the case to the Superior Court. Granville's husband formally adopted Isabelle and Natalie.

The Washington Court of Appeals reversed the lower court's visitation order and dismissed the Troxels' petition for visitation, holding that nonparents lack standing to seek visitation under Section 26.10.160(3) unless a custody action is pending. In the Court of Appeals' view, that limitation on nonparental visitation actions was consistent with the constitutional restrictions on state interference with parents' fundamental liberty interest in the care, custody, and management of their children.

The Washington Supreme Court granted the Troxels' petition for review and affirmed. The Washington Supreme Court agreed with the Court of Appeals' ultimate conclusion that the Troxels could not obtain visitation of Isabelle and Natalie pursuant to Section 26.10.160(3). The court rested its decision on the Federal Constitution, holding that Section 26.10.160(3) unconstitutionally infringes on the fundamental right of parents to rear their children.

We granted certiorari and now affirm the judgment. Specifically, we are asked to decide whether Section 26.10.160(3), as applied to Tommie Granville and her family, violates the Federal Constitution. The Fourteenth Amendment provides that no State shall "deprive any person of life, liberty, or property, without due process of law."

The liberty interest at issue in this case—the interest of parents in the care, custody, and control of their children—is perhaps the oldest of the fundamental liberty interests recognized by this Court.

We have recognized the fundamental right of parents to make decisions concerning the care, custody, and control of their children.

Section 26.10.160(3), as applied to Granville and her family in this case, unconstitutionally infringes on that fundamental parental right. The Washington nonparental visitation statute is breathtakingly broad. According to the statute's text, any person may petition the court for visitation rights at any time, and the court may grant such visitation rights whenever visitation may serve the best interest of the child. 26.10.160(3). That language effectively permits any third party seeking visitation to subject any decision by a parent concerning visitation of the parent's children to state-court review. Once the visitation petition has been filed in court and the matter is placed before a judge, a parent's decision that visitation would not be in the child's best interest is

accorded no deference. Section 26.10.160(3) contains no requirement that a court accord the parent's decision any presumption of validity or any weight whatsoever. Instead, the Washington statute places the best-interest determination solely in the hands of the judge. Should the judge disagree with the parent's estimation of the child's best interests, the judge's view necessarily prevails. Thus, in practical effect, in the State of Washington a court can disregard and overturn any decision by a fit custodial parent concerning visitation whenever a third party affected by the decision files a visitation petition, based solely on the judge's determination of the child's best interests.

Turning to the facts of this case, the record reveals that the Superior Court's order was based on precisely the type of mere disagreement we have just described and nothing more. The Superior Court's order was not founded on any special factors that might justify the State's interference with Granville's fundamental right to make decisions concerning the rearing of her two daughters.

The Troxels did not allege, and no court has found, that Granville was an unfit parent. That aspect of the case is important, for there is a presumption that fit parents act in the best interests of their children. Accordingly, so long as a parent adequately cares for his or her children (i.e., is fit), there will normally be no reason for the State to inject itself into the private realm of the family to further question the ability of that parent to make the best decisions concerning the rearing of that parent's children.

We note that there is no allegation that Granville ever sought to cut off visitation entirely. Rather, the present dispute originated when Granville informed the Troxels that she would prefer to restrict their visitation with Isabelle and Natalie to one short visit per month and special holidays.

In the Superior Court proceedings Granville did not oppose visitation but instead asked that the duration of any visitation order be shorter than that requested by the Troxels. While the Troxels requested two weekends per month and two full weeks in the summer, Granville asked the Superior Court to order only one day of visitation per month (with no overnight stay) and participation in the Granville family's holiday celebrations.

The combination of these factors demonstrates that the visitation order in this case was an unconstitutional infringement on Granville's fundamental right to make decisions concerning the care, custody, and control of her two daughters. Accordingly, we hold that Section 26.10.160(3), as applied in this case, is unconstitutional.

Agency, Employment, and Immigration Law

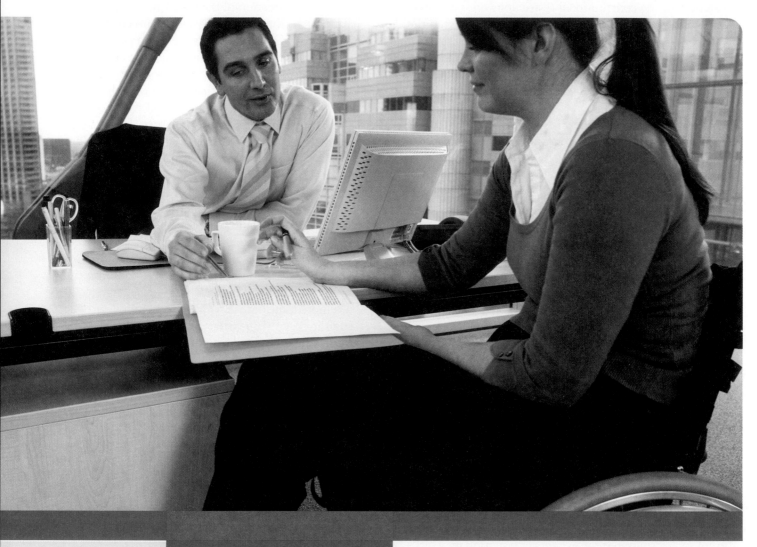

LEARNING OBJECTIVES

After studying this chapter, you should be able to:

1. Recognize the professional opportunities for paralegals in the employment law area.

2. Describe how express, implied, and apparent agencies are created.

3. Identify and describe the principal's liability for the tortious conduct of an agent.

4. Explain how state workers' compensation programs work and describe the benefits available.

5. Describe the scope of coverage of Title VII of the Civil Rights Act of 1964.

6. Describe the scope of coverage of the Age Discrimination in Employment Act.

7. Describe the protections afforded by the Americans with Disabilities Act.

8. Describe how a labor union is organized and employers' rights to strike and picket.

9. Understand immigration laws that apply to employment law.

10. Explain a paralegal's duty to disclose his or her paralegal status.

Paralegals at Work

You are a paralegal for Ms. Francis Brown, a renowned attorney in the area of employment law. You have been Ms. Brown's paralegal for more than ten years. One day Ms. Brown calls you into her office to sit in on a conference with a new client, Ms. Maria Rodriquez. Ms. Rodriquez has hired Ms. Brown to determine whether she has an employment law case against her employer, Retro Bank, N.A., a private bank that has hundreds of branch offices across the United States. During the conference, Ms. Rodriquez explains her situation.

Ms. Rodriquez has worked for Retro Bank for fifteen years. She started as an assistant branch manager and was promoted to Branch Manager and Assistant Vice President seven years ago. Ms. Rodriquez is still an Assistant Vice President and branch manager in a branch office located in the Hispanic community. Ms. Rodriquez explains that she had earned a bachelor's degree in business administration from the Wharton School, University of Pennsylvania, just before starting with the bank.

Several months ago Ms. Rodriquez applied for a promotion to District Manager of a region of the bank. The bank advertised this open position. One other candidate applied for the position. Mr. Rich Huntington, a white male, had graduated with a master in Business Administration (MBA) degree from a university and has worked as a branch manager for three years.

The candidate to be promoted to the new District Manager position would be in charge of at least ten branch offices, and the promotion to this position would include the title "Vice President" and a salary increase of $50,000 per year. The requirements for the new position were a bachelor's degree, experience as a bank branch manager for three or more years, passing a financial analysis test, and an interview with the President and the Board of Directors of the bank. Ms. Rodriquez and Mr. Huntington both passed the financial test.

At the interview, the president and board members of the bank asked Ms. Rodriquez questions about her job experience and management style. Ms. Rodriquez found several questions somewhat troubling—questions about the ages of her two children (4 and 6), whether she would be willing to attend charity events on some evenings to promote the bank, and whether traveling on bank business would cause any problems with her family. Later, Ms. Rodriquez was told that she did not receive the promotion, that Mr. Huntington had received the promotion.

Ms. Rodriquez wants to know if she has any cause to sue Retro Bank. She said she had heard that the bank promoted majority-race males over minority-race females in the past, particularly for positions as District Managers, including oversight of bank branches in primarily white areas. Currently the bank has forty District Managers. Only four of the District Managers are females, and none of them are minorities.

Consider the issues involved in this scenario as you read this chapter.

INTRODUCTION FOR THE PARALEGAL

Paralegals often work for lawyers who specialize in employment law matters. Lawyers in this area of practice negotiate and draft employment contracts, advise businesses on compliance with federal and state worker protection and antidiscrimination laws, and represent businesses and employees in the litigation of employment law disputes. Paralegals who work in this area must have an understanding of agency law, federal and state employment statutes, and administrative law that affects the employment relationship.

If individuals and businesses had to conduct all of their business personally, the scope of their activities would be severely curtailed. The use of agents (or agency), which allows one person to act on behalf of another, solves this problem. Among the many examples of agency relationships are a salesperson who sells goods for a store, an executive who works for a corporation, a partner who acts on behalf of a partnership, an attorney who is hired to represent a client, and a real estate broker who is employed to sell a house. Agency is governed by a large body of common law, known as *agency law*.

The United States Congress has enacted many federal statutes that provide protections and benefits for employees. For example, Congress has enacted federal statutes establishing worker safety rules, providing for the payment of minimum wages, and prohibiting discrimination based on race, sex, religion, age, disability, and other protected classes. States have enacted similar laws.

Another area of the law that is becoming more important is that of immigration law. Immigration law includes issues of becoming a citizen of the United States. In the employment law area, immigration law includes advising employers as to how to comply with immigration laws. It also includes assisting employers and employees obtain foreign worker visas.

Employment law is a burgeoning area of the law. Paralegals will be called on to conduct research, assist lawyers in the preparation and review of employment contracts, and prepare for litigation in this exciting area of the law.

CAREER OPPORTUNITIES FOR PARALEGALS IN EMPLOYMENT AND IMMIGRATION LAW

The paralegal who works in the employment law area can be involved in many different areas. Employment law consists of an array of state and federal laws. A paralegal who works in the employment law field must have good knowledge of the state and federal laws that apply to employers and employees in the state in which they work.

The law of agency applies to employers and employees, as well as to other employment relationships. Principals generally are liable for the torts of their agents, and usually are liable for the contracts entered into by agents on behalf of the principal while the agent is acting within the scope of his or her employment.

Employers often are sued by third parties either to recover for the negligence and other torts committed by employees, or to enforce contracts that their employees have entered. Agency law is an area of the law in which paralegals are needed to support attorneys, particularly when an attorney is representing the employer, employee, or third party in lawsuits involving agency and employment law matters.

In the employment law area, attorneys are called upon to negotiate and draft employment contracts. Attorneys sometimes are hired by corporations and other businesses to draft form employment contracts that the employer requires employees to sign. In other cases, attorneys represent either the executive or the employer in negotiating complex employment law agreements—bonuses, stock option plans, and the like. Paralegals usually prepare drafts of these employment contracts for the attorneys.

Paralegals often work for attorneys who represent clients who must comply with complex federal and state worker safety and protection statutes. These include workers' compensation laws, the federal Occupational Safety and Health Act, the federal Fair Labor Standards Act, and other state and federal laws.

Attorneys represent employers and employees in administrative proceedings and lawsuits involving these safety laws. Paralegals must understand these laws and regulatory procedures. Paralegals often draft documents required to comply with these laws, conduct research, and perform other tasks for lawyers involved in this area of employment law.

One exciting area of employment law for paralegals is the compliance and enforcement of equal opportunity in employment laws. A major federal statute in this area is Title VII of the Civil Rights Act of 1964, which prohibits employment discrimination based on race, national origin, color, religion, and sex. Other federal antidiscrimination statutes include the Equal Pay Act, the Age Discrimination in Employment Act, and the Americans with Disabilities Act, among others. States also have statutes that prohibit job discrimination.

In the area of equal opportunity in employment laws, paralegals may be engaged in researching statutes, regulations, or case law, preparing documents to be submitted to government administrative agencies that enforce these laws, or preparing for lawsuits involving equal opportunity in employment laws. If there is an administrative hearing or a lawsuit, a paralegal is called upon by his or her attorney to help prepare the case for the hearing or lawsuit.

Another growing area of employment opportunities for paralegal professionals is in immigration law. Many paralegals do a substantial amount of the work in preparing documents and assisting attorneys in representing clients who have immigration law issues.

The area of employment law covers a vast array of employment opportunities for paralegals. This is a growing area of the law, so there will be even more need in the future for paralegals who are qualified for positions in employment law.

Agency Law

Agency relationships are formed by the mutual consent of a principal and an agent. Section 1(1) of the Restatement (Second) of Agency defines *agency* as a *fiduciary relationship* "which results from the manifestation of consent by one person to another that the other shall act in his behalf and subject to his control, and consent by the other so to act." The Restatement (Second) of Agency is the reference source of the rules of agency. A party who employs another person to act on his or her behalf is called a **principal**. A party who agrees to act on behalf of another is called an **agent**. The principal–agent relationship is commonly referred to as an **agency**. This relationship is depicted in Exhibit 17.1.

Any person who has the capacity to contract can appoint an agent to act on his or her behalf. Generally, persons who lack contractual capacity, such as insane persons and minors, cannot appoint an agent. But, the court can appoint a legal guardian or other representative to handle the affairs of insane persons, minors, and others who lack capacity to contract. With court approval, these representatives can enter into enforceable contracts on behalf of the persons they represent.

An agency can be created only to accomplish a lawful purpose. Agency contracts that are created for illegal purposes or are against public policy are void and unenforceable.

> **Example** A principal cannot hire an agent to kill another person. Some agency relationships are prohibited by law.

> **Example** Unlicensed agents cannot be hired to perform the duties of certain licensed professionals (e.g., doctors and lawyers).

Kinds of Employment Relationships

Businesses usually have three kinds of employment relationships: (1) employer–employee relationships; (2) principal–agent relationships; and (3) principal–independent contractor relationships.

Employer–Employee Relationship

An **employer–employee relationship** exists when an employer hires an employee to perform some form of physical service.

> **Example** A welder on General Motors Corporation's assembly line is employed in an employer–employee relationship because he performs a task.

An employee is not an agent unless he or she is specifically empowered to enter into contracts on the principal employer's behalf. Employees may enter into only the contracts that are within the scope of their employment.

Principal A party who employs another person to act on his or her behalf.

Agent A party who agrees to act on behalf of another.

Agency A principal-agent relationship; the fiduciary relationship "which results from the manifestation of consent by one person to another that the other shall act in his behalf and subject to his control, and consent by the other so to act."

Employer–employee relationship A relationship that results when an employer hires an employee to perform some form of physical service.

Exhibit 17.1 The principal-agent relationship

Principal → *Agency contract* → Agent → *Contract with third party* → Third Party

on behalf of the principal

Principal's obligation to perform the contract

Example The welder in the prior example is not an agent, because he cannot enter into contracts on behalf of General Motors Corporation. If the company empowers him to enter into contracts, he becomes an agent.

Principal–Agent Relationship

A **principal–agent relationship** is formed when an employer hires an employee and gives that employee authority to act and enter into contracts on his or her behalf. The extent of this authority is governed by any express agreement between the parties and implied from the circumstances of the agency.

Examples The president of a corporation usually has the authority to enter into major contracts on the corporation's behalf, but a supervisor on the corporation's assembly line may have the authority only to purchase the supplies necessary to keep the line running.

Principal–Independent Contractor Relationship

A **principal–independent contractor relationship** exists when principals employ outsiders—persons and businesses who are not employees—to perform certain tasks on their behalf. These persons and businesses are called **independent contractors**. Professionals and tradespeople who typically act as independent contractors include doctors, dentists, stockbrokers, architects, certified public accountants, real estate brokers, and plumbers.

A principal can authorize an independent contractor to enter into contracts. Principals are bound by the authorized contracts of their independent contractors.

Example If a client authorizes an attorney to settle a case within a certain dollar amount and the attorney does so, the settlement agreement is binding.

Formation of the Agency Relationship

An agency and the resulting authority of an agent can arise in any of four ways: (1) express agency, (2) implied agency, (3) apparent agency, and (4) agency by ratification. Each of these types of agencies is discussed in the following pages.

Express Agency

The most common form of agency is **express agency**. In an express agency, the agent has the authority to contract or otherwise act on the principal's behalf as expressly stated in the agency agreement. In addition, the agent may possess certain implied or apparent authority to act on the principal's behalf (as discussed later in this chapter).

Express agency occurs when a principal and an agent expressly agree to enter into an agency agreement with each other. Express agency contracts can be either oral or written unless the Statute of Frauds stipulates that they must be written.

Example In most states a real estate broker's contract to sell real estate must be in writing.

If the principal and agent enter into an **exclusive agency contract**, the principal cannot employ any agent other than the exclusive agent. If the principal does so, the exclusive agent can recover damages from the principal. If an agency is not an exclusive agency, the principal can employ more than one agent to try to accomplish a stated purpose. When multiple agents are employed, the agencies with all of the agents terminate when any one of the agents accomplishes the stated purpose.

Power of Attorney. A **power of attorney** is one of the most formal types of express agency agreements. It is often used to give an agent the power to sign legal documents, such as deeds to real estate, on behalf of the principal. The two kinds of powers of

EMPLOYMENT-AT-WILL

Employees who are offered express employment contracts for a definite term cannot be discharged in violation of the contract. Most employees, however, do not have employment contracts; their status is termed employment-at-will.

Under common law, an at-will employee could be discharged by an employer at any time for any reason. This laissez-faire doctrine gave the employer great flexibility in responding to its changing needs. It also caused unfair results for some employees. Today, there are many statutory, contract, public policy, and tort exceptions to the at-will doctrine. These exceptions are:

- **Statutory exception.** Some federal and state statutes restrict the employment-at-will doctrine.

  Examples Federal labor laws that prohibit employers from discharging employees who are members of labor unions in violation of labor laws or collective bargaining agreements. Title VII and other federal and state antidiscrimination laws that prohibit employers from engaging in race, sex, religious, age, disability, or other forms of discrimination are additional examples of such laws.

- **Contract exception.** The courts have held that an implied-in-fact contract can be created between an employer and an employee. Implied-in-fact contracts develop from the conduct of the parties.

Examples A company bulletin, handbook, or personnel policy might mention that employees who do their jobs properly will not be discharged. This can be construed as an implied promise that an employee can be discharged only for good cause. Thus, the employer's ability to discharge an employee at will is removed. An employee who is discharged in violation of an implied-in-fact contract can sue the employer for breach of contract.

- **Public policy exception.** The most used common- law exception to the employment-at-will doctrine is the *public policy exception.* This rule states that an employee cannot be discharged if such discharge violates the public policy of the jurisdiction.

  Examples Violations of public policy are discharging an employee for serving as a juror, refusing to do an act in violation of the law (e.g., refusing to engage in dumping of toxic wastes in violation of environmental protection laws), refusing to engage in illegal research (e.g., research that violates patent laws or animal protection laws), and refusing to distribute defective products.

An employee who has been wrongfully discharged can sue his or her employer for damages and other remedies (reinstatement, back pay, and such). Punitive damages may be recovered if the employer has engaged in fraud or other intentional conduct.

---

attorney are (1) **general power of attorney**, which confers broad powers on the agent to act in any matters on the principal's behalf; and (2) **special power of attorney**, which limits the agent to acts specifically enumerated in an agreement. The agent is called an **attorney-in-fact** even though he or she does not have to be a lawyer. Powers of attorney must be written, and usually they must be notarized. A general power of attorney is shown in Exhibit 17.2.

Implied Agency

In many situations, a principal and an agent do not expressly create an agency. Instead, the agency is implied from the conduct of the parties. This type of agency is referred to as **implied agency**. The extent of the agent's authority is determined from the facts and circumstances of the particular situation. Implied authority can be conferred by

1. industry custom,
2. prior dealing between the parties,
3. the agent's position, and
4. the acts deemed necessary to carry out the agent's duties.

The court may deem other factors relevant as well. Implied authority cannot conflict with express authority or with stated limitations on express authority. Often, even

Exhibit 17.2 Sample general power of attorney

POWER OF ATTORNEY

Know All Men by These Presents: That _____ the undersigned (jointly and severally, if more than one) hereby make, constitute and appoint _____ My true and lawful Attorney for me and in my name, place and stead and for my use and benefit:

(a) To ask, demand, sue for, recover, collect and receive each and every sum of money, debt, account, legacy, bequest, interest, dividend, annuity and demand (which now is or hereafter shall become due, owing or payable) belonging to or claimed by me, and to use and take any lawful means for the recovery thereof by legal process or otherwise, and to execute and deliver a satisfaction or release therefor, together with the right and powers to compromise or compound any claim or demand;

(b) To exercise any or all of the following powers as to real property, any interest therein and/or any building thereon: To contract for, purchase, receive and take possession thereof and of evidence of title thereto; to lease the same for any term or purpose, including leases for business, residence, and oil and/or mineral development; to sell, exchange, grant or convey the same with or without warranty; and to mortgage, transfer in trust, or otherwise encumber or hypothecate the same to secure payment of a negotiable or non-negotiable note or performance of any obligation or agreement;

(c) To exercise any or all of the following powers as to all kinds of personal property and goods, wares and merchandise, chosen in action and other property in possession or in action: To contract for, buy, sell, exchange, transfer and in any legal manner deal in and with the same and to mortgage, transfer in trust, or otherwise encumber or hypothecate the same to secure payment of a negotiable or non-negotiable note or performance of any obligation or agreement;

(d) To borrow money and to execute and deliver negotiable or non-negotiable notes therefor with or without security, and to loan money and receive negotiable or non-negotiable notes therefor with such security as said Attorney shall deem proper;

(e) To create, amend, supplement and terminate any trust and to instruct and advise the trustee of any trust wherein I am or may be trustor or beneficiary; to represent and vote stock, exercise stock rights, accept and deal with any dividend, distribution or bonus, join in any corporate financing reorganization, merger, liquidation, consolidation or other action and the extension, compromise, conversion, adjustment, enforcement or foreclosure, singly or in conjunction with others of any corporate stock, bond, note, debenture or other security; to compound, compromise, adjust, settle and satisfy any obligation secured or unsecured, owing by or to me and to give or accept any property and/or money whether or not equal to or less in value than the amount owing in payment, settlement or satisfaction thereof;

(f) To transact business of any kind or class and as my act and deed to sign, execute, acknowledge and deliver any deed, lease, assignment of lease covenant, indenture, indemnity, agreement, mortgage, deed of trust, assignment of mortgage or of the beneficial interest under deed of trust, extension or renewal of any obligation, subordination or waiver or priority, hypothecation, bottomry, charter-party, bill of lading, bill of sale, bill, bond, note, whether negotiable or non-negotiable, receipt, evidence of debt, full or partial release or satisfaction of mortgage, judgment and other debt, request for partial or full reconveyance of deed of trust and such other instruments in writing of any kind or class as may be necessary or proper in the premises.

Giving and Granting unto my said Attorney full power and authority to do and perform all and every act and thing whatsoever, requisite, necessary or appropriate to be done in and about the premises as fully to all intents, and purposes as I might or could do it personally present, hereby ratifying all that my said Attorney shall lawfully do or cause to be done by virtue of these presents. The powers and authority hereby conferred upon my said Attorney shall be applicable to all real and personal property or interests therein now owned or hereafter required by me and whenever situate.

My said Attorney is empowered hereby to determine in said Attorney's sole discretion the time when, purpose for and manner in which any power herein conferred upon said Attorney shall be exercised, and the conditions, provisions and covenants of any instrument or document which may be executed by said Attorney pursuant hereto and in the acquisition or disposition of real or personal property, my said Attorney shall have exclusive power to fix the terms thereof for cash, credit and/or property, and if on credit with or without security.

The undersigned, if a married person, hereby further authorizes and empowers my said Attorney, as my duly authorized agent, to join in my behalf, in the execution of any instrument by which any community real property or any interest therein, now owned or hereafter acquired by my spouse and myself, or either of us, is sold, leased, encumbered, or conveyed.

When the context to requires, the masculine gender includes the feminine and/or neuter, and the singular number includes the plural.

Witness my hand this _____ day of _____ 20_____
STATE OF CALIFORNIA, COUNTY OF _____ SS.
On _____ before me, the undersigned, a Notary Public
in and for said State personally appeared _____

_____   _____

personally known to me (or proved to me on the basis of satisfactory evidence) to be the person _____ whose name _____ subscribed to the within instrument and acknowledge that _____ executed the same.
WITNESS my hand and official seal.

Signature _____

Name (*Typed or Printed*) _____   *(This area for official seal)*

FORMATION OF AGENCY RELATIONSHIPS

SIDEBAR

Type of Agency	Definition	Enforcement of the Contract
Express	Authority is expressly given to the agent by the principal.	Principal and third party are bound to the contract.
Implied	Authority is implied from the conduct of the parties, custom and usage of trade, or act incidental to carrying out the agent's duties.	Principal and third party acts are bound to the contract.
Apparent	Authority created when the principal leads a third party into believing that the agent has authority.	Principal and third party are bound to the contract.
By ratification	Acts of the agent committed outside the scope of his or her authority.	Principal and third party are not bound to the contract unless the principal ratifies the contract.

Apparent agency Agency that arises when a principal creates the appearance of an agency that in actuality does not exist.

Agency by ratification An agency that occurs when (1) a person misrepresents himself or herself as another's agent when in fact he or she is not and (2) the purported principal ratifies the unauthorized act.

an express agency agreement does not provide enough detail to cover all contingencies that may arise in the future regarding the performance of the agency. In this case, the agent possesses certain implied authority to act. This implied authority sometimes is referred to as *incidental authority*. Certain emergency situations may arise in the course of an agency. If the agent cannot contact the principal for instructions, the agent has implied emergency powers to take all actions reasonably necessary to protect the principal's property and rights.

Apparent Agency

Apparent agency, or **agency by estoppel**, arises when a principal creates the appearance of an agency that in actuality does not exist. Where an apparent agency is established, the principal is estopped from denying the agency relationship and is bound to contracts entered into by the apparent agent while acting within the scope of the apparent agency. Note that the principal's action—not the agent's action—is what creates an apparent agency.

Example Suppose Georgia Pacific, Inc., interviews Albert Iorio for a sales representative position. Mr. Iorio, accompanied by Jane Franklin, the national sales manager, visits retail stores located in the open sales territory. While visiting one store, Jane tells the store manager, "I wish I had more sales reps like Albert." Nevertheless, Albert is not hired. If Albert later enters into contracts with the store on behalf of Georgia Pacific and Jane has not controverted the impression of Albert she left with the store manager, the company will be bound to the contracts.

Agency by Ratification

Agency by ratification occurs when (1) a person misrepresents himself or herself as another's agent when in fact he or she is not, and (2) the purported principal ratifies (accepts) the unauthorized act. In such cases, the principal is bound to perform and the agent is relieved of any liability for misrepresentation.

Example Bill Levine sees a house for sale and thinks his friend Sherry Maxwell would want it. Bill enters into a contract to purchase the house from the seller and signs the contract "Bill Levine, agent for Sherry Maxwell." Because Bill is not Sherry Maxwell's agent, she is not bound to the contract. If, however, Sherry agrees to purchase the house, there is an agency by ratification. The ratification "relates back" to the moment Bill Levine entered into the contract. Upon ratification of the contract, Sherry Maxwell is obligated to purchase the house.

Tort Liability of Principals and Agents to Third Parties

The principal and the agent are each personally liable for their own tortious conduct. The principal is liable for the tortious conduct of an agent who is acting within the scope of his or her authority. The agent, however, is liable only for the tortious conduct of the principal if he or she directly or indirectly participates in or aids and abets the principal's conduct.

The courts have applied a broad and flexible standard in interpreting scope of authority in the context of employment. Although other factors also may be considered, the courts rely on the following factors to determine whether an agent's conduct occurred within the scope of his or her employment:

- Was the act specifically requested or authorized by the principal?
- Was it the kind of act that the agent was employed to perform?
- Did the act occur substantially within the time period of employment authorized by the principal?
- Did the act occur substantially within the location of employment authorized by the employer?
- Was the agent advancing the principal's purpose when the act occurred?

Where liability is found, tort remedies are available to the injured party. These remedies include recovery for medical expenses, lost wages, pain and suffering, and emotional distress, and, in some cases, punitive damages.

Intentional Torts

Intentional torts include acts such as assault, battery, false imprisonment, and other intentional conduct that causes injury to another person. Most jurisdictions apply the **work-related test**, which holds that if an agent commits an intentional tort within a work-related time or space the principal is liable for any injuries caused by the agent's intentional torts.

> **Work-related test** A test that says if an agent commits an intentional tort within a work-related time or space, the principal is liable for any injury caused by the agent's intentional tort.

Example   If an employee commits battery on another employee during working hours or on the principal's premises under the work-related test, the employer would be held liable.

If a state follows the **motivation test** instead of the work-related test, the court must determine the motivation of the perpetrator for committing the intentional tort.

Example   If an employee commits the tort of battery on a customer because of a personal dispute with the customer, then the employer would not be liable under the motivation test.

A principal is not liable for the intentional torts of agents and employees that are committed outside the principal's scope of business.

Example   If an employee attends a sporting event after working hours and gets into a fight with another spectator at the event, the employer is not liable.

Negligence

Principals are liable for the negligent conduct of agents acting within the scope of their employment. This liability for **negligence** is based on the common-law doctrine of *respondeat superior* ("let the master answer"), which, in turn, is based on the legal theory of **vicarious liability** (liability without fault). The principal is liable because of his or her employment contract with the negligent agent, not because the principal was personally at fault.

> **Respondeat superior** A rule that says an employer is liable for the tortious conduct of its employees or agents while they are acting within the scope of its authority.

This doctrine rests on the principle that if someone (i.e., the principal) expects to derive certain benefits from acting through others (i.e., an agent), that person also should bear the liability for injuries caused to third persons by the negligent conduct of an agent who is acting within the scope of his or her employment.

Frolic and Detour

Agents sometimes do things during the course of their employment to further their own interests rather than the principal's interests.

Example An agent might take a detour to run a personal errand while on assignment for the principal. This is commonly referred to as a **frolic and detour**. Agents always are personally liable for their tortious conduct in such situations. Principals generally are relieved of liability if the agent's frolic and detour is substantial. If the deviation is minor, however, the principal is liable for the injuries caused by the agent's tortious conduct.

Examples A salesperson stops home for lunch while on an assignment for his principal. While leaving his home, the agent hits and injures a pedestrian with his automobile. The principal is liable if the agent's home was not too far out of the way from the agent's assignment. But the principal would not be liable if an agent who is supposed to be on assignment to Los Angeles, California, drives to Irvine, California (50 miles away), to meet a friend and is involved in an accident. Negligence actions stemming from frolic and detour are examined on a case-by-case basis.

The "Coming and Going" Rule

Under the common law, a principal generally is not liable for injuries caused by its agents and employees while they are on their way to or from work. This so-called **"coming and going" rule** applies even if the principal supplies the agent's automobile or other transportation or pays for gasoline, repairs, and other automobile operating expenses. This rule is quite logical. Because principals do not control where their agents and employees live, they should not be held liable for tortious conduct of agents on their way to and from work.

Dual-Purpose Mission

Sometimes principals request that agents run errands or conduct other acts on their behalf while the agent or employee is on personal business. In this case, the agent is on a **dual-purpose mission**. That is, he or she is acting partly for himself or herself and partly for the principal. Most jurisdictions hold both the principal and the agent liable if the agent injures someone while on such a mission.

Example Suppose a principal asks an employee to drop off a package at a client's office on the employee's way home. If the employee negligently injures a pedestrian while on this dual-purpose mission, the principal is liable to the pedestrian.

Independent Contractor

Section 2 of the Restatement (Second) of Agency defines an independent contractor as "a person who contracts with another to do something for him [or her] who is not controlled by the other nor subject to the other's right to control with respect to his [or her] physical conduct in the performance of the undertaking." Independent contractors usually work for a number of clients, have their own offices, hire employees, and control the performance of their work.

TORT LIABILITY OF PRINCIPALS AND AGENTS TO THIRD PARTIES

Agent's Conduct	Agent Liable	Principal Liable
Intentional tort	Yes	Motivation test: The principal is liable if the agent's motivation in committing the intentional tort was to promote the principal's business.
Intentional tort	Yes	Work-related test: The principal is liable if the agent committed the intentional tort within work-related time and space.
Negligence	Yes	The principal is liable under the doctrine of *respondeat superior* if the agent's negligent act was committed within his or her scope of employment.

Merely labeling someone an "independent contractor" is not enough. The crucial factor in determining whether someone is an employee or an independent contractor is the *degree of control* the employer has over the agent. Critical factors in determining independent contractor status include:

- Whether the worker is engaged in a distinct occupation or an independently established business
- The length of time the agent has been employed by the principal
- The amount of time the agent works for the principal
- Whether the principal supplies the tools and equipment used in the work
- The method of payment, whether by time or by the job
- The degree of skill necessary to complete the task
- Whether the worker hires employees to assist him or her
- Whether the employer has the right to control the manner and means of accomplishing the desired result

If an examination of these factors shows that the principal asserts little control, the person is an independent contractor. Substantial control indicates an employer–employee relationship.

Torts of Independent Contractors

Generally, a principal is not liable for the torts of its independent contractors. Independent contractors are personally liable for their own torts. The rationale behind this rule is that principals do not control the means by which the results are accomplished.

Example A client employs an attorney who is an independent contractor to represent him in a lawsuit. While driving to the courthouse in her automobile the attorney negligently causes an automobile accident that causes severe injury to another person. Here, the attorney is liable to the injured person. However, the client is not liable to the injured person.

Nevertheless, this rule has several exceptions where a principal is held liable for the torts of an independent contractor it has employed. These are:

- **Nondelegable duties.** Certain duties, called **nondelegable duties**, may not be delegated.

  Example Railroads owe a duty to maintain safe railroad crossings. They cannot escape this liability by assigning the task to an independent contractor.

- **Special risks.** Principals cannot avoid strict liability for dangerous activities assigned to independent contractors.

  Example The use of explosives, clearing land by fire, crop dusting, and such involve special risks that are shared by the principal.

- **Negligence in the selection of an independent contractor.** A principal who knowingly hires an unqualified or dangerous person as an independent contractor is liable if that person injures someone while on the job.

Termination of an Agency

An agency contract is similar to other contracts in that it can be terminated either by an act of the parties or by operation of law. These different methods of termination are discussed next. Note that once an agency relationship is terminated, the agent no longer can represent the principal or bind the principal to contracts.

Web Exploration

Go to http://en.wikipedia.org/wiki/Walt_Disney_World. Read the information about how the Walt Disney Company used dummy corporations to acquire much of the land in central Florida for its Walt Disney World Resort.

Termination by Acts of the Parties

The parties to an agency contract can terminate an agency contract by agreement or by their actions. The four methods of termination of an agency relationship by acts of the parties are:

1. *Mutual agreement.* As with any contract, the parties to an agency contract can mutually agree to terminate their agreement. By doing so, the parties relieve each other of any further rights, duties, obligations, or powers provided for in the agency contract. Either party can propose the termination of an agency contract.

2. *Lapse of time.* Agency contracts are often written for a specific period of time. The agency terminates when the specified time period elapses.

   Example Suppose that a principal and agent enter into an agency contract "beginning January 1, 2002, and ending December 31, 2005." The agency automatically terminates on December 31, 2005. If the agency contract does not set forth a specific termination date, the agency terminates after a reasonable time has elapsed. The courts often look to the custom of an industry in determining the reasonable time for termination of the agency.

3. *Purpose achieved.* A principal can employ an agent for the time it takes to accomplish a certain task, purpose, or result. Such agencies automatically terminate once they are completed.

   Example Suppose a principal employs a licensed real estate broker to sell his house. The agency terminates when the house is sold and the principal pays the broker the agreed-upon compensation.

4. *Occurrence of a specified event.* An agency contract can specify that the agency exists until a specified event occurs. The agency terminates when the specified event happens.

   Example If a principal employs an agent to take care of her dog until she returns from a trip, the agency terminates when the principal returns from the trip.

Wrongful Termination of an Agency or Employment Contract

Generally, agency and employment contracts that do not specify a definite time for their termination can be terminated at will by either the principal or the agent without liability to the other party. When a principal terminates an agency contract, it is called a *revocation of authority*. When an agent terminates an agency, it is called a *renunciation of authority*.

Unless an agency is irrevocable, both the principal and the agent have an individual power to unilaterally terminate any agency contract. Note that having the power to terminate an agency agreement is not the same as having the right to terminate it. The unilateral termination of an agency contract may be wrongful. If the principal's or agent's termination of an agency contract breaches the contract, the other party can sue for damages for **wrongful termination of an agency.**

Wrongful termination of an agency The termination of an agency contract in violation of the terms of the agency contract. In this situation, the nonbreaching party may recover damages from the breaching party.

Example A principal employs a licensed real estate agent to sell his house. The agency contract gives the agent an exclusive listing for three months. After one month, the principal unilaterally terminates the agency. The principal has the power to do so, and the agent can no longer act on behalf of the principal. Because the principal did not have the right to terminate the contract, however, the agent can sue him and recover damages (i.e., lost commission) for wrongful termination.

Workers' Compensation

Many types of employment are dangerous, and each year many workers are injured on the job. At common law, employees who were injured on the job could sue their employer for negligence. This time-consuming process placed the employee at odds with his or her employer. In addition, there was no guarantee that the employee would win the case. Ultimately, many injured workers—or the heirs of deceased workers—were left uncompensated.

Workers' compensation acts were enacted in response to the unfairness of that result. These acts create an administrative procedure for workers to receive compensation for injuries that occur on the job—**workers' compensation.** First, the injured worker files a claim with the appropriate state government agency (often called the workers' compensation board or commission). Next, that entity determines the legitimacy of the claim. If the worker disagrees with the agency's findings, he or she may appeal the decision through the state court system. Workers' compensation benefits are paid according to preset limits established by statute or regulation. The amounts that are recoverable vary from state to state.

Exhibit 17.3 shows a state complaint form that must be filed to claim workers' compensation benefits.

Workers' compensation acts Laws that compensate workers and their families if workers are injured in connection with their jobs.

Workers' Compensation Insurance

States usually require employers to purchase insurance from private insurance companies or state funds to cover workers' compensation claims. Some states permit employers to self-insure if they demonstrate that they have the ability to pay workers' compensation claims. Many large companies self-insure. Workers can sue an employer in court to recover damages for employment-related injuries if the employer does not carry workers' compensation insurance or does not self-insure if permitted to do so.

Web Exploration

Go to http://www.dir.ca.gov/dwc/WCFaqIW.html#1 to learn more about workers' compensation. Read the first four questions and answers.

Employment-Related Injury

To be compensable under workers' compensation, the claimant must prove that the injury arose out of and in the course of his or her employment, that it is an **employment-related injury.** An accident that occurs while an employee is actively working is clearly within the scope of this rule. Accidents that occur at a company cafeteria or while on a business lunch for an employer are covered. Accidents that happen while the employee is at an off-premises restaurant during his or her personal lunch hour are not covered. Many workers' compensation acts include stress as a compensable work-related injury.

Web Exploration

Go to http://www.ohiobwc.com/basics/guidedtour/generalinfo/empgeneralinfo22.asp "Fraud Red Flags." Read the section "Spotting injured worker claim fraud."

Exclusive Remedy

Workers' compensation is an **exclusive remedy.** Thus, workers cannot sue their employers in court for damages. The one exception to this rule is: If an employer intentionally injures a worker, the worker can collect workers' compensation benefits and sue the employer. Workers' compensation acts do not bar injured workers from suing responsible third parties to recover damages.

Occupational Safety and Health Act

In 1970, Congress enacted the **Occupational Safety and Health Act** to promote safety in the workplace. Virtually all private employers are within the scope of the act, but federal, state, and local governments are exempt. Industries regulated by other federal safety legislation are also exempt. The act also established the **Occupational**

Occupational Safety and Health Act A federal act enacted in 1970 that promotes safety in the workplace.

Exhibit 17.3   Workers' compensation complaint form

State of California
Department of Industrial Relations
DIVISION OF WORKERS' COMPENSATION

WORKERS' COMPENSATION CLAIM FORM (DWC 1)

PRINT   CLEAR

Estado de California
Departamento de Relaciones Industriales
DIVISION DE COMPENSACIÓN AL TRABAJADOR

PETITION DEL EMPLEADO PARA DE COMPENSACIÓN DEL TRABAJADOR (DWC 1)

Employee: Complete the **"Employee"** section and give the form to your employer. Keep a copy and mark it **"Employee's Temporary Receipt"** until you receive the signed and dated copy from your employer. You may call the Division of Workers' Compensation and hear recorded information at **(800) 736-7401**. An explanation of workers' compensation benefits is included as the cover sheet of this form.

You should also have received a pamphlet from your employer describing workers' compensation benefits and the procedures to obtain them.

Empleado: Complete la sección "Empleado" y entregue la forma a su empleador. Quédese con la copia designada "Recibo Temporal del Empleado" hasta que Ud. reciba la copia firmada y fechada de su empleador. Ud. puede llamar a la Division de Compensación al Trabajador al (800) 736-7401 para oir información gravada. En la hoja cubierta de esta forma esta la explicación de los beneficios de compensación al trabjador.

Ud. también debería haber recibido de su empleador un folleto describiendo los benficios de compensación al trabajador lesionado y los procedimientos para obtenerlos.

Any person who makes or causes to be made any knowingly false or fraudulent material statement or material representation for the purpose of obtaining or denying workers' compensation benefits or payments is guilty of a felony.

Toda aquella persona que a propósito haga o cause que se produzca cualquier declaración o representación material falsa o fraudulenta con el fin de obtener o negar beneficios o pagos de compensación a trabajadores lesionados es culpable de un crimen mayor "felonia".

Employee—complete this section and see note above   *Empleado—complete esta sección y note la notación arriba.*

1.   Name. *Nombre.* _____   Today's Date. *Fecha de Hoy.* _____

2.   Home Address. *Dirección Residencial.* _____

3.   City. *Ciudad.* _____   State. *Estado.* _____   Zip. *Código Postal.* _____

4.   Date of Injury. *Fecha de la lesión (accidente).* _____   Time of Injury. *Hora en que ocurrió.* _____ a.m. _____ p.m.

5.   Address and description of where injury happened. *Dirección/lugar dónde occurió el accidente.* _____
_____

6.   Describe injury and part of body affected. *Describa la lesión y parte del cuerpo afectada.* _____
_____

7.   Social Security Number. *Número de Seguro Social del Empleado.* _____

8.   Signature of employee. *Firma del empleado.* _____

Employer—complete this section and see note below. *Empleador—complete esta sección y note la notación abajo.*

9.   Name of employer. *Nombre del empleador.* _____

10. Address. *Dirección.* _____

11. Date employer first knew of injury. *Fecha en que el empleador supo por primera vez de la lesión o accidente.* _____

12. Date claim form was provided to employee. *Fecha en que se le entregó al empleado la petición.* _____

13. Date employer received claim form. *Fecha en que el empleado devolvió la petición al empleador.* _____

14. Name and address of insurance carrier or adjusting agency. *Nombre y dirección de la compañía de seguros o agencia adminstradora de seguros.* _____

15. Insurance Policy Number. *El número de la póliza de Seguro.* _____

16. Signature of employer representative. *Firma del representante del empleador.* _____

17. Title. *Título.* _____   18. Telephone. *Teléfono.* _____

Employer: You are required to date this form and provide copies to your insurer or claims administrator and to the employee, dependent or representative who filed the claim within **one working day** of receipt of the form from the employee.

SIGNING THIS FORM IS NOT AN ADMISSION OF LIABILITY

*Empleador: Se requiere que Ud. feche esta forma y que provéa copias a su compañía de seguros, administrador de reclamos, o dependiente/representante de reclamos y al empleado que hayan presentado esta petición dentro del plazo de **un día hábil** desde el momento de haber sido recibida la forma del empleado.*

EL FIRMAR ESTA FORMA NO SIGNIFICA ADMISION DE RESPONSABILIDAD

☐ Employer copy/*Copia del Empleador*   ☐ Employee copy/ *Copia del Empleado*   ☐ Claims Administrator/*Administrador de Reclamos*   ☐ Temporary Receipt/*Recibo del Empleado*

7/1/04 Rev.

Safety and Health Administration (OSHA), a federal administrative agency within the Department of Labor that is empowered to enforce the act. The act imposes record keeping and reporting requirements on employers and requires them to post notices in the workplace, informing employees of their rights under the act.

Specific and General Duty Standards

OSHA is empowered to adopt rules and regulations to interpret and enforce the Occupational Safety and Health Act. OSHA has adopted thousands of regulations to enforce the safety standards established by the act. These include the following:

- **Specific duty standards.** Many of the OSHA standards address safety problems of a **specific duty** nature.

  Example OSHA standards establish safety requirements for equipment (e.g., safety guards), set maximum exposure levels to hazardous chemicals, regulate the location of machinery, establish safety procedures for employees, and the like.

- **General duty standards.** The act imposes a general duty on an employer to provide a work environment free from recognized hazards that are causing or are likely to cause death or serious physical harm to employees. This is so even if no specific regulation applies to the situation.

OSHA is empowered to inspect places of employment for health hazards and safety violations. If a violation is found, OSHA can issue a *written citation* that requires the employer to abate or correct the situation. Contested citations are reviewed by the Occupational Safety and Health Review Commission. Its decision is appealable to the Federal Circuit Court of Appeals. Employers who violate the act, OSHA rules and regulations or OSHA citations are subject to both civil and criminal penalties. Exhibit 17.4 shows a safety and health poster that must be posted in workplaces in the state of Arizona. Exhibit 17.5 shows a federal OSHA poster that must be posted in workplaces.

Fair Labor Standards Act

In 1938, Congress enacted the **Fair Labor Standards Act (FLSA)** to protect workers. The FLSA applies to private employers and employees engaged in the production of goods for interstate commerce.

Child Labor

The FLSA forbids the use of oppressive **child labor** and makes it unlawful to ship goods produced by businesses that use oppressive child labor. The Department of Labor has adopted the following regulations that define lawful child labor.

1. Children under the age of 14 cannot work except as newspaper deliverers.
2. Children ages 14 and 15 may work limited hours in nonhazardous jobs approved by the Department of Labor (e.g., restaurants and gasoline stations).
3. Children ages 16 and 17 may work unlimited hours in nonhazardous jobs.

The Department of Labor determines which occupations are hazardous (e.g., mining, roofing, working with explosives). Children who work in agricultural employment and child actors and performers are exempt from these restrictions. Persons age 18 and older may work at any job, whether it is hazardous or not.

Web Exploration
Go to http://www.osha.gov/html and find the address of the office of the federal Occupational Safety and Health Administration (OSHA) that serves your area.

Web Exploration
Go to the website www.dol.gov/esa/minwage/america.htm. What is the minimum wage for your state?

Fair Labor Standards Act (FLSA) A federal act enacted in 1938 to protect workers that prohibits child labor and establishes minimum wage and overtime pay requirements.

Exhibit 17.4 OSHA English poster

EMPLOYEE SAFETY AND HEALTH PROTECTION

The Arizona Occupational Safety and Health Act of 1972 (Act), provides safety and health protection for employees in Arizona. The Act requires each employer to furnish his employees with a place of employment free from recognized hazards that might cause serious injury or death. The Act further requires that employers and employees comply with all workplace safety and health standards, rules and regulations promulgated by the Industrial Commission. The Arizona Division of Occupational Safety and Health (ADOSH), a division of the Industrial Commission of Arizona, administers and enforces the requirements of the Act.

As an employee, you have the following rights:

You have the right to notify your employer or ADOSH about workplace hazards. You may ask ADOSH to keep your name confidential.

You have the right to request that ADOSH conduct an inspection if you believe there are unsafe and/or unhealthful conditions in your workplace. You or your representative may participate in the inspection.

If you believe you have been discriminated against for making safety and health complaints, or for exercising your rights under the Act, you have a right to file a complaint with ADOSH within 30 days of the discriminatory action. You are also afforded protection from discrimination under the Federal Occupational Safety and Health Act and may file a complaint with the U.S. Secretary of Labor within 30 days of the discriminatory action.

You have the right to see any citations that have been issued to your employer. Your employer must post the citations at or near the location of the alleged violation.

You have the right to protest the time frame given for correction of any violation.

You have the right to obtain copies of your medical records or records of your exposure to toxic and harmful substances or conditions.

Your employer must post this notice in your workplace.

The Industrial Commission and ADOSH do not cover employers of household domestic labor, those in maritime activities (covered by OSHA), those in atomic energy activities (covered by the Atomic Energy Commission) and those in mining activities (covered by the Arizona Mine Inspector's office). To file a complaint, report an emergency or seek advice and assistance from ADOSH, contact the nearest ADOSH office:

Phoenix:	Tucson:
800 West Washington	2675 East Broadway
Phoenix AZ. 85007	Tucson, AZ. 85716
602-542-5795	520-628-5478

Industrial Commission web site: www.ica.state.az.us

Note: Persons wishing to register a complaint alleging inadequacy in the administration of the Arizona Occupational Safety and Health plan may do so at the following address:

U.S. Department of Labor – OSHA
3221 N. 16th St., Suite 100
Phoenix, AZ 85016
Telephone: 1-800-475-4020

Revised 11/01

Exhibit 17.5 OSHA Spanish poster

Seguridad y Salud en el Trabajo
¡Es la Ley!

OSHA
Administración de Seguridad y Salud Ocupacional

Departamento del Trabajo de los Estados Unidos

EMPLEADOS:

- Usted tiene el derecho de notificar a su empleador o a la OSHA sobre peligros en el lugar de trabajo. Usted también puede pedir que la OSHA no revele su nombre.

- Usted tiene el derecho de pedir a la OSHA que realice una inspección si usted piensa que en su trabajo existen condiciones peligrosas o poco saludables. Usted o su representante pueden participar en esa inspección.

- Usted tiene 30 días para presentar una queja ante la OSHA si su empleador llega a tomar represalias o discriminar en su contra por haber denunciado la condición de seguridad o salud o por ejercer los derechos consagrados bajo la Ley OSH.

- Usted tiene el derecho de ver las citaciones enviadas por la OSHA a su empleador. Su empleador debe colocar las citaciones en el lugar donde se encontraron las supuestas infracciones o cerca del mismo.

- Su empleador debe corregir los peligros en el lugar de trabajo para la fecha indicada en la citación y debe certificar que dichos peligros se hayan reducido o desaparecido.

- Usted tiene derecho de recibir copias de su historial o registro médico y el registro de su exposición a sustancias o condiciones tóxicas o dañinas.

- Su empleador debe colocar este aviso en su lugar de trabajo.

- Usted debe cumplir con todas las normas de seguridad y salud ocupacionales expedidas conforme a la Ley OSH que sean aplicables a sus propias acciones y conducta en el trabajo.

EMPLEADORES:

- Usted debe proporcionar a sus empleados un lugar de empleo libre de peligros conocidos.

- Usted debe cumplir con las normas de seguridad y salud ocupacionales expedidas conforme a la Ley OSH.

Los empleadores pueden obtener ayuda gratis para identificar y corregir las fuentes de peligro y para cumplir con las normas, sin citación ni multa, por medio de programas de consulta respaldados por la OSHA en cada estado del país.

1-800-321-OSHA
www.osha.gov

OSHA 3167-01-07R

Web Exploration

Go to http://www.eeoc.gov/
offices/html and click on your
state on the map to find the
address of the federal Equal
Employment Opportunity
Commission (EEOC) that serves
your area.

Minimum Wage and Overtime Pay Requirements

The FLSA establishes minimum wage and overtime pay requirements for workers. Managerial, administrative, and professional employees are exempt from the act's wage and hour provisions. As outlined in the following paragraphs, the FLSA requires employers to pay covered workers at least the minimum wage for their regular work hours and to provide overtime pay:

- **Minimum wage.** The **minimum wage** is set by Congress and can be changed. As of 2009, it was set at $7.25 per hour. The Department of Labor permits employers to pay less than the minimum wage to students and apprentices. An employer may reduce minimum wages by an amount equal to the reasonable cost of food and lodging provided to employees.
- **Overtime pay.** Under the FLSA, an employer cannot require nonexempt employees to work more than 40 hours per week unless they are paid one-and-a-half times their regular pay for each hour worked in excess of 40 hours. Each week is treated separately.

    Example   If an employee works 50 hours one week and 30 hours the next, the employer owes the employee 10 hours of **overtime pay** for the first week.

Title VII of the Civil Rights Act of 1964

Title VII of the Civil Rights Act of 1964 A title of a federal statute enacted to eliminate job discrimination based on five protected classes: *race, color, religion, sex, and national origin.*

After substantial debate, Congress enacted the **Civil Rights Act of 1964. Title VII** of that act (entitled the Fair Employment Practices Act) was intended to eliminate job discrimination based on the following **protected classes:** (1) *race*, (2) *color*, (3) *national origin*, (4) *religion*, or (5) *sex*. Title VII provides in pertinent part that: It shall be an unlawful employment practice for an employer

1. To fail or refuse to hire or to discharge any individual, or otherwise to discriminate against any individual with respect to his compensation, terms, conditions, or privileges of employment, because of such individual's race, color, religion, sex, or national origin; or
2. To limit, segregate, or classify his employees or applicants for employment in any way which would deprive or tend to deprive any individual of employment opportunities or otherwise adversely affect his [or her] status as an employee, because of such individual's race, color, religion, sex, or national origin.

Equal Employment Opportunity Commission (EEOC)

Equal Employment Opportunity Commission (EEOC) A federal administrative agency responsible for enforcing most federal antidiscrimination laws.

The **Equal Employment Opportunity Commission (EEOC)** is a federal agency responsible for enforcing most federal antidiscrimination laws. Members of the EEOC are appointed by the U.S. President. The EEOC is empowered to conduct investigations, interpret the statutes, encourage conciliation between employees and employers, and bring suit to enforce the law. The EEOC also can seek injunctive relief. Exhibit 17.6 shows a map of the fifteen districts of the EEOC.

Scope of Coverage of Title VII

Title VII prohibits discrimination in hiring, decisions regarding promotion or demotion, payment of compensation and fringe benefits, availability of job training and apprenticeship opportunities, referral systems for employment, decisions regarding dismissal, work rules, and any other "term, condition, or privilege" of employment. Any employee of covered employers, including undocumented aliens, may bring actions for employment discrimination under Title VII.

Exhibit 17.6   Fifteen districts of the Equal Employment Opportunity Commission (EEOC)

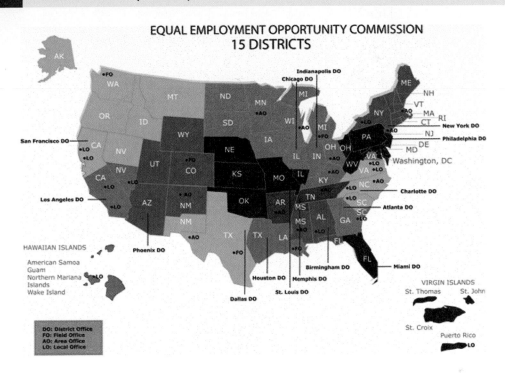

District Offices

Atlantic District Office	Memphis District Office
Birmingham District Office	Miami District Office
Charlotte District Office	New York District Office
Chicago District Office	Philadelphia District Office
Dallas District Office	Phoenix District Office
Houston District Office	San Francisco District Office
Indianapolis District Office	St. Louis District Office
Los Angeles District	

Source: Equal Employment Opportunity Commission (EEOC)

Race, Color, and National Origin Discrimination

Title VII of the Civil Rights Act of 1964 was enacted primarily to prohibit **race discrimination, color discrimination,** and **national origin discrimination** in employment.

Race refers to broad categories such as Black, Caucasian, Asian, and Native American.

Example   If an employer refuses to hire someone because he or she is a member of a minority race this would constitute illegal race discrimination in violation of Title VII.

Color refers to the color of a person's skin.

Example If light-skinned members of a race refuse to hire dark-skinned members of the same race, this would be color discrimination in violation of Title VII.

National origin refers to the country of a person's ancestors or cultural characteristics.

Example If an employer refuses to hire Hispanics or persons of Irish descent, this would be national origin discrimination that violates Title VII.

Religious Discrimination

Title VII prohibits employment discrimination based on a person's religion. Religions include traditional religions, other religions that recognize a supreme being, and religions based on ethical or spiritual tenets. Many **religious discrimination** cases involve a conflict between an employer's work rule and an employee's religious beliefs (e.g., when an employee is required to work on his or her religious holiday).

The right of an employee to practice his or her religion is not absolute. Under Title VII, an employer is under a duty to *reasonably accommodate* the religious observances, practices, or beliefs of its employees if it does not cause an *undue hardship* on the employer. The courts must apply these general standards to specific fact situations. In making their decisions, the courts must consider factors such as the number of employees of the employer, the importance of the employee's position, and the availability of alternative workers.

Sex Discrimination

Sex discrimination Discrimination against a person solely because of his or her sex.

Although the prohibition against **sex discrimination** applies equally to men and women, the overwhelming majority of Title VII sex discrimination cases are brought by women. An example of such discrimination is the old airline practice of ignoring the marital status of male flight attendants but hiring only single female flight attendants.

In 1978, the **Pregnancy Discrimination Act** was enacted as an amendment to Title VII. This amendment forbids employment discrimination because of "pregnancy, childbirth, or related medical conditions." Thus, a work rule that prohibits the hiring of pregnant women violates Title VII.

Sexual Harassment

Sexual harassment Lewd remarks, touching, intimidation, posting of pinups, and other verbal or physical conduct of a sexual nature that occur on the job.

In the modern work environment, coworkers sometimes become sexually interested or involved with each other voluntarily. On other occasions, though, a coworker's sexual advances are not welcome.

Refusing to hire or promote someone unless he or she has sex with the manager or supervisor is sex discrimination that violates Title VII. Other forms of conduct, such as lewd remarks, touching, intimidation, posting pinups, and other verbal or physical conduct of a sexual nature, constitute **sexual harassment** and violate Title VII. To determine what conduct creates a hostile work environment, the U.S. Supreme Court stated [*Harris v. Forklift Systems, Inc.*, 510 U.S. 17, 114 S. Ct. 367, 126 L.Ed.2d 295, 1999 U.S. Lexis 7155 (1993)]:

> We can say that whether an environment is "hostile" or "abusive" can be determined only by looking at all the circumstances. These may include the frequency of the discriminatory conduct; its severity; whether it is physically threatening or humiliating, or a mere offensive utterance; and whether it unreasonably interferes with an employee's work performance.

Exhibit 17.7 sets forth the EEOC's description of sexual harassment. Exhibit 17.8 sets forth a company's policy against sexual harassment.

Exhibit 17.7	Sexual harassment

Sexual harassment is a form of sex discrimination that violates Title VII of the Civil Rights Act of 1964.

Unwelcome sexual advances, requests for sexual favors, and other verbal or physical conduct of a sexual nature constitutes sexual harassment when submission to or rejection of this conduct explicitly or implicitly affects an individual's employment, unreasonably interferes with an individual's work performance, or creates an intimidating, hostile, or offensive work environment.

Sexual harassment can occur in a variety of circumstances, including but not limited to the following:

- The victim as well as the harasser may be a woman or a man. The victim does not have to be of the opposite sex.
- The harasser can be the victim's supervisor, an agent of the employer, a supervisor in another area, a coworker, or a non-employee.
- The victim does not have to be the person harassed but could be anyone affected by the offensive conduct.
- Unlawful sexual harassment may occur without economic injury to or discharge of the victim.
- The harasser's conduct must be unwelcome.

It is helpful for the victim to directly inform the harasser that the conduct is unwelcome and must stop. The victim should use any employer complaint mechanism or grievance system available.

When investigating allegations of sexual harassment, EEOC looks at the whole record: the circumstances, such as the nature of the sexual advances, and the context in which the alleged incidents occurred. A determination on the allegations is made from the facts on a case-by-case basis.

Prevention is the best tool to eliminate sexual harassment in the workplace. Employers are encouraged to take steps necessary to prevent sexual harassment from occurring. They should clearly communicate to employees that sexual harassment will not be tolerated. They can do so by establishing an effective complaint or grievance process and taking immediate and appropriate action when an employee complains.

Source: Equal Employment Opportunity Commission (EEOC)

Bona Fide Occupational Qualification (BFOQ)

Discrimination based on protected classes (other than race or color) is permitted if it is shown to be a **bona fide occupational qualification (BFOQ)**. To be legal, a BFOQ must be both *job-related* and a *business necessity*.

> **Bona fide occupational qualification (BFOQ)** Lawful employment discrimination that is based on a protected class (other than race or color) and is *job-related* and a *business necessity*. This exception is narrowly interpreted by the courts.

Examples Allowing only women to be locker-room attendants in a women's gym is a valid BFOQ, but prohibiting males from being managers or instructors at the same gym would not be a BFOQ.

The Ethical Perspective discusses a paralegal's duty to report sexual harassment conduct that he or she is being subjected to at work.

Equal Pay Act

Discrimination often takes the form of different pay scales for men and women performing the same job. The **Equal Pay Act of 1963** protects both sexes from pay discrimination based on sex. This act covers all levels of private-sector employees and state and local government employees. Federal workers are not covered, however.

> **Equal Pay Act of 1963** A federal statute that protects both sexes from pay discrimination based on sex. It extends to jobs that require equal skill, equal effort, equal responsibility, and similar working conditions.

The act prohibits disparity in pay for jobs that require *equal skill* (i.e., equal experience), *equal effort* (i.e., mental and physical exertion), *equal responsibility* (i.e., supervision and accountability), or *similar working conditions* (e.g., dangers of injury, exposure to the elements). To make this determination, the courts examine the actual requirements of jobs to determine whether they are equal and similar. If two jobs are determined to be equal and similar, an employer cannot pay disparate wages to members of different sexes.

Employees can bring a private cause of action against an employer for violating the act. Back pay and liquidated damages are recoverable. In addition, the employer

Exhibit 17.8 Company's policy against sexual harassment

Many businesses have taken steps to prevent sexual harassment in the workplace. For example, some businesses have explicitly adopted policies (see below) forbidding sexual harassment, implemented procedures for reporting incidents of sexual harassment, and conducted training programs to sensitize managers and employees about the issue.

Statement of Prohibited Conduct

The management of Company considers the following conduct to illustrate some of the conduct that violates Company's Sexual Harassment Policy:

A. Physical assaults of a sexual nature, such as

   1. Rape, sexual battery, molestation, or attempts to commit these assaults.

   2. Intentional physical conduct that is sexual in nature, such as touching, pinching, patting, grabbing, brushing against another employee's body, or poking another employee's body.

B. Unwanted sexual advances, propositions, or other sexual comments, such as

   1. Sexually oriented gestures, noises, remarks, jokes, or comments about a person's sexuality or sexual experience directed at or made in the presence of any employee who indicates or has indicated in any way that such conduct is unwelcome in his or her presence.

   2. Preferential treatment or promises of preferential treatment to an employee for submitting to sexual conduct, including soliciting or attempting to solicit any employee to engage in sexual activity for compensation or reward.

   3. Subjecting, or threats of subjecting, an employee to unwelcome sexual attention or conduct or intentionally making performance of the employee's job more difficult because of the employee's sex.

C. Sexual or discriminatory displays or publications anywhere in Company's workplace by Company employees, such as

   1. Displaying pictures, posters, calendars, graffiti, objects, promotional materials, reading materials, or other materials that are sexually suggestive, sexually demeaning, or pornographic, or bringing into Company's work environment or possessing any such material to read, display, or view at work.

     A picture will be presumed to be sexually suggestive if it depicts a person of either sex who is not fully clothed or in clothes that are not suited to or ordinarily accepted for the accomplishment of routine work in and around the workplace and who is posed for the obvious purpose of displaying or drawing attention to private portions of his or her body.

   2. Reading or otherwise publicizing in the work environment materials that are in any way sexually revealing, sexually suggestive, sexually demeaning, or pornographic.

   3. Displaying signs or other materials purporting to segregate an employee by sex in any area of the workplace (other than restrooms and similar semi-private lockers/changing rooms).

must increase the wages of the discriminated-against employee to eliminate the unlawful disparity of wages. The wages of other employees may not be lowered.

The Equal Pay Act expressly provides four criteria that justify a differential in wages. These defenses include payment systems that are based on

1. Seniority
2. Merit (as long as there is some identifiable measurement standard)
3. Quantity or quality of product (commission, piecework, or quality-control–based payment systems are permitted)
4. "Any factor other than sex" (including shift differentials, i.e., night versus day shifts) The employer bears the burden of proving these defenses.

ETHICAL PERSPECTIVE

Paralegal's Duty to Report Sexual Harassment Conduct

Ms. Heath is hired as a paralegal for the law firm of White, Cassel, and Smith, a large law firm. Ms. Heath is assigned as a paralegal professional to assist Mr. White, a partner of the law firm. During the first couple of weeks on the job, on numerous occasions when Ms. Heath was in attorney Mr. White's office on legal and paralegal matters, Mr. White made rude comments such as talking about people having sex, how good he is in bed, making obscene gestures, and touching Ms. Heath on the shoulder. After several weeks of being subjected to such conduct, Ms. Heath is distressed about coming to work because she may face continuing similar conduct by Mr. White.

What should Ms. Heath do?

In this case there is a clear pattern of sexual harassment by Mr. White that is creating a hostile work environment for Ms. Heath that violates Title VII of the Civil Rights Act of 1964. Ms. Heath should go to the Human Resource Department of the law firm, if it has one, or to the managing partner or partners of the law firm, and disclose Mr. White's conduct and how it is affecting her at work. She should file a written complaint so there is evidence of her disclosure of the problem.

The law firm is under the duty to correct the situation, by reprimanding Mr. White and notifying him that his conduct violates the law firm's policy against sexual harassment, if need be reassign Ms. Heath to be a paralegal for a partner of the firm that is of equal status as Mr. White, or dismiss Mr. White if his conduct rises to a level that would warrant such dismissal.

Ms. Heath could also report this matter to the local office of the state equal opportunity commission or to the office of the Equal Employment Opportunity Commission (EEOC). If the law firm retaliates against Ms. Heath for reporting this matter, the firm has engaged in conduct that further violates Title VII, for which Ms. Heath could seek redress. If the EEOC gives Ms. Heath a right-to-sue letter, she can bring a civil lawsuit under Title VII to recover damages for the sexual harassment and retaliation.

If a paralegal is being sexually harassed on the job, she or he should immediately report such conduct, and if the law firm does not immediately correct the situation, the paralegal should notify the proper government authorities, state and federal, to obtain redress. The paralegal may also hire an attorney to represent her or him in a civil lawsuit against the law firm.

Family and Medical Leave Act

In February 1993, Congress enacted the **Family and Medical Leave Act.** This law guarantees workers unpaid time off from work for medical emergencies. The act, which applies to companies with 50 or more workers as well as federal, state, and local governments, covers about half of the nation's workforce. To be covered by the act, an employee must have worked for the employer for at least one year and have performed more than 1,250 hours of service during the previous 12-month period.

Covered employers are required to provide up to 12 weeks of unpaid leave during any 12-month period as a result of the

1. birth of, and care for, a son or daughter.
2. placement of a child for adoption or in foster care.
3. serious health condition that makes the employee unable to perform his or her duties.
4. care for a spouse, child, or parent with a serious health problem.

Paralegals *in* Practice

Jaxine L. Wintjen is a board certified paralegal (CP) with 30 years of experience. She specializes in employee benefits, an area that combines employment law and tax law. Jaxine is a member and past chair of the Paralegal/Legal Assistants Section of the State Bar of Michigan. She is also a member of the Employee Benefits Committee of the Michigan State Bar Taxation Section. Jaxine currently works in the Labor, Employment and Benefits Practice Group of Foster, Swift, Collins & Smith in Lansing, Michigan.

Technology plays a major role in my everyday work. For example, I use the Internet extensively for legal research and e-discovery. Online services, such as Accurint® and KnowX®, help me find current addresses of pension plan participants who no longer work for a client. Other frequently-used online materials include Internal Revenue Service (IRS) code/regulations and Department of Labor (DOL) regulations/rulings. During a recent litigation case, I gathered online data to compare retirement plans offered by both the plaintiff's former employer and current employer. This information was used to prove that the plaintiff was not disadvantaged by the loss of his 401(k) benefit when he was discharged from his former employer.

Pension plans are normally long, complex documents that involve a series of supplemental resource files. Working with our in-house programmer, I helped design a document preparation system that uses macros in Microsoft® Word. The system can draw from nearly 3,000 different provisions, and assemble the various paragraphs into an individualized plan for a client. This plan is then merged with the client's employee database to quickly produce a large number of customized documents. I also use Microsoft Excel spreadsheets to perform annual mathematical tests on pension plans.

Finally, all IRS forms for obtaining benefit plan approvals and filing annual returns are computer generated using Relius Government Forms software. Beginning in 2010, we will be required to electronically file all Form 5500 returns. This process will include electronically obtaining author, signer, and transmitter credentials from the IRS and DOL.

Leave because of the birth of a child or the placement of a child for adoption or foster care cannot be taken intermittently unless the employer agrees. Other leaves may be taken on an intermittent basis. The employer may require medical proof of claimed serious health conditions.

An eligible employee who takes leave must, upon returning to work, be restored to either the same or an equivalent position with equivalent employment benefits and pay. The restored employee is not entitled to the accrual of seniority during the leave period, however. A covered employer may deny restoration to a salaried employee who is among the highest-paid 10 percent of that employer's employees if the denial is necessary to prevent "substantial and grievous economic injury" to the employer's operations.

Age Discrimination in Employment Act

In the past, some employers discriminated against employees and prospective employees based on their age. For example, employers often refused to hire older workers. The **Age Discrimination in Employment Act (ADEA)**, which prohibits certain age discrimination practices, was enacted in 1967.

ADEA prohibits age discrimination in all employment decisions, including hiring, promotions, payment of compensation, and other terms and conditions of employment. Originally, ADEA prohibited employment discrimination against persons between 40 and 65 years of age. In 1978, its coverage was extended to persons up to 70 years of age. Further amendments completely eliminated an age ceiling, so ADEA now applies to employees who are age 40 and older.

Americans with Disabilities Act

The **Americans with Disabilities Act (ADA),** signed into law on July 26, 1990, is the most comprehensive piece of civil rights legislation since the Civil Rights Act of 1964. ADA imposes obligations on employers and providers of public transportation,

Age Discrimination in Employment Act (ADEA) A federal statute that prohibits age discrimination practices against employees who are age 40 and older.

Americans with Disabilities Act (ADA) A federal statute that imposes obligations on employers and providers of public transportation, telecommunications, and public accommodations to accommodate individuals with disabilities.

telecommunications, and public accommodations to accommodate individuals with disabilities.

Title I of ADA prohibits employment discrimination against qualified individuals with disabilities in regard to job application procedures, hiring, compensation, training, promotion, and termination. It requires an employer to make *reasonable accommodations* to individuals with disabilities that do not cause undue hardship to the employer. Reasonable accommodations may include making facilities readily accessible to individuals with disabilities, providing part-time or modified work schedules, acquiring equipment or devices, modifying examination and training materials, and providing qualified readers or interpreters.

Employers are not obligated to provide accommodations that would impose an *undue burden*, or actions that would require significant difficulty or expense. The courts consider factors such as the nature and cost of accommodation, the employer's overall financial resources, and the employer's type of operation. Obviously, what may be a significant difficulty or expense for a small employer may not be an undue hardship for a large employer.

Civil Rights Act of 1866

The **Civil Rights Act of 1866** was enacted after the Civil War. **Section 1981** of this act states that all persons "have the same right . . . to make and enforce contracts . . . as is enjoyed by white persons." This law was enacted to give African Americans, just freed from slavery, the same right to contract as Caucasians. Section 1981 expressly prohibits racial discrimination; it also has been held to forbid discrimination based on national origin.

Employment decisions are covered by Section 1981 because the employment relationship is contractual. Although most racial and national origin employment discrimination cases are brought under Title VII, there are two reasons that a complainant would bring the action under Section 1981:

1. A private plaintiff can bring an action without going through the procedural requirements of Title VII.
2. There is no cap on the recovery of compensatory or punitive damages.

Civil Rights Act of 1866 A federal statute enacted after the Civil War that says all persons "have the same right . . . to make and enforce contracts . . . as is enjoyed by white persons." It prohibits racial and national origin employment discrimination.

Labor Union Law

Prior to the Industrial Revolution, employees and employers had somewhat equal bargaining power. Once the country became industrialized in the late 1800s, large corporate employers had much more bargaining power than their employees. In the early 1900s, members of the labor movement lobbied Congress to pass laws to protect their rights to organize and bargain with management. During the Great Depression of the 1930s, several statutes were enacted to give workers certain rights and protections. Other statutes have been added since then. The major federal statutes in this area are:

- **Norris-LaGuardia Act.** Enacted in 1932, this act stipulates that it is legal for employees to organize and form labor unions.
- **National Labor Relations Act (NLRA).** This act, also known as the Wagner Act, was enacted in 1935. The NLRA establishes the right to employees to form, join, and assist labor organizations; to bargain collectively with employers; and to engage in concerted activity to promote these rights.
- **Labor–Management Relations Act.** In 1947, Congress enacted the Labor–Management Relations Act (the Taft-Hartley Act). This act (1) expands the activities that labor unions can engage in, (2) gives employers the right to engage in free speech efforts against unions prior to a union election, and (3) gives the president of the United States the right to seek an injunction (for up to 80 days) against a strike that would create a national emergency.

- **Labor–Management Reporting and Disclosure Act.** Congress enacted the Labor–Management Reporting and Disclosure Act of 1959 (the Landrum-Griffin Act). This act regulates internal union affairs and establishes the rights of union members.
- **Railway Labor Act.** The Railway Labor Act of 1926, as amended in 1934, covers employees of railroad and airline carriers.

Today, approximately 10 percent of private-sector wage and salary workers belong to labor unions: Many government employees also belong to unions.

National Labor Relations Board (NLRB)

The NLRA created the **National Labor Relations Board (NLRB)**. The NLRB is an administrative body composed of five members appointed by the President and approved by the Senate. The NLRB oversees union elections, prevents employers and unions from engaging in illegal and unfair labor practices, and enforces and interprets certain federal labor laws. The decisions of the NLRB are enforceable in court.

Organizing a Union

Section 7 of the NLRA gives employees the right to join together and form a union. Section 7 provides that employees shall have the right to self-organization; to form, join, or assist labor organizations; to bargain collectively through representatives of their own choosing; and to engage in other concerted activities for the purpose of collective bargaining or other mutual aid protection.

Section 8(a) of the NLRA makes it an **unfair labor practice** for an employer to interfere with, coerce, or restrain employees from exercising their statutory right to form and join unions.

> **Examples** Threats of loss of benefits for joining the union, statements such as "I'll close this plant if a union comes in here," and the like are unfair labor practices. Also, an employer may not form a company union. Section 8(b) of the NLRA prohibits unions from engaging in unfair labor practices that interfere with a union election. Coercion, physical threats, and such are unfair labor practices.

Once a union has been elected, the employer and the union discuss the terms of employment of union members and try to negotiate a contract that embodies these terms. The act of negotiating is called **collective bargaining**, and the resulting contract is called a **collective bargaining agreement**. The employer and the union must negotiate with each other in good faith.

Strikes and Picketing

The NLRA gives union management the right to recommend that the union call a **strike** if a collective bargaining agreement cannot be reached. Before there can be a strike, though, a majority vote of the union's members must agree to the action.

Striking union members often engage in **picketing** in support of their strike. Picketing usually takes the form of the striking employees and union representatives walking in front of the employer's premises carrying signs announcing their strike. Picketing is used to put pressure on an employer to settle a strike. The right to picket is implied from the NLRA.

Picketing is lawful unless it

1. is accompanied by violence,
2. obstructs customers from entering the employer's place of business,
3. prevents nonstriking employees from entering the employer's premises, or
4. prevents pickups and deliveries at the employer's place of business.

An employer may seek an injunction against unlawful picketing.

Illegal Strikes

Several types of strikes have been held to be illegal and are not protected by federal labor laws, Illegal strikes take the form of:

- **Violent strikes.** In **violent strikes**, striking employees cause substantial damage to property of the employer or a third party. Courts usually tolerate a certain amount of isolated violence before finding that the entire strike is illegal.
- **Sit-down strikes.** In **sit-down strikes**, striking employees continue to occupy the employer's premises. Such strikes are illegal because they deny the employer's statutory right to continue its operations during the strike.
- **Partial or intermittent strikes.** In **partial** or **intermittent strikes,** employees strike part of the day or workweek and work the other part. This type of strike is illegal because it interferes with the employer's right to operate its facilities at full operation.

A union is required to give an employer a 60-day notice before commencing a strike. This is called **cooling-off period**. This mandatory cooling-off period is designed to give the employer and the union time to negotiate a settlement of the union grievances and avoid a strike. Any strike without a proper 60-day notice is illegal. Illegal strikers may be discharged by the employer, with no rights to reinstatement.

Crossover and Replacement Workers

Individual members of a union do not have to honor a strike. They may (1) choose not to strike, or (2) return to work after joining the strikers for a time. Employees who choose either of these two options are known as **crossover workers**.

Once a strike begins, the employer may continue operations by using management personnel and hiring **replacement workers** to take the place of the striking employees. Replacement workers can be hired on either a temporary or a permanent basis. If replacement workers are given permanent status, they do not have to be dismissed when the strike is over.

Immigration Law

Many immigrants arrive in the United States daily. Many of these immigrants have come here legally and can obtain employment. Other immigrants are here illegally and cannot legally work. The **Immigration Reform and Control Act of 1986 (IRCA)** and the **Immigration Act of 1990** are federal statutes administered by the **U.S. Immigration and Customs Enforcement (ICE)**. These acts make it unlawful for employers to hire illegal immigrants.

U.S. Immigration and Customs Enforcement (ICE) The federal administrative agency that enforces federal immigration laws.

Employment Eligibility Verification

Employers have an affirmative duty to verify that the employees they hire are authorized to work in the United States. Employers are required to have prospective employees complete **Form I-9 "Employment Eligibility Verification."** Employers must obtain a completed Form I-9 for every employee, regardless of citizenship or national origin. Employers must examine evidence of prospective employees' identity and employment eligibility. A state-issued driver's license is not sufficient. Employers must review other documents to establish eligibility, such as social security cards, birth certificates, and such.

Employers must maintain records and post in the workplace notices of the contents of the law. Violators are subject to both civil and criminal penalties.

Exhibit 17.9 shows Form I-9 Employment Eligibility Verification.

Form I-9 "Employment Eligibility Verification" A form that must be completed by prospective employees.

H-1B Foreign Guest Worker Visa

An **H-1B visa** is a nonimmigrant visa that allows U.S. employers to employ foreign nationals in the United States that are skilled in specialty occupations. Foreign guest workers under an H-1B visa must have a bachelor's degree or higher and have a

H-1B visa A nonimmigrant visa that allows U.S. employers to employ foreign nationals in the United States that are skilled in specialty occupations.

Exhibit 17.9 **Form I-9, Employment Eligibility Verification**

OMB No. 1615-0047; Expires 06/30/09

Department of Homeland Security
U.S. Citizenship and Immigration Services

**Form I-9, Employment
Eligibility Verification**

Please read instructions carefully before completing this form. The instructions must be available during completion of this form.

ANTI-DISCRIMINATION NOTICE: It is illegal to discriminate against work eligible individuals. Employers CANNOT specify which document(s) they will accept from an employee. The refusal to hire an individual because the documents have a future expiration date may also constitute illegal discrimination.

Section 1. Employee Information and Verification. To be completed and signed by employee at the time employment begins.

Print Name: Last	First	Middle Initial	Maiden Name

Address (Street Name and Number)	Apt. #	Date of Birth (month/day/year)

City	State	Zip Code	Social Security #

I am aware that federal law provides for imprisonment and/or fines for false statements or use of false documents in connection with the completion of this form.

I attest, under penalty of perjury, that I am (check one of the following):

☐ A citizen or national of the United States
☐ A lawful permanent resident (Alien #) A _____
☐ An alien authorized to work until _____
(Alien # or Admission #) _____

Employee's Signature	Date (month/day/year)

Preparer and/or Translator Certification. (To be completed and signed if Section 1 is prepared by a person other than the employee.) I attest, under penalty of perjury, that I have assisted in the completion of this form and that to the best of my knowledge the information is true and correct.

Preparer's/Translator's Signature	Print Name

Address (Street Name and Number, City, State, Zip Code)	Date (month/day/year)

Section 2. Employer Review and Verification. To be completed and signed by employer. Examine one document from List A OR examine one document from List B and one from List C, as listed on the reverse of this form, and record the title, number and expiration date, if any, of the document(s).

	List A	OR	List B	AND	List C
Document title:					
Issuing authority:					
Document #:					
Expiration Date (if any):					
Document #:					
Expiration Date (if any):					

CERTIFICATION - I attest, under penalty of perjury, that I have examined the document(s) presented by the above-named employee, that the above-listed document(s) appear to be genuine and to relate to the employee named, that the employee began employment on (month/day/year) _____ and that to the best of my knowledge the employee is eligible to work in the United States. (State employment agencies may omit the date the employee began employment.)

Signature of Employer or Authorized Representative	Print Name	Title

Business or Organization Name and Address (Street Name and Number, City, State, Zip Code)	Date (month/day/year)

Section 3. Updating and Reverification. To be completed and signed by employer.

A. New Name (if applicable)	B. Date of Rehire (month/day/year) (if applicable)

C. If employee's previous grant of work authorization has expired, provide the information below for the document that establishes current employment eligibility.

Document Title:	Document #:	Expiration Date (if any):

I attest, under penalty of perjury, that to the best of my knowledge, this employee is eligible to work in the United States, and if the employee presented document(s), the document(s) I have examined appear to be genuine and to relate to the individual.

Signature of Employer or Authorized Representative	Date (month/day/year)

Form I-9 (Rev. 06/16/08) N

Exhibit 17.9 **Form I-9, Employment Eligibility Verification** *(continued)*

LISTS OF ACCEPTABLE DOCUMENTS

LIST A	LIST B	LIST C
Documents that Establish Both Identity and Employment Eligibility OR	**Documents that Establish Identity** AND	**Documents that Establish Employment Eligibility**
1. U.S. Passport (unexpired or expired)	1. Driver's license or ID card issued by a state or outlying possession of the United States provided it contains a photograph or information such as name, date of birth, gender, height, eye color and address	1. U.S. Social Security card issued by the Social Security Administration *(other than a card stating it is not valid for employment)*
2. Permanent Resident Card or Alien Registration Receipt Card (Form I-551)	2. ID card issued by federal, state or local government agencies or entities, provided it contains a photograph or information such as name, date of birth, gender, height, eye color and address	2. Certification of Birth Abroad issued by the Department of State *(Form FS-545 or Form DS-1350)*
3. An unexpired foreign passport with a temporary I-551 stamp	3. School ID card with a photograph	3. Original or certified copy of a birth certificate issued by a state, county, municipal authority or outlying possession of the United States bearing an official seal
4. An unexpired Employment Authorization Document that contains a photograph (Form I-766, I-688, I-688A, I-688B)	4. Voter's registration card	4. Native American tribal document
	5. U.S. Military card or draft record	5. U.S. Citizen ID Card *(Form I-197)*
5. An unexpired foreign passport with an unexpired Arrival-Departure Record, Form I-94, bearing the same name as the passport and containing an endorsement of the alien's nonimmigrant status, if that status authorizes the alien to work for the employer	6. Military dependent's ID card	6. ID Card for use of Resident Citizen in the United States *(Form I-179)*
	7. U.S. Coast Guard Merchant Mariner Card	
	8. Native American tribal document	7. Unexpired employment authorization document issued by DHS *(other than those listed under List A)*
	9. Driver's license issued by a Canadian government authority	
	For persons under age 18 who are unable to present a document listed above:	
	10. School record or report card	
	11. Clinic, doctor or hospital record	
	12. Day-care or nursery school record	

Illustrations of many of these documents appear in Part 8 of the Handbook for Employers (M-274)

"specialty occupation" such as engineering, mathematics, computer science, physical sciences, medicine, and such.

The **foreign guest worker** must be sponsored by a U.S. employer. Employers apply for an H-1B visa for proposed foreign guest workers. The number of H-1B visas are limited, usually to less than 100,000 per year, so the competition is fierce to obtain such a visa. H-1B visa holders are allowed to bring their immediate family members (spouse and children under 21) to the United States under the **H4 visa** category as dependents. An H4 visa holder may remain in the United States as long as the H-1B visa holder remains in legal status. An H4 visa holder is not eligible to work in the United States.

The duration of stay for a worker on an H-1B visa is three years, which can usually be extended another three years. During this time an employer may sponsor an H-1B holder for a green card, which if issued permits the foreign national to eventually obtain U.S. citizenship.

ETHICAL PERSPECTIVE
Duty to Disclose Paralegal Status

Ms. Abigail Knight works as a paralegal for a small law firm. Ms. Knight works directly for Mr. Abdul Farid, one of the two partners in the law firm. In her capacity as a paralegal, Ms. Knight conducts legal research, and prepares drafts of agreements and documents for review by Mr. Farid. Because the law firm is small, Ms. Knight also is the business manager of the firm. In this capacity, Ms. Knight is responsible for bookkeeping and ordering supplies for the law firm.

The law firm hires a consultant to redesign the law firm's name and create a marketing strategy for the firm. The new design for the name of the law firm is completed and approved by the two lawyers of the firm. Ms. Knight is to order new business cards using the new design for the two attorneys and her. On the business cards of the two attorneys she places their names and the words "Attorney at Law." Ms. Knight is also to have a business card with her name and the law firm's name and address on it.

Does Ms. Knight owe a duty to disclose her status as a paralegal on the business cards she orders for herself?

Many model and state paralegal professional codes of ethics and responsibility require that a paralegal properly identify himself or herself as a paralegal on business cards, letterhead, brochures, and such. In addition, fraudulent failure to include such title obviously violates paralegal ethical standards and could possibly subject the paralegal to disciplinary actions of the licensing agency of the state.

PARALEGAL'S ETHICAL DECISION

Thus, Ms. Knight owes an ethical duty to disclose her position as a paralegal professional on the business cards she is ordering for herself. This ethical duty is designed to avoid confusion that a paralegal may be holding himself or herself out as an attorney. Therefore, Ms. Knight must include the word "Paralegal" on her business cards to avoid this confusion.

Concept Review *and* Reinforcement

LEGAL TERMINOLOGY

Age Discrimination in Employment Act (ADEA) 638	Agent 618	Bona fide occupational qualification (BFOQ) 635
Agency 618	Americans with Disabilities 1Act (ADA) 638	Child labor 629
Agency by estoppel 622	Apparent agency 622	Civil Rights Act of 1866 639
Agency by ratification 622	Attorney-in-fact 620	Collective bargaining 640

SUMMARY OF KEY CONCEPTS

Agency Law

Definition	Agency is a fiduciary relationship that results from the manifestation of consent by one person to act on behalf of another person with that person's consent.
Parties	1. *Principal:* Party who employs another person to act on his or her behalf. 2. *Agent:* Party who agrees to act on behalf of another person.
Kinds of Employment Relationships	*Employer–employee relationship:* An employer hires an employee to perform some form of physical service. An employee is not an agent unless the principal authorizes him or her to enter into contracts on the principal's behalf. *Principal–agent relationship:* An employer hires an employee and authorizes the employee to enter into contracts on the employer's behalf. *Principal–independent contractor relationship:* A principal employs a person who is not an employee of the principal. The independent contractor has authority to enter into only those contracts authorized by the principal.

Formation of the Agency Relationship	1. *Express agency:* The principal and the agent expressly agree in words to enter into an agency agreement. The agency contract may be oral or written unless the Statute of Frauds requires it to be in writing.
	2. *Implied agency:* An agency is inferred from the conduct of the parties.
	3. *Apparent agency:* A principal creates an appearance of an agency that in actuality does not exist. Also called *agency by estoppel* or *ostensible agency*.
	4. *Agency by ratification:* A person misrepresents himself or herself as another's agent when he or she is not and the purported principal ratifies (accepts) the unauthorized act.

Tort Liability of Principals and Agents to Third Parties

Description	Principals are liable for the *tortious conduct* of an agent who is acting within the *scope of his or her authority*. Liability is imposed for misrepresentation, negligence, and intentional torts.
Intentional Torts	States apply one of the following rules: 1. *Motivation test:* The principal is liable if the agent's intentional tort was committed to promote the principal's business. 2. *Work-related test:* The principal is liable if the agent's intentional tort was committed within a work-related time or space. Agents are personally liable for their own tortious conduct.
Negligence	Principals are liable for the negligent conduct of agents acting within the scope of their employment. Special negligence doctrines include: 1. *Frolic and detour:* Principals are generally relieved of liability if the agent's negligent act occurred on a substantial frolic and detour from the scope of employment. 2. *"Coming and going" rule:* Principals are not liable if the agent's tortious conduct occurred while on the way to or from work. 3. *Dual-purpose mission:* If the agent is acting on his or her own behalf and on behalf of the principal, the principal is generally liable for the agent's tortious conduct.

Independent Contractor

Independent Contractor	Generally, principals are not liable for the tortious conduct of independent contractors. Exceptions to the rule are for: 1. *Nondelegable duties.* 2. *Special risks.* 3. *Negligence in selecting an independent contractor.* Independent contractors are personally liable for their own torts.

Termination of an Agency

Termination by Acts of the Parties	The following *acts of the parties* terminate agency contracts: 1. *Mutual agreement* 2. *Lapse of time* 3. *Purpose achieved* 4. *Occurrence of a specified event*
Wrongful Termination of an Agency Contract	If an agency is for an agreed-upon term or purpose, the *unilateral termination* of the agency contract by either the principal or the agent constitutes the *wrongful termination* of the agency. The breaching party is liable to the other party for damages caused by the breach.

Workers' Compensation

Workers' Compensation Acts	Workers' compensation acts are state statutes that create an administrative procedure for workers to receive payments for job-related injuries.

Workers' Compensation Insurance	Most states require employers to carry private or government-sponsored *workers' compensation insurance*. Some states permit employers to self-insure.
Employment-Related Injury	To be compensable under workers' compensation, the claimant must prove that the injury arose out of and in the course of his or her employment.
Exclusive Remedy	Workers' compensation is an exclusive remedy. Thus, workers cannot sue their employers to recover damages for job-related injuries.

Occupational Safety and Health Act

Descriptions	1. *Occupational Safety and Health Act:* A federal statute that requires employers to provide safe working conditions. 2. *Occupational Safety and Health Administration (OSHA):* Federal administrative agency that administers and enforces the Occupational Safety and Health Act.
Duty Standards	OSHA enforces the following duty standards on employers: 1. *Specific duty standards:* OSHA safety standards established for specific equipment (e.g., chain saw) or a specific industry (e.g., mining). 2. *General duty standards:* OSHA standards that impose a general duty on employers to provide safe working conditions.

Fair Labor Standards Act (FLSA)

Description Protections	*Fair Labor Standards Act (FLSA):* Federal statute that protects workers. 1. *Child labor:* The FLSA forbids the use of illegal child labor. The U.S. Department of Labor defines illegal child labor. 2. *Minimum wage:* Workers must be paid a minimum wage. The federal minimum wage is $7.25 per hour. The minimum wage can be changed by Congress. 3. *Overtime pay:* An employer cannot require employees to work more than 40 hours per week unless they are paid 1.5 times their regular pay for each hour worked in excess of 40 hours.

Title VII of the Civil Rights Act of 1964

Description	Title VII of the Civil Rights Act of 1964 is a federal statute that prohibits job discrimination based on the (1) race, (2) color, (3) religion, (4) sex, or (5) national origin of the job applicant.
Scope of Coverage of Title VII	*Employment decisions subject to Title VII:* Decisions regarding hiring; promotion; demotion; payment of salaries, wages, and fringe benefits; job training and apprenticeships; work rules; or any other "term, condition, or privilege of employment."
Protected Classes	Title VII prohibits employment discrimination based on the following protected classes: 1. *Race:* Broad class based on common physical characteristics 2. *Color:* Skin color 3. *National origin:* A person's national heritage 4. *Sex:* Male or female 5. *Religion:* Discrimination solely because of a person's religious beliefs or practices. An employer has a duty to *reasonably accommodate* an employee's religious beliefs if it does not cause an *undue hardship* on the employer.
Sexual Harassment	Sexual harassment consists of lewd remarks, touching, intimidation, posting pinups, and other verbal or physical conduct of a sexual nature that occurs on the job. Sexual harassment that creates a *hostile work environment* violates Title VII [*Meritor Savings Bank v. Vinson*, 477 U.S. 57 (1986)].

Equal Pay Act

Description	The Equal Pay Act is a federal statute that forbids pay discrimination for the same job based on the sex of the employee performing the job, where the job requires equal skill, effort, responsibility, and working conditions.
Criteria that Justify a Differential in Wages	The Equal Pay Act expressly provides the following four criteria that justify a differential in wages for the same job: 1. Seniority 2. Merit (based on a measurable standard) 3. Quantity or quality of product (e.g., commission, piecework) 4. "Any factor other than sex" (e.g., night shift)

Family and Medical Leave Act

Description	The Family and Medical Leave Act is a federal statute that guarantees covered workers unpaid time off from work for the birth or adoption of a child, serious health problems of the worker, and serious health problems of a spouse, child, or parent.

Age Discrimination in Employment Act (ADEA)

Description	ADEA is a federal statute that prohibits employment discrimination against applicants and employees who are 40 years of age and older.

Americans with Disabilities Act (ADA)

Description	ADA is a federal law that imposes obligations on employers and providers of public transportation, telecommunications, and public accommodations to accommodate individuals with disabilities.
Title I of ADA	Title I of ADA is a federal law that prohibits employment discrimination against qualified individuals with disabilities. It requires employers to make *reasonable accommodations* for employees with disabilities that do not cause *undue hardship* to the employer.

Civil Rights Act of 1866

Section 1981	Section 1981 of the Civil Rights Act of 1866, enacted after the Civil War, states that all persons "have the same right . . . to make and enforce contracts . . . as enjoyed by white persons."
Protected Class	Section 1981 prohibits discrimination because of *race* or *national origin* concerning employment contracts.
Remedies	A successful plaintiff can recover compensatory and punitive damages. There is no monetary cap on compensatory and punitive damages.

Labor Union Law

National Labor Relations Act (NLRA)	The NLRA is a federal statute that established the right of employees to form, join, and assist labor unions.
National Labor Relations Board (NLRB)	The NLRB is a federal administrative agency empowered to administer federal labor law, oversee union elections, and decide labor disputes.
Unfair Labor Practice	1. *Employer:* Section 8(a) of the NLRA makes it an *unfair labor practice* for an employer to interfere with, coerce, or restrain employees exercising their right to form and join unions. 2. *Labor union:* Section 8(b) makes it an *unfair labor practice* for a union to interfere with a union election.

Collective Bargaining	1. *Collective bargaining:* A process whereby a union and an employer negotiate the terms and conditions of employment for the covered employee union members.
	2. *Collective bargaining agreement:* A contract between an employer and a labor union that results from collective bargaining.
Strikes and Picketing	1. *Strike:* A strike is cessation of work by union members in obtaining economic benefits, correcting for the purpose of an unfair labor practice, or preserving their work. The NLRA gives employees the right to strike.
	2. *Cooling-off period:* A labor union must give an employer at least 60 days' prior notice of a strike—called the *cooling-off period.*
	3. *Picketing:* Striking employees and union organizers may picket—walk around the employer's premises, usually carrying signs, notifying the public of their grievance against the employer.
	4. *Illegal strikes and picketing:* The following types of picketing and strikes are illegal:
	a. *Illegal picketing:* Picketing that is accompanied by violence, or obstructs customers, nonstriking workers, or suppliers from entering the employer's premises.
	b. *Violent strike:* A strike in which striking employees cause substantial damage to the employer's or a third party's property.
	c. *Sit-down strike:* A strike in which the striking employees occupy and refuse to leave the employer's premises.
	d. *Partial or intermittent strike:* A strike in which the striking employees strike for only parts of each day or week.

Immigration Law

Federal Immigration Law	1. *Federal statutes:* The Immigration Reform and Control Act of 1986 (IRCA) and the Immigration Act of 1990 are federal statutes that make it unlawful for employers to hire illegal immigrants.
	2. *U.S. Immigration and Customs Enforcement (ICE):* The federal administrative agency that enforces federal immigration laws.
	3. *Form I-9 "Employment Eligibility Verification":* A form that must be completed by prospective employees. Employers must examine evidence of prospective employees' identity and employment eligibility.
	4. *H-1B visa:* A nonimmigrant visa that allows U.S. employers to employ foreign nationals in the United States that are skilled in specialty occupations.

WORKING THE WEB

1. Visit the website http://www.eeoc.gov/html, the website of the federal Equal Employment Opportunity Commission (EEOC). Under the category "Discrimination by Types," find the description of "Pregnancy Discrimination." Write a one-page report on pregnancy discrimination.

2. Visit the website http://www.osha.gov/html, the website of the federal Occupational Safety and Health Administration (OSHA). Find an OSHA workplace safety rule that interests you. Write a one-page report that describes the rule.

3. Visit the website http://www.nlrb.gov/html, the website of the federal National Labor Relations Board (NLRB). Find a recent decision of the NLRB for the current year and write a one-page report summarizing the facts of the case and the NLRB's decision in the case.

4. Visit the website http://www.eeoc.gov/html, the website of the federal Equal Employment Opportunity Commission (EEOC). Click on the category "News." Find a current case or news event that interests you and write a one-page report on the case or news item.

5. Visit the website http://www.dol.gov/html, the website of the U.S. Department of Labor (DOL). Click on "Wages." On the next page click on "minimum wage." On the next page click on "states." On the next page click on "Current State Minimum Wage Rates." On the map that is shown, click on your state. Based on federal and state law, what is the minimum wage for your state?

CRITICAL THINKING & WRITING QUESTIONS

1. Define an agency, a principal, and an agent.
2. Define an independent contractor. What elements are examined to determine if a person or party is an independent contractor?
3. What is an employee-at-will? Can an at-will employee be easily terminated? Explain.
4. Describe the differences among the following: (1) express agency, (2) implied agency, and (3) agency by ratification.
5. What is an apparent agency? Give an example.
6. What is power of attorney? What is the difference between a general power of attorney and a special power of attorney? Who is an attorney-in-fact?
7. Describe the tort liability of a principal for the intentional torts of an agent under each of the following tests: (1) motivation test, and (2) work-related test.
8. Define the term *respondeat superior*. Describe vicarious liability.
9. What is the principal's liability for an agent's negligence? What does "scope of authority" mean?
10. Describe a principal's liability for the torts of an agent under the following special doctrines: (1) frolic and detour, (2) "coming and going" rule, and (3) dual-purpose mission.
11. Describe the wrongful termination of an agency. Give an example.
12. What is workers' compensation? Describe the following: (1) work-related injury, and (2) exclusive remedy.
13. What does the Occupational Safety and Health Act require? Describe the difference between specific duty standards and general duty standards.
14. What are the Fair Labor Standards Act (FLSA) requirements concerning (1) child labor, (2) minimum wage, and (3) overtime pay?
15. What does Title VII of the Civil Rights Act of 1964 provide? What are the protected classes under Title VII?
16. What is the difference between race discrimination and national heritage discrimination? Give an example of each.
17. What is a bona fide occupational qualification (BFOQ)? Give an example.
18. Define sexual harassment. Give an example.
19. Define religious discrimination prohibited by Title VII. What is the duty of an employer concerning protecting the religious preferences of employees? Give an example.
20. What does the Equal Pay Act provide? Give an example.
21. What is age discrimination? What age group is protected by the Age Discrimination in Employment Act?
22. What does the Americans with Disabilities Act (ADA) provide? What is the duty of an employer concerning protecting employees under this ADA? Give an example.
23. What benefits does the Family Medical Leave Act provide? Explain.
24. What does the Civil Rights Act of 1866 provide? Elaborate.
25. Define a labor union. What benefit does the National Labor Relations Act (NLRA) provide to workers?
26. Describe the following: (1) unfair labor practice, (2) collective bargaining, (3) strike, (4) cooling-off period, and (5) picketing.

Building Paralegal Skills

VIDEO CASE STUDIES

Mechanic's Deposition: Duties of the Agent and Liability of the Principal

The mechanic who worked on the brake system of the truck involved in an accident reveals during his deposition/trial testimony that he bought cheaper replacement parts and disposed of the original parts when he fixed the truck after the accident.

After viewing the video case study at www.pearsonhighered.com/goldman answer the following:

1. When does a mechanic have the authority to purchase repair parts?
2. Is it reasonable for a salesperson to believe that a mechanic working in a trucking company would have the authority to act on behalf of the trucking company?
3. What are the potential consequences of the mechanic throwing out the original brake parts?

Truck Driver's Deposition: Agent on a Detour and Liability of the Principal

A truck driver during his deposition admits that he left his assigned route to attend to personal business before going on his lunch break, during which he was involved in the accident in which his brakes failed.

After viewing the video case study at pearsonhighered .com/goldman answer the following:

1. Is an employer liable for the actions of the employee when the employee deviates from an assigned route?
2. If an employee deviates from his assigned route when he is deemed to be on business for the employer, is the employee liable for his behavior?
3. Is the employer liable for everything the employee does during the working day?

ETHICS ANALYSIS & DISCUSSION QUESTIONS

1. What ethical issues may be involved when a paralegal acts under a power of attorney for a client of the firm?
2. Is a paralegal who is investigating the facts of a case acting as an agent for the client or for the law firm? Does the answer change the ethical obligations of the paralegal?
3. A corporate client is concerned about testimony that an employee may give in a pending civil action even though the corporation has not been named as a defendant [Colorado Bar Association Ethics Opinion 79.] May a paralegal attend depositions for the sole purpose of taking notes on testimony given or taken in the action?

DEVELOPING YOUR COLLABORATION SKILLS

With a group of other students, selected by you or assigned by your instructor, review the "Paralegals at Work" scenario at the beginning of the chapter. As a group, discuss the following questions.

1. What are the protected classes under Title VII of the Civil Rights Act of 1964? Does Ms. Rodriquez fall under any of these protected classes? If so, which one(s)?
2. Does Ms. Rodriquez have a legitimate Title VII sex discrimination claim against her employer, Retro Bank? Explain.
3. Does Ms. Rodriquez have a legitimate Title VII national origin discrimination claim against her employer, Retro Bank? Explain.

PARALEGAL PORTFOLIO EXERCISE

Using the website http://google.com/html or similar Internet website, or the Internet legal services Westlaw or Lexis-Nexis, or law books, find a sample general power of attorney for your state. Complete this form as if you are the principal and someone you choose is the attorney-in-fact. Complete the form, meeting all of the state's requirements for creating a valid general power of attorney.

LEGAL ANALYSIS & WRITING CASES

Edgewater Motels, Inc. v. Gatzke and Walgreen Co.

277 N.W.2d 11, Web 1979 Minn. Lexis 1381

Supreme Court of Minnesota

Arlen Gatzke (Gatzke) was a district manager for the Walgreen Company (Walgreen). Gatzke was sent to Duluth, Minnesota, to supervise the opening of a new Walgreen store. In Duluth, Gatzke stayed at the Edgewater Motel (Edgewater). While in Duluth, Gatzke was "on call" 24 hours a day to other Walgreen stores located in his territory.

At midnight several days later, Gatzke, after working 17 hours that day, went with several other Walgreen employees to a restaurant and bar to drink. Within one hour's time, Gatzke had consumed three "doubles" and one single brandy Manhattan. About 1:30 A.M., he went back to the Edgewater Motel and filled out his expense report. Soon thereafter a fire broke out in Gatzke's motel room. Gatzke escaped, but the fire spread and caused extensive damage to the motel. Evidence showed that Gatzke smoked two packs of cigarettes a day. An expert fire reconstruction witness testified that the fire started from a lit cigarette in or next to the wastepaper basket in Gatzke's room.

Edgewater Motels, Inc. sued Gatzke and Walgreen. The parties stipulated that the damage to the Edgewater Motel was $330,360. The jury returned a verdict against defendants Gatzke and Walgreen. The court granted Walgreen's posttrial motion for judgment notwithstanding the verdict. Plaintiff Edgewater and defendant Gatzke appealed.

Question

1. Was Gatzke's act of smoking within his "scope of employment," making his principal, the Walgreen Company, vicariously liable for his negligence?

International Union, United Automobile, Aerospace and Agricultural Implement Workers of America, UAW v. Johnson Controls, Inc.

499 U.S. 187, 111 S.Ct. 1196, 113 L.Ed.2d 158, Web 1991 U.S. Lexis 1715

Supreme Court of the United States

Johnson Controls, Inc. (Johnson Controls), manufactures batteries. Lead is the primary ingredient in the manufacturing process. Exposure to lead entails health risks, including risk of harm to any fetus carried by a female employee. To protect unborn children from such risk, Johnson Controls adopted an employment rule that prevents pregnant women and women of childbearing age from working at jobs involving lead exposure. Only women who were sterilized or could prove they could not have children were not affected by the rule. Consequently, most female employees were relegated to lower-paying clerical jobs at the company.

Several female employees field a class action suit, challenging Johnson Controls's fetal-protection policy as sex discrimination in violation of Title VII. The District Court held that the policy was justified as a bona fide occupational qualification (BFOQ) and granted summary judgment to Johnson Controls. The Court of Appeals affirmed. The plaintiffs appealed to the U.S. Supreme Court.

Question

1. Is Johnson Controls's fetal-protection policy a BFOQ?

PGA Tour, Inc. v. Martin

532 U.S. 661, 121 S.Ct. 1879, 149 L.Ed.2d 904, Web 2001 U.S. Lexis 4115

Supreme Court of the United States

The PGA Tour, Inc., is a nonprofit entity that sponsors professional golf tournaments. The PGA has adopted a set of rules that apply to its golf tour. One rule requires golfers to walk the course during PGA-sponsored tournaments. Casey Martin is a talented amateur golfer who won many high school and university golf championships. Martin has contracted Klippel-Trenaunay-Weber syndrome, a degenerative circulatory disorder that obstructs the flow of blood from his right leg to his heart. The disease is progressive and has atrophied his right leg. Walking causes Martin pain, fatigue, and anxiety, with significant risk of hemorrhaging.

When Martin turned professional, he qualified for the PGA Tour. He made a request to use a golf cart while playing in PGA tournaments. When the PGA denied his request, Martin sued the PGA for violation of the Americans with Disabilities Act (ADA) for not making reasonable accommodations for his disability. The District Court sided with Martin and ordered the PGA to permit Martin to use a golf cart. The Court of Appeals affirmed. The U.S. Supreme Court agreed to hear the PGA's appeal.

Question

1. Does the ADA require PGA Tour, Inc., to accommodate Casey Martin, a professional golfer with a disability, by permitting him to use a golf cart while playing in PGA-sponsored golf tournaments?

Largey v. Intrastate Radiotelephone, Inc.

136 Cal.App.3d 660, 186 Cal.Rptr. 520, Web 1982 Cal.App. Lexis 2049

Court of Appeal of California

Intrastate Radiotelephone, Inc., a public utility, supplies radiotelephone utility service to the general public for radiotelephones, pocket pagers, and beepers. Robert Kranhold, an employee of Intrastate, was authorized to use his personal vehicle on company business. On the morning of March 9, 1976, when Kranhold was driving his vehicle to Intrastate's main office, he negligently struck a motorcycle driven by Michael S. Largey, causing severe and permanent injuries to Largey. The accident occurred at the intersection where Intrastate's main office is located.

Evidence showed that Kranhold acted as a consultant to Intrastate, worked both in and out of Intrastate's offices, had no set hours of work, often attended meetings at Intrastate's offices, and went to Intrastate's offices to pick up things or drop off things. Largey sued Intrastate for damages.

Question

1. Is Intrastate liable?

Huddleston v. Roger Dean Chevrolet, Inc.

845 F.2d 900, Web 1988 U.S. App. Lexis 6823

United States Court of Appeals for the Eleventh Circuit

Shirley Huddleston became the first female sales representative of Roger Dean Chevrolet, Inc. (RDC) in West Palm Beach, Florida. Shortly after she began working at RDC, Philip Geraci, a fellow sales representative, and other male employees began making derogatory comments to and about her, expelled gas in her presence, called her a whore, and

such. Many of these remarks were made in front of customers. The sales manager of RDC participated in the harassment. On several occasions, Huddleston complained about this conduct to RDC's general manager.

Question

1. Was Title VII violated?

Dothard, Director, Department of Public Safety of Alabama v. Rawlinson

433 U.S. 321, 97 S. Ct. 2720, 53 L.Ed.2d 786, Web 1977 U.S. Lexis 143

Supreme Court of the United States

Dianne Rawlinson, 22 years old, is a college graduate whose major course of study was correctional psychology. After graduation, she applied for a position as a correctional counselor (prison guard) with the Alabama Board of Corrections. Her application was rejected because she failed to meet the minimum 120-pound weight requirement of an Alabama statute that also established a height minimum of 5 feet 2 inches. In addition, the Alabama Board of Corrections adopted Administrative Regulation 204, which established gender criteria for assigning correctional counselors to maximum-security prisons for "contact positions." These are correctional counselor positions that require continual close physical proximity to inmates. Under this rule,

Rawlinson did not qualify for contact positions with male prisoners in Alabama maximum-security prisons.

Rawlinson brought this class action lawsuit against Dothard, who was the director of the Department of Public Safety of Alabama.

Question

1. Does either the height–weight requirement or the contact position rule constitute a bona fide occupational qualification that justifies the sexual discrimination in this case? Does society owe a duty of social responsibility to protect women from dangerous job positions? Or is this "romantic paternalism"?

WORKING WITH THE LANGUAGE OF THE COURT CASE

District of Columbia v. Howell

607 A.2d 501, Web 1992 D.C. App. Lexis 109
United States Court of Appeals for the District of Columbia

Read the following case, excerpted from the Court of Appeals opinion. Review and brief the case. In your brief, answer the following questions:

1. Was A. Louis Jagoe hired by the District of Columbia as an employee or as an independent contractor?
2. Describe the accident. Who was injured?
3. Normally, an employer is not liable for the tortious conduct of an independent contractor it has hired. What is the "special risks" exception to this rule?
4. What damages were awarded to the plaintiff?

Farrell, Associate Judge

The Murch School Summer Discovery Program was designed to provide hands-on education for gifted and talented eight- and nine-year-old children. The program originated in 1985 when Mrs. Gill, the Murch School principal, attended a reception at Mount

Vernon College arranged by Greg Butta, a Ph.D. candidate at the American University, to advertise the success of a summer program he had conducted at Mount Vernon. The program interested Mrs. Gill, and after several discussions Butta sent her a formal proposal for conducting a similar program at the Murch School. Gill proposed changes to the proposal, then solicited

(continued)

and received approval for the program from the Assistant Superintendent for the District of Columbia Public Schools.

Butta hired the staff for the summer program, including some of the instructors who had taught in the Mount Vernon program. Mrs. Gill, however, reviewed all of the instructors' resumes, had veto authority over their hiring, and interviewed most of the staff, including A. Louis Jagoe, before the hiring was made final. Jagoe, who was hired to teach chemistry to the eight- and nine-year-olds in the program, held a master's degree in chemistry and was a Ph.D. candidate at the American University. Before the first general staff meeting, he told Butta that as part of the class he would do a luminescence experiment and a "cold-pack" experiment and wanted to make sparklers with the children. Jagoe and Butta discussed the safety of the sparkler experiment only in regard to the location where the children would be allowed to light the sparklers.

On August 1, 1985, a staff meeting was held at which Gill, Butta, and all instructors and counselors were present. Each instructor gave a brief talk about what he or she intended to do in class. Several instructors testified that Jagoe told the group, including Mrs. Gill, that he planned to make sparklers as one of the chemistry experiments. Gill, who was in and out of the meeting, did not remember hearing Jagoe discuss the experiment, although notes she took at the meeting reflect that she heard him discuss the luminescence and cold-pack experiments and asked him questions about these. Gill spoke and emphasized the "hands-on" nature of the program and her hopes for its success.

One child attending the program was nine-year-old Dedrick Howell, whose parents enrolled him after receiving the school brochure in the mail. The accident occurred on August 12, 1985. At the beginning of the chemistry class, Jagoe distributed his "recipe" for sparklers to the children and also wrote it on the blackboard. Along with other chemical ingredients, the recipe called for the use of potassium perchlorate as the oxidizing agent. Potassium perchlorate was described at trial as an extremely unstable and highly volatile chemical often used to make rocket fuel. Commercially made sparklers are not made with potassium perchlorate.

The children scooped the chemicals, including the potassium perchlorate, out of jars and, using pestles, ground up the mixture in mortars. While they were combining the chemicals, Jagoe ignited three different chemical mixtures at the front of the room with a butane lighter. Butta was present for one of the ignitions when he entered the room to drop off metal hangers for use in the experiment. Mrs. Gill also entered the room at one point, and saw the children working at tables wearing goggles or glasses. She also saw Jagoe at the front of the room lighting the chemicals with a fire extinguisher on the table next to him.

The children continued to grind the material while a counselor, Rebecca Seashore, distributed pieces of metal hangers to be dipped into the mixture at a later time. Dedrick Howell was specifically told not to dip the hanger into the material until instructed to do so. Moments later the chemicals exploded in front of Dedrick. The chemicals burned at 5000 degrees Fahrenheit, and Dedrick was burned over 25% of his body including his hands, arms, chest, and face.

An employer generally is not liable for injuries to third parties caused by an independent contractor over whom (or over whose work) the employer has reserved no control. There are exceptions to the rule, however, one of which is that one who employs an independent contractor to do work involving a special danger to others which the employer knows or has reason to know to be inherent in or normal to the work, or which he contemplates or has reason to contemplate when making the contract, is subject to liability for physical harm caused to such others by the contractor's failure to take reasonable precautions against such danger.

It is sufficient that work of any kind involves a risk, recognizable in advance, of physical harm to others which is inherent in the work itself, or normally to be expected in the ordinary course of the usual or prescribed way of doing it, or that the employer has special reason to contemplate such a risk under the particular circumstances under which the work is to be done.

The sparkler experiment combined flammable, combustible chemicals, open flames, and children; for that very reason, presumably, the children had been equipped with goggles. Though sparklers are explosives of a lesser order, conducting controlled explosions is a textbook example of an inherently dangerous activity. It was not unreasonable for the jury to conclude that the manufacture of sparklers by nine-year-old children was an inherently dangerous activity.

Therefore, the jury was well within its authority in finding that Jagoe was an independent contractor performing inherently dangerous work of which the District had actual or constructive knowledge.

The judgment is affirmed as to liability and as to the award of $8 million in damages both for pain and suffering and for past medical expenses.

Business Organizations and Bankruptcy Law

DIGITAL RESOURCES

Chapter 18 Digital Resources at *www.pearsonhighered.com/goldman*

- Video Case Studies:
  - A Corporate Officer Seeks Legal Counsel: Conflict of Interest
- Chapter Summary • Web Links • Court Opinions • Glossary • Comprehension Quizzes
- Technology Resources

> " The biggest corporation, like the humblest private citizen, must be held to strict compliance with the will of the people. "
>
> *Theodore Roosevelt*

Paralegals at Work

As a paralegal, you work for Mr. Abraham Weinstein, a well-known business attorney. One day Mr. Weinstein asks you to come into the conference room for a meeting with him. During the meeting, Mr. Weinstein informs you that he has been retained by new clients, Ms. Sophia Lopez and four other persons, who want to form a new business venture.

Mr. Weinstein informs you that the five prospective owners each will invest $300,000 in the new business. The business will open and operate a new men's clothing store called Victor's Secret. The store will sell upscale casual clothes, formal clothes, undergarments, perfume, and other accessories for men. The owners plan to open the first store six months from now, and then plan to expand and open one additional store each year for the next five years.

Mr. Weinstein explains to you that the owners would like to form a type of business organization in which they will have limited liability—that is, they will have no personal liability beyond their capital in the business. They also want to have flow-through taxation—that is, the entity will pay no taxes and all of the gains and losses of the business will flow-through to their individual tax returns. In addition, the five owners want two of the owners, Ms. Lopez and Ms. Genevieve Cross, to manage the business; the other three owners do not want to manage the business but only want to remain owners and investors.

Mr. Weinstein asks you to compare the different forms of business organizations available and determine which type or types of organizations best meet the owners' requirements.

Consider the issues involved in this scenario as you read the chapter.

After studying this chapter, you should be able to:

1. Recognize the professional opportunities for paralegals in the business organizations and corporation law area.
2. Define a *sole proprietorship* and explain the liability of a sole proprietor.
3. Define *general partnership* and describe how general partnerships are formed.
4. Define *limited partnership* and distinguish between limited and general partners.
5. Define *limited liability partnership (LLP)* and describe the limited liability of partners of an LLP.
6. Define *limited liability company (LLC)* and describe the limited liability of owners of an LLC.
7. Define *corporation* and describe the process of forming a corporation.
8. Explain the functions of shareholders, directors, and officers in managing the affairs of a corporation.
9. Recognize the professional opportunities for paralegals in the bankruptcy law area.
10. Identify the major forms of bankruptcy permitted under federal bankruptcy law.
11. Describe types of personal bankruptcy.
12. Describe business reorganization bankruptcy.
13. Describe the major changes to federal bankruptcy law made by the Bankruptcy Abuse Prevention and Consumer Protection Act of 2005.
14. Explain a paralegal's duty not to use confidential information.

INTRODUCTION FOR THE PARALEGAL

Many paralegals work for lawyers who represent various forms of businesses. These consist of lawyers who represent entrepreneurs and other small business owners, as well as lawyers who represent the largest multinational corporations in the world. Corporations and other forms of business employ lawyers to represent the business in all sorts of matters ranging from starting the entity, to advising the business as to compliance with the law, to representing the business and their owners or managers in bringing or defending lawsuits.

Among the many different types of business organizations are *sole proprietorships*, *general partnerships*, *limited partnerships*, *limited liability partnerships (LLPs)*, *limited liability companies (LLCs)*, and *corporations*. These are collectively referred to as *business organizations*. An entrepreneur must make a choice as to which type of business to form and operate. Once formed, these business organizations employ lawyers to represent them in their ongoing business transactions.

Paralegals often assist lawyers in representing corporations and other business organizations. This ranges from drafting the original documents to form a business, as well as assisting the lawyer in representing businesses and their management in many other ways. Therefore, a paralegal working in this field must have knowledge of the law of business organizations. This chapter covers the law regarding the formation and operation of corporations and other forms of business.

Sole Proprietorship

Sole proprietorship A form of business in which the owner is actually the business; the business is not a separate legal entity.

The **sole proprietorship** is the simplest form of **business organization.** The owner, called a **sole proprietor,** is the business; there is no separate legal entity. Sole proprietorships are the most common form of business organization in the United States. Many small businesses—and a few large ones—operate this way.

Operating a business as a sole proprietorship has these advantages:

1. Ease and low cost of formation.
2. The owner's right to make all management decisions concerning the business, including those involving hiring and firing employees.
3. The sole proprietor owns all of the business, with the right to receive all of the ownership of business's profits.
4. Ease of transfer or sale if and when the owner desires to do so; no other approval (such as from partners or shareholders) is necessary.

This business form has disadvantages, too, among them:

1. The sole proprietor's access to capital is limited to personal funds plus any loans he or she can obtain.
2. The sole proprietor is legally responsible for the business's contracts and the torts he or she or any of his or her employees commits in the course of employment.

Web Exploration

Go to http://www.powerhomebiz .com/vol144/starbucks.htm and read the article "Learning from Starbucks: 10 Lessons for Small Businesses."

Creation of a Sole Proprietorship

It is easy to create a sole proprietorship. There are no formalities, and no federal or state government approval is required. Some local governments require all businesses, including sole proprietorships, to obtain a license to do business within the city. If no other form of business organization is chosen, the business is a sole proprietorship by default.

d.b.a. ("Doing Business As")

A sole proprietorship can operate under the name of the sole proprietor or a *trade name.* For example, the author of this book can operate a sole proprietorship under the

CAREER OPPORTUNITIES FOR PARALEGALS IN SMALL BUSINESS LAW

Many paralegals work for lawyers who represent small businesses and their owners. Small businesses are everywhere in this country. For example, most businesses in small towns and cities are operated by local businesspersons. This includes the local department store, restaurants, insurance agencies, automobile repair shops, the local bank, plumbers, and so forth. The small businesses in local communities comprise a substantial amount of work for lawyers.

In addition, thousands of small businesses operate in large cities. These include small businesses serving specific areas of the larger metropolitan area in which they are located. In large cities, many of the small businesses serve ethnic communities as well. Thousands of small businesses located in large cities require the services of lawyers.

In smaller communities, small businesses are more likely to rely on local attorneys to handle their legal needs. These attorneys tend to be sole practitioners or attorneys who work for smaller law firms. The attorneys are members of the local community and are well known, often friends or acquaintances of their clients. Small businesses in large cities tend to rely on smaller law firms to handle their legal affairs, although some use larger law firms as well.

Small businesses often require the services of lawyers. For instance, to get started, entrepreneurs need advice as to the type of legal form under which their business should operate. Some of these businesses are sole proprietorships, general partnerships, limited partnerships, limited liability companies, limited liability partnerships, or small corporations. The lawyer representing such clients must advise these clients as to the form of organization that would best suit the clients' needs, and the paralegal must have knowledge of these different forms of organization as well.

Paralegals for small law firms that represent small businesses are often called upon to draft the necessary legal documents to start the business. If it is to be a small corporation or a limited liability company, the paralegal will draft the initial articles of incorporation or articles of organization, plus other documents such as bylaws, minutes of the first meeting of the owners, and such. If a type of partnership is chosen, the paralegal will draft the articles of partnership.

Once established, small businesses often rely on their lawyer to represent them in other transactions. If contracts are required for the operation of the business, the business will employ the attorney to draft these contracts. Here, the paralegal often is the first person to complete a draft of the contract. If a sale or purchase of real estate is required by the business, the attorney is looking to represent the small business and to complete or review the necessary documents. Again, the paralegal for these attorneys often is called upon to prepare drafts of these documents.

In addition, small businesses sometimes sue or are sued. The lawyer will represent the small business in these lawsuits. Most of these lawsuits are in state court, although some are tried in federal court. Because these lawyers are sole practitioners or work for small law firms, they often need the assistance of a paralegal to prepare the law case.

Thus, paralegals often work in smaller law firms representing local businesses and individuals. The paralegals in these law firms usually are involved in all aspects of the legal services provided to small-business clients. Work in small law firms will continue to be a substantial source of jobs for paralegals, particularly those who live in small communities across the country, as well as those who work for smaller law firms in metropolitan areas that derive a substantial amount of their work representing small businesses and their owners.

name "Henry R. Cheeseman" or under a trade name such as "The Big Cheese." Operating under a trade name is commonly designated as a **d.b.a. (doing business as)** (e.g., Henry R. Cheeseman, doing business as "The Big Cheese").

Most states require all businesses that operate under a trade name to file a **fictitious business name statement** (or *certificate of trade name*) with the appropriate government agency. The statement must contain the name and address of the applicant, the trade name, and the address of the business. Most states also require that notice of the trade name be published in a newspaper of general circulation serving the area in which the applicant does business.

These requirements are intended to disclose the real owner's name to the public. Noncompliance can result in a fine. Some states prohibit violators from maintaining lawsuits in the state's courts. A sample fictitious business name statement is shown in Exhibit 18.1.

 Web Exploration

Go to http://www.business.gov/guides/business_law/dba.html. Scroll down to the name of your state and read the requirements for obtaining a d.b.a. in your state. If there is an online link for your state, go to that link for further information.

Exhibit 18.1 **Sample fictitious business name statement**

Return To:	PUBLISH IN:
Name: Kerry Fields, Esq. Address: 115 S. Chaparral Court City: Anaheim, CA 92808 Telephone # (714) 283-0140 Cust. Ref. # 53247	COUNTY CLERK'S FILING STAMP
☒ First Filing ☐ Renewal Filing Current Registration No.	

FICTITIOUS BUSINESS NAME STATEMENT

THE FOLLOWING PERSON(S) IS (ARE) DOING BUSINESS AS:

1 Fictitious Business Name(s)
The Big Cheese

2 Street address & Principal place of Business in California
1000 Exposition Boulevard   Los Angeles   California   Zip Code 90089

3 Full name of Registrant   (if corporation - incorporated in what state)
Henry R. Cheeseman

Residence Address	City	State	Zip Code
575 Barrington Ave.	Los Angeles	California	90049

Full Name of Registrant   (if corporation - incorporated in what state)

Residence Address	City	State	Zip Code

Full name of Registrant   (if corporation - incorporated in what state)

Residence Address	City	State	Zip Code

Full name of Registrant   (if corporation - incorporated in what state)

Residence Address	City	State	Zip Code

4 This Business is
conducted by:
(check one only)
(X) an Individual   ( ) a general partnership   ( ) joint venture   ( ) a business trust
( ) co-partners   ( ) husband and wife   ( ) a corporation   ( ) a limited partnership
( ) an unincorporated association other than a partnership   ( ) other—(*please specify*)

5 The registrant commenced to transact business under the fictitious business name or names listed above on _____

6
a. Signed:
Henry R. Cheeseman
SIGNATURE   Henry R. Cheeseman
TYPE OR PRINT NAME

_____ SIGNATURE   _____ TYPE OR PRINT NAME

_____ SIGNATURE   _____ TYPE OR PRINT NAME

b. If Registrant a corporation sign below:
_____ CORPORATION NAME
_____ SIGNATURE & TITLE
_____ TYPE OR PRINT NAME

This statement was filed with the County Clerk of ____ Los Angeles ____ County on date indicated by file stamp above.

NOTICE THIS FICTITIOUS NAME STATEMENT EXPIRES FIVE YEARS FROM THE DATE IT WAS FILED IN THE OFFICE OF THE COUNTY CLERK. A NEW FICTITIOUS BUSINESS NAME STATEMENT MUST BE FILED BEFORE THAT TIME. THE FILING OF THIS STATEMENT DOES NOT OF ITSELF AUTHORIZE THE USE IN THIS STATE OF A FICTITIOUS BUSINESS NAME IN VIOLATION OF THE RIGHTS OF ANOTHER UNDER FEDERAL, STATE, OR COMMON LAW (SEE SECTION 14400 ET SEQ., BUSINESS AND PROFESSIONS CODE).

I HEREBY CERTIFY THAT THIS COPY IS A CORRECT COPY OF THE ORIGINAL STATEMENT ON FILE IN MY OFFICE.
_____ Helen Pitts
COUNTY CLERK
BY _____ Deborah Cantrell   DEPUTY
FILE NO. ____ 081646

Personal Liability of Sole Proprietors

The sole proprietor bears the entire risk of loss of the business; the owner will lose his or her entire capital contribution if the business fails. In addition, the sole proprietor has unlimited **personal liability** (see Exhibit 18.2). Therefore, creditors may recover claims against the business from the sole proprietor's personal assets (e.g., home, automobile, bank accounts).

Example   Suppose Ken Smith opens a clothing store called The Rap Shop and operates it as a sole proprietorship. Smith files the proper statement and publishes the necessary notice of the use of the trade name. He contributes $25,000

Exhibit 18.2 Sole proprietorship

Exhibit 18.3 General partnership

of his personal funds to the business and borrows $100,000 in the name of the business from a bank. Assume that after several months Smith closes the business because it was unsuccessful. At the time it is closed, the business has no assets, owes the bank $100,000, and owes rent, trade credit, and other debts of $25,000. Here, Smith is personally liable to pay the bank and all of the debts from his personal assets.

General Partnership

General, or ordinary, partnerships have been recognized since ancient times. The English common law of partnerships governed early U.S. partnerships. The individual states expanded the body of partnership law.

A **general partnership**, or **partnership**, is a voluntary association of two or more persons for carrying on a business as co-owners for profit. The formation of a partnership creates certain rights and duties among partners and with third parties. These rights and duties are established in the **partnership agreement** and by law. **General partners**, or **partners**, are personally liable for the debts and obligations of the partnership (see Exhibit 18.3).

General partnership A voluntary association of two or more persons for carrying on a business as co-owners for profit. Also called a *partnership*.

General partner A partner of a general partnership who is liable for the debts and obligations of the general partnership.

Uniform Partnership Act

In 1914, the National Conference of Commissioners on Uniform State Laws (a group of lawyers, judges, and legal scholars) promulgated the **Uniform Partnership Act (UPA)**, which codifies partnership law. Its goal was to establish consistent partnership law that would be uniform throughout the United States. The UPA has been adopted in whole or in part by 48 states, the District of Columbia, Guam, and the Virgin Islands.

The UPA covers most problems that arise in the formation, operation, and dissolution of ordinary partnerships. Other rules of law or equity govern if there is no applicable provision of the UPA [UPA § 5].

The UPA adopted the **entity theory** of partnership, which considers partnerships as separate legal entities. As such, partnerships can hold title to personal and real property, transact business in the partnership name, and the like.

Formation of a Partnership

A business must meet four criteria to qualify as a partnership under the Uniform Partnership Act [UPA Section 6(1)]. It must be

1. an association of two or more persons.
2. carrying on a business.
3. as co-owners.
4. for profit.

Partnerships are voluntary associations of two or more persons. All partners must agree to the participation of each co-partner. A person cannot be forced to be a partner or to accept another person as a partner. The UPA definition of "person" includes natural persons, partnerships (including limited partnerships), corporations, and other associations. A business—trade, occupation, or profession—must be carried on. To qualify as a partnership, the organization or venture must have a profit motive even though the business does not actually have to make a profit.

A general partnership may be formed with little or no formality. Co-ownership of a business is essential to create a partnership. The most important factor in determining co-ownership is whether the parties share the business's profits and management responsibility.

Receipt of a share of business profits is *prima facie* evidence of a partnership because nonpartners usually are not given the right to share in the business's profits. No inference of the existence of a partnership is drawn if profits are received in payment of

1. a debt owed to a creditor in installments or otherwise,
2. wages owed to an employee,
3. rent owed to a landlord,
4. an annuity owed to a widow, widower, or representative of a deceased partner,
5. interest owed on a loan, or
6. consideration for the sale of goodwill of a business [UPA Section 7].

An agreement to share losses of a business is strong evidence of a partnership.

The right to participate in the management of a business is important evidence for determining the existence of a partnership, but it is not conclusive evidence because the right to participate in management is sometimes given to employees, creditors, and others. If a person is given the right to share in profits, losses, and management of a business, it is compelling evidence of the existence of a partnership.

The Partnership Agreement

The agreement to form a partnership may be oral, written, or implied from the conduct of the parties. It may even be created inadvertently. No formalities are necessary, although a few states require general partnerships to file certificates of partnership with an appropriate government agency. Partnerships that exist for more than one year or are authorized to deal in real estate must be in writing under the Statute of Frauds. It is good practice for partners to put their partnership agreement in writing. A written document is important evidence of the terms of the agreement, particularly if a dispute arises among the partners.

A written partnership agreement is called a partnership agreement or **articles of partnership**. The partners can agree to almost any terms in their partnership agreement, except terms that are illegal. The articles of partnership can be short and simple or long and complex. If the agreement fails to provide for an essential term or contingency, the provisions of the UPA control. Thus, the UPA acts as a gap-filling device to the partners' agreement.

Contract Liability

As a legal entity, a partnership must act through its agents—that is, its partners. Contracts entered into with suppliers, customers, lenders, or others on the partnership's behalf are binding on the partnership.

Under the UPA, partners have **joint liability** for the contracts and debts of the partnership [UPA Section 15(b)]. This means that a third party who sues to recover on a partnership contract or debt must name all of the partners in the lawsuit. If the lawsuit is successful, the plaintiff can collect the entire amount of the judgment against any or all of the partners. If the third party's suit does not name all of the partners, the judgment cannot be collected against any of the partners or the partnership assets. Similarly, releasing any partner from the lawsuit releases them all. A partner who is made to pay more than his or her proportionate share of contract liability may seek **indemnification** from the partnership and from those partners who have not paid their share of the loss.

Tort Liability

While acting on partnership business, a partner or an employee of the partnership may commit a tort that causes injury to a third person. This tort could be caused by a negligent act, a breach of trust (such as embezzlement from a customer's account), a breach of fiduciary duty, defamation, fraud, or other intentional tort. The partnership is liable if the act is committed while the person is acting within the ordinary course of partnership business or with the authority of his or her co-partners.

Under the UPA partners have **joint and several liability** for torts and breaches of trust [UPA Section 15(a)]. This is so even if a partner did not participate in commission of the act. This type of liability permits a third party to sue one or more of the partners separately. Judgment can be collected only against the partners who are sued. The partnership and partners who are made to pay tort liability may seek indemnification from the partner who committed the wrongful act. A release of one partner does not discharge the liability of other partners.

> **Example**   Suppose Nicole, Jim, and Maureen form a partnership. Assume that Jim, while on partnership business, causes an automobile accident that injures Kurt, a pedestrian. Kurt suffers $100,000 in injuries. At his option, Kurt can sue Nicole, Jim, or Maureen separately, or any two of them, or all of them.

Dissolution of Partnerships

The duration of a partnership can be for a fixed term (e.g., five years) or until a specific undertaking is accomplished (e.g., until a real estate development is completed), or it can be for an unspecified term. A partnership with a fixed duration is called a **partnership for a term**. A partnership with no fixed duration is called a **partnership at will**.

Although a partner has the *power* to withdraw and dissolve the partnership at any time, he or she may not have the *right* to do so. For example, a partner who withdraws from a partnership before expiration of the term stated in the partnership agreement

PARTNERSHIP AGREEMENT

The partnership agreement should contain the following information:

- the firm name
- names and addresses of the partners
- principal office of the partnership
- nature and scope of the partnership business
- duration of the partnership
- capital contributions of each partner
- the division of profits and losses among the partners
- the salaries, if any, to be paid to partners
- duties of the partners regarding management of the partnership
- limitations, if any, on the authority of partners to bind the partnership
- provisions for the admission and withdrawal of partners from the firm and the terms, conditions, and notices required for withdrawal
- provisions for continuing the partnership upon withdrawal of a partner, death of a partner, or other dissolution of the partnership
- any other provisions deemed relevant by the partners

Joint and several liability   Tort liability where general partners are liable as a group or separately. This means that the plaintiff can sue one or more of the partners separately. If successful, the plaintiff can recover the entire amount of the judgment from any or all of the defendant-partners.

Paralegals *in* Practice

PARALEGAL PROFILE
Kelly A. LaGrave

Kelly A. LaGrave specializes in business/corporate law. Her credentials include a Bachelor of Arts Degree in International Relations from Michigan State University, and the Certified Legal Assistant Specialty designation from the National Association of Legal Assistants (NALA) in both Intellectual Property and Real Estate. She also earned the Advanced Paralegal Certification (ACP) from NALA in Contract Management/Contract Administration. During her 25-year paralegal career, Kelly has served on various professional boards including the Advisory Committee for Lansing Community College's Paralegal Program. She is currently employed by the law firm of Foster, Swift, Collins & Smith in Lansing, Michigan.

In my area of practice, it is vital that a paralegal understands the various types of business entities allowed under the state's statutes. Some specific tasks that I do on a regular basis include drafting all documentation necessary to form, dissolve, or merge business entities; performing due diligence such as obtaining and reviewing Uniform Commercial Code documents (affidavits, notices, financing statements, etc.), litigation dockets, and government agency certified documents; completing copyright applications; and preparing documentation for the purchase/sale of businesses.

One of my most interesting experiences in corporate law occurred when I was asked to set up and maintain an electronic data room. This "room" is actually a dedicated Web site that allows approved users to search hundreds of due diligence documents. Technology has definitely changed the way we handle transactions!

What I find most rewarding about my job is the variety of work, and the opportunity to take a project from start to completion. I have also been given the chance to learn new areas of the law. A new paralegal entering my practice area needs to have a willingness to learn, an extreme attention to detail, the ability to organize and track many tasks at once, and fearlessness when it comes to using technology in the workplace.

does not have the right to do so. The partner's action causes a **wrongful dissolution** of the partnership. The partner is liable for damages caused by wrongful dissolution of the partnership.

Limited Partnership

Limited partnership A special form of partnership that is formed only if certain formalities are followed. A limited partnership has both general and limited partners.

Limited partnerships are statutory creations that have been used since the Middle Ages. They include both general (manager) and limited (investor) partners. Today, all states have enacted statutes that provide for the creation of limited partnerships. In most states these partnerships are called **limited partnerships** or *special partnerships*. Limited partnerships are used for business ventures such as investing in real estate, drilling oil and gas wells, investing in movie productions, and the like.

Revised Uniform Limited Partnership Act

In 1916 the National Conference of Commissioners on Uniform State Laws, a group composed of lawyers, judges, and legal scholars, promulgated the **Uniform Limited Partnership Act (ULPA).** The ULPA contains a set of provisions for the formation, operation, and dissolution of limited partnerships. Most states originally enacted this law.

Revised Uniform Limited Partnership Act (RULPA) A 1976 revision of the ULPA that provides a more modern, comprehensive law for the formation, operation, and dissolution of limited partnerships.

In 1976, the National Conference on Uniform State Laws promulgated the **Revised Uniform Limited Partnership Act (RULPA),** which provides a more modern comprehensive law for the formation, operation, and dissolution of limited partnerships. This law supersedes the ULPA in the states that have adopted it. The RULPA provides the basic foundation for our discussion of limited partnership law.

General and Limited Partners

Limited partnerships have two types of partners:

1. General partners, who invest capital, manage the business, and are personally liable for partnership debts.

Exhibit 18.4   Limited partnership

2. **Limited partners,** who invest capital but do not participate in management and are not personally liable for partnership debts beyond their capital contribution.

Exhibit 18.4 illustrates a limited partnership. A limited partnership must have at least one or more general partners and one or more limited partners [RULPA Section 101 (7)]. There are no restrictions on the number of general or limited partners allowed in a limited partnership. Any person may be a general or limited partner. This includes natural persons, partnerships, limited partnerships, trusts, estates, associations, and corporations. A person may be both a general and a limited partner in the same limited partnership.

Limited partners Partners in a limited partnership who invest capital but do not participate in management and are not personally liable for partnership debts beyond their capital contribution.

Formation of Limited Partnerships

The creation of a limited partnership is formal and requires public disclosure. The entity must comply with the statutory requirements of the Revised Uniform Limited Partnership Act or other state statutes.

Under the RULPA, two or more persons must execute and sign a **certificate of limited partnership** [RULPA Sections 201 and 206]. The certificate must contain the following information:

1. name of the limited partnership
2. general character of the business
3. address of the principal place of business, and name and address of the agent to receive service of legal process
4. name and business address of each general and limited partner
5. the latest date upon which the limited partnership is to dissolve
6. amount of cash, property, or services (and description of property or services) contributed by each partner, and any contributions of cash, property, or services promised to be made in the future
7. any other matters that the general partners determine to include

The certificate of limited partnership must be filed with the secretary of state of the appropriate state and, if required by state law, with the county recorder in the county or counties in which the limited partnership carries on business. The limited partnership is formed when the certificate of limited partnership is filed.

Limited Partnership Agreement

Although not required by law, the partners of a limited partnership often draft and execute a **limited partnership agreement** (also called the **articles of limited partnership**) that sets forth the rights and duties of the general and limited partner(s), terms and conditions regarding the operation, termination, and dissolution of the partnership, and so on. Where there is no such agreement, the certificate of limited partnership serves as the articles of limited partnership.

The limited partnership agreement may specify how profits and losses from the limited partnership are to be allocated among the general and limited partners. If there is no such agreement, the RULPA provides that profits and losses from a limited partnership are shared on the basis of the value of the partner's capital contribution [RULPA Section 503]. A limited partner is not liable for losses beyond his or her capital contribution.

In addition, it is good practice to establish voting rights in the limited partnership agreement or certificate of limited partnership. The limited partnership agreement can provide which transactions must be approved by which partners (i.e., general, limited, or both). General and limited partners may be given unequal voting rights. A sample limited partnership agreement is set forth in Exhibit 18.5.

Liability of General and Limited Partners

The general partners of a limited partnership have **unlimited liability** for the debts and obligations of the limited partnership. This liability extends to debts that cannot be satisfied with the existing capital of the limited partnership. Generally, limited partners are liable only for the debts and obligations of the limited partnership up to their capital contributions.

As a trade-off for **limited liability,** limited partners give up their right to participate in the control and management of the limited partnership. This means, in part, that limited partners have no right to bind the partnership to contracts or other obligations. Under the RULPA, a limited partner is liable as a general partner if his or her participation in the control of the business is substantially the same as that of a general partner, but the limited partner is liable only to persons who reasonably believed him or her to be a general partner [RULPA Section 303(a)].

Limited Liability Partnership (LLP)

Many states have enacted legislation to permit the creation of **limited liability partnerships (LLPs).** An LLP does not have to have a general partner who is personally liable for the debts and obligations of the partnership. Instead, *all* partners are limited partners who stand to lose only their capital contribution if the partnership fails. None of the partners is personally liable for the debts and obligations of the partnership beyond his or her capital contribution (see Exhibit 18.6).

LLPs enjoy the "flow-through" tax benefit of other types of partnerships; that is, no tax is paid at the partnership level and all profits and losses are reported on the individual partners' income tax returns. LLPs must be created formally by filing **articles of limited liability partnership** with the secretary of state of the state in which the LLP is organized. This is a public document.

The LLP is a domestic LLP in the state in which it is organized. The **Uniform Limited Liability Partnership Act (ULLPA)** is a model act that codifies the law governing LLPs. Many states have adopted all or part of the ULLPA to govern LLPs. The limited liability partnership law of the state governs the operation of the LLP. An LLP

Exhibit 18.5 Sample limited partnership agreement

LIMITED PARTNERSHIP AGREEMENT

1. Introduction. This agreement of Limited Partnership dated January 2, 2007 by and between John Weston, Wai Chan, and Susan Martinez (General Partners) and Shari Berkowitz, Raymond Wong, and Harold Johnson (Limited Partners).

The General Partners and Limited Partners agree to form a Limited Partnership (Partnership) pursuant to the provisions of the California Revised Limited Partnership Act on the terms and conditions hereinafter set forth.

2. Name of Partnership. The name of the Partnership shall be "The Wilshire Investment Company, a California Limited Partnership." The business of the Partnership shall be conducted in that name.

3. Principal Place of Business. The principal office of the Partnership shall be at 4000 Wilshire Boulevard, Los Angeles, California 90010 or at such other place within California as may be determined from time to time by the General Partners.

4. Purpose of the Partnership. The Partnership shall be engaged in the business of buying, selling, and developing commercial and industrial real estate and such activities as are related or incidental thereto.

5. Agent for Service of Process. The name of the agent for service of process is Frederick Friendly, whose address is 2500 Century Park East, Suite 600, Los Angeles, California 90067.

6. Term of Partnership. The term of the Partnership shall commence on the date on which the Partnership's Certificate of Limited Partnership is filed by the Secretary of State of California and shall continue until it terminates in accordance with the provisions of this Agreement.

7. Certificate of Limited Partnership. The General Partners shall immediately execute a Certificate of Limited Partnership and cause that Certificate to be filed in the office of the secretary of state of California. The General Partners shall also record a certified copy of the Certificate in the office of the county recorder of every county in which the Partnership owns real property.

8. Members of the Partnership.

   (a) The names and addresses of each original General Partner are as follows:

NAME	John Weston	ADDRESS	500 Ocean Boulevard, Los Angeles, California
	Wai Chan		700 Apple Road, Seattle, Washington
	Susan Martinez		800 Palm Drive, Miami, Florida

   (b) The names and addresses of each original Limited Partner are as follows:

NAME	Shari Berkowitz	ADDRESS	700 Apple Street, New York, New York
	Raymond Wong		900 Flower Avenue, San Francisco, California
	Harold Johnson		300 Oil Field Road, Houston, Texas

9. General Partners' Capital Contributions. The General Partners shall make the following contributions to the Partnership's capital no later than January 2, 2007.

CASH	John Weston	$60,000
PROPERTY	Wai Chan	$30,000
	Susan Martinez	$30,000

   No interest will be paid on any balances in the General Partners' capital accounts.

10. Limited Partners' Capital Contributions. The Limited Partners shall make the following contributions to the Partnership's capital no later than January 2, 2007.

CASH	Shari Berkowitz	$100,000
	Raymond Wong	$ 50,000
	Harold Johnson	$ 50,000

    No interest will be paid on any balances in the Limited Partners' capital accounts.

11. Additional Capital Contributions from Limited Partners. The General Partners may call for additional cash contributions to the Partnership's capital from the Limited Partners. The aggregate of all additional capital contributions made by the Limited Partners pursuant to this Paragraph shall not exceed 100 percent of the original capital contributions made by them pursuant to Paragraph 10 of this Agreement. Notice of the call shall be made by registered mail, return receipt requested, and shall be deemed made when posted. The Limited Partners' additional capital contribution must be made no later than 60 days following the call.

12. Division of Profits. Each Partner shall receive the following share of the net profits of the Partnership:

	PARTNER	PERCENT
General Partners:	John Weston	30%
	Wai Chan	15%
	Susan Martinez	15%
Limited Partners:	Shari Berkowitz	20%
	Raymond Wong	10%
	Harold Johnson	10%

(continued)

Exhibit 18.5 **Sample limited partnership agreement** *(continued)*

13. Sharing of Losses. Each Partner shall bear a share of the losses of the Partnership equal to the share of the profits to which he or she is entitled. The share of the losses of each Partner shall be charged against his contribution to the capital of the Partnership.

   The Limited Partners will not be liable for any Partnership debts or losses beyond the amounts to be contributed to them pursuant to Paragraphs 10 and 11 of this Agreement.

   After giving effect to the share of losses chargeable against the capital contributions of Limited Partners, the remaining Partnership losses shall be borne by the General Partners in the same proportions in which, between themselves, they are to share profits.

14. Management of Partnership. The General Partners shall have the sole and exclusive control of the Limited Partnership.

   The General Partners shall have an equal voice in the management of the Partnership, and each shall devote his or her full time to the conduct of the Partnership's business.

   The General Partners shall have the power and authority to take such action from time to time as they may deem to be necessary, appropriate, or convenient in connection with the management and conduct of the business and affairs of the Partnership, including, without limitation, the power to

   (a) Acquire property, including real and personal property.

   (b) Dispose of Partnership property.

   (c) Borrow or lend money.

   (d) Make, deliver, or accept commercial paper.

   (e) Pledge, mortgage, encumber, or grant a security interest in the Partnership properties as security for repayment of loans.

   (f) Take any and all other action permitted by law that is customary in or reasonably related to the conduct of the Partnership business or affairs.

15. Limited Partners Not to Manage Business. The Limited Partners will not manage the business of the Partnership or assist in its management.

16. Partnership Books and Records. The Partnership books of account will be kept in accordance with generally accepted accounting principles. The books and supporting records will be maintained at the Partnership's principal office and will be examined by the Partnership's certified public accountants at least annually. The Partnership's fiscal year shall start on January 1 and close on December 31.

17. General Partners' Salaries. The General Partners shall each receive a salary of $60,000 per annum, payable in monthly installments, as compensation for managing the Partnership. No increases shall be made in the General Partners' salaries without the written consent of a majority of the Limited Partners.

18. Admission of New General Partners. No new General Partners will be admitted to the Partnership without the written consent of all the General Partners and Limited Partners as to both his or her admission and the terms on which the new General Partner is admitted.

19. Admission of New Limited Partners. No new Limited Partners will be admitted to the Partnership without the written consent of all the General Partners and Limited Partners as to both his or her admission and the terms on which the new Limited Partner is admitted.

20. No Sale or Assignment of or Granting Lien on Partnership Interest by General Partner. Without the written consent of all the General Partners and Limited Partners, no General Partner shall assign, mortgage, or give a security interest in his or her Partnership interest.

21. Right of Limited Partner to Assign Partnership Interest or Substitute New Limited Partner. Upon 30 days' written notice to the General Partners, a Limited Partner can assign his or her interest in the Partnership's profits to a third party. Such assignment shall not constitute a substitution of the third party as a new Limited Partner in the place of the assignor. A Limited Partner may substitute a third party in his or her place as a new Limited Partner only with the consent in writing of all the General Partners and Limited Partners.

22. Effect of Death, Disability, or Retirement of a General Partner. The death, retirement, or permanent disability of a General Partner (the withdrawing General Partner) that makes it impossible for him or her to carry out his or her duties under this Agreement shall terminate the Partnership.

   If a General Partner survives, the remaining General Partners may continue the Partnership business and may purchase the interest of the withdrawing General Partner in the assets and goodwill of the Partnership. The remaining General Partners have the option, exercisable by them at any time within 30 days after the date on which the withdrawing General Partner ceases to be a General Partner, to purchase the withdrawing General Partner's interest by paying to the person legally entitled thereto the value of that interest as shown on the last regular accounting of the Partnership preceding the date on which the General Partner ceased to be a General Partner, together with the full unwithdrawn portion of the withdrawing General Partner's distributive share of any net profits earned by the Partnership between the date of that accounting and the date on which the withdrawing General Partner ceased to be a General Partner of the Partnership.

Exhibit 18.5 Sample limited partnership agreement *(continued)*

23. Duties of Remaining Purchasing General Partners. Upon the purchase of a withdrawing General Partner's interest, the remaining General Partners shall assume all obligations of the Partnership and shall hold the withdrawing General Partner, the personal representative and estate of the withdrawing General Partner, and the property of the withdrawing General Partner free and harmless from all liability for those obligations.

The remaining General Partners shall immediately amend the Certificate of Limited Partnership and shall file such amendment with the office of the Secretary of State, and shall cause to be prepared, filed, served, and published all other notices required by law to protect the withdrawing General Partner or the personal representative and estate of the withdrawing General Partner from all liability for the future obligations of the Partnership business.

24. Effect of Death of Limited Partner or Substitution of Limited Partner. The death of a Limited Partner or the substitution of a new Limited Partner for a Limited Partner shall not affect the continuity of the Partnership or the conduct of its business.

25. Voluntary Dissolution. A General Partner may terminate the Partnership at any time upon 120 days written notice to each Limited Partner. Upon termination of the Partnership, it shall be liquidated in accordance with Paragraph 26 of this Agreement.

26. Liquidation of Partnership. If the Partnership is liquidated, its assets, including its goodwill and name, shall be sold in the manner designed to produce the greatest return. The proceeds of the liquidation shall be distributed in the following order:

    (a) To creditors of the Partnership including Partners who are creditors to the extent permitted by law, in satisfaction of liabilities of the Partnership

    (b) To Partners in payment of the balances in their income accounts

    (c) To Partners in payment of the balances in their capital accounts

    (d) To Partners in payment of the remainder of the proceeds

27. Certificate of Dissolution. Upon dissolution of the Partnership, the General Partners shall execute and file in the office of the Secretary of State a Certificate of Dissolution. If dissolution occurs after a sole General Partner ceases to be a General Partner, the Limited Partners conducting the winding up of the Partnership's affairs shall file the Certificate of Dissolution.

28. Entire Agreement. This Agreement contains the entire understanding among the Partners and supersedes any prior written or oral agreements between them respecting the subject matter contained herein. There are no representations, agreements, arrangements, or understandings, oral or written, between and among the Partners relating to the subject matter of this Agreement that are not fully expressed herein.

29. Controlling Law. This Agreement shall be interpreted under the law of the State of California. Further, each Partner consents to the jurisdiction of the courts of the State of California.

30. Service of Notices. Service of notice upon the Partnership will be made by registered or certified mail, return receipt requested, addressed to the Partnership's principal place of business.

Service of notice upon any or all Partners will be made by certified mail, return receipt requested, addressed to the addresses given in this Agreement or such other addresses as a Partner may from time to time give to the Partnership.

31. Severability. If any provisions of this Agreement shall be declared by a court of competent jurisdiction to be invalid, void, or unenforceable, the remaining provisions shall continue in full force and effect.

32. Arbitration of Disputes. Any controversy concerning this Agreement will be settled by arbitration according to the rules of the American Arbitration Association, and judgment upon the award may be entered and enforced in any court.

GENERAL PARTNER _____ LIMITED PARTNER _____

GENERAL PARTNER _____ LIMITED PARTNER _____

---

may do business in other states, however. To do so, the LLP must register as a foreign LLP in any state in which it wants to conduct business.

> **Example** An accounting firm has 20 partners and other employees. The accounting firm organizes itself as a limited liability company (LLP). When one of the partners is managing an audit of a client corporation, the auditors fail to discover a large fraud being perpetrated by the owners and executives of the corporation. The corporation has a "cooked" set of fraudulent financial reports that is provided to the auditors. Subsequently, the corporation fails, ruining the shareholders of the corporation and leaving many of the creditors of the corporation unpaid. The shareholders and creditors sue the accounting firm, alleging it is liable because of the

 Web Exploration

Using http://google.com.html or other Internet search engine, locate the website for your state's limited liability partnership (LLP) law and make a note of this website.

Exhibit 18.6 Limited liability partnership (LLP)

negligence of one of its partners. Here, the negligent partner is personally liable because he was the tortfeasor. The injured plaintiffs can recover against the accounting firm itself. However, because the accounting firm was formed as an LLP the other partners of the accounting firm are not personally liable.

Limited Liability Company (LLC)

Limited liability company (LLC) An unincorporated business entity that combines the most favorable attributes of general partnerships, limited partnerships, and corporations.

Member An owner of an LLC.

A majority of states have approved a new form of business entity called a **limited liability company (LLC).** An LLC is an unincorporated business entity that combines the most favorable attributes of general partnerships, limited partnerships, and corporations. An LLC may elect to be taxed as a partnership. The owners, usually called **members,** can manage the business and have limited liability. Many entrepreneurs who begin new businesses choose the LLC as their legal form for conducting business.

Uniform Limited Liability Company Act

Uniform Limited Liability Company Act (ULLCA) A model act that provides comprehensive and uniform laws for the formation, operation, and dissolution of LLCs.

In 1995, the National Conference of Commissioners on Uniform State Laws (a group of lawyers, judges, and legal scholars) issued the **Uniform Limited Liability Company Act (ULLCA).** The ULLCA codifies limited liability company law. Its goal is to establish comprehensive LLC law that is uniform throughout the United States.

The ULLCA covers most problems that arise in the formation, operation, and termination of LLCs. The ULLCA is not law unless a state adopts it as its LLC statute. Many states have adopted all or part of the ULLCA as their limited liability company law.

Limited liability companies are creatures of state law, not federal law. Limited liability companies can be created only pursuant to the laws of the state in which the LLC is being organized. These statutes, commonly referred to as limited liability company codes, regulate the formation, operation, and dissolution of LLCs. The state legislature may amend its LLC statute at any time. The courts interpret state LLC statutes to decide LLC and member disputes.

Web Exploration

Using http://google.com.html or other Internet search engine, locate the website for your state's limited liability company (LLC) law and make a note of this website.

Members' Limited Liability

The general rule is that members are not personally liable to third parties for the debts, obligations, and liabilities of an LLC beyond their capital contribution. Members are said to have limited liability (see Exhibit 18.7). The debts, obligations, and liabilities of

Exhibit 18.7   Limited liability company (LLC)

an LLC, whether arising from contracts, torts, or otherwise, are solely those of the LLC [ULLCA Section 303(a)].

> **Example**   Jasmin, Shan-Yi, and Vanessa form an LLC and each contributes $25,000 in capital. The LLC operates for a period of time during which it borrows money from banks and purchases goods on credit from suppliers. After some time, the LLC experiences financial difficulty and goes out of business. If the LLC fails with $500,000 in debts, each of the members will lose her capital contribution of $25,000 but will not be personally liable for the rest of the unpaid debts of the LLC.

Formation of an LLC

Forming an LLC is similar to organizing a corporation. Two or more persons (which include individuals, partnerships, corporations, and associations) may form an LLC for any lawful purpose. To form an LLC, **articles of organization** must be filed with the appropriate state office, usually the Secretary of State's office (see Exhibit 18.8). The articles of organization must state the LLC's name, duration, and other information required by statute or that the organizers deem important to include. The name of an LLC must contain the words Limited Liability Company or the abbreviation *L.L.C.* or *L.C.*

Articles of organization The formal document that must be filed with the secretary of state to form an LLC.

The owners of an LLC usually are called members, although in some states they are referred to as shareholders. Members of an LLC may enter into an **operating agreement** that regulates the affairs of the company and the conduct of its business and governs relations among the members, managers, and company [ULLCA Section 103(a)]. The operating agreement may be amended by the approval of all members unless otherwise provided in the agreement. The operating agreement and amendments may be oral but usually are written.

Operating agreement An agreement entered into by members that governs the affairs and business of the LLC and the relations among members, managers, and the LLC.

Partnership Taxation for LLCs

A federal tax default rule provides that LLCs are treated as partnerships with flow-through taxation unless an election is made to be taxed as a corporation. This election to be taxed as a corporation is made by filing Form 8832 with the IRS and must be signed by all owners or a manager who is given authority to sign such an election. Most states automatically apply the federal classification rules for state income tax purposes, although a few do not.

Exhibit 18.8 **Sample LLC articles of organization**

ARTICLES OF ORGANIZATION
FOR FLORIDA LIMITED LIABILITY COMPANY

ARTICLE I – NAME

The name of the Limited Liability Company is

iCitrusSystems.com

ARTICLE II – ADDRESS

The mailing address and street address of the principal office of the Limited Liability Company is

3000 Dade Boulevard

Suite 200

Miami Beach, Florida 33139

ARTICLE III – DURATION

The period of duration for the Limited Liability Company shall be

50 years

ARTICLE IV – MANAGEMENT

The Limited Liability Company is to be managed by a manager and the name and address of such manager is

Susan Escobar

1000 Collins Avenue

Miami Beach, Florida 33141

Thomas Blandford

Pam Rosales

Corporation

Corporation A fictitious legal entity that is created according to statutory requirements.

Shareholders The owners of corporations, whose ownership interests are evidenced by stock certificates.

Corporations are the dominant form of business organization in the United States, generating more than 85 percent of the country's gross business receipts. Corporations range in size from one owner to thousands of owners. Owners of corporations are called **shareholders**.

A corporation is a separate *legal entity* (or *legal person*) for most purposes. Corporations are treated, in effect, as artificial persons created by the state that can sue or be sued in their own names, enter into and enforce contracts, hold title to and transfer property, and be found civilly and criminally liable for violations of law. Corporations cannot be put in prison, so the normal criminal penalty is the assessment of a fine, loss of a license, or other sanction.

Corporations have the following unique characteristics:

- **Limited liability of shareholders.** As separate legal entities, corporations are liable for their own contracts and debts. Generally, the shareholders have only limited liability. They are liable only to the extent of their capital contributions.
- **Free transferability of shares.** Corporate shares are freely transferable by the shareholder, by sale, assignment, pledge, or gift, unless they are

issued pursuant to certain exemptions from securities registration. Shareholders may agree among themselves on restrictions on the transfer of shares. National securities markets, such as the New York Stock Exchange, the American Stock Exchange, and NASDAQ, have been developed for the organized sale of securities.

- **Perpetual existence.** Corporations exist in perpetuity unless a specific duration is stated in the corporation's articles of incorporation. The existence of a corporation can be terminated voluntarily by the shareholders. Corporations may be terminated involuntarily by the corporation's creditors if an involuntary petition for bankruptcy against the corporation is granted. The death, insanity, or bankruptcy of a shareholder, a director, or an officer of the corporation does not affect its existence.

- **Centralized management.** The board of directors makes policy decisions concerning the operation of the corporation. Members of the board of directors are elected by the shareholders. The directors, in turn, appoint **corporate officers** to run the corporation's day-to-day operations. Together, the directors and the officers form the corporate "management."

Exhibit 18.9 depicts the hierarchy of a corporation and shows the limited liability of shareholders.

Revised Model Business Corporation Act

The Committee on Corporate Laws of the American Bar Association drafted the Model Business Corporation Act (MBCA) in 1950. The model act was intended to provide a uniform law regulating the formation, operation, and termination of corporations.

In 1984, the committee completely revised the MBCA and issued the **Revised Model Business Corporation Act (RMBCA).** Certain provisions of the RMBCA have been amended since 1984. The RMBCA arranged the provisions of the act more logically, revised the language of the act to be more consistent, and made substantial changes in the provisions of the model act.

Web Exploration

Using http://google.com.html or other Internet search engine, locate the website for your state's corporation law and make a note of this website.

Revised Model Business Corporation Act (RMBCA) A 1984 revision of the MBCA that arranged the provisions of the original act more logically, revised the language to be more consistent, and made substantial changes in the provisions.

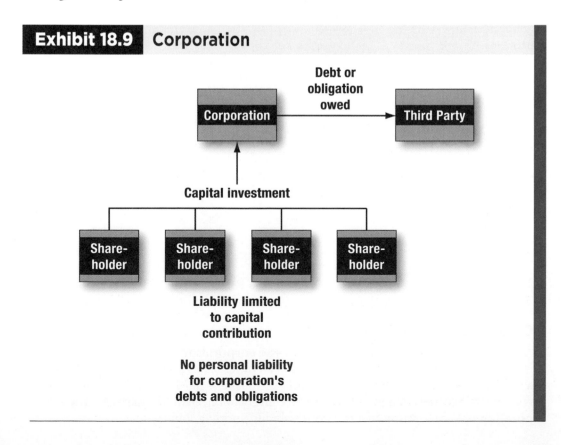

Exhibit 18.9 Corporation

CAREER OPPORTUNITIES FOR PARALEGALS IN CORPORATION LAW

Many paralegals work for large law firms that represent corporate America. Major corporations operate across America, and transnational corporations operate throughout the world. These corporations are huge, and they control an enormous proportion of the economy. Large corporations usually hire large law firms to represent them in all types of legal work. Sometimes large corporations hire boutique law firms to represent them in specialized areas of the law—for instance, patent law.

The largest law firms of America have hundreds of lawyers. The law firm itself typically is divided into different practice groups, including transactional work, real estate, securities regulation, environmental law, employment law, mergers and acquisitions, and so forth. Therefore, corporations can find most of the law talent they need in large law firms that serve corporate clients.

Paralegals who work for large law firms typically are assigned to one of the areas of the law practiced by the law firm. Therefore, the paralegals who work for these large law firms often become experts in one area of law—the type of law practiced by the attorney or attorneys to whom they have been assigned.

Transactional work takes up most of large firms' legal services provided to clients. This may consist of drafting the complex contracts the client needs. These contracts generally are negotiated with the help of the lawyers, then drafted by the lawyers. The contracts may be sales contracts, purchase contracts, service contracts, licenses, leases, and other contracts and agreements.

Major corporations need securities lawyers to represent them in issuing securities to the public, lawyers to represent them in negotiating collective bargaining agreements with labor unions, drafting the agreements for stock option and pension plans, consummating mergers with other corporations, and the like. Paralegals who work for these lawyers acquire expertise in these areas of practice.

Corporations also require lawyers to represent them in proceedings at administrative agencies, such as the federal Environmental Protection Agency (EPA), the federal Food and Drug Administration (FDA), the Securities and Exchange Commission (SEC), the Equal Employment Opportunity Commission, and other federal and state administrative agencies. Paralegals who work in these areas must acquire knowledge of administrative law that is practiced before these administrative agencies.

Many corporations operate in foreign markets. These law firms have lawyers who are experts in import law and export law, as well as specialists representing multinational corporations in their dealings in individual countries. Large law firms have international groups in America that provide these services. Large law firms also have opened offices in other countries to provide these services. Therefore, large law firms that represent multinational corporations offer an opportunity for paralegals in the international law area.

For paralegals, then, these large law firms offer tremendous employment opportunities. These large law firms seem to pay the highest salaries but also tend to demand the most hours of work from paralegals. Because large law firms are located almost solely in urban areas, these employment opportunities can be expected to be found in large cities.

Corporations themselves usually have a corporate law department; the corporation has its own legal department consisting of lawyers who are employees of the corporation. These in-house attorneys provide all sorts of legal services to the large corporation. In many instances, a large corporation uses its own attorneys to handle many of its legal needs.

In-house legal departments of corporations offer another employment opportunity for paralegals: Paralegals who work in legal departments of large corporations are employees of the corporation and, therefore, often participate in special employee benefits such as stock option plans. Corporate legal departments will continue to offer excellent employment opportunities for paralegals. Again, though, many corporate legal offices are located at the head office of the corporation in urban areas.

Corporate America will continue to employ substantial numbers of paralegals. These paralegals may work for the large law firms that represent corporate America or for the large national and multinational corporations themselves.

Many states have adopted all or part of the RMBCA as their corporation codes. The RMBCA serves as the basis for our discussion of corporation law in this book.

Classifications of Corporations

Domestic corporation A corporation in the state in which it was formed.

A private, for-profit corporation is a **domestic corporation** in the state in which it is incorporated. It is a **foreign corporation** in all other states and jurisdictions. Suppose a corporation is incorporated in Texas and does business in Montana. The corporation is a domestic corporation in Texas and a foreign corporation in Montana. An **alien corporation** is a corporation that is incorporated in another country.

Incorporation Procedure

Corporations are creatures of statute. Thus, the organizers of the corporation must comply with the state's incorporation statute to form a corporation. Although relatively similar, the procedure for **incorporation** varies somewhat from state to state.

A corporation can be incorporated in only one state even though it can do business in all other states in which it qualifies to do business. In choosing a **state of incorporation,** the incorporators, directors, and/or shareholders must consider the corporation law of the states under consideration.

For the sake of convenience, most corporations (particularly small ones) choose as the state for incorporation the state in which the corporation will be doing most of its business. Large corporations generally opt to incorporate in the state with the laws that are most favorable to the corporation's internal operations.

Articles of Incorporation

The **articles of incorporation,** or **corporate charter,** are the basic governing document of the corporation. They must be drafted and filed with, and approved by, the state before the corporation can be officially incorporated. Under the RMBCA [§ 2.02(a)], the articles of incorporation must include:

(1) the name of the corporation
(2) the number of shares the corporation is authorized to issue
(3) the address of the corporation's initial registered office and the name of the initial registered agent
(4) the name and address of each incorporator

The articles of incorporation also may include provisions concerning

1. the period of duration, which may be perpetual
2. the purpose or purposes for which the corporation is organized
3. limitation or regulation of the powers of the corporation
4. regulation of the affairs of the corporation
5. any provision that otherwise would be contained in the corporation's bylaws.

The RMBCA provides that corporate existence begins when the articles of incorporation are filed. The secretary of state's filing of the articles of incorporation is *conclusive proof* that the incorporators satisfied all conditions to incorporation. The corollary to this rule is that failure to file articles of incorporation is conclusive proof of the nonexistence of the corporation.

The articles of incorporation can be amended to contain any provision that could have been lawfully included in the original document. After the amendment is approved by the shareholders, the corporation must file articles of amendment with the secretary of state [RMBCA Section 10.06]. Exhibit 18.10 shows sample articles of incorporation.

Corporate Bylaws

In addition to the articles of incorporation, corporations are governed by their **corporate bylaws**. Either the incorporators or the initial directors can adopt the bylaws of the corporation. The **bylaws** are much more detailed than are the articles of incorporation. Bylaws may contain any provision for managing the business and affairs of the corporation that are not inconsistent with law or the articles of incorporation [RMBCA Section 2.06]. They do not have to be filed with any government official. The bylaws are binding on the directors, officers, and shareholders of the corporation.

The bylaws govern the internal management structure of the corporation. Typically, they specify the time and place of the annual shareholders' meeting, how special meetings of shareholders are called, the time and place of annual and monthly board of directors' meetings, how special meetings of the board of directors are called, the notice

Web Exploration

Go to the website of the Department of State of Delaware, Division of Corporations, at http://corp .delaware.gov/faqs.shtml. Read information about incorporating a corporation in Delaware.

Articles of incorporation The basic governing document of the corporation. This document must be filed with the secretary of state of the state of incorporation.

Web Exploration

Go to www.microsoft.com/ about/companyinformation/ corporategovernance/ articlesincorp.mspx to view the articles of incorporation of Microsoft Corporation.

Corporate bylaws A detailed set of rules that are adopted by the board of directors after the corporation is incorporated, containing provisions for managing the business and the affairs of the corporation.

Exhibit 18.10 **Sample articles of incorporation**

ARTICLES OF INCORPORATION

OF

THE BIG CHEESE CORPORATION

ONE: The name of this corporation is:

THE BIG CHEESE CORPORATION

TWO: The purpose of this corporation is to engage in any lawful act or activity for which a corporation may be organized under the General Corporation Law of California other than the banking business, the trust company business, or the practice of a profession permitted to be incorporated by the California Corporations Code.

THREE: The name and address in this state of the corporation's initial agent for service of process is:

Nikki Nguyen, Esq.   1000 Main Street, Suite 800
                       Los Angeles, California 90010

FOUR: This corporation is authorized to issue only one class of shares which shall be designated common stock. The total number of shares it is authorized to issue is 1,000,000 shares.

FIVE: The names and addresses of the persons who are appointed to act as the initial directors of this corporation are:

Shou-Yi Kang	100 Maple Street	Los Angeles, California 90005
Frederick Richards	200 Spruce Road	Los Angeles, California 90006
Jessie Quian	300 Palm Drive	Los Angeles, California 90007
Richard Eastin	400 Willow Lane	Los Angeles, California 90008

SIX: The liability of the directors of the corporation from monetary damages shall be eliminated to the fullest extent possible under California law.

SEVEN: The corporation is authorized to provide indemnification of agents (as defined in Section 317 of the Corporations Code) for breach of duty to the corporation and its stockholders through bylaw provisions or through agreements with the agents, or both, in excess of the indemnification otherwise permitted by Section 317 of the Corporations Code, subject to the limits on such excess indemnification set forth in Section 204 of the Corporations Code.

IN WITNESS WHEREOF, the undersigned, being all the persons named above as the initial directors, have executed these Articles of Incorporation.

_____

_____

_____

Dated: January 2, 2007

Web Exploration

Go to www.microsoft.com/about/companyinformation/corporategovernance/bylaws.mspx to view the bylaws of Microsoft Corporation.

required for meetings, the quorum necessary to hold a shareholders' or board of directors' meeting, the required vote necessary to enact a corporate matter, the corporate officers and their duties, committees of the board of directors and their duties, where the records of the corporation are to be kept, directors' and shareholders' inspection rights of corporate records, procedure for transferring shares of the corporation, and such.

The board of directors has the authority to amend the bylaws unless the articles of incorporation reserve that right for the shareholders. The shareholders of the corporation have the absolute right to amend the bylaws even though the bylaws also may be amended by the board of directors. Sample provisions of corporate bylaws are set forth in Exhibit 18.11.

Exhibit 18.11 Sample provisions from corporate bylaws

BYLAWS OF
THE BIG CHEESE CORPORATION

ARTICLE I Offices

Section 1. Principal Executive Office. The corporation's principal executive office shall be fixed and located at such place as the Board of Directors (herein called the "Board") shall determine. The Board is granted full power and authority to change said principal executive office from one location to another.

Section 2. Other Offices. Branch or subordinate offices may be established at any time by the Board at any place or places.

ARTICLE II Shareholders

Section 1. Annual Meetings. The annual meetings of shareholders shall be held on such date and at such time as may be fixed by the Board. At such meetings, directors shall be elected and any other proper business may be transacted.

Section 2. Special Meetings. Special meetings of the shareholders may be called at any time by the Board, the Chairman of the Board, the President, or by the holders of shares entitled to cast not less than ten percent of the votes at such meeting. Upon request in writing to the Chairman of the Board, the President, any Vice President or the Secretary by any person (other than the Board) entitled to call a special meeting of shareholders, the officer forthwith shall cause notice to be given to the shareholders entitled to vote that a meeting will be held at a time requested by the person or persons calling the meeting, not less than thirty-five nor more than sixty days after the receipt of the request. If the notice is not given within twenty days after receipt of the request, the persons entitled to call the meeting may give the notice.

Section 3. Quorum. A majority of the shares entitled to vote, represented in person or by proxy, shall constitute a quorum at any meeting of shareholders. If a quorum is present, the affirmative vote of a majority of the shares represented and voting at the meeting (which shares voting affirmatively also constitute at least a majority of the required quorum) shall be the act of the shareholders, unless the vote of a greater number or voting by classes is required by law or by the Articles, except as provided in the following sentence. The shareholders present at a duly called or held meeting at which a quorum is present may continue to do business until adjournment, notwithstanding the withdrawal of enough shareholders to leave less than a quorum, if any action taken (other than adjournment) is approved by at least a majority of the shares required to constitute a quorum.

ARTICLE III Directors

Section 1. Election and Term of Office. The directors shall be elected at each annual meeting of the shareholders, but if any such annual meeting is not held or the directors are not elected thereat, the directors may be elected at any special meeting of shareholders held for that purpose. Each director shall hold office until the next annual meeting and until a successor has been elected and qualified.

Section 2. Quorum. A majority of the authorized number of directors constitutes a quorum of the Board for the transaction of business. Every act or decision done or made by a majority of the directors present at a meeting duly held at which a quorum is present shall be regarded as the act of the Board, unless a greater number be required by law or by the Articles. A meeting at which a quorum is initially present may continue to transact business notwithstanding the withdrawal of directors, if any action taken is approved by at least a majority of the required quorum for such meeting.

Section 3. Participation in Meetings by Conference Telephone. Members of the Board may participate in a meeting through use of conference telephone or similar communications equipment, so long as all members participating in such meeting can hear one another.

Section 4. Action Without Meeting. Any action required or permitted to be taken by the Board may be taken without a meeting if all members of the Board shall individually or collectively consent in writing to such action. Such consent or consents shall have the same effect as a unanimous vote of the Board and shall be filed with the minutes of the proceedings of the Board.

Organizational meeting A meeting that must be held by the initial directors of the corporation after the articles of incorporation are filed.

Organizational Meeting

An **organizational meeting** of the initial directors of the corporation must be held after the articles of incorporation are filed. At this meeting the directors must adopt the bylaws, elect corporate officers, and transact other business that may come before the meeting [RMBCA Section 2.05]. The latter category includes matters such as accepting share subscriptions, approving the form of the stock certificate, authorizing issuance of the shares, ratifying or adopting promoters' contracts, selecting a bank, choosing an auditor, forming committees of the board of directors, fixing the salaries of officers, hiring employees, authorizing the filing of applications for government licenses to transact the business of the corporation, and empowering corporate officers to enter into contracts on behalf of the corporation. Exhibit 18.12 contains sample **corporate resolutions** from an organizational meeting of the board of directors of a corporation.

S Corporations

S corporation A corporation that has elected S corporation status. An S corporation pays no federal income tax at the corporate level. The gains or losses of an S corporation flow-through to the shareholders.

In 1982, Congress enacted the Subchapter S Revision Act. The act divided all corporations into two groups: **S corporations,** which are those that elect to be taxed under Subchapter S, and **C corporations,** which are all other corporations [26 U.S.C. Sections 6242 et seq.].

If a corporation elects to be taxed as an S Corporation, it pays no federal income tax at the corporate level. As in a partnership, the corporation's income or loss flows to the shareholders' individual income tax returns. Thus, this election is particularly advantageous if (1) the corporation is expected to have losses that can be offset against other income of the shareholders, or (2) the corporation is expected to make profits and the shareholders' income tax brackets are lower than the corporation's. Profits are taxed to the shareholders even if the income is not distributed. The shares retain other attributes of the corporate form, including limited liability.

Corporations that meet the following criteria can elect to be taxed as S corporations:

1. The corporation must be a domestic corporation.
2. The corporation cannot be a member of an affiliated group of corporations.
3. The corporation can have no more than 100 shareholders.
4. Shareholders must be individuals, estates, or certain trusts. Corporations and partnerships cannot be shareholders.
5. Shareholders must be citizens or residents of the United States. Nonresident aliens cannot be shareholders.
6. The corporation cannot have more than one class of stock. Shareholders do not have to have equal voting rights.

Web Exploration

Go to www.irs.gov/pub/irs-pdf/ f2553.pdf to view IRS Form 2553 that must be filed by a corporation selecting Subchapter S status.

An S corporation election is made by filing a **Form 2553** with the Internal Revenue Service (IRS). The election can be rescinded by shareholders who collectively own at least a majority of the shares of the corporation. If the election is rescinded, however, another S Corporation election cannot be made for five years. The duty of a paralegal to file corporate documents on time is discussed in the Ethical Perspective feature on page 681.

Shareholders

Common stock A type of equity security that represents the residual value of the corporation.

Common stockholder A person who owns common stock.

Common stock is an equity security that represents the residual value of the corporation. Common stock has no preferences. That is, creditors and preferred shareholders must receive their required interest and dividend payments before **common shareholders** receive anything. Common stock does not have a fixed maturity date. If the corporation is liquidated, the creditors and preferred shareholders are paid the value of their interests first, and the common shareholders are paid the value of their interest

Exhibit 18.12   **Sample corporate resolutions from an organizational meeting**

MINUTES OF FIRST MEETING
OF
BOARD OF DIRECTORS
OF
THE BIG CHEESE CORPORATION
January 2, 2007
10:00 A.M.

The Directors of said corporation held their first meeting on the above date and at the above time pursuant to required notice.

The following Directors, constituting a quorum of the Board of Directors, were present at such meeting:

Shou-Yi Kang

Frederick Richards

Jessie Quian

Richard Eastin

Upon motion duly made and seconded, Shou-Yi was unanimously elected Chairman of the meeting and Frederick Richards was unanimously elected Secretary of the meeting.

1. Articles of Incorporation and Agent for Service of Process

The Chairman stated that the Articles of Incorporation of the Corporation were filed in the office of the California Secretary of State. The Chairman presented to the meeting a certified copy of the Articles of Incorporation. The Secretary was directed to insert the copy in the Minute Book. Upon motion duly made and seconded, the following resolution was unanimously adopted.

RESOLVED, that the agent named as the initial agent for service of process in the Articles of Incorporation of this corporation is hereby confirmed as this corporation's agent for the purpose of service of process.

2. Bylaws

The matter of adopting Bylaws for the regulation of the affairs of the corporation was next considered. The Secretary presented to the meeting a form of Bylaws, which was considered and discussed. Upon motion duly made and seconded, the following recitals and resolutions were unanimously adopted:

WHEREAS, there has been presented to the directors a form of Bylaws for the regulation of the affairs of this corporation; and

WHEREAS, it is deemed to be in the best interests of this corporation that said Bylaws be adopted by this Board of Directors as the Bylaws of this corporation;

NOW, THEREFORE, BE IT RESOLVED, that Bylaws in the form presented to this meeting are adopted and approved as the Bylaws of this corporation until amended or repealed in accordance with applicable law.

RESOLVED FURTHER, that the Secretary of this corporation is authorized and directed to execute a certificate of the adoption of said Bylaws and to enter said Bylaws as so certified in the Minute Book of this corporation, and to see that a copy of said Bylaws is kept at the principal executive or business office of this corporation in California.

3. Corporate Seal

The secretary presented for approval a proposed seal of the corporation. Upon motion duly made and seconded, the following resolution was unanimously adopted:

RESOLVED, that a corporate seal is adopted as the seal of this corporation in the form of two concentric circles, with the name of this corporation between the two circles and the state and date of incorporation within the inner circle.

4. Stock Certificate

The Secretary presented a proposed form of stock certificate for use by the corporation. Upon motion duly made and seconded, the following resolution was unanimously adopted:

RESOLVED, that the form of stock certificate presented to this meeting is approved and adopted as the stock certificate of this corporation. The secretary was instructed to insert a sample copy of the stock certificate in the Minute Book immediately following these minutes.

5. Election of officers

The Chairman announced that it would be in order to elect officers of the corporation. After discussion and upon motion duly made and seconded, the following resolution was unanimously adopted:

RESOLVED, that the following persons are unanimously elected to the offices indicated opposite their names

Title	Name
Chief Executive Officer	Shou-Yi Kang
President	Frederick Richards
Secretary and Vice President	Jessie Quian
Treasurer	Richard Eastin

There being no further business to come before the meeting, on motion duly made, seconded and unanimously carried, the meeting was adjourned.

DELAWARE CORPORATION LAW

The state of Delaware is the corporate haven of the United States. More than 50 percent of the publicly traded corporations in America, including 60 percent of the Fortune 500 companies, are incorporated in Delaware. In total, over 500,000 business corporations are incorporated in Delaware. But why?

Remember, whatever state that a corporation is incorporated in then that state's corporation code applies to such things as election of directors, voting and other requirements for a merger to occur, laws for fending over corporate raiders, and such. So, even if a corporation does no business in Delaware, it can obtain the benefits of Delaware incorporation law by incorporating in Delaware.

On the legislative side, Delaware has enacted the **Delaware General Corporation Law.** This law is the most advanced corporation law in the country. And the statute is particularly written to be of benefit to large corporations. For example, the Delaware corporation code provides for the ability of corporations incorporated in Delaware to adopt "poison pills" that make it virtually impossible for another company to take over a Delaware corporation unless the board of directors of the target corporation agrees and removes such poison pills. In addition, the legislature keeps amending the corporation code as the demands of big business warrant or need such changes. For instance, the legislature has enacted a state antitakeover statute that makes it legally impossible to take over a

Delaware corporation unless the corporation's directors wave the state's antitakeover law and agree to be taken over.

On the judicial side, Delaware has a special court—the Court of Chancery—that hears and decides business cases. This court has been around for over 200 years. In that time it has interpreted Delaware corporation law favorably to large corporations in such matters as electing corporate boards of directors, eliminating negligence liability of outside directors, upholding the antitakeover provisions of the Delaware corporation code, and such. And there are no emotional juries to worry about. The decisions of the Chancery Court are made by judges who are experts at deciding corporate law disputes. The court is known for issuing decisions favorable to large corporations as the court applies Delaware corporation law to decide disputes. Appeals from the Court of Chancery are brought directly to the Supreme Court of Delaware. Thus, Delaware courts have created a body of precedent of legal decisions that provides more assurance to Delaware corporations in trying to decide whether they will be sued and what the outcome would be if they do get sued.

The state of Delaware makes a substantial sum of money each year on fees charged to corporations incorporated within the state. The state of Delaware is the "business state," providing advanced corporate laws and an expert judiciary for deciding corporate disputes.

(if any) last. Corporations may issue different classes of common stock [RMBCA Section 6.01 (a) and (b)].

Rights and Duties of Common Shareholders

Persons who own common stock are called common shareholders. A common stockholder's investment in the corporation is represented by a common stock certificate. Common shareholders have the right to elect directors and to vote on mergers and other important matters. In return for their investment, common shareholders receive dividends declared by the board of directors.

A corporation's shareholders *own* the corporation. Nevertheless, they are not agents of the corporation (i.e., they cannot bind the corporation to any contracts), and the only management duties they have are the right to vote on matters such as the election of directors and the approval of fundamental changes in the corporation.

Disregard of the Corporate Entity

Piercing the corporate veil
A doctrine that says that if a shareholder dominates a corporation and misuses it for improper purposes, a court of equity can disregard the corporate entity and hold the shareholder personally liable for the corporation's debts and obligations.

Shareholders of a corporation generally have limited liability (i.e., they are liable for the debts and obligations of the corporation only to the extent of their capital contribution). But if a shareholder or shareholders dominate a corporation and misuse it for improper purposes, a court of equity can **disregard the corporate entity** and hold the shareholders of a corporation personally liable for the corporation's debts and obligations. This doctrine, commonly referred to as **piercing the corporate veil**, is often resorted to by unpaid creditors who are trying to collect from shareholders a debt owed

ETHICAL PERSPECTIVE

Paralegal's Duty to File Corporate Documents on Time

Ms. Nguyen is a paralegal for a law firm. Her supervising attorney is Mr. Arnold. Several persons come into the law office to have a meeting with Mr. Arnold to represent them in incorporating a new corporation. Mr. Arnold asks Ms. Nguyen to be present at the meeting. After explaining their plan, the organizers employ Mr. Arnold to form the corporation for them and to draft and file the necessary documents. At the meeting, Mr. Arnold obtains the necessary information to prepare the articles of incorporation, bylaws, and other documents for the corporation. The meeting adjourns.

Mr. Arnold instructs Ms. Nguyen to prepare the articles of incorporation for the new corporation, which she does. After Mr. Arnold reviews the articles and approves them, he instructs Ms. Nguyen to send the articles to the incorporators for their signatures. Ms. Nguyen does so and the articles are returned to the law office signed by the incorporators. Mr. Arnold then instructs Ms. Nguyen to immediately file the articles of incorporation electronically with the state's division of corporations' office. Ms. Nguyen agrees to file the articles of incorporation electronically. However, Ms. Nguyen fails to do so.

One week later, Ms. Nguyen discovers a note that she had made to herself to file the articles of incorporation. She now realizes that she has failed to do so. At that time Ms. Nguyen electronically files the articles of incorporation with the state's division of corporations.

Ms. Nguyen's failure to file the articles of incorporation on time could easily cause serious problems for the organizers. If the incorporators had entered into contracts on behalf of the corporation during this one-week period, they would be personally bound to those contracts if the corporation did not later ratify these contracts as its own or if the corporation does ratify these contracts but fails to pay them.

Also, if one of the organizers had injured someone during this one-week period while on company business, for example, negligently causing an automobile accident that causes injury to another person, the organizers would be personally liable for the damages. This is because the corporation had not yet been in existence and therefore the organizers are not shareholders who would have been sheltered from personal liability, but instead are considered general partners of a general partnership who would be held personally liable.

Thus, a paralegal's failure to file articles of incorporation on time could cause serious financial consequences to the organizers of the corporation. Also, such negligence could lead to a lawsuit against the law firm to recover damages caused by such negligence.

by the corporation. The piercing the corporate veil doctrine is also called the **alter-ego doctrine** because the corporation has become the alter ego of the shareholder.

Courts will pierce the corporate veil if (1) the corporation has been formed without sufficient capital—called *thin capitalization*—or (2) the corporation and its shareholders have not maintained separateness (e.g., commingling of personal and corporate assets, failure to hold required shareholders' meetings, failure to maintain corporate records and books). The courts examine this doctrine on a case-by-case basis.

Board of Directors

The **board of directors** of a corporation is responsible for formulating the policy decisions affecting the management, supervision, and control of the operation of the corporation [RMBCA Section 8.01]. Such policy decisions include deciding the business or businesses in which the corporation should be engaged, selecting and removing the

Board of directors A panel of decision makers, the members of which are elected by a corporation's shareholders.

top officers of the corporation, determining the capital structure of the corporation, declaring dividends, and the like.

Typically, boards of directors are composed of inside directors and outside directors. An **inside director** is a person who is also an officer of the corporation. For example, the president of a corporation often sits as a director of the corporation. An **outside director** is a person who sits on the board of directors of a corporation but is not an officer of that corporation. Outside directors often are officers and directors of other corporations, bankers, lawyers, professors, and others. Outside directors usually are selected for their business knowledge and expertise.

The directors can act only as a board. They cannot act individually on the corporation's behalf. Every director has the right to participate in any meeting of the board of directors. Each director has one vote. Directors cannot vote by proxy.

Regular meetings of the board of directors are held at the times and places established in the bylaws. Such meetings can be held without notice. The board can call special meetings as provided in the bylaws [RMBCA Section 8.20(a)]. They typically are convened for reasons such as issuing new shares, considering proposals to merge with other corporations, adopting maneuvers to defend against hostile takeover attempts, and the like.

The board of directors may act without a meeting if all of the directors sign written consents that set forth the actions taken. Such consent has the effect of a unanimous vote. The RMBCA permits meetings of the board to be held via conference calls.

Corporate Officers

Officers Employees of a corporation who are appointed by the board of directors to manage the day-to-day operations of the corporation.

The board of directors has the authority to appoint the **officers of the corporation.** The officers are elected by the board of directors at such time and by such manner as prescribed in the corporation's bylaws. The directors can delegate certain management authority to the officers of the corporation.

At minimum, most corporations have the following officers: (1) a president, (2) one or more vice presidents, (3) a secretary, and (4) a treasurer. The bylaws or the board of directors can authorize duly appointed officers the power to appoint assistant officers. The same individual may simultaneously hold more than one office in the corporation [RMBCA Section 8.40]. The duties of each officer are specified in the bylaws of the corporation. Officers of the corporation have such authority as may be provided in the bylaws of the corporation or as determined by resolution of the board of directors.

The hierarchy of the ownership, and control of a corporation, is set forth in Exhibit 18.13.

Directors' and Officers' Duty of Loyalty

Duty of loyalty A responsibility of directors and officers not to act adversely to the interests of the corporation and to subordinate their personal interests to those of the corporation and its shareholders.

The **duty of loyalty** requires directors and officers to subordinate their personal interests to those of the corporation and its shareholders. Justice Benjamin Cardozo defined this duty of loyalty as follows:

> A corporate director or officer owes loyalty and allegiance to the corporation—a loyalty that is undivided and an allegiance that is influenced by no consideration other than the welfare of the corporation. Any adverse interest of a director or officer will be subjected to scrutiny rigid and uncompromising. He may not profit at the expense of his corporation and in conflict with its rights; he may not for personal gain divert unto himself the opportunities that in equity and fairness belong to the corporation.
>
> Many forms of conduct permissible in a workaday world for those acting at arm's length are forbidden to those bound by fiduciary ties. Not honesty alone, but the punctilio of an honor the most sensitive, is then the standard of behavior. As to this there has developed a tradition that is unbending and inveterate. [*Meinhard v. Salmon*, 164 N.E. 545, 546 (N.Y. App. 1928)]

One of the common breaches of the duty of loyalty is a corporate director or officer competing with the corporation without board of directors' approval, secretly

Exhibit 18.13 Hierarchy of corporation

E-CORPORATION

Most states have amended their corporation codes to permit the use of electronic communications to shareholders and among directors. For example, the Delaware General Corporation law recognizes the following uses of electronic technology:

- Delivery of notices to stockholders may be made electronically if the stockholder consents to the delivery of notices in this form.
- Proxy solicitation for shareholder votes may be made by electronic transmission.
- The shareholder list of a corporation that must be made available during the 10 days prior to a stockholder meeting may be made available either at the principal place of business of the corporation or by posting the list on an electronic network.

- Stockholders who are not physically present at a meeting may be deemed present, participate in, and vote at the meeting by electronic communication; a meeting may be held solely by electronic communication, without a physical location.
- The election of directors of the corporation may be held by electronic transmission.
- Directors' actions by unanimous consent may be taken by electronic transmission.

The use of electronic transmissions, electronic networks, and communications by e-mail will make the operation and administration of corporate affairs more efficient.

dealing with the corporation, secretly usurping a corporate opportunity, or making secret profits from bribes. If a director or officer breaches his or her duty of loyalty and makes a secret profit on a transaction, the corporation can sue the director or officer to recover the secret profit.

Directors' and Officers' Duty of Care

The **duty of care** requires corporate directors and officers to use *care and diligence* when acting on behalf of the corporation. To meet this duty, the directors and officers must discharge their duties (1) in good faith, (2) with the care that an *ordinary prudent person* in a like position would use under similar circumstances, and (3) in a manner that he or she reasonably believes to be in the best interests of the corporation [RMBCA Sections 8.30 (a) and 8.42(a)].

Duty of care A responsibility of corporate directors and officers to use care and diligence when acting on behalf of the corporation.

Negligence Failure of a corporate director or officer to exercise the duty of care while conducting the corporation's business.

A director or officer who breaches this duty of care is personally liable to the corporation and its shareholders for any damages caused by the breach. Such breaches, which normally are caused by **negligence**, often involve a director's or officer's failure to (1) make a reasonable investigation of a corporate matter, (2) attend board meetings on a regular basis, (3) properly supervise any subordinate who causes a loss to the corporation through embezzlement and such, or (4) stay adequately informed about corporate affairs. Breaches are examined by the courts on a case-by-case basis.

The determination of whether a corporate director or officer has met his or her duty of care is measured as of the time the decision is made. The benefit of hindsight is not a factor. Therefore, the directors and officers are not liable to the corporation or its shareholders for honest mistakes of judgment. This is called the **business judgment rule**.

Business judgment rule A rule stating that directors and officers are not liable to the corporation or its shareholders for honest mistakes of judgment.

> **Example** Suppose, after conducting considerable research and investigation, the directors of a major automobile company decide to produce a large, expensive automobile. When the car is introduced to the public for sale, few of the automobiles are sold because the public is interested in buying smaller, less expensive automobiles. Because this was an honest mistake of judgment on the part of corporate management personnel, their judgment is shielded by the business judgment rule.

Sarbanes-Oxley Act

In the late 1990s and early 2000s, many large corporations in the United States were found to have engaged in massive financial frauds. Many of these frauds were perpetrated by the chief executive officers and other senior officers of the companies. Financial officers, such as chief financial officers and controllers, were also found to have been instrumental in committing these frauds.

In response, Congress enacted the **Sarbanes-Oxley Act of 2002 (SOX)**, which makes certain conduct by public companies and their directors and officers illegal and establishes criminal penalties for violations. SOX also prompts public companies to adopt a code of ethics. Section 406 of the Sarbanes-Oxley Act requires a public company to disclose whether it has adopted a code of ethics for senior financial officers, including its principal financial officer and principal accounting officer. In response, public companies have adopted codes of ethics for their senior financial officers. Many public companies have included all officers and employees in the coverage of their codes of ethics.

A typical code of ethics is illustrated in Exhibit 18.14.

Bankruptcy

The extension of credit from creditors to debtors in commercial and personal transactions is important to the viability of the U.S. and world economies. On occasion, however, borrowers become overextended and are unable to meet their debt obligations. Federal bankruptcy law provides methods for debtors to be relieved of some debt in order to obtain a "fresh start."

Prior to 2005, the most recent overhaul of federal bankruptcy law occurred in 1978. The 1978 law was structured to make it easier for debtors to be relieved of much of their debt by declaring bankruptcy. The 1978 act was deemed "debtor friendly" because it allowed many debtors to escape from their unsecured debts.

Bankruptcy Abuse Prevention and Consumer Protection Act of 2005 A federal act that substantially amended federal bankruptcy law. It makes it more difficult for debtors to file for bankruptcy and have their unpaid debts discharged.

After a decade of lobbying by credit card companies and banks, Congress enacted the **Bankruptcy Abuse Prevention and Consumer Protection Act of 2005**. The 2005 act makes it much more difficult for debtors to escape from their debts under federal bankruptcy law. The 2005 act, which has been criticized by consumer groups for being too "creditor friendly," has been praised by many businesses, banks, and credit card issuers.

Exhibit 18.14	**Code of ethics**

Big Cheese Corporation
Code of Ethics

Big Cheese Corporation's mission includes the promotion of professional conduct in the practice of general management worldwide. Big Cheese's Chief Executive Officer (CEO), Chief Financial Officer (CFO), corporate Controller, and other employees of the finance organization and other employees of the corporation hold an important and elevated role in the corporate governance of the corporation. They are empowered and uniquely capable to ensure that all constituents' interests are appropriately balanced, protected, and preserved.

This Code of Ethics embodies principles to which we are expected to adhere and advocate. The CEO, CFO, finance organization employees, and other employees of the corporation are expected to abide by this Code of Ethics and all business conduct standards of the corporation relating to areas covered by this Code of Ethics. Any violation of the Code of Ethics may result in disciplinary action, up to and including termination of employment. All employees will:

- Act with honesty and integrity, avoiding actual or apparent conflicts of interest in their personal and professional relations.
- Provide stakeholders with information that is accurate, fair, complete, timely, objective, relevant, and understandable, including in our filings with and other submissions to the U.S. Securities and Exchange Commission.
- Comply with rules and regulations of federal, state, provincial, and local governments and other appropriate private and public regulatory agencies.
- Act in good faith, responsibly, with due care, competence, and diligence, without misrepresenting material facts or allowing one's independent judgment to be subordinated.
- Respect the confidentiality of information acquired in the course of one's work, except when authorized or otherwise legally obligated to disclose. Confidential information acquired in the course of one's work will not be used for personal advantage.
- Share knowledge and maintain professional skills important and relevant to stakeholders' needs.
- Proactively promote and be an example of ethical behavior as a responsible partner among peers, in the work environment and the community.
- Achieve responsible use, control, and stewardship over all Big Cheese's assets and resources that are employed or entrusted to us.
- Not unduly or fraudulently influence, coerce, manipulate, or mislead any authorized audit or interfere with any auditor engaged in the performance of an internal or independent audit of Big Cheese's financial statements or accounting books and records.

If you are aware of any suspected or known violations of this Code of Ethics or other Big Cheese policies or guidelines, you have a duty to promptly report such concerns either to your manager, another responsible member of management, a Human Resources representative, or the Director of Compliance or the 24-hour Business Conduct Line.

If you have a concern about a questionable accounting or auditing matter and wish to submit the concern confidentially or anonymously, you may do so by sending an e-mail to (bc.codeofethics@bigcheese.cc) or calling the Business Conduct Line 24-hour number at 1-888-666-BIGC (2442).

Big Cheese will handle all inquiries discreetly and make every effort to maintain, within the limits allowed by law, the confidentiality of anyone requesting guidance or reporting questionable behavior and/or a compliance concern.

It is Big Cheese's intention that this Code of Ethics to be its written code of ethics under Section 406 of the Sarbanes-Oxley Act of 2002 complying with the standards set forth in Securities and Exchange Commission Regulation S-K Item 406.

Types of Bankruptcy

Four special chapters of the Bankruptcy Code provide different types of bankruptcy under which individual and business debtors may be granted remedy. These four types of bankruptcies established by the 2005 act are:

Chapter	Type of Bankruptcy
Chapter 7	Liquidation
Chapter 11	Reorganization
Chapter 12	Adjustment of debts of a family farmer or fisherman with regular income
Chapter 13	Adjustment of debts of an individual with regular income

Congress created a system of federal **bankruptcy courts.** These special courts are necessary because the number of bankruptcies would overwhelm the federal district courts. The bankruptcy courts are part of the federal court system, and one bankruptcy court is attached to each of the 96 U.S. district courts located across the country.

Bankruptcy courts Special federal courts that hear and decide bankruptcy cases.

CAREER OPPORTUNITIES FOR PARALEGALS IN BANKRUPTCY LAW

For years, many paralegals have worked in the area of federal bankruptcy law. In the past, the majority of bankruptcy filings were for Chapter 7 liquidation bankruptcy. This type of bankruptcy was easy to file, and debtors were usually able to walk away from most of their unsecured credit such as credit card debt. This type of bankruptcy was "debtor friendly." Chapter 7 bankruptcy required the completion of forms, and was procedurally oriented. Paralegals were important in completing these forms and assisting in the completion of the bankruptcy proceeding.

However, the Bankruptcy Abuse Prevention and Consumer Protection Act of 2005 was enacted to make it more difficult for debtors to obtain Chapter 7 liquidation bankruptcy. The new act establishes detailed income and means tests that must be met before a debtor qualifies for Chapter 7 bankruptcy. The new law is designed to force many debtors into Chapter 13 bankruptcy, a form of rehabilitation bankruptcy that requires debtors to use part of their future income to pay off some of their preexisting debts. The 2005 act also establishes certain requirements that must be met by a debtor before qualifying for Chapter 13 bankruptcy. The 2005 act is said to be "creditor friendly."

The 2005 act provides for Chapter 12 bankruptcy, a special type of rehabilitation bankruptcy designed for family farmers and family fisherman. In addition, the 2005 act also made some changes to Chapter 11 bankruptcy, a form of bankruptcy usually used by large corporations to reorganize their financial structure. Chapter 11 is a very complicated form of bankruptcy, and requires a special knowledge of debtor and creditor rights. The 2005 act also made some procedural changes to federal bankruptcy law.

What does this mean for paralegals either working in or interested in working in the bankruptcy field? The area of federal bankruptcy law is more complex than before. This will require that the paralegal learn substantive knowledge of the different forms of bankruptcy and how to determine who qualifies for each form of bankruptcy. Second, the procedures for filing and maintaining a bankruptcy are also more detailed. Therefore, paralegals who work in the bankruptcy field will be required to acquire a greater knowledge of bankruptcy procedures than before.

In the future, many paralegals will find opportunities to work in the field of bankruptcy law. Lawyers and paralegals will be called upon to assist debtors as well as creditors in bankruptcy proceedings. The bankruptcy field will continue to offer jobs for the well-educated and well-trained paralegal professional.

Bankruptcy Procedure

The Bankruptcy Code provides procedures and requirements for filing petitions for bankruptcy, defines the bankruptcy estate, provides certain protections to debtors during the course of bankruptcy, and establishes the rights of creditors.

The 2005 act added a new provision that requires an individual filing for bankruptcy to receive prepetition and postpetition credit and financial counseling. The debtor must receive prepetition credit counseling within 180 days prior to the debtor filing his or her petition for bankruptcy. In addition, the 2005 act requires that before an individual debtor receives a discharge in a Chapter 7 or Chapter 13 bankruptcy, the debtor must attend a personal financial management course.

Petition A document filed with the bankruptcy court that starts a bankruptcy proceeding.

A bankruptcy case is commenced when a **petition** is filed with the bankruptcy court. A debtor can file a **voluntary petition** in Chapter 7 (liquidation), Chapter 11 (reorganization), Chapter 12 (family farmer or fisherman), and Chapter 13 (adjustment of debts) bankruptcy cases.

A creditor or creditors can file an **involuntary petition** and place a debtor into bankruptcy in Chapter 7 (liquidation) and Chapter 11 (reorganization) cases if certain requirements are met. An involuntary petition cannot be filed in Chapter 12 (family farmer or fisherman) or Chapter 13 (adjustment of debts).

The 2005 act places a new burden on attorneys who represent debtors in bankruptcy. The 2005 act requires the attorney to certify the accuracy of the information contained in the bankruptcy petition and the schedules, under penalty of perjury. If there are any factual discrepancies, the attorney is subject to monetary fines and sanctions. Many attorneys may no longer be willing to represent debtors in bankruptcy because of this rule.

A creditor must file a **proof of claim** stating the amount of his or her claim against the debtor. The proof of claim must be timely filed, which generally means within six months of the first meeting of the creditors. A secured creditor whose claim exceeds the value of the collateral may submit a proof of claim and become an unsecured claimant as to the difference. An equity security holder (e.g., a shareholder of a corporation) must file a **proof of interest.**

A **trustee** must be appointed in the following types of bankruptcy cases: Chapter 7 (liquidation), Chapter 12 (family farmer or family fisherman), and Chapter 13 (adjustment of debts). A trustee may be appointed in a Chapter 11 (reorganization) case upon a showing of fraud, dishonesty, incompetence, or gross mismanagement of the affairs of the debtor by current management. Once appointed, a trustee becomes a legal representative of the debtor's estate.

Exhibit 18.15 sets forth a voluntary petition for bankruptcy that would be filed by a debtor. Exhibit 18.16 sets forth a proof of claim form that would be filed by a creditor.

The Bankruptcy Estate

The **bankruptcy estate** is created upon the commencement of a bankruptcy case. It includes all the debtor's legal and equitable interests in real, personal, tangible, and intangible property, wherever located, that exist when the petition is filed, and all interests of the debtor and the debtor's spouse in community property. Gifts, inheritances, life insurance proceeds, and property from divorce settlements that the debtor is entitled to receive within 180 days after the petition is filed become part of the bankruptcy estate.

Earnings from services performed by an individual debtor are not part of the bankruptcy estate in a Chapter 7 (liquidation) bankruptcy. However, the 2005 act provides that a certain amount of postpetition earnings from services performed by the debtor may be required to be paid as part of the completion of Chapter 12 (family farmer or family fisherman), Chapter 11 (reorganization), and Chapter 13 (adjustment of debts) cases.

Because the Bankruptcy Code is not designed to make the debtor a pauper, certain property is exempt from the bankruptcy estate. The debtor may retain exempt property. **Exempt property** is property of the debtor that he or she can keep and that does not become part of the bankruptcy estate. The creditors cannot claim this property. Federal bankruptcy law establishes federal exemptions, but permits states to enact their own exemptions.

The federal Bankruptcy Code permits homeowners to claim a **homestead exemption** in their principal residence. The 2005 act limits abusive homestead exemptions. The 2005 act provides that a debtor may not exempt an amount greater than $125,000 if the property was acquired by the debtor within 1,215 days (approximately three years and four months) before the filing of the petition for bankruptcy.

The 2005 act gives the bankruptcy court the power to void certain **fraudulent transfers** of the debtor's property and obligations incurred by the debtor within two years of the filing of the petition for bankruptcy.

Chapter 7: Liquidation

Chapter 7 liquidation bankruptcy (also called **straight bankruptcy**) is a familiar form of bankruptcy. In this type of bankruptcy proceeding, the debtor is permitted to keep a substantial portion of his or her assets (*exempt assets*), the debtor's nonexempt property is sold for cash and the cash is distributed to the creditors, and any of the debtor's unpaid debts are discharged. The debtor's future income cannot be reached to pay the discharged debt. Thus, a debtor would be left to start life anew without the burden of his or her prepetition debts.

The 2005 act substantially restricts the ability of many debtors to obtain a Chapter 7 liquidation bankruptcy. The 2005 act added certain *median income* and dollar-based *means* tests that must be met before a debtor is permitted to obtain a

Trustee A legal representative of a debtor's estate.

Bankruptcy estate A debtor's property and earnings that comprise the estate of a bankruptcy proceeding.

Exempt property Property that may be retained by a debtor pursuant to federal or state law that does not become part of the bankruptcy estate.

Homestead exemption Equity in a debtor's home that the debtor is permitted to retain.

Chapter 7 liquidation A form of bankruptcy in which the debtor's nonexempt property is sold for cash, the cash is distributed to the creditors, and any unpaid debts are discharged.

Exhibit 18.15 Voluntary petition for bankruptcy

B 1 (Official Form 1) (1/08)

AZB

United States Bankruptcy Court	**Voluntary Petition**

Name of Debtor (if individual, enter Last, First, Middle):	Name of Joint Debtor (Spouse) (Last, First, Middle):
All Other Names used by the Debtor in the last 8 years (include married, maiden, and trade names):	All Other Names used by the Joint Debtor in the last 8 years (include married, maiden, and trade names):
Last four digits of Soc. Sec. or Indvidual-Taxpayer I.D. (ITIN) No./Complete EIN (if more than one, state all):	Last four digits of Soc. Sec. or Indvidual-Taxpayer I.D. (ITIN) No./Complete EIN (if more than one, state all):
Street Address of Debtor (No. and Street, City, and State): ZIP CODE	Street Address of Joint Debtor (No. and Street, City, and State): ZIP CODE
County of Residence or of the Principal Place of Business:	County of Residence or of the Principal Place of Business:
Mailing Address of Debtor (if different from street address): ZIP CODE	Mailing Address of Joint Debtor (if different from street address): ZIP CODE
Location of Principal Assets of Business Debtor (if different from street address above): ZIP CODE	

Type of Debtor
(Form of Organization)
(Check **one** box.)

☐ Individual (includes Joint Debtors)
    See Exhibit D on page 2 of this form.
☐ Corporation (includes LLC and LLP)
☐ Partnership
☐ Other (If debtor is not one of the above entities, check this box and state type of entity below.)

_____

Nature of Business
(Check **one** box.)

☐ Health Care Business
☐ Single Asset Real Estate as defined in 11 U.S.C. § 101(51B)
☐ Railroad
☐ Stockbroker
☐ Commodity Broker
☐ Clearing Bank
☐ Other

Tax-Exempt Entity
(Check box, if applicable.)

☐ Debtor is a tax-exempt organization under Title 26 of the United States Code (the Internal Revenue Code).

Chapter of Bankruptcy Code Under Which the Petition is Filed (Check **one** box.)

☐ Chapter 7
☐ Chapter 9
☐ Chapter 11
☐ Chapter 12
☐ Chapter 13
☐ Chapter 15 Petition for Recognition of a Foreign Main Proceeding
☐ Chapter 15 Petition for Recognition of a Foreign Nonmain Proceeding

Nature of Debts
(Check one box.)

☐ Debts are primarily consumer debts, defined in 11 U.S.C. § 101(8) as "incurred by an individual primarily for a personal, family, or household purpose."
☐ Debts are primarily business debts.

Filing Fee (Check one box.)

☐ Full Filing Fee attached.

☐ Filing Fee to be paid in installments (applicable to individuals only). Must attach signed application for the court's consideration certifying that the debtor is unable to pay fee except in installments. Rule 1006(b). See Official Form 3A.

☐ Filing Fee waiver requested (applicableto chapter 7 individuals only). Must attach signed application for the court's consideration. See Official Form 3B.

Chapter 11 Debtors

Check one box:
☐ Debtor is a small business debtor as defined in 11 U.S.C. § 101(51D).
☐ Debtor is not a small business debtor as defined in 11 U.S.C. § 101(51D).

Check if:
☐ Debtor's aggregate noncontingent liquidated debts (excluding debts owed to insiders or affiliates) are less than $2,190,000.
- -
Check all applicable boxes:
☐ A plan is being filed with this petition.
☐ Acceptances of the plan were solicited prepetition from one or more classes of creditors, in accordance with 11 U.S.C. § 1126(b).

Statistical/Administrative Information

☐ Debtor estimates that funds will be available for distribution to unsecured creditors.
☐ Debtor estimates that, after any exempt property is excluded and administrative expenses paid, there will be no funds available for distribution to unsecured creditors.

THIS SPACE IS FOR COURT USE ONLY

Estimated Number of Creditors

☐	☐	☐	☐	☐	☐	☐	☐	☐	☐
1-49	50-99	100-199	200-999	1,000-5,000	5,001-10,000	10,001-25,000	25,001-50,000	50,001-100,000	Over 100,000

Estimated Assets

☐	☐	☐	☐	☐	☐	☐	☐	☐	☐
$0 to $50,000	$50,001 to $100,000	$100,001 to $500,000	$500,001 to $1 million	$1,000,001 to $10 million	$10,000,001 to $50 million	$50,000,001 to $100 million	$100,000,001 to $500 million	$500,000,001 to $1 billion	More than $1 billion

Estimated Liabilities

☐	☐	☐	☐	☐	☐	☐	☐	☐	☐
$0 to $50,000	$50,001 to $100,000	$100,001 to $500,000	$500,001 to $1 million	$1,000,001 to $10 million	$10,000,001 to $50 million	$50,000,001 to $100 million	$100,000,001 to $500 million	$500,000,001 to $1 billion	More than $1 billion

Exhibit 18.15 **Voluntary petition for bankruptcy** *(continued)*

B 1 (Official Form 1) (1/08)

Voluntary Petition *(This page must be completed and filed in every case.)*	**Name of Debtor(s):**

All Prior Bankruptcy Cases Filed Within Last 8 Years (If more than two, attach additional sheet.)

Location Where Filed:	Case Number:	Date Filed:
Location Where Filed:	Case Number:	Date Filed:

Pending Bankruptcy Case Filed by any Spouse, Partner, or Affiliate of this Debtor (If more than one, attach additional sheet.)

Name of Debtor:	Case Number:	Date Filed:
District:	Relationship:	Judge:

<table>
<tr><td align="center">Exhibit A

(To be completed if debtor is required to file periodic reports (e.g., forms 10K and 10Q) with the Securities and Exchange Commission pursuant to Section 13 or 15(d) of the Securities Exchange Act of 1934 and is requesting relief under chapter 11.)

☐   Exhibit A is attached and made a part of this petition.</td><td>Exhibit B
(To be completed if debtor is an individual whose debts are primarily consumer debts.)

I, the attorney for the petitioner named in the foregoing petition, declare that I have informed the petitioner that [he or she] may proceed under chapter 7, 11, 12, or 13 of title 11, United States Code, and have explained the relief available under each such chapter. I further certify that I have delivered to the debtor the notice required by 11 U.S.C. § 342(b).

X _____
    Signature of Attorney for Debtor(s) (Date)</td></tr>
</table>

Exhibit C

Does the debtor own or have possession of any property that poses or is alleged to pose a threat of imminent and identifiable harm to public health or safety?

☐   Yes, and Exhibit C is attached and made a part of this petition.

☐   No.

Exhibit D

(To be completed by every individual debtor. If a joint petition is filed, each spouse must complete and attach a separate Exhibit D.)

☐   Exhibit D completed and signed by the debtor is attached and made a part of this petition.

If this is a joint petition:

☐   Exhibit D also completed and signed by the joint debtor is attached and made a part of this petition.

Information Regarding the Debtor - Venue
(Check any applicable box.)

☐   Debtor has been domiciled or has had a residence, principal place of business, or principal assets in this District for 180 days immediately preceding the date of this petition or for a longer part of such 180 days than in any other District.

☐   There is a bankruptcy case concerning debtor's affiliate, general partner, or partnership pending in this District.

☐   Debtor is a debtor in a foreign proceeding and has its principal place of business or principal assets in the United States in this District, or has no principal place of business or assets in the United States but is a defendant in an action or proceeding [in a federal or state court] in this District, or the interests of the parties will be served in regard to the relief sought in this District.

Certification by a Debtor Who Resides as a Tenant of Residential Property
(Check all applicable boxes.)

☐   Landlord has a judgment against the debtor for possession of debtor's residence. (If box checked, complete the following.)

_____
(Name of landlord that obtained judgment)

_____
(Address of landlord)

☐   Debtor claims that under applicable nonbankruptcy law, there are circumstances under which the debtor would be permitted to cure the entire monetary default that gave rise to the judgment for possession, after the judgment for possession was entered, and

☐   Debtor has included with this petition the deposit with the court of any rent that would become due during the 30-day period after the filing of the petition.

☐   Debtor certifies that he/she has served the Landlord with this certification. (11 U.S.C. § 362(l)).

Exhibit 18.15 **Voluntary petition for bankruptcy** *(continued)*

AZB

B 1 (Official Form) 1 (1/08)	Page 3
Voluntary Petition *(This page must be completed and filed in every case.)*	Name of Debtor(s):

Signatures

Signature(s) of Debtor(s) (Individual/Joint)	**Signature of a Foreign Representative**

Signature(s) of Debtor(s) (Individual/Joint)

I declare under penalty of perjury that the information provided in this petition is true and correct.

[If petitioner is an individual whose debts are primarily consumer debts and has chosen to file under chapter 7] I am aware that I may proceed under chapter 7, 11, 12 or 13 of title 11, United States Code, understand the relief available under each such chapter, and choose to proceed under chapter 7.

[If no attorney represents me and no bankruptcy petition preparer signs the petition] I have obtained and read the notice required by 11 U.S.C. § 342(b).

I request relief in accordance with the chapter of title 11, United States Code, specified in this petition.

X _____
    Signature of Debtor

X _____
    Signature of Joint Debtor

_____
Telephone Number (if not represented by attorney)

_____
Date

Signature of a Foreign Representative

I declare under penalty of perjury that the information provided in this petition is true and correct, that I am the foreign representative of a debtor in a foreign proceeding, and that I am authorized to file this petition.

(Check only **one** box.)

☐ I request relief in accordance with chapter 15 of title 11, United States Code. Certified copies of the documents required by 11 U.S.C. § 1515 are attached.

☐ Pursuant to 11 U.S.C. § 1511, I request relief in accordance with the chapter of title 11 specified in this petition. A certified copy of the order granting recognition of the foreign main proceeding is attached.

X _____
    (Signature of Foreign Representative)

_____
(Printed Name of Foreign Representative)

_____
Date

Signature of Attorney*

X _____
    Signature of Attorney for Debtor(s)

_____
Printed Name of Attorney for Debtor(s)

_____
Firm Name

_____
Address
_____
_____

_____
Telephone Number

_____
Date

*In a case in which § 707(b)(4)(D) applies, this signature also constitutes a certification that the attorney has no knowledge after an inquiry that the information in the schedules is incorrect.

Signature of Debtor (Corporation/Partnership)

I declare under penalty of perjury that the information provided in this petition is true and correct, and that I have been authorized to file this petition on behalf of the debtor.

The debtor requests the relief in accordance with the chapter of title 11, United States Code, specified in this petition.

X _____
    Signature of Authorized Individual

_____
Printed Name of Authorized Individual

_____
Title of Authorized Individual

_____
Date

Signature of Non-Attorney Bankruptcy Petition Preparer

I declare under penalty of perjury that: (1) I am a bankruptcy petition preparer as defined in 11 U.S.C. § 110; (2) I prepared this document for compensation and have provided the debtor with a copy of this document and the notices and information required under 11 U.S.C. §§ 110(b), 110(h), and 342(b); and, (3) if rules or guidelines have been promulgated pursuant to 11 U.S.C. § 110(h) setting a maximum fee for services chargeable by bankruptcy petition preparers, I have given the debtor notice of the maximum amount before preparing any document for filing for a debtor or accepting any fee from the debtor, as required in that section. Official Form 19 is attached.

_____
Printed Name and title, if any, of Bankruptcy Petition Preparer

_____
Social-Security number (If the bankruptcy petition preparer is not an individual, state the Social-Security number of the officer, principal, responsible person or partner of the bankruptcy petition preparer.) (Required by 11 U.S.C. § 110.)

_____
Address

_____

X _____

_____
Date

Signature of bankruptcy petition preparer or officer, principal, responsible person, or partner whose Social-Security number is provided above.

Names and Social-Security numbers of all other individuals who prepared or assisted in preparing this document unless the bankruptcy petition preparer is not an individual.

If more than one person prepared this document, attach additional sheets conforming to the appropriate official form for each person.

A bankruptcy petition preparer's failure to comply with the provisions of title 11 and the Federal Rules of Bankruptcy Procedure may result in fines or imprisonment or both. 11 U.S.C. § 110; 18 U.S.C. § 156.

Exhibit 18.16 Proof of claim

B 10 (Official Form 10) (12/08)

UNITED STATES BANKRUPTCY COURT _____ DISTRICT OF _____	**PROOF OF CLAIM**
Name of Debtor:	Case Number:

NOTE: *This form should not be used to make a claim for an administrative expense arising after the commencement of the case. A request for payment of an administrative expense may be filed pursuant to 11 U.S.C. § 503.*

Name of Creditor (the person or other entity to whom the debtor owes money or property):	☐ Check this box to indicate that this claim amends a previously filed claim.
Name and address where notices should be sent:	**Court Claim Number:**_____ *(If known)*
Telephone number:	Filed on:_____
Name and address where payment should be sent (if different from above):	☐ Check this box if you are aware that anyone else has filed a proof of claim relating to your claim. Attach copy of statement giving particulars.
Telephone number:	☐ Check this box if you are the debtor or trustee in this case.

1. Amount of Claim as of Date Case Filed: $_____

If all or part of your claim is secured, complete item 4 below; however, if all of your claim is unsecured, do not complete item 4.

If all or part of your claim is entitled to priority, complete item 5.

☐ Check this box if claim includes interest or other charges in addition to the principal amount of claim. Attach itemized statement of interest or charges.

2. Basis for Claim: _____
  (See instruction #2 on reverse side.)

3. Last four digits of any number by which creditor identifies debtor: _____

   3a. Debtor may have scheduled account as: _____
      (See instruction #3a on reverse side.)

4. Secured Claim (See instruction #4 on reverse side.)
   Check the appropriate box if your claim is secured by a lien on property or a right of setoff and provide the requested information.

   Nature of property or right of setoff: ☒ Real Estate   ☒ Motor Vehicle   ☒ Other
   Describe:

   Value of Property:$_____   **Annual Interest Rate**___%

   Amount of arrearage and other charges as of time case filed included in secured claim,

   if any: $_____   **Basis for perfection:** _____

   Amount of Secured Claim: $_____   **Amount Unsecured: $**_____

6. Credits: The amount of all payments on this claim has been credited for the purpose of making this proof of claim.

7. Documents: Attach redacted copies of any documents that support the claim, such as promissory notes, purchase orders, invoices, itemized statements of running accounts, contracts, judgments, mortgages, and security agreements. You may also attach a summary. Attach redacted copies of documents providing evidence of perfection of a security interest. You may also attach a summary. (*See instruction 7 and definition of "redacted" on reverse side.*)

DO NOT SEND ORIGINAL DOCUMENTS. ATTACHED DOCUMENTS MAY BE DESTROYED AFTER SCANNING.

If the documents are not available, please explain:

5. Amount of Claim Entitled to Priority under 11 U.S.C. §507(a). If any portion of your claim falls in one of the following categories, check the box and state the amount.

Specify the priority of the claim.

☒ Domestic support obligations under 11 U.S.C. §507(a)(1)(A) or (a)(1)(B).

☒ Wages, salaries, or commissions (up to $10,950*) earned within 180 days before filing of the bankruptcy petition or cessation of the debtor's business, whichever is earlier – 11 U.S.C. §507 (a)(4).

☒ Contributions to an employee benefit plan – 11 U.S.C. §507 (a)(5).

☒ Up to $2,425* of deposits toward purchase, lease, or rental of property or services for personal, family, or household use – 11 U.S.C. §507 (a)(7).

☐ Taxes or penalties owed to governmental units – 11 U.S.C. §507 (a)(8).

☒ Other – Specify applicable paragraph of 11 U.S.C. §507 (a)(___).

Amount entitled to priority:

$_____

Amounts are subject to adjustment on 4/1/10 and every 3 years thereafter with respect to cases commenced on or after the date of adjustment.

Date:	**Signature:** The person filing this claim must sign it. Sign and print name and title, if any, of the creditor or other person authorized to file this claim and state address and telephone number if different from the notice address above. Attach copy of power of attorney, if any.	**FOR COURT USE ONLY**

Penalty for presenting fraudulent claim: Fine of up to $500,000 or imprisonment for up to 5 years, or both. 18 U.S.C. §§ 152 and 3571.

Chapter 7 discharge The termination of the legal duty of a debtor to pay unsecured debts that remain unpaid upon the completion of a Chapter 7 proceeding.

discharge of debts under Chapter 7. If these tests are not met, the 2005 act provides that the debtor's Chapter 7 proceeding may, with the debtor's consent, be dismissed or be converted to a Chapter 13 or Chapter 11 bankruptcy proceeding.

In a Chapter 7 bankruptcy, the property of the estate is sold and the proceeds are distributed to satisfy allowed claims. The remaining unpaid debts that the debtor incurred prior to the date of the order for relief are discharged. **Chapter 7 discharge** means that the debtor is no longer legally responsible for paying those claims. Only individual debtors may be granted discharge. Unsecured claims are to be satisfied out of the bankruptcy estate in order of their statutory priority, as established by the Bankruptcy Code.

> **Example** Annabelle finds herself overburdened with debt, particularly credit card debt. At the time she files for Chapter 7 bankruptcy her unsecured credit is $100,000. Annabelle has few assets, and most of those are exempt property (e.g., her clothes, some furniture, and such). Her nonexempt property is $10,000, which will be sold to raise cash. The $10,000 in cash will be distributed to her debtors on a prorata basis, that is, each creditor receives ten cents for every dollar of debt owed. The other $90,000 is *discharged*, that is, the creditors have to absorb this loss. Annabelle is free from this debt forever. Annabelle is given a "fresh start" and her future earnings are hers.

Chapter 13 adjustment of debts of an individual with regular income A rehabilitation form of bankruptcy that permits bankruptcy courts to supervise the debtor's plan for the payment of unpaid debts in installments over the plan period.

Chapter 13 discharge A discharge in a Chapter 13 case that is granted to the debtor after the debtor's plan of payment is completed (which could be up to three or up to five years).

Chapter 13: Adjustment of Debts of an Individual with Regular Income

Chapter 13, which is called **adjustment of debts of an individual with regular income,** is a rehabilitation form of bankruptcy for individuals. Chapter 13 permits qualified debtors to propose a plan to pay all or a portion of the debts that he or she owes in installments over a specified period of time, pursuant to the requirements of Chapter 13. The bankruptcy court supervises the debtor's plan for the payment. A Chapter 13 proceeding can be initiated only by the voluntary filing of a petition by an individual debtor with regular income. The 2005 act establishes dollar limits on the secured and unsecured debt that a debtor may have in order to qualify to file for Chapter 13 bankruptcy.

The debtor must file a plan of payment and information about his or her finances, including a budget of estimated income and expenses during the period of the plan. The Chapter 13 plan may be either up to three years or up to five years, depending on requirements established by the 2005 act. A Chapter 13 plan of payment may modify the rights of unsecured creditors and some secured creditors.

The court will grant an order discharging the debtor from all unpaid unsecured debts covered by the plan after all the payments required under the plan are completed (which could be up to three years or up to five years). This is called a **Chapter 13 discharge**.

> **Example** Annabelle owes unsecured credit of $100,000. Annabelle earns too high an income to qualify for Chapter 7 bankruptcy, so she files for Chapter 13 bankruptcy. Her plan of payment is accepted by the court whereby she will pay $700

DISCHARGE OF STUDENT LOANS

During college and other professional schools, many students borrow money for their tuition and living expenses. Upon graduation, when a student might have large student loans and very few assets, the student might be inclined to file for bankruptcy in an attempt to have his or her student loans discharged.

To prevent such abuse of bankruptcy law, Congress amended the Bankruptcy Code to make it more difficult for students to have their student loans discharged in bankruptcy. Student loans are defined by the Bankruptcy Code to include loans made by or guaranteed by governmental units. The 2005 act added student loans made by nongovernmental commercial institutions, such as banks, as well as funds for scholarships, benefits, or stipends granted by educational institutions.

The Bankruptcy Code now states that student loans can be discharged in bankruptcy only if the nondischarge would cause an "undue hardship" to the debtor and his or her dependants. Undue hardship is construed strictly and would be difficult for a debtor to prove unless he or she could show severe physical or mental disability or that he or she is unable to pay for the basic necessities of food or shelter for himself or herself and any dependents.

Cosigners (e.g., parents who guarantee their child's student loan) must also meet the heightened undue hardship test to discharge their obligation.

disposable income each month for five years toward her prepetition debts. During the five-year period, Annabelle's lifestyle will be reduced considerably because she is paying her disposable income to pay off her prepetition debt. At the end of five years she has paid $42,000 (60 months $\times$ $700) toward her debt; at that time her unpaid prepetition debt of $58,000 ($100,000 − $42,000) is discharged.

Chapter 11: Reorganization

Chapter 11 of the Bankruptcy Code provides a method for reorganizing a debtor's financial affairs under the supervision of the bankruptcy court. The goal of Chapter 11 is to reorganize the debtor with a new capital structure so that it will emerge from bankruptcy as a viable concern. This option is referred to as **reorganization bankruptcy.** The majority of Chapter 11 proceedings are filed by corporations that want to reorganize their capital structures by receiving discharge of a portion of their debts, obtain relief from burdensome contracts, and emerge from bankruptcy as going concerns.

In a Chapter 11 proceeding, the court will appoint a **creditors' committee** composed of representatives of the class of unsecured claims. The court may also appoint a committee of secured creditors and a committee of equity holders. Committees may appear at bankruptcy court hearings, participate in the negotiation of a plan of reorganization, assert objections to proposed plans of reorganization, and the like.

The debtor has the exclusive right to file a **plan of reorganization** with the bankruptcy court within the first 120 days after the date of the order for relief. Under the 2005 act, this period may be extended up to 18 months. If the debtor fails to do so, any party of interest (e.g., a trustee, a creditor, an equity holder) may propose a plan.

A debtor in a Chapter 11 bankruptcy has the following benefits:

1. *Automatic stay.* The filing of a Chapter 11 petition stays (i.e., suspends) actions by creditors to recover the debtor's property. This **automatic stay** suspends legal actions against the debtor or the debtor's property, including the ability of creditors to foreclose on assets given as collateral for their loans to the debtor. An automatic stay is extremely important to a business trying to reorganize under Chapter 11 because the debtor needs to keep its assets to stay in business.

   Example Big Oil Company owns a manufacturing plant and has borrowed $50 million from a bank and used the plant as collateral for the loan. If Big Oil Company files for Chapter 11 bankruptcy, the automatic stay prevents the bank from foreclosing and taking the property. Once out of bankruptcy, Big Oil Company must pay the bank any unpaid arrearages and begin making the required loan payments again.

2. *Executory contract or unexpired lease.* Another major benefit of Chapter 11 bankruptcy is that the debtor is given the opportunity to accept or reject certain executory contracts and unexpired leases. An **executory contract or unexpired lease** is a contract or lease that has not been fully performed.

   Example Big Oil Company enters into a three-year contract to sell oil to another company, and there is two years to go on the contract when the oil company files for Chapter 11 bankruptcy. This is an *executory contract.* Big Oil Company has leased an office building for 20 years from a landlord to use as its headquarters, and there is 15 years left on the lease when the oil company declares bankruptcy. This is an *unexpired lease.* In the Chapter 11 reorganization proceeding, Big Oil Company can reject (get out of) either the executory

Chapter 11 reorganization A bankruptcy method that allows the reorganization of the debtor's financial affairs under the supervision of the bankruptcy court.

Plan of reorganization A plan that sets forth a proposed new capital structure for the debtor to have when it emerges from Chapter 11 reorganization bankruptcy.

Executory contract or unexpired lease A contract or lease that has not been fully performed. With the bankruptcy court's approval, executor contracts and unexpired leases may be rejected by a debtor in bankruptcy.

contract or the unexpired lease without any liability; it can keep either one if it is in its best interests to do so.

3. *Discharge.* In its plan of reorganization, the debtor will propose reducing its unsecured debt so that it can come out of bankruptcy with fewer debts to pay than when it filed for bankruptcy. If the plan is approved by the creditors and the court, the court will confirm the plan of reorganization. Any unsecured debt that is not carried forward with the reorganized firm is **discharged**, that is, the creditors have to absorb this loss.

Example Big Oil Company has $100 million secured debts (e.g., real estate mortgages and personal property secured transactions) and $100 million unsecured credit when it files for Chapter 11 bankruptcy. In its plan of reorganization, Big Oil Company proposes to eliminate 60 percent—$60 million—of unsecured credit. If the unsecured creditors agree and the court approves, then Big Oil will emerge from bankruptcy owing only $40 million of prepetition unsecured debt. The other $60 million is discharged and the creditors can never recover these debts in the future.

Confirmation The bankruptcy court's approval of a plan of reorganization.

There must be **confirmation** of the plan of reorganization by the bankruptcy court for the debtor to be reorganized under Chapter 11. The bankruptcy court will confirm a plan of reorganization under the acceptance method if the plan is feasible (that is, the new reorganized company is likely to succeed if other necessary requirements are met). If a class of creditors does not accept the plan, the plan can still be confirmed by the court, using the Bankruptcy Code's **cram-down provision.** In order for the court to confirm a plan over the objection of a class of creditors, certain requirements as established by bankruptcy law must be met.

Chapter 12: Family Farmer and Family Fisherman Bankruptcy

The 2005 act establishes special definitions and rules that allow family farmers and family fisherman to file for bankruptcy reorganization under **Chapter 12—adjustment of debts of a family farmer or fisherman with regular income**. *Family farmer* and *family fisherman* are defined by the 2005 act.

Chapter 12—adjustment of debts of a family farmer or family fisherman with regular income A form of bankruptcy reorganization permitted to be used by family farmers and family fishermen.

The family farmer or family fisherman debtor must file a plan of reorganization. Generally, the plan may provide for payments to creditors over a period no longer than three years, but the court can increase the period to up to five years based on a showing of cause. The plan of reorganization must be confirmed by the court before it becomes operable. The plan of reorganization can modify the rights of secured creditors and unsecured creditors.

Once the family farmer or family fisherman debtor has completed making all payments required by the plan (which is usually three years but could be up to five years), the bankruptcy court will grant the debtor discharge of all debts provided for by the plan. This is called a **Chapter 12 discharge**.

Chapter 12 discharge A discharge in a Chapter 12 case that is granted to a family farmer or family fisherman debtor after the debtor's plan of payment is completed (which is usually three years but could be up to five years).

Example If a Chapter 12 plan calls for the debtor to pay 55 percent of the outstanding unsecured debt to the unsecured creditors and this amount has been paid by the debtor during the plan period, the court will grant discharge of the unpaid 45 percent of this unsecured debt. A paralegal's duty not to use confidential information is discussed in the Ethical Perspective Feature on page 695.

ETHICAL PERSPECTIVE

Duty Not to Use Confidential Information

Mr. Drovski is a paralegal who works at a very large law firm that represents major corporate clients. Mr. Drovski works directly for Ms. Ross, a senior partner of the law firm and an expert in mergers and acquisitions law.

One day Ms. Ross asks Mr. Drovski to accompany her to a meeting at the corporate offices of MicroHard Corporation, a client of the law firm. The corporation is one of the largest multinational corporations in the United States. Ms. Wong, the Chief Executive Officer (CEO) of MicroHard Corporation, and other top corporate officers of the corporation, attend the meeting.

At the meeting, Ms. Wong and the other executives disclose that they want MicroHard Corporation to make a secret tender offer to purchase the stock of Quail Technology Inc. from the shareholders of Quail Technology Inc. Ms. Wong explains that Quail Technology Inc. holds many patents that would be beneficial to MicroHard Corporation. Ms. Wong discloses that it wants Ms. Ross and her law firm to draft the documents necessary to make this secret tender offer. The drafting of these documents will take three weeks. Ms. Ross agrees, on behalf of her law firm, to represent MicroHard Corporation and draft the legal documents necessary for MicroHard Corporation's acquisition of Quail Technology Inc.

Ms. Wong further discloses that the purchase price that MicroHard Corporation will offer for each share of Quail Technology Inc. stock in the tender offer will be $50 per share. Quail Technology Inc.'s stock is currently priced at $30 per share on the New York Stock Exchange.

Ms. Wong states that preparation of the legal documents for the tender offer is an utmost secret and must remain so while Ms. Ross and her law firm prepare the necessary documents for the tender offer. Ms. Ross assures Ms. Wong that she and the personnel of her law firm will keep the tender offer secret while they draft the necessary legal documents for the tender offer. Mr. Drovski, the paralegal, has sat through the entire meeting and has heard everything that has been said.

Later that day, Mr. Drovski, the paralegal, is tempted to call a securities broker and purchase 4,000 shares of stock of Quail Technology Inc.

Does Mr. Drovski owe a duty not to use this confidential information to benefit himself?

Many model and state paralegal professional codes of ethics and responsibility provide that a paralegal should not use confidential information obtained while he or she is working as a paralegal. A violation could lead to the paralegal being censored or other disciplinary actions by paralegal licensing agencies, cause pecuniary loss to the law firm's clients, cause loss to the law firm such as losing the trust of a client and possibly losing the client, and the paralegal could be sued for violating the law, in this case both state and federal securities laws.

PARALEGAL'S ETHICAL DECISION

Thus, Mr. Drovski owes an ethical duty not to use the confidential information that he has heard regarding MicroHard Corporation's proposed tender offer for shares of Quail Technology Inc. stock. To do so would violate paralegal ethical and social responsibility codes, the law firm's rules, and the law. Mr. Drovski must refrain from using the confidential information for his own benefit or that of others.

Concept Review *and* Reinforcement

LEGAL TERMINOLOGY

Alien corporation 674

Alter-ego doctrine 681

Articles of incorporation 675

Articles of partnership 663

Articles of limited liability partnership 666

Articles of limited partnership 666

Articles of organization 671

Automatic stay 693

Bankruptcy Abuse Prevention and Consumer Protection Act of 2005 684

Bankruptcy court 685

Bankruptcy estate 687

Board of directors 681

Business judgment rule 684

Business organizations 658

Bylaws 675

C corporation 678

Certificate of limited partnership 665

Chapter 7 liquidation (straight bankruptcy) 694

Chapter 11 reorganization 693

Chapter 12 adjustment of debts of a family farmer or family fisherman with regular income 694

Chapter 12 discharge 694

Chapter 13 adjustment of debts for an individual with regular income 692

Chapter 13 discharge 692

Common stock 678

Common stockholder (common shareholders) 678

Confirmation 694

Corporate bylaws 675

Corporate charter 675

Corporate officers 673

Corporate resolutions 678

Corporation 672

Cram-down provision 694

Creditors' committee 693

d.b.a. (doing business as) 659

Delaware General Corporation Law 680

Discharge 692

Disregard of the corporate entity 680

Domestic corporation 674

Duty of care 683

Duty of loyalty 682

Entity theory 662

Executory contract or unexpired lease 693

Exempt property 687

Fictitious business name statement 659

Foreign corporation 674

Form 2553 678

Fraudulent transfer 687

General partner 661

General partnership 661

Homestead exemption 687

Incorporation 675

Indemnification 663

Inside director 682

Involuntary petition 686

Joint liability 663

Joint and several liability 663

Limited liability 666

Limited liability company (LLC) 670

Limited liability partnership (LLP) 666

Limited partner 665

Limited partnership 664

Limited partnership agreement 666

Member 670

Negligence 684

Officer of the corporation 682

Operating agreement 671

Organizational meeting 678

Outside director 682

Partner 661

Partnership 661

Partnership agreement 661

Partnership at will 663

Partnership for a term 663

Personal liability 660

Petition for bankruptcy 686

Piercing the corporate veil 680

Plan of reorganization 693

Proof of claim 687

Proof of interest 687

Reorganization bankruptcy 693

Revised Model Business Corporation Act (RMBCA) 673

Revised Uniform Limited Partnership Act (RULPA) 664

S corporation 678

Sarbanes-Oxley Act of 2002 (SOX) 684

Shareholder 672

Sole proprietor 658

Sole proprietorship 658

State of incorporation 675

Trustee 687

Uniform Limited Liability Company Act (ULLCA) 670

Uniform Limited Liability Partnership Act (ULLPA) 666

Uniform Limited Partnership Act (ULPA) 664

Uniform Partnership Act (UPA) 662

Unlimited liability 666

Voluntary petition 686

Wrongful dissolution 664

SUMMARY OF KEY CONCEPTS

Sole Proprietorship

Definition	A sole proprietorship is a form of business in which the owner and the business are one; the business is not a separate legal entity.
Business Name	A sole proprietorship can operate under the name of the sole proprietor, or a *trade name*. Operating under a trade name is commonly designated as *d.b.a. (doing business as)*. If a trade name is used, a *fictitious business name statement* must be filed with the appropriate state government office.
Liability	The sole proprietor is personally liable for the debts and obligations of the sole proprietorship.

General Partnership

Definition	A general partnership is an association of two or more persons to carry on as co-owners of a business for profit [UPA Section 6(1)].
Uniform Partnership Act (UPA)	The UPA is a model act that codifies partnership law. Most states have adopted all or part of the UPA.
Entity Theory of Partnerships	The entity theory holds that partnerships are *separate legal entities* that can hold title to personal and real property, transact business in the partnership name, and the like.
Taxation of Partnerships	Partnerships do not pay federal income taxes; the income and losses of partnerships flow onto individual partners' federal income tax returns.
Partnership Agreement	The partnership agreement establishes a general partnership and sets forth terms of the partnership. It is good practice to have a written partnership agreement that the partners sign.
Partners' Contract Authority	A contract entered into by a partner with a third party on behalf of a partnership is binding on the partnership.
Tort Liability	1. *Tort:* A partner causes injury to a third party by his or her negligent act, breach of trust, breach of fiduciary duty, or intentional tort. 2. *Partnership liability:* The partnership is liable to third persons who are injured by torts committed by a partner while he or she is acting within the ordinary course of partnership business. 3. *Joint and several liability of partners:* Partners are personally liable for torts committed by partners acting on partnership business. This liability is *joint and several*, which means that the plaintiff can sue one or more of the partners separately. If successful, the plaintiff can recover the entire amount of the judgment from any or all of the defendant-partners.
Dissolution of Partnerships	Dissolution is a change in the relation of the partners caused by any partner ceasing to be associated in carrying on the business [UPA Section 29]. Wrongful dissolution occurs when a partner withdraws from a partnership without having the *right* to do so at the time. The partner is liable for damages caused by wrongful dissolution of the partnership.

Limited Partnership

Uniform Limited Partnership Act (ULPA)	The ULPA is a 1916 model act that contains a uniform set of provisions for the formation, operation, and dissolution of limited partnerships.
Revised Uniform Limited Partnership Act (RULPA)	The RULPA is a 1976 revision of the ULPA that provides a more modern, comprehensive law for the formation, operation, and dissolution of limited partnerships.
General and Limited Partnerships	1. *General partners:* Partners in a limited partnership who invest capital, manage the business, and are personally liable for partnership debts. 2. *Limited partners:* Partners in a limited partnership who invest capital but do not participate in management and are not personally liable for partnership debts beyond their capital contributions.
Formation of Limited Partnerships	1. *Certificate of limited partnership:* A document that two or more persons must execute and sign that establishes a limited partnership. The certificate of limited partnership must be filed with the secretary of state of the appropriate state. 2. *Limited partnership agreement:* A document that sets forth the rights and duties of general and limited partners, the terms and conditions regarding the operation, termination, and dissolution of the partnership, and so on.
Liability of General and Limited Partners	1. *General partners:* General partners of a limited partnership have *unlimited personal liability* for the debts and obligations of the limited partnership. 2. *Limited partners:* Limited partners of a limited partnership are liable only for the debts and obligations of the limited partnership up to their capital contributions. 3. *Limited partners and management:* Limited partners have no right to participate in the management of the partnership. A limited partner is *liable as a general partner* if his or her participation in the control of the business is substantially the same as that of a general partner, but the limited partner is liable only to persons who reasonably believed him or her to be a general partner.

Limited Liability Partnership (LLP)

Definition	The LLP is a form of business in which there does not have to be a general partner who is personally liable for debts and obligations of the partnership. All partners are limited partners and stand to lose only their capital contribution should the partnership fail. LLPs are formed by accountants and other professionals as allowed by LLP law.
Partners	The partners are owners of an LLP.
Articles of Partnership	Articles of partnership constitute a document that the partners of an LLP must execute, sign, and file with the secretary of state of the appropriate state to form an LLP.
Taxation	An LLP does not pay federal income taxes unless it elects to do so. If an LLP is taxed as a partnership, the income and losses of the LLP flow onto individual partners' federal income tax returns.

Limited Liability Company (LLC)

Definition	The LLC is a special form of unincorporated business entity that combines the tax benefits of a partnership with the limited personal liability attribute of a corporation.
Members	Members are owners of an LLC.
Articles of Organization	Articles of organization constitute a document that owners of an LLC must execute, sign, and file with the secretary of state of the appropriate state to form an LLC.

Operating Agreement	An operating agreement is entered into among members that govern the affairs and business of the LLC and the relations among partners, managers, and the LLC.
Taxation	An LLC does not pay federal income taxes unless it elects to do so. If an LLC is taxed as a partnership, the income and losses of the LLP flow onto individual members' federal income tax returns.

Corporation

Definition	A corporation is a legal entity created pursuant to the laws of the state of incorporation. A corporation is a separate legal entity—an *artificial person*—that can own property, sue and be sued, enter into contracts, and such.
Characteristics of Corporations	1. *Limited liability of shareholders:* Shareholders are liable for the debts and obligations of the corporation only to the extent of their capital contributions. 2. *Free transferability of shares:* Shares of a corporation are freely transferable by the shareholders unless they are expressly restricted. 3. *Perpetual existence:* Corporations exist in perpetuity unless a specific duration is stated in the corporation's articles of incorporation. 4. *Centralized management: Board of directors* of the corporation makes policy decisions of the corporation. Corporate *officers* appointed by the board of directors run the corporation's day-to-day operations. Together, the directors and officers form the corporation's management.
Business Corporation Acts	1. *Model Business Corporation Act (MBCA):* A model act drafted in 1950 that was intended to provide a uniform law for the regulation of corporations. 2. *Revised Model Business Corporation Act (RMBCA):* A revision of the MBCA promulgated in 1984 that arranged the provisions of the model to act more logically, revised the language to be more consistent, and made substantial changes that modernized the provisions of the act.
Classifications of Corporations	1. *Domestic corporation:* A corporation in the state in which it is incorporated. 2. *Foreign corporation:* A corporation in any state other than the one in which it is incorporated. A domestic corporation often transacts business in states other than its state of incorporation; hence, it is a foreign corporation in these other states. A foreign corporation must obtain a *certificate of authority* from these other states to be able to transact intrastate business in those states. 3. *Alien corporation:* A corporation that is incorporated in another country. Alien corporations are treated as foreign corporations for most purposes.
Incorporation Procedure	Incorporation is the process of incorporating (forming) a new corporation. A corporation can be incorporated in only one state, although it can conduct business in other states.
Articles of Incorporation	1. The basic governing document of a corporation; must be filed with the secretary of state of the state of incorporation. This is a public document, also called the *corporate charter.* 2. The corporation code of each state sets out the information that must be included in the articles of incorporation. Additional information may be included in the articles of incorporation as deemed necessary or desirable by the incorporators.
Corporate Bylaws	Corporate bylaws are a detailed set of rules adopted by the board of directors after the corporation is formed, containing provisions for managing the business and affairs of the corporation. This document does not have to be filed with the secretary of state.

Organizational Meeting	An organizational meeting must be held by the initial directors of the corporation after the articles of incorporation are filed. At this meeting the directors adopt the bylaws, elect corporate officers, ratify promoters' contracts, adopt a corporate seal, and transact such other business as may come before the meeting.
Common Stock	Common stock is a type of equity security that represents the *residual value* of the corporation. Common stock has no preferences, and its shareholders are paid dividends and assets upon liquidation only after creditors and preferred shareholders have been paid. 1. *Common stockholder:* A person who owns common stock. 2. *Common stock certificate:* A document that represents the common shareholders' investment in the corporation.
Liability of Shareholders	1. Shareholders of corporations typically have *limited liability*; that is, they are liable for the debts and obligations of the corporation only to the extent of their capital contribution to the corporation. 2. Shareholders may be found *personally liable* for the debts and obligation of the corporation under the doctrine called *piercing the corporate veil*. Courts can disregard the corporate entity and hold shareholders personally liable for the debts and obligations of the corporation if (a) the corporation has been formed without sufficient capital (*thin capitalization*), or (b) separateness has not been maintained between the corporation and its shareholders (e.g., commingling of personal and corporate assets, failure to hold required shareholders' meetings, and such). Also called the *alter-ego doctrine*.
Board of Directors	The board of directors is a panel of decision makers for the corporation, the members of which are elected by the shareholders. The directors of a corporation are responsible for formulating the policy decisions affecting the corporation, such as deciding what businesses to engage in, determining the capital structure of the corporation, selecting and removing top officers of the corporation, and the like. 1. *Inside director:* A member of the board of directors who is also an officer of the corporation. 2. *Outside director:* A member of the board of directors who is not an officer of the corporation.
Meetings of the Board of Directors	1. *Regular meeting:* A meeting of the board of directors held at the time and place scheduled in the bylaws. 2. *Special meeting:* A meeting of the board of directors convened to discuss an important or emergency matter, such as a proposed merger, a hostile takeover attempt, and such. 3. *Written consents:* The board of directors acting without a meeting if all of the directors sign written consents that set forth the action taken.
Corporate Officers	*Officers:* Employees of the corporation who are appointed by the board of directors to manage the *day-to-day operations* of the corporation. 1. *Duties of loyalty:* A duty that directors and officers have not to act adversely to the interests of the corporation and to subordinate their personal interests to those of the corporation and its shareholders. 2. *Duty of care:* A duty that corporate directors and officers have to use care and diligence when acting on behalf of the corporation. This duty is discharged if they perform their duties (a) in good faith, (b) with the care that an *ordinary prudent person* in a like position would use under similar circumstances, and (c) in a manner they reasonably believe to be in the best interests of the corporation. 　a. *Negligence:* Failure of a corporate director or officer to exercise this duty of care when conducting the corporation's business. 　b. *Business judgment rule:* A rule that says directors and officers are not liable to the corporation or its shareholders for honest mistakes of judgment.

Sarbanes-Oxley Act (SOX)	A federal statute that makes certain conduct by public companies and their officers and directors illegal and establishes criminal penalties for violations. The act also prompts public companies to adopt a code of ethics.

Bankruptcy

Bankruptcy Law	1. *Bankruptcy Reform Act of 1978, as amended:* This federal statute establishes the requirements and procedures for filing for bankruptcy. 2. *Bankruptcy Abuse Prevention and Consumer Protection Act of 2005:* This federal act substantially amends federal bankruptcy law. The 2005 act makes it more difficult for debtors to file for bankruptcy and have their unpaid debts discharged. 3. *Bankruptcy courts:* Bankruptcy courts have exclusive jurisdiction to hear bankruptcy cases. A bankruptcy court is attached to each federal district court. Bankruptcy judges are appointed for 14-year terms.

Bankruptcy Procedure	1. *Filing of a petition:* The filing of a petition commences a bankruptcy case.
	  a. *Voluntary petition:* A voluntary petition is filed by a debtor.
	  b. *Involuntary petition:* An involuntary petition is filed by a creditor or creditors.
	2. *Proof of claims:* Each unsecured creditor must file proof of claim, stating the amount of its claim against the debtors.

The Bankruptcy Estate	The *bankruptcy estate* includes: 1. All the debtor's legal and equitable interests in real, personal, tangible, and intangible property at the time the petition is filed. 2. Gifts, inheritances, life insurance proceeds, and property from divorce settlements that the debtor is entitled to receive within 180 days after the petition is filed.
Exempt Property	The Bankruptcy Code permits the debtor to retain certain property that does not become part of the bankruptcy estate. Exemptions are stipulated in federal and state law.

Types of Bankruptcy	1. *Chapter 7—Liquidation bankruptcy:* A form of bankruptcy where the debtor's nonexempt property is sold for cash, the cash is distributed to the creditors, and unpaid debts are discharged.
	  a. *Median income and means tests:* The 2005 act establishes certain median income and means tests that a debtor must meet in order to qualify for Chapter 7 liquidation relief.
	  b. *Discharge of student loans:* A student loan may be discharged after it is due only if nondischarge would cause an *undue hardship* on the debtor or his or her family.
	2. *Chapter 13—Adjustment of debts by an individual with regular income:* A rehabilitation form of bankruptcy that permits bankruptcy courts to supervise the debtor's plan for the repayment of unpaid debts by installment. Called *consumer debt adjustment.* The court will grant an order discharging the debtor from all unpaid debts covered by the plan only after all the payments required under the plan are completed.
	3. *Chapter 11—Reorganization bankruptcy:* A form of bankruptcy for reorganizing the debtor's financial affairs under the supervision of the bankruptcy court. The debtor files a plan of reorganization that sets forth the debtor's proposed new capital structure. A plan of reorganization must be confirmed by the bankruptcy court before it becomes effective. Upon confirmation of a plan of reorganization, the debtor is granted a discharge of all claims not included in the plan. The debtor's legal obligation to pay the discharged debts is terminated.
	4. *Chapter 12—Family farmer and family fisherman bankruptcy:* A rehabilitation form of bankruptcy that provides a method for reorganizing the family farmer or family fisherman debtor's financial affairs under the supervision of the bankruptcy court.

WORKING THE WEB

1. Use the website http://google.com.html or similar Internet search engine to find an Internet business that provides services to incorporate a corporation. Read the website you found and write a one-half page report on what you found, answering questions such as how fast a corporation can be formed and how much it costs.

2. Go to the website http://www.microsoftcorporation.com.html. Type the search term "Board of Directors." How many directors does the Microsoft Corporation have? Make a list of these directors and identify which directors are inside directors and which directors are outside directors.

3. Visit the website http://www.business.gov/html. Where the words "Access Additional Information by" appear on the screen, click on "Region." On the map that appears, click on your state, then click on "Starting a Business." Find out how to reserve a business or corporate name in your state. Write a one-page report about this process.

4. Visit the website http://www.sba.gov/regions/states.html. Whose website is this? Click on your state on the map. Read "About Us." Write a one-half page report on what this organization does.

CRITICAL THINKING & WRITING QUESTIONS

1. Define *sole proprietorship*. Describe the liability of a sole proprietor.

2. What does the term *d.b.a. (doing business as)* mean? How is it obtained?

3. Define *general partnership*. Describe the liability of general partners.

4. What is the difference between *joint liability* and *joint and several liability*? Explain.

5. Define *limited partnership*. What is the liability exposure of a (a) general partner, and (b) a limited partner? Explain.

6. Define *limited liability partnership (LLP)*. Describe the liability of its partners.

7. Define *limited liability company (LLC)*. Describe the liability of its members.

8. Define *corporation*. Describe the liability of shareholders.

9. Describe the difference between a (a) domestic corporation, (b) foreign corporation, and (c) alien corporation.

10. Describe the following: (a) articles of incorporation, (b) bylaws, (3) organizational meeting.

11. Explain the difference between a C corporation and an S corporation. How is S corporation status obtained?

12. Describe the function of the board of directors of a corporation. What is the difference between an *inside director* and an *outside director*?

13. Define a corporate officer's and a director's duty of loyalty. Give examples of breaches of this duty.

14. Define a corporate officer's and a director's duty of care. When is this duty breached?

Building Paralegal Skills

VIDEO CASE STUDIES

A Corporate Officer Seeks Legal Counsel: Conflict of Interest

 A client, the owner of a trucking company that is experiencing financial difficulty, is meeting with his attorney to investigate potential alternatives for continuing with the business. He is concerned because he has been told that the court may try to pierce the corporate veil and hold him personally responsible for a judgment for which there is not enough insurance.

After viewing the video case study at www.pearsonhighered.com/goldman answer the following:

1. Are the stockholders or officers of a corporation liable for the debts of the corporation?

2. What are the different kinds of legal entities that may be used to offer some protection from personal liability?

3. Is it ethical or legal to transfer a potential asset of the corporation to a new company owned by an officer or stockholder of the original corporation?

ETHICS ANALYSIS & DISCUSSION QUESTIONS

1. May a paralegal be a partner in a law firm?
2. May a paralegal be a partner with a client of the law firm?
3. Because of the volume of work and an impending deadline, you are hired as a temporary paralegal in a large Wall Street law firm to work on a case involving a major corporate client. One of the lawyers tells you that the client soon will announce a major breakthrough that will lead to a highly profitable business opportunity. May a paralegal take advantage of inside information learned about a public corporate client to trade in stock of the client?

DEVELOPING YOUR COLLABORATION SKILLS

With a group of other students, selected by you or assigned by your instructor, review the "Paralegals at Work" scenario at the beginning of the chapter. As a group, discuss the following questions.

1. What is a sole proprietorship? Does this form of business satisfy the owners' requirements? Why or why not?
2. What is a general partnership? Does this form of business satisfy the owners' requirements? Why or why not?
3. What is a limited partnership? Does this form of business satisfy the owners' requirements? Why or why not?
4. What is a limited liability partnership (LLP)? Does this form of business satisfy the owners' requirements? Can this form of business be used by the owners?
5. What is a limited liability company (LLC)? Does this form of business satisfy the owners' requirements? Can this form of business be used by the owners?
6. What is a corporation? What is the difference between a C corporation and an S corporation? Does either of these satisfy the owners' requirements?

PARALEGAL PORTFOLIO EXERCISE

Locate on the Internet or in the library a source that explains the requirements for preparing the articles of incorporation for a new corporation to be formed in your state. Prepare the articles of incorporation to form a new corporation in your state. Select a corporate name, and make up other information that is needed to complete the articles of incorporation.

LEGAL ANALYSIS & WRITING CASES

Kinney Shoe Corp. v. Polan   939 F.2d 209, 1991 U.S. App. Lexis 15304 United States

Court of Appeals for the Fourth Circuit

Lincoln M. Polan formed Industrial Realty Company (Industrial), a West Virginia corporation. Polan was the sole shareholder of Industrial. Although a certificate of incorporation was issued, no organizational meeting was held and no officers were elected. Industrial issued no stock certificates because nothing was ever paid in to the corporation. Other corporate formalities were not observed.

Polan, on behalf of Industrial, signed a lease to sublease commercial space in a building controlled by Kinney Shoe Corporation (Kinney). The first rental payment to Kinney was made out of Polan's personal funds, and no further payments were made on the lease. Kinney filed suit against Industrial and obtained a judgment of $66,400 for unpaid rent. When the amount was unpaid by Industrial, Kinney sued Polan individually and sought to pierce the corporate veil to collect from Polan.

The District Court held for Polan. Kinney appealed.

Question

1. Is Polan personally liable for Industrial's debts?

National Lumber Co. v. Advance Development Corp.

732 S.W.2d 840, 1987 Ark. Lexis 2225

Supreme Court of Alabama

Pat McGowan, Val Somers, and Brent Robertson were general partners of Vermont Place, a limited partnership formed for the purpose of constructing duplexes on an undeveloped tract of land in Fort Smith, Arkansas. The general partners appointed McGowan and his company, Advance Development Corporation, to develop the project, including contracting with material men, mechanics, and other suppliers. None of the limited partners took part in the management or control of the partnership.

Eight months later, Somers and Robertson discovered that McGowan had not been paying the suppliers. They removed McGowan from the partnership and took over the project. The suppliers sued the partnership to recover the money owed them. The partnership assets were not sufficient to pay all of their claims.

Question

1. Who is liable to the suppliers?

Singer v. Microhard.com, LLC et al.

Hypothetical Case

Harold, Jasmine, Caesar, and Yuan form "Microhard.com, LLC," a limited liability company, to sell computer hardware and software over the Internet. Microhard.com, LLC hires Heather, a recent graduate of the University of Chicago and a brilliant software designer, as an employee. Heather's job is to design and develop software that will execute a computer command when the computer user thinks of the next command he or she wants to execute on the computer.

Using Heather's research, Microhard.com, LLC, develops the "Third Eye" software program that does this. Microhard.com, LLC, sends Heather to the annual Comdex Computer Show in Las Vegas, Nevada, to unveil this revolutionary software. Heather goes to Las Vegas and, while there, rents an automobile to get from the hotel to the computer show and to meet interested buyers at different locations in Las Vegas.

While Heather is driving from her hotel to the site of the Comdex Computer Show, she negligently causes an accident and runs over Harold Singer, a pedestrian. Singer, who suffers severe personal injuries, sues Microhard.com, LLC as well as Heather, Harold, Jasmine, Caesar, and Yuan to recover monetary damages for his injuries.

Question

1. Who is liable?

Billy v. Consolidated Mach. Tool Corp.

51 N.Y.2d 152, 412 N.E.2d 934, 432 N.Y.S.2d 879, 1980 N.Y. Lexis 2638

Court of Appeals of New York

Joseph M. Billy was an employee of the USM Corporation, a publicly held corporation. Billy was at work when a 4,600-pound ram from a vertical boring mill broke loose and crushed him to death. Billy's widow brought suit against USM, alleging that the accident was caused by certain defects in the manufacture and design of the vertical boring mill and in the two moving parts directly involved in the accident, a metal lifting arm and the 4,600-pound ram.

Question

1. If Mrs. Billy's suit is successful, can the shareholders of USM Corporation be held personally liable for any judgment against USM?

Vernon v. Schuster, d/b/a Diversity Heating and Plumbing

688 N.E.2d 1172 (1997)

Supreme Court of Illinois

James Schuster was a sole proprietor doing business as (d.b.a.) Diversity Heating and Plumbing. Diversity Heating was in the business of selling, installing, and servicing heating and plumbing systems. George Vernon and others (Vernon) owned a building that needed a new boiler. Vernon hired Diversity Heating to install a new boiler in the building. Diversity Heating installed the boiler and gave a warranty that the boiler would not crack for 10 years.

Four years later James Schuster died. On that date, James's son, Jerry Schuster, inherited his father's business and thereafter ran the business as a sole proprietorship under the d/b/a "Diversity Heating and Plumbing." One year later the boiler installed in Vernon's building broke and could not be repaired. Vernon demanded that Jerry Schuster honor the warranty and replace the boiler. When Jerry Schuster refused to do so Vernon had the boiler replaced at the cost of $8,203 and sued Jerry Schuster to recover this amount for breach of warranty.

The Trial Court dismissed Vernon's complaint, but the Appellate Court reinstated the case. Jerry Schuster appealed to the Supreme Court of Illinois.

Question
1. Is Jerry Schuster liable for the warranty made by his father?

Chelsea Industries, Inc. v. Gaffney   449 N.E.2d 320, 1983 Mass. Lexis 1413

Supreme Judicial Court of Massachusetts
Lawrence Gaffney was the president and general manager of Ideal Tape Co. Ideal, a subsidiary of Chelsea Industries, Inc., was engaged in the business of manufacturing pressure-sensitive tape. Gaffney recruited three other Ideal executives to join him in starting a tape-manufacturing business. The four men remained at Ideal for the two years it took them to plan the new enterprise. During this time they used their positions at Ideal to travel around the country to gather business ideas, recruit potential customers, and purchase equipment for their business. At no time did they reveal to Chelsea their intention to open a competing business.

The new business was incorporated as Action Manufacturing Co. When executives at Chelsea discovered the existence of the new venture, Gaffney and the others resigned from Chelsea. Chelsea sued them for damages.

Question
1. Who wins?

Kawaauhau v. Geiger   523 U.S. 57, 118 S.Ct. 974, 140 L.Ed.2d 90, 1998 U.S. Lexis 1595

Supreme Court of the United States
Margaret Kawaauhau sought treatment from Dr. Paul Geiger for a foot injury. Dr. Geiger examined Kawaauhau and admitted her to the hospital to attend to the risks of infection. Although Dr. Geiger knew that intravenous penicillin would have been a more effective treatment, he prescribed oral penicillin, explaining that he thought that his patient wished to minimize the cost of her treatment. Dr. Geiger then departed on a business trip, leaving Kawaauhau in the care of other physicians. When Dr. Geiger returned, he discontinued all antibiotics because he believed that the infection had subsided. Kawaauhau's condition deteriorated over the next few days, requiring the amputation of her right leg below the knee. Kawaauhau and her husband sued Dr. Geiger for medical malpractice. The jury found Dr. Geiger liable and awarded the Kawaauhaus $355,000 in damages. Dr. Geiger, who carried no malpractice insurance, filed for bankruptcy in an attempt to discharge the judgment. The bankruptcy court denied discharge, and the district court agreed. The Court of Appeals reversed and allowed discharge. The Kawaauhaus appealed to the U.S. Supreme Court.

Question
1. Is a debt arising from a medical malpractice judgment that is attributable to negligent or reckless conduct dischargeable in bankruptcy?

WORKING WITH THE LANGUAGE OF THE COURT CASE

United States v. WRW Corporation

986 F.2d 138 1993 U.S. App. Lexis 2307
United States Court of Appeals, Sixth Circuit

Read the following case, excerpted from the Court of Appeals opinion. Review and brief the case. In your brief, answer the following questions.

1. Who was the plaintiff? What was it suing for?
2. Who were the defendants?
3. What is the doctrine of piercing the corporate veil?
4. Did the court find the defendants personally liable?

(continued)

Peck, Judge

In 1985, civil penalties totaling $90,350 were assessed against WRW Corporation (WRW), a Kentucky corporation, for serious violations of safety standards under the Federal Mine Safety and Health Act (the Act) which resulted in the deaths of two miners. Following the imposition of civil penalties, WRW liquidated its assets and went out of business.

Three individual defendants, who were the sole shareholders, officers, and directors of WRW, were later indicted and convicted for willful violations of mandatory health and safety standards under the Act. Roger Richardson, Noah Woolum, and William Woolum each served prison sentences and paid criminal fines. After his release from prison, Roger Richardson filed for bankruptcy under Chapter 7 of the Bankruptcy Code.

The United States (the Government) brought this action in May of 1988 against WRW and Roger Richardson, Noah Woolum, and William Woolum to recover the civil penalties previously imposed against WRW. The District Court denied the individual defendants' motion to dismiss and granted summary judgment to the Government, piercing the corporate veil under state law and holding the individual defendants liable for the civil penalties assessed against WRW. For the reasons discussed herein, we affirm.

Having determined that the imposition of a $90,350 sanction upon the defendants does not violate principles of double jeopardy, we turn to the defendants' argument that the district court erred in holding the individual defendants liable for the penalty by piercing the corporate veil of WRW under Kentucky law.

The district court held that it was appropriate to pierce WRW's corporate veil under either an equity theory or an alter-ego theory, both of which are recognized under Kentucky law. Under either theory, the following factors must be considered when determining whether to pierce the corporate veil: (1) undercapitalization; (2) a failure to observe the formalities of corporate existence; (3) nonpayment or overpayment of dividends; (4) a siphoning off of funds by dominant shareholders; and (5) the majority shareholders having guaranteed corporate liabilities in their individual capacities.

The court first found that WRW was undercapitalized because it was incorporated with only $3,000 of capital, which the record indicates was insufficient to pay normal expenses associated with the operation of a coal mine. The District Court next found that WRW failed to observe corporate formalities, noting that no bylaws were produced by the defendants, and that all corporate actions taken by the individual defendants were without corporation authorization. Finally, although WRW never distributed any dividends to the individual defendants, and there was no evidence that the individual defendants siphoned off corporate funds, these factors alone do not mitigate against piercing the corporate veil in this case because WRW was never sufficiently capitalized and operated at a loss during its two years of active existence.

In addition to holding that the equities of this case support piercing the corporate veil, the District Court held that the corporate veil should be pierced under the "alter ego" theory, because WRW and the defendants did not have separate personalities. In light of the lack of observance of corporate formalities or distinction between the individual defendants and the corporation, we agree with the district court's conclusion that "there was a complete merger of ownership and control of WRW with the individual defendants."

The specific factual findings made by the District Court amply support piercing the corporate veil of WRW and holding the individual defendants liable for the penalty assessed against the corporate entity. For all of the foregoing reasons, the judgment of the district court is AFFIRMED.

Crimes

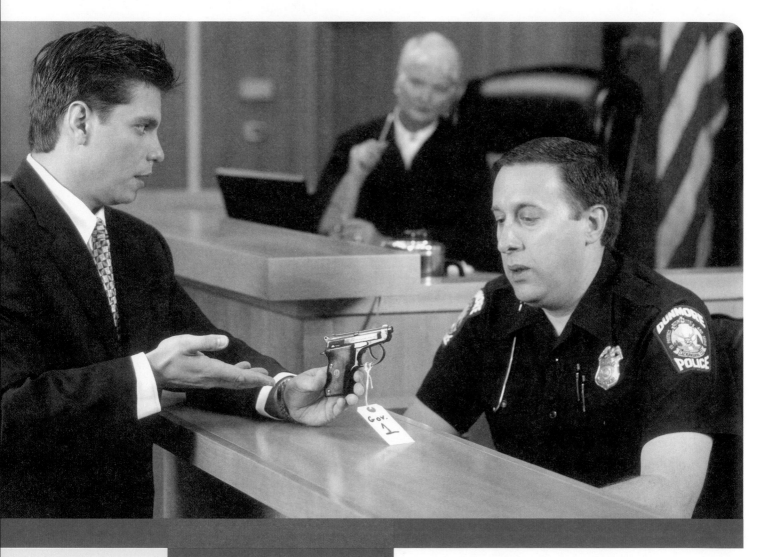

Law cannot persuade, where it cannot punish. "

Thomas Fuller
Gnomologia (1732)

LEARNING OBJECTIVES

After studying this chapter, you should be able to:

1. Recognize the professional opportunities for paralegals in the criminal law area.
2. Define and list the essential elements of a crime.
3. Describe the most important common crimes.
4. Define and describe the most prevalent business crimes.
5. Describe identity theft and the laws that make identity theft a crime.
6. Explain a paralegal's duty to report criminal activity.

Paralegals at Work

You are a paralegal who works for a law firm that does criminal defense work. The law firm specializes in defending executives in white-collar criminal law matters. You work for Ms. Chen, a renowned attorney in the area of white-collar criminal defense. Ms. Chen informs you that the law firm has been retained to represent Mr. Johnson, an executive now facing criminal charges for alleged white-collar crimes. Ms. Chen informs you that you will assist her in preparing the defense of Mr. Johnson.

Ms. Chen explains the following facts and issues to you: Mr. Johnson was the founder and Chief Executive Officer (CEO) of the Financial Corporation. The Financial Corporation was one of the largest financial companies in the United States and operated an investment business. Mr. Johnson has been served a complaint, *United States v. Johnson*, wherein Mr. Johnson has been charged by the federal government with various crimes.

Mr. Johnson, as well as Ms. Matthews, Financial Corporation's Chief Financial Officer (CFO), and other corporate executives agreed with each other to "cook the books" of the corporation to make the corporation seem like it was making huge profits when it was not. Mr. Johnson and the other executives used these financial statements to raise money from investors who purchased stock in Financial Corporation.

Mr. Johnson, Ms. Matthews, and other corporate executives stole money that the investors had invested in the corporation and diverted the money to their own personal bank accounts. Mr. Johnson purchased a restaurant and used the restaurant to hide and move the stolen money through it to make it seem that he had another business that generated the stolen money for him. Mr. Johnson then used the money to purchase a large house, invested some of the money to purchase real estate, and spent money living a lavish lifestyle. He also moved millions of dollars of the money to an offshore bank in the Cayman Islands in a bank account in his name. Mr. Johnson used the mail, telephones, and computers to implement and operate the entire scheme.

When these misdeeds were discovered, the Financial Corporation failed and had to declare bankruptcy. The investors lost their entire investment, and the creditors of the corporation were not paid.

Consider the issues involved in this scenario as you read the chapter.

INTRODUCTION FOR THE PARALEGAL

For members of society to coexist peacefully and commerce to flourish, people and their property must be protected from injury by other members of society. Federal, state, and local governments' criminal laws are intended to accomplish this by providing an incentive for persons to act reasonably in society and imposing penalties on persons who violate them.

Many crimes are common crimes that involve property, such as misappropriating another's personal property through robbery, burglary, larceny, and other forms of theft. Other common crimes involve injury or death to other persons, such as the crimes of murder, rape, assault, and battery. Many crimes that are committed in society involve these crimes against persons and property.

Another category of crimes are called white-collar crimes. They are given this name because these crimes are often committed by persons who are executives or employees of businesses. Several of these crimes are bribery, civil fraud, and securities fraud. Businesses are liable for the crimes committed by their employees on behalf of the business.

Organized crime commits many crimes in this country. Organized crime members can be prosecuted for these crimes. In addition, the federal government has enacted several statutes that are primarily directed at organized crime, although these crimes can also be committed by others. Two of these crimes are racketeering and money laundering.

In today's Information Age, many crimes are committed using computer and digital technology. The computer makes it easier for criminals to reach a substantial number of potential victims in a very short period of time. One of the most prevalent crimes committed using the computer and the Internet is identity theft. Congress has enacted statutes that make identity theft and other crimes committed using the computer and the Internet federal crimes.

Criminal law is an important area of the law. Paralegals will be called on to conduct research and otherwise assist lawyers in preparing for litigation in this exciting area of the law. This chapter covers state and federal crimes.

Crimes

Crime A violation of a statute for which the government imposes a punishment.

A **crime** is defined as any act by an individual in violation of those duties that he or she owes to society and for the breach of which the law provides that the wrongdoer shall make amends to the public. Many activities have been considered crimes throughout the ages, whereas other crimes are of recent origin.

CAREER OPPORTUNITIES FOR PARALEGALS IN CRIMINAL LAW

The job opportunities for paralegals are quite varied in the area of criminal law. The criminal law system in this country is extremely large and requires the services of thousands of lawyers and, thus, thousands of paralegals. The area of criminal law provides abundant opportunities for jobs for paralegals.

Many crimes involve violations of state laws. When a defendant is charged with a state-law crime, the state brings the lawsuit against the alleged criminal. The lawsuits are brought by prosecutors of the local jurisdiction where the crime has been alleged to have been committed. The prosecutors are lawyers who are state government employees. Paralegals have job opportunities to work for the state government assisting prosecuting attorneys in bringing and pursuing criminal charges.

Many defendants in criminal cases cannot afford their own attorneys, so the government provides defense attorneys to represent the defendant in the criminal case. The defense attorneys frequently are government employees who often are referred to as public defenders. Sometimes the court will appoint an attorney in private practice to represent a criminal defendant and the government pays the private attorney's fees. Paralegals have job opportunities to work for the state government or other defense attorneys assisting in the defense of criminally charged defendants.

In addition, some defendants are charged with violating federal criminal laws. The lawyers who prosecute a case on behalf of the federal government are U.S. attorneys. These are federal government employees. The defendant is represented by a defense attorney who is a private attorney if the defendant can afford his or her own attorney, or is either a government or court-appointed attorney if the defendant cannot afford an attorney.

There are excellent opportunities for paralegals in the criminal law area. Paralegals work for private law firms that specialize in criminal law. In addition, paralegal professionals can be employed by state and federal governments in the criminal law area.

There will always be criminals; therefore, there will always be a need for attorneys to represent the government on one side of the case and the defendant on the other side of the case. In a parallel fashion, there will always be a need for paralegals on the government prosecutor's side of the case, as well as the defendant's side of the case. The area of criminal law will remain an important source of employment for paralegals.

Penal Codes and Regulatory Statutes

Statutes are the primary source of criminal law. Most states have adopted comprehensive **penal codes** that define in detail the activities considered to be crimes within their jurisdiction and the penalties that will be imposed for committing these crimes.

A comprehensive federal criminal code defines federal crimes (Title 18 of the U.S. Code). In addition, state and federal **regulatory statutes** often provide for criminal violations and penalties. The state and federal legislatures are adding to the list of crimes continually.

The penalty for committing a crime may consist of the imposition of a fine, imprisonment, both, or some other form of punishment (e.g., probation). Generally, imprisonment is imposed to (1) incapacitate the criminal so he or she will not harm others in society, (2) provide a means to rehabilitate the criminal, (3) deter others from similar conduct, and (4) inhibit personal retribution by the victim.

Penal codes Statutes that define crimes.

Regulatory statutes Statutes, such as environmental laws, securities laws, and antitrust laws that provide for criminal violations and penalties.

Parties to a Criminal Action

In a criminal lawsuit, the government (not a private party) is the **plaintiff**. A lawyer called the **prosecutor, district attorney**, or, in the federal system, **United States Attorney** represents the government. The accused is the **defendant**. The **defense attorney** represents the accused. If the accused cannot afford a defense lawyer, the government will provide one free of charge, called a **public defender**.

Classification of Crimes

All crimes can be classified as *felonies*, *misdemeanors*, or *violations*.

- **Felonies. Felonies** are the most serious kinds of crimes. They include crimes that are **mala in se**—inherently evil. Most crimes against the

PARTIES AND ATTORNEYS INVOLVED IN A CRIMINAL CASE

Parties to a Criminal Lawsuit

Government (plaintiff)	Person or Business (defendant)

Attorneys Representing the Parties

Prosecutor (government attorney)	Defense Attorney (private attorney or public defender)

SIDEBAR

CLASSIFICATION OF CRIMES

Classification	Description
Felony	The most serious kinds of crimes. They are *mala in se* (inherently evil), and they are usually punishable by imprisonment.
Misdemeanor	Crimes that are less serious than felonies. They are *mala prohibita* (prohibited by society), and they are usually punishable by fine and/or imprisonment for less than one year.
Violation	Crimes that are neither felonies nor misdemeanors. Violations are generally punishable by a fine.

person (murder, rape, and the like) and certain business-related crimes (such as embezzlement and bribery) are felonies in most jurisdictions.

Felonies usually are punishable by imprisonment. In some jurisdictions, certain felonies (e.g., first-degree murder) are punishable by death. Federal law and some state laws require mandatory sentencing for specified crimes. Many statutes define different degrees of crimes (e.g., first-, second-, and third-degree murder) with each degree earning different penalties.

- **Misdemeanors. Misdemeanors** are less serious than felonies. They are crimes *mala prohibita*—not inherently evil but prohibited by society. This category includes many crimes against property, such as robbery, burglary, and violations of regulatory statutes. Misdemeanors carry lesser penalties than felonies; they usually are punishable by fine and/or imprisonment for one year or less.
- **Violations.** Crimes such as traffic violations and jaywalking are neither felonies nor misdemeanors. Called **violations,** these crimes usually are punishable by a fine. Occasionally, a few days of imprisonment are imposed.

Intent Crimes

For a person to be found guilty of most crimes, a *criminal act* and *criminal intent* must be proven.

Criminal Act

Actus reus "Guilty act"—the actual performance of the criminal act.

To commit a **criminal act,** the defendant must have actually performed the prohibited act. Under the common law, actual performance of the criminal act is called the **actus reus (guilty act).** Under the Model Penal Code, the prohibited act may be analyzed in terms of conduct, circumstances, and results.

Example Killing someone without legal justification is an example of *actus reus*. Sometimes the omission of an act constitutes the requisite *actus reus*.

Example A crime has been committed if a taxpayer who is under a legal duty to file a tax return fails to do so. Merely thinking about committing a crime is not a crime, because no action has been taken.

Criminal Intent

Mens rea "Evil intent"—the possession of the requisite state of mind to commit a prohibited act.

To be found guilty of a crime, the accused must be found to have possessed the requisite subjective state of mind, or **criminal intent** (i.e., specific or general intent) when the act was performed. This is called the **mens rea (evil intent)** under the traditional common law analysis and *culpable mental state* under the Model Penal Code. The Model Penal Code has four levels of culpable mental state:

1. Purposeful (or intentional)
2. Knowingly
3. Recklessly
4. With criminal negligence

Web Exploration

Go to http://wings.buffalo.edu/law/bclc/web/website/allcodes2.htm and find the penal code of the state in which your college or university is located. Find and read your state's definition of murder.

Specific intent is found where the accused purposefully, intentionally, or with knowledge commits a prohibited act. **General intent** is found where there is a showing of recklessness or a lesser degree of mental culpability. The individual criminal statutes state whether the crime requires a showing of specific or general intent. Juries may infer an accused's intent from the facts and circumstances of the case. There is no crime if the requisite *mens rea* cannot be proven. Thus, no crime is committed if one person accidentally injures another person.

Non-Intent Crimes

Most states provide for certain **non-intent crimes.** The crime of **involuntary manslaughter** is often imposed for reckless conduct.

> **Example**   If a driver of an automobile drives too fast (e.g., 20 miles over the speed limit) on a city street and hits and kills a pedestrian, the driver most likely would be found guilty of the crime of involuntary manslaughter and be sentenced to jail.

Criminal Acts as Basis for Tort Actions

An injured party may bring a **civil tort action** against a wrongdoer who has caused the party injury during the commission of a criminal act. Civil lawsuits are separate from the government's criminal action against the wrongdoer. In many cases, a person injured by a criminal act will not sue the criminal to recover civil damages. This is because the criminal is often **judgment-proof**—that is, the criminal does not have the money to pay a civil judgment.

Common Crimes

Many crimes are committed against persons and property. The most important types of crimes against persons and property are discussed in the following paragraphs.

Crimes Against the Person

Crimes against the person are the most heinous of crimes. The most common forms of crimes against the person are:

- **Assault**: threat of immediate harm or offensive conduct toward another person coupled with apparent present ability to execute the attempt. Actual physical contact is not necessary.
- **Battery**: harmful or offensive physical contact with another person without his or her consent (e.g., punching someone in the face without just cause).
- **Mayhem**: depriving another person of a member of his or her body (e.g., cutting off a person's finger).
- **Rape**: sexual relations with a person by another person forcibly and against the other person's will.
- **Kidnapping**: the abduction and detention of a person against his or her will.
- **False imprisonment**: confinement or restraint of another person without authority or justification and without his or her consent.

Murder

Murder is the unlawful killing of a human being by another with intent. There are several degrees of murder—such as *first degree*, *second degree*, and *third degree*—depending on the circumstances of the case. The convicted perpetrators of murder generally receive the harshest jail sentences for committing these crimes.

Sometimes a murder is committed during the commission of another crime even though the criminal did not originally intend to commit murder. Most state laws hold the perpetrator liable for the crime of murder in addition to the other crime. This is called the **felony murder rule**. The intent to commit the murder is inferred from the

Non-intent crime A crime that imposes criminal liability without a finding of *mens rea* (intent).

Web Exploration

Go to www.fbi.gov and find the "Ten Most Wanted" fugitives in the United States. Who is number one and what crime is he or she wanted for?

Murder The unlawful killing of a human being by another with intent.

Paralegals *in* Practice

PARALEGAL PROFILE
Debra K. Jennings

Debra K. Jennings is an Advanced Certified Paralegal in Trial Practice who works for the Campbell County Attorney's Office in Gillette, Wyoming. Of her 18 years as a paralegal, the first 11 were spent in civil practice and the last seven in criminal prosecution. Debra is a member of the National Association of Legal Assistants and currently serves on its Advanced Paralegal Certification board.

I'd like to share the following case description to help illustrate the various skills and knowledge needed by a criminal prosecution paralegal: A man slammed head-on into another vehicle while driving intoxicated at three times the legal limit. At impact, he was driving over 90 mph in a 65-mph zone, on a hill in a no-passing zone, while going around a double tractor-trailer. In the other car, the female driver and her young son were severely injured, and her mother died instantly. The drunk driver also sustained serious injuries. All three survivors eventually recovered.

The man was charged with one count of Aggravated Vehicular Homicide and two counts of Driving Under the Influence with Serious Bodily Injury. As the prosecuting attorney's paralegal, I first coordinated the gathering of information, materials, documents, reports, and evidence. This included researching the defendant's criminal history and identifying applicable laws and judicial decisions as they pertained to the case facts. All relevant information was analyzed and organized.

Next, my writing and communication skills were called into play. I prepared written explanatory material on laws and recommended courses of action. I then helped the prosecutor prepare legal arguments and write pleadings, traverses, motions, and briefs. I also assisted with hearing and pre-trial groundwork. This included communicating with other agencies and law enforcement, interviewing and preparing witnesses, performing background checks of the potential jury pool, preparing exhibits and trial notebooks, as well as discussing legal issues with the prosecutor.

In the end, the evidence and arguments presented were overwhelming. The driver responsible for the crash eventually pleaded guilty. He was sentenced to 18 to 20 years on Count I and 9 to 10 years each on Counts II and III, all to run consecutively with one another. As you can see from this case, the key to any paralegal's success is being organized and able to multi-task. Educationally, the social sciences provide a great background. The bottom line: remember your real client is the attorney for whom you work.

---

intent to commit the other crime. Many states also hold accomplices liable under this doctrine.

The statutory definition of first-degree murder from the Florida Penal Code is set forth in Exhibit 19.1.

Robbery

Robbery The taking of personal property from another person by the use of fear or force.

In common law, **robbery** is defined as the taking of personal property from another person or business by the use of fear or force. Robbery with a deadly weapon is generally considered aggravated robbery (or armed robbery) and carries a harsher penalty.

> **Examples** If a robber threatens the victim with a gun unless the victim surrenders her purse, this is the crime of robbery. If a person pickpockets somebody's wallet, it is not robbery because there has been no use of force or fear. This is the crime of theft.

Burglary

Burglary The taking of personal property from another's home, office, or commercial or other type of building.

In common law, **burglary** is defined as "breaking and entering a dwelling at night" with the intent to commit a felony. Modern penal codes have broadened this definition to include daytime thefts from homes, offices, commercial, and other buildings. In addition, the "breaking in" element has been abandoned by most modern definitions of burglary. Thus, unauthorized entering of a building through an unlocked door is sufficient. Aggravated burglary (or armed burglary) carries stiffer penalties.

| **Exhibit 19.1** | **Florida penal code (excerpts)** |

782.04 Murder
(I)(a) The unlawful killing of a human being:

First Degree Murder
(1) When perpetrated from a premeditated design to effect the death of the person killed or any human being;
(2) When committed by a person engaged in the perpetration of, or in the attempt to perpetrate, any: trafficking offense prohibited by s. 893.135(1), arson, sexual battery, robbery, burglary, kidnapping, escape, aggravated child abuse, aggravated abuse of an elderly person or disabled adult, aircraft piracy, unlawful throwing, placing, or discharging of a destructive device or bomb, carjacking, home-invasion robbery, aggravated stalking, murder of another human being, resisting an officer with violence to his or her person, felony that is an act of terrorism or is in furtherance of an act of terrorism; or . . .
(3) Which resulted from the unlawful distribution of any substance controlled under s. 893.03(1), cocaine as described in s. 893.03(a)4.,or opium or any synthetic or natural salt, compound, derivative, or preparation of opium by a person 18 years of age or older, when such drug is proven to be the proximate cause of the death of the user, is murder in the first degree and constitutes a capital felony, punishable as provided in s. 775.082.
(b) In all cases under this section, the procedure set forth in s. 921.141 shall be followed in order to determine sentence of death or life imprisonment.

Example   Harold breaks into Sharon's home and steals jewelry and other items. Harold is guilty of the crime of burglary because he entered a dwelling and committed theft.

Larceny

In common law, **larceny** is defined as the wrongful and fraudulent taking of another person's personal property that is not robbery or burglary. Most personal property—including tangible property, trade secrets, computer programs, and other business property—is subject to larceny. Neither the use of force nor the entry of a building is required.

Larceny The taking of another's personal property other than from his or her person or building.

Examples   Stealing of automobiles and car stereos, pickpocketing, and such are larceny. Some states distinguish between grand larceny and petit larceny. This distinction depends on the value of the property taken.

Theft

Some states have dropped the distinction among the crimes of robbery, burglary, and larceny. Instead, these states group these crimes under the general crime of **theft**. Most of these states distinguish between grand theft and petit theft. The distinction depends on the value of the property taken.

Receiving Stolen Property

It is a crime for a person to (1) knowingly **receive stolen property** and (2) intend to deprive the rightful owner of that property. Knowledge and intent can be inferred from the circumstances. The stolen property can be any tangible property (e.g., personal property, money, negotiable instruments, and stock certificates).

 Web Exploration

Go to http://newsinfo.inquirer .net/breakingnews/world/view/ 20080211-118178/UPDATE and read about the theft of $168 million of paintings from a museum. Use www.google.com to find out if any of these paintings have been recovered.

Example   David is walking down the street and is approached by a man who offers to sell David a Rolex watch "at a cheap price." David looks at the 20 Rolex watches that the man has, chooses one that would normally sell in a retail store for $2000 and pays $250 for it. It is an actual Rolex. David is guilty of the crime of receiving stolen property because it could easily be proven by circumstantial evidence that he had knowledge that the watch was stolen property.

Arson

In common law, **arson** is defined as the malicious or willful burning of the dwelling of another person. Modern penal codes have expanded this definition to include the burning of all types of private, commercial, and public buildings.

> **Example** An owner of a motel that is not doing well financially burns down the motel to collect insurance proceeds. The owner is guilty of the crime of arson. If arson is found, the insurance company does not have to pay the proceeds of any insurance policy on the burned property.

Forgery

Forgery The fraudulent making or alteration of a written document that affects the legal liability of another person.

The crime of **forgery** occurs if a written document is fraudulently made or altered and that change affects the legal liability of another person.

> **Examples** Counterfeiting, falsifying public records, and materially altering legal documents are forgery. One of the most common forms of forgery is the signing of another person's signature to a check or changing the amount of a check. Note that signing another person's signature without intent to defraud is not forgery. For instance, forgery has not been committed if one spouse signs the other spouse's payroll check for deposit in a joint checking or savings account at the bank.

Extortion

Extortion Threat to expose something about another person unless that other person gives money or property. Often referred to as "blackmail."

The crime of **extortion** means the obtaining of property from another, with his or her consent, induced by wrongful use of actual or threatened force, violence, or fear.

> **Example** Extortion occurs when a person threatens to expose something about another person unless that other person gives money or property. The truth or falsity of the information is immaterial. Extortion of private persons is commonly called **blackmail**. Extortion of public officials is called *extortion "under color of official right."*

White-Collar Crimes

White-collar crimes Crimes usually involving cunning and deceit rather than physical force.

Certain types of crimes are prone to be committed by businesspersons. These crimes are often referred to as **white-collar crimes**. These crimes usually involve cunning and deceit rather than physical force. Many business and white-collar crimes are discussed in the paragraphs that follow.

Embezzlement

Embezzlement The fraudulent conversion of property by a person to whom that property was entrusted.

Unknown at common law, the crime of **embezzlement** is now a statutory crime. Embezzlement is the fraudulent conversion of property by a person to whom that property was entrusted. Typically, embezzlement is committed by an employer's employees, agents, or representatives (e.g., accountants, lawyers, trust officers, treasurers). Embezzlers often try to cover their tracks by preparing false books, records, or entries.

The key element here is that the stolen property was *entrusted* to the embezzler. This differs from robbery, burglary, and larceny, in which property is taken by someone not entrusted with the property.

> **Example** Embezzlement has been committed if a bank teller absconds with money that was deposited by depositors. The employer (the bank) entrusted the teller to take deposits from its customers.

Criminal Fraud

Obtaining title to property through deception or trickery constitutes the crime of **criminal fraud**, also known as *false pretenses* or *deceit*. To prove fraud, the following elements must be shown:

1. *The wrongdoer made a false representation of material fact.* To be actionable as fraud, the misrepresentation must be of a past or existing material fact. Statements of opinion or predictions about the future generally do not form the basis for fraud.
2. *The wrongdoer intended to deceive the innocent party.* Thus, the person making the misrepresentation must either have had knowledge that the representation was false or made it without sufficient knowledge of the truth. This is called **scienter** ("guilty mind").
3. *The innocent party justifiably relied on the misrepresentation.* A misrepresentation is not actionable unless the innocent party to whom the misrepresentation was directed acted upon it.
4. *The innocent party was injured.* To recover damages, the innocent party must prove that the fraud caused economic injury. The measure of damages is the difference between the value of the property as represented and the actual value of the property.

Example Robert Anderson, a stockbroker, promises Mary Greenberg, a prospective investor, that he will use any money she invests to purchase interests in oil wells. Based on this promise, Ms. Greenberg decides to make the investment. Mr. Anderson never intended to invest the money. Instead, he used the money for his personal needs. This is criminal fraud. A paralegal's duty not to engage in fraudulent conduct is discussed in the following Ethical Perspective feature.

ETHICAL PERSPECTIVE

Paralegal's Duty Not to Engage in Fraudulent Conduct

Mr. Barr is a paralegal for the law firm of Jonas, Carlson, and Smith, a medium-size law firm. Mr. Barr is assigned as a paralegal professional to assist Ms. Jonas, a partner of the law firm. Mr. Barr is also the bookkeeper who keeps track of the income and expenses of the law firm and prepares the financial records of the law firm.

Ms. Jonas has run into financial difficulty and thinks that the best way to come up with sufficient funds to pay her immediate debts is to steal money from the partnership. To do so, Ms. Jonas needs the help of Mr. Barr to produce fake financial records. Ms. Jonas proposes this to Mr. Barr, telling Mr. Barr that she will shortly return the money to the law firm when she sells some property that she owns and therefore no one will be financially hurt by her defalcation.

What should Mr. Barr do?

Model and state paralegal codes of ethics and responsibility prohibit a paralegal professional from engaging in fraudulent conduct.

PARALEGAL'S ETHICAL DECISION

In this case, Mr. Barr should refuse Ms. Jonas's request that he manipulate the financial records of the law firm to allow Ms. Jonas to steal money from the law firm. The fact that Ms. Jonas has promised to return the money shortly must have no effect on Mr. Barr's decision not to participate in the fraudulent conduct proposed by Ms. Jonas.

Mail and Wire Fraud

Federal law prohibits the use of mails or wires (e.g., telegraph or telephone) to defraud another person. These crimes are called **mail fraud** and **wire fraud**, respectively. The government often prosecutes a suspect under these statutes if there is insufficient evidence to prove the real crime that the criminal was attempting to commit or did commit. Wire fraud statutes also are used sometimes to prosecute Internet fraud.

Bribery

Bribery A crime in which one person gives another person money, property, favors, or anything else of value for a favor in return. Often referred to as a payoff or *kickback*.

Bribery is one of the most prevalent forms of white-collar crime. A bribe can be in the form of money, property, favors, or anything else of value. The crime of commercial bribery prohibits the payment of bribes to private persons and businesses. This type of bribe is often called a **kickback** or a **payoff**. Intent is a necessary element of this crime. The offeror of a bribe commits the crime of bribery when the bribe is tendered. The offeree is guilty of the crime of bribery when he or she accepts the bribe. The offeror can be found liable for the crime of bribery even if the person to whom the bribe is offered rejects the bribe.

> **Example** Harriet Landers, as the purchasing agent for the ABCD Corporation, is in charge of purchasing equipment to be used by the corporation. Neal Brown, sales representative of a company that makes equipment that can be used by the ABCD Corporation, offers to pay her a 10 percent kickback if she buys equipment from him. She accepts the bribe and orders the equipment. Both parties are guilty of bribery.

At common law, the crime of bribery was defined as the giving or receiving of anything of value in corrupt payment for an "official act" by a public official. Public officials include legislators, judges, jurors, witnesses at trial, administrative agency personnel, and other government officials. Modern penal codes also make it a crime to bribe public officials.

> **Example** A real estate developer who is constructing an apartment building cannot pay the building inspector to overlook a building code violation.

Foreign Corrupt Practices Act

Foreign Corrupt Practices Act A federal statute that makes it illegal for U.S. companies, or their officers, directors, agents, or employees, to bribe a foreign official or foreign political party official to influence the awarding of new business or the retention of continuous business activity.

It is well known that the payment of bribes is pervasive in conducting international business. To prevent U.S. companies from engaging in this type of conduct, the U.S. Congress enacted the **Foreign Corrupt Practices Act** of 1977 (FCPA) [15 U.S.C. Section 78m]. The FCPA makes it illegal for U.S. companies, or their officers, directors, agents, or employees, to bribe a foreign official, a foreign political party official, or a candidate for foreign political office. A bribe is illegal only where it is meant to influence the awarding of new business or retaining a continuing business activity.

The FCPA imposes criminal liability where a person pays the illegal bribe himself or herself, or supplies a payment to a third party or an agent, knowing that it will be used as a bribe. A firm can be fined up to $2 million, and an individual can be fined up to $100,000 and imprisoned for up to five years for violations of the FCPA.

Amendments to the FCPA created two defenses. One excuses a firm or person charged with bribery under the FCPA if the firm or person can show that the payment was lawful under the written laws of that country. The other allows a defendant to show that a payment was a reasonable and *bona fide* expenditure related to the furtherance or execution of a contract. This latter exemption is difficult to interpret.

Some people argue that U.S. companies are placed at a disadvantage in international markets where commercial bribery is commonplace and firms from other countries are not hindered by laws similar to the FCPA.

Identity Theft

Identity theft—or **ID theft**—is where one person steals information about another person to pose as that person and take the innocent person's money or property or to purchase goods and services using the victim's credit information. The advent of the computer and the Internet has made this type of crime easier to commit. By using the computer and the Internet, criminals are able to obtain the information they need to commit identity theft.

To commit ID theft, thieves must first obtain certain information about the victim. This could be the victim's name, social security number, credit card numbers, bank account information, and other personal information. The **Federal Trade Commission (FTC)**, the federal administrative agency primarily charged with handling ID theft matters, lists the following methods criminals use to obtain your information.

1. *Dumpster Diving.* Thieves rummage through trash looking for bills or other paper with the victim's personal information on it.
2. *Skimming.* Thieves steal credit/debit card numbers by using a special storage device when processing the victim's card.
3. *Phishing.* Thieves pretend to be financial institutions or companies and send spam or pop-up messages to victims by Internet to get the victims to reveal their personal information.
4. *Changing Your Address.* Thieves divert a person's billing statements to another location by completing a change of address form.
5. *Old-Fashioned Stealing.* Thieves steal wallets and purses; mail, including bank and credit card statements; preapproved credit offers; and new checks or tax information. They steal personnel records, or bribe employees who have access.
6. *Pretexting.* Thieves use false pretenses to obtain your personal information from financial institutions, telephone companies, and other sources.

Credit card fraud is one of the most commonly committed crimes by identity thieves. The thief may open new credit card accounts in the victim's name and purchase goods and services with these credit cards. Or the thief may change the billing address on the victim's existing credit cards so that the victim no longer receives bills and the thief then runs up charges on the victim's account. Because bills are now sent to a different address, it may be some time before the victim realizes there's a problem. When they use the cards and don't pay the bills, the delinquent accounts appear on your credit report.

A victim of identity theft often does not find out about the ID theft until a debt collection agency contacts the victim about overdue debts, when the victim applies for a car loan or a home mortgage and it is discovered when the bank or creditor conducts a credit check, or the victim receives something in the mail about an apartment he or she never rented, a house he or she did not buy, or a job he or she never had.

A victim of ID theft can lose money or property to the thieves. It is often impossible to trace the identity of the thieves or to recover the lost money or property if the thief is found. In addition, ID theft often destroys the victim's credit rating and makes it difficult to obtain credit in the future.

If you have been a victim of ID theft there are several things you should do. You should file an **Identity Theft Report** with the police, cancel certain credit cards, change bank accounts, change security and stock accounts, notify the credit reporting agencies of the items on your credit report that are not yours and that have been created by ID thieves, and have an extended fraud alert placed on your credit report so that credit agencies will notify you of questionable activity. In some cases of ID theft the victim may not suffer too much loss or not have to do much work to repair his or her credit rating after the ID theft. In other cases, the innocent victim may suffer

Identity theft A crime where one person steals information about another person and poses as that person and takes the innocent person's money or property or purchases goods and services using the victim's credit information.

Web Exploration

To test your knowledge about ID theft, go to the FTC's website http://onguardonline.gov/quiz/idtheft_quiz.html and take the online quiz.

Identity Theft and Assumption Deterrence Act A federal statute that makes identity theft a felony that is punishable by a prison sentence.

substantial financial loss and have to spend thousands of dollars and countless hours trying to straighten out his or her credit history and financial life.

To combat such fraud, Congress passed the **Identity Theft and Assumption Deterrence Act of 1998**. This act criminalizes identity fraud, making it a federal felony punishable with prison sentences ranging from 3 to 25 years. The act also appoints a federal administrative agency, the Federal Trade Commission (FTC), to help victims restore their credit and erase the impact of the imposter.

Law enforcement officials suggest the following steps to protect against identity fraud: Never put your Social Security number on any document unless it is legally required, obtain and review copies of your credit report at least twice each year, and use safe passwords (e.g., other than family names and birthdays) on bank accounts and other accounts that require personal identification numbers (PINs).

Organized Crime

Organized crime has a pervasive influence on many parts of the U.S. economy. **Organized crime** consists of a criminal organization and its members who engage in crime on a routine basis. Obviously, organized crime members can always be found guilty for committing crimes.

> **Example** A member of a criminal organization who commits extortion is guilty of the crime of extortion.

However, in an attempt to thwart organized crime, the federal government has enacted two federal statutes that are primarily aimed at organized crime. These are the crimes of racketeering and money laundering.

Racketeer Influenced and Corrupt Organizations Act (RICO)

Racketeer Influenced Corrupt Organizations Act (RICO) A federal statute that defines the crime of racketeering and provides for both criminal and civil penalties for racketeering.

In 1980, Congress enacted the Organized Crime Control Act. The **Racketeer Influenced and Corrupt Organizations Act (RICO)** is part of this act [18 U.S.C. Sections 1961–1968]. RICO, which provides for both criminal and civil penalties, is one of the most important laws affecting business today.

Criminal RICO

Criminal RICO makes it a federal crime to acquire or maintain an interest in, use income from, or conduct or participate in the affairs of an "enterprise" through a "pattern" of "racketeering activity." An "enterprise" is defined as a corporation, a partnership, a sole proprietorship, another business or organization, and the government.

The definition of *racketeering* consists of two major elements. First, the RICO statute lists certain specifically enumerated federal and state crimes, including crimes such as gambling, arson, robbery, counterfeiting, dealing in narcotics, criminal fraud, bribery, embezzlement, mail fraud, wire fraud, and the like. Second, to prove a **pattern of racketeering,** the defendant must commit at least two of these crimes within a 10-year period. If these requirements are met, the defendant has committed the crime of raketeering.

> **Example** Assume a person commits two crimes, criminal fraud and arson, whether at the same time and against the same victim, or at different times and against different victims. If these two crimes have been committed within 10 years of each other this would be considered a pattern and the perpetrator is guilty of a third crime of racketeering.

Individual defendants found criminally liable for RICO violations can be fined or imprisoned or both. In addition, RICO provides for the **forfeiture** of any property or business interests (even interests in a legitimate business) that were gained because of RICO violations. This provision allows the government to recover investments made with monies derived from racketeering activities. The government also may seek civil penalties for RICO violations. These include injunctions, orders of dissolution, reorganization of business, and divestiture of the defendant's interest in an enterprise.

Civil RICO

Persons injured by a RICO violation can bring a private **civil action** against the violator to recover injury to business or property. A successful plaintiff may recover **treble damages** (three times actual loss) plus attorneys' fees.

> **Example**   Suppose a mobster tries to extort protection money from a bar owner, but the bar owner refuses to pay. That night the mobster burns down the bar. Here there have been two substantive crimes, extortion and arson, committed by the mobster within 10 years. Therefore, the third crime of racketeering has been committed by the mobster. Suppose the bar was valued at $1 million. The bar owner can recover treble damages—$3 million—from the mobster.

Originally, RICO was intended to apply only to organized crime, but the broad language of the RICO statute has been used against nonorganized crime defendants as well, such as securities firms, commercial banks, and other businesses.

Money Laundering Control Act

When criminals make money from illegal activities, they often are faced with the problem of having large sums of money and no record of how this money was earned. This could easily tip off the government to their illegal activities. To "wash" the money and make it look as though it was earned legitimately, many criminals purchase legitimate businesses and run the money through that business to clean it before the criminal receives the money. The legitimate business has "cooked the books," showing faked expenditures and receipts, in which the illegal money is buried.

> **Example**   Restaurants, motels, and other cash businesses make excellent money laundries.

To address the problem of **money laundering**, the federal government enacted the **Money Laundering Control Act** [18 U.S.C. Section 1957]. This act makes it a crime to:

- knowingly engage in a *monetary transaction* through a financial institution involving property worth more than $10,000.

  > **Example**   This would include making deposits, making withdrawals, conducting transactions between accounts, or obtaining monetary instruments such as cashiers' checks, money orders, and travelers' checks from a bank or other financial institution.

- knowingly engage in a *financial transaction* involving the proceeds of an illegal activity.

  > **Example**   This would include buying real estate, automobiles, personal property, intangible assets, or anything else of value with money obtained from illegal activities.

Money Laundering Control Act A federal statute that makes it a crime to (1) knowingly engage in a *money transaction* through a financial institution involving property worth more than $10,000 and (2) knowingly engage in a *financial transaction* involving the proceeds of an illegal activity.

Thus, money laundering itself is now a federal crime. The money that is washed could have been made from illegal gambling operations, drug dealing, fraud, and other crimes, including white-collar crimes. Persons convicted of money laundering can be fined or imprisoned or both. In addition, violation of the act subjects any property involved in or traceable to the offense to forfeiture to the government.

Inchoate Crimes

In addition to the substantive crimes discussed, a person can be held criminally liable for committing an **inchoate crime,** which includes incomplete crimes and crimes committed by nonparticipants. The most important inchoate crimes are discussed in the following paragraphs.

Criminal Conspiracy

Criminal conspiracy A crime in which two or more persons enter into an agreement to commit a crime and an overt act is taken to further the crime.

When two or more persons enter into an *agreement* to commit a crime, it is termed **criminal conspiracy.** To be liable for a criminal conspiracy, the conspirators must take an **overt act** to further the crime. The crime itself does not have to be committed, however. The government usually brings criminal conspiracy charges if (1) the defendants have been thwarted in their efforts to commit the substantive crime, or (2) insufficient evidence is available to prove the substantive crime.

Example   Two securities brokers agree by telephone to commit a securities fraud. They also obtain a list of potential victims and prepare false financial statements necessary for the fraud. Because they entered into an agreement to commit a crime and took overt action, the brokers are guilty of the crime of criminal conspiracy even if they didn't carry out the securities fraud.

Attempt to Commit a Crime

The **attempt to commit a crime** is itself a crime.

Example   Suppose a person wants to kill his neighbor. He shoots at her but misses. The perpetrator is not liable for the crime of murder, but he is liable for the crime of attempted murder.

Aiding and Abetting the Commission of a Crime

Sometimes persons assist others in the commission of a crime. The act of **aiding and abetting** the commission of a crime is itself a crime. This concept, which is broad, encompasses rendering support, assistance, or encouragement to the commission of a crime.

Example   Harboring a criminal after he or she has committed a crime is considered aiding and abetting.

Corporate Criminal Liability

A corporation is a fictitious legal person that is granted legal existence by the state only after meeting certain requirements. A corporation cannot act on its own behalf. Instead, it must act through *agents* such as managers, representatives, and employees.

The question of whether a corporation can be held criminally liable has intrigued legal scholars for some time. Originally, under the common law, it was generally held that corporations lacked the criminal mind (*mens rea*) to be held criminally liable. Modern courts, however, are more pragmatic. These courts have held that corporations are criminally liable for the acts of their managers, agents, and employees. In any event, because corporations cannot be put in prison, they usually are sanctioned with fines, loss of a license or franchise, and the like.

Corporate directors, officers, and employees are individually liable for crimes they personally commit, whether for personal benefit or on behalf of the corporation. In addition, under certain circumstances a corporate manager can be held criminally liable for the criminal activities of his or her subordinates. To be held criminally liable, the manager must have failed to supervise the subordinate appropriately. This is an evolving area of the law. A paralegal's duty to report criminal activity is discussed in the Ethical Perspective feature on page 723.

ETHICAL PERSPECTIVE

Duty to Report Criminal Activity

Ms. Gutierrez is a paralegal who works at a white-collar criminal defense law firm. Ms. Gutierrez works directly for Mr. Darrow, a partner at the law firm.

One day Mr. Darrow requests that Ms. Gutierrez sit in on a meeting with him and a client of the firm. The client, Mr. Elliot, owns Securities Corporation. Mr. Elliot explains that he and Securities Corporation are under investigation by the federal government for engaging in criminal fraud, insider trading, wire fraud, and mail fraud. Mr. Elliot has hired Mr. Darrow and his law firm to represent him and the company during the federal investigation and possible criminal lawsuit. At the meeting, Mr. Elliot discloses that he wants to get cash out of Securities Corporation before the federal government goes any further with its investigation.

Mr. Darrow, who is an expert in white-collar criminal matters, tells Mr. Elliot he can accomplish this if Mr. Elliot starts another business that is secretly owned by Mr. Elliot through a front, transfers the cash from Securities Corporation to this new business, and then transfers the cash to a bank located in the Bahamas in a bank account in Mr. Elliot's name. Mr. Darrow explains that the Bahamas has bank secrecy laws that prevent any party, including the United States government, from discovering the owner of and the amount of money in bank accounts that are located in the Bahamas.

Mr. Elliot asks Mr. Darrow if he will help him do this, and Mr. Darrow agrees. The actions that Mr. Elliot proposes, and Mr. Darrow has agreed to help accomplish, would constitute criminal conspiracy, criminal fraud, money laundering, and other federal crimes. Ms. Gutierrez has been a witness to this conversation and agreement.

What should Ms. Gutierrez do?

Model and state paralegal codes of ethics and professional responsibility provide that a paralegal who possesses knowledge of future criminal activity must report this fact to the appropriate authorities. This is so even if the paralegal has become aware of the information in a situation where the attorney–client privilege or the work-product rule would normally protect such information from being disclosed.

PARALEGAL'S ETHICAL DECISION

Ms. Gutierrez owes an ethical duty to report the criminal conspiracy between Mr. Elliot and attorney Mr. Darrow to the appropriate authorities. This decision is a difficult decision for a paralegal professional to make because it would implicate her supervising attorney. Even so, Ms. Gutierrez owes an ethical duty to report the criminal conspiracy to the government authorities.

Concept Review *and* Reinforcement

LEGAL TERMINOLOGY

SUMMARY OF KEY CONCEPTS

Crimes

Definition	A crime is any act done by a person in violation of those duties that he or she owes to society and for the breach of which the law provides a penalty.
Penal Codes and Regulatory Statutes	Penal codes are state and federal statutes that define many crimes. Criminal conduct also is defined in many regulatory statutes.
Parties to a Criminal Lawsuit	1. *Plaintiff:* The government, which is represented by the prosecuting attorney or prosecutor or district attorney in the state court systems. In the federal system this attorney is called the United States Attorney. 2. *Defendant:* The person or business accused of the crime, who is represented by a defense attorney. If the defense attorney is a government attorney the attorney is called a public defender.
Classification of Crimes	1. *Felonies:* The most serious kinds of crimes; *mala in se* (inherently evil); usually punishable by imprisonment. 2. *Misdemeanors:* Less serious crimes; *mala prohibita* (prohibited by society); usually punishable by fine and/or imprisonment for less than one year. 3. *Violations:* Not a felony or a misdemeanor; generally punishable by a fine.
Elements of a Crime	Intent crimes require the following elements: 1. *Actus reus:* Guilty act 2. *Mens rea:* Evil intent
Non-Intent Crimes	Crimes that do not require intent. An example is the crime of involuntary manslaughter that can be found based on reckless conduct.

Common Crimes

Crimes Against the Person	Crimes against the person include: 1. Assault 2. Battery 3. Mayhem 4. Rape 5. Kidnapping 6. False imprisonment
Murder	Murder is the unlawful killing of another human being with intent.
Robbery	Robbery is the taking of personal property from another by fear or force.
Burglary	Burglary is the unauthorized entering of a building to commit a felony.
Larceny	Larceny is the wrongful taking of another's property other than from his or her person or building.
Theft	Theft is the wrongful taking of another's property, whether by robbery, burglary, or larceny.
Receiving Stolen Property	Receiving stolen property is (1) knowingly receiving stolen property and (2) intending to deprive the rightful owner of that property.
Arson	Arson is the malicious and willful burning of another's building.
Forgery	Forgery is the fraudulent making or altering of a written document that affects the legal liability of another person.
Extortion	Extortion is the threat to expose something about another person unless that person gives up money or property. Also called *blackmail*.

White-Collar Crimes

Definition	White-collar crimes are those that are prone to be committed by businesspersons and involve cunning and trickery rather than physical force.
Embezzlement	Embezzlement is the fraudulent conversion of property by a person to whom the property was entrusted.
Criminal Fraud	Criminal fraud involves obtaining title to another's property through deception or trickery. Also called *false pretenses* or *deceit*.
Mail Fraud	Mail fraud is the use of mail to defraud another person.
Wire Fraud	Wire fraud is the use of wire (telephone or telegraph) to defraud another person.
Bribery	Bribery is the offer of payment of money or property or something else of value in return for an unwarranted favor. The payor of a bribe also is guilty of the crime of bribery. 1. *Commercial bribery* is the offer of a payment of a bribe to a private person or a business. This often is referred to as a *kickback* or *payoff*. 2. Bribery of a public official for an "official act" is a crime.
Foreign Corrupt Practices Act	A federal statute that makes it illegal for U.S. companies, or their officers, directors, agents, or employees, to bribe a foreign official or foreign political party official to influence the awarding of new business or the retention of continuous business activity.

Identity Theft

Identity Fraud	A crime where one person steals information about another person and poses as that person and takes the innocent person's money or property or purchases goods and services using the victim's credit information.
Identity Theft and Assumption Deterrence Act	A federal statute that makes identity theft a federal crime and provides for prison sentences for violating the act.

Organized Crime

Definition	Organized crime consists of a criminal organization and its members who engage in crime on a routine basis.
Racketeer Influenced and Corrupt Organizations Act (RICO)	RICO makes it a federal crime to acquire or maintain an interest in, use income from, or conduct or participate in the affairs of an "enterprise" through a "pattern" of "racketeering activity." Criminal penalties include the *forfeiture* of any property or business interests gained by a RICO violation. 1. *Criminal RICO:* Permits the government to bring criminal actions against violators of RICO and obtain jail sentences against convicted violators. 2. *Civil RICO:* Permits persons injured by a RICO violation to sue the violator and recover treble damages for injury caused to their business or property.
Money Laundering Control Act	A federal statute that makes money laundering a federal crime.

Inchoate Crimes

Definition	Inchoate crimes are crimes that are incomplete or are committed by nonparticipants.
Criminal Conspiracy	A criminal conspiracy consists of two or more persons entering into an *agreement* to commit a crime and taking some *overt act* to further the crime.
Attempt to Commit a Crime	The attempt to commit a crime is a crime even if the commission of the intended crime is unsuccessful.
Aiding and Abetting the Commission of a Crime	Aiding and abetting refer to rendering support, assistance, or encouragement to the commission of a crime, or knowingly harboring a criminal after he or she has committed a crime.

Corporate Criminal Liability

Definition	Corporations are criminally liable for the acts of their managers, employees, and agents. Punishment is usually the assessment of fines, loss of license, or other sanctions.

WORKING THE WEB

1. Go to the website of the Federal Bureau of Investigation (FBI) at http://www.fbi.gov/. Read one of the articles that appear under the section "Breaking News." What is the subject matter of this article?
2. Go to the website of the Internet Crime Complaint Center (IC3) at http://www.ic3.gov/default.aspx. What is the IC3? Read the section "Filing a Complaint with IC3."
3. Go to www.google.com or other Internet search engine and find the website for the prosecuting attorney's office for the county in which you are located. Read the

information that is available that describes the functions of the county prosecutor.
4. Go to the website of the U.S. Attorney at http://www.usdj.gov/usao/. What is the mission of the United States Attorneys. Find the address and telephone number of the U.S. Attorney's office closest to you.
5. Go to www.google.com or other Internet search engine and find the definition of the crime of bribery for the state you live in. Read this definition. What are the elements of the crime of bribery?

1. What is a penal code? Give an example of a crime defined by the penal code. What types of crimes are prohibited by regulatory statutes? Give an example of such a crime.
2. Describe the difference between the following classifications of crimes: felonies, misdemeanors, violations.
3. Define *actus reus*. Define *mens rea*. What is a non-intent crime? Give an example.
4. What are the differences between a criminal law and civil law? What is the jury vote required for each? What is the standard of proof required for each?
5. Define the following common crimes: (a) robbery, (b) burglary, (c) larceny, and (d) receiving stolen property.
6. Describe the crime of murder. What is the crime of involuntary manslaughter?
7. Describe each of the following crimes: (a) forgery, (b) extortion, (c) bribery, and (d) embezzlement.
8. Define criminal fraud. What is mail fraud? What is wire fraud?
9. Describe the crime made unlawful by the Foreign Corrupt Practices Act. Give an example.
10. Describe the crime made unlawful by the Identity Theft and Assumption Deterrence Act.
11. Describe the crime made unlawful by the Racketeer Influenced and Corrupt Organizations Act (RICO). Give an example.
12. Describe the crime made unlawful by the Money Laundering Control Act. Give an example of money laundering.
13. Describe the criminal liability of corporations.
14. Describe the following inchoate crimes: (a) criminal conspiracy, (b) attempt to commit a crime, and (c) aiding and abetting the commission of a crime.

Building Paralegal Skills

Attorney–Client Privilege: Confidentiality Issue

In a meeting between a paralegal and a client, the client reveals to the paralegal conduct that may be criminal in nature.

After viewing the video case study at www.pearsonhighered.com/goldman answer the following:

1. Does the paralegal have a duty to disclose fraudulent activity?
2. Is the paralegal protected under the attorney–client privilege?
3. Is the information of commission of a crime covered under the duty of confidentiality?

1. As a paralegal you work for a white-collar criminal defense firm. A client of the firm is a corporate executive who has "cooked the books" of his corporation and defrauded investors out of millions of dollars, some who were elderly persons who lost their life savings. You are incensed by the client's actions. As a paralegal, do you owe a duty to assist your supervising attorney in preparing the criminal defense for the executive?
2. You are a paralegal who works for the state government assisting a public defender attorney, your supervising attorney, in the defense of common criminals. One defendant is accused of attempted murder of his spouse. It is obvious the defendant is guilty of this charge. Can you report this fact to the judge overseeing the case?
3. In the prior example, you are at a meeting with the public defender and the defendant and the defendant says, "I may have missed killing her before, but if I get off she's dead!" Do you have a duty to report this statement to the judge overseeing the case or other government official?

DEVELOPING YOUR COLLABORATION SKILLS

With a group of other students, selected by you or assigned by your instructor, review the "Paralegals at Work" scenario at the beginning of the chapter. As a group, discuss the following questions.

1. What are the elements of criminal fraud? Is Mr. Johnson, the defendant, guilty of criminal fraud?
2. What is embezzlement? Is Mr. Johnson guilty of the crime of extortion?
3. What is the crime of money laundering? Does it violate any federal laws? Has Mr. Johnson engaged in money laundering?
4. What is mail fraud? What is wire fraud? What is computer fraud? Is Mr. Johnson guilty of any of these crimes?
5. If Mr. Johnson is found guilty of a crime, can he keep his house and other real estate purchased with his ill-gotten gains?

PARALEGAL PORTFOLIO EXERCISE

Using the website http://google.com/html or similar Internet website, or the Internet legal services Westlaw or LexisNexis, or law books, find a copy of the jury instruction for first-degree murder in your state. Write a two-page report discussing the elements necessary to prove first-degree murder in your state.

LEGAL ANALYSIS & WRITING CASES

People v. Shaw 10 Cal.App.4th 969, 12 Cal Rptr.2d 665, Web 1992 Cal.App. Lexis 1256

Court of Appeal of California

Leo Shaw, an attorney, entered into a partnership agreement with three other persons to build and operate an office building. From the outset, it was agreed that Shaw's role was to manage the operation of the building. Management of the property was Shaw's contribution to the partnership; the other three partners contributed the necessary capital.

Ten years later, the other partners discovered that the loan on the building was in default and that foreclosure proceedings were imminent. Upon investigation, they discovered that Shaw had taken approximately $80,000 from the partnership's checking account. After heated discussions, Shaw repaid $13,000. When no further payment was forthcoming, a partner filed a civil suit against Shaw and notified the police. The state filed a criminal complaint against Shaw. Shaw repaid the remaining funds as part of a civil settlement. At his criminal trial, Shaw argued that the repayment of the money was a defense to the crime of embezzlement.

Question

1. Is Shaw guilty of the crime of embezzlement?

United States v. Cloud 872 F.2d 846, Web 1989 U.S. App. Lexis 4534

United States Court of Appeals for the Ninth Circuit

Ronald V. Cloud purchased the Cal-Neva Lodge, a hotel and casino complex located in the Lake Tahoe area near the California–Nevada border, for $10 million. Cloud was a sophisticated 68-year-old entrepreneur who was experienced in buying and selling real estate and had real estate holdings valued at more than $65 million. He also had experience in banking and finance, having been the founder and chairman of Continental National Bank of Fresno. After two years of mounting operation losses, Cloud closed the Cal-Neva Lodge and actively began seeking a new buyer. Cloud met with Jon Perroton and orally agreed to transfer the lodge to Perroton for approximately $17 million. Perroton met with an executive of Hibernia Bank (Hibernia) to discuss a possible loan to finance the purchase of the lodge. Perroton made multiple false representations and presented false documents to obtain a $20 million loan from Hibernia. In particular, Perroton misrepresented the sale price for the lodge ($27.5 million) and stated that $7.5 million had already been paid to Cloud. An escrow account was opened with Transamerica Title Company (Transamerica).

Cloud and his attorney and Perroton met at Transamerica to sign mutual escrow instructions. Cloud reviewed the instructions and noticed that the sale price and down payment figures were incorrectly stated at $27.5 million and $7.5 million, respectively, and that the Hibernia loan was for $20 million, almost $3 million above what he knew to be the true sale price. Cloud signed the escrow instructions. Later, Cloud signed a settlement statement containing the same false figures and signed a grant deed to the property. The sale closed on January 23, 1985, with Hibernia making the $20 million loan to Perroton. Subsequently, when the loan went into default, Continental Insurance Company (Continental) paid Hibernia its loss of $7.5 million on the bank's blanket bond insurance policy. The United States sued Cloud for aiding and abetting a bank fraud in violation of federal law (18 U.S.C. Sections 2 and 1344). The jury convicted Cloud of the crime and ordered him to make restitution of $7.5 million to Continental. Cloud appealed.

Question

1. Is Cloud guilty of aiding and abetting a bank fraud?

Dixon and Hinton v. United States   465 U.S. 482, 104 S.Ct. 1172, 79 L.Ed.2d 458, Web 1984 U.S. Lexis 35

Supreme Court of the United States

The city of Peoria, Illinois, received federal funds from the Department of Housing and Urban Development (HUD) to be used for housing rehabilitation assistance. The city of Peoria designated United Neighborhoods, Inc. (UNI), a corporation, to administer the funds. Arthur Dixon was UNI's executive director, and James Lee Hinton was its housing rehabilitation coordinator. In these capacities, they were responsible for contracting with suppliers and tradespeople to provide the necessary goods and services to rehabilitate the houses. Evidence showed that Dixon and Hinton used their positions to extract 10 percent payments back on all contracts they awarded.

Question

1. What crime has been committed?

State of Utah v. Roberts   711 P.2d 235, Web 1985 Utah Lexis 872

Supreme Court of Utah

Miriam Marlowe's husband purchased a life insurance policy on his own life, naming his wife as the beneficiary. Three years later, after Marlowe's husband died in a swimming accident, Marlowe received payment on the life insurance policy. Marlowe later met John Walton, a friend of a friend. He convinced her and her representative that he had a friend who worked for the State Department and had access to gold in Brazil and that the gold could be purchased in Brazil for $100 an ounce and sold in the United States for $300 an ounce. Walton convinced Miriam to invest $25,000. Instead of investing the money in gold in Brazil, Walton opened an account at Tracy Collins Bank in the name of Jeffrey McIntyre Roberts and deposited Miriam's money in the account. He later withdrew the money in cash.

Question

1. What crime is Walton guilty of?

WORKING WITH THE LANGUAGE OF THE COURT CASE

Commonwealth v. Benjamin Serrano

74 Mass.App.Ct. 1, 903 N.E.2d 247, 2009 Mass. App. Lexis 384
Appeals Court of Massachusetts

Read the following case, excerpted from the appeals court's opinion. Review and brief the case. In your brief, answer the following questions:

1. What crime was the defendant tried for?
2. What crime was the co-defendant convicted of in a separate trial?
3. Do you think the jury instruction given by the judge on the aspect of joint venture was appropriate?
4. Was the defendant found guilty of the crime charged?

(continued)

Brown, Judge

The defendant appeals from his conviction of murder in the second degree. He seeks a new trial on the grounds that (1) the judge improperly refused to give instructions on withdrawal from a joint venture, (2) the judge improperly instructed the jury on an aspect of joint venture not pursued by the Commonwealth at trial, (3) the judge erred in allowing the prosecution to present evidence that the defendant was incarcerated prior to the murder, and (4) the prosecutor wrongfully argued facts not in evidence.

Facts. The jury could have found the following facts. In October of 2003, while the defendant was in jail, his girlfriend at the time broke up with him. In January of 2004, she began dating the victim. During the remainder of the defendant's incarceration, the now ex-girlfriend received many letters from the defendant, pleading with her to resume the relationship. After he got out of prison in February of 2004, the defendant began to harass the ex-girlfriend and her new boyfriend, the victim, on the telephone and by confronting them in person, on multiple occasions. At these encounters, he threatened to kill her, members of her family, and the victim.

At around 9 P.M., April 1, 2004, the fatal confrontation between the victim and defendant occurred. The defendant went to the ex-girlfriend's apartment with a companion, Luis Penn, the codefendant. [Penn was found guilty after a separate jury trial of murder in the first degree.] When the defendant knocked at the door, he was told that the ex-girlfriend was not there. The defendant then went outside, where he saw the victim's car. The two occupants of the car, neither of whom was the victim, got out and questioned the defendant as to why he was following them. The defendant took out a gun and told the two men to leave, and that "it's not with you." One of the men told him to put down the gun and use his hands, pulling up his shirt to show the defendant that he was unarmed. Shortly thereafter the victim emerged from the ex-girlfriend's home.

The victim stepped between the defendant and the two men; an argument ensued about the ex-girlfriend. One of the men continued to yell at the defendant to "fight like a man." The defendant summoned the codefendant over and gave him the gun. After the defendant punched the victim, a fight erupted between the two; all the while the codefendant pointed the gun at the other two men, one of whom left the scene to call the police. The fight moved up the street. The victim broke away from the defendant. A man who was pumping gasoline about a block away saw the codefendant and the victim engage in a face-to-face argument for about thirty

seconds, and then he saw the codefendant shoot the victim in the head. He did not see the defendant. The man called 911 on his cellular telephone; he then followed the codefendant to see if he recognized him.

Withdrawal instruction. The defendant argues that there was insufficient evidence of a joint venture, and that the codefendant was solely responsible for the victim's death. He requested an instruction on withdrawal from a joint venture. In light of the lack of evidence demonstrating that the defendant communicated to the codefendant his intention to withdraw from the enterprise, the judge, apparently concluding that there was an insufficient basis to support the withdrawal theory, declined to give the instruction at the close of the case.

Assuming that the defendant properly preserved all issues relating to the withdrawal instruction,[2] we think there was insufficient evidence at trial to warrant a withdrawal instruction. We conclude, as did the trial judge, that the events immediately leading to the victim's death happened very quickly, and no "appreciable interval between the alleged termination and the fatal shooting, a detachment from the enterprise before the shooting has become so probable that it cannot reasonably be stayed, and such notice or definite act of detachment that [the] other principal [] in the attempted crime [had] opportunity also to abandon it" occurred here.

Joint venture instructions. During deliberations, the jury sent the judge a note asking: "Does [the defendant] have to be present at the time of actual 'murder'?" In response, the judge instructed that "a joint venturer . . . has to be present at or near the scene. But . . . you don't have to be right at the location." "[T]he Commonwealth does not have to prove that the defendant was actually present at the scene at the time that the gun was shot, as long as the Commonwealth shows that the defendant was present; that is, was at or near the general vicinity of the crime, at—at some point during the joint venture. The joint venturer does not have to be there at the culmination of the crime."

There was no substantial risk of a miscarriage of justice. By describing "presence" to mean "at or near the general vicinity of the crime . . . at some point during the joint venture," the judge correctly stated the law.

[S]ince the defendant here (1) initiated the animosity between himself and the victim; (2) brought the gun to the altercation; (3) threatened on multiple occasions to kill the victim, even stating, "This is how I want to catch you," as he pointed the gun at the victim's head; (4) proceeded to beat up the victim after handing the gun to his companion; and (5) did not engage in any other "withdrawal" behavior, his presence at the time of the fatal shot is of no consequence in a determination whether he was a joint venturer. Furthermore, the defendant "acted with knowledge of the [crime] and with the intent to assist in the commission of that crime so as to accomplish [*6] its objective," which was to harm the victim. Moreover, as already mentioned, the jury were warranted in finding that the defendant made no communication to the codefendant of his lack of intent to kill or cause grievous bodily harm to the victim. In short, his willingness and availability to help his companion (or in this case, his acquiescing to his companion's shooting of the victim) have been established on the record.

Judgment affirmed.

CHAPTER
20

Intellectual Property and Digital Law

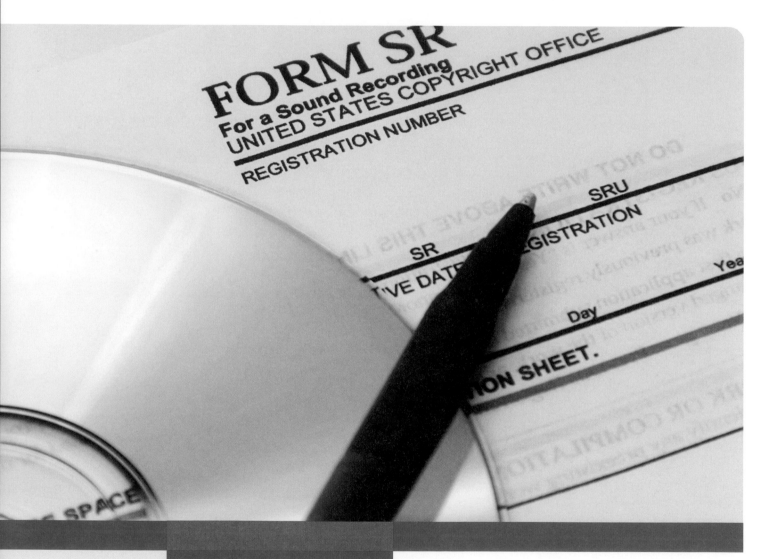

DIGITAL RESOURCES

Chapter 20 Digital Resources at *www.pearsonhighered.com/goldman*

- Video Case Studies:
  - Confidentiality Issue: Need-to-Know Circle
- Chapter Summary • Web Links • Court Opinions • Glossary • Comprehension Quizzes
- Technology Resources

> "The Congress shall have the power . . . to promote the Progress of Science and useful Arts, by securing for limited Times to Authors and Inventors the exclusive Right to their respective Writings and Discoveries."

Article 1, Section 8, Clause 8,
U.S. Constitution

After studying this chapter, you should be able to:

1. Recognize the professional opportunities for paralegals in digital and intellectual property law.
2. Describe the business tort of misappropriating a trade secret.
3. Describe how an invention can be patented under patent laws and the penalties for patent infringement.
4. List the writings and other works that can be copyrighted, and describe the penalties for copyright infringement.
5. Describe the legal rights that computer and software designers have in their works.
6. Define *trademarks* and *service marks,* and describe the penalties for trademark infringement.
7. Describe Internet law.
8. Explain the process for obtaining Internet domain names.
9. Describe the protections provided by the federal Anticybersquatting Act.
10. Describe important digital laws.
11. Explain a paralegal's duty to disclose his or her paralegal status and conflict of interest.

Paralegals at Work

You are a paralegal for a boutique law firm that specializes in intellectual property and Internet law. The lawyers of the firm are known for their expertise in this area of the law. As a paralegal, you often work for different partners of the law firm, depending upon the needs of the firm.

One day, Ms. Maria Rodriquez, an intellectual property lawyer and partner at the firm, calls you into her office. Waiting in the office is a client, Mr. Geek Einstein. Ms. Rodriquez introduces you to Mr. Einstein and asks you to sit in on a meeting between them. Ms. Rodriquez cautions you that everything said is highly confidential.

Mr. Einstein goes on to explain that he has invented a new digital basketball shoe that will allow wearers of the shoe to jump at least 8 inches higher in the air than if they wore competing nondigital basketball shoes. Mr. Einstein describes his digital technology that, if imbedded in a shoe, allows a user to jump this high. Mr. Einstein goes on to explain that he believes no such digital technology exists, and that he is the first inventor of this technology.

Further, Mr. Einstein explains that he has determined a name he would like to call the basketball shoe—"Einstein+2." He also shows you a design he has drawn that he wants to be used as the logo for the shoe. The logo is an "E" with a "2" superimposed over it, using script writing. He also tells you that he has a new slogan—"Plus 2"—for the advertising campaign for the shoe.

Mr. Einstein shows you a ten-page *User's Manual* he has written that is to be inserted into each shoebox explaining how to use his new digital basketball shoe. In addition, Mr. Einstein explains that he would like to sell the shoe not only in stores but also over the Internet, using the website name "Einstein+2."

Consider the issues involved in this scenario as you read the chapter.

INTRODUCTION FOR THE PARALEGAL

Intellectual property Patents, copyrights, trademarks, trade secrets, trade names, domain names, and other valuable business assets. Federal and state laws protect intellectual property rights from misappropriation and infringement.

Often, a paralegal will work in an area of the law that requires a unique and special expertise of statutory law. One of these areas is cyber law and intellectual property. Many boutique law firms or departments of large law firms specialize in **intellectual property** such as patents, copyrights, trademarks, trade secrets, and domain names. Other lawyers specialize in e-commerce and Internet law. A paralegal who works for lawyers in these areas must have knowledge of the major statutes, cases, and issues of these law subjects.

The American economy is based on the freedom of ownership of property. In addition to real estate and personal property, intellectual property rights have value to both businesses and individuals. This is particularly the case in the modern Information Age, computers, and the Internet.

Trade secrets form the basis of many successful businesses, which are protected from misappropriation. Federal law provides protections for intellectual property rights, such as patents, copyrights, and trademarks. In addition, businesses and individuals may register domain names to use on the Internet. Anyone who infringes on these rights may be stopped from doing so and is liable for damages. Computers and computer software are accorded special protections from infringement.

The use of the Internet and the World Wide Web, along with the sale of goods and services through e-commerce, has exploded. Large and small businesses sell goods and services over the Internet through websites and registered domain names. Consumers and businesses can purchase almost any good or service they want over the Internet. Businesses and individuals may register domain names to use on the Internet. Anyone who infringes on these rights may be stopped from doing so and is liable for damages.

Intellectual property rights and digital law are important developing areas of the law. Therefore, a paralegal has to acquire knowledge of these important areas of the law to search government websites, conduct research in the areas of intellectual property rights and digital law, and help prepare documents for the creation and transfer of intellectual property rights. This chapter covers trade secrets, patents, copyrights, trademarks, digital law, and domain names.

Trade Secret

Trade secret A product formula, pattern, design, compilation of data, customer list, or other business secret.

Many businesses are successful because their **trade secrets** set them apart from their competitors. Trade secrets may be product formulas, patterns, designs, compilations of data, customer lists, or other business secrets. Many trade secrets do not qualify to be— or simply are not—patented, copyrighted, or trademarked. Many states have adopted the Uniform Trade Secrets Act to give statutory protection to trade secrets.

Web Exploration

Use www.google.com and see if you can find the purported secret recipe for original Coca-Cola posted on someone's website.

Example The most famous trade secret is the formula for Coca-Cola. This secret recipe, which is referred to by the code name "Merchandise 7X," is kept in a bank vault in Atlanta, Georgia. The formula is supposedly known by only two executives who have signed nondisclosure agreements.

CAREER OPPORTUNITIES FOR PARALEGALS IN INTELLECTUAL PROPERTY AND DIGITAL LAW

Paralegals can work in one of the most explosive areas of the law today: intellectual property rights. Lawyers and paralegals both have been able to find excellent positions in this dynamic area of the law, provided, however, that they learn significant knowledge of intellectual property laws and procedures.

Who does not recognize the business names "McDonald's Corporation" or "Microsoft Corporation"? And who does not know the famous phrases, "Diamonds are Forever" or, "Just Do It." These are examples of famous trademarks. Paralegals who work for lawyers that practice in the trademark field must know how to search for available names at the U.S. Patent and Trademark Office, as well as how to complete the necessary documents for obtaining or renewing trademarks.

The copyright area is similar in requiring paralegals who know how to work with copyright lawyers. Copyrights are an extremely important intellectual property right. Movies, books, screenplays, paintings, sculptures, and software can be copyrighted. Therefore, a paralegal must know how the U.S. Copyright Office works, how to check on the availability of proposed names and phrases, and how to complete the documentation for obtaining a copyright.

Of the intellectual property rights areas, the area of patent law is the most complex for lawyers and paralegals alike. Lawyers who practice in this area must pass a separate patent law examination. The determination of whether an invention, drug, biomedicine, or other innovation is patentable, or whether a patent exists on these, requires significant skill and knowledge. Drafting the patent application to be filed with the U.S. Patent and Trademark office is extremely complicated. Paralegals with science, biology, chemistry, engineering, or related education are indispensable in assisting patent lawyers.

A new form of intellectual property has developed with the advent of the Internet and the World Wide Web. Businesses and individuals can now sell and purchase goods and services using the Internet. Cyber law provides that businesses and individuals can operate using Web addresses and domain names. Domain names sometimes are valuable property rights. Many federal and state laws protect business and privacy rights involving the Internet. This area of the law offers paralegals a new avenue in which to apply their skills.

In addition, paralegals support lawyers who are engaged in lawsuits and arbitration proceedings that allege infringement of trademarks, copyrights, patents, or domain names. Paralegals support lawyers involved on both sides of these infringement cases. Therefore, paralegals who provide support in litigation and arbitration of intellectual property rights must know the area of the law involved as well as the procedures, pleadings, documents, discovery, and other issues involved in the dispute.

Intellectual property and digital law is a growing area of the law for lawyers and paralegals. Paralegals have a great opportunity to join this complex, yet dynamic area of the law.

Misappropriation of a Trade Secret

State unfair competition laws allow the owner of a trade secret to bring a civil lawsuit for **misappropriation** against anyone who steals a trade secret. To be actionable, the defendant (often an employee of the owner or a competitor) must have obtained the trade secret through unlawful means such as theft, bribery, or industrial espionage. No tort has occurred if there is no misappropriation.

Example A competitor can lawfully discover a trade secret by performing *reverse engineering* (i.e., taking apart and examining a rival's product).

The owner of a trade secret is obliged to take all reasonable precautions to prevent others from discovering that secret. These precautions include fencing in buildings, placing locks on doors, hiring security guards, and the like. If the owner fails to take such actions, the secret is no longer subject to protection under state unfair competition laws.

Generally, a successful plaintiff in a trade secret action can:

1. recover the profits made by the offender from the use of the trade secret,
2. recover for damages, and
3. obtain an injunction prohibiting the offender from divulging or using the trade secret.

Web Exploration

Go to http://www.usatoday.com/money/industries/food/2005-07-22-kfc-secret-recipe_x.htm and read how KFC protects its secret recipe.

Economic Espionage Act

Economic Espionage Act A federal statute that makes it a crime for any person to convert a trade secret for his or another's benefit, knowing or intending to cause injury to the owners of the trade secret.

Until recently—although stealing trade secrets exposes the offender to a civil lawsuit by the injured party to recover economic damages—the offender seldom faced criminal charges except under a few state laws. All of that changed with enactment of the federal **Economic Espionage Act** of 1996 [18 U.S.C. Sections 1831–1839], which makes it a federal crime to steal another's trade secrets.

Under the Espionage Act, it is a federal crime for any person to convert a trade secret to his or her benefit or for the benefit of others, knowing or intending that the act would cause injury to the owner of the trade secret. Under the Espionage Act, the definition of *trade secret* is broad and covers any economic, business, financial, technical, scientific, or engineering information, including processes, software programs, and codes.

One of the major reasons for passing the Espionage Act was to address the ease of stealing trade secrets through espionage and using the Internet. For example, hundreds of pages of confidential information can be downloaded onto a small computer disk, placed in someone's pocket, and taken from the legal owner.

Patent

Federal Patent Statute A federal statute that establishes the requirements for obtaining a patent and protects patented inventions from infringement.

Pursuant to the express authority granted in the U.S. Constitution [Article I, Section 8, clause 8, Congress enacted the **Federal Patent Statute** of 1952 [35 U.S.C. Sections 10 et seq.]. This law is intended to provide an incentive for inventors to invent and make their inventions public and to protect patented inventions from infringement. Federal patent law is exclusive; there are no state patent laws. The United States Court of Appeals for the Federal Circuit in Washington, D.C., was created in 1982 to hear patent appeals. The court was established to promote uniformity in patent law.

Patenting an Invention

For an inventor to be granted a **patent**, a patent application must be filed with the **United States Patent and Trademark Office (PTO)**. To be patented, the **invention** must be *novel*, *useful*, and *nonobvious*. In addition, only certain subject matters can be patented. Patentable subject matter includes (1) machines, (2) processes, (3) compositions of matter, (4) improvements to existing machines, processes, or compositions of matter, (5) designs for an article of manufacture, (6) asexually reproduced plants, and (7) living material invented by a person. Abstractions and scientific principles cannot be patented unless they are part of the tangible environment.

Example Einstein's theory of relativity ($E = MC^2$) cannot be patented.

Patent applicants must file a **patent application** containing a written description of the invention with the United States Patent and Trademark Office in Washington, D.C. If a patent is granted, the invention is assigned a patent number. Patent holders usually affix the word *Patent* or *Pat.* and the patent number to the patented article. If a patent application is filed but a patent has not yet been issued, the applicant usually places the words **patent pending** on the article. Any party can challenge either the issuance of a patent or the validity of an existing patent.

Requirements for Obtaining a Patent

As stated above, to be patented, an invention must be (1) novel, (2) useful, and (3) nonobvious:

1. *Novel.* An invention is novel if it is new and has not been invented and used in the past. If the invention has been used in "prior art," it is not novel and cannot be patented.

   Example College and professional football games are often televised on television and cable stations. Inventors received a patent for a system whereby a yellow line is digitally drawn across the football field on television at the distance that a team has to go to obtain a first down. This "yellow line" invention is novel.

Web Exploration

Go to the website of the U.S. Patent and Trademark Office (PTO) at www.uspto.gov. Read the basic facts about patents. What is the approximate cost for filing a patent application with the PTO?

2. *Useful.* An invention is useful if it has some practical purpose. If an invention has only theoretical benefit, and no useful purpose, it cannot be patented.

> **Example** An inventor received a patent for "forkchops," which are a set of chopsticks where one chopstick has a spoon at the handle-end and the other chopstick has a fork on the handle-end. This invention is novel.

3. *Nonobvious.* If the invention is nonobvious, it qualifies for a patent; if the invention is obvious, then it does not qualify for a patent.

> **Example** Inventors received a patent for a cardboard or heavy paper sleeve that can be placed over the outside of a paper coffee cup so that the cup will not be as hot as if there were no sleeve. This invention serves a useful purpose.

To be patented, an invention must meet all three of these requirements. If an invention is found to not meet any one of these requirements, it cannot be patented. The PTO provides for the online submission of patent applications and documents through its EFS-Web system.

Exhibit 20.1 shows the patent for Thomas Edison's electric lightbulb.

Patent Period

In 1995, in order to bring the U.S. patent system into harmony with the systems of the majority of other developed nations, Congress made the following important changes in U.S. patent law:

1. Patents for inventions are valid for *20 years* (instead of the previous term of 17 years). Design patents are valid for 14 years.
2. The patent term begins to run from the date the patent application is *filed* (instead of when the patent is issued, as was previously the case).

First-to-Invent Rule

The United States still follows the *first-to-invent rule* rather than the *first-to-file rule* followed by some other countries. Thus, in the United States, the first person to invent an item or a process is given patent protection over another party who was first to file a patent application.

> **Example** On January 3, 2010, Nerdette, a straight-A student in college, invents "smork," a chemical formula that can be released into the air and eliminate air pollution. Smork causes no harmful effects to humans, any other living being, or the environment. She keeps her discovery secret, however. Two years later, Nerd, who is a straight-C student in college, invents "dork," which is the same chemical formula as previously invented by Nerdette. The next day Nerd rushes out and files a patent application with the U.S. Patent and Trademark Office. Subsequently, Nerd is issued a patent for Dork. Nerdette later discovers this fact and challenges Nerd's patent since she wishes to patent Smork. Nerdette will win her patent challenge against Nerd because she was the first to invent the invention. Nerd, although he was the first to file for a patent, loses his patent.

Public-Use Doctrine

Under the **public-use doctrine**, a patent may not be granted if the invention was used by the public for more than one year prior to filing of the patent application. This doctrine forces inventors to file their patent applications at the proper time.

> **Example** Suppose Cindy Parsons invents a new invention on January 1. She allows the public to use this invention and does not file a patent application until February of the following year. She has lost the right to patent her invention.

Web Exploration
Go to www.uspto.gov. Click on "5 Search Patents." Click on "Database Contents." Click on "Pat Num." Look up the following two patents by entering their seven-digit patent numbers in the box. Click on "Search." Patent numbers 5205473 and 6863644.

Web Exploration
Go to www.uspto.gov. Click on "5 Search Patents." Click on "Database Contents." Click on "Pat Num." Type the Patent number 3741662 in the open box. Click on "Search." Read the information about this patent.

Exhibit 20.1 Thomas Edison's patent for the electric lightbulb

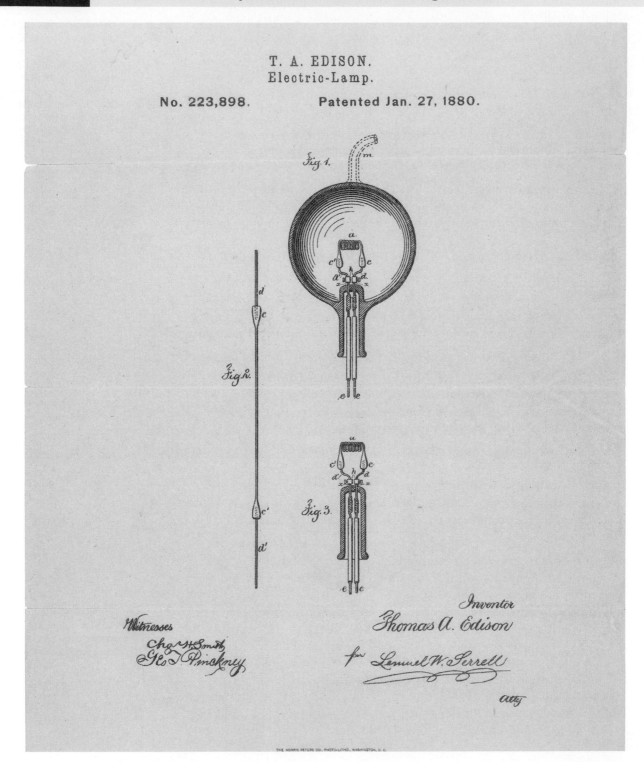

Patent Expiration and Public Domain

After the patent period runs out, the invention or design enters the **public domain**, which means that anyone can produce and sell the invention without paying the prior patent holder.

Example   A patent application for a prescription drug is filed on June 1, 2000, and the invention is subsequently granted a patent. When the 20-year patent period expires on June 1, 2020, any other manufacturer can make this prescription drug. Note: The new manufacturer cannot use the trademark name of the patent holder.

The American Inventors Protection Act

In 1999, Congress enacted the **American Inventors Protection Act**. This statute does the following:

1. Permits an inventor to file a **provisional application** with the PTO, pending the preparation and filing of a final and complete patent application. This part of the law grants "provisional rights" to an inventor for three months, pending the filing of a final application.
2. Requires the PTO to issue a patent within three years after the filing of a patent application unless the applicant engages in dilatory activities.
3. Provides that non-patent holders may challenge a patent as being overly broad by requesting a contested reexamination of the patent application by the PTO. This provides that the reexamination will be within the confines of the PTO; the decision of the PTO can be appealed to the U.S. Court of Appeals for the Federal Circuit in Washington, D.C.

American Inventors Protection Act A federal statute that permits an inventor to file a *provisional application* with the U.S. Patent and Trademark Office (PTO) three months before the filing of a final patent application, among other provisions.

Patent Infringement

Patent holders own exclusive rights to use and exploit their patent. **Patent infringement** occurs when someone makes unauthorized use of another's patent. In a suit for patent infringement, a successful plaintiff can recover:

1. money damages equal to a reasonable royalty rate on the sale of the infringed articles,
2. other damages caused by the infringement (such as loss of customers),
3. an order requiring the destruction of the infringing article, and
4. an injunction preventing the infringer from such action in the future.

The court has the discretion to award up to treble damages if the infringement was intentional.

Exhibit 20.2 shows Google Inc.'s international patent application filed with the World Intellectual Property Organization (WIPO) for "Recognizing Text in Images."

Patent infringement Unauthorized use of another's patent. A patent holder may recover damages and other remedies against a patent infringer.

 Web Exploration

Go to the website of the U.S. Court of Appeals for the Federal Circuit in Washington, DC at wwwfedcir.gov. Click on "About the Court." Read about the authority of this court.

Copyright

A **copyright** is the exclusive legal right to reproduce, publish, and sell a literary, musical, or artistic work. Congress enacted a federal copyright law pursuant to an express grant of authority in the U.S. Constitution [Article I, Section 8, clause 8]. This law protects the work of authors and other creative persons from the unauthorized use of their copyrighted materials and provides a financial incentive for authors to write, thereby increasing the number of creative works available in society. The **Copyright Revision Act** of 1976 governs copyright law [17 U.S.C. Sections 101 et seq.]. Federal copyright law is exclusive; there are no state copyright laws.

Only **tangible writings**—writings that can be physically seen—are subject to copyright registration and protection. The term *writing* has been defined broadly to include books, periodicals, and newspapers; lectures, sermons, and addresses; musical compositions; plays, motion pictures, radio and television productions; maps; works of art, including paintings, drawings, sculpture, jewelry, glassware, tapestry, and lithographs; architectural drawings and models; photographs, including prints, slides, and filmstrips; greeting cards and picture postcards; photoplays, including feature films, cartoons, newsreels, travelogues, and training films; and sound recordings published in the form of tapes, cassettes, compact disks, and phonograph albums. Software also can be copyrighted.

Copyright Revision Act A federal statute that (1) establishes the requirements for obtaining a copyright and (2) protects copyrighted works from infringement.

(12) INTERNATIONAL APPLICATION PUBLISHED UNDER THE PATENT COOPERATION TREATY (PCT)

(19) World Intellectual Property Organization
International Bureau

(43) International Publication Date
3 January 2008 (03.01.2008)

PCT

(10) International Publication Number
WO 2008/003095 A3

(51) International Patent Classification:
G06F 17/30 (2006.01)

(21) International Application Number:
PCT/US2007/072578

(22) International Filing Date: 29 June 2007 (29.06.2007)

(25) Filing Language: English

(26) Publication Language: English

(30) Priority Data:
11/479,957   29 June 2006 (29.06.2006)   US
11/479,155   29 June 2006 (29.06.2006)   US
11/479,115   29 June 2006 (29.06.2006)   US

(71) Applicant *(for all designated States except US)*:
GOOGLE INC. [US/US]; 1600 Amphitheatre Parkway, Mountain View, California 94043 (US).

(72) Inventors; and

(75) Inventors/Applicants *(for US only)*: VINCENT, Luc [US/US]; 4237 Manuela Avenue, Palo Alto, California 94306 (US). ULGES, Adrian [DE/DE]; Ehrlichsweg 15, 56130 Bad Ems (DE).

(74) Agent: GUSTAFSON, Brian, J.; Fish & Richardson P.C., P.O. Box 1022, Minneapolis, Minnesota 55440-1022 (US).

(81) Designated States *(unless otherwise indicated, for every kind of national protection available)*: AE, AG, AL, AM, AT, AU, AZ, BA, BB, BG, BH, BR, BW, BY, BZ, CA, CH, CN, CO, CR, CU, CZ, DE, DK, DM, DO, DZ, EC, EE, EG, ES, FI, GB, GD, GE, GH, GM, GT, HN, HR, HU, ID, IL, IN, IS, JP, KE, KG, KM, KN, KP, KR, KZ, LA, LC, LK, LR, LS, LT, LU, LY, MA, MD, ME, MG, MK, MN, MW, MX, MY, MZ, NA, NG, NI, NO, NZ, OM, PG, PH, PL, PT, RO, RS, RU, SC, SD, SE, SG, SK, SL, SM, SV, SY, TJ, TM, TN, TR, TT, TZ, UA, UG, US, UZ, VC, VN, ZA, ZM, ZW.

(84) Designated States *(unless otherwise indicated, for every kind of regional protection available)*: ARIPO (BW, GH, GM, KE, LS, MW, MZ, NA, SD, SL, SZ, TZ, UG, ZM, ZW), Eurasian (AM, AZ, BY, KG, KZ, MD, RU, TJ, TM), European (AT, BE, BG, CH, CY, CZ, DE, DK, EE, ES, FI, FR, GB, GR, HU, IE, IS, IT, LT, LU, LV, MC, MT, NL, PL,

[Continued on next page]

(54) Title: RECOGNIZING TEXT IN IMAGES

100

FOX WARFIELD 104
102 SBC
106

(57) Abstract: Methods, systems, and apparatus including computer program products for using extracted image text are provided. In one implementation, a computer-implemented method is provided. The method includes receiving an input of one or more image search terms and identifying keywords from the received one or more image search terms. The method also includes searching a collection of keywords including keywords extracted from image text, retrieving an image associated with extracted image text corresponding to one or more of the image search terms, and presenting the image.

Paralegals *in* Practice

PARALEGAL PROFILE
Kathleen D. Kasiorek

Kathleen D. Kasiorek, a Certified Paralegal, is a graduate of Ferris State University with a Bachelor's Degree in Business Administration and an Associate's Degree in Legal Assisting. She is currently employed as a Senior Paralegal at the law firm of Warner Norcross & Judd, in Grand Rapids, Michigan. Kathleen is also an active participant in several professional associations including the Council of the State Bar of Michigan's Paralegal/Legal Assistant Section.

Most of my 13-year paralegal career has been spent working in intellectual property. In my position, tasks include performing trademark and patent research, filing documents with the U.S. Patent and Trademark Office, maintaining a docketing system and electronic database, communicating with clients and their attorneys, registering and maintaining domain names, tracking time and billing clients, and preparing various reports.

Additional responsibilities include assisting with trademark oppositions and cancellation proceedings, which are administered by the U.S. Patent and Trademark Office, Trademark Trial and Appeal Board, and similar agencies in other countries. I also assist in cases in which counterfeit goods are intercepted by customs officials here and abroad. It is very interesting work and always rewarding when we can successfully stop the "bad guys" from stealing our clients' intellectual property.

My advice to new paralegals is: make an effort to continue learning throughout your career. Things are constantly changing in this field, so it is imperative to stay current on the latest changes and issues. For example, to help keep myself up-to-date, I regularly read journals and periodicals. I also attend seminars and conferences related to the intellectual property practice area. A large part of my work involves collaborating with attorneys from all over the world. In order to communicate more effectively with them, I try to learn as much as I can about other countries and their cultures.

To be protected under federal copyright law, a work must be the original work of the author. A copyright is created when an author produces his or her work.

Example   When a student writes a term paper for her class, she owns a copyright to her work.

Published and unpublished works may be registered with the **United States Copyright Office** in Washington, D.C. **Registration** is permissive and voluntary and can be affected at any time during the term of the copyright.

Copyright Term and Notice

In 1989, the United States signed the **Berne Convention**, an international copyright treaty. This law eliminated the need to place the symbol © or the word "copyright" or "copr." on a copyrighted work. Although notice is now permissive, it is recommended that notice be placed on copyrighted works to defeat a defendant's claim of innocent infringement.

Example   The author of this book would place the following on his manuscripts written in the year 2011:

"Henry Richard Cheeseman © 2011"

Under the **Sonny Bono Copyright Term Extension Act of 1998**, copyright protection is provided for the following time periods:

1. Individuals are granted copyright protection for their life plus 70 years.
2. Copyrights owned by businesses are protected for the shorter of either
   a. 95 years from the year of first publication
   b. 120 years from the year of creation

Example At age 30, Ernst writes the great novel "To Save a Hummingbird." Ernst lives until he is 70. The copyright period of Ernst's great novel is 120 years, which includes the 40 years of his life and 70 years after he is deceased. Thus, Ernst's heirs will receive royalties or other payments due for the publication of the novel for 70 years after Ernst's death.

Copyright Expiration and Public Domain

After the copyright period runs out, the work enters the public domain, which means that anyone can publish the work without paying the prior copyright holder.

Example In the previous example, 70 years after Ernst's death his copyrighted work enters the public domain. This means that anyone can publish Ernst's book and compete with his heirs in selling their book to the public. After that date, you could find several versions of Ernst's book for sale in a bookstore. The consumer can choose to buy whoever's book they like the best.

Copyright Infringement

Copyright infringement An act in which a party copies a substantial and material part of the plaintiff's copyrighted work without permission. A copyright holder may recover damages and other remedies against the infringer.

Copyright infringement occurs when a party copies a substantial and material part of the plaintiff's copyrighted work without permission. The copying does not have to be either word-for-word or the entire work. A successful plaintiff can recover:

1. the profit made by the infringer from the copyright infringement,
2. damages suffered by the plaintiff,
3. an order requiring the impoundment and destruction of the infringing works, and
4. an injunction preventing the infringer from doing so in the future.

The court, at its discretion, can award statutory damages for willful infringement in lieu of actual damages.

NET Act: Criminal Copyright Infringement

No Electronic Theft Act (NET Act) A federal statute that makes it a crime for a person to willfully infringe on a copyright work that exceeds $1,000 in retail value.

A copyright holder owns a valuable right and may sue an infringer in a civil lawsuit to recover damages and obtain injunctions and other remedies for copyright infringement. In 1997, Congress enacted the **No Electronic Theft Act (NET Act),** which criminalizes certain copyright infringement as well.

Congress passed the NET Act to directly criminalize copyright infringement. The NET Act prohibits any person from willfully infringing a copyright for the purpose of commercial advantage or financial gain, or by reproduction or distribution even without commercial advantage or financial gain, including by electronic means. The act provides for criminal penalties including fines and imprisonment.

Fair-Use Doctrine

Fair-use doctrine A doctrine that permits certain limited use of a copyright by someone other than the copyright holder without the permission of the copyright holder.

The copyright holder's rights in the work are not absolute. The law permits certain limited unauthorized use of copyrighted materials under the **fair-use doctrine**. Protected under this doctrine are:

1. quotation of the copyrighted work for review or criticism or in a scholarly or technical work,
2. use in a parody or satire,
3. brief quotation in a news report,
4. reproduction by a teacher or student of a small part of the work to illustrate a lesson,
5. incidental reproduction of a work in a newsreel or broadcast of an event being reported, and
6. reproduction of a work in a legislative or judicial proceeding.

Examples A college student is assigned to write a paper on the history of the Statue of Liberty. The student finds many sources on the Internet about the history of the Statue of Liberty. If the student uses two paragraphs from a copyrighted Internet article in her paper and places the materials in quotation marks and cites the source and author in a footnote, this is fair use for academic purposes. If, however, the student copies and uses three pages from the article, this would not be fair use and would constitute copyright infringement whether she footnotes the author or not.

Digital Millennium Copyright Act

The Internet makes it easier for people to illegally copy and distribute copyrighted works. To combat this, software and entertainment companies developed "wrappers" and encryption technology to protect their copyrighted works from unauthorized access. Not to be outdone, software pirates and other Internet users devised ways to crack these wrappers and protection devices.

Seeing that they were losing the battle, software companies and the entertainment industry lobbied Congress to enact legislation that made illegal the cracking of their wrappers and selling of technology to do so. In 1998, Congress responded by enacting the **Digital Millennium Copyright Act (DMCA)** [17 U.S.C. Section 1201], which does the following:

- Prohibits unauthorized *access* to copyrighted digital works by circumventing the wrapper or encryption technology that protects the intellectual property.
- Prohibits the manufacture and distribution of technologies, products, or services designed primarily for the purpose of circumventing wrappers or encryption protection.

The DMCA imposes civil and criminal penalties. A successful plaintiff in a civil action can recover actual damages from first-time offenders and treble damages from repeat offenders, costs and attorney's fees, an order for the destruction of illegal products and devices, and an injunction against future violations by the offender. Criminal penalties include fines and imprisonment.

Digital Millennium Copyright Act (DMCA) A federal statute that prohibits unauthorized access to copyrighted digital works by circumventing encryption technology or the manufacture and distribution of technologies designed for the purpose of circumventing encryption protection of digital works.

Trademark

Trademark law is intended to (1) protect the owner's investment and goodwill in a mark, and (2) prevent consumers from being confused as to the origin of goods and services. In 1946, Congress enacted the **Lanham Trademark Act** to provide federal protection to trademarks, service marks, and other marks [15 U.S.C. Sections 1114 et seq.]. Congress passed the **Trademark Law Revision Act of 1988**, which amended trademark law in several respects. The amendments made it easier to register a trademark but harder to maintain it. States also may enact trademark laws.

Lanham Trademark Act A federal statute that (1) establishes the requirements for obtaining a federal mark, and (2) protects marks from infringement.

Registration of Trademarks

Trademarks are registered with the United States Patent and Trademark Office in Washington, D.C. The original **registration** of a mark is valid for 10 years and can be renewed for an unlimited number of 10-year periods. The registration of a trademark, which is given nationwide effect, serves as constructive notice that the mark is the registrant's personal property. The registrant is entitled to use the registered trademark symbol ® in connection with a registered trademark or service mark. Use of the symbol is not mandatory. Note that the frequently used notations "TM" and "SM" have no legal significance.

Web Exploration

Go to http://www.coca-cola .com/template1/index.jsp to see trademarks of the Coca-Cola Corporation.

Example McDonald's Corporation owns the trademark "I'm lovin' it." McDonald's received an initial trademark period of 10 years, but must renew its trademark "I'm lovin' it" every 10 years to keep the trademark.

An applicant can register a mark if (1) it was in use in commerce (e.g., actually used in the sale of goods or services), or (2) the applicant verifies a bona fide intention to use the mark in commerce and actually does so within six months of its registration. Failure to do so during this period causes loss of the mark to the registrant. A party other than the registrant can submit an opposition to a proposed registration of a mark or to the cancellation of a previously registered mark.

Distinctiveness of a Mark

To qualify for federal protection, a mark must be either (1) **distinctive** or (2) have acquired a **"secondary meaning."** A distinctive mark would be a word or design that is unique. Ordinary words that are descriptive can qualify as a mark if they have taken on a secondary meaning. Words that are *descriptive* but have no secondary meaning cannot be trademarked.

Examples Marks such as *Xerox* and *Acura* are *distinctive*. These words do not appear in the dictionary, and are therefore distinctive. Nike, Inc. has taken the ordinary words "*Just Do It*" and trademarked the slogan, which has taken on a secondary meaning when it is used in connection with its sporting apparel and goods. When most people see the "Just Do It" language associated with athletic wear and clothing, they think of Nike. The word *cola* alone is descriptive and has not taken on a secondary meaning, so it could not be trademarked.

Types of Marks

Mark The collective name for trademarks, service marks, certification marks, and collective marks.

The word **mark** collectively refers to *trademarks, service marks, certification marks*, and *collective marks*. Each of these types of marks is described following:

Trademark A distinctive mark, symbol, name, word, motto, or device that identifies the goods of a particular business.

- **Trademarks.** A **trademark** is a distinctive mark, symbol, name, word, motto, or device that identifies the *goods* of a particular business.

  Examples "*Coca-Cola*" (The Coca-Cola Company), "*Big Mac*" (McDonald's Corporation), "*mac*" (Apple Computer), "*intel inside*" (Intel Corporation), *Better Ingredients. Better Pizza.* (Pizza Hut) are trademarks.

Service mark A mark that distinguishes the services of the holder from those of its competitors.

- **Service marks.** A **service mark** is used to distinguish the *services* of the holder from those of its competitors.

  Examples *FedEx* (FedEx Corporation), *The Friendly Skies* (United Air Lines, Inc.), *Big Brown* (UPS Corporation), and *Weight Watchers* are service marks.

- **Certification marks.** A **certification mark** is a mark that is used to certify that goods and services are of a certain quality or originate from particular geographical areas. The owner of the mark is usually a nonprofit corporation that licenses producers that meet standards or conditions to use the mark.

  Examples The Underwriters Laboratories (UL) certifies that products meet certain safety requirements. The Good Housekeeping Seal of Approval certifies the products meet certain quality specifications.

- **Collective marks.** A **collective mark** is owned by an organization (such as an association) whose members use it to identify themselves with a level of quality or accuracy, geographical origin, or other characteristic set by the organization.

  Examples *Washington Apple* (Washington Apple Commission), *FTD Florist* (FTD, Inc.), and *Grown in Idaho* (The Idaho Potato Commission) are examples of collective marks.

Certain marks cannot be registered. They include (1) the flag or coat of arms of the United States, any state, municipality, or foreign nation; (2) marks that are immoral or scandalous; (3) geographical names standing alone (e.g., "South"); (4) surnames standing alone (note that a surname can be registered if it is accompanied by a picture or fanciful name, such as *Smith Brothers cough drops*); and (5) any mark that resembles a mark already registered with the Federal Patent and Trademark Office.

Trademark Infringement

The owner of a mark can sue a third party for the unauthorized use of a mark. To succeed in a **trademark infringement** case, the owner must prove that (1) the defendant infringed the plaintiff's mark by using it in an unauthorized manner, and (2) such use is likely to cause confusion, mistake, or deception of the public as to the origin of the goods or services. A successful plaintiff can recover:

1. the profits made by the infringer by the unauthorized use of the mark,
2. damages caused to the plaintiff's business and reputation,
3. an order requiring the defendant to destroy all goods containing the unauthorized mark, and
4. an injunction preventing the defendant from such infringement in the future.

The court has discretion to award up to treble damages where intentional infringement is found.

Trademark infringement Unauthorized use of another's mark. The holder may recover damages and other remedies from the infringer.

Generic Names

When filing for a trademark, if a word, name, or slogan is too generic, it cannot be registered as a trademark. If a word is not generic, it can be trademarked.

Examples   The word "apple" cannot be trademarked because it is a generic name. However, the brand name "Apple Computer" is permitted to be trademarked because it is not a generic name. The word "secret" cannot be trademarked because it is a generic name. However, the brand name "Victoria's Secret" is permitted to be trademarked because it is not a generic name.

Once a company has been granted a trademark or service mark, the company usually uses the mark as a brand name to promote its goods or services. However, sometimes a company may be *too* successful in promoting a mark and at some point in time the public begins to use the brand name as a common name to denote the type of product or service being sold, rather than as the trademark or service mark of the individual seller. A trademark that becomes a common term for a product line or type of service is called a **generic name**. Once a trademark becomes a generic name, the term loses its protection under federal trademark law.

Generic name A term for a mark that has become a common term for a product line or type of service and therefore has lost its trademark protection.

Example   Sailboards are surfboards that have sails mounted on them and are used by one person to glide on water such as oceans and lakes. There were many manufacturers and sellers of sailboards. The most successful brand was "Windsurfer." However, the word "windsurfing" was used so often by the public for all brands of sailboards that the trademarked name "Windsurfer" was found to be a generic name and its trademark was canceled.

Exhibit 20.3 lists names that at one time were trademarked but lost trademark protection because the trademarked name became overused and generic. Exhibit 20.4 lists trademarked names that are at some risk of becoming generic names.

Internet

The **Internet**, or **Net**, is a collection of millions of computers that provide a network of electronic connections between the computers. Hundreds of millions of computers are connected to the Internet. The Internet's evolution helped usher in the Information

Internet A collection of millions of computers that provide a network of electronic connections between the computers.

Exhibit 20.3   **Generic names**

The following once-trademarked names have been so overused to designate an entire class of products that they have been found to be generic and have lost their trademark status.

Windsurfer	Frisbee
Laser	Trampoline
Escalator	Cornflakes
Kerosene	Yoyo
Formica	Raisin bread
Thermos	Toll house cookies
Linoleum	Nylon

Exhibit 20.4   **Brand names at risk of becoming generic**

Certain trademarks and service marks are often used improperly and have some risk in the future of becoming generic names. Several of these marks are listed below, with their proper use and typical misuse also noted.

Mark	Proper Use	Misuse
Xerox	"Copy this document on a Xerox-brand copier."	"Go Xerox this."
Google	"Use the Google search engine and find information about him."	"Just google him."
FedEx	"Use FedEx overnight delivery service to send this package."	"Please fedex this."
Rollerblade	"Let's go inline skating on our Rollerblade inline skates."	"Let's go rollerblading."

Age of today. Individuals and businesses use the Internet for communication of information and data.

World Wide Web

The **World Wide Web** consists of millions of computers that support a standard set of rules for the exchange of information called Hypertext Transfer Protocol (HTTP). Web-based documents are formatted using common coding languages. Businesses and individuals can hook up to the Web by registering with a service such as America Online (AOL).

Individuals and businesses can have their own websites. A website is composed of electronic documents known as Web pages. Websites and pages are stored on servers throughout the world, which are operated by Internet service providers (ISPs). They are viewed by using Web browsing software such as Microsoft Internet Explorer and Netscape Navigator. Each website has a unique online address.

The Web has made it extremely attractive to conduct commercial activities online. Companies such as Amazon.com and eBay are e-commerce powerhouses that sell all sorts of goods and services. Existing brick-and-mortar companies, such as Wal-Mart, Merrill Lynch, and Dell Computers, sell their goods and services online as well. E-commerce over the Web will continue to grow dramatically each year.

Electronic Mail

Electronic mail, or **email**, is one of the most widely used applications for communication over the Internet. Using email, individuals around the world can instantaneously communicate in electronic writing with one another. Each person can have an

CHECKLIST Types of Intellectual Property Protected by Federal Law

Type	Subject Matter	Term
Patent	Inventions (e.g., machines; processes; compositions of matter; designs for articles of manufacture; and improvements to existing machines, processes). Invention must be: 1. Novel 2. Useful 3. Nonobvious *Public-use doctrine:* Patent will not be granted if the invention was used in public for more than one year prior to filing of the patent application.	Patents on articles of manufacture and processes: 20 years: design patents: 14 years.
Copyright	Tangible writing (e.g., books, magazines, newspapers, lectures, operas, plays, screenplays, musical compositions, maps, works of art, lithographs, photographs, postcards, greeting cards, motion pictures, newsreels, sound recordings, computer programs, and mask works fixed to semiconductor chips). Writing must be the original work of the author.	Author (individual registrant): life of author plus 70 years.
	Fair-use doctrine: It permits use of copyrighted material without consent for limited uses (e.g., scholarly work, parody or satire, and brief quotation in news reports).	Work for hire (business registrant) for the shorter of either (1) 120 years from the date of creation or (2) 95 years from the date of first publication.
Trademark	Marks (e.g., name, symbol, word, logo, or device). Marks include trademarks, service marks, certification marks, and collective marks. Mark must be distinctive or have acquired a secondary meaning. *Generic name:* A mark that becomes a common term for a product line or type of service loses its protection under federal trademark law.	Original registration: 10 years. Renewal registration: unlimited number or renewals for 10-year terms.

email address that identifies him or her by a unique address. Email will continue to grow in use in the future as it replaces some telephone and paper correspondence and increases new communication between persons.

Domain Name

Most businesses conduct e-commerce by using websites that can be located on the Internet under domain names. Each website is identified by a unique Internet **domain name**.

Domain name A unique name that identifies an individual's or a company's website.

> **Examples** The domain name for the publisher of this book—Prentice Hall Publishing Company—is www.prenhall.com. The domain name for Microsoft Corporation is www.microsoft.com. The domain name for McDonald's Corporation is www.mcdonalds.com.

Domain names can be registered. The first step in **registering** a domain name is to determine whether any other party already owns the name. For this purpose, InterNIC

ETHICAL PERSPECTIVE

Paralegal's Duty to Keep a Client's Intellectual Property Confidential

Mr. Edwards is hired as a paralegal for the law firm of Berkowitz, Brown, and McGregor, a law firm specializing in intellectual property law. Mr. Edwards is assigned as a paralegal professional to assist Mr. Berkowitz, a partner of the law firm. One day a new client, Ms. Newton, comes into the office to see Mr. Berkowitz about representing her in obtaining trademarks for her company's name, a new product, and a slogan that will be used for selling the product.

Mr. Berkowitz invites Mr. Edwards to attend the meeting with Ms. Newton. At the meeting, Ms. Newton discloses the names that she would like to have trademarked. Mr. Berkowitz introduces Mr. Edwards as the paralegal professional who will be assisting him in applying for the trademarks for Ms. Newton. Ms. Newton employs the law firm to obtain the trademarks.

Mr. Edwards realizes that the proposed name for the product is an extremely unique name that would have a large commercial value. Mr. Edwards has an idea of telling a friend about the name with the proposition that he and his friend would share any monetary gain from obtaining a trademark on the name. If his friend obtained the trademark before Ms. Newton, then Ms. Newton would have to buy the name from the friend if she wanted the name, or forgo using the name. Mr. Edwards realizes that the name has potential value for use by others than just Ms. Newton.

What should Mr. Edwards do?

PARALEGAL'S ETHICAL DECISION

In this case, it is clear that Mr. Edwards cannot act upon his thoughts about this matter. A paralegal professional owes an ethical duty not to misuse confidential information obtained in his or her employment and cannot make a monetary gain by the misuse of this information. Therefore, even though he is tempted to disclose the name to his friend and share in the possible profits from doing so, Mr. Edwards must make the ethical decision to keep the information confidential.

Web Exploration

Go to www.networksolutions.com. See if your name is available in the .com and .name extensions. Think up a name that you would like to use for a business. Check to see if this business name is available in the .com extension.

maintains a "Whois" database that contains the domain names that have been registered. The InterNIC website is located online at www.internic.net.

Domain names can also be registered at Network Solutions, Inc.'s website, which is located at www.networksolutions.com, as well as at other sites. An applicant must complete a registration form, which can be done online. It usually costs less than $50 to register a domain name for one year, and the fee may be paid by credit card online. There are other domain name extensions available. Countries have country-specific extensions assigned to the country. Some countries make these domain name extensions available for public purchase. Country-specific domain names are often more expensive to register.

The most commonly used top-level extensions for domain names are set forth in Exhibit 20.5.

Anticybersquatting Consumer Protection Act

In November 1999, the U.S. Congress enacted, and the president signed, the **Anticybersquatting Consumer Protection Act (ACPA)** [15 U.S.C. Section 1125(d)]. The act was specifically aimed at cybersquatters who register Internet domain names of famous companies and people and hold them hostage by demanding ransom payments from the famous company or person.

In the past, trademark law was of little help in this area, either because the famous person's name was not trademarked or because, even if the name was trademarked,

IN THE WORDS OF THE COURT

Reno v. American Civil Liberties Union

521 U.S. 844, 117 S.CT. 2329, 138 L.ED.2D 874,
WEB 1997 U.S. LEXIS 4037
SUPREME COURT OF THE UNITED STATES

The Internet is an international network of interconnected computers. The Internet has experienced extraordinary growth. Individuals can obtain access to the Internet from many different sources, generally hosts themselves or entities with a host affiliation. Most colleges and universities provide access for their students and faculty; many corporations provide their employees with access through an office network. Several major national "online services" offer access to their own extensive proprietary networks as well as a link to the much larger resources of the Internet.

Anyone with access to the Internet may take advantage of a wide variety of communication and information retrieval methods. These methods are constantly evolving and difficult to categorize precisely. But, as presently constituted, those most relevant to this case are electronic mail ("e-mail"), automatic mailing list services ("mail exploders," sometimes referred to as "listservs"), "newsgroups," "chat rooms," and the "World Wide Web." All of these methods can be used to transmit text; most can transmit sound, pictures, and moving video images. Taken together, these tools constitute a unique medium—known to its users as "cyberspace"—located in no particular geographical location but available to anyone, anywhere in the world, with access to the Internet.

Each medium of expression may present its own problems. Thus, some of our cases have recognized special justifications for regulation of the broadcast media that are not applicable to other speakers. In these cases, the Court relied on the history of extensive government regulation of the broadcast medium, the scarcity of available frequencies at its inception, and its "invasive" nature. Those factors are not present in cyberspace. Moreover, the Internet is not as "invasive" as radio or television. The District Court specifically found that "communications over the Internet do not invade an individual's home or appear on one's computer screen unbidden. Users seldom encounter content by accident."

Unlike the conditions that prevailed when Congress first authorized regulation of the broadcast spectrum, the Internet can hardly be considered a "scarce" expressive commodity. It provides relatively unlimited, low-cost capacity for communication of all kinds. This dynamic, multifaceted category of communication includes not only traditional print and news services, but also audio, video, and still images, as well as interactive, real-time dialogue. Through the use of chat rooms, any person with a phone line can become a town crier with a voice that resonates farther than it could from any soapbox. Through the use of Web pages, mail exploders, and newsgroups, the same individual can become a pamphleteer. As the District Court found, "the content on the Internet is as diverse as human thought."

---

trademark laws required distribution of goods or services to find infringement, and most cybersquatters did not distribute goods or services but merely sat on the Internet domain name.

The 1999 act has two fundamental requirements: (1) The name must be famous and (2) the domain name must have been registered in bad faith. Thus, the law prohibits the act of **cybersquatting** itself if it is done in *bad faith*.

The first issue in applying the statute is whether the domain name is someone else's famous name. Trademarked names qualify; nontrademarked names—such as those of famous actors, actresses, singers, sports stars, politicians, and such—are also protected. In determining bad faith, the law provides that courts may consider the extent to which the domain name resembles the holder's name or the famous person's

Exhibit 20.5   Domain name extensions

The most common **domain name extensions** include the following.

Extension	Used by
.com	represents the word *commercial*, and is the most widely used extension in the world. Most businesses prefer a .com domain name because it is a highly recognized business symbol.
.net	represents the word *network*, and is used most commonly by Internet service providers, Web-hosting companies, and other businesses that are involved directly in the infrastructure of the Internet. Some businesses also choose domain names with a .net extension.
.org	represents the word *organization* and is used primarily by nonprofit groups and trade associations.
.info	signifies a "resource" website. This unrestricted global name may be used by businesses, individuals, and organizations.
.biz	used for small-business websites.
.us	for U.S. websites. Many businesses choose this extension, which is a relatively new extension.
.cc	originally was the country code for Coco Keeling Islands but now is unrestricted and may be registered by anyone from any country. It often is registered by businesses.
.bz	originally was the country code for Belize but now is unrestricted and may be registered by anyone from any country. It is commonly used by small businesses.
.name	new extension for individuals, who can use it to register personalized domain names.
.museum	enables museums, museum associations, and museum professionals to register their own websites.
.coop	represents the word *cooperative* and may be used by cooperative associations around the world.
.aero	reserved exclusive for the aviation community. It enables organizations and individuals to reserve websites.
.pro	available to professionals, such as doctors, lawyers, consultants, and other professionals.
.edu	for educational institutions.

name, whether goods or services are sold under the name, the holder's offer to sell or transfer the name, and whether the holder has acquired multiple Internet domain names of famous companies and persons.

The act provides for the issuance of cease-and-desist orders and injunctions by the court. In addition, the law adds monetary penalties: A plaintiff has the option of seeking statutory damages in lieu of proving damages. The Anticybersquatting Consumer Protection Act gives owners of trademarks and persons with famous names a new weapon to attack the kidnapping of Internet domain names by cyberpirates.

Digital Law

With the advent of the Information Age, the government has had to develop laws that apply to and regulate the use of computers, the Internet, and other electronic mediums. These laws are sometimes collectively referred to as **digital law**. Some of the major digital laws that have been enacted are discussed in the following paragraphs.

Controlling the Assault of Non-Solicited Pornography and Marketing Act (CAN-SPAM Act)

Americans are being bombarded in their email accounts by "spam"—unsolicted commercial advertising. Spammers try to sell you literally anything. Spam accounts for approximately three-quarters of all business email traffic. In addition, many spam messages are fraudulent and deceptive, including misleading headers in their subject lines. It takes time and money to sort through, review, and discard unwanted spam.

In 2003, Congress enacted the federal **Controlling the Assault of Non-Solicited Pornography and Marketing Act (CAN-SPAM Act)** [15 U.S.C. Sections 7701–7713]. The act (1) prohibits spammers from using falsified headers in email messages, including the originating domain name and email address, (2) prohibits deceptive subject lines that mislead a recipient of the contents or subject matter of the message, (3) requires that recipients of spam be given the opportunity to opt out and not have the spammer send email to the recipient's address, and (4) requires spammers who send sexually oriented email to properly label it as such. The Federal Trade Commission (FTC) is empowered to enforce the CAN-SPAM Act.

In effect, the CAN-SPAM Act does not can spam, but instead approves businesses to spam as long as they do not lie. The act expressly provides that victims of spam do not have a right to bring civil lawsuits against spammers. The CAN-SPAM Act does not regulate spam sent internationally to Americans from other countries. In essence, the CAN-SPAM Act is very weak to help consumers ward off the spam that deluges them on a daily basis.

In 2004, the FTC adopted a rule which requires that sexually explicit spam email contain a warning on the subject line reading "SEXUALLY EXPLICIT." The FTC rule also prohibits the messages themselves from containing graphic material. The graphic material can only appear after the recipient has opened the email message.

Electronic Communications Privacy Act (ECPA)

Email, computer data, and other electronic communications are sent daily by millions of people using computers and the Internet. Recognizing how the use of computer and electronic communications raise special issues of privacy, the federal government enacted the **Electronic Communications Privacy Act (ECPA)** [18 U.S.C. Section 2510].

The ECPA makes it a crime to intercept an electronic communication at the point of transmission, while in transit, when stored by a router or server, or after receipt by the intended recipient. An electronic communication includes any transfer of signals, writings, images, sounds, data, or intelligence of any nature. The ECPA makes it illegal to access stored email as well as email in transmission.

Example Henry owns a computer on which he sends and receives email. Harriet learns Henry's access code to his email account. Harriet opens Henry's email and reads his emails. Harriet has violated the Electronic Communications Privacy Act (ECPA).

DOMAIN NAMES SOLD FOR MILLIONS

SIDEBAR

What is a domain name worth? In some case, plenty. Take the case of the domain name www.business.com. This name, which was originally registered as a domain name for less than $50, was sold to another purchaser for $150,000 in 1996. Many people at the time thought this was an outrageous sum to pay for a domain name—that is, until the second purchaser turned around and resold the name to ECompanies for $7.5 million. Subsequently, www.business.com was sold to RH Donnelley for $350 million. RH Donnelly beat out the New York Times and Dow Jones in the bidding for the domain name. The sale was in stock.

Other domain names have been sold at high prices too. The domain name www.wine.com sold for $3 million, www.bingo.com for $1.1 million, www.wallstreet.com for $1 million, www.drugs.com for $800,000, www.pizza.com for $2.6 million, and www.vip.com sold for $1.4 million. Gary Kremen had purchased the domain name www.sex.com in 1996 for next to nothing. In 2006, Kremen sold the name to Escom for the price of $14 million.

As commerce over the Internet increases, unregistered memorable domain names become harder to find. The sale of the better domain names has increased, with multimillion dollar price tags being paid for the most desirable names—which were originally registered for less than $100.

Controlling the Assault of Non-Solicited Pornography and Marketing Act (CAN-SPAM Act) A federal statute that prohibits certain deceptive and misleading email. The act is administered by the Federal Trade Commission (FTC).

Electronic Communications Privacy Act (ECPA) A federal statute that makes it a crime to intercept an electronic communication at the point of transmission, while in transit, when stored by a router or server, or after receipt by the intended recipient.

The ECPA provides that stored electronic communications may be accessed without violating the law by the following:

1. The party or entity providing the electronic communication service. The primary example would be an employer who can access stored email communications of employees using the employer's service.
2. Government and law enforcement entities that are investigating suspected illegal activity. Disclosure would be required only pursuant to a validly issued warrant.

The ECPA provides for criminal penalties. In addition, the ECPA provides that the injured party may bring a civil lawsuit to recover monetary damages from the violator.

Information Infrastructure Protection Act (IIP Act)

The Internet and Information Age ushered in a whole new world for education, business, and consumer transactions. But what followed was a rash of cyber crimes. Prosecutors and courts wrestled over how to apply existing laws written in a nondigital age to new Internet-related abuses.

In 1996, Congress responded by enacting the **Information Infrastructure Protection Act (IIP Act)** [18 U.S.C. Section 1030]. In this federal law, Congress addressed computer-related crimes as distinct offenses. The IIP Act provides protection for any computer attached to the Internet.

The IIP Act makes it a federal crime for anyone to intentionally access and acquire information from a protected computer without authorization. The IIP Act does not require that the defendant accessed a protected computer for commercial benefit. Thus, persons who transmit a computer virus over the Internet or hackers who trespass into Internet-connected computers may be criminally prosecuted under the IIP Act. Even merely observing data on a protected computer without authorization is sufficient to meet the requirement that the defendant has accessed a protected computer. Criminal penalties for violating the IIP Act include imprisonment and fines.

The IIP Act gives the federal government a much-needed weapon for directly prosecuting cyber-crooks, hackers, and others who enter, steal, destroy, or look at others' computer data without authorization.

Counterfeit Access Device and Computer Fraud and Abuse Act (CFAA)

The **Counterfeit Access Device and Computer Fraud and Abuse Act (CFAA)**, as amended, makes it a federal crime to access a computer knowingly to obtain (1) restricted federal government information, (2) financial records of financial institutions, and (3) consumer reports of consumer reporting agencies. The act also makes it a crime to use counterfeit or unauthorized access devices, such as cards or code numbers, to obtain things of value or transfer funds or to traffic in such devices [18 U.S.C. Section 1030]. The duty of paralegals to disclose their paralegal status and any conflicts of interest are discussed in the Ethical Perspective Feature on page 753.

Information Infrastructure Protection Act (IIP Act) A federal statute that makes it a federal crime for anyone to intentionally access and acquire information from a protected computer without authorization.

Counterfeit Access Device and Computer Fraud and Abuse Act (CFAA) A federal statute that makes it a federal crime to access a computer knowingly to obtain (1) restricted federal government information, (2) financial records of financial institutions, and (3) consumer reports of consumer reporting agencies.

ETHICAL PERSPECTIVE

Duty to Disclose Paralegal Status and Conflict of Interest

Mr. Frederick Aston, a paralegal, leaves his current employment at the law firm at which he has been working for years, to take a new paralegal position at a new law firm. Upon joining the new law firm, the firm provides Mr. Aston with a list of clients that the firm represents, and a list of the lawsuits and other matters in which the law firm represents clients, including the names of the adversarial party and opposing law firms that represent these clients.

As Mr. Aston reviews the list, he identifies a pending lawsuit where his prior law firm represents a client in a case against a client that is represented by his new law firm. Mr. Aston worked on that case during his previous employment.

Does Mr. Aston owe a duty to disclose this conflict of interest to the new law firm? Does Mr. Aston owe a duty not to work on the case where it would involve a conflict of interest?

Model and state paralegal professional codes of ethics and responsibility require that a paralegal disclose any conflict of interest that has been identified, not to work on matters where a conflict of interest has been identified, and not to disclose any information from his or her previous employment from which the conflict of interest arises.

PARALEGAL'S ETHICAL DECISION

Mr. Aston, as a paralegal professional, owes an ethical duty to disclose to his new employer the fact that he has worked on a case that the firm is involved in when he was employed by a prior law firm. Mr. Aston cannot work on this case if it would cause a conflict of interest for him to do so. Mr. Aston also must not disclose to his new employer any information that he had learned at his prior employment about the case.

Concept Review *and* Reinforcement

LEGAL TERMINOLOGY

SUMMARY OF KEY CONCEPTS

Trade Secret

Definition	A *trade secret* is a product formula, pattern, design, compilation of data, customer list, or other business secret that makes a business successful. The owner of a trade secret must take reasonable precautions to prevent its trade secret from being discovered by others.
Misappropriation	Misappropriation is a tort in which another's trade secret is obtained through unlawful means such as theft, bribery, or espionage. A successful plaintiff can recover profits, damages, and an injunction against the offender.
Economic Espionage Act	The Federal Economic Espionage Act makes it a crime for any person to convert a trade secret for his or another's benefit, knowing or intending to cause injury to the owners of the trade secret.

Patent

Federal Patent Statute	Patent law is exclusively federal law; there are no state patent laws.
Scope	Patentable subject matter includes inventions such as machines; processes; compositions of matter; improvements to existing machines, processes, or compositions of matter; designs for articles of manufacture; asexually reproduced plants; and living matter invented by humans.
Criteria	To be patented an invention must be: 1. Novel 2. Useful 3. Nonobvious
Patent Application	An application containing a written description of the invention must be filed with the United States Patent and Trademark Office in Washington, D.C.
Term	Patents are valid for 20 years.
Public-Use Doctrine	A patent may not be granted if the invention was used by the public for more than one year prior to filing the patent application.
The American Inventors Protection Act	The American Inventors Protection Act: 1. Permits an inventor to file a *provisional application* with the U.S. Patent and Trademark Office three months pending the filing of a final patent application to gain "provisional rights." 2. Requires the PTO to issue a patent within three years after the filing of a patent application.

Patent Infringement	The patent holder may recover damages and other remedies against a person who makes unauthorized use of the holder's patent.
Patent Appeal	The United States Court of Appeals for the Federal Circuit in Washington, D.C., hears patent appeals.

Copyright

Scope	Copyright law is exclusively federal law; there are no state copyright laws. Only tangible writings can be copyrighted. These include books, newspapers, addresses, musical compositions, motion pictures, works of art, architectural plans, greeting cards, photographs, sound recordings, computer programs, and mask works fixed in semiconductor chips.
Requirements for Copyright	The writing must be the original work of the author.
Copyright Registration	Copyright registration is permissive and voluntary. Published and unpublished works may be registered with the United States Copyright Office in Washington, D.C. Registration itself does not create the copyright.
Term	Copyrights are for the following terms: 1. *Individual holder:* Life of the author plus 70 years 2. *Corporate holder:* Either (1) 95 years from the date of publication, or (2) 120 years from the date of creation, whichever is shorter.
Copyright Infringement	The copyright holder may recover damages and other remedies against a person who copies a substantial and material part of a copyrighted work without the holder's permission.
No Electronic Theft Act (NET Act)	The federal NET Act makes it a crime for a person to willfully infringe a copyright work, even without commercial advantages or financial gain.
Fair-Use Doctrine	The fair-use doctrine permits use of copyrighted material without the consent of the copyright holder for limited uses (e.g., scholarly work, parody or satire, and brief quotation in news reports).
Digital Millennium Copyright Act (DMCA)	The federal DMCA, enacted in 1998, provides civil and criminal penalties that 1. Prohibit the manufacture and distribution of technologies, products, or services primarily designed for the purpose of circumventing wrappers or encryption protection. 2. Prohibit unauthorized *access* to copyrighted digital works by circumventing the wrapper or encryption technology that protects the intellectual property.

Trademark

Mark	Referred to collectively as trademarks, a mark consists of the trade name, symbol, word, logo, design, or device that distinguishes the owner's good or services.
Registration of Trademarks	Marks are registered with the United States Patent and Trademark Office in Washington, D.C.
Types of Marks	1. *Trademark:* Identifies goods of a particular business 2. *Service mark:* Identifies services of a particular business 3. *Certification mark:* Certifies that goods or services are of a certain quality or origin 4. *Collective mark:* Used by cooperatives, associations, and fraternal organizations

Requirements for a Trademark	The mark must either (1) be *distinctive*, or (2) have acquired a *secondary meaning*. The mark must have been used in commerce or the holder must intend to use the mark in commerce and actually do so within six months after registering the mark.
Term	The original registration of a mark is valid for 10 years and can be renewed for an unlimited number of 10-year periods.
Trademark Infringement	The mark holder may recover damages and other remedies from a person who makes unauthorized use of another's registered mark.
Generic Name	A generic name is a mark that becomes a common term for a product line or type of service and loses its protection under federal trademark law.

Internet

Internet	The Internet is a collection of millions of computers that provide a network of electronic connections between computers.
World Wide Web	The www is an electronic connection of computers that support a standard set of rules for the exchange of information called hypertext transfer protocol (HTTP).
Electronic Mail (Email)	Email is electronic written communication between individuals using computers connected to the Internet.

Domain Name

Domain Name	The domain name is a unique name that identifies an individual's or company's website.
Anticybersquatting Consumer Protection Act	The Anticybersquatting Consumer Protection Act (ACPA) is a federal statute that permits a court to issue cease-and-desist orders and injunctions and to award monetary damages against anyone who has registered a domain name (1) of a famous name (2) in bad faith.

Digital Law

Controlling the Assault of Non-Solicited Pornography and Marketing Act (CAN-SPAM Act)	A federal statute that prohibits certain deceptive and misleading email. The act is administered by the Federal Trade Commission (FTC).
Electronic Communications Privacy Act (ECPA)	A federal statute that makes it a crime to intercept an electronic communication at the point of transmission, while in transit, when stored by a router or server, or after receipt by the intended recipient.
Information Infrastructure Protection Act (IIP Act)	A federal statute that makes it a federal crime for anyone to intentionally access and acquire information from a protected computer without authorization.
Counterfeit Access Device and Computer Fraud and Abuse Act (CFAA)	A federal statute that makes it a federal crime to access a computer knowingly to obtain (1) restricted federal government information, (2) financial records of financial institutions, and (3) consumer reports of consumer reporting agencies.

WORKING THE WEB

1. Go to the website http://networksolutions.com.html. Pick an Internet domain name you would be interested in registering. Check to see if this name is available. What is the cost of registering an Internet domain name?

2. Visit the website http://www.uspto.gov/html. Select "Trademarks" and click on "search." Select a name in which you are interested to determine whether a trademark or service mark is available for that name. Select "New User Form Search" and search to see if this name is available. What are the results of your search?

3. Visit the website http://1web.loc.gov/copyright/html. Click on "Frequently Asked Questions (FAQ)." Click on "What is a copyright?" Write a one-page report on what a copyright is and what protection is afforded a copyright.

4. Visit the website http://www.inta.org/html. Describe this association and the mission of the association. Read about the E-Learning courses this association offers.

5. Visit the website http://coca-cola.com.html. Search this website and find the history of the "Coca-Cola" trademark. Write a half-page history of the trademark. Find and list five other trademarks that the Coca-Cola Company owns.

CRITICAL THINKING & WRITING QUESTIONS

1. What is intellectual property?
2. What is a trade secret? How is a trade secret protected? For how long a time is protection available? Explain.
3. What does the Economic Espionage Act provide? What does the Digital Millennium Copyright Act (DMCA) provide?
4. What is a patent? What can be patented? What are the statutory requirements for a patent? How is a patent obtained?
5. Explain patent infringement. What types of remedies are available for patent infringement?
6. Explain the public-use doctrine. Give an example.
7. What is a copyright? What can be copyrighted? How is a copyright obtained?
8. Explain copyright infringement. What types of remedies are available for copyright infringement?
9. Explain the fair-use doctrine. Give an example.
10. What is a mark? What are the requirements for obtaining a mark?
11. Describe the difference between: (1) trademark, (2) service mark, (3) certification mark, and (4) collective mark.
12. What is a generic name? Give an example.
13. What is the Internet? What is email? What does the Electronic Communications Privacy Act (ECPA) do?
14. What is an Internet domain name? How is a domain name registered?

Building Paralegal Skills

VIDEO CASE STUDIES

Confidentiality Issue: Need-to-Know Circle

Two paralegals working in the same law firm meet in the coffee room of the office. They begin to discuss a case which one of the paralegals is working on.

After viewing the video case study at www.pearsonhighered.com/goldman answer the following:

1. Can every matter being handled within the firm be discussed with everyone in the law firm? Why or why not?

2. Will disclosure of information about intellectual property jeopardize the client's rights?

3. How is a paralegal supposed to know with whom he or she may discuss a case?

ETHICS ANALYSIS & DISCUSSION QUESTIONS

1. Does a paralegal working in the area of intellectual property law have any ethical obligation to obtain specialized training or education?

2. Are memoranda of law and other reports prepared by a paralegal protected by copyright law? To whom do the rights belong—the paralegal, the client, or the firm?

3. You are not a lawyer but, under regulations issued by the Commissioner of Patents with the approval of the Secretary of Commerce pursuant to 35 U.S.C. Section 31, you are authorized to practice before the United States Patent Office [*Sperry v. Florida ex rel. Florida Bar*, 373 U.S. 379, 83 S.Ct. 1322, 10 L.Ed.2d 428, 1963 U.S. Lexis 2486 (1963)]. May you represent patent applicants, prepare and prosecute their applications, and advise them in connection with their applications in Florida?

DEVELOPING YOUR COLLABORATION SKILLS

With a group of other students, selected by you or assigned by your instructor, review the "Paralegals at Work" scenario at the beginning of the chapter. As a group, discuss the following questions.

1. What type of protection can Mr. Einstein obtain for his new invention? How is this protection obtained? How long does this protection last?

2. What type of protection can Mr. Einstein obtain for the name of the shoe, the logo he has designed, and the slogan he has developed? How is this protection obtained? How long does this protection last?

3. What type of protection can Mr. Einstein obtain for his *User's Manual*? How is this protection obtained? How long does this protection last?

4. What type of protection is available to protect Mr. Einstein's proposed website name? How is this protection obtained? How long does this protection last?

PARALEGAL PORTFOLIO EXERCISE

Go to the website http://www.loc.gov/copyright.html. Find and print out the proper form and instructions for obtaining a copyright for a nondramatic literary work. Read the instructions for completing this form. Complete the form as if you are the writer of the nondramatic literary work to be registered. Make up whatever information is necessary to complete the form. Search the website and determine where the form is to be submitted and the fee that must be paid to submit the form.

LEGAL ANALYSIS & WRITING CASES

J.E.M. Ag Supply, Inc., dba Farm Advantage, Inc. v. Pioneer Hi-Bred International, Inc.

534 U.S. 124, 122 S.Ct. 593, 151 L.Ed.2d 508, Web 2001 U.S. Lexis 10949

Supreme Court of the United States

Pioneer Hi-Bred International, Inc. (Pioneer) has obtained seventeen patents that cover the company's inbred and hybrid corn and corn seed products. A hybrid plant patent protects the plant, its seeds, variants, mutants, and modifications of the hybrid. Pioneer sells its patented hybrid seeds under a limited label license that provides: "License is granted solely to produce grain and/or forage." The license states that it "does not extend to the use of seed from such crop or the progeny thereof for propagation or seed multiplication." The license strictly prohibits "the use of such seed or progeny thereof for propagation or seed multiplication or for production or development of a hybrid or different variety of seed."

J.E.M. Ag Supply, Inc., doing business as Farm Advantage, Inc., purchased patented hybrid seeds from Pioneer in bags bearing this license agreement. Pioneer sued Farm Advantage, alleging that Farm Advantage infringed its patent and violated the license by creating seed from the hybrid corn products it grew from Pioneer's patented hybrid seed. Farm Advantage filed a counter-claim of patent invalidity, arguing that Pioneer hybrid plant seed patents are not patentable subject matter. The District Court granted summary judgment to Pioneer, and the Court of Appeals affirmed. The U.S. Supreme Court agreed to hear the appeal.

Question

1. Are sexually reproducing hybrid plants patentable subject matter?

Castle Rock Entertainment, Inc. v. Carol Publishing Group, Inc.   150 F.3d 132 (1998)

United States Court of Appeals, Second Circuit

Castle Rock Entertainment, Inc., is the producer and copyright owner of the successful "Seinfeld" television series. For years, Seinfeld was the highest-rated show on television. The series revolved around petty tribulations in the lives of four single, adult friends in New York: Jerry Seinfeld, George Costanza, Elaine Benes, and Cosmo Kramer.

To take advantage of the public interest in Seinfeld, Carol Publishing Group, Inc. published a book written by Beth Golub, entitled *The Seinfeld Aptitude Test* (SAT). The 132-page book contained 643 questions and answers about events and characters in 84 TV episodes of Seinfeld. These included 211 multiple-choice questions, 93 matching questions, and a number of short-answer questions. The correct answers to these questions have as their source fictional moments in Seinfeld episodes, and 41 questions contain exact dialogue from Seinfeld. The name "Seinfeld" appears prominently on front and back covers of the SAT, and pictures of the principal actors in Seinfeld appear on the cover and throughout the book.

Castle Rock filed an action against Carol Publishing and Golub alleging federal copyright infringement. Castle Rock made a motion for summary judgment, alleging that no facts were in dispute and that the court could make a decision as a matter of law whether copyright infringement occurred. The trial court agreed that no facts were in dispute that required a jury's determination. The court, therefore, considered the undisputed evidence that the defendants had violated Castle Rock's copyrights of Seinfeld, and awarded damages and issued an injunction enjoining the defendants from publishing *The Seinfeld Aptitude Test*. The court granted Castle Rock's motion for summary judgment. The defendants appealed.

Question

1. Is Castle Rock entitled to a summary judgment on its copyright infringement claim?

Elsmere Music, Inc. v. National Broadcasting Co., Inc.   623 F.2d 252, Web 1980 U.S. App. Lexis 16820

United States Court of Appeals for the Second Circuit

Once in the past, when the City of New York teetered on the brink of bankruptcy, on the television screens of America there appeared an image of a top-hatted Broadway showgirl, backed by an advancing phalanx of dancers, chanting: "I-I-I-I-I-I Love New Yo-o-o-o-o-o-o-rk." As an ad campaign for an ailing city, it was an unparalleled success. Crucial to the campaign was a brief but exhilarating musical theme written by Steve Karmin called "I Love New York." Elsmere Music, Inc. owned the copyright to the music. The success of the campaign did not go unnoticed. The popular weekly variety program *Saturday Night Live (SNL)* performed a comedy sketch over National Broadcasting Company's network (NBC). In the sketch, the cast of *SNL*, portraying the mayor and members of the chamber of commerce of the biblical city of Sodom, were seen discussing Sodom's poor public image with out-of-towners and its effect on the tourist trade. In an attempt to recast Sodom's image in a more positive light, a new advertising campaign was revealed, with the highlight of the campaign being a song "I Love Sodom" sung a cappella by a chorus line of *SNL* regulars to the tune of "I Love New York." Elsmere Music did not see the humor of the sketch and sued NBC for copyright infringement.

Question

1. Has SNL engaged in copyright infringement?

Coca-Cola Company v. Francis Net

Hypothetical Case

Francis Net, a freshman in college and computer expert, browses websites for hours each day. One day she thinks to herself, "I can make money registering domain names and selling them for a fortune." She recently saw an advertisement for Classic Coke, a cola drink produced and marketed by the Coca-Cola Company. The Coca-Cola Company has a famous trademark for the term *Classic Coke* and has spent millions of dollars advertising this brand and making the term famous throughout the United States and the world.

Francis goes to the website www.networksolutions.com, an Internet domain name registration service, to see if the Internet domain name classiccoke.com has been taken. She discovers that it is available, so she immediately registers the Internet domain name classiccoke.com for herself and pays the $70 registration fee with her credit card.

Coca Cola Company decides to register the Internet domain name classiccoke.com but discovers that Francis Net has already registered the domain name. Coca Cola Company contacts Francis, who demands $500,000 for the name. Coca Cola Company sues Francis to prevent Francis from using the Internet domain name classiccoke.com and to recover it from her under the federal Anticybersquatting Consumer Protection Act.

Question

1. Who wins?

Macy's Department Stores et al. v. BluePeace.org

Hypothetical Case

BluePeace.org is a new environmentalist group that has decided that expounding its environmental causes over the Internet is the best and most efficient way to spend its time and money to advance its environmental causes. To draw attention to its websites, BluePeace.org comes up with catchy Internet domain names. One is macyswearus.org; another is exxonvaldezesseals.org; and another is generalmotorscrashesdummies.org.

The macyswearus.org website first shows beautiful women dressed in mink coats sold by Macy's Department Stores, and then goes into graphic photos of minks being slaughtered and skinned and made into the coats. The exxonvaldezesseals.org website first shows a beautiful pristine bay in Alaska with the Exxon Valdez oil tanker quietly sailing through the waters, and then shows photos of the ship breaking open and spewing forth oil, and then seals who are covered with oil suffocating and dying on the shoreline. The website generalmotorscrashesdummies.org shows a General Motors automobile involved in normal crash tests with dummies, followed by photographs of automobile accident scenes where people lie bleeding and dying after accidents involving General Motors automobiles.

Macy's Department Stores, the Exxon Oil Company, and the General Motors Corporation sue BluePeace.org for violating the federal Anticybersquatting Consumer Protection Act.

Question

1. Who wins? Has BluePeace.org acted unethically in this case?

WORKING WITH THE LANGUAGE OF THE COURT CASE

Feist Publications, Inc. v. Rural Telephone Service Co., Inc.

499 U.S. 340, 111 S.Ct. 1282, 113 L.Ed.2d 358, Web 1991 U.S. Lexis 1856
Supreme Court of the United States

Read the following case, excerpted from the U.S. Supreme Court's opinion. Review and brief the case. In your brief, answer the following questions.

1. Who was the plaintiff? Who was the defendant?
2. What had the defendant done that caused the plaintiff to sue?
3. What is the issue in this case?
4. What was the decision of the U.S. Supreme Court?

O'Connor, S., delivered the opinion of the Court.

Rural Telephone Service Company is a certified public utility that provides telephone service to several communities in northwest Kansas. It is subject to a state regulation that requires all telephone companies operating in Kansas to issue annually an updated telephone directory. Accordingly, as a condition of its monopoly franchise, Rural publishes a typical telephone directory, consisting of white pages and yellow pages. The white pages list in alphabetical order the names of Rural's subscribers, together with their towns and telephone numbers. The yellow pages list Rural's business subscribers alphabetically by category and feature classified advertisements of various sites. Rural distributes its directory free of charge to its subscribers, but earns revenue by selling yellow pages advertisements.

Feist Publications, Inc. is a publishing company that specializes in areawide telephone directories. Unlike a typical directory, which covers only a particular calling area, Feist's areawide directories cover a much larger geographical range, reducing the need to call directory assistance or consult multiple directories. The Feist directory that is the subject of this litigation covers 11 different telephone service areas in 15 counties and contains 46,878 white pages listings—compared to Rural's approximately 7,700 listings.

Of the 11 telephone companies, only Rural refused to license its listings to Feist. Rural's refusal created a problem for Feist, as omitting these listings would have left a gaping hole in its areawide directory, rendering it less attractive to potential yellow pages advertisers. Unable to license Rural's white pages listings, Feist used them without Rural's consent.

Rural sued for copyright infringement in the District Court for the District of Kansas, taking the position that Feist, in compiling its own directory, could not use the information contained in Rural's white pages. The District Court granted summary judgment to Rural, explaining that "courts have consistently held that telephone directories are copyrightable" and citing a string of lower court decisions. In an unpublished opinion, the Court of Appeals for the Tenth Circuit affirmed "for substantially the reasons given by the district court."

This case concerns the interaction of two well-established propositions. The first is that facts are not copyrightable; the other, that compilations of facts generally are. The key to resolving the tension lies in understanding why facts are not copyrightable. The sine qua non of copyright is originality. To qualify for copyright protection, a work must be original to the author. Original, as the term is used in copyright, means only that the work was independently created by the author (as opposed to copied from other works), and that it possesses at least some minimal degree of creativity.

Originality is a constitutional requirement. The source of Congress' power to enact copyright laws is Article 1, Section 8, C. 8, of the Constitution, which authorizes Congress to "secure for limited Times to Authors . . . the exclusive Right to their respective Writings." It is this bedrock principle of copyright that mandates the law's seemingly disparate treatment of facts and factual compilations. No one may claim originality as to facts. This is because facts do not owe their origin to an act of authorship. The distinction is one between creation and discovery: The first person to find and report a particular fact has not created the fact; he or she has merely discovered its existence.

If the selection and arrangement of facts are original, these elements of the work are eligible for copyright protection. No matter how original the format, however, the facts themselves do not become original through association.

There is no doubt that Feist took from the white pages of Rural's directory a substantial amount of factual information. At a minimum, Feist copied the names, towns, and telephone numbers of 1,309 of Rural's subscribers. Not all copying, however, is copyright infringement. Two elements must be proven: (1) ownership of a valid copyright, and (2) copying of constituent elements of the work that are original. The first element is not at issue here: Feist appears to concede that Rural's directory, considered as a whole, is subject to a valid copyright because it contains some foreword text, as well as original material in its yellow pages advertisements.

The question is whether Rural has proven the second element. In other words, did Feist, by taking 1,309 names, towns, and telephone numbers from Rural's white pages, copy anything that was "original" to Rural? Certainly, the raw data do not satisfy the originality requirement. Rural may have been the first to discover and report the names, towns, and telephone numbers of its subscribers, but these data do not "owe their origin" to Rural. The question that remains is whether Rural selected, coordinated, or arranged these copyrightable facts in an original way. The selection, coordination, and arrangement of Rural's white pages do not satisfy the minimum constitutional standards for copyright protection. Rural's selection of listings could not be more obvious: It publishes the most basic information—name, town, and telephone number—about each person who applies to it for telephone service. This is "selection" of a sort, but it lacks the modicum of creativity necessary to transform mere selection into copyrightable expression. Rural extended sufficient effort to make the white pages directory useful, but insufficient creativity to make it original.

The judgment of the Court of Appeals is Reversed.

How to Brief a Case

CRITICAL LEGAL THINKING

Judges apply legal reasoning in reaching a decision in a case. In doing so, the judge must specify the issue presented by the case, identify the key facts in the case and the applicable law, and then apply the law to the facts to come to a conclusion that answers the issue presented. This process is called **critical legal thinking.** Skills of analysis and interpretation are important in deciding legal cases.

Key Terms

Before embarking upon the study of law, the student should be familiar with the following key legal terms:

Plaintiff　The party who originally brought the lawsuit.

Defendant　The party against whom the lawsuit has been brought.

Petitioner or Appellant　The party who has appealed the decision of the trial court or lower court. The petitioner may be either the plaintiff or the defendant, depending on who lost the case at the trial court or lower court level.

Respondent or Appellee　The party who must answer the petitioner's appeal. The respondent may be either the plaintiff or the defendant, depending upon which party is the petitioner. In some cases, both the plaintiff *and* the defendant may disagree with the trial court's or lower court's decision and both parties may appeal the decision.

Briefing a Case

"Briefing" a case is important to clarify the legal issues involved and to gain a better understanding of the case.

The student must summarize (brief) the court's decision in no more than 400 words (some professors may shorten or lengthen this limit). The format is highly structured, consisting of five parts, each of which is numbered and labeled:

Part	Maximum Words
1. Case name and citation	25
2. Summary of key facts in the case	125
3. Issue presented by the case, stated as a one-sentence question answerable only by *yes* or *no*	25
4. Holding—the court's resolution of the issue	25
5. A summary of the court's reasoning justifying the holding	200
Total words	400

1. Case Name and Citation

The name of the case is placed at the beginning of each briefed case. The case name usually contains the names of the parties to the lawsuit. If there are multiple plaintiffs or defendants, however, some of the names of the parties may be omitted from the case name. Abbreviations often are used in case names.

The case citation—which consists of a number plus the year in which the case was decided, such as "126 L.Ed.2d 295 (1993)"—is set forth below the case name. The case citation identifies the book in the law library in which the case may be found. For example, the case in the above citation may be found in volume 126 of the *Supreme Court Reporter Lawyer's Edition (Second)*, page 295. The name of the court that decided the case appears below the case name.

2. Summary of Key Facts in the Case

The important facts of a case are stated briefly. Extraneous facts and facts of minor importance are omitted from the brief. The facts of the case usually can be found at the beginning of the case, but not necessarily. Important facts may be found throughout the case.

3. Issue Presented by the Case

It is crucial in briefing a case to identify the issue presented to the court to decide. The issue on appeal is most often a legal question, although questions of fact sometimes are the subject of an appeal. The issue presented in each case usually is quite specific and should be asked in a one-sentence question that is answerable only by a *yes* or *no*. For example, the issue statement, "Is Mary liable?" is too broad. A more proper statement of the issue would be, "Is Mary liable to Joe for breach of the contract made between them based on her refusal to make the payment due on September 30?"

4. Holding

The holding is the decision reached by the present court. It should be *yes* or *no*. The holding also states which party won.

5. Summary of the Court's Reasoning

When an appellate court or supreme court issues a decision—which often is called an *opinion*—the court normally states the reasoning it used in reaching its decision. The rationale for the decision may be based on the specific facts of the case, public policy, prior law, or other matters. In stating the reasoning of the court, the student should reword the court's language into the student's own language. This summary of the court's reasoning should pick out the meat of the opinions and weed out the nonessentials.

Following are two U.S. Supreme Court opinions for briefing. The case is presented in the language of the U.S. Supreme Court. A "Brief of the Case" follows each of the two cases. A third case, from the New York State Court of Appeals, also is included for briefing.

CASE 1

For Briefing

Harris v. Forklift Systems, Inc. **CASE NAME**
510 U.S. 17, 114 S.Ct. 367, 126 L.Ed.2d 295 **CITATION** *1993 U.S. LEXIS 7155 (1993)*
                                              COURT *Supreme Court of the United States*

OPINION OF THE COURT. O'CONNOR, JUSTICE

FACTS. Teresa Harris worked as a manager at Forklift Systems, Inc., an equipment rental company, from April 1985 until October 1987. Charles Hardy was Forklift's president. Throughout Harris's time at Forklift, Hardy often insulted her because of her gender and often made her the target of unwanted sexual innuendos. Hardy told Harris on several occasions, in the presence of other employees, "You're a woman, what do you know" and "We need a man as the rental manager"; at least once, he told her she was "a dumb-ass woman." Again in front of others, he suggested that the two of them "go to the Holiday Inn to negotiate Harris' raise." Hardy occasionally asked Harris and other female employees to get coins from his front pants pocket. He threw objects on the ground in front of Harris and other women, and asked them to pick the objects up. He made sexual innuendos about Harris' and other women's clothing.

In mid-August 1987, Harris complained to Hardy about his conduct. Hardy said he was surprised that Harris was offended, claimed he was only joking, and apologized. He also promised he would stop and based on his assurance Harris stayed on the job. But in early September, Hardy began anew: While Harris was arranging a deal with one of Forklift's customers, he asked her, again in front of other employees, "What did you do, promise the guy some sex Saturday night?" On October 1, Harris collected her paycheck and quit.

LOWER COURTS' OPINIONS. Harris then sued Forklift, claiming that Hardy's conduct had created an abusive work environment for her because of her gender. The United States District Court for the Middle District of Tennessee found this to be "a close case," but held that Hardy's conduct did not create an abusive environment. The court found that some of Hardy's comments offended Harris, and would offend the "reasonable woman," but that they were not "so severe as to be expected to seriously affect Harris' psychological well-being." A reasonable woman manager under like circumstances would have been offended by Hardy, but his conduct would not have risen to the level of interfering with that person's work performance. The United States Court of Appeals for the Sixth Circuit affirmed in a brief unpublished decision.

ISSUE. We granted certiorari to resolve a conflict among the Circuits on whether conduct, to be actionable as "abusive work environment" harassment, must "seriously affect an employee's psychological well-being" or lead the plaintiff to "suffer injury."

STATUTE BEING INTERPRETED. Title VII of the Civil Rights Act of 1964 makes it "an unlawful employment practice for an employer . . . to discriminate against any individual with respect to his compensation, terms, conditions, or privileges of employment, because of such individual's race, color, religion, sex, or national origin." 42 U.S.C. §2000e-2(a)(1).

U.S. SUPREME COURT'S REASONING. When the workplace is permeated with discriminatory intimidation, ridicule, and insult that is sufficiently severe or pervasive to alter the conditions of the victim's employment and create an abusive working environment, Title VII is violated. This standard takes a middle path between making actionable any conduct that is merely offensive and requiring the conduct to cause a tangible psychological injury. Mere utterance of an epithet which engenders offensive feelings in an employee does not sufficiently affect the conditions of employment to implicate Title VII. Conduct that is not severe or pervasive enough to create an objectively hostile or abusive work environment—an environment that a reasonable person would find hostile or abusive—is beyond Title VII's purview. Likewise, if the victim does not subjectively perceive the environment to be abusive, the conduct has not actually altered the conditions of the victim's employment, and there is no Title VII violation.

But Title VII comes into play before the harassing conduct leads to a nervous breakdown. A discriminatorily abusive work environment, even one that does not seriously affect employees' psychological well-being, can and often will detract from employees' job performance, discourage employees from remaining on the job, or keep them from advancing in their careers. Moreover, even without regard to these tangible effects, the very fact that the discriminatory conduct was so severe or pervasive that it created a work environment abusive to employees because of their race, gender, religion, or national origin offends Title VII's broad rule of workplace equality.

HOLDING. We therefore believe the district court erred in relying on whether the conduct "seriously affected plaintiff's psychological well-being" or led her to "suffer injury." Such an inquiry may needlessly focus the factfinder's attention on concrete psychological harm, an element Title VII does not require. So long as the environment would reasonably be perceived, and is perceived, as hostile or abusive, there is no need for it also to be psychologically injurious. This is not, and by its nature cannot be, a mathematically precise test. But we can say that whether an environment is "hostile" or "abusive" can be determined only by looking at all the circumstances.

We therefore reverse the judgment of the Court of Appeals, and remand the case for further proceedings consistent with this opinion.

CONCURRING OPINION. GINSBURG, JUSTICE
The critical issue, Title VII's text indicates, is whether members of one sex are exposed to disadvantageous terms or conditions of employment to which members of the other sex are not exposed. The adjudicator's inquiry should center, dominantly, on whether the discriminatory conduct has reasonably interfered with the plaintiff's work performance. To show such interference, the plaintiff need not prove that his or her tangible productivity has declined as a result of the harassment.

Brief of the Case: *Harris v. Forklift Systems, Inc.*

1. Case Name, Citation, and Court

Harris v. Forklift Systems, Inc.

126 L.Ed.2d. 295 (1993)

United States Supreme Court

2. Summary of the Key Facts

A. While Harris worked at Forklift, Hardy continually insulted her because of her gender and made her the target of unwanted sexual innuendos.

B. This conduct created an abusive and hostile work environment, causing Harris to terminate her employment.

C. Harris sued Forklift, alleging sexual harassment in violation of Title VII of the Civil Rights Act of 1964, which makes it an unlawful employment practice for an employer to discriminate in employment because of an individual's sex.

3. The Issue

Must an employee prove that she suffered psychological injury before she can prove a Title VII claim for sexual harassment against her employer?

4. The Holding

No. The Supreme Court remanded the case for further proceedings consistent with its opinion.

5. Summary of the Court's Reasoning

The Supreme Court held that a workplace that is permeated with discriminatory intimidation, ridicule, and insult so severe that it alters the conditions of the victim's employment creates an abusive and hostile work environment that violates Title VII. The Court held that the victim is not required to prove that she suffered tangible psychological injury to prove her Title VII claim. The Court noted that Title VII comes into play before the harassing conduct leads the victim to have a nervous breakdown.

CASE 2

For Briefing

PGA Tour, Inc. v. Martin
121 S.Ct. 1879, 149 L.Ed.2d 904 (2001)

CASE NAME
CITATION   *2001 U.S. LEXIS 4115*
COURT   *Supreme Court of the United States*

OPINION OF THE COURT. STEVEN, JUSTICE

ISSUE. This case raises two questions concerning the application of the Americans with Disabilities Act of 1990 [42 U.S.C. § 12101 *et seq.*] to a gifted athlete: first, whether the Act protects access to professional golf tournaments by a qualified entrant with a disability; and second, whether a disabled contestant may be denied the use of a golf cart because it would "fundamentally alter the nature" of the tournaments to allow him to ride when all other contestants must walk.

FACTS. Petitioner PGA TOUR, Inc., a nonprofit entity formed in 1968, sponsors and cosponsors professional golf tournaments conducted on three annual tours. About 200 golfers participate in the PGA TOUR; about 170 in the NIKE TOUR; and about 100 in the SENIOR PGA TOUR. PGA TOUR and NIKE TOUR tournaments typically are 4-day events, played on courses leased and operated by petitioner. The revenues generated by television, admissions, concessions, and contributions from cosponsors amount to about $300 million a year, much of which is distributed in prize money. The "Conditions of Competition and Local Rules," often described as the "hard card," apply specifically to petitioner's professional tours. The hard cards for the PGA TOUR and NIKE TOUR require players to walk the golf course during tournaments, but not during open qualifying rounds. On the SENIOR PGA TOUR, which is limited to golfers age 50 and older, the contestants may use golf carts. Most seniors, however, prefer to walk.

RESPONDENT. Casey Martin is a talented golfer. As an amateur, he won 17 Oregon Golf Association junior events before he was 15, and won the state championship as a high school senior. He played on the Stanford University golf team that won the 1994 National Collegiate Athletic Association (NCAA) championship. As a professional, Martin qualified for the NIKE TOUR in 1998 and 1999, and based on his 1999 performance, qualified for the PGA TOUR in 2000. In the 1999 season, he entered 24 events, made the cut 13 times, and had 6 top-10 finishes, coming in second twice and third once.

Martin is also an individual with a disability as defined in the Americans with Disabilities Act of 1990 (ADA or Act). Since birth he has been afflicted with Klippel-Trenaunay-Weber Syndrome, a degenerative circulatory disorder that obstructs the flow of blood from his right leg back to his heart. The disease is progressive; it causes severe pain and has atrophied his right leg. During the latter part of his college career, because of the progress of the disease, Martin could no longer walk an 18-hole golf course. Walking not only caused him pain, fatigue, and anxiety, but also created a significant risk of hemorrhaging,

developing blood clots, and fracturing his tibia so badly that an amputation might be required.

When Martin turned pro and entered the petitioner's Qualifying-School, the hard card permitted him to use a cart during his successful progress through the first two stages. He made a request, supported by detailed medical records, for permission to use a golf cart during the third stage. Petitioner refused to review those records, or to waive its walking rule for the third stage. Martin therefore filed this action.

DISTRICT COURT'S DECISION 994 F.SUPP. 1242 [DISTRICT: OREGON (1998)]. At trial, petitioner PGA TOUR did not contest the conclusion that Martin has a disability covered by the ADA, or the fact that his disability prevents him from walking the course during a round of golf. Rather, petitioner asserted that the condition of walking is a substantive rule of competition, and that waiving it as to any individual for any reason would fundamentally alter the nature of the competition. Petitioner's evidence included the testimony of a number of experts, among them some of the greatest golfers in history. Arnold Palmer, Jack Nicklaus, and Ken Venturi explained that fatigue can be a critical factor in a tournament, particularly on the last day when psychological pressure is at a maximum. Their testimony makes it clear that, in their view, permission to use a cart might well give some players a competitive advantage over other players who must walk.

The judge found that the purpose of the rule was to inject fatigue into the skill of shot-making, but that the fatigue injected "by walking the course cannot be deemed significant under normal circumstances." Furthermore, Martin presented evidence, and the judge found, that even with the use of a cart, Martin must walk over a mile during an 18-hole round, and that the fatigue he suffers from coping with his disability is "undeniably greater" than the fatigue his able-bodied competitors endure from walking the course. As a result, the judge concluded that it would "not fundamentally alter the nature of the PGA Tour's game to accommodate him with a cart." The judge accordingly entered a permanent injunction requiring petitioner to permit Martin to use a cart in tour and qualifying events.

COURT OF APPEALS DECISION 204 F.3D 994 [9TH CIRCUIT (2000)]. The Court of Appeals concluded that golf courses remain places of public accommodation during PGA tournaments. On the merits, because there was no serious dispute about the fact that permitting Martin to use a golf cart was both a reasonable and a necessary solution to the problem of providing him access to the tournaments, the Court of Appeals regarded the central dispute as whether such permission would "fundamentally alter" the nature of the PGA TOUR or NIKE

TOUR. Like the District Court, the Court of Appeals viewed the issue not as "whether use of carts generally would fundamentally alter the competition, but whether the use of a cart by Martin would do so." That issue turned on "an intensively fact-based inquiry," and, the court concluded, had been correctly resolved by the trial judge. In its words, "all that the cart does is permit Martin access to a type of competition in which he otherwise could not engage because of his disability."

FEDERAL STATUTE BEING INTERPRETED. Congress enacted the ADA in 1990 to remedy widespread discrimination against disabled individuals. To effectuate its sweeping purpose, the ADA forbids discrimination against disabled individuals in major areas of public life, among them employment (Title I of the Act), public services (Title II), and public accommodations (Title III). At issue now is the applicability of Title III to petitioner's golf tours and qualifying rounds, in particular to petitioner's treatment of a qualified disabled golfer wishing to compete in those events.

U.S. SUPREME COURT'S REASONING. It seems apparent, from both the general rule and the comprehensive definition of "public accommodation," that petitioner's golf tours and their qualifying rounds fit comfortably within the coverage of Title III, and Martin within its protection. The events occur on "golf courses," a type of place specifically identified by the Act as a public accommodation. Section 12181(7)(L). In this case, the narrow dispute is whether allowing Martin to use a golf cart, despite the walking requirement that applies to the PGA TOUR, the NIKE TOUR, and the third stage of the Qualifying-School, is a modification that would "fundamentally alter the nature" of those events.

As an initial matter, we observe that the use of carts is not itself inconsistent with the fundamental character of the game of golf. From early on, the essence of the game has been shot-making—using clubs to cause a ball to progress from the teeing ground to a hole some distance away with as few strokes as possible. Golf carts started appearing with increasing regularity on American golf courses in the 1950's. Today they are everywhere. And they are encouraged. For one thing, they often speed up play, and for another, they are great revenue producers. There is nothing in the Rules of Golf that either forbids the use of carts, or penalizes a player for using a cart.

Petitioner, however, distinguishes the game of golf as it is generally played from the game that it sponsors in the PGA TOUR, NIKE TOUR, and the last stage of the Qualifying-School—golf at the "highest level." According to petitioner, "the goal of the highest-level competitive athletics is to assess and compare the performance of different competitors, a task that is meaningful only if the competitors are subject to identical substantive rules." The waiver of any possibly "outcome-affecting" rule for a contestant would violate this principle and therefore, in petitioner's view, fundamentally alter the nature of the highest level athletic event. The walking rule is one such rule, petitioner submits, because its purpose is "to inject the element of fatigue into the skill of shot-making," and thus its effect may be the critical loss of a stroke. As a consequence, the reasonable modification Martin seeks would fundamentally alter the nature of petitioner's highest level tournaments.

The force of petitioner's argument is, first of all, mitigated by the fact that golf is a game in which it is impossible to guarantee that all competitors will play under exactly the same conditions or that an individual's ability will be the sole determinant of the outcome. For example, changes in the weather may produce harder greens and more head winds for the tournament leader than for his closest pursuers. A lucky bounce may save a shot or two. Whether such happenstance events are more or less probable than the likelihood that a golfer afflicted with Klippel-Trenaunay-Weber Syndrome would one day qualify for the NIKE TOUR and PGA TOUR, they at least demonstrate that pure chance may have a greater impact on the outcome of elite golf tournaments than the fatigue resulting from the enforcement of the walking rule.

Further, the factual basis of petitioner's argument is undermined by the District Court's finding that the fatigue from walking during one of petitioner's 4-day tournaments cannot be deemed significant. The District Court credited the testimony of a professor in physiology and expert on fatigue, who calculated the calories expended in walking a golf course (about five miles) to be approximately 500 calories—"nutritionally less than a Big Mac." What is more, that energy is expended over a 5-hour period, during which golfers have numerous intervals for rest and refreshment. In fact, the expert concluded, because golf is a low intensity activity, fatigue from the game is primarily a psychological phenomenon in which stress and motivation are the key ingredients. And even under conditions of severe heat and humidity, the critical factor in fatigue is fluid loss rather than exercise from walking. Moreover, when given the option of using a cart, the majority of golfers in petitioner's tournaments have chosen to walk, often to relieve stress or for other strategic reasons. As NIKE TOUR member Eric Johnson testified, walking allows him to keep in rhythm, stay warmer when it is chilly, and develop a better sense of the elements and the course than riding in a cart. As we have demonstrated, the walking rule is at best peripheral to the nature of petitioner's athletic events, and thus it might be waived in individual cases without working a fundamental alteration.

HOLDING AND REMEDY. Under the ADA's basic requirement that the need of a disabled person be evaluated on an individual basis, we have no doubt that allowing Martin to use a golf cart would not fundamentally alter the nature of petitioner's tournaments. As we have discussed, the purpose of the walking rule is to subject players to fatigue, which in turn may influence the outcome of tournaments. Even if the rule does serve that purpose, it is an uncontested finding of the District Court that Martin "easily endures greater fatigue even with a cart than his able-bodied competitors do by walking." The purpose of the walking rule is therefore not compromised in the slightest by allowing Martin to use a cart. A modification that provides an exception to a peripheral tournament rule without impairing its purpose cannot be said to "fundamentally alter" the tournament. What it can be said to do, on the other hand, is to allow Martin the chance to qualify for and compete in the athletic events petitioner offers to those members of the public who have the skill and desire to enter. That is exactly what the ADA requires. As a result, Martin's request for a waiver of the walking rule should have been granted.

The judgment of the Court of Appeals is affirmed. It is so ordered.

DISSENTING OPINION. SCALIA, JUSTICE

In my view, today's opinion exercises a benevolent compassion that the law does not place it within our power to impose. The judgment distorts the text of Title III, the structure of the ADA, and common sense. I respectfully dissent.

The Court, for its part, assumes that conclusion for the sake of argument, but pronounces respondent to be a "customer" of the PGA TOUR or of the golf courses on which it is played. That seems to me quite incredible. The PGA TOUR is a professional sporting event, staged for the entertainment of a live and TV audience. The professional golfers on the tour are no more "enjoying" (the statutory term) the entertainment that the tour provides, or the facilities of the golf courses on which it is held, than professional baseball players "enjoy" the baseball games in which they play or the facilities of Yankee Stadium. To be sure, professional baseball players *participate* in the games, and *use* the ballfields, but no one in his right mind would think that they are *customers* of the American League or of Yankee Stadium. They are themselves the entertainment that the customers pay to watch. And professional golfers are no different. A professional golfer's practicing his profession is not comparable to John Q. Public's frequenting "a 232-acre amusement area with swimming, boating, sun bathing, picnicking, miniature golf, dancing facilities, and a snack bar."

Having erroneously held that Title III applies to the "customers" of professional golf who consist of its practitioners, the Court then erroneously answers—or to be accurate simply ignores—a second question. The ADA requires covered businesses to make such reasonable modifications of "policies, practices, or procedures" as are necessary to "afford" goods, services, and privileges to individuals with disabilities; but it explicitly does not require "modifications that would fundamentally alter the nature" of the goods, services, and privileges. Section 12182(b)(2)(A)(ii). In other words, disabled individuals must be given *access* to the same goods, services, and privileges that others enjoy.

A camera store may not refuse to sell cameras to a disabled person, but it is not required to stock cameras specially designed for such persons. It is hardly a feasible judicial function to decide whether shoe stores should sell single shoes to one-legged persons and if so at what price, or how many Braille books the Borders or Barnes and Noble bookstore chains should stock in each of their stores. Eighteen-hole golf courses, 10-foot-high basketball hoops, 90-foot baselines, 100-yard football fields—all are arbitrary and none is essential. The only support for any of them is tradition and (in more modern times) insistence by what has come to be regarded as the ruling body of the sport—both of which factors support the PGA TOUR's position in the present case. One can envision the parents of a Little League player with attention deficit disorder trying to convince a judge that their son's disability makes it at least 25% more difficult to hit a pitched ball. (If they are successful, the only thing that could prevent a court order giving a kid four strikes would be a judicial determination that, in baseball, three strikes are metaphysically necessary, which is quite absurd.)

Agility, strength, speed, balance, quickness of mind, steadiness of nerves, intensity of concentration—these talents are not evenly distributed. No wild-eyed dreamer has ever suggested that the managing bodies of the competitive sports that test precisely these qualities should try to take account of the uneven distribution of God-given gifts when writing and enforcing the rules of competition. And I have no doubt Congress did not authorize misty-eyed judicial supervision of such revolution. The year was 2001, and "everybody was finally equal." K. Vonnegut, Harrison Bergeron, in *Animal Farm and Related Readings* 129 (1997).

Brief of the Case: *PGA TOUR, Inc. v. Martin*

1. Case Name, Citation, and Court

PGA TOUR, Inc. v. Martin

121 S.Ct. 1879, 2001 LEXIS 415 (2001)

Supreme Court of the United States

2. Summary of the Key Facts

A. PGA TOUR, Inc. is a nonprofit organization that sponsors professional golf tournaments.

B. The PGA establishes rules for its golf tournaments. A PGA rule requires golfers to walk the golf course, and not use golf carts.

C. Casey Martin is a professional golfer who suffers from Klippel-Trenaunay-Weber Syndrome, a degenerative circulatory disorder that atrophied Martin's right leg and causes him pain, fatigue, and anxiety when walking.

D. When Martin petitioned the PGA to use a golf cart during golf tournaments, the PGA refused.

E. Martin sued the PGA, alleging discrimination against a disabled individual in violation of the American with Disabilities Act of 1990, a federal statute.

3. Issue

Does the Americans with Disabilities Act require the PGA to accommodate Martin by permitting him to use a golf cart while playing in PGA golf tournaments?

4. Holding

Yes. The Supreme Court held that the PGA must allow Martin to use a golf cart when competing in PGA golf tournaments. Affirmed.

5. Court's Reasoning

The Supreme Court held that:

A. Martin was disabled and covered by the Act.
B. Golf courses are "public accommodations" covered by the Act.
C. The use of golf carts is not a fundamental characteristic of the game of golf.
D. Other than the PGA rule, no Rule of Golf forbids the use of golf carts.
E. It is impossible to guarantee all players in golf will play under the exact same conditions, so allowing Martin to use a golf cart gives him no advantage over other golfers.
F. Martin, because of his disease, will probably suffer more fatigue playing golf using a golf cart than other golfers will suffer without using a cart.
G. The PGA's "walking rule" is only peripheral to the game of golf and not a fundamental part of golf.
H. Allowing Martin to use a golf cart will not fundamentally alter the PGA's highest-level professional golf tournaments.

CASE 3

For Briefing

Palsgraf v. Long Island R.R. Co.	**CASE NAME**	
248 N.Y. 339 (1928)	**CITATION**	*162 N.E. 99*
	COURT	*Court of Appeals of the State of New York*

OPINION OF THE COURT. CARDOZO, Ch. J.

FACTS. Plaintiff was standing on a platform of defendant's railroad after buying a ticket to go to Rockaway Beach. A train stopped at the station, bound for another place. Two men ran forward to catch it. One of the men reached the platform of the car without mishap, though the train was already moving. The other man, carrying a package, jumped aboard the car, but seemed unsteady as if about to fall. A guard on the car, who had held the door open, reached forward to help him in, and another guard on the platform pushed him from behind. In this act, the package was dislodged, and fell upon the rails. It was a package of small size, about fifteen inches long, and was covered by a newspaper. In fact it contained fireworks, but there was nothing in its appearance to give notice of its contents. The fireworks when they fell exploded. The shock of the explosion threw down some scales at the other end of the platform, many feet away. The scales struck the plaintiff, causing injuries for which she sues.

The conduct of the defendant's guard, if a wrong in its relation to the holder of the package, was not a wrong in its relation to the plaintiff, standing far away. Relatively to her it was not negligence at all. Nothing in the situation gave notice that the falling package had in it the potency of peril to persons thus removed. Negligence is not actionable unless it involves the invasion of a legally protected interest, the violation of a right. "Proof of negligence in the air, so to speak, will not do" (Pollock, *Torts* [11th ed.], p. 455; *Martin v. Herzog*, 228 N.Y. 164, 170; cf. Salmond, Torts [6th ed.], p.24). "Negligence is the absence of care, according to the circumstances" (WILLES, J., in *Vaughan v. Taff Vale Ry. Co.*, 5 H. & N. 679, 688; 1 Beven, Negligence

[4th ed.], 7; *Paul v. Consol. Fireworks Co.*, 212 N.Y. 117; *Adams v. Bullock*, 227 N.Y. 208, 211; *Parrott v. Wells-Fargo Co.*, 15 Wall. [U.S.] 524). The plaintiff as she stood upon the platform of the station might claim to be protected against intentional invasion of her bodily security. Such invasion is not charged. She might claim to be protected against unintentional invasion by conduct involving in the thought of reasonable men an unreasonable hazard that such invasion would ensue. These, from the point of view of the law, were the bounds of her immunity, with perhaps some rare exceptions, survivals for the most part of ancient forms of liability, where conduct is held to be at the peril of the actor (*Sullivan v. Dunham*, 161 N.Y. 290 Page 342). If no hazard was apparent to the eye of ordinary vigilance, an act innocent and harmless, at least to outward seeming, with reference to her, did not take to itself the quality of a tort because it happened to be a wrong, though apparently not one involving the risk of bodily insecurity, with reference to some one else. "In every instance, before negligence can be predicated of a given act, back of the act must be sought and found a duty to the individual complaining, the observance of which would have averted or avoided the injury" (McSHERRY, C.J., in *W. Va. Central R. Co. v. State*, 96 Md. 652, 666; cf. *Norfolk & Western Ry. Co. v. Wood*, 99 Va. 156, 158, 159; *Hughes v. Boston & Maine R.R. Co.*, 71 N.H. 279, 284; *U.S. Express Co. v. Everest*, 72 Kan. 517; *Emry v. Roanoke Nav. Co.*, 111 N.C. 94, 95; *Vaughan v. Transit Dev. Co.*, 222 N.Y. 79; *Losee v. Clute*, 51 N.Y. 494; *DiCaprio v. N.Y.C.R.R. Co.*, 231 N.Y. 94; 1 Shearman & Redfield on Negligence, § 8, and cases cited; Cooley on Torts [3d ed.], p. 1411; Jaggard on Torts, vol. 2, p. 826; Wharton, *Negligence*, § 24; Bohlen, *Studies in the Law of Torts*, p. 601). "The ideas of negligence and duty are strictly correlative" (BOWEN, L.J., in *Thomas v. Quartermaine*, 18 Q.B.D. 685, 694). The plaintiff sues in her own right for a wrong personal to her, and not as the vicarious beneficiary of a breach of duty to another.

A different conclusion will involve us, and swiftly too, in a maze of contradictions. A guard stumbles over a package which has been left upon a platform. It seems to be a bundle of newspapers. It turns out to be a can of dynamite. To the eye of ordinary vigilance, the bundle is abandoned waste, which may be kicked or trod on with impunity. Is a passenger at the other end of the platform protected by the law against the unsuspected hazard concealed beneath the waste? If not, is the result to be any different, so far as the distant passenger is concerned, when the guard stumbles over a valise which a truckman or a porter has left upon the walk? The passenger far away, if the victim of a wrong at all, has a cause of action, not derivative, but original and primary. His claim to be protected against invasion of his bodily security is neither greater nor less because the act resulting in the invasion is a wrong to another far removed. In this case, the rights that are said to have been violated, the interests said to have been invaded, are not even of the same order. The man was not injured in his person nor even put in danger. The purpose of the act, as well as its effect, was to make his person safe. If there was a wrong to him at all, which may very well be doubted, it was a wrong to a property interest only, the safety of his package. Out of this wrong to property, which threatened injury to nothing else, there has passed, we are told, to the plaintiff by derivation or succession a right of action for the invasion of an interest of another order, the right to bodily security. The diversity of interests emphasizes the futility of the effort to build the plaintiff's right upon the basis of a wrong to some one else. The gain is one of emphasis, for a like result would follow if the interests were the same. Even then, the orbit of the danger as disclosed to the eye of reasonable vigilance would be the orbit of the duty. One who jostles one's neighbor in a crowd does not invade the rights of others standing at the outer fringe when the unintended contact casts a bomb upon the ground. The wrongdoer as to them is the man who carries the bomb, not the one who explodes it without suspicion of the danger. Life will have to be made over, and human nature transformed, before prevision so extravagant can be accepted as the norm of conduct, the customary standard to which behavior must conform. The argument for the plaintiff is built upon the shifting meanings of such words as "wrong" and "wrongful," and shares their instability. What the plaintiff must show is "a wrong" to herself, i.e., a violation of her own right, and not merely a wrong to some one else, nor conduct "wrongful" because unsocial, but not "a wrong" to any one. We are told that one who drives at reckless speed through a crowded city street is guilty of a negligent act and, therefore, of a wrongful one irrespective of the consequences. Negligent the act is, and wrongful in the sense that it is unsocial, but wrongful and unsocial in relation to other travelers, only because the eye of vigilance perceives the risk of damage. If the same act were to be committed on a speedway or a race course, it would lose its wrongful quality. The risk reasonably to be perceived defines the duty to be obeyed, and risk imports relation; it is risk to another or to others within the range of apprehension (Seavey, Negligence, Subjective or Objective, 41 H.L. Rv. 6; *Boronkay v. Robinson & Carpenter*, 247 N.Y. 365). This does not mean, of course, that one who launches a destructive force is always relieved of liability if the force, though known to be destructive, pursues an unexpected path. "It was not necessary that the defendant should have had notice of the particular method in which an accident would occur, if the possibility of an accident was clear to the ordinarily prudent eye" (*Munsey v. Webb*, 231 U.S. 150, 156; *Condran v. Park & Tilford*, 213 N.Y. 341, 345; *Robert v. U.S.E.F. Corp.*, 240 N.Y. 474, 477). Some acts, such as shooting, are so imminently dangerous to any one who may come within reach of the missile, however unexpectedly, as to impose a duty of prevision not far from that of an insurer. Even today, and much oftener in earlier stages of the law, one acts sometimes at one's peril (Jeremiah Smith, Tort and Absolute Liability, 30 H.L. Rv. 328; Street, *Foundations of Legal Liability*, vol. 1, pp. 77, 78). Under this head, it may be, fall certain cases of what is known as transferred intent, an act willfully dangerous to A resulting by misadventure in injury to B (*Talmage v. Smith*, 101 Mich. 370, 374) These cases aside, wrong is defined in terms of the natural or probable, at least when unintentional (*Parrot v. Wells-Fargo Co.* [The Nitro-Glycerine Case], 15 Wall. [U.S.] 524). The range of reasonable apprehension is at times a question for the court, and at times, if varying inferences are possible, a question for the jury. Here, by concession, there was nothing in the situation to suggest to the most cautious mind that the parcel wrapped in newspaper would spread wreckage through the station. If the guard had thrown it down knowingly and willfully, he would not have threatened the plaintiff's safety, so far as appearances could warn him. His conduct would not have involved, even then, an unreasonable probability of invasion of her bodily security. Liability can be no greater where the act is inadvertent.

Negligence, like risk, is thus a term of relation. Negligence in the abstract, apart from things related, is surely not a tort, if indeed it is understandable at all (BOWEN, L.J., in *Thomas v. Quartermaine*, 18 Q.B.D. 685, 694). Negligence is not a tort unless it results in the commission of a wrong, and the commission of a wrong imports the violation of a right, in this case, we are told, the right to be protected against interference with one's bodily security. But bodily security is protected, not against all forms of interference or aggression, but only against some. One who seeks redress at law does not make out a cause of action by showing without more that there has been damage to his person. If the harm was not willful, he must show that the act as to him had possibilities of danger so many and apparent as to entitle him to be protected against the doing of it though the harm was unintended. Affront to personality is still the keynote of the wrong. Confirmation of this view will be found in the history and development of the action on the case. Negligence as a basis of civil liability was unknown to mediaeval law (8 Holdsworth, *History of English Law*, p. 449; Street, *Foundations of Legal Liability*, vol. 1, pp. 189, 190). For damage to the person, the sole remedy was trespass, and trespass did not lie in the absence of aggression, and that direct and personal (Holdsworth, op. cit. p. 453; Street, op. cit. vol. 3, pp. 258, 260, vol. 1, pp. 71, 74.) Liability for other damage, as where a servant without orders from the master does or omits something to the damage of another, is a plant of later growth (Holdsworth, op. cit. 450, 457; Wigmore, *Responsibility or Tortious Acts*, vol. 3, *Essays in Anglo-American Legal History*, 520, 523, 526, 533). When it emerged out of the legal soil, it was thought of as a variant of trespass, an offshoot of the parent stock. This appears in the form of action, which was known as trespass on the case (Holdsworth, op. cit. p. 449; cf. *Scott v. Shepard*, 2 Wm. Black. 892; Green, *Rationale of Proximate Cause*, p. 19). The victim does not sue derivatively, or by right of subrogation, to vindicate an interest invaded in the person of another. Thus to view his cause of action is to ignore the fundamental difference between tort and crime (Holland, *Jurisprudence* [12th ed.], p. 328). He sues for breach of a duty owing to himself.

The law of causation, remote or proximate, is thus foreign to the case before us. The question of liability is always anterior to the question of the measure of the consequences that go with liability. If there is no tort to be redressed, there is no occasion to consider what damage might be recovered if there were a finding of a tort. We may assume, without deciding, that negligence, not at large or in the abstract, but in relation to the plaintiff, would entail liability for any and all consequences, however novel or extraordinary (*Bird v. St. Paul F. & M. Ins. Co.*, 224 N.Y. 47, 54; *Ehrgott v. Mayor, etc., of N.Y*, 96 N.Y. 264; *Smith v. London & S.W. Ry. Co.*, L.R. 6 C.P. 14; 1 Beven, Negligence, 106; Street, op. cit. vol. 1, p. 90; Green, *Rationale of Proximate Cause*, pp. 88, 118; cf. *Matter of Polemis*, L.R. 1921, 3 K.B. 560; 44 *Law Quarterly Review*, 142). There is room for argument that a distinction is to be drawn according to the diversity of interests invaded by the act, as where conduct negligent in that it threatens an insignificant invasion of an interest in property results in an unforeseeable invasion of an interest of another order, as, e.g., one of bodily security. Perhaps other distinctions may be necessary. We do not go into the question now. The consequences to be followed must first be rooted in a wrong.

HOLDING. The judgment of the Appellate Division and that of the Trial Term should be reversed, and the complaint dismissed, with costs in all courts.

DISSENTING OPINION. ANDREWS, J.
Assisting a passenger to board a train, the defendant's servant negligently knocked a package from his arms. It fell between the platform and the cars. Of its contents the servant knew and could know nothing. A violent explosion followed. The concussion broke some scales standing a considerable distance away. In falling they injured the plaintiff, an intending passenger.

Upon these facts may she recover the damages she has suffered in an action brought against the master? The result we shall reach depends upon our theory as to the nature of negligence. Is it a relative concept—the breach of some duty owing to a particular person or to particular persons? Or where there is an act which unreasonably threatens the safety of others, is the doer liable for all its proximate consequences, even where they result in injury to one who would generally be thought to be outside the radius of danger? This is not a mere dispute as to words. We might not believe that to the average mind the dropping of the bundle would seem to involve the probability of harm to the plaintiff standing many feet away whatever might be the case as to the owner or to one so near as to be likely to be struck by its fall. If, however, we adopt the second hypothesis we have to inquire only as to the relation between cause and effect. We deal in terms of proximate cause, not of negligence.

Negligence may be defined roughly as an act or omission which unreasonably does or may affect the rights of others, or which unreasonably fails to protect oneself from the dangers resulting from such acts. Here I confine myself to the first branch of the definition. Nor do I comment on the word "unreasonable." For present purposes it sufficiently describes that average of conduct that society requires of its members.

There must be both the act or the omission, and the right. It is the act itself, not the intent of the actor, that is important. (*Hover v. Barkhoof*, 44 N.Y. 113; *Mertz v. Connecticut Co.*, 217 N.Y. 475.) In criminal law both the intent and the result are to be considered. Intent again is material in tort actions, where punitive damages are sought, dependent on actual malice—not on merely reckless conduct. But here neither insanity nor infancy lessens responsibility. (*Williams v. Hays*, 143 N.Y. 442.)

As has been said, except in cases of contributory negligence, there must be rights which are or may be affected. Often though injury has occurred, no rights of him who suffers have been touched. A licensee or trespasser upon my land has no claim to affirmative care on my part that the land be made safe. (*Meiers v. Koch Brewery*, 229 N.Y. 10.) Where a railroad is required to fence its tracks against cattle, no man's rights are injured should he wander upon the road because such fence is absent. (*DiCaprio v. N.Y.C.R.R.*, 231 N.Y. 94.) An unborn child may not demand immunity from personal harm. (Drobner v. Peters, 232 N.Y. 220.)

But we are told that "there is no negligence unless there is in the particular case a legal duty to take care, and this duty must be one which is owed to the plaintiff himself and not merely to others." (Salmond Torts [6th ed.], 24.) This, I think too narrow a conception. Where there is the unreasonable act, and some right that may be affected there is negligence whether damage does or does not result. That is immaterial. Should we drive down Broadway at a reckless speed, we are negligent whether we strike an approaching car or miss it by an inch. The act itself is wrongful. It is a wrong not only to those who happen to be within the radius of danger but to all who might have been there—a wrong to the public at large. Such is the language of the street. Such the language of the courts when speaking of contributory negligence. Such again and again their language in speaking of the duty of some defendant and discussing proximate cause in cases where such a discussion is wholly irrelevant on any other theory. (*Perry v. Rochester Line Co.*, 219 N.Y. 60.) As was said by Mr. Justice HOLMES many years ago, "the measure of the defendant's duty in determining whether a wrong has been committed is one thing, the measure of liability when a wrong has been committed is another." (*Spade v. Lynn & Boston R.R. Co.*, 172 Mass. 488.) Due care is a duty imposed on each one of us to protect society from unnecessary danger, not to protect A, B or C alone.

It may well be that there is no such thing as negligence in the abstract. "Proof of negligence in the air, so to speak, will not do." In an empty world negligence would not exist. It does involve a relationship between man and his fellows. But not merely a relationship between man and those whom he might reasonably expect his act would injure. Rather, a relationship between him and those whom he does in fact injure. If his act has a tendency to harm some one, it harms him a mile away as surely as it does those on the scene. We now permit children to recover for the negligent killing of the father. It was never prevented on the theory that no duty was owing to them. A husband may be compensated for the loss of his wife's services. To say that the wrongdoer was negligent as to the husband as well as to the wife is merely an attempt to fit facts to theory. An insurance company paying a fire loss recovers its payment of the negligent incendiary. We speak of subrogation—of suing in the right of the insured. Behind the cloud of words is the fact they hide, that the act, wrongful as to the insured, has also injured the company. Even if it be true that the fault of father, wife or insured will prevent recovery, it is because we consider the original negligence not the proximate cause of the injury. (Pollock, *Torts* [12th ed.], 463.)

In the well-known *Polemis* case (1921, 3 K.B. 560), SCRUTTON, L.J., said that the dropping of a plank was negligent for it might injure "workman or cargo or ship." Because of either possibility the owner of the vessel was to be made good for his loss. The act being wrongful the doer was liable for its proximate results. Criticized and explained as this statement may have been, I think it states the law as it should be and as it is. (*Smith v. London & Southwestern Ry. Co.*, [1870-71] 6 C.P. 14; *Anthony v. Slaid*, 52 Mass. 290; *Wood v. Penn. R.R.Co.*, 177 Penn. St. 306; *Trashansky v. Hershkovitz*, 239 N.Y. 452.)

The proposition is this. Every one owes to the world at large the duty of refraining from those acts that may unreasonably threaten the safety of others. Such an act occurs. Not only is he wronged to whom harm might reasonably be expected to result, but he also who is in fact injured, even if he be outside what would generally be thought the danger zone. There needs be duty due the one complaining but this is not a duty to a particular individual because as to him harm might be expected. Harm to some one being the natural result of the act, not only that one alone, but all those in fact injured may complain. We have never, I think, held otherwise. Indeed in the Di Caprio case we said that a breach of a general ordinance defining the degree of care to be exercised in one's calling is evidence of negligence as to every one. We did not limit this statement to those who might be expected to be exposed to danger. Unreasonable risk being taken, its consequences are not confined to those who might probably be hurt.

If this be so, we do not have a plaintiff suing by "derivation or succession." Her action is original and primary. Her claim is for a breach of duty to herself—not that she is subrogated to any right of action of the owner of the parcel or of a passenger standing at the scene of the explosion.

The right to recover damages rests on additional considerations. The plaintiff's rights must be injured, and this injury must be caused by the negligence. We build a dam, but are negligent as to its foundations. Breaking, it injures property down stream. We are not liable if all this happened because of some reason other than the insecure foundation. But when injuries do result from our unlawful act we are liable for the consequences. It does not matter that they are unusual, unexpected, unforeseen and unforeseeable. But there is one limitation. The damages must be so connected with the negligence that the latter may be said to be the proximate cause of the former.

These two words have never been given an inclusive definition. What is a cause in a legal sense, still more what is a proximate cause, depend in each case upon many considerations, as does the existence of negligence itself. Any philosophical doctrine of causation does not help us. A boy throws a stone into a pond. The ripples spread. The water level rises. The history of that pond is altered to all eternity. It will be altered by other causes also. Yet it will be forever the resultant of all causes combined. Each one will have an influence. How great only omniscience can say. You may speak of a chain, or if you please, a net. An analogy is of little aid. Each cause brings about future events. Without each the future would not be the same. Each is proximate in the sense it is essential. But that is not what we mean by the word. Nor on the other hand do we mean sole cause. There is no such thing.

Should analogy be thought helpful, however, I prefer that of a stream. The spring, starting on its journey, is joined by tributary after tributary. The river, reaching the ocean, comes from a hundred sources. No man may say whence any drop of water is derived. Yet for a time distinction may be possible. Into the clear creek, brown swamp water flows from the left. Later, from the right comes water stained by its clay bed. The three may remain for a space, sharply divided. But at last, inevitably no trace of separation remains. They are so commingled that all distinction is lost.

As we have said, we cannot trace the effect of an act to the end, if end there is. Again, however, we may trace it part of the way. A murder at Sarajevo may be the necessary antecedent to an assassination in London twenty years hence. An overturned lantern may burn all Chicago. We may follow the fire from the shed to the last building. We rightly say the fire started by the lantern caused its destruction.

A cause, but not the proximate cause. What we do mean by the word "proximate" is, that because of convenience, of public policy, of a rough sense of justice, the law arbitrarily declines to trace a series of events beyond a certain point. This is not logic. It is practical politics. Take our rule as to fires. Sparks from my burning haystack set on fire my house and my neighbor's. I may recover from a negligent railroad. He may not. Yet the wrongful act as directly harmed the one as the other. We may regret that the line was drawn just where it was, but drawn somewhere it had to be. We said the act of the railroad was not the proximate cause of our neighbor's fire. Cause it surely was. The words we used were simply indicative of our notions of public policy. Other courts think differently. But somewhere they reach the point where they cannot say the stream comes from any one source.

Take the illustration given in an unpublished manuscript by a distinguished and helpful writer on the law of torts. A chauffeur negligently collides with another car which is filled with dynamite, although he could not know it. An explosion follows. A, walking on the sidewalk nearby, is killed. B, sitting in a window of a building opposite, is cut by flying glass. C, likewise sitting in a window a block away, is similarly injured. And a further illustration. A nursemaid, ten blocks away, startled by the noise, involuntarily drops a baby from her arms to the walk. We are told that C may not recover while A may. As to B it is a question for court or jury. We will all agree that the baby might not. Because, we are again told, the chauffeur had no reason to believe his conduct involved any risk of injuring either C or the baby. As to them he was not negligent.

But the chauffeur, being negligent in risking the collision, his belief that the scope of the harm he might do would be limited is immaterial. His act unreasonably jeopardized the safety of any one who might be affected by it. C's injury and that of the baby were directly traceable to the collision. Without that, the injury would not have happened. C had the right to sit in his office, secure from such dangers. The baby was entitled to use the sidewalk with reasonable safety.

The true theory is, it seems to me, that the injury to C, if in truth he is to be denied recovery, and the injury to the baby is that their several injuries were not the proximate result of the negligence. And here not what the chauffeur had reason to believe would be the result of his conduct, but what the prudent would foresee, may have a bearing. May have some bearing, for the problem of proximate cause is not to be solved by any one consideration.

It is all a question of expediency. There are no fixed rules to govern our judgment. There are simply matters of which we may take account. We have in a somewhat different connection spoken of "the stream of events." We have asked whether that stream was deflected—whether it was forced into new and unexpected channels. (*Donnelly v. Piercy Contracting Co.*, 222 N.Y. 210.) This is rather rhetoric than law. There is in truth little to guide us other than common sense.

There are some hints that may help us. The proximate cause, involved as it may be with many other causes, must be, at the least, something without which the event would not happen. The court must ask itself whether there was a natural and continuous sequence between cause and effect. Was the one a substantial factor in producing the other? Was there a direct connection between them, without too many intervening causes? Is the effect of cause on result not too attenuated? Is the cause likely, in the usual judgment of mankind, to produce the result? Or by the exercise of prudent foresight could the result be foreseen? Is the result too remote from the cause, and here we consider remoteness in time and space. (*Bird v. St. Paul F. & M. Ins. Co.*, 224 N.Y. 47, where we passed upon the construction of a contract—but something was also said on this subject.) Clearly we must so consider, for the greater the distance either in time or space, the more surely do other causes intervene to affect the result. When a lantern is overturned the firing of a shed is a fairly direct consequence. Many things contribute to the spread of the conflagration—the force of the wind, the direction and width of streets, the character of intervening structures, other factors. We draw an uncertain and wavering line, but draw it we must as best we can.

Once again, it is all a question of fair judgment, always keeping in mind the fact that we endeavor to make a rule in each case that will be practical and in keeping with the general understanding of mankind.

Here another question must be answered. In the case supposed it is said, and said correctly, that the chauffeur is liable for the direct effect of the explosion although he had no reason to suppose it would follow a collision. "The fact that the injury occurred in a different manner than that which might have been expected does not prevent the chauffeur's negligence from being in law the cause of the injury." But the natural results of a negligent act—the results which a prudent man would or should foresee—do have a bearing upon the decision as to proximate cause. We have said so repeatedly. What should be foreseen? No human foresight would suggest that a collision itself might injure one a block away. On the contrary, given an explosion, such a possibility might be reasonably expected. I think the direct connection, the foresight of which the courts peak, assumes prevision of the explosion, for the immediate results of which, at least, the chauffeur is responsible.

It may be said this is unjust. Why? In fairness he should make good every injury flowing from his negligence. Not because of tenderness toward him we say he need not answer for all that follows his wrong. We look back to the catastrophe, the fire kindled by the spark, or the explosion. We trace the consequences—not indefinitely, but to a certain point. And to aid us in fixing that point we ask what might ordinarily be expected to follow the fire or the explosion.

This last suggestion is the factor which must determine the case before us. The act upon which defendant's liability rests is knocking an apparently harmless package onto the platform. The act was negligent. For its proximate consequences the defendant is liable. If its contents were broken, to the owner; if it fell upon and crushed a passenger's foot, then to him. If it exploded and injured one in the immediate vicinity, to him also as to A in the illustration. Mrs. Palsgraf was standing some distance away. How far cannot be told from the record—apparently twenty-five or thirty feet. Perhaps less. Except for the explosion, she would not have been injured. We are told by the appellant in his brief "it cannot be denied that the explosion was the direct cause of the plaintiff's injuries." So it was a substantial factor in producing the result—there was here a natural and continuous sequence—direct connection. The only intervening cause was that instead of blowing her to the ground the concussion smashed the weighing machine which in turn fell upon her. There was no remoteness in time, little in space. And surely, given such an explosion as here it needed no great foresight to predict that the natural result would be to injure one on the platform at no greater distance from its scene than was the plaintiff. Just how no one might be able to predict. Whether by flying fragments, by broken glass, by wreckage of machines or structures no one could say. But injury in some form was most probable.

Under these circumstances I cannot say as a matter of law that the plaintiff's injuries were not the proximate result of the negligence. That is all we have before us. The court refused to so charge. No request was made to submit the matter to the jury as a question of fact, even would that have been proper upon the record before us.

The judgment appealed from should be affirmed, with costs.

National Federation of Paralegal Associations, Inc.

Model Code of Ethics and Professional Responsibility and Guidelines for Enforcement

PREAMBLE

The National Federation of Paralegal Associations, Inc.("NFPA") is a professional organization comprised of paralegal associations and individual paralegals throughout the United States and Canada. Members of NFPA have varying backgrounds, experiences, education, and job responsibilities that reflect the diversity of the paralegal profession. NFPA promotes the growth, development, and recognition of the paralegal profession as an integral partner in the delivery of legal services.

In May 1993 NFPA adopted its Model Code of Ethics and Professional Responsibility ("Model Code") to delineate the principles for ethics and conduct to which every paralegal should aspire.

Many paralegal associations throughout the United States have endorsed the concept and content of NFPA's Model Code through the adoption of their own ethical codes. In doing so, paralegals have confirmed the profession's commitment to increase the quality and efficiency of legal services, as well as recognized its responsibilities to the public, the legal community, and colleagues.

Paralegals have recognized, and will continue to recognize, that the profession must continue to evolve to enhance their roles in the delivery of legal services. With increased levels of responsibility comes the need to define and enforce mandatory rules of professional conduct. Enforcement of codes of paralegal conduct is a logical and necessary step to enhance and ensure the confidence of the legal community and the public in the integrity and professional responsibility of paralegals.

In April 1997 NFPA adopted the Model Disciplinary Rules ("Model Rules") to make possible the enforcement of the Canons and Ethical Considerations contained in the NFPA Model Code. A concurrent determination was made that the Model Code of Ethics and Professional Responsibility, formerly aspirational in nature, should be recognized as setting forth the enforceable obligations of all paralegals.

The Model Code and Model Rules offer a framework for professional discipline, either voluntarily or through formal regulatory programs.

§1 NFPA Model Disciplinary Rules and Ethical Considerations

1.1 A Paralegal Shall Achieve and Maintain a High Level of Competence.

Ethical Considerations

EC-1.1 (a) A paralegal shall achieve competency through education, training, and work experience.

EC-1.1 (b) A paralegal shall aspire to participate in a minimum of twelve (12) hours of continuing legal education, to include at least one (1) hour of ethics education, every two (2) years in order to remain current on developments in the law.

EC-1.1 (c) A paralegal shall perform all assignments promptly and efficiently.

1.2 A Paralegal Shall Maintain a High Level of Personal and Professional Integrity.

Ethical Considerations

EC-1.2 (a) A paralegal shall not engage in any ex parte communications involving the courts or any other adjudicatory body in an attempt to exert undue influence or to obtain advantage or the benefit of only one party.

EC-1.2 (b) A paralegal shall not communicate, or cause another to communicate, with a party the paralegal knows to be represented by a lawyer in a pending matter without the prior consent of the lawyer representing such other party.

EC-1.2 (c) A paralegal shall ensure that all timekeeping and billing records prepared by the paralegal are thorough, accurate, honest, and complete.

EC-1.2 (d) A paralegal shall not knowingly engage in fraudulent billing practices. Such practices may include, but are not limited to: inflation of hours billed to a client or employer; misrepresentation of the nature of tasks performed; and/or submission of fraudulent expense and disbursement documentation.

EC-1.2 (e) A paralegal shall be scrupulous, thorough, and honest in the identification and maintenance of all funds, securities, and other assets of a client and shall provide accurate accounting as appropriate.

EC-1.2 (f) A paralegal shall advise the proper authority of non-confidential knowledge of any dishonest or fraudulent acts by any person pertaining to the handling of the funds, securities or other assets of a client. The authority to whom the report is made shall depend on the nature and circumstances of the possible misconduct, (e.g., ethics committees of law firms, corporations and/or paralegal associations, local or state bar associations, local prosecutors, administrative agencies, etc.). Failure to report such knowledge is in itself misconduct and shall be treated as such under these rules.

1.3 A Paralegal Shall Maintain a High Standard of Professional Conduct.

Ethical Considerations

EC-1.3 (a) A paralegal shall refrain from engaging in any conduct that offends the dignity and decorum of proceedings before a court or other adjudicatory body and shall be respectful of all rules and procedures.

EC-1.3 (b)   A paralegal shall avoid impropriety and the appearance of impropriety and shall not engage in any conduct that would adversely affect his/her fitness to practice. Such conduct may include, but is not limited to: violence, dishonesty, interference with the administration of justice, and/or abuse of a professional position or public office.

EC-1.3 (c)   Should a paralegal's fitness to practice be compromised by physical or mental illness, causing that paralegal to commit an act that is in direct violation of the Model Code/Model Rules and/or the rules and/or laws governing the jurisdiction in which the paralegal practices, that paralegal may be protected from sanction upon review of the nature and circumstances of that illness.

EC-1.3 (d)   A paralegal shall advise the proper authority of non-confidential knowledge of any action of another legal professional that clearly demonstrates fraud, deceit, dishonesty, or misrepresentation. The authority to whom the report is made shall depend on the nature and circumstances of the possible misconduct (e.g., ethics committees of law firms, corporations and/or paralegal associations, local or state bar associations, local prosecutors, administrative agencies, etc.). Failure to report such knowledge is in itself misconduct and shall be treated as such under these rules.

EC-1.3 (e)   A paralegal shall not knowingly assist any individual with the commission of an act that is in direct violation of the Model Code/Model Rules and/or the rules and/or laws governing the jurisdiction in which the paralegal practices.

EC-1.3 (f)   If a paralegal possesses knowledge of future criminal activity, that knowledge must be reported to the appropriate authority immediately.

1.4 A Paralegal Shall Serve the Public Interest by Contributing to the Improvement of the Legal System and Delivery of Quality Legal Services, Including Pro Bono Publico Services.

Ethical Considerations

EC-1.4 (a)   A paralegal shall be sensitive to the legal needs of the public and shall promote the development and implementation of programs that address those needs.

EC-1.4 (b)   A paralegal shall support efforts to improve the legal system and access thereto and shall assist in making changes.

EC-1.4 (c)   A paralegal shall support and participate in the delivery of Pro Bono Publico services directed toward implementing and improving access to justice, the law, the legal system or the paralegal and legal professions.

EC-1.4 (d)   A paralegal should aspire annually to contribute twenty-four (24) hours of Pro Bono Publico services under the supervision of an attorney or as authorized by administrative, statutory or court authority to:

1. persons of limited means; or
2. charitable, religious, civic, community, governmental and educational organizations in matters that are designed primarily to address the legal needs of persons with limited means; or
3. individuals, groups or organizations seeking to secure or protect civil rights, civil liberties or public rights.

The twenty-four (24) hours of Pro Bono Publico services contributed annually by a paralegal may consist of such services as detailed in this EC-1.4(d), and/or administrative matters designed to develop and implement the attainment of this aspiration as detailed above in EC-1.4(a) or (c), or any combination of the two.

1.5 A Paralegal Shall Preserve all Confidential Information Provided by the Client or Acquired from Other Sources Before, During, and After the Course of the Professional Relationship.

Ethical Considerations

EC-1.5 (a) A paralegal shall be aware of and abide by all legal authority governing confidential information in the jurisdiction in which the paralegal practices.

EC-1.5 (b) A paralegal shall not use confidential information to the disadvantage of the client.

EC-1.5 (c) A paralegal shall not use confidential information to the advantage of the paralegal or of a third person.

EC-1.5 (d) A paralegal may reveal confidential information only after full disclosure and with the client's written consent; or, when required by law or court order; or, when necessary to prevent the client from committing an act that could result in death or serious bodily harm.

EC-1.5 (e) A paralegal shall keep those individuals responsible for the legal representation of a client fully informed of any confidential information the paralegal may have pertaining to that client.

EC-1.5 (f) A paralegal shall not engage in any indiscreet communications concerning clients.

1.6 A Paralegal Shall Avoid Conflicts of Interest and Shall Disclose any Possible Conflict to the Employer or Client, as Well as to the Prospective Employers or Clients.

Ethical Considerations

EC-1.6 (a) A paralegal shall act within the bounds of the law, solely for the benefit of the client, and shall be free of compromising influences and loyalties. Neither the paralegal's personal or business interest, nor those of other clients or third persons, should compromise the paralegal's professional judgment and loyalty to the client.

EC-1.6 (b) A paralegal shall avoid conflicts of interest that may arise from previous assignments, whether for a present or past employer or client.

EC-1.6 (c) A paralegal shall avoid conflicts of interest that may arise from family relationships and from personal and business interests.

EC-1.6 (d) In order to be able to determine whether an actual or potential conflict of interest exists, a paralegal shall create and maintain an effective record-keeping system that identifies clients, matters, and parties with which the paralegal has worked.

EC-1.6 (e) A paralegal shall reveal sufficient non-confidential information about a client or former client to reasonably ascertain if an actual or potential conflict of interest exists.

EC-1.6 (f) A paralegal shall not participate in or conduct work on any matter where a conflict of interest has been identified.

EC-1.6 (g) In matters where a conflict of interest has been identified and the client consents to continued representation, a paralegal shall comply fully with the implementation and maintenance of an Ethical Wall.

1.7 A Paralegal's Title Shall be Fully Disclosed.

Ethical Considerations

EC-1.7 (a)   A paralegal's title shall clearly indicate the individual's status and shall be disclosed in all business and professional communications to avoid misunderstandings and misconceptions about the paralegal's role and responsibilities.

EC-1.7 (b)   A paralegal's title shall be included if the paralegal's name appears on business cards, letterhead, brochures, directories, and advertisements.

EC-1.7 (c)   A paralegal shall not use letterhead, business cards or other promotional materials to create a fraudulent impression of his/her status or ability to practice in the jurisdiction in which the paralegal practices.

EC-1.7 (d)   A paralegal shall not practice under color of any record, diploma, or certificate that has been illegally or fraudulently obtained or issued or which is misrepresentative in any way.

EC1.7 (e)   A paralegal shall not participate in the creation, issuance, or dissemination of fraudulent records, diplomas, or certificates.

1.8 A Paralegal Shall Not Engage in the Unauthorized Practice of Law.

Ethical Considerations

EC-1.8 (a)   A paralegal shall comply with the applicable legal authority governing the unauthorized practice of law in the jurisdiction in which the paralegal practices.

§2 NFPA Guidelines for the Enforcement of the Model Code of Ethics and Professional Responsibility

2.1 Basis for Discipline

2.1(a)   Disciplinary investigations and proceedings brought under authority of the Rules shall be conducted in accord with obligations imposed on the paralegal professional by the Model Code of Ethics and Professional Responsibility.

2.2 Structure of Disciplinary Committee

2.2(a)   The Disciplinary Committee ("Committee") shall be made up of nine (9) members including the Chair.

2.2(b)   Each member of the Committee, including any temporary replacement members, shall have demonstrated working knowledge of ethics/professional responsibility-related issues and activities.

2.2(c)   The Committee shall represent a cross-section of practice areas and work experience. The following recommendations are made regarding the members of the Committee.

     1. At least one paralegal with one to three years of law-related work experience.

     2. At least one paralegal with five to seven years of law related work experience.

     3. At least one paralegal with over ten years of law related work experience.

     4. One paralegal educator with five to seven years of work experience; preferably in the area of ethics/professional responsibility.

     5. One paralegal manager.

     6. One lawyer with five to seven years of law-related work experience.

     7. One lay member.

2.2(d)   The Chair of the Committee shall be appointed within thirty (30) days of its members' induction. The Chair shall have no fewer than ten (10) years of law-related work experience.

2.2(e)   The terms of all members of the Committee shall be staggered. Of those members initially appointed, a simple majority plus one shall be appointed to a term of one year, and the remaining members shall be appointed to a term of two years. Thereafter, all members of the Committee shall be appointed to terms of two years.

2.2(f)   If for any reason the terms of a majority of the Committee will expire at the same time, members may be appointed to terms of one year to maintain continuity of the Committee.

2.2(g)   The Committee shall organize from its members a three-tiered structure to investigate, prosecute, and/or adjudicate charges of misconduct. The members shall be rotated among the tiers.

2.3 Operation of Committee

2.3(a)   The Committee shall meet on an as-needed basis to discuss, investigate, and/or adjudicate alleged violations of the Model Code/Model Rules.

2.3(b)   A majority of the members of the Committee present at a meeting shall constitute a quorum.

2.3(c)   A Recording Secretary shall be designated to maintain complete and accurate minutes of all Committee meetings. All such minutes shall be kept confidential until a decision has been made that the matter will be set for hearing as set forth in Section 6.1 below.

2.3(d)   If any member of the Committee has a conflict of interest with the Charging Party, the Responding Party, or the allegations of misconduct, that member shall not take part in any hearing or deliberations concerning those allegations. If the absence of that member creates a lack of a quorum for the Committee, then a temporary replacement for the member shall be appointed.

2.3(e)   Either the Charging Party or the Responding Party may request that, for good cause shown, any member of the Committee not participate in a hearing or deliberation. All such requests shall be honored. If the absence of a Committee member under those circumstances creates a lack of a quorum for the Committee, then a temporary replacement for that member shall be appointed.

2.3(f)   All discussions and correspondence of the Committee shall be kept confidential until a decision has been made that the matter will be set for hearing as set forth in Section 6.1 below.

2.3(g)   All correspondence from the Committee to the Responding Party regarding any charge of misconduct and any decisions made regarding the charge shall be mailed certified mail, return receipt requested, to the Responding Party's last known address and shall be clearly marked with a "Confidential" designation.

2.4 Procedure for the Reporting of Alleged Violations of the Model Code/Disciplinary Rules

2.4(a)   An individual or entity in possession of non-confidential knowledge or information concerning possible instances of misconduct shall make a confidential written report to the Committee within thirty (30) days of obtaining same. This report shall include all details of the alleged misconduct.

2.4(b)   The Committee so notified shall inform the Responding Party of the allegation(s) of misconduct no later than ten (10) business days after receiving the confidential written report from the Charging Party.

2.4(c)   Notification to the Responding Party shall include the identity of the Charging Party, unless, for good cause shown, the Charging Party requests anonymity.

2.4(d)   The Responding Party shall reply to the allegations within ten (10) business days of notification.

2.5 Procedure for the Investigation of a Charge of Misconduct

2.5(a)   Upon receipt of a Charge of Misconduct ("Charge"), or on its own initiative, the Committee shall initiate an investigation.

2.5(b)   If, upon initial or preliminary review, the Committee makes a determination that the charges are either without basis in fact or, if proven, would not constitute professional misconduct, the Committee shall dismiss the allegations of misconduct. If such determination of dismissal cannot be made, a formal investigation shall be initiated.

2.5(c)   Upon the decision to conduct a formal investigation, the Committee shall:
1. mail to the Charging and Responding Parties within three (3) business days of that decision notice of the commencement of a formal investigation. That notification shall be in writing and shall contain a complete explanation of all Charge(s), as well as the reasons for a formal investigation and shall cite the applicable codes and rules;
2. allow the Responding Party thirty (30) days to prepare and submit a confidential response to the Committee, which response shall address each charge specifically and shall be in writing; and
3. upon receipt of the response to the notification, have thirty (30) days to investigate the Charge(s). If an extension of time is deemed necessary, that extension shall not exceed ninety (90) days.

2.5(d)   Upon conclusion of the investigation, the Committee may:
1. dismiss the Charge upon the finding that it has no basis in fact;
2. dismiss the Charge upon the finding that, if proven, the Charge would not constitute Misconduct;
3. refer the matter for hearing by the Tribunal; or
4. in the case of criminal activity, refer the Charge(s) and all investigation results to the appropriate authority.

2.6 Procedure for a Misconduct Hearing Before a Tribunal

2.6(a)   Upon the decision by the Committee that a matter should be heard, all parties shall be notified and a hearing date shall be set. The hearing shall take place no more than thirty (30) days from the conclusion of the formal investigation.

2.6(b)   The Responding Party shall have the right to counsel. The parties and the Tribunal shall have the right to call any witnesses and introduce any documentation that they believe will lead to the fair and reasonable resolution of the matter.

2.6(c)   Upon completion of the hearing, the Tribunal shall deliberate and present a written decision to the parties in accordance with procedures as set forth by the Tribunal.

2.6(d)   Notice of the decision of the Tribunal shall be appropriately published.

2.7 Sanctions

2.7(a)   Upon a finding of the Tribunal that misconduct has occurred, any of the following sanctions, or others as may be deemed appropriate, may be imposed upon the Responding Party, either singularly or in combination:
1. letter of reprimand to the Responding Party; counseling;
2. attendance at an ethics course approved by the Tribunal; probation;
3. suspension of license/authority to practice; revocation of license/authority to practice;
4. imposition of a fine; assessment of costs; or
5. in the instance of criminal activity, referral to the appropriate authority.

2.7(b)   Upon the expiration of any period of probation, suspension, or revocation, the Responding Party may make application for reinstatement. With the application for reinstatement, the Responding Party must show proof of having complied with all aspects of the sanctions imposed by the Tribunal.

2.8 Appellate Procedures

2.8(a)   The parties shall have the right to appeal the decision of the Tribunal in accordance with the procedure as set forth by the Tribunal.

DEFINITIONS

"Appellate Body" means a body established to adjudicate an appeal to any decision made by a Tribunal or other decision-making body with respect to formally-heard Charges of Misconduct.

"Charge of Misconduct" means a written submission by any individual or entity to an ethics committee, paralegal association, bar association, law enforcement agency, judicial body, government agency, or other appropriate body or entity, that sets forth non-confidential information regarding any instance of alleged misconduct by an individual paralegal or paralegal entity.

"Charging Party" means any individual or entity who submits a Charge of Misconduct against an individual paralegal or paralegal entity.

"Competency" means the demonstration of: diligence, education, skill, and mental, emotional, and physical fitness reasonably necessary for the performance of paralegal services.

"Confidential Information" means information relating to a client, whatever its source, that is not public knowledge nor available to the public.("Non-Confidential Information" would generally include the name of the client and the identity of the matter for which the paralegal provided services.)

"Disciplinary Hearing" means the confidential proceeding conducted by a committee or other designated body or entity concerning any instance of alleged misconduct by an individual paralegal or paralegal entity.

"Disciplinary Committee" means any committee that has been established by an entity such as a paralegal association, bar association, judicial body, or government agency to: (a) identify, define, and investigate general ethical considerations and concerns with respect to paralegal practice; (b) administer and enforce the Model Code and Model Rules and; (c) discipline any individual paralegal or paralegal entity found to be in violation of same.

"Disclose" means communication of information reasonably sufficient to permit identification of the significance of the matter in question.

"Ethical Wall" means the screening method implemented in order to protect a client from a conflict of interest. An Ethical Wall generally includes, but is not limited to, the following elements: (1) prohibit the paralegal from having any connection with the matter; (2) ban discussions with or the transfer of documents to or from the paralegal; (3) restrict access to files; and (4) educate all members of the firm, corporation, or entity as to the separation of the paralegal (both organizationally and physically) from the pending matter. For more information regarding the Ethical Wall, see the NFPA publication entitled "The Ethical Wall—Its Application to Paralegals."

"Ex parte" means actions or communications conducted at the instance and for the benefit of one party only, and without notice to, or contestation by, any person adversely interested.

"Investigation" means the investigation of any charge(s) of misconduct filed against an individual paralegal or paralegal entity by a Committee.

"Letter of Reprimand" means a written notice of formal censure or severe reproof administered to an individual paralegal or paralegal entity for unethical or improper conduct.

"Misconduct" means the knowing or unknowing commission of an act that is in direct violation of those Canons and Ethical Considerations of any and all applicable codes and/or rules of conduct.

"Paralegal" is synonymous with "Legal Assistant" and is defined as a person qualified through education, training, or work experience to perform substantive legal work that requires knowledge of legal concepts and is customarily, but not exclusively, performed by a lawyer. This person may be retained or employed by a lawyer, law office, governmental agency, or other entity or may be authorized by administrative, statutory, or court authority to perform this work.

"Pro Bono Publico" means providing or assisting to provide quality legal services in order to enhance access to justice for persons of limited means; charitable, religious, civic, community, governmental, and educational organizations in matters that are designed primarily to address the legal needs of persons with limited means; or individuals, groups or organizations seeking to secure or protect civil rights, civil liberties or public rights.

"Proper Authority" means the local paralegal association, the local or state bar association, Committee(s) of the local paralegal or bar association(s), local prosecutor, administrative agency, or other tribunal empowered to investigate or act upon an instance of alleged misconduct.

"Responding Party" means an individual paralegal or paralegal entity against whom a Charge of Misconduct has been submitted.

"Revocation" means the recision of the license, certificate or other authority to practice of an individual paralegal or paralegal entity found in violation of those Canons and Ethical Considerations of any and all applicable codes and/or rules of conduct.

"Suspension" means the suspension of the license, certificate or other authority to practice of an individual paralegal or paralegal entity found in violation of those Canons and Ethical Considerations of any and all applicable codes and/or rules of conduct.

"Tribunal" means the body designated to adjudicate allegations of misconduct.

Model Standards and Guidelines for Utilization of Legal Assistants— Paralegals

Table of Contents:

INTRODUCTION

The purpose of this annotated version of the National Association of Legal Assistants, Inc. Model Standards and Guidelines for the Utilization of Legal Assistants (the "Model," "Standards" and/or the "Guidelines") is to provide references to the existing case law and other authorities where the underlying issues have been considered. The authorities cited will serve as a basis upon which conduct of a legal assistant may be analyzed as proper or improper.

The Guidelines represent a statement of how the legal assistant may function. The Guidelines are not intended to be a comprehensive or exhaustive list of the proper duties of a legal assistant. Rather, they are designed as guides to what may or may not be proper conduct for the legal assistant. In formulating the Guidelines, the reasoning and rules of law in many reported decisions of disciplinary cases and unauthorized practice of law cases have been analyzed and considered. In addition, the provisions of the American Bar Association's Model Rules of Professional Conduct, as well as the ethical promulgations of various state courts and bar associations, have been considered in the development of the Guidelines.

These Guidelines form a sound basis for the legal assistant and the supervising attorney to follow. This Model will serve as a comprehensive resource document and as a definitive, well-reasoned guide to those considering voluntary standards and guidelines for legal assistants.

I
PREAMBLE

Proper utilization of the services of legal assistants contributes to the delivery of cost-effective, high-quality legal services. Legal assistants and the legal profession should be assured that measures exist for identifying legal assistants and their role in assisting attorneys in the delivery of legal services. Therefore, the National Association of Legal Assistants, Inc., hereby adopts these Standards and Guidelines as an educational document for the benefit of legal assistants and the legal profession.

Comment

The three most frequently raised questions concerning legal assistants are (1) How do you define a legal assistant; (2) Who is qualified to be identified as a legal assistant; and (3) What duties may a legal assistant perform? The definition adopted in 1984 by the National Association of Legal Assistants answers the first question. The Model sets forth minimum education, training, and experience through standards which will assure that an individual utilizing the title "legal assistant" or "paralegal" has the qualifications to be held out to the legal community and the public in that capacity. The Guidelines identify those acts which the reported cases hold to be proscribed and give examples of services which the legal assistant may perform under the supervision of a licensed attorney.

These Guidelines constitute a statement relating to services performed by legal assistants, as defined herein, as approved by court decisions and other sources of authority. The purpose of the Guidelines is not to place limitations or restrictions on the legal assistant profession. Rather, the Guidelines are intended to outline for the legal profession an acceptable course of conduct. Voluntary recognition and utilization of the Standards and Guidelines will benefit the entire legal profession and the public it serves.

II
DEFINITION

The National Association of Legal Assistants adopted the following definition in 1984:

> Legal assistants, also known as paralegals, are a distinguishable group of persons who assist attorneys in the delivery of legal services. Through formal education, training, and experience, legal assistants have knowledge and expertise regarding the legal system and substantive and procedural law which qualify them to do work of a legal nature under the supervision of an attorney.

In recognition of the similarity of the definitions and the need for one clear definition, in July 2001, the NALA membership approved a resolution to adopt the definition of the American Bar Association as well. The ABA definition reads as follows:

> A legal assistant or paralegal is a person qualified by education, training or work experience who is employed or retained by a lawyer, law office, corporation, governmental agency or other entity who performs specifically delegated substantive legal work for which a lawyer is responsible. (Adopted by the ABA in 1997)

Comment

These definitions emphasize the knowledge and expertise of legal assistants in substantive and procedural law obtained through education and work experience. They further define the legal assistant or paralegal as a professional working under the supervision of an attorney as distinguished from a non-lawyer who delivers services directly to the public without any intervention or review of work product by an attorney. Such unsupervised services, unless authorized by court or agency rules, constitute the unauthorized practice of law.

Statutes, court rules, case law, and bar association documents are additional sources for legal assistant or paralegal definitions. In applying the Standards and Guidelines, it is important to remember that they were developed to apply to the legal assistant as defined herein. Lawyers should refrain from labeling those as paralegals or legal assistants who do not meet the criteria set forth in these definitions and/or the definitions set forth by state rules, guidelines or bar associations. Labeling secretaries and other administrative staff as legal assistants/paralegals is inaccurate.

For billing purposes, the services of a legal secretary are considered part of overhead costs and are not recoverable in fee awards. However, the courts have held that fees for paralegal services are recoverable as long as they are not clerical functions, such as organizing files, copying documents, checking docket, updating files, checking court dates, and delivering papers. As established in *Missouri v. Jenkins*, 491 U.S.274, 109 S.Ct. 2463, 2471, n.10 (1989) tasks performed by legal assistants must be substantive in nature which, absent the legal assistant, the attorney would perform.

There are also case law and Supreme Court Rules addressing the issue of a disbarred attorney serving in the capacity of a legal assistant.

III
STANDARDS

A legal assistant should meet certain minimum qualifications. The following standards may be used to determine an individual's qualifications as a legal assistant:

1. Successful completion of the Certified Legal Assistant (CLA)/Certified Paralegal (CP) certifying examination of the National Association of Legal Assistants, Inc.;
2. Graduation from an ABA approved program of study for legal assistants;
3. Graduation from a course of study for legal assistants which is institutionally accredited but not ABA approved, and which requires not less than the equivalent of 60 semester hours of classroom study;
4. Graduation from a course of study for legal assistants, other than those set forth in (2) and (3) above, plus not less than six months of in-house training as a legal assistant;
5. A baccalaureate degree in any field, plus not less than six months in-house training as a legal assistant;
6. A minimum of three years of law-related experience under the supervision of an attorney, including at least six months of in-house training as a legal assistant; or
7. Two years of in-house training as a legal assistant.

For purposes of these Standards, "in-house training as a legal assistant" means attorney education of the employee concerning legal assistant duties and these Guidelines. In addition to review and analysis of assignments, the legal assistant should receive a reasonable amount of instruction directly related to the duties and obligations of the legal assistant.

Comment

The Standards set forth suggest minimum qualifications for a legal assistant. These minimum qualifications, as adopted, recognize legal related work backgrounds and formal education backgrounds, both of which provide the legal assistant with a broad base in exposure to and knowledge of the legal profession. This background is necessary to assure the public and the legal profession that the employee identified as a legal assistant is qualified.

The Certified Legal Assistant (CLA) /Certified Paralegal (CP) examination established by NALA in 1976 is a voluntary nationwide certification program for legal assistants. (*CLA and CP are federally registered certification marks owned by NALA.*) The CLA/CP designation is a statement to the legal profession and the public that the legal assistant has met the high levels of knowledge and professionalism required by NALA's certification program. Continuing education requirements, which all certified legal assistants must meet, assure that high standards are maintained. The CLA/CP designation has been recognized as a means of establishing the qualifications of a legal assistant in supreme court rules, state court and bar association standards, and utilization guidelines.

Certification through NALA is available to all legal assistants meeting the educational and experience requirements. Certified Legal Assistants may also pursue advanced certification in specialty practice areas through the APC, Advanced Paralegal Certification, credentialing program. Legal assistants/paralegals may also pursue certification based on state laws and procedures in California, Florida, Louisiana, and Texas.

IV
GUIDELINES

These Guidelines relating to standards of performance and professional responsibility are intended to aid legal assistants and attorneys. The ultimate responsibility rests with an attorney who employs legal assistants to educate them with respect to the duties they are assigned and to supervise the manner in which such duties are accomplished.

Comment

In general, a legal assistant is allowed to perform any task which is properly delegated and supervised by an attorney, as long as the attorney is ultimately responsible to the client and assumes complete professional responsibility for the work product.

ABA Model Rules of Professional Conduct, Rule 5.3 provides:

With respect to a non-lawyer employed or retained by or associated with a lawyer:

a. a partner in a law firm shall make reasonable efforts to ensure that the firm has in effect measures giving reasonable assurance that the person's conduct is compatible with the professional obligations of the lawyer;
b. a lawyer having direct supervisory authority over the non-lawyer shall make reasonable efforts to ensure that the person's conduct is compatible with the professional obligations of the lawyer; and
c. a lawyer shall be responsible for conduct of such a person that would be a violation of the rules of professional conduct if engaged in by a lawyer if:
   1. the lawyer orders or, with the knowledge of the specific conduct ratifies the conduct involved; or
   2. the lawyer is a partner in the law firm in which the person is employed, or has direct supervisory authority over the person, and knows of the conduct at a time when its consequences can be avoided or mitigated but fails to take remedial action.

There are many interesting and complex issues involving the use of legal assistants. In any discussion of the proper role of a legal assistant, attention must be directed to what constitutes the practice of law. Proper delegation to legal assistants is further complicated and confused by the lack of an adequate definition of the practice of law.

Kentucky became the first state to adopt a Paralegal Code by Supreme Court Rule. This Code sets forth certain exclusions to the unauthorized practice of law:

> For purposes of this rule, the unauthorized practice of law shall not include any service rendered involving legal knowledge or advice, whether representation, counsel or advocacy, in or out of court, rendered in respect to the acts, duties, obligations, liabilities or business relations of the one requiring services where:
> a. The client understands that the paralegal is not a lawyer;
> b. The lawyer supervises the paralegal in the performance of his or her duties; and
> c. The lawyer remains fully responsible for such representation including all actions taken or not taken in connection therewith by the paralegal to the same extent as if such representation had been furnished entirely by the lawyer and all such actions had been taken or not taken directly by the attorney. Paralegal Code, Ky.S.Ct.R3.700, Sub-Rule 2.

South Dakota Supreme Court Rule 97-25 Utilization Rule a(4) states:

> The attorney remains responsible for the services performed by the legal assistant to the same extent as though such services had been furnished entirely by the attorney and such actions were those of the attorney.

GUIDELINE 1

Legal assistants should:

1. Disclose their status as legal assistants at the outset of any professional relationship with a client, other attorneys, a court or administrative agency or personnel thereof, or members of the general public;
2. Preserve the confidences and secrets of all clients; and
3. Understand the attorney's Rules of Professional Responsibility and these Guidelines in order to avoid any action which would involve the attorney in a violation of the Rules, or give the appearance of professional impropriety.

Comment

Routine early disclosure of the paralegal's status when dealing with persons outside the attorney's office is necessary to assure that there will be no misunderstanding as to the responsibilities and role of the legal assistant. Disclosure may be made in any way that avoids confusion. If the person dealing with the legal assistant already knows of his/her status, further disclosure is unnecessary. If at any time in written or oral communication the legal assistant becomes aware that the other person may believe the legal assistant is an attorney, immediate disclosure should be made as to the legal assistant's status.

The attorney should exercise care that the legal assistant preserves and refrains from using any confidence or secrets of a client, and should instruct the legal assistant not to disclose or use any such confidences or secrets.

The legal assistant must take any and all steps necessary to prevent conflicts of interest and fully disclose such conflicts to the supervising attorney. Failure to do so may jeopardize both the attorney's representation of the client and the case itself.

Guidelines for the Utilization of Legal Assistant Services adopted December 3, 1994 by the Washington State Bar Association Board of Governors states:

> Guideline 7: A lawyer shall take reasonable measures to prevent conflicts of interest resulting from a legal assistant's other employment or interest insofar as such other employment or interests would present a conflict of interest if it were that of the lawyer.

In Re Complex Asbestos Litigation, 232 Cal. App. 3d 572 (Cal. 1991), addresses the issue wherein a law firm was disqualified due to possession of attorney-client confidences by a legal assistant employee resulting from previous employment by opposing counsel.

In Oklahoma, in an order issued July 12, 2001, in the matter of *Mark A. Hayes, M.D. v. Central States Orthopedic Specialists, Inc.*, a Tulsa County District Court Judge disqualified a law firm from representation of a client on the basis that an ethical screen was an impermissible device to protect from disclosure confidences gained by a non-lawyer employee while employed by another law firm. In applying the same rules that govern attorneys, the court found that the Rules of Professional Conduct pertaining to confidentiality apply to nonlawyers who leave firms with actual knowledge of material, confidential information, and a screening device is not an appropriate alternative to the imputed disqualification of an incoming legal assistant who has moved from one firm to another during ongoing litigation and has actual knowledge of material, confidential information. The decision was appealed and the Oklahoma Supreme Court determined that, under certain circumstances, screening is an appropriate management tool for non-lawyer staff.

In 2004 the Nevada Supreme Court also addressed this issue at the urging of the state's paralegals. The Nevada Supreme Court granted a petition to rescind the Court's 1997 ruling in *Ciaffone v. District Court*. In this case, the court clarified the original ruling, stating "mere opportunity to access confidential information does not merit disqualification." The opinion stated instances in which screening may be appropriate, and listed minimum screening requirements. The opinion also set forth guidelines that a district court may use to determine if screening has been or may be effective. These considerations are:

1. substantiality of the relationship between the former and current matters
2. the time elapsed between the matters
3. size of the firm
4. number of individuals presumed to have confidential information
5. nature of their involvement in the former matter
6. timing and features of any measures taken to reduce the danger of disclosure
7. whether the old firm and the new firm represent adverse parties in the same proceeding rather than in different proceedings.

The ultimate responsibility for compliance with approved standards of professional conduct rests with the supervising attorney. The burden rests upon the attorney who employs a legal assistant to educate the latter with respect to the duties which may be assigned and then to supervise the manner in which the legal assistant carries out such duties. However, this does not relieve the legal assistant from an independent obligation to refrain from illegal conduct. Additionally, and notwithstanding that the Rules are not binding upon non-lawyers, the very nature of a legal assistant's employment imposes an obligation not to engage in conduct which would involve the supervising attorney in a violation of the Rules.

The attorney must make sufficient background investigation of the prior activities and character and integrity of his or her legal assistants.

Further, the attorney must take all measures necessary to avoid and fully disclose conflicts of interest due to other employment or interests. Failure to do so may jeopardize both the attorney's representation of the client and the case itself.

Legal assistant associations strive to maintain the high level of integrity and competence expected of the legal profession and, further, strive to uphold the high standards of ethics.

NALA's Code of Ethics and Professional Responsibility states "A legal assistant's conduct is guided by bar associations' codes of professional responsibility and rules of professional conduct."

GUIDELINE 2

Legal assistants should not:

1. Establish attorney-client relationships; set legal fees; give legal opinions or advice; or represent a client before a court, unless authorized to do so by said court; nor
2. Engage in, encourage, or contribute to any act which could constitute the unauthorized practice of law.

Comment

Case law, court rules, codes of ethics and professional responsibilities, as well as bar ethics opinions now hold which acts can and cannot be performed by a legal assistant. Generally, the determination of what acts constitute the unauthorized practice of law is made by state supreme courts.

Numerous cases exist relating to the unauthorized practice of law. Courts have gone so far as to prohibit the legal assistant from preparation of divorce kits and assisting in preparation of bankruptcy forms and, more specifically, from providing basic information about procedures and requirements, deciding where information should be placed on forms, and responding to questions from debtors regarding the interpretation or definition of terms.

Cases have identified certain areas in which an attorney has a duty to act, but it is interesting to note that none of these cases state that it is improper for an attorney to have the initial work performed by the legal assistant. This again points out the importance of adequate supervision by the employing attorney.

An attorney can be found to have aided in the unauthorized practice of law when delegating acts which cannot be performed by a legal assistant.

GUIDELINE 3

Legal assistants may perform services for an attorney in the representation of a client, provided:

1. The services performed by the legal assistant do not require the exercise of independent professional legal judgment;
2. The attorney maintains a direct relationship with the client and maintains control of all client matters;
3. The attorney supervises the legal assistant;
4. The attorney remains professionally responsible for all work on behalf of the client, including any actions taken or not taken by the legal assistant in connection therewith; and
5. The services performed supplement, merge with, and become the attorney's work product.

Comment

Paralegals, whether employees or independent contractors, perform services for the attorney in the representation of a client. Attorneys should delegate work to legal assistants commensurate with their knowledge and experience and provide appropriate instruction and supervision concerning the delegated work, as well as ethical acts of their employment. Ultimate responsibility for the work product of a legal assistant rests with the attorney. However, a legal assistant must use discretion and professional judgment and must not render independent legal judgment in place of an attorney.

The work product of a legal assistant is subject to civil rules governing discovery of materials prepared in anticipation of litigation, whether the legal assistant is viewed as an extension of the attorney or as another representative of the party itself. Fed.R.Civ.P. 26 (b) (3) and (5).

GUIDELINE 4

In the supervision of a legal assistant, consideration should be given to

1. Designating work assignments that correspond to the legal assistant's abilities, knowledge, training, and experience;
2. Educating and training the legal assistant with respect to professional responsibility, local rules and practices, and firm policies;
3. Monitoring the work and professional conduct of the legal assistant to ensure that the work is substantively correct and timely performed;
4. Providing continuing education for the legal assistant in substantive matters through courses, institutes, workshops, seminars and in-house training; and
5. Encouraging and supporting membership and active participation in professional organizations.

Comment

Attorneys are responsible for the actions of their employees in both malpractice and disciplinary proceedings. In the vast majority of cases, the courts have not censured attorneys for a particular act delegated to the legal assistant, but rather, have been critical of and imposed sanctions against attorneys for failure to adequately supervise the legal assistant. The attorney's responsibility for supervision of his or her legal assistant must be more than a willingness to accept responsibility and liability for the legal assistant's work. Supervision of a legal assistant must be offered in both the procedural and substantive legal areas. The attorney must delegate work based upon the education, knowledge, and abilities of the legal assistant and must monitor the work product and conduct of the legal assistant to insure that the work performed is substantively correct and competently performed in a professional manner.

Michigan State Board of Commissioners has adopted Guidelines for the Utilization of Legal Assistants (April 23, 1993). These guidelines, in part, encourage employers to support legal assistant participation in continuing education programs to ensure that the legal assistant remains competent in the fields of practice in which the legal assistant is assigned.

The working relationship between the lawyer and the legal assistant should extend to cooperative efforts on public service activities wherever possible. Participation in pro bono activities is encouraged in ABA Guideline 10.

GUIDELINE 5

Except as otherwise provided by statute, court rule or decision, administrative rule or regulation, or the attorney's rules of professional responsibility, and within the preceding parameters and proscriptions, a legal assistant may perform any function delegated by an attorney, including, but not limited to the following:

1. Conduct client interviews and maintain general contact with the client after the establishment of the attorney-client relationship, so long as the client is aware of the

status and function of the legal assistant, and the client contact is under the supervision of the attorney.

2. Locate and interview witnesses, so long as the witnesses are aware of the status and function of the legal assistant.
3. Conduct investigations and statistical and documentary research for review by the attorney.
4. Conduct legal research for review by the attorney.
5. Draft legal documents for review by the attorney.
6. Draft correspondence and pleadings for review by and signature of the attorney.
7. Summarize depositions, interrogatories and testimony for review by the attorney.
8. Attend executions of wills, real estate closings, depositions, court or administrative hearings and trials with the attorney.
9. Author and sign letters providing the legal assistant's status is clearly indicated and the correspondence does not contain independent legal opinions or legal advice.

Comment

The United States Supreme Court has recognized the variety of tasks being performed by legal assistants and has noted that use of legal assistants encourages cost-effective delivery of legal services, *Missouri v. Jenkins*, 491 U.S.274, 109 S.Ct. 2463, 2471, n.10 (1989). In *Jenkins*, the court further held that legal assistant time should be included in compensation for attorney fee awards at the market rate of the relevant community to bill legal assistant time.

Courts have held that legal assistant fees are not a part of the overall overhead of a law firm. Legal assistant services are billed separately by attorneys, and decrease litigation expenses. Tasks performed by legal assistants must contain substantive legal work under the direction or supervision of an attorney, such that if the legal assistant were not present, the work would be performed by the attorney.

In *Taylor v. Chubb*, 874 P.2d 806 (Okla. 1994), the Court ruled that attorney fees awarded should include fees for services performed by legal assistants and, further, defined tasks which may be performed by the legal assistant under the supervision of an attorney including, among others: interview clients; draft pleadings and other documents; carry on legal research, both conventional and computer aided; research public records; prepare discovery requests and responses; schedule depositions and prepare notices and subpoenas; summarize depositions and other discovery responses; coordinate and manage document production; locate and interview witnesses; organize pleadings, trial exhibits and other documents; prepare witness and exhibit lists; prepare trial notebooks; prepare for the attendance of witnesses at trial; and assist lawyers at trials.

Except for the specific proscription contained in Guideline 1, the reported cases do not limit the duties which may be performed by a legal assistant under the supervision of the attorney.

An attorney may not split legal fees with a legal assistant, nor pay a legal assistant for the referral of legal business. An attorney may compensate a legal assistant based on the quantity and quality of the legal assistant's work and value of that work to a law practice.

CONCLUSION

These Standards and Guidelines were developed from generally accepted practices. Each supervising attorney must be aware of the specific rules, decisions, and statutes applicable to legal assistants within his/her jurisdiction.

ADDENDUM

For further information, the following cases may be helpful to you:

Duties

Taylor v. Chubb, 874 P.2d 806 (Okla. 1994)

McMackin v. McMackin, 651 A.2d 778 (Del.Fam Ct 1993)

Work Product

Fine v. Facet Aerospace Products Co., 133 F.R.D. 439 (S.D.N.Y. 1990)

Unauthorized Practice of Law

Akron Bar Assn. v. Green, 673 N.E.2d 1307 (Ohio 1997)

In Re Hessinger & Associates, 192 B.R. 211 (N.D. Calif. 1996)

In the Matter of Bright, 171 B.R. 799 (Bkrtcy. E.D. Mich)

Louisiana State Bar Assn v. Edwins, 540 So.2d 294 (La. 1989)

Attorney/Client Privilege

In Re Complex Asbestos Litigation, 232 Cal. App. 3d 572 (Calif. 1991)

Makita Corp. v. U.S., 819 F.Supp. 1099 (CIT 1993)

Conflicts

In Re Complex Asbestos Litigation, 232 Cal. App. 3d 572 (Calif. 1991)

Makita Corp. v. U.S., 819 F.Supp. 1099 (CIT 1993)

Phoenix Founders, Inc., v. Marshall, 887 S.W.2d 831 (Tex. 1994)

Smart Industries v. Superior Court, 876 P.2d 1176 (Ariz. App. Div.1 1994)

Supervision

Matter of Martinez, 754 P.2d 842 (N.M. 1988)

State v. Barrett, 483 P.2d 1106 (Kan. 1971)

Hayes v. Central States Orthopedic Specialists, Inc., 2002 OK 30, 51 P.3d 562

Liebowitz v. Eighth Judicial District Court of Nevada Nev Sup Ct., No 39683, November 3, 2003 clarified in part and overrules in part *Ciaffone v. District Court*, 113 Nev 1165, 945. P2d 950 (1997)

Fee Awards

In Re Bicoastal Corp., 121 B.R. 653 (Bktrcy.M.D.Fla. 1990)

In Re Carter, 101 B.R. 170 (Bkrtcy.D.S.D. 1989)

Taylor v. Chubb, 874 P.2d 806 (Okla.1994)

Missouri v. Jenkins, 491 U.S. 274, 109 S.Ct. 2463, 105 L.Ed.2d 229 (1989) 11 U.S.C.A.§ 330

McMackin v. McMackin, Del.Fam.Ct. 651 A.2d 778 (1993)

Miller v. Alamo, 983 F.2d 856 (8th Cir. 1993)

Stewart v. Sullivan, 810 F.Supp. 1102 (D.Hawaii 1993)

In Re Yankton College, 101 B.R. 151 (Bkrtcy. D.S.D. 1989)

Stacey v. Stroud, 845 F.Supp. 1135 (S.D.W.Va. 1993)

Court Appearances

Louisiana State Bar Assn v. Edwins, 540 So.2d 294 (La. 1989)

In addition to the above referenced cases, you may contact your state bar association for information regarding guidelines for the utilization of legal assistants that may have been adopted by the bar, or ethical opinions concerning the utilization of legal assistants. The following states have adopted a definition of "legal assistant" or "paralegal" either through bar association guidelines, ethical opinions, legislation or case law:

Legislation

California
Florida
Illinois
Indiana
Maine
Pennsylvania

Supreme Court Cases or Rules

Kentucky
New Hampshire
New Mexico
North Dakota
Rhode Island
South Dakota
Virginia

Cases

Arizona
New Jersey
Oklahoma

Cases (Cont.)

South Carolina
Washington

Guidelines

Colorado
Connecticut
Georgia
Idaho
New York
Oregon
Utah
Wisconsin

Bar Association Activity

Alaska
Arizona
Colorado
Connecticut
Florida
Illinois

Bar Association Activity (Cont.)

Iowa
Kansas
Kentucky
Massachusetts
Michigan
Minnesota
Missouri
Nevada
New Mexico
New Hampshire
North Carolina
North Dakota
Ohio
Oregon
Rhode Island
South Carolina
South Dakota
Tennessee
Texas
Virginia
Wisconsin

Federal Court Name Abbreviations

Court	Abbrev.
United States Supreme Court	U.S.

UNITED STATES COURTS OF APPEALS

First Circuit	1st Cir.
Second Circuit	2d Cir.
Third Circuit	3d Cir.
Fourth Circuit	4th Cir.
Fifth Circuit	5th Cir.
Sixth Circuit	6th Cir.
Seventh Circuit	7th Cir.
Eighth Circuit	8th Cir.
Ninth Circuit	9th Cir.
Tenth Circuit	10th Cir.
Eleventh Circuit	11th Cir.
D.C. Circuit	D.C. Cir.
Federal Circuit	Fed. Cir.

UNITED STATES DISTRICT COURTS

Middle District of Alabama	**M.D. Ala.**
Northern District of Alabama	**N.D. Ala.**
Southern District of Alabama	**S.D. Ala.**
District of Alaska	**D. Alaska**
District of Arizona	**D. Ariz.**
Eastern District of Arkansas	**E.D. Ark.**
Western District of Arkansas	**W.D. Ark.**
Central District of California	**C.D. Cal.**
Eastern District of California	**E.D. Cal.**

(Note: The D.C.Z. ceased to exist on March 31, 1982.)

Reprinted with permission of Aspen Publishers, from ALWD Citation Manual: A Professional System of Citation.

Court	Abbrev.
Northern District of California	N.D. Cal.
Southern District of California	S.D. Cal.
District of the Canal Zone	D.C.Z.
District of Colorado	D. Colo.
District of Connecticut	D. Conn.
District of Delaware	D. Del.
District of D.C.	D.D.C.
Middle District of Florida	M.D. Fla.
Northern District of Florida	N.D. Fla.
Southern District of Florida	S.D. Fla.
Middle District of Georgia	M.D. Ga.
Northern District of Georgia	N.D. Ga.
Southern District of Georgia	S.D. Ga.
District of Guam	D. Guam
District of Hawaii	D. Haw.
District of Idaho	D. Idaho
Central District of Illinois	C.D. Ill.
Northern District of Illinois	N.D. Ill.
Southern District of Illinois	S.D. Ill.
Northern District of Indiana	N.D. Ind.
Southern District of Indiana	S.D. Ind.
Northern District of Iowa	N.D. Iowa
Southern District of Iowa	S.D. Iowa
District of Kansas	D. Kan.
Eastern District of Kentucky	E.D. Ky.
Western District of Kentucky	W.D. Ky.
Eastern District of Louisiana	E.D. La.
Middle District of Louisiana	M.D. La.
Western District of Louisiana	W.D. La.
District of Maine	D. Me.
District of Maryland	D. Md.
District of Massachusetts	D. Mass.
Eastern District of Michigan	E.D. Mich.
Western District of Michigan	W.D. Mich.
District of Minnesota	D. Minn.
Northern District of Mississippi	N.D. Miss.
Southern District of Mississippi	S.D. Miss.
Eastern District of Missouri	E.D. Mo.
Western District of Missouri	W.D. Mo.
District of Montana	D. Mont.
District of Nebraska	D. Neb.

Court	Abbrev.
District of Nevada	**D. Nev.**
District of New Hampshire	**D.N.H.**
District of New Jersey	**D.N.J.**
District of New Mexico	**D.N.M.**
Eastern District of New York	**E.D.N.Y.**
Northern District of New York	**N.D.N.Y.**
Southern District of New York	**S.D.N.Y.**
Western District of New York	**W.D.N.Y.**
Eastern District of North Carolina	**E.D.N.C.**
Middle District of North Carolina	**M.D.N.C.**
Western District of North Carolina	**W.D.N.C.**
District of North Dakota	**D.N.D.**
District of the Northern Mariana Islands	**D.N. Mar. I.**
Northern District of Ohio	**N.D. Ohio**
Southern District of Ohio	**S.D. Ohio**
Eastern District of Oklahoma	**E.D. Okla.**
Northern District of Oklahoma	**N.D. Okla.**
Western District of Oklahoma	**W.D. Okla.**
District of Oregon	**D. Or.**
Eastern District of Pennsylvania	**E.D. Pa.**
Middle District of Pennsylvania	**M.D. Pa.**
Western District of Pennsylvania	**W.D. Pa.**
District of Puerto Rico	**D.P.R.**
District of Rhode Island	**D.R.I.**
District of South Carolina	**D.S.C.**
District of South Dakota	**D.S.D.**
Eastern District of Tennessee	**E.D. Tenn.**
Middle District of Tennessee	**M.D. Tenn.**
Western District of Tennessee	**W.D. Tenn.**
Eastern District of Texas	**E.D. Tex.**
Northern District of Texas	**N.D. Tex.**
Southern District of Texas	**S.D. Tex.**
Western District of Texas	**W.D. Tex.**
District of Utah	**D. Utah**
District of Vermont	**D. Vt.**
Eastern District of Virginia	**E.D. Va.**
Western District of Virginia	**W.D. Va.**
District of the Virgin Islands	**D.V.I.**
Eastern District of Washington	**E.D. Wash.**
Western District of Washington	**W.D. Wash.**
Northern District of West Virginia	**N.D.W. Va.**

Court	Abbrev.
Southern District of West Virginia	**S.D.W. Va.**
Eastern District of Wisconsin	**E.D. Wis.**
Western District of Wisconsin	**W.D. Wis.**
District of Wyoming	**D. Wyo.**

MILITARY COURTS

Court	Abbrev.
United States Court of Appeals for the Armed Forces	**Armed Forces App.**
United States Court of Veterans Appeals	**Vet. App.**
United States Air Force Court of Criminal Appeals	**A.F. Crim. App.**
United States Army Court of Criminal Appeals	**Army Crim. App.**
United States Coast Guard Court of Criminal Appeals	**Coast Guard Crim. App.**
United States Navy-Marine Corps Court of Criminal Appeals	**Navy-Marine Crim. App.**

BANKRUPTCY COURTS

Each United States District Court has a corresponding bankruptcy court. To cite a bankruptcy court, add Bankr. to the district court abbreviation.

Examples:

Bankr. N.D. Ala.

Bankr. D. Mass.

OTHER FEDERAL COURTS

Court	Abbrev.
Court of Federal Claims	**Fed. Cl.**
Court of Customs and Patent Appeals	**Cust. & Pat. App.**
Court of Claims	**Ct. Cl.**
Claims Court	**Cl. Ct.**
Court of International Trade	**Ct. Intl. Trade**
Tax Court	**Tax**

Effective Learning
How to Study

Everyone learns differently. Some people seem to absorb information like a sponge while others must work hard to soak up any information. Although some people truly do have photographic memories, they are few and far between. Most likely, the people who seem to absorb information "like a sponge" have learned how to maximize their learning experiences. Most of us do not take the time to figure out how we learn best and, as a result, probably spend more time than necessary to achieve the same results as more proficient learners.

Have you ever wondered how some people who are just average students seem to always get A's? If you were to ask them, they probably would tell you that they spend more time than most people studying and preparing, or that they have learned how to study more effectively and efficiently in the time they have available. A good starting point is to determine how you learn best and work out methods to maximize the time and effort you have available.

LEARNING STYLES

A learning style is the way you learn most effectively. Everyone has his or her own learning style, and there are no "better" or "correct" ways to learn. Somewhere in your school career you may have been given tests—such as the Hogan/Champagne Personal Style Indicator or the Kolb Learning Style Inventory—to determine your personal learning styles. These and similar assessments are available through most school advisors and guidance counselors. If you want help in determining your learning styles, take the initiative for your own success and make an appointment with someone who can administer an assessment.

Learning styles fall into these categories:

- independent (competitive) versus collaborative
- structured versus unstructured
- auditory versus visual
- spatial versus verbal
- practical versus creative
- applied versus conceptual
- factual versus analytical
- emotional versus logical

This sounds like a lot to consider, but taking a few minutes to determine which learning style best suits you can save you countless hours of frustration—hours that could be better devoted to studying or other activities.

Independent Versus Collaborative

Do you prefer to work with a group or independently? Some people like to avoid all distractions by working alone. Others prefer to work in a study group and share information.

If you prefer to work independently, you may want to obtain additional course information from study guides and computer-assisted instruction. You may prefer lecture-format classes to small discussion courses. If you prefer to work collaboratively, you may wish to form study groups early in the semester or find a tutor to work with, and you should choose courses that include small discussion groups or group projects.

Structured Versus Unstructured

Structured learners feel more comfortable when they formalize their study habits—for example, by selecting a definite time and place in which to study every day. If you are a structured learner, you may find it useful to create "to-do" lists and keep a written schedule of classes, study times, and activities.

Unstructured learners tend to resist formalizing their study plan and try to avoid feeling "locked-in." They tend to procrastinate. Procrastinators need to find ways to give more structure to their learning activities. One method is to join a study group of students who are more organized.

Auditory Versus Visual

Auditory learners learn best by listening. Visual learners learn best from what they see. Visual learners cannot always learn everything by listening to lectures or by reading and watching video presentations. Auditory learners may find it more efficient to listen to lectures and then read related material. Visual learners may do better reading the book first, and then attending lectures. Auditory learners may also find group discussion and study group activities beneficial.

Spatial Versus Verbal

Spatial learners are better then verbal learners at reading and interpreting maps, charts, and other graphics. Verbal learners prefer to read words than to interpret graphics. Spatial learners need to create and incorporate their own diagrams, maps, timelines, and other graphics into their notes.

Verbal learners need to translate or obtain translations of graphics into words. A useful technique for verbal learners is to take notes that describe the material, including the graphics, in such a way that a visually impaired student could understand the graphic representation from the verbal description. Teaming up with a visually impaired student may be mutually beneficial.

Practical Versus Creative

Practical learners tend to be methodical and systematic. They prefer specific instruction that is directed and focused. Creative learners prefer experimentation and creative activities. Practical learners may benefit from creating an organized study plan for each course, including detailed "to-do" lists and a calendar. For creative learners, courses that allow writing and other creative approaches may be more satisfying.

Applied Versus Conceptual

Applied learners want to know how information can be transferred to given situations. Conceptual learners are not so much concerned with the application as with the underlying concepts. Applied learners need to focus on ways in which the ideas presented in courses and lectures can be applied. Taking notes that include examples for applying the concepts helps them recall the concepts later. Conceptual learners may find it useful to consider the concepts in a broader context than that of the narrow lecture presentation.

Factual Versus Analytical

Factual learners are good with details and enjoy learning interesting and unusual facts. They prefer objective tests. Analytical learners like to break down a topic into its component parts to understand how the parts relate to each other. Analytical learners prefer essay exams that allow them to demonstrate how their knowledge relates to the question. Factual learners may want to make lists of facts, which they can associate with prior knowledge. Analytical learners may want to analyze the organization as they read a textbook, looking for trends and patterns.

Emotional Versus Logical

Emotional learners tend to prefer human-interest stories to material that presents just facts and logic. Logical learners want to understand the factual basis, including statistics, of an argument. Emotional learners may find that reading biographical sketches helps them understand factual subjects.

PUTTING IT ALL TOGETHER

1. *Understand yourself.* From the previous list of types of learners, select the descriptions in each category that best fit your style of learning. Look back at courses and classes you have taken in which you have done well or that you enjoyed the most. You may see a pattern that will help you understand your learning style.

2. *Set goals.* Determine your personal and occupational goals. Do you want a career working with people or with things? Do you want a professional career working directly with people or behind the scenes supporting others? What courses will help you acquire the skills and knowledge you need to achieve these goals?

3. *Make a plan.* Your educational path should lead to a goal. It may be a personal goal to be an outstanding parent or partner, or it may be a goal to be a generalist or a specialist in an occupation or profession. To achieve these goals, you will have to focus on courses that give you the necessary skills and knowledge. Within the courses may be options that accommodate your learning style, such as large lecture classes versus small-group discussion classes, face-to-face courses versus distance-learning courses, and so on.

   Create a personal plan that allows for flexibility as your goals or interests change. A good foundation will allow you more flexibility in courses and curriculum. Don't be afraid to admit that you did not enjoy some courses you expected to enjoy or that you enjoyed some classes you didn't think would give you pleasure. These insights may help you fine-tune your personal and professional goals.

4. *Check your progress.* Periodically assess how well you are doing in individual classes, as well as in your overall program of study. Use the opportunity to assess why you are doing better than you expected in some classes and not as well in others. You may have to adjust your overall plan or merely your learning methods. Or outside influences such as work, family, or personal issues may be interfering with your learning. Periodic self-assessment is the first step in modifying your goals.

5. *Make adjustments.* As your goals change, so will your plan. Don't be afraid to make the adjustments necessary to achieve your goals or to change your goals as your interests change. Life rarely follows a straight path. Be adaptable and make adjustments when necessary.

SCHEDULING TIME

Most people use a calendar to keep track of information such as birthdays, appointments, or upcoming events. Calendars may include vacations, concerts, and other special events or activities. Depending on your personal style, you might include "to-do" lists or an hour-by-hour schedule of classes and other activities. Scheduling school and study time is helpful to most students.

Whichever method works best for you, use it to track the amount of time you spend in all of your activities so you can budget your time more accurately. When scheduling, keep in mind that the power of concentration has a limitation for everyone. Don't schedule so many activities that they exceed your mental or physical abilities.

SUPPLEMENTAL LEARNING AIDS

1. *Study guides*. Many textbooks have a study guide that will give you additional information, including sample tests and quizzes. Your instructor may or may not require the use of a study guide. If you need additional reinforcement, you may want to purchase a study guide even if it is not a required part of the course.

2. *Flash cards*. Flash cards are available in college bookstores for many courses. But you will learn more by preparing your own and customizing them to the course you are taking. On the front side of an index card, write a word, phrase, or concept, and write the definition or explanation on the reverse side. With a properly prepared set of flash cards, you may not have to refer to the text or your notes when studying for a test.

3. *Companion websites*. Many publishers offer companion websites for their textbooks. These websites frequently are available on the publisher's website without cost or for a nominal fee. Often these websites are the equivalent of an online study guide. Others offer self-tests. The publisher may post information that has become available since the publication of the textbook.

4. *Outlining*. Few people have a photographic memory or the ability to absorb material on one reading. The following approach can help you use your textbook effectively.

   a. *How long is the chapter?* Before you start, check the length of the chapter and your reading assignment. Most textbooks are filled with graphics and illustrations that reduce the amount of actual reading time to a manageable level.

   b. *Scan the chapter.* Look over the material quickly to get a sense of what will be covered.

   c. *Chapter objectives.* At the beginnings of each chapter, most textbooks list what you should learn from reading the chapter. These chapter objectives help you focus on important topics, information, and themes.

   d. *Read the chapter.* Quickly read through the chapter to get an overall sense of the material and how the sections relate to each other.

   e. *Underline the important items.* After you have done this go back over the material and underline in pencil the items you believe are important.

   f. *Go to class.* From the instructor's lecture and class discussion, you may find that what you think is important changes.

   g. *Highlight the important material.* After class, use a highlighter to highlight what you now believe to be the important information in the text. You probably will find that it is substantially less than what you underlined in pencil.

   h. *Make your flash cards.* From the highlighted information, create a set of flash cards for each chapter.

5. *Tutors.* Not everyone can afford the luxury of a personal tutor, but most colleges and universities have a tutoring center or offer some form of tutoring assistance. If you are having difficulty, don't be afraid to ask for help before it is too late. At the beginning of the semester determine what personalized help is available for each course. You may not need to use this information, but having it available will reduce your anxiety and panic if you realize that you need some help.

Don't be afraid to ask your instructor for help. Your instructor wants you to succeed. If you are doing everything you can to be successful in a class, the instructor should be more than happy to help you or direct you for help.

6. *Study groups.* If you are the type of learner who benefits from working with others, form a study group at the beginning of each semester in each course. After the first class, ask if others wish to form a study group, or post a notice on the course bulletin board website.

One advantage of study groups is the opportunity to share class notes as well as ideas. Verbal learners can benefit from having visual learners in the study group to interpret and explain charts, graphs, and maps. Study groups can motivate procrastinators to complete tasks on time.

7. *Tests.* Most students suffer from some form of test anxiety. At the beginning of each course, ask the instructor for the exam schedule and the type of tests he or she will be giving. Some schools maintain copies of all tests that students can use for practice. If your school does not maintain these, ask your instructors if they will make available sample tests and quizzes. Practice tests may be available in the study guide for the text or on a companion website. If you are in a study group, members can prepare practice tests as part of test preparation.

For more detailed information about study skills, see *Effective Study Skills: Maximizing Your Academic Potential*, by Judy M. Roberts (Prentice Hall, 1998).

The Constitution of the United States of America

PREAMBLE

We the People of the United States, in Order to form a more perfect Union, establish Justice, insure domestic Tranquility, provide for the common defense, promote the general Welfare, and secure the Blessings of Liberty to ourselves and our Posterity, do ordain and establish this Constitution for the United States of America.

ARTICLE I

Section 1. All legislative Powers herein granted shall be vested in a Congress of the United States, which shall consist of a Senate and House of Representatives.

Section 2. The House of Representatives shall be composed of Members chosen every second Year by the People of the several States, and the Electors in each State shall have the Qualifications requisite for Electors of the most numerous Branch of the State Legislature.

No Person shall be a Representative who shall not have attained to the Age of twenty five Years, and been seven Years a Citizen of the United States, and who shall not, when elected, be an Inhabitant of that State in which he shall be chosen.

Representatives and direct Taxes shall be apportioned among the several States which may be included within this Union, according to their respective Numbers, which shall be determined by adding to the whole Number of free Persons, including those bound to Service for a Term of Years, and excluding Indians not taxed, three fifths of all other Persons. The actual Enumeration shall be made within three Years after the first Meeting of the Congress of the United States, and within every subsequent Term of ten Years, in such Manner as they shall by Law direct. The Number of Representatives shall not exceed one for every thirty Thousand, but each State shall have at Least one Representative; and until such enumeration shall be made, the State of New Hampshire shall be entitled to chuse three, Massachusetts eight, Rhode Island and Providence Plantations one, Connecticut five, New York six, New Jersey four, Pennsylvania eight, Delaware one, Maryland six, Virginia ten, North Carolina five, South Carolina five, and Georgia three.

When vacancies happen in the Representation from any State, the Executive Authority thereof shall issue Writs of Election to fill such Vacancies.

The House of Representatives shall chuse their Speaker and other Officers; and shall have the sole Power of Impeachment.

Section 3. The Senate of the United States shall be composed of two Senators from each State, chosen by the Legislature thereof for six Years; and each Senator shall have one Vote.

Immediately after they shall be assembled in Consequence of the first Election, they shall be divided as equally as may be into three Classes. The Seats of the Senators of the first Class shall be vacated at the Expiration of the second Year, of the second Class at the Expiration of the fourth Year, and of the third Class at the Expiration of the sixth Year, so that one third may be chosen every second Year; and if Vacancies happen by Resignation, or otherwise, during the Recess of the Legislature of any State, the Executive thereof may make temporary Appointments until the next Meeting of the Legislature, which shall then fill such Vacancies.

No Person shall be a Senator who shall not have attained to the Age of thirty Years, and been nine Years a Citizen of the United States, and who shall not, when elected, be an Inhabitant of that State for which he shall be chosen.

The Vice President of the United States shall be President of the Senate, but shall have no Vote, unless they be equally divided.

The Senate shall chuse their other Officers, and also a President pro tempore, in the Absence of the Vice President, or when he shall exercise the Office of President of the United States.

The Senate shall have the sole Power to try all Impeachments. When sitting for that Purpose, they shall be on Oath or Affirmation. When the President of the United States is tried, the Chief Justice shall preside: And no Person shall be convicted without the Concurrence of two thirds of the Members present.

Judgment in Cases of Impeachment shall not extend further than to removal from Office, and disqualification to hold and enjoy any Office of honor, Trust or Profit under the United States: but the Party convicted shall nevertheless be liable and subject to Indictment, Trial, Judgment and Punishment, according to Law.

Section 4. The Times, Places and Manner of holding Elections for Senators and Representatives, shall be prescribed in each State by the Legislature thereof; but the Congress may at any time by Law make or alter such Regulations, except as to the Places of chusing Senators.

The Congress shall assemble at least once in every Year, and such Meeting shall be on the first Monday in December, unless they shall by Law appoint a different Day.

Section 5. Each House shall be the Judge of the Elections, Returns and Qualifications of its own Members, and a Majority of each shall constitute a Quorum to do Business; but a smaller Number may adjourn from day to day, and may be authorized to compel the Attendance of absent Members, in such Manner, and under such Penalties as each House may provide.

Each House may determine the Rules of its Proceedings, punish its Members for disorderly Behaviour, and, with the Concurrence of two thirds, expel a Member.

Each House shall keep a Journal of its Proceedings, and from time to time publish the same, excepting such Parts as may in their Judgment require Secrecy; and the Yeas and Nays of the Members of either House on any question shall, at the Desire of one fifth of those Present, be entered on the Journal.

Neither House, during the Session of Congress, shall, without the Consent of the other, adjourn for more than three days, nor to any other Place than that in which the two Houses shall be sitting.

Section 6. The Senators and Representatives shall receive a Compensation for their Services, to be ascertained by Law, and paid out of the Treasury of the United States. They shall in all Cases, except Treason, Felony and Breach of the Peace, be privileged from Arrest during their Attendance at the Session of their respective Houses, and in going to and returning from the same; and for any Speech or Debate in either House, they shall not be questioned in any other Place.

No Senator or Representative shall, during the Time for which he was elected, be appointed to any civil Office under the Authority of the United States, which shall have been created, or the Emoluments whereof shall have been encreased during such time; and no Person holding any Office under the United States, shall be a Member of either House during his Continuance in Office.

Section 7. All Bills for raising Revenue shall originate in the House of Representatives; but the Senate may propose or concur with Amendments as on other Bills.

Every Bill which shall have passed the House of Representatives and the Senate, shall, before it become a Law, be presented to the President of the United States: If he approve he shall sign it, but if not he shall return it, with his Objections to that House in which it shall have originated, who shall enter the Objections at large on their Journal, and proceed to reconsider it. If after such Reconsideration two thirds of that House shall agree to pass the Bill, it shall be sent, together with the Objections, to the other House, by which it shall likewise be reconsidered, and if approved by two thirds of that House, it shall become a Law. But in all such Cases the Votes of both Houses shall be determined by yeas and Nays, and the Names of the Persons voting for and against the Bill shall be entered on the Journal of each House respectively. If any Bill shall not be returned by the President within ten Days (Sundays excepted) after it shall have been presented to him, the Same shall be a Law, in like Manner as if he had signed it, unless the Congress by their Adjournment prevent its Return, in which Case it shall not be a Law.

Every Order, Resolution, or Vote to which the Concurrence of the Senate and House of Representatives may be necessary (except on a question of Adjournment) shall be presented to the President of the United States; and before the Same shall take Effect, shall be approved by him, or being disapproved by him, shall be repassed by two thirds of the Senate and House of Representatives, according to the Rules and Limitations prescribed in the Case of a Bill.

Section 8. The Congress shall have Power To lay and collect Taxes, Duties, Imposts and Excises, to pay the Debts and provide for the common Defence and general Welfare of the United States; but all Duties, Imposts and Excises shall be uniform throughout the United States;

To borrow Money on the credit of the United States;

To regulate Commerce with foreign Nations, and among the several States, and with the Indian Tribes;

To establish an uniform Rule of Naturalization, and uniform Laws on the subject of Bankruptcies throughout the United States;

To coin Money, regulate the Value thereof, and of foreign Coin, and fix the Standard of Weights and Measures;

To provide for the Punishment of counterfeiting the Securities and current Coin of the United States;

To establish Post Offices and post Roads;

To promote the Progress of Science and useful Arts, by securing for limited Times to Authors and Inventors the exclusive Right to their respective Writings and Discoveries;

To constitute Tribunals inferior to the supreme Court;

To define and punish Piracies and Felonies committed on the high Seas, and Offences against the Law of Nations;

To declare War, grant Letters of Marque and Reprisal, and make Rules concerning Captures on Land and Water;

To raise and support Armies, but no Appropriation of Money to that Use shall be for a longer Term than two Years; To provide and maintain a Navy;

To make Rules for the Government and Regulation of the land and naval Forces;

To provide for calling forth the Militia to execute the Laws of the Union, suppress Insurrections and repel Invasions;

To provide for organizing, arming, and disciplining, the Militia, and for governing such Part of them as may be employed in the Service of the United States, reserving to the States respectively, the Appointment of the Officers, and the Authority of training the Militia according to the discipline prescribed by Congress;

To exercise exclusive Legislation in all Cases whatsoever, over such District (not exceeding ten Miles square) as may, by Cession of particular States, and the Acceptance of Congress, become the Seat of the Government of the United States, and to exercise like Authority over all Places purchased by the Consent of the Legislature of the State in which the Same shall be, for the Erection of Forts, Magazines, Arsenals, dockYards, and other needful Buildings;—And

To make all Laws which shall be necessary and proper for carrying into Execution the foregoing Powers, and all other Powers vested by this Constitution in the Government of the United States, or in any Department or Officer thereof.

Section 9. The Migration or Importation of such Persons as any of the States now existing shall think proper to admit, shall not be prohibited by the Congress prior to the Year one thousand eight hundred and eight, but a Tax or duty may be imposed on such Importation, not exceeding ten dollars for each Person.

The Privilege of the Writ of Habeas Corpus shall not be suspended, unless when in Cases of Rebellion or Invasion the public Safety may require it.

No Bill of Attainder or ex post facto Law shall be passed.

No Capitation, or other direct, Tax shall be laid, unless in Proportion to the Census or enumeration herein before directed to be taken.

No Tax or Duty shall be laid on Articles exported from any State.

No Preference shall be given by any Regulation of Commerce or Revenue to the Ports of one State over those of another; nor shall Vessels bound to, or from, one State, be obliged to enter, clear, or pay Duties in another.

No Money shall be drawn from the Treasury, but in Consequence of Appropriations made by Law; and a regular Statement and Account of the Receipts and Expenditures of all public Money shall be published from time to time.

No Title of Nobility shall be granted by the United States: And no Person holding any Office of Profit or Trust under them, shall, without the Consent of the Congress, accept of any present, Emolument, Office, or Title, of any kind whatever, from any King, Prince, or foreign State.

Section 10. No State shall enter into any Treaty, Alliance, or Confederation; grant Letters of Marque and Reprisal; coin Money; emit Bills of Credit; make any Thing but gold and silver Coin a Tender in Payment of Debts; pass any Bill of Attainder, ex post facto Law, or Law impairing the Obligation of Contracts, or grant any Title of Nobility.

No State shall, without the Consent of the Congress, lay any Imposts or Duties on Imports or Exports, except what may be absolutely necessary for executing it's inspection Laws: and the net Produce of all Duties and Imposts, laid by any State on Imports or Exports, shall be for the Use of the Treasury of the United States; and all such Laws shall be subject to the Revision and Controul of the Congress.

No State shall, without the Consent of Congress, lay any Duty of Tonnage, keep Troops, or Ships of War in time of Peace, enter into any Agreement or Compact with another State, or with a foreign Power, or engage in War, unless actually invaded, or in such imminent Danger as will not admit of delay.

ARTICLE II

Section 1. The executive Power shall be vested in a President of the United States of America. He shall hold his Office during the Term of four Years, and, together with the Vice President, chosen for the same Term, be elected, as follows:

Each State shall appoint, in such Manner as the Legislature thereof may direct, a Number of Electors, equal to the whole Number of Senators and Representatives to which the State may be entitled in the Congress: but no Senator or Representative, or Person holding an Office of Trust or Profit under the United States, shall be appointed an Elector.

The Electors shall meet in their respective States, and vote by Ballot for two Persons, of whom one at least shall not be an Inhabitant of the same State with themselves. And they shall make a List of all the Persons voted for, and of the Number of Votes for each; which List they shall sign and certify, and transmit sealed to the Seat of the Government of the United States, directed to the President of the Senate. The President of the Senate shall, in the Presence of the Senate and House of Representatives, open all the Certificates, and the Votes shall then be counted. The Person having the greatest Number of Votes shall be the President, if such Number be a Majority of the whole Number of Electors appointed; and if there be more than one who have such Majority, and have an equal Number of Votes, then the House of Representatives shall immediately chuse by Ballot one of them for President; and if no Person have a Majority, then from the five highest on the List the said House shall in like Manner chuse the President. But in chusing the President, the Votes shall be taken by States, the Representation from each State having one Vote; A quorum for this purpose shall consist of a Member or Members from two thirds of the States, and a Majority of all the States shall be necessary to a Choice. In every Case, after the Choice of the President, the Person having the greatest Number of Votes of the Electors shall be the Vice President. But if there should remain two or more who have equal Votes, the Senate shall chuse from them by Ballot the Vice President.

The Congress may determine the Time of chusing the Electors, and the Day on which they shall give their Votes; which Day shall be the same throughout the United States.

No Person except a natural born Citizen, or a Citizen of the United States, at the time of the Adoption of this Constitution, shall be eligible to the Office of President; neither shall any Person be eligible to that Office who shall not have attained to the Age of thirty five Years, and been fourteen Years a Resident within the United States.

In Case of the Removal of the President from Office, or of his Death, Resignation, or Inability to discharge the Powers and Duties of the said Office, the Same shall devolve on the Vice President, and the Congress may by Law provide for the Case of Removal, Death, Resignation or Inability, both of the President and Vice President, declaring what Officer shall then act as President, and such Officer shall act accordingly, until the Disability be removed, or a President shall be elected.

The President shall, at stated Times, receive for his Services, a Compensation, which shall neither be increased nor diminished during the Period for which he shall have been elected, and he shall not receive within that Period any other Emolument from the United States, or any of them.

Before he enter on the Execution of his Office, he shall take the following Oath or Affirmation:—"I do solemnly swear (or affirm) that I will faithfully execute the Office of President of the United States, and will to the best of my Ability, preserve, protect and defend the Constitution of the United States."

Section 2. The President shall be Commander in Chief of the Army and Navy of the United States, and of the Militia of the several States, when called into the actual Service of the United States; he may require the Opinion, in writing, of the principal

Officer in each of the executive Departments, upon any Subject relating to the Duties of their respective Offices, and he shall have Power to grant Reprieves and Pardons for Offences against the United States, except in Cases of Impeachment.

He shall have Power, by and with the Advice and Consent of the Senate, to make Treaties, provided two thirds of the Senators present concur; and he shall nominate, and by and with the Advice and Consent of the Senate, shall appoint Ambassadors, other public Ministers and Consuls, Judges of the supreme Court, and all other Officers of the United States, whose Appointments are not herein otherwise provided for, and which shall be established by Law: but the Congress may by Law vest the Appointment of such inferior Officers, as they think proper, in the President alone, in the Courts of Law, or in the Heads of Departments.

The President shall have Power to fill up all Vacancies that may happen during the Recess of the Senate, by granting Commissions which shall expire at the End of their next Session.

Section 3. He shall from time to time give to the Congress Information of the State of the Union, and recommend to their Consideration such Measures as he shall judge necessary and expedient; he may, on extraordinary Occasions, convene both Houses, or either of them, and in Case of Disagreement between them, with Respect to the Time of Adjournment, he may adjourn them to such Time as he shall think proper; he shall receive Ambassadors and other public Ministers; he shall take Care that the Laws be faithfully executed, and shall Commission all the Officers of the United States.

Section 4. The President, Vice President and all civil Officers of the United States, shall be removed from Office on Impeachment for, and Conviction of, Treason, Bribery, or other high Crimes and Misdemeanors.

ARTICLE III

Section 1. The judicial Power of the United States shall be vested in one supreme Court, and in such inferior Courts as the Congress may from time to time ordain and establish. The Judges, both of the supreme and inferior Courts, shall hold their Offices during good Behaviour, and shall, at stated Times, receive for their Services a Compensation, which shall not be diminished during their Continuance in Office.

Section 2. The judicial Power shall extend to all Cases, in Law and Equity, arising under this Constitution, the Laws of the United States, and Treaties made, or which shall be made, under their Authority;—to all Cases affecting Ambassadors, other public Ministers and Consuls;—to all Cases of admiralty and maritime Jurisdiction;—to Controversies to which the United States shall be a Party;—to Controversies between two or more States;—between a State and Citizens of another State;—between Citizens of different States;—between Citizens of the same State claiming Lands under Grants of different States, and between a State, or the Citizens thereof, and foreign States, Citizens or Subjects.

In all Cases affecting Ambassadors, other public Ministers and Consuls, and those in which a State shall be Party, the supreme Court shall have original Jurisdiction. In all the other Cases before mentioned, the supreme Court shall have appellate Jurisdiction, both as to Law and Fact, with such Exceptions, and under such Regulations as the Congress shall make.

The Trial of all Crimes, except in Cases of Impeachment, shall be by Jury; and such Trial shall be held in the State where the said Crimes shall have been committed; but when not committed within any State, the Trial shall be at such Place or Places as the Congress may by Law have directed.

Section 3. Treason against the United States, shall consist only in levying War against them, or in adhering to their Enemies, giving them Aid and Comfort. No Person shall be convicted of Treason unless on the Testimony of two Witnesses to the same overt Act, or on Confession in open Court.

The Congress shall have Power to declare the Punishment of Treason, but no Attainder of Treason shall work Corruption of Blood, or Forfeiture except during the Life of the Person attainted.

ARTICLE IV

Section 1. Full Faith and Credit shall be given in each State to the public Acts, Records, and judicial Proceedings of every other State. And the Congress may by general Laws prescribe the Manner in which such Acts, Records and Proceedings shall be proved, and the Effect thereof.

Section 2. The Citizens of each State shall be entitled to all Privileges and Immunities of Citizens in the several States.

A Person charged in any State with Treason, Felony, or other Crime, who shall flee from Justice, and be found in another State, shall on Demand of the executive Authority of the State from which he fled, be delivered up, to be removed to the State having Jurisdiction of the Crime.

No Person held to Service or Labour in one State, under the Laws thereof, escaping into another, shall, in Consequence of any Law or Regulation therein, be discharged from such Service or Labour, but shall be delivered up on Claim of the Party to whom such Service or Labour may be due.

Section 3. New States may be admitted by the Congress into this Union; but no new State shall be formed or erected within the Jurisdiction of any other State; nor any State be formed by the Junction of two or more States, or Parts of States, without the Consent of the Legislatures of the States concerned as well as of the Congress.

The Congress shall have Power to dispose of and make all needful Rules and Regulations respecting the Territory or other Property belonging to the United States; and nothing in this Constitution shall be so construed as to Prejudice any Claims of the United States, or of any particular State.

Section 4. The United States shall guarantee to every State in this Union a Republican Form of Government, and shall protect each of them against Invasion; and on Application of the Legislature, or of the Executive (when the Legislature cannot be convened), against domestic Violence.

ARTICLE V

The Congress, whenever two thirds of both Houses shall deem it necessary, shall propose Amendments to this Constitution, or, on the Application of the Legislatures of two thirds of the several States, shall call a Convention for proposing Amendments, which, in either Case, shall be valid to all Intents and Purposes, as Part of this Constitution, when ratified by the Legislatures of three fourths of the several States, or by Conventions in three fourths thereof, as the one or the other Mode of Ratification may be proposed by the Congress; Provided that no Amendment which may be made prior to the Year One thousand eight hundred and eight shall in any Manner affect the first and fourth Clauses in the Ninth Section of the first Article; and that no State, without its Consent, shall be deprived of its equal Suffrage in the Senate.

ARTICLE VI

All Debts contracted and Engagements entered into, before the Adoption of this Constitution, shall be as valid against the United States under this Constitution, as under the Confederation.

This Constitution, and the Laws of the United States which shall be made in Pursuance thereof; and all Treaties made, or which shall be made, under the Authority of the United States, shall be the supreme Law of the Land; and the Judges in every State shall be bound thereby, any Thing in the Constitution or Laws of any State to the Contrary notwithstanding.

The Senators and Representatives before mentioned, and the Members of the several State Legislatures, and all executive and judicial Officers, both of the United States and of the several States, shall be bound by Oath or Affirmation, to support this Constitution; but no religious Test shall ever be required as a Qualification to any Office or public Trust under the United States.

ARTICLE VII

The Ratification of the Conventions of nine States, shall be sufficient for the Establishment of this Constitution between the States so ratifying the Same.

AMENDMENTS TO THE CONSTITUTION OF THE UNITED STATES

[Amendments I–X make up the Bill of Rights]

AMENDMENT I

Congress shall make no law respecting an establishment of religion, or prohibiting the free exercise thereof; or abridging the freedom of speech, or of the press; or the right of the people peaceably to assemble, and to petition the Government for a redress of grievances.

AMENDMENT II

A well regulated Militia, being necessary to the security of a free State, the right of the people to keep and bear Arms, shall not be infringed.

AMENDMENT III

No Soldier shall, in time of peace be quartered in any house, without the consent of the Owner, nor in time of war, but in a manner to be prescribed by law.

AMENDMENT IV

The right of the people to be secure in their persons, houses, papers, and effects, against unreasonable searches and seizures, shall not be violated, and no Warrants shall issue, but upon probable cause, supported by Oath or affirmation, and particularly describing the place to be searched, and the persons or things to be seized.

AMENDMENT V

No person shall be held to answer for a capital, or otherwise infamous crime, unless on a presentment or indictment of a Grand Jury, except in cases arising in the land or naval forces, or in the Militia, when in actual service in time of War or public danger; nor shall any person be subject for the same offence to be twice put in jeopardy of life or limb; nor shall be compelled in any criminal case to be a witness against himself, nor be deprived of life, liberty, or property, without due process of law; nor shall private property be taken for public use, without just compensation.

AMENDMENT VI

In all criminal prosecutions, the accused shall enjoy the right to a speedy and public trial, by an impartial jury of the State and district wherein the crime shall have been committed, which district shall have been previously ascertained by law, and to be informed of the nature and cause of the accusation; to be confronted with the witnesses against him; to have compulsory process for obtaining witnesses in his favor, and to have the Assistance of Counsel for his defence.

AMENDMENT VII

In suits at common law, where the value in controversy shall exceed twenty dollars, the right of trial by jury shall be preserved, and no fact tried by a jury, shall be otherwise reexamined in any Court of the United States, than according to the rules of the common law.

AMENDMENT VIII

Excessive bail shall not be required, nor excessive fines imposed, nor cruel and unusual punishments inflicted.

AMENDMENT IX

The enumeration in the Constitution, of certain rights, shall not be construed to deny or disparage others retained by the people.

AMENDMENT X

The powers not delegated to the United States by the Constitution, nor prohibited by it to the States, are reserved to the States respectively, or to the people.

AMENDMENT XI

The Judicial power of the United States shall not be construed to extend to any suit in law or equity, commenced or prosecuted against one of the United States by Citizens of another State, or by Citizens or Subjects of any Foreign State.

AMENDMENT XII

The Electors shall meet in their respective states and vote by ballot for President and Vice-President, one of whom, at least, shall not be an inhabitant of the same state with themselves; they shall name in their ballots the person voted for as President, and in distinct ballots the person voted for as Vice-President, and they shall make distinct lists of all persons voted for as President, and of all persons voted for as Vice-President, and of the number of votes for each, which lists they shall sign and certify, and transmit sealed to the seat of the government of the United States, directed to the President of the Senate;—the President of the Senate shall, in the presence of the Senate and House of Representatives, open all the certificates and the votes shall then be counted;—The person having the greatest number of votes for President, shall be the President, if such number be a majority of the whole number of Electors appointed; and if no person have such majority, then from the persons having the highest numbers not exceeding three on the list of those voted for as President, the House of Representatives shall choose immediately, by ballot, the President. But in choosing the President, the votes shall be taken by states, the representation from each state having one vote; a quorum for this purpose shall consist of a member or members from two-thirds of the states, and a majority of all the states shall be necessary to a choice. [And if the House of Representatives shall not choose a President whenever the right of choice shall devolve upon them, before the fourth day of March next following, then the Vice-President shall act as President, as in case of the death or other constitutional disability of the President.—]* The person having the greatest number of votes as Vice-President, shall be the Vice-President, if such number be a majority of the whole number of Electors appointed, and if no person have a majority, then from the two highest numbers on the list, the Senate shall choose the Vice-President; a quorum for the purpose shall consist of two-thirds of the whole number of Senators, and a majority of the whole number shall be necessary to a choice. But no person constitutionally ineligible to the office of President shall be eligible to that of Vice-President of the United States.

AMENDMENT XIII

Section 1. Neither slavery nor involuntary servitude, except as a punishment for crime whereof the party shall have been duly convicted, shall exist within the United States, or any place subject to their jurisdiction.

Section 2. Congress shall have power to enforce this article by appropriate legislation.

AMENDMENT XIV

Section 1. All persons born or naturalized in the United States, and subject to the jurisdiction thereof, are citizens of the United States and of the State wherein they reside. No State shall make or enforce any law which shall abridge the privileges or immunities of citizens of the United States; nor shall any State deprive any person of life, liberty, or property, without due process of law; nor deny to any person within its jurisdiction the equal protection of the laws.

Section 2. Representatives shall be apportioned among the several States according to their respective numbers, counting the whole number of persons in each State, excluding Indians not taxed. But when the right to vote at any election for the choice of electors for President and Vice-President of the United States, Representatives in Congress, the

Executive and Judicial officers of a State, or the members of the Legislature thereof, is denied to any of the male inhabitants of such State, being twenty-one years of age,* and citizens of the United States, or in any way abridged, except for participation in rebellion, or other crime, the basis of representation therein shall be reduced in the proportion which the number of such male citizens shall bear to the whole number of male citizens twenty-one years of age in such State.

Section 3. No person shall be a Senator or Representative in Congress, or elector of President and Vice-President, or hold any office, civil or military, under the United States, or under any State, who, having previously taken an oath, as a member of Congress, or as an officer of the United States, or as a member of any State legislature, or as an executive or judicial officer of any State, to support the Constitution of the United States, shall have engaged in insurrection or rebellion against the same, or given aid or comfort to the enemies thereof. But Congress may by a vote of two-thirds of each House, remove such disability.

Section 4. The validity of the public debt of the United States, authorized by law, including debts incurred for payment of pensions and bounties for services in suppressing insurrection or rebellion, shall not be questioned. But neither the United States nor any State shall assume or pay any debt or obligation incurred in aid of insurrection or rebellion against the United States, or any claim for the loss or emancipation of any slave; but all such debts, obligations and claims shall be held illegal and void.

Section 5. The Congress shall have the power to enforce, by appropriate legislation, the provisions of this article.

AMENDMENT XV

Section 1. The right of citizens of the United States to vote shall not be denied or abridged by the United States or by any State on account of race, color, or previous condition of servitude—

Section 2. The Congress shall have the power to enforce this article by appropriate legislation.

AMENDMENT XVI

The Congress shall have power to lay and collect taxes on incomes, from whatever source derived, without apportionment among the several States, and without regard to any census or enumeration.

AMENDMENT XVII

The Senate of the United States shall be composed of two Senators from each State, elected by the people thereof, for six years; and each Senator shall have one vote. The electors in each State shall have the qualifications requisite for electors of the most numerous branch of the State legislatures.

When vacancies happen in the representation of any State in the Senate, the executive authority of such State shall issue writs of election to fill such vacancies:

Provided, That the legislature of any State may empower the executive thereof to make temporary appointments until the people fill the vacancies by election as the legislature may direct.

This amendment shall not be so construed as to affect the election or term of any Senator chosen before it becomes valid as part of the Constitution.

AMENDMENT XVIII

Section 1. After one year from the ratification of this article the manufacture, sale, or transportation of intoxicating liquors within, the importation thereof into, or the exportation thereof from the United States and all territory subject to the jurisdiction thereof for beverage purposes is hereby prohibited.

Section 2. The Congress and the several States shall have concurrent power to enforce this article by appropriate legislation.

Section 3. This article shall be inoperative unless it shall have been ratified as an amendment to the Constitution by the legislatures of the several States, as provided in the Constitution, within seven years from the date of the submission hereof to the States by the Congress.

AMENDMENT XIX

The right of citizens of the United States to vote shall not be denied or abridged by the United States or by any State on account of sex.

Congress shall have power to enforce this article by appropriate legislation.

AMENDMENT XX

Section 1. The terms of the President and the Vice President shall end at noon on the 20th day of January, and the terms of Senators and Representatives at noon on the 3d day of January, of the years in which such terms would have ended if this article had not been ratified; and the terms of their successors shall then begin.

Section 2. The Congress shall assemble at least once in every year, and such meeting shall begin at noon on the 3d day of January, unless they shall by law appoint a different day.

Section 3. If, at the time fixed for the beginning of the term of the President, the President elect shall have died, the Vice President elect shall become President. If a President shall not have been chosen before the time fixed for the beginning of his term, or if the President elect shall have failed to qualify, then the Vice President elect shall act as President until a President shall have qualified; and the Congress may by law provide for the case wherein neither a President elect nor a Vice President shall have qualified, declaring who shall then act as President, or the manner in which one who is to act shall be selected, and such person shall act accordingly until a President or Vice President shall have qualified.

Section 4. The Congress may by law provide for the case of the death of any of the persons from whom the House of Representatives may choose a President whenever the right of choice shall have devolved upon them, and for the case of the death of any of the persons from whom the Senate may choose a Vice President whenever the right of choice shall have devolved upon them.

Section 5. Sections 1 and 2 shall take effect on the 15th day of October following the ratification of this article.

Section 6. This article shall be inoperative unless it shall have been ratified as an amendment to the Constitution by the legislatures of three-fourths of the several States within seven years from the date of its submission.

AMENDMENT XXI

Section 1. The eighteenth article of amendment to the Constitution of the United States is hereby repealed.

Section 2. The transportation or importation into any State, Territory, or Possession of the United States for delivery or use therein of intoxicating liquors, in violation of the laws thereof, is hereby prohibited.

Section 3. This article shall be inoperative unless it shall have been ratified as an amendment to the Constitution by conventions in the several States, as provided in the Constitution, within seven years from the date of the submission hereof to the States by the Congress.

AMENDMENT XXII

Section 1. No person shall be elected to the office of the President more than twice, and no person who has held the office of President, or acted as President, for more than two years of a term to which some other person was elected President shall be elected to the office of President more than once. But this Article shall not apply to any person holding the office of President when this Article was proposed by Congress, and shall not prevent any person who may be holding the office of President, or acting as President, during the term within which this Article becomes operative from holding the office of President or acting as President during the remainder of such term.

Section 2. This article shall be inoperative unless it shall have been ratified as an amendment to the Constitution by the legislatures of three-fourths of the several States within seven years from the date of its submission to the States by the Congress.

AMENDMENT XXIII

Section 1. The District constituting the seat of Government of the United States shall appoint in such manner as Congress may direct:

A number of electors of President and Vice President equal to the whole number of Senators and Representatives in Congress to which the District would be entitled if it were a State, but in no event more than the least populous State; they shall be in addition to those appointed by the States, but they shall be considered, for the purposes of the election of President and Vice President, to be electors appointed by a State; and they shall meet in the District and perform such duties as provided by the twelfth article of amendment.

Section 2. The Congress shall have power to enforce this article by appropriate legislation.

AMENDMENT XXIV

Section 1. The right of citizens of the United States to vote in any primary or other election for President or Vice President, for electors for President or Vice President, or for Senator or Representative in Congress, shall not be denied or abridged by the United States or any State by reason of failure to pay poll tax or other tax.

Section 2. The Congress shall have power to enforce this article by appropriate legislation.

AMENDMENT XXV

Section 1. In case of the removal of the President from office or of his death or resignation, the Vice President shall become President.

Section 2. Whenever there is a vacancy in the office of the Vice President, the President shall nominate a Vice President who shall take office upon confirmation by a majority vote of both Houses of Congress.

Section 3. Whenever the President transmits to the President pro tempore of the Senate and the Speaker of the House of Representatives his written declaration that he is unable to discharge the powers and duties of his office, and until he transmits to them a written declaration to the contrary, such powers and duties shall be discharged by the Vice President as Acting President.

Section 4. Whenever the Vice President and a majority of either the principal officers of the executive departments or of such other body as Congress may by law provide, transmit to the President pro tempore of the Senate and the Speaker of the House of Representatives their written declaration that the President is unable to discharge the powers and duties of his office, the Vice President shall immediately assume the powers and duties of the office as Acting President.

Thereafter, when the President transmits to the President pro tempore of the Senate and the Speaker of the House of Representatives his written declaration that no inability exists, he shall resume the powers and duties of his office unless the Vice President and a majority of either the principal officers of the executive department or of such other body as Congress may by law provide, transmit within four days to the President pro tempore of the Senate and the Speaker of the House of Representatives their written declaration that the President is unable to discharge the powers and duties of his office. Thereupon Congress shall decide the issue, assembling within forty-eight hours for that purpose if not in session. If the Congress, within twenty-one days after receipt of the latter written declaration, or, if Congress is not in session, within twenty-one days after Congress is required to assemble, determines by two-thirds vote of both Houses that the President is unable to discharge the powers and duties of his office, the Vice President shall continue to discharge the same as Acting President; otherwise, the President shall resume the powers and duties of his office.

AMENDMENT XXVI

Section 1. The right of citizens of the United States, who are eighteen years of age or older, to vote shall not be denied or abridged by the United States or by any State on account of age.

Section 2. The Congress shall have power to enforce this article by appropriate legislation.

AMENDMENT XXVII

No law, varying the compensation for the services of the Senators and Representatives, shall take effect, until an election of representatives shall have intervened.

Internet Resources

Courts—Alternative Dispute Resolution—Government

U.S. Courts	www.uscourts.gov
U.S. Tax Court	www.ustaxcourt.gov/ustcweb.htm
U.S. Court of Federal Claims	www.uscfc.uscourts.gov/
U.S. Court of International Trade	www.uscit.gov/
U.S Court for the Federal Circuit	www.fedcir.gov/
U.S. Supreme Court	www.supremecourtus.gov
National Mediation Board	www.nmb.gov
American Arbitration Association	www.adr.org
Pacer System	http://pacer.psc.uscourts.gov/
U.S. Court of Appeals	www.uscourts.gov/courtsofappeals.html
Internal Revenue Service	www.irs.gov
Government Printing Office	www.gpo.gov/
Code of Federal Regulations	www.access.gpo.gov/nara/cfr/index.html

Legal Research

VersusLaw	www.versuslaw.com/
Lexis	www.lexisnexis.com/
Westlaw	www.westlaw.com/
Library of Congress	www.loc.gov
Loislaw	www.loislaw.com
Cornell University LII	www.law.cornell.edu/citation
ALWD Manual	www.alwd.org

Legal Organizations

American Bar Association	www.abanet.org
National Federation of Paralegal Associations, Inc.	www.paralegals.org
National Association of Legal Assistants	www.nala.org
American Association of Legal Administrators	www.alanet.org/home.html
American Association for Paralegal Education	www.aafpe.org
ABA Standing Committee on Legal Assistants	www.abanet.org/legalassts
Legal Nurse Consultants	www.aalnc.org

State Bar Associations

Alabama	www.alabar.org
Alaska	www.alaskabar.org
Arizona	www.azbar.org.org
Arkansas	www.arkbar.org
California	www.calbar.org
Colorado	www.cobar.org
Connecticut	www.ctbar.org
Delaware	www.dsba.org
District of Columbia	www.dcbar.org
Florida	www.flabar.org
Georgia	www.gabar.org
Hawaii	www.hsba.org
Idaho	www2.state.id.us/isb/
Illinois	www.isba.org
Indiana	www.inbar.org
Iowa	www.iowabar.org
Kansas	www.ksbar.org
Kentucky	www.kybar.org
Louisiana	www.lsba.org
Maine	www.maine.org
Maryland	www.msba.org
Massachusetts	www.massbar.org
Michigan	www.michbar.org
Minnesota	www.mnbar.org
Mississippi	www.msbar.org
Missouri	www.mobar.org
Montana	www.montanabar.org
Nebraska	www.nebar.org
Nevada	www.nvbar.org
New Hampshire	www.nhbar.org
New Jersey	www.njsba.com
New Mexico	www.nmbar.org
New York	www.nysba.org
North Carolina	www.ncbar.com
North Dakota	www.sband.org
Ohio	www.ohiobar.org
Oklahoma	www.okbar.org
Oregon	www.osbar.org
Pennsylvania	www.pa-bar.org
Rhode Island	www.ribar.com
South Carolina	www.scbar.org

South Dakota	www.sdbar.org
Tennessee	www.tba.org
Texas	www.texasbar.com
Utah	www.utahbar.org
Vermont	www.vtbar.org
Virginia	www.vsb.org
Washington	www.wsba.org
West Virginia	www.wvbar.org
Wisconsin	www.wisbar.org
Wyoming	www.wyomingbar.org

Other

Religious calendar	www.interfaithcalendar.org/
AOL	www.aol.com
Compuserve	www.compuserve.com
The Affiliate	www.futurelawoffice.com/practice.html
Adobe Systems	www.adobe.com
Mapquest	www.mapquest.com

Internet Search Engines

AltaVista	www.altavista.com
Ask Jeeves	www.askjeeves.com
Dogpile	www.dogpile.com
Excite	www.excite.com
Google	www.google.com
Metacrawler	www.metacrawler.com
Netscape	www.netscape.com
Yahoo!	www.yahoo.com
Findlaw	www.findlaw.com

Glossary of Spanish Equivalents for Important Legal Terms

A

a priori   Desde antes, del pasado.

AAA   Siglas para **American Arbitration Association** Asociación de Arbitraje.

ABA   Siglas para **American Bar Association** Colegio de Abogados Estadounidenses.

accept   Aceptar, admitir, aprobar, recibir reconocer.

accession   Accesión, admisión, aumento, incremento.

accord   Acuerdo, convenio, arreglo, acordar, conceder.

acquittal   Absolución, descargo, veredicto de no culpable.

act   Acto, estatuto, decreto, actuar, funcionar.

actionable   Justiciable, punible, procesable.

adjourn   Levantar, posponer, suspender la sesión.

adjudicate   Adjudicar, decidir, dar fallo a favor de, sentenciar, declarar.

administrative   Administrativo, ejecutivo.

administrative agency   Agencia administrativa.

administrative hearing   Juicio administrativo.

administrative law   Derecho administrativo.

administrative law judge   Juez de derecho, Administrativo.

administrator   Administrador.

admit   Admitir, conceder, reconocer, permitir entrada, confesar, asentir.

adverse   Adverso, contrario, opuesto.

adverse possession   Posesión adversa.

advice   Consejo, asesoramiento, notificación.

affected class   Clase afectada, grupo iscriminado.

affidavit   Declaración voluntaria, escrita y bajo uramento, afidávit, atestiguación, testificata.

affirmative action   Acción positiva.

affirmative defense   Defensa justificativa.

after acquired property   Propiedad adquirida con garantía adicional.

against   En contra.

agency   Agencia, oficina, intervención.

agent   Agente, representante autorizado.

aggrieved party   Parte dañada, agraviada, perjudicada.

agreement   Acuerdo, arreglo, contrato, convenio, pacto.

alibi   Coartada.

alien   Extranjero, extraño, foráneo.

annul   Anular, cancelar, invalidar, revocar, dejar sin efecto.

answer   Contestación, réplica, respuesta, alegato.

antecedent   Antecedente, previo, preexistente.

appeal   Apelar, apelación.

appear   Aparecer, comparecer.

appellate court   Tribunal de apelaciones.

appellate jurisdiction   Competencia de apelación.

applicable   Aplicable, apropiado, pertinente a, lo que puede ser aplicado.

arraign   Denunciar, acusar, procesar, instruir de cargos hechos.

arrears   Retrasos, pagos atrasados, decursas.

arrest   Arresto, arrestar, aprehensión, aprehender, detener.

arson   Incendio intencional.

articles of incorporation   Carta de organización corporativa.

assault   Agresión, asalto, ataque, violencia carnal, agredir, atacar, acometer.

assault and battery   Amenazas y agresión, asalto.

assign   Asignar, ceder, designar, hacer cesión, traspasar, persona asignada un derecho.

attachment   Secuestro judicial.

attorney   Abogado, consejero, apoderado.

award   Fallo, juicio, laudo, premio.

B

bail   Caución, fianza.

bail bondsman   Fiador, fiador judicial.

bailee   Depositario de bienes.

bailment   Depósito, encargo, depósito mercantil, depósito comercial.

bailment   For hire, depósito oneroso.

bailor   Fiador.

bankruptcy   Bancarrota, quiebra, insolvencia.

battery   Agravio, agresión.

bearer bond   Título mobiliario.

bearer instrument   Título al portador.

bench   Tribunal, los jueces, la magistratura.

beneficiary   Beneficiario, legatario.

bequeath   Legar.

bilateral contract   Contrato bilateral.

bill of lading   Póliza de embarque, boleto de carga, documento de tránsito.

bill of rights   Las primeras diez enmiendas a la Constitución de los Estados Unidos de América.

binder   Resguardo provisional, recibo para garantizar el precio de un bien inmueble.

birth certificate   Acta de nacimiento, partida de nacimiento, certificado de nacimiento.

blue sky laws   Estatutos para prevenir el fraude en la compraventa de valores.

bond   Bono, título, obligación, deuda inversionista, fianza.

booking   Término dado en el cuartel de policía al registro de arresto y los cargos hechos al arrestado.

breach of contract   Violación, rotura, incumplimiento de contrato.

brief   Alegato, escrito memorial.

burglary   Escalamiento, allanamiento de morada.

buyer   Comprador.

bylaws   Estatutos sociales, reglamentos internos.

C

capacity to contract   Capacidad contractual.

case   Causa, caso, acción legal, proceso, proceso civil, asunto, expediente.

case law   Jurisprudencia.

cashier's check   Cheque bancario.

cease and desist order   Orden judicial de cese.

censure   Censura.

certificate of deposit   Certificado de depósito.

certified check   Cheque certificado.

certify   Certificar, atestiguar.

charge   Cobrar, acusar, imputar.

charitable trust   Fideicomiso caritativo.

chattel   Bienes muebles, bártulos.

cheat   Fraude, engaño, defraudador, trampa, tramposo, estafar.

check   Cheque, talón, comprobación.

cite   Citación, citar, referir, emplazar.

citizenship   Ciudadanía.

civil action   Acción, enjuiciamiento civil, demanda.

civil law   Derecho civil.

Claims Court   Tribunal federal de reclamaciones.

client   Cliente.

closing arguments   Alegatos de clausura.

closing costs   Gastos ocasionados en la venta de bienes raíces.

clue   Pista, indicio.

codicil   Codicilo.

coercion   Coerción, coacción.

collateral   Colateral, auxiliar, subsidiario, seguridad colateral, garantía prendaria.

collect   Cobrar, recobrar, recaudar.

collision   Choque, colisión.

common law   Derecho consuetudinario.

comparative negligence   Negligencia comparativa.

compensatory damages   Indemnización compensatoria por daños y perjuicios, daños compensatorios.

competency   Competencia, capacidad legal.

concurrent conditions   Condiciones concurrentes.

concurrent jurisdiction   Jurisdicción simultanea, conocimiento acumulativo.

concurrent sentences   Sentencias que se cumplen simultáneamente.

concurring opinion   Opinión coincidente.

condemn   Condenar, confiscar, expropiar.

condition precedent   Condición precedente.

condition subsequent   Condición subsecuente.

confession   Confesión, admisión.

confidential   Confidencial, íntimo, secreto.

confiscation   Confiscación, comiso, decomiso.

consent decree   Decreto por acuerdo mutuo.

consequential damages   Daños especiales.

consideration   Contraprestación.

consolidation   Consolidación, unión, concentración.

constructive delivery   Presunta entrega.

contempt of court   Desacato, contumacia o menosprecio a la corte.

contract   Contrato, convenio, acuerdo, pacto.

contributory negligence   Negligencia contribuyente.

conversion   Conversión, canje.

conviction   Convicción, fallo de culpabilidad, convencimiento, sentencia condenatoria, condena.

copyright   Derecho de autor, propiedad literaria, propiedad intelectual, derecho de impresión.

corroborate   Corroborar, confirmar.

counterclaim Contrademanda, excepción de compensación.

counteroffer Contra oferta.

courts Cortes o tribunales establecidas por la constitución.

covenant for quiet enjoyment Convenio de disfrute y posesión pacífica.

creditor Acreedor.

crime Crimen, delito.

criminal act Acto criminal.

criminal law Derecho penal.

cross examination Contrainterrogatorio, repregunta.

cure Curar, corregir.

D

damages Daños y perjuicios, indemnización pecuniaria.

DBA Sigla para **doing business as** En negociación comercial.

deadly force Fuerza mortífera.

debt Deuda, débito.

debtor Deudor.

decision Decisión judicial, fallo, determinación auto, sentencia.

deed Escritura, título de propiedad, escritura de traspaso.

defamation Difamación, infamación.

default Incumplir, faltar, no comparecer, incumplimiento.

defendant Demandado, reo, procesado, acusado.

delinquent Delincuente, atrasado en pagos, delictuoso.

denial Denegación, negación, denegatoria.

deponent Deponente, declarante.

deportation Deportación, destierro.

deposition Deposición, declaración bajo juramento.

detain Detener, retardar, retrasar.

devise Legado de bienes raíces.

direct examination Interrogatorio directo, interrogatorio a testigo propio.

directed verdict Veredicto expedido por el juez, veredicto por falta de pruebas.

disaffirm Negar, rechazar, repudiar, anular.

discharge Descargo, cumplimiento, liberación.

disclose Revelar.

discovery Revelación de prueba, exposición reveladora.

discriminate Discriminar.

dismiss Despedir, desechar, desestimar.

dissenting opinion Opinión en desacuerdo.

dissolution Disolución, liquidación.

diversity of citizenship Diversidad de ciudadanías, ciudadanías diferentes.

dividend Acción librada, dividendo.

divorce Divorcio, divorciar.

docket Orden del día, lista de casos en la corte.

double jeopardy Non bis in idem.

driving under the influence Manejar bajo los efectos de bebidas alcohólicas o drogas.

duress Coacción.

E

earnest money Arras, señal.

easement Servidumbre.

edict Edicto, decreto, auto.

embezzlement Malversación de fondos.

eminent domain Dominio eminente.

encroachment Intrusión, usurpación, invasión, uso indebido.

encumbrance Gravamen, afectación, cargo.

enforce Hacer cumplir, dar valor, poner en efecto.

entitlement Derecho, título.

equal protection clause Cláusula de protección de igualdad ante la ley.

equal protection of the law Igualdad ante la ley.

equity Equidad. Derecho equitativo.

escheat Reversión al estado al no haber herederos.

estate Bienes, propiedad, caudal hereditario, cuerpo de la herencia, caudal, derecho, título, interés sobre propiedad.

estop Impedir, detener, prevenir.

ethics Sistema ético.

eviction Evicción, desalojo, desalojamiento, desahucio, lanzamiento.

evidence Testimonio, prueba, pruebas documentales, pieza de prueba.

examination Examen, reconocimiento, interrogatorio.

executed contract Contrato firmado, contrato ejecutado.

execution Ejecución, desempeño, cumplimiento.

executory contract Contrato por cumplirse.

executory interests Intereses futuros.

exempt Franquear, exentar, exencionar, eximir, libre, franco, exento, inmune.

exoneration Exoneración, descargo, liberación.

expert witness Testigo perito.

express contract Contrato explícito.

expropriation Expropiación, confiscación.

eyewitness Testigo ocular o presencial.

F

fact Hecho falsificado.

failure to appear Incomparecencia.

fault Falta, defecto, culpa, negligencia.

fee Honorarios, retribución, cuota, cargo, derecho, dominio, asesoría, propiedad, bienes raíces.

fee simple estate Propiedad en dominio pleno.

felon Felón, autor de un delito.

felony Delito mayor o grave.

fiduciary Fiduciario.

find against Fallar o decidir en contra.

find for Fallar o decidir a favor.

finding Determinación de los hechos.

fine Multa, castigo.

fixture Accesorio fijo.

foreclose Entablar juicio hipotecario, embargar bienes hipotecados.

forgery Falsificación.

franchise Franquicia, privilegio, patente, concesión social, derecho de votar.

fraud Fraude, engaño, estafa, trampa, embuste, defraudación.

full disclosure Revelación completa.

G

garnishment Embargo de bienes.

gift Regalo, dádiva, donación.

gift causa mortis Donación de propiedad en expectativa de muerte.

gift inter vivos Donación entre vivos.

gift tax Impuesto sobre donaciones.

good and valid consideration Causa contractual válida.

good faith Buena fe.

goods Mercaderías, bienes, productos.

grace period Período de espera.

grantee Concesionario, cesionario.

grantor Otorgante, cesionista.

grievance Agravio, injuria, ofensa, queja formal.

gross negligence Negligencia temeraria, negligencia grave.

H

habitation Habitación, lugar donde se vive.

harassment Hostigamiento.

hearing Audiencia, vista, juicio.

hearsay Testimonio de oídas.

holder Tenedor, poseedor.

holding Decisión, opinión, tenencia posesión, asociación, grupo industrial.

holographic will Testamento hológrafo.

homeowner Propietario, dueño de casa.

homestead Casa, solariega, hogar, heredad, excepción de embargo, bien de familia.

hung jury Jurado sin veredicto.

I

identify Identificar, verificar, autenticar.

illegal Ilegal, ilícito, ilegítimo.

illegal entry Entrada ilegal.

illegal search Registro domiciliario, allanamiento ilegal, cacheo ilegal.

immunity Inmunidad, exención.

implied warranty Garantía implícita.

impossibility of performance Imposibilidad de cumplimiento.

impound Embargar, incautar, confiscar, secuestrar.

inadmissible Inadmisible, inaceptable.

income Ingreso, ganancia, entrada, renta, rédito.

incriminate Incriminar, acriminar.

indictment Procesamiento, acusación por jurado acusatorio, inculpatoria.

indorsement Endose, endoso, respaldo, garantía.

informant Informador, denunciante, delator.

information Información, informe, acusación por el fiscal, denuncia.

informed consent Conformidad por información.

inherit Heredar, recibir por herencia.

injunction Mandato judicial, amparo, prohibición judicial, interdicto.

innocent Inocente, no culpable.

inquiry Indagatoria judicial, pesquisa.

insufficient evidence Prueba insuficiente.

interrogation Interrogación.

interstate commerce Comercio interestatal.

intestate Intestado, intestar, sin testamento.

intestate succession Sucesión hereditaria.

investigation Investigación, indagación, encuesta.

issue Emisión, cuestión, punto, edición, número, tirada, sucesión, descendencia, resultado, decisión.

J

jail Cárcel, calabozo, encarcelar.

joint tenancy Condominio.

judge Magistrado, juez, juzgar, adjudicar, enjuiciar, fallar.

judgment Sentencia, fallo, juicio, decisión, dictamen, criterio.

judicial proceeding Proceso o diligencia judicial.

judicial review Revisión judicial.

jump bail Fugarse bajo fianza.

jurisdiction Jurisdicción, fuero competencia.

jury Jurado

L

landlord Arrendatario, propietario.

larceny Hurto, latrocinio, ladronicio.

law Ley, derecho.

lease Contrato de arrendamiento, arrendamiento, arriendo, contrato de locación, arrendar, alquilar.

leasehold estate Bienes forales.

legatee Legatario, asignatario.

lender   Prestamista.

lessee   Arrendatario, locatario, inquilino.

lessor   Arrendatario, arrendador, arrendante, locador.

letter of credit   Letra de crédito.

liability   Responsiva, responsabilidad.

libel   Libelo por difamación por escrito.

license   Licencia, permiso, privilegio, matrícula, patente, título, licenciar, permitir.

lien   Gravamen, derecho prendario o de retención, embargo preventivo.

life estate   Hipoteca legal, dominio vitalicio.

limited liability company   Sociedad de responsabilidad limitada.

limited partnership   Sociedad en comandita, sociedad comanditaria.

litigated   Pleiteado, litigado, sujeto a litigación.

M

majority opinion   Opinión que refleja la mayoría de los miembros de la corte de apelaciones.

maker   Otorgante, girador.

malice   Malicia, malignidad, maldad.

malpractice   Incompetencia profesional.

manslaughter   Homicidio sin premeditación.

material witness   Testigo esencial.

mechanics lien   Gravamen de construcción.

mediation   Mediación, tercería, intervención, interposición.

medical examiner   Médico examinador.

merger   Fusión, incorporación, unión, consolidación.

minor   Menor, insignificante, pequeño, trivial.

misdemeanor   Delito menor, fechoría.

mitigation of damages   Mitigación de daños, minoración, atenuación.

monetary damages   Daños pecuniarios.

mortgage   Hipoteca, gravamen, hipotecar, gravar.

motion to dismiss   Petición para declaración sin lugar.

motion to suppress   Moción para suprimir, reprimir o suspender.

motive   Motivo.

murder   Asesinato, asesinar, homicidio culposo.

N

naturalization   Naturalización.

negligence   Negligencia, descuido, imprudencia.

negotiable   Negociable.

negotiate   Negociar, agenciar, hacer efectivo, traspasar, tratar.

net assets   Haberes netos.

notice   Aviso, notificación, advertencia, conocimiento.

novation   Novación, delegación de crédito.

nuisance   Daño, molestia, perjuicio.

nuncupative will   Testamento abierto.

O

oath   Juramento.

objection   Objeción, oposición, disconformidad, recusación, impugnación, excepción, réplica, reclamación.

obstruction of justice   Encubrimiento activo.

offer   Oferta, ofrecimiento, propuesta, ofrecer, proponer.

omission   Omisión, falla, falta.

opinion   Opinión, dictamen, decisión de la corte.

oral argument   Alegato oral.

order instrument   Instrumento de pago a la orden.

owe   Deber, estar en deuda, adeudo.

owner   Dueño, propietario, poseedor.

P

pain and suffering   Angustia mental y dolor físico.

pardon   Perdón, indulto, absolución, indultar, perdonar.

parol evidence rule   Principio que prohíbe la modificación de un contrato por prueba verbal.

parole   Libertad vigilada.

partnership   Sociedad, compañía colectiva, aparcería, consorcio, sociedad personal.

patent   Patente, obvio, evidente, aparente, privilegio de invención, patentar.

penalty   Pena, multa, castigo, penalidad, condena.

pending   Pendiente, en trámite, pendiente de, hasta que.

per capita   Por cabeza.

performance   Cumplimiento, desempeño, ejecución, rendimiento.

perjury   Perjurio, testimonio falso, juramento falso.

personal property   Bienes personales, bienes mobiliarios.

plea bargain   Declaración de culpabilidad concertada.

plea of guilty   Alegación de culpabilidad.

pleadings   Alegatos, alegaciones, escritos.

pledge   Prenda, caución, empeño, empeñar, dar en prenda, pignorar.

police power   Poder policial.

policy   Póliza, escritura, práctica política.

possession   Posesión, tenencia, goce, disfrute.

possibility of reverter   Posibilidad de reversión.

power of attorney   Poder de representación, poder notarial, procura.

precedent   Precedente, decisión previa por el mismo tribunal.

preemptive right   Derecho de prioridad.

prejudicial   Dañoso, perjudicial.

preliminary hearing   Audiencia preliminar.

premeditation   Premeditación.

presume   Presumir, asumir como hecho basado en la experiencia, suponer.

prevail   Prevalecer, persuadir, predominar, ganar, triunfar.

price discrimination   Discriminación en el precio.

principal   Principal, jefe, de mayor importancia, valor actual.

privileged communication   Comunicación privilegiada.

privity   Coparticipación, intereses comunes.

procedural   Procesal.

proceeds   Ganancias.

profit   Ganancia, utilidad, lucro, beneficio.

prohibited   Prohibido.

promise   Promesa.

promissory estoppel   Impedimento promisorio.

promissory note   Pagaré, vale, nota de pago.

proof   Prueba, comprobación, demostración.

prosecutor   Fiscal, abogado público acusador.

proximate cause   Causa relacionada.

proxy   Poder, delegación, apoderado, mandatario.

punishment   Pena, castigo.

punitive damages   Indemnización punitiva por daños y perjuicios, daños ejemplares.

Q

qualification   Capacidad, calidad, preparación.

qualified indorsement   Endoso limitado endoso con reservas.

quasi contract   Cuasicontrato.

query   Pregunta, interrogación.

question of fact   Cuestión de hecho.

question of law   Cuestión de derecho.

quiet enjoyment   Uso y disfrute.

quitclaim deed   Escritura de traspaso de finiquito.

R

race discrimination   Discriminación racial.

rape   Estupro, violación, ultraje, rapto, violar.

ratification   Ratificación, aprobación, confirmación.

ratify   Aprobar, confirmar, ratificar, convalidar, adoptar.

real property   Bienes raíces, bienes inmuebles, arraigo.

reasonable doubt   Duda razonable.

rebut   Rebatir, refutar, negar, contradecir.

recognizance   Obligación impuesta judicialmente.

recordation   Inscripción oficial, grabación.

recover   Recobrar, recuperar, obtener como resultado de decreto.

redress   Reparación, compensación, desagravio, compensar, reparar, satisfacer, remediar.

regulatory agency   Agencia reguladora.

reimburse   Reembolsar, repagar, compensar, reintegrar.

rejoinder   Respuesta, réplica, contrarréplica.

release   Descargo, liberación, librar, relevar, descargar, libertar.

relevance   Relevancia.

remainder   Resto, restante, residuo, derecho expectativo a un bien raíz.

remedy   Remedio, recurso.

remuneration   Remuneración, compensación.

reply   Réplica, contestación, contestar, responder.

reprieve   Suspensión de la sentencia, suspensión, indulto, indultar, suspender.

reprimand   Reprender, regañar, reprimenda, reprensión.

repudiate   Repudiar, renunciar, rechazar.

rescission   Rescisión, abrogación, cancelación de un contrato.

respondeat superior   Responsabilidad civil al supervisor.

respondent   Apelado, demandado.

restitution   Restitución, devolución.

restraining order   Inhibitoria, interdicto, orden de amparo.

retain   Retener, emplear, guardar.

reversion   Reversión, derecho de sucesión.

revocation   Revocación, derogación, anulación.

reward   Premio.

right of first refusal   Retracto arrendaticio.

right of subrogation   Derecho de sustituir.

right of survivorship   Derecho de supervivencia entre dueños de propiedad mancomunada.

right to work laws   Leyes que prohíben la filiación sindical como requisito para poder desempeñar un puesto, derecho de trabajo.

rights   Derechos.

robbery   Robo, atraco.

ruling   Determinación oficial, auto judicial.

S

sale   Venta.

sale on approval   Venta por aprobación.

satisfaction   Satisfacción, liquidación, cumplimiento, pago, finiquito.

scope of authority   Autoridad explícitamente otorgada o implícitamente concedida.

search and seizure   Allanamiento, registro e incautación.

search warrant   Orden de registro o de allanamiento.

secured party   Persona con interés asegurado.

secured transaction   Transacción con un interés asegurado.

securities   Valores, títulos, obligaciones.

security agreement   Acuerdo que crea la garantía de un interés.

security deposit   Deposito de seguridad.

seize   Arrestar, confiscar, secuestrar, incautar.

settlement   Arreglo, composición, ajuste, liquidación, componenda, acomodo.

sex discrimination   Discriminación sexual.

sexual harassment   Acoso sexual.

shoplifting   Ratería en tiendas.

signature   Firma.

slander   Calumnia, difamación oral, calumniar.

source of income   Fuente de ingresos.

specific performance   Prestación específica contractual.

split decision   Decisión con opiniones mixtas.

spousal abuse Abuso conyugal.

stare decisis Vinculación con decisiones judiciales anteriores.

state of mind Estado de ánimo, estado mental.

statement Alegación, declaración, relato, estado de cuentas.

statutory foreclosure Ejecución hipotecaria estatutaria.

statutory law Derecho estatutario.

statutory rape Estupro, violación de un menor de edad.

steal Robar, hurtar, robo, hurto.

stock Acciones, capital, existencias, semental.

stock option Opción de comprar o vender acciones.

stop payment order Suspensión de pago.

strict liability Responsabilidad rigurosa.

sublease Subarriendo, sublocación, subarrendar.

subpoena Citación, citatorio, comparendo, cédula de citación, citación judicial, subpoena.

sue Demandar, procesar.

summary judgment Sentencia sumaria.

summon Convocar, llamar, citar.

suppress Suprimir, excluir pruebas ilegalmente obtenidas, reprimir, suspender.

surrender Rendir, entregar, entrega, rendirse, entregarse.

surviving spouse Cónyuge sobreviviente.

suspect Sospecha, sospechar, sospechoso.

T

tangible evidence Prueba real.

tangible property Propiedad tangible, bienes tangibles.

tenancy at sufferance Tenencia o posesión por tolerancia.

tenancy at will Tenencia o inquilinato sin plazo fijo.

tenancy by the entirety Tenencia conyugal.

tenancy for life Tenencia vitalicia.

tenancy for years Inquilinato por tiempo fijo.

tender Propuesta, oferta, presentar.

testator Testador.

testify Atestar, atestiguar, dar testimonio.

theft Hurto.

title Título, derecho de posesión, rango, denominación.

tort Agravio, torticero, entuerto, daño legal, perjuicio, acto ilícito civil.

Totten trust Fideicomiso bancario Totten.

trade name Nombre comercial, marca de fábrica, marca comercial.

trademark Marca registrada, marca industrial.

transgression Ofensa, delito, transgresión.

trespass Transgresión, violación de propiedad ajena, translimitación, traspasar, violar, infringir, transgredir.

trial court Tribunal de primera instancia.

trust Fideicomiso, confianza, confidencia, confianza, crédito, combinación, consorcio, grupo industrial.

truth Verdad, verdadero, veracidad.

try Probar, juzgar.

U

ultra vires Mas allá de la facultad de actuar.

unanimous verdict Veredicto unánime.

unbiased Imparcial, neutral.

unconditional pardon Perdón, amnistía, indulto incondicional.

unconscionable Reprochable, repugnante, desmedido.

under arrest Arrestado, bajo arresto.

underwrite Subscribir, asegurar, firmar.

undisclosed Escondido, no revelado.

undue influence Influencia indebida, coacción, abuso de poder.

unenforceable Inejecutable.

unilateral contract Contrato unilateral.

unlawful Ilegal, ilícito, ilegítimo.

unsound mind Privado de razón, de mente inestable.

usury Usura, agiotaje, logrería.

V

vagrancy Vagancia, vagabundeo.

validity Validez, vigencia.

valuable consideration Causa contractual con cierto valor, causa contractual onerosa.

venue Partido judicial.

verbal contract Contrato verbal.

verbatim Al pié de la letra.

verdict Veredicto, fallo, sentencia, decisión.

victim Víctima.

voidable Anulable, cancelable.

W

wage Salario, jornal, sueldo.

waive Renunciar, ceder, suspender, abdicar.

waiver Renunciar, desistir, ceder, suspender, abdicar, renuncia.

warrant Autorización, resguardo, comprobante, certificado, justificación, decisión judicial.

warranty Garantía, seguridad.

warranty of habitability Garantía de habitabilidad.

welfare Asistencia pública.

will Testamento, voluntad.

willful misconduct Mala conducta intencional.

withhold Retener, detener.

witness Testigo, declarante, atestar, testificar, atestiguar.

writ of attachment Mandamiento de embargo.

writ of certiorari Pedimento de avocación.

writ of execution Auto de ejecución, ejecutoria.

Glossary

ABA Model Rules of Professional Conduct   A recommended set of ethics and professional conduct guidelines for lawyers, prepared by American Bar Association, originally released in 1983; prior release was Model Code of Professional Conduct.

Abandoned property   Property that an owner has discarded with the intent to relinquish his or her rights in it; mislaid or lost property that the owner has given up any further attempts to locate.

Abatement   If the property the testator leaves is not sufficient to satisfy all the beneficiaries named in a will and there are both general and residuary bequests, the residuary bequest is abated first (i.e., paid last).

Acceptance   A manifestation of assent by the offeree to the terms of the offer in a manner invited or required by the offer as measured by the objective theory of contracts.

Actus reus   "Guilty act"—the actual performance of the criminal act.

Ademption   A principle that says if a testator leaves a specific devise of property to a beneficiary, but the property is no longer in the estate when the testator dies, the beneficiary receives nothing.

Administrative agencies   Agencies that the legislative and executive branches of federal and state governments establish.

Administrative law   Substantive and procedural law that governs the operation of administrative agencies.

Administrative law judge (ALJ)   A judge who presides over an administrative proceeding and who decides the questions of law and fact that arise in the proceeding.

Administrative Procedure Act (APA)   An act that establishes certain administrative procedures that federal administrative agencies must follow in conducting their affairs.

Admitted   A possible response of the defendant to the complaint which accepts the facts of the averment are true.

Adoption   A situation in which a person becomes the legal parent of a child who is not his or her biological child.

Adverse possession   A situation in which a person who wrongfully possesses someone else's real property obtains title to that property if certain statutory requirements are met.

Affirm   The appellate court agrees with the outcome of trial and can find no reversible error and the decision of the trial court stands.

Age Discrimination in Employment Act (ADEA)   A federal statute that prohibits age discrimination practices against employees who are age 40 and older.

Agency   A principal–agent relationship; the fiduciary relationship "which results from the manifestation of consent by one person to another that the other shall act in his

behalf and subject to his control, and consent by the other so to act."

Agency adoption   An adoption that occurs when a person adopts a child from a social service organization of a state.

Agency by ratification   An agency that occurs when (1) a person misrepresents himself or herself as another's agent when in fact he or she is not and (2) the purported principal ratifies the unauthorized act.

Agent   A party who agrees to act on behalf of another.

Agreement   The manifestation by two or more persons of the substance of a contract.

Aiding and abetting the commission of a crime   Rendering support, assistance, or encouragement to the commission of a crime; harboring a criminal after he or she has committed a crime.

Alien corporation   A corporation that is encorporated in another country.

ALS (Acredited Legal Secretary)   The basic certification for legal professionals from NALS.

Alternative dispute resolution (ADR)   Methods of resolving disputes other than litigation.

American Arbitration Association (AAA)   A private nonprofit organization providing lists of potential arbitrators for the parties to select from and a set of rules for conducting the private arbitration.

American Association for Paralegal Education (AAfPE)   National organization of paralegal educators and institutions offering paralegal education programs.

American Bar Association (ABA)   Largest professional legal organization in the United States.

American Inventors Protection Act   A federal statute that permits an inventor to file a *provisional application* with the U.S. Patent and Trademark Office (PTO) three months before the filing of a final patent application, among other provisions.

Americans with Disabilities Act (ADA)   A federal statute that imposes obligations on employers and providers of public transportation, telecommunications, and public accommodations to accommodate individuals with disabilities.

Amicus curia   Briefs submitted by interested parties who do not have standing in the action as a "friend of the court."

Annulment   An order of the court declaring that a marriage did not exist.

Answer   Document by which the defendant responds to the allegations contained in the plaintiff's complaint.

Antenuptial agreement   A contract entered into after marriage to specify how property will be distributed upon termination of the marriage.

Apparent agency   Agency that arises when a principal creates the appearance of an agency that in actuality does not exist.

Appeal   The act of asking an appellate court to overturn a decision after the trial court's final judgment has been entered.

Appellant   The appealing party in an appeal. Also known as *petitioner*.

Appellate courts   Courts which review the record from the trial court to determine if the trial judge made an error in applying the procedural or substantive law.

Appellee   The responding party in an appeal. Also known as *respondent*.

Applications software   Applications programs are software that perform generic tasks such as word processing.

Arbitration   A form of ADR in which the parties choose an impartial third party to hear and decide the dispute.

Arbitration clause   A clause in contracts that requires disputes arising out of the contract to be submitted to arbitration. A clause contained in many international contracts that stipulates that any dispute between the parties concerning the performance of the contract will be submitted to an arbitrator or arbitration panel for resolution.

Arraignment   A hearing during which the accused is brought before a court and is (1) informed of the charges against him or her and (2) asked to enter a plea.

Arrest warrant   A document for a person's detainment based upon a showing of probable cause that the person committed the crime.

Arson   Willfully or maliciously burning another's building.

Article 2 (Sales) of the Uniform Commercial Code (UCC)   An article of the UCC that governs the sale of goods.

Article 2A (Leases) of the Uniform Commercial Code (UCC)   An article of the UCC that governs the lease of goods.

Articles of incorporation   The basic governing document of the corporation. This document must be filed with the secretary of state of the state of incorporation.

Articles of limited liability partnership   A public document that must be filed with the secretary of state to form a limited liability partnership.

Articles of organization   The formal document that must be filed with the secretary of state to form an LLC.

Assault   The threat of immediate harm or offensive contact or (2) any action that arouses reasonable apprehension of imminent harm. Actual physical contact is unnecessary.

Associate's degree   A college degree in science (AS) arts (AA), or applied arts (AAS), generally requiring two years of full-time study.

Association of Legal Writing Directors (ALWD)   A society for professors who coordinate legal writing instruction.

Assumption of the risk   A defense a defendant can use against a plaintiff who knowingly and voluntarily enters into or participates in a risky activity that results in injury.

Attachment   A popular method of transmitting text files and graphic images by attaching the file to an email.

Attempt to commit a crime   When a crime is attempted but not completed.

Attestation   The action of a will being witnessed by the required number of competent people.

Attestation clause   Section of a will where witnesses sign to acknowledge testation of the will.

Attorney–client privilege   A client's right to have anything told to a lawyer while seeking legal advice, kept confidential in most instances.

Automatic stay   The result of the filing of a voluntary or involuntary petition; the suspension of certain actions by creditors against the debtor or the debtor's property.

Bachelor's degree   A college degree generally requiring four years of full-time study.

Backup of data   Making a copy of critical files and programs in case of a loss of the original computer files.

Bailee   A holder of goods who is not a seller or a buyer (e.g., a warehouse or common carrier).

Bailment   A transaction in which an owner transfers his or her personal property to another to be held, stored, delivered, or for some other purpose. Title to the property does not transfer.

Bailor   The owner of property in a bailment.

Bankruptcy Abuse Prevention and Consumer Protection Act of 2005   A federal act that substantially amended federal bankruptcy law. It makes it more difficult for debtors to file for bankruptcy and have their unpaid debts discharged.

Bankruptcy courts   Special federal courts that hear and decide bankruptcy cases.

Bankruptcy estate   A debtor's property and earnings that comprise the estate of a bankruptcy proceeding.

Battery   Unauthorized and harmful or offensive physical contact with another person. Direct physical contact is not necessary.

Bench opinions   The initial version of a decision issued from the bench of the court.

Beneficiary   A person or organization designated in the will that receives all or a portion of the testator's property at the time of the testator's death.

Bequest   A gift of personal property by will. Also known as a legacy.

Best interests of the child   A legal doctrine used by the court to decide what is best for the child.

Bicameral   In the American system a legislature of a house of representatives and a senate.

Bill of Rights   The first 10 amendments to the Constitution. They were added to the U.S. Constitution in 1791.

Board of directors   A panel of decision makers, the members of which are elected by a corporation's shareholders.

Bona fide occupational qualification (BFOQ)   Lawful employment discrimination that is based on a protected class (other than race or color) and is *job-related* and a *business necessity*. This exception is narrowly interpreted by the courts.

Breach of contract   A contracting party's failure to perform an absolute duty owed under a contract.

Breach of duty of care   Failure to exercise care or to act as a reasonable person would act.

Bribery   A crime in which one person gives another person money, property, favors, or anything else of value for a favor in return. Often referred to as a payoff or *kickback*.

Briefs   Documents submitted by the parties' attorneys to the judge that contain legal support for their side of the case.

Building   A structure constructed on land.

Burden of proof   The level of proof required to establish an entitlement to recovery.

Burglary   The taking of personal property from another's home, office, or commercial or other type of building.

Business judgment rule   A rule stating that directors and officers are not liable to the corporation or its shareholders for honest mistakes of judgment.

Bylaws   A detailed set of rules adopted by the board of directors after the corporation is incorporated that contains provisions for managing the business and the affairs of the corporation.

Candor   A duty of honesty to the court.

Case and litigation management software   Case and litigation management programs are used to manage documents and the facts and issues of cases.

Case syllabus   In a court opinion a headnote for the convenience of the reader.

Causation   The two types of causation that must be proven are (1) causation in fact (actual cause) and (2) proximate cause (legal cause)

Causation in fact or **actual cause**   The actual cause of negligence. A person who commits a negligent act is not liable unless causation in fact can be proven.

Central processing unit (CPU)   The computer chip and memory module that perform the basic computer functions.

Certificate   A recognition of the completion of a program of study that requires less than that needed for a degree.

Certificate of limited partnership   A document that two or more persons must execute and sign that makes the limited partnership legal and binding.

Certified Legal Assistant (CLA)   Designation by National Association of Legal Assistants for those who take and pass NALA certification program two-day comprehensive examination.

Chain of distribution   All manufacturers, distributors, wholesalers, retailers, lessors, and subcomponent manufacturers involved in a transaction.

Chapter 7 discharge   The termination of the legal duty of a debtor to pay unsecured debts that remain unpaid upon the completion of a Chapter 7 proceeding.

Chapter 7 liquidation   A form of bankruptcy in which the debtor's nonexempt property is sold for cash, the cash is distributed to the creditors, and any unpaid debts are discharged.

Chapter 11 reorganization   A bankruptcy method that allows the reorganization of the debtor's financial affairs under the supervision of the bankruptcy court.

Chapter 12 adjustment of debts of a family farmer or family fisherman with regular income   A form of bankruptcy reorganization permitted to be used by family farmers and family fishermen.

Chapter 12 discharge   A discharge in a Chapter 12 case that is granted to a family farmer or family fisherman debtor after the debtor's plan of payment is completed (which is usually three years but could be up to five years).

Chapter 13 adjustment of debts of an individual with regular income   A rehabilitation form of bankruptcy that permits bankruptcy courts to supervise the debtor's plan for the payment of unpaid debts in installments over the plan period.

Chapter 13 discharge   A discharge in a Chapter 13 case that is granted to the debtor after the debtor's plan of payment is completed (which could be up to three or up to five years).

Charitable trust   A trust for the benefit of a charity.

Child custody   The awarding of legal custody of a child to a parent based on the best interests of the child. The parent awarded custody is called the *custodial parent*.

Child neglect   Failure to provide necessities to a child for whom one is legally responsible.

Child support   Payments made by the noncustodial parent to help pay for the financial support of his or her children.

Choice-of-law clause   Clause in an international contract that designates which nation's laws will be applied in deciding a dispute.

Chronological resume format   Presents education and job history in chronological order with the most recent experience listed first.

Citation   A reference to the source of the information.

Citator   An index of cases.

Cite checking   The process of verifying proper citation format in a document.

Civil litigation   Resolution of legal disputes between parties seeking a remedy for a civil wrong or to enforce a contract.

Civil Rights Act   A federal statute that prohibits racial discrimination in the transfer of real property.

Civil Rights Act of 1866   A federal statute enacted after the Civil War that says all persons "have the same right . . . to make and enforce contracts . . . as is enjoyed by white persons." It prohibits racial and national origin employment discrimination.

Closing arguments   The last opportunity for the attorneys to address the jury, summing up the client's case and persuading the jury to decide in his client's favor.

Codicil   A separate document that must be executed to amend a will. It must be executed with the same formalities as a will.

Collective bargaining   The act of negotiating contract terms between an employer and the members of a union.

Collective bargaining agreement   The resulting contract from a collective bargaining procedure.

"Coming and going" rule   A rule that says a principal is generally not liable for injuries caused by its agents and employees while they are on their way to and from work.

Commerce Clause   A clause of the U.S. Constitution that grants Congress the power "to regulate commerce with foreign nations, and among the several states, and with Indian tribes."

Commercial speech   Speech used by businesses, such as advertising. It is subject to time, place, and manner restrictions.

Common carrier   A firm that offers transportation services to the general public. The bailee. Owes a duty of strict liability to the bailor.

Common interest privilege   To permit a client to share confidential information with the attorney for another who shares a common legal interest.

Common law   Developed by judges who issue their opinions when deciding cases. The principles announced in these cases became precedent for later judges deciding similar cases.

Common law of contracts   Contract law developed primarily by state courts.

Common stock   A type of equity security that represents the residual value of the corporation.

Common stockholder (common shareholders)   A person who owns common stock.

Common-law marriage   A type of marriage recognized in some states where a marriage license has not been issued but certain requirements are met.

Community property   A form of ownership in which each spouse owns an equal one-half share of the income of both spouses and the assets acquired during the marriage.

Comparative negligence   A doctrine under which damages are apportioned according to fault.

Compensatory damages   An award of money intended to compensate a nonbreaching party for loss of the bargain. Compensatory damages place the nonbreaching party in the same position as if the contract had been fully performed by restoring the "benefit of the bargain."

Competence/competent   The minimum level of knowledge and skill required of a professional.

Complaint   The document the plaintiff files with the court and serves on the defendant to initiate a lawsuit.

Complete performance   A situation in which a party to a contract renders performance exactly as required by the contract. Complete performance discharges that party's obligations under the contract.

Complex litigation   Cases involving many parties as in a class action or multiple or complex legal issues.

Computer addresses and locations   The modern equivalent of a person's telephone number is the email address. Pages on the Internet also have addresses known as the Uniform Resource Locator (URL), made up of three parts: protocol, computer, and path.

Computer hardware   Hardware is the term that encompasses all of the tangible or physical items including computers, monitors, printers, fax machines, duplicators, and similar items that usually have either an electrical connection or use batteries as a power source.

Computer network   A set of workstations connected together.

Computer system   A combination of an input device, a processor, and an output device.

Computer viruses   Viruses are programs that attack and destroy computer programs, internal computer operating systems, and occasionally the hard disk drives of computers.

Conciliation   A form of dispute resolution in which a conciliator transmits offers and counteroffers between the disputing parties in helping to reach a settlement of their dispute.

Conciliator   A third party in a conciliation proceeding who assists the disputing parties in reaching a settlement of their dispute. The conciliator cannot make a decision or an award.

Concurrent jurisdiction   Jurisdiction shared by two or more courts.

Concurrent ownership (co-ownership)   When two or more persons own a piece of real property.

Condition precedent   A condition that requires the occurrence of an event before a party is obligated to perform a duty under a contract.

Condominium   A common form of ownership in a multiple-dwelling building in which the purchaser has title to the individual unit and owns the common areas as a tenant in common with the other condominium owners.

Confidentiality   A duty imposed on the attorney to enable clients to obtain legal advice by allowing the client to freely and openly give the attorney all the relevant facts.

Confirmation   The bankruptcy court's approval of a plan of reorganization.

Conflict checking   Verifying that the attorneys in the firm do not have a personal conflict and have not previously represented and are not currently representing any party with an adverse interest or conflict with the potential client.

Conflict of interest   The representation of one client being directly adverse to the interest of another client.

Connectors   Instructions in a search query on how to treat the words in the query.

Consequential damages   Foreseeable damages that arise from circumstances outside the contract. To be liable for these damages, the breaching party must know or have reason to know that the breach will cause special damages to the other party.

Consideration   Something of legal value given in exchange for a promise.

Consolidation   The act of a court to combine two or more separate lawsuits into one lawsuit. Occurs when two or more corporations combine to form an entirely new corporation.

Constitution of the United States of America   The supreme law of the United States. The Constitution of the United States of America establishes the structure of the federal government, delegates powers to the federal government, and guarantees certain fundamental rights.

Constructive trust   An equitable trust that is implied by law to avoid fraud, unjust enrichment, and injustice.

Contract   An agreement entered by two parties for valid consideration.

Contracts contrary to public policy   Contracts that have a negative impact on society or that interfere with the public's safety and welfare.

Contributory negligence   An affirmative defense which states there is no recovery where the plaintiff's negligence contributed to his injuries.

Controlling the Assault of Non-Solicited Pornography and Marketing Act (CAN-SPAM Act)   A federal statute that prohibits certain deceptive and misleading email. The act is administered by the Federal Trade Commission (FTC).

Conversion of personal property   A tort that deprives a true owner of the use and enjoyment of his or her personal property by taking over such property and exercising ownership rights over it.

Cooling-off period   Requires a union to give an employer at least 60 days' notice before a strike can commence.

Cooperative   A form of coownership of a multiple-dwelling building in which a corporation owns the building and the residents own shares in the corporation.

Co-ownership (concurrent ownership)   A situation in which two or more persons own a piece of real property. Also called *concurrent ownership.*

Copyright infringement   An act in which a party copies a substantial and material part of the plaintiff's copyrighted work without permission. A copyright holder may recover damages and other remedies against the infringer.

Copyright Revision Act　A federal statute that (1) establishes the requirements for obtaining a copyright and (2) protects copyrighted works from infringement.

Corporate bylaws　A detailed set of rules that are adopted by the board of directors after the corporation is incorporated, containing provisions for managing the business and the affairs of the corporation.

Corporation　A fictitious legal entity that is created according to statutory requirements.

Cost-benefit analysis　Process by which a litigant determines the costs of pursuing litigation and compares that to what is likely to be gained.

Counterfeit Access Device and Computer Fraud and Abuse Act (CFAA)　A federal statute that makes it a federal crime to access a computer knowingly to obtain (1) restricted federal government information, (2) financial records of financial institutions, and (3) consumer reports of consumer reporting agencies.

Counteroffer　A response by an offeree that contains terms and conditions different from or in addition to those of the offer. A counteroffer terminates an offer.

Court accounting　An accounting with the local court that administers or supervises trust and estate matters. These reports are designed to show that the fiduciary has properly administered the estate or trust.

Court of Appeals for the Federal Circuit　A court of appeals in Washington, DC, that has special appellate jurisdiction to review the decisions of the Claims Court, the Patent and Trademark Office, and the Court of International Trade.

Court of Chancery　Court that granted relief based on fairness. Also called *equity court*.

Courts of record　Those courts in which the testimony and evidence presented are recorded and preserved.

Covenant　An unconditional promise to perform.

Cover letter　A brief letter sent with a document identifying the intended recipient and the purpose of the attachment.

Creditors' committee　The creditors holding the seven largest unsecured claims are usually appointed to the creditors' committee. Representatives of the committee appear at Bankruptcy Court hearings, participate in the negotiation of a plan of reorganization, assert objections to proposed plans and so on.

Crime　An act done by an individual in violation of those duties that he or she owes to society and for the breach of which the law provides that the wrongdoer shall make amends to the public.

Criminal conspiracy　A crime in which two or more persons enter into an agreement to commit a crime and an overt act is taken to further the crime.

Criminal fraud (false pretenses or deceit)　Obtaining title to property through deception or trickery. Also known as false pretenses or deceit.

Criminal laws　A violation of a statute for which the government imposes a punishment.

Criminal trial　A trial to determine if a person has violated a statue for which the government imposes a penalty.

Critical legal thinking　The process of identifying the issue, the material facts, and the applicable law and applying the law to come to a conclusion.

Cross-complaint　Filed by the defendant against the plaintiff to seek damages or some other remedy.

Cross-examination　Opportunity of defense (opposing) counsel to question a witness after the direct examination of the witness.

Crossover worker　A person who does not honor a strike who either (1) chooses not to strike or (2) returns to work after joining the strikers for a time.

Cruel and unusual punishment　A clause of the Eighth Amendment that protects criminal defendants from torture or other abusive punishment.

Custodial parent　The parent to whom physical custody of the child is legally given.

Damages　Compensation for loss suffered.

Database program　A database program is an electronic repository of information of all types that can be sorted and presented in a meaningful manner.

Deathbed will　Oral will that is made dying declaration before a witness during the testator's last illness.

Decree of divorce　A court order that terminates a marriage.

Deed　A writing that describes a person's ownership interest in a piece of real property.

Defamation of character　False statement(s) made by one person about another. In court, the plaintiff must prove that (1) the defendant made an untrue statement of fact about the plaintiff and (2) the statement was intentionally or accidentally published to a third party.

Default judgment　Judgment obtained by the plaintiff against the defendant where the defendant has failed to respond in a timely fashion to the complaint.

Defect　Something wrong, inadequate, or improper in manufacture, design, packaging, warning, or safety measures of a product.

Defect in design　A flaw that occurs when a product is improperly designed.

Defect in manufacture　A defect that occurs when the manufacturer fails to (1) properly assemble a product, (2) properly test a product, or (3) adequately check the quality of the product.

Defect in packaging　A defect that occurs when a product has been placed in packaging that is insufficiently tamperproof.

Defendant　The party who files the answer.

Defendant's case　Process by which the defendant calls witnesses and introduces evidence to (1) rebut the plaintiff's evidence, (2) prove affirmative defenses, and (3) prove allegations made in a cross-complaint.

Defense of Marriage Act (DOMA)　A federal statute banning same sex couples from federal benefits given heterosexual couples.

Delegation doctrine　A doctrine that says when an administrative agency is created, it is delegated certain powers; the agency can only use those legislative, judicial, and executive powers that are delegated to it.

Denied　A possible response of the defendant to the complaint which asserts the facts of the averment are not true.

Deponent　Party who gives his or her deposition.

Deposition   Oral testimony given by a party or witness prior to trial. The testimony is given under oath and is transcribed.

Devise   A gift of real estate by will.

Dicta   Court comments on issues not directly related to the holding and therefore not having precedential effect.

Digital format   A computerized format utilizing a series of 0's and 1's.

Digital Millennium Copyright Act (DMCA)   A federal statute that prohibits unauthorized access to copyrighted digital works by circumventing encryption technology or the manufacture and distribution of technologies designed for the purpose of circumventing encryption protection of digital works.

Digital (or electronic) signature   Some electronic method that identifies an individual.

Direct examination   Questions addressed to a witness by the attorney who has called that witness to testify on behalf of his client.

Disaffirm   The act of a minor to rescind a contract under the infancy doctrine. Disaffirmance may be done orally, in writing, or by the minor's conduct.

Discharge   Actions or events that relieve certain parties from liability on negotiable instruments. There are three methods of discharge: (1) payment of the instrument; (2) cancellation; and (3) impairment of the right of recourse. The termination of the legal duty of a debtor to pay debts that remain unpaid upon the completion of a bankruptcy proceeding. Creditors' claims that are not included in a Chapter 11 reorganization are discharged. A discharge is granted to a debtor in a Chapter 13 consumer debt adjustment bankruptcy only after all the payments under the plan are completed by the debtor.

Discovery   A legal process during which both parties engage in various activities to elicit facts of the case from the other party and witnesses prior to trial.

Diversity of citizenship   A case between (1) citizens of different states, (2) a citizen of a state and a citizen or subject of a foreign country, and (3) a citizen of a state and a foreign country where a foreign country is the plaintiff.

Divorce   An order of the court that terminates a marriage.

Doctrine of Equity   A doctrine that permits judges to make decisions based on fairness, equality, moral rights, and natural law.

Doctrine of strict liability   A tort doctrine that makes manufacturers, distributors, wholesalers, retailers, and others in the chain of distribution of a defective product liable for the damages caused by the defect irrespective of fault.

Doctrine of transferred intent   An offender may be held responsible for an intent crime or intentional tort when someone other than the intended victim is injured.

Domain name   A unique name that identifies an individual's or a company's Web site.

Domestic corporation   A corporation in the state in which it was formed.

Dominant easement   The land that benefits from the easement.

Donee   A person who receives a gift.

Donor   A person who gives a gift.

Double Jeopardy Clause   A clause of the Fifth Amendment that protects persons from being tried twice for the same crime.

Dram Shop Act   Statute that makes taverns and bartenders liable for injuries caused to or by patrons who are served too much alcohol.

Dual-purpose mission   An errand or another act that a principal requests of an agent while the agent is on his or her own personal business.

Due Process Clause   A clause that provides that no person shall be deprived of "life, liberty, or property" without due process of the law.

Duty not to willfully or wantonly injure   The duty an owner or renter of real property owes a trespasser to prevent intentional injury or harm to the trespasser when the trespasser is on his or her premises.

Duty of candor   Honesty to the court.

Duty of care   The obligation we all owe each other not to cause any unreasonable harm or risk of harm. A responsibility of corporate directors and officers to use care and diligence when acting on behalf of the corporation.

Duty of loyalty   A responsibility of directors and officers not to act adversely to the interests of the corporation and to subordinate their personal interests to those of the corporation and its shareholders.

Duty of ordinary care   The duty an owner or renter of real property owes an invitee or a licensee to prevent injury or harm when the invitee or licensee steps on the owner's premises.

Duty of reasonable care   The duty that a reasonable bailee in like circumstances would owe to protect the bailed property.

Duty of utmost care   A duty of care that goes beyond ordinary care that says common carriers and innkeepers.

Easement   A given or required right to make limited use of someone else's land without owning or leasing it.

Easement by grant   One party gives another party an easement across his or her property.

Easement by implication   A right erected on division of land to allow each owner use.

Easement by necessity   Right to access another's property in order to reach one's landlocked property.

Easement by reservation   A retained right to use land after a transfer.

E-commerce   The sale of goods and services by computer over the Internet.

Economic Espionage Act   A federal statute that makes it a crime for any person to convert a trade secret for his or another's benefit, knowing or intending to cause injury to the owners of the trade secret.

E-contract   A contract that is entered into by email and over the World Wide Web.

E-discovery   The discovery of emails, electronically stored data, e-contracts, and other electronically stored records.

E-filing   The electronic filing of pleadings, briefs, and other documents related to a lawsuit with the court.

Elder law   Advocacy for the elderly.

Electronic Communications Privacy Act (ECPA)   A federal statute that makes it a crime to intercept an electronic communication at the point of transmission, while in transit, when stored by a router or server, or after receipt by the intended recipient.

Electronic Mail (email)   Electronic written communication between individuals using computers connected to the Internet.

Electronic repository   A secure protected file server to which everyone authorized has access over the internet.

Electronic Signature in Global and National Commerce Act (E-SIGN Act)   A federal statute that recognizes that electronic contracts, or e-contracts, meet the writing requirement of the Statute of Frauds and gives electronic signatures, or e-signatures, the same force and effect as peninscribed signatures on paper.

E-license   A contract that transfers limited rights in intellectual property and informational rights.

Emancipation   When a minor voluntarily leaves home and lives apart from his or her parents.

Embezzlement   The fraudulent conversion of property by a person to whom that property was entrusted.

Eminent domain   The government's power to take private property for public use, provided that just compensation is paid to the private property holder.

Employer–employee relationship   A relationship that results when an employer hires an employee to perform some form of physical service.

Encryption   Encryption is technology that allows computer users to put a "lock" around information to prevent discovery by others.

Engagement   (1) A formal entrance into a contract between a client and an accountant; (2) the period between acceptance of offer to marry and the marriage.

Entity theory   A theory that holds that partnerships are separate legal entities that can hold title to personal and real property, transact business in the partnership name, sue in the partnership name, and the like.

Enumerated powers   Certain powers delegated to the federal government by the states.

Environmental law   An area of the law dealing with the protection of the environment.

Equal Access to Justice Act   An act that was enacted to protect persons from harassment by federal administrative agencies.

Equal Employment Opportunity Commission (EEOC)   A federal administrative agency responsible for enforcing most federal antidiscrimination laws.

Equal Pay Act of 1963   A federal statute that protects both sexes from pay discrimination based on sex. It extends to jobs that require equal skill, equal effort, equal responsibility, and similar working conditions.

Equal Protection Clause   A clause that provides that state, local, and federal governments cannot deny to any person the "equal protection of the laws."

Equitable distribution   A law used by many states where the court orders a *fair distribution* of marital property to the divorcing spouses.

Equitable remedies   Used where no amount of monetary damages can make the injured party whole.

Escheat   When property goes to the state in the absence of claim by heir.

Establishment Clause   A clause to the First Amendment that prohibits the government from either establishing a state religion or promoting one religion over another.

Estate (estate in land)   Ownership rights in real property; the bundle of legal rights of the owner to possess, use, and enjoy the property.

Ethical wall   An environment in which an attorney or a paralegal is isolated from a particular case or client to avoid a conflict of interest or to protect a client's confidences and secrets.

Exclusionary rule   A rule that says evidence obtained from an unreasonable search and seizure can generally be prohibited from introduction at a trial or administrative proceeding against the person searched.

Exclusive agency contract   A contract a principal and agent enter into that says the principal cannot employ any agent other than the exclusive agent.

Exculpatory evidence   Evidence which tends to prove the innocence of the accused or prove the facts of the defendant's case.

Executed contract   A contract that has been fully performed on both sides; a completed contract.

Executive branch   One of the three co-equal branches of government represented by the president and administrative agencies.

Executor/executrix (male/female)   A person representative named in a will.

Executory contract or unexpired lease   A contract or lease that has not been fully performed. With the bankruptcy court's approval, executor contracts and unexpired leases may be rejected by a debtor in bankruptcy.

Exempt property   Property that may be retained by a debtor pursuant to federal or state law that does not become part of the bankruptcy estate.

Expert witness   A person qualified by education or experience to render an opinion based on a set of facts.

Express agency   An agency that occurs when a principal and an agent expressly agree to enter into an agency agreement with each other.

Express contract   An agreement that is expressed in written or oral words.

Express trust   A trust created voluntarily by the settlor.

Extension of time to respond   Request by the defendant to enlarge the time to respond to the complaint beyond that which is permitted under the rules.

Extortion   Threat to expose something about another person unless that other person gives money or property. Often referred to as "blackmail."

Fact pleading   Pleadings required to include all relevant facts in support of all claims asserted.

Facts   Information or details.

Failure to provide adequate instructions   A defect that occurs when a manufacturer does not provide detailed directions for safe assembly and use of a product.

Failure to warn   A defect that occurs when a manufacturer does not place a warning on the packaging of products that could cause injury if the danger is unknown.

Fair Housing Act   A federal statute that makes it unlawful for a party to refuse to rent or sell a dwelling to any person because of his or her race, color, national origin, sex, or religion.

Fair Labor Standards Act (FLSA)   A federal act enacted in 1938 to protect workers that prohibits child labor and establishes minimum wage and overtime pay requirements.

Fair-use doctrine   A doctrine that permits certain limited use of a copyright by someone other than the copyright holder without the permission of the copyright holder.

False imprisonment   The intentional confinement or restraint of another person without authority or justification and without that person's consent.

Father's registry   Where a male may register as the father of a child.

Federal administrative agencies   Agencies established by legislative and executive branches of federal and state governments.

Federal Arbitration Act (FAA)   A federak statute that provides that arbitration agreements in commercial contracts are valid, irrevocable, and enforceable unless some legal or equitable (fraud, duress) grounds exist to invalidate them.

Federal Patent Statute   A federal statute that establishes the requirements for obtaining a patent and protects patented inventions from infringement.

Federal question   A case arising under the U.S. Constitution, treaties, or federal statutes and regulations.

Federal Trade Commission (FTC)   Federal government agency empowered to enforce federal franchising rules. Federal administrative agency empowered to enforce the Federal Trade Commission Act and other federal consumer protection statutes.

Federalism   The U.S. form of government; the federal government and the 50 state governments share powers.

Fee simple absolute (fee simple)   A type of ownership of real property that grants the owner the fullest bundle of legal rights that a person can hold in real property.

Fee simple defeasible (qualified fee)   A type of ownership of real property that grants the owner all the incidents of a fee simple absolute except that it may be taken away if a specified condition occurs or does not occur.

Felony   The most serious type of crime; inherently evil crime. Most crimes against the person and some business-related crimes are felonies.

Fiduciary relationship   A relationship under which one party has a duty to act for the interest and benefit of another while acting within the scope of the relationship.

File attachment   The attachment is a popular method for transmitting text files, and occasionally graphic images, by attaching the file to an email.

File extension   When a file is saved, a file extension (a period followed by three characters) is added to the end of the filename to identify the program or format in which the file has been saved.

Finding tools   Publications used to find primary and secondary sources.

Firewalls   Programs designed to limit access to authorized users and applications.

Fixtures   Goods that are affixed to real estate so as to become part thereof.

Foreign corporation   A corporation in any state or jurisdiction other than the one in which it was formed.

Foreign Corrupt Practices Act (FCPA)   A federal statute that makes it illegal for U.S. companies, or their officers, directors, agents, or employees, to bribe a foreign official or foreign political party official to influence the awarding of new business or the retention of continuous business activity.

Forgery   The fraudulent making or alteration of a written document that affects the legal liability of another person.

Form I-9 "Employment Eligibility Verification"   A form that must be completed by prospective employees.

Formal will   A will that meets all the requirements of the state will statute.

Forum-selection clause   Contract provision that designates a certain court to hear any dispute concerning nonperformance of the contract.

Foster care   Parent care, sponsored by the state, by those not the adoptive or biological parents.

Fraud   A knowing misrepresentation or concealment of a material fact to induce another to act to their detriment.

Fraudulent transfer   Occurs when (1) a debtor transfers property to a third person within one year before the filing of a petition in bankruptcy and (2) the transfer was made by the debtor with an intent to hinder, delay, or defraud creditors.

Free Exercise Clause   A clause to the First Amendment that prohibits the government from interfering with the free exercise of religion in the United States.

Freedom of Information Act   A law that was enacted to give the public access to most documents in the possession of federal administrative agencies.

Freedom of speech   The right to engage in oral, written, and symbolic speech protected by the First Amendment.

Freehold estate   An estate in which the owner has a present possessory interest in the real property.

Frolic and detour   A situation in which an agent does something during the course of his or her employment to further his or her own interests rather than the principal's interests.

Functional resume format   Lists a summary of the individual's qualifications with current experience and education without any emphasis on dates of employment.

Future interest   The interest that the grantor retains for him- or herself or a third party.

General denial   In some jurisdictions, the word "Denied" alone is insufficient and the averment of the complaint is treated as if it were "Admitted."

General gift   A gift that does not identify the specific property from which the gift is to be made.

General government regulation   Government regulation that applies to many industries collectively.

General law practice   A general law practice is one that handles all types of cases.

General partner   A partner of a general partnership who is liable for the debts and obligations of the general partnership. Also, Partners in a limited partnership who invest capital, manage the business, and are personally liable for partnership debts.

General partnership   A voluntary association of two or more persons for carrying on a business as co-owners for profit. Also called a *partnership*.

General-jurisdiction trial court (courts of record)   A court that hears cases of a general nature that are not within the jurisdiction of limited-jurisdiction trial courts.

Generally known dangers   A defense that acknowledges that certain products are inherently dangerous and are known to the general population to be so.

Generic name   A term for a mark that has become a common term for a product line or type of service and therefore has lost its trademark protection.

Gift   A voluntary transfer of title to property without payment of consideration by the donee. To be a valid gift, three elements must be shown: (1) *donative intent*, (2) *delivery*, and (3) *acceptance*.

Gift *causa mortis*   A gift that is made in contemplation of death.

Gift *inter vivos*   A gift made during a person's lifetime that is an irrevocable present transfer of ownership.

Gift promise   A promise that is unenforceable because it lacks consideration.

GlobalCite   Loislaw's tool for searching cases containing references to another case.

Good Samaritan law   A state statute that relieves medical professionals from liability for ordinary negligence when they stop and render aid to victims in emergency situations.

Goods   Tangible things that are movable at the time of their identification to the contract.

Government employment   Working for federal, state, and local government agencies and authorities.

Government in the Sunshine Act   An act that was enacted to open certain federal administrative agency meetings to the public.

Grantee   The party to whom an interest in real property is transferred.

Grantor   The party who transfers an ownership interest in real property.

Grantor (trustor)   The person who creates a living trust. Also called the *trustor*.

Graphic user interface (GUI)   A set of screen presentations and metaphors that utilize graphic elements such as icons in an attempt to make an operating system easier to operate.

H-1B visa   A nonimmigrant visa that allows U.S. employers to employ foreign nationals in the United States that are skilled in specialty occupations.

Hacking   Unauthorized access to a computer or computer network.

Hardcopy   Paper copies of documents.

Headnotes   The syllabus or summary of the points of law prepared by the editorial staff of a publisher.

Health care agent   One designated by a person in a health care directive to act for a person in making health care decisions.

Health care directive (health care proxy)   A document in which the maker should name someone to be his or her health care agent to make all health care decisions in accordance with his or her wishes in the living will.

Heir   One who receives property from a deceased relative under intestacy statute.

Highest state court   The top court in a state court system; it hears appeals from intermediate state courts and certain trial courts.

Holding   The actual decision on the specific point of law the court was asked to decide.

Holographic will   Will that is entirely handwritten and signed by the testator.

Homestead exemption   Equity in a debtor's home that the debtor is permitted to retain.

Hot spot   A wireless access point, generally in a public area.

Hung jury   A jury that does not come to a unanimous decision about the defendant's guilt. The government may choose to retry the case.

Identity theft (ID theft)   A crime where one person steals information about another person and poses as that person and takes the innocent person's money or property or purchases goods and services using the victim's credit information.

Identity Theft and Assumption Deterrence Act   A federal statute that makes identity theft a felony that is punishable by a prison sentence.

Illegal contract   A contract to perform an illegal act. Cannot be enforced by either party to the contract.

Immaterial facts   A fact not essential to the matter or issue at hand.

Immigration Reform and Control Act of 1986 (IRCA)   A federal statute that makes it unlawful for employers to hire illegal immigrants.

Immunity from prosecution   The government agrees not to use any evidence given by a person granted immunity against that person.

Implied agency   An agency that occurs when a principal and an agent do not expressly create an agency, but it is inferred from the conduct of the parties.

Implied attorney—client relationship   Implied attorney–client relationship may result when a prospective client divulges confidential information during a consultation with an attorney for the purpose of retaining the attorney, even if actual employment does not result.

Implied warranty of habitability   A warranty that provides that leased premises must be fit, safe, and suitable for ordinary residential use.

Implied-in-fact contract   A contract in which agreement between parties has been inferred from their conduct.

In personam (personal) jurisdiction   Jurisdiction over the parties to a lawsuit.

In rem jurisdiction   Jurisdiction to hear a case because of jurisdiction over the property of the lawsuit.

Income beneficiary   Person or entity to be paid income from the trust.

Indemnification   Right of a partner to be reimbursed for expenditures incurred on behalf of the partnership.

Independent adoption   An adoption in which there is a private arrangement between the biological parents and adoptive parents.

Independent contractor   A person or business that is not an employee and is employed by a principal to perform a certain task on his or her behalf.

Independent Medical Examination (IME)   Term formerly used to describe a defense medical evaluation.

Indictment   The charge of having committed a crime (usually a felony), based on the judgment of a grand jury.

Infancy doctrine   A doctrine that allows minors to disaffirm (cancel) most contracts they have entered into with adults.

Inferior performance   A situation in which a party fails to perform express or implied contractual obligations and impairs or destroys the essence of the contract.

Information The charge of having committed a crime (usually a misdemeanor), based on the judgment of a judge (magistrate).

Information Infrastructure Protection Act (IIP Act) A federal statute that makes it a federal crime for anyone to intentionally access and acquire information from a protected computer without authorization.

Injunction A court order that prohibits a person from doing a certain act.

Injury The plaintiff must suffer personal injury or damage to his or her property to recover monetary damages for the defendant's negligence.

Innkeeper The owner of a facility that provides lodging to the public for compensation.

Inside director A member of the board of directors who is also an officer of the corporation.

Intangible property Rights that cannot be reduced to physical form such as stock certificates, certificates of deposit, bonds, and copyrights.

Intellectual property and information rights Patents, copyrights, trademarks, trade secrets, trade names, domain names, and other valuable business assets. Federal and state laws protect intellectual property rights from misappropriation and infringement.

Intentional infliction of emotional distress A tort that occurs when a person's extreme and outrageous conduct intentionally or recklessly causes severe emotional distress to another person. Also known as the *tort of outrage*.

Intentional torts A category of torts that requires that the defendant possessed the intent to do the act that caused the plaintiff's injuries.

***Inter vivos* trust** A trust that is created while the settlor is alive.

Intermediate appellate court An intermediate court that hears appeals from trial courts.

Intermediate scrutiny test Test that is applied to classifications based on protected classes other than race (e.g., sex or age).

International Paralegal Management Association (IPMA) A North American association for legal assistant managers.

Internet A collection of millions of computers that provide a network of electronic connections between the computers.

Internet (Web) browsers An Internet or Web browser is a software program that allows a person to use a computer to access the Internet. The two most popular Web browsers are Microsoft Internet Explorer and AOL.

Internet search engine An Internet search engine is a program designed to take a word or set of words and locate websites on the Internet.

Internet service provider (ISP) The company providing the connection between the user and the Internet.

Interpretive rules Rules issued by administrative agencies that interpret existing statutory language.

Interrogatories Written questions submitted by one party to another party. The questions must be answered in writing within a stipulated time.

Interstate commerce Commerce that moves between states or that affects commerce between states.

Intervention The act of others to join as parties to an existing lawsuit.

Intestacy statute A state statute that specifies how a deceased's property will be distributed if he or she dies without a will or if the last will is declared void and there is no prior valid will.

Intestate The state of having died without leaving a will.

Intoxicated person A person who is under contractual incapacity because of ingestion of alcohol or drugs to the point of incompetence.

Invasion of the right to privacy A tort that constitutes the violation of a person's right to live his or her life without being subjected to unwarranted and undesired publicity.

Invitee One expressly or by implication invited onto the premises of the owner for mutual benefit.

Involuntary petition A petition filed by creditors of the debtor; alleges that the debtor is not paying his or her debts as they become due.

IOLTA account Where the amount is too small to earn interest, court rules require the funds be deposited into a special interest-bearing account, and the interest generally paid to support legal aid projects (Interest on Lawyers Trust Accounts).

Irreconcilable differences The legal matter in dispute.

Joint and several liability Tort liability where general partners are liable as a group or separately. This means that the plaintiff can sue one or more of the partners separately. If successful, the plaintiff can recover the entire amount of the judgment from any or all of the defendant–partners.

Joint custody Custody given to both parents with each having a period of physical custody and shared decision making power.

Joint liability Partners are jointly liable for contracts and debts of the partnership. This means that a plaintiff must name the partnership and all of the partners as defendants in a lawsuit.

Joint tenancy A form of co-ownership that includes the right of survivorship.

Joint will A will that is executed by two or more testators.

Judgment The official decision of the court.

Judicial branch The court system.

Judicial decision A ruling about an individual lawsuit issued by federal and state courts.

Jurisdiction The authority of the court to hear disputes and impose resolution of the dispute upon the litigants.

Jurisprudence The philosophy or science of law.

Jury deliberation The process where the jury meets to discuss and resolve the dispute.

Jury instructions (charges) Instructions given by the judge to the jury that informs them of the law to be applied in the case.

Jury selection Process by which a group of six or more people is chosen to serve on the jury.

Just Compensation Clause A clause of the U.S. Constitution that requires the government to compensate the property owner, and possibly others, when the government takes property under its power of eminent domain.

KeyCite Westlaw's tool for searching cases containing references to another case.

Land   The most common form of real property; includes the land and buildings and other structures permanently attached to the land.

Landlord/lessor   An owner who transfers a leasehold.

Landlord-tenant relationship   A relationship created when the owner of a freehold estate (landlord) transfers a right to exclusively and temporarily possess the owner's property to another (tenant).

Land-use control or **land-use regulation**   The collective term for the laws that regulate the possession, ownership, and use of real property.

Lanham Trademark Act   A federal statute that (1) establishes the requirements for obtaining a federal mark, and (2) protects marks from infringement.

Larceny   The taking of another's personal property other than from his or her person or building.

Large law offices   Large law offices are an outgrowth of traditional law offices that have expanded over the years, adding partners and associates along the way.

Law   That which must be obeyed and followed by citizens subject to sanctions or legal consequences; a body of rules of action or conduct prescribed by controlling authority, and having binding legal force.

Law court   A court that developed and administered a uniform set of laws decreed by the kings and queens after William the Conqueror; legal procedure was emphasized over merits at this time.

Leading question   A question which suggests the answer.

Lease   A transfer of the right to the possession and use of real property for a set term in return for certain consideration; the rental agreement between a landlord and a tenant.

Leasehold estate/leasehold   A tenant's interest in property.

Legal assistant   See *Paralegal.*

Legal research   The process for finding the answer to a legal question.

Legally enforceable   A contract in which if one party fails to perform as promised, the other party can use the court system to enforce the contract and recover damages or other remedy.

Legislative branch   The part of the government that consists of Congress (the Senate and the House of Representatives).

Lessee   The person who acquires the right to possession and use of goods under the lease.

Lessor   The person who transfers the right of possession and use of goods under the lease.

Libel   A false statement that appears in a letter, newspaper, magazine, book, photograph, movie, video, or other media.

License   A contract that transfers limited rights in intellectual property and information rights. Grants a person the right to enter upon another person's property for a specified and usually short period of time.

Licensee   A party who is granted limited rights in or access to intellectual property or informational rights owned by a licensor.

Licensing agreement   A detailed and comprehensive written agreement between a licensor and a licensee that sets forth the express terms of their agreement.

Licensor   An owner of intellectual property or informational rights who transfers rights in the property or information to the licensee.

Life estate   An interest in land for a person's lifetime; upon that person's death, the interest will be transferred to another party.

Limited liability   Members are liable for the LLC's debts, obligations, and liabilities only to the extent of their capital contributions. Liability that shareholders have only to the extent of their capital contribution. Shareholders are generally not personally liable for debts and obligations of the corporation.

Limited liability company (LLC)   An unincorporated business entity that combines the most favorable attributes of general partnerships, limited partnerships, and corporations.

Limited liability partnership (LLP)   A form of partnership in which all partners are limited partners and there are no general partners.

Limited partners   Partners in a limited partnership who invest capital but do not participate in management and are not personally liable for partnership debts beyond their capital contribution.

Limited partnership   A special form of partnership that is formed only if certain formalities are followed. A limited partnership has both general and limited partners.

Limited partnership agreement   A document that sets forth the rights and duties of the general and limited partners, the terms and conditions regarding the operation, termination, and dissolution of the partnership, and so on.

Limited-jurisdiction trial courts   Courts authorized to hear certain types of disputes such as divorce or bankruptcy.

Lineal descendants   The testator's children, grandchildren, great-grandchildren, and so on.

Liquidated damages   Damages to which parties to a contract agree in advance should be paid if the contract is breached.

Litigation   The process of bringing, maintaining, and defending a lawsuit.

Living trust   A method for holding property during a person's lifetime and distributing the property upon that person's death. Also called a *grantor's trust* and a *revocable trust.*

Living will   A document that states which life-saving measures the signor does and does not want, and can specify that he or she wants such treatments withdrawn if doctors determine that there is no hope of a meaningful recovery.

Local area network (LAN)   A network of computers at one location.

Long-arm statute   A statute that extends a state's jurisdiction to nonresidents who were not served a summons within the state.

Lost property   Property that the owner leaves somewhere because of negligence, carelessness, or inadvertence.

Mainframe   A large computer system used primarily for bulk processing of data and financial information.

Malicious prosecution   A lawsuit in which the original defendant sues the original plaintiff for bringing a lawsuit without probable cause and with malice.

Mandatory authority   Court decisions that are binding on all lower courts.

Marital property   Property acquired during the course of marriage using income earned during the marriage, and separate property that has been converted to marital property.

Mark   The collective name for trademarks, service marks, certification marks, and collective marks.

Marketable title   Title to real property that is free from any encumbrances or other defects that are not disclosed but would affect the value of the property. Also called *good title*.

Marriage   A legal union between two people that confers certain legal rights and duties upon the parties and upon the children born of the marriage.

Marriage ceremony   A mutual exchange of intent to be married.

Marriage license   A legal document issued by a state certifying that two people are married.

Marriage requirements   Minimum standards for marriage under state law.

Material breach   A breach that occurs when a party renders inferior performance of his or her contractual duties.

Material facts   A fact significant or essential to the issue.

Mediation   A form of negotiation in which a neutral third party assists the disputing parties in reaching a settlement of their dispute.

Mediator   A neutral third party who assists the disputing parties in reaching a settlement of their dispute. The mediator cannot make a decision or an award.

Member   An owner of an LLC.

Memorandum   A working legal document for the legal team for use in preparation and presentation of a case.

Mens rea   "Evil intent"—the possession of the requisite state of mind to commit a prohibited act.

Merchant protection statute   A state statute that allows merchants to stop, detain, and investigate suspected shoplifters without being held liable for false imprisonment if (1) there are reasonable grounds for the suspicion, (2) suspects are detained for only a reasonable time, and (3) investigations are conducted in a reasonable manner.

Mineral rights (subsurface rights)   Rights to the earth located beneath the surface of the land.

Minitrial   A voluntary private proceeding in which the lawyers for each side present a shortened version of their case to representatives of the other side, and usually to a neutral third party, in an attempt to reach a settlement of the dispute.

Minor   A person who has not reached the age of majority.

Minor breach   A breach that occurs when a party renders substantial performance of his or her contractual duties.

Miranda rights   Rights that a suspect must be informed of before being interrogated, so that the suspect will not unwittingly give up his or her Fifth Amendment right.

Mirror image rule   A rule that states that for an acceptance to exist, the offeree must accept the terms as stated in the offer.

Misappropriation of the right to publicity   A tort in which one party appropriates a person's name or identity for commercial purposes.

Misdemeanor   A less serious crime; not inherently evil but prohibited by society. Many crimes against property are misdemeanors.

Mislaid property   Property that an owner voluntarily places somewhere and then inadvertently forgets.

Mitigation of damages   A nonbreaching party's legal duty to avoid or reduce damages caused by a breach of contract.

Model Guidelines for the Utilization of Legal Assistant Services   A set of guidelines by ABA policymaking body, the House of Delegates, intended to govern conduct of lawyers when utilizing paralegals or legal assistants.

Modem   A device to translate electrical signals to allow computers to communicate with each other.

Monetary damages   An award of money.

Money Laundering Control Act   A federal statute that makes it a crime to (1) knowingly engage in a *money transaction* through a financial institution involving property worth more than $10,000 and (2) knowingly engage in a *financial transaction* involving the proceeds of an illegal activity.

Moral obligation   An obligation based on one's own conscience.

Motion for judgment on the pleadings   A motion that alleges that if all the facts presented in the pleadings are taken as true, the party making the motion would win the lawsuit when the proper law is applied to these asserted facts.

Motion for summary judgment   A motion that asserts that there are no factual disputes to be decided by the jury and that the judge can apply the proper law to the undisputed facts and decide the case without a jury. These motions are supported by affidavits, documents, and deposition testimony.

Motion to dismiss   A motion that alleges that the plaintiff's complaint fails to state a claim for which relief can be granted. Also called a *demurrer*.

Motivation test   A test to determine the liability of the principal; if the agent's motivation in committing the intentional tort is to promote the principal's business, then the principal is liable for any injury caused by the tort.

Murder   The unlawful killing of a human being by another with intent.

Mutual benefit bailment   A bailment for the mutual benefit of the bailor and bailee. The bailee owes a duty of ordinary care to protect the bailed property.

Mutual (reciprocal) will   Occurs where two or more testators execute separate wills that leave their property to each other on the condition that the survivor leave the remaining property on his or her death as agreed by the testators.

Narrative opportunity   A question that allows the giving of a full explanation.

National Association of Legal Assistants (NALA)   Professional organization for legal assistants that provides continuing education and professional certification for paralegals, incorporated in 1975.

National Association of Legal Secretaries (NALS)   Since 1999, an association for legal professionals, originally formed in 1949 as an association for legal secretaries.

National Federation of Paralegal Associations (NFPA)   Professional organization of state and local paralegal associations founded in 1974.

National Labor Relations Board (NLRB)   A federal administrative agency that oversees union elections, prevents employers and unions from engaging in illegal and unfair labor practices, and enforces and interprets certain federal labor laws.

Necessaries of life   A minor must pay the reasonable value of food, clothing, shelter, medical care, and other items considered necessary to the maintenance of life.

Negligence   Failure of a corporate director or officer to exercise the duty of care while conducting the corporation's business.

Negligence *per se* Tort where the violation of a statute or ordinance constitutes the breach of the duty of care.

Negligent infliction of emotional distress A tort that permits a person to recover for emotional distress caused by the defendant's negligent conduct.

Negotiation A procedure in which the parties to a dispute engage in negotiations to try to reach a voluntary settlement of their dispute.

Network administrator The network administrator usually is the person with the highest-level access to the network file server.

Network file server A separate computer in a network that acts as the traffic cop of the system controlling the flow of data.

Network rights and privileges Rights or privileges determine who has access to the server, the data stored on the server, and the flow of information between connections.

Networking The establishment of contact with others with whom questions and information are shared.

No Electronic Theft Act (NET Act) A federal statute that makes it a crime for a person to willfully infringe on a copyright work that exceeds $1,000 in retail value.

No-fault divorce A divorce recognized by the law of a state whereby neither party is blamed for the divorce.

Noncupative will Oral will that is made before a witness during the testator's last illness.

Nonfreehold estate An estate in which the tenant has a right to possession of the property but not title to the property.

Non-intent crime A crime that imposes criminal liability without a finding of *mens rea* (intent).

Notice pleading Pleadings required to include sufficient facts to put the parties on notice of the claims asserted against them.

Nurse paralegals Nurses who have gained medical work experience and combine it with paralegal skills. Also referred to as *legal nurse consultants.*

Objective rule A rule stating that if an engagement is broken off, the prospective bride must return the engagement ring, regardless of which party broke off the engagement.

Obscene speech Speech that (1) appeals to the prurient interest, (2) depicts sexual conduct in a patently offensive way, and (3) lacks serious literary, artistic, political, or scientific value.

Occupational Safety and Health Act A federal act enacted in 1970 that promotes safety in the workplace.

Offensive speech Speech that is offensive to many members of society. It is subject to time, place, and manner restrictions.

Offer The manifestation of willingness to enter into a bargain, so made as to justify another person in understanding that his assent to that bargain is invited and will conclude it.

Offeree The party to whom an offer to enter into a contract is made.

Offeror The party who makes an offer to enter into a contract.

Office software suites This software consists of commonly used office software programs that manage data and database programs; manipulate financial or numeric information, spreadsheet programs; or display images and presentation graphics programs.

Officers of the corporation Employees of a corporation who are appointed by the board of directors to manage the day-to-day operations of the corporation.

One-year rule An executory contract that cannot be performed by its own terms within one year of its formation must be in writing.

Online collaboration Using the internet to conduct meetings and share documents.

Open adoption Where biological and adoptive parents are known to each other.

Open-ended question A question that usually does not have a yes or no answer.

Opening brief The first opportunity for the attorneys to address the jury and describe the nature of the lawsuit.

Operating agreement An agreement entered into by members that governs the affairs and business of the LLC and the relations among members, managers, and the LLC.

Operating system The operating system is a basic set of instructions to the computer on how to handle basic functions— how to process input from "input devices" such as the keyboard and mouse, the order in which to process information, and what to show on the computer monitor.

Opinion letter A formal statement of advice based on the lawyers expert knowledge.

Order Decision issued by an administrative law judge.

Ordinances Laws enacted by local government bodies such as cities and municipalities, countries, school districts, and water districts.

Organizational meeting A meeting that must be held by the initial directors of the corporation after the articles of incorporation are filed.

Outside director A member of the board of directors who is not an officer of the corporation.

Outsourcing Use of persons or services outside of the immediate office staff.

Paperless office The paperless office is one in which documents are created and stored electronically.

Paralegal A person qualified by education, training, or work experience who is employed or retained by a lawyer, law office, corporation, governmental agency, or other entity who performs specifically delegated substantive legal work for which a lawyer is responsible. Also referred to as *legal assistant.*

Paralegal Advanced Competency Exam (PACE) National Association of Paralegal Association's certification program that requires the paralegal to have two years of experience and a bachelor's degree and have completed a paralegal course at an accredited school.

Paralegal manager Someone who hires, supervises, trains, and evaluates paralegals.

Parallel citation The citation to the same case in a different publication.

Parent A person who by adoption or as the biological parent is legally responsible for a child.

Partnership Two or more natural (human) or artificial (corporation) persons who have joined together to share ownership and profit or loss.

Partnership agreement A written partnership agreement that the partners sign. Also called articles of partnership.

Partnership at will A partnership with no fixed duration.

Partnership for a term A partnership with a fixed duration.

Patent infringement   Unauthorized use of another's patent. A patent holder may recover damages and other remedies against a patent infringer.

Paternity action   A legal proceeding that determines the identity of the father of a child.

Penal codes   Statutes that define crimes.

Per capita **distribution**   A distribution of the estate that makes each grandchild and greatgrandchild of the deceased inherit equally with the children of the deceased.

Per stirpes **distribution**   A distribution of the estate that makes grandchildren and greatgrandchildren of the deceased inherit by representation of their parent.

Periodic tenancy   A tenancy created when a lease specifies intervals at which payments are due but does not specify the length of the lease.

Permanent (lifetime) alimony   Payments of spousal support paid until remarriage or death of recipient.

Personal jurisdiction   Requires the court to have authority over the persons as well as the subject matter of the lawsuit.

Personal property   Tangible property such as automobiles, furniture, and equipment, and intangible property such as securities, patents, and copyrights.

Personal representative   The person(s) appointed by the court to administer an estate.

Persuasive authority   Court decisions the court is not required to follow but are well reasoned and from a respected court.

Petition for bankruptcy   A document filed with the bankruptcy court that starts a bankruptcy proceeding.

Petition for *certiorari*   A petition asking the Supreme Court to hear one's case.

Petition for divorce   A document filed with the proper state court that commences a divorce proceeding.

Petitioner   The party appealing the decision of an administrative agency.

Physical and mental examination   A form of discovery that permits the physical or mental examination of a party by a qualified expert of the opposing party's choosing where the physical or mental condition of the party is at issue in the lawsuit.

Picketing   The action of strikers walking in front of the employer's premises carrying signs announcing their strike.

Piercing the corporate veil   A doctrine that says that if a shareholder dominates a corporation and misuses it for improper purposes, a court of equity can disregard the corporate entity and hold the shareholder personally liable for the corporation's debts and obligations.

Plaintiff   The party who files the complaint.

Plaintiff's case   Process by which the plaintiff calls witnesses and introduces evidence to prove the allegations contained in his or her complaint.

Plan of reorganization   A plan that sets forth a proposed new capital structure for the debtor to have when it emerges from Chapter 11 reorganization bankruptcy.

Plant life and vegetation   Real property that is growing in or on the surface of the land.

Plea bargain agreement   An agreement in which the accused admits to a lesser crime than charged. In return, the government agrees to impose a lesser sentence than might have been obtained had the case gone to trial.

Pleadings   The paperwork that is filed with the court to initiate and respond to a lawsuit.

Pocket parts   An update to a book that is a separate document that slips into a pocket in the back of the main volume.

Police power   The power of states to regulate private and business activity within their borders.

Pour-over will   A will that, upon the grantor's death, distributes the grantor's property that is not in the living will.

Power of attorney   An express agency agreement that is often used to give an agent the power to sign legal documents on behalf of the principal.

Precedent   Prior case law that is controlling.

Preemption doctrine   The concept that federal law takes precedence over state or local law.

Pregnancy Discrimination Act   Amendment to Title VII that forbids employment discrimination because of "pregnancy, childbirth, or related medical conditions."

Prenuptial agreement   A contract entered into prior to marriage that specifies how property will be distributed upon the termination of the marriage or death of a spouse. Also referred to as a *premarital agreement.*

Pretrial hearing   A hearing before the trial in order to facilitate the settlement of a case. Also called a settlement conference.

Pretrial motion   A motion a party can make to try to dispose of all or part of a lawsuit prior to trial.

Primary authority   The actual law itself.

Primary source of law   The actual law itself.

Principal   A party who employs another person to act on his or her behalf.

Principal–agent relationship   A relationship in which an employer hires an employee and gives that employee authority to act and enter into contracts on his or her behalf.

Privacy Act   An act stipulating that federal administrative agencies can maintain only information about an individual that is relevant and necessary to accomplish a legitimate agency purpose.

Privilege   A special legal right.

Privileged communication   A communication that the person has a right to be kept confidential based on the relationship with the other part such as attorney and client.

Pro bono   Working without compensation on behalf of individuals and organizations that otherwise could not afford legal assistance.

Pro se   Parties represent themselves.

Probate (settlement of estate)   The process of a deceased's property being collected, debts and taxes being paid, and the remainder of the estate being distributed.

Procedural due process   Due process that requires the respondent to be given (1) proper and timely notice of the allegations or charges against him or her and (2) an opportunity to present evidence on the matter.

Procedural law   Law which realtes to how the trial is conducted and is usually based upon Rules of Court and Rules of Evidence.

Production of documents   Request by one party to another party to produce all documents relevant to the case prior to the trial.

Products liability The liability of manufacturers, sellers, and others for the injuries caused by defective products.

Professional Legal Secretary (PLS) The advanced certification for legal professionals from NALS.

Professional malpractice The liability of a professional who breaches his or her duty of ordinary care.

Professional Paralegal (PP) Certification from NALS for those performing paralegal duties.

Promise to marry An offer to marry that is accepted.

Proof of claim A document required to be filed by unsecured creditors that states the amount of their claim against the debtor.

Proprietary school Private, as opposed to public, institution, generally for profit, offering training and education.

Protocol In a URL the required format of the Web address.

Proximate cause A point along a chain of events caused by a negligent party after which this party is no longer legally responsible for the consequences of his or her actions. Also referred to as *legal cause*.

Published opinion A court's written explanation of its decision on a case intended to be relied upon as a statement of the law based on the facts of the case.

Punitive damages Damages that are awarded to punish the defendant, to deter the defendant from similar conduct in the future, and to set an example for others.

Quasi in rem (attachment) jurisdiction Jurisdiction allowed a plaintiff who obtains a judgment in one state to try to collect the judgment by attaching property of the defendant located in another state.

Quasi-contract (implied-in-law contract) An equitable doctrine whereby a court may award monetary damages to a plaintiff for providing work or services to a defendant even though no actual contract existed.

Quiet title An action brought by a party seeking an order of the court declaring who has title to disputed property. By its decision, the court "quiets title."

Racketeer Influenced Corrupt Organizations Act (RICO) A federal statute that defines the crime of racketeering and provides for both criminal and civil penalties for racketeering.

Random access memory (RAM) Temporary computer memory that stores work in processs.

Rational basis test Test that is applied to classifications not involving a suspect or protected class.

Real property The land itself as well as buildings, trees, soil, minerals, timber, plants, and other things permanently affixed to the land.

Reasonable person standard Acting as a responsible, prudent person would act under the same or similar circumstances.

Reasonable professional standard Acting as a responsible, prudent professional would act as measured by other similar professionals.

Rebuttal Phase of the trial that gives the plaintiff the chance to address or respond to information contained in the defendant's case-in-chief.

Receiving stolen property A person (1) knowingly receives stolen property and (2) intends to deprive the rightful owner of that property.

Recording statute A state statute that requires a mortgage or deed of trust to be recorded in the county recorder's office of the county in which the real property is located.

Recross examination Permits opposing counsel to again challenge the credibility of the witness but only as to matters questioned on redirect examination.

Redirect examination After cross-examination, counsel who originally called the witness on direct examination may ask the witness additional questions.

Reformation An equitable doctrine that permits the court to rewrite a contract to express the parties' true intentions.

Registrar of Deeds A public official with whom property deeds are filed and maintained.

Regulatory statutes Statutes, such as environmental laws, securities laws, and antitrust laws that provide for criminal violations and penalties.

Rejection Express words or conduct by the offeree that rejects an offer. Rejection terminates the offer.

Relevant facts Facts crucial to the case and having legal significance.

Religious discrimination Discrimination against a person solely because of his or her religion or religious practices.

Remainder (remainderman) A right of possession that returns to a third party upon the expiration of a limited or contingent estate.

Remainder beneficiary Person or entity to receive the trust *corpus* upon termination of the trust.

Remand When the basis of federal jurisdiction is resolved and only state claims remain to be litigated, the federal court must send the matter back to the state trial court. Also, when the appellate court disagrees with the outcome of the trial court but sends the matter back to the trial court for further proceeding in accordance with its opinion, which may include additional proceedings or a new trial to correct the error, in accordance with the appellate court's decision.

Remote collaboration Working on a common document utilizing remote access by two or more parties.

Renounce an inheritance A beneficiary rejection of a bequest or right to take property.

Replacement workers Workers who are hired to take the place of striking workers. They can be hired on either a temporary or permanent basis.

Reply Filed by the original plaintiff to answer the defendant's cross-complaint.

Request for admission A form of discovery in which written requests are made to the opposing party asking him to admit the truth of certain facts or liability.

Res ipsa loquitur Tort where the presumption of negligence arises because (1) the defendant was in exclusive control of the situation, and (2) the plaintiff would not have suffered injury but for someone's negligence. The burden switches to the defendant(s) to prove they were not negligent.

Residuary gift A gift of the estate left after the debts, taxes, and specific and general gifts have been paid.

Respondeat superior A rule that says an employer is liable for the tortious conduct of its employees or agents while they are acting within the scope of its authority.

Respondent   The party who must respond to the appeal, usually the verdict winner at trial.

Restatement of the Law Third, Torts   A legal treatise with suggested rules of laws relating to torts.

Restraining order   A court order directing one party to avoid contact with another.

Resulting trust   A trust that is implied from the conduct of the parties.

Resume   A short description of a person's education, a summary of work experience, and other related and supporting information that potential employers use in evaluating a person's qualifications for a position in a firm or an organization.

Retainer   A payment at the beginning of the handling of a new matter for a client. This amount may be used to offset the fees for services rendered or costs advanced on behalf of the client.

Reverse   The appellate court disagrees with the outcome of the trial and finds reversible error was made and judgment should be overturned and entered in favor of the appellant.

Reversion   A right of possession that returns to the grantor after the expiration of a limited or contingent estate.

Revised Model Business Corporation Act (RMBCA)   A 1984 revision of the MBCA that arranged the provisions of the original act more logically, revised the language to be more consistent, and made substantial changes in the provisions.

Revised Uniform Limited Partnership Act (RULPA)   A 1976 revision of the ULPA that provides a more modern, comprehensive law for the formation, operation, and dissolution of limited partnerships.

Revocation   Withdrawal of an offer by the offeror which terminates the offer.

Robbery   The taking of personal property from another person by the use of fear or force.

Rules of court   A court's rules for the processing and presentation of cases.

S corporation   A corporation that has elected S corporation status. An S corporation pays no federal income tax at the corporate level. The gains or losses of an S corporation flow-through to the shareholders.

Sale   The passing of title from a seller to a buyer for a price. Also called a *conveyance.*

Sales contract under UCC   A passage of the title to goods for a price.

Scienter   Means international conduct. Scienter is required for there to be a violation of Section 10(b) and Rule 10b-5.

Screening interview   Limited first contact with a prospective new client.

Search query   Specific words used in a computerized search.

Search warrant   A warrant issued by a court that authorizes the police to search a designated place for specified contraband, articles, items, or documents. The search warrant must be based on probable cause.

Secondary authority   Writings that explain the law.

Secondary meaning   When an ordinary term has become a brand name.

Secondary source of law   Writings about the law.

Section 7 of the NLRA   A law that gives employees the right to join together and form a union.

Section 8(a) of the NLRA   A law that makes it an unfair labor practice for an employer to interfere with, coerce, or restrain employees from exercising their statutory right to form and join unions.

Self-employment   Working independently either as a freelance paralegal for different lawyers or, when authorized by state or federal law, performing services for the public.

Self-incrimination   The Fifth Amendment states that no person shall be compelled in any criminal case to be a witness against himor herself.

Separate property   Property owned by a spouse prior to marriage, as well as inheritances and gifts received by a spouse during the marriage.

Service mark   A mark that distinguishes the services of the holder from those of its competitors.

Service of process settlement agreement   A summons is served on the defendant to obtain personal jurisdiction over him or her.

Servient easement   The land that is used by dominant easement.

Settlement agreement   An agreement voluntarily entered into by the parties to a dispute that settles the dispute. In a divorce, a written document signed by divorcing parties that evidences their agreement settling property rights and other issues of their divorce.

Settlor, trustor, or **transferor**   Person who creates a trust. Also referred to as *trustor* or *transferor.*

Sex discrimination   Discrimination against a person solely because of his or her sex.

Sexual harassment   Lewd remarks, touching, intimidation, posting of pinups, and other verbal or physical conduct of a sexual nature that occur on the job.

Shareholders   The owners of corporations, whose ownership interests are evidenced by stock certificates.

Slander   Oral defamation of character.

Slip opinion   A copy of the opinion sent to the printer.

Small offices   Small-office arrangements range from individual practitioners sharing space to partnerships.

Small-claims court   A court that hears civil cases involving small dollar amounts.

Software   Refers to programs containing sets of instructions that tell the computer and the other computer-based electronic devices what to do and how to do it.

Sole proprietorship   A form of business in which the owner is actually the business; the business is not a separate legal entity.

Solo practice   One lawyer practicing alone without the assistance of other attorneys.

Special federal courts   Federal courts that hear matters of specialized or limited jurisdiction.

Specialty application programs   Specialty programs combine many of the basic functions found in software suites, word processing, database management, spreadsheets, and graphic presentations to perform law office, case, and litigation management.

Specialty practice   A specialty practice is involved in practice in one area of law.

Specific duty   An OSHA standard that addresses a safety problem of a specific duty nature (e.g., requirement for a safety guard on a particular type of equipment.)

Specific gift   A gift of a specifically named piece of property.

Specific government regulation   Government regulation that applies to individual industries.

Specific performance   A remedy that orders the breaching party to perform the acts promised in the contract. Specific performance usually is awarded in cases where the subject matter is unique, such as in contracts involving land, heirlooms, and paintings.

Spendthrift trust   A trust for a beneficiary with limits on the use of the funds to prevent claims of the beneficiary's creditors.

Spoliation of evidence   Destruction of evidence.

Spousal support   Payments made by one divorced spouse to the other divorced spouse. Also called *alimony*.

Spreadsheet programs   Programs that permit the calculation and presentation of financial information in a grid format of rows and columns.

Standing to sue   The plaintiff must have some stake in the outcome of the lawsuit.

Stare decisis   Latin: "to stand by the decision." Adherence to precedent. The legal principle that prior case law should apply unless there is a substantial change in society necessitating a change in the case law.

State administrative agencies   Administrative agencies that states create to enforce and interpret state law.

Statement of policy   A statement issued by administrative agencies announcing a proposed course of action that an agency intends to follow in the future.

Statute   Written law enacted by the legislative branch of the federal and state governments that establishes certain courses of conduct that the covered parties must adhere to.

Statute of Frauds   A state statute that requires certain types of contracts to be in writing.

Statute of limitations   A time limit within which a case must be brought or lose the right to seek redress in court.

Statute of repose   A statute that limits the seller's liability to a certain number of years from the date when the product was first sold.

Statute of Wills   A state statute that establishes the requirements for making a valid will.

Strict liability   A tort doctrine that makes manufacturers, distributors, wholesalers, retailers, and others in the chain of distribution of a defective product liable for the damages caused by the defect *irrespective of fault*. Also, liability without fault.

Strict scrutiny test   Test that is applied to classifications based on race.

Strike   Cessation of work by union members to obtain economic benefits or correct an unfair labor practice.

Subject-matter jurisdiction   Jurisdiction over the subject matter of a lawsuit.

Subpoena   A court order compelling a witness to attend and testify, must accompany a Notice of deposition served on a non-party witness.

Substantial performance   Performance by a contracting party that deviates only slightly from complete performance.

Substantive due process   Due process that requires that the statute or rule that the respondent is charged with violating be clearly stated.

Substantive law   Law which relates to the law of the case, such as the law of negligence or contract.

Substantive rule   A rule issued by an administrative agency that has much the same power as a statute: It has the force of law and must be adhered to by covered persons and businesses.

Subsurface rights (mineral rights)   Rights to the earth located beneath the surface of the land.

Summons   A court order directing the defendant to appear in court and answer the complaint.

Superseding (or intervening) event   A defendant is not liable for injuries caused by a superseding or intervening event for which he or she is not responsible.

Supervising attorney   The member of the legal team to whom all others on the team report and who has the ultimate responsibility for the actions of the legal team.

Supremacy Clause   A clause of the U.S. Constitution that establishes that the federal Constitution, treaties, federal laws, and federal regulations are the supreme law of the land.

Tangible property   All real property and physically defined personal property such as buildings, goods, animals, and minerals.

Teleworker   People who work from remote locations, typically home.

Temporary (rehabilitation) alimony   Spousal support paid for a limited period of time.

Tenancy at sufferance   A tenancy created when a tenant retains possession of property after the expiration of another tenancy or a life estate without the owner's consent.

Tenancy at will   A tenancy created by a lease that may be terminated at any time by either party.

Tenancy by the entirety   A form of co-ownership of real property that can be used only by married couples.

Tenancy for years   A tenancy created when the landlord and the tenant agree on a specific duration for a lease.

Tenancy in common   A form of co-ownership in which the interest of a surviving tenant in common passes to the deceased tenant's estate and not to the co-tenants.

Tenant   The party to whom a leasehold is transferred.

Tender of performance   Tender is an unconditional and absolute offer by a contracting party to perform his or her obligations under the contract. Occurs when a party who has the ability and willingness to perform offers to complete the performance of his or her duties under the contract.

Testamentary trust   A trust created by will: the trust comes into existence when the settlor dies.

Testator or **testatrix**   The person who makes a will.

Thin client   A computer system where programs and files are maintained on a centralized server.

Third-party documents   Documents prepared by a third party in the ordinary course of business that would have been prepared in similar form if there was no litigation.

Title III of the Americans with Disabilities Act   A federal statute that prohibits discrimination on the basis of disability in places of public accommodation by private entities.

Title VII of the Civil Rights Act of 1964   A title of a federal statute enacted to eliminate job discrimination based on five protected classes: *race, color, religion, sex,* and *national origin*.

Title insurance   Insurance that owners of real property purchase to insure that they have clear title to the property.

Tort   A wrong. There are three categories of torts: (1) intentional torts, (2) unintentional torts (negligence), and (3) strict liability.

Totten trust   Typically a bank account payable to a benefactor only on death of the person opening the account.

Track Changes   Track Changes, as found in MS Word, shows the original text, the deleted text, and the new text as well as a strike through for deleted text, underlining or highlighting of new text, as well as margin notes on the document.

Trade secret   A product formula, pattern, design, compilation of data, customer list, or other business secret.

Trademark   A distinctive mark, symbol, name, word, motto, or device that identifies the goods of a particular business.

Trademark infringement   Unauthorized use of another's mark. The holder may recover damages and other remedies from the infringer.

Treaty   A compact made between two or more nations.

Trespass to land   A tort that interferes with an owner's right to exclusive possession of land.

Trespass to personal property   A tort that occurs whenever one person injures another person's personal property or interferes with that person's enjoyment of his or her personal property.

Trial brief   Document presented to the court setting forth a legal argument to persuade the court to rule in a particular way on a procedural or substantive legal issue.

Trial notebook   A summary of the case tabbed for each major activity, witness, or element of proof.

Trier of facts   The trier of facts decides what facts are to be accepted and used in making the decision. It is usually a jury, but may be a judge who hears a case without a jury and decides the facts and applies the law.

Trust   A legal arrangement established when one person transfers title to property to another person to be held and used for the benefit of a third person.

Trust account   The funds of the client.

Trust *corpus* or trust *res*   The property and assets held in trust.

Trustee   Person or entity that holds legal title to the trust *corpus* and manages the trust for the benefit of the beneficiary or beneficiaries.

Trustee in bankruptcy   A legal representative of a debtor's estate.

UCC Statute of Frauds   A rule that requires all contracts for the sale of goods costing $500 or more and lease contracts involving payments of $1,000 or more to be in writing.

U.S. Courts of Appeals   The federal court system's intermediate appellate courts.

U.S. District Courts   The federal court system's trial courts of general jurisdiction.

U.S. Immigration and Customs Enforcement (ICE)   The federal administrative agency that enforces federal immigration laws.

U.S. Supreme Court   The Supreme Court was created by Article III of the U.S. Constitution. The Supreme Court is the highest court in the land. It is located in Washington, DC.

Unauthorized Practice of Law (UPL)   Giving legal advice, if legal rights may be affected, by anyone not licensed to practice law.

Undue influence   Occurs where one person takes advantage of another person's mental, emotional, or physical weakness and unduly persuades that person to make a will; the persuasion by the wrongdoer must overcome the free will of the testator.

Uniform Arbitration Act   A uniform act adopted by more than half of the states, similar to the Federal Arbitration Act it describes procedures that must be followed for arbitration to be initiated, how the panel of arbitrators is to be selected, and the procedures for conducting arbitration hearings.

Uniform Commercial Code (UCC)   A comprehensive statutory scheme that includes laws covering aspects of commercial transactions.

Uniform Computer Information Transactions Act (UCITA)   A model state law that creates contract law for the licensing of information technology rights.

Uniform Gift to Minors Act or Revised Uniform Gift to Minors Act   Acts that establish procedures for adults to make gifts of money and securities to minors.

Uniform Limited Liability Company Act (ULLCA)   A model act that provides comprehensive and uniform laws for the formation, operation, and dissolution of LLCs.

Uniform Partnership Act (UPA)   A model act that codifies partnership law. Most states have adopted the UPA in whole or in part.

Uniform Probate Code (UPC)   A model law promulgated to establish uniform rules for the creation of wills, the administration of estates, and the resolution of conflicts in settling estates.

Uniform resource locator (URL)   The address of a site on the Internet.

Uniform Simultaneous Death Act   An act that provides that if people who would inherit property from each other die simultaneously, each person's property is distributed as though he or she survived.

Unintentional tort/negligence   The omission to do something which a reasonable person would do or doing something a reasonable person would refrain from doing.

Uninterruptable power supply (UPS)   A battery system that can supply power to a computer or computer peripheral for a short period of time.

Universal Citation Format   A system for citation relying on the courts to number the paragraphs in their opinions.

Unprotected speech   Speech that is not protected by the First Amendment and may be forbidden by the government.

Unpublished opinions   Cases which the court does not feel have precedential effect and are limited to a specific set of facts.

Unreasonable search and seizure   Any search and seizure by the government that violates the Fourth Amendment.

V. Cite   VersusLaw's tool for searching cases containing references to another case.

Variance   An exception that permits a type of building or use in an area that would not otherwise be allowed by a zoning ordinance.

Vendor-specific citation format   Citation format of a legal publisher adopted by a court.

Venue   A concept that requires lawsuits to be heard by the court with jurisdiction that is nearest the location in which the incident occurred or where the parties reside.

Verdict   Decision reached by the jury.

Videoconferencing   Conferencing from multiple locations using high speed Internet connections to transmit sound and images.

Violation   A crime that is neither a felony nor a misdemeanor that is usually punishable by a fine.

Visitation rights   A time period for visitation by non-custodial parent with the child.

Voice recognition   Computer programs for converting speech into text or commands without the use of other inout devices such as keyboards.

VoIP   Voice over internet protocol is a computer internet replacement for traditional telephone connections.

Voir dire   Process whereby prospective jurors are asked questions by the judge and attorneys to determine if they would be biased in their decision.

Voluntary petition   A petition filed by the debtor; states that the debtor has debts.

White-collar crimes   Crimes usually involving cunning and deceit rather than physical force.

Wide area network   A wide area network is a network of networks. Each network is treated as if it were a connection on the network.

Will   A declaration of how a person wants his or her property to be distributed upon death.

Wire fraud   The use of telephone or telegraph to defraud another person.

Wireless computer networks   A wireless network uses wireless technology in place of wires for connecting to the network.

Wireless network   A wireless network uses wireless technology instead of wires for connecting to the network.

Workers' compensation acts   Laws that compensate workers and their families if workers are injured in connection with their jobs.

Work-product doctrine   A qualified immunity from discovery for "work product of the lawyer" except on a substantial showing of "necessity or justification" of certain written statements and memoranda prepared by counsel in representation of a client, generally in preparation for trial.

Work-related test   A test that says if an agent commits an intentional tort within a work-related time or space, the principal is liable for any injury caused by the agent's intentional tort.

Workstation   A computer connected to a network that is used for access consisting of a monitor, input device, and computer.

World Wide Web   An electronic connection of millions of computers that support a standard set of rules for the exchange of information.

Writ of certiorari   An official notice that the Supreme Court will review one's case.

Wrongful death action   Lawsuit seeking compensation for damage caused by death of a relative.

Wrongful dissolution   When a partner withdraws from a partnership without have the right to do so at that time.

Wrongful termination of an agency   The termination of an agency contract in violation of the terms of the agency contract. In this situation, the nonbreaching party may recover damages from the breaching party.

Zoning commission   A local administrative body that formulates zoning ordinances, conducts public hearings, and makes recommendations to the city council.

Zoning ordinances   Local laws that are adopted by municipalities and local governments to regulate land use within their boundaries.

Case Index

Subject Index